English Literature in Context

This is the second edition of *English Literature in Context*, a popular textbook which provides an essential resource and reference tool for all English Literature students. Designed to accompany students throughout their degree course, it offers a detailed narrative survey of the diverse historical and cultural contexts that have shaped the development of English literature, from the Anglo-Saxon period to the present day. Carefully structured for undergraduate use, the eight chronological chapters are written by a team of expert contributors who are also highly experienced teachers. Each chapter includes a detailed chronology, contextual readings of selected literary texts, annotated suggestions for further reading, a rich range of illustrations and textboxes, and thorough historical and literary overviews. This second edition has been comprehensively revised, with a new chapter on postcolonial literature, a substantially expanded chapter on contemporary literature, and the addition of over 200 new critical references. Online resources include: textboxes; chapter samples; study questions and chronologies.

Formerly of the University of Leicester, where he was Director of Studies at Vaughan College and Senior Lecturer in English, Paul Poplawski now lives and works as an independent scholar in Austria.

English Literature in Context

PAUL POPLAWSKI
General Editor

VALERIE ALLEN, Medieval English, 500–1500

ANDREW HISCOCK, The Renaissance, 1485–1660

LEE MORRISSEY, The Restoration and Eighteenth Century, 1660–1780

PETER J. KITSON, The Romantic Period, 1780–1832

MARIA FRAWLEY, The Victorian Age, 1832–1901

PAUL POPLAWSKI, The Twentieth Century, 1901–1939

JOHN BRANNIGAN, The Twentieth and Twenty-First Centuries, 1939–2015

PAUL POPLAWSKI, Postcolonial Literature in English

CAMBRIDGE UNIVERSITY PRESS

CAMBRIDGE
UNIVERSITY PRESS

University Printing House, Cambridge CB2 8BS, United Kingdom

One Liberty Plaza, 20th Floor, New York, NY 10006, USA

477 Williamstown Road, Port Melbourne, VIC 3207, Australia

314-321, 3rd Floor, Plot 3, Splendor Forum, Jasola District Centre, New Delhi – 110025, India

79 Anson Road, #06–04/06, Singapore 079906

Cambridge University Press is part of the University of Cambridge.

It furthers the University's mission by disseminating knowledge in the pursuit of education, learning, and research at the highest international levels of excellence.

www.cambridge.org
Information on this title: www.cambridge.org/9781107141674
10.1017/9781316493779

First published 2017
Reprinted 2017

Printed in the United Kingdom by TJ International Ltd. Padstow Cornwall

A catalogue record for this publication is available from the British Library.

ISBN 978-1-107-14167-4 Hardback
ISBN 978-1-316-50663-9 Paperback

Contents

Illustrations

2 The Renaissance, 1485–1660

3 The Restoration and Eighteenth Century, 1660–1780

4 The Romantic Period, 1780–1832

5 The Victorian Age, 1832–1901

6 The Twentieth Century, 1901–1939

Images 2, 3, 4, 6, 7 and 8 reproduced courtesy of Getty Images

7 The Twentieth and Twenty-First Centuries, 1939–2015

All the above images courtesy of Getty Images

8 Postcolonial Literature in English

Notes on Contributors

VALERIE ALLEN is Professor of Literature at John Jay College of Criminal Justice at the City University of New York. She was educated at Trinity College Dublin, and taught in Scotland and Florida before moving to New York. Recent publications include a co-edited collection, *Roadworks: Medieval Britain, Medieval Roads* (Manchester University Press, 2016), and essays on Chaucer, Nicholas Love, Old English compensation law, medieval piety, Margery Kempe, and the Bayeux Tapestry.

JOHN BRANNIGAN is Professor of English in University College Dublin. His publications include *Literature, Culture and Society in Postwar England, 1945–1965* (2002), *Orwell to the Present: Literature in England, 1945–2000* (2003), *Pat Barker* (2005), and *Archipelagic Modernism: Literature in the Irish and British Isles, 1890–1970* (2015).

MARIA FRAWLEY is a professor of English at George Washington University, where she teaches courses in nineteenth-century British literature and directs the University Honors Program. She is the author of three books: *A Wider Range: Travel Writing by Women in Victorian England, Anne Brontë* and, most recently, *Invalidism and Identity in Nineteenth-Century Britain*. In addition, she has prepared an edition of Harriet Martineau's *Life in the Sick-Room* for Broadview Press. She is currently working on a variety of projects related to Victorian literary and medical history and is also writing a book titled *Keywords of Jane Austen's Fiction*.

ANDREW HISCOCK is Professor of English Literature at Bangor University, Wales and Marie Skłodowska-Curie Research Fellow at the *Institut de recherches sur la Renaissance, l'Age Classique et les Lumières* (IRCL), Université Paul Valéry III, Montpellier. He is English Literature editor of the academic journal *MLR*, series co-editor of *Arden Early Modern Drama Guides* and a Fellow of the English Association. He has published widely on English and French early modern literature and his most recent monograph is *Reading Memory in Early Modern Literature* (Cambridge University Press).

PETER J. KITSON is Professor of English at the University of East Anglia. He has taught and published widely in the field of Romantic period literature and culture and is the author of *Forging Romantic China: Sino-British Cultural Exchange, 1760–1840* (2013), *Romantic Literature, Race and Colonial Encounter* (2007) and (with D. Lee and T. Fulford), *Romantic Literature, Science and Exploration in the Romantic Era: Bodies of Knowledge* (2004). He is also the editor (with D. Lee) of the multi-volume editions of *Slavery, Abolition and Emancipation: Writings from the British Romantic Period* (1999) and (with T. Fulford), *Travels, Explorations and Empires: Writings from the Era of Imperial Expansion 1770–1835* (2001–2). He has served as the Chair and President of the

English Association (2004–10) and President of the British Association for Romantic Studies (2007–11) and has held fellowships from the Leverhulme Trust, the AHRC, The Japan Society for the Promotion of Science, The Huntington Library, and the Australian National University.

LEE MORRISSEY, Professor and Chair of English at Clemson University, is the author of *From the Temple to the Castle: An Architectural History of British Literature, 1660–1760*, and of *The Constitution of Literature: Literacy, Democracy, and Early English Literary Criticism*. He is the editor of *The Kitchen Turns Twenty: A Retrospective Anthology*, and *Debating the Canon: A Reader from Addison to Nafisi*, and Associate Editor of the three-volume *Encyclopedia of British Literature, 1660–1789*. His work has been published in *New Literary History*, *College Literature*, *Women's Writing*, and *Shakespeare*. He has been a Fulbright Scholar at the National University of Ireland-Galway, and a McCarthy Fellow at Marsh's Library, Dublin.

Preface

> Don't want your drum and trumpet history – no fear … Don't want to know who was who's mistress, and why so-and-so devastated such a province; that's bound to be all lies and upsy-down anyhow. Not my affair. Nobody's affair now. Chaps who did it didn't clearly know … What I want to know is, in the middle ages Did they Do Anything for Housemaid's Knee? What did they put in their hot baths after jousting, and was the Black Prince – you know the Black Prince – was he enamelled or painted, or what? I think myself, black-leaded – very likely – like pipe-clay – but *did* they use blacking so early?
>
> (H. G. Wells, *Tono-Bungay* (1909), p. 214)

As Edward Ponderevo's rambling comments from Wells's novel humorously illustrate, literature regularly asks questions about history and about the processes by which historical knowledge and understanding are shaped. What is somewhat less common is to see historical questions asked of literature – questions, for example, such as how and why particular types of literature should emerge from particular sets of historical circumstances. The academic study of literature usually takes for granted the idea that literature should function as a critical reflection on people and society in history, and on the ways in which people make historical sense of their lives, but it often glosses over the fact that literature (in both its material and symbolic aspects) is itself always actively part of the historical process and inextricably bound up with its surrounding historical contexts.

There has certainly been a growing trend among critics and scholars in recent years to place increased emphasis on the precise historical contextualisation of literature, and this trend has to some extent been reflected within degree programmes in English. However, it remains the case that undergraduate literature students often have only a fairly limited sense of relevant historical contexts, and this is partly because of the relative dearth of appropriate and accessible study materials within this field. By its very nature, relevant historical information for the whole sweep of English literature tends to be widely scattered in a number of different sources, and, in any case, historical information of itself does not *necessarily* illuminate literary study without further interpretation and contextualisation of its own – and students often need guidance with this. There are many helpful general histories of English literature, of course, and these can go some way towards providing such guidance, but they usually deal mainly with the 'internal' development of literature through the ages and only briefly, if at all, with the broader historical contexts which have helped to shape that development. At the other end of the spectrum, there are also many useful books of specialised historical literary criticism which deal in close detail with specific periods, and these are certainly valuable resources for a focused historical understanding of literature. However, broad-based books dedicated to introducing students to the systematic study of literature in context, with historical and literary material relevant to all periods of literature, are very few and far between, and it is this particular gap in provision for students that the present book seeks to address.

English Literature in Context has been written and designed specifically for undergraduates to provide a detailed and accessible source of contextual reference material to support the study of English literature from the Middle Ages to the present. The book offers a wide-ranging introduction to the key historical and cultural contexts in which literature has been produced through the ages and it explores the complex interactions between literature and its contexts through focused discussions of particular literary trends, movements, texts and issues within each period. Each chapter of the book provides a comprehensive overview of one broad period of English literature, outlining important historical and literary events and examining the ways in which the diverse social, economic, political and cultural aspects of the period have informed its literary activity. To consolidate and enhance the reader's understanding of the period and its literature, a range of illustrations and 'break-out' textboxes also feature in each chapter.

As indicated above, the book has been written as an introductory text for undergraduates and, in particular, the authors have tried to maintain a clear, lively and accessible style of writing without any assumption of prior specialist knowledge on the part of the reader. At the same time, however, we hope that the book's detailed treatment of particular trends, texts and contexts within each period will make it suitable as a source of reference and stimulus for more advanced study too. It should perhaps be noted that the authors are all experienced teachers of literature with a clear grasp of the learning needs of students as they progress through degree programmes in English, and the book has been designed to cater flexibly for those needs.

Using This Book

The chapters of the book have a common structure of five main sections which move the focus gradually from the general to the particular as they each develop the dialogue between history and literature, contexts and texts. These five sections are as follows:

 i. Historical Overview
 ii. Literary Overview
 iii. Texts and Issues
 iv. Readings
 v. Reference

In each chapter, the 'Historical Overview' is preceded by a brief introductory paragraph and a chronology which covers the period in question, listing all major historical and cultural events alongside key literary developments. Among other things, the chronologies are intended to provide a quick reference guide to the literature and history of each period and to enable readers to make some critical observations of their own about the period, both before and after reading the main part of the related chapter. The first two sections then lay narrative foundations for each chapter by broadly surveying the historical and literary trends of the relevant period and by drawing attention to key points of conjunction between the two. The third section, 'Texts and Issues', looks more closely at such points of conjunction and expands on the interrelations between texts and contexts by considering some of the dominant issues or themes which can be seen to permeate the period, both in its literature and in its broader social and cultural contexts. The 'Readings' section then narrows the focus further by providing short contextualised readings of a small group of representative texts from the period. In their attention to textual and contextual detail, these critical readings are intended to draw together specific elements of the preceding historical, literary and thematic overviews while also serving as practical examples of how to discuss individual texts in close relation to their historical contexts. The final 'Reference' section in each chapter provides readers with structured and annotated suggestions for further reading and research, as well as full references for all works cited in the main text. This section has three main subsections which are common to all chapters – A: Primary texts and anthologies of primary sources; B: Introductions and overviews; and C: Further reading.

Within the common broad structure outlined above, there are different types of emphasis from chapter to chapter and many individual variations in how material is organised within each of the five main sections (and it should be noted that Chapter 8, which is not defined solely by period, has a somewhat different nature from the other chapters and diverges from the standard pattern above by treating sections ii and iii together). These variations reflect the different characteristics of each particular period (including their differences in length) as well as the different interests of individual authors – for, while we have aimed at a certain degree of standardisation of style and structure across chapters, we have wanted to avoid a narrow uniformity and have done our best to retain a clear sense of our own individual voices, along with a lively feel for the distinctiveness of our periods.

It should be made clear that the focus of the book is primarily on literature from the United Kingdom and that American literature and other literatures in English are not dealt with in any detail by seven of the book's eight chapters (the exception is Chapter 8 which, while also not discussing American literature, provides a broad introduction to postcolonial literature in English). Having said that, variable historical circumstances over the centuries inevitably mean that authors have had to make their own critical judgements for their specific periods as to how narrowly or broadly to apply the book's main focus and how far to trace literary developments and influences beyond the United Kingdom at any particular point. Similarly, although several chapters touch on critical questions about how we define and delimit literary periods in the first place, and also about how we decide on what constitutes a relevant historical context, we have not felt it appropriate in a practically oriented book like this to dwell too much on such matters. We certainly want readers to reflect on these things for themselves, and we have tried in our discussions to retain a degree of flexibility and open-endedness to encourage this, but, equally, in organising our material we have each had to make some clear-cut decisions and selections – and in the main these have been guided by a pragmatic sense of the broad requirements of undergraduate studies in English and of the sorts of literary traditions, periods and texts that are widely taught and studied in universities and colleges around the world. We are aware, of course, that there is no neat consensus on such matters and that English degrees are as many and various as the institutions which offer them, but we hope our coverage is sufficiently broad and balanced to meet the requirements of at least some parts of most degree programmes. It should be stressed, moreover, that much of the discussion in the book (especially in the 'Texts and issues' and 'Readings' sections) is only intended to be *illustrative* of a general approach to the study of literature in its historical contexts. We are by no means trying to prescribe particular programmes of study of our own, or indeed to narrow the possibilities of analysis and interpretation to the ones presented here. Our hope is simply that we can provide a firm foundation for historically contextualised literary study, along with sufficiently stimulating examples of such study to encourage readers to make their own critical explorations in this field according to their own circumstances and interests.

For this second edition of *English Literature in Context*, a completely new chapter has been added on the important field of 'Postcolonial literature in English', while the book's existing chapter on contemporary literature has now been substantially revised and expanded to bring the story up to the present date. The 'Reference' sections of all the chapters have been carefully reviewed, revised and updated to reflect the latest developments in the subject for each different period, and, as a result, over two hundred new items have been added to the book's annotated lists of critical references. In order to make space for all this extra material without unduly increasing the physical size of the book, a number of selected textboxes from the first edition have not been reprinted here but have instead been moved to the book's accompanying website, which should also be consulted for a range of other relevant online resources (see www.cambridge.org/poplawski2). Apart from Chapter 7, the substance of most of the other original chapters remains largely unchanged here from the first edition, although there have been some small additions and amendments to the text of Chapter 4 and a slightly more extensive revision of the text of Chapter 1.

Sources for all quotations and references are cited in abbreviated form in the main text and full details of such citations can be found in the relevant 'Reference' section at the end of each chapter. For ease of orientation within that section, citations are always keyed to its various subsections (A, Bi, Cii, etc.) – for example:

Stephen Constantine, *Unemployment in Britain between the Wars*, pp. 1–2 [Bi]

Acknowledgements

First edition

The editor and contributors would like to thank current and former colleagues at Cambridge University Press for their invaluable support and encouragement throughout the whole period of this book's planning, development and production. In particular, we would like to thank Rachel de Wachter and Sarah Stanton for initiating the project; Pat Maurice and Juliet Davis-Berry for their help in planning and developing the book's overall design; Paul Stevens for his help with shepherding the illustrations; our wonderfully sharp-eyed copy-editor, Margaret Berrill, who made innumerable and invaluable improvements to the book in its later stages; Mike Leach for the index and Alison Powell for efficiently steering us through the final production process; Sarah Stanton again for overseeing the whole project from beginning to end; and last, but certainly not least, Rebecca Jones for her detailed editorial and organisational work throughout, and for her enthusiastic good cheer in helping us to bring the book to completion.

Second edition

For this second edition, we have again received wonderful support from colleagues at Cambridge University Press and we would once more like to give them our warmest thanks. We are particularly grateful to Sarah Stanton for proposing the new edition in the first place and for setting it firmly on its way, and to Rosemary Crawley for her superbly efficient editorial direction thereafter and for seeing the whole project smoothly through to publication. We are also indebted to Valerie Appleby for her invaluable groundwork in the initial planning of the edition; to Martin Thacker for his eagle-eyed, insightful and thoroughly engaged copy-editing of the text; to Isobel Cowper-Coles and to Tim Mason for their friendly administrative help; to Chantal Hamill for the book's new index and to Caroline Mowatt for her careful management of the final production process. We would, in addition, like to take this opportunity to record our deep gratitude to the many readers, students, teachers and scholars who have kindly provided feedback on the book at different stages in its development from its initial inception through to this second edition. As editor, I would like to thank the other contributors for their professionalism and support throughout the many years we have worked together on this book, and for their great perseverance and friendly good humour in the face of my seemingly endless requests for revisions, additions, amendments, corrections and 'just one more thing'! I would like to express my love and gratitude to my wife, Angie, for *her* great perseverance and support throughout this time. My love and thanks also go to the rest of my family for their support over the years and especially to my grandchildren, Poppy, Oscar and Charlie, for keeping me (literally) on my toes.

I am grateful to the University of Leicester for granting a period of study leave during which I undertook some of the initial research and writing for Chapter 6 – and grateful, too, to Cynthia Brown for helpful advice on the illustrations for that chapter. Susan Reid gave generously of her time to read and comment on a draft of Chapter 8, and I am indebted to her for many helpful suggestions. My thanks are also due to David Cox for his excellent maps. For helping to inform the whole of my contribution to this book, I thank all the students and colleagues I have worked with in the past for making *my* contexts for the study of literature so congenial.

Valerie Allen would like to thank Ares Axiotis and Michael Sargent for help with her chapter.

John Brannigan would like to thank colleagues and students at University College Dublin, especially the teaching team and students of *Literature in Context* who have given very valuable feedback on this volume. He would also like to thank Professor Tony Roche, for a fruitful discussion of Larkin; Professor Andrew Carpenter for supporting a period of research leave which helped with the completion of the chapter for the first edition; and Dr Fionnuala Dillane, for many insightful conversations about the relationship between this volume and teaching undergraduate English. He would also like to acknowledge the love, support, distractions and replenishments afforded by his wife, Moyra, and three children, Conor, Owen, and Laura.

Maria Frawley would like to thank her research assistants from the George Washington University Honors Program, Liza Blake and Taylor Asen, for their generous help both with researching material for her chapter and for reading portions of the chapter in draft.

Andrew Hiscock is grateful to the many colleagues with whom he has discussed his chapter and he wishes particularly to thank Professor Tony Claydon (Bangor University), Professor Heather Easterling (Gonzaga University) and Dr Ceri Sullivan (Cardiff University) for their invaluable advice and comments.

Peter J. Kitson would like to thank his colleague at the University of Dundee, Dr David Robb, for help with the photography for his chapter and also Rebecca Jones for her advice and help with the illustrations.

Lee Morrissey gratefully acknowledges Clemson University's College of Architecture, Arts and Humanities Research Grants for supporting his contribution to this book.

1 Medieval English, 500–1500

VALERIE ALLEN

What should we call this period of 'medieval literature' that straddles nearly a millennium and two languages? The 'Dark' and 'Middle Ages' (of which 'medieval' is simply the Latinate form), were terms applied retrospectively and pejoratively by writers in the seventeenth century to describe the period between classical and Renaissance learning; the 'medievals' generally perceived themselves as modern, sometimes even corruptly sophisticated in comparison to earlier, simpler days. 'Literature' is equally problematic, not existing as a word in English until the fourteenth century. For most of the period, that body of writing containing what we now call 'literature' encompassed without division texts that today we categorise as religious, historical, legal and medical.

Furthermore, how do we name a period that so lacks internal coherence? It moves from a Germanic tribal economy to late Old English feudalism, to the 'high' feudalism of the Normans, to the emergence of the state bureaucracy, centralisation of power, and urban economy that brought England to the eve of its precociously early capitalism. It starts at a moment when the essentially urbanised experience of guild-organised mystery plays is inconceivable, and ends at a time when Old English heroic poetry is largely unintelligible both culturally and linguistically. Taking this medieval period as a discrete historical epoch in its own right, we must ask what its literature distinctively meant. History and literature are divided in modern disciplinary parlance and then united in an artificial synthesis imposed on a body of medieval writing that recognised no such distinction in the first place. Literature is not some constant that progresses unchanged through the eras; its very meaning changes according to the epoch in which it occurs. We must ask what made its dominant genres – heroic poetry, romance, saint's life, mystery play – assume the form they did when they did. We must consider the possibility that literature as we understand it today simply does not map onto the medieval landscape of poetic and scribal production. To read medieval literature well is thus to read medieval literature historically.

Chronology

Key

AS   Anglo-Saxon, the collective term for the inhabitants of England after the immigration of the Germanic tribes from the fifth century. The name comes from the two most populous tribes, the Angles and the Saxons. Used more precisely, the term is distinguished from the native Britons, inhabiting the island prior to invasion, and from the Danes, who invaded from the eighth to eleventh centuries.

fl.   'Flourished'.

IF   Insular French, referring to the predominantly Norman-influenced dialect of French that developed in England after 1066. Also refers broadly to any French written in England.

L.   Latin, the language of learning and of the Church; in use continuously throughout the medieval period and across western Europe.

ME   Middle English, referring to the English language from the thirteenth to late fifteenth centuries. English from the twelfth and late eleventh centuries is transitional, and can be understood as either late OE or early ME.

OE   Old English, referring to the conglomeration of dialects used in England from the earliest written vernacular (roughly early seventh century) until the Norman invasion. Most OE writing is in the West-Saxon dialect.

OF   Old French, language of continental France, as distinct from its insular counterpart, Insular French.

Unless designated otherwise, all texts are in English (whether Old or Middle).

Note

There is often a lag between when a work was composed and the date of its earliest surviving manuscript. Anglo-Saxon poetry is particularly vulnerable to this kind of delayed date of record. *The Dream of the Rood*, for example, is known to have existed in some form by the late seventh century, but the manuscript in which it exists dates from some three hundred years later.

	HISTORY AND CULTURE	LITERATURE
449	Bede's date for arrival of Germanic mercenaries. King Arthur possibly a British resistance leader fighting the invaders	
Late C. 5th / early C. 6th		Gildas, *The Ruin of Britain* (L.), source for Bede
597	St Augustine brings Roman Christianity (and script) to Kent	
c. 602–3	Æthelbert, king of Kent, first Anglo-Saxon ruler to convert	Æthelbert establishes written law, first known OE writing (preserved only in later manuscripts)
616	Edwin (–633), king of Northumbria, converts to Christianity	
c. 625	Sutton Hoo ship burial	
c. 632	Penda (–655), pagan king of Mercia	
635	Cynegisl, first West-Saxon king baptised	
642	Oswald, king of Northumbria, killed by Penda	
643		Earliest original date for *Widsith* and *Deor* (in Exeter Book, c. 950), although a later date is more likely

	HISTORY AND CULTURE	LITERATURE
656	Mercia converts to Christianity	
657		(–680) 'Cædmon's Hymn', and possibly *Genesis A, Exodus* and *Daniel* (in Junius manuscript, c. 950)
664	Synod of Whitby establishes supremacy of Roman Christianity	
674	Monastery of Monkwearmouth founded. Bede educated there as child within the decade	
c. 678	English Christian missions to the Continent	Earliest original date for *Beowulf*, latest ninth century; also *Battle of Finnsburgh*
682	Monastery of Jarrow founded near Monkwearmouth	
687	Death of St Cuthbert	
688		Ine (–726), king of Wessex, establishes law code
c. 698		Lindisfarne Gospels (L.); *Dream of the Rood*
730	(–750) Ruthwell Cross	
731		Bede, *Ecclesiastical History of the English People* (L.)
757	Offa (–96), king of Mercia	
c. 782		Poetic elegies, including: *Wanderer, Seafarer, Wife's Lament* and *Ruin* (all in Exeter Book, c. 950)
780s	Alcuin of York teaches and writes in Charlemagne's court	
793	First Danish invasions. Monastery at Lindisfarne sacked	
796		*fl.* Nennius, *History of the Britons* (L.); early reference to historical Arthur
c. 800	Four remaining kingdoms: Northumbria, Mercia, East Anglia, Wessex	'Cynewulf' poems (from runic signature): *Juliana, Christ II* (in Exeter Book, c. 950), *Fates of the Apostles, Elene* (in Vercelli Book, c. 950). OE riddles
c. 851		*Genesis B*
869	Danes kill Edmund, king of East Anglia	Edmund venerated as saint
871	Alfred the Great, king of Wessex, then of Anglo-Saxons	Possible date of *Andreas*
875	York becomes separate Scandinavian kingdom	
878	Defeat of Danish leader Guthrum at Edington (Wilts.). Treaty of Wedmore. Guthrum baptised	
c. 880	Kingdom of the Anglo-Saxons. Boundaries of Danelaw established: Dane and Englishman given equal legal value (or wergild)	Alfredian law-code and translations. *Anglo-Saxon Chronicle* begun
899	Edward the Elder, son of Alfred, king of Anglo-Saxons	
924	Æthelstan, son of Edward, king of Anglo-Saxons, then of English (927)	
937	Battle of Brunanburh: Æthelstan defeats Norsemen and Scots	*Battle of Brunanburh* recorded as poem in *Anglo-Saxon Chronicle*
939	Edmund, first king to succeed to all England	
946	King Eadred, brother of Edmund	
c. 950		Exeter Book (–c. 1000), Vercelli Book (containing earliest homilies), Junius manuscript. *Beowulf* manuscript probably late tenth or early eleventh century
955	King Eadwig, son of Edmund	
959	Edgar, brother of Eadwig, king of England Dunstan (–988), Archbishop of Canterbury	Monastic Benedictine Revival
961	Oswald (–992), Bishop of Worcester, Archbishop of York from 971	Oswald major figure in Benedictine Revival

	HISTORY AND CULTURE	LITERATURE
963		Æthelwold (–984), Bishop of Winchester, teacher of Wulfstan and Ælfric, translates *Rule* of St Benedict (L.) into OE; writes *Regularis Concordia* (L.), standardising monastic, liturgical observance
c. 971		Blickling Homilies, anonymous
975	King Edward 'the Martyr', son of Edgar	His murder in 978 lamented by *Anglo-Saxon Chronicle*, Byrhtferth of Ramsey and Wulfstan (1014); venerated as a saint
978	Æthelræd II, 'the Unready', half-brother of Edward the Martyr	
c. 980	Second wave of Viking invasion (–1066)	
985–7		Abbo of Fleury at Ramsey; commemorates death of Edmund (d. 869)
c. 991		*Apollonius of Tyre*, only OE romance, in manuscript with Wulfstan's homilies
990–2		Ælfric, *Catholic Homilies*
991	Battle of Maldon. Danegeld first paid	*Battle of Maldon* composed within twenty years
c. 996		Ælfric, *Lives of the Saints*
997		Byrhtferth of Ramsey, *Life of St Oswald* (L.) (Archbishop of York, d. 992)
c. 998		Ælfric, Latin *Grammar* in OE, *Colloquy* (L.), and Old Testament translations and paraphrases
1011		Byrhtferth of Ramsey's *Enchiridion*, scientific treatise
1013–14	Swein Forkbeard, king of Denmark, deposes Æthelræd	
1014	Æthelræd reinstated	Wulfstan, Archbishop of York, '"Wolf's" Sermon to the English' *Sermo Lupi ad Anglos*
1016	King Edmund Ironside, son of Æthelræd and Ælfgifu; defeated by (Danish) Cnut; murdered same year King Cnut; king of Denmark from 1018	
1035–7	Kingdom divided between Harold Harefoot and Harthacnut, sons of Cnut by different mothers	
1037	King Harold Harefoot	
1040	King Harthacnut	
1042	King Edward the Confessor, son of Æthelræd II and Emma of Normandy	
1066	Harold II	
1066	Battle of Hastings: William of Normandy defeats Harold	*Song of Roland* (OF) allegedly sung to the Normans before battle. Earliest record of poem dates from twelfth-century IF version
1066	William I	
1070–1	Hereward the Wake, rebellion in East Anglia	
1086	Domesday land survey completed. Oath of Salisbury: main landowners swear fealty to William	
1087	William II, son of William I	
1096–9	First Crusade. William II attends. Jerusalem stormed 1099	
1100	Henry I, son of William I	(–1125) *Gesta Herewardi*, L. translation of (lost) English account of outlaw Hereward the Wake
1125		William of Malmesbury, L. writings, including *History of the Kings of the English* and *Life of St Dunstan*
1128	First Cistercian abbey in England (order founded 1098 in reaction to Benedictine opulence)	
c. 1133		Henry of Huntingdon, *History of the English* (L.)

	HISTORY AND CULTURE	LITERATURE
1135	Stephen, Henry I's nephew, claims throne from Matilda, Henry's daughter Intermittent civil war	
c. 1137		Geoffrey of Monmouth, *History of the Kings of Britain* (L.); first sustained account of King Arthur
c. 1140		Geoffrey Gaimar, *Estoire des Engleis* (IF), includes account of Havelok the Dane
1147–9	Second Crusade	
1147		Ælred (–1167), Abbot of Rievaulx, later canonised. L. spiritual and historical works, including life of Edward the Confessor
c. 1150		Play *Mystère d'Adam* (IF) probably composed in England
1153	Treaty of Winchester (or Wallingford): Stephen retains throne, Matilda's son Henry heir	
1154	Henry II, grandson of Henry I	OE Peterborough Chronicle ends
1155	Pope allegedly grants Henry lordship of Ireland	Wace, *Roman de Brut* (IF), based on Geoffrey of Monmouth, *Roman de Rou* (c. 1160)
1159		*fl.* John of Salisbury; L. treatises on political theory (*Policraticus*) and logical arts (*Metalogicon*)
1164	Constitutions of Clarendon: Henry seeks control over Church	
1166	Assize of Clarendon: Henry lays foundation of trial by jury of English common law	
c. 1167	(–1170) Oxford halls of residence for English scholars founded; scholars previously had studied at University of Paris	*Cnut's Song, Poema morale, Proverbs of Alfred*, verses of St Godric, *Paternoster* poem (first use of extended rhyming couplets in English)
1169–71	Invasion of Ireland led by Richard of Clare ('Strongbow')	
1170	Thomas Becket murdered after years of conflict with Henry over jurisdiction of Church and state (canonised 1173)	Approximate date for *Vie d'Edouard le Confesseur* (IF) by the Nun of Barking
1174	Treaty of Falaise; William I of Scotland pays homage to Henry	
1176	Assize of Northampton further increases administration of centralised royal justice	
c. 1177		Richard FitzNigel, *Dialogus de Scaccario* (L.), on methods of government. Nigel Wireker, *Mirror of Fools* (L.), satire on manners and clerical vices
c. 1180		William Fitzstephen (L.). *Life of Thomas Becket* (includes account of London). Marie de France at English court; writes *Fables* and *Lais* (IF). Drama, *La Seinte Resureccion* (IF)
1180–6		John of Forde, *Life of St Wulfric of Haselbury* (L.) (d. 1154)
1181–92		Walter Map, *Trifles of Courtiers* (L.), satire of court life
1187	Jerusalem retaken by Saladin	
1189–92	Third Crusade	
1189	Richard I, son of Henry II; leads Crusade to Holy Land (1190)	Approximate date for *Owl and the Nightingale*
c. 1190		(–1225) Katherine Group (alliterative prose): *Seinte Marherete, Seinte Iuliene, Seinte Katerine, Sawles Warde* and *Hali Meiðhad* (MS. Bodley 34) Laȝamon's *Brut*, derived from Bede and Wace

	HISTORY AND CULTURE	LITERATURE
c. 1196–8		William of Newburgh, *History of English Matters* (L.)
1199	John I, brother of Richard	
c. 1200		Marian lyrics. Ælfric's *Grammar* transcribed Religious elegies: *The Grave* and *Soul's Address to the Body*. Geoffrey of Vinsauf, *Poetria Nova* (L.)
1202–4	Fourth Crusade	
1204–6	Philip Augustus of France retakes Normandy, Anjou and other territories	
c. 1205		*Ormulum*, metrical paraphrase of gospels; develops unique phonetic spelling system
1209	Cambridge halls of residence established	
1210		*Roman de Waldef* (IF), apparently based on an English source
1215	Pope Innocent III, Fourth Lateran Council: requires annual confession for Christians, and distinctive garb for Jews; clarifies doctrine of transubstantiation; establishes marriage as sacrament; increases penalties against heretics John signs Magna Carta, grants concessions to barons, liberties to towns Civil war; Prince Louis of France besieges Rochester	
1216	Henry III, son of John, nine years old	
1217	Jews to wear yellow badges marking alien status	
c. 1220		*Ancrene Riwle* (or *Ancrene Wisse*)
1221	Dominican (Blackfriars) order established in England; founded 1216 to combat heresy	
1224	Franciscan friars (Greyfriars) in England	
c. 1225		'Wooing Group', prose prayers to Christ: *Wohung of Ure Lauerd, On Lofsong of ure Louerde, On Ureisun of ure Louerde*
1227	Order of St Clare founded – female mendicants Henry III achieves majority	
1228–9	Fifth Crusade	
1230–1		*Genesis and Exodus* (metrical paraphrase of Old Testament books). *Vices and Virtues* (prose dialogue)
1235		*fl.* Matthew Paris, monk of St Albans, illustrated *Chronicles* (L.)
1237	Treaty of York, Anglo-Scottish borders fixed	
c. 1240	*Curia Regis* (King's Grand Council of barons and prelates) as embryonic *Parlement*	Walter Bibbesworth, *Tretiz* (IF). *Roman de Gui de Warewic* (IF)
c. 1242		*fl.* Bartholomaeus Anglicus, *De Proprietatibus Rerum* (L.) (encyclopaedic treatise)
1248–54	Sixth Crusade	
c. 1250		First English (metrical) romances: *King Horn, Floris and Blauncheflur. Physiologus* (L.), allegorical interpretation of animal natures 'Sumer is icomen in', musical round for six voices

	HISTORY AND CULTURE	LITERATURE
1258	Provisions of Oxford, Simon de Montfort attempts regulation of King's finances	
1259	Treaty of Paris. Henry III acknowledges French claim to territories in France	
c. 1260		(–1300) Robert of Gloucester, metrical chronicle of England
1264	Feast of Corpus Christi instituted	
1265	Battle of Evesham, Simon de Montfort killed	
c. 1265		Duns Scotus (–1308), Scots philosopher of logic
1270	Seventh Crusade. Prince Edward attends	
1272	Edward I, son of Henry III	
1275	First formal meeting of Parliament	Approximate date for English fabliaux, *Dame Sirith, Fox and the Wolf*
c. 1280		*South English Legendary*, versified saints' lives and miracles
1282–3	Edward invades Wales, establishes himself as ruler, proclaims son Edward Prince of Wales (1301)	
c. 1285		Hereford *Mappa Mundi*
1290	Jews expelled from England Statute (*Quia Emptores*) bars granting of new feudal rights (sub-infeudation), except by the Crown, and makes land held in 'fee simple' (fully 'owned') freely transferable	
c. 1290s?		*Of Arthour and of Merlin* (in Auchinleck manuscript), non-alliterative romance *Harrowing of Hell*, semi-dramatic verse dialogue Metrical romances: *Havelok the Dane, Arthour and Merlin, Kyng Alisaunder, Sir Tristrem, Amis and Amiloun*
1297	Battle of Stirling Bridge, William Wallace defeats Edward; Wallace defeated at Falkirk (1298), executed 1305	
c. 1300		*Cursor Mundi*, biblical poem *Lay Folks' Catechism* *Land of Cockaigne* Richard Rolle (–1349), devotional writing (L. and vernacular)
1303		Robert Mannyng of Brunne, *Handlyng Synne* (verse translation of IF penitential treatise)
1307	Edward II, son of Edward I	
c. 1310?		*William of Palerne*, early romance of Alliterative Revival. *Lay le Freine*
1314	Battle of Bannockburn, Robert Bruce defeats English; ends English control in Scotland	
1315–17	Great famine	
1320s		*The Simonie*, protest poem on the evil times of Edward II's reign
1320	Declaration of Arbroath: letter to pope from Scottish barons, declaring right to self-rule	
1326–7	Edward II deposed and murdered	Approximate date of *Bevis of Hampton*

	HISTORY AND CULTURE	LITERATURE
1327	Edward III, son of Edward II	
c. 1330		Auchinleck manuscript (London): large miscellany of religious and didactic poetry, including the *Assumption of the Blessed Virgin* and *A Pennyworth of Wit*; romances, including: *Sir Orfeo, Kyng Alisaunder, Floris and Blaunchefleur, Sir Degaré, Of Arthour and of Merlin, Horn Childe and Maiden Rimnild* Harley lyrics, large collection of lyrics, religious, amatory, satiric, political
1333		*fl.* Laurence Minot, political (particularly anti-Scots) verse
1337	Hundred Years' War begins	
1338		Robert Mannyng, *Chronicle* (translation of Peter of Langtoft's IF *Chronicle*)
1340		Dan Michel of Northgate, *Ayenbite of Inwit* (*Remorse of Conscience*), Kentish prose translation of French confessional treatise
1340		(–1370) *fl.* Dafydd ap Gwilym, Welsh poet
1344		Richard of Bury, *Philobiblon*: L. treatise in praise of books
1346	Battle of Crécy	
1348	Order of the Garter established	
1348–50	Black Death, estimated population loss at one-third to one-half	
c. 1350	First paper-mill built in England	*Pride of Life*, morality play Romances: *Tale of Gamelyn, Athelston, William of Palerne, Stanzaic Morte Arthur, Sir Isumbras, Sir Eglamour of Artois, Octavian, Sir Amadace; Lybeaus Desconus; Joseph of Arimathie*
		Richard Ledred, L. account of witch trial of Alice Kyteler, Kilkenny, Ireland
1350–1400		Romances, including *Sege of Melayne, Emaré, Sir Gowther, Sir Firumbras, Sir Degrevant, Gest Historyale of the Destruction of Troy; Erle of Tolous*
1351	Statute of Labourers fixes wages	
c. 1352		*Winner and Waster*, alliterative poem
1356	Battle of Poitiers	
1360	Treaty of Brétigny, nine-year peace between England and France	*Pricke of Conscience*, long devotional poem in rhyming couplets
c. 1360		*The Book of John Mandeville* translated from IF
1361	Black Death Jean Froissart in England (–1367)	
1362	English declared official language of law courts	Approximate date, *Piers Plowman*, A-text
c. 1370		(–1387) Geoffrey Chaucer, early writings: dream visions, translations, *Troilus and Criseyde*
c. 1373		(–1393) Julian of Norwich, *Revelations of Divine Love* (short and long versions)
c. 1374–9		John Gower, *Mirour de l'Omme* (IF)
c. 1375		*Northern Homily Cycle* being expanded from early fourteenth-century version

	HISTORY AND CULTURE	LITERATURE
1376	'Good' Parliament attempts reform of court corruption John Wyclif preaches disendowment of clergy Black Prince dies	John Barbour's (Scots) poem, *The Bruce*
1377	'Bad' Parliament, flat-rate poll tax Richard II, grandson of Edward III	Earliest record of York mystery plays Approximate date of *Piers Plowman*, B-text
1378	Great Schism (–1417), rival popes in Rome and Avignon	
1379	Income-differentiated poll tax	John Wyclif, *De Eucharistia* (L.) (on transubstantiation)
1380	Flat-rate poll tax	
c. 1380		*Cloud of Unknowing* Romances: *Apollonius of Tyre*; Thomas Chestre, *Sir Launfal; Athelston*
1381	Peasants' Revolt, now renamed Great Revolt University of Oxford condemns Wyclif's teachings	
1382		Complete translation of Bible into Middle English
1384		ME *Speculum Vitae* investigated for heresy
c. 1385		Thomas Usk (d. 1388), *Testament of Love* John Gower, *Vox Clamantis* (L.) Sir John Clanvowe, *Boke of Cupide*
c. 1386–90		John Gower, *Confessio Amantis* (ME)
1387		*fl.* John Trevisa, translates *Polychronicon* and *On the Properties of Things*
c. 1387		Geoffrey Chaucer (–1400), *Canterbury Tales*
1388	'Merciless' Parliament impeaches Richard's advisers	
c. 1390		*Piers Plowman*, C-text Alliterative *Parlement of the Thre Ages* and *St Erkenwald* Alliterative *Morte Arthure; The Awntyrs off Arthure*
1390s		*Sir Gawain and the Green Knight, Pearl, Patience, Cleanness* Vernon manuscript, compilation of earlier vernacular religious works: *Ancrene Riwle, Speculum Vitae*, Walter Hilton's *Scale of Perfection, Piers Plowman* A-text, *Northern Homily Cycle, South English Legendary* *Siege of Jerusalem*
c. 1392		Earliest mention of Coventry plays
c. 1395		*Pierce the Ploughman's Crede*
1399	Richard deposed and murdered. Henry IV, cousin of Richard II	(–1406) *Richard the Redeless* and *Mum and the Soþsegger*
c. 1400		*fl.* John Mirk, *Festial* (sermons); verse treatise, *Instructions for Parish Priests*
Early 1400s		*A Tretis of Miraclis Pleyinge*, a Wycliffite tract criticising drama *Castle of Perseverance*
1400–9	Welsh rebellion led by Owain Glyndŵr	
1401	Thomas Arundel, Archbishop of Canterbury, establishes Lollard heresy inquisitions	
1402		Thomas Hoccleve (–1421): *Letter of Cupid, Regiment of Princes*, 'Lament for Chaucer'

	HISTORY AND CULTURE	LITERATURE
c. 1404–5		Christine de Pisan, OF works, including *Cite des Dames*
c. 1405–10		*Dives and Pauper*, long prose dialogue on Ten Commandments
1409–15		*The Lanterne of Light*, anticlerical, Lollard treatise
c. 1408		*fl.* John Lydgate (–c. 1438): *Troy Book, Life of Our Lady, Siege of Thebes, Fall of Princes, Pilgrimage of the Life of Man, Mumming plays*
c. 1410		Edward, Duke of York, *The Master of Game*, hunting treatise Nicholas Love, *Mirrour of the Blessed Lyf of Jesu Christ*
1413	Henry V, son of Henry IV	
c. 1413		Margery Kempe (–c. 1439), religious experiences and writings
1414	Sir John Oldcastle, Lollard revolt; executed 1417	
1415	Battle of Agincourt	
1418		(–c. 1509) Paston letters
1420	Treaty of Troyes. Henry acknowledged Duke of Normandy and heir to French throne	
c. 1422		Earliest record of Chester plays
1422	Henry VI, son of Henry V (nine months old)	
c. 1424		James I of Scotland, *Kingis Quair*
1428–9	Joan of Arc lifts siege of Orléans; turning point of Hundred Years' War	
1431	English burn Joan of Arc as witch in Rouen	
1445		Osbern Bokenham, *Legendys of Hooly Wummen*
1449–51	English lose Normandy and Gascony	
1450	Jack Cade's rebellion	
c. 1450		*Weddynge of Sir Gawen and Dame Ragnell*, prose *Merlin*, prose *Siege of Thebes, Ipomedon, Squyr of Lowe Degree, Turnement of Totenham* *Jacob's Well*, sermon collection
1450–70		*The Prologue and Tale of Beryn*
1453	Fall of Constantinople to Turks; Eastern Roman empire ends Hundred Years' War ends; English retain only Calais	
1455	First book printed in Europe using movable lead type – the 42-line Bible, printed in Mainz, Germany, by Johannes Gutenberg (c. 1400–68)	
1455–85	Wars of the Roses	
c. 1456		William Dunbar (–c. 1513), Scots poet
c. 1460		John Skelton (–1529)
c. 1460–80		*Floure and the Leaf; Assembly of Ladies*
1461	Edward IV, House of York	
c. 1461		(–1500) Croxton, *Play of the Sacrament*
1461–82		*The Freiris of Berwik*, written in Scotland
c. 1463		Sir John Fortescue, *De Monarchia: The Difference between an Absolute and a Limited Monarchy*
1464		John Capgrave, *Chronicle of England*

HISTORY AND CULTURE		LITERATURE
1468		*N-Town* plays
c. 1470		Sir Thomas Malory, *Morte Darthur* Morality plays: *Wisdom, Mankind*
1470–1	Henry VI briefly reinstated; deposed and murdered 1471; Edward IV resumes reign	
c. 1470–90		Scots poet Robert Henryson, *Testament of Cresseid, Morall Fabillis of Esope, Orpheus and Eurydice*
c. 1473		Sir John Fortescue, *On the Governance of England*
c. 1475		Gavin Douglas (–1522)
c. 1477		Blind Harry, *The Wallace*
1477	William Caxton (c. 1420–91) introduces printing to England	Caxton's printed works (–1485) include *Reynard the Fox, Canterbury Tales, Order of Chivalry, The Golden Legend, Morte Darthur, Eneydos*
1483	Edward V, son of Edward IV, murdered Richard III, brother of Edward IV	
1485	Battle of Bosworth Field; Henry VII	
c. 1485		Towneley plays (–c. 1530). Manuscript dates from mid-sixteenth century
c. 1490		Sir David Lindsay (–1555), Scots poet
1497		Henry Medwall, *Fulgens and Lucrece*

Historical Overview

Introduction

In a charter of 1058, Bishop Ealdred granted land in Worcestershire to his minister Dodda, with reversion to the bishopric after Dodda's death (see box). The charter itself is written and signed in Latin, but instead of including a map, it describes the boundaries in OE as a survey of the metes and bounds. Such a survey requires a walkabout, and in medieval England, these walkabouts around the community's parishes were performed as public events still called today in places the 'beating of the bounds'. The purposes of such occasions were multiple: verification of local testimony, whether oral or written; affirmation of the community's spatial identity; and a chance to party. The name comes from a quite literal beating of the bounds, in which critical intersections and landmarks – trees, streams, large stones, etc. – would be whipped and beaten with sticks, as if to impress the division of the land into the earth itself. Custom alleges that the children of the parish would receive a dunking in the streams and other such untender reminders of where communities coexisted and divided; feasting, fighting and horseplay all marked occasions. In the later Middle Ages, these perambulations were often performed on Rogation Sunday in May, with prayers for blessing of people and the land itself. For a small rural parish, unable to afford dramatic spectacles such as the Corpus Christi processions of York or Coventry, perambulations such as this were an occasion for a community to celebrate its own identity in a performance as theatrical as any play (Justice, *Writing and Rebellion*, pp. 165–7 [Ci]).

An Old English Land Charter

Ðis is ðære twegra hida boc and anre gyrde æt
norðtune and ða feower æceras ðærto of ðære
styfecunge into ðam twam hidan and ða mæde.
and ðone graf ðe þærto midrihte toligeð. and
ða ðry æceras mæde on afan hamme. þe sancte
oswald geaf bercstane into ðam lande. and ðiss
synd þa land gemæro into ðam grafe. Ærost of ðære
dune andlang þære rode oð hit cymð beneoðan
stancnolle þanon ongerihte to cwenn hofoton.
of cwenn hofoton benorðon þam mere þanon
ongerihte eft up on þa dune.

[This is the charter of the two hides [of land], and
one yardland at Northtown [Norton], and the four
acres of that clearing land [belong] to the two
hides, and the meadow, and the grove that [also]
belongs to it; and the three acres of meadow in
the Avon region that St Oswald added to the land
for Bercstan. And these are the boundary lands
[belonging] to the grove: First, from the hill and
along the road until it comes beneath the stone
knoll [Bredon Hill], thence straight on to Cwenn
Hofoton [?Queenscourttown, possibly Queen Hills
Lays]; from Cwenn Hofoton north of the mere
thence straight back up to the hill.]
(Hooke, *Worcestershire Anglo-Saxon Charter Bounds*,
pp. 368–70 [Ci]; throughout this chapter,
all translations given in square brackets are my own)

Although we do not know whether the bounds of this eleventh-century charter would have been beaten in this festive way, the survey of the metes and bounds of the land performs the boundaries rather than fixing them in a static map as a cartographer would.

Secure boundaries were essential to the well-being and effective functioning of the community, for these people lived close to the land. The stealthy moving of a boundary marker could result in a legal dispute that might sunder the peace for years; Avarice or *Coueitise*, one of the seven deadly sins, enacts itself in a man who ploughs another man's strip of land into his own (Langland, C. vi.267–71 [A]). When these boundaries ran between kingdoms, it was no longer a question of litigation but of war. The horseplay by which the authority of the boundaries was forcibly impressed on children's memories (not to mention their hides) illustrates in the local and benign instance the lesson of subjection to power, a lesson learnt by entire peoples. When a ruler erected a landmark, it stood as a forceful visual reminder of his presence, a local embodiment of his power. Thus it was that Emperor Hadrian in 122 built his wall across the north of England to repel the harrying Picts in Scotland, that the Romans built Watling Street, running from Dover past London to Wroxeter near Shrewsbury (now the A2/M2 and A5 roads), that Offa built his dyke across the Welsh border, and that William the Conqueror built castles, dozens of them. As the *Anglo-Saxon Chronicle* records for 1068, when the north of England rose in rebellion against William, he directly marched on Nottingham and built a castle there, two more in York, another at Lincoln (Swanton, p. 202 [A]). The White Tower, the great central keep of the Tower of London, begun c. 1077, was in dressed stone, never used in AS England for secular buildings; small wonder that in an English commemorative poem at his death in 1087, the first line should read, 'Castelas he let wyrcean' [He caused castles to be built] (Clark, pp. 13–14 [A]; Lerer, 'Old English', pp. 15–16 [Ci]). The bounds of the White Tower's Liberties, an area under the jurisdiction of the Tower and independent of the City of London, were ritually beaten (and still are, although the practice is only ceremonial). Such an edifice and practice made authority a palpable reality, one that that left its mark on physical bodies. How did a society understand power that could stake its claim on flesh itself? If one's body was so easily subject to another, what did it really feel like in this period to be an individual, a woman, a celibate, a poet, a man, a Jew? How did one think of 'oneself' when bodily obligation was for most a daily reality? These issues are as 'historical' as the laws, taxes and battles that comprise the stuff of archives, and it is out of them that literature arises.

The Backdrop

By the time the fifth-century Germanic invaders – those tribes that gave us 'Old English' – had begun to settle in earnest, Britain had already been invaded by Caesar's Roman armies in 55 BC, who by this time were well integrated with the indigenous Celts, known as Britons. Rome abandoned formal occupation of Britain shortly after the sack of Rome in 410, a deep blow to imperial sensibility. To Christian historian Augustine of Hippo, Rome brought downfall upon itself by its own corruption, and for the later English monk Bede, the same logic led the barbarians to invade the Britons for their rebelliousness against God. A power divided within cannot withstand force from without, observes Gildas, writing in the late fifth or early sixth century (James, p. 98 [B]). Roman occupation left a sturdy material infrastructure of roads, walls, dykes and agricultural settlements that the invading Anglo-Saxons simply took over (Postan, *The Medieval Economy and Society*, pp. 10–11 [B]). Perhaps it is some of these abandoned buildings that inspire the poet of *The Wanderer* (ll. 76–7) to speak so hauntingly of 'winde biwaune, weallas stondaþ, / hrime bihrorene. Hryðge þa ederas' [wind-blown, walls stand, rime-covered, the ramparts storm-beaten] (Marsden, *The Cambridge Old English Reader*, p. 380 [A]).

In his *Ecclesiastical History of the English People*, Bede adds detail to the story of the first Germanic tribes, under the leadership of Hengest and Horsa, who were invited as mercenaries by King Vortigern, a Briton, to fight Picts in the north and Scots in Ireland. The allies soon turned invaders, and what is remarkable about their coming is the completeness of their linguistic takeover. General opinion of the numbers of the invading settlers is that they were small, perhaps a few tens of thousands – too many to repel, but themselves not enough to eradicate an indigenous population, suggesting some sort of accommodation between the Britons and the Germanic tribes (James, p. 114 [B]).

They came from different places: the Jutes apparently from 'Jutland' in northern Denmark, settling in Kent, the Isle of Wight and parts of Hampshire; the Angles from the southern part of the Danish peninsula, settling in the Midlands, comprising the East Angles (hence East Anglia), the 'west' Angles (in Mercia), and the Angles north of the Humber estuary (hence Northumbria); and the Saxons from west of the Elbe and east of the Rhine, settling in Wessex (the West Saxons), Sussex (the South Saxons), and Essex (the East Saxons). These were northern seafarers, their social organisation more purely tribal than the Franks and Goths, touched by Roman rule. These 'Germanic' tribes did not regard themselves as related, and, with differing customs and languages, they were as interested in war with each other as they were with the

1.1 Anglo-Saxon England. In this chapter, the Roman-derived name 'Britain' is used to refer to the island before the consolidation of the peoples into the Anglo-Saxons. Medieval chroniclers such as Geoffrey of Monmouth used the name in similar fashion. The legend of Arthur, not belonging to any conventional time-line, is usually set in 'Britain' also. This should not be confused with the modern usage, which refers to the political construct of a unified England, Scotland and Wales. 'England' (as distinct from Scotland or Wales) is the more frequently used term in this chapter, denoting the land ruled by Anglo-Saxon, Norman and then 'English' kings. However, the map shows the unstable, contested boundaries between the three territories in this period.

indigenous Britons. We call them 'Anglo-Saxon', splicing together the names of only the largest invading tribes, and include their related languages under the umbrella term 'Old English'.

Tacitus' *Germania*, written in the first century about the 'barbarian' hordes of the north, describes many cultural features that ring true for these late tribal settlers. Tacitus describes a rural rather than urban people; for whom war constitutes their main activity and a central source of wealth; who circulate wealth by gift-giving rather than by trade; whose kin are central to personal identity; whose king governs by the consent of the clan rather than by divine right; who decide matters by open debate and lack the bureaucratic baggage of Romanised state formation. This description tempts us to picture the Germanic tribes as more egalitarian than the later hierarchies of Norman feudalism, but as the earliest OE laws (of Æthelbert, c. 602–3) demonstrate, society was highly stratified, and more complex than the mere division into free men and slaves: *læt* denoted a class between freeman and slave; a *ceorl* (cf. modern churl) is a freeman of the lowest class; and slaves seemed to subdivide into at least three categories. The redemption value of a *ceorl*'s slave (in the event of being raped, maimed or killed) was less than that of the slave of an *ealdorman*, a much higher rank of freeman.

As ties with continental overlords loosened, the settling tribes gained increasing independence and with it more powerful kingship. The kingdoms of early AS England were multiple and fleeting. The division of them in the twelfth century by Henry of Huntington into the 'Heptarchy' (of Northumbria, Mercia, East Anglia, Essex, Kent, Sussex and Wessex) does not do justice to the complexity of the matter: Northumbria was originally composed of two distinct kingdoms, Deira and Bernicia; Kent divided into West and East Kent in the eighth century; and Mercia in the seventh and eighth centuries absorbed sub-kingdoms of the Hwicce, the Magonsæte, Middle Angles, Lindsey and Surrey. There was no sense of a united England, and kingship was a matter of local leadership. The welter of sub-kingships gradually coalesced into more substantial kingdoms, although the provincial nature of peoples did not change. Not until the eighth century can we talk meaningfully of kings such as Ine, under whose reign the term 'West Saxon' first appears, who through conquest united disparate peoples and territories into the larger AS kingdoms.

Kingship

Today, we speak of the 'monarchy' or of the 'Crown' as an abstract idea, to which belong designated powers, rights of heredity and an administrative apparatus. Being a king in earlier AS England meant being the 'first among equals', as the Latin phrase *primus inter pares* goes; it was more to do with strong leadership skills and military success than with any superior right. After the death of a strong king a kingdom's fortunes could quickly wane, as did those of Wessex once Ine died, and pre-eminence shift to another kingdom. By the middle of the eighth century, we see perhaps the first king with aggressively expansionist policies – Offa, King of Mercia. Force was only part of the reason for his success: the establishment of a new coinage; patronage

King Alfred on the English Language

Swæ clæne hio wæs oðfeallenu on Angelcynne
ðæt swiðe feawa wæron behionan Humbre ðe
hiora ðeninga cuðen understondan on Englisc
oððe furðum an ærendgewrit of Lædene on
Englisc areccean, ond ic wene ðætte noht monige
begiondan Humbre næren.

[So complete was its [scholarship's] decay in
England that very few this side of the Humber were
able to understand their services in English, or even
translate a letter from Latin to English; and I imagine
that there were not many beyond the Humber.]

(Marsden, p. 68 [A])

It's a glum scenario, but here in the Preface to his
translation of St Gregory's *Pastoral Care*, Alfred begins
to remedy the situation with an ambitious educational
programme of translating Latin classics into English: his
own translations of St Augustine's *Soliloquies*, Gregory's
Pastoral Care, Boethius' *Consolation of Philosophy* and
Psalms 1–50, and commissioned translations of Bede's
Ecclesiastical History, Gregory's *Dialogues*, and Orosius'
History against the Pagans. He also indicates that sons of
free men should learn to read English, and afterwards, if
they wish to continue in study, Latin. Setting such a high
value on vernacular literacy was a remarkable statement
in its day. Alfred and his scribes wrote in the West-Saxon
dialect of English; together they 'translated' texts not only
from Latin but also from other OE dialects. Alfred was
promoting a literary standard dialect that would serve as
the norm for all copying and writing. Such confidence in the
vernacular and vision of linguistic unity was rare at the time
in Europe and subsequently lost under Normanisation.

of monasteries placed strategically throughout his kingdom; and his physical imprint on the landscape – the long dyke along the west of Herefordshire, deterring Welsh attacks – all combined to increase his lasting influence. Whatever Offa's real aspirations, in his time he was regarded as a political groundbreaker. Alcuin, the Northumbrian scholar living in Charlemagne's court (780s), spoke warmly of Offa's attempts to reinvent Mercian kingship according to the Carolingian model. Offa influenced Alfred's law-code; he was chronicled as 'an extraordinary man' (*uir mirabilis*); and in 1014 Æthelstan bequeathed a sword to his brother Edmund Ironside that had apparently belonged to Offa (Lapidge, pp. 347–8 [B]). Strong kingship was remembered and emulated.

Power shifted over the span of the OE ascendancy from Northumbria in the seventh century, to Mercia under Offa, into the kingdom of Wessex, where perhaps the most famous king, Alfred (871–99), became, by the end of his reign, king of all Anglo-Saxons. To some extent, his vision of political unity was driven by notions of empire and of Christian kingship explicitly embodied in Charlemagne's rule; but unity also came about from the experience of having a common enemy and external threat in the Danes, also called 'Vikings', 'Northmen' or just plain 'heathens'. Their debut – the sack of Lindisfarne in 793 – was a relatively isolated incident, but it foreshadowed a devastating stream of attacks from the mid years of the ninth century onwards.

The Anglo-Saxons were poorly armed in comparison to the Vikings, and it was not until Alfred's reign that they levied significant resistance. The 'year of battles', 871, marked rock bottom for AS fortunes, after which, under Alfred's leadership, the English rallied and forced the Danes to make peace. From this time on, England was roughly bisected: AS England to the south and west and along Watling Street to Chester; the Danelaw to the north and east, occupied primarily by the Danes. The cultural price of the Danish attacks was high, and the chronicles register repeated sackings of monasteries, whose libraries and scriptoria formed the backbone of learning.

Alfred's successors made good on his gains, and the period 900–75 marks the reconquest of the Danelaw, which nevertheless retained much of its Scandinavian character at the level of language, custom and appearance. From 954 to 980 the chronicles make no mention of any Viking invasions, and it is significant that Edgar, great-grandson of Alfred, reigned during that period. He was called the 'peacemaker', suggesting that the absence of Viking activity resulted directly from his policies. Certainly the chroniclers thought so:

> Næs se flota swa rang,
> Ne se here swa strong,
> þæt on Angel cynne
> æs him gefetede
> Þa hwile þe se æþela cyning
> Cyne stol gerehte.

> [There was no fleet proud enough,
> No host strong enough,
> That it could win booty for itself
> In England, while that noble king
> Held the royal throne.]

(*Anglo-Saxon Chronicle*, 1:121 [A])

In 973, he was recrowned in Bath by Archbishop Dunstan; with its fine symbolic juxtaposition of Christian and Roman foundations, Bath invoked the notion of Christian empire. Two centuries earlier in France, Charlemagne had set such juxtapositions into play. With groundwork laid by Alfred in the ninth century, Edgar made explicit in the symbols of his investiture a theologised notion of kingship and a sovereign realm, however unstable its boundaries. Coinage, an assertion of sovereign value that one could literally hold in the hand, was recalled and reminted periodically under Edgar. Cultural as well as fiscal achievements also ensured stability and unity: the Benedictine Revival, galvanised by Dunstan, fostered a programmatic intellectual reform in the Church; gradually, England began to recover the cultural wealth it had lost during generations of sackings. At the beginning of Edgar's reign, Glastonbury was the only fully established Benedictine foundation; at its end, there were twenty-two.

Monastic reform played a crucial role in consolidating AS supremacy over the Danish threat and in enforcing internal control of power. Ælfric defends aggression as a *rihtlic gefeoht* (just war) waged 'wið ðe reðan flot-menn, oþþe wið oðre þeoda þe eard willað fordon' [against the cruel seamen or against other people who want to destroy the land] (Skeat, p. 114.708 [A]). It is easy enough to characterise the Danes as marauding thugs, but remember that *Beowulf* is set in the very lands from which these *reðan flot-menn* came. In terms of culture and geography, it is not an 'English' poem. Most likely, had it not been for the patronage by some English king (perhaps Æthelræd II in the eleventh century) of a 'skald', a Scandinavian poet, there would be no *Beowulf* in English literature.

If we measure the strength of England solely by its ability to fend off Danes, then things disintegrated quickly after the death of Edgar, who left two young sons from different mothers at a time when no fixed rules of succession were in place.

Æthelræd II, who has gone down in history as 'the Unready', failed to withstand the Danes, who, by 1013, had conquered all England, and in 1016 the monarchy passed into Danish hands with Cnut. But with many Danes now Christian, and Danish settlers thoroughly ensconced, it was less easy to demonise the Vikings as the grisly 'other', despite their negative depictions in '"Wolf's" Sermon to the English' in 1014 by Wulfstan, Archbishop of York. The need was for strong kings with administrative as well as martial skills, and these were provided by Cnut, whose reign, secured by military strength, diplomacy and legal administration, began a brief Anglo-Danish empire. For all his anti-Danish rhetoric, Wulfstan evidently cooperated with Cnut in his law- and policymaking. Cnut's queen, Emma, widow of Æthelræd, daughter of the Duke of Normandy, and mother of both an English and a Danish king, more accurately represents the complex reality of international connection than do the binary opposites offered in the poetry and sermons. Things might have turned out rather differently had not Cnut's sons died early, leaving Emma's son by Æthelræd, Edward the Confessor, as heir. On Edward's death, William of Normandy laid claim to the throne from Harold. The year 1066 saw the Battle of Hastings, the death of the current king, Harold, and the beginning of a permanent Norman occupation of England.

Hastings is looked to as the moment of Normanisation, but it was a one-day battle fought in the south-eastern corner of England. How did a handful of Normans assume power? Within ten weeks of the battle, William had been crowned, so England was his at least in name, but resistance remained for years: Hereward the Wake was only the most well known of many rebels who now welcomed those Danish fleets coming from the east. William's policy of conquest was vicious and effective. Wherever there was uprising, the Norman armies slaughtered the people and destroyed their infrastructure of livestock, fields and ploughs, thereby ensuring starvation for any survivors. When they left, they left a castle, hastily erected in wood, later made permanent in stone. Whenever William returned to Normandy, he took England's most valued men with him as hostages. Whenever he returned, he ousted English *ealdormen* and bishops to replace them with his own Norman men. Finally, he exercised bureaucratic power in the form of a massive stock-take of England's resources: the Domesday Book, completed in one year (1086), inventorying every piece of land with its monetary dues and chattels down to the last piglet.

William also set up a schematic system of obligations by which his barons and churchmen provided him with some 5,000 mounted knights on demand. This is the core of the English feudal system in its formal aspect. Royal estates under William were doubled in contrast to Edward the Confessor's holdings, and in this William strengthened the Crown against his own barons, who themselves had to be watched. In his laws, he claimed to be holding to the law of Edward the Confessor, and even though he conquered by force, there was remarkable continuity maintained with existing AS administrative and legislative structures. William, illegitimate son of a duke, understood power and the importance of bureaucratised control, even though he himself was quite illiterate. It would have made King Alfred turn in his grave.

This promise of the restoration of the laws of Edward the Confessor was reaffirmed by Henry I in his Coronation Charter of 1100. Like his father William I, Henry styled himself as a perpetuator rather than destroyer of AS custom. Conversely, Edward the Confessor is implicitly refashioned as an Anglo-Norman before his time – a political spin neatly capitalising on his Norman half (on his mother's side) and on the fact that he had spent half his life in exile in Normandy. The crisis of succession following Henry I speaks volumes about the equivocal place of women in the feudal system. Matilda (also known as Maud), named successor after Henry's sons drowned in 1120, was the rightful ruler when Henry died in 1135, yet she lost the throne to her cousin Stephen, whose mother was William's daughter. Who had the better claim – the daughter of the son of William the Conqueror or the son of his daughter? Civil war was the inevitable outcome of such an undecidable situation, resolved only in 1153 by Matilda's concession to Stephen on condition that her son Henry should succeed him as heir. The solution may have worked, but it only reinforced the underlying belief that a woman cannot be sovereign, a belief not dislodged in historical fact until four centuries later.

Henry II's reign (1154–89) is rightly regarded as a critical point in the construction of monarchy for three reasons: the assertion of the state's power over the Church (a conflict acted out between Henry himself and his archbishop, Thomas Becket); the expansion of Anglo-Norman territorial interest through inheritance of Anjou and marriage with Eleanor of Aquitaine into a vast 'Angevin empire'; and the formation of English common law, brought about as the result of strengthening centralised royal courts that ruled by legal principle, as opposed to the regional seigneurial courts that ruled by custom. The common law means just what it says – law applied commonly throughout the king's realm.

Two of Henry's sons reigned, Richard and John, though it is the latter who is remembered in political history, albeit in no complimentary way, for two things: the humiliating loss of French territories in 1204–6; and the signing of Magna Carta (1215), the charter of liberties conceded to his English barons, a document much touted as an early triumph of English democracy over despotism. In truth, its democratic influence extended primarily to baronial self-interest and barely touched the life of the little person. It belongs to the ongoing story throughout the twelfth

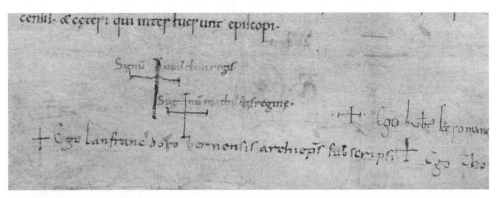

1.2 'The sign of King William' and 'the sign of Queen Matilda', marked by crosses. Detail from the Accord of Winchester 1072.

and thirteenth centuries of tension between feudal devolution of power through regional seigneurial control and the centrist tendencies of monarchy. By alienating his barons, John was unable to maintain control despite his concessions in the Magna Carta, and his reign ended in civil war. His notoriety was sealed in the later, popular Robin Hood legends, although historical evidence for the familiar story of good King Richard, bad Prince John and loyal Robin Hood is scant indeed.

Most of the rest of the thirteenth century, occupied by the long reign of Henry III, was marked at the political level by conflict between Crown and barons. Henry's relentless taxations sparked unsuccessful baronial attempts to regulate royal expenditures, and eventually the civil war known as the Barons' Revolt, which ended only with the death in 1265 of its leader, Simon de Montfort. Where the twelfth century saw England and France never before or since so closely allied, the thirteenth saw France reclaiming its territories, and Henry having to renounce his claims to Normandy and Anjou before the King of France in 1259. Although French culture continued to dominate, we note a growing sense of Englishness, measured inversely by anti-French sentiment, and resentment of the French favourites of both John and Henry.

The tensions between Crown and barons can be understood variously. On the one hand, they tell the story of the emergence of a strong, centralised monarchy through the erosion of baronial feudal privilege; on the other hand, they reveal the dangers of tyranny, held in check by that same baronial feudal privilege. The balance was struck in a parliamentary structure by which the sovereign's wishes (a euphemism for taxes to finance his latest project) had first to be ratified by the consent of his subjects. The *Curia Regis*, already in place by the mid-thirteenth century, used to serve this purpose, but under Edward I, Parliament assumed a more formal and representative aspect, including all three estates: clergy, nobility and commoners. It is from his reign that parliamentary records or *rotuli* (rolls) came to be kept, from 1272 onwards, an indication of the sense of the importance of its work.

A certain pattern seems to establish itself through the reigns of Edward I, and his son, grandson and great-great-grandson: Edward II, Edward III and Richard II, respectively, who between them reigned from 1272 to 1399. That pattern is one of oscillation between unity brought about by waging national war (Edward I and Edward III), and internal strife between king and barons (Edward II and Richard II). Its national wars indicate a growing sense of England as a sovereign kingdom; yet its internal troubles indicate that the feudal relationship between king and vassal was developing into a structure better suited to English national autonomy, one with a sovereign monarch whose power was balanced by a fully representative parliamentary system. For better or worse, feudal organisation was changing in the face of new political realities.

We look to the Peasants' Revolt of 1381 for how it articulates the political awareness of the times. Richard II, only ten on being crowned in 1377, inherited many royal headaches: France had regained most of the territories lost in the Hundred Years' War; taxation was crippling; and the demographic ravages from the Black Death (a general estimate has the casualties anywhere from one-third to one-half of the population) had created a severe labour shortage. The effect of this shortage was to empower the peasant workers, enabling them to sell their labour to the highest bidder in a market ethic that flew in the face of all feudal notions of fixed estate and domain. The Statute of Labourers (1351) attempted to restrict these opportunities by fixing earnings to pre-plague rates and reaffirming the obligation of serfs to stay on their estates. Three decades of this treatment had taken its toll, and the peasantry, already angry, was pressed past the limit with three hefty poll taxes from 1377 to 1380. John Gower's contemporary *Vox Clamantis* expresses upper-class anxiety provoked by such sedition against established authority; and it is notable how Chaucer's Ploughman pays his taxes – those taxes that drove the nation to rebellion – and would gladly work *withouten hire* if he could afford it, as if in deliberate contrast to the historical workers of 1381. Bands of them marched on London, joined by the urban poor; they burned John of Gaunt's Savoy Palace, liberated prisoners, and killed many London Flemings, immigrant wool traders who provoked deep resentment among the locals. The rebels'

Medieval Jews

Jews make their first appearance in England after William I's assumption of power, and within a generation they had settled in London, York, Bristol and Canterbury. So embedded was Christianity in public culture, their 'unbelief' made them outsiders in many ways: they were, for example, unable to participate in legal processes such as trial by ordeal or oath-taking. Barred equally from feudal vassalage, and therefore from extensive landholding, they thrived in trade and money-lending, in which latter activity they provided apt service to the Crown, the gentry and religious houses. Punitively taxed, they were a valuable source of revenue, and this, rather than theological tolerance, secured them charters of immunity. But their money-lending was always open to accusations of usury (something like loan-sharking), and their persons were vulnerable to anti-Jewish purges, which were not infrequent, even during the twelfth century, when their presence was most secure. In 1144 in Norwich came the first public accusation of the ritual murder by the Jews of a Christian child (a similar accusation in 1255 of the murder of Hugh of Lincoln providing the inspiration for Chaucer's *Prioress' Tale*). A new low was reached in 1190 in York, in Clifford's Tower, one of William I's many monuments to Norman dominion, where the Jews had gathered to take refuge from the mob outside, who offered them death or baptism. Many opted for a third solution, mass suicide, and the rest were burned or murdered. Reprisals for continued money-lending eventually resulted in wholesale expulsion from England in 1290, during Edward I's reign. The majority left, fleeing to France, and any remaining had to convert.

rage was also vented on manorial records of feudal obligations to their overlord, a gesture that says much about where their real discontent lay.

Although the eye of the storm was in London, there were uprisings in York, Scarborough and Beverley in northern England, and in Bury St Edmunds, Norfolk and St Albans in eastern England. Several of the rebels' slogans appear in sermon literature prior to 1381, suggesting a literature of protest that went higher up the social scale than the rural peasantry to include small landowners, craftsmen and lesser clergy. By convention, we call the rebellion the 'Peasants' Revolt', although the name ignores the role of these other social groups, for which reason historians now refer to it as the 'Great Revolt'. John Ball, one of the leaders, was himself a priest. Not least, the citing of *Piers Plowman* by the rebels gives an unusually direct example of convergence between literature and politics (Dobson, pp. 380–1 [A]). The chroniclers record the famous slogan of the crowd: 'Whan Adam dalf, and Eve span / Wo was thanne a gentilman?' This class-conscious challenge to the hereditary system of estates ideology was roundly rebuffed by Richard's reassertion of the destiny of blood: 'Rustics you were and rustics you are still; you will remain in bondage, not as before but incomparably harsher' (Dobson, pp. 374, 311 [A]).

On Friday 14 June 1381, King Richard met the rebels at Mile End, who pledged their allegiance to Richard, and petitioned for the following privileges: the abolition of villeinage, labour services based on free contracts, and the right to rent land at fourpence an acre. Richard acceded. The rioters, however, were neither well organised nor disciplined. That same day, some of them entered the Tower of London and executed the man held responsible for the poll tax, Simon of Sudbury, Archbishop of Canterbury and Chancellor. Having either sated their anger or sensed that they had gone too far, many subsequently dispersed.

The next day, Richard met the Kentish rebels at Smithfield. Their demands had by now taken a form bound to fail: an end to all lordship (lay and ecclesiastical) save that of the King and a prelate, and that the Church's estates be returned to the people. Once more, however, the King agreed. Things turned tense when Wat Tyler, the rebel leader, who had spoken insolently to the King, was killed by one of Richard's attendants. Outright hostilities seemed inevitable, but Richard persuaded the rebels to disperse and granted them pardon.

London was quiet again, but not the same. Were the King's promises made simply to buy time, or was there a common bond between the King and his humbler subjects? The bloody reprisals and revocations over the subsequent months of all agreements and pardons would suggest the former; yet Richard throughout his reign would find that his pesky barons were in a real sense an enemy shared by king and commons. It is also difficult to gauge the extent of the punishments: judicial records show little evidence of mass reprisals; yet the contemporary chronicles (admittedly, never given to impartiality or understatement) record retribution on thousands of offenders, real and suspected. Although the Revolt was thoroughly squashed, no poll tax was again imposed on the peasantry, subsequent legislation allowed some flexibility in wage levels and serfdom declined rapidly thereafter.

The fifteenth century has traditionally been fashioned as one of transition, too late to be fully medieval, too early to be early modern. In 1415, Henry V won an important victory at Agincourt against the French, but it was a moment that still looked backward to the preoccupations of the fourteenth century. By 1453, France had reclaimed everything except Calais, and England was sucked into a dynastic civil war between Lancastrian and Yorkist claimants to the throne, all descendants of Edward III, all claiming prior birthright. Defining national identity in relation to France no longer made the sense it once had. The English language flourished within administration, scribal culture and, by the end of the century, print culture. The mounted knight, a figure that in earlier centuries symbolised both military might and manorial law, was a waning force on the fifteenth-century battlefield, where infantry and cannon were on the rise. Baronial monopoly was giving way to an upwardly mobile class of merchants and burghers with aspirations to gentrification. What England needed was centralised leadership, and its civil strife registered that need acutely. When Henry Tudor won the crown from Richard III at Bosworth in 1485, he effectively ended the Wars of the Roses, and, in the eyes of posterity, the Middle Ages. It would be a mistake to think that Henry VII was somehow a modern 'Renaissance' man in

1.3 Wat Tyler killed by Lord Mayor Walworth in front of Richard II. Note that the manuscript itself dates from nearly a century after the events depicted. *Chroniques de France et d'Angleterre.* S. Netherlands, c. 1460–80.

contrast to his royal predecessors; he was as interested as they in renewing the war with France, and his energies were also absorbed in repressing rebellion, this time from Yorkist sympathisers and pretenders to the throne. The historical forces changing England went deeper than any one man's vision of the future. True, we have considered a period where political theory explicitly defined itself in relation to that one man, the sovereign king, but political theory – the very notion of what it meant to be an English subject – was itself in the act of change.

Feudalism and Social Status

The *Colloquy* of Ælfric of Eynsham, dating from the last quarter of the tenth century, is a schoolroom exercise written in Latin to teach Latin conversation and vocabulary to the young scholar. Cast for a number of parts, the *Colloquy* ranges through the lives of a monk, ploughman, baker, cook, shoemaker, hunter, shepherd, oxherd, merchant, fisherman, fowler, salter, blacksmith and a counsellor. At some point in the mid-eleventh century, a scribe inserted the English words above the Latin words as an interlinear gloss – an indication of the loss of Latinity in his readers. It is these *ad hoc* prompts that got lifted out of the context of their manuscript, arranged into plausible OE syntax by nineteenth-century philologist Henry Sweet, and offered to students of OE literature as a 'vernacular' composition (Scragg, 'Secular Prose', pp. 274–5 [Ci]).

A classroom exercise, the *Colloquy* nonetheless raises questions worthy of Plato's *Republic*. What makes a society? What is its most important profession? What is the ideal balance between autonomy and social obligation? The *Colloquy* portrays an essentially rural economy, with the ploughman as the embodiment of rural labour: because he is unfree, he is legally bound to the land and his labour is his obligatory service to his lord. No less busy, but with a degree more self-determination, are the craftsmen. 'Labour' does not properly describe the merchant's trade, for instead of producing he invests, buying goods at a low price and selling them at a higher. Over and above the secular occupations, the *Colloquy*'s counsellor judges the life of the monk to be the most superior, for service to God is the highest calling. Ælfric's dialogue asserts the interdependence of the occupations, and exhorts everyone to do their job gladly 'swa mæsseprest, swa munuc, swa ceorl, swa kempa' [whether priest, monk, peasant or soldier] (Garmonsway, p. 41 [A]), and not to desire another's position – reflecting a political theory of society that seeks to conserve rather than change the status quo, that presents its model as an achieved ideal rather than as a dynamic, ongoing process.

We have here an embryonic division of society into groups that subsequently came to be known as the three estates: those who pray, those who fight, and those who labour, the king himself overseeing all. Honorius of Autun in the twelfth century gives these divisions ideological justification by deriving them from Noah's three sons: from Shem come freemen (*liberi*); from Japhet, knights (*milites*); and from Ham, serfs (*servi*). As late as the fourteenth century, *Piers Plowman* pictures the same social order that Ælfric delineates (Langland, B.Prol.116–22 [A]).

Even at this point in the tenth century, the division of labour into churchman, fighter and worker was too simple a model to describe the complexities of English economy – for example, the description of a merchant as a labourer is deeply misleading – yet its broad strokes well sum up categories that both produced social cohesion and generated tension between its elements: the Church, whose interests often conflicted with those of the state and whose privilege was resented by the peasant class; the military, an essential resource in defence and the maintenance of law and order; and the huge number of labourers needed to cultivate the land, the backbone of the economy.

AS England was already shaped into large estates, often following old tribal contours, and worked by unfree labourers; the inequity between landed nobility or rich monasteries and impoverished serfs was no Norman invention. Moreover, the exchange of military service in lieu of land was also a staple of the Anglo-Saxon *fyrd* (army). The linkage William I established after 1066 between land tenure and military service was not new, just more systematic than what was in place before; and the personnel had changed from AS *ealdormen* to Norman tenants-in-chief.

What was different was the kind of elite warrior. The Battle of Hastings has been regarded as the best infantry of Europe (the English) fighting the best cavalry of Europe (the Normans). The increasing dependence on horsed soldiers required adapted armour and weaponry, and the image of the axe-wielding OE *huscarl* on foot as the king's elite fighter came to be replaced by the Norman knight on horseback. William's immediate vassals supplied him with these armed and mounted knights in exchange for lands. The *Anglo-Saxon Chronicle* for 1086 recounts the knighting of William's son (Henry I), but simply uses the OE phrase *to ridere* (as a mounted soldier) (Clark, p. 9 [A]); in time, and in order to indicate the new order of special military servant, the general OE word *cniht* (youth) became imbued with distinctive social meaning to denote a 'knight'.

The Domesday survey divided England into knights' fees, each of which represented a unit of land considered sufficient to support one mounted and armed knight. There never was a sense of the fee as a standard unit of measurement, but six hundred acres might be taken as the roughest of guides. The barons, who held monster estates containing many knights' fees, themselves then sub-let their lands to men of lesser rank, and that process, called 'subinfeudation', continued down to the poorest free men, beneath whom remained only bondmen, unfree serfs who, along with livestock, buildings and tools, were chattels of the estate. This is the so-called feudal pyramid, with the king at the apex, followed by a narrow band of barons, and continuing down the social scale of lesser landholders to the wide base, the majority of the population, the bondmen. The baronial class of great landowners, roughly equivalent to the OE class of *ealdorman*, or 'earl' (in the eleventh century) was too small to be an estate in itself; so together with the lesser landowners, they constituted a hereditary class of knights, the second estate, below whom the free peasants, even prosperous ones, existed in a world apart – the third estate.

No doubt this structure arose out of the need of William, a foreigner with no command over English hearts, for an organised system of devolved military control. But it would be overstating the case to describe the story of Norman feudalism as the story of war. The elegance of the feudal scheme fused agrarian economy not only to

Demography of England, c. 1200

In 1200, England had an estimated population of about 4 million, with an average life expectancy of about twenty-five years, someone in their forties being considered old. About 80 per cent of that 4 million comprised the 'third estate', the tenant farmers, labourers and serfs along with their families who worked the land and lived outside the towns in small villages scattered throughout England. The remaining 20 per cent accounted for everyone else – the nobility (the 'second estate'), the religious (the 'first estate') and the townsfolk. Although many new towns were founded in England between 1100 and 1300 – some 140 or so – most were small. Even London at its strength before the Black Death never rose above 100,000. As a result of the founding of monastic orders in the twelfth century, 1200 saw some 700–800 monastic communities throughout England. In addition, there were the numerous parish priests and chaplains who constituted the secular clergy. The religious orders comprised some 2 per cent of the entire population. The term 'baron' is an elastic one, but might be supposed to refer to some 250 men in the early 1200s, who were the large landholders and of noble birth. Beneath them come the knightly class of some thousands, a group that could contain men barely richer than well-off peasants and those whose wealth exceeded that of the poorer barons.

(Given-Wilson, pp. 5–6 [B]).

military control but also to legal and political governance. On continental Europe as well as England, the lord's manorial estate became the 'component cell' of society, the state itself in miniature (Postan, p. 87 [B]). The manorial estate contained both the lord's personal dwelling along with its 'demesne' lands, and land rented out to tenants, semi-free and unfree, whose involuntary obligations ensured cultivation of the land. The business of civil governance – resolving disputes about boundaries, securing the lord's permission to marry or bequeath property, a contested inheritance, land conveyance – all such matters were conducted in the manorial courts and juries. The land held together the two estates of those who laboured and those who fought.

Governing estates as extensive as those of the barons, the Church fitted neatly enough into this feudal scheme. Although early Norman churchmen, such as William's half-brother Odo, Bishop of Bayeux, were themselves fighters, and although some military orders, such as the Knights Templar and Hospitaller, had presence in England, the Church for the most part kept a distance from military obligation, which was easily commuted to money payments, with which the king could hire mercenaries. Thus the Church assumed an independent place in society, the estate of those whose labour was prayer, according to the Latin tag *orare est laborare*.

The fisherman in Ælfric's *Colloquy* remarks that he sells his fish in the cities, and when we remember that William I ruled that trading of livestock could only be conducted in the cities (*English Historical Documents*, 2:399, §5 [A]), we see the essential connection between urban life, mercantilism and cash; hence the distinctive role that cities played in this largely agrarian economy. The German saying *Stadtluft macht frei* (city air makes one free) testifies to the special legal position cities later held in the feudal scheme, with their free citizenry, exemption from tenurial labour, trade guilds and self-government; a serf who fled to the town was said to have gained his freedom after a year and a day, and was not obliged to return to the manor.

Since military service lay so close to the heart of the feudal relation, it becomes at once apparent that woman holds an uneasy position in this schema, for if she cannot promise military service, how can she in the fullest sense inherit? In reality, women routinely inherited, but their position was always in some sense indirect. When she inherited, her husband did homage to the king for her land. Cnut's law (c. 1023) stipulated that 'neither a widow nor a maiden is ever to be forced to marry a man whom she herself dislikes' (*English Historical Documents*, 1:429, §74 [A]); by 1100, Henry I in his Coronation Charter declared that if an unmarried woman inherits as daughter the lands of her baron father, 'I will dispose of her in marriage and of her lands according to the counsel given me by my barons' (2:401, §3). The phrasing is subtly different, and points to a diminishment in the position of women in post-Conquest England. It is ironic that rules of inheritance during the twelfth and thirteenth centuries should have affected noblewomen more adversely than it did peasant women; the more land at stake, the more conservative the law-making and the less latitude she had. For an aristocratic woman, her identity was in the most fundamental legal and economic sense mediated through that of her father or husband.

The heyday of the manorial estate occurred during the twelfth and thirteenth centuries, but after the mid-fourteenth century, the system dissolved rapidly. The reason for this was in part an increased need for ready cash among manorial lords.

By leasing their lands to free workmen rather than by supporting serfs, they could generate money; and hired workers motivated by cash bought a better quality of service on demesne lands than did serfs performing the same labour as their tenurial obligation. The Statute of *Quia Emptores* (1290) enabled greater freedom of land conveyance, and thereby implicitly severed the tenure of land from any personal relationship between lord and vassal, marking an increasing monetisation of social relations. The labour shortage in the fourteenth century rapidly sped up the dissolution of manorial power, for the massive workforce of unfree peasants – on which the manorial system wholly depended – was no longer as readily available to the lord for the maintenance of his estate. The centralising movement of law and administration also sapped the energy of the manor as a political entity. The economic shape of England was changing, and although the three estates continued to be invoked as late as 1483 at the opening of Parliament (Given-Wilson, p. 181 [B]), anyone who stopped to think about it must have wondered about its usefulness as any real picture of society.

A more realistic sense of societal divisions comes from the wealth categories determined by the graduated poll tax of 1379 (*English Historical Documents*, 4:125–6 [A]), the diversity of which suggests that the classification of a large proportion of society in terms of military function no longer fitted social reality. Fighting was turning into an occupation just like any other, no longer the (perceived) *raison d'être* of an entire estate, no longer the cornerstone of an economy we call feudal. Chaucer's presentation of the Canterbury pilgrims in the *General Prologue* seems to fall into the bipartite division between 'gentles' (ending with the Franklin) and 'commons' (beginning with the Guildsmen) (Morgan, pp. 291–2 [Ci]), and the division shows how the lines between second and third estate were blurring at the edges, and how class antagonisms, motivated by money, were fracturing the supposedly integrated third estate. In relation to the orthodox disposition of society into three estates evident in *Piers Plowman* or books 3 and 4 of Gower's *Vox Clamantis*, Chaucer's motley pilgrims represent more contemporary class interests that were fast turning estates ideology into an antiquated model.

The Church

Christianity offered the petty AS kings a theory of authority in which hierarchy became divinely sanctioned, a model of sovereignty that combined Romanised political theology with Germanic tribal leadership into a powerful hybrid. It also brought writing, and the bureaucratic control that it promised. Motives for conversion ranged from sincerity to expediency; the progress of Christianity in AS England is inextricable from achieving dominion within local kingdoms and subjugation of competing 'pagan' kingdoms. When Oswald, first OE royal saint, stood sponsor to Cynegisl, King of the West Saxons in 635, his spiritual motives doubtless had a political agenda: Christian alliances to contain the power of pagan King Penda of Mercia.

Christianity did not democratise AS social structure. Slavery remained common after Christianisation, and the main reason for its disappearance was that it became more economically viable to have peasants who fed themselves (or starved) than to keep slaves, who lived at the owner's expense. Although wealthy *ealdormen* and kings frequently in their wills granted land to the Church and 'freedom' to their slaves, that freedom meant little more than changing from being slaves of ealdormen into serfs of bishops. The endowment of these large estates for religious foundations was particularly prevalent, so much so that by the eleventh century the Church was in possession of possibly as much as one-third of England's occupied surface (Postan, p. 86 [B]). The fact that these lands were held in perpetuity (and therefore could not be wrested back by the king or his successor) indicates the might of the Church and explains the later tense relations between it and the state.

The connection between Church and state ran deep throughout the AS period, and, as a result, so did the bond between the papacy and the English kings. Churchmen sat alongside laymen in the king's council and at all levels of law and administration. Heavily involved in missionary work (first in England and then on the Continent) and charity, the Church may have commanded more respect and less satire than it did in the later Middle Ages, although we glimpse another side of the story in King Edgar's rebuke to the clergy in 969 for their decadence and penchant for the low-brow entertainment of actors (L. *histriones*) and entertainers (L. *mimi*) (Davidson, p. 10 [A]).

This mingling of church and state business changed considerably under William I, who replaced Stigand, Archbishop of Canterbury, with his own man Lanfranc, who in turn replaced many AS church leaders with Normans. Lanfranc was as interested in separate jurisdictions for Church and state as was his king. Bishops ceased to sit on the local courts of justice and assumed sole authority over suits that concerned the rule of the soul; this was the first and formative step in the establishment of full ecclesiastical courts. The 'Writ of William I Concerning Spiritual and Temporal Courts' (c. 1072) set forth the guidelines whereby ecclesiastical business was taken out of the civil and criminal courts. The English judicial system would not be a unified body again until the sixteenth century. The separation was agreeable to king and Church alike, giving each autonomy.

But what happened when the two did not cooperate? The stand-off between Thomas Becket, Archbishop of Canterbury, and Henry II illustrated the tensions implicit in the relationship between Church and state. With the Constitutions of Clarendon (1164), Henry II subjugated the authority of church law to secular by requiring clerics to answer summons to appear before the king's court as well as the ecclesiastical court. To Becket this amounted to double jeopardy, being tried twice for the same offence, and he opposed it forcibly. Not even Becket's martyrdom and Henry II's public repentance enabled the pope to reverse entirely the shift of power represented by the legislation of 1164.

Papal authority was at its strongest from the late eleventh century to the early thirteenth, its most powerful assertion of authority seen in the Fourth Lateran Council of 1215. The effects of the Council were felt immediately in many aspects of life. For example, it forbade ecclesiastical participation in the ordeal, one of the main ways in which legal evidence was attained. Without an officiating priest, there could be no ordeal, and its loss from English law directly resulted in the increased use of the jury, which remains with us today. The gradual decline of papal authority in England had

most to do with an increasing nationalisation of the Church, which itself
depended on the powerful administrative bureaucratic structures put
in place by the twelfth-century monarchs, Henrys I and II most especially.
It is too easy to attribute the power of
the Church simply to the greed and
political aspirations of prelates. If the
Church as a political institution was
as self-serving as the state, it also was
the patron of some of the most beautiful art and architecture in England.
If political tensions between Church
and Crown mark the twelfth and
thirteenth centuries, so also does
religious revival, and the foundation of many religious communities
and monastic orders – Cistercian,

1.4 Henry II argues with Thomas Becket. From Peter of
Langtoft's *Chronicle of England*, c. 1300–25. Note that
the manuscript itself dates from about 150 years after
the events depicted.

Carthusian and, later, Dominican and Franciscan. Instead of inhabiting the already
richly monastic area of the Severn Valley, many of these new establishments sought
an ascetic life in the remotest places of England. The north, not yet recovered from
William I's purges, offered ideal locations for retreats such as Rievaulx Abbey.

Shaping everybody's business – their working week, familial and sexual relations, pocket and diet – the Church intervened in all aspects of life … and death.
The Norman separation of jurisdiction between secular and ecclesiastical law may
suggest that the Church took care of sins and the state took care of crimes, but the
Church's control extended into anything pertaining to the care of the soul, including
family law and the probating of wills. For reasons as economic as they were spiritual,
dying intestate was as shameful and dangerous as dying unconfessed, because it left
possessions vulnerable to the three interested claimants: the Church, the overlord
and the family. Will-making and distribution of gifts were understood as part of the
art of dying well. Indeed entire 'arts of dying' (*artes moriendi*) were written to prepare
the sinner for the hereafter.

As the distinction between secular and ecclesiastical law blurred, will-making
had become largely a matter of secular law by the sixteenth century. Yet medieval
wills attest to the powerful presence of the Church when thoughts turned to death.
Custom required that most of a person's chattels be distributed to the remaining
spouse and offspring, perhaps one-half or three-quarters. The remaining 'dead man's
part' was considered one's own, to bequeath as one wished. To whom did it go? Not
to the cat, but to funeral services, candles, tomb, masses and prayers, to the repair
of common roads and charitable works, and to the upkeep and beautification of the
church. In 1417, Thomas Broke of Holditch, Thorncombe, Devon, wealthy enough to
have bequeathed £100 to the blind and lame, wants no coffin for himself but just a
'grete Clothe to hely [cover] my foule Caryin [corpse]' to be buried under a 'flat playne

stone', so that people will step on the engraved gravestone entering the church and say a prayer for him (Furnivall, p. 27 [A]). What is striking is the public nature of religious devotion, the commitment to charitable acts and the way in which individual death was experienced as a communal event.

Such piety, and on such a widespread scale, represents a challenge to the modern reader in terms of imaginative sympathy. It can perhaps best be understood by the extent of the opposite passions it aroused in late medieval England. The demands of the rebels in 1381 spoke volumes about the intensity of anticlerical feeling at grass-roots level of the population.

The Church struck back against anti-ecclesiastical critique, identifying and punishing an unusual phenomenon in medieval England – heresy, or as the contemporaries called it, Lollardy. The origins of Lollardy lie in the writings of John Wyclif in the 1370s, whose call for the disendowment of corrupt clergy initially sounded as music in the ears of an impoverished royal government. But further teachings against church lordship and its right to possessions, and then against the Eucharistic doctrine of transubstantiation itself, managed to offend all dignitaries in some way. The 'Earthquake Council' of 1382 judged many points of Wyclif's teaching heretical, yet it continued to spread at all levels of society. So widespread and sustained was Lollardy that it embodies much more than Wyclif's teachings alone. It represents a massive proliferation of vernacular theological prose, an expansion of lay literacy, and an involvement of the laity in theological debate. Although the Peasants' Revolt of 1381 was driven by its own economic agenda, it is clear that Wycliffite objection to the mediation of the Church and the rebels' call for the overthrow of lesser lords belonged to the same community of political dissent. Seeing to it that such dissent was caricatured as the grossest acts of impiety, chronicler Henry Knighton recounts how two Lollards in the 1380s subjected a statue of St Katherine to their own version of the ordeal by fire by chopping her into firewood to boil cabbages (Knighton, pp. 294–9 [A]). For the devout, who often felt a personal connection with particular saints and statues, such an action must have seemed like martyrdom all over again.

Political critique and theological dissent were hard to distinguish in these decades, and with the Lollard inquisition spearheaded by Thomas Arundel, Archbishop of Canterbury, treason and heresy were elided. After Sir John Oldcastle's failed rising of 1414, it became impossible to be both a Lollard and respectable; yet the writings and intellectual legacy would live on into the next century to provide a receptive host for the Protestant reformist ideas entering England from continental Europe.

Literary Overview

Language

England's physical and linguistic contours go hand in hand, with rivers such as the Humber (as in 'Northumbria') and the Thames providing political boundaries, maintaining the integrity of the different tongues, and creating the differing OE dialects.

Northumbrian was the first dialect in which early literature flowered, and it contains our first written record of OE poetry. Bede records in 731 how Cædmon, a worker in the monastery of Whitby, Yorkshire, was inspired with the gift of composing religious poetry in Germanic heroic alliterative verse (Bede, IV.24, pp. 414–17 [A]). Bede records Cædmon's hymn in Latin, and apologises for the 'loss of beauty and dignity' in the translation – a comment in itself on the prestige of the vernacular. Later scribes inserted the Northumbrian words into the margins of Bede's text, although most of the surviving manuscripts standardised the Northumbrian into West Saxon.

If we can be guided by Bede's account, poetic composition was a spontaneous, communal production, and poetic performance frequent. The *scop* or poet was often simply the man who had the harp in his hands and the best story to tell. What made OE verse so easy to extemporise was its alliterative quality, with its formulaic phrases, compound words and circumlocutions (kennings) – all flexible units of thought, capable of endless variation, which the poet recited from memory. Much harder to compose, end-rhyme, in contrast, yields fewer verbal options. Other metrical features lent themselves to extemporisation: repetition through alternative epithets, adaptable line-length with its unfixed syllabic count, and unalliterated last stress, which gives a conversational quality – all such made poetry come 'naturally' to an essentially oral community; and in each recitation the poem changed subtly, an endlessly mobile expression of the mood of the moment. Paradoxically, it is writing that gives us our only access to that oral poetry, and the act of committing a poem to the page inevitably fixes and alters it. Transcription also brings its own kind of experimentation; in the Exeter Book (later tenth century), we find the *Rhyming Poem*, the only pre-Conquest example of sustained end-rhyme in English, and evidence that the opposition between (English) alliteration and (French) end-rhyme is too reductive. By Chaucer's time, the awareness of poetry as something to be read as much as it was to be heard is discernible in his 'eye rhyme' between 'Rome' and 'to me' (Chaucer, I.671–2 [A]).

Where does OE end and ME begin? The answer lies in a confluence of factors: Frenchification of

---

Old English Poetic Metre

A strict metrical protocol differentiates alliterative verse from the (still rhythmic) alliterative prose that is ubiquitous in OE (and later) literature: medicinal recipes, wills, land charters, laws and sermons. The OE alliterative unit, which can contain any number of syllables (rather than a set number of feet or syllables), determines the shape of the poetic line, which falls into two half-lines, each containing two stressed sounds. The first stressed syllable of the second half-line provides the alliterative (and often semantic) key for the line, while the second stressed syllable of the second half-line never alliterates: 'Syllic wæs se sigebeam, and ic synnum fah' (Wondrous was the victory-cross, and I stained with sins) (*Dream of the Rood*, l. 13 [A]). The rules of alliterative variation were categorised into different metrical types (Scragg, 'The Nature of Old English Verse' [Ci]) although a more basic key to the metre is provided in the following mnemonic, where the underlined letters mark the stressed words in the two half-lines (Alexander, p. 62 [B]):

One or other | of the opening stresses
Must alliterate | with the leading syllable
In the second half-line; | sometimes both do,
In triple front-rhyme; | the fourth is different.

English; grammatical simplification of OE; and the point by which tenth-century writing is largely unintelligible to later medieval readers. These points occurred at different times in different parts of England, and at different paces among the different levels of society, creating a long period of transition that stretched to the end of the twelfth century.

OE was already changing before the arrival of the Normans. Danish – with its initial *sk-* and final *-g* sounds – had already influenced spelling and vocabulary in the northern dialects. Most particularly, OE was slowly losing its inflectional structure, a process accelerated by the Norman Conquest, which, by dislodging West Saxon as the scribal linguistic standard, returned OE to its regional diversity and local spellings. The result, notes Trevisa in the fourteenth century, was a lamentable hotch-potch of 'straunge wlafferynge, chiterynge, harrynge, and garrynge grisbayting' [strange stammering, jabbering, snarling, and teeth-gnashing chattering] (Babington, 2:159 [A]).

Loss of OE case-endings resulted in two main changes: fixed word order to clarify relationships between (now uninflected) subjects and objects, and a proliferation of prepositions now needed to denote relationships between nouns. Verbs such as OE *weaxan* (to grow) simplified by generally forming their past tense with an *–ed* suffix, and adjective case-endings generally simplified into an undifferentiated *–e*. The *Anglo-Saxon Chronicle* charts the quick deterioration of the suffix for the phrase 'in this year': *on þisum geare* (in 1083), *on þison geare* (1116), *on þis geare* (1122), *on þis gær* (1140) (Clark, pp. 7, 38, 41, 57 [A]). The same erosion occurred in grammatical gender, which was fast turning into the natural gender we now observe; and in plurals, which today we form by simply adding an *s*, although a few forms retain some of the complexity of the OE system – mouse/mice (mūs/mȳs), foot/feet (fōt/fēt), ox/oxen (oxa/oxan).

But the most radical change was undoubtedly the systematic unseating of English by Insular French as the language of legal and historical record. The twelfth-century anchorite (a hermit living in an enclosed cell) Wulfric of Haselbury, having miraculously healed a mute, incurred the anger of his priest Brictric, who complained that Wulfric had blessed a stranger with French but withheld it from him, his servant, whose humble English was itself a kind of dumbness (John of Forde, p. 115 [A]). By the late thirteenth century, however, Robert of Gloucester expresses a beginning sense of the possibilities of English.

> Vor bote a man conne frenss me telþ of him lute
> Ac lowe men holdeþ to engliss, and to hor owe speche ȝute
> Ich wene þer ne beþ in al þe world contreyes none
> Þat ne holdeþ to hor owe speche, bote engelond one
> Ac wel me wot uor to conne boþe wel it is
> Vor þe more þat a mon can, þe more wurþe he is
>
> [For unless a man knows French, people think little of him. But low men stick still to English, to their own tongue. I think that in all the world there are no countries except England that keep to their own speech. But it is well known that it is good to know both, for the more a man knows, the worthier he is.]
>
> (Wright, *The Metrical Chronicle of Robert of Gloucester*, p. 544; ll. 7542–7 [A])

Written English continued to flourish in monasteries, where scribes copied OE homilies for liturgical and educational purposes. The poetry that does survive reflects this religious, gnomic sensibility (*Poema morale, Pater-Noster Poem, Proverbs of Alfred*, verses of St Godric) (c. 1167); yet as *Cnut's Song* attests, religious singing could inspire any kind of poetic composition.

> Merie sungen ðe muneches binnen Ely
> Þa Cnut ching reu ðer by
> Roweþ cnites noer the lant
> And here we þes muneches sæng.
> [Merrily sang the monks in Ely when Cnut the king rowed by. 'Row, knights, near the land, and let's hear the monks sing there.']
>
> (Fairweather, *Liber Eliensis*, p. 182 [A])

Cnut then apparently composed a song on the spot, as the record says. That this was the sole stanza the writer chose to record says much about how little English poetry was recorded. Yet at the oral level it was creatively absorbing French into its structure and rhythms. French words flooded into English, the period of greatest borrowing being 1200–1350. Under the influence of IF spelling conventions, OE consonant clusters shifted to the now familiar forms: *fn–* (*fnastian*, sneeze) to *sn–*; *hw–* (*hwæt*) to *wh–* (what), and *hl–* (*hleahtor*, laughter) to *l–*. Middle English was refashioning itself out of languages that had thrown shadows over English for centuries (Cannon, p. 70 [Ci]).

In contrast to Modern English, OE and ME have unique status as vernaculars, for the true language of prestige was Latin. To learn grammar was to learn Latin grammar, leaving it more the wonder that OE could attain the complexity, elegance and stability it did without any formal structural rule. Ælfric's *Grammar* (c. 998) – a Latin grammar but written in OE – is a precocious achievement in the history of European vernaculars, for we know of no other such attempt until centuries later. For the grammatical term preposition (*præpositio*), literally meaning 'placed before', Ælfric translates *foresetnyss* (Zupitza, pp. 10.15 [A]); for interjection (*interiectio*), something 'thrown between', he translates *betwuxaworpennyss* (pp. 10.20–11.1), managing in this way to echo Latin even as he creates a new word in English. These 'translations' of the constituent parts of a word are called calques, and OE is full of

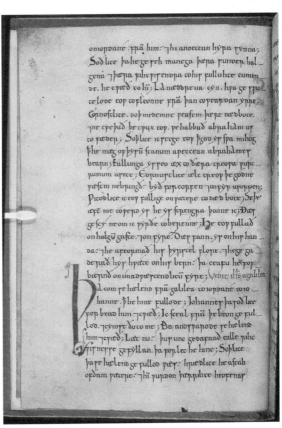

1.5 The West-Saxon Gospel. 1000–50. Translation of Matthew 3.13.

them, a measure of the language's imitativeness and creativity: *eorþcræft* (geo-metry), *wiþsprecan* (contra-dict), *godspel* (*evangelium* or 'good news').

However, Ælfric's confidence as translator falters somewhat when it comes to translating the Old Testament, for a vernacular translation reveals both too much truth and not enough. The Old Testament needs to be explained and a translation can only translate – it cannot paraphrase, gloss or expound. How then can full meaning be communicated in translation? How can English recreate the verbal density of Latin? Latin, for Ælfric, is already a *menigfeald* tongue, with 'manifold' meaning. He understands 'ðæt Leden and ðæt Englisc nabbað na ane wisan on þære spræce fadunge' [that Latin and English never have exactly the same idiom (Marsden, p. 263 [A])], and so he attempts to echo the Latin in OE. Ælfric's vernacular is more wordy, repetitive and plainer than his Latin, as if English itself is qualitatively different from Latin, a language of concreteness and of surface that must recreate Latin's close texture as verbal volume, its depth as breadth.

It is ironic that one could be commanded to translate the Bible into English in the eleventh century, yet burned for doing so in the fifteenth. It was going to be three centuries before the Bible would be translated into English again and Latin taught through English. In 1485, John Trevisa observes how 'in alle þe gramere scoles of Engelond, children leueþ Frensche and construeþ and lerneþ an Englische' (Babington, 2:161 [A]). It is possible that Chaucer learned Latin through English and that Langland was himself a grammar master, teaching schoolboys to construe between English and Latin, possibly with absurd sentences like the following:

> I saw þe drunkyn while þu were sobere
> Ego vidi te ebrius dum fuisti sobrius

> (Orme, p. 50 [A])

The moral is to follow Latin agreement rather than its word order, for the English sentence ought to read: 'I drunken saw thee while thou wast sober.' In such exercises, the schoolboy understands that English and Latin have different shapes; that Latin can delay meaning by putting the verb at the end of the sentence, while English possesses a linear straightforwardness of subject, verb, object. The writer of the General Prologue to the Bible in Middle English similarly understands how the convolutions of Latin syntax need to be 'straightened out' in English (Forshall and Madden, 1:57 [A]). What is compressed in Latin is in English dilated and ironed out. English is straighter, more simple, wordier and plainer than Latin.

This growing awareness of the structural possibilities of English is evident in an increasing presence of grammatical metaphor to speak of political relationships: 'The mydlonde peple is be-twix þe norþyn & þe sowþirne, as is a participle bee-twix Nowne & Verbe' [The midland people are [positioned] between the northerners and southerners just as a participle is between a noun and a verb] (Bokenham, p. 32, chap. 16 [A]); the Duke of Exeter comments to Henry V that Scotland is 'like a noun adjective that cannot stand without a substantive' (Hall, p. 55 [A]). The geographical metaphors of Bokenham and Exeter arrange the nations into their rightful political syntax, with England as the self-standing, newly eloquent subject.

That independence of English is heralded by the adoption of English in 1362 as the language of the courts, opening the way for its fostering as the language of the nation. Hitherto perceived as plain and unadorned, English began to be spoken of as beautiful and elegant, as Lydgate in his *Life of Our Lady* celebrates Chaucer's 'golde dewe, dropes, of speche and eloquence' (1633 [A]); or as Hoccleve claims in *Regiment of Princes*, when he calls Chaucer the 'firste fyndere of our fair langage' (4978 [A]), inaugurating a centuries-long tradition of assumption that Chaucer was, as Dryden puts it, the 'Father of English Poesye' and even of the English language.

> **Semantic Change**
>
> Over the course of the centuries, original meanings can alter dramatically or get lost from view through change of form. The etymological resources of the *Oxford English Dictionary* can tell us much about the original social contexts of words. Consider, for example, that *lord* used to mean 'keeper of bread'; *lady* 'kneader of bread'; *silly* 'holy'; *daft* 'meek'; *lewd* 'non-clerical'; *buxom* 'obedient'; *hussy* 'housewife'; *gossip* 'baptismal sponsor'; *to worry* 'to strangle'; *wan* 'black'; *to blush* 'to glance'; *curfew* 'cover fire'; *umpire* 'without equal'; *humble pie* 'pie made of deer's entrails'.

The fifteenth century saw the rise of a standard English – essentially London English – distributed through the machinery of scribal norms, just as West Saxon was centuries before. That machinery was the English written by the king's clerks in Chancery, or 'Chauncelrie' (Langland, B.Prol.93 [A]) at Westminster, his official secretariat. For example, where fourteenth-century English distinguished between singular and plural second personal pronoun (*thou, yow*), which also served (respectively) as informal and formal terms of address, Chancery fixed both as *yow*. Similar decisions to conventionalise spelling helped to create a national standard, at least at the level of administration and, subsequently, in printing.

What turned the so-called 'Middle Ages' into the so-called 'Early Modern Period'? The labels, imposed retroactively, do little to explain how changing circumstances felt at the time. The (humiliating) end of the Hundred Years' War reshaped English identity, which had for centuries been cast in terms of its relationship with France. At the linguistic level, standardisation of spelling and what is known as the Great Vowel Shift made the literature of the recent past seem antique and remote, and the present new. Beginning early in the fifteenth century and continuing well into the sixteenth, the Great Vowel Shift affected all ME long, stressed monophthongs (as opposed to diphthongs), moving them generally to the front and top of the mouth. For example, the $\bar{a}$ of ME *name* (phonetic /a/ sounded like German *Mann* or as in 'fa-la-la') becomes pronounced as it is today /eɪ/; the $\bar{u}$ in ME *toune* (sounded like r*u*de) acquires its modern sound /aʊ/; and the $\bar{\imath}$ of ME *shire* (sounded like mach*ine*) becomes pronounced /ʌɪ/ as in today's pronunciation. By enunciating the sounds consecutively, the movement of the tongue forward and upward is evident. As spelling became fixed, it no longer phonetically measured how people spoke, it acquired the mark of correctness and learning, and the experiences of reading or writing and of speaking became increasingly divorced from each other. Chaucer spelled *knyght* and *nyght* differently because they were pronounced differently (the *k* being sounded); by the sixteenth century, the words sounded the same, and the difference in spelling was a convention only. 'Proper' writing became more artificial, and reading an act increasingly separated from speaking aloud, increasingly silent and private. By such subtle but definitive changes in the relationship between self and the book, we mark the end of the 'Middle Ages'.

From Epic to Romance

The 'epic' poetry of the OE period, more often known as 'heroic', is too often compartmentalised into a category that ends abruptly with 1066. Yet the loose definition of heroic poetry – a long, narrative celebration of a military ethos, and of courageous individuals who risk life and limb to protect both their own honour and that of their people – works just as well for many a medieval romance as it does for the OE genre, save that the heroic battlefield shrinks in focus to the lone knight in quest of adventure, that communal mentality shifts towards private, psychological interiority. Yet for most readers epic and romance are simply separate genres from separate eras. One of the reasons for this is the terminology. 'Romance', from OF *romans*, means 'a story told in French', so the initial difference was sometimes largely a matter of the language of record rather than the kind of story told.

In truth, only *Beowulf* perfectly fits the definition of a long narrative poem that recounts a hero's exploits, for the OE heroic genre also includes hybrids such as *Deor*, a short, gnomic poem, in which the narrator thinks back on the faded glories of past heroes and on his own present misfortunes, punctuating each thought with the sad refrain: 'þæs ofereode; þisses swa mæg' [That passed away, so may this] (Hill, p. 37, l. 7 [A]). Lacking a plot, and foregrounding grief, the poem is more elegiac than heroic, and exposes the artificial limits of self-contained genres. Conversely, the brooding quality of the OE elegies such as we find in *The Wanderer* is remarkably close to passages in *Beowulf* (2247–70). The 'religious' *Dream of the Rood* figures Christ as a warrior-hero, and the commemorative *Battle of Maldon*, belonging to local and recent history, nonetheless casts the defeated English as heroes. *Maldon*'s early patriotism and the *Rood*'s Christianity represent distinctive, revisionary adaptations of the heroic theme to devotional and chronicle material. The extant OE heroic poetry survives in manuscripts compiled in the late tenth and early eleventh centuries, yet poems such as *Widsith* clearly originate in much older events, probably historical, but embellished and mythologised over centuries as they changed through retelling. We cannot know how the earliest oral versions compare with the written version that survives, or how they changed in the retelling.

If, as William of Malmesbury claims, the Normans went into battle at Hastings singing the *Song of Roland*, it is clear that heroic literature was a living tradition for Normans as much as for Anglo-Saxons, and its heroes offered immediate ethical models. Roland and Beowulf display superhuman courage in the face of impossible odds, stirring fighters to feel that in their skirmishes and local battles they too are making history and great songs. OE heroic poetry is traditionally regarded as deeply masculinist, celebrating a military ethic in which women play no part, and its most notable expression is in the presence of what Tacitus calls the *comitatus*, the king's retinue of young fighting elite, who slept and ate in the great hall – constant companions, and unswervingly loyal. Wiglaf would have been such a companion of Beowulf, as were the retainers of King Cynewulf in 755, who preferred to die fighting for their slain lord than accept his murderer as their new king. For outstanding services, the king might award land rather than treasure to one of his band; land elevated that young retainer's status, entailed residence on his new estate, and facilitated marriage. Still serving the king in counsel and in times of need, the promoted retainer would acquire hearth-companions of his own. In such a masculinist, militaristic ethos, it is hard to see where women fit in, except to bear children; yet one of Beowulf's opponents was a vengeful woman, and the same manuscript that records *Beowulf* also contains the exploits of Judith (*Judith*), no less heroic for being biblical. Furthermore, a woman does not need to swashbuckle to have heroic presence. Hrothgar's queen Wealtheow gives counsel in her own right, and dispenses gifts to reward brave feats (*Klaeber's 'Beowulf'*, 1216–31 [A]). And a kenning for 'lady', *freoðu-webbe* (peace-weaver) (1942), demonstrates her political role in warfare, for in marrying to seal pacts between tribes, she carries in her body the union between former enemies.

In heroic literature kingship and military prowess are intimately connected. The image of a warrior-king who actually fights on the battlefield is one we associate with medieval monarchs, less so with early modern, and not at all with modern English monarchs. The need for a strong protector also influenced hereditary custom in the Germanic tribes. Where post-Conquest monarchs observed a line of strict succession through primogeniture (the entire inheritance going to the eldest son), AS succession had more flexibility, balancing the claims of blood against the need for a military leader, for the bureaucratic machine was rarely powerful enough to hold affairs together should the king prove weak. Consequently, loyalty was more to the king than to a nation – a sentiment echoed by Ealdorman Byrhtnoth that he will defend the 'ealdres mines / folc and foldan' [people and land of my prince] (*Battle of Maldon*, 53–4 [A]). Although our records of heroic poetry date from no earlier than the tenth century, we might call it the dominant cultural expression of earlier tribal identity.

The bond between king and war band cuts across tribal distinction, for a powerful king will attract followers from other regions and tribes. Bede records how noblemen from every

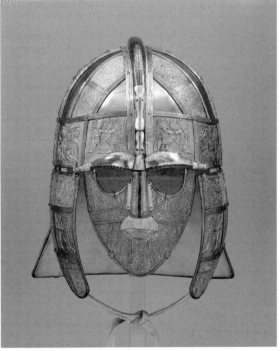

1.6 *Heaþosteapa Helm* (The High Battle-Helmet) (*Beowulf*, 1245 [A]). Reconstructed from actual helmet in Sutton Hoo, early C.7th.

Beowulf (2009–69) and *Troilus and Criseyde* (II.1653–722) illustrate the continuities and differences beween OE heroic poetry and ME romance. Both passages employ the device of the precious object as a point of recognition to engineer a dramatic reversal of fortune. In *Beowulf*, the heirloom won in battle turns Ingeld's festive wedding into a bloody fight; in *Troilus*, it turns battle victory into the heartbreak caused by a lover's infidelity. The contrast between the two recognitions highlights the shift in affective investment. In *Beowulf*, the heroic ethos is stronger, and the bond between men, whether comradeship or enmity, holds more sway than that between a man and a woman. Ingeld's love for Freawaru cools as the passion of battle mounts (2064–6). In *Troilus*, martial passion yields to the heartbreak of infidelity. The space of some four hundred years brings a significant shift in the psychic topography of a nobleman's deepest emotions and loyalties. In those centuries, epic has given way to romance as the literature of an age.

province would come to serve King Oswine of Deira (a sub-kingdom of Northumbria) who ruled in the mid-seventh century (Bede, III.14, pp. 256–9 [A]); and Beowulf, who comes to Denmark to serve Hrothgar (temporarily), owes allegiance to Hygelac, king of the Geats. The fact that Beowulf went in spite of Hygelac's wish for him to remain (1987–98) indicates the limits of the authority of early kings. Long disregarded among the Geats as unpromising, Beowulf reverses his misfortune and gains stature in their eyes by his exploits at Heorot. He also fosters peaceful relations between the two kingdoms (1855–65). Beowulf both augments his own stature and represents the court from which he came; in this, he shares much with the knight of medieval romance, such as Gawain in *Sir Gawain and the Green Knight*. What heroic poetry is to Old English, so chivalric romance is to Middle English.

Late heroic poetry, historical chronicle and early English romance overlap variously. Chronicle was connected to the mathematical art of computing years and setting dates for movable feasts such as Easter, and historical events were noted against the years as terse entries such as we get for the battle at Maldon in 991. Yet chronicle also proved apt to recount heroic stories (as in the Cynewulf and Cyneheard episode for 755); to record heroic poetry (as in the *Battle of Brunanburh* for 937) and to bring together historical commentary, critique and commemoration. The poems recording the deaths of Edward the Confessor (1065) and of William I (1087) contrast sharply between the good rulership of Edward and the tyranny of William.

> [K]yningc kystum god, clæne and milde,
> Eadward se æðela, eðel bewerode,
> land and leode.

> [A king of excellent virtues, pure and benign,
> Edward the noble protected his fatherland,
> His realm and people.]

(*Anglo-Saxon Chronicle*, 1:194 [A])

> Castelas he let wyrcean,
> 7 earme men swiðe swencean.
> Se cyng wæs swa swiðe stearc,
> 7 benam of his underþeoddan manig marc
> goldes 7 ma hundred punda seolfres.
> Ðet he nam be wihte

7 mid mycelan unrihte
Of his landleode,
For littelre neode.

[Castles he had built, and greatly oppressed poor men. The king was very severe, and he seized many marcs of gold and hundreds of pounds of silver in addition from his subjects. This he took from the people and with great injustice from his subjects out of petty desire.]

(Clark, *The Peterborough Chronicle*, pp. 13–14 [A])

The question of kingship underlies *Beowulf*, chronicle, and Laʒamon's (or Lawman's) late-twelfth-century *Brut*, the earliest English narrative that celebrates King Arthur. It is hard to categorise Laʒamon's poem, something between heroic narrative and metrical chronicle, yet with the motifs that characterise later romance. Like ME romance generally, Laʒamon's poem emerges out of IF literature (specifically, Wace's IF *Brut*). These IF writers chronicled their stories in a French that was self-consciously insular, and that insular culture forged out of French and English a new identity distinct from both. From this synthesis comes the choice to write about King Arthur, or what French poet Jean Bodel called the 'matter of Britain', as distinct from the 'matter of Rome' with its stories of Alexander, the Trojan wars and Thebes, and from the 'matter of France', with its stories of Charlemagne and Roland. Here in Laʒamon's *Brut* is still the OE alliterative line, but now conglomerated with rhyme, syllabic rhythm and assonance, for English prosody was rapidly expanding into new forms. *Brut* lacks the courtly apparatus of distressed damsels and the feminine presence of later romance, for Guinevere gets short shrift in comparison to the way she dominates later stories, such as Malory's *Morte Darthur*. Laʒamon's female presence better recollects OE heroic poetry, as (the Saxon) Rowenne bears the wine-cup at the feasting (Barron and Weinberg, ll. 7135–57 [A]). The influence of French *chansons de geste* such as the *Song of Roland* is discernible in the central role treachery plays as the cardinal sin, while honour – the cardinal chivalric virtue – is everywhere celebrated in the swearing of oaths on relics. We get a sense of the legal, religious and emotional importance of oath-taking from the Bayeux Tapestry's depiction of Earl Harold's swearing on sacred relics to William of Normandy. In vouching on holy relics, he swears in the immediate presence of God himself – something not done lightly in an age when the very elements were called on to 'witness' to the guilt or innocence of a person through the ordeals by fire and water. The Tapestry's message is clear: in subsequently claiming the crown of England, Harold broke that oath to William, who fought a just war to claim a throne that was rightfully his.

Arthur's arming scene in *Brut* (10542–62), in which each piece bears its own name and genealogy, is a narrative sequence that looks both backwards to *Beowulf* (1441–72) and forwards to *Sir Gawain and the Green Knight* (566–669) or the alliterative *Morte Arthure* (Benson, ll. 900–19 [A]). Such descriptions, along with those of fights and tournaments, as in Chaucer's *Knight's Tale*, re-enact martial rituals of deep cultural importance. These affirmations of manly prowess connect directly to the question of good rulership. A king must be as brave as the best of his men, yet also be something more, the repository of justice, administrator of law, mediator between warring factions and peacemaker, despite his fighting renown. The short reign of Aurelie well

1.7 Harold swears an oath to William. Detail from the Bayeux Tapestry. C.11th.

displays the qualities of good kingship: he listened to wise counsellors; respected the voice of the people through hustings; established Christian observance; had churches and halls built and lands tilled and administered the law (Barron and Weinberg, ll. 8433–71 [A]). As if reversing the description of William I's oppression in the *Anglo-Saxon Chronicle*, the poem celebrates his true kingly conduct.

> He letten stronge walles, he lette bulden halles,
> and rihte al þa workes þe ær weore tobrokene,
> and aȝef heom alle þa laȝen þe stoden bi heore ælderne dæȝen;
> he makede þer reuen þan uolke to reden.

> [He had the walls strengthened, halls built, and all the buildings restored that were formerly broken; and gave them back all the laws that stood in the days of their elders; and he appointed magistrates there, to rule the folk.]

> (Barron and Weinberg, ll. 8459–62 [A]).

This interest in good rulership continues throughout the more thoughtful examples of medieval romance. Where Havelok in *Havelok the Dane* rules both by right and by consent, and is a consensus builder, the usurpers Godrich and Godard act autocratically out of self-interest, the sure mark of the tyrant. By accepting oaths of fealty (*mandrede*) from the entire people (*Havelok*, 2252–73 [A]), Havelok interrupts the devolved system of feudal mutual obligation and directly commands loyalty from the heart of each subject.

The preoccupation with right rule and with public integrity, if a constant, also reflects political circumstances of the period. One of the most popular Arthurian episodes refers to how the young boy proved his birthright as rightful king of England by pulling the sword from the stone. Malory elaborates the episode from his French sources, and in doing so obliquely comments on the dynastic conflicts between Lancastrian and Yorkist, Plantagenet and Tudor, and on the civil war that oppressed fifteenth-century England. And in Mordred's treachery against Arthur, Malory's commentary becomes explicit:

Lo ye all Englysshemen, se ye nat what a myschyff here was? For he [Arthur] that was the moste kynge and nobelyst knyght of the worlde ... and yet myght nat thes Englyshemen holde them contente with hym.

(Malory, 3:1229 [A])

Old stories these may be – indeed, romance delights in the antique nature of its material – yet their very antiquity provokes for romance writers an awareness of historical tension between the past, usually idealised, and the corrupt present: 'And ryght so faryth the love nowadayes, sone hote sone colde. Thys ys no stabylyté. But the olde love was not so' (Malory, 3:1120 [A]). '[F]or such custom was used in tho dayes: for favoure, love, nother affinité there sholde be none other but ryghtuous jugemente' (2:1055).

For all the continuity between epic and romance in its masculinist interests, romance's more feminine preoccupation with courtliness, love and marriage is central to the genre. Love interest is often wrapped into tales of marvels and faerie such as *Sir Orfeo* and *Sir Launfal*; yet even these stories retain their interest in kingship and courtly integrity. Romance also shares striking parallels to hagiographic stories with their adventures of young Christian women as victims of lust or malice: the blurred line between saint's life and romance is evident in Gower's *Tale of Constance* in *Confessio Amantis* (II.587–1598) (Gower, 2:146–73 [A]). *Apollonius of Tyre*, dating remarkably early, from the tenth and eleventh centuries, survives in a manuscript containing sermons. The juxtaposition suggests that 'romance' stories, sketched briefly as *exempla*, could comfortably stand adjacent to rather than in opposition to religious material (Scragg, 'Secular Prose', pp. 268–9 [Ci]), that the distinction between sacred and secular often fades in medieval literature.

It is a puzzling paradox that an economy such as feudalism, so unfriendly to female agency, should express itself in a literature in which the lady is pre-eminent and the knight her 'vassal', for the feudal model of homage is explicitly invoked and made erotic. Romance's reverence for the lady both reflects and is energised by hymns of Marian devotion, which can sound like a wooing lover: 'Swete levedi, of me thu reowe, / And have merci of thin knicht' (Saupe, p. 52.15–16 [A]). Not only does woman inform the content of romance as the inevitable marriage prize, and not only does the narrator identify with the woman's perspective; she also often, historically, constitutes the audience of the genre. Eleanor of Aquitaine, queen of Henry II, was a renowned patron of the arts and the dedicatee of Wace's *Roman de Brut* (Barron and Weinberg, ll. 19–23 [A]). Norman land-inheritance foregrounded primogeniture as the preferred custom of descent, and this need for heirs placed woman at the centre of the maintenance of landed estates, despite her lack of access to outright possession. In one sense, romance inversely reflects woman's feudal disenfranchisement by celebrating her power over the chivalric knight; in another, romance offers woman, absented from the sphere of political control, an alternative 'real' world of cultural capital in the patronage and production of arts and letters.

Yet from the evidence of later medieval private libraries and commissioned manuscripts, fifteenth-century owners of English romances were most likely to be men (Cooper, p. 703 [Ci]). Such owners were not royal or even baronial. The 'consumers' of later English romance included lesser knights, provincial men, burghers and the mercantile class, from which Chaucer's own family originated. Romance promised a code of courtliness resulting from nurture as well as from birthright, an education of the soul available to the 'free' and 'gentle' man, who finds in the tales a mirror to his aspirations. The terms are loaded. The *fredom* of Chaucer's *Franklin's Tale* and the *gentilesse* of the *Wife of Bath's Tale* are virtues supposedly attainable by all, but 'free' and 'gentle' are also terms of designated social rank, automatically excluding serfs and commoners. For all the indisputable virtue of Chaucer's pilgrim Parson and Plowman, we will search in vain for any reference to their *fredom, gentilesse* or *curteisye*. For them such terms are inappropriate; medieval romance remains the ultimate form of chivalric self-representation, the literature of an estate that, by the end of the fifteenth century, could no longer be defined in terms of military function, and that fast was becoming a badge of social prestige available to whoever could afford it.

The Rise of Theatre

Without purpose-built playhouses such as the Globe in London, medieval drama could happen anywhere: town streets, churchyards, manorial halls, and so on. What counts as drama is similarly diverse, for with no strict definition of 'theatre', royal processions, performing acrobats and even sermons fairly qualify as performance art. Where the large-scale guild pageants constitute an essentially urban experience – requiring the resources of personnel, community audience, large public fora and cash – much smaller operations might be staged by individual parishes or a collective of them. Some productions, such as Henry Medwall's *Fulgens and Lucrece*, were clearly for a more elevated and private audience, performed in a banqueting hall. Its preoccupation with whether a Roman low-born man can be 'nobler' (i.e. more virtuous) than a patrician betrays its genteel orientation. John Lydgate's mummings for the goldsmiths and mercers of London similarly address a dedicated audience, and demonstrate the thin line between theatre and narrative poetry, which was so often read aloud publicly rather than silently.

Surviving dramatic texts come predominantly from the mid-fifteenth century, but stray references – including that to Absalom in Chaucer's *Miller's Tale* playing Herod 'upon a scaffold hye' – point to the plays being performed in the previous century. The plays continued into the second half of the sixteenth century, and by their lateness undo the neat boundaries we set between the late medieval and early modern periods, which cluster around the close of the fifteenth century. The procession of the seven deadly sins in Marlowe's *Faustus* and the characterisation of the king in Shakespeare's *Richard III* are just two of the most obvious examples of a theatrical tradition that is continued rather than overturned.

Whether morality, saints', miracle or mystery play, the Church dominates most medieval drama. The mystery plays, so called because each pageant was performed by a separate town guild or 'mystery', are thought to have gained momentum from the public celebration, established by the pope in 1311, of Corpus Christi (the body of Christ) every year in May or June, on which occasion the clergy processed through the community following the Eucharistic host. But medieval religious drama was played throughout the year, and has much earlier origins than the feast of Corpus Christi. The oldest assumption is that it developed from liturgical drama, from dramatised tropes or embellishments at special points in church services. One such trope – the *Quem Quæritis* (whom seek ye?) for the Easter office – dates from Æthelwold's late tenth-century *Regularis Concordia*, and entails a semi-dramatic exchange of question and response between the angel at the sepulchre and the women who come seeking Christ's (risen) body. Certainly, there are suggestive links between such moments and the mystery cycles, especially those pageants that deal with the resurrection and where the vernacular drama includes song, such as the well-known Coventry Carol from the Coventry *Shearmen and Taylors' Pageant*, but the evolution of boisterous vernacular street theatre is long, and includes other formative influences. The slapstick humour of the devils in the morality play *Mankind* evokes much stronger associations with professional entertainers such as Langland describes (Langland, B.xiii.231–4 [A]) than with any religious source; while the early fabliau *Dame Sirith* points to a secular side of medieval theatre.

The evidence of the York mystery cycle, both text and civic records, is so full that from it we can reconstruct at least in this instance how the play took place. Divided into multiple short episodes taken from biblical history, the cycle was performed by the civic guilds, each guild claiming responsibility for one pageant (or play episode). Where possible, the guilds would act a pageant that advertised their trade in some way: thus, the York butchers performed the Crucifixion, the bakers the Last Supper, the shipwrights the Building of the Ark and so on. With so many pageants to perform, the show started early, at daybreak. In contrast to the *Castle of Perseverance*, for example, which would have been performed in a fixed location, these pageants were performed along staging points through the city. In the case of York, there were between twelve and sixteen stations, and by the time the twelfth or sixteenth pageant wagon had begun to play, the city's streets were resounding with theatre. Beginning at Holy Trinity Priory in Micklegate and ending at the Pavement, the pageants traced successive episodes from the Fall of the Angels to the Last Judgement. Walking down Micklegate, it must have seemed as if the whole holy story was taking place in a perpetual present.

Central to mystery-cycle drama is the community life and locality it celebrates. For those with advantageously appointed dwellings, they could watch the pageants from their own doorway, and rent out a window seat. The involvement of the community was evident at every level of participation – patronage and sponsorship, the building of the wagons, supply of props, actors and audience. The pageant wagons, by processing through the town, connected its disparate parts, unifying place as well as people.

The doctrine of the Eucharistic real presence, celebrated and commemorated in the feast of Corpus Christi, would come under direct attack in the sixteenth-century Reformation. Yet Wyclif first challenged the reality of transubstantiation back in 1379, and the celebration of Corpus Christi should be understood in the light of Lollard scepticism. This scepticism is played out – and roundly answered – in the Croxton *Play of the Sacrament*, in which Jonathas, a Jewish merchant, procures the sacramental Host and subjects it to tortures similar to those the Jews inflicted on Christ's body: he and his companions stab the Host with daggers, whereupon it bleeds. Finally, they roast it in the oven, but the oven shatters and Jesus appears, chastising them for their blasphemy. Faced with such incontrovertible proof, Jonathas overcomes his scepticism, represented by his mercantile materialism, and becomes a believer. Although such a story is unusual in theatrical form, it is common enough in sermons, and it is not only Jews who show unbelief. In a fifteenth-century sermon collection, *Festial*, preacher John Mirk recounts the story of the woman Lasma, who smiled when the Pope offered her the Host in mass. Stopping the service, the Pope inquires after her reason, to which she replies that she smiled 'For þou callest þat

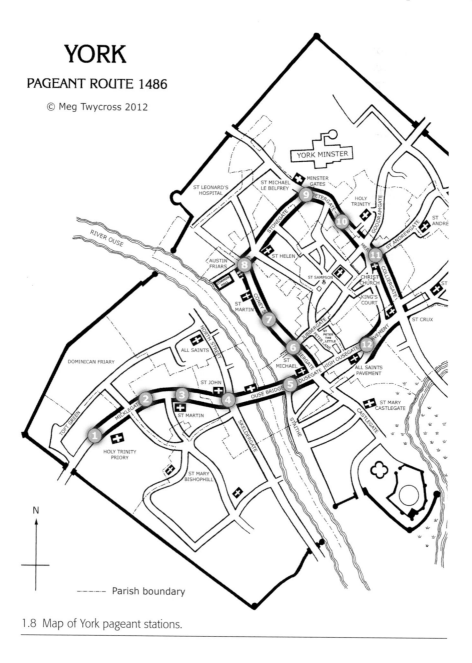

1.8 Map of York pageant stations.

Goddys body þat I made wyth myne owne handes' [because what you call God's body I baked with my own hands]. The Pope prays, the bread changes to throbbing flesh, and Lasma finally repents of her unbelief (Mirk, p. 159 [A]). The Eucharist itself is for this period the most dramatic performance of all.

Texts and Issues

In the above section, we considered the dominant connection between the political economy of medieval England and its literary expression, and in doing so examined the central role heroic poetry, romance and theatre play in the changing culture of the period. That connection is mediated through the Church, which was as political an institution as the state yet also the central matrix of cultural production, the bringer of writing itself, the provider of monastic scriptoria and schools, and the inspiration for much medieval literary output. After considering its role, we turn to the intersection between economic and literary worlds in the depiction of money and wealth, and finally to gender, and some of the less highbrow aspects of medieval literature.

The Church and Literature

The oldest OE poetry might be most accurately thought of as a kind of music. Its alliterative, rhythmic pattern is delivered in a semi-chanting, sing-song voice, *hlude be hearpan* (loudly to the accompaniment of the lyre) as Widsith attests in singing of warrior-kings (Hill, p. 35, l. 105 [A]). Yet, ironically, the earliest extant OE poetry is Christian in content. Whatever we know of OE oral poetry relies ultimately on written transmission, and because monastic houses monopolised literary production and copying of manuscripts, it is impossible to separate the story of writing from the story of Christianity and of Latinity. Alcuin's famous rebuke to the monks of Lindisfarne in 797, 'What has Ingeld to do with Christ?' attests simultaneously to the commingling of 'pagan' and Christian culture and its attempted

The Ruthwell Cross

The Ruthwell cross, preserved in Dumfries, Scotland, was built in the late seventh or early eighth century for the purposes of Christian devotion or commemoration. Its rectilinear tapered shaft has biblical scenes, elaborately carved, on its four faces. Four sentences from *The Dream of the Rood* are etched on the cross in AS runes, in early Northumbrian. Although *The Dream of the Rood* exists in a late tenth-century manuscript, the Ruthwell cross shows the poem to be much older, and reveals how early heroic and Christian themes and imagery intertwined. Spoken in the first person, the lines make the sculpture come to life as a real cross. Reading the runes in sequence requires motion around the cross and interconnection with the biblical scenes, which typologically foreshadow Christ's perpetual presence in the Eucharist. In this way, the cross enacts the liturgy, which moves beyond its formal confines of organised service to become sacramental art in the viewer-reader's personal experience of a poetic and sculptural performance.

Bismærædu uŋket men ba ætgadre (Ruthwell cross runes; *The Dream of the Rood*, p. 94 [A])

Bysmeredon hie unc butu ætgædere (*The Dream of the Rood*, l. 48 [A])

[They mocked the two of us together]

separation. Despite these cautions from Church leaders, evidence is clear of the coexistence among common folk of superstition, pagan material, popular religion and Christianity. In metrical charms, for example, it is often impossible to discriminate between incantatory spell and Christian blessing or exorcism.

Prior to the spread of writing in the seventh century, an AS alphabet of sorts did exist; this was the runic alphabet, or *futhark* – used primarily for inscriptional use on stone, metal and wood – which coexisted with Roman script as late as the eighth century, given the evidence of the Ruthwell cross, and whose traces remained in medieval script as the runes þ (*þorn*, thorn) and ƿ (*wynn*, joy) for *th* and *w* respectively.

Each rune was an ideogram, named by a common object; thus þ was called *þorn* (thorn), which *byþ ðearle scearp* (is cruelly sharp), as the '*Rune' Poem* says (6–8) (Halsall, p. 86 [A]). Employing only the rune itself rather than the full word, the poem becomes a kind of riddle in which we guess the name of the rune from the definition. That riddling, runic sense pervades *The Dream of the Rood* when the cross suddenly starts speaking (l. 28).

Until the rise of professional scribes serving court and universities, monasteries remained the primary place of scribal production, one of their crucial moments being the twelfth century, during which OE devotional texts were transcribed, probably for an unlearned audience whose only access was to English. These monasteries maintained a continuity of written vernacular that would be invisible were we only looking for evidence of 'literature' in its strictly aesthetic sense. Their work was of deep cultural importance, and the very forms of worship, supposedly timeless, themselves embody the politics of the moment; consider the way in which racial tension between Norman and English resulted in bloodshed at Glastonbury in 1083, when the abbot imposed a newer form of liturgy from Dijon on the monks, who adhered to the Gregorian tradition (Swanton, p. 214 [A]).

Epic and romance heroes come and go, but the one narrative staple throughout the medieval period is the saint's life, a genre that celebrates as many if not more women as it does men. In these saints and martyrs, the faithful found an ethical model, a comforter, a friend, and learned the redemptive nature of pain. The pilgrimage trade with its relics gave economic foundation to the cult of saints; in many ways, the saint was worth more dead than alive, more valuable in small pieces scattered along pilgrimage routes than physically entire. The bodies of saints seem endlessly divisible, and such holy fragmentation cancels out the swarming multiplicity of the demons that inhabit the air. The departure of the blessed from earth is traditionally marked by the presence of sweet fragrance and shining light, such as is recounted in the OE *Life of St Guthlac* (*Anglo-Saxon Prose*, p. 60 [A]). These narrative motifs attest to the powerful faith in the resurrection of flesh and to the belief that decay is the consequence of sin; for this reason, saints' dying flesh does not stink like that of lesser mortals. In the ornate reliquaries of medieval art, which housed the withered limbs of the saint, we see the same principle enacted: noble metal that does not tarnish or decay touches the shrunken flesh of the saint as if to make it whole again. That incorruptibility emerges in hagiography as miracle: in Ælfric's description of how King Edmund's severed head calls out to his followers who are searching for it; in St Christina the Astonishing's ability to survive boiling water and hot ovens intact; and in Chaucer's *litel clergeon* who sings his *Alma Redemptoris Mater* despite having had his throat fatally slit. In such miracles we see the dead made present again among the living. Fashion and politics affect the fortunes of saints also, who are often of noble breeding just like the protagonists of romance. The difference between seventh-century St Oswald, who died at the hands of pagan Penda on the battlefield, and the ninth-century St Edmund, who refused to raise a weapon against the Danes, says much about a growing sense in OE political theology of the king as a lover of peace. After Normanisation, the veneration of a king as saint seemed unlikely – Edward the Confessor being the last royal saint. And in the thirteenth-century lives of the female saints such as St Margaret, we see a new direction towards a personal relationship with God.

Reigning supreme above the saints and apostles stands Mary, the prized object of devotion. From the twelfth century, we see a marked increase in the veneration of her, and in the common perception of her as negotiator between Christ and sinners.

By the early Middle Ages, Saturdays and several feast days were devoted to her, and the Lateran Council of 1215 made the Ave Maria compulsory learning for all layfolk. Throughout England, pilgrims visited Marian shrines and Lady chapels at Winchester, Ely, Walsingham, Ipswich, Lincoln and Newark, to note only the most famous. For many visitors, these life-sized images seemed as if they were the Virgin Mary herself. For many Lollards, this was idolatry. Others sought a compromise between God and a piece of wood by a ticklish distinction between adoration of

1.9 Mary bares her breast before Christ on behalf of sinners. Hereford *Mappa Mundi*. c. 1285.

the living God and veneration of holy objects (*Dives and Pauper*, p. 108 [A]). Care was taken 'so þat þou knele, ȝyf þou wylt, *aforn* [before] þe ymage nought *to* þe ymage' (p. 85, emphasis added). The emotional connection with Mary is expressed through the many lyric poems and songs in her honour. In the following thirteenth-century lyric, the economy of Latin and the expansiveness of English counterpoint each other to create contrasting lines of singular beauty:

> Of on þat is so fayr and briȝt
> *velud maris stella*,
> Briȝter þan þe dayis liȝt
> *parens et puella*,
> Ic crie to þe, þou se to me,
> Leuedy, preye þi sone for me,
> *tam pia*
> þat Ic mote come to þe,
> *Maria.*

> [Of one who is so fair and bright,
> Just as a star of the sea,
> Brighter than the day's light
> Mother and virgin.
> I cry to thee, you look favourably on me,
> Lady, pray to your son for me,
> So very affectionately,
> That I may come to thee,
> Maria.]
>
> (Bennett and Smithers (eds.), *Early Middle English Verse and Prose*, p. 129; ll. 1–9 [A])

Dense theological meaning is compressed into the short Latin lines: the theological paradox of *parens et puella* (parent and virgin); and in another stanza the reversed spellings of *Eva* and *Ave* recall how paradise was lost through one woman (Eve) and regained through another (Mary, invoked through Gabriel's salutation *Ave Maria*). The poem manages to enhance the vernacular in its juxtaposition with Latin and to embellish the Latin through vernacular elaboration and paraphrase.

What we see in the long arc from *The Dream of the Rood* to late medieval devotional literature (frequently in prose), is a shift of interest from resurrection to crucifixion, a change in the role of Christ from the hero-warrior in the OE poem to the abject creature we meet in the meditational literature of the fourteenth and early fifteenth centuries: Julian of Norwich's eighth revelation 'of the last petivous peynes of Christe deyeng' (Watson and Jenkins, p. 395 [A]), *The Book of Margery Kempe*, and Richard Rolle's *Meditations on the Passion*, in which Rolle has a vision of Christ bloodied and riven, his hair matted with gore, moving in the wind, his face swollen and bruised (Allen, p. 95 [A]). More boisterous than the others, Margery Kempe has visions of biblical events in which she sometimes actively participates. The grotesque detail of Christ's sufferings brings her a cathartic excess of grief, matching pain with pain:

> Than sey sche wyth hyr gostly eye how þe Iewys festenyd ropis on þe oþer hand, for þe senwys & veynys wer so schrynkyn wyth peyne þat it myth not come to þe hole þat þei had morkyn þerfor, & drowyn þeron to makyn it mete wyth þe hole. & so her peyne & hir sorwe euyr encresyd … And þan sche wept & cryid passyngly sor.

[Then she saw, with her spiritual eye, how the Jews fastened ropes on to the other hand – for the sinews and veins were so shrunken with pain that it would not reach to the hole that they had drilled for it – and they pulled on it to make it reach the hole. And so her pain and her sorrow ever increased ... Then she wept and cried most pitifully.]

(Meech, *Book*, chap. 80, p. 192; ll. 16–21, 31 [A])

The luridness of the description is also captured in the crucifixion plays of medieval drama – for example, the York pageant of the crucifixion – rendering such scenes not only the material of private visions but also of public, collective experience. The deeply affective quality of much late medieval devotional writing is matched by equally deep anger more publicly directed against church abuse or expressed in the desecration of images. Both the piety and the righteous anger register the violent intensity of religious experience in this period.

At the end of *The Parson's Tale*, Chaucer offers a paragraph commonly called 'The Retraction', so unusual it has often been considered not to be a proper part of *The Canterbury Tales* (Chaucer, *Canterbury Tales* in *Riverside Chaucer*, X.1081–92 [A]). In it, he asks Christ's forgiveness for his 'translacions and enditynges of worldly vanities', such Canterbury tales 'that sownen into synne', and 'many a song and lecherous lay'; he takes pride only in his worthy works, such as 'legendes of seintes, and omelies, and moralitee, and devocioun'. It is unlikely that this statement is ironic, for the speaking voice seems to have lost its narrative masks, signalled by the use of prose rather than of poetry. We are not free, however, to dismiss the lines as a fit of piety in Chaucer's dotage. They pose a problem to us as an apparent betrayal of poetic integrity, for he speaks as a poet about his poetry, commending some, disparaging other by the sublime standard of eternity. If art should be free of dogma (of whatever persuasion), then Chaucer's 'confession' of literary sin thus seems like an act of bad faith. Medieval literature is not artistically 'free' in the modern aesthetic sense of the term. 'The Retraction' brings us to the terminal limits of poetry, to the 'death' of the aesthetic, and rests on the supposition that art, however polished and beautiful, is only fleeting and partial. From the local vantage point of imminent death, then, such *enditynges* should be retracted, but that is not to say they should never have been written; what seems true at death may not have been so in health and youth.

Wealth and Wages

The word 'chattel', deriving from central OF *chattel*, means 'property' in general, or 'movable assets'; what we may not know is that 'cattle' derives from the same word in its IF form (*catel*). Similar connection is displayed in 'pecuniary', which derives ultimately from L. *pecu* (money, cattle), and in 'fee', from OE *feoh* (cattle, money, property). In today's society where money represents the pure exchange value between commodities, we forget that cattle once used to be a more meaningful kind of 'money' for earlier societies, entering vocabulary variously in indication of its strong symbolic value; for example, a 'hide' was a measurement of land (around 120 acres), which imaginatively if not in reality represented as much land as could be encompassed by a thong cut from a hide. Laȝamon recounts the story of how Hengest tricked King Vortigern

1.10 The Desborough necklace. C.7th. Gold and garnet. The cross indicates that it belonged to a convert.

into granting him a hide of land that turned out big enough to become the city of Lancaster (Barron and Weinberg, ll. 7073–109 [A]).

Durable, recyclable, uniform, divisible, efficiently compact and more portable than a cow, gold attained the status of money early on as the ideal medium of measure and circulation. Although coins were a recognised standard of price throughout the OE period, and coinage bearing the imprint of the reigning king a powerful assertion of monarchical control, the daily transactions of most people were effected by payments in kind, and heroic poetry invoked a more elevated and ancient form of value – treasure.

War in Germanic tribal culture filled coffers and kept busy thegns who might otherwise become restive and rebellious; war was a given, circulating women, treasure and land among tribes just as they circulated more peacefully within the tribe. Although muted, that same ethic of the fighting estate – idealised in chivalric romance, and driven by the sense that war was necessary and profitable – would persist in the later Middle Ages and inform tensions between Richard II's barons, eager to continue the Hundred Years' War, and himself. Without a strong king to lead the (AS) people, the fortunes of a kingdom could quickly wane. *Beowulf* again demonstrates this truth powerfully as Wiglaf predicts a time of battle, oppression and exile for the Geats once foreign peoples hear about the cowardice of the retainers in the face of their king's death (2886–91). There is no more shameful thing to say of a thegn in heroic literature than that he was a coward, or of a king that he was niggardly in distributing wealth.

In *Widsith*, Eormanric, King of the Goths, gives the poet Widsith a costly gold 'ring' (*beag*) (Hill, p. 34, ll. 88–98 [A]), which was probably an armlet or a torque such as the Desborough necklace (see Figure 1.10). In turn the circlet is offered by Widsith to his lord Eadgils, lord of the Myrgingas, and this act of homage is rewarded doublefold both by another one given him by Ealhhild, Eadgils's queen and by Eadgils's own gift of land. Compare with this the torque or collar (*hælsbeag*) that Beowulf receives from

Queen Wealtheow after Grendel is killed (1192–6). Such a precious object marks elevated status, royal favour and, on the part of the giver, munificence. Evident for all to see, it is a visual affirmation of loyalty rewarded, homage and gratitude. Just as Widsith passed on the treasure to his lord, so Beowulf offers the torque to Hygelac upon his return to the Geats. Treasure circulates.

These gifts, often a necklet or fine sword, are invested with meaning in and of themselves. Although they approximate to what we now understand as payment, they are essentially gifts, offered freely rather than obligated by contract. Although money was long already a part of the AS economy, precious objects – primarily armour, war gear and jewellery – have a central status as a chief form of wealth. Even money, at the level of gold and silver coins, possesses the status of treasure. Treasure possesses a material presence and uniqueness that 'cash' in its most abstract sense does not. For these reasons, gifts are described in luxuriant detail, and in an epic work such as *Beowulf*, become important points of transition and digression in the narrative. As Wealtheow bestows the precious collar on Beowulf, the poet looks forward in time to anticipate how that same collar would be snatched from the neck of Hygelac, Beowulf's lord, by his Frisian slayer on the battlefield (1202–13). We do not find out until later that Beowulf gave the collar to Hygd, Hygelac's queen, who presumably gave it to Hygelac before battle as a good-luck gift. A complex cluster of assumptions and narrative manipulations surround this single necklace. Such digressions and extended descriptions of heirlooms (compare 2009–69) add to the dark mood of *Beowulf*, foreshadowing future grief; but apart from this, the sheer importance of 'stuff' dominates the narrative. Where 'plot' – at least any Aristotelian definition of it – commonly denotes an abstract conception of action that meshes together episodes linked causally, these narrative riffs take their origin in concrete objects: a collar, war booty, a scar on a leg, a shield. Such 'stuff' has a visual presence that dictates its own pictorial logic as opposed to the causal logic of plot, and creates descriptions that have a life of their own. With it, we might compare the loving precision with which certain objects are described in wills. In the will of Æthelstan, son of Æthelræd (1015), in which he bequeaths his armour to the Church, alliteration and repetition echo the musicality of poetry, and suggest that objects are not only described for the purpose of identification but also enjoyed in their own right:

> 7 þæs swurdes mid þam sylfrenan hiltan. Þe Wulfric worhte. 7 þone gyldenan fetels. 7 þæne beh þe Wulfric worhte.

> (And the sword with the silver hilt that Wulfric made, and the gold belt and the armlet that Wulfric made.)

> (Whitelock, *Anglo-Saxon Wills*, pp. 56–7 [A])

Anglo-Saxon wills are a particularly apt source of information in this respect because they are all about gift-giving. One word in particular links poetry and these legal acts. *Brucan* – to make use of, to enjoy – occurs regularly in *Beowulf* in connection with treasure (894, 1487, 2162). The noun (*bryce*) occurs in Anglo-Saxon wills with a precise meaning, best captured in the legal term 'usufruct', which means 'temporary possession', literally 'use' (or enjoyment) as opposed to ownership. Thus

Brihtric Grim (in 964–80) grants his land to Winchester Cathedral, on condition that he have 'usufruct' (*bryce*) of it 'as long as his time [on earth] lasts' (Whitelock, *Anglo-Saxon Wills*, pp. 18–19 [A]). 'Usufruct' splices together the concepts of use (L. *usus*) and enjoyment (*fructus*), where *brucan* has flexible range and application, from use and enjoyment to consumption, for it also literally means 'to eat'. When Beowulf exhorts Hygelac to use his gifts well – *Bruc ealles well* (2162) – the implication is that the treasure is not to be 'owned' by hoarding but 'used', 'enjoyed' and 'consumed' by redistribution. Wealth is enjoyed when it is shared rather than when amassed as surplus.

The imaginative importance of gift-giving can scarcely be over-emphasised in OE literature, in particular, in the heroic world. In post-Conquest England, it remains as the basis of the reciprocal exchange of tenurial obligation between lord and vassal. By gift-giving, the king circulates wealth within his kingdom and, in the case of his gifts to Beowulf, seals the bond of peace between Scylding and Geat (1855–65). In contrast to this open-handed circulation of wealth stand both the niggardliness of bad kingship (1719–20; 1748–51) and the extreme hoarding of the dragon, who guards jealously the useless wealth, though 'ne byð him wihte ðy sel' [he will not be one whit the better for it] (2277). The ancient association between gold and immortality seems to preserve the dragon, who nursed the hoard for three hundred years (2278). Conversely, the readiness to give gifts covertly acknowledges one's mortal limits and the interdependence between self and community. Treasure is no good stockpiled; it must pass from hand to hand. That said, coin hoards have been excavated often enough to establish that they served during the OE period as the ordinary man's banking system; but the high number of hoards found in distressed areas – for example, from Sussex in 1066 – shows that they were used to shelter wealth that was endangered rather than simply to amass surplus.

Ready giving was an ethical norm, and in the king a positive virtue (*Beowulf*, 1484–7 [A]). At the end of the poem, Beowulf, mortally wounded, expresses his last wish that Wiglaf bring him the dragon's gold so that with his dying eyes he can gaze on the treasure his life has bought (2743–51; 2792–801). To a strictly Christian ethic, this constitutes avarice; but to the warrior-king it is visual evidence of his provision for the people he leaves behind, an affirmation that he died well. Heroic and elegiac poetry depict a world in which mobile assets rather than land form the primary measure of status and wealth. Wealth must be portable or buriable, and the place it holds in OE society registers its cultural roots in wandering.

The gift requires an implied counter-gift, which, at the very least, must be the responsible use of that gift. In accepting a gift, one accepts those reciprocal obligations. Thus Wulfric leaves his estate to the monastery at Burton after the death of his impoverished daughter, who has the use (*bryce*) of it as long as she 'knows how to deserve' it (*geearnigean cann*) (Whitelock, *Anglo-Saxon Wills*, pp. 46–8 [A]). This reciprocity between giving and receiving has to do with the centrality of the gift in the economies of our most ancient societies, and is reflected in grammar itself; the Latin dative case is governed by verbs of giving *and* receiving. For a society centred on war, the central gift from a 'treasure-giving' lord to his thegn is armour and weapons. On the thegn's death, that war gear (or some other form of wealth) was returned, and in receiving it back, the lord agreed to execute the dead man's wishes.

So regularly was a thegn's military equipment ceremonially returned to his lord that the term for war gear, *heregeatu*, came to denote a general death duty, and evolved into the term 'heriot', the medieval death-tax. To the Norman fiscal administrators who compiled the Domesday Book, the *heregeatu* seemed to approximate to their 'relief' or inheritance tax. In accordance with the successful strategy of assimilation they adopted wherever possible, they thus retained the external form of an AS custom, but imbued it with new meaning, for the *heregeatu* quickly shed its military association and degenerated over time in meaning from an earl's rich war trappings to a peasant's inheritance tax of a farm animal. In this form the heriot continued for some centuries as the requirement of tenurial succession, a faint memory of bonds forged on the battlefield between lord and thegn fighting shoulder to shoulder.

Early banking was alive and well among society's more mobile classes from the twelfth century onwards; merchant banking arose out of the use of bills of exchange cashed in at different points along trade routes without any shipping of actual coin. This, along with the ubiquity of tally sticks, fostered a ready enough sense of symbolic currency. And lending at interest was done by goldsmiths using monies deposited by other clients. There was a sense that money, apart from being the most elegantly apt form of universal exchange, could itself be put to work by earning interest. Alongside this awareness of money's abstract possibility, there nonetheless prevailed a residual and conservative sense that money must have value in itself. The bullion content of coins was supposed to represent their face value; paper banknotes, with their negligible intrinsic value, did not exist; minting false coin under the law of Cnut would cost a man his hand, and coin clipping – shaving the (unmilled) edges of coins for reuse – was a treasonable offence in the later Middle Ages, punishable even by execution. Usury – the loan of money at unreasonably high interest rates – was both preached against and punishable by law. Jews figure large in the economic role played by money-lending, although they by no means stood alone in extending credit for profit. There

> ### The Statute of Labourers, 1351
>
> Against the malice of servants who were idle and unwilling to serve after the pestilence without taking outrageous wages it was recently ordained by our lord the king, with the assent of the prelates, nobles and others of his council, that such servants, both men and women, should be obliged to serve in return for the salaries and wages which were customary (in those places where they ought to serve) during the twentieth year of the present king's reign (1346–7) or five or six years previously. It was also ordained that such servants who refused to serve in this way should be punished by imprisonment … But now our lord the king has been informed in this present parliament, by the petition of the commons, that such servants completely disregard the said ordinance in the interests of their own ease and greed and that they withhold their service to great men and others unless they have liveries and wages twice or three times as great as those they used to take in the said twentieth year of Edward III and earlier, to the serious damage of the great men and impoverishment of all members of the said commons … Wherefore … the following things were ordained to prevent the malice of the said servants:
>
> … [That] those who refuse to take such oath, or to fulfil what they have sworn or undertaken shall be put in the stocks for three days or more … or sent to the nearest gaol, there to remain until they are willing to submit to justice. For this purpose stocks are to be constructed in every vill between now and Whitsunday.
> (Dobson, pp. 64–5 [A]).

was a delicate balance between the fluidity, abstraction and anonymity of money and the concrete reality of having to show up in person to fight, plough or mend a road for an overlord. If a cash economy over-dominates, it begins to blur the boundaries between social castes and undermine the demography of the feudal base, which distributes workers throughout manorial estates, and regulates the size and number of towns. That undermining becomes evident in the fourteenth century, and everyone was talking about it, in sermons, in Parliament, and even in dream visions.

In the alliterative poem, *Pearl*, the narrator, grieving for his lost daughter of two years, has a vision in which he meets her, now crowned a queen of heaven. In the ensuing dialogue between them, he marvels that one so young, so unproven in spiritual maturity, should hold so elevated a place in heaven. Reprimanding him sharply, the young creature, Pearl, reminds him of the parable in Matthew 20.1–16 of the vineyard owner and the labourers (Andrew and Waldron, ll. 493–576 [A]). Some were hired early in the morning, more in the middle of the day, and others just before its close, all for a penny a day. As the labourers line up for payment, those hired in the early morning complain that they had worked more for the same money, but the lord holds them to their contract, warning them not to challenge his authority. About forty years before *Pearl* was written, the Statute of Labourers attempted to control the escalating price of labour in the wake of the demographic decimation of plague. Landowners found themselves hoist with their own petard: by encouraging a cash economy through commutation of tenurial service in kind to money, they had yielded to the logic of market conditions that no longer worked in their favour. Despite this change in market conditions, wages were fixed at pre-plague prices (haymakers earning no more than a penny a day), and labourers had to take an oath to observe the statute. Although *Pearl*'s parable alludes to spiritual rather than earthly wages, the analogy must have resonated with those who remembered the enforcement of the Statute. The parable's moral – to respect the fixed agreement of lordly authority rather than to compete for reward – applied as aptly to economic as it did to spiritual welfare.

The thin line between fair wages and extortion (capitalising on the need of another) is explored in the figure of Mede in *Piers Plowman*, whose name, 'Meed' is ambiguous, ranging in meaning from wages or just reward (Usk, III. 139–40 [A]) to bribery, although Langland consistently interprets the word pejoratively. Rescuing her from a marriage with Fals Fikel-tonge (passus iii), the King unsuccessfully attempts to pair her with Conscience, who will have none of her on account of her falseness. Conscience distinguishes between meed and right reward for virtue, and his example is telling:

> That laborers and lowe [lewede] folk taken of hire maistres,
> It is no manere mede but a mesurable hire.

> [That which labourers and lay folk take from their masters is in no way meed but a fair wage.]

> (Langland, B.iii.255–6 [A])

In the context of the Statute of Labourers, it is hard to know what exactly the words mean. In charging higher rates, were labourers simply asking for *mesurable hire* or for meed, in its ominous sense? Langland's fourteenth-century England was a place where wage-earning had increasingly replaced the old system of payment in kind or of wages established by custom that bore little relation to actual market value; serfs had either become money-paying tenants or, by moving into the towns, had become wage-labourers. A world where everything is on sale to the highest bidder is the world of Mede, which, for Langland, spelled the destruction of values without which the community would founder – justice, charity and a divinely ordained division of labour.

Men Writing about Women

> Chit te ant cheoweð þe ant scheomeliche schent te, tukeð þe to bismere as huler his hore, beateð þe ant busteð þe as his ibohte þrel ant his eðele þeowe ... Bisih þe, seli wummon; beo þe cnotte icnut eanes of wedlac, beo he cangun oðer crupel, beo he hwuch se he eauer beo, þu most to him halden ... Ah nu iwurðe hit al þet ha habb hire wil of streon þet ha wilneð, ant loki we hwuch wunne þrof hire iwurðe... Inwið i þi wombe, swel in þi butte þe bereð þe forð as a weater-bulge, þine þearmes þralunge ant stiches i þi lonke, ant i þi lendene sar eche riue... Ant hwet, þe cader fulðen, ant bearmes umbe stunde... Ant lokin efter al þis hwenne hit forwurðe, ant bringe on his moder sorhe upo sorhe.

> He rails at you and scolds you and abuses you shamefully, treats you disgracefully as a lecher does his whore, beats you and thrashes you like his bought slave and his born serf. Consider, innocent woman: once the knot of wedlock is tied, even if he is an idiot or cripple, whatever he may be like, you must be faithful to him ... But now suppose that it turns out that she has all she wanted in the child that she longs for, and let us see what happiness she gets from it ... Inside, in your belly, a swelling in your womb which bulges you out like a water-skin, discomfort in your bowels and stitches in your side, and often painful backache ... And all the filth in the cradle and your lap sometimes ... And anticipating after all this time when it will go astray and bring all kinds of unhappiness to its mother.
>
> (Millett and Wogan-Browne, *Medieval English Prose for Women*, pp. 28–33 [A])

This is a remarkably accurate and graphic account of the hardships of wifely subservience, so it comes as a surprise to learn that it is the work of a priest in the twelfth or thirteenth century, writing a treatise on virginity, *Hali Meiðhad* (*Holy Maidhood*), for a small group of anchoresses. The relationship between the author and his female audience seems affectionate, yet the priest's exhortation to virginity does ultimately participate in an institutional discourse that subordinates woman; indeed most anti-feminist writing in the Middle Ages came from the clerical establishment. Despite this institutional complicity, the passage portrays an acute psychological insight into and awareness of female anger, an awareness shown in other contexts (*Owl and the Nightingale*, 1491–570 [A]). It is hard to know whether to value the words for their sympathetic insight or be cynical of their designs to prescribe female sexuality and regulate women's bodies.

1.11 Gossiping women surrounded by demons.
c. 1325–40.

In another text written by a man, the French *Roman de la Rose*, we meet an Old Woman (La Vieille), who speaks at length about the deceitful and lascivious nature of her own sex. Women, she says, need to know every trick in the book, including faking an orgasm, 'so that he will think that she is taking with gratitude what she doesn't think worth a chestnut' (14305–10, Dahlberg, p. 244 [A]). The author of this part of the *Roman*, Jean de Meun, was possibly a cleric, and his depiction of female deceitfulness only confirms the suspicion that women don't get a fair deal from men, especially clerks, who alone are the social group most responsible for the written word. Anyone familiar with Chaucer's *Wife of Bath's Prologue* will recognise the influence of La Vieille on his characterisation of Alison, who, married off at twelve to a succession of old men, or old bacon, as she describes them, relates how she made a *feyned appetit* of enjoying sex with them (Chaucer, III.417–18 [A]). In embodying such allegations about women, she herself colludes with misogynist discourse, yet in the same breath attests to the common enough experience of being with a man she does not desire and having to fulfil the 'marital debt' like it or not.

Feigning an appetite might be the only way to protect private feelings that have no sanctioned outlet. The Wife of Bath is such a manifold of textual allusion that it is impossible to separate tonal ironies from sincerities; misogynist axioms uttered in all apparent sincerity assume an ironic cast from their new context. Although Alison often seems lifelike and psychologically authentic, we do well to remember that she is a construct of texts, a jumble of (mis)quotations assembled by someone who does not even share her sex. Not only that, there are a number of lines in her prologue that, although they exist in some manuscripts, may not have been Chaucer's, or if they were, may have been afterthoughts or an early draft, later revised. Cambridge University Library MS. Dd.4.24, here referred to as 'Dd', is authoritative enough, copied within twenty years of Chaucer's death, one of the six earliest manuscripts of the *Prologue* out of fifty-eight in all. Dd includes lines that significantly add to the image of the Wife as every man's nightmare:

> Blessed be god that I haue wedded fyue
> Of whiche I haue pyked out the beste
> Bothe of here nether purs and of here cheste.

> [Blessed be God that I have wedded five (husbands), whom I picked clean in both the purse they have 'down there' and the one in their pocket.]
> (Robinson, *Wife of Bath's Prologue*, Dd, fol. 67v, 44–44B [A])

I ne loved neuere by no discrecioun
But euere folwed myn appetite
Al were he short long blak or whiʒt.

[I never did show discrimination in love, but always indulged my appetites whether he
was tall or short, dark or blond.]

(Robinson, *Wife of Bath's Prologue*, Dd, fol. 74r, 604D–F [A])

Whether the scribe of Dd inserted these lines or copied them from his exemplar we
will probably never know, but we can know his opinion of them readily enough.
When it comes to the lines, 'For half so boldly there can no man / sweren and lyen as
a womman can' (fol. 69v, lines 227–8), the copyist sourly inserted *verum est* (it is true)
in the margin. Other such editorial lemon drops throughout the prologue reveal how
invested he was in what he was transcribing. Whether the lines originally came from
Chaucer or someone else only matters to a certain degree; what is important is the
extent to which the copyist impressed himself upon the text, making this new manuscript, this new incarnation of Chaucer's work, assume the local colour of his own
beliefs and interests. In manuscript culture, the copier or reproducer of a text is also
its reader and editor. Save in the instance of the survival of a work solely in the original manuscript, a medieval text represents the work and intentions not only of the
original author but also of all subsequent copyists. The Wife of Bath may have considerably rattled the scribe of Dd, prompting him to add a few lines of his own to exag-
gerate her voraciousness and make her cruder than Chaucer had originally depicted
her; or maybe he thought it high time that women were exposed for the wicked creatures they were, and his scribal exuberances are his way of applauding what he read
in his exemplar. He was not alone in so characterising women. In William Dunbar's
satiric *Tretis of the Twa Mariit Women and the Wedo* [*Treatise of the Two Married Women and
the Widow*], one of the wives echoes the Wife of Bath's strategy of making her husband
pay for sex: 'His purse pays richely in recompense efter' (Dunbar, *Tretis*, l. 136 [A]).

Men did not have it all their own way. A counter-tradition flourished, and much
of this came from the pens of women. Christine de Pisan (c. 1364–c. 1431), a prolific
writer in French whose career overlapped that of Chaucer, wrote extensively about the
slander done to women by these misogynist writings, most particularly the *Romance
of the Rose*. In her 'God of Love's Letter' (1399) (Blumenfeld-Kosinski and Brownlee,
pp. 15–29 [A]), Cupid castigates clerks for damning women. Ventriloquising through
Cupid, Christine poses her objections: how can universal female nature be logically
predicated on the evidence of one bad woman (185–209)? The truth of what is written
is relative to the author – in other words, if women had been doing the writing, the
story would have been quite different (407–30). Clerks write what they write out of
sexual frustration (471–508); as Aesop's fable relates, when the fox found he couldn't
reach the grapes he claimed they were sour.

We find a similar literary device in Chaucer's 'Prologue' to the *Legend of Good
Women*, in which he dreams he meets the God of Love, who chastises Chaucer the
narrator for having written such awful things about women, *Troilus and Criseyde*
and his translation of the *Romance of the Rose* being singled out for specific rebuke.
Chaucer's participation in the intellectual debate over anti-feminism does not only

rely on such mannered literary devices. After the Wife of Bath has had enough of listening to Jankyn's excerpts from his book of wicked wives, she grabs the volume and tears it up, earning for herself a blow to the head that permanently impairs her hearing. It is interesting that Christine de Pisan should place her protest in the mouth of a male, for in the Wife of Bath Chaucer voices his most cutting questions to clerkly misogyny, as does his contemporary, Thomas Usk, when Usk defends women through the voice of Lady Love (Usk, ll. 226–97 [A]). The Wife's question, provoked by Jankyn's anti-feminist pronouncements – 'Who peyntede the leon, tel me who?' (Chaucer, III.692 [A]) – alludes to a popular fable of the painting depicting a lion defeated by a man. By asking whether it was the lion or the man who painted the picture, the lion insinuates authorial bias. This hotchpotch of quotations we call the Wife of Bath manages to affirm female depravity even as she questions the truth of the belief. Chaucer's text is complex and layered, his position impossible to pin down, his tone inscrutably ironic. Master of indirection, he refuses to nail his colours to the mast in a gesture that fuses complicity with critique. There is no easy way to align ideological sympathies when medieval men write about women.

Two fifteenth-century poems, the *Floure and the Leaf* and the *Assembly of Ladies*, add a different dimension to the debate: a female narrator. In the *Floure and the Leaf*, the sleepless narrator walks to an arbour and there witnesses two bands of courtly lords and ladies, one faithful to the flower and the other to the leaf. The flower represents youth and beauty, which fade fast, while the leaf represents constancy in love and maidenliness. The narrator pledges her allegiance to the leaf. In the more explicitly allegorical *Assembly of Ladies*, the narrator dreams that she and four female companions present their bills of complaint at the court of Lady Loyalty. Both narrators draw us, and are themselves drawn, into a world where women's perspective dominates. Whether the authors of the poems were actually female we do not know; the impact of the literary device remains whatever their sex.

And Now for Something Completely Different: *Harlotrie*

Despite its stories of devout saints, brave warriors and faithful lovers, medieval English literature was far from high-minded and encompassed a good deal of obscene material. It is hard to put a label on such a diverse body of writing, for its energies were often politically invested, in, for example, anti-ecclesiastical or anti-Scots invective; and it may only be a question of a few words or lines rather than the entire document. In the following verse, the anti-ecclesiastical invective is disguised in dog Latin and in code (by writing the next alphabet letter to the intended letter):

> Fratres Carmeli navigant in a bothe apud Eli.
> Non sunt in celi, quia gxddbov xxkxzt pg ifmk.
> Omnes drencherunt, quia sterisman non habuerunt.
> Fratres cum knyvys goth about and txxkxzv nfookt xxzxkt.

> (Carmelite friars sail in a boat in Ely.
> They are not heavenly/miserable

Because they fuck the women of Ely.
They all drowned, because they had no steersman.
Friars with knives go about and screw [swyve] men's wives.)
(Fletcher, 'Chaucer the Heretic', pp. 88–9 [Ci])

What we are really talking about, then, is writing that offends against morals in some way, and we might simply borrow Chaucer's own terms when excusing himself to his audience for recounting *The Miller's Tale*:

Blameth nat me if that ye chese amys.
The Millere is a cherl; ye knowe wel this.
So was the Reve eek and othere mo,
And harlotrie they tolden bothe two.

(Chaucer, I.3181–4 [A])

Harlotrie maybe better captures the unfixed nature of what might count as offensive literature, for the term 'fabliau' both excludes too much and has been so overworked that it inculcates a misleading habit of thinking in terms of a rigid genre. It is debatable whether Chaucer consciously wrote *The Miller's Tale* as a fabliau in the same way that he wrote *The Tale of Sir Thopas* as a romance; the references within *Thopas* to other contemporary texts – *Horn Child, Bevis of Hamptown, Guy of Warwick, Lybeaus Desconus* and *Ypotis* – attest to a conscious sense of the genre, although *Ypotis*, a dialogue, hardly qualifies for the classification.

The term fabliau nonetheless does have some specificity, appearing in French and IF manuscripts from the late twelfth to thirteenth centuries (and even later), which contain some raucously rude short narratives, composed in verse (usually octosyllabic couplets). The IF header for the ME 'fabliau' *Dame Sirith* uses just such a term: 'Ci comence le fablel e la cointise de dame Siriz' [Here begins the short story and cunning of Dame Sirith]. The derivation of *fablel* from 'fable' supplies a useful reminder of the connection between fabliau and *exemplum*, for fabliaux offer a jaundiced moral, explicit or implied, such as: 'don't marry young girls if you're an old man', or 'all wives deceive their husbands' or 'all friars live in Satan's arsehole'. The surprise is how close the spirit of the fabliaux is to the *exempla* and anecdotes that pepper sermons. There was, for example, a popular connection in Lollard writing between friars and the tail of Antichrist (Fletcher, *Preaching and Politics*, pp. 281–303 [Ci]). The connection, however, between fabliau and sermon only stretches so far, for their contexts are entirely distinct. French fabliaux delight in obscene terms. The ruder the title, quite possibly, the more popular the tale: 'Le Chevalier qui fist parler les cons' [The Knight Who Made Cunts Talk] exists in seven manuscript copies; and 'Cele qui se fist foutre sur las fosse de son mari' [The Woman Who Got Fucked on the Tomb of her Husband] in six (Hines, p. 19 [Ci]).

In relation to the French fabliaux, which number over a hundred, there are remarkably few ME poems that have come close to fitting the genre: *Dame Sirith* and *The Fox and the Wolf* (c. 1275), and from the Auchinleck manuscript, *A Pennyworth of Wit*. This last – the story of a smart and loyal wife whose cunning eventually brings her unfaithful husband to his senses – is just as legitimately a moral *exemplum* or a romance in the mode of Chaucer's *Clerk's Tale*. Chaucer's *Miller's, Reeve's, Cook's, Summoner's, Friar's, Merchant's* and *Shipman's Tales*, which show remarkable skill in the

1.12 Man defecates before praying nun. *Romance of Alexander*. French and English, C.14th–15th.

detail of characterisation, dramatic dialogue and craft of storytelling, comprise the bulk of English fabliaux. The fifteenth-century *Prologue* to the *Tale of Beryn*, a spurious continuation of the *Canterbury Tales*, creates a fabliau-like story out of the encounter between the Pardoner and Kit, the Tapster at the inn in Canterbury. And *The Freiris of Berwik*, written in Scotland in the second half of the fifteenth century, matches Chaucer's talent for well-paced narration.

This list raises two points of debate: the lack of any obvious source for Chaucer's fabliaux, and the overall lack of English fabliaux prior to Chaucer, a lack only partially explained by the general predominance of French as the scribal vernacular of choice in the twelfth and thirteenth centuries. By broadening the terms of the question, however, we see on the one hand a much wider continental tradition of rude stories (for example, the closest analogue we have to *The Miller's Tale* is the Middle Dutch *Heile van Beersele*); and on the other, a loosening of the generic hold of 'fabliau' (a term appropriate to French literature) to reveal affinities with debate poetry, sermon *exempla*, invective, riddles and dramatic farce.

In *Dame Sirith* the early 'fabliau' – a term we guardedly retain – we notice a debate-like structure, implying that the text was performed rather than read (Bennett and Smithers, pp. 77–95 [A]). The manuscript clearly shows this in its use of marginal letters to designate change of the four different interlocutors: the lover, the wife, Dame Sirith and the narrator. When compared with a very similar English dramatic piece, *Interludium de clerico et puella* [Interlude Concerning a Clerk and a Girl] (Bennett and Smithers, pp. 196–200 [A]), *Dame Sirith* seems to have been a performance piece, perhaps an interlude at a feast, whether courtly or more popular. Like *Sirith*, the *Interludium* opens with the clerk declaring his love for a girl, who spurns his advances. This rejection drives him to seek help from Mome Elwis (corresponding to

Dame Sirith in the other poem) in procuring help to change the girl's mind. Mome Elwis also refuses him, asserting her devoutness (*Interludium*, 65–84); Dame Sirith initially does exactly the same thing, denying all interest in procuration and witchcraft (*Dame Sirith*, 193–216), but is eventually persuaded by the clerk, whereupon she devises a trick that reverses the wife's decision. Dame Sirith feeds her dog pepper and mustard making the animal's eyes water, then takes her dog to the wife, saying that her daughter, who spurned a clerk's advances, was turned into a bitch for her hard-heartedness, and this is why the dog weeps. Horrified at the prospect of being turned into a bitch, the wife changes her mind and takes the clerk as lover.

Unlike pure debate, *Dame Sirith* involves narrative action alongside its alternating speeches, and it is this trickster element that most obviously identifies it with fabliaux, and distinguishes it from the *Interludium*, which entirely comprises speeches and lacks action. *Dame Sirith* attests to the dramatic, performative quality of poetry, to bawdiness as communal entertainment, and suggests how the fabliau-like farce of Gil and Mak in the Towneley *Second Shepherds' Play* might have come about, which is hard to explain by any appeal to liturgical origins.

Dame Sirith is also explicitly crude, at least at one point. The trick executed, Dame Sirith offers some words of advice to the clerk, now on the point of conquest (440–1):

> And loke þat þou hire tille
> And strek out hire þes.

> [Make sure to plough her, and spread out her thighs.]

Avoiding any actual obscene word, the remark is nonetheless crude enough. In general, and certainly in comparison to its French counterparts, English bawdy tends to be sparing with sexual vocabulary, often preferring euphemisms such as *jewellys* (*Mankind*, 381, Eccles, p. 166 [A]) or *hangers* (Malory, 2:643 [A]) for 'testicles'. The comparative lack of sexual obscenity is generously compensated by scatological reference. In *Owl and the Nightingale*, the refined affectation of courtly love is soundly debunked by juxtaposition of toilets and courtship. One of the Owl's strongest arguments against the Nightingale is that she sings her songs of love in the bushes where people go to relieve themselves, that where there is the bedchamber there is the privy and the nightingale:

> Wan ich flo niʒtes after muse,
> I mai þe uinde ate rumhuse,
> Among þe wode, among þe netle.
> Þu sittest & singst bihinde þe setle:
> Þar me mai þe ilomest finde –
> Þar men worpeþ hore bihinde.

> [Whenever I fly at night mousing, I can find you at the privy, among the weeds, among the nettles. You sit and sing behind the toilet-seat. That's where men most often find you – where people stick out their backsides.]

> (*Owl and the Nightingale*, 591–6 [A])

This anti-courtly strain is one of the most important aspects of fabliau, and the opposition between romance and fabliau, courtly and uncourtly love is evident in the *quyting* of the Knight by the Miller in Chaucer's *Canterbury Tales*. Possibly the notion of obscenity itself takes definition in relation to discourses that constrain or sanitise the body, that is, to clerical and courtly discourse. Where courtly language idealises and elevates chivalry, fabliau parodies it. *Dame Sirith*'s courtly phrases – *in priuite* (84), *swete lemmon* (127), *derne loue* (130), 'dame Siriz þe hende' (154) – parody the refined locutions of courtliness and romance, and anticipate the strikingly similar diction of Chaucer's *Miller's Tale*. Further parody is gained by the reduction of the courtly lover's travail to (implied manual) labour through the word *swynk*, used three times in *Dame Sirith*; while in Chaucer's *Reeve's Tale*, the degradation is complete, as the courtly lover's honourable efforts morally diminish to the sweaty exertions of Aleyn's all-night sexathon: 'myn heed is toty of my swynk to-nyght' (Chaucer, I.4253 [A]). It might be observed, however, that for all the anti-courtly parody of fabliaux, their constant targets of sometimes vicious derision are the 'lower' orders of society: merchants affecting gentility, lesser churchmen, women and peasants. Class- and estates-consciousness are as present in this literature as they are in anything else.

The fascination demonstrated by such literature in the naming of things, whether by directly naming the unmentionable (*cunte, fert, ballockes, pyntel* [penis], *swyven* [to screw, have sex with]) or by euphemism – giving crude meanings to ordinary language – participates in its own way with contemporary philosophical enquiry into the relationship between language and reality, names and things. That enquiry, usually referred to as the debate between realism and nominalism, hinges on the status of ideas and on the words that denoted them. Does a universal idea actually exist in the same way that individual entities do? French fabliaux offer a spectacularly rich and satiric meditation on this problem of what it is that we name, particularly women's genitals or the act of sex. Punning furiously, and taking quite literally the notion of the 'unmentionable' and 'ignominious' (a word that means 'loss of name'), the fabliaux go far beyond slapstick humour to offer a profound consideration of the extent to which the words we utter passively reflect or actively construct reality. In ways less outrageously obscene than the French fabliaux, Chaucer's poetry shows similar preoccupations: in the *fert(h)yng* pun of *The Summoner's Tale*, the gap between seeming and reality in *The Merchant's Tale*, and the distinction between figurative and literal meanings in *The Friar's Tale*. The author referred to as the 'Wakefield Master' of the Towneley Plays demonstrates a similar interest in language's power to represent and misrepresent.

Alongside the philosophical parody of naming reality persists the exuberant delight medieval bawdy takes in wordplay and linguistic inventiveness. The remarkable L. colloquies of Ælfric Bata, Ælfric of Eynsham's student, demonstrate the creative energy that went into medieval invective: 'Fox shit! Cat turd! Chicken shit! You ass turd! … I would like you to be totally beshat and bepissed for all these words of yours. Have shit in your beard! May you always have shit in your beard, and shit and turds in your mouth' (Gwara, p. 139 [A]). Middle English can rival the Latin any day. Compare *Mankind*'s 'I have schetun yowr mowth full of turdys' [I have shat you a mouthful of turds] (*Mankind*, 132, Eccles, p. 158 [A]). Flyting – an insult-competition fought between medieval poets or between enemies as a preliminary to battle – was clearly a cherished part of cultural exchange; oratorical ability and the power of commanding laughter could make or break reputations. The flyting associated with heroic poetry was probably, in its historical reality, a rumbustious affair, demonstrating how derisory humour might find a place on the battleline, how laughter itself is a weapon. Although by the fifteenth century flyting had essentially lost this military aspect, Scots poet William Dunbar keeps the stylistic tradition alive in the 'Flyting of Dunbar and Kennedie', in which invective between two poets proves as inventive as any other literary endeavour.

> Thow hes na breik to latt thy bellokis gyngill,
>
> [You have no breeches to stop your bollocks from jingling.]
>
> (119)

> Herretyk, lunatyk, purspyk, carlingis pet,
> Rottin crok, dirtin dok, cry cok, or I sall quell the!
>
> [Heretic, lunatic, pick-purse, old woman's fart, liver-rotted old ewe, filthy arse, confess defeat, or I shall destroy you.]
>
> (247–8)

The fabliau-type story, which invariably involves narrative action, some kind of trick or poetic justice, and rudeness, is only one kind of scurrilous exercise in medieval English literature, though perhaps the most overtly poetic or 'literary'. The parodic sermon emerged in the later Middle Ages, a form borrowed from the French *sermons joyeux* (Jones, 'Parodic Sermon', pp. 94–114 [Ci]). Peppered with rude names (*Kateryn Fyste*, 'Katherine Wet-Fart') (Jones, 'Parodic Sermon', p. 105 [Ci]), the parodic sermon employs a madcap logic that pokes fun at scholastic disputation and reason as the privileged mark of human nature. In one such sermon, St Peter asks Adam a 'full greyt dowtfull' question, namely, why Adam ate the apple unpeeled (p. 101). Adam's answer, because he didn't have any fried pears, defeats all expectation of a sensible response. Late as the parodic sermon is, and derived from French models, it partakes in a perverse humour that dates back to Anglo-Saxon riddles, some of which are as rude and suggestive as anything that came later. The riddle is actually linked to wisdom literature, and the very word 'riddle' (OE *rædels*) is related to *rædan* (to advise), whence comes 'to read'.

> Staþol min is steapheah, stonde ic on bedde,
> neoþan ruh nathwær. Neþeð hwilum
> ful cyrtenu ceorles dohtor,
> modwlonc meowle, þæt heo on mec gripeð
>
> [My stem is erect, I stand up in bed, hairy somewhere below. Sometimes a ceorl's daughter, most comely, a proud maiden dares to lay hold of me.]
>
> (Marsden, p. 361 [A])

Deliberately double in meaning, the answer nonetheless is innocuous enough: an onion. Riddles pose an enigma that makes us think about language and reality differently, that defamiliarises the seemingly self-evident, and brings a new consciousness of things. They belong to a persistent thread of absurdity that informs medieval art and literature, perhaps most evident in the visual arts, where manuscript marginalia and sculpture delight both in rudeness and in a topsy-turvy world in which women beat their husbands, animals preach to a human congregation and baboons read.

Like *The Land of Cockaigne* with its rivers 'gret and fine / Of oile, melk, honi, and wine' (45–6, Bennet and Smithers, pp. 136–44 [A]), the artwork revels in turning authority on its head. Much of such humour is benignly employed, and sanctioned by authorities that are not above laughing at themselves. Yet humour notoriously masks its own intentions, and there is ultimately little to differentiate between the 'literary' world-turned-upside-down and that drawn in 1381 by rebel John Ball's letter to the Essex Commons.

> Iohan the Mullere hath ygrounde smal, smal, smal;
> The Kynges sone of heuene schal paye for al.
> Be war or ye be wo;
> Knoweth your freend fro your foo;
> Haueth ynow, and seith 'Hoo'.

> [John the Miller has ground small, small, small. The King's son of heaven will pay for all. Be wary or be full of woe; know your friend from your foe. Have sufficient, and say 'Ho!']

> (Dobson, p. 381 [A])

Although Chaucer's fabliaux tend to steal the limelight when considering medieval English bawdy, laughter, absurdity and rudeness find their way into all discourse, wounding, healing, dividing, uniting. If we have not understood their centrality in medieval literature then neither have we understood the nature of medieval religious and political power, for where there is belief there is laughter.

Readings

The Battle of Maldon

Maldon, Essex, August 991: Byrhtnoth, Ealdorman of Essex, faces the Danish army that have already looted in Kent and Suffolk, and, perhaps in hopes of good pickings such as they got in Ipswich, have sailed into the deep estuary of the River Blackwater. Byrhtnoth stands on the southern bank, the Danes on Northey Island, where they have moored their boats. The Blackwater, called Panta in the poem (*The Battle of Maldon*, ed. D. G. Scragg, ll. 68, 97 [A]), is at low tide, leaving exposed a narrow causeway called Northey Hard, which links island to mainland. Byrhtnoth controls the causeway; his men pick off any Danes who try to cross (72–83); battle is about to begin.

From the poem's evidence, this is how we think the forces were arrayed. All the historical documents record is that Byrhtnoth died in a battle fought at Maldon. Vividly described as the poem is, there is no evidence that it is an eyewitness account, or based on one. The poem reads as heroic poem rather than chronicle, yet it implies choices of action and outcomes that were real enough for a kingdom trying to survive. Although the battle was a resounding defeat for the English, the poet turns the disaster into the occasion of celebration of the outstanding courage and loyalty of Byrhtnoth's army.

The heroic world to which the poem belongs is revealed in its kennings and special poetic vocabulary, invoking an other-worldly atmosphere of larger-than-life feats of courage. In this respect, Byrhtnoth belongs in the same world as Beowulf. The poem's heroism is most exaggeratedly portrayed in Byrhtnoth's thegns, who stood

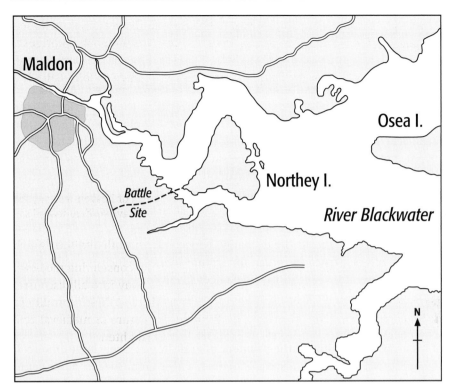

1.13 Map of Maldon, Essex.

The Maldon Manuscript

Antiquarian Sir Robert Cotton (1571–1631) collected a huge library of medieval manuscripts, readily available since Henry VIII's dissolution of the monasteries. A catalogue of 1696 describes a poem, even then a fragment, made up of three folded pages making a six-page booklet. Since medieval bookmakers regularly sewed four such pages together to make a 'quire', it is possible that only the first and last pages of the poem were lost. It is also possible that the poem had itself been used to form the inner binding of a more expensive book, and Cotton, who often dismantled and reassembled medieval books, may have come across it thus. All that was known before then about the battle at Maldon came from the *Anglo-Saxon Chronicle*, and some monastic and Latin records. In 1731, a huge fire burnt the poem and hundreds of other manuscripts 'to a crust'. Previously, deputy-keeper David Casley of the Cotton library (formerly thought to be John Elphinston) had transcribed the poem, and this transcription wound up in the possession of diarist Thomas Hearne, who, fortunately for us, never threw out anything. Our knowledge of this poem, a blank for the first seven centuries of its existence, thus depends on the survival of an eighteenth-century transcription, by an inexperienced copyist, of a fragment, subsequently burnt.

fighting after he fell. Disgusted by Godric's flight, Leofsunu, an Essexman, sums up the ethic of loyalty:

> Ne þurfon me embe Sturmere stedefæste hælæð
> Wordum ætwitan, nu min wine gecranc,
> Þæt ic hlafordleas ham siðie,
> wende fram wige.

[The steadfast men around Sturmer [village in Essex] will not need to reproach me with their words, now that my dead lord has fallen, that I return home lordless, and turn back from battle.]

(249–52)

Commendable though such loyalty be, it was not the historical norm in AS England for an ealdorman's thegns, who were landed and powerful in their own right, to die alongside their lord as a matter of principle (Woolf, p. 68 [Ci]). Hyperbole elevates the known historical defeat at Maldon into an epic loss borne with epic honour.

By contrast, note the laconic entry for the same year in the *Anglo-Saxon Chronicle*: 'Here Ealdorman Byrhtnoth was killed at Maldon, and in the same year it was first decided that tax be paid to the Danish men because of the enormities which they wrought along the sea coast. That was at first ten thousand pounds. Archbishop Sigeric decided on the decision' (Swanton, p. 126 [A]).

It is ironic that *Maldon* records the exchange between Byrhtnoth and the Danish messenger, who offers a truce in return for tribute money, which the ealdorman bluntly refuses. Alliteration heightens the choices involved: the Danish messenger offers peace for gold (*wið þam golde, grið*) (35), to which Byrhtnoth responds that he will send spears instead (*to gafole, garas*) (46). King Æthelræd, to whom Byrhtnoth is stoutly loyal (51–4, 151, 203), chose differently from his ealdorman, and at the advice of his archbishop initiated the payment of graft in punitively large amounts. At least by Byrhtnoth's moral standards, Æthelræd, whose name means 'noble counsel', was rightly called by posterity *Unrǣdig* (Ill-Counselled). The lives of Byrhtnoth and his men paid for little in the long run. That the advice to pay tribute should come from an ecclesiastic says much about the differing attitudes among English factions towards the Danish threat: diplomacy, opposition, pay-off, intermarriage, conversion and sponsorship at baptism, easy and uneasy cohabitation – all describe the conflicted nature of English reaction to Danish presence.

Nor was it simply a question of mixed opinion. Mixed parentage is also reflected in the English host. The three cowardly sons who flee the field of battle after Byrhtnoth's death – Godric, Godwine and Godwig – share Anglo-Saxon names, but the name of their father, Odda, is Danish (185–94). Their bad blood tells in premature flight. Yet other Anglo-Danes are loyal: Maccus fell early in the battle, defending the causeway (79–83); Wistan, son of Thurstan, killed three Danes before he was cut down (297–300); and the Northumbrian hostage Æscferth, whose father's name, Ecglaf, suggests Danish parentage, pitched in bravely (265–72). Northumbria, being within the Danelaw, was ambivalent in its loyalties, for which reason, presumably, Æscferth was brought along to fight. There is no easy opposition between English and Danish. Byrhtnoth's defiant words to the Danish messenger exhibit a loyalty to land and king rather than to any abstract concept of English nationality. His message is:

Þæt her stynt unforcuð eorl mid his werode,
Þe wile gealgean eþel þysne,
Æþelredes eard, ealdres mines
folc and foldan.

[That here stands, undaunted, a nobleman with his host, who will defend this homeland, the country of Æthelræd, the people and land of my prince.]

(51–4)

Byrhtnoth fights for the 'country of Æthelræd' rather than for 'England'. The naming of each Saxon warrior, and the recitation of his brave speech before falling alongside his lord, give us a strong sense of the bonds of loyalty that tie men together
and thegn to lord. In contrast, the Danish fighters are unnamed, their collectivity
suggesting lack of identity rather than unity. They are preying wolves (*wælwulfas*)
(96); they proceed by guile rather than by honour (86). The continued epithet of 'wanderer' – *brimliþendra* (27), *sælida* (45), *flotan* (72) – renders them landless and parasitic,
despite the fact that they also had a homeland. Although we speak of England as
united under one king by the tenth century, its 'national' identity is best explained
in terms of local affinity to land and to overlord. Northumbria belonged to the kingdom, yet the fighter from that region was a 'hostage' (*gysel*) (265). 'National' identity,
whether before or after 1066, is measured in terms of bodily relationship to the land
and to one's lord.

At the beginning of the poem, or at least of what survives, Byrhtnoth instructs his
men to dismount and drive away their horses (2–4); he himself remains mounted,
moving among the men as he pre-
pares them for battle; this done, he
also dismounts and stands with his
chosen band of retainers (17–24).
These details accord with what we
know about Anglo-Saxon military
strategy: the 'shield-wall' formed
the core of the English army (Abels,
p. 147 [Ci]). Standing in wedge-for-
mation, the fighters overlapped
their round wooden shields,
thereby creating secure protection
from arrows and a cavalry charge.
Spears and swords were the basic
offensive weapons, long- and short-
range. With the shield-wall as the
backbone of the army, and the
spear and sword the main instruments of missile and shock combat, cavalry was generally ancillary
and under-utilised, horses being
used more for travelling from one
place to another. Lacking buildings, neighbours and familiar terrain, the invading Danes tended
to be more heavily armed than

The Danegeld

The Danish raids were coming so thick and fast by
1010 that English unity and morale were shattered.
Shires no longer helped each other and none could
be found to gather an army (Swanton, pp. 140–1
[A]). In 1011 Æthelræd attempted peace on the
promise of tribute, and some of the Danes, led by
Thorkell the Tall, switched allegiance to the English.
Thus was born the Danegeld, at the time called the
heregeld (army-payment) to pay off the Scandinavian
mercenaries and finance the war. The Danegeld was
levied on owners of land, and was in effect an early
property tax, abolished and reinstated intermittently
until it eventually disappears from the Rolls in 1163.
The idea of paying off the Danes first appears in 991,
after Maldon, when Æthelræd paid them £10,000 – a
large sum, but one that rose exponentially: in 994
£16,000, in 1002 £24,000, in 1007 £36,000 and in
1012 £48,000. These tributes were not collected in a
systematic way as the Danegeld was, and no doubt
made use of money hoards containing coins no longer
in currency. It is no surprise that during his reign
Æthelræd increased the number of mints from about
fifty to over seventy. Burdensome as the tributes and
Danegeld were, they bought some respite and, at
least in the instance of Thorkell, effectively split the
loyalties of the Danes. Did Æthelræd have any other
alternatives?

1.14 Norman cavalry and English shieldwall. Detail from the Bayeux Tapestry. C.11th.

the Saxons, using chain mail, arrows and axes along with the statutory spear. They also understood the value of horses, which enabled mobility and a fast getaway. At the Battle of Ringmere (1010), the victorious Danes, seizing the horses, 'thereafter had possession of East Anglia, and for three months raided and burned that country; they even travelled into the wild fens, and they killed men and cattle, and burned throughout the fens' (Swanton, p. 140 [A]). Where ships enabled lightning raids upon water-accessible dwellings, stolen horses were land-ships, enabling access to the hinterland. This presumably is why Byrhtnoth commands all the horses to be driven away, a courageous decision, for it also put paid to any possibility of retreat for his own men; the one horse remaining, his own, was taken by the spineless Godric, who took to his heels on Byrhtnoth's death; many in the army, seeing their leader's horse in retreat, thought it was Byrhtnoth himself, and they fled too, thereby breaking the ranks of the Saxon defence and ensuring defeat for the remaining cadre (237–43).

Looking ahead to 1066, the 'Northmen' who conquered England under William had one materially different weapon: the horse. Their cavalry unit proved crucial in hewing down the English once they unwisely broke ranks. 'Chivalry', etymologically related to 'cavalry', enters ME from OF *chevalerie* (the art of horsemanship). The Bayeux Tapestry makes much of the contrast between William's horsed fighters (despite the fact that cavalry only formed one part of the Norman army) and the English, all on foot, including King Harold, just as Byrhtnoth and the Danes fought seventy-five years earlier.

The contrast is greatly exaggerated, yet in the minds of these needleworkers of history, the Normans introduced *chevalerie* to England. Cavalry would have its own moment, at the close of the Middle Ages, of being outmoded by more effective military technology – artillery – but in the tenth and eleventh centuries, it was coming into its own on the battlefield, and Byrhtnoth's infantry tactics were soon to be an outmoded technology. Courage and loyalty, so celebrated by the poem, could not do the job alone.

On all fronts, Byrhtnoth demonstrates exemplary leadership, instructing his forces meticulously and fighting alongside them (17–24). In his negotiations with the Danish messenger, he is fiery and resolute (42–4), and eloquent in flyting (45–61). *Anræd*, literally 'single-minded', is a word particularly apt to describe courage in the face of danger; twelve years after Maldon, in 1003, the Danes, seeing the English no longer resolute (*anræd*) once their leader had abandoned them, seize the advantage

(Swanton, p. 134 [A]). *Anræd* also ironically reminds us of the epithet subsequently applied to Byrhtnoth's king, Æthelræd the *Unrædig*. Byrhtnoth shows strategic planning, holding his tactical advantage on the mainland by keeping the Danes in a bottleneck on the causeway (72–83). Even in the thick of fighting, he praises individuals for particularly brave and vengeful efforts (113–21). Wounded, he fights on until he can no longer hold his sword or stay standing, but even then, emphasises the poet, he heartens his men and commends his soul to God (159–80).

So if Byrhtnoth is such a great leader, why on earth does he throw away his territorial advantage on the mainland by letting the Danes cross the causeway?

> Þa hi þæt ongeaton and georne gesawon,
> Þæt hi þær bricgweardas bitere fundon,
> ongunnon lytegian þa laðe gystas:
> bædon þæt hi upgangan agan moston,
> ofer þone ford faran, feþan lædan.
> Ða se eorl ongan for his ofermode
> alyfan landes to fela laþere ðeode.

> [When they perceived this and clearly saw that they had encountered grim guardians of the causeway there, the hateful strangers began to get crafty; they asked that they be allowed access to the land, to cross the ford, leading their foot-soldiers. Then the earl, because of his pride, began to yield too much land to the hateful people.]

> (84–90)

In his catalogue of virtues, *ofermod* strikes a jarring note. It seems to mean 'pride', but more charitable interpretations place the meaning closer to 'great-spiritedness'. If great-spiritedness, it could be argued that in holding the Danes off the causeway, Byrhtnoth had only achieved stalemate rather than checkmate (Abels, p. 148 [Ci]). This same army had already looted in Kent at Folkstone and Sandwich, and in Suffolk at Ipswich (Swanton, p. 126 [A]); if Byrhtnoth did not actively inflict damage on the enemy army, even at the cost of his own, they would continue unhindered to ravage the coastline and possibly the interior.

Yet considered alongside the phrase *landes to fela, ofermod* seems to suggest a reprehensible rashness, although that need not detract overmuch from his heroism: Homer's Achilles was quick-tempered and Odysseus proud, and Beowulf does not escape the taint of pride either ('*Beowulf*', 1758–61 [A]). Byrhtnoth's example differs from the others, however, in that he alone was a local historical personage, and the battle he fought a real and recent loss for the English. To that extent, the poem has more in common with contemporary chronicle than with *Beowulf*. In contrast to Byrhtnoth and his *ofermod* stands Godric the 'cowardly' (*earh*) (238). The poem's inner dynamics set up the contrast between the rashness of one and the fearfulness of the other. Godric's shameful example is echoed by that of Ealdorman Ælfric in the battle of 1003:

> Then a great army was gathered; and then Ealdorman Ælfric should have led the army, but he took to his old tricks; as soon as they were so close at hand that each of them looked on the other, then he pretended to vomit, and said that he was ill, and thus betrayed the people. Then when Swein saw that they were not resolute [*hi anræde*

næron], he led his raiding-army into Wilton, and burned down the settlement, and then went to Salisbury and from there back to the sea.

(Swanton, p. 134 [A])

Ealdorman Ælfric (not our homilist Ælfric of Eynsham) held the same rank as Byrhtnoth. An *ealdorman* was of first rank beneath the king, and controlled a number of shires. Semi-independent rulers in their own right, they were comparable to the great dukes on the continent. Historical chronicle itself offers a stark contrast between Ealdorman Byrhtnoth who, perhaps unnecessarily, died fighting the Dane, and Ealdorman Ælfric whose cowardice before the Dane robs him of all dignity. In a time peopled with too many Ælfrics and Godrics, the poet points to England's need for a great leader. Between Byrhtnoth's *ofermod* and the lack of resolution brought about by Ælfric's cowardice, what chance was there against the Danes? Byrhtnoth chose to stand and fight. His king, Æthelræd, chose to pay the Danes off, perhaps even as a consequence of the losses at Maldon – for if Byrhtnoth could not fend off the Danes, what chance had anyone else? As Aristotle points out in his *Nicomachean Ethics* (II.viii), the virtue of courage strikes a mean between the vice of excess, rashness, and of deficiency, cowardice; sometimes courage means knowing when to walk away from a fight and cut a deal. Viewed from the wider angle, maybe Æthelræd the Unready wasn't so ill advised after all.

Ancrene Wisse (c. 1220)

Ancrene Wisse (*Guide for Anchoresses*) was commissioned, we believe, by three well-born young sisters, who had taken anchoritic vows. The term 'anchoress' or its masculine form, 'anchorite', refers to a very specific kind of hermit life. Unlike nuns who lived as a community, anchoresses lived alone in an enclosed cell that usually abutted a church – solitary, but curiously public in the middle of community life. In a ceremony closest to funeral rites, extreme unction was administered as she was 'buried' in her cell, from which she would only exit as a corpse. References throughout the *Ancrene* suggest the basic features of this cell, which sported three windows: through the church window, the anchoress could participate remotely in the services; through the external parlour window, the anchoress could 'speak' (OF *parler*) with the public; a third, 'house', window overlooked an adjacent space where her two maids slept. Smaller anchorholds might only have two windows, an external one and one opening onto the church. It is possible that anchoritic cells were built alongside each other, perhaps with a shared window through which anchoresses might communicate. If a guest stayed briefly, her maid would entertain her (a male guest being out of the question) in the anchoress's place; the anchoress herself only waving cheerfully at her through the house window (*Ancrene Wisse*, ed. Hasenfratz, 2.259–65, p. 114 [A]).

Although we speak of the author as male, we might consider the involvement of the women about and for whom *Ancrene* is written. Composed over so many months, *Ancrene* may well have been read in part to the anchoresses, shaped by their reactions and requests even as it was under 'composition'. In a culture in which reading aloud to others was a daily social occurrence, authorial agency was dispersed through a community that included writer, scribe, reader and audience. We do not know how the arrangement of *Ancrene*'s eight parts came to be, but the initial attention to liturgical first principles in the first part bespeaks a practical orientation shaped directly by the needs and directives of the anchoresses.

The last brick in place, the world at bay, what now? *Ancrene* was a guide, something fuller than, say, St Benedict's rule, which simply enumerates external observation of duties and office. This 'lady rule', however, probes her innermost feelings and thoughts. Only the first and eighth parts of *Ancrene* discuss the 'outer' rule; the core of the work is devoted to the inner rule of her selfhood. Where the monk had labours to perform, the anchoress's sole duty was fixed devotion on God. In fact, she is warned against too much activity: against instructing children; making elaborate lace, even as gifts; owning property that would involve her in worldly business; and socialising. As an anchoress, she has become dead to the world, and in the silence of death, her purpose is to find God.

Ancrene circulated widely from its earliest appearance, each version suggesting a different kind of readership: monastic, female, lay, mixed and so on. How could the lonely, Spartan life of the recluse have appealed to so many, and have such value to the community at large? Evidently, the book, a scribal labour of love, was a precious gift for the anchoress, read and reread constantly. Teaching about temptation, the writer directs her to turn back to a passage dealing with Christ's own torments (4.126–30, p. 213). Certain passages, loved more than others, were turned to daily for comfort and wisdom. If the anchoress were asked to name her most precious possession, this book might well have been it. Plainly beautiful, compact and neat; maybe the object itself was a source of temptation for her, making her overly proud and possessive of it, reluctant to share or lend it (or some sections of it) to a scribe for copying. In the recluse's life of relentless soul-searching, even good things can bring evil outcomes. Reading a book was no leisurely pursuit. Although silent reading was not unknown, the anchoress probably mumbled aloud as she read. Vocalising her prayers and readings thus for hours a day was physically demanding, yet it also filled her cell with sound and presence. Always in her hands (4.1326, p. 298), the book must have felt like a living comforter.

A day empty of all busyness stretches long, and so the outer rule gives directives from the minute the anchoress awakes to the minute before sleep. The anchoress's day might have included about five hours for prayer, perhaps a couple of hours for private reading and meditation, and some time for instructing servants, sewing vestments and so on. On waking, she is to kneel on her bed, greet the Lord, the Virgin Mary and the saints as if they were her husband and immediate family, cross and bless herself, recite a hymn, recite the Lord's Prayer while dressing and throughout the day. The regulations continue – what to say after this or that prayer if it is a Sunday, how to genuflect on a workday and so on. The sheer act of internalising these rules until they become habitual requires months and years; quiet and empty her day may appear to be from the outside, but inside it is a fury of busyness, a constant battle of the will to master straying thoughts and fill the mind with God.

1.15 The enclosing of a recluse. c. 1397–1435.

The outer rule continues and concludes in the eighth and last part of *Ancrene*. The writer forbids the anchoress from overly harsh penances without her confessor's explicit permission: wearing hair shirts or hedgehog skins, flogging herself with nettles, holly or lead-tipped scourges, cutting herself until she bleeds (8.99–107, p. 404). 'Me is leovere thet ye tholien wel an heard word, then an heard here' [I would rather that you well endure a harsh word than a rough haircloth] (8.115–16, p. 405). Twelfth-century anchorite Wulfric of Haselbury wore an iron coat of mail next to his skin. In contrast, the priest's recommendation of penances is light – ten or twelve Our Fathers and Hail Marys or some other *lutles i-hweat* (little thing) (5.528–9, p. 345) – because the anchoritic life is already a penance. Instead, she is to find redemption in Christ's pain rather than in hers. Such mutilation indicates to us self-hatred and emotional disturbance rather than piety. The imaginative challenge of understanding this text lies in how such self-abasement can be desirable not only to the anchoress herself, but also to the entire community for whom she stands as a spiritual 'anchor' (3.268–70, pp. 175–6). Even in medieval times, the anchoritic life seemed harsh. To the lay person, such extreme penance could seem unbalanced, and create a contradiction between a loving God and one who required physical affliction. Without denying the justice of these objections, the writer defends the special arduousness of the anchoritic life. In the paragraphs ahead, we will consider how such ascetic practice makes sense in its time, and offers a model of selfhood that reveals how historical difference shapes consciousness itself.

With a life so bare of human interaction and ornament, one might wonder in what way an anchoress could be tempted, yet by far the longest sequence in *Ancrene*, part 4, forming its physical and moral core, is on temptation. Although temptations were many and various, the ultimate temptation for a woman, most especially for one who had taken a vow of celibacy, was sex; lust figures large in this treatise for virgins. The chances of actual sexual contact between an anchoress and a man were remote, but that does not remove desire, which lasts longer and holds the mind more than the act itself. In a solitary day that stretches long in front of her, one look or touch through the window can arouse a torment of passion. Lack of interaction only makes the tiniest stimulation more dangerous; for this reason, she keeps the window veiled. Desire and the act itself blur at the point where lust would prevail 'yef ther were eise to fulle the dede' [if opportunity to do the deed arose] (4.1349–50, p. 300). The anchoress was even counselled against looking at her *ahne hwite honden* [own white hands] (2.814, p. 154). Why? The context suggests she might be tempted to vanity and romantic fancies, but another possibility suggests itself. Nowhere in *Ancrene* does the writer mention either sexual desire between women or masturbation. In itself, this is unsurprising, for like many confessional treatises, *Ancrene* declines to name the most secret and shameful of sins:

> Ich ne dear nempnin the uncundeliche cundles of this deofles scorpiun, attri i-teilet. Ah sari mei ha beon the bute fere, other with, haveth swa i-fed cundel of hire galnesse – thet ich ne mei speoken of for scheome ne ne dear for drede, leste sum leorni mare uvel then ha con ant beo th'rof i-temptet.

[I dare not name the unnatural offspring of this poison-tailed devil's scorpion. How sorry she may be who, with or without a companion, has so fed the offspring of her lechery, of which I can neither speak for shame nor dare for fear, lest someone learn more evil than they are aware of and become tempted by it.]

(4.341–5, p. 229)

These most private aspects of the anchoress's life remain undiscussed, but the writer's pained delicacy suggests that some women indeed knew what it was to wrestle with desires for which they did not even have a name, stopping their tongues in the confessional with incomprehension added to shame. The solitary life brought every kind of temptation, brought the anchoress up against her darkest side.

Against these dark thoughts, the anchoress is urged to dwell on more positive images of sanctity, licensed fantasies in which she plays a role that gratifies without spiritual endangerment, such as that offered by St Margaret (4.795–6, p. 261).

The Long Work of Transcription

The writer of *Ancrene* ends his work admitting he would rather go on pilgrimage to Rome than begin the book again. We can appreciate his reluctance, for composition could have taken years. Subsequent scribes of *Ancrene* similarly devoted possibly a year, maybe more of their lives to copying this one work, depending on the scribe's other duties, and the availability of light, parchment, ink and transcription exemplars. Certainly the transcription of *Ancrene* represented a major commitment of time. Sometime in the 1220s, cramped and with eyes strained, the scribe finally finishes: 117 pages, measuring 21.5 cm by 14.8 cm. The writing is neat and plain, elaborate lettering minimal, no illustration. This is his gift to a group of women living as recluses nearby. Large enough to enable reading aloud by one woman to her fellow recluses, small and light enough to be held in her hands and pored over alone, this is Cambridge, Corpus Christi College MS. 402. A later scribe makes a copy so tiny – 10 cm by 6.7 cm – it must have been made for solitary reading (the Caius manuscript). Later manuscripts attest to the changing nature of the audience: the elaborate, fourteenth-century Vernon manuscript weighs 48 lbs and was destined for the lectern; a fifteenth-century version of *Ancrene* changes the forms of address for a monastic or clerical audience. Modern print culture both mass produces for an anonymous audience, and replicates a 'work' that remains essentially unchanged by publication. In medieval scribal culture, however, one can almost say that there are as many versions of a 'work' as there are manuscripts of it – a radical idea when dealing with a work such as *Piers Plowman*.

Þet milde meiden Margarete grap þet grisliche þing, þet hire ne agras nawiht, ant het-eueste toc him bi þet eateliche top ant hef him up ant duste him dunriht to þer eorðe, ant sette hire riht fot on his ruhe swire … Wið þis, þa þudde ha o þe þurs feste wið hire fot wið euchan of þeose word.

The gentle maiden Margaret seized that frightful creature, who frightened her not at all, and grasped him firmly by his hideous hair and swung him upwards and threw him down again straight to the ground, and set her right foot on his rough neck … With this, she stamped hard with her foot on the demon at every sentence.

(Millett and Wogan-Browne, pp. 62–5 [A])

This is a favourite scene in lives of St Margaret. So real is the devil's presence that the anchoress lashes out at him physically, spitting, thrashing him, swinging the cross around her to fight him as St George fought the dragon. The fouler the temptation, the fouler her language, and if she cannot get rid of the devil's presence, she may resort to flagellation (4.1358–417, pp. 300–5). The violence of her actions against a bodiless reality strikes us as strange, even deranged behaviour, but in a life with-drawn from sensory stimulation and human contact, the immaterial world seems more real than the physical.

The inner temptations are the most deadly; if the anchoress feels no temptation, then she is most endangered. The seven deadly sins (pride, avarice, gluttony, lust, wrath, sloth, envy), so popular in medieval sermons (not to mention appearances in the Auchinleck manuscript, Gower's poetry, Chaucer's *Parson's Tale, Piers Plowman*, and Dunbar's 'Dance of the Seven Deadly Sins'), figure large in the writer's exposi-tion. All wrongdoing can be subsumed under one of the seven deadlies (4.392–5, p. 232). His analysis is astute: did she lick her eyebrows to shape them? Pride. Did she damage a book she borrowed? Neglect, a form of sloth. Did she skim a little from her tithing? Avarice. There is no sin that does not originate in the seven deadly sins, and thus the writer's call to her is to recognise and identify herself in these pages, to name her wrongdoing. Realising the hopelessness of trying to name every tiny sin, he urges her to study the pages carefully, pausing longest where the analysis is most dense (4.253–5, pp. 222–3). These few pages contain a lifetime of self-examination, a never-ending probing of intention and testing of sincerity.

In keeping with many other religious texts and movements in the later medieval period, *Ancrene* measures piety in terms of emotional authenticity. Despite the pre-scription of the Fourth Lateran Council (1215), requiring annual oral confession for all layfolk, the author nonetheless emphasises the 'inner' repentance of contrition rather than the 'outer' act of oral confession. Once more, we see emotion rather than doctrinal rectitude as the guarantee of authentic spirituality.

Empiricism derives all knowledge and concepts from the formative power of the senses, so it is arresting that *Ancrene* should urge sensory denial as the path to self-knowledge. In discussing the dangers of sight, the writer speaks of the subtlest danger, which is not of seeing but of being seen through the parlour window. Even if she is unaware of it, a woman who causes a man who looks at her to sin is responsi-ble for his lapse (2.114–15, p. 103). What this amounts to is a call to the anchoress not to impress herself on anyone, to be invisible, as if by shutting out her own sensory awareness she diminishes in the sight of others. While this may seem to represent a desire not to exist, it is rather an attempt to turn all energy away from external sensation to internal. Sensory stimulation must be minimal in order for her life to remain focused inward.

The monastic ideal emphasises the community at every point, exclusion and solitude generally being considered a punishment. So the life of a recluse is an extraordinary existence; a self-imposed penance, it is a withdrawal for contemplation, for God shows himself most to those in solitude (3.391–3, p. 185). We are used today to identifying being alone with being fully oneself, yet anchoritic solitude leads to a denial of *singularite* – a form of pride – to a shedding of all the baggage of personality and egocentric desire for uniqueness and specialness. The importance of the confessional from the thirteenth century onwards increasingly offers a model for introspection; we might even say that the structure of self-reflection, self-analysis and self-knowledge enabled by medieval cultural experience is essentially a Christian one.

Ancrene is written as a mirror of the soul in which the anchoress sees herself for who she really is, yet she also seeks to go beyond self-knowledge to lose self in God. Rousseau and Romantic ideals place the self prior to society, but the anchoress avoids self-absorption and seeks a state of being prior to selfhood. What could compel young women to lead such a life? Perhaps some took vows in the absence of any marriage prospects, but for many, being a bride of Christ was preferable to becoming an earthly wife, an estate offering little opportunity for the depth of reflection gained by a lifetime of reading and prayer.

Sir Gawain and the Green Knight (1390s)

Widely considered the treasure of medieval English romance, *Sir Gawain and the Green Knight* (henceforth, *Gawain*) is an elegantly structured and morally complex piece of storytelling. Existing in a unique manuscript (British Library, MS. Cotton Nero A. x), *Gawain* finishes the collection, and is preceded by *Pearl, Cleanness* and *Patience*. As such, the manuscript is perhaps the single most valuable document of fourteenth-century alliterative verse. At first glance, the poem seems to epitomise the values habitually associated with the genre: Arthurian romance; alliterative 'Englishness' (as opposed to the dominance of French rhyming schemes); and rusticity (the dialect is associated with the north-west Midlands of England, and the setting involves Wales, Anglesey and the Wirral).

When Chaucer complains of the scarcity of rhymes in English ('Complaint of Venus', 80), he no doubt alludes to a popular sense of French as the ideal language of end-rhyme, with all its *–aunce* and *–esse* endings, and English as naturally suited to the internal structure of alliteration. That the two key alliterative poets – William Langland and the unnamed *Gawain*-poet, who is believed to have authored the manuscript's other poems – seem to come from provinces north and west of London has played an important role in an implied opposition between Englishness, rusticity and alliterative form on the one hand, and French, court, London culture and

1.16 Map of Arthurian Britain.

end-rhyme on the other. With Chaucer's only sustained use of alliterative poetry being *Sir Thopas*, whose 'drasty rhyming is nat worth a toord' (Chaucer, VII.930), and his Parson's claim to be a southerner, who knows nothing of *rum, ram, ruf*, it is easy enough to see how alliterative poetry has come to be understood as the 'Other of Chaucerian verse' (Hanna, p. 508 [Ci]).

The closer one looks at the whole spectrum of alliterative poetry, however, the harder it is to sustain the polarity except in the broadest way. *Richard the Redeless*, using an epithet for Richard II that resurrects the slur of Æthelræd the *Unrædig*, can hardly be called provincial; much of the alliterative poetry combined alliteration with end-rhyme; and alliterative prose further breaks down the generic oppositions. With reference to *Gawain*, the closer we look at it, the more it seems to belong to the court rather than the country. The rustic 'quaintness' of alliterative poetry may well be little more than a caricature, possibly fostered during the reign of Lancastrian Henry IV, in an effort to displace Richard's prodigious cultural programme with his own by setting Gower, Lydgate and Chaucer in the centre of poetic achievement where the *Gawain*-poet might have been.

A connection with court would certainly explain a curious coda written in the manuscript at the end of the poem: 'Hony soyt qui mal pence'. This is the motto of the Order of the Garter, founded by Edward III in 1348, although chronicler Jean Froissart confuses it with the Round Table society established by Edward four years earlier. Both orders were originally established by the 'Lord Arthur, formerly King of England', as chronicler Adam of Murimuth (c. 1274–1347) records (Boulton, pp. 101–17 [Ci]). In addition to the manuscript's coda of the motto, what conjoins the poem and the Order is the story of the alleged founding of the Order of the Garter. King Edward III, the story goes, attended a feast, and during the dancing a lady (in some accounts, the Countess of Salisbury) accidentally dropped a garter. Edward picked it up and attached it to his own clothes, chastising the snickering courtiers with the words 'hony soit qui mal y pense' (shame on whoever thinks evil of it), which subsequently became the Order's official motto (Boulton, pp. 155–7 [Ci]). The resonance with Camelot's fraternity, which adopts the girdle as its own, is clear:

> Vche burne of þe broþerhede, a bauderyk schulde haue,
> A bende abelef hym aboute, of a bryȝt grene,
> And þat, for sake of þat segge, in swete to were.
> For þat watz accorded þe renoun of þe Rounde Table
> And he honoured þat hit hade, euermore after,
> As hit is breued in þe best boke of romaunce.

> [Each knight of the brotherhood [of the Round Table] should have a baldric, a band of bright green worn diagonally about him, to wear following suit for the sake of that man [Gawain]. Thus it was designated as the glory of the Round Table, and whoever wore it was honoured ever after, as it is recounted in the greatest authorities of romance.]
> (*Sir Gawain and the Green Knight*, ed. Andrew and Waldron, ll. 2516–21 [A])

Despite differences in colour and type of garment, the general resemblance remains: a mark of shame transforms into a badge of chivalric honour, worn by the worthiest of the land.

It is this preoccupation with chivalry and its attendant ethics – courtesy, shame, honour, courage, loyalty to one's word – that lies at the centre of the poem, and demonstrates the dominance of both the second estate or knightly class at an economic and cultural level, and of romance as the main genre through which it finds self-expression. Looking strictly at the historical conditions of England in the late fourteenth century – rebellion in the rank and file of the labouring class, the advanced erosion of the feudal infrastructure of manorial management, the rise of the archer on the battlefield and the increasing power of artillery – we would be justified in thinking that chivalry was a dying art, and romance a thing of the past. Yet the contemporary literature shows no sign of this; English romance burgeoned in the fourteenth and fifteenth centuries, and the establishment of the Court of Chivalry in the fourteenth century, which regulated the use of coats of arms, registers the jealousy and energy with which families guarded their badges of chivalric identity. In one sense, the gap between historical conditions and culture registers the lag between actuality and consciousness, and even suggests that the dominant literature of an era by definition looks backward rather than forward. Yet in another, we can understand the lateness of romance and the interest in chivalry as peculiarly English, as a recently legitimated vernacular flexing its muscles at the highest levels of cultural expression. *Gawain* thus expresses the chivalric consciousness of its time, bringing a psychological depth and ethical complexity not often found in the genre.

That ethical complexity is evident in the third day of Gawain's exchange with Bertilak. Much of the interest of the poem hinges on the moral status of Gawain's acceptance and retention of the girdle, and on whether or not he made a true confession on the third day. Was Gawain right to accept the girdle? Did he mean to hand it over to Bertilak but then kept it in accordance with the lady's wishes? Did his promise to the lady to hide it from her husband compromise his earlier oath to Bertilak to hand over everything he won? If not, why not, since the two promises are so patently in conflict? If so (and it certainly seems so), then did he understand this when he confessed? And if this be the case, then he made a false confession by intending a sin not yet committed (namely, withholding the girdle from Bertilak). The questions are speculative and unanswerable, yet they are directly invited by the text, which carefully distinguishes the stages of the moral problematic, from initial refusal (of the girdle), to acceptance, to promise, to confession, to withholding. While it is proper in this context to leave these questions open, we might note that Gawain initially refuses the girdle until he hears of its magical virtues. He seems to accept the girdle with the express intention of using it the next day.

> Þan kest þe knyȝt, and hit come to his hert
> Hit were a juel for þe jopardé þat hym jugged were:
> When he acheued to þe chapel his chek for to fech,
> Myȝt he haf slypped to be vnslayn þe sleȝt were noble.

> [Then the knight considered, and it occurred to him that it would be a gem for the danger that was decreed for him. When he made his way to the chapel to get checkmated, if he could escape being slain, the device would be precious.]

(1855–8)

Is he deliberately planning to violate his agreement with Bertilak, or is he planning to give it to Bertilak and then ask for it back? Neither seems likely. For all his 'casting', Gawain seems at this point to fudge thinking through the consequences of his decision to accept the girdle, namely, necessarily breaking troth with his host. The lady's subsequent request that he keep it from her husband allows him to sustain that momentary fudge under the guise of fidelity to a subsidiary oath, blinding him to the conflict of interest (the legal term is not overstated here) between the two promises.

As to what blinded him, Gawain himself identifies it later, after hearing Bertilak's chastisement: *cowarddyse and couetyse bobe* (2374). *Couetyse* might be understood in this context as wrongful withholding of another man's property, for we already know that Gawain did not desire it for its material value because he initially refused it along with the precious ring. His *cowardyse* represents the momentary failing of his habitual courage or *belde* (650), the virtue represented by the fourth 'pentad' or group of five virtues on his shield. That courage is at its lowest ebb on the third morning (1748–54), and the *þro þoȝt* ('constant thought'; 645, 1751, *þoȝtes*) that preoccupies him is not of Mary, his personal protector, but of his imminent death. Distracted from dwelling on the source of his courage (Mary's image being depicted on the inside of his shield), Gawain's mortal fear dominates his mind and temporarily blinds him to the compromise of his promise to Bertilak. But to use a scholastic distinction, this is a sin of weakness rather than of malice; fear of death is a natural emotion, and even Bertilak admits that inasmuch as Gawain acted from it, 'þe lasse I yow blame' (2368).

Much as we might wish to minimise the gravity of Gawain's fault, we still must account for the intensity of Gawain's reaction to Bertilak's criticism. He stands deep in thought for some time; then,

> Alle þe blode of his brest blende in his face,
> þat al he schrank for schome þat þe schalk talked.

> [All the blood from his heart rushed to his face, so that he completely shrank in shame at what the man said.]

(2371–2)

He relives that shame when subsequently relating his adventures to the court at Camelot (2503–4). For a tale about such manly adventures, male blushes appear with some frequency. When the Green Knight derides Arthur's court, 'þe blod schot for scham into his schyre face / and lere' (his bright face / and cheek) (317–18), for the honour of Camelot is at stake. In Gawain's case also, shame arises from the slight to chivalric identity. In his own eyes, he has disgraced his arms and standing as a knight. Cowardice or fear of the Green Knight's death-blow conspired with covetousness 'my kynde to forsake / þat is larges and lewté, þat longez to knyȝtez' [to forsake my nature, the generosity and fidelity that belong to knights] (2380–1).

For Gawain, to be is to be a knight, and to be a knight requires an ethical code that extends beyond the battlefield or lists into the bedroom and private thought. Chivalry cultivates an entire psychology of shame at and fear of disgrace, and in this tale presents a knight who feels as much as he acts, and whose thoughts occupy the centre of the narrative. Inasmuch as the girdle betokens

---

Ordinance Concerning Trial by Battle (Late C.14th)

And than the conestable [Constable] shalle make calle by the marchalle the appellaunt agayne, and shalle make hym ley his hande as he did afore vpon the masseboke, and shalle say: 'A. de K., thou swerest that thou ne hauest … ne stone of virtue, ne herbe of virtue, ne charme, ne experiment, ne carocte [talisman], ne other inchauntment by the, ne for thee, by the which thou trusteth the the bettir to ovircome the foresaide C. de B. thyne aduersarie … ne that thou trustith in noon other thynge, but oonly in god and thi body, and on thy rightfulle quarelle.'

(Lester, 'Gawain's Fault in Terms of Contemporary Law of Arms', p. 393 [Ci])

his shame, he might be said to wear his feelings on his sleeve, to turn affect into a badge of chivalric identity.

The pentangle depicted on his shield further elaborates this public emblazoning of inner worth, for each of its points symbolises his personal virtues. Most of all, the portrayal of Mary on the inside of his shield demonstrates perfectly the alignment of inner spiritual and outer chivalric values. Beyond being a key piece of armour, the shield bears the arms of the knight, identifying him for all to see (since a helmet blocks his face). Literally backed by Christian devotion, Gawain's shield sums up the knight's public function and standing. It makes a statement that he goes to fight in God's name, and trusts to providence to award the just outcome.

Against this empowerment of the knight by the image of Mary stands the talismanic virtue of the girdle. Although its magical powers may appear to be so much romance paraphernalia, the wearing of artificial aids in combat was regarded as seriously then as sports performance-enhancing drugs are now.

Talismans give the knight an unfair advantage and detract from the pitching of skill against skill that is the essence of fair sport and of the chivalric ideal. At the beginning of the poem, Arthur eagerly awaits the challenge of some knight to joust with him, 'in jopardé to lay, / Lede, lif for lyf' [a man to hazard life against life] (97–8). This is the measure of manly endeavour, and it is telling that inasmuch as the girdle disables manly courage, it comes from the 'wyles of wymmen' (2415). The enemy of Camelot is not the Green Knight but Morgan le Faye, engineer of the entire plot.

The ethic of chivalry goes beyond the mere appreciation of fair sportsmanship and a level playing field. As the ordinance above demonstrates, the outcome is assumed to lie in God's hands and in the intrinsic justice of one's cause. The belief in the power of talismans is matched by the belief that the outcome of trial by battle is ultimately a judgement of God, that God himself witnesses to the truth by intervening in the action. Whoever wins is right. Gawain does not undergo a trial by battle in any formal way, but the solemnity of the terms upon which he contracts to the Green Knight and later to Bertilak indicates the gravity of this Christmas *gomen*. So writing-oriented is our culture that we deem no agreement legally binding unless it exists in a signed document; but in a culture where events of great legal import were often enacted orally and without documentation, the terms of the contract spelled out in public between Bertilak and Gawain have the binding force of law, over and above any moral or sporting obligation. In such a world, a broken promise and perjury mean much the same thing. The poem disallows us to separate systematically the gravity of the ordeal from the jollity of a Christmas wager.

This fusion of what Chaucer elsewhere calls *ernest* and *game* sums up the business of the second estate. The tournament, a loose term for a meeting in which knights fight variously, on horseback as well as on foot, originated as peacetime training for war. As the Middle Ages progressed, the English tournament became less functional and more decorative, and, during Richard's reign, became increasingly the grounds for grumbling against monarchical frivolity. It did not sit well with the veterans of the glory days of the Hundred Years' War – most notably, Thomas of Gloucester – that young Richard seemed more interested in jousting with the French than fighting them. It is hard to know, relying as we do on the accounts from Lancastrian chroniclers, whether Richard was indeed as irresponsible as they say he was, or whether he was evading the haemorrhage of war by defusing battle into the martial play of tournament. What is clear from this poem, however, is that Gawain's trial of chivalric mettle, his moral ordeal, the test of his worth both in his own right and as representative of Camelot, is a grave matter, yet entirely conducted in the guise of *game* or *gomen* – the word occurs repeatedly throughout the poem. In the terms laid out by the poem, life itself can depend on courteous behaviour, and honour to a promise made even without witnesses. Itself a polished metrical piece and a work of great beauty, the poem celebrates courtliness as a cult of excellence and aesthetic ideal. If apparently an escape from the baser realities of court politics and war, it suggests that deep things can lie on the surface, and, as Gawain learned so well, that one can be never more serious than when at 'play'.

The Towneley *Second Shepherds' Play (Secunda Pastorum)* (c. 1485–1530)

We do not know for sure in the way we can be sure with the York cycle of plays where the Towneley plays were performed, but general opinion is that they come from the West Riding of Yorkshire, Wakefield being the most well-known suggestion, and quite likely the origin of some of the plays. The text is known as the 'Towneley' manuscript because it was for many years in the possession of the Towneley family of Towneley Hall, in Lancashire. Compiled as a cycle, the manuscript probably represents an accretion of individual plays and clusters of plays collected over time. Where the manuscript of the York cycle is clearly a civic register, a practical document recording ongoing changes in performance, the Towneley manuscript (Huntington Library, MS. HM 1) is a finished thing, and – given its good-quality decoration – an aesthetically pleasing object in its own right, perhaps a presentation copy for the lord of the manor (Stevens, pp. 91–4 [Ci]). Although sixteenth-century marginal inscriptions identify certain trade guilds with certain pageants (e.g., the Tanners played *The Creation*, the Glovers *The Killing of Abel*), we know little about which parish, guild, or community might have staged the individual plays. Perhaps because none of the play authors is known by name, and because of the communally performative nature of the genre, we tend to think of these 'authors' as compilers rather than as poets, but poets they are. The unknown person identified by past critics as the 'Wakefield Master' may be simply an editorial fiction, but the distinctive metrical shape of five of the thirty-two plays shows conscious poetic crafting, whether the result of sole or collective authorship: *Noah and his Sons, First Shepherds' Play, Second Shepherds' Play, Herod the Great* and *Buffeting*. In this reading, we will concentrate on the *Second Shepherd's Play* and to a lesser degree *The Killing of Abel*, with wider reference to other plays.

Even for medieval drama, already a late phenomenon in the Middle Ages, the Towneley plays are late. A number of its pageants are so similar to their counterparts in the York cycle that it is clear that many of Towneley's elements were borrowed from the model of York, which supported plays as early as the last quarter of the fourteenth century. In contrast to York, however, Towneley's many references to exploitative overlords and tyrants (such as Herod the Great) keeps rural life and the power of the gentry constantly to the fore. The Towneley plays seem quintessentially modern,

1.17 Annunciation to the shepherds. Holkham Picture Bible.

despite the biblical content of the narrative. They do not look backward to an antique past, as does romance; rather, they relocate ancient history into the present. Bethlehem seems only a stone's throw from Mak and Gill's house. Cain and Abel's story is transposed to the West Riding of Yorkshire, with its local tensions between ploughmen and sheep-farmers, and with its struggles to graze animals in a period known for its enclosure of common pastureland.

This fix on the here and now is reflected in the language of the pageant. In an exchange between Mak, the local scoundrel, and the shepherds, Mak affects a southern accent, and pretends to be a yeoman of the king, sent by a great lord. The Gallicisms and allusions to great men tellingly convey the northern perception of the South as the place of privilege, wealth and power. And common perception of the northern dialect is registered in the late fourteenth century in John Trevisa's digression on the state of English in his translation of Ranulph Higden's *Polychronicon*:

> Al þe longage of þe Norþhumbres, and specialliche at ȝork, is so scharp, slitting, and frotynge and vnschape, þat we souþerne men may þat longage vnneþe vnderstonde.
>
> [The language of the people of Northumbria, specially at York, is so grating and badly formed, that we southerners can barely understand it.]
>
> (Babington, 2:163 [A])

It is hard to think of any modern English locution to rival the shepherd's put-down to Mak's affected accent: 'Now take outt that Sothren tothe, / And sett it in a torde!' ['Now take out that Southern tooth, and stick it in a turd!'] (*Second Shepherds' Play*, ll. 311–12, in Stevens and Cawley, *The Towneley Plays*, 1:135 [A]). The pageant grounds its world in hardship, theft, wrangling between economic factions and clashing dialects; this is the world into which Christ is born.

The *Second Shepherds' Play* opens with three shepherds out in the open at night, tending their flocks. They bemoan their hard life – the cold, the endless labour, their hunger and poverty, the meanness of their overlord, and the tribulations of marriage to a nagging wife. They are joined by Mak, who gains more by stealing than by any honest occupation, and after some conversation the three shepherds fall asleep. Mak, staying awake, steals a sheep, hides it with his wife Gill, and together they hatch a plan to evade questions from the shepherds once they discover their loss. Mak then rejoins the shepherds and pretends to have been asleep all along. On waking, he announces that his wife has been in labour, and returns home to await with Gill the visit of the shepherds seeking restoration of their lost sheep. Gill has wrapped the sheep in swaddling clothes and laid him in a crib, pretending that he is her newborn son. Initially duped, the shepherds offer their good wishes to the infant boy, only to discover that the baby is their lost sheep. The trick exposed, the shepherds let Mak off lightly by tossing him in a canvas, and then they return to the fields. An angel appears to them and sends them to Bethlehem, where, on arriving, they worship the Christ child, and close the pageant in song.

Song is an integral and crucial part of the dramatic presentation, and the angel's annunciation to the shepherds takes song beyond the ordinary level to the meeting of heavenly and earthly languages; as a narrative event, it is featured in many contemporary representations. The Holkham Picture Bible depicts the shepherds listening to the angel's *Gloria in excelsis* as the meeting not simply between Latin and vernacular, but between sacred and profane, truth and nonsense, as the shepherds speak the following gobbledy-gook: 'Glum glo ceo ne est rien. Allums la, nous la severums bien.'

Compare the corresponding moment in the *Chester Paynters' Playe of the Shepherds* (*Chester Mystery Cycle*, pp. 125–56 [A]) in which the shepherds attempt to decipher the angel's message:

> *Tertius Pastor.* What songe was this, say yee
> that he sange to us all three?
> Expounded shall yt bee ...
> hit was 'grorus glorus' with a 'glee' ...
> *Garcius.* Nay, yt was 'glorus glarus, glorius' ...
> *Primus Pastor.* Nay, yt was 'glorus, glarus' with a 'glo,' ...
> *Secundus Pastor.* Nay, by God, yt was a 'gloria,'
> sayde Gabryell when hee sayde soe.
>
> (376–8, 382, 384, 388, 404–5)

The message of the Incarnation is incomprehensible without revealed grace. When the Latin words of the divine liturgy are brought down to earth, as it were, the shepherds cannot fully fathom their meaning without revelation. The wrangling between local dialects that we saw in the initial exchange between Mak and the shepherds transmutes to a realignment of the vernacular to reflect, in its humble way, the presence of divinity.

Mak and Gill steal the show in the pageant, with Mak's southern affectations and the farcical sheep/newborn baby episode. These narrative dilations stand in their own right as entertainment value, and, in terms of the biblical account, are entirely extraneous to the plot, such as it is, of the shepherds coming to visit the newborn Jesus, which would have made a very short pageant if presented without embellishment. But the sheep-stealing episode has clear thematic relevance, as a parody of the birth of Christ, the sacrificial Lamb of God. That sacrificial lamb is prefigured as the stolen wether; Mary, who addresses the shepherds in the play, is prefigured by the duplicitous scold Gill; and the angel who gives the message to the shepherds is prefigured by the scoundrel Mak, who tells them that Gill 'was lyght [delivered] / Of a knaue-childe this nyght' (487–8). Apart from the structural parallel, many comments in the pageant alert us to the sacred meaning that underlies the slapstick: Mak pretends to the shepherds that he dreamt during the night that Gill had given birth to a boy 'for to mend oure floke' [to augment/atone for our flock] (560); Gill promises to 'swaddle' (*swedyll*) the sheep in her cradle (*credyll*) (623–4); and when accused by the shepherds, she prays to God so mild, 'If euer I you begyld, / That I ete this chylde / That lygys in this credyll' (774–6) – a direct allusion to the Eucharistic eating of Christ's body, the event celebrated in the feast of Corpus Christi.

The pageant thus establishes the action on two levels of meaning – sacred and profane – and two levels of chronology – prefigurement and fulfilment; that duality was most likely theatrically realised on a stage constructed with differing platforms to represent the different localities. For medieval exegetes of scripture, such doubleness pervaded reality: everything mundane, that is, everything in the world, could be understood figuratively as an allegorical sign of a sacred reality; and by the same logic, mundane history prefigured the future reality when Judgement Day brings us to the end of history. Such a hermeneutic system, called 'typology', was at its clearest when applied to the relationship between Old and New Testaments: the Old Testament story of Jonah being in the belly of the whale for three days and nights foreshadows the New Testament's account of Christ's three days of death; the paradox of the burning bush in the desert that appeared to Moses prefigures the mystery of a virgin giving birth (*First Shepherds' Play*, 517–31, Stevens and Cawley, 1.120–1 [A]); the drowning of the Egyptians in the Red Sea anticipates the washing away of sin in baptism; Abraham's sacrifice of the ram in substitution of his own son Isaac prefigures God's sacrifice of his own son, the Lamb of God. Thus proceeded the recitation of Old Covenant history as anticipation of New Covenant revelation. These meanings were expounded regularly in sermons, and so the audience would readily have understood the comic reworking of the shepherds' visitation as the fulfilment of the profane story of Mak and the stolen sheep.

Comic inversion of such sacred events is part and parcel of what cultural historian Mikhail Bakhtin, in his study of François Rabelais's writing, calls carnivalesque humour, popular festive entertainment in which all arenas of sanctioned authority – monarchical, divine, clerical, marital and legal – are ritually debunked, often in highly obscene ways. It seems disrespectful, to say the least, to reduce the Lamb of God to a stolen sheep in a crib, but there are worse examples. Chaucer's resolution of the problem of the equal division of the fart in *The Summoner's Tale* – in which each brother has to lay his nose at the end of the spoke of a cartwheel while Thomas the churl sits atop the wheel's hub and farts – has been understood as a grotesque parody of Pentecost, in which the Holy Spirit comes upon the assembled disciples like a *greet wynde*, as the Middle English Bible states (Acts, 2.2) (Levitan, pp. 236–46 [Ci]). And in the Towneley *Killing of Abel* (Stevens and Cawley, 1.12–25 [A]), Cain flagrantly thumbs his nose at God, who has just rebuked him for the sub-standard tithe Cain has passed off as an offering:

> Whi, who is that hob [hobgoblin] ouer the wall?
> We! who was that that piped so small?
> Com, go we hens, for parels [perils] all –
> God is out of hys wit!

(299–302)

The Killing of Abel stands out in the Towneley plays for its scatological language. Where Abel rebukes Cain in the mildest terms ('this is not worth oone leke [leek]' (287)), Cain's language is peppered with curses and profanity: 'Com kys myne ars!' (61), 'Kys the dwillis toute [devil's arsehole]!' (65), 'Not as mekill [much], grete ne small, / As he [God] myght wipe his ars withall' (239–40), 'Yei, kys the dwills [devil's] ars behynde' (268), 'Comm kys the dwill [devil] right in the ars!' (289), 'Bi all men set I not a fart' (371). Such language is commonplace enough in medieval drama, and particularly associated with the devil, whether in collections such as the *N-Town* or morality plays such as *Mankind*.

How do we explain the fact that such popular entertainment occurs not outside church worship but within it? For a society that so reverenced the passage of meaning from the literal to the spiritual, from concrete matter to abstract spirit, it seems equally to delight in reversing that process, detransubstantiating the Holy Spirit to a peasant's fart or the Son of God to a stolen sheep somewhere in the West Riding. It has long been recognised that such carnival moments, taking place within officially sanctioned festivals in this way, function as licensed comedy, as 'letting off some steam'; and in doing so, serve an ultimately conservative function, maintaining the status quo by means of benign subversion by the lower ranks of society. While this conservative agenda of festive comedy is no doubt in part the case, it only explains how the lower classes get to laugh at the upper classes. It does not explain how degradation can itself constitute an integral part of worship, in its broadest sense. Mere inversion or opposition between sacred and profane does not explain the way in which, in such moments, profanity itself becomes a kind of devotion. Against all expectation, the ritual desacralisation enjoyed by medieval drama creates rather than abolishes mystery. When Gill, in feigned indignation, claims she will eat the child that lies in the cradle, she speaks truth in a punning way, for the central event of the Eucharist celebrates the eating of the body of Christ. The irreverent literalisation of mystery, the reductive pun, the emphasis on bodily functions, all perform the work of in-corporating the holy, of making the salvation event a local thing, of taking Christ into one's body. More than any other genre, drama enacts religious observance by its inherent performativity and communality; it personates God and the characters of the sacred story, it renders the events of centuries before a present reality, visually and aurally evident, happening even as the crowd watches.

Reference

A Primary Texts and Anthologies of Primary Sources

Note

The following abbreviations are used in this section:

EETS   Early English Text Society
ES   Extra series
OS   Original series
SS   Supplementary series

Allen, Rosamund S., ed. and trans. *Richard Rolle: The English Writings*. Mahwah, NJ: Paulist Press, 1988.

Ancrene Wisse. Ed. Robert Hasenfratz. Kalamazoo, MI: Medieval Institute Publications, 2000. The full text, with glossary and full critical infrastructure, of Cambridge, Corpus Christi College, MS. 402.

Andrew, Malcolm, and Ronald Waldron, eds. *Poems of the 'Pearl' Manuscript: 'Pearl', 'Cleanness', 'Patience' and 'Sir Gawain and the Green Knight'*. 5th edn. Liverpool University Press, 2007.

Anglo-Saxon Chronicle: Two of the Saxon Chronicles Parallel. Ed. John Earle; rev. Charles Plummer. 2 vols. Oxford: Clarendon Press, 1892, 1899.

Anglo-Saxon Prose. Trans. and ed. Michael Swanton. London: Dent, 1975. A useful miscellany of AS prose, ranging from chronicle, homilies and saints' lives to medical recipes and laws.

Babington, Churchill, ed. *Polychronicon Ranulphi Higden Together with English Translations of John Trevisa*. Vol. 2. London: Longman, 1869.

Barron, W. R. J. and S. C. Weinberg, eds. and trans. [Laȝamon's] *Brut*. Harlow: Longman, 1995. This dual-text edition provides both critical apparatus and a translation for Laȝamon's text.

The Battle of Maldon. Ed. D. G. Scragg. Manchester University Press, 1981. The value of this edition is the detailed linguistic analysis along with a full introduction. Its usefulness has not been displaced by subsequent editions.

The Bayeux Tapestry Digital Edition. Ed. Martin K. Foys. Leicester: Scholarly Digital Editions, 2003. This digital reproduction contains commentary on each scene, review of critical research, translation of Latin inscriptions, sources and analogues (visual and written), and maps. High resolution enables scrutiny of stitchwork.

Bede. *Bede's Ecclesiastical History of the English People*. Ed. Bertram Colgrave and R. A. B. Mynors. Oxford: Clarendon Press, 1969. This dual-text edition enables the reader to check the original Latin.

Bennett, J. A. W. and G. V. Smithers, eds. *Early Middle English Verse and Prose*. 2nd edn. Oxford University Press, 1982. With its detailed linguistic introduction, this anthology, still in print, bridges the gap between OE and late ME literature, and represents the classics of the period: *Owl and the Nightingale, Dame Sirith, Land of Cockaigne*, Laȝamon's *Brut* and *Floris and Blauncheflour*.

Benson, Larry D., ed. Rev. Edward E. Foster. *King Arthur's Death: The Middle English 'Stanzaic Morte Arthur' and 'Alliterative Morte Arthure'*. Kalamazoo, MI: Medieval Institute Publications 1994. For translation, see Brian Stone.

Blumenfeld-Kosinski, Renate, and Kevin Brownlee, eds. and trans. *The Selected Writings of Christine de Pizan*. New York: Norton, 1997. A well-selected miscellany of Christine's work, along with useful critical essays.

Bokenham, Osbern. *Mappula Anglie*. Ed. C. Horstmann. *Englische Studien* 10 (1887): 1–34.

Brook, G. L. and R. F. Leslie, eds. *Laȝamon: Brut*. 2 vols. EETS OS 250, 277. Oxford University Press, 1963, 1978. The standard scholarly edition of the poem.

Chaucer, Geoffrey. *The Riverside Chaucer*. Ed. Larry D. Benson. 3rd edn. Boston: Houghton Mifflin, 1987. Rev. 2008. The standard scholarly edition of Chaucer's complete works. Its text of the *Canterbury Tales* is based on the famous Ellesmere manuscript, though many scholars consider the Hengwrt manuscript more authoritative.

The Chester Mystery Cycle. Vol. 1. Ed. R. M. Lumiansky and David Mills. EETS SS 3. Oxford University Press, 1974.

Clark, Cecily, ed. *The Peterborough Chronicle 1070–1154*. 2nd edn. Oxford: Clarendon Press, 1970. The only chronicle to be maintained so late, this is a critical document for recovering an OE 'voice', and charting changes in the language during the first century after the conquest. Clark edits only the later section.

A Concise Anglo-Saxon Dictionary. Ed. J. R. Clark Hall. 4th edn. Toronto, Buffalo and London: University of Toronto Press, 1960. Affordable and useful for basic dictionary reference, with standardised spellings – most notably, the collapse of thorn (Þ), the unvoiced *th* sound, to eth (ð), the voiced *th*. For detailed word searches, consult the online Bosworth-Toller and online *Dictionary of Old English* [Cii].

Dahlberg, Charles, trans. *The 'Romance of the Rose' by Guillaume de Lorris and Jean de Meun*. 3rd edn. Princeton University Press, 1995. An authoritative translation of this poem, much read in its own day, and influential on writers such as Geoffrey Chaucer and Christine de Pisan.

Davidson, Clifford, ed. *A Tretise of Miraclis Pleyinge*. Rev. edn. Kalamazoo, MI: Medieval Institute Publications, 2011. Edition, with useful introduction, of Wycliffite tract criticising devotional drama.

Dives and Pauper. Ed. Priscilla Heath Barnum. Vol. 1, Part 1. EETS OS 275. Oxford University Press, 1976.

Dobson, R. B. *The Peasants' Revolt of 1381*. 2nd edn. London and Basingstoke: Macmillan Press, 1983. Dobson assembles translated texts and records of the rebellion – an essential starting and reference point for the events of 1381.

The Dream of the Rood. Ed. Michael Swanton. Rev. edn. University of Exeter Press, 1987.

Dunbar, William. *The Poems of William Dunbar*. Ed. Priscilla Bawcutt. 2 vols. Glasgow: Association for Scottish Literary Studies, 1998.

Eccles, Mark, ed. *The Macro Plays: 'The Castle of Perseverance', 'Wisdom', 'Mankind'*. EETS 262. Oxford University Press, 1969.

English Historical Documents. Oxford University Press, 1953–69. *Vol. I: 500–1042*. Ed. D. Whitelock. *Vol. II: 1042–1189*. Ed. David C. Douglas and George Greenaway. *Vol. III: 1189–1327*. Ed. Harry Rothwell. *Vol. IV: 1327–1485*. Ed. A. R. Myers. These volumes draw from a huge range of materials: laws, letters, decrees, sermons, parliamentary records, chronicles, poetry, etc.; they offer a comprehensive context for all periods of medieval literature.

Fairweather, Janet, trans. *Liber Eliensis: A History of the Isle of Ely from the Seventh Century to the Twelfth Compiled by a Monk of Ely in the Twelfth Century*. Woodbridge: Boydell Press, 2005.

Forshall, Josiah, and Frederic Madden, eds. *The Holy Bible, containing the Old and New Testaments, with the Apocryphal books, in the earliest English versions made from the Latin Vulgate by John Wycliffe and his followers*. 4 vols. Oxford University Press, 1850.

Furnivall, Frederick J., ed. *The Fifty Earliest English Wills in the Court of Probate London: A.D. 1387–1439; with a priest's of 1454*. EETS OS 78. Oxford University Press, 1882. Rptd 1964.

Garmonsway, G. N., ed. *Ælfric's Colloquy*. Rev. edn. University of Exeter Press, 1991.

Goldie, Matthew. *Middle English Literature: A Historical Sourcebook*. Maldon, MA and Oxford: Blackwell, 2003. Brings together a useful selection of texts from the later Middle Ages, including letters of Margaret Paston and Ranulf Higden's comments about the English language (as translated by John Trevisa).

Gower, John. *Complete Works of John Gower*. Ed. G. C. Macaulay. 4 vols. Oxford: Clarendon Press, 1899–1902. At present, the only complete edition, but TEAMS Middle English Texts Series [Cii] has published substantial parts of his works.

Gwara, Scott, ed., David Porter, trans. *Anglo-Saxon Conversations: The Colloquies of Ælfric Bata*. Woodbridge: Boydell Press, 1997.

Hall, Edward. *Hall's chronicle; containing the history of England, during the reign of Henry the Fourth … in which are particularly described the manners and customs of those periods. Carefully collated with the editions of 1548 and 1550*. London: J. Johnson, 1809.

Halsall, Maureen, ed. *The Old English 'Rune' Poem: A Critical Edition*. University of Toronto Press, 1981.

Havelok [the Dane]. Ed. G. V. Smithers. Oxford: Clarendon Press, 1987.

Heaney, Seamus, ed. and trans. *Beowulf: A New Verse Translation*. New York: Norton, 2001. This parallel-text edition of the poem offers the original along with the kind of translation that recreates in modern English how the original must have sounded to its audience.

Hill, Joyce, ed. *Old English Minor Heroic Poems*. 3rd edn. Durham University Centre for Medieval and Renaissance Studies, and Toronto: Pontifical Institute for Mediaeval Studies, 2009.

Hoccleve, Thomas. *The Regiment of Princes*, ed. Charles R. Blyth. Kalamazoo, MI: Medieval Institute Publications, 1999.

John of Forde. *The Life of Wulfric of Haselbury, Anchorite*. Trans. Pauline Matarasso. Collegeville, MN: Liturgical Press, 2011.

Klaeber's 'Beowulf' and the 'Fight at Finnsburg'. Ed. R. D. Fulk, Robert E. Bjork, and John D. Niles. 4th edn. University of Toronto Press, 2008. Originally edited by Friedrich Klaeber, this remains the classic version and has a comprehensive critical apparatus.

Knight, Stephen, and Thomas Ohlgren, eds. *Robin Hood and Other Outlaw Tales*. Kalamazoo, MI: Medieval Institute Publications, 1997. Gathers in one volume the late medieval and early modern documents, whether chronicle or popular poetry, pertaining to Robin Hood. Translated or modernised, the texts provide a complete study of the legend.

Knighton, Henry. *Knighton's Chronicle 1337–1396*. Ed. and trans. G. H. Martin. Oxford: Clarendon Press, 1995.

Langland, William. *Piers Plowman: A Parallel-Text Edition of the A, B, C, and Z Versions*. 2nd edn. 2 vols (2nd vol. in 2 parts). Ed. A. V. C. Schmidt. Kalamazoo, MI: Medieval Institute Publications, 2011. This parallel-text edition enables instant comparison between all versions.

Lydgate, John. *Life of Our Lady*. Ed. J. Lauritis, R. Klinefelter and V. Gallagher. Pittsburg: Duquesne University Press, 1961.

Malory, Thomas. *The Works of Sir Thomas Malory*. Ed. Eugène Vinaver. 2nd edn. 3 vols. Oxford: Clarendon Press, 1967. This remains the standard edition of the eight books collectively referred to as *Morte Darthur*.

Marsden, Richard. *The Cambridge Old English Reader*. 2nd edn. Cambridge University Press, 2015. Suitable for the beginner, this book also includes enough grammatical detail to guide more advanced readers. Excerpts offer a sampler of a wide range of Old English literature.

Meech, Sanford Brown, ed. *The Book of Margery Kempe*. EETS 212. Oxford University Press, 1940.

Millett, Bella, and Jocelyn Wogan-Browne, eds. *Medieval English Prose for Women: Selections from the Katherine Group and 'Ancrene Wisse'*. Oxford: Clarendon Press, 1990. Rptd 1992. A useful parallel-text edition with the full version of *Hali Meðhad* and *Sawles Warde*.

Mirk, John. *John Mirk's 'Festial': Edited from British Library MS Cotton Claudius A.II, Part 1*. Ed. Susan Powell. EETS OS 34. Oxford University Press, 2009.

Orme, Nicholas. 'Latin and English Sentences in Fifteenth-Century Schoolbooks Followed by a Transcript of the English and Latin Sentences in Beinecke Library MS. 3 (34), Fol. 5'. *Yale University Library Gazette* 60 (1985): 47–57.

Owl and the Nightingale. Ed. Neil Cartlidge. Exeter University Press, 2001. Brings together the complete text, critical apparatus, commentary on recent criticism, parallel-text original with paraphrase and glossary.

The Play of the Sacrament. In *Non-Cycle Plays and Fragments*. Ed. Norman Davis. EETS SS 1. Oxford University Press, 1970, pp. 58–89. Known as the *Croxton Play of the Sacrament*, this work is neither a mystery pageant nor a morality play; in its anti-Semitic and miraculous interest, its plot is reminiscent of many sermon *exempla*.

Robinson, Peter, ed. *Chaucer: The 'Wife of Bath's Prologue' on CD-ROM*. Cambridge University Press, 1996. Each word of the *Prologue* is hyperlinked to the same word in the fifty-seven other manuscript witnesses that record the *Prologue*. The act of reading becomes multi-dimensional, moving both *across* the text in linear, progressive fashion from start to finish, and *through* fifty-eight texts.

Salisbury, Eve, ed. *The Trials and Joys of Marriage*. Kalamazoo, MI: Medieval Institute Publications, 2002. This well-conceived selection of texts addresses the theme of marriage, which was culturally, economically and theologically of huge importance in this era. Genres range through satire, instructional *exempla* and lyrics, including 'A Henpecked Husband's Complaint'.

Savage, Anne, and Nicholas Watson, eds. *Anchoritic Spirituality: 'Ancrene Wisse' and Associated Works*. New York: Paulist Press, 1991. A careful translation of *Sawles Warde, Hali Meiðhad* (Holy Maidenhood), the *Wooing of Our Lord*, and the lives of Saints Katherine, Margaret and Juliana. The introduction gives an excellent sense of the anchoritic life, and of the circumstances in which these texts were composed and became so popular.

Saupe, Karen, ed. *Middle English Marian Lyrics*. Kalamazoo, MI: Medieval Institute Publications, 1998.

Skeat, W. W., ed. *Ælfric's Lives of Saints*. EETS OS 94. London: Kegan Paul, Trench, Trübner, 1890.

Stevens, Martin, and A. C. Cawley, eds. *The Towneley Plays*. 2 vols. EETS SS 13, 14. Oxford University Press, 1994.

Stone, Brian, trans. *King Arthur's Death: Morte Arthure, Le Morte Arthur*. London: Penguin, 1988. Stone's translation, being versified, inevitably takes some liberties.

Swanton, Michael, trans. *The Anglo-Saxon Chronicle*. London: J. M. Dent, 1996. This translation of all seven chronicles, maintained at different times and places, makes readily accessible an essential set of contemporary documents for the late Old English period and early post-Conquest years.

Usk, Thomas. *The Testament of Love*. Ed. R. Allen Shoaf. Kalamazoo, MI: Medieval Institute Publications, 1998.

Watson, Nicholas, and Jacqueline Jenkins, eds. *The Writings of Julian of Norwich: A Vision Showed to a Devout Woman and A Revelation of Love*. Turnhout: Brepols, 2006.

Whitelock, Dorothy, ed. *Anglo-Saxon Wills*. Cambridge University Press, 1930.

Wright, William Aldis, ed. *The Metrical Chronicle of Robert of Gloucester*. Vol. 2. London: Published by the authority of the Lords Commissioners of Her Majesty's Treasury, under the Direction of the Master of the Rolls, 1887.

The York Corpus Christi Plays. Ed. Clifford Davidson. Kalamazoo, MI: Medieval Institute Publications, 2011.

Zupitza, Julius, ed. *Ælfrics Grammatik und Glossar: Text und Varianten*. 4th edn with introduction by Helmut Gneuss. Hildesheim: Weidmann, 2003.

B   Introductions and Overviews

Alexander, Michael. *A History of Old English Literature*. Peterborough, Ontario: Broadview Press, 2002. Divides material into the familiar categories of heroic poetry, riddles, ecclesiastical writing, elegies, prose, saints' lives and biblical poetry, and the Benedictine Revival. It omits discussion of legal and medical texts, which can modify the orthodox Christianity that for Alexander defines the period.

Bartlett, Robert. *England under the Norman and Angevin Kings 1075–1225*. Oxford University Press, 2000. This comprehensive study focuses on the important period immediately after the Norman conquest and before the reassertion of English as official language of record.

Beadle, Richard, and Alan J. Fletcher, eds. *The Cambridge Companion to Medieval English Theatre*. 2nd edn. Cambridge University Press, 2008.

Brown, Peter, ed. *A Companion to Medieval English Literature and Culture c.1350–c.1500*. Oxford: Blackwell, 2007. This companion, like many others, covers literary genres and individual authors or texts. Its particular strength lies in its integration of literary with historical issues.

Dinshaw, Carolyn, and David Wallace, eds. *The Cambridge Companion to Medieval Women's Writing*. Cambridge University Press, 2003. Rptd 2006. Women were constantly involved with writing: through patronage, dictation, transcription, or ownership. Many authored work, yet could not write: a distinction our vocabulary of 'writing' cannot accommodate. The anthology charts the estates of women – virginity, marriage and widowhood – and offers individual chapters on Margery Kempe and Julian of Norwich.

Edwards, A. S. G., ed. *A Companion to Middle English Prose*. Cambridge and Rochester, NY: Brewer, 2004. Pbk 2010. Sidelining Chaucer, Malory and *Ancrene Wisse*, this collection considers sermons, Wycliffite writings, letters, travel literature, prose romances, mystical and devotional writings, autobiography, saints' lives, historiography, translations and letters.

Given-Wilson, Chris, ed. *An Illustrated History of Late Medieval England*. Manchester University Press, 1996. Liberally illustrated, this historical overview of English politics and culture from the thirteenth to fifteenth centuries is both wide-ranging and informative.

Godden, Malcolm, and Michael Lapidge, eds. *The Cambridge Companion to Old English Literature*. 2nd edn. Cambridge University Press, 2013. Appearing twenty-two years after the first, this second edition both updates current essays and commissions new ones.

James, Edward. *Britain in the First Millennium*. London: Arnold, 2001. Integrates historical, linguistic and archaeological evidence to animate the story of the making of England, from Roman Britain to the unification of the English kingdom as a result of Viking invasions, explaining how diverse tribes eventually coalesced into one people.

Lapidge, Michael, et al., eds. *The Wiley Blackwell Encyclopedia of Anglo-Saxon England*. 2nd edn. Chichester: Wiley Blackwell, 2014. This volume contains a wealth of historical and cultural reference material, and appendices of maps and lists of all the rulers of the English from c. 450 to 1066. The second edition includes entries on important new finds, such as the Staffordshire Hoard.

Lerer, Seth. *Inventing English: A Portable History of the Language*. Rev. edn. New York: Columbia University Press, 2015. Engaging and informed overview of the history of English from its beginnings to the present.

Lass, Roger. *Old English: A Historical Linguistic Companion*. Cambridge University Press, 1994. Rptd 1998. Provides a thorough grammar of OE, more detailed than the (necessarily) compact grammatical overviews supplied in most combined readers and anthologies. Includes a useful chapter on the morphological features that characterise the transition from Old to Middle English.

Lupack, Alan. *Oxford Guide to Arthurian Literature and Legend*. 2nd edn. Oxford University Press, 2007. This handy overview helps readers get their bearings in the labyrinth of Arthurian traditions.

Mortimer, Ian. *The Time Traveler's Guide to Medieval England: A Handbook for Visitors to the Fourteenth Century*. London: The Bodley Head, 2008. An informative and engaging 'visitor's' guide to the fourteenth century.

Pearsall, Derek. *Arthurian Romance: A Short Introduction*. Malden, MA: Blackwell, 2003. Traces the origins, inasmuch as we know them, of the 'real' Arthur, the influence of Chrétien de Troyes, Arthurian literature on the Continent and then in England. Without taking into account such influences, especially French, it is impossible to understand the context of English Arthurian romance.

Postan, M. M. *The Medieval Economy and Society: An Economic History of Britain in the Middle Ages*. London: Penguin, 1972. Rptd 1986. Focusing on the thirteenth century, Postan's study reveals the centrality of the manor and the village in this period. Trade, industry, towns and guilds are also considered, although the role of the Church is marginalised.

Pulsiano, Phillip, and Elaine Treharne, eds. *A Companion to Anglo-Saxon Literature*. 2nd edn. Oxford: Blackwell, 2008. Surveys the landscape of OE literary production. Rather than focusing on individual works, authors or sub-genres (heroic poetry, elegies, etc.), it treats topics broadly: authorship, audience, manuscript production, liturgical texts, legal texts, secular and religious prose, secular and religious poetry.

Rubin, Miri. *The Hollow Crown: A History of Britain in the Late Middle Ages*. London: Allen Lane, 2005. This new version of the Penguin History of Britain series covers the fourteenth and fifteenth centuries. In comparison to the earlier series, it emphasises the life of the commoner and pays less attention to the governmental structures of the land, its courts and its law-making and parliamentary bodies.

Saunders, Corinne, ed. *A Companion to Medieval Poetry*. Chichester: Wiley-Blackwell, 2010. Essays offer in-depth consideration of medieval English poetry with some consideration of its connections with continental and Latin traditions.

Scanlon, Larry, ed. *The Cambridge Companion to Medieval English Literature 1100–1500*. Cambridge University Press, 2009. Essays from leading authorities on general genres and individual authors.

C Further Reading

i Books

Abels, Richard. 'English Tactics, Strategy and Military Organization in the Late Tenth Century'. In D. G. Scragg, ed., *The Battle of Maldon A.D. 991*, pp. 143–55.

Bakhtin, Mikhail. *Rabelais and His World* (1965). Trans. Hélène Iswolsky. Bloomington: Indiana University Press, 1984. This study of the sixteenth-century French writer immediately became a classic on account of its radical recuperation of popular and bawdy humour, which is seen to belong to an ancient ritual of mocking authority. These two worlds – near-blasphemous levelling and hierarchical power – coexist interdependently.

Barber, Richard. *The Knight and Chivalry*. 3rd edn. Woodbridge, Suffolk: Boydell, 1995.

Barker, Juliet. *England, Arise: The People, the King, and the Great Revolt of 1381*. London: Little, Brown, 2014. The protesters' complaints are given serious consideration in this highly readable narrative of the conventionally named 'Peasants' Revolt'.

Bennett, Michael J. *Community, Class and Careerism: Cheshire and Lancashire Society in the Age of 'Sir Gawain and the Green Knight'*. Cambridge University Press, 1983.

Boulton, D'Arcy Jonathan Dacre. *The Knights of the Crown: The Monarchical Orders of Knighthood in Later Medieval Europe 1325–1520*. New York: St Martin's Press, 1987.

Cannon, Christopher. *The Making of Chaucer's English: A Study of Words*. Cambridge University Press, 1998.

Cooper, Helen. 'Romance after 1400'. In Wallace, ed., *Cambridge History*, pp. 690–719 [Ci].

Fletcher, Alan J. 'Chaucer the Heretic'. *Studies in the Age of Chaucer* 25 (2003): 53–121.
    Preaching and Politics in Late-Medieval England. Dublin: Four Courts Press, 1998.

Hanna, Ralph. 'Alliterative Poetry'. In Wallace, ed., *Cambridge History*, pp. 488–512 [Ci].

Hines, John. *The Fabliau in English*. London and New York: Longman, 1993. Hines argues that despite its relative scarcity, the English fabliau is an independent tradition. Chapters cover Chaucer's work, *Dame Sirith* and fifteenth-century fabliaux.

Hooke, Della. *Worcestershire Anglo-Saxon Charter Bounds*. Woodbridge: Boydell Press, 1990.

Jones, Malcolm. *The Secret Middle Ages*. Stroud: Sutton, 2002. Not limited to English culture, this book takes a look at the unofficial side of medieval culture: popular religion, superstitions, absurdity, proverbs, rudeness both sexual and scatological. Wide in scope and very accessible, the book supplies an important supplement to overly selective depictions of the Middle Ages as orthodox.
    'The Parodic Sermon in Medieval and Early Modern England'. *Medium Aevum* 66 (1997): 94–114. A useful overview of a popular literature in late medieval England. Jones's article contains the text of one such sermon.

Jones, Terry, et al. *Who Murdered Chaucer? A Medieval Mystery*. London: Methuen, 2003. A former member of the Monty Python team and some academics argue that Geoffrey Chaucer was bumped off during Archbishop Thomas Arundel's ideological counter-revolution against political dissenters and critics. This imaginative if unprovable thesis unsettles the long-held belief that Chaucer was a 'safe' poet, eschewing politics in his poetry.

Justice, Steven. *Writing and Rebellion: England in 1381*. Rev. edn. Berkeley, Los Angeles and London: University of California Press, 1996. Far from being the barking mob depicted by Gower and contemporary chroniclers, many of the rebels were literate and politically articulate, argues Justice.

Knight, Stephen. *Reading Robin Hood: Content, Form and Reception in the Outlaw Myth*. Manchester University Press, 2015. Reviews early Robin Hood materials and assesses the cultural impact of the centuries-long tradition.

Lerer, Seth. 'Old English and its Afterlife'. In Wallace, ed., *Cambridge History*, pp. 7–34 [Ci].

Lester, G. A. 'Gawain's Fault in Terms of Contemporary Law of Arms'. *Notes and Queries* NS 23 (1976): 392–3.

Levitan, Alan. 'The Parody of Pentecost in Chaucer's *Summoner's Tale*'. *University of Toronto Quarterly* 40 (1971): 236–46.

Morgan, Gerald. 'Moral and Social Identity and the Idea of Pilgrimage in the *General Prologue*'. *Chaucer Review* 37 (2003): 285–314.

Scragg, D. G., ed. *The Battle of Maldon A. D. 991*. Oxford: Blackwell, 1991. Contains a photographic reproduction of the Casley transcription. The essays cover the poem from all angles: military formation and battle tactics, politics, the heroic poetic tradition, chronicle evidence, etc.

    'The Nature of Old English Verse'. In Godden and Lapidge, eds., *The Cambridge Companion to Old English Literature*, pp. 50–65 [B].

    'Secular Prose'. In Pulsiano and Treharne, eds., *A Companion to Anglo-Saxon Literature*, pp. 268–80. [B].

Stevens, Martin. *Four Middle English Mystery Cycles: Textual, Contextual, and Critical Interpretations*. Princeton University Press, 1987. Covers the four play collections of York, Wakefield, N-Town and Chester. With detailed chapters on each collection, it combines textual and critical scholarship, and conveys a sense of both the generic links and the distinction of each collection.

Wallace, David, ed. *The Cambridge History of Medieval English Literature*. Pbk edn. Cambridge University Press, 2002. OE is not included, but early ME is well represented, and continuities with pre-Norman England are emphasised throughout. Individual essays listed separately.

Woolf, Rosemary. 'The Ideal of Men Dying with their Lord in the *Germania* and in *The Battle of Maldon*'. *Anglo-Saxon England* 5 (1976): 63–81.

ii   Websites

The Auchinleck Manuscript. Ed. David Burnley and Alison Wiggins. National Library of Scotland. www.nls.uk/auchinleck. A wonderful online edition of the famous Auchinleck manuscript, with the history of the manuscript, edited text, facsimile of every page and critical apparatus.

Bosworth-Toller Anglo-Saxon Dictionary. Charles University in Prague. http://bosworth.ff.cuni.cz/. *The Dictionary of Old English* (below) is gradually updating and replacing Bosworth-Toller, which, until then, remains an essential resource.

Chaucer Metapage. Ed. Edward Duncan and Joseph Wittig. www.unc.edu/depts/chaucer/index.html. This resource includes Chaucer's texts as well as links to other Chaucer bibliographies and course home pages.

De Re Militari. http://deremilitari.org. An essential resource for anyone researching medieval warfare. Contents mostly comprise scholarly articles rather than images, videos or teaching aids.

Dictionary of Old English. Ed. Antonette diPaolo Healey. University of Toronto. http://doe.utoronto.ca/pages/index.html. Currently only complete from A to G, but for those letters, much the best Old English dictionary to use.

Early Manuscripts at Oxford University. http://image.ox.ac.uk. High resolution digital images of complete manuscripts enable close investigation of these volumes, which range from the workaday to the sumptuously illustrated, such as the *Romance of Alexander*, found in Bodleian 264.

The Electronic Beowulf. Ed. Kevin S. Kiernan. The British Library and the University of Kentucky. http://ebeowulf.uky.edu/gettingstarted/overview. A fascinating story of digital editing that offers the *Beowulf* manuscript page by page with facing transcription.

The Labyrinth: Resources for Medieval Studies. Ed. Deborah Everhart and Martin Irvine. Georgetown University. https://blogs.commons.georgetown.edu/labyrinth/. The Labyrinth covers many aspects of medieval life and learning, with citations for articles, maps and discussion threads.

Medieval Warfare: Sources and Approaches. James Ross and Adrian Jobson. The National Archives. http://media.nationalarchives.gov.uk/index.php/medieval-warfare-sources-and-approaches/. This is one of a number of excellent podcasts about how the documentary records at the National Archives help us understand medieval armies and fighting. Other podcasts cover topics such as medieval queens, criminals and the Magna Carta.

Medieval Writing. Ed. Dianne Tillotson. http://medievalwriting.50megs.com/writing .htm. This website introduces the reader to the world of manuscript writing, known as paleography. Interactive exercises offer hands-on experience in deciphering script.

Medievalists.net. Peter Konieczny and Sandra Alvarez. http://www.medievalists.net. This engaging website offers up-to-date coverage of recent archaeological finds and miscellaneous features of interest, treating the Middle Ages as if it were today's news.

The Middle English Compendium. Ed. Frances McSparran. University of Michigan. http://quod.lib.umich.edu/m/mec/. Excellent database of medieval texts with free access to the *Middle English Dictionary*.

Middle English Dictionary. University of Michigan, 2001. Essential for all research in Middle English, 1100–1500. Used in conjunction with the *Dictionary of Old English* and the *Oxford English Dictionary*, it offers a comprehensive historical analysis of the English language.

Regia Anglorum. Roland Williamson and Kim Skiddorn. http://regia.org/about.php. An excellent website with an emphasis on historical reconstruction and material culture, covering all things to do with pre-Conquest and Norman England.

Robbins Library Digital Project. University of Rochester. http://d.lib.rochester.edu/home. This major site houses a number of projects that are of immediate interest to the student of medieval England, namely: *The Camelot Project*. Ed. Alan Lupack and Barbara Tepa Lupack. A database of Arthurian texts and information from throughout the centuries. *The Robin Hood Project*. Ed. Alan Lupack and Barbara Tepa Lupack. A database of texts and information about Robin Hood from throughout the centuries. *TEAMS Middle English Texts Series*. Ed. Medieval Institute Publications. An invaluable collection of carefully edited Middle English texts.

iii   Films

The Advocate or *The Hour of the Pig*. Dir. Leslie Megahey, 1993. An amusing and disturbing tale about the murder trial of a pig. Animal trials did occur in later medieval France (and elsewhere), and for all its satiric presentation of absurdity, the film contains a powerful defence of such strange justice in a courtroom speech delivered by Donald Pleasance.

Anchoress. Dir. Chris Newby (1993). Set in fourteenth-century England, and loosely based on a story of such a girl, the film tells of a young girl whose visions lead her to become an anchoress. Without discrediting belief, the film well displays the disenchantments of the anchoritic life and its entanglements with human weakness.

Becket. Dir. Peter Glenville (1964). Based on Jean Anouilh's play, this powerful film depicts the story of the (implicitly homosexual) relationship between Henry II of England and his 'turbulent priest' Thomas Becket. Whatever the accuracy of its portrayal of their relationship, the film brings to life the conflicts between Church and state.

Beowulf. Dir. Robert Zemeckis (2007). An array of famous actors are here motion captured to make this computer-animated film that gives life to many features of the poem, as for example when Grendel speaks his few words in Old English.

Braveheart. Dir. Mel Gibson (1995). Historians object to its depiction of the Battle of Stirling Bridge, success in which depended on Wallace's unchivalric attack on the English before they had finished crossing the bridge. The film depicts no bridge, but well conveys the grit of battle engagement, and the divisive politicking of the Scottish barons.

Canterbury Tales. Dir. John McKay (2003). In this BBC mini-series, six of Chaucer's tales (by the Miller, Wife of Bath, Knight, Shipman, Pardoner, and Man of Law) are cleverly adapted and modernised.

Excalibur. Dir. John Boorman (1981). Visually beautiful, the film has a storyline that sprawls like the book it is based on – Malory's *Morte Darthur*. The fidelity to much of the original comes at the price of continuity of plot and characterisation, but the film remains well worth watching.

The Fisher King. Dir. Terry Gilliam (1991). A medieval romance about a quest for a grail set in modern-day New York. A comic study, it is an intelligent imitation of the romance form with its themes of providential design, the quest, faith, love and forgiveness.

The Hollow Crown. Dir. Rupert Goold et al. (2012, 2016). Shakespeare's history plays about the kings of late medieval England are televised in this fine mini-series made for TV. The first season covers *Richard II, Henry IV* Parts 1 and 2, and *Henry V*; the second season *Henry VI* Parts 1 and 2, and *Richard III*.

A Knight's Tale. Dir. Brian Helgeland (2001). With its vaguely punk heroine and accompanying rock music, this film makes no attempt at all to recreate historical authenticity, yet curiously manages in a lighthearted way to reinvent Chaucer and medieval popular culture.

Lancelot du Lac. Dir. Robert Bresson (1974). A brooding and tragic anti-romance, the film exposes the sinfulness, doubt and weakness of Camelot's heroes.

The Last Kingdom. Dir. Nick Murphy et al. (2015–). Set in ninth-century England, this TV series features Uhtred as its conflicted hero, born Saxon, raised Danish. Although faux-historical details mix with authentic, the story and acting imaginatively dramatise King Alfred's England.

The Lion in Winter. Dir. Anthony Harvey (1968). Depicts the aging Henry II (Peter O'Toole) and his 'turbulent' family. Eschews anachronistic luxury of castle life, exposes the draughty, dirty existence of medievals, even royalty, and reveals the complex connections between England and France, the instability of the throne and the uncertainty of hereditary succession.

Medieval Lives. Mini-series. Dir. Nigel Miller (2004). Presented and played by Terry Jones, this is an excellent and entertaining documentary about medieval lives. The episode on 'The Peasant' is particularly good.

Le moine et la sorcière (The Sorceress). Dir. Suzanne Schiffman (1987). Based on an actual story about a French village that had a dog for its local saint, this film is a powerful *exemplum* about forgiveness and mercy. It is especially interesting for its depiction of the tensions between church dogma and popular faith.

Monty Python and the Holy Grail. Dir. Terry Gilliam and Terry Jones (1975). The usual bizarre Pythonesque humour focused around the quest for the grail. As all good parodies do, it provides keen observation on the (romance) form it imitates, and employs many authentically medieval motifs.

The Name of the Rose. Dir. Jean-Jacques Annaud (1986). Based on the detective mystery by medieval scholar Umberto Eco, this film inevitably loses the novel's historical and philosophical nuance yet works very well on screen. Sean Connery and Christian Slater ably act the lead roles.

Pope Joan (Die Päpstin). Dir. Sönke Wortmann (2009). The legend of a woman who became pope first appeared in the late Middle Ages and remained popular, despite its unlikely historical basis. This film convincingly recreates the scandal that captured medieval imaginations.

Robin and Marion. Dir. Richard Lester (1976). Sean Connery and Audrey Hepburn play an aging Robin Hood and Maid Marion; his merry men are exhausted and want to go home. There are many Robin Hood films and this is probably the most complex and thoughtful of them.

Se7en. Dir. David Fincher (1995). This grim morality tale and thriller tells a story about a psychotic killer who murders his victims according to the seven deadly sins. It raises critical questions about the difference between sin and crime, and about the role of retribution in relation to the contrast between medieval and modern justice.

The Seventh Seal (Det Sjunde Inseglet). Dir. Ingmar Bergman (1957). A knight returning from the Crusades plays a game of chess with Death in a bid to escape the Black Death. Haunting imagery makes for a powerful meditation on death. After half a century, still a classic.

Tristan and Isolde. Dir. Kevin Reynolds (2006). The story of these unhappy lovers lies at the heart of medieval romance, and was told in many versions across Europe, including Thomas Malory's *Morte Darthur*. Reynolds's screen production is epic and visually beautiful.

2   The Renaissance, 1485–1660

ANDREW HISCOCK

This chapter explores the strategic historical and literary contexts for understanding Renaissance England. This was a period of enormous transition in religious, political and social terms. At the end of the fifteenth century, England might be seen as a rather marginal European kingdom governed in many ways by semi-feudal political relationships and local allegiances. By the end of Cromwell's Protectorate and the return of the Stuart monarchy in 1660, a sequence of wide-sweeping religious, political and economic changes had thrust the realm much more centrally into the arena of European affairs and had often traumatised the native population into the bargain. Unsurprisingly, Renaissance writers engaged tightly with the radically changing cultural landscape which their audiences were experiencing and often explored in new and challenging ways the directions which this developing nation might take.

Chronology

	HISTORY AND CULTURE	LITERATURE
1485	Battle of Bosworth Field. Death of Richard III. Accession of Henry VII	William Caxton, England's first printer of books (since 1477), publishes Sir Thomas Malory's *Morte Darthur* (c. 1470) (Caxton had printed 100 books by his death in 1491)
1492	Arrival of Columbus in the Caribbean Jews expelled from Spain Rodrigo Borgia becomes Pope Alexander VI	
c. 1495		Anon., *Everyman* Henry Medwall, *Fulgens and Lucres*
1497	Vasco da Gama begins journey round Africa to India (–1499)	
1499		John Skelton, *Bowge of Court*
1503	Leonardo da Vinci paints *The Mona Lisa* Pope Julius II	
1508	Michelangelo begins work on the Sistine Chapel	Scottish poet Gavin Douglas completes translation of *Aeneid*
1509	Accession of Henry VIII	Desiderius Erasmus, *In Praise of Folly*
1513	Portuguese explorers begin contact with China	Niccolò Machiavelli, *The Prince* Sir Thomas More, *History of Richard III*

	HISTORY AND CULTURE	LITERATURE
1515	Birth of humanist Roger Ascham	Performance of Skelton's *Magnyfycence*
1516	Erasmus's Latin translation of the New Testament published in Basle	More, *Utopia* (in Latin) Ludovico Ariosto, *Orlando Furioso*
1517	Martin Luther, *Wittenberg Theses*	John Rastell, *Four Elements*
1518	Cardinal Wolsey appointed Papal Legate	
1519	Invasion of Mexico by Cortés and defeat of Aztec empire (–1521) Magellan begins his voyage around the world (–1522) Charles V becomes Holy Roman Emperor	Erasmus, *Colloquies*
1521	Luther excommunicated	Skelton, *Speak Parrot; Colin Clout*
1524	The Peasants' Revolt (–1525)	
1525		William Tyndale, *New Testament*
1527	Sack of Rome	
1528		Castiglione, *Il Libro del Cortegiano* (trans. into English 1561)
1529	Thomas More becomes Chancellor	
1531		Sir Thomas Elyot, *The Book Named the Governor*
1532	Henry VIII divorces Katherine of Aragon Pizarro conquers the Inca empire (–1536)	François Rabelais, *Pantagruel* W. Thynne edition, *The Works of Geoffrey Chaucer Newly Printed*
1533	The English Church separates from Rome and Henry VIII is excommunicated Henry VIII marries Anne Boleyn	Death of Ariosto
1534	Henry VIII becomes head of the Church (Act of Supremacy) Ignatius Loyola founds the Society of Jesus (Jesuits)	Rabelais, *Gargantua*
1535	Executions of Sir Thomas More and Bishop Fisher	The first entire translation of the Bible in English published by Miles Coverdale, building on earlier work of William Tyndale
1536	Calvin, *The Institutes of the Christian Religion* (trans. into English 1561) Guicciardini begins *The History of Italy* Execution of Anne Boleyn The dissolution of the monasteries begins Pilgrimage of Grace, Northern rebellions (–1537) Union of England and Wales	Death of Erasmus
1538		John Bale, *Three Laws, John the Baptist Preachyng, God's Promises*
1539		*The Great Bible* Anon., *Godly Queen Hester*
1541	Henry VIII now named King of Ireland and Head of the Church in Ireland	
1542	Portuguese explorers begin contact with Japan Death of James V of Scotland and birth of daughter Mary, who becomes the next Scottish monarch Inquisition established in Rome	Edward Hall, *The Union of the two noble and illustrious families of Lancaster and York* Death of Sir Thomas Wyatt
1543	Copernicus, *On the Revolutions of the Heavenly Spheres*	
1547	Death of Henry VIII. Accession of Edward VI Western Rebellion (–1549) Death of Francis I of France	Execution of Henry Howard, Earl of Surrey

	HISTORY AND CULTURE	LITERATURE
1548	Council of Trent	
1549		The Book of Common Prayer (principally by Thomas Cranmer)
1550	Giorgio Vasari, *Lives of the Most Excellent Painters, Sculptors and Architects*	
1552	First Jesuit College opened in Rome	Nicholas Udall, *Ralph Roister Doister* Birth of Edmund Spenser
1553	Edward VI dies. Accession of Mary I Wyatt's rebellion (–1554)	William Baldwin, *Beware the Cat* Thomas Wilson, *The Art of Rhetoric* Performances of *Gammer Gurton's Needle* and Udall, *Respublica*
1554	The marriage of Mary and Philip of Spain in Winchester Execution of Lady Jane Grey English Church returns to Rome with Mary retaining title of Supreme Head	
1555	Burning of Latimer and Ridley Charles V abdicates as Holy Roman Emperor	
1556	Burning of Cranmer	John Foxe, *Christus Triumphans*
1557		Richard Tottel, *Songes and Sonnettes* More, *Works*
1558	Calais surrendered to France Death of Mary. Accession of Elizabeth I	Marguerite de Navarre, *Heptameron* Jane Lumley, *Iphigenia in Aulis* (trans.)
1559	Acts of Uniformity Mary, Queen of Scots marries the Dauphin	First edition in Latin of Foxe, *Acts and Monuments of the Christian Church* William Baldwin, George Ferrers et al., *Mirror for Magistrates*
1561		Sir Thomas Hoby's translation of Castiglione's *The Courtier* John Heywood, *Hercules Furens* (trans.) Birth of Francis Bacon
1562	Slaving operations to Africa begun by John Hawkins First 'War of Religion' in France	Thomas Norton and Thomas Sackville, *Gorboduc*
1563	Thirty-Nine Articles of Anglican Church Birth of John Dowland, composer	First edition in English of Foxe, *Acts and Monuments* Alexander Neville, *Oedipus* (trans.)
1564	Death of Calvin and Michelangelo Birth of Galileo	Birth of William Shakespeare and Christopher Marlowe R. B., *Apius and Virginia*
1565		Arthur Golding's translation of Ovid's *Metamorphoses* I–IV
1567	Opening of the Red Lion theatre in London Birth of Monteverdi, composer	Isabella Whitney, *The Copy of a Letter*
1568	Dutch Revolt against Spanish rule Slavery abolished in the Portuguese empire Flight of the Scottish queen Mary into England	*Bishop's Bible*
1569	The Northern Rebellion (–1570) Munster Rebellions begin in Ireland	
1570	Excommunication of Elizabeth I	Roger Ascham, *The Schoolmaster*
1571	Ridolfi plot to set Mary, Queen of Scots upon the English throne Battle of Lepanto	
1572	St Bartholomew's Day massacre of Huguenots in France Duke of Norfolk executed	

	HISTORY AND CULTURE	LITERATURE
1573		George Gascoigne, *A Hundred Sundry Flowers*
1575		Pierre de Ronsard, *Sonnets pour Hélène* Gascoigne, *Glass of Government*
1576	The Theatre – purpose-built playhouse in London	Gascoigne, *The Steel Glass*
1577	Sir Francis Drake begins his circumnavigation of the globe (–1581)	First edition of Raphael Holinshed, *The Chronicles of England, Scotland and Ireland* (–1578)
1578	Marriage proposal received by Elizabeth I from Francis, Duke of Alençon	John Lyly, *Euphues: The Anatomy of Wit*
1579		Sir Thomas North's translation of Plutarch's *Lives* Edmund Spenser, *The Shepherd's Calendar*
1580	Union of Spanish and Portuguese crowns	Torquato Tasso, *Gerusalemme Liberata* Michel de Montaigne, *Essais* I–II John Stow, *The Chronicles of England*
1582		Richard Hakluyt, *Diverse Voyages*
1584	First English colony in America established by Sir Walter Ralegh at Roanoke Island, Virginia Assassination of William of Orange in the Netherlands	Lyly, *Campaspe, Sappho and Phao*
1587	Execution of Mary, Queen of Scots Pope proclaims crusade against England	Performances of Thomas Kyd, *The Spanish Tragedy*; Marlowe, *Tamburlaine* I; George Peele, *David and Bethshabe*; Robert Greene, *Alphonsus, King of Aragon* William Camden, *Britannia*
1588	Defeat of the Spanish Armada Marprelate Tracts (–1599)	Lyly, *Endymion* Anon., *Mucedorus*
1589	Henry of Navarre named as Henri IV of France	George Puttenham, *The Art of English Poesy* Performance of Marlowe, *The Jew of Malta*
1590		Sir Philip Sidney, *Countess of Pembroke's Arcadia* Spenser, *The Faerie Queene* I–III
1591		Sidney, *Astrophil and Stella* Shakespeare, *Henry VI* pts II and III
1592		Performances of Marlowe, *Dr Faustus* and Shakespeare, *Comedy of Errors* Mary Sidney, *Tragedy of Antony* published
1593		Shakespeare, *Venus and Adonis* Performances of Shakespeare, *Richard III*; *The Two Gentlemen of Verona* Death of Marlowe
1594	Beginning of the Nine Years' War in Ireland led by Hugh O'Neil, Earl of Tyrone (–1603)	Richard Hooker, *Of the Laws of the Ecclesiastical Polity* I–IV Thomas Nashe, *The Unfortunate Traveller* Shakespeare, *The Rape of Lucrece*
1595		Sidney, *An Apology for Poetry* (or *The Defence of Poesy*) Spenser, *Amoretti*
1596	Essex attacks Cadiz Birth of René Descartes	Spenser, *The Faerie Queene* IV–VI
1597	New Poor Law Early opera productions in Europe Dowland, *First Book of Songs*	First edition of Sir Francis Bacon's *Essays*

	HISTORY AND CULTURE	LITERATURE
1598	Edict of Nantes offers some guarantees of safety and toleration to French Huguenots Death of Philip II	Performance of Ben Jonson, *Every Man In His Humour* John Stow, *A Survey of the Cities of London and Westminster*
1599	The Globe theatre built	Death of Spenser Performance of Shakespeare, *Julius Caesar*
1600	East India Company founded	
1601	Execution of Essex after his rebellion is quashed	'War of the Theatres' – Jonson, Thomas Dekker, John Marston
1602		Thomas Campion, *Observations in the Art of English Poesy*
1603	Death of Elizabeth I. Accession of James VI of Scotland to English throne as James I Millenary Petition presented to James by Puritans	John Florio's translation of Montaigne, *Essais* Jonson, *Sejanus*
1604	Peace negotiated with Spain Hampton Court conference	Performance of Shakespeare, *Othello*
1605	The Gunpowder Plot	Bacon, *The Advancement of Learning* Cervantes, *Don Quixote*, pt 1 Jonson, *The Masque of Blackness*
1606	Birth of Rembrandt	Performances of Jonson, *Volpone*; Shakespeare, *King Lear*; Cyril Tourneur, *The Revenger's Tragedy*
1607	Founding of Jamestown, Virginia	Francis Beaumont and John Fletcher, *The Knight of the Burning Pestle* George Chapman, *Bussy D'Ambois*
1608	Plantation of Ulster begins	Birth of John Milton
1609		Shakespeare, *Sonnets* Jonson, *Epicoene*
1610	Complaints in Parliament about 'impositions' Galileo, *The Starry Messenger*	Performances of Jonson, *The Alchemist*; Beaumont and Fletcher, *The Maid's Tragedy* Campion, *Two Books of Airs*
1611	Gustavus Adolphus, King of Sweden (–1632)	Authorised Version of the Bible Chapman, translation of Homer's *Iliad* Performance of Shakespeare, *The Tempest* Aemilia Lanyer, *Salve Deus Rex Judaeorum*
1612	Death of Robert Cecil and Prince Henry	Performance of John Webster, *The White Devil*
1613		Performance of Webster, *The Duchess of Malfi* Elizabeth Cary, *Tragedy of Mariam*
1614	Globe theatre rebuilt after fire in previous year	Chapman, translation of Homer's *Odyssey* (–1615) Ralegh, *The History of the World* Jonson, *Bartholomew Fair*
1615		Cervantes, *Don Quixote*, pt 2
1616	Lectures on the circulation of the blood by William Harvey in London	Jonson, *Works* Death of Shakespeare Death of Cervantes
1618	Beginning of the Thirty Years' War Execution of Ralegh Elector Palatine becomes King of Bohemia	Jonson, *Pleasure Reconciled to Virtue*

	HISTORY AND CULTURE	LITERATURE
1620	The Pilgrim Fathers sail to America in the *Mayflower* Battle of the White Mountain	Bacon, *Novum Organum*
1621	Donne becomes Dean of St Paul's Cathedral	Robert Burton, *The Anatomy of Melancholy* Mary Wroth, *The Countess of Montgomerie's Urania, Part I* Performances of Philip Massinger, *A New Way to Pay Old Debts*; Thomas Middleton, *Women Beware Women*
1622		Performance of Middleton, *The Changeling*
1623	Birth of Blaise Pascal	Shakespeare, *First Folio*
1624	Act of Parliament to restrict the sale of monopolies War declared on Spain Ascendancy of Cardinal Richelieu in France until 1642	John Donne, *Devotions upon Emergent Occasions*
1625	Accession of Charles I. Charles marries Henrietta Maria of France	Samuel Purchas, *Hakluyt Posthumous, or Purchas his Pilgrimes, Containing a History of the world; in Sea Voyages and Land Travels*
1626	The 'Forced Loan' (1626–7) War with France	Death of Bacon
1628	Petition of Right presented Laud appointed Bishop of London Buckingham assassinated	
1629	After protracted disagreements, Charles has Parliament dissolved and Sir John Eliot among other leaders imprisoned Personal Rule of Charles I commences and lasts for eleven years Peace with France	Lancelot Andrewes, *XCVI Sermons*
1630	Massachusetts Bay Colony established	
1631		Death of John Donne
1633	Laud appointed Archbishop of Canterbury	John Ford, *'Tis Pity She's a Whore* George Herbert, *The Temple* Posthumous publication of Donne, *Poems*
1634	Charles insists upon payment of Ship Money without agreement of Parliament	Performance of Milton, *Comus*
1635	Founding of the Académie Française	Francis Quarles, *Emblems*
1637	Trial of John Hampden for non-payment of Ship Money Papal ambassador welcomed at court Action to impose new Prayer Book on Scottish Church led by Charles	Milton, *Lycidas* René Descartes, *Discours de la méthode*
1639	First Bishops' War	
1640	Parliament recalled on advice of Strafford. The Long Parliament operating until 1653 Second Bishops' War Impeachment proceedings begun by Parliament against Strafford and Laud	
1641	Triennial Act – ensuring that Parliament will be called at least every three years Execution of Strafford Parliamentary Act declaring Ship Money illegal and presentation to Charles of the Grand Remonstrance Rebellion in Ireland Breakdown of censorship	
1642	Attempt to arrest MPs. Charles leaves London and Parliament reorganises London militia. Henrietta Maria sails to France for financial and military assistance. Charles at Nottingham calls for volunteers to the royalist cause. Battle of Edgehill	

	HISTORY AND CULTURE	LITERATURE
1643	Sieges of Gloucester and Hull preventing royalist attack on London Scots ally with Parliament Reign of child Louis XIV begins (–1715)	Sir Thomas Browne, *Religio Medici*
1644	Battle of Marston Moor means that North of England is secured for Parliament	Milton, *Areopagitica*
1645	New Model Army established. Main royalist army destroyed at Battle of Naseby Prayer Book abolished and Laud executed	Edmund Waller, *Poems*
1646	Charles surrenders to the Scots	Milton, *Poems* James Shirley, *Poems* Richard Crashaw, *Steps to the Temple* Henry Vaughan, *Poems* …
1647	Charles delivered over to Parliament. Putney Debates. Charles escapes to Isle of Wight	Folio of Beaumont and Fletcher, *Comedies and Tragedies* Abraham Cowley, *The Mistress*
1648	Second Civil War: Scots now side with the king. Thirty Years' War ends	Robert Herrick, *Hesperides*
1649	Trial and execution of Charles I. Abolition of monarchy and England declared a commonwealth	Richard Lovelace, *Lucasta: Epodes*
1650	Defeat of Scots at Battle of Dunbar. Cromwell replaces Fairfax as Lord General	Anne Bradstreet, *The Tenth Muse Lately Sprung Up in America* Andrew Marvell, 'An Horatian Ode' First edition of Henry Vaughan, *Silex Scintillans*
1651	Charles II crowned at Scone. His forces are defeated at the Battle of Worcester	Marvell, 'Upon Appleton House' John Cleveland, *Poems* Thomas Hobbes, *Leviathan*
1652		Crashaw, *Carmen Deo Nostro: Sacred Poems*
1653	Cromwell named as Lord Protector	An Collins, *Divine Songs and Meditations* Margaret Cavendish, *Poems and Fancies* Izaak Walton, *The Compleat Angler*
1654	First Parliament of the Protectorate in session	
1655	War with Spain (–1659)	
1656		John Bunyan, *Some Gospel-Truths Opened* Sir William D'Avenant, *The Siege of Rhodes* James Harrington, *The Commonwealth of Oceana* Cowley, *Poems*
1657	Cromwell refuses the crown	Henry King, *Poems, Elegies, Paradoxes and Sonnets*
1658	Death of Cromwell. His son Richard is proclaimed Lord Protector	Sir Thomas Browne, *Hydriotaphia, or Urn Burial; The Garden of Cyrus* Anna Trapnel, *Voice for the King of Saints and Nations*
1659	Richard Cromwell resigns. Army leaders recall the Rump Parliament	Bunyan, *The Doctrine of the Law and Grace Unfolded*
1660	Monck's army marches into England. Declaration of Breda Parliament votes that government should be by King, Lords and Commons Charles Stuart returns as Charles II Royal Society founded	Milton, *A Ready and Easy Way to Establish a Free Commonwealth* John Dryden, *Astraea Redux*

Historical Overview

Tudor Sovereignty, 1485–1603

After the defeat of Richard III at the Battle of Bosworth Field in 1485, the reign of Henry VII (1485–1509) effectively brought to an end the bitter and bloody divisions between the Houses of York and Lancaster. However, at the time it would have been difficult to arrive at this conclusion, for recent Yorkist monarchs (such as Edward IV and Richard III) had also seized the crown in violent and unexpected ways, and these actions had not led to sustained periods of national peace and security. The Wars of the Roses had been unfolding since at least the middle of the fifteenth century when the increasingly weak Lancastrian king, Henry VI, sank further into mental illness and the Yorkists defeated the royal forces of Queen Margaret and the Duke of Somerset at the Battle of St Albans in 1455. The 28-year-old Henry VII married Elizabeth of York (daughter of Edward IV, niece of Richard III) in January 1486, five months after his accession. By delaying the marriage, Henry was determined to show that his sovereignty did not in any way depend upon it, but nonetheless this act performed a symbolic union of the two houses and would considerably strengthen his rather weak claim to the English crown.

Having spent much of his life in exile in Brittany (1471–85), the new king was very inexperienced in political and financial government. However, this meant that he had made few enemies and, in addition, he did not have any brothers to challenge his claim to the crown. During his reign, Yorkist sympathisers continued to rally around impostors (such as Lambert Simnel and Perkin Warbeck), who were promoted as royal pretenders. Henry was capable of spending extravagantly on occasions in the area of court decoration, plate and ceremonial in the desire to impress upon his various audiences the grandeur of his sovereignty – and, equally importantly, its legitimacy and permanence. More generally, his government was shaped by his instinctive mistrust of anyone with political influence (either at home or abroad) and his ruthless financial control of his realm. His son, Henry VIII, was not born to be king and only became the heir apparent on the death of his brother Arthur in 1502. The reign of the second Tudor monarch (1509–47) ushered in a quite different period of political experience characterised by a much more hedonistic court culture, more belligerent foreign policies and religious ferment, particularly in its later years. When the handsome seventeen-year-old Henry VIII acceded to the throne he was ambitious to make his mark on the European stage as a chivalric prince and a formidable military commander – in the event, it was the implications of his sexual career (spanning six wives and numerous mistresses) which were all too often to attract and sometimes perplex the minds of European courts during his lifetime. Henry frequently proved himself to be more susceptible to flattery than his father had ever been. His early devotion to the pleasures of hunting, feasting and love-making meant that he left much of the political work to his advisers. He allowed trusted figures, like Cardinal Wolsey and Thomas Cromwell, to wield enormous political power in a manner which would

Renaissance

The term 'Renaissance' means rebirth in French and derives originally from the Latin 'renascentia'. This label was first employed in the sixteenth century to describe a period in which the recovery and/or renewal of interest in texts from Ancient Greek and Roman culture became a significant focus of intellectual attention. More generally, 'Renaissance' is now used by historians and literary critics to refer to a whole host of different cultural movements (artistic, political, religious, literary) which began in fourteenth-century Italy and whose influence radiated out across Europe in the succeeding centuries. It is generally agreed that the influence of this significant period of cultural change in Europe did not reach the shores of the rather insular kingdom of England in any substantial manner until the arrival of the Tudors on the throne. The accession of Henry VII marked an end to an extended period of civil unrest (the Wars of the Roses) and thus facilitated greater cultural dialogue and exchange with European neighbours. Since the late twentieth century, the term 'Renaissance' has met with a number of challenges on the part of scholars who question whether it was only male members of certain political and intellectual elites who profited from a period of 'cultural renewal'. As a result, the term 'early modern' has had increasing currency among those studying this period.

have horrified Henry VII. By the late 1520s, a more assertive sovereign emerged, but his irascibility also grew progressively as he found his ambitions for influence abroad and his desires to contain religious controversy at home repeatedly thwarted. In the later years of his reign, Henry's bids to replenish royal funds and to consolidate his political support were centrally linked to the sale of ecclesiastical properties to eager subjects.

The reign of Edward VI (1547–53) was dominated by a much more vigorous engagement with Protestant doctrine than had hitherto been witnessed in the realm. Edward ascended to the throne at the age of nine and, as a consequence, political authority was expressed in his name mostly by ambitious relatives: the 'Lord Protector', the Duke of Somerset; and by the close of 1549 by the 'Lord President of the Council', the Earl of Warwick (named Duke of Northumberland in 1551). Much of this short reign was focused upon responses to Scotland's changing allegiances, to demands to eradicate persisting Catholic practices in the national Church and to economic unrest. If the Edwardian court was never free from bitter factionalism among the Protestant nobility, it maintained in general a much more sober and restrained atmosphere than had been in evidence in previous decades under Henry VIII. Edward's death in the spring of 1553 was followed immediately by an attempted coup d'état led by the Northumberland party and centring upon the Protestant Lady Jane Grey (granddaughter of Henry VIII's sister Mary, Duchess of Suffolk) – Grey had been compelled to marry Northumberland's son earlier that year. In the event, Northumberland's strategy could count upon no popular support of any substance and it was Edward's half-sister, Mary (daughter of the Spanish princess, Katherine of Aragon) who ascended to the throne at the age of thirty-seven. Unsurprisingly, the reign of the Catholic Mary I (1553–8) heralded a period of radical political and religious realignment for the kingdom. Some eight hundred reformists went into exile on the Continent shortly after her accession, anticipating that Mary would be eager to re-establish the 'old faith' in her land. Indeed, she welcomed papal representatives to her shores and accepted the marriage proposal of Philip II of Spain. These initiatives combined with the energetic persecution of Protestant heretics meant that the goodwill which had carried her to the throne was quickly squandered. Her distrust of the

2.1 Isaac Oliver, *A Miniature Depicting an Allegory of Virtue Confronting Vice*, c.1590 (detail). In all aspects of its cultural life, the Renaissance displayed a compulsive interest in the tension between competing values and beliefs.

2.2 Lucas De Heere (1534–84), *The Family of Henry VIII: an Allegory of the Tudor Succession*. A symbolic representation of Henry VIII and his childless offspring, Edward VI, Elizabeth I and Mary I (with her husband, Philip II of Spain): a dynasty dogged by anxieties of succession.

previous political elite, her failure to produce an heir and the progressive onset of ill health also ultimately contributed to Mary's inability to strengthen the power base of her support during her short reign.

When Mary died in November 1558, her Protestant half-sister Elizabeth accepted the crown of an exhausted and weakened nation. The reign of the last Tudor monarch (1558–1603) offered at least the prospect of conciliation and stability. If Elizabeth was frequently guilty of short-termist thinking, excessive caution and parsimonious-ness, she proved to be a vigilant, intelligent and effective political leader who could rally popular support when necessary in a more successful manner than any of her Tudor predecessors. This achievement is all the more remarkable in a world deeply unsympathetic to female rule of any kind. Fearing any loss of political control and, indeed, the prospect of her own mortality, Elizabeth was never able to respond ade-quately to abiding national anxieties concerning the succession. In religious matters, if she had approximately the same number of religious heretics executed as Mary had done (just under 300), she did so over a much longer period. In general, her gov-ernment was much more concerned with the threat of political dissent than with the private devotions of subjects. Elizabeth had her father's weakness for favourites (who managed to gain political influence), but she never lost sight of the fact during her reign that her own authority often depended upon maintaining a balance of power between factions at home and abroad.

The Early Stuarts and the Interregnum, 1603–1660

James VI of Scotland nurtured relations with Elizabeth's advisers as the century drew to a close and a tacit agreement was forged whereby he would claim the crown directly after Elizabeth's death. In the event, Sir Robert Cecil proclaimed the Stuart monarch as king in March 1603 directly on Elizabeth's demise and the 36-year-old Scottish king left Edinburgh the next month. However, it is important not to under-estimate the political upheaval which still surrounded the arrival of the Stuarts on the English throne. James was foreign. He was the first male to wear the English crown in fifty years. Unlike his Tudor predecessors, he also had responsibility for three separate kingdoms (England with Wales, Scotland and Ireland), each with their own parliaments and codes of law – yet none of these rivalled the wealth and power of their major European neighbours. In addition, James inherited a costly history of hostilities with Spain, ongoing financial difficulties for the administration, and social and religious tensions. His pretensions to be a theologian, a scholar-king and the peace-loving arbiter abroad (*rex pacificus*) also marked a noticeable change in the political climate – one of the first decisions upon taking up his new throne was to end the war with Spain. The fact that he had two sons was also welcomed among his new subjects after so many years of anxiety surrounding the succession under Elizabeth. Whatever hopes were raised at his accession among hitherto disaffected religious communities, he soon proved to Catholics and Puritans alike that he was no more minded to introduce radical religious reform than his predecessor had been. Despite his lack of enthusiasm for the finer details of government, James was shrewd enough to draw talented political servants about him to steer the administration. It was only in the final years of his reign from 1618 onwards, when the continental powers were drawn into the Thirty Years' War (after his son-in-law, the Elector Palatine, accepted the crown of Bohemia), that his control of political events grew progressively weaker.

During his intrepid adventure with Villiers, the Duke of Buckingham, to Spain in 1623 to win the hand of the *infanta*, the heir Charles Stuart had been much impressed with the ceremonial and formality of the Habsburg court. When he ascended to the throne in 1625 at the age of twenty-four he wished to replicate this in England. His aloofness, desire for privacy and attention to administrative procedure all served to create a very different atmosphere at court from that which had been witnessed during his father's reign. Whereas James had promoted individuals of merit from a range of religious persuasions, Charles often concentrated upon advancing the careers of those who had Arminian sympathies and/or supported the vigorous assertion of royal authority. As his reign unfolded, Charles was often misunderstood, but the country began increasingly to view him in autocratic terms. It became clear that he had none of his father's pragmatism or Elizabeth's skilful diplomacy with her subjects. In the opening years of his reign Charles showed himself determined to restore to health the royal finances and raised funds by extending schemes of taxation. In response to opposition at Westminster, Charles dissolved Parliament in 1629 and the eleven-year period (known as 'the Personal Rule') began.

The effectiveness of this period of political rule has been vigorously debated by generations of historians but whatever expressions there may have been of dissent and opposition in the country, serious political unrest and disorder were only triggered in 1637 when Charles attempted to impose the English Prayer Book on Scotland. Violent uprisings then broke out in Ireland in 1641 and in England in 1642. There has been growing dissatisfaction among scholars surrounding the theses that the Civil War was the inevitable result of increasing conflict between a tyrant and a democratic Parliament, or centred on ongoing economic frictions and financial competition between the ruling elite and rising middling classes. National divisions and regicide were viewed with horror throughout the early modern period and it is clearly wrong to view any social class or grouping as homogeneous in its political and/or religious allegiances. Internal divisions and unwanted conflict across the political spectrum are increasingly being seen as responses to a developing narrative in the 1630s of rather high-handed government across the three kingdoms of England, Scotland and Ireland. Much of the disaffection was rooted in the

Arminianism

The Dutch theologian Jacob Arminius (1560–1609) rejected Calvinist doctrines of predestination, promoting instead the view that God's redeeming grace was open to all who sought it in His church and that divine judgement could be affected by the decisions made by human free will. With their commitment to church ceremonial and decoration, to an enhanced status for good works in the Christian's quest for salvation, to the privileged standing of the clergy, to government by bishops and to an emphasis upon worship in terms of the rituals of sacrament rather than the moral instruction of the sermon, Arminians represented for their Protestant critics a dangerous return to Catholic practices of worship.

2.3 Van Dyck, c. 1632, *Charles I and Queen Henrietta Maria with Their Two Eldest Children*.

following issues: growing political mistrust in the nation about the unwillingness of government to submit itself to public scrutiny; the sourcing of ultimate political sovereignty; the nomination of royal advisers; the financing of government; the political and legal status of those of differing religious persuasions; and the policing of social control across the nations. By February 1642 Charles had moved the court to York and his queen had sailed to France to seek assistance. The Battle of Naseby in 1645 saw the decisive blow to the royalist forces and the interventions of Parliament's recently organised New Model Army brought the hostilities to a close in 1646. At the beginning of 1649 the Commons called for the trial of the King and after being found guilty he was executed on 30 January. In March of that year the monarchy and the House of Lords were abolished and in May, England was declared a commonwealth.

2.4 *The Execution of Charles I*, c. 1649–50.

The Interregnum regimes 1649–60 (occurring between the execution of Charles I in 1649 and the 'Restoration' of his son Charles II to the throne in 1660) continued to discover that widespread popular support could not be counted upon at any point. Moreover, during this period continuing anxieties were provoked by royalists abroad and radical groups at home, such as the Levellers. By 1654, the Commonwealth was replaced by a military Protectorate led by Cromwell assisted by a Council of State and parliaments elected every three years. Cromwell could number Henry VIII's minister, Thomas Cromwell, among his forefathers. His personality and example of inspirational leadership during times of conflict meant that he could control the army as well as return some measure of stability to civilian life. However, when his eldest son succeeded him in 1658 the weakness of the political structure which depended upon the character of one individual was revealed. Richard Cromwell withdrew from public life in 1659 and Parliament was recalled to deal with the crisis. A new future was assured when the commander of the republic's forces in Scotland, General George Monck, marched south preparing the way for the return of Charles II and the Stuart monarchy in 1660.

The British Nations

While the dominant focus of this volume is upon the English experience, it is also important to consider interrelations with the Scots, Irish and Welsh as well as those with continental Europe and beyond. Whereas in previous ages Britain succumbed to various degrees to the invasions of the Romans, Angles, Saxons, Jutes, Danes and Normans, the early modern period saw Britain confronting the great dangers of invasion and warfare, but also responding keenly to cultural movements from abroad.

In the case of Wales, under the Statute of Rhuddlan (1284) Edward I had finally established political continuity between England and Wales, moving in English political administrators at the highest level, encouraging the colonising of Welsh communities with English settlers and establishing English governance from Caernarvon and Carmarthen. The English king's eldest son was named henceforth the Prince of Wales. Wales continued to be viewed as a realm culturally distinct in terms of its language, legal traditions and history during this period and as resistant to the 'civilising' influence (religious and political) of its English neighbour. Ongoing problems of unrest and sedition occurring outside the lands of royal lordship in Wales were addressed in an Act of 1536 whereby England and Wales were united politically. The latter was divided up into shires and overseen by justices in accordance with the English model.

Political life in England and Wales continued to be governed throughout the Renaissance by events beyond their borders. Scotland was a distinct kingdom with its own government and legal system during the Tudor period and would not become politically 'engaged' with England until the union of the crowns in 1603, when James VI of Scotland acceded to the English throne as James I. England and Scotland had always been extremely jittery about each other's political life and had often supported certain factions and causes (for example, through marriage alliances, the sheltering of political fugitives, and diplomatic and military interventions) for their own strategic purposes. The 'Auld Alliance' between the Scottish and French nations constituted a continual political pressure upon English policy-making at home and abroad. At the beginning of Edward VI's reign, Somerset was determined to continue a policy of bullying the northern neighbour (the so-called 'rough wooing'): in this instance, he attempted to compel the young Catholic Mary, Queen of Scots to marry the Protestant Edward by organising armed raids along the Scottish border. Despite an English victory outside Edinburgh in 1547, the Scottish forces would not submit. In 1548, a large contingent of French troops landed, occupied Edinburgh and removed Mary to France where she would ultimately marry the future Francis II. Marie de Guise was left as regent, but in 1561, after the death of her husband, Mary returned to Scotland. The political consequences of her subsequent marriages to Darnley and Bothwell forced her to flee as a deposed monarch south of the border in 1568. Her son acceded to the Scottish throne in 1567 – and to the English one in 1603.

The Early Stuart kings failed to respond in any substance to Scottish resentments about the centralised nature of government from London. James attempted to pursue his project of an empire of Great Britain, signifying the unification of the British nations under one rule. Despite the fact that the Westminster parliament threw this out, James did manage to restrain the Scottish ruling elite during his reign. His son Charles I was less astute in this area and by 1637 expressed his expectations of Scottish obedience by proclaiming that a version of the English Book of Common Prayer, revised by Scottish prelates with Laudian sympathies, was to be used by Scottish churches. In so doing, Charles managed to unite a politically and religiously divided kingdom against him. In 1643 Parliament signed a decisive treaty with the Scots securing military assistance in return for the imposition of Presbyterian structures in the Church of England. The Scots were subsequently shocked by the execution of Charles in 1649 and the failure of the English to honour promises to introduce Presbyterianism throughout the realm. By 1650 Scottish forces in support of Charles II marched south but were defeated finally at the Battle of Worcester in the following year. During the 1650s Cromwell maintained military control over the northern kingdom. The failure of the republic to respond to Scottish demands for religious reform and political status meant that the return of Charles II was welcomed widely north of the border.

Since the early fourteenth century, English control in Ireland had only extended around the city of Dublin (the Pale). In the area outside this domain (the Irishry), the English were forced to treat with powerful noble families and clans. The majority of native Irish and Old English settlers (belonging to the period following the Anglo-Norman invasion in the twelfth century) were Catholic. The prospect of sustained control of Ireland by military means continued to be prohibitively expensive for English monarchs and the island remained a potential centre of political and religious opposition. When Henry VIII broke with Rome, the Fitzgerald family led a revolt against him in Ireland. In 1535, an English force was sent out and the resisting garrison at Maynooth was slaughtered. This uprising opened the way for more vigorous direct rule from England to be funded by confiscation of the Fitzgerald estates and the dissolution of the Irish monasteries. In 1541, the Irish Parliament recognised Henry as King of Ireland and chieftains were invited to surrender their lands, to pay homage to their sovereign and to have these same lands regranted as fiefs ('surrender and regrant') – and some families like the O'Neills did so.

Nonetheless, unrest continued on the island throughout the decade, particularly in response to the more energetic Protestantism of the Edwardian settlement. In reality, there were never enough English troops sent to Ireland to subdue it in any adequate fashion and Ireland, dominated by the rivalries of the Irish chieftains, remained only nominally under English control. During Edward VI's reign, the policy of cultural and territorial 'plantation' was implemented which involved English colonists being settled on territories previously belonging to native clans. During Mary I's reign, further areas of English influence ('Queen's County' and 'King's County') were established outside the Pale. Under Elizabeth, particular attention was devoted to Ulster and Munster, with this policy of plantation often engendering local uprisings. In 1585, Hugh O'Neill, Earl of Tyrone, fearing further English expansionism

Laudians

These clerics were sympathetic to the ecclesiastical policies of Charles I's Archbishop of Canterbury William Laud (1573–1645) during the 1630s. Laud was seen by his adversaries as leading the 'Arminian faction'. His policies included: the releasing of the Church and its courts from secular control; a determination to secure regular church funding through royal financing and tithe payments from landowners; the establishment of an educated and morally scrupulous clergy; the outlawing of unlicensed (mostly Puritan) preachers; a greater emphasis upon the aesthetics of worship (especially in terms of ceremonial, clerical adornment, church decoration); a resulting loss of status for preaching (which was particularly cherished by those of Calvinist sympathies); and the locating of the communion table at the east end of the church (reviving the Catholic custom of worship, rather than placing the table more centrally and closer to the congregation as the more radical Protestants desired).

as a result of changes in European politics, led an attack on English forces. By the mid-1590s, the province of Ulster was up in arms against Tudor governorship and in 1596, Philip of Spain sent another Armada to support the rebels. As with the first Spanish Armada of 1588, this again was beset by bad weather and had to turn back – the same experience was repeated in 1597. By 1598 the situation had reached crisis point as insurrection in Munster and Connacht spread across the whole island, and Elizabeth sent out a force of 17,000 men under the command of her favourite Essex in April 1599. His inept campaign, compounded by his decision to undertake unauthorised peace talks with the Irish rebels, led to his disgrace. His successor, Charles Blount, Lord Mountjoy, eventually was able with much violence to quell the revolt (despite the continuing context of largely ineffectual Spanish assistance to the rebels) and the so-called Nine Years' War was brought to a close just days after Elizabeth's death in 1603.

The situation was little better for the population at large with the arrival of the Stuarts on the English throne. As soon as Sir Arthur Chichester replaced Mountjoy in 1604 as Deputy in Ireland, he embarked upon a policy of confiscating arms among the population and insisted that loyalty should now be pledged to the Crown rather than to any local chieftain. With the prospect of their political authority gradually ebbing away, the Irish leaders (led by Tyrone and Rory O'Donnell, Earl of Tyrconnell) left for the European continent in 1607 ('the Flight of the Earls'). The remaining, mostly Catholic population was left to survive upon an exhausted island, while the Crown confiscated most of the leaders' estates with a view to welcoming further English and Scottish settlers into Ulster. During the 1630s Charles's Deputy in Ireland, Strafford, came to be vilified by all sections of the landed classes for his policies of promoting Laudian Anglicanism and further 'plantation'. By 1641 Ireland was in rebellion against the Puritan 'Long Parliament' as a result of ongoing resentment against anti-Catholic legal restrictions, evictions and confiscations implemented by English rule. By 1649 news of the King's execution united Irish feeling, and Cromwell landed with some 12,000 soldiers in July in the fear that the island might prove an important base for a Stuart uprising. Cromwell brutally repressed resistance at Drogheda and Wexford and was able to return to England by the spring of 1650. By 1652, with the native leaders either killed or in exile, the invaders were able to impose their own terms of rule and thousands of Catholic landowners found their properties confiscated or handed over in repayment deals to soldiers and government investors. Cromwell left his younger son Henry in charge as Lord Deputy and by the end of the 1650s the number of Ireland's Catholic landowners had been radically reduced to less than one-fifth of the total.

Culture and Society

The vast majority of the British population in the Renaissance was engaged in small-scale agriculture. While the southern counties were very much focused upon arable farming, elsewhere the dominant occupation was pastoral agriculture supplemented by activities such as spinning and localised activities of mining (domestic coal, iron, copper, tin), quarrying and the preparation of wools for sale. Wool was virtually the major export in demand in Europe, constituting about three-quarters at least of England's foreign trade – the emphasis being upon finished cloth rather than raw wool for export in the latter half of the sixteenth century. Naturally, fishing and trade were often found to dominate coastal areas. There were areas of common grazing land and peasant farming strips around agricultural settlements but these were increasingly under pressure from the 'enclosing' ambitions of great landowners (approximately 0.5 per cent of the population) seeking to maximise upon profits by renting land to tenant farmers. Greater emphasis upon the poten-

Enclosure

This was the enclosing of fields by landowners so that the farming of livestock could be practised more profitably. This process of economic change replaced more traditional labour-intensive systems of farming, and land conversions often resulted in hardship for many rural workers. Violent responses to the enclosure of common or waste ground could mean angry protesters tearing down the offending fences and hedges which prevented grazing and the collection of fuel. Most unrest in the Tudor period centred on the area of the Midlands. In 1517 Cardinal Wolsey launched an enquiry into the growing population of the landless and this question became an abiding concern of the Earl of Somerset during Edward VI's reign. Indeed, successive Tudor administrations continued to pass legislation to prevent large-scale enclosures during the sixteenth century, but the agents and magistrates required to implement these measures were often those owners who were doing the enclosing!

tially lucrative and more stable business of sheep farming encouraged many owners to abandon arable farming, leading to great loss of employment and indeed livelihood in certain areas among sections of the lower orders. Until the sixteenth century there was relatively little opportunity for land ownership as little came up for sale in an economy based around inherited fortune. However, sale of Crown lands by cash-strapped monarchs, the dissolution of monastic and church estates and new legal possibilities of inheritance schemes not based solely on primogeniture changed this situation.

In many ways the Renaissance describes a period of enormous economic transition in the movement away from feudal economies based on land ownership and the obligations and rights that it involved, to a structure (more familiar to modern experience) involving private ownership and investment, profit-seeking and competition, credit systems and speculation – what has come to be known as capitalism. The fact that members of the highest social elite were often ceasing to live in the midst of communities and buying up land (and buying out rural dwellers and thus clearing villages) for the purposes of private estates had some enormous repercussions on individual communities. As the testimony of Shakespeare's Corin indicates in *As You Like It*, the lot of the rural dweller could leave much to be desired:

> But I am shepherd to another man
> And do not shear the fleeces that I graze.
> My master is of churlish disposition
> And little recks to find the way to heaven
> By doing deeds of hospitality.
> Besides, his cote, his flocks, and bounds of feed
> Are now on sale, and at our sheepcote now,
> By reason of his absence there is nothing
> That you will feed on.
>
> (*As You Like It*, II.iv.77–85, ed. Juliet Dusinberre, Arden Shakespeare, 2007)

For rural settlements, there may have been some common land available for the grazing of animals, but the movement towards enclosures in certain regions by many landowners meant that such areas were under increasing pressure.

Among the poorer sections of society, farm animals often lived in close proximity with their owners; and this, in turn, meant it was not uncommon in the period for the poor to be compared with their own beasts by their social superiors – and they could be treated accordingly as 'brutish'. The more urban societies constituted the markets for agricultural labour and the sale of produce. It was in the towns that wealth was spent and the possibilities (albeit meagre or non-existent for the very poor) of recourse to the law, medical assistance, entertainment, training and education were on offer. At the beginning of Henry VII's reign under one-tenth of the population lived in cities, while poorer families on the land farmed to pay rent and to generate a little income to feed themselves.

London had a population of about 50,000 but its influence at this time was much slighter than it would be at the end of the sixteenth century. After decades of increasing importance being accorded to the capital in a host of different areas (political, courtly, mercantile, artistic), London's population was perhaps as much as 200,000 at the turn of the century and it became a source of ongoing political concern for successive regimes. In contrast, other cities like Norwich and Bristol could claim perhaps populations of between 10,000 and 20,000. Dublin could not rival these settlements in size and development during this period and it is useful to remember that European cities such as Naples or Paris dwarfed London at this time. More generally across the country, there were notable plague epidemics at the close of the century in 1584–5, 1589–93, 1597 and 1603–4 with numbers of mortalities increasing to 30,000 in the latter case. Problems of disease, crime, vagrancy and poverty were evident to those at the time who lived and travelled through both town and country. The Renaissance city was often a grubby and squalid place to inhabit; indeed, in 1578 Queen Elizabeth avoided London because of its 'noisome smells'.

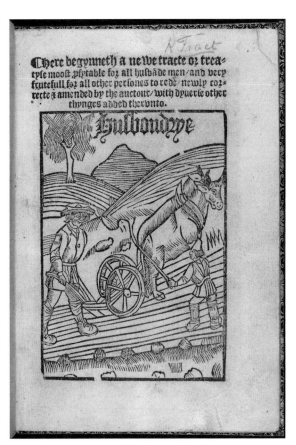

2.5 Title page from John Fitzherbert's *Here Begynneth a Newe Tract or Treatyse Moost Profitable for All Husbandmen* (1532).

Economic problems were in many cases associated with inadequate political responses to a number of factors: demographic growth; unemployment and vagrancy; disease; harvest failure; price inflation; currency depreciations at home and abroad; continental wars and so on. In general contrast to the economic experience during much of the medieval period, the cost of living continued to rise during the sixteenth century (most dramatically in 1540–50). Indeed, in the final decade of Elizabeth's reign the price of corn more than doubled. Sustained periods of continental conflict (such as the Dutch Revolt or the Thirty Years' War) also inevitably inhibited trade and networks of production in Britain. With poor harvests (1586–8 and 1594–7), the price of corn (and thus bread) inevitably escalated astronomically and famine (1596–7) and rioting were in evidence in the final decade of the sixteenth century. During such times xenophobia tended to increase and foreign merchants and visitors could find themselves the targets of unruly crowds fired up by the experience of harsh conditions. With continuing demographic rise, demand exceeded supply in an economy with little technological innovation in agriculture and insufficient schemes of land reclamation. The inevitable results were all too frequently price rises, lower wages and higher rents.

In an attempt to counteract the effects of a decaying wool industry, later Tudor and Early Stuart administrations from the middle of the sixteenth century stimulated interest in overseas trade by granting royal charters for a number of different companies to have trading privileges: for example, the Muscovy Company (1555), the Spanish Company (1577), the Baltic Company (1579), the Turkey Company (1581), the East India Company (1600), the Virginia Company (1606) and the Massachusetts Bay Company (1629). Governments rewarded favourites with privileges over such bodies and invariably insisted upon cash benefits in return for the privileges awarded. Apart from the lure of financial gain and commercial opportunity, it was thought that ventures of this nature could have political rewards: these new lands might furnish England with strategic power bases or at least allies against hostile European powers. In reality, by the beginning of the seventeenth century the most attractive known territories had already been 'scrambled' over by European neighbours. Walter Ralegh, among others, attempted to secure a territory in the New World, 'Virginia', for his queen, but it was not until the reign of James I that a permanent colony would be established there. Indeed, colonial settlement of any substance would not take place until the 1620s when religious persecution, economic hardship and/or political disaffection encouraged groups and individuals to seek a new life across the seas. By the end of that decade, the Pilgrim Fathers were turning their attention to New England as a refuge from religious persecution. While it has been estimated that some 60,000 emigrated during the Caroline period, one-third of the emigrants ultimately chose to return across the Atlantic. It should also be noted that from the 1620s onwards schemes of colonisation were also being introduced for Barbados and other West Indian islands linked to the production of cotton, tobacco and, later, sugar. More generally during this decade, currency depreciation on the Continent, stiffer competition from Mediterranean cloth industries and the effects of the Thirty Years' War, in addition to ongoing problems of piracy, continued to depress economic markets at home. Furthermore, the slide into civil war had an inevitably large impact on English patterns of trade and agriculture.

Poverty and Crime

It has been estimated that by the close of the sixteenth century approximately 30 per cent of any given urban population in England was of no fixed abode and that about the same percentage of the rural population was compelled to resort to begging. Poverty was frequently associated with idleness in the Tudor mind and by an Act of 1531 convicted vagrants might be stripped and whipped and then returned forcibly to their parish of origin. The 1536 Poor Law distinguished the 'deserving' or 'impotent' (unable to work, for example, through illness or advanced age) from the 'undeserving' or 'idle' poor. The dissolution of the monasteries did not inhibit private and communal schemes for charitable work (which extended to the endowment of schools, almshouses and hospitals across the country), but neither was there a marked increase in charitable actions in response to the withdrawal of ecclesiastical provision which had been strategic in some areas. There was, however, a growing awareness that unemployment might not be a choice.

In 1547, London brought in a compulsory Poor Rate for the wealthier inhabitants and other towns and cities quickly followed suit. In 1552 Parliament established alms collectors to record the numbers of the poor and the funds distributed to them. By the 1560s Parliament was insisting upon the levying of taxes at a local level ('poor rates') to support the 'deserving poor'. The 1572 Poor Relief Act insisted upon compulsory parish donations to assist the 'deserving' poor and established 'workhouses' in communities funded by local taxes in which the residents were required to work (e.g. by spinning) as payment for the 'benefits' of dwelling there. This measure was brought in to quell criticism in some quarters that the poor were doing nothing to assist their community. The conditions of the workhouses would remain for centuries so unpleasant as to deter only the most destitute from entering. By 1597 disastrous harvests caused such hardship that systems of relief in regions such as the north and the west collapsed under excessive pressure. Previous legislation was brought together in the Great Poor Law Acts of 1598 and 1601: these maintained the distinction between the undeserving and deserving poor, confirming the establishment of 'convenient Houses of Dwelling' for the latter supported by a compulsory Poor Rate. In 1631 under Charles I's Personal Rule, 'Books of Orders' were issued to Justices stipulating the duties which should be levied to ensure the financing of local policing, the upkeep of highways and the Poor Law, for example. This eased communal life to a great degree for the five years or so following this date.

The level of crime in early modern English society is hard to assess given that the recorded figures only represent the reported felonies. There was no police force and the local constable was for the most part employed upon a part-time basis. However, punishment was often excessive when the perpetrators were caught. To avoid inflicting capital punishment upon the criminal, victims might not report crimes or undervalue the nature of the violation. For similar reasons, juries might reduce the value of goods taken in the crime. Pregnant women could postpone, sometimes indefinitely, their punishment; and in claiming benefit of clergy (the reading of a verse of Psalm 51 in Latin) as Ben Jonson did in 1598, the criminal might also evade capital punishment.

Mercy could also be granted by magistrates so that only about one-quarter of those condemned to death might actually meet their punishment. The 1547 Vagrancy Act proclaimed that those who had left their parish or were found to be unwilling to work would be branded with a 'V' and put to hard labour for two years. The 1563 Statute of Artificers introduced whipping for vagrants. By 1572, Parliament proclaimed that vagrants could be whipped, put to hard labour and for a third offence, hanged.

Politics, Power and Ideologies

The cultural mindset of the period we are considering was influenced by a host of different factors. Many of the enquiries which we might now term as political theory explored (and sometimes questioned) the ways in which ideas of hierarchy and sovereignty might be seen to organise society. The majority of people across Europe from the late fifteenth to the mid-seventeenth centuries would be most likely to express a feeling of belonging in terms of family, household, the community in which they worked and indeed, most importantly for the time, religion. Appeals by the political elite to larger ideas of the 'country', so common in more modern periods of conflict and triumph, could never be widely successful in societies often bound by local, economic loyalties.

It is becoming increasingly evident that there was some geographical movement by families and groups to and from different communities, prompted often by economic hardship and unemployment. For the mid-sixteenth century, for example, it has been estimated that less than one-fifth of the London population was actually born in the capital, while by the beginning of the next century it is thought that one in eight adults lived there at some time in their lives. Nonetheless, in whatever community you happened to reside, one feature of Renaissance society would be immediately apparent to the modern observer: the power relationships were firmly patriarchal in nature. This is a social vision in which it is perceived as 'natural' and commonplace that men (as fathers, employers, monarchs) should control the dominant positions of power. In his speech to the Commons at the Palace of Whitehall in March 1609, James I insisted that 'a Father may dispose of his Inheritance to his children, at his pleasure; yea, even disinherit the eldest upon just occasions, and prefer the youngest, according to his liking ... So may the king deal with his subjects.'

Drawing upon lines of thinking inherited from classical writers and the Bible, many (mostly male-authored) texts from the period frequently testify to the fact that women were considered as 'the weaker vessel'. When women such as Elizabeth Tudor or Mary, Queen of Scots did gain access to significant political power, they encountered opposition or vigorous forms of manipulation from rival political factions. Interestingly, such was the pervasive influence of patriarchy in the early modern society that these female leaders (and their supporters) often promoted themselves in terms of their 'masculine' strengths and virtues.

As many of the literary texts from the Renaissance indicate, the role of the court was key in the area of political decision-making as well as a central arena for ceremonial, literary production and entertainment. It could often move between a number of royal palaces, or, during Elizabeth's reign, for example, it famously went on 'progresses' away from the capital, staying at the great houses of courtiers and eminent servants of the Crown. The court was often riven with bitter rivalries and this situation was made worse by the fondness of monarchs such as Henry VIII, Elizabeth and James I for favourites. Nonetheless, such men could fall from high positions of power in spectacular and indeed violent ways, like Thomas More and Thomas Cromwell during the reign of Henry VIII; and Robert Devereux, Earl of Essex, who finally led a short-lived revolt against Elizabeth in 1601. In general, the court was frequently associated with human vices, as in George Wither's *Britains Remembrancer* (1628), for example, where there is a remorseless tirade against this elite community which was 'fraught with bribery and hate, / With envy, lust, ambition and debate'. Throughout the Tudor and Early Stuart reigns there was an enduring concern (particularly in prose and drama) with court corruption and the positions held by self-seeking flatterers. As a consequence, much attention was devoted to the role of the good courtier as a potential source of wise advice, loyalty and knowledge about the needs of the larger nation. During Henry VIII's reign, for example, Sir Thomas Elyot begins the final chapters of *The Book Named the Governor* (1531) with the assertion that 'The end of all doctrine and study is good counsel … wherein virtue may be found.' In the same period the distinguished humanist scholar Erasmus urged in his *Education of a Christian Prince* (1516) that 'you cannot be a king unless reason completely controls you; that is, unless under all circumstances you follow advice and judgement. You cannot rule over others until you yourself have obeyed the course of honour.' Later in the century in his essay 'Of Counsel', Francis Bacon insisted that 'The greatest Trust, betweene Man and Man, is the Trust of *Giving Counsell* … The Wisest *Princes*, need not thinke it any diminution to their Greatnesse, or derogation to their Sufficiency, to rely upon *Counsell, God* himselfe is not without: But hath made it one of the great Names, of his blessed Sonne; *The Counsellor.*'

In the event, the political realities occasioned by weak, flawed and tyrannous monarchs continued to figure prominently in literature throughout the Renaissance. Nonetheless, the privileged community of courtiers under the Tudors and the Stuarts attracted many others (including writers) who were spurred on with hopes of financial gain and political and social advancement, as well as the possibility of gaining access to the elite society of the land. It is surprising to note that the nobility of England during the Tudor period remained relatively small, numbering around fifty – with the execution of the Duke of Norfolk in 1572, for example, there were no more dukes created for the rest of the century. The situation changed radically with the accession of James I. Henry VIII had been happy to sell off church lands in the aftermath of the dissolution of the monasteries but it was not linked to any systematic policy of ennobling the new owners. At the turn of the century the newly acclaimed Stuart King of England created over three hundred knights just on his journey down from Edinburgh for his coronation, and decided to sell off noble titles, including the newly invented one of 'baronet', in order to generate funds for the royal purse. Indeed, in his first four months as English monarch he created more knights than Elizabeth had done in the whole of her long reign. It is all too possible that the Scottish king's largesse was designed to win him friends across the elite of his new realm. James was notable also for introducing a much more informal atmosphere to the proceedings of his court, as well as a determination to spend lavishly on ceremony and entertainment. Indeed, this custom of informality meant that courtly society in the Jacobean period could be given over to some rather gross displays, as on the occasion of the visit of Christian IV of Denmark to the Jacobean court. After the death of James in 1625 a more moral tone was struck by Charles I in his court culture, though great energy continued to be devoted to opulent display and costly entertainment. Interestingly, even during the English Republic when dramatic production was for the most part suppressed, Cromwell's interest in music, art and sculpture meant that visiting dignitaries and ambassadors were received by the English government surrounded by many of the former trappings of royal society.

In the context of this largely pre-industrial society we need to think about communities being organised around concepts of rank, birthright, obligation and ownership rather than 'class' – large groups of people engaged in similar forms of labour. It is true that in towns and cities across Europe organised bodies (representing artisans and merchants) frequently had much influence in civic government; nonetheless, even by the end of our period, over three-quarters of the English population was still living and working outside urban communities. Higher social station could be evident from the estates that an individual owned, the kind of residence in which he or she lived and even by the fabrics that they wore. During the sixteenth and early seventeenth centuries, English monarchs introduced a sequence of 'sumptuary laws' which sought to regulate who might be allowed to wear silk or velvet, for example. It was clearly in the interests of the ruling powers to maintain a rigorous attention to all forms of social order and decorum. Revolt and dissent were demonised in official literature and the prevailing political systems of hierarchy and monarchy were promoted as 'fixed' and as the most legitimate forms of government. The state-commissioned homily *Concerning Good Order and Obedience to Rulers and Magistrates* (1559), for example,

> ### A Lively Encounter at the Jacobean Court
>
> One day, a great feast was held, and, after dinner, the representation of Solomon his Temple, and the coming of the Queen of Sheba was made, or (as I may better say) was meant to have been made, before their Majesties ... But, alas! as all earthly thinges do fail to poor mortals in enjoyment, so did prove our presentation thereof. The lady who did play the Queens part ... forgetting the steppes arising to the canopy, overset her caskets into his Danish Majesties lap, and fell at his feet ... His Majesty then got up and would dance with the Queen of Sheba; but he fell down ... and was carried to an inner chamber and laid on a bed of state; which was not a little defiled with the presents of the Queen which had been bestowed on his garments; such as wine, cream, jelly, beverage, cakes, spices, and other good matters. The entertainment and show went forward, and most of the presenters went backward, or fell down; wine did so occupy their upper chambers. Now did appear, in rich dress, Hope, Faith, and Charity: Hope did assay to speak, but wine rendered her endeavours so feeble that she withdrew ... Faith ... left the court in a staggering condition: Charity came to the King's feet ... in some sorte she made obeysance and brought giftes ... She returnd to Hope and Faith, who were both sick and spewing in the lower hall.
>
> (Sir John Harington to a friend, 1606, cited in Thomas Park (ed.), *Nugæ Antiquæ: Being a Miscellaneous Collection of Original Papers* (London, 1804), 1:349–51)

was one of a number of texts which was to be read aloud on a regular basis to church congregations – and this, it should be remembered, was in an age of compulsory church attendance. The sermon clearly argues that the existing political order is part of a divinely appointed, universal, system of government. Elsewhere, in his *Archeion, or a Discourse upon the High Courts of Justice in England* (completed c. 1591), a more musically minded William Lambarde affirmed that the political structure of the nation was 'natural' in that 'it hath an imitation of the natural "Body" of man, truly called a little World … and Harmonicall, because from, as so well-tuned a Base, Meane, and Treble, there proceedeth a most exquisite *consort*, and delicious melodie.'

This emphasis upon the unchanging nature of this social order noticeably failed to take into account widespread evidence of social mobility (both ascent and decline) during this period. Indeed, throughout the Renaissance there had been for a number of different reasons (religious, economic, political) a reluctance to submit to official declarations of reassurance. If much sixteenth-century political statement often concentrated upon the benefits of the present system of government, this was not universally the case. In *Concerning True Obedience* (1553), for example, the Catholic Stephen Gardiner argued that 'obedience is due, but how far the limits of requiring obedience extend, that is the whole question that can be demanded'. But when questioning 'extended' to more deliberate actions against the existing political office-holders, the response was frequently swift, unambiguous and violent. The 1571 sermon *Against Disobedience and Wilful Rebellion* reserves greatest scorn for such political ill-doers: 'A rebel is worse than the worst prince, and rebellion worse than the worst government of the worst prince.' As we shall see in subsequent sections, poets and dramatists also are often found to acknowledge and indeed *unsettle* prevailing theories of power.

There had been some promotion of a divinely appointed monarchy during the Tudor period, but when James I acceded to the English throne in 1603 he gave much greater emphasis to the ('absolutist') role of the monarch as God's lieutenant on earth. As the century unfolded, he and his successor Charles I would find it increasingly difficult to put these political visions into practice. One of the main reasons for this was that

Government Ideas on Social Order

Almighty God hath created and appointed all thinges, in heauen, earth, and waters, in a most excellente and perfect ordre. In heauen, he hath appointed distincte or seuerall orders and states of Archangels and Angels. In earth he hath assigned and appoynted kinges, princes, with other gouernours vnder them, all in good and necessary order … Euerye degree of people, in their vocacion, callying and office hath appoynted to them, theyr duety and ordre. Some are in hygh degree, some in lowe … and euery one haue nede of other: so yt in all thinges is to bee lauded and praised the goodly order of god wythoute the whiche, no house, no citie, no common wealth, can continue and indure or laste … Take away kinges, princes, rulers, magistrates, iudges, and such estates of gods order, no man shall ride or go by the high waye vnrobbed, no man shall slepe in his own house or bed vnkilled, no man shall kepe hys wife, children & possessions in quietnes …

('An exhortation concerning good ordre and obedience, vnto rulers and Magistrates', in *Certayne sermons appoynted by the Quenes Maiestie, to be declared and read, by all persones, vicars, and curates, euery Sondaye and holy daye in theyr churches* … (London, 1559), sig. R4r–R4v)

by the sixteenth century England had developed a complex constitutional system of checks and balances combining the authorities of monarch and national representation – this structure is frequently promoted in terms of the power of 'King-in-Parliament'. This form of 'mixed government' came to be celebrated by a number of political theorists of the time such as Sir Thomas Smith, who in his *De Republica Anglorum* (1565) affirmed that a parliamentary Act 'is the Prince's and the whole realm's deed' and that Parliament itself 'representeth and hath the power of the whole realm both the head and the body. For every Englishman is entended to be

> ### Debating Renaissance Kingship
>
> It is Atheisme and blasphemie to dispute what God can doe: good Christians content themselues with his will reuealed in his word. So, it is presumption and high contempt in a Subiect to dispute what a King can doe, or say that a King cannot doe this, or that …
> (James I, speech to the Star Chamber, 1616, in McIlwain, *Political Works*, p. 333 [A])
>
> Kings are stiled Gods upon Earth, not absolute, but *Dixi dii estis*, and the next words are, *sed moriemini sicut homines*; they shall die like men, and then their thoughts perish; they cannot possibly see all things with their own eyes, nor hear all things with their own ears; they must commit many great trusts to their ministers. Kings must be answerable to God Almighty (to whom they are but vassals) for their actions, and for their negligent omissions.
> (Francis Bacon, 1616 letter to royal favourite George Villiers, in *Works*, ed. Spedding et al., 13:15 [A])

there present … from the Prince to the lowest person.' Parliament (a grouping of peers in the Lords and mostly gentry of one kind or another in the Commons) had survived into the Renaissance standing by its right to have an all-important political role of approval: debating and participating in the monarch's law-making and taxation plans, for example, as well as more acutely divisive issues of religious reform, foreign policy and, in the case of Elizabeth, royal marriage. Henry VIII recognised that this theory of power (King-in-Parliament) was key to his own sovereignty and Elizabeth often coaxed and seduced her parliaments into performing her wishes. James and his son Charles I encountered growing dissent when they gave increasing emphasis to the idea that the national law included provision for kings to overrule statute in certain (usually extreme) situations.

A further level of complexity to the political situation is that when James I accepted the crown of England he was already James VI of Scotland. A monarch having two or more titles of sovereignty was not unheard of and indeed the situation would recur in British history when William of Orange arrived in England from the Netherlands to be named joint ruler with his Stuart wife Mary in 1688, and later in the eighteenth century, for example, when the Hanoverian Elector was crowned George I in 1714. Nonetheless, from 1603 James and his successors continued to rule over both England (with Wales) and Scotland according to their different political systems. Much to the growing discontent of the Scots, London emerged as principal centre of government for the British Isles. James attempted to placate his subjects with energetic plans for unification: he proposed himself as sovereign of 'Great Britain' and instituted new designs for the coinage and the flag. The first coin of his reign hailed him as Emperor of Britain. Such schemes won over few supporters either side of the border. Francis Bacon's *Discourse touching the Happy Union* published in the year of James's accession to the English throne cautioned the new sovereign that he 'was hastening to a mixture of both Kingdoms and nations, faster perhaps than policy would conveniently bear'. James only visited his native land once more, in 1617; Charles honoured his father's custom by making a single visit in 1633.

Belief and Thought

When Henry VII ascended to the throne in 1485, England was part of Catholic Europe. Pilgrims travelled to shrines in Britain and abroad, religious drama such as miracle, mystery and saints' plays (see pp. 42–5) were being energetically supported by religious, civic and parish authorities as extensions of worship on particular saints' days and festivals, such as that of the Corpus Christi. Mass was celebrated up and down the land in churches and recalled the Passion of Christ. The consecrated bread and wine used in the service was thought to undergo a miraculous transformation (transubstantiation): when raised above the priest's head ('elevation of the host'), they became the flesh and blood of the crucified Christ returned to earth to wash away the sins of the praying congregation. Only rarely was this larger congregation or laity allowed to take communion of the consecrated bread and they never tasted the wine. For the most part, these privileges were reserved for the priest who recited in Latin the words of the ceremony at the altar which was set behind a rood screen – the rood being the crucified figure of Christ. This was a world in which requiem masses were said for the dead to ensure that they should not lie trapped (like Shakespeare's Old Hamlet) in Purgatory – a limbo state of torment for the dead who still sought spiritual peace and required purification. Appeals to saints and, most particularly, to the Virgin Mary figured prominently in the worship of many and were strongly supported through church rituals, images, festivals, shrines and narratives of miracles. Spiritual blessings were dispensed through sacraments such as baptism, marriage, ordination and extreme unction (the last rites administered to the dying). There were also practices such as the sale of indulgences or pardons which were sanctioned by the Church and granted the remission of sins for the living and sometimes for the dead (such as those thought to be suffering in Purgatory).

The sale of indulgences, along with other issues such as the enormous wealth of the Church, the sale of church offices, the poor education of many priests, the decline in sermonising and the violation of vows of celibacy by some clergy, for example, had been the target of vigorous criticism and satire during the medieval period by figures within the Church as well as those without, as can be seen in Chaucer's Canterbury Tales. Nevertheless, it would be quite wrong to think of Catholic culture as decaying during the reigns of Henry VII and Henry VIII: whatever its faults, for the vast majority of the population there could be no possibility of spiritual redemption outside its bounds. The Church penetrated all aspects of people's lives, sanctifying births, deaths and marriages, instructing the faithful and judging the sinning in its own courts. In a society governed by a very congested church calendar, services might be attended on a number of different days apart from Sunday and indeed perhaps on two or more occasions on the same day. It was not unknown for Henry VIII to hear five masses in one day. Furthermore, it has been estimated that there were more men being recruited into the priesthood (perhaps as many as 4 per cent of the total male population) at the end of the 1520s than at any time since the mid-fourteenth century. However, by the beginning of the sixteenth century evidence of corruption in the practices and structures of the Catholic Church was once again incurring mounting criticism.

The beginning of the sixteenth-century Reformation in Europe (led by 'Reformist' or 'Protestant' thinkers) is usually linked to the crises of faith, and angry outbursts against such practices as indulgence-selling, of an Augustinian monk called Martin Luther, who was working as an academic at the German university of Wittenberg. He soon developed his ideas into the '95 Theses' on indulgences which in 1517 he posted on the door of the castle church at Wittenberg. However, his most mature and radical views were made public in 1520 with *The Babylonian Captivity, The Freedom of a Christian Man* and *To the Christian Nobility of the German Nation*: in these tracts he affirmed (in opposition to Catholic doctrine) that salvation could not be bought, that true faith (rather than good works) was the most important commitment of the Christian wishing to be saved, that the Bible rather than the pope was the source of religious authority and, for example, that only the sacraments of baptism and communion were sanctioned in the Bible. Such revolutionary ideas were inevitably going to lead to conflict with the Catholic Church and he was eventually condemned as a heretic in the same year and was excommunicated in 1521. Nonetheless, Luther's ideas were interpreted and published; and they inspired many other leading European intellectuals who had similar misgivings about Catholic practices and ideology (such as Martin Bucer and Philipp Melanchthon) to voice their own criticisms. Unsurprisingly, the first place in which the Reformist ideas took hold was the German states, but soon their influence was being felt across Northern Europe.

In England the call for religious reform appears initially to have moved more slowly. Lutheran ideas were beginning to attract the attention of certain individuals and particular groups in the 1520s, and as a consequence the hostility of Henry VIII and his counsellors, such as Sir Thomas More. Indeed, Henry was awarded the title of *Fidei Defensor* ('Defender of the Faith') by the pope for his anti-Lutheran tract *Assertio Septem Sacramentorum* ('In Defense of the Seven Sacraments') published in 1521. By the mid-1520s Henry's anxiety over his wife's (the Spanish princess Katherine of Aragon) inability to produce a male heir led him to convince himself that God disapproved of his marriage to his brother's widow. As a consequence, he began to explore the possibility of divorcing a wife who was nearing the end of her child-bearing years in favour of the Duke of Norfolk's niece, Anne Boleyn, with whom he had become infatuated. By the beginning of the 1530s Henry had implemented a number of initiatives to pressurise those in the church hierarchy to accept the idea of a royal divorce. In addition, he identified and promoted politically a number of individuals who criticised church practices and sought reform. Henry increasingly forged a league with figures who sought religious reform not through any crisis of faith on his own part, but because his dynastic ambitions were being repeatedly thwarted by the authority of Rome.

When the pope agreed in 1529 to hear Katherine's appeal in Rome against the divorce proceedings, Henry dismissed one of the judges of the proceedings (and his close personal adviser) Cardinal Wolsey. The pace of change now gathered momentum. In 1530 Henry dispatched academics from Oxford and Cambridge to European universities to plead his cause, but by 1531 he was demanding that the clergy in his land should acknowledge him as the 'sole protector and supreme head' of the Church. In 1532 Thomas Cranmer, a cleric with Reformist leanings but great devotion to the Crown, was named Archbishop of Canterbury and at the beginning of 1533 Henry married secretly the pregnant Anne Boleyn. The Act of Supremacy of the following year endowed him with the power to control and implement reform in the English Church; and in 1536 the process of the dissolution of the monasteries began. The English Crown and nobility would prove the greatest beneficiaries in the subsequent sales of monastic land and properties. In the years which followed, there were Catholic uprisings and centres of resistance – and it should be stressed that in regions further away from the political centre of London many communities continued to worship according to traditional Catholic practices. However, during Henry's son's (Edward VI's) short reign a more radical programme of Protestant reform was introduced. In 1547 there was the publication of *Certain Sermons, or Homilies, Appointed by the King's Majesty, to Be Declared and Read, by All Parsons, Vicars, or Curates, Every Sunday in their Churches*. In the same year chantries (chapels devoted to the celebration of masses for the dead in Purgatory) were finally abolished and their property was confiscated. In 1549 Cranmer introduced a new Book of Common Prayer (in English) for use in religious services throughout the land. Church images continued to be destroyed, candles could only be lighted on the altar and praying with rosary beads was outlawed.

Of enormous importance for the period we are considering in England is the emergence of another European figure in the next generation of Reformist thinkers, John Calvin (1509–64). Although Calvin was French by birth, he moved to the Swiss city of Geneva, where he became more of a radical thinker and international leader than Luther; and he initiated a fundamental rethinking of the role of the Church. He was beginning to have his ideas published by the 1530s. Like Luther, he affirmed the importance of biblical (rather than papal) authority, the irrelevance of such things as indulgences for personal salvation, the spiritual equality of priest and layman, and the crucial significance of the Christian understanding that God's grace was the sole source of redemption. However, unlike Lutherans and Catholics, Calvin insisted that the Church should serve God's will rather than make its followers believe that it could assist them on their journey to salvation. He believed that all the sacraments were 'commemorative' in nature (but also a communication of God's grace) and, for example, that Christian worship should be purified by putting aside distractions such as church music, decoration, devotions to saints, etc. Most importantly for many of his followers, Calvin believed that human beings were already predestined to be damned or saved when they entered this world. When the Catholic Mary Tudor ascended to the throne in 1553 some hundreds of English Reformists went into exile on the Continent and many became profoundly influenced by Calvin's doctrines. The return of these 'Marian exiles', many of them with radical ideas, in the years following Mary's death in 1558 would continue to pose problems for Elizabeth. The new and embattled queen was anxious to win friends at home and abroad and to heal the rifts between Catholics and Protestants in her realm with a religious settlement that involved compromise on all sides: the 1559 Book of Common Prayer, for example, tried to drive a middle course, asking the minister during the communion service to celebrate 'the body of our Lord Jesus Christ' (suggesting a rapprochement with the Catholic doctrine of transubstantiation) and then asking the communicant to 'take, and eat this, in remembrance that Christ died for thee ... ' (supporting the Calvinist belief that the sacrament was symbolic or commemorative in nature).

Elizabeth herself was clearly influenced by the nation's complex religious inheritance: she shared Reformist beliefs in the primacy of scripture and the irrelevance of the cults of saints to personal redemption, and quickly on her accession forbade the elevation of the host by the minister during the communion service. Nonetheless, she evidently cherished church music and church decoration such as candles and crucifixes (which were associated with the 'old faith') and disapproved strongly of marriage for the clergy, for example. Most importantly, however, despite the religious divisions of her subjects Elizabeth was determined to assert her control as 'Supreme Head' over the English Church. In the first decade of her reign, public celebration of the Catholic mass was outlawed and recusancy laws were brought in to compel church attendance for everyone. In Rome these decisions inevitably brought with them growing hostility. By 1567 the pope was urging English Catholics not to attend church services and in 1570 Elizabeth was excommunicated. As her reign progressed, there were uprisings and political plots forged by discontented Catholics at home; and abroad Philip II of Spain, for example, was clearly able to draw upon Catholic support in his venture to launch an Armada against Elizabeth's realm in 1588.

However, from the beginning of Elizabeth's reign there was also biting criticism from her more radical Protestant subjects who felt her religious settlement was too 'Catholic'. By 1570 a prominent Cambridge professor, Thomas Cartwright, was calling for the abolition of bishops and for the institution of church government and doctrines such as those in operation in Calvin's Geneva. Elizabeth saw in this a thinly veiled attack upon her position as 'Supreme Head' of the Church. Cartwright was exiled and other figures in Parliament who raised similar criticisms found themselves in prison. It should be remembered that 'Puritan' was originally a term of abuse. It came to be associated with radical Protestants who wished to eradicate any traces of Catholicism from English patterns of worship, to abolish the rule of bishops and to assert that the true Christian should pursue an individual path of faith governed by scripture. If such figures are extravagantly represented and ridiculed in some of Ben Jonson's comedies such as *The Alchemist* and *Bartholomew Fair*, for example (and indeed Shakespeare informs us that the foolish steward Malvolio in *Twelfth Night* is 'a kind of puritan'), this should not blind us to the fact that they were to become an enormously important (if not cohesive) political pressure group in England throughout the final decades of the sixteenth century and the whole of the Early Stuart period. Although on his accession to the English throne James revoked the recusancy laws, the Gunpowder Plot in 1605 did very little to weaken his suspicions of Catholic political ambitions; neither did he offer much hope to those with more radical Protestant sympathies. Like Elizabeth, James saw the Church principally as a vehicle for political unity and sponsored a new translation of the Bible (the Authorised, or 'King James' Version) with this in mind. In general, he proceeded with caution in both Scotland and England and was determined to give no faction the opportunity to challenge his control over religious affairs. Charles I was less inclined to pursue the tactful approach of his father in such matters. The complex role which religion played in the evolution of opposition to Charles's government and the establishment of a republican administration is beyond the scope of this discussion, but suggestions for further reading are given at the end of the chapter. However, as we shall see in later sections, the conflict between Catholic and Reformist ideologies which raged across Europe was to have a crucial influence upon the life and work of a host of Renaissance English writers.

Another strategic influence upon spiritual and intellectual life in England was the increasing interest being devoted to scientific advances. The sixteenth and seventeenth centuries are often associated by scholars with the establishment of the ideas, systematic analysis and institutions necessary for the growth in modern scientific thinking. However, the term most frequently employed for what we might now term scientific enquiry into the physical world was 'natural philosophy'. The 'natural philosophy' inherited from the classical period and mediated through the medieval centuries was particularly influenced by the writings of Aristotle (384–322 BC) and the Greek-Egyptian astronomer Claudius Ptolemy (90–168) as well as traditions of Hebrew and Christian thinking – and for large numbers of physicians, astronomers, thinkers and so on, this body of knowledge continued to govern in their daily practices. Aristotle had proposed that the cosmos was geocentric (having the Earth as its central point and the focus for the orbits of all other heavenly spheres) – indeed, it was geostatic. From this perspective, the motionless Earth was orbited by a number of planets (made of a crystalline substance) which were thought widely to be propelled by angelic bodies each sounding a different, perfect note from a celestial octave ('the music of the spheres'). Beyond this cosmic zone was a realm of fire ('Empyrean') and the heavenly home of divine harmony, of the Aristotelian Prime Mover or, for later Hebrew–Christian cosmologists, Jehovah or God. The whole of creation was ordered into a 'Great Chain of Being' extending from God to the lowliest creature. Matter within the zone of the orbit of the moon (the 'sublunary') was deemed to be in its primary form composed of the four elements of earth, air, fire and water, and condemned to change and decay. Those bodies existing elsewhere (in the 'superlunary') were thought to be composed of a perfect fifth substance of 'essence' (or 'quintessence') which was incorruptible. The experience of the material world was thus intimately bound up with considerations of hierarchy, government and theology – for a contemporary exploration of these ideals, see, for example, Sir John Davies's poem, 'Orchestra' (in Brooks-Davies [A]), or John Donne's verse.

What is clear from the most cursory appreciation of currents of thinking across Europe is that a number of theories were increasingly competing in later sixteenth-century intellectual society for attention. Occult philosophy, a belief in magical phenomena, the identification of mystical patternings at work in the universe, the ability of certain individuals to summon up demonic forces ... all these lines of thinking continued to have assured readers throughout the period. The term 'magic' could also be broadened out to include the modern classification of bodies of knowledge such as astrology, astronomy and alchemy. The enormous expansion in the Renaissance of trade, colonisation, diplomacy and exploration meant that Europeans were increasingly being asked to conceive of their world according to alternative modes of thinking. The encounters with new species of animal and plant and with non-European races in new lands, for example, could lead to a questioning of the 'Great Chain of Being' theories inherited from the past and to an undermining of the belief that the universe was constructed wholly upon principles of resemblance and association. The growth of more sophisticated methods of surveying, navigation, map-making and measurement, as well as emphases in humanist scholarship (upon reassessing primary sources and searching out lost texts) meant that a greater appetite was being triggered in many intellectual circles to investigate the material world in more detail.

Literary Overview

Literacy and Education

Literacy levels in Renaissance Britain continue to be a source of lively debate among historians. Naturally, among the poorer sections of the population, children could often not be spared from the family's labour activities. It is also difficult to assess the abilities of many because writing skills were taught at six or seven after reading skills had been acquired, and again this was exactly the age when poorer families might withdraw their children from schooling in order to enlarge the income. It can only be affirmed with certainty that by the beginning of the Early Stuart period literacy was assured 'with few exceptions' among the gentry and that it was more and more evident among those in the higher and more affluent echelons of society. If it has been estimated that by the Restoration at least 20 per cent of the male population on average could sign their names (and that the figure would be less for women), the picture of a largely illiterate society is difficult to repress.

The Church had an enormous influence upon parents in the medieval and Renaissance centuries, urging them to place children where they might gain instruction. In this instance, the instruction

Humanism

This was an intellectual movement which had its roots in fourteenth-century Italy and is particularly associated with the scholar and poet Petrarch (1304–74). After centuries of learning and philosophical debate being dominated by the Church, a new generation of intellectuals emerged in European universities and courts during the Renaissance whose ambitions and imaginations were fired by the rediscovery of texts from Greek and Roman civilisation. These figures involved themselves enthusiastically in the translation and critical commentary of these texts and of scripture. As a result, they established rigorous standards which would be adopted by succeeding generations. Their profound veneration for the cultures of antiquity frequently led them to try to imitate what they perceived as the superlative achievements of the ancients in the areas of philosophical debate, political reasoning, pedagogic practice and literary composition, for example; and many went on to have distinguished careers in this period in the worlds of secular or ecclesiastical affairs where expert advisers and administrators were in great demand.

being promoted is most particularly of a moral and spiritual nature; however, any conception of child learning in this period frequently meant learning *by heart*. It should be remembered that until the Reformation close textual study of the Bible was reserved for those who were able to decipher Latin. As a consequence, large sections of the population were left alienated or dependent upon popular (often oral) accounts of scriptural narratives or representations of them in church art. It was in the 1520s that biblical translations in English by the humanist scholar William Tyndale started to be smuggled into Britain – and a large number of them were burned publicly at the order of the Bishop of London. However, by the second half of the sixteenth century it has been estimated that up to half a million Bibles in English were circulating among a population of some 6 million inhabitants. As the period unfolded, there also emerged another lively debate among those in intellectual and government circles about who should and should not be educated. At the beginning of the seventeenth century, for example, Francis Bacon was advising a restriction in educational opportunities; and by the Restoration, many of the upheavals associated with the effects of radical political thinking were frequently blamed by some conservative commentators upon the recent developments in the education system.

Education, of course, might take place for children in the home or in the more formal settings of a tutor's or cleric's room, a master's lodgings or, more rarely, a designated school building. Reading aloud and group reading (particularly of religious texts) continued to be common practices. Even when silent reading had become more fashionable among certain sections of the leisured classes, there often remained great emphasis upon communal reading of scripture among families, households and communities in the Great Houses, for example. It appears that reading might be undertaken while standing or indeed, like Hamlet, while walking! Educational choices (such as they were) were often dictated by the financial circumstances and geographical location of the parents. There are many references in the period to initial skills being gained in 'petty' schools with 'hornbooks' which contained an alphabet, the Lord's Prayer and perhaps other equally basic religious texts. In fact, it is widely apparent that the Bible itself was a central text in the acquisition of literacy skills for both girls and boys in the later Tudor and Early Stuart periods. In general, girls were only expected to be taught reading. While the boys later occupied themselves with writing and numeracy, the girls were expected to devote themselves to such 'useful' occupations as needlework. Nonetheless, if girls' education was supposed to be dominated by the acquisition of reading, it is clear from the later diverse cultural roles that they played in the economic life of the nation that many women were numerate and sometimes managed family business interests.

However, for those from better-off families aspiring to more formal educational careers for their offspring, there were in the large towns and cities endowed grammar schools. Sometimes these establishments were under the direction of humanist scholars such as John Colet at St Paul's, for example, and during Elizabeth's reign William Camden at Westminster School. Here, the more literary skills of reading and writing (anchored firmly around the study of classical texts) predominated over anything we might now call arithmetical skills. From the middle of the sixteenth century, more and more grammar schools were being founded across the country, often supported by funds donated by local clerics, civic corporations and monied patrons. The study, translation, dissection and memorisation of Latin texts occupied the vast majority of the boys' school days, supplemented by some learning of prayers, the catechism and so on. After three years or so spent in the company of William Lily's Latin *Grammar* (instituted by Henry VIII's government as the standard textbook for schools), boys would then turn to studying rhetoric (the linguistic arts of persuasion) and to composition in Latin, and they began Greek. Later studies might involve comparative grammar between classical languages, oratory and the use of commonplace books – the latter were personal collections of proverbs, opinions and wise sayings which pupils noted separately in their own book from their classical reading matter. This practice was continued into adulthood by many.

Moreover, as the sixteenth century progressed, the increased population of educated students emanating from the growing number of grammar schools clearly had an influence upon the founding of new colleges at Oxford and Cambridge. After a number of years in a grammar school or with a personal tutor, a small number of boys (a few benefiting like Christopher Marlowe from a scholarship) would be sent to complete their education at a particular college of the universities of Oxford or Cambridge. Here, a knowledge of Latin and sometimes Greek would have been taken for granted for a new student about to commence a university career. There would have been no possibility of studying contemporary literature in the curriculum – although evidence from diaries, letters, pamphlets and university plays, for example, clearly indicates that this formed an important pursuit outside the formal structure of classes for many students. While some of the wealthier students came to these institutions to complete their formal education, the majority were preparing for later careers in law, civil administration or the Church. Like other members of the population, students were compelled to attend church services on a regular basis. However, after Henry VIII established the Act of Supremacy they and their tutors were also required to record formally their acceptance of the articles of the new religion and the monarch as the Supreme Head. For many Catholic families, such as that of John Donne, this meant that they would not allow their children to matriculate and thus complete their course of study.

At the beginning of the early modern period, the universities of Oxford and Cambridge were admitting about 300 students between them each year. These admission figures continued to rise and peaked in the 1580s and 1630s with over 400 new students welcomed annually by each university in these decades. The curriculum continued to be based around the trivium (grammar, dialectics, rhetoric) and the quadrivium (arithmetic, geometry, astronomy, music). University experience might be followed by attendance at the law schools in London, the Inns of Court. Here, there were all kinds of temptations on offer to the aspiring gentleman: the acquisition of necessary cultural knowledge and access to important social, political and economic networks; an invaluable 'finishing school' environment where social skills might be polished, and important acquaintances of one's generation made. The Inns were also, of course, a central location for the performance of significant legal transactions. Gray's Inn, Middle Temple, Inner Temple and Lincoln's Inn were admitting about a hundred students annually at the beginning of Elizabeth's reign and over twice this number during the reign of James. These communities were more exclusive than those of the universities: they accommodated a larger proportion of gentlemen than the universities and had no provision for poor students. Some students employed tutors in music and other liberal disciplines and the Inns frequently staged theatrical events of one kind or another. About 15 per cent of the students actually went on to practise law as a profession.

Despite the fact that there is every evidence in documents from the period, such as diaries, autobiographical writings, religious chronicles and legal examinations, that women often played a striking role in the educational, intellectual and religious life of their societies, grammar school and university were reserved for males only. Intellectual life in any period can take on a number of different guises, being pursued through written and visual documents (diaries, letters, manuscripts, paintings, sculpture and so on) as well as in conversation and more formal debate. While artistic patrons like monarchs and aristocrats such as Mary Sidney, Countess of Pembroke, her brother Philip Sidney and their uncle, Robert Dudley, Earl of Leicester, attracted writers and scholars (variously in search of an income, protection and recognition), intellectual enquiry was not solely dominated by the activities of an elite society or the Church. If the theatre did not have the same social esteem that poetry commanded, it is clear that such upwardly mobile figures as Shakespeare (son of a Warwickshire glover), Jonson (stepson of a bricklayer), Marlowe (son of a cobbler) and Webster (son of a coachbuilder) were able to participate strategically in cultural debates in new and seductive ways for contemporary audiences from all walks of life.

Continuities, Innovations, Influences

If universities and aristocratic households across Britain emerged increasingly as centres of intellectual life, many of the Renaissance texts which are most frequently studied now are often closely related to the metropolitan life of the capital (most especially the drama) and to the expectations surrounding patronage and recognition at the Tudor and Early Stuart courts. The court was mostly populated by well-connected men and women, who had gained (or who sought) royal favour, and a body of political office-holders of one kind or another – sometimes individuals might indeed belong to both categories. The possibilities of financial reward, desirable employment, enhanced social status and access to political power meant that the community immediately surrounding the sovereign generated a whole network of followers all seeking advancement. Thus, the so-called 'court culture' affected a large community of people, some of whom might reside at great distances from the royal palaces but who were anxious to endear themselves by performing services, acquiring regular information, maintaining 'useful' contacts and following court fashions (in music, dance, sports, clothes and literary fashions – both in terms of reading and composition).

Across Europe the cult of 'courtliness' meant that manuals and handbooks came to be published to instruct the aspirant in the ways of this rarefied society – one of the most influential of these was Castiglione's *Il Cortegiano* which was translated as

The Book of the Courtier by Sir Thomas Hoby in 1561. Writers frequently dedicated their productions (printed texts, manuscripts and performances) to eminent aristocrats in the hope of gaining or maintaining particular favour – it is clear, for example, that in the Elizabethan period, pastorals, romances and erotic lyrics and translations from classical and living European languages were particularly to the taste of courtly audiences. Some writers might be associated (or wish to be associated) at points in their careers with certain social circles or coteries: Spenser with the Sidney and Ralegh households; Shakespeare with Henry Wriothesley, the Earl of Southampton; Samuel Daniel with Mary Sidney; and Francis Bacon with Robert Devereux, the Earl of Essex. There were often lavish entertainments organised for the court and performances might be commissioned for particular festivities such as Twelfth Night from companies playing at the public playhouses. Alternatively, certain entertainments might be designed especially for the more restricted audience of the monarch's entourage, such as Sidney's pastoral *The Lady of May* or the formal masque texts written for the Early Stuart courts by Samuel Daniel, Ben Jonson and Thomas Carew, for example. Equally, royal society might be presented with pageants on arriving at a particular city, or with large-scale entertainments of music, song and chivalric performances, such as those designed by Robert Dudley for Elizabeth at Kenilworth Castle in 1575. In the area of the visual arts, Hans Holbein during the Henrician period and the later miniaturists Nicholas Hilliard and Isaac Oliver are particularly notable for their representations of the courtier and courtly society in England. When Charles I came to the throne in 1625 he gained a reputation across Europe as a connoisseur of fine art. He offered Van Dyck repeated commissions and requested Rubens to paint the interior of his palace of Whitehall when the latter arrived as part of a diplomatic mission from the Low Countries.

In 1576 a wood joiner-cum-actor, James Burbage, had a permanent building constructed for theatrical performance in Shoreditch to the north of the city of London, just outside the city walls. This was quite possibly the first purpose-built structure of its kind in Britain since Roman times – although recent research is now pointing towards evidence of a playhouse ('The Red Lion') in Whitechapel from about 1567. Burbage's structure was named the Theatre and, following on its success, the Curtain was built nearby in 1577. As we have seen, there were all kinds of possibilities for performance in the preceding decades: at court and in the 'Great Houses', in religious and secular processions, during civic and church festivals, at educational establishments, in taverns and street theatricals. Dramatic performance was perceived in terms of popular entertainment and there is no evidence until Jonson's ground-breaking publication of his own theatre texts in the early years of the seventeenth century that anyone was willing to attribute to it any elevated artistic status. Indeed, the fact that later theatres like the Globe, the Rose and the Swan were located outside the city on the South Bank amid communities devoted to equally lively trades such as bear-baiting, prostitution and crime did little to change this perception. The City authorities were clearly anxious about the possibilities of sedition when large groups gathered together in this way on its boundaries; and they were similarly unimpressed by what they perceived as the invitations to their customers, embedded in the theatre companies' performances, to get involved in political debate, sexual immorality

2.6 A detail from Wenceslas Hollar's engraving 'Long View of London' (1644). The attributions of 'The Globe' and 'Beere Bayting' are not accurate and should be reversed.

and idleness. It appears that Francis Bacon was also made anxious by this industry of pretence when he wrote 'it is not good to stay too long in the theatre'.

Interestingly, Londoners might even be entertained by comic versions of themselves as in Jonson's *The Alchemist* and *Bartholomew Fair*, Dekker's *The Shoemaker's Holiday* or Francis Beaumont's *The Knight of the Burning Pestle*. There were also boys' companies playing, often in more stylised, satirical pieces in indoor theatres such as Blackfriars; however, we should also be mindful of contemporary appetites for religious instruction which may indeed be seen to surpass that for the theatre. On a regular basis, more Elizabethans and Jacobeans listened to sermons in church than visited a London theatre and the crowds which sermons attracted at St Paul's Cross, for example, could clearly rival, if not exceed, the numbers squeezing through entrances to the Globe or the Rose at the end of the sixteenth century.

Elsewhere, large publications such as John Stow's *Survey of the Cities of London and Westminster* (1598, 1603) again indicate the growing desire of the city to have itself memorialised in print. Striking a rather different note, the printing of ballads increased enormously. These ballads ranged in subject matter from courtship, political crisis and legend to extravagant crimes and they reached an extremely wide and diverse audience. The appeal that such tales in verse might have is clearly demonstrated by Shakespeare in *The Winter's Tale* with his clowning pedlar Autolycus. In addition, there was clearly a growing market from the middle of the sixteenth century for the sensational prose descriptions of the ravages made by plague and most particularly of the antics of the criminal underworld ('cony-catching' pamphlets) in the capital.

> **Crime and the City**
>
> A roging mate, & such another with [him] there were there got vpon a stal singing of balets, which belike was some prety toy, for very many gathered about to heare it, & diuers buying, as their affections serued, drew to their purses, & paid the singers for them. The slie mate and his fellowes, who were dispersed among them that stood to hear the songs well noted where euerie man that bought, put vp his purse againe … and as they were scatred by shouldring, thrusting, feining to let fall somthing, and other wilie tricks fit for their purpose: heere one lost his purse, there another had his pocket pickt, & to say all in briefe, at one instant, vpon the complaint of one or two that saw their purses were gone, eight more in the same companie, found themselues in like predicament … But one angry fellow, more impacient then all the rest, he fals vpon the ballad singer, and beating him with his fists well fauouredly, sayes, if he had not listned his singing, he had not lost his purse … The rest that had lost their purses likewise … [they] begin to tug & hale the ballad singers when one after one, the false knaues began to shrink away with the purses … let this forewarne those that listen singing in the streets.
>
> (Robert Greene, *The Third and Last Part of Conny-catching With the new deuised knauish arte of foole-taking* … (London, 1592), sigs. C4r–C4v)

Intellectual Influences

It has already been shown that Protestant writing on the Continent brought about enormous changes in the spiritual life of the nation. Nevertheless, before examining cultural change, it is as well to recognise that there were significant continuities in the Renaissance with habits of writing, reading (for literate society) and performance from the medieval period. Medieval practices of dramatising scriptural narrative and allegorising the struggles of the soul between sin and virtue for public performance continued until the 1580s and beyond in certain, more secluded corners of the country. Scriptural translation and commentary, sermons, accounts of spiritual confession, extended poetic and prose narratives of popular romance, legendary and chivalric exploits, didactic verse and social satires … all these survived into the Renaissance with assured audiences. The ever increasing publication across Europe of classical texts (a movement driven by humanist scholars) meant that the educated (not just clerical and university communities) were exposed to challenging avenues of philosophical speculation and models for writing (e.g. the essay, the dialogue, the letter, the epic, pastoral poetry, satire and verse drama).

We should remember that international intellectual life in the Renaissance was dominated by Latin and so an examination of cultural influences in Britain should not be limited to those publications appearing in English. Only one dialogue associated with Plato, for example, was translated into English by the end of the sixteenth century (*Axiochus*, 1592), but Latin and French versions circulated in intellectual society. Only a small section of English scholars achieved great fluency in Greek – someone like Ben Jonson is notable for his great classical learning. Earlier in the century we have an account from Lady Jane Grey's tutor of her extensive learning. However, if John Donne, for example, appears to have had very little command of

Greek, his knowledge of Hebrew must be seen as exceptional in this society. Greek texts had their most substantial influence among the wider reading public in Latin translation. In the case of Plato, the Italian humanist Marsilio Ficino's translations and commentaries were crucial in disseminating his ideas across Europe. While it is not possible here to consider the roll-call of important classical writers for Renaissance readers, it is important to outline some of the main currents of thinking which had particular influence upon writers and intellectuals. In addition, it should be added that this influence may be felt at one or two removes from the original source as the reader may encounter Platonic ideas, for example, by means of later texts such as Ficino's translations of Plotinus, the meditations of the Roman Cicero or those of the fourteenth-century Italian humanist Petrarch. From a literary perspective, (neo-) Platonic thinking is often expressed in terms of the association of earthly beauty with a higher spiritual beauty, the imaging of the human soul as motivated by intellectual (non-erotic) love. In such writing earthly realities are often perceived as being merely shadows of a higher unchanging spiritual realm and the whole order of creation is thought to be organised in systems of hierarchy which ascend towards the world of the divine. Such emphases are notably explored at some length in sonnet sequences (Spenser's *Amoretti* (1595), Sidney's *Astrophil and Stella* (1591)), court masques and epic narratives such as Spenser's *Faerie Queene* (1590–6). Platonic thinking was often a source of interest for its potential affinities with Christian beliefs and this became a consuming interest for many European scholars.

The writings of Plato and other Ancient Greek thinkers were also significant for the ways in which Roman writers digested and reinterpreted them for later generations. Among these Roman writers, Cicero (or Tully as he was often known at the time) held an exalted status for Renaissance scholars and readers and was valued especially for his ornate, elegant diction, his commitment to public life, his ethical enquiries and his analysis of philosophical thinking. Cicero was particularly important in the Renaissance as a widely available source of sceptical thinking: he is often associated with intellectual enquiries which are governed

THE
Third and laſt part of Conny-catching.

With the new deuiſed knauiſh arte of
Foole-taking.

The like coofnages and villanies neuer before diſcouered.

By R. G.

Printed by *T. Scarlet* for *C. Burby*, and are to be ſolde at
his ſhop vnder S. Mildreds Church in the
Poultrie.   1592.

2.7 Robert Greene's *The Third and Last Part of Conny-Catching*, 1592.

by initial attitudes of doubt, disbelief and interrogation. A further extension of this philosophy from texts earlier than Cicero's came in the shape of Pyrrhonian Scepticism: this mode of reasoning had some currency among certain intellectual circles and placed in question the possibility of *any* secure human knowledge. The importance of this intellectual approach may be witnessed, for example, in some aspects of Marlowe's dramas, Montaigne's and Bacon's essays and Donne's poetry. Another extremely strategic philosophical legacy from the classical period was that of Stoicism. Once again Cicero was significant as a source for this philosophy for Renaissance readers, but the dialogues, essays and dramas of Seneca were also notable places in which these ideas might be encountered. An emphasis upon strength of character and fortitude in the face of misfortune, a disdain for earthly cares, a commitment to moderation and virtuous life ... these all represent common modes of Stoical thinking. Indeed, these ideas were often combined with affirmations of emotional restraint, the determining power of Fate and the worthy course of suicide in certain circumstances. (The latter propositions were more difficult commitments to negotiate for Renaissance Christian readers.) These ideas are explored centrally in Shakespeare's *Julius Caesar, Hamlet* and *King Lear*, for example, in Jonson's poetry and in Milton's epic narratives.

In addition to these Graeco-Roman philosophical legacies, readers of Renaissance literature should also be aware of another intellectual tradition inherited from antiquity which asserted that the universe had been constructed harmoniously according to numerical principles (numerology). Such a belief in cosmic unity and symmetry was particularly associated with Pythagoras ('The world is built upon the power of numbers'), although the work of a host of different figures (such as the Greek-Egyptian astronomer Ptolemy, St Augustine and the fifth-century writer Boethius) meant that this rather mystical faith in the different properties of numbers gathered importance for succeeding generations. In a variety of forms, the intellectual tradition continued to have a powerful influence throughout the medieval and Renaissance centuries; and for literary scholars it has been a particularly rich source of investigation in the study of Spenser's and Milton's schemes of composition, for example, quite apart from the large number of numerological analyses of scripture from the period. However, it is clear that a fascination with numerological principles may be identified widely in Renaissance society. The poet Thomas Campion, for example, argues in his *Observations in the Art of English Poesy* (1602) that 'The world is made by symmetry and proportion, and is in that respect compared to music, and music to poetry ... '; and Sir Thomas Browne's *The Garden of Cyrus* (1658) is a notable example of a study which devotes much time and energy to numerological analysis – in this case, the recurring influence of the number five and its related form, the quincunx, upon diverse areas of human experience and knowledge.

In terms of more contemporary cultural and philosophical influence, the work of the humanists has previously been noted, but particular reference should be made to humanist history writing for its influence upon the changing attitudes to politics. Machiavelli (1469–1527), author of *The Prince* and *The Discourses*, was often demonised in literature from the period as an agent spreading 'devilish', 'vicious', 'atheistical' thinking, though few of his critics across Europe appear to have read his works. His unsentimental analyses of the strategies of political craft and domination were clearly building upon insights afforded by the historical narratives of classical historians such as Tacitus and Plutarch, if not the spectacle of political life as witnessed in all ages. If Marlowe's *The Jew of Malta* and Shakespeare's *Richard III*, for example, clearly exploit to some extent popular prejudices about the ruthless political motives, fondness for violence and effortless guile of the 'Machiavel', it is becoming clear that by the end of the sixteenth century the tide was just beginning to turn in some intellectual circles towards a more measured approach to his writings. The Flemish humanist Lipsius (1547–1606) proposed in his *Six Bookes of Politickes or Civil Doctrine* (published in Latin in 1589) that the relationship between deceit and political control needed to be understood more carefully, and late sixteenth-century essayists, such as the French scholar Michel de Montaigne and, in Britain, Francis Bacon, clearly believed that Machiavelli's ideas merited intellectual debate.

Writing: Production, Consumption and the Marketplace

As we have seen so far in this chapter, there were any number of ways in which a poem or essay might find its way to a reader during the Renaissance. It might be read aloud, printed abroad or smuggled into the country. It might reach you on paper in the writer's own hand, in a copy made by a scribe, in a cheap printed octavo edition or in an elaborate and expensively produced folio collection. A given text might be passed on within defined scholarly, student, family or social groupings (coteries) such as those in noble households and courtly circles. And, of course, a play-text was often in a constant state of change … written, revised, performed, revised for performance, perhaps stolen by certain ones for the purposes of publication, or indeed prepared precisely with a view to publication.

The author might, but frequently would not, have a hand in the dissemination of his or her work. The modern fascination with the unique figure of the creative author has meant that audiences and readers since at least the nineteenth century have often been uncomfortable with the idea of collaborative writing, which was in fact a common practice in the theatre world of Renaissance London. In the frantic world of theatrical performance where there was a constant appetite for new material and no possibility of long 'runs' of performing a single text night after night, acts and scenes could quite easily have been divided up among two or more writers. Partially finished texts might be completed by another, or a writer might revise, edit and reshape the work of his fellow dramatists. Many figures like Ben Jonson, John Fletcher and Francis Beaumont are known to have written both collaborative and single-authored plays. Indeed, Shakespeare at the end of his career worked together with John Fletcher on plays such as *Henry VIII* and *The Two Noble Kinsmen*. The identity of his collaborator(s) in the earlier *Pericles* is open to speculation, but scholars agree that the play is not solely by Shakespeare.

The opposition between manuscript and print culture in this period is far from clear-cut: some writers, like Ben Jonson, exploited both forms of textual transmission to publicise their work. Equally intriguingly, there is evidence that writers and patrons could in some cases have manuscripts imitate print format, having them prepared with pagination, indexes, titles and dedications ... all clearly with a larger readership in mind. During the Renaissance, manuscript circulation was often more significant than printed works in targeting certain elite patrons or social groups. Whereas manuscripts might be destined for a select audience and reinforce bonds and dialogues within it, publication meant that the writer had no control over the pairs of eyes that read his or her work. In addition, he or she might incur the wrath of censors or biting criticism from rivals. Ben Jonson remarked, for example, in his conversations with the Scottish poet Drummond of Hawthornden that his fellow poet Donne had tried to recall copies of his secular verse when he became Dean of St Paul's. Another related difficulty which may have led writers to refrain from publication is that there was in some of the higher echelons of society a perceived vulgarity associated with publication: none of Sir Thomas Wyatt's or Sir Philip Sidney's texts, for example, were published during their lifetimes. Nevertheless, it should be added that while such notions of social stigma may perhaps have influenced Sir Walter Ralegh's circulation of his poetry, for example, it did not affect his publishing ambitions for the *Discoverie of ... Guiana* (1595) or his *History of the World* (1614). Indeed, if the world of print was associated with lowly commercialism it does not seem to have prevented even more socially eminent figures such as Edward De Vere, Earl of Oxford, from publishing some of their works. Moreover, from a different perspective, some writers (like those of religious and political controversy) often wished precisely to gain access through print to the widest possible audience.

Once a manuscript was sold to a publisher, the author had no further rights over it. Publications came in a number of different sizes. Those in which large printers' sheets were folded only once creating four pages of print ('folio') were expensive and in general designed as presentation copies or prestigious volumes of scholarly value. For the smaller, cheaper 'quarto', the printing sheet

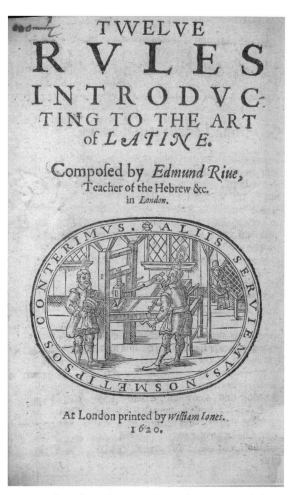

2.8 Woodcut displaying an early modern print workshop from the title page of Edmund Reeve's *Twelve Rules Introducting to the Art of Latine* (1620).

was folded twice to produce eight pages of printed text and accommodated all kinds of writing by classical and contemporary authors. The even smaller 'octavo' format in which the printer's sheet was folded three times creating sixteen pages of printed text was the most convenient size for easy transport and frequent reference. Some writers, as we can see from the extracts regarding publications by Elizabeth Cary and Samuel Daniel, argued that manuscripts had been obtained without their consent or that only under duress had the writer agreed to publication. The truth of the matter in these instances remains open to speculation, but the statement is so widespread as to become a commonplace gesture of modesty in many cases. It was perhaps a necessary submission prefacing works by women, nobles and divines who might not be expected to enter the public hurly-burly of the publishing world.

The fear of censorship is more apparent in the Renaissance than the reality of any rigorous surveillance by the authorities. At the beginning of Elizabeth's reign, decrees were issued insisting that new publications should be submitted initially for the sanction of Privy Councillors or the Archbishop of Canterbury and the Bishop of London (or the Vice Chancellors of Oxford or Cambridge if printed at these locations). However, there is little evidence for a coherent policy of censorship during the period and particular examples of (partially) censored texts or the recalling of copies such as in the cases of Gascoigne's *A Hundreth Sundrie Flowers* (1573) or Wroth's *Urania* (1621) appear to be the result of individual circumstances surrounding questions of libel and, more rarely, political anxiety. As far as the drama goes, in the final decades of the sixteenth century the Master of the Revels (which up until the 1580s had traditionally been an office associated with organising court entertainments) was given a more official role by Elizabeth's government in censoring plays designed for public performance. Initially, companies might be asked to act plays before this official; however, later, just play-texts were submitted to his office for permission to perform. In reality, the Master of the Revels was just one figure among a number of others (noblemen patronising theatre companies, city authorities, magistrates, political officials) who intervened at different points in controversies concerning debates over the drama.

Presenting the (Reluctant?) Renaissance Author

From this time she writ many things for her private recreation, on several subjects, and occasions, all in verse (out of which she scarce ever writ anything that was not translations). One of them was after stolen out of that sister-in-law's (her friend's) chamber and printed, but by her own procurement was called in.

(*The Lady Falkland, Her Life by one of her daughters.*
Possibly referring to Elizabeth Cary's *Tragedy of Mariam*, pp. 189–90 [A])

Right honorable, although I rather desired to keep in the private passions of my youth, from the multitude, as things vtterd to my selfe, and consecrated to silence: yet seeing I was betraide by the indiscretion of a greedie Printer, and had some of my secrets bewraide to the world, vncorrected: doubting the like of the rest, I am forced to publish that which I neuer ment.

(Samuel Daniel, Prefatory letter to Mary Sidney in his sonnet collection
Delia (1592), sig. A2r)

Language

In direct contrast with the status of English in more modern times, it quickly becomes apparent from the writings of the period that the native speech of the inhabitants of Renaissance Britain would have been of little value in the wider world. Latin was the international language of scholarship and intellectual dialogue. Among the living languages, Italian and French were infinitely more useful than English for the trader and traveller overseas; however, even the continental languages were negotiating what was referred to at the time as the 'Questione della Lingua' – a lively cultural debate by native scholars who were re-evaluating the status and purposes of vernacular writing. This was just one facet of contemporary debate which indicated a growing cultural self-consciousness among European nations during the Renaissance. Writers like Philip Sidney and Samuel Daniel were clearly aware of the low esteem in which their native language was held. In the sixteenth century, many thought that this situation could be remedied with lexical expansion: among the scholars and intellectuals who did involve themselves in this debate in England, some favoured importing words from continental languages as well as dead classical ones, whereas the opposing party wished to draw upon a more native resource by exploiting the neglected riches of Anglo-Saxon and Middle English. In the larger scheme of things it seems that the 'European' party won the day. Interestingly, in the later seventeenth century the proliferation of printed grammars, orthographies and 'proto'-dictionaries indicates a greater cultural concern with standardisation. Nevertheless, at the beginning of our period, Sir Thomas More wrote *Utopia* first in Latin in order to secure an international audience for his treatise, and, at the beginning of the seventeenth century, Sir Francis Bacon had some of his works translated into Latin in order once again to access a European readership for his theories of scientific thinking. In England, the 'Questione della Lingua' was never engaged with in quite the formal manner that is in evidence in sixteenth-century France or Italy. Nonetheless, the

---

Welcoming a Literature in English

… our language gyueth vs great occasion, beeing indeed capable of any excellent exercising of it. I know, some will say it is a mingled language. And why not so much the better, taking the best of both the other? Another will say it wanteth Grammer. Nay truly, it hath that prayse, that it wanteth not Grammer: for Grammer it might haue, but it needes it not; beeing so easie of it selfe, & so voyd of those cumbersome differences of Cases, Genders, Moodes, and Tenses, which I thinke was a peece of the Tower of *Babilons* curse, that a man should be put to schoole to learne his mother-tongue.

(Sir Philip Sidney, *An apologie for poetrie. Wrtten by the right noble, vertuous, and learned, Sir Phillip Sidney, Knight* (London, 1595), sig. L1v. Written c. 1579)

Now when so many pennes (like Speares) are charg'd,
To chace away this tyrant of the North:
Gross Barbarism, whose powre growne far inlarg'd,
Was lately by thy valiant Brothers worth,
First found, encountred, and prouoked forth:
Whose onset made the rest audacious,
Whereby they likewise haue so well discharg'd,
Vpon that hidious Beast incroching thus.

(Samuel Daniel, dedication to Mary Sidney in his *Delia and Rosamond augmented Cleopatra* (London, 1594), n.p.)

cultural anxieties and political ambitions of this frequently beleaguered realm on the edge of Europe often converged to encourage writers to promote the English language as worthy of literary composition, philosophical enquiry and political debate.

We also need to take into account that the mother tongues of many Britons were considerably more diverse than at the present time. There were large sections of the population in the south-west peninsula who spoke only Cornish. After the Acts of Union with Wales in 1536, the English Crown made specific provisions barring Welsh speakers from appealing through the justice system or from holding public office. Nonetheless, Welsh remained the dominant language of the population. Similar initiatives were taken to try to suppress Scots Gaelic and Irish Gaelic by the English authorities. In Ireland, colonisation by settlers often established greater usage of English in certain communities. In Scotland, Scots English (drawing its roots, like Northern English dialects, from the language of Anglo-Saxon Northumbria) was the language most widely used among the inhabitants. Linguistically, early modern English ranges over the period 1400–1700. Printed texts demonstrate that much of the substance of the language is understandable to modern eyes despite initial stumbling blocks such as 'loue' instead of 'love', 'vpper' instead of 'upper', 'ſhee' instead of 'she' and 'Lōdon' for 'London'. For our ears, there would be additional surprises if we were to listen to speakers from the period. Conclusions can only be arrived at from the texts which survive and, most importantly, we should not believe that everybody pronounced words in an identical fashion, but it becomes clear when Cassius in *Julius Caesar* declares 'Now is it Rome indeed, and room enough, / When there is in it but one only man', for example, that the close pronunciation of room/Rome allowed for punning in a way that is no longer possible.

The Renaissance was clearly a time of transition for the language as it moved towards standardisation driven by the demands of the new print culture. Equally importantly, the changes in the ways in which vowels were being pronounced by some communities in the South (the Great Vowel Shift) means that a more familiar pronunciation of words like 'frown', 'house', 'sky' and 'part' was emerging from older forms which would have sounded something like 'froown', 'hoose', 'skee' and 'parrt' – these are still current in some Northern English dialects and Scots English. These changes had begun towards the end of the Middle English period and continued to develop gradually, at different speeds and in very localised ways; so the pattern is extremely complex for the period. However, this transformation in pronunciation is largely seen by scholars as 'completed' across much of the nation by the close of the sixteenth century. Interestingly, competing forms of pronunciation did mean that poets and dramatists had extraordinary possibilities for rhyme and rhythmic experimentation at their disposal, if they desired. Moreover, we find writers moving between the forms of 'he desireth' and 'he desires' which are identical in meaning, for example, and exploring different usages for strategic building blocks for the language such as the verbs 'to be', 'to have' and 'to do': Doth thou look at me?/Lookest thou at me?; he hath need of me/he has need of me/he needeth me … Increasingly, the importance of word order (rather than the more heavily inflected language that we witness in Old English) was making its impact as a dominant structure for communication.

Any reader of early modern literature is made immediately aware of the employment of 'thou' for equals, inferiors and enemies, for example, and 'you' for groups, those in authority, or perhaps for equals of high rank. The modulations in usage across a dialogue or a given scene in a play can often reveal fascinating information about the power relations being dramatised. Inevitably, poets and dramatists like Spenser, Shakespeare and Donne pay particular attention to questions of rhythm, rhyme and the harmonies of their verse: as a consequence, they will exploit widely different language sources (sometimes turning back to archaic, obscure or rare forms) in order to achieve their ends. The formulation of new words and borrowings of one kind or another from other languages had been going on in English at least since invaders and traders first reached British shores. This movement constitutes the most dynamic change in language use during the period and was inevitably nourished by the very varied commitments of the population to economic expansion, trade, exploration, religious reform, diplomacy, travel and learning. The impact of biblical translation upon the development of the English language was very significant and is discussed in a later section. In the world of the arts, a linguistically innovative dramatist like Shakespeare clearly often tried to seduce his audiences with new, extravagant and archaic language forms. Interestingly, however, affectation involving excessive use of French, Italian or Latinate vocabulary often became a source of energetic criticism in all kinds of writing. Moreover, any theatrical representation of a foreigner was liable to be extravagantly comic and draw much scornful laughter from the London audiences.

Forms, Genres, Styles

While the range of genres potentially on offer to the Renaissance writer was very diverse indeed, choices were made in response to a number of factors: e.g., the desired means of transmission; the likely readership or audience; the particular tastes of a patron or coterie; the ambition and indeed, in some cases, the sex of the writer. Certain forms of writing were appropriate for particular relationships or particular forms of self-advertisement. A woman writer would hardly endear herself to potentially hostile audiences by writing sexually explicit comic dramas – it would require the very different cultural climate of the Restoration for Aphra Behn to effect this and she nevertheless still incurred much social disapproval. And a Protestant divine wishing to gain access to a wider readership is more likely to be tempted by prose narrative (influenced by existing traditions of the sermon, the letter, the spiritual confession and so on) rather than Petrarchan poetics or the pastoral.

As mentioned earlier, medieval traditions of composition and the increasing awareness of classical texts exerted extremely important influences over the business of writing. This is not to say that there were no generic innovations at all: the history play, for example, and the texts of the formal Early Stuart masques clearly had their roots in earlier forms, but they also marked significant changes of direction in writing. Looking back to inherited traditions, however, personal accounts of faith remained an important form of authorship from the medieval period.

Elsewhere, the influence of widely taught texts by Pliny, Cicero and Seneca meant that the oration, the letter, the philosophical essay, for example, were held in high esteem within intellectual circles across Europe. Indeed, the majority of published material on what we may now call literary theory concentrated upon the questions of the textual precedents established by classical writers and the didactic functions of these modes. The widespread study of Tacitus, Livy and Plutarch rendered history an increasingly common focus for discussion for the 'gentleman' author. Similarly, the numerous pedagogic exercises focused on Horace's odes, the satires of Martial, Juvenal and Catullus, the epic and pastoral verse of Virgil, the comedies of Terence and Plautus (and later at university, upon the tragedies of Seneca), meant that all these genres became familiar and represented possible avenues of composition for an aspiring author. While the tragic, the epic and the philosophic were promoted often as the most desirable modes for the ambitious author, leads given by the erotic verse of Ovid, for example, caused greater consternation for the authorities when poets like Shakespeare and Marlowe decided to imitate its thematic and narrative emphases in *Venus and Adonis* and *Hero and Leander*.

There is also much discussion concerning diction and generic expectation – the appropriate styles, conventions and registers of language for a given text. Famously, Philip Sidney deplored the hybrid genre of tragi-comedy as 'mingling kings and clowns … hornpipes and funerals'. However, one of the most challenging aspects of Renaissance literature is the Age's taste for difficulty. This meant that often the most esteemed texts were those which refused to yield easy access and interpretation on first reading. We have already noted the influence of numerology for the understanding of such texts as Spenser's lyrics and Milton's *Paradise Lost*. However, other complex schemes of textual interpretation were commonplace and emerge as a habit of reading and, indeed, of thinking for contemporaries. Preachers appear to have pursued lengthy programmes of scriptural interpretation on a regular basis from the pulpit: these might involve expositions of the differing levels of meaning (literal, moral, allegorical, eschatological) of a given parable. Indeed, in 'A Prologue into the Second Book of Moses Called Exodus' (1530), the Reformist translator of the Bible into English, William Tyndale cautions his readers to 'beware of subtle allegories'. Nonetheless, allegory (the interpretation of a text according to different levels of meaning of which the literal is the least important) remained a favourite strategy to be adopted by those poets, intellectuals and artists who were addressing the courtly and scholarly reader (even if theological allegory was being gradually dispensed with in the drama as the period progressed). Such schemes of interpretation fed a much larger appetite for writing which required the pleasures of careful deciphering and most particular attention to allusiveness, irony, textual voice, wit and concealed meaning.

For many writers, the pastoral was firmly linked with the themes and modes employed in the widely available texts of Virgil's *Eclogues*, and Spenser's *Shepheardes Calendar* (1579) clearly bears witness to this literary heritage. The figuring of a rural idyll populated by shepherds and shepherdesses given over to the discussion of competing sets of cultural values offered rich possibilities to the writer interested in cultural critique, as Philip Sidney acknowledged in his *Apology for Poetry*: 'Sometimes under the pretty tale of wolves and sheep, can include the whole considerations of wrong doing and patience' (Sidney, p. 119 [A]). The most familiar epic narrative from the classical period to the vast majority of educated readers in the Renaissance would have been Virgil's *Aeneid*. Until Chapman's translations of Homer's *Iliad* (1611) and *Odyssey* (1614–15) were published, exposure to Homer would mostly have been through Latin, Italian or French translation for contemporary audiences. English translators of Greek epic existing before Chapman often relied upon a combination of these, having no knowledge of the original tongue themselves. This genre of extended verse narrative which concentrates upon the heroics of given individuals and communicates the complex drama of watershed moments in the political or spiritual fates of enormous populations was reserved conventionally for the most ambitious and most able poetic talents – according to Sidney, the epic poet 'teacheth and moveth to the most high and excellent truth'. During the period we are considering in this chapter, Spenser's *The Faerie Queene* is the outstanding example of epic poetry in English. However, it should be remembered Spenser was as

Reading Strategies and Renaissance Literature

Spenser's 'Whole Intention' in *The Faerie Queene*

Sir knowing how doubtfully all Allegories may be construed, and this booke of mine, which I have entituled the *Faery Queene*, being a continued Allegory, or darke conceit, I have thought good as well for avoiding of gealous opinions and misconstructions, as also for your better light in reading therof ... to discover unto you the general intention and meaning ... I labour to pourtraict in Arthure, before he was king, the image of a brave knight, perfected in the twelve private morall vertues ... To some I know this Methode will seeme displeasaunt, which had rather have good discipline delivered plainly in way of precepts, or sermoned at large, as they use, then thus clowdily enwrapped in Allegoricall devises.

(Edmund Spenser, letter to Sir Walter Ralegh, in *Norton Anthology*, pp. 716–17[A])

Sir John Harington on His *Orlando Furioso*

The ancient Poets haue indeed wrapped as it were in their writings diuers and sundry meanings, which they call the sences or mysteries thereof. First of all for the litterall sence ... as a second rine and somewhat more fine, as it were nearer to the pith and marrow, they place the Morall sence ... Manie times also vnder the selfsame words they comprehend some true vnderstanding of naturall Philosophie, or sometimes of politike gouernment, and now and then of diuinitie: and these same sences that comprehend to excellent knowledge we call the Allegorie ... Now let any iudge if it be a matter of meane art or wit to containe in one historicall narration either true or fained, so many, so diuerse, and so deepe conceits ... [allegories were used in antiquity] that they might not be rashly abused by prophane wits, in whom science is corrupted, like good wine in a bad vessell ... For the weaker capacities will feed themselues with the pleasantnes of the historie and sweetnes of the verse, some that haue stronger stomackes will as it were take a further taste of the Morall sence, a third sort more high conceited then they, will digest the Allegorie ...

(Lodovico Ariosto, *Orlando furioso in English heroical verse, by Iohn Harington* (London, 1591), sigs. 4r–4v)

conscious of the earlier achievements by medieval writers of chivalric exploits and near-contemporary Italian writers such as Tasso and Ariosto as he was of his classical forebears. He draws upon a number of different influences to create a complex allegory which transports the reader through meandering narratives of romance, knightly questing, supernatural events, scriptural symbolism and coded political analysis.

Among other major generic modes adopted by writers, different forms of lyric and satirical production will be considered later in the chapter. However, precedents of tragic and comic writing are of obvious concern to the students of Renaissance drama. While Aristotle's theorising of tragedy in his tract of *Poetics* is invariably the departure point for a consideration of the development of thinking about the genre, this is not a text which has been found to influence English dramatists widely, except perhaps at several removes. Aristotelian ideas became apparent in Renaissance England through the study of texts such as Horace's *Ars Poetica* at schools and colleges. The imitation of the Roman dramatist Seneca's tragic structures also communicated that the genre involved certain conventions: grand narratives of misfortunes for socially eminent characters, violations of cultural or sacred laws, agonised moral dilemmas for the protagonists, choric interventions, supernatural apparitions … and in the case of Seneca, a taste for bloodthirsty detail. There was some translation and study of Greek drama, but knowledge was not widespread. Equally important as a formative influence upon tragic narrative are the widely studied texts of classical history and more contemporary chronicle writing which focused upon the fall of figures from the political and social elite of a society (critically termed as the *de casibus* tradition derived from the Italian Renaissance writer Boccaccio's work *De casibus illustrium virorum*). Narrative collections such as *The Mirror for Magistrates*, Holinshed's *Chronicles* and North's translation of Plutarch's *Lives* provided a rich fund of heroic and plaintive tales of the adversities of cultural leaders and were near at hand when Shakespeare turned his attention to composing *Macbeth, King Lear, Antony and Cleopatra* and *Coriolanus*.

In contrast to tragedy, comedy often deals with less socially elevated characters and emphasises the much reduced (if not entirely absent) role of the supernatural in human affairs. This world is frequently organised by the forces of chance rather than the more formidable government of tragedy's 'Fate' and audiences are exposed to (largely resolvable) crises of love, money and ownership which often involve forms of disguise and deception. Here, as we see in Shakespeare's knowledge of Plautus's *Menaechmi* when composing *The Comedy of Errors*, comic dramatists might once again be profoundly influenced by the heritage of Roman writers – in this case, Terence and Plautus who were widely studied in Tudor schools as a method of teaching Latin. The conventions of Roman comedy often drew upon familiar stock characters like the lovers, the witty and resourceful slave and the tyrannical father, and indeed in the case of *Menaechmi*, twins who generate endless situations of mistaken identity in congested and often frenzied urban settings. If Jonson's comedies, like *Volpone* and *The Alchemist*, have no clear parent texts, such as does Shakespeare's *Comedy of Errors*, among the canon of Roman drama, these city comedies have affinities with them in terms of theme, characterisation and intrigue. The influence of knockabout humour and slapstick antics of interludes and entertainments from the later medieval period and earlier Tudor moral plays also has to be accounted for when considering the servant pranks dramatised in Marlowe's *Dr Faustus*, for example.

Despite the evocation of urban landscapes in the farcical *Comedy of Errors* or the more bitter comedies of *The Merchant of Venice* and *Measure for Measure*, Shakespeare characteristically gravitated to courtly and pastoral environments for the dramatisation of comic narratives: these frequently concentrate on issues of mistaken or disguised identity, erotic adventure and (thwarted) persecution. In general, his comedies unfold during a provisional 'festive' time of release from customary cultural restraints (represented mostly by rulers, parents, the law or the demands of work). The pursuit of unexpected 'liberties' on the part of the characters in such plays not only brings forth scenes involving farce, romance, comic reversals and possibilities for linguistic duelling and punning. Such narratives also offer audiences ample opportunity to ponder the unequal power relations which normally govern the lives of Portia, Viola and Shylock and their fellow citizens.

Authors, Texts, Subjects

As we have seen, many of the most famous dramatists of the Renaissance were from non-aristocratic backgrounds. Towards the end of the period it became more possible for the titled to consider dramatic composition as the worlds of the court, theatrical performance and dramatic composition began to converge to a greater extent. However, figures like Sir William D'Avenant, Sir John Suckling and William Cavendish, Duke of Newcastle, were mostly targeting a courtly or aristocratic audience rather than the public playhouse in their dramatic writing and Newcastle's wife, Margaret Cavendish, admitted that she never expected her plays to be produced publicly at all. In contrast to dramatic composition, poetry and prose writing appears to have attracted interest from writers from nearly all sections of society.

There are a number of publications which indicate the very diverse ways in which reading matter arrived before the eyes of its audiences. Let us take the example of the English Bible. Until the committed Reformist William Tyndale (1494?–1536) began his venture in the 1520s, there had been no published version of the complete Bible in English; and when it was published, it became the central document for the development of Protestant faith in England. Tyndale's rendering of scripture would live on in different revisions and permeate idiomatic English right to the present day with phrases such as 'the spirit is willing but the flesh is weak'. Because of the opposition of the Henrician Catholic administration in the 1520s to the *dangerous* prospect of a translated Bible which might be read and pondered over by every subject, Tyndale was forced to go overseas to the German states to pursue his project and there he met Luther in Wittenberg. Despite being denounced by the English authorities, copies of his translations of the New Testament (1525) based on the Greek text of Erasmus did make their way over the Channel, but on the orders of the bishops they were seized and burned. Miles Coverdale (1488?–1569) completed Tyndale's

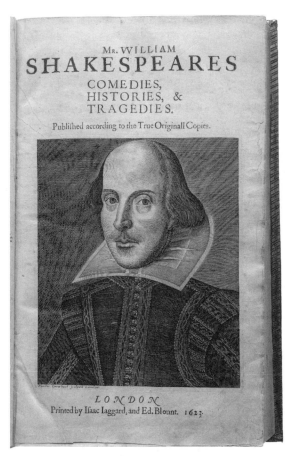

Mr. WILLIAM
SHAKESPEARES
COMEDIES,
HISTORIES, &
TRAGEDIES.

Publiſhed according to the True Originall Copies.

LONDON
Printed by Iſaac Iaggard, and Ed. Blount. 1623.

2.9 Title page from the 1623 'First Folio' of Shakespeare's dramatic works.

translation of the Bible and it was published in Antwerp in 1535. Tyndale was finally betrayed to Spanish forces in the Low Countries in 1536. He was strangled and burnt as a heretic in the Netherlands: his last words at the stake were reported by the martyrologist John Foxe as being 'Lord, open the King of England's eyes.' However, the 1530s represented a political and religious climate in England very different from that of previous decades; and Miles Coverdale would finally oversee the publication in English of the 'Great Bible' (1539) which was officially sanctioned by Henry's administration.

Two other publications had enormous influence upon religious life in Renaissance England. The Reformist John Foxe (1516–87) first began to prepare his huge volume *Acts and Monuments of the Christian Church* (familiarly known as Foxe's *Book of Martyrs*) while in exile in Europe during Mary's reign. He was determined to give accounts of the persecution of Protestant English martyrs, though this project came to expand as he included narratives of the trials and tribulations of the Early Church, histories of European persecution and the punishments of English critics of the Catholic Church in the medieval centuries. Foxe wanted to establish the legitimacy and spiritual roots of the Protestant faith by revealing a continuity of doctrine and worship with the very earliest Christians. The first version of this project was published in Latin in 1559, and was expanded after further research and published in English in 1563, dedicated to Elizabeth. By 1570 it had expanded to two volumes of hundreds and hundreds of pages supplemented by woodcut illustrations. It would go through further editions and was at the time the largest book ever published in English. The collection would have been far too costly for the ordinary man and woman to purchase, but the bishops did order it to be made available for the reading public in cathedrals and church libraries up and down the land. As the centuries went by, it was often placed in private libraries and parishes with the Bible as a revered monument to the reformed faith (and indeed to national identity) in England. The other lasting legacy of religious publication was the 'Authorised Version' of the Bible (the King James Bible) published in 1611. Tyndale's translation formed a central core of this

Lord opē the king of Englands eies.

2.10 Woodcut from Foxe's *Acts And Monuments* illustrating the martyrdom of William Tyndale.

volume. The 'new' translation was commissioned by James to represent the cohesive religious settlement of his reign. Interestingly, it was only at the Restoration when other translations ceased to be published that the 'King James Version' established a central formative place in the worship (and indeed the rhythms and phrases of everyday speech) of many.

Another important publication, this time for the development of new poetic styles in Renaissance England, occurred during the reign of Mary Tudor: the printer Richard Tottel published *Songes and Sonnettes, written by the ryght honorable Lorde Henry Haward late Earle of Surrey, and other* in 1557 – otherwise known as *Tottel's Miscellany*. The poetry of Sir Thomas Wyatt and Henry Howard, Earl of Surrey, marks the first significant engagement with Petrarchan poetics in English verse and yet, until this date, it had only circulated in manuscript form. Surrey's experimental translation of the second and fourth books of Virgil's *Aeneid* in what is now known as blank verse (unrhymed iambic pentameter – the metre of Shakespeare's plays) was also edited and republished here. Tottel brought together for the first time a wide selection of Wyatt's and Surrey's work along with that of some other contemporaries such as Nicholas Grimald, who himself also had a hand in compiling the *Miscellany*, and this anthology was influential for the next generation of Elizabethan poets. It was so popular that it went through numerous editions up until 1587. Moreover, the collection was one of the few to be considered worthy of comment by critics such as Philip Sidney in his *Apology for Poetry* and George Puttenham, author of *The Art of English Poesy* (1589); and it was certainly greatly instrumental in promoting models of courtliness and courtly poetics for the second half of the century.

Philip Sidney (1554–86) is an exceptionally important figure in the English Renaissance as the author of the first sonnet sequence in English, *Astrophil and Stella*, of an essay of literary criticism, *An Apology for Poetry*, and of an extremely popular prose romance, *Arcadia*. However, none of these were published in his lifetime and circulated in manuscript among a select readership. When they were published in the 1590s under the stewardship of his sister Mary, Countess of Pembroke, or his friend Fulke Greville (whose own verse was not published until after his death), in his choices of styles, genres and themes Sidney became a model of authorship for a whole generation of writers for the next decades. In stark contrast to the apparent carelessness, or courtly *sprezzatura*, with which Sidney regarded the circulation of his literary works is the career of Isabella Whitney (c. 1548?–1600?) who is credited as being the first professional woman writer in English. Unlike Sidney, she came from a rather modest landowning family in Cheshire. Little is known about her or the publication of works such as *The Copy of a Letter* (1567) or *A Sweet Nosegay* (1573), although it appears from textual evidence alone that she and some of her siblings were employed in some form of 'service' in London. Clearly encountering cultural prejudices surrounding her sex and her relatively low social station, Whitney lamented her vulnerable place in society in her verse but, most unusually for the period, was also clearly intent upon entering the public world of print.

Texts and Issues

Political Structures

The issue which dominated political debate and theorising throughout the period was that of sovereignty: on what basis was royal authority established? Within which parameters should the sovereign operate? What status did Parliament have in political decision-making? In which circumstances might the sovereign be resisted? Furthermore, the very subject of what we might now term 'politics' was intimately bound up with issues of religious allegiance. Indeed, for many modern historians and literary critics, religion has become the defining discourse for understanding questions of identity, motivation and action in the Renaissance. The very ideas of political obedience and resistance were explored frequently at the time with questions of religious belonging (Protestant or Catholic) uppermost in people's minds. In the increasingly politically polarised world of the Renaissance, to affirm membership of a Catholic or radical Protestant/Puritan congregation was to make a very public statement of your feelings towards the existing social hierarchy. Catholics, for example, were often considered suspect in official circles in that they belonged to a Church which was opposed to the Elizabethan administration – theirs was a Church which was challenging across Europe the authority of Protestant monarchs and actively urging the faithful to resist such governments.

Building upon ideas which had been developed during the medieval centuries, there was political interest during the Tudor and Early Stuart periods in the idea of the monarch as divinely appointed leader. Throughout the sixteenth and seventeenth centuries political debate was often strategically organised around examples drawn from scripture: in the Old Testament those wishing to further this cause could cite such proofs as 'By me Kings reign, and Princes decree justice' (Proverbs 8.15); and there were supporting texts in the New Testament, such as the instance when Jesus informs Pilate, 'Thou couldest have no power at all against me, except it were given thee from above' (John 19.11). James I (as James VI of Scotland) explored these lines of thinking at great length in order to consolidate his own position at the apex of the political structure in *The Trew Law of Free Monarchies* (1598):

> I grant that a wicked king is sent by God for a curse to his people, and a plague for their sins. But that it is lawful to them to shake off that curse at their own hand, which God has laid on them, that I deny, and may so do justly.

In fact, in a later 1610 speech at Whitehall to Parliament, James argued unambiguously that 'kings are not only God's lieutenants on earth, and sit upon God's throne, but even by God himself they are called gods'. If such theological emphases had been struck in royal pronouncements by members of the previous Tudor dynasty, they remained implicit rather than explicit. Nonetheless, throughout the Renaissance there was regular discussion of the idea that after the Fall from Eden, God had ordained a rigidly hierarchical social order ('the Great Chain of Being'): this order extended not only across the whole of human society from ruler to peasant, but shaped perceptions of the universe with a narrative which ranged from God himself to the lowliest stone, and beyond to the depths of Hell. Monarchs, priests and judges

2.11 *Elizabeth I Receiving Dutch Emissaries*, c. 1585.

were promoted as the cornerstones of this divinely appointed hierarchy and each living thing had its designated place in the cosmic order.

Exploiting theories which had been devised to justify papal authority during the medieval period, there was also much discussion concerning the possibility that the sovereign might be worthy *in office*, if not *in person*. Elizabeth I clearly relied upon such thinking (what has come to be termed 'the King's Two Bodies') when she spoke before her troops at Tilbury awaiting the arrival of the Spanish Armada in 1588. The tension between the undying respect owed to God's lieutenant on earth and the spectacle of a fallible human being trying to maintain control over the political structure of a nation remained a rich field of enquiry for writers and thinkers alike. It is clear that Renaissance writers and thinkers did not hesitate to analyse the potential flaws in the prevailing systems of government. If hereditary monarchy was the prevailing mode of political government in countries such as England, Scotland, France, Denmark and Portugal, it never ceased to be a theme of controversial debate across Europe as a whole. In France, for example, Jean Bodin's pro-monarchical *Les six livres de la République* (1576, translated into English in 1606) found a match in his fellow-countryman's equally widely read anti-monarchist tract, François Hotman's *Francogallia* (1573). Moreover, the study of Roman history opened up discussion of a bewildering array of modes of political government, as did contemporary interest in travel writing.

The political importance of those of noble rank in advising the monarch is pondered throughout the literature of the period. In his essay 'Of Nobility' (1625), Francis Bacon contended that 'A monarchy where there is no nobility at all is ever a pure and absolute tyranny, as that of the Turks.' However, he subsequently concedes in the same discussion,

> It is well when nobles are not too great for sovereignty, nor for justice, and yet maintained in that height, as the insolency of inferiors may be broken upon them, before it come on too fast upon the majesty of kings ... Certainly, kings that have able men of their nobility shall find ease in employing them, and a better slide into their business; for people naturally bend to them as born in some sort to command.

(Cited in *Major Works*, ed. Vickers, pp. 364–5[A])

In terms of political administration, nobles could be called upon to perform tasks of great weight and responsibility, but there was also a large community of political servants drawn from humbler origins at court.

If it is relatively easy in the dramas, essays, poetic narratives and sermons from the sixteenth and seventeenth centuries to identify lively political debate and enquiry, it is much more difficult than some have believed in the past to fix upon a world-picture of a political system which the society at large supported. The lower orders of society are not infrequently depicted as being variously: dangerous and violent; emotionally uncontrollable; cunning or incapable of reasoning; and useful only as a source of labour, cannon-fodder and tax revenue. However, even a brief excursion into the worlds of *Coriolanus*, *Henry V* and *The Tempest* indicates that this is not the whole story and, indeed, that brutality, irrationality and exploitative behaviour are not the monopoly of those at the bottom of the social ladder.

Gender Roles and Relations

An interest in gender, the cultural representation of femininity and masculinity, constitutes one of the liveliest centres of enquiry for students and scholars alike of Renaissance literature. This area of study offers some clear perspectives on the ways in which cultural power was articulated and distributed in the society and to some extent the ways in which individuals chose to define themselves. While, as we have seen, Renaissance society clearly attributed superior status to the male, it had also inherited from the medieval period an ongoing debate about the role of women. This debate (*la querelle des femmes*) was conducted mostly by male authors and debaters – eloquence and public debate being perceived since classical times as pre-eminently a male preserve. There were some exceptional women with high social status and authority such as Elizabeth Tudor and Mary Sidney, Countess of Pembroke, but these were 'exceptional' – and it is difficult to estimate how such anomalous cases might be seen to undermine gender expectations in the society at large.

Many of the expectations concerning male and female behaviour in the Renaissance were governed by thinking inherited from culturally strategic texts

Gender and Power

I am assured that God hath reueled to some in this our age, that it is more then a monstre in nature, that a woman shall reigne and haue empire aboue man … And where no repentance is founde, there can be no entrie to grace. And therfore I say, that of necessitie it is, that this monstriferouse empire of women, (which amongest all enormities, that this day do abound vpon the face of the hole earth, is most detestable and damnable) be openlie reueled and plainlie declared to the world, to the end that some may repent and be saued.

(John Knox, *The First Blast of the Trumpet against the Monstruous Regiment of Women* (Geneva, 1558), pp. 3–4, 5)

… an absolute Quéene, an absolute Dutches or Countesse … These I say haue the same authoritie although they be women or children in that kingdome, dutchie or erledome, as they should haue had if they had bin men of full age. For the right and honour of the bloud, and the quietnes and suretie of the realme, is more to be considered, than either the tender age as yet impotent to rule, or the sex not accustomed (otherwise) to intermeddle with publicke affaires, being by common intendment vnderstood, that such personages neuer doe lacke the counsell of such graue and discréete men as be able to supplie all other defectes.

(Sir Thomas Smith, *The common-welth of England and the maner of gouernment thereof* … (London, 1589), p. 28)

I haue set down vnto you (which are of mine owne Sex) the subtil dealings of vntrue meaning men: not that you should contemne al men, but to the end that you may take hed of the false hearts of al & stil reproue the flattery which remaines in all … heare euery thing that they say, (& afford them nodes which make themselues Noddies) but beleeue very little therof or nothing at all, and hate all those, who shall speake any thing in the dispraise or to the dishonor of our sex.

(Jane Anger, *Jane Anger her Protection for women* … (London, 1589), sigs. C4r–C4v)

which dated back centuries. In the narratives of Aristotle as well as those from the Bible, for example, audiences were confronted on a regular basis with clearly differentiated ('essentialist') expectations relating to each of the sexes. The differences between male and female were frequently expressed in terms of binary oppositions: reason/passion; knowledge/ignorance; active/passive; superior/inferior; governor/governed. The common appearance of cross-dressing characters on stage (indeed, the very convention of male actors taking on female roles) often serves to point up codes of gender expectation and, indeed, to indicate how arbitrary they were. In his *On the Generation of Animals*, Aristotle had associated the physically weaker woman with mental weakness, whereas in the Bible woman is often restricted to the roles of sinner or (more rarely) redemptress. She is described unequivocally at I Peter 3.7 as 'the weaker vessel'. If some (and only some) thinkers of the period chose to emphasise the equality of man and woman before God (' … there is neither male nor female: for ye are all one in Jesus Christ', Galatians 3.28), there is precious little evidence that men and women occupied an equal footing in their daily lives. At the limit of our period in Milton's *Paradise Lost* (1667), the description of Adam and Eve reminds us that they were 'Not equal, as their sex not equal seemed' (4.296).

Those violating social expectations of femininity were demonised in terms of unruly women. The chaotic cultural potential of woman was often linked in the minds of contemporaries to the seemingly mysterious and mutable nature of the woman's body. From the time of Aristotle and Galen, medicine and anatomy had taken the male body as the model for examining human life – indeed, Aristotle viewed woman as a 'defective male'. Those women who sought to ape men in their habits and dress were thought to undermine the very power structure of the divinely ordered society and thus became monstrous and requiring of discipline. Most famously, there was a pamphlet war concerning the cultural role of women which unfolded at the beginning of the seventeenth century and was given particular impetus by Joseph Swetnam's *Arraignment of Lewd, Idle, Froward Women* (1615). There

Renaissance Marriage

The duty of an honest faythful woman vnto her husband is, to [ac]knowledg her husband to be her head, to be subiecte vnto hym, to reuerence him, to obey him, quietly to learne of him, to lead a blameles life, to vse much silence, peaceably and circumspectly to looke vnto her householde, and to tyer her selfe with such apparell as becommeth a sober Christian woman.

('The dutie of wiues vnto their husbandes', in Thomas Becon, *The principles of Christian religion* … (London, 1553), sig. L7v)

… Saint Peter doth better iudge [than 'the common sort of men'] what shoulde be semying to a man, and what he shuld most reasonably performe. For he saith, reasoning should be vsed, and not fighting. Yea he sayth more, that the woman ought to haue a certayne honor attributed to her, that is to say, she must be spared and borne with, the rather for that she is the weaker vessel, of a frayle harte, inconstant, and with a worde sone stirred to wrath. And therfore considering these her freylties, she is to be the rather spared … Now as concernyng the wyues duetie … as S. Paule expresseth it in this fourme of wordes: Let women be subiect to theyr husbandes as to the Lorde. For the husband is the head of the woman, as Christ is the head of the Church.

('An homely of matrimonie', in *The seconde tome of homelyes of such matters* … set out by the aucthoritie of the Quenes Maiestie … (London, 1563), sigs. LLL4r, LLL4v, LLL5r–LLL5v)

had been publications feeding this debate across Europe throughout the period. However, Swetnam's ranting was followed by a number of published responses, including Rachel Speght's *A Muzzle for Melastomus*, Ester Sowernam's *Ester Hath Hang'd Haman* and Constantia Munda's *Worming of a Mad Dog* in 1617 alone.

Much women's writing was focused during the Renaissance upon genres of autobiography destined for their children, spiritual confession, prayer, household government, recipes and remedies, midwifery and so on. Only relatively rarely do figures such as Isabella Whitney, Mary Wroth, Elizabeth Cary and Margaret Cavendish at the end of our period emerge, who author texts not primarily linked to faith or mothering roles.

Gender Politics

Constabarus to His Wife Salome Who Seeks a Divorce

What are Hebrew women now transformed to men?
Why do you not as well our battles fight,
And wear our armour? Suffer this, and then
Let all the world be topsy-turvèd quite.
Let fishes graze, beasts [swim], and birds descend,
Let fire burn downwards whilst the earth aspires …

(Elizabeth Cary, The Tragedy of Mariam, I.vi.421–6[A])

Household Government

And therefore it is impossible for a man to vnderstand how to gouerne the common-wealth, that doth not know to rule his owne house, or order his owne person; so that he that knoweth not to gouerne, deserueth not to reigne.

(John Dod and Robert Cleaver,
A Godlie Forme of Householde Government (London, 1612), p. 16)

The Happy Creation

It appeareth by that Soueraignty which God gaue to *Adam* ouer all the Creatures of Sea and Land, that man was the end of Gods creation, wherevpon it doth necessarily, without all exception follow, that *Adam*, being the last worke, is therefore the most excellent worke of creation: yet *Adam* was not so absolutely perfect, but that in the sight of God, he wanted an Helper: Wherevpon God created the woman his last worke, as to supply and make absolute that imperfect building which was vnperfected in man, as all Diuines do hold, till the happy creation of the woman.

(Ester Sowernam, Ester hath hang'd Haman: or An answere to a lewd pamphlet,
entituled, The arraignment of women … Written by Ester Sowernam,
neither maide, wife nor widdowe, yet really all,
and therefore experienced to defend all (London, 1617), pp. 5–6)

The Man-Woman

For since the daies of *Adam* women were neuer so Masculine … Masculine in Moode, from bold speech, to impudent action … for (without redresse) they were, are, and will be still most Masculine, most mankinde, and most monstrous.

(Hic mulier: or, The man-woman (London, 1620), sig. A3r)

Love and Sexuality

Modern discussions of desire and sexual behaviour have been shaped in many cases by medical and scientific enquiries which began in the nineteenth century. The contemporary fascination with classifying sexual identities (e.g. heterosexual, homosexual, lesbian, bisexual) and attributing certain expectations and cultural behaviours to them are mostly unhelpful for the Renaissance when these subjects were often approached from radically different perspectives from our own.

When sexual behaviour is discussed at all in documents of the period, it is most frequently in the context of marriage. The account of sexual congress and reproduction often relied upon the Aristotelian oppositions outlined in the section above. Activity, heat and creativity were associated with the male body and fathering; the woman's body often emerged in this discourse as a vessel for incubating and birthing the child. Elsewhere, it was believed that both the woman and the man contributed 'seed' to create an infant. A cause of great anxiety appears to have been the contention in much medical theorising that the controlling element in the anatomy of the adult female was the womb which was given to unruliness if not 'occupied' with childbearing. It quickly becomes apparent in such discussions that the sexually uncontrolled or 'naughty' woman was thought to have potentially a powerful disruptive force upon the economic and power networks of the society around her. As we see in *The Winter's Tale*, even the pregnant woman needed to be watched over lest she warped the mind of the infant with the fantastical 'humours' and lack of restraint to which her sex was supposedly prey. In Europe some contemporary writers argued that the female body was in fact an inversion (indeed, lesser version) of the male body – the male genitalia appearing in 'inverted' fashion inside the woman.

As far as the business of courtship and sexual initiative was concerned, it was once again the male who would be expected to take the lead and Shakespeare pokes fun energetically at such cultural expectations in his narrative poem *Venus and Adonis*. If his heroines such as Rosalind in *As You Like It* are often seen to be very far from prudish in their sexual bantering, they clearly challenge their male counterparts by adopting assertive 'masculinised' roles. The comic play on the differing meaning of the same word or 'punning' is particularly in evidence in both the drama and the poetry when dealing with sexual humour. A favourite which recurs in Shakespearean drama and Donne's erotic verse, for example, is the pun focusing on 'death', meaning both demise and sexual orgasm. Feste, the clown in *Twelfth Night*, is clearly allowed to enjoy this pun in the song 'Come away, come away death', as is the reader of Donne's 'A Valediction of Weeping' and 'The Expiration'.

The legacy of courtly love conventions (see pp. 36–42) was still very much alive for poets in the sixteenth and seventeenth centuries in their readings of Chaucer's *Troilus and Criseyde*, for example. Themes and motifs derived from classical poetry also continued to shape poetic developments: of particular interest is the *carpe diem* ('seize the day') motif which concentrated traditionally upon the lover attempting to seduce the mistress (and, at one remove, the reader) with an urgent appeal to make the very most of her (transient) physical beauty … by jumping into bed with him!

Marlowe, Ralegh, Donne and Marvell are among the most notable poets of the age to respond to (and often to mock) these conventions. The *Canzoniere* by the Italian poet Petrarch (1304–74) served as the dominant reference for love poetry for much of the Renaissance: imitations and translations (and sometimes exaggerations and gross distortions) of his poetic language of desire sprang up across Europe. Love poetry also came to be associated most particularly with the fourteen-line poem known as the sonnet. Despite Chaucer's passing interest in the Petrarchan sonnet form, it is with the verse of Wyatt and Surrey during the reign of Henry VIII that its influence was first felt in any substance among its courtly audiences. It is in the second half of the sixteenth century that the form attracts widespread interest. In 1560 Anne Vaughan Lok's short devotional sonnet sequence *A Meditation of a Penitent Sinner* was published, and, by the beginning of the seventeenth century, a dynamic relationship between the conventions of erotic poetry and the expression of crises of religious faith came to dominate much of the poetic output of figures such as Donne and Herbert. In terms of erotic verse sequences, Philip Sidney's *Astrophil and Stella* (pub. posthumously 1591) has been seen to have triggered a fashion for Petrarchan sonnet collections which includes Spenser's *Amoretti*, Daniel's *Delia*, Watson's *Hecatompathia*, Drayton's *Idea*, Constable's *Diana*, Barnes's *Parthenophil and Parthenope* and Shakespeare's *Sonnets*. (The use to which Mary Wroth puts this lyric tradition in her *Pamphilia to Amphilanthus* will be discussed in the Readings section (see pp. 177–9).) The vast majority of this poetry concentrates upon the drama of the agonies and (often narcissistic) psychological dilemmas of the alienated male lover who makes suit to an unobtainable or unresponsive mistress (the 'cruel fair'). This male lover is often seen to luxuriate in the textual staging of his own heroic anguish. While it was by no means certain that the Petrarchan sonneteers were going to win the day at the end of Henry VIII's reign, by the 1590s it had become almost impossible to write love poetry without paying at least some lip service to Petrarchan diction and employing the sonnet. Increasingly, Petrarch's use of antitheses, of the idealisation of the woman's appearance, of the figurative language of lovers as sailors, hearts as ships … was extended and often exaggerated by his imitators. We also find an emphasis in such poetry upon the poet's power to 'eternise' the loved one in verse.

From a range of contemporary evidence, it is apparent that same-sex relations (ranging from familiar acquaintance to great intimacy) might be expressed in much more demonstrative terms in public than may be the case today. The opening poems in Shakespeare's *Sonnets* were addressed to a young man and certainly seem to have worried numbers of editors and readers down the centuries. When we encounter much more explicitly homoerotic verse (such as that found in Richard Barnfield's collection *The Affectionate Shepherd*, 1594), we must take into account not only the narrative of male same-sex desire but also other possible (and competing) influences of authorship, including desires for patronage, classical models of diction, parody and particular expectations of certain audiences. Quite simply we should beware of carelessly imposing twenty-first-century models of sexual identity upon a radically different society which existed four hundred years ago. Equally important when dealing with any representation of erotic desire in texts we study from the Renaissance must be a care not to confuse the textual speaker with the author. Indeed, in the

2.12 Miniature by Nicholas Hilliard, *Young Man against a Flame Background.*

introduction to his poetry collection *Licia* (1593) Giles Fletcher helpfully underlined, 'a man may write of Love and not be in love'.

Shakespeare's recurring fascination with the cultural implications of close male relationships in *The Two Gentlemen of Verona, The Merchant of Venice* and *Twelfth Night*, for example, must clearly have engaged at differing levels with experiences and expectations which had currency among his audiences at the end of the sixteenth century. More generally, we find that there is less credence given to the exclusivity of sexual identities than is often the case in modern Western societies. Among their immediate society, emotional (and perhaps physical) intimacy between men in the upper echelons of Renaissance society appears often to have been a concern only if it began to prove a bar to marriage – kin might often be concerned more about the economic transferral of power and estates than moral condemnation in such instances. In fact, excessive heterosexual desire on the part of the male could emerge a far greater source of concern for close ones: such a desire may 'un-man' the lover and render him 'womanish' as we see in the dramatic debate surrounding the conduct of Antony in Shakespeare's tragedy. The study of the representation of lesbian desire in the Renaissance is only now emerging as a significant source of scholarly interest and is drawing upon evidence from medical documents, diaries, treatises on midwifery and the female anatomy as well as evidence from the drama and poetry. The extent to which female same-sex relations were discussed in terms of physical intimacy during this period is still being explored and debated by critics. Many of the texts which are examined in literary studies of female relationships (such as Katherine Philips's poetry) belong to the period after the Restoration, which lies outside the parameters of this chapter. Unlike *Twelfth Night*, for example, which deals (at least at one level) with the attraction of Olivia for another (disguised) female, Donne's epistolary poem 'Sappho to Philaenis' does not explore this relationship in comic terms. It is all too possible that his male-authored poem expresses intimacy between women to titillate an implied male reader, but the emotional investment and urgent feelings of Sappho are communicated in many ways just as poignantly and persuasively as those found in Lanyer's poetry or Shakespeare and Fletcher's *The Two Noble Kinsmen*. While same-sex relations between women appear not to have been awarded cultural recognition in terms of law-making at least, it is very clear from the writing and jurisdiction of the period that homosexual acts by men (mostly condemned as 'sodomy') were demonised in this society. However, it should be added that on the relatively rare occasions when accusations of sodomy were made in court, they were frequently linked with a host of others suggesting forms of treachery to the state in one form or another – conspiracy, rebellion, Catholicism ... In England, the crime of sodomy was often thus intimately associated with acts of religious and political subversion.

> **Poetry and Desire**
>
> How oft have I, my dear and cruel foe,
> With my great pain to get some peace or truce,
> Given you my heart; but you do not use
> In so high things, to cast your mind so low.
> (Sir Thomas Wyatt, Sonnet 23, ll. 1–4, in
The Complete Poems, ed. R. A. Rebholz
(Harmondsworth: Penguin, 1978), p. 83)
>
> My mistress' eyes are nothing like the sun;
> Coral is far more red, than her lips red ...
> And yet by heaven, I think my love as rare,
> As any she belied with false compare.
> (William Shakespeare, Sonnet 130, ll. 1–4,
Norton Anthology, p. 1074 [A])

Nationhood, Race, Colonialism and Empire

The larger geography of the world was often drawn up by Europeans in theological terms during the medieval centuries in which biblical narratives might form the central interest of maps and 'heathen' populations occupied the periphery of the field of vision. Despite the trade routes established into Asia by earlier explorers such as Marco Polo, the accounts passed down about Viking discoveries to the West and the exotic riches to be found on the African continent, the main focus of English life with its international neighbours concentrated upon the area from the German states to the Mediterranean basin in the opening decades of the Renaissance.

By the second decade of the fifteenth century, the Portuguese explorations of the coasts of Africa and further out into the Atlantic were particularly associated with the leadership of Prince Henry 'the Navigator' (1394–1460). Such initiatives led to a greater commerce in exotic goods such as ivory and gold and the establishment of the European role in enslaving African natives. (It was in 1562 that John Hawkins (1532–95) set out on the first English slaving voyage, transporting his cargo of three hundred Native Africans from the Guinea coast to the West Indies for sugar, animal skins and silver. If there were some condemnation of the trade in the period, it appears not to have prevented even Elizabeth from investing in such lucrative ventures.) In the final decade of the fifteenth century, Columbus crossed the Atlantic with a small Spanish-funded expedition to arrive in the Bahamas in 1492. In the following years he placed Cuba, Haiti and Trinidad on European maps in his search for conquest and treasure. Meanwhile, in 1498 the expedition of the Portuguese sailor Vasco da Gama arrived in India, having charted a course via what would now be known as the Cape Verde islands, South Africa, Mozambique and Kenya. From

1519 the Portuguese Magellan travelled with five Spanish-funded ships in search of a short passage to the Spice islands. He travelled round Cape Horn (through the Magellan Straits) on to the Philippines where he was killed by native inhabitants. The remaining company sailed on past the Cape of Good Hope and returned to Spain in 1522, three years after their departure. While Spain and Portugal sought to divide these new-found horizons for themselves, Henry VII advised one John Cabot based in Bristol (but probably of Genoese origin) to sail north in exploration and thus carefully to avoid giving offence to the Iberian nations. In 1497, crossing the Atlantic with just one ship, he sighted land of the new American continent (now thought to be either Nova Scotia or Newfoundland). He descended along the coast, believing that he had arrived in Asia. In 1509 his son Sebastian set out in search of the North West Passage to Asia; he seems to have sighted Labrador and entered Hudson Bay, but turned back to an England now ruled by Henry VIII where there was little appetite for future expeditions of this type. For the next decades, if English sailors crossed the Atlantic it was with the ambition of cod fishing.

However, as the period unfolded, it became increasingly apparent that the British Isles were no longer seen as marginal kingdoms set on the edge of the map. The growth in the lucrative Atlantic trade and voyages down the African coast began to place these islands (with their many harbours and seafaring traditions) much more centrally in this growing field of commerce. Commercial ambitions which governed overseas trade were further consolidated in subsequent decades with the founding of the Muscovy Company, for example, in 1555, the Cathay Company in 1576, the Levant Company in 1592, the East India Company in 1600, the Virginia Company in 1606 and the Massachusetts Bay Company in 1629. However, the riches that Spain was to bring from its New World possessions certainly stimulated Sir Francis Drake (1541–96) to circumnavigate the globe in 1577–80, claiming California for the English Crown en route and returning laden with looted Spanish treasure and a rich cargo of spices.

In the years which followed, Sir Martin Frobisher renewed the search for a North West Passage to the East and arrived at Baffin Island. Sir John Davis sailed to Greenland and also discovered the Falkland Islands, while Sir Walter Ralegh (1552–1618) travelled to what is now known as Venezuela in search of treasure, and most famously to Virginia in 1583. This latter venture led to the founding of a colony at Roanoke Island in the following year. Many of the explorers like Drake, Frobisher and Hawkins died during their travels to foreign lands. However, when ships did return, they might also bring back native people from these new-found lands – unsurprisingly, it was rare for these displaced persons to survive in their new surroundings. Nonetheless, they remained valuable curiosities even in death and were clearly seen as lucrative investments – as can be witnessed from the servants' responses to Caliban in *The Tempest*. The English endeavours to found an American colony in the late 1580s collapsed owing to a dearth of necessary provisions and medical supplies. Later attempts during the reign of James I to establish plantations in Virginia remained uncertain because of poor management, poor relations with many native communities and the dissatisfaction of investors at home looking for a quick return for their money. Greater success was achieved with those fleeing religious persecution in the closing years of James I's reign, like the Pilgrim Fathers who voyaged in the *Mayflower* in 1620 and established communities in New England.

The term 'race' was used in a number of different ways in this period. It could refer frequently to relations of kinship ('blood') or more generally to genealogy and lineage. Elsewhere, it might refer to individual worth or behaviour, status of birth (and thus rights of inheritance), religious confession, geographical residence as well as, on occasion, skin colour. Frequently, populations of distant lands were perceived either as being savage or as more primitive, childlike versions of Europeans. If English writers and statesmen are found to promote their native land in imperial terms (indeed James I styled himself as the sovereign over the 'Empire of Great Britain'), such claims remained most powerful for their textual persuasiveness rather than the reality of overseas possessions – the 'empire' was made up of conceptual space rather than geographical fact.

Readings

Sir Thomas More, *Utopia* (1516)

Utopia has excited reader attention down the centuries for a number of different reasons and has been enlisted to support the causes of often diametrically opposed political groups. Sir Thomas More's (1478–1535) imaginative and deceptively complex prose narrative clearly invites comparison with earlier narratives of ideal societies to be found in Plato's *Republic*, biblical narratives and classical evocations of the Golden Age. This is quite apart from examples of travel literature and records of colonial exploits popular across Europe in the opening decades of the sixteenth century. Most provocatively, *Utopia* challenges the reader to ponder alternative modes of social organisation, ranging across such subject areas as politics, religion, economics, jurisprudence, imperialism and education. More was targeting primarily, it seems, an international audience of scholars and intellectuals and thus naturally for the period, as we have seen in previous discussions, he wrote in Latin. The publication of *Utopia* was overseen in the Low Countries by his friend and fellow humanist Erasmus in 1516. The work became enormously popular and was translated into English by Ralph Robinson in 1551 (who found it to be a 'fruitful, pleasant and witty work'), and indeed by others into many European languages. Its narrative complexities and ambiguities clearly exercised the minds of subsequent generations of European writers such as François Rabelais and Francis Bacon.

More was deeply involved in the political life of Henrician society, rising to fame as Henry's Privy Councillor, the Lord Chancellor (he was knighted in 1521), and then, equally famously, falling victim to Henry's wrath when he refused to take any oath impugning papal authority or confirming the legitimacy of the divorce from Katherine of Aragon: he was beheaded in 1535. As an under-sheriff of London, he distinguished himself in the eyes of many for his sympathetic response to the needs

2.13 Illustration depicting the Moghul emperor Jahangir preferring a Sufi sheikh to kings (including James I), c. 1615–18.

of the poor in the capital. However, in more elevated political offices, he participated energetically in the Henrician struggle against and persecution of the Lutherans. Much earlier in his career, he had begun to sketch out some ideas for an island of Utopia during a diplomatic mission in 1515 in Flanders. In reading *Utopia* it is important to guard against the common mistake of paying principal attention to 'Book Two', which describes the landscape, history and society of the island. 'Book One' is much more than a framing device or stepping stone for a subsequent travel narrative. In Book One More expertly guides us into an all-too-plausible intellectual world of dialogue, debate and interpretation which characterised the commitment of humanist scholars across Europe. Indeed, More and his fellow humanists such as Peter Giles and Erasmus, among many others, conspired to convince the wider European audience (with letters, poems and testimonials attached to editions of the work) of the authenticity of this account of a distant island – Giles even formulated an Utopian alphabet! These efforts paid off and the hoax had a great deal of success at the time. However, as we read on, we may like to compare the individual inventiveness and the lively intellectual society being depicted in Antwerp with the carefully circumscribed level of debate sanctioned among the Utopians.

The degree to which More blended his account of the island with satirical social critique has been the subject of heated discussion down the centuries, but what becomes immediately evident in the opening pages of the work is the care which is being devoted to the (persuasively) specific details of the meeting with Raphael Hythloday. It may be instructive to compare More's initial strategies (of verisimilitude) with those of the opening pages of Behn's *Oroonoko* which is discussed in the next chapter. In both texts there is an urgent emphasis at the beginning of the narratives upon convincing (or seducing) the reader into believing that these are the accounts of true events. The distinctions between fiction and fact are blurred as we enter the world of identifiable places and people. Indeed, some of the earlier editions of *Utopia* even included accompanying maps of the island.

All More's efforts are being organised to make us submit to the 'truth' of the narrative which will follow: the formal opening with his own title as Sheriff of London; biographical details of his own stay in Flanders; references made to other actual events, such as the voyages of Vespucci; the naming of 'real' people such as Henry VIII, Cuthbert Tunstall, Georges de Themsecke, Peter Giles, John Morton; the evocation of the city of Antwerp; the classical knowledge of the scholars; detailed portraits of the main speakers; and the apparently faithful accounts of conversations occurring between them … the authority of all these elements prepare us to contemplate Utopia later with the same assurance that we may credit the details of the Antwerp encounters. Interestingly, in this Flemish city we are introduced into a company greedy for knowledge of the wider world, but we must never let our guard down in our own journey into this fiction for we are in the company of Hythloday (meaning 'expert in nonsense') and More, or *Morus* (punning on the Latin *moria*, meaning 'folly'), who are talking about Utopia (meaning 'no-place').

Frequently in Hythloday's accounts we are drawn into societies in which many Eurocentric cultural expectations (e.g., marriage, family life, patterns of labour, political hierarchy, patriarchy, operations of colonisation, even shipping design) still operate, even if certain details render them somewhat unfamiliar – consider, for example, how prospective brides and grooms on the island are presented for inspection to each other completely naked. It becomes increasingly apparent that the distances (geographical, moral, religious, legal, political and so on) between Utopia and its European counterparts may be illusory. More (hereafter in the discussion referring to the character, rather than the writer) makes the point early on that some of the customs of the societies Hythloday visits are 'ill-considered' but others warrant further reflection in Europe – the difficulty for us is to identify which belong to which category ... Nevertheless, a spirit of intellectual enquiry and interrogation is evoked in the opening pages which will set the mood for the narrative as a whole. In direct comparison with humanist discussions being pursued across Europe, early on the reader is asked to consider the role of the scholar in the secular world and how the merits of study should be rewarded. More urges Hythloday to share his wisdom with the larger society and to enter the service of a ruler as an adviser. Unlike the author, Hythloday shows himself sceptical about the value of service to those in power, who, he believes, are mostly uninterested in the arts of peace. In Hythloday's descriptions of debates at the house of John Morton we are firmly drawn into the business of cultural analysis, reflecting upon gross inequalities in the justice system, the exploitation of agricultural workers by their ruthless masters, the sufferings endured in societies where warfare is a commonplace, the nature of political sovereignty, and the need to recognise our moral obligations to our fellow men and women. The most famous discussion in Book One concerns the harmful effects of land enclosures upon the tenants who may not only lose their livelihoods but their homes as a consequence of their masters' search for profits in the thriving wool trade. The image of a horde of sheep gobbling up the riches of the nation has struck a chord with readers down the centuries. Strategically, Cardinal Morton is seen to silence the pompous lawyer who wishes to challenge Hythloday's analyses. Indeed, the latter is given full rein to elaborate upon his remedies for a flawed society: he concentrates particularly in this instance upon fault-lines in the criminal justice system, noting that in Utopia penalties are exacted through the confiscation of the criminal's property and his or her compulsory participation in projects for the benefit of the community, rather than imitating the present European regime which relies upon sentences of harsh labour or execution. Here, Hythloday may cite examples from the societies of the Polylerites ('much nonsense') in Persia or the Anchorians ('people without place') who live near Utopia, but most importantly from these very earliest conversations we as readers are being urged to question received cultural thinking and to formulate alternative modes of social organisation.

We must remember that our introduction to Utopia begins in Book One. Hythloday recounts that Utopia is a land of plenty where there is no private property. Neither More nor Giles is convinced that such a system could operate in Europe without eroding the key cultural concept of hierarchy, which they view as the cornerstone of social cooperation and government. Hythloday reminds them that Utopia *is* thriving and that its civilisation pre-dates anything known in Europe. The Utopians had had some contact centuries earlier with Roman and Egyptian survivors from shipwrecks and learned much from them. Thus, with the same cultural influences that

Europe enjoyed at the beginning of its history, the island has nevertheless evolved into a much more complex and apparently prosperous society than any in evidence in sixteenth-century Europe. Suitably tantalised with the prospect of further information about this wonderful island, More, Giles and the reader encourage Hythloday on in his description of the island (in Book Two) – More even implores the traveller not to be brief in his account.

In Book Two we finally arrive on the shores of an island whose population appears largely given over to moderation, reasonable debate and civic obedience. Among this population with its seemingly rather 'bourgeois' fondness for wine-drinking, public service and studious application, we find that there are a large number of urban communities, all divided

2.14 Woodcut image of the island of Utopia from the 1518 Basle edition of More's *Utopia*.

rigorously into households under the supervision of a phylarch (an elected official representing thirty households; every group of ten phylarchs is under the command of a head phylarch). At the summit of this political structure is an elected prince who remains in place for life, unless he displays tyrannical behaviour. Each household changes its abode every ten years according to the results of a collective lottery. There is compulsory agricultural work experience for everyone (apart from certain exceptions such as the phylarchs) – indeed, physical and/or intellectual work appears to be the key to gaining merit on the island. However, only the ancestor King Utopus has any semblance of individuality in Hythloday's account, elsewhere the community has little human specificity ... clothes and meal times and even hours of sleep, for example, are unrelieved by personal detail. Leisure hours are carefully regulated, precious metals are uniformly despised by citizens of Utopia and everyone wears a cloak of exactly the same colour. Travel is closely supervised to ensure that no one shirks his or her labour obligations. Idleness, like the aspiration for privacy, is vigorously addressed and indeed repressed among the Utopian population.

The price of Utopian peace and prosperity has seemed rather high to many readers since the sixteenth century. There are heartening emphases upon the importance of questions of public health and assistance for the sick and needy which would have enormously improved the life of urban communities if they had been taken up by contemporaries. Moreover, the religion of the Utopians appears to be most energetically focused upon practical ethics and the relief of social ills, rather than anything to do with faith. Nonetheless, this seemingly effortless model of social cohesion powered by a class of scholars and expressed in terms of patriarchal authority can appear a rather passionless and unequal vision of what human existence could be. There is very little evidence of individual creativity (or even liberty) or the possibility of innovation. Women are repeatedly viewed as the 'weaker sex' and defined in terms of domestic and familial duties – the most important Utopian women are wives of priests. We are informed that it is very rare indeed for a woman herself to be chosen to be a priest – and then they are invariably widows! It is unclear what mechanism is in place to decide when the prince has become a tyrant. The uses to which slaves and mercenaries are put raise more than a few questions about the moral, paternalist project of the nation as a whole. Utopian colonial initiatives are mostly a response, it appears, to overpopulation on the island; and if natives refuse to join with the colonists and live under Utopian laws, they are driven away. Each generation of readers will bring its own value systems, prejudices and cultural appetites to *Utopia*. In its gender expectations, descriptions of colonial strategies, veneration for social hierarchies, and its accounts of warfare, for example, Utopian society participates in cultural practices widely in evidence in sixteenth-century Europe. Of course, how far the reader is invited to subscribe to these practices is a quite different matter ... The famously arch comment in Book Two that European rulers invariably respect treaties, leaders always keep their word and popes only promise what they are able to perform is an extravagant example of how *Utopia* repeatedly teases and unsettles the reader with thorny questions such as those of social inequality, euthanasia and imperialism, provoking him or her into thoughtful reflection. If *Utopia* offers at many points an acute diagnosis of the ailing condition of early sixteenth-century society, we may find the prospect of joining the regimented ranks of Utopians equally uninviting.

At the end of his account, Hythloday concludes that the societies which 'flourish' in his native continent are mostly structured by the ruthless greed of those who belong to the economic elite. However, More strikes a rather different note insisting that the Utopians' rejection of private property and their commitment to collective living and ownership pose the greatest stumbling block to their achieving the nobility and sophistication of European cultures. At least irony is not in short supply in Antwerp ... Above all, we should remember that More never dismisses the traveller as foolish and his objections (like those of the pompous lawyer at the Cardinal's house) to the traveller's propositions are never voiced – on this occasion because Hythloday appears tired after his marathon bout of storytelling. So once again, it seems, the debate stands unresolved. However, the knowledge that More has been a resisting listener is invaluable as the final piece of information in this intricately constructed tale of competing ideals.

Elizabeth Cary, *The Tragedy of Mariam* (1613)

Elizabeth Cary's dramatic text *The Tragedy of Mariam* has come to be celebrated critically as the first original dramatic work by a woman to be published in England. It was entered in the Stationers' Register for December 1612 and published in 1613; it was probably written at some point during the preceding ten years. *The Tragedy of Mariam* clearly was not written with the public playhouses of London in mind, but rather works within the conventions of a dramatic sub-genre called 'closet drama'. This form of writing was substantially influenced by the dramas of the Roman Seneca which were enjoying renewed interest in the second half of the sixteenth century owing to the publication of translations into English. It is important to note that Seneca's dramas were not thought to have been penned for theatrical performance. They are highly rhetorical in style, frequently focus upon the agonies associated with political dilemmas and are sustained more by the intricate inward speculations of the characters than by their dynamic action. As vehicles for foregrounding political analysis and cultural debate (most particularly that of tyranny and, more generally, of misgovernment at all levels) they seem to have appealed to many of the members of the Sidney circle, for example.

Given the attachment of many of the writers of closet dramas to coteries and noble households, there may be every reason to widen our understanding of 'performance' to the possibility of *ensemble* readings and 'verbal' enactments by members of these communities. More generally, for an aspiring female dramatist in this period (and we have the evidence from her biography written by one of her daughters that Cary loved plays 'extremely') the composition of closet drama had much to recommend it. The often volatile theatre world in the capital (where, it should be remembered, performing was monopolised by men and boys) was regularly associated by its many detractors with all kinds of immorality. The only space afforded 'respectable' women in such an environment might be among the ranks of the audience. Indeed, as we have seen, women seeking to make themselves a focus of public attention were invariably a source of cultural anxiety. Cary's own chorus underlines that the cloistered virtue of chastity should govern all aspects of female behaviour: for there was every reason to equate in a woman a 'common body' with a 'common mind' (Cary, *The Tragedy of Mariam*, III.iii.244 [A]).

Interestingly, *The Tragedy of Mariam* connects with the narrative of Antony and Cleopatra which preoccupied so many writers of the Sidney circle. The drama unfolds in Palestine in the aftermath of Antony's defeat at the Battle of Actium and its principal source material is Josephus' *Antiquities of the Jews*. However, unlike her source material and many other 'Mariam' plays written across Europe during the

Renaissance which often foreground the role of Herod, Cary concentrates most particularly upon female political and emotional experience and upon the implications of viewing political crises from the perspective of Christian ideology. Cary's drama draws its particular energy from a heroine who actively seeks a role for herself in the public world of royal politics. Mariam is keenly conscious that her society will accord no 'public' identity to her distinct from that of her husband: indeed, at the end of Act Three the rather irascible chorus enquires 'When to their husbands they themselves do bind, / Do they not wholly give themselves away?' (III.iii.233–4). Her ambition to participate fully in the world of the court means that she is trespassing into a cultural forum reserved for male decision-making. As a consequence, the narrative begins with the anguished Queen of Palestine believing that she has transgressed in making apparent her opposition to her husband's regime. It soon becomes clear that Herod's absence in Rome has disclosed multiple fissures in the society's power structure and appears to have unleashed all the subversive energies previously held in check by his ruthless government. In the case of the heroine, her finely textured moral consciousness acknowledges the crises brought about by political subterfuge ('How oft have I with public voice run on / To censure Rome's last hero for deceit' I.i.1–2), and yet at the same time she clearly submits to the limitation and denigration of women in her fiercely patriarchal society ('Mistaking is with us but too too common' I.i.8). The heightened sensibilities of the tragic heroine mean that she is unable to stifle the competing voices of personal fulfilment and cultural obligation; and thus is rendered more complex than any of the other characters who inhabit this dramatic world.

In a manner reminiscent of the dramatic structure of Shakespeare's *Hamlet*, Cary's *Tragedy of Mariam* urges its readers repeatedly to set the actions of the protagonist against those of individual members of the surrounding society. One of the first comparisons to be made is between Herod's first wife Doris and his second, the heroine herself. Doris seeks political power by affirming the claims of her son Antipater as Herod's successor. Mariam also legitimises herself as a political player in the dangerous court world of Palestine by asserting her status as a matron: '[Herod] not a whit his first-born son esteem'd, / Because as well as his he was not mine' (I.ii.135–6). As so often in Renaissance literature, in this instance we witness female characters laying claim to significant cultural identities by stressing their relationships with men. Subsequently, Mariam is so desperate to triumph over her adversary Salome that she quickly discloses her own racial prejudices: 'Thou parti-Jew, and parti-Edomite, / Thou mongrel' (I.iii.235–6). Such prejudices are in fact widely in evidence throughout this society which is obsessed with tales of bloodlines and heroic action as a means of legitimising expressions of political might. A very different figure who appears to be wholly the creation of Cary is the mistress of Herod's brother Pheroras, Graphina (meaning 'writing'). This submissive, indeed mostly silent, young woman may embody, as many critics have pointed out, the only acceptable character for female-authored writing in Renaissance society and the only acceptable mode in which a woman can engage in an erotic relationship in this dramatised patriarchy. However, like so many of the feelings, appetites and ambitions experienced in Palestine, this relationship has had to remain clandestine owing to Herod's overt disapproval. In direct contrast with the ways in which the meek Virgilia is greeted in Shakespeare's *Coriolanus*, Graphina's silence becomes a source of anxiety for the menfolk who seek reassurance that it does not signify an expression of cultural resistance: 'Move thy tongue, / For silence is a sign of discontent' (II.i.41–2).

The other two female characters with whom the heroine is explicitly compared are very far from being submissive, silent women. Herod's sister Salome is perhaps the most dramatically arresting creation in the piece. Her irrepressible determination to construct her own sexual and political careers in Herod's absence constitutes a central context with which to assess the heroine's initiatives and value systems. However, Salome's moral depravity, like that of her brother, must not be allowed to obscure the fact that she (like Mariam) is seeking cultural independence; and it must be underlined that her unashamedly self-interested stratagems are markedly more successful in political terms than those of the conscience-ridden heroine. Significantly, it is Salome's decision to institute her own 'separating bill' (of divorce) from her present husband which excites the most extreme reaction to her actions in Cary's narrative: Constabarus declares, 'Are Hebrew women now transformed to men? … Let thistles grow on vines, and grapes on briars, / Set us to spin or sew' (I.vi.419, 428–9 [A]). Finally, in this dramatic kaleidoscope of female cultural profiles, Mariam's mother Alexandra emerges as one of the most irresolvable elements in Cary's narrative. As one of the sole remaining members of the displaced royal house which ruled in the period directly preceding Herod's rise to power, she is eaten up with long-standing animosities and unfulfilled ambitions. She speculates early on in the play how different Rome's imperial fortunes would have been if Antony had chosen her daughter rather than the 'brown Egyptian' Cleopatra. However, her remorseless criticism of every aspect of her environment (including the anguished actions of her daughter) and her apparently insatiable appetite for violence inevitably render her a hopelessly estranged figure and she is progressively placed beyond the sympathies of Cary's readers.

Ultimately, the fineness of Mariam's moral and cultural understanding of the acutely fragmented world around her prevents her from imitating any of these female models. Her role as a resisting subject of her husband's erotic and political government is placed in keen dramatic relief with the subplot centring on Constabarus' concealment of the political rebels, Babas' sons. In the power vacuum created by Herod's absence the emotionally fragile Mariam is repeatedly discovered wracked with guilt and indecision, whereas the male role of political rebel can be articulated, it seems, in positive terms of undying comradeship and heroic commitment: 'Command and you shall see yourself esteem'd' (II.ii.89). An analogous exposure of the radically unequal schemes of gender expectation at work in this dramatic society is also offered in the clash between Salome's rival lovers, Constabarus and Silleus. Here, the anarchic potential of the female malcontent is occluded, if not neutralised (at least for a time), by the staging of male chivalry: 'Had not my heart and tongue engag'd me so, / I would from thee no foe, but friend depart' (II.iv.391–2). Rendering Salome little more than a sack of goods, Constabarus replies, 'I willingly to thee resign my right' (II.iv.361). However, Salome herself has little time to devote to obsolete fixations with honour and reputation: 'Why stand I now / On honourable points? 'Tis long ago / Since shame was written on my tainted brow' (I.vi.281–3).

Despite the rumours of his death, Herod returns to Jerusalem to confront a court wholly given over to conspiracies and betrayal. If we fail to encounter the awesome tyrant we have been led to believe has ruled this kingdom with an iron grip, Cary's often rather clownish Herod responds to his own sense of wild disorientation and the reality of political crisis with a suitably stunted vocabulary of violence. The painful inadequacy of his political and emotional understanding is made clear when he insists that the erring Mariam must be silenced with an axe. Most perplexingly, she meets this fate after being decried in public by her own mother: 'She told her that her death was too too good, / And that already she had liv'd too long' (V.i.41–2). Excluded from the world of classical heroism which Babas' sons are allowed to inhabit as political traitors executed by the state, Mariam's death is finally articulated through a Christian (indeed Christological) discourse of martyrdom: 'By three days hence, if wishes could revive, / I know himself would make me oft alive' (V.i.77–8). The grandeur of Herod's subsequent Othello-like remorse ('I'll muffle up myself in endless night', V.i.247) is rather punctured by his previous 'idle' fancy that Mariam's head might somehow be magically restored to her living trunk!

The conclusion of the play, like each of its individual acts, is voiced by Cary's chorus. If at different turns this dramatic body is found to contradict itself, misread and misrepresent situations and to express simple-minded aphorisms, it also enacts important textual functions in communicating the society's schemes of cultural expectation, in provoking the reader to reassess the implications of the narrative to date and in exciting an awareness that the events have much wider repercussions in the political order and cultural narrative of the kingdom as a whole. Its continuing role in questioning and undermining the moral and political sympathies of the reader at strategic points in the narrative is emblematic of the larger undertaking of this carefully structured and often enigmatic text.

William Shakespeare, *Hamlet* (Written c. 1600)

For many generations of readers and audiences *Hamlet* represents the most familiar point of contact with Shakespeare's work. It was entered in the Stationers' Register in July 1602 but is thought to have been composed in or about the year 1600. Written in the same period as *Julius Caesar, Hamlet* stands at the beginning of the central phase (1600–8) of Shakespeare's career as a dramatist which was predominantly focused upon tragic writing and would include *King Lear, Macbeth, Othello* and *Antony and Cleopatra*. Before considering the dynamics of the play itself, it is worth pausing a moment to reflect upon the difficulties associated with the shaping of the play in modern times. The first text that we have of the tragedy ('First Quarto') dates from 1603 and it has been speculated that this is a text which had been pirated by those wishing to make a profit from the play's success or that it was an abridged version designed for touring. Here, for example, we have the Polonius character called Corumbis and Reynaldo called Montano; and there are scenes, such as a meeting between Gertrude and Horatio, which occur in no other version. The 'enlarged' 'Second Quarto' (1604–5) is about 1,500 lines longer (totalling approximately 3,800 lines) and claims on its front page to be printed 'according to the true and perfect Coppie'. Certainly, features of this text have suggested to scholars that this version may be based on access to Shakespeare's own written copy ('foul papers') which no longer survives. The quarto texts might also be placed beside the version available in the 1623 First Folio which is comparable in size to the 'Second Quarto' but has over 200 lines not found in that earlier quarto. Many modern editions of the play draw upon both the 'Second Quarto' *and* the 'Folio' to yield the most 'complete' *Hamlet*. However, it should be remembered that editions of *Hamlet* that we mostly study would require some five hours of performance in a modern theatre, whereas it has been estimated that the playing times in Elizabethan and Jacobean theatres would normally have been

2.15 Copy of a drawing of the Swan Theatre originally made in 1596 by Johannes De Witt.

restricted to somewhere between two or three hours. It might also be added that even when we are armed with our 'enlarged' texts of the tragedy, we still know too little for many critics about the Gertrude–Hamlet relationship, the sovereignty of Old Hamlet, the processes of political succession in Denmark, the origins of the ghost and the veracity of Hamlet's memory, for example.

Whereas modern audiences unthinkingly associate the figure of Hamlet with Shakespeare's pen, those entering the theatre at the beginning of the seventeenth century to see the play for the first time may not have arrived at this opinion so readily. Thomas Nashe refers mysteriously in a preface published in 1589 to an 'English *Seneca*' who 'will afford you whole *Hamlets*'. The Lord Admiral's Men and Lord Chamberlain's Men performed a *Hamlet* in 1594 and the latter company appears to have performed another version of it (or possibly the same one) which is referred to by Thomas Lodge in 1596. This *Hamlet* or one of the *Hamlets* being performed (none of them has survived) *may* have been written by Thomas Kyd, but the admittedly sketchy evidence that remains of these 1590s productions suggests that they encompassed acts of revenge and violence, supernatural apparitions and a generally 'tragic' narrative. As we have seen in earlier discussions, the writing of tragedy in Renaissance

England was often influenced by expectations aroused by Senecan drama, history and chronicle writing, religious narratives and discussions about literary genre inherited from classical and medieval texts. In the often brief analyses of tragedy by contemporaries we can identify recurring emphases emerging: the portrayal of human failing and social/political injustice; the experience of adversity and dire misfortune by a socially elevated (often royal) personage; the impact of this downfall upon a larger (often dependent) community; and a human environment which for whatever reasons is bound on a course of destruction and harrowing violence. Renaissance critics appear to have drawn heavily didactic conclusions from these spectacles of human misery. In 1591, for example, Elizabeth I's godson Sir John Harington insisted in his preface to his translation of Ariosto's *Orlando Furioso* that tragedy represented the 'cruell and lawless proceedings of Princes, moving nothing but pitie and detestation ... I may boldly say that Tragedies well handled be a most worthy kinde of Poesie ... [enough to] terrifie all tyrannous minded men from following their foolish humours.' Furthermore, in *Hamlet* Shakespeare is clearly testing the conventions of revenge tragedy as it had developed in the final decade of the sixteenth century. He had already explored the possibilities of this bloodthirsty sub-genre in an earlier play, *Titus Andronicus*, as well as allowing the theme of vengeance to take centre-stage in many of his history plays of the 1590s. However, unlike *Titus Andronicus* or Kyd's *The Spanish Tragedy* (pub. 1594), *Hamlet* moves away from the spectacular and often plot-driven narratives of betrayal and butchery to a much more meditative and poignant evocation of a painfully introspective hero who finds himself supplanted in the affections of others and who ultimately discovers that he is unequal to the demands of a corrupt society in which violence is a commonplace.

At the very beginning of the play we are transported to the eerie environment of the ramparts of Elsinore, the centre of a nation on the edge of war. Here, the grave political insecurity described by the soldiers is more than matched by the mental turmoil being experienced on stage in anticipation of another appearance of the ghost. Unlike the initially sceptical and hitherto stoically minded Horatio, the imagination of Hamlet is excited by the prospect of an encounter with an other-worldly presence, most particularly with one who appears in the shape of the warrior-king, his dead father. How far the words of the ghost (imprisoned soul, demonic spirit, devious tempter or cosmic messenger) should be believed comes to preoccupy the hero more and more. Indeed, the later performance of *The Murder of Gonzago* at court (which the prince stage-manages) may indicate that he continues to *re-member* the ghost's words but, equally plausibly, that he needs to 'verify' the ghost's testimony by investigating the new king's reactions to it. Old Hamlet has apparently departed from an 'undiscovered country from whose bourn no traveller [should] return'. He is supposedly 'forbid[den] to tell the secrets of [his] Prison-House', yet this does not prevent him from conjuring up the image of being 'confin'd to fast in Fires' (I.v.). Far from being a repentant soul cleansed by purgatorial flames, this ghost seeks vengeance but only, it appears, in certain respects: Gertrude is not to suffer at Hamlet's hand, he urges. If Hamlet shows himself later to be mindful that God has set 'his canon 'gainst self-slaughter', he is understandably perplexed by this most particular call to arms from beyond the grave when scripture insists that God alone has the power over human life – 'Vengeance is mine, saith the Lord. I will repay.' If the prince is keenly aware of the responsibility of *bearing witness* to the ghost's tidings, he must gain our sympathy in his demands for more time to interpret their meaning: we should remember that the bereaved Laertes responds passionately to the news of his father's death in the final stages of the play and soon falls prey to the self-interested plans of others; the more calculating Fortinbras avenges the humiliation of a father and secures the Danish crown by deftly biding his time on the outskirts of a crisis-ridden nation.

The anxieties and uncertainties so apparent on the ramparts at the beginning of the play are clearly in evidence in the proceedings of the new Danish court where the memory of Old Hamlet is still 'green'. The silver-tongued Claudius works inordinately hard to appease a potentially hostile assembly by insisting upon the reverence owed to the former king, the political continuity ensured through marriage to 'our sometimes sister, now our queen', the adoption of Hamlet as heir and upon his expert diplomatic dealings with Norway. A startling contrast is established between the profile of this intelligent and strategically minded Renaissance prince and his dead brother who appears to have expressed his sovereignty mostly through acts of slaughter. (Nevertheless, as the play as a whole unfolds, it becomes increasingly a moot point whether the present regime's preoccupation with control and destruction is so very different in its achievements from those of the war-like state of Old Hamlet.) In the event, the new king has little need to worry about any uneasiness or moral scrupulousness on the part of his most eminent subjects; not even Horatio or Ophelia express any discomfort about the hastiness of the royal marriage. It is left to Hamlet himself to pursue this theme and to fashion from it an irrepressible psychological obsession. Like some earlier Shakespearean heroes such as Richard II, Hamlet appears in many ways to realise his full emotional and intellectual potential on stage by embracing vigorously the identity of victim. The prince is clearly unmatched in this dramatic world in terms of his acute sensitivities, his capacity for passionate investment and his intellectual sophistication. However, if this is a tragedy of state (as well as a revenge tragedy with a heroic protagonist), the prospect of being governed by such a self-preoccupied man as Hamlet may fill us with a sense of disquiet for the nation's well-being. The play does not allow us to forget that Claudius is clearly a capable ruler even if he is morally flawed.

The news of how Claudius 'popped in between th'election and my hopes' is only imparted in the fifth act and does not appear to have weighed heavily on the prince's mind at any stage. Hamlet's soliloquies (the most analysed performances in the play by generations of modern critics) are fascinating not only for the details they betray about the hero's agonies of displacement and the debilitating violence of his feeling about the injustices of the world to which he is condemned, they may also thwart our expectations in arresting ways: where is the evidence of affection (past or present) which he has cherished for Ophelia? Did he have any hopes of gaining the crown? Would this have responded to his ambitions? What is the status of his childhood memories which gravitate obsessively towards the image of Gertrude and Old Hamlet as lovers rather than parents? Is the prince outraged more by murder, usurpation or the presence of an uncle in his mother's bed? The irresolvable nature of such enquiries has mostly excited rather than exasperated readers and audiences, but it remains nevertheless important to signal that the extended nature of the protagonist's soliloquising is exceptional even for Shakespearean tragedy (indeed it is noticeable for its absence in a later tragedy like *Coriolanus*). Moreover, these soliloquies function as important structuring devices for the play as a whole, establishing the protagonist's changing mental landscape in response to the developing events of the tragic narrative.

Operating frequently as an echoing chamber for the mental anguish of the hero, the Danish court reveals itself to be a place of expert subterfuge, surveillance and, ultimately, unharnessed brutality. The narrative of mental cruelty, arbitrary government, ruthless duplicity and impulsive action which characterises so much of the life of the royal family and, indeed, the nation as a whole is played out in miniature form in the internal dealings of the courtly family of Polonius, Ophelia and Laertes. Like Rosencrantz and Guildenstern, they are often called upon to define themselves publicly in terms of unfailing service to the monarch. However, the destructive results of the role-playing (which they are all repeatedly forced to adopt) is amply witnessed in their many and various fates. In addition, the sobering spectacle of emotional vacancy and moral decline at the court is only poorly masked by this society's fondness for all kinds of ritual (the changing of the guard on the ramparts, court ceremonial, rhetorical performance, cannons 'bruiting', Ophelia's 'maimed' funeral rites, dramatic entertainment, duelling etiquettes and so on) and by the enforced revelry of a king seeking consolation (and perhaps oblivion) in the bottom of a drained goblet: 'No jocund health that Denmark drinks today / But the great cannon to the clouds shall tell' (I.ii). (Interestingly, it appears that Denmark was popularly associated with extravagant drinking habits in the period.)

The visitors to this rather frantic world are the players who are themselves perfectly conversant with the disorders or 'innovations' brought about by 'inhibitions' (II.ii) and well trained in the arts of pretence. Their various performances of Trojan defeat and royal crimes connect intimately with the larger thematic concerns of deception, political corruption, revenge and national collapse in the play as a whole. Hamlet's enthusiastic engagement with them indicates admirably that even the most sensitive spectator brings his or her own prejudices, appetites and ambitions to the business of play-making. Always more willing to duel with words than with swords, *The Murder of Gonzago* answers many of the present needs of the company's new director who wishes to 'catch the conscience of the King' rather than 'smite' him 'in an angry parle' as his father would have done (I.i). In the first encounter with these visitors, Hamlet urges them to summon up once again for his ears the figure of the 'rugged Pyrrhus like th'Hyrcanian Beast' which appears to have marked him so deeply. This dynamic revenger, seemingly crazed by a blood lust, renews Hamlet's relations with the violent past, most especially that which the ghost has just described. The discrepancy between his own responses and those of the Greek prince (and indeed between his own and the impassioned declamation of the player) only contribute further to his growing realisation that the only way he can address the violation of his own family and the ethical decay of the realm as a whole is through violence. The black mass which takes place at the end of the play (with its poisoned 'chalice' and rather unruly congregation) more than satisfies any hunger which the Renaissance (or modern) audience might have for a large body count at the end of a tragedy. With Fortinbras (who may be seen to resemble Old Hamlet more than anyone else in the play), sovereignty is re-established in this exhausted world on the basis of political might rather than anything to do with a divinely appointed authority. Hamlet has finally embraced the calling of a killer, but this has led in one way and another to the wiping out of most of the ruling elite of Denmark. Furthermore, it might give us pause that the prince's final decision to take the life of Claudius would seem to have rather more to do with the untimely death of his mother than that of his much lamented father:

> Here thou incestuous, murderous, damned Dane,
> Drink off this potion. Is thy union here?
> Follow my mother.

> (V.ii)

Philip Sidney and Mary Wroth

The Sidneys emerge as key players in the development of English literature in the final decades of the sixteenth century and into the Jacobean period. Sir Philip Sidney (1554–86), his sister Mary Sidney Herbert, Countess of Pembroke (1561–1621) and his niece, Lady Mary Wroth (1586/7–c. 1653) became important figures not only as prose writers, dramatists and poets in their own right, but as patrons, translators, imitators and, in the case of Mary, as editor of her brother's work; and Philip also made a significant contribution to what we might now term literary theory with his essay *An Apology for Poetry* (pub. 1595). Indeed, there appears no end to the literary talents of the family: Philip's brother Sir Robert Sidney (1563–1626) penned a manuscript collection of poetry (which was only fully edited and published in 1984); and Ben Jonson insisted that Philip's daughter Elizabeth rivalled her father in poetic talent. If Philip's enthusiasm for introducing Latin poetry metres into English verse and Mary Sidney's interest in neo-classical closet drama did not bear fruit in the works of subsequent generations, their translations of the Psalms were much admired by those readers who had access to the manuscripts (published for the wider public for the first time in 1823) and by poets such as John Donne and George Herbert. None of Philip's writing was published before his untimely death as a result of wounds received at the Battle of Zutphen in 1586. It was left to others, principally Mary Sidney, to oversee the publication of his influential work in the 1590s.

It is now becoming clear with such discoveries as Ann Vaughan Lok's sacred sonnet sequence of 1560, for example, that Sidney's *Astrophil and Stella* ('star-lover and star') was not the first of the genre to be written in English. However, the collection, which extends to 108 sonnets and 11 songs, was certainly the most influential and seems to have triggered a fashion for such collections in the 1590s. As we have seen in earlier discussions of Renaissance erotic verse, the influence of Petrarch's *Canzoniere* had become so pervasive in aristocratic circles across Europe that it became inconceivable to write love poetry without enlisting the help of the sonnet form and presenting familiar tableaux from his poetic landscapes: most particularly, the outpourings of the rejected and thus anguished male lover whose imagination is excited (if not titillated) by the experience of pain; the idealisation of a beautiful, desirable woman in hyperbolic terms of golden hair, pearl-like teeth, alabaster skin, coral lips and so on; the accompanying portrait of an unattainable and mostly unresponsive mistress, the *cruel fair*; the transformation of the mistress from an alluring physical presence to an ethereal, spiritual guide and/or poetic muse. Petrarch himself had inherited a rich tradition of erotic verse and poetry of courtship from earlier centuries, but for Renaissance Europe he became the perceived inspiration and model for such composition.

There is every reason to be careful not to impose more modern (seemingly irrepressible) novel-reading habits upon Renaissance sonnet collections. *Astrophil and Stella* certainly offers a kaleidoscope of human experience: the role of narcissism and gullibility in our dealings with others; angst-ridden debates about the legitimacy of erotic desire and, indeed, the business of putting pen to paper; how we may construct identity through the axes of suffering and victimisation as well as those of personal achievement and ambition; the relationship between the demands of faith and our involvement in sexual politics; the ways in which we exploit the textual and philosophical inheritances from the past for our present needs; the competition between political, literary and erotic desire. There has been much critical focus upon the biographical interest of Astrophil/Philip staging his poetic devotions to Stella, who may represent at points Penelope Devereux: she had once been betrothed to Sidney but went on to marry Lord Rich in 1581. As many readers have observed, there is a good deal of punning on the word 'rich' in a number of the poems. Nevertheless, whereas many generations of readers have felt that *Astrophil and Stella* actively encourages us to organise its poetic snapshots in terms of Sidney's (heavily abridged!) biography, there is every evidence that our own modern appetite for reading extended texts or collections in a linear, cumulative manner (searching for developing narratives of characterisation, thematic development and narrative structure) may not have played a dominant part in Renaissance reading strategies. With *Astrophil and Stella*, such 'novelisation' can easily render us inattentive to the competing dramas unfolding independently in each poem and prevent us from appreciating the central importance of contradiction, ambivalence and reversal which lie at the very heart of Sidney's understanding of human desire.

Despite the (comic) arrogance with which Astrophil can sometimes articulate his desires ('I saw and liked, I liked but loved not'), it is as the vacillating, insecure and vulnerable lover that he appears to have captured the imaginations of successive generations of readers. The dynamic moral and spiritual struggle vividly realised in the fourth sonnet, 'Virtue, alas, now let me take some rest', or the fourteenth, 'Alas, have I not pain enough, my friend', create a powerful sense of drama. Indeed, they offer the possibility of a heroic dimension to this commitment to love, which remains unpunctured by the witty self-reflexiveness or the extravagant parody widely in evidence elsewhere in the collection:

If that be sin which in fixed hearts doth breed
A loathing of all loose unchastity,
Then Love is sin, and let me sinful be.

As many critics have pointed out, it is very difficult to read *Astrophil and Stella* without encountering the Protestant grave suspicion towards worldly (most especially carnal) desires and, indeed, any act of writing which is not focused upon sacred meditation. The voice of conscience barks in sonnet 34 'Art not ashamed to publish thy disease?' This is an anxiety which haunts the acutely sensitive and thoughtful Astrophil throughout: 'Thus write I while I doubt to write … ' Elsewhere in the collection Sidney distinguishes himself from later poets of erotic verse such as Shakespeare or Donne, for example, in his determination to conjure up an animated backdrop of mythological narrative, historical referencing, political events, comic interludes and clownish exclamations for his main narrative: 'But (God wot) wot not what they mean by it … ' An account of Cupid's escapades is updated regularly throughout the collection. We are treated to a brief insight into Edward IV's private passions in sonnet 75, political asides in sonnet 30, and a mocking address to a sparrow called Philip ('in her neck you did love-ditties peep') in sonnet 83 which looks back to similar models established by Skelton and indeed earlier by Catullus: 'Leave that, sir Phip, lest off your neck be wrung.'

Mary Wroth's collection *Pamphilia to Amphilanthus* appeared with her prose romance *Urania* in 1621. The published sequence contained eighty-three sonnets and twenty songs, but it is clear that parts of it were being read at least from 1613 onwards in one surviving manuscript version which contains more lyrics. While there is evidence of the thematic and stylistic influence of a number of her family members in this publication, that of her uncle Philip remains apparent throughout. If she is often found to be less given to technical experiment than her uncle, who is more at ease in complex rhyme schemes and varied metres, Wroth is interested in exploring the formal possibilities of staging poetic selves through alternating sonnet structures from the Italian (ending in two tercets) to the English (ending in a couplet).

This collection describes the desire of one Pamphilia (all-loving) to her rather wayward Amphilanthus (lover of two) and once again has often been discussed critically in terms of a biographical emphasis of Wroth's passionate relationship with her married and rather philandering cousin William Herbert, Earl of Pembroke – one of the dedicatees of Shakespeare's First Folio of 1623. It is interesting to compare and contrast Astrophil and Pamphilia in terms of their overwhelming self-preoccupation and their engagement with mythological narrative in the analysis of their mental struggles triggered by devotion to a largely unresponsive object of desire. Indeed, in Wroth's collection Amphilanthus emerges mostly as a rather abstract presence or is absent altogether. In this context we should not overlook the difficulties for a woman writer of writing love poetry in a society which often showed itself hostile to women writing *per se* and had persisting anxieties over the potentially unruly nature of female sexuality. The fact that the published sequence appeared alongside her very substantial prose romance may have served to deflect potential criticism. In the event, it appears that the perceived satirical nature of the character portraits in *Urania* (which came to be seen by contemporaries as a *roman-à-clef*) excited most interest among her Jacobean readers.

Unlike *Astrophil and Stella, Pamphilia to Amphilanthus* takes little interest in narrative or the summoning up of a larger cultural backdrop for the drama of thwarted human desire. The opening sonnet describes Pamphilia's defeat before the combined forces of Venus and Cupid. Whereas Astrophil is often discovered in the (comic) frenzy of sexual repression ('My mouth doth water, and my breast doth swell, / My tongue doth itch, my thoughts in labour be'), the more solemn (and socially restrained) Pamphilia is left to enact a more intimate and elegiac drama of emotional torment and powerlessness: 'Then I alas with bitter sobs, and pain / Privately groan'd, my Fortune's present ill.' Interestingly, Pamphilia's most poignant engagements in the sequence are with the more anonymous forces of memory, nature and night than with any image or presence of Amphilanthus. (Here, we may wish to draw parallels with another patrician heroine, this time in Shakespeare's narrative poem *The Rape of Lucrece*, who, in the aftermath of her violation, directs her mental outpourings not against her aggressor Tarquin but primarily against the forces of time, opportunity and night.) In both instances, we may find that the female protagonists are trying to establish a heroic (rather than a purely carnal) context in which their desires may be dissected: 'If ever love had force on human breast … Then look on me.' However, some of the most memorable lyrics in Wroth's sequence depart from reliance on techniques of apostrophe, personification or abstraction and seek to flesh out the drama of emotional

2.16 Nicholas Hilliard's famous miniature of an Elizabethan lover, entitled *Young Man among the Roses.*

alienation with textual detail ('Like to a ship, on Goodwin's cast by wind / The more she strives, more deep in sand is pressed') and tightly focused imagery:

> Like to the Indians, scorched with the sun,
>   The sun which they do as their God adore
>   So am I us'd by love, for ever more
>   I worship him, less favours have I won.

In such lyrics Wroth creates a vivid drama of rejection by anchoring individual poetic narratives firmly in highly wrought figurative language.

John Donne

John Donne (1572–1631) was a writer of religious polemic and, after his ordination in 1615, he went on to become a distinguished preacher for court and city audiences in the opening decades of the seventeenth century. Despite the high esteem in which his published sermons continue to be held (160 of them survive), it is for his secular and devotional verse that he is most widely known to modern readers. After enduring centuries of neglect, Sir Herbert Grierson and T. S. Eliot at the beginning of the twentieth century returned attention once again to Donne as a poet of major interest. Since that time he has enjoyed continuing popularity among generations of readers who have been seduced by the arresting rhythms and dramatic disharmonies of his experimental poetics and the restless, unpredictable nature of his narratives.

    In general, Donne's poems remained in manuscript form during his own lifetime: initially at least, they appear to have circulated among select audiences (coteries) such as his acquaintance at the Inns of Court where he trained as a lawyer during the 1590s. Most of his poems are difficult to date: if many critics down the years have preferred to have a rake-like Donne writing secular poetry in the 1590s and then a devout, if often angst-ridden, believer taking up the pen in the seventeenth century, there is surprisingly little evidence to support the theory. We have already touched upon the appetite for difficulty which many Renaissance readers shared and, on many occasions, the riddling Donne would appear to have such readers in mind when he puts pen to paper. Quick-wittedness, intellectual flexibility and a talent for flamboyant performance were useful skills for lawyers to have at their disposal and they were sure to appreciate expertise in these areas.

    Donne's verse can often seem rather cryptic at first blush, presenting itself as a kind of conundrum and demanding energetic mental gymnastics on the part of the reader. In recent times, his obsessive poetic fascinations with marginality, failure, transience, transcendence and irresolvable contradiction have rendered him very much to the taste of modernist and indeed post-modern critics. However, the often beguilingly colloquial terms in which Donne establishes his poetic narratives have meant that many critics and readers down the generations have been all too eager to identify the poetic voices in the collection *Songs and Sonets* with that of the poet himself. Such a response can only serve to underplay the considerable potential for irony, comedy, provocation and self-conscious performance in these complex lyrics. Nonetheless, this is not to discount completely the importance of acquainting ourselves more closely with the man in order to understand some of the contexts of his poetry. Donne grew up in a Catholic family, attended university, trained in the law, participated in Essex's ventures to Cadiz and the Azores, worked as a secretary for the Lord Keeper, was elected as an MP in 1601, became Dean of St Paul's, attended court on certain occasions ... All these biographical facts can be significant when considering his poetry because it becomes increasingly evident that his narratives and diction are intimately related to the London of his day.

One of the most striking features of his poems which continues to excite students and scholars alike is its tremendous variety and its unfailing sense of the dramatic nature of human life which is communicated in vivid, almost cinematic terms in some of the lyrics. In general, it is often useful to think of a Donne poem in terms of a script for performance: 'Spit in my face, you Jews, and pierce my side, / Buffet, and scoff, scourge, and crucify me' (Holy Sonnet XI, *Complete English Poems*, ed. Smith, p. 313 [A]). In many of the erotic poems (and in some of the devotional ones), the extravagant gestures, the often heady emotional states of the speakers, the highly charged figurative language and the provocative challenges thrown down to the mistress and/ or reader are both arresting and seductive: see, for example, the opening line of 'The Canonization' – 'For God's sake hold your tongue, and let me love' (p. 47). Donne was clearly deeply versed in the poetry of previous generations, most particularly that of the Petrarchans. Rather than rejecting this poetic mode altogether as some critics have proposed, it may be more insightful to view him as imaginatively interrogating its premises. The legacy of such a tradition is often as visible in the devotional poetry as it is in the erotic verse, as we see in the third 'Holy Sonnet', for example: 'O! might those sighs and tears return again / Into my breast and eyes, which I have spent, / ... To poor me is allow'd / No ease; for long, yet vehement grief hath been / Th'effect and cause, the punishment and sin' (p. 310).

Later in the seventeenth century, Dryden famously claimed that Donne 'affects the metaphysics, not only in his satires, but in his amorous verses, where nature only should reign; and perplexes the minds of the fair sex with nice speculations of philosophy, when he should engage their hearts, and entertain them with the softnesses of love'. The quicksilver wit of many of Donne's poems certainly means that they can indeed lead every reader (not just the members of the 'fair sex') on into 'speculations of philosophy'. However, it is often in the irregular metres, staccato rhythms and unexpected 'conceits' (or highly wrought metaphors bringing together usually dissimilar ideas) that his poetic writing can seem the most challenging and dynamic. Earlier in this chapter we noted how complex patterns of patronage could be in Renaissance society: we have the image of many individuals like writers and musicians, for example, vying with each other in soliciting protection, funding, advancement and/or employment from members of the wealthy social elite. There may be every reason in many of Donne's poems to scrutinise the privileging of the erotic experience of the lovers: it may be intimately linked to the larger disappointment of the speaker's more political ambitions in the wider world of the court and government. Donne's recurring fascination with isolating the lovers from a hostile society may point to the 'heroic' achievement of these members of 'love's clergy', but it could equally disclose deep-seated anxieties about the modest social perceptions and punctured worldly aspirations of the lovers.

Striking a very different note in 'The First Anniversary', the poetic voice famously argues that the 'new philosophy calls all in doubt, / ... 'Tis all in pieces, all coherence gone' (p. 276). Donne's keen enthusiasm for keeping up with what we might now term 'scientific' thinking is clearly in evidence throughout the poem. For Donne, the consequence of such developments was that the perfect nature of God's creation was being questioned and, as we witness in his sermons, he became accustomed to viewing his society as bound on a course of decay. This is not to say, however, that there was no place in his writing for redemption. In 'Good Friday, 1613, Riding Westward', for example, his poetic conceit invites us on this occasion to figure 'man's soul [to] be a sphere': then we are reassured that 'in this, / Th'intelligence that moves, devotion is'. In due course such speculations make way for the larger drama of the soul encountering the majesty of God's grace: 'That spectacle of too much weight for me' (*Complete English Poems*, ed. Smith, p. 330 [A]).

The recurring motif of the dislocated speaker attempting to make a virtue of his ex-centricity is played out movingly in this poem and may indeed connect, as many critics have proposed, with the wider experience of cultural displacement and intellectual disorientation being felt at the time by many contemporaries. This fascination with reorientation and reappraisal surfaces in his poems in a number of different guises: see, once again, 'The Canonization' as an example of this – 'Take you a course, get you a place / ... what you will, approve, / So you will let me love.' The desperate need of the lover for an existence of uninterrupted intimacy may be a desperate attempt to arrest the march of time, to reinstate permanence of experience and epistemological truth, but it also indicates that dialogue with society cannot be suppressed. In 'The Canonization', such protestations are frequently accompanied by strategic punning of the kind noted earlier in the chapter on contemporary meanings of 'death': 'We die, and rise the same, and prove / Mysterious by this love ... ' (p. 47). Elsewhere in 'The Relic', the transcendental nature of the lovers' erotic commitment as well as a witty re-membering of sexual coupling is proposed as the speaker imagines his grave being broken into and the discovery of 'a bracelet of bright hair about the bone' (p. 76).

The desire for control and advancement and the recurring experience of powerlessness come increasingly to dominate Donne's poetic writing; and they can serve as a larger lens with which to consider the textual identities of his speakers. During the Renaissance, Petrarchan poetry across Europe often imitated Petrarch's own model of neo-Platonic thinking in the *Canzoniere*: here, the beloved Laura is seen to transcend the earthly and to become for the speaker a source of spiritual guidance. This dualistic approach which draws clear distinctions between the worlds of the body and the soul appears to have held few attractions for Donne. Indeed, his poetic imagination is constantly excited by the possibility of expressing profound human fulfilment in terms of physical engagement: 'Batter my heart, three-personed God; for, you / As yet but knock, breathe, shine, and seek to mend ...' (Holy Sonnet XIV, p. 314); 'Only thine image, in my heart, doth sit / ... Hand to strange hand, lip to lip none denies; / Why should they breast to breast, or thigh to thighs?' ('Sappho to Philaenis', pp. 127–8). In direct comparison with many other Donne lyrics, in the 'Heroical Epistle: Sappho to Philaenis' we should not exclude the possibility that the harmonious physical intimacy desired by the speaker may also be designed as a kind of witty titillation for the reader.

Elsewhere, the fine-grained sensibilities and compulsive narcissism of the conventional Petrarchan lover are often radically mocked in lyrics such as 'The Indifferent': 'I can love both fair and brown ... / I can love her, and her, and you, and you, / I can love any, so she be not true' (p. 61). (However, in this particular case, Venus has her revenge upon this erotic 'heretic' by compelling fidelity upon him.) It is clear Donne vigorously interrogated the conventions of Petrarchan poetics which sought to celebrate in detail the seemingly unique physical beauties of the unresponsive mistress. Nonetheless, the Petrarchan model of power relationships between the sexes is often left intact when Donne's speakers are found to 'instruct' their erotic partners in what their emotional, spiritual and social ambitions should be. Famously in the nineteenth elegy 'To His Mistress Going to Bed', for example, the beloved is even given advice (in comic detail) upon how to undress, in order, it seems, to arouse fully her voyeuristic lover. Whereas the sixteenth-century poetry of the blazon focused upon itemising the physical charms of the mistress, Donne is here found to stage a kind of 'anti-blazon' in which the mistress is 'un-pieced' stage by stage in a sexual fantasy in order to render her more amenable to his desires. Even poems such as 'The Extasie', with its celebration of superlative, mutual love, can emerge as a fashioning from the male perspective of how the relationship must be perceived and, indeed, experienced ...

Elsewhere, Donne expertly orchestrates dramas of rejection and misogynistic feeling, such as that found in 'Woman's Constancy': 'Now thou hast lov'd me one whole day. / Tomorrow when thou leav'st, what wilt thou say? / Wilt thou then antedate some new-made vow?' (p. 92). Interestingly, in the religious poetry the reader may witness surprisingly analogous anxieties of devotion and powerlessness, narratives of frustration and unbridled speculation. In the eighteenth 'Holy Sonnet' these thematic interests are played out on the broader stage of Renaissance politics. Here, the reader is made to confront the anguished dilemma which has become a central focus of this chapter: the bitter conflict of an age which has fallen victim to competing religious allegiances.

> Show me dear Christ, thy spouse, so bright and clear.
> What, is it she, which on the other shore
> Goes richly painted? Or which robbed and tore
> Laments and mourns in Germany and here?
>
> (*Complete English Poems*, ed. Smith, p. 316 [A])

Reference

A Primary Texts and Anthologies of Primary Sources

Note

Unless otherwise stated, all the contemporary texts cited in this chapter may be found in the searchable database, EEBO: Early English Books Online (http://eebo .chadwyck.com/), available at most institutions of Higher Education.

Aughterson, K., ed. *Renaissance Woman. Constructions of Femininity in England*. London: Routledge, 1995. A lively and wide-ranging resource for further study into this area.

    The English Renaissance. London: Routledge, 2001. This collection constitutes an invaluable introduction to the mindset of the period with excerpts from important documents.

Bacon, Francis. *The Major Works*. Ed. Brian Vickers. Rptd. Oxford University Press, 2002. See also the ongoing publication of Bacon's works as part of the Oxford Francis Bacon series, http://www.cems.ox.ac.uk/ofb/

    Works. Ed. James Spedding, Robert Leslie Ellis and Douglas Denon Heath. 14 vols. London: Longman, 1857–74.

Bevington, David, et al., eds. *English Renaissance Drama*. New York: Norton, 2002.

Black, Joseph, et al., eds. *Broadview Anthology of British Literature. Vol. 2: The Renaissance and the Early Seventeenth Century*. Peterborough, Ontario: Broadview Press, 2006. This excellent volume offers some concise introductions to a variety of early modern texts, including poetry and drama as well as substantial extracts from prose narratives.

Brooks-Davies, Douglas, ed. *Silver Poets of the Sixteenth Century*. London and Rutland, VT: J. M. Dent/Charles E. Tuttle, 1992.

Cary, Elizabeth, Lady Falkland. *'The Tragedy of Mariam, The Fair Queen of Jewry' with 'The Lady Falkland: Her Life' – by one of her daughters*. Ed. Barry Weller and Margaret W. Ferguson. Berkeley: University of California Press, 1994.

Cressy, David, and Lori Anne Ferrell, eds. *Religion and Society in Early Modern England: A Sourcebook*. New York: Routledge, 1996.

Donne, John. *The Complete English Poems*. Ed. A. J. Smith. Harmondsworth: Penguin, 1980.

Jonson, Ben. *The Cambridge Edition of the Works of Ben Jonson*. Cambridge University Press, 2012.

Keeble, N. H. *The Cultural Identity of Seventeenth-Century Woman*. London: Routledge, 1994. Another very informative introduction to the subject organised around excerpts of documents from the period.

Luminarium (http://www.luminarium.org/lumina.htm). A freely accessible web resource which gives some excellent introductions to writers from the early modern period with plentiful examples of their writing.

McIlwain, C. H., ed. *The Political Works of James I* (1918). Rptd. New York: Russell and Russell, 1965.

Middleton, Thomas. *Thomas Middleton: The Collected Works*. Gary Taylor and John Lavagnino, gen. eds. Oxford University Press, 2007.

More, Thomas. *Utopia*. Ed. and trans. Robert M. Adams. New York and London: Norton, 1992.

Nichols, John. *John Nichols's The Progresses and Public Processions of Queen Elizabeth I*. Ed. Elizabeth Goldring et al. Oxford University Press, 2014.

Norbrook, David, and H. R. Woudhuysen, eds. *The Penguin Book of Renaissance Verse 1509–1659*. Harmondsworth: Penguin, 1992.

The Norton Anthology of English Literature. Vol. 1. Ed. M. H. Abrams and Stephen Greenblatt. 8th edn. New York and London: Norton, 2006.

Ostovich, Helen, et al., eds. *Reading Early Modern Women: An Anthology of Texts in Manuscript and Print, 1550–1700*. New York: Routledge, 2004. This collection constitutes a stimulating and wide-ranging introduction to early modern women's writing.

Rumrich, John P., and Gregory Chaplin, eds. *Seventeenth-Century British Poetry 1603–1660*. New York: Norton, 2006.

Salzman, Paul, ed. *An Anthology of Elizabethan Prose Fiction*. World's Classics, Oxford University Press, 1987.

   An Anthology of Seventeenth-Century Fiction. World's Classics. Oxford University Press, 1991.

Shakespeare, William. *The Arden Shakespeare. Complete Works*. Ed. Richard Proudfoot et al. London: Arden/Thomson Learning, 2001. Rev. edn. London: Bloomsbury, 2011.

Sidney, Philip. *Sir Philip Sidney*. Ed. Katherine Duncan-Jones. Oxford University Press, 1994.

Stater, Victor. *The Political History of Tudor and Stuart England: A Sourcebook*. London and New York: Routledge, 2002.

Vickers, Brian, ed. *English Renaissance Literary Criticism*. Oxford: Clarendon Press, 1999.

Women Writers Project (http://www.wwp.northeastern.edu/). A fascinating research project which offers to subscribers access to pre-Victorian women's writing along with critical introductions by leading scholars in the field.

Wroth, Mary. *The Poems of Lady Mary Wroth*. Ed. Josephine A. Roberts. Baton Rouge and London: Louisiana State University Press, 1983. This is a key critical collection for understanding Wroth's poetics.

B   Introductions and Overviews

Barnard, T. *The English Republic, 1649–1660*. 2nd edn. London: Longman, 1997.

Bennett, M. *The English Civil War, 1640–1649*. London: Longman, 1995. An accessible and informative introduction to a complex historical narrative.

Blank, Paula. *Broken English: Dialects and the Politics of Language in Renaissance Writing*. London: Routledge, 1996. A clear introduction to linguistic developments.

Brigden, Susan. *New Worlds, Lost Worlds: The Rule of the Tudors, 1485–1603*. Oxford University Press, 2000. This is an excellent introduction to the Tudor century with particular strengths in explaining the changing religious climate.

Briggs, J. *This Stage-Play World: English Literature and its Background 1580–1625*. Oxford University Press, 1983. A very readable account of cultural contexts for literary study.

Cameron, Euan, ed. *Early Modern Europe: An Oxford History*. Oxford University Press, 1999.

Demers, Patricia, ed. *Women's Writing in English: Early Modern England*. University of Toronto Press, 2005.

Dillon, Janette. *The Cambridge Introduction to Early English Theatre*. Cambridge University Press, 2006. One of the most accessible and informative introductions to the subject for the student reader.

Dutton, Richard. *Licensing, Censorship and Authorship in Early Modern England*. Basingstoke: Palgrave, 2000.

ed. *The Oxford Handbook of Early Modern Theatre*. Oxford University Press, 2011. A wide-ranging overview of all the many and various aspects of playmaking in the sixteenth and seventeenth centuries.

Grazia, M. de, and S. Wells, *The Cambridge Companion to Shakespeare*. Cambridge University Press, 2001. A wide-ranging collection giving illuminating angles of vision on Shakespeare and his culture.

Gurr, Andrew. *The Shakespearean Stage 1574–1642*. Cambridge University Press, 2009. Orig. pub. 1992. An outstanding introduction to the field.

Guy, John. *The Tudor Monarchy*. London: Hodder Arnold, 1997. An excellent introduction to the political climate of the period.

Hadfield, Andrew. *Literature, Politics, and National Identity: Reformation to Renaissance*. Cambridge University Press, 1994. An excellent study of the ways in which literature engaged with the volatile political climate of the sixteenth century.

Happé, Peter. *English Drama before Shakespeare*. London: Longman, 1999.

Hattaway, Michael, ed. *Companion to English Renaissance Literature and Culture*. Oxford: Blackwell, 2000.

Hiscock, Andrew, and Lisa Hopkins, eds. *Teaching Shakespeare and Early Modern Dramatists*. Basingstoke: Palgrave MacMillan, 2007. A collection designed to assist the lecturer, schoolteacher and student in their encounters with familiar and not-so-familiar texts on the curriculum.

Hiscock, Andrew, and Stephen Longstaffe, eds. *The Shakespeare Handbook*. London: Continuum, 2009. This is conceived as a broad introduction to Shakespeare and the variety of ways in which the critics have engaged with him down the generations.

Jordan, Constance. *Renaissance Feminism. Literary Texts and Political Models*. Ithaca and London: Cornell University Press, 1990. This study helpfully places the area of gender expectations in a Europe-wide framework.

Kinney, Arthur F., ed. *The Oxford Handbook to Shakespeare*. Oxford University Press, 2012.

Kishlansky, M. *A Monarchy Transformed: Britain, 1603–1714*. Harmondsworth: Penguin, 1996. A very readable and accessible introduction to the seventeenth century as a whole.

Knoppers, Laura Lunger, ed. *The Cambridge Companion to Early Modern Women's Writing*. Cambridge University Press, 2009.

Loewenstein, David, and Janel Mueller, eds. *The Cambridge History of Early Modern English Literature*. Cambridge University Press, 2002. Particular strengths in this collection on the production, circulation and consumption of texts during the period.

Mousley, Andrew. *Renaissance Drama and Contemporary Literary Theory*. London: Macmillan, 2000. This collection remains one of the most stimulating and accessible contributions to the field.

Nevalainen, Terttu. *An Introduction to Early Modern English*. Oxford University Press, 2006.

Pacheco, Anita, ed. *A Companion to Early Modern Women's Writing*. Oxford: Blackwell, 2002.

Parry, Graham. *The Seventeenth Century. The Intellectual and Cultural Context of English Literature, 1603–1700*. London: Longman, 1989. A good introduction to the ways in which literature and the visual arts can be seen as part of the larger cultural context of the period.

Pincombe, Mike, and Cathy Shrank, eds. *The Oxford Handbook of Tudor Literature, 1485–1603*. Oxford University Press, 2009.

Rivers, Isabel. *Classical and Christian Ideas in English Renaissance Poetry*. London and New York: Routledge, 1994. This remains an invaluable initial introduction into key concepts for the early modern period.

Rutherford, Donald, ed. *The Cambridge Companion to Early Modern Philosophy*. Cambridge University Press, 2006. An accessible and illuminating introduction to thinking and thinkers in the early modern period.

Salzman, Paul. *English Prose Fiction 1558–1700*. Oxford: Clarendon Press, 1986.

Whitlock, Keith, ed. *The Renaissance in Europe: A Reader*. New Haven, CT: Yale University Press, 2000.

Wilcox, Helen, ed. *Women and Literature in Britain, 1500–1700*. Cambridge University Press, 1996.

C Further Reading

Amussen, Susan. *An Ordered Society: Gender and Class in Early Modern England*. Oxford University Press, 1988.

Baldwin, Anna, and Sarah Hutton, eds. *Platonism and the English Imagination*. Cambridge University Press, 1994.

Barber, Charles. *The English Language: A Historical Introduction*. Cambridge University Press, 1993.

Bernard, G. W. *Power and Politics in Tudor England*. Aldershot: Ashgate, 2000.

Canny, N., ed. *The Origins of Empire: British Overseas Enterprise to the Close of the Seventeenth Century*. Oxford University Press, 1998. A very useful study of a relatively neglected subject area.

Cartwright, K. *Theatre and Humanism*. Cambridge University Press, 1999.

Clare, J. *'Art Made Tongue-Tied by Authority': Elizabethan and Jacobean Dramatic Censorship*. Manchester University Press, 1990. Accessible and lively study of the development of censorship.

Coffey, J. *Persecution and Toleration in Protestant England, 1558–1689*. London: Longman, 2000.

Coombs, Katherine. *The Portrait Miniature in England*. London: V & A Publications, 1989.

Coster, W. *Family and Kinship in England, 1450–1800*. London: Longman, 2001. An accessible and economical insight into social change during the period.

Cressy, David. *Birth, Marriage and Death: Ritual, Religion, and the Life-Cycle in Tudor and Stuart England*. Oxford University Press, 1997.

Cummins, Juliet, and David Burchell, eds. *Science, Literature and Rhetoric in Early Modern England*. Aldershot: Ashgate, 2007.

Donawerth, Jane. *Shakespeare and the Sixteenth-Century Study of Language*. Urbana: University of Illinois Press, 1984.

Fennell, Barbara A. *A History of English: A Sociolinguistic Approach*. Oxford: Blackwell, 2001.

Friedrichs, Christopher R. *The Early Modern City, 1450–1750*. London and New York: Longman, 1995. This remains an invaluable historical introduction to anyone with an interest in cities and urban culture in early modern Europe.

Fuller, Mary C. *Remembering the Early Modern Voyage: English Narratives in the Age of European Expansion*. New York: Palgrave Macmillan, 2008.

Gurr, Andrew. *Playgoing in Shakespeare's London*. Cambridge University Press, 2004 reprint. A key study of the theatre-going world in London.

Haigh, Christopher. *English Reformations: Religion, Politics, and Society Under the Tudors*. Oxford University Press, 1993.

Hindle, S. *The State and Social Change in Early Modern England, 1550–1640*. Basingstoke: Palgrave, 2000.

Holland, Peter, and Stephen Orgel, eds. *From Script to Stage in Early Modern England*. New York: Palgrave Macmillan, 2004.

Houlbrooke, Ralph A. *The English Family 1450–1700*. London: Longman, 1999. Orig. pub. 1984.

Kinney, A. F., ed. *The Cambridge Companion to English Literature 1500–1600*. Cambridge University Press, 2000.

Lamb, Julian. *Rules of Use: Language and Instruction in Early Modern England*. London: Bloomsbury, 2014.

Loades, D. M. *Politics and the Nation 1450–1660*. London: Fontana, 1982. Orig. pub. 1974. A particularly useful analysis of the ways in which religious change impacted on the court culture and the mechanism of government in the period.

Lenman, B. *Britain's Colonial Wars, 1550–1688*. Harlow: Longman, 2001.

Marotti, Arthur, and Michael D. Bristol, eds. *Print, Manuscript, Performance: The Changing Relations of the Media in Early Modern England*. Columbus: Ohio State University Press, 2000.

Matz, Robert. *Defending Literature in Early Modern England: Renaissance Literary Theory in Social Context*. Cambridge University Press, 2000.

Nauert, Charles G. *The A to Z of the Renaissance*. Maryland, Toronto and Oxford: Scarecrow Press, 2006.

Norbrook, David. *Poetry and Politics in the English Renaissance*. Oxford University Press, 2002.

Pendergast, John S. *Religion, Allegory and Literacy in Early Modern England, 1560–1640: The Control of the Word*. Burlington VT: Ashgate, 2006.

Pocock, J. G. A. *The Varieties of British Political Thought 1500–1800*. Cambridge University Press, 1993.

Ruggiero, Guido, ed. *A Companion to the Worlds of the Renaissance*. Oxford: Blackwell, 2002. This is a most stimulating collection, asking the reader to consider the early modern period in a wide range of historical, intellectual and political contexts.

Sharpe, Kevin, and Steven N. Zwicker, eds. *Reading, Society and Politics in Early Modern England*. Cambridge University Press, 2003.

Smith, Nigel. *Literature and Revolution in England, 1640–1660*. New Haven, CT: Yale University Press, 1994.

Spiller, Michael R. G. *The Development of the Sonnet*. London: Routledge, 1992.

Spurr, John. *English Puritanism, 1603–1689*. New York: Palgrave, 1998.

Stern, Tiffany. *Documents of Performance in Early Modern England*. Cambridge University Press, 2009. A revelatory study into the cultures of early modern playmaking.

Straznicky, Marta, ed. *The Book of the Play: Playwrights, Stationers, and Readers in Early Modern England*. Amherst, MA: University of Massachusetts Press, 2006.

Walker, Greg. *Writing Under Tyranny. English Literature and the Henrician Reformation*. Oxford University Press, 2005. A key study of literary writing under Henry VIII and how it engaged tightly with crises of political direction.

Waller, Gary. *English Poetry of the Sixteenth Century*. London: Longman, 1986.

Wilding, Michael. *Dragon's Teeth: Literature in the English Revolution*. Oxford: Clarendon Press, 1987.

Worden, Blair. *Stuart England*. Oxford University Press, 1986.

Wroughton, J. *The Longman Companion to the Stuart Age, 1603–1714*. London: Longman, 1997. A systematic discussion which supports all of the areas of study covered in this chapter.

3 The Restoration and Eighteenth Century, 1660–1780

LEE MORRISSEY

At first glance, the period from the second half of the seventeenth century to the latter decades of the eighteenth can seem very foreign to us today. One only has to think of the fashions of the time – men and women wearing wigs, men with stockings over calves made visible by short trousers, and women in expansive hoop skirts, carrying fans – to realise how other-worldly it can all appear. Nevertheless, despite major differences between those times and ours, Britain was undergoing a dramatic process of modernisation during this period. Britain was becoming increasingly urbanised, and London, during the eighteenth century, would become the largest city in Europe and one of the largest in the world. There was a burgeoning consumer culture, led by newly available products such as coffee, tea and porcelain; and Britain saw the development of its political parties (Whig and Tory) and had its first prime minister. Indeed, the entity of Great Britain itself was created during the period, through the 1707 Act of Union between the kingdoms of England and Scotland. The terms of modern political philosophy in English were both developed and implemented in the period, as contractual government went from theory to practice in the form of a constitutional monarchy, with a monarch brought to England from Germany (despite being more than fiftieth in line to the throne). Francis Bacon's insights for modern science – advocating the use of empirical induction and instruments – were institutionalised in the Royal Society (chartered 1662), which sponsored scientific investigation and published the results. The early 1660s also saw the creation of what would come to be known as the Royal Africa Company, which would organise Britain's participation in the transatlantic African slave trade. This involvement would be intimately bound up with the history of the thirteen colonies, many of them settled during this period, on the western edge of the Atlantic, and later known as the United States of America, which itself emerged during the eighteenth century. The early seventeenth-century creation of the East India Company similarly organised British trade with India, an involvement that would lead within a century to Britain ruling the entire Indian subcontinent.

Alongside these developments, British literature acquired several of its most enduring fictional characters, including Robinson Crusoe and Lemuel Gulliver, while their authors participated in one of the most important literary developments of the Restoration and eighteenth century: the rise of the novel in English. At the same time, it was during this period that literary criticism began to take its modern, institutional form, partly through the growth of book reviewing in periodical publications (which was a response to the increasing number of books being published). When read in context, though, it can be seen that the early novels and early literary criticism were addressing, responding to and even shaping the historic events of their day.

Chronology

	HISTORY AND CULTURE	LITERATURE
1660	Restoration of Charles II	Theatre patents granted to Thomas Killigrew and Sir William D'Avenant
1662	The Act of Uniformity Royal Society chartered	
1663	Company of Royal Adventurers to Africa, later known as Royal Africa Company	
1665	Plague in London	
1665–7	Second Dutch War	
1666	Fire of London	
1667	Thomas Sprat, *History of the Royal Society*	John Dryden, *Annus Mirabilis* John Milton, *Paradise Lost*
1668		Dryden made Poet Laureate Dryden, *An Essay of Dramatic Poesy.*
1673	Duke of York (later James II) marries a Roman Catholic Test Act excludes Catholics from public office	
1675		William Wycherley, *The Country Wife*
1676		George Etherege, *The Man of Mode* (first performed)
1677		Aphra Behn, *The Rover* (first performed)
1678–81	Exclusion Crisis	
1678	Popish Plot	John Bunyan, *Pilgrim's Progress*
1679	Exclusion Bill introduced	
1681	Charles II dissolves Parliament	Dryden, *Absalom and Achitophel*
1682		Dryden, *MacFlecknoe*
1685	Charles II dies, James II accedes Monmouth's Rebellion	
1687	Isaac Newton, *Principia*	
1688	Glorious Revolution	Behn, *Oroonoko*
1688–1702	William and Mary	
1689	War of the League of Augsburg begins John Locke, *A Letter Concerning Toleration* Toleration Act (Dissenters can build their own churches and practise in them) James II invades Ireland Henry Purcell, *Dido and Aeneas* (opera)	
1690	Battle of the Boyne: William defeats James II Locke, *An Essay Concerning Human Understanding, Two Treatises of Government*	

	HISTORY AND CULTURE	LITERATURE
1694	Bank of England	
1697		Sir John Vanbrugh, *The Provok'd Wife*
1698		Jeremy Collier, *A Short View of the Immorality and Profaneness of the English Stage*
1700		William Congreve, *The Way of the World* (first performed)
1701	The Act of Settlement War of Spanish Succession (–1713)	Dryden dies
1702	William dies; Queen Anne accedes	
1704	England captures Gibraltar Battle of Blenheim	Daniel Defoe, *The Review* (–1713) Jonathan Swift, *Tale of A Tub, The Battle of the Books*
1707	Act of Union between England and Scotland	
1708	James Francis Edward Stuart ('Old Pretender') tries to invade Scotland	
1709	The Sacheverell Affair	Nicholas Rowe publishes edition of Shakespeare *The Tatler* begins (–1711)
1711	Act of Occasional Conformity	Lord Shaftesbury, *Characteristics* *The Spectator* begins (–1712) Alexander Pope, *An Essay on Criticism*
1713	Treaty of Utrecht ends War of Spanish Succession	
1714	Queen Anne dies, without any surviving heir. George I accedes	Bernard de Mandeville, *Fable of the Bees* (first published as *The Grumbling Hive*, 1705)
1715	James Stuart, Old Pretender, fails in Jacobite uprising from Scotland	
1716	Septennial Act, insulating Parliament	
1717	George Frideric Handel, *Water Music*	
1719		Defoe, *Robinson Crusoe*
1720	South Sea Bubble Sir Robert Walpole rises to power	Pope, translation of Homer's *Iliad*
1722	Atterbury Plot – Francis Atterbury, Bishop of Rochester, attempts to restore Jacobites (–1723) Johann Sebastian Bach, *Well-Tempered Clavier*, Book I	Defoe, *Moll Flanders* and *A Journal of the Plague Year*
1723	Bach, *Magnificat*	
1724		Defoe, *Roxana* and *A Tour through the Whole Island of Great Britain*
1725	Antonio Vivaldi, *The Four Seasons*	
1726		Swift, *Gulliver's Travels*
1727	George I dies; George II accedes	
1728		Pope, *The Dunciad* John Gay, *Beggar's Opera* (first performed)
1729	Bach, *The Passion According to St Matthew* Chambers *Cyclopedia, or An Universal Dictionary of Arts and Science*	
1730		Henry Fielding, *Tragedy of Tragedies; or, The Life and Death of Tom Thumb the Great* (first performed)
1731		George Lillo, *The London Merchant* (first performed)
1732	The Excise Crisis: Walpole tries to lower land tax and increase tobacco tax, almost losing his parliamentary majority in the process William Hogarth, *The Harlot's Progress*	Covent Garden Theatre opens

	HISTORY AND CULTURE	LITERATURE
1733		Pope, *An Essay on Man* (–1734)
1734		Voltaire, *Letters on England*
1735		Pope, 'Epistle to Dr Arbuthnot'
1737	The Theatre Licensing Act	
1738		Samuel Johnson, 'London'
1739	War of Jenkins' Ear	
1739–48	War of Austrian Succession	
1740		Samuel Richardson, *Pamela*
1741	Foundling Hospital opens in London	Fielding, *Shamela* David Garrick begins acting
1742	Walpole loses majority; resigns Handel, *Messiah*	Fielding, *Joseph Andrews* Pope, *New Dunciad*
1743	French Invasion Fleet (10,000 men) for Charles Edward Stuart	Fielding, *Jonathan Wild*
1744		Sarah Fielding, *David Simple* Johnson, *Life of Richard Savage* Joseph Warton, 'The Enthusiast'
1745	Charles Edward Stuart ('Young Pretender') leads Jacobite Rebellion in Scotland Hogarth, *Marriage à la Mode*.	
1746	Battle of Culloden – Jacobites defeated	William Collins, *Odes*
1747	Hogarth, *Industry and Idleness*	Richardson, *Clarissa* (–1748)
1748	Treaty of Aix-la-Chapelle, ends War of Austrian Succession	Tobias Smollett, *Roderick Random* John Cleland begins publishing *Fanny Hill*
1749		Johnson, 'The Vanity of Human Wishes' Fielding, *Tom Jones*
1750	Hogarth, *Beer Street, Gin Lane*	Johnson, *The Rambler* (–1752)
1751	Frederick, Prince of Wales, dies *Encyclopédie, ou Dictionnaire raisonné des sciences, des arts, et des métiers par une société de gens de lettres* begins (–1772)	Thomas Gray, *An Elegy Written in a Country Churchyard* Smollett, *Peregrine Pickle*
1752	Great Britain switches from the Julian to the modern 'Gregorian' calendar	Fielding, *Amelia* Charlotte Lennox, *The Female Quixote*
1753	Riots over the 'Jew Bill', which would increase civil liberties for Jews British Museum opens	Smollett, *The Adventures of Ferdinand Count Fathom*
1754		Richardson, *Sir Charles Grandison*
1755		Johnson, *A Dictionary of the English Language* Smollett, translation of *Don Quixote*
1756	Britain and Prussia ally against France 'Black Hole of Calcutta' – English held captive in small cell, Fort William, Calcutta, by Siraj-ad-Daulah; England takes Calcutta in 1757	
1757	Seven Years' War (–1763) Battle of Plassey, India; Clive becomes Governor of Bengal	Edmund Burke, *A Philosophical Inquiry into the Origin of Our Ideas of the Sublime and Beautiful* Smollett co-founds *The Critical Review* (–1760)
1758		Johnson, *Idler* (–1760)
1759	France loses India, Canada, Martinique and Guadaloupe	Johnson publishes *Rasselas* Laurence Sterne begins publishing *Tristram Shandy* Voltaire, *Candide* Adam Smith, *A Theory of Moral Sentiments*

	HISTORY AND CULTURE	LITERATURE
1760	George II dies; George III accedes	Smollett, *The Life and Adventures of Sir Launcelot Greaves* (serial)
1763	British debt at £123 million Riots against Cider Tax	John Wilkes, *The North Briton*, no. 45 James Boswell meets Johnson
1764		Horace Walpole, *The Castle of Otranto* Voltaire, *Philosophical Dictionary*
1765–6	American Stamp Act opposition	Smollett, *Travels in France and Italy*
1765	East India Company acquires *Diwani*, the power to collect taxes, in Bengal (marking its shift from expanding trade to expanding governance in India)	
1766		Oliver Goldsmith, *The Vicar of Wakefield*
1768	Captain Cook begins first of three voyages to the South Seas *Encyclopaedia Britannica* begins (–1771)	Sterne, *A Sentimental Journey*
1769	Joshua Reynolds, *Discourses*	
1770		Goldsmith, 'The Deserted Village'
1771		Smollett, *The Expedition of Humphrey Clinker* Henry Mackenzie, *The Man of Feeling*
1772	Mansfield, Lord Chief Justice of the King's Bench, rules that slaves are free on English soil	
1773	Jew Bill Riots	Goldsmith, *She Stoops to Conquer*
1774	Warren Hastings, first Governor-General of India	
1776	American War for Independence begins Smith, *The Wealth of Nations*	
1777		Richard Brinsley Sheridan, *The School for Scandal*
1778	Founding of Royal Academy Scottish court rules slavery illegal	Fanny Burney, *Evelina*
1780	Gordon Riots, June 2–10; 300 people killed; more damage done to London property than to Paris during storming of Bastille	
1787	Wolfgang Amadeus Mozart, *Don Giovanni*	

Historical Overview

The Monarchy, 1660–1745: Restoration, Renovation or Innovation?

Charles II's arrival in England (from exile in France) and his subsequent accession as king in May 1660 are taken as the beginning of a new period in British history: the Restoration. With Charles II on the throne, England had a king for the first time in eleven years, ending the period between kings, known by its Latinate name, the Interregnum. In the process, the lineage of the Stuarts was restored to the English monarchy, their position there having been severed by an executioner's axe in 1649. Thus, 1660 saw a Restoration in several senses. Both monarchy and the particular family of the preceding monarch were restored. At the same time, though, the concept of Restoration more broadly was equally important for England in the 1660s.

Historiography of Seventeenth-Century British Politics

The five decades between 1640 and 1689 are among the richest in British political history. The execution of one king, the creation of a commonwealth, the Restoration of the family deposed at the execution, the failed bid to block the next person in line in that family, his tumultuous term as monarch, and his flight to France make for an extraordinarily complicated period. The record of historians on the period – its historiography – is equally dense as well. How one tells the story can automatically, even if unintentionally, align one with one or the other side of events. As this historiography also creates its own context for understanding the literature of the period, it is important to have at least a schematic sense of it too. In the nineteenth century, historians treated the Civil Wars of the 1640s as a Puritan revolution, and the Revolution of 1688 as 'Glorious'. By the mid-twentieth century, Marxist historians downplayed the role of religion and read the same events in terms of changes in modes of production (from feudal farming to early modern mercantilism), and related conflicts between classes (represented, for example, by the Lords and the Commons). More recently, the religious variety of the period has been recovered and reasserted against both the nineteenth-century vision of a single monolithic 'Puritan' opposition and the Marxist vision of an economic struggle. Some have argued that there was no revolution at all in the seventeenth century, while others have pointed to the relatively narrow band within which religious disagreements occurred. An important development over the past few decades has been to see the seventeenth century internationally, first as a war of three kingdoms, then as part of a larger European conflict and, most recently, globally, in relation to European colonial ventures largely in the Americas. There is probably a complicated calculus that could represent the new possibilities of a synthetic approach: wars within and among three kingdoms in which differences among the religious perspectives of the participants reflect and shape differing attitudes towards increasing modernity. By the early eighteenth century, as positions are consolidated and political parties coalesce, the work of roughly contemporary authors such as Defoe, Pope and Swift will create the impression of a correlation between at least some of these variables.

The Restoration of Charles II ended nearly two decades of Civil Wars across Britain and army coups at Parliament in London. The numerous bonfires seen by Samuel Pepys as he stood on London Bridge in February 1660 indicated a profound hope that peace might be restored along with Charles. In this way, 'The Restoration' is the name of a period and of an act that initiated a lengthy process of attempting to address the causes and consequences of the Civil Wars. For the next quarter-century, until his death in 1685, Charles II would provide England with stability at the top of the political system. Therefore, this historical overview of the period will begin with political history, reviewing the monarchy and its relationship with Parliament in the decades from 1660 to the middle of the eighteenth century, precisely because the return of the king to the throne gave the period its name, and also gave a high political cast to much that was written about it from that time on.

Upon his return to England and his Restoration to the throne, and although welcomed after some of the excesses of the Interregnum governments, Charles II ruled without the various causes of British political instability having been resolved. There were still conflicts between the three kingdoms, radical differences in religious and political affiliation and an international chess match of colonial expansion still unfolding. In the twentieth century, almost three hundred years after the return of Charles, T. S. Eliot would argue, suggestively, that 'The Civil War is not ended' ('Milton II' p. 148 [A]). In 1660, the question, in the aftermath of the Civil Wars and the Interregnum, was whether the Restoration could overcome the destabilising effects of that earlier, defining upheaval. As it turned out, new versions of the old debates over the relationship between religious and political diversity would persist and events repeatedly provoked questions over the permanency of the restoration (in its broadest sense). In events such as the Exclusion Crisis (1678–81), the Glorious Revolution (1688), the Act of Settlement (1701), the accession of George I (1714), and the Jacobite Rebellions by supporters of Stuart monarchy (1689, 1715 and 1745), we can see a repeated pattern of concern over the religion of the King, and over the relationship between the various kingdoms united by the Stuarts. At the same time, the relatively peaceable treatment of these issues during and after the Restoration contrasts with their handling in the 1640s and 1650s, leading some historians to talk about this period in terms of a growth in political stability.

Restoration

In the Declaration at Breda (1660) made prior to his being offered the monarchy, Charles II recognised 'liberty to tender consciences'. That is, Charles granted religious toleration, which was the watchword of the radical Protestants who had played such an important role in the 1640s (most importantly within Cromwell's New Model Army). But Parliament was not ready to make such a grant, and in 1662 they passed the Act of Uniformity, which required, among other things, that ministers agree to an Episcopalian form of church government (with bishops running the Church, as opposed to a 'Presbyterian' form run by the congregations' memberships). The theological differences between the Episcopalians and the Presbyterians were compounded by the differences between the three kingdoms that were combined by the Stuarts: Ireland had a majority Roman Catholic population administered by an Anglican settler minority; Scotland had a Presbyterian church structure, and was not tolerant of other religions; and England had an Episcopalian church structure in a country with a substantial number of Presbyterians and Catholics. Parliament's 1662 Act of Uniformity excluded both the radical Protestants (such as the Presbyterians) and the Roman Catholics.

Charles II tried to overturn the Act, but Parliament made it law in 1663. The process basically created a new category of Protestants. Those who refused to accept the new dispensation came to be known as Dissenters, because they 'dissented' from the Episcopalian structure of the Anglican, or English, Church (and therefore from the Act of Uniformity). It soon became clear that Charles II – like Charles I before him (and James II after, as it turned out) – meant to extend toleration to Roman Catholicism. Indeed, although many in England did not know it at the time, by 1670, Charles II had made a secret alliance (the Treaty of Dover) with Louis XIV, the Catholic King of Catholic France. In other words, Charles II had waded into the same controversy that had ended his father's life and reign a little over two decades earlier.

The Exclusion Crisis

In 1673, just ten years after the Act of Uniformity, Parliament passed the Test Act, also designed to exclude Roman Catholics and dissenting Protestants from any government office (except the House of Lords). This law required government officials to swear that they, unlike Catholics, believed that no transubstantiation occurs during communion at church. Transubstantiation refers to the Roman Catholic belief that the bread consecrated during communion *becomes* the body of Jesus Christ. Therefore, the Test Act would require Catholics either to denounce their own religion or to lose their public office. One of those who relinquished their position rather than forswear their Catholicism was none other than James, the Duke of York, brother of Charles II, an avowed Catholic since 1670, and next in line to be king of England. Subsequently, the 1670s saw various conspiracy theories about the religious future of the English state, as people feared that the Duke of York might be an agent of Catholic Rome. In 1678, Titus Oates came forward saying he had been witness to a conspiracy (known as the Popish Plot) developed by the Jesuits to bring a Roman Catholic back to the English throne. It was a well-told story, and, although not true, resonated with the English public, which took to massive 'Pope Burnings' in crowds as large as 200,000 to demonstrate their dislike for Catholicism. Anthony Ashley Cooper, the first Earl of Shaftesbury and a member of the House of Commons, saw this development as an opportunity to make sure that the next monarch would not be Catholic. In 1679, he put forward an Exclusion Act that would have 'excluded' James from the throne. Thus, the political events of these years are known as the Exclusion Crisis.

Three times between 1679 and 1681 Shaftesbury's 'Whig' majority in the Commons passed Exclusion Bills, only to be refused or dissolved by Charles II. But in 1681, the story of the Popish Plot collapsed as its originators admitted they had invented it. Cautious Shaftesbury, who had never pressed his advantage to the point of revolution or civil war, was accused of high treason for his possible role in the forged plot. Acquitted, he nonetheless fled to Holland, an action that did not represent the best defence of his position. In 1683, the year of Shaftesbury's death, a few of his disappointed followers plotted to murder Charles II and his brother James and thereby to put Charles's illegitimate – but Protestant – son, the Duke of Monmouth, on the throne. With the discovery and subsequent beheading of two

The Development of Political Parties

At stake in the Exclusion Crisis were some of the same questions from the Civil Wars more than three decades earlier: what is the religious orientation of the English monarchy? what does it mean to be an Episcopalian and a Protestant church? and where does the king's authority come from? Some of the answers to those questions from the 1680s would have been familiar to participants in the debate of the 1640s, although in the 1680s it is as if the various positions in the Civil Wars had been boiled down to two contrasting essences. As had his father before him, Charles II argued that he had inherited a divine right to rule. Shaftesbury's side, represented most famously by John Locke's *Second Treatise of Government* (written around 1681; published 1690), argued that the relationship between the king and the people is contractual. Consequently in these two opposing views of authority, England had the makings of another constitutional crisis. This time around, though, instead of civil war, England saw the formation of political parties on either side of the divide. Those on Charles II's side were called 'Tories' by their opponents. Shaftesbury's allies were labelled 'Whigs' by those they called Tories. Although this is a crisis involving differences of religious belief and political philosophy, it is a telling sign of the tensions between the three kingdoms that the English political parties pejoratively named each other after different sides of Scottish and Irish politics. The Tories were named after the Irish, and therefore implicitly Catholic, word for bandit, *toraighe*, and the Whigs after the Scottish, and therefore implicitly Presbyterian, Whigamores.

participants, Charles II had exactly the evidence that he needed to make the case that there were powerful forces out to undermine the English constitution, and the Stuarts' role in it. Making that case allowed Charles to secure the throne.

James II

In 1685, Charles II died. Technically, it can be said that the Restoration also came to a close with his passing, although the need for a restoration in the larger sense continued. Charles's brother, the Catholic James II of England (also James VII of Scotland) ascended to the English throne at this point, precisely the prospect that Shaftesbury and the Whigs had found so threatening just a few years earlier. James's actions and sentiments confirmed the worst fears of those who had tried to exclude him from the throne. During his first year on the throne, James appointed Catholics to be officers of the army, in violation of the 1673 Test Act; and, for the first time since the 1530s, he also normalised England's diplomatic relations with Rome, the very seat of the Roman Catholic Church. By 1687, James II had issued a 'Declaration of Indulgence', which suspended all the preceding requirements for participation in and allegiance to the Church of England (such as the Test Act of 1673), and offered the 'free exercise of religion'. The king was offering religious toleration, cognisant of the diversity of religious opinion. But the king also explained in the same document that he 'cannot but heartily wish … that all the people of our dominions were members of the Catholic Church'. In other words, his toleration of religious diversity appeared to have been a cover for expanding the role of the Catholic Church, long controversial in England, but particularly so just eight years earlier, when the country was aflame with 'Pope Burnings'. James II was stirring those embers again. His Protestant daughter, Mary, by then married to Protestant William of Orange (in Holland), joined her husband in publishing a declaration of their support for the Test Act. In 1688, James amended his Declaration of Indulgence and required that it be read in every church one Sunday in May. Seven bishops refused. Put on trial for that refusal, they were acquitted, indicating that public sympathy was not on the king's side.

The Glorious Revolution

In June 1688 James's wife Queen Mary gave birth to a son, James Francis Edward. James II made it clear that he would be raising his son as a Roman Catholic. James's determination that his son would be Catholic precipitated yet another constitutional crisis, with features that would be familiar not only to participants in the Exclusion Crisis of the late 1670s and early 1680s but also to those who had been involved in the tumultuous events of the 1640s. But the differences between the Exclusion Crisis and the Civil Wars are what make the events of 1688 so important that they are often known as the Glorious Revolution. Unlike the Exclusion Crisis, it was no longer just the Whigs in opposition to the monarch. This time even the Tories, defenders of the Stuart monarchy, could not accept James's approach. There was thus agreement across the political spectrum that James had gone too far. But in contrast to the crisis which led to the Civil Wars of the 1640s, the result this time was not widespread violence. Instead, on 30 June, seven members of the House of Lords opposed to James II invited William of Orange and his wife Mary Stuart (daughter of James II), to intervene in English political life. By December, James II had fled London for Kent, and from there to France. Early in 1689, a Convention Parliament decided James's flight constituted abdication, and installed William and Mary on the throne as rulers of England and Ireland, for the length of their lives only. With what was called the Declaration of Right, William and Mary accepted the throne in a ceremony at the Banqueting House in London's Whitehall, the building outside which Charles I had been executed in 1649. (This Declaration of Right became the Bill of Rights.) The events of 1688 are sometimes known as the Bloodless Revolution. But when William and Mary landed in England in November 1688, they were backed by about 600 ships with approximately 15,000 Dutch and German soldiers, and it took battles in Ireland and Scotland to bring those kingdoms under their control.

The Bill of Rights

In December 1689, William's Declaration of Right was passed as an Act of Parliament, and thereby known as the Bill of Rights. One of the most important documents in the political history of Britain, the Bill of Rights was, as its full title indicated, 'An act declaring the Rights and Liberties of the Subject and Settling the Succession of the Crown'. By specifying a series of limits on the power of the monarchy, the Bill of Rights made it clear that government was now to be understood as a form of contract. The monarch could not suspend laws, raise funds or keep a standing army without the consent of Parliament, nor could the monarch curtail the free speech of Parliament or prevent subjects from petitioning it. By itself, the Act represents a new step in the relationship between Parliament and the monarchy, with Parliament newly empowered. Later, and in ways that could not have been anticipated in 1689, the same document would be cited by colonists in thirteen British colonies in North America asserting their rights to representation in Parliament. As far as 1689 is concerned, the very fact that there could be a document contractually prescribing the role of the monarch pointed to another, maybe larger issue: monarchy itself was understood contractually. Succession could be settled by a document written by Parliament. The Whig argument from the Exclusion Crisis – and the radicals' argument from the Civil Wars – had carried the day. The Stuart position which ran, backwards, from James II through Charles II to Charles I, that the monarch inherited the throne by divine right, would now seem to have been discredited. Consequently, tradition treats the events of 1688 as perhaps the most signal event in the development of a Whiggish vision of British history – a narrative of increasing rights and stability.

Succession Crises and the Act of Union

With James II in France, the Catholics in Ireland and the northern clans of Scotland conquered, and with an act for settling the succession of the monarchy passed into law, one might have expected the conflict over the English throne to have subsided. As it turned out, the monarchy continued to be contested for decades to come, though more intermittently than during the seventeenth century. The Catholic side of the Stuart family survived to press their claims to the throne and Stuart sympathisers became known as 'Jacobites' after the Latin for James, 'Jacobus'. And the 1689 Bill of Rights, whose subtitle had claimed that it was for 'Settling the Succession of the Crown', would be revised just thirteen years later. In 1694, Queen Mary died, childless, and the throne was occupied by her husband, William III. Mary's sister, Princess Anne, became the last remaining Protestant Stuart. Anne, however, was unable to produce an heir: she had twelve miscarriages, and five children who died in infancy, the last, William, dying in 1700. In 1701, Parliament passed the Act of Settlement, so that after the death of Anne's last child, the English monarchy would pass to the family of Sophia, Duchess of Hanover (in Germany), provided that the descendant was Protestant and not married to a Catholic. The arrangement formalised Parliament's role in deciding on the next monarch.

In the following year, 1702, William died, and Anne became Queen of England. Her accession precipitated another crisis between the kingdoms, for in 1703, with the Act of Security, Scotland declared its own right to name its next monarch. Although the principle was similar to that defended by the English Parliament with the 1701 Act of Settlement, the likely effect would have been starkly different. Presumably, the Scots would have chosen James Francis Edward Stuart (known as the 'Old Pretender'), son of James II, and member of the family that had ruled Scotland since 1371. Several years of parliamentary negotiations, bribery, and even some massing of troops on the English–Scottish border resulted in the Act of Union (1707), whereby England and Scotland merged parliaments, with the Scottish to be represented in London. It is this new combination of England, Wales and Scotland that made Britain 'great', or Great Britain. In the process, Queen Anne became the first ruler of Great Britain. There was, though, still the matter of her half-brother, the Old Pretender, James Francis Edward. His followers in a court-in-exile in France had already declared him king upon the death in 1701 of his father, James II. France recognised him as king, thus siding with him against William, and later Anne. In 1708, James Francis Edward Stuart sailed with a fleet into the Firth of Forth, just north of Edinburgh, but was turned back to France by the Royal Navy.

In 1713, Bolingbroke, the new Tory leader, negotiated the Treaty of Utrecht, ending the War of Spanish Succession (a war fought in Europe and North America to prevent a French–Spanish alliance on the Continent). Through this treaty, from France Britain secured its Canadian activities in the Hudson's Bay Company, and took possession of Acadia, a section of eastern Canada that then stretched from Newfoundland

Ireland and Scotland after the Glorious Revolution

Contrary to the Whiggish sense that the divine right of monarchy was now discredited, opinion in the rest of the kingdoms did not come around so easily. Indeed, William would intervene militarily in largely Catholic Ireland, where James, the French and the Catholic Irish came together in hopes of launching an attack against the new English government. They were defeated at the Battle of the Boyne in June 1690 by William's larger force. It is this victory that is still commemorated each July in Northern Ireland by the Orange Order in what is sometimes called the marching season. In other words, the effects of this battle are still felt in the volatile present of Northern Ireland. In Scotland, the situation was quite similar. There, it would also take a military invasion to subdue the northern Highland section. The Stuarts, after all, were a Scottish family, and had ruled Scotland since 1371. Just forty years earlier, in London, by executing Charles I, one could say that the English had killed the Scottish king. In 1688, they had chased off another one, and now the Highlanders rose up against the new government. The showdown occurred at Glencoe, where the Macdonald clan welcomed Williamite soldiers but were slow to confirm their loyalty to the new king. Early in the morning of 13 February 1692, thirty-eight of the village's men were murdered in what has come to be known as the Massacre of Glencoe. The town was ransacked, and forty additional people – women and children – died from exposure as they were left without shelter. The message was clear, and Scotland was now to go through several hard years of transition.

The Jacobite Rebellion of 1715

In 1715, after the ascension of George I, with dissension facing the new, German monarch, James Francis Edward Stuart thought that the time was right for his being installed as the king of Great Britain. James planned to invade England through Scotland, where discontent ran comparatively high. Scottish supporters there, such as the Earl of Mar (recently removed from his post by the new king), opened a military campaign in Scotland in September 1715. A small number of troops and horses were raised in Northern England, and headed south, converging on Preston in Lancashire, but their numbers could not compensate for the training and determination of the government's army. The English Jacobites surrendered at Preston on 13 November. The Scottish troops, though, continued to march, inconclusively, against the English forces. James himself did not arrive in Scotland until 22 December, months after the – granted, slow-moving and fairly small – uprising had begun. By the time James arrived, the English Jacobites had already surrendered, and the Scottish had not been able to win against the English troops. So, six weeks after he arrived in Scotland, James headed back to France. In the process, the Jacobites learned that there was a difference between opposition to the new king and support for the Stuarts; they should not assume they could rely on a surge in popular support to carry James to the throne. If there were to be a next attempt, it would require foreign support as well. But even that was not enough in itself. In 1719, for example, Spain sent 5,000 soldiers to Scotland for another attempt at an invasion. The ships were damaged by a storm in transit. With squabbling among their commanders (about whether or not the diminished force ought to return to Spain), the invaders were defeated by the English artillery soon after arrival. It would be almost thirty years before a Stuart would make another attempt on England.

maritime province islands south to Pennsylvania. The Acadians were required either to swear allegiance to Great Britain or leave within one year. (Later, in 1755, Britain would revisit this same question, forcing out thousands of Acadians; many of them headed south, to French Louisiana, where they came to be known as Cajuns). From Spain, Britain acquired Gibraltar and Minorca, and also a concession – the *Asiento* – allowing access to the lucrative slave trade to Spanish colonies. Settling this foreign entanglement seemed to leave Bolingbroke in a very strong position, with Queen Anne favourably disposed to him and his party, the Tories. But in 1714 Queen Anne died, and although she had believed that James Francis Edward Stuart ought to be the next in line, the 1701 Act of Settlement was clear: the next monarch must be Protestant. And James Francis Edward Stuart was not about to renounce Catholicism. So, George, Prince Elector of Hanover, son of Sophia, was crowned King of Great Britain and Ireland, although he was fifty-seventh in line genealogically, and spoke no English, only German. The Tories demonstrated against him on his arrival, which, among other things, meant that they did not endear themselves to the new king.

The South Sea Bubble Bursts and Walpole Rises

The South Sea Bubble takes its name from the 1720 collapse of the South Sea Company, which had been created in 1711 to trade in the South Seas, largely to the ports of the Spanish colonies in the New World. The motivation for the Company's charter involved the possibility that it could be a new source of revenue for the government and maybe a counterbalance to the Bank of England (1694) and the East India Company (1600). Some of the Company's revenues were to be used to pay down the national debt. The presumption was that Britain would be successful in the War of Spanish Succession and that the South Sea Company would have a monopoly advantage on the Spanish *Asiento*, giving it access to slave-trading in Spanish ports. However, the war dragged on and the Treaty of Utrecht was not signed until 1713, delaying the Company's operations. In anticipation of future profits, the Company raised money by taking on government bonds in exchange for company stock. Unfortunately, though, the future profits did not materialise. The Company did not make any shipments until 1717, and soon tensions between the Spanish and the English meant that port authorities in the New World were not necessarily recognising the South Sea Company's claim to the *Asiento*. The result was that the Company was shipping slaves to these ports, and, in some cases, unable to bring them ashore legally, was basically dumping them on the coast to fend for themselves. Convinced that the Company would soon turn the corner, investors lined up to purchase its shares. In the process, the South Sea Company became more of a stock-printing organisation than a trading company in the usual sense. It tried to keep pace with, and stimulate, demand for its stock, as prices shot up. Between January and June 1720, the value of South Sea Company stock rose from £128 to more than £1,000. Eventually, some started to believe that the Company's future performance could not justify such a valuation, and a few sold. A broad sell-off began, the price collapsed, and bankruptcies followed. Some investors lost as much as £50,000, at a time when a family could live well on a few hundred pounds annually. The person who was able to devise a solution that stemmed the bleeding and restored confidence was Robert Walpole, who managed to get the Bank of England and the East India Company to take over £9 million in South Sea stock. By the end of the year, South Sea stock was back up to £200. And Walpole was on his way to becoming Britain's first *de facto* prime minister.

The Last Jacobite Rebellion

In August 1745, the Young Pretender, Charles Stuart, son of James Francis Edward Stuart, the Old Pretender, and grandson of James II, arrived in Scotland to mount another Jacobite rebellion. On the way to Scotland, the British navy had engaged the Jacobite fleet, separating Charles from the guns and swords with which he had intended to pursue his cause. Charles was able to pull together a thousand supporters for an attack on England. Somehow, in September 1745 that small force was able to defeat the Scottish army at Prestonpans, outside Edinburgh. Charles had retaken the capital of Scotland for the Stuarts. After a debate over strategy at Holyrood Palace in Edinburgh, Charles decided that the campaign – now bolstered by several thousand more Scottish troops – ought to head south, quickly. Soon, the Jacobites had taken a series of northern English cities, including Manchester – without firing a shot. By December, the Jacobites had arrived within about 130 miles of London, and were faced with a decision: press on, hoping that support would materialise, take the capital and achieve a new Restoration; or see their quick march as something like a trap, as they could soon be surrounded by English forces. Only Charles voted for pressing on. The retreat north began. The French, who had begun to mobilise support, decided not to sail. Tories, who had begun to think that this might be the moment

Robert Walpole: First and Longest-Serving Prime Minister

In the 1720s, Robert Walpole brought an important measure of political and financial stability to Britain, which is surprising given his tumultuous history in public until then. Secretary of War and MP, Walpole was impeached for corruption, found guilty, and expelled from Parliament in 1712, only to be re-elected by his constituents in 1713. Chancellor of the Exchequer in 1715, he had resigned from the Cabinet by 1717, only to be reappointed in 1719. In that year, Walpole had brokered a peace between King George I and the Prince of Wales, the future George II. This truce brought King and Prince together, and Walpole back into the Cabinet. It was in this capacity, and also with this insider knowledge and proximity, that Walpole was able to respond to the South Sea Bubble of 1720 (see Figure 3.1 and 'South Sea Bubble' in 'Historical Overview', above). Something like an early version of a stock market crash, the South Sea Bubble wiped out vast amounts of wealth. Walpole was able to understand and describe what had happened in terms that reassured his audience both in Parliament and among investors. He was also able to protect some influential people from prosecution. He became, consequently, invaluable to both Parliament and the king. From 1721, with his appointment as the First Lord of the Treasury, until his resignation in 1742 he would be de facto the first prime minister (and after 1732 the first person in such a position to occupy 10 Downing Street). Strictly speaking, the position of prime minister did not exist yet, nor did its name. But Walpole fulfilled its function. A country squire from Norfolk, Walpole naturally represented landed interests; married to the daughter of a city merchant, he also understood the needs of London business. A Whig pragmatist, he was able to balance both sets of interests, while still maintaining a Whig defence of the Glorious Revolution, Hanoverian succession, religious toleration and an extravagant consumerist pursuit of pleasure. The country squire from Norfolk built himself one of the largest homes in England, Houghton Hall, and spared no expense on his lavish entertainments for himself and his guests. In the process, he contributed to the political – or perhaps more accurately government – stability Britain would enjoy through the middle of the eighteenth century. Of course, that stability would also be a source of great frustration, as the Tories were a party out of power for four decades, thanks in part to the powerful political legacy Walpole was able to build over his two decades in power.

for a Jacobite return, stood down as well. By April 1746, Charles had retreated as far as Culloden, in Scotland. There, for the first time, the Hanoverian troops defeated the Jacobites. It was decisive. Sloppy Jacobite strategy and a new technology – the bayonet – on the Hanoverian side combined for a lopsided loss. Charles literally fled the battlefield, making his way back to France disguised as his own maid.

With the failure of the 1745 Jacobite Rebellion, the Jacobite cause was lost, permanently: the question of the British monarchy had finally been settled. The period of the Restoration ended with the death of Charles II, the Stuart who had been restored to the English throne in 1660. But in a larger political sense, Britain was haunted for the next six decades by an attempt at a new Restoration. To the extent that any of the Stuarts – James II, the Old Pretender, or the Young Pretender – were able to mobilise any support for their position, all the same questions recurred across this time period, long after the end of the Restoration *per se*. Who is really the king? How can his status be known? Where does legitimacy come from? What is the role of religion in Great Britain? What is to be the political relationship between the three kingdoms? How will the continental powers try to intervene in Britain? By 1746, though, at least one such question had been answered: there would not be a Restoration after 1688.

3.1 Hogarth, *The South Sea Scheme* (1721). With Trade asleep in the lower right corner, Honesty is beaten on a broken wheel of Fortune, and Honour is flogged to the right, while ministers and priests gamble (lower left corner). Inscription on Wren's monument to Fire of London has been changed: now, the South Sea has destroyed the City.

Social and Cultural History

Introduction

With so many British political institutions and arrangements tracing their origins to the eighteenth century, several generations of historians have understood the period as a smaller version of modern Great Britain – well-organised, developing, expanding and trading. Pointing to the Enlightenment, historians have shown how the emergence of modern science combined with an early consumer culture to spread a wide range of material benefits to a growing cross-section of the population. For some, the first third of the eighteenth century is known as the Augustan Age, a comparison between early eighteenth-century Britain and the early Roman empire, when, under Augustus, authors such as Horace, Ovid and Virgil wrote some of Rome's most important works. For others, the circulation of information in periodicals and in public spaces such as coffee houses makes the eighteenth century seem representative of modernity itself. Most influential in this vision of the eighteenth century is the work of twentieth-century German philosopher Jürgen Habermas, who sees in early eighteenth-century London an early modern 'public sphere' ('The Public Sphere' [B]). It is a different picture, however, when we look at the social circumstances of eighteenth-century Britain. Britain's involvement in transatlantic slave-trading and allowing slavery within its own borders make it difficult to see eighteenth-century Britain as having the best possible public sphere. The fact that, according to Joseph Massie's 1759 survey, one-half of the English lived on less than £23 a year while there were ten families who had incomes of at least £27,000 a year suggests a country much more late feudal than early modern. And the persistence of popular, regular Sunday attendance at church is at odds with the secularising implications associated with Enlightenment rationalism.

Because they seem to undermine the picture of an enlightened, august, modern eighteenth-century Britain, and suggest an eighteenth-century Britain tied to the traditions of the past rather than contributing to the important innovations that would shape its future, the statistics of eighteenth-century British social history can accidentally involve us in debates over how to understand the period more generally. The progressive vision of increasing stability and democratic access is known as the 'Whig' view of history: the countervailing focus on persistence of older traditions, or the continuing importance of religion, is sometimes considered a 'Tory' vision. Although these two sides of eighteenth-century historiography are often in conflict over which of them provides the more complete, accurate and significant picture of the time, in fact both sides are plausible, because there was a confusing interplay of the old and the new in the eighteenth century. If there had not been a dramatic need for them, several of the changes that unfolded during the eighteenth century would not have been so important. In the eighteenth century, infant mortality (the percentage of babies who die before the end of their first year) was running at approximately 20 per cent and something like 30 per cent died before turning five years old. With life expectancy in the early thirties in the first third of the century, most parents would not live to see their children grow up. In such a context, even small scientific improvements could have a significant impact. So even as this section mentions progressive social and cultural developments in Britain during the period, it is important to remember that these changes took place within a society that would nonetheless strike us today as more agricultural and more medieval than modern.

Agriculture

Although Britain would become increasingly urban during the period (and occupations would begin to change accordingly), agriculture employed the most people during the eighteenth century, a fact with significant consequences for how life was lived during the period, both in the rural areas and in the growing city of London. Around 1700, it is estimated, approximately 50 per cent of the population was employed in agriculture. Over the course of the century, farming increasingly occurred on large farms. English inheritance laws helped prevent family farms from splitting into smaller pieces, but there was also a decades-long process of land enclosure in the eighteenth century. Initially done through individual land acquisition and then agreements between neighbouring owners, this process of combining open fields into new, much larger farms really took off in the second half of the century with parliamentary Enclosure Acts. The consequences of enclosure were far-reaching. It is estimated that after 1750, 24 per cent of the land in England and Wales was affected by enclosure. In 'The Deserted Village' (1770), Oliver Goldsmith painted a picture of rural England passing away: 'Sweet smiling village, loveliest of the lawn, / Thy sports are fled, and all thy charms withdrawn' (*Norton Anthology*, p. 2485 [A]). During the 1760s poor rates did shoot up, probably reflecting the effects of displacing small farmers from their traditional, subsistence farms. Others see enclosure as part of a longer process of improving agriculture that goes back to the sixteenth century. For example, the larger farms made it easier to rotate crops and avoid depleting the soil. From the seventeenth to the eighteenth century, there is a shift from the small, independent farmer to the larger tenant farmer; consequently, there is a new need for distribution, transportation and merchandising the products of the larger, eighteenth-century farm. It may also be that the Enclosure Acts contributed to Britain's urbanisation, not only in that fewer workers would be needed for more modern farming, but also in the new interconnections the farming represented. A country that had 50 per cent of the population in farming at the turn of the eighteenth century had two-thirds of its population in wage-earning jobs by 1800. Still, there was extraordinary money to be made from the land. The wealthiest landowners – who leased to farmers, who in turn hired farm workers, sometimes daily, sometimes annually – could take in anything from £10,000 to £50,000 per year. There may have been fewer than two hundred noble families with 10,000 acres, able to bring in the upper end of that spectrum in annual revenue. Beneath this level were the gentry, maybe 15,000 families whose smaller acreage could bring in somewhere between £2,000 and £10,000 a year.

London's Restorations

Within a few years of the Restoration, London suffered extraordinary devastation: a plague in 1665 and a massive fire in 1666. It is estimated that at least 100,000 people died in the Plague of 1665, or approximately one out of every six Londoners, a total equal to the combined populations of the next several largest towns in England at the time. It may be that the later Fire helped to suppress the Plague, which had by then already begun to subside, but that did not much ease the blow levelled by the Fire's destructive power. For four days in early September 1666, from Sunday 2 until Wednesday 5, medieval London – 'the City' – burned out of control. Four hundred streets, 13,000 houses, nearly ninety parish churches, and the Royal Exchange were among the structures completely destroyed by the Fire. Other structures, such as St Paul's Cathedral, some of the city's gates, and the Inner Temple (one of the Inns of Court in which lawyers were housed and trained) were significantly damaged. More than 100,000 people were left homeless, and approximately 430 acres were affected. At the time, the Fire, devastating though it clearly must have been, was taken as both a symbol and an opportunity. Symbolically, it seemed to represent the possibility of a new, second restoration – a physical restoration to accompany and complete the prior political Restoration.

While some of London was being rebuilt to a plan, an equally important if much more haphazard development of London unfolded across the Restoration and eighteenth century: London was booming. By the eighteenth century, it was pioneering what is today known as urban sprawl. 'It is the disaster of London … that it is thus stretched out in buildings, just at the pleasure of every builder, or undertaker of buildings … whether for trade or otherwise; and this has spread the face of it in a most straggling, confused manner, out of all shape, uncompact, and unequal', Daniel Defoe fretted in *A Tour Through the Whole Island of Great Britain* (1724; I:314–15[A]). It was a horizontal city, spreading its streets into what had hitherto been farmland. Around plots of this fertile land, London developers created a new form of up-market

3.2 Canaletto, view of St Paul's Cathedral, façade (c. 1747).

urban living, as a multi-storeyed residential form built around new parks serving as central 'squares' became established. This new, eighteenth-century type of domestic architecture was called a 'town house', because it was built for the wealthy landowners who would come to London from the country for the annual 'Season', generally from November to June.

Bloomsbury and Grosvenor Squares, among the most famous of these town house developments, were both completed in the first few decades of the eighteenth century. 'And', Defoe asked, 'how much farther it may spread, who knows? New squares, and new streets rising up every day to such a prodigy of buildings, that nothing in the world does, or ever did, equal it' (p. 314). Actually, Defoe has answered his own question: by the middle of the eighteenth century, the result of London's growth was a city among the largest and most populous the world had known. At the time, only Constantinople (Istanbul), Peking (Beijing) and Edo (Tokyo) might have been bigger than London. And London's dominance of England was even more outsized. In 1500, London's population 'equaled that of the six largest provincial towns put together; by 1680 it exceeded the *sixty* largest' (Porter, *London*, p. 131 [Civ]).

3.3 Hogarth, *Harlot's Progress*, Plate I (1732). Arriving from York, a country girl is welcomed to London by a procuress and a lecherous older man, while the country parson looks away. Front right, the girl's 'goose is cooked'; front left, there is going to be a 'fall'.

Urbanisation and Interconnection

Between 1700 and 1800, England's population nearly doubled, from 5.4 to 9.2 million, although it is important to note that most of that growth occurred in the second half of the eighteenth century. (Indeed, life expectancy actually *fell* from 37 to 33 between the first and the fourth decades of the century.) Even as London grew, the country became increasingly urbanised, as other cities around England increased in size and became more closely connected by transportation systems as well. In 1650 only 8.8 per cent of the British population lived in cities with 10,000 or more inhabitants; between 1650 and 1750, that percentage practically doubled, to 16.7 per cent (De Vries, pp. 36, 38 [Civ]). Bath's population grew from 3,000 in 1700 to 35,000 in 1800. Cities in the Midlands and North, such as Birmingham, Leeds, Manchester and Sheffield, tripled in population from 1700 to the 1770s. As Britain's urbanisation grew in the late eighteenth and nineteenth centuries, so did new service-related jobs. Transportation and lodging, for example, both increased. In this way, canals and turnpikes are the most important manifestations of the integration of the British economy. Turnpikes were a form of toll road, the fees for which meant better construction and regular maintenance, and therefore higher speeds and greater comfort in travel. The first turnpike road was begun in 1693; by 1700 there were 519. Travel times fell dramatically, more in fact between the 1730s and the 1750s than at any point prior to the development of the railways. Consequently, Britain became more interconnected. In 1680, there were coaches

3.4 Hogarth, *Idle Prentice Executed at Tyburn* (1747). With fruit, drink and a viewing gallery, executions at Tyburn were popular spectacles. Note the skeletons Hogarth hangs on the frame.

from London to 88 towns daily; by 1715, that number had risen to more than 200. A similar increase in the miles of canals – from 700 in 1660 to 2,200 in 1790 – had a complementary integrative effect. The products of Britain's regionally differentiated economies could now be shipped across the country to new markets, serving the newly urbanising locales.

With urbanisation came other service institutions of modernity: libraries, hospitals, schools and museums. London's Guy's Hospital opened in 1726, its Foundling Hospital in 1741, the British Museum in 1753, and Library Societies in Leeds, Bristol, Bradford and Hull in 1768, 1773, 1774 and 1775, respectively. However, it is important (although perhaps not as easy or pleasant), therefore, to remember how squalid eighteenth-century cities would seem to us today. In London, the streets were covered in a layer of composting filth so deep that women wearing heels would find it dangerous to walk. The water was piped under those same filthy streets in wooden tubes that leaked fresh water out and pulled seepage back in about every 7 feet. And executions were staged in public, on a gallows with stadium bleachers at Tyburn (near today's Marble Arch) as they had been since the twelfth century. The convicted were paraded through the streets of London on their way to Tyburn. By the end of the eighteenth century, there were nearly two hundred crimes that were punishable by death. (Similarly, cows were marched through the streets to slaughterhouses in central London.) Dogs 'baiting' or attacking confined bulls provided popular entertainment, and cockfights were both common and popular. It was, in other words, not simply an august age.

Consumer Culture

With its growth, London came to contain great extremes of wealth and poverty, from the city's 'Gin Lanes', memorialised in Hogarth's famous print (see Figure 3.5), to the pleasure gardens on the south bank of the Thames, such as Vauxhall and Ranelagh (see

3.5 Hogarth, *Gin Lane* (1751). The city collapses, a child dies, and possessions are pawned, all in pursuit of gin. The Gin Act is passed weeks after Hogarth publishes this print.

3.6 Ranelagh Gardens, interior.

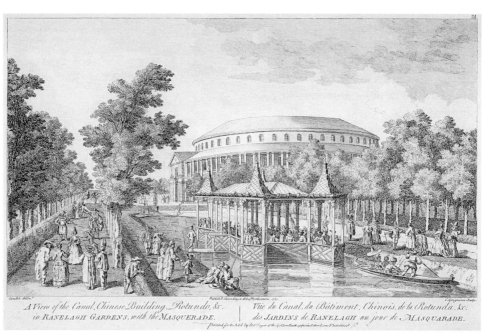

3.7 Ranelagh Gardens, exterior.

Figures 3.6 and 3.7). For some historians, what tied these seemingly different sides together is an emerging 'consumer culture', devoted to the buying and selling of leisure goods and services to a degree never seen before. To this way of thinking, Mandeville's *Fable of the Bees* (1714) provides the era's key equation in its subtitle: 'Private Vices, Public Benefits'. Using the vast volume of filth that lay in the London streets as his example, Mandeville argues, 'what offends … is the result of the plenty' that traverses those streets. As bothersome as that filth might be, clean streets would be a more important problem, because they would represent a lack of commercial activity and material goods. Historian John Brewer and others point to print advertisements, fashions in clothing, Josiah Wedgwood's porcelain and, even, shaving to show the relationship between marketing and modernity. Class, of course, played a role within this consumer culture. In mid-eighteenth-century London, at the lowest end of the socio-economic scale, the consumer product of choice was gin, an alcoholic beverage distilled from grain. Between 1720 and 1750, gin consumption exploded, as it was sold from wheelbarrows in the streets, individual homes, even through pipes from bar to street. In 1730, such gin consumption as was recorded totalled 6,658,788 gallons; by 1750, that figure had topped 11 million gallons. The Gin Act, passed in June 1751 – just four months after Hogarth published *Gin Lane* – limited who could sell gin, and thereby cut consumption dramatically.

Towards the other end of the class spectrum, London was developing what we might call an entertainment and tourist industry. During the summer months, at Vauxhall and Ranelagh, patrons could wander across paved paths through gardens, listening to music, seeing and being seen, and enjoying a cross between a semi-permanent carnival and the London equivalent of a casual evening *passeggiata* (or 'promenade'). Before the completion of the Westminster and Blackfriars Bridges (1750 and 1769, respectively), both parks were accessible only by boat, which no doubt added to the visitors' sense of being transported to another place. Vauxhall featured regularly arranged paths (the further ends of which were suggestively and suspiciously dark); Ranelagh, by contrast, included a huge circular indoor space, 150 feet across, with a bandstand in the middle and box seats all the way around; outside, there was a 'canal' with gondolas on it. Samuel Johnson went there regularly, and the young Mozart visited during his stay in London in the 1760s.

In Twickenham, the same other-worldly effect took hold as authors Alexander Pope and Horace Walpole each developed stylised homes on riverfront sites. In Pope's case, he designed an Italianate, symmetrical building, which he thought of as his villa. On the reverse of the translations of Homer that would make it possible for him to afford this new home, he sketched his design. A few years later, Horace Walpole arrived and rented a home neighbouring Pope's. By the late 1740s, Walpole and a group of friends he called the 'Committee of Taste' had begun to transform that house into a playful set of variations on medieval architectural themes. In the change from Pope's to Walpole's homes, it is possible to see, at least from this vantage point, the beginning of a shift away from a neo-classical aesthetic and towards the fragmentary cragginess preferred by the Romantic sublime. The possible lessons of these homes were not lost on contemporaries, and, not long after Walpole's home, Strawberry Hill, was completed, tours of the houses were initiated. These visits were added to

3.8 Horace Walpole's Strawberry Hill, exterior.

an existing circuit of massive eighteenth-century country houses also open to visitors. In *Tom Jones* (1749), Henry Fielding lovingly parodies these great homes with his description of 'Paradise Hall': 'the Gothick stile of building could produce nothing nobler than Mr Allworthy's house. There was an air of grandeur in it, that struck you with awe, and rival'd the beauties of the best Grecian architecture; and it was as commodious within, as venerable without' (p. 30 [A]). From Ranelagh's pleasure dome to Twickenham's domestic tourism, there is the sense by the middle of the eighteenth century that Britain now believed it had the resources within itself to educate and entertain an increasing number of its citizens. The figure of the magnificent country house will continue to play an important, beneficent role in the English novel at least through the early nineteenth century (e.g., Darcy's estate in Jane Austen's *Pride and Prejudice*, 1813) before it would become something overwhelming and haunted (e.g., Miss Havisham's home in Charles Dickens's *Great Expectations*, 1860–61).

Education

Throughout this period, women could not attend colleges or universities. But the educational situation for both sexes in the eighteenth century is somewhat surprising. Oxford and Cambridge, England's only universities at the time, were in decline, with Oxford taking in only about two hundred new students annually in the middle of the eighteenth century. Contrary to the image of the eighteenth century as a period of increasing access to information, funding for students to study at Oxford and Cambridge declined, and the percentage of university students drawn from the aristocracy increased. Over the eighteenth century, the role and influence of commercial or 'public' – as opposed to home – schooling also increased. By 1800, nearly 70 per cent of aristocratic children were educated at Eton, Harrow, Westminster and Winchester. There, they would study the classics, Latin and Greek, participate in organised team sports, and, notoriously, be subjected to harsh discipline from the older students. While these children of the wealthy could continue their classical learning in a sumptuous Oxbridge setting, the value of such an education was increasingly under question in a time of modern science. As part of their education in architecture, art, history and languages, the sons of the wealthy often opted for a two- or three-year 'Grand Tour' of the European continent, travelling from England through France to Italy and back. For girls, schools were just beginning to be started, especially in the second half of the eighteenth century. However, the kind of education they offered differed from that available to boys and men, even those young men shut out for financial and religious reasons from the universities, with women's education generally focused on providing them with a set of appropriately feminine 'accomplishments', such as dancing, music and needlepoint. During the century, many charitable schools (run neither by the state nor the Church but rather by independent governing boards) were set up to teach reading to the children of the poor.

It is estimated that in the middle of the eighteenth century, one-third of the men and two-thirds of the women were illiterate. Still, there were important countervailing democratising forces. Circulating libraries, for example, were starting to be set up in the 1740s, and they spread to the provinces: Bradford, Bristol, Leeds and Hull all acquired their library societies within a decade starting in the late 1760s. In the latter half of the century, new colleges were started, known as Dissenting Academies (because they were organised by those who did not subscribe to the Anglican religion required for attendance at Oxford and Cambridge). These colleges were less expensive than Oxford or Cambridge, and also featured a different curriculum. The faculties at these Dissenting Academies were more committed to the physical sciences than those at the more classics-oriented Universities. Early chemist, Joseph Priestley, for example, taught at the dissenting Warrington Academy. However, few of these Dissenting Academies survived for long. One descendent of Warrington, Manchester, relocated several times before setting up in Oxford during the last decade of the nineteenth century, although it would be another century before Harris Manchester College would be accepted as a full college within the University of Oxford. Some wags might see this as fairly quick given the span of Oxford history and the complexity of its administration. But it might also be an important example of how long it took to diffuse what are often represented as some of the most progressive aspects of the Enlightenment, such as access to education and scientific knowledge.

Marriage

Especially after the influential work of social historian Lawrence Stone (e.g., *The Family, Sex and Marriage in England 1500–1800*, 1977 [Civ]), there is a positive story told about developments in relationships between men and women over the eighteenth century: a rising sense of companionate marriages, and a combination of affection and individualism. During the eighteenth century, there was a significant development in the understanding of family, as it went from being a genealogical, biological unit to being more like a matter of choice. That is certainly the case in the novelistic, narrative depictions of relationships, where young women fought against being forced into marriages arranged by their families. But even by the end of the century women were still at a distinct legal disadvantage. Women could not vote, held no property within marriage, and were excluded from the trades and the guilds. Generally, women needed to look to marriage for security, and to keeping a home as an occupation, although how that played itself out would tend to vary along class lines. We could say that among the upper classes, the wedding itself had commercial benefits, while among the working classes, the marriage did. In both cases, the married woman was said to have disappeared into the marriage as far as the law was concerned. For the working classes, marriage involved working together. Couples did not marry until the man had completed his apprenticeship and was able to support a family. Therefore, marriages typically occurred relatively late. It is estimated that 40 per cent married after 35, although marriages generally took place around 25 or 26 for women and 27 or 28 for men. Until the Hardwicke Marriage Act of 1753, a wedding need not occur in church in order to make a marriage. Divorce, on the other hand, required an Act of Parliament, and only a handful of such acts were passed during the period. If working-class women gained protection, status and access to their husbands' earnings, men gained the labour of their wives. As housewives, working-class women would have had cows to feed and milk, wool to spin and candles to make, along with perhaps tailoring, or keeping a bed-and-breakfast inn for additional income. At the beginning of the eighteenth century, women would still work with men in the fields, although that would change over the century. Men began to take over work traditionally associated with women, such as midwifery, and women's agricultural work was increasingly marginalised. Among the wealthier classes, household tasks would be given to domestic servants who were managed by the housewife.

'Affective Individualism'

Historian Lawrence Stone traces a shift in the basic patterns of family life during the eighteenth century, from a 'restricted patriarchal nuclear' family at the turn of the century to a 'closed domesticated nuclear' family by the end. In the latter form, the home is increasingly private, and the relationships within increasingly affectionate, what Stone calls the companionate marriage. Increasingly, marrying for love is not only acceptable, but it is also respected, even among those families whose concern a few generations earlier had been solely for a suitable match, by which they would have meant a well-connected, wealthy match. In a way, Richardson's *Clarissa* (1747–8 [A]) records the tension between these modes of marriage as a tragedy that descends on Clarissa, who is prevented by her parents from achieving the independence she wants (and that her grandfather's will would make possible for her). For Stone, four eighteenth-century developments make companionate marriages possible (and thereby make Clarissa's story a tragedy), all of them subsets of what he sees as an overarching rise of individualism: new levels of emotional bonding between men and women, increasing individual autonomy, a desire for physical privacy and a lessening of the association between sensuality, sexuality and sin. Indeed, for Stone the period between the Puritans of the seventeenth century and the Evangelicals of the nineteenth represents remarkable openness and permissiveness in matters of sexuality.

Greenwich and the Political Science of Geography

At Greenwich, a town on the south side of the Thames about 6 miles east of central London, buildings such as Inigo Jones's Queen's House, Christopher Wren and Robert Hooke's Royal Observatory, and Wren's Royal Naval Hospital were built between the early 1600s and the early 1700s. The combination of architectural and historical significance in these buildings makes Greenwich among the most important developments in or near London during the Restoration and eighteenth century. The new development of Greenwich was pioneered by Inigo Jones's Queen's House (begun 1616–19), one of the earliest examples of Italian classical architecture in England. In 1675–6, during the Restoration and after the Royal Society had started to develop some of the institutions of modern science, Christopher Wren and Robert Hooke placed the Royal Observatory on a hill overlooking the Queen's House from the other side of Greenwich Park. The first Astronomer Royal, John Flamsteed, conducted astronomical experiments and observations there from 1675 until his death in 1719. Flamsteed, named a member of the Royal Society in 1676, would predict the existence of planets and study the surface of the moon (so closely that a Moon crater is named after him).

In 1695, funds were raised for a Royal Naval Hospital, to be designed largely by Christopher Wren (working with Nicholas Hawksmoor), and to be located in Greenwich. This building sits on land between the Queen's House and the Thames, and would serve as something like a retirement community for those who had served in the navy. When seen from the water, the new buildings frame the Queen's House, creating the impression of one massive, linked classical villa and arcade. On either side of the axis that runs from the Thames to the Queen's House there is one building, each with a dome-topped tower on the inner, water-side corner. The second to be built, Queen Mary Court, was not finished until 1751 (meaning that, owing to a host of financial problems, the whole Wren design took over fifty years to complete). Each domed tower stands on top of a large, public space, one a chapel and the other a formal dining hall. The dining hall, known as the Painted Hall, features one of the most important

Longitude

Astronomers, such as John Flamsteed, at the Royal Observatory, Greenwich, mapped the heavens for a very practical reason: to facilitate global travel and exploration. At the time, navigators faced the problem of how to measure their distances in east–west travel. Conceptually, it should have been possible to compare the time in the ship with the time at a fixed position and thus learn at which degree of the earth's turning one found oneself. However, neither an initial or 'prime' line for establishing longitude, nor a clock that could keep accurate time while in a rocking ship, had yet been created. The Longitude Act of 1714, though, aimed to spur the creation of a timepiece that could work reliably at sea by offering a £20,000 prize (at a time when a gentleman might live quite comfortably on £300 per annum) for an onboard timepiece that would allow for a calculation accurate to within half a degree of longitude. After building four different clocks, each more accurate than the one before, and after years of conflict with the Longitude Board, English clockmaker John Harrison was awarded the prize by Parliament in 1773. Captain Cook took Harrison's clock on his second voyage to the South Seas (1772–5), a trip commissioned by the Royal Society. The Royal Observatory subsequently served as the zero point on all British maps. In the late nineteenth century, treaties agreed that this zero point would become the Prime Meridian, internationally.

works by an eighteenth-century English painter, James Thornhill. Working in two stages through the mid-1720s, Thornhill added to the ceiling a fresco that commemorated William and Mary, the Protestant Succession, John Flamsteed and British naval power. It was immediately added to that domestic Grand Tour mentioned above with Walpole's Strawberry Hill, as tourists lined up to see the space and its painting, a Baroque celebration of the combination of knowledge and power.

Evangelism and Methodism

The eighteenth century is often understood as the period of the Enlightenment, an age of science, reason and increasing religious toleration. Often, this perception is based on a contrast between the eighteenth-century Enlightenment and the religious wars of the seventeenth century. However, the fact of the matter is that the eighteenth century provides significant new religious developments. Some have described an Evangelical Awakening in London during the 1720s and 1730s, one that apparently coincided with the arrival of the Moravians in London in 1728. Moravians were Protestant followers of John Hus, and had come to England from the Moravia region of central Europe (in today's Czech Republic). In London, their outreach, their Evangelism and their emphasis on music in religious services engaged other Christians. Perhaps their biggest influence was to be felt through Charles and John

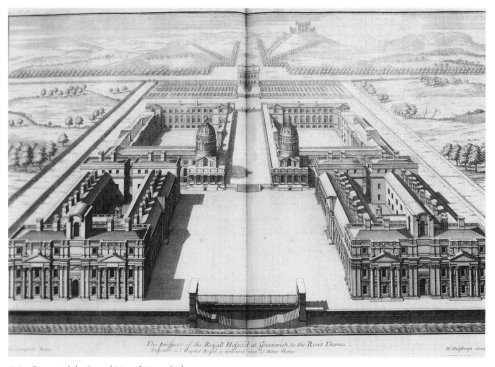

3.9 Greenwich, Royal Naval Hospital.

3.10 Greenwich Hospital, Painted Hall, James Thornhill.

Wesley, who accompanied some of the Moravians on a voyage to Savannah, Georgia, in October 1735. Charles was back in England by the following August, but John spent about two years in the colony, returning to England in early 1738. Upon their return, the Wesleys committed themselves to the Evangelical spread of Christianity: Charles wrote 7,000 songs; John travelled 250,000 miles and preached 40,000 times. John Wesley never had his own parish; rather, most of this work would fall under the heading 'field preaching', as Wesley reached out to the working classes beyond the existing churches. Perhaps it is not so surprising that the spread of an Evangelical form of Christianity during the period associated with the Enlightenment might wind up being known as Methodism.

Literary Overview

Literature and Letters

A literary overview of the Restoration and eighteenth century can provide only the barest outlines of such a rich and complicated period. Indeed, the difference between the little that even scholars read from any particular historical period and the great volume of titles published in the period has led at least one literary historian to complain about 'the slaughter house of literature', as so many titles are left behind in the march of literary study (Moretti [Ci]). In addition to the many titles that cannot fit into this overview, there is also the related tension between what was popular at the time and what has come to be regarded as valuable for subsequent literary history. This can be seen most clearly with the novel. The novel became a popular form during the Restoration and the eighteenth century, but it emerged in a context in which other genres were thought to be more important, and in which more short works, such as ballads and broadsheets of current events, were published. So, to focus on the novel, especially in the early years of the eighteenth century, is to trace an emerging form. Unless we are attentive to how the novel engaged other models of writing and knowing, we will miss the central tensions about its novelty. Moreover, contrary to the familiar literary history about the rise of the novel, many of the most popular novelists until 1740 were women, e.g., Aphra Behn, Delarivière Manley and Eliza Haywood. Again, it will be important to notice how the novels written by men reflect self-consciousness about the novel as a female-gendered genre.

In considering a period known as 'The Restoration and the Eighteenth Century', one point that needs to be addressed initially is whether we are looking at one cultural period or two. Of course, distinct periodisation is always difficult. Cultural and intellectual history is cumulative. Rather than breaks, it is more likely that there are gradations, tendencies, shifts and overlaps. But with the overall period being named after two shorter ones – both the Restoration *and* the eighteenth century – we are almost invited to consider questions of continuity and discontinuity across the time period. To the extent that we can accurately make broad sketches of the two periods, there are important differences between the Restoration and the eighteenth century. Indeed, these developments in literary history are part of what make this period as interesting as it is. For example, the court culture of the Restoration was quite distinct from that of the eighteenth century; the Anglo-Scottish Stuarts, who had lived in exile in France after the execution of Charles I, brought a Bourbon sense of opulence with them to London, very different from what would be brought from Hanover by the German Georges in the eighteenth century. The pursuit of pleasure in the Restoration court is replaced in the eighteenth century by a diffusion of taste. The intensity and immediacy of contact in late seventeenth-century London is replaced in the eighteenth century by a sense of politeness and sociability. As Anthony Ashley Cooper, the third Earl of Shaftesbury, put it in *Characteristics* (1711), 'a public spirit can come only from a social feeling or sense of partnership with humankind'

(p. 50). Later, by the middle of the century, this will become what is known as sensibility, through which sentiment and sympathy engage our fellow-feeling for others. Literary life in the 1690s and the early decades of the eighteenth century centred on friendly 'circles' and clubs, such as the Whiggish Kit-Kat club, whose members included Addison, Congreve, Steele and Vanbrugh, and the Scriblerus Club, including Alexander Pope, John Gay and Jonathan Swift. The British pursuit of continental – largely French and Italian – models in the arts (e.g., drama and opera) during the Restoration is replaced by the middle of the eighteenth century by an increasing confidence in native British artistic productions in arts and architecture. And it has often been noted that the Restoration's Baroque aesthetic (perhaps a vestige of what has come to be known as the Metaphysical style of the earlier seventeenth century) is replaced by an ease and simplicity across the culture of the eighteenth century – in architecture, fashion and writing.

During this period, the idea and role of the modern author were solidifying: authors were identified with works; copyrights were instituted protecting the work of those authors; bookselling spread to cities other than London; with the related development of a literary marketplace, bookselling and publication by subscription came to replace the role formerly played by the aristocratic patron; and periodical essays and review criticism in newspapers and magazines spread the word about, evaluated and selected new books. The period is also characterised by an important shift from a literary manuscript culture to a literary print culture. By the late seventeenth century, of course, the technology of printing with movable type had been in use for more than two centuries in England. During the Restoration, in which the court and 'circles' of friends dominated the literary scene, many literary works circulated in manuscript or handwritten form. This is in a sense consistent with the patronage system then in place. By the eighteenth century, authorship came to mean publication, the product of the mechanical processes of print rather than of handwriting. Samuel Johnson's life and work stands as a metaphor for these developments in authorship and in the diffusion of print. The son of a provincial bookseller, Johnson broke with his potential aristocratic patron Lord Chesterfield, and worked with booksellers instead, developing both a kind of English literary canon (*The Lives of the English Poets*) and the best English dictionary that had been published until then.

In the eighteenth century, the word 'literature' still referred to something like its root meaning of 'letters' and could include a wide range of printed materials. But it was also a period in which letters, in the sense of written correspondence with others, were important, often published by authors themselves in multi-volume series. Lord Chesterfield's *Letters to his Son*, for example, are among the most famous writings from the eighteenth century. Alexander Pope published his letters in 1735. (It must be said, though, that neither Pope nor Chesterfield fared altogether well among critics, Pope because he revised his letters for publication, and Chesterfield because of the sometimes Machiavellian tone of his advice.) Lady Mary Wortley Montagu's *Letters* were published within a year of her death, and stretch in their modern edition to four substantial volumes. But most prolific of eighteenth-century letter writers is Horace Walpole, whose letters take up forty-eight volumes in a modern, scholarly edition (an edition begun in 1937 and completed in 1983, a time frame that also indicates the scale of letter writing in the eighteenth century). Such garrulousness is often taken as yet another sign of a clubbable, friendly period, where people were reaching out and making connections. It could also have something to do, though, with how the stagecoach and toll-road system was bringing far-flung parts of the United Kingdom into closer contact. These transportation developments increased the speed and ease with which mail could be sent around the country. At the same time, then, the familiar letter was also used as a vehicle in essays and fiction. By the mid-century, writers such as Samuel Richardson so relied on letters for conveying action that such a form came to be known as the 'epistolary' novel (from Latin *epistola*, 'letter').

Poetry

These days, poetry is not the most popular form of writing left to us from the Restoration and eighteenth century. Novels of the eighteenth century may be among the best-loved works in English, and the literary critics of the eighteenth century may be among the most influential, but the poetry of the period is generally overlooked and undervalued. It is strange that the poetry written by contemporaries of Addison, Defoe, Fielding and Swift should find itself in this compromised critical

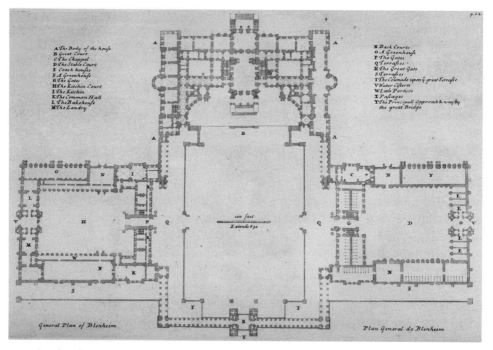

3.11 [Vanbrugh,] *General Plan of Blenheim*. Commissioned by Parliament in gratitude for the Duke of Marlborough's 1704 defeat of the French at Blenheim, the Great Court of this home extends 850 feet according to the plan (1705–22).

position. In part, Restoration and eighteenth-century poetry has suffered by comparison with the poetry – and literary-critical assumptions – of the periods that preceded and followed it. The poetry of the early seventeenth century, the work of the Metaphysical poets, has the difficulty appreciated by the high modernists and the density of metaphor appreciated by post-structuralist literary theory. The poetry of the late eighteenth and early nineteenth centuries, the period associated with Romanticism, redefined nature itself, contributing among other things a vocabulary for what would come to be known today as environmentalism. Between these two, the poetry of the eighteenth century is remembered for being too formal, too simple and too topical. When Wordsworth claimed in the 'Preface' to the *Lyrical Ballads* that his poetry aimed 'to adopt the very language of men', one can interpret Wordsworth as criticising the work of the earlier eighteenth century, which, he implies, used a more elevated and therefore unnatural language.

The poets of the Restoration and eighteenth century saw the poetry of the early seventeenth century as excessive, even unrefined. They associated the intensity of the tropes in Metaphysical poetry with political and epistemological instability. Although the eighteenth-century valued sociability, the 'spontaneous overflow of powerful feelings' that for Wordsworth defined good poetry would no doubt have struck eighteenth-century poets as unnecessarily impulsive. Between these two periods and the styles associated with them, the poets of the eighteenth century aimed for a balance. Formally, this balance was best achieved in the work of Alexander Pope, as we shall see. But the quest for balance had consequences across the poetry of the period. Stylistically, Restoration and eighteenth-century poetry was dominated by the heroic couplet. This form features pairs or 'couplets' of iambic pentameter lines. That is, each line is composed of ten syllables arranged into five groups or 'feet' of unstressed and stressed syllables; both lines in the pair end with the same sound. Each line, then, can represent a kind of balance within itself. Moreover, the prevalence of this pattern also created an expectation in readers, an expectation against which the poet could play unexpected rhythms and rhymes. The topicality of Restoration poetry, which today makes the poetry seem inaccessible, represents its own kind of balance – an attempt to counterbalance the political pull of powerful contemporaries. Over the course of the Restoration and eighteenth century, poetry became increasingly balanced demographically as well. During the Restoration, classically educated males distributed poems in manuscript among court and aristocratic circles. By the middle of the eighteenth century, working-class poets, male and female, were able to get their works published. For the best-known working-class poets of the eighteenth century, balance between genders was at issue, as Mary Collier, washerwoman, reacts to Stephen Duck, thresher. In a related process, the themes and settings of English poetry go from urban (and focused on London at that) in the Restoration to rural by the mid-eighteenth century.

Poetry was dominated by two poets during this period: John Dryden in the Restoration and Alexander Pope through at least the first third of the eighteenth century. Both of them, though, were engaged with the precedent and influence of John Milton (1608–74). For several reasons, Milton is not usually thought of as a Restoration poet, but as his most important poems were all published after 1660 he certainly fits in any consideration of Restoration literature. Because the bulk of his public career spans the English Civil Wars of the 1640s and the Interregnum of the 1650s, Milton is treated, understandably, as a writer from a generation before that of the Restoration authors. In that sense of the Restoration, Milton is not a Restoration poet. But on another level, Milton is also associated with the republican, Puritan and Parliamentary side during the Civil Wars, even publishing papers defending the execution of Charles I. During the 1650s, Milton worked for Cromwell's government, and published an essay against Restoration just weeks before Charles II returned to the throne. In this more important sense of actively opposing the Restoration of the Stuart monarchy, Milton is again not usually considered a Restoration poet either. Nonetheless, Milton's most important poems were published during the Restoration, including *Paradise Lost*, one of the most influential poems in English (1667, revised 1674). These poems can certainly be read as Milton's engagement with the Restoration that he had opposed; in this way, then, Milton is still a Restoration poet.

Although it is discussed in greater detail in the 'Texts and Issues' section, it is important to note for the literary overview of the period that *Paradise Lost*'s status as the first English epic was too important for an ambitious poet such as Dryden to ignore, despite the differences in their political orientation and affiliations. Three years after *Paradise Lost* was published, Dryden produced *The State of Innocence and the Fall of Man* (1677), which reflects Dryden's engagement with the themes of Milton's epic. It may also be that Dryden found inspiration in Milton's lifelong engagement with politics, although Dryden chose a different approach from that of Milton. Dryden sided with successive monarchs where Milton successively rejected them. John Dryden had a varied career as a writer and often wrote on highly topical subjects – so topical, in fact, that Dryden could write a poem mourning the death of Cromwell in 1658 and a poem, *Astraea Redux*, celebrating Charles II in 1660, just two years later. The poem that earned Dryden his reputation for turning the contemporary into poetry is *Annus Mirabilis* (1667), concerned with the events of 1666, the Fire of London and the defeat of the Dutch navy. In the following year, Dryden was appointed Poet Laureate (1668) and published *Of Dramatic Poesy*, a prose essay on English drama. Over the next decade Dryden would make a name for himself in the Restoration theatre, writing and presenting many plays, including *The Conquest of Granada* (1670), *Marriage à la Mode* (1673), *Aureng-Zebe* (1675), and *All for Love* (1678). But it is the remarkably productive three- or four- year period around the Exclusion Crisis in the late 1670s and early 1680s that resulted in some of Dryden's most important poetic achievements: *Absalom and Achitophel, MacFlecknoe, The Medall*, and *Religio Laici*. Along with *The Hind and the Panther*, they are also among the most inscrutable of Dryden's works, because, again, of their coded topical references.

Traditionally, there is a tendency to see literature and the other arts as having a tenuous connection to politics at most. The aesthetic, the argument goes, is above the political, meaning not only 'better than' but 'beyond' and having little to do with the political. In this model, the critic tends to look at the organisation and appeal of the formal attributes of the poem, often pointing to its representation of universal themes. Steeped in the politics of its moment, the poetry of the Restoration confounds this model of criticism. Dryden's poetry perfectly illustrates this late seventeenth-century combination of the literary and the political. Depending on the poem, literary issues represent politics and political issues can represent literary ones. *Absalom and Achitophel* (1681) was published just before the treason trial of Shaftesbury, leader of the opposition to James's possible succession, and cast Charles as the biblical David, Shaftesbury as Achitophel and the Duke of Monmouth (Charles's illegitimate son) as Absalom. Understanding the poem, then, requires familiarity with the biblical story and the principal players and stakes in the Exclusion Crisis. Removing this poem from the Exclusion Crisis would leave us with a 1,000-line poem on the Bible (as opposed to a 1,000-line poem which uses the Bible for a defence of the king's position in the Exclusion Crisis). With *MacFlecknoe*, published 1682 (but probably circulated in manuscript form in the late 1670s), Dryden invokes the same anxiety over valid succession ('to settle the succession of the state'), but this time directs his attention toward literary succession, skewering Thomas Shadwell: 'for anointed dullness he was made' (*Norton Anthology*, pp. 1816, 1817, ll. 10, 64 [A]). Ironically, and unfortunately for Shadwell, it is through *MacFlecknoe* that he is remembered, if at all, today. At the time, though, Shadwell had recently taken up Shaftesbury's side and published a work criticising Dryden's defence of the court. In other words, again, the literary and the political merge in any consideration of late seventeenth-century poetry. In this way, it is understandable that the period has on the one hand resisted the universalist claims often made for great literature while on the other proved such a fruitful area for historicist approaches to literature.

Like Dryden, Alexander Pope could certainly write satirical poetry. In its focus on dullness, Pope's *Dunciad* (1728, 1729, 1744, 1745), for instance, owes a debt to Dryden's *MacFlecknoe*. However, Pope's 'essays', such as *An Essay on Criticism* (1711) and *An Essay on Man* (1733–4) also mark an important shift away from the often topical poetry of the Restoration and towards the general and universal claims associated with the Enlightenment. In *An Essay on Criticism*, Pope sets out to describe what is required for good literary criticism. Against the familiar opposition between critics and authors he argues that the best critics will be the best writers, and vice versa. For Pope, writers and critics ought to follow Nature. On the one hand, Pope's 'Nature' combines a late Renaissance classicism with Newtonian mechanical physics. Following from Newton's discovery of universal mathematical formulae to explain natural phenomena, Pope's Nature is a function of and compatible with rules: 'Nature Methodiz'd' as he describes it ('Essay on Criticism', *Norton Anthology*, p. 2218, l. 89 [A]). For Pope, Homer, too, had discovered the same rules long ago; thus, Pope counsels writers and critics to read Homer: 'Nature and Homer were, he found, the same' (p. 2219, l. 135). The Romantics will later pick up on Pope's focus on nature. But where Pope's 'Nature' is 'standard', 'unerring', 'clear, unchang'd, and Universal' (p. 2218, ll. 69, 70, 71), Nature for the Romantics will be vales, thorns, babbling brooks, and mountain ridges. With an analogy to 'Some well-proportion'd Dome' (p. 2222, l. 247), Pope offers a vision of criticism that is consistent with his sense of the relationship between nature, rules and standardisation. The dome, like a poem, might be composed of many smaller pieces, but when surveyed at an appropriate distance 'all comes united to th' admiring eyes' (p. 2222, l. 250). Such unity, symmetry and balance go a long way to explaining why the period was for so long known as Augustan, although it is important to remember that Pope thinks such symmetry is best seen at a distance. Implicit in this analogy is a kind of reading, one that pays attention to the overall structure rather than the details. This distinction between the structure and the details (not to mention the combination of the classical and the universal) will have important consequences for emerging English literary criticism.

With *An Essay on Man*, the symmetry of Pope's form is brought to bear on some of the same questions Milton had addressed in a different way in *Paradise Lost*. Like Milton in *Paradise Lost*, Pope begins with a 'Garden, tempting with forbidden fruit' (*Norton Anthology*, p. 2264, l. 8[A]). But everything about the form has been changed. Rather than an epic, Pope's poem is an epistle, a letter. Rather than blank (or unrhymed) verse, Pope uses the heroic couplet, rhyming pairs of iambic pentameter lines. Pope found a form for 'steering betwixt the extremes of doctrines seemingly opposite', as he describes it in 'The Design'. This steering between is also a way of finding a balance, a point with implications at once epistemological, ontological, poetical and political. Where *An Essay on Criticism* seems to have understood literary criticism in Newtonian terms, *An Essay on Man* understands Newtonian philosophy through a carefully symmetrical poetic form. Nearly every line of *An Essay on Man* is balanced with five syllables on either side of a break called a 'caesura' (and in this case often represented by a comma or some other punctuation). Such balance within each line is complemented by the lines' rhyming in pairs. Most importantly, this symmetry, this steering between, represented by the shape of nearly every line in the poem, creates a poetic form for representing how Pope understands Newton's vision of the universe, with an equal and opposite reaction sustaining a balanced whole.

During the middle years of the eighteenth century, there was, perhaps in reaction against the relatively static balanced universe envisioned by Pope, a new emphasis on the pastoral, a sometimes self-conscious return to the rural and earthy and away from the urban and conceptual. This mid-century poetry has always been hard to categorise, sometimes described as the poetry of sensibility, sometimes as 'pre-Romanticism'. But sensibility means something quite particular (something closer to our use of 'sensitivity'); it is not clear that the poetry of the period shared this 'sensibility', nor that pastoral poetry of other periods lacked it. 'Pre-Romanticism' fares little better, because it is by definition anachronistic, as the term implies that the poets of the mid-century were writing in anticipation of something they actually did not know was going to develop. Still it is tempting when reading, say, Mark Akenside's *Pleasures of the Imagination* (1744 [A]), to think that his focus on 'ever-blooming sweets', 'rural honours', 'lucid leaves', and 'autumn tinges' marks a change away from Pope's and towards the Romantics' idea of Nature ('Love of Nature', ll. 4, 15, 21, 22).

If there is one poem that is usually taken to represent this shift it is Gray's *Elegy Written in a Country Church Yard* (1749–51). In it, a narrator is left alone at evening in a church graveyard, where the narrator can read 'the short and simple annals of the poor' (*Norton Anthology*, p. 2459, l. 32). In what seems to be a reflection of the exclusion of the poor from accomplishment, the narrator wonders whether there is a 'village-Hampden', 'some mute inglorious Milton', or 'some Cromwell' buried, unknown. But the narrator's sense of loss is ambivalent, as it is possible that 'their sober wishes never learn'd to stray' (*Norton Anthology*, p. 2460, l. 74) here, so 'far from the madding crowd' (a phrase to which Thomas Hardy would allude with the title of his 1874 novel). In other words, maybe it would have been better for England to have kept to its rural course, and, relatedly, not to have experienced the Civil Wars and Interregnum. It is interesting to note that in the manuscript version of the poem, the English names Hampden, Milton, and Cromwell were originally 'Cato', 'Tully', and 'Caesar'. This poem, then, traces many important changes in England's understanding of itself by the middle of the eighteenth century. The shift from the classical Roman names in the original to the seventeenth-century English names in the published version might indicate a sense of regret that England's urbanisation coincided with political violence and developing empire. It also indicates, though, a new, tentative sense that English history can now stand on its own. Thus the importance of 'The Epitaph' for a deceased 'Youth to Fortune and to Fame unknown' (*Norton Anthology*, p. 2461, l. 118) with which the poem ends, and supposedly engraved on a tombstone in this churchyard: it stands for the passage of time (including our resistance through stone to the passage of time) and for something like the work of a native English bard, all of which would become important in the second half of the eighteenth century.

Drama

More than was the case for other areas of cultural history, the Stuart Restoration was a restoration for drama. The theatre had been made illegal by Parliament in 1642; upon his arrival in England from France, where Corneille and Molière were active, Charles II restored drama to the English stage. Charles allowed two theatres in London: the King's and the Duke's. And in an innovation rather than a restoration, women were allowed to act for the first time as well. Some of these women, such as Nell Gwynn, joined the ranks of the best-known actresses and actors of the English stage. Nonetheless, there is the sense that the English stage was still finding its way during the first years after the restoration of drama. In this, Dryden's 1668 *An Essay of Dramatic Poesy* is a turning point. There, Dryden 'staged' a debate over contemporary drama, English and French. In it, he recorded but also created the terms for a critical discussion of the new phenomenon: English drama. Dryden turns the differences between English drama and classical and French precedents into an advantage, and in so doing gives English drama a vision of how it could be more self-confident than it had been, at least since the Restoration. Three years later, George Villiers, Duke of Buckingham, was confident enough to satirise the anxieties of early Restoration drama by giving them a name and a theatrical form in *The Rehearsal* (1671). The play features an author unsure of how to write a play, and actors unaware of how to act. The author within the play, Bayes, exclaims, 'I must tell you, Sir, it is a very difficult matter to pen a whisper well', a predicament made all the more acute by actors who say, 'I don't understand how it is to be spoken' (Harris, ed., *Restoration Plays*, pp. 17, 8 [A]). Villiers was satirising the current state of the English stage, but such satire would presumably have been possible on the stage only with some distance from the painful reality.

The Rehearsal also introduces us to a tension that would animate the London stage until the end of the century: the role and influence of the city and the differences between it and the country. Theatre, in general, can raise questions about whether identity is innate or enacted, whether identity is 'performed'. Through the Restoration stage, London was able to examine a range of identity issues: e.g., whether London's emergence as a centre for international trade would have a corrosive effect on its citizens, turning them into consumers; and whether even sexual identities could be changed through performance. All of these issues can be seen in Wycherley's play, *The Country Wife* (1675) and George Etherege's *The Man of Mode, Or, Sir Fopling Flutter* (1676). When the latter play opens, Horner explains that he has just had word spread around town that he is a eunuch, in the belief that this rumour will make him non-threatening as he begins affairs with other men's wives. One female character spends part of the play dressed as a man, known and unknown to different characters. Different areas of London, for instance St James's Park and Covent Garden, are placed on stage, and in the process it is implied that London itself has become a kind of theatre, with people performing during strolls in certain parts of the city.

By the 1690s, female playwrights, such as Susanna Centlivre, Charlotte Clarke, Elizabeth Cooper, Eliza Haywood, Delarivière Manley and Mary Pix, started to come into their own. In 1697, Sir John Vanbrugh defended the actions of 'the provoked wife' in his play of the same name. One male character goes so far as to argue, on behalf of the provoked wife, that 'where laws dispense with equity, equity should dispense with laws'. It is perhaps not a surprise, then, that the theatre should come under attack, as it did in 1698 with Jeremy Collier's *Short View of the Immorality and Profaneness of the English Stage*. With its concern about plays' 'smuttiness of expression; their swearing, profaneness, and lewd application of Scripture; their abuse of the clergy, their making their top characters libertines and giving them success in their debauchery', Collier's argument brought the Puritan objections to the theatre back, almost four decades after the theatres had been reopened. Other critics, such as John Dennis, rushed to the theatre's defence. But they were probably less successful than plays and playwrights in reclaiming authority for the stage. Particularly important in this regard would be *The Way of the World* (1700) by William Congreve. Published two years after Collier's *Short View*, Congreve's play is so intricate – and humorous – in the complexity of the relationships depicted it can be read as a parody of Collier's wish for clarity and distinctions: such clarity is not 'the way of the world'. At the same time, the printed version of this play included prefatory material that solicited the protection of a powerful patron – the tradition of high art. Rejecting critics, 'that they very often let fly their censure, when through their rashness they have mistaken their aim', Congreve claims 'it is only by the countenance of your Lordship, and the *few* so qualified, that such who write with care and pains can hope to be distinguished; for the prostituted name of *poet* promiscuously levels all that bear it'. In this formulation, Congreve asserts that the correct understanding of the play ought to be left to the few, and coincidentally rejects the gendered implications of selling the labour of one's body that Aphra Behn had taken up with the sign of Angellica Bianca. There is a way in which Congreve, with this letter, is

3.12 Hogarth, *Masquerades and Operas, or The Taste of the Town* (1724). French and Italian architecture and theatre are popular while English authors are 'waste paper for shops'. Banner shows stage of Vanbrugh's Queen's/Haymarket Theatre.

contributing as much to the history of criticism, and the related development of an English canon, as he is to the London stage.

Ironically, despite Congreve's defence, drama after 1700 is not as influential culturally as it was between 1660 and 1700. There are many reasons to account for this relative decline: the importance of Italian opera; changes in theatre design; less tension over life in the city and over differences between the city and the country; and the rise of the novel. Still, the eighteenth century would see the production of several plays that would join Britain's most influential. John Gay's *The Beggar's Opera* (1728), for example, combined play and music in a form that was then called ballad opera and today might strike us as musical theatre. In the early years of Walpole's being prime minister, the play's references to well-to-do thieves took on an added political significance. In 1730, Fielding presented *The Life and Death of Tom Thumb the Great*, which explored the physical limits of what could be presented on stage, while the footnotes included in the printed version parodied pedantic scholarly concerns. The Licensing Act of 1737 tried to rein the theatre in, pulling it back to just two London theatres, the Covent Garden and the Drury Lane, and requiring that plays be approved in advance by the Lord Chamberlain. One of the most famous actors of the day, Colley Cibber, published an autobiography, *An Apology for the Life of Colley Cibber* in 1740, providing historians with tremendous insights into the workings of the eighteenth-century stage. The 1770s saw two of the best-loved plays in the English language produced for the first time: Goldsmith's *She Stoops to Conquer* (1773) and Sheridan's *The Rivals* (1775), the latter of which included a character given to awkward turns of phrase, Mrs Malaprop (after whom funny, mangled idioms have come to be known as 'malapropisms').

The Novel

Perhaps the most important development in literary genres in English during the Restoration and eighteenth century is the emergence of the novel, which would go on to become the most popular and influential literary genre. When viewed through the familiar lens of the nineteenth-century novels by Anne, Charlotte and Emily Brontë, Charles Dickens, George Eliot and Thomas Hardy, the novels of the Restoration and eighteenth century can seem quite odd, almost as if they are not at all novels in the nineteenth-century sense of the term. In the best-known nineteenth-century novels, for example, the focus is on tensions between city and country, or between poor residents of the provinces and wealthier city residents, or on the lonely consequences of living in the landscape (recently animated by the Romantics). Many of the major nineteenth-century novels are domestic in the largest sense, set in the great country house and in a changing British countryside. In these nineteenth-century novels, Britain's relation to the outside world and to its colonies is consigned to the attic, so to speak. There is often in the nineteenth-century novel a sprawling assortment of native British voices assembled from across the socio-economic spectrum. The major eighteenth-century novels, by contrast, are often engaged globally, rather than domestically; the most famous eighteenth-century novels are populated by world explorers such as Robinson Crusoe and Lemuel Gulliver. Where the nineteenth-century novel is often a lengthy polyphonic collection of overlapping narratives (the openness and heteroglossia that Mikhail Bakhtin, the Russian literaty theorist, associates with all novels), the Restoration and eighteenth-century novel can often be fairly slim and often does not include the same range of voices. Especially in the novels from the earlier part of the period, the landscape of the Restoration and eighteenth-century novel is the *terra incognita* of colonial locations, the New World that Britain was increasingly engaging.

The Restoration and eighteenth-century English novel is as flexible, fluid, and open a genre as the novel would be in the nineteenth century. Both can accommodate all sorts of issues and participate in a dialogue with a range of contemporary genres and uses of print. But the contemporary issues and the contemporary uses of print differ in the Restoration and eighteenth century from those of the nineteenth. This difference between the novels of different historical periods raises this question, then: what is the novel? If there are such differences, what makes them all novels? Generally, novels are thought to be extended, prose, fictional narratives – although this definition raises even more questions: what is extended; how is prose different from poetry; what is the relation between fiction and the real? It will be necessary to address these general questions. Related to these questions is the equally vexed issue of why the English novel emerges during the Restoration and eighteenth century. This complicated issue has absorbed the attention of several generations of literary historians.

Classical and medieval precedents are important for a consideration of the novel as a genre, as the novel is often engaged in a dialogue with these older forms. For example, *Don Quixote* (1605, 1615), a book many take to be the first modern European novel, is in many ways a parody of the medieval romance genre. The medieval romance, represented by books such as Thomas Malory's fifteenth-century English work *Morte Darthur* and the early sixteenth-century Spanish *Amadis de Gaul* (1508), also features extended prose narrative. In the romance, there is usually a knight who travels out in search of adventure, while observing a series of honourable conventions represented by the chivalric code, with the hope that he might in the end win the love of a particular princess whose virtue would be as pure as his valour. Inspired – or, according to other characters in the book, deranged – by the sheer number of medieval romances he has been reading (including *Amadis de Gaul*), the title character and protagonist of the story, *Don Quixote*, decides one day to become a knight errant, a wandering knight, on the model of all the characters he has seen in his books. So, he puts a basin on his head for a helmet, mounts a decrepit horse, and heads out of the back gate of his house in search of adventure and the love of his life, Dulcinea, whom, of course, he has never met. *Don Quixote* illustrates the complicated relationship that the early novel would have with romance (and, by extension, with other, existing major genres). *Don Quixote* is indebted to the medieval romance genre that its protagonist attempts to embody. By showing the unfortunate consequences of trying to enact the romance genre, *Don Quixote* also makes fun of the romance and its readers: they are out of touch, and relying on a code that apparently does not fit the modern world. This complicated relationship with the romance helps account for the fact that in the continental European languages, the extended prose fictional narrative is called a 'roman'. In English a terminological distinction is made between 'romance' and 'novel'.

The epic is another genre with which the novel is often compared. Simply in terms of the familiar attributes of the form, the comparison is perhaps unavoidable. The epic is a long, fictional narrative in verse, the novel a long, fictional narrative in prose. Some therefore see the novel as a prose epic. The connection between the novel and the epic is more than just a matter of comparison or analogy. Consistent with his sense that the epic is part of the past and the novel of the present, Bakhtin believes that continuing evolution is an important feature of the novel as a genre. For Bakhtin, the novel's invocation of the epic (and any other existing genre) is part of the process of its unfolding development, a process that will continue through the history of the genre as it engages with other narrative modes contemporary with it (including those that pre-exist it). At the same time, though, the novel's process of narrative adoption and adaptation makes it seem like a 'colonising' genre: it takes other genres over for itself, remaking them in the process. Such appropriation might explain why the novel seems to re-emerge when it does in European and then, later, in British history. That is, *Don Quixote* was published about a century after Spain had arrived on the western edge of the Atlantic. We might even understand the story's central metaphor of the delusional Crusader as a critical reflection on the ideology

The Ancient Novel

The novel is usually considered a modern form, but there are ancient and non-Western examples of the novel as well. It is true that the novel has flourished internationally in the modern period, over the last three centuries or so. Indeed, its English development is but one example of this modern internationalising of the form. But it is also important to remember that the novel has a pre-modern history as well. There are, for example, Greek and Roman novels from their classical periods. Although these novels are not as well known as novels in the modern languages, nor as well known as the epics or tragedies of Graeco-Roman classicism, works such as *The Golden Ass* by the Roman writer Apuleius can also fit the definition of the novel as extended, prose, fictional narratives. Similarly, the eleventh-century Japanese story, *The Tale of Genji*, could also fit the bill. And while its episodic storytelling within a frame means that it does not have the sustained narrative development characteristic of the novel, Boccaccio's fourteenth-century collection of a hundred short stories, the *Decameron*, shares with the later development of the novel a similar ambitious scale.

that shaped Spanish colonialism in America. Similarly, Britain sees its first novels approximately a century into its Atlantic colonial experience. Early English novels such as Aphra Behn's *Oroonoko* (1688), Defoe's *Robinson Crusoe* (1719) and Swift's *Gulliver's Travels* (1726) represent and debate this new colonial adventure. If epics recount stories of national origins, providing an imagined community, the emergence of the novel seems to coincide, cyclically, with shifts from nation to a sense of empire (e.g. Ancient Greece, classical Rome, early seventeenth-century Spain, early eighteenth-century Britain, etc.).

The early novel in English, that of the Restoration and eighteenth century, profoundly engages with 'history', in several senses of the word. As we have already seen, the novel engages the emerging British colonies, and is thus historical in that sense. But the fact that most early 'novels' had subtitles that called them a 'history' is just as important for the development of the genre in English. The full titles of *Oroonoko, or the History of the Royal Slave* (1688) by Behn, *Clarissa, or The History of a Young Lady* (1747–8) by Samuel Richardson and *The History of Tom Jones, A Foundling* (1749) by Henry Fielding show this seventeenth- and eighteenth-century connection between the novel and history. The question of course is why these fictional prose narratives should be called histories. One possibility is that the British were simply using an Anglicised version of the French word for story: 'histoire'. But there are many early novels, such as Defoe's *A Journal of the Plague Year* (1722) and Swift's *Gulliver's Travels*, that claimed to be true stories 'never made public before', as the full title of *A Journal of the Plague Year* puts it. Through such connections to history, early English novels implied that the events recorded within them were true. 'I do not pretend' are, for example, the first four words of Behn's *Oroonoko*. This claim to truth is crucial for the early novel, and certainly part of why so many were subtitled 'a history'.

For many critics, the fact that the early novel raises questions about its own status as fiction is precisely what makes it 'novel'. The particular kind of claim to truth in the early modern English prose narrative is new (thus, novel). For some, the early novel has a connection to the then-emerging newspapers; both claimed to provide true 'news' in a prose narrative format. For others, the early modern English novel assumes an empiricist's sense of objectivity. To these critics, early modern science helps shape the plain-spoken prose of the early novel. Others, though, wonder whether the prose is actually as plain as it may seem (and whether any prose can be without the metaphors early modern science wishes to avoid). In *The Origins of the English Novel, 1600–1740* [Ci], Michael McKeon takes these possibilities and treats them dialectically, in relation to one another. For McKeon, the novel provides a range of ways of addressing both the questions of virtue implicit in the older romance tradition and questions of truth more contemporary with the early modern circumstances. Where novel criticism has often focused on the dialogic heteroglossia of different voices within novels, McKeon focuses on a dialogue *between* novels. Thus, in a complicated dance, the empiricism of Defoe and later Richardson is countered by the scepticism of Swift and Fielding. There is also another sense in which many major Restoration and eighteenth-century novels are histories, related to Bakhtin's sense of the novel as tied to the contemporary. By paying attention to the often careful dating included in them, it is possible to read several of the period's most important novels as ambiguous allegories regarding the period's political events. In *Robinson Crusoe*, for example, Crusoe is trapped on his island from 1659 to 1687, or basically the entire Restoration, returning to England just in time for the Glorious Revolution. Similar use of different dates, and thus references to different political events, can be traced in *Gulliver's Travels* as well.

Perhaps nothing makes the novel more 'novel' than the role of women in the writing and reading of novels. It is not a coincidence that the first professional female author in England, Aphra Behn, wrote romances and novels. To a degree not represented by the usual list of major novels from the Restoration and eighteenth century, the novel genre had a gender: female. In part, this might be attributed to the novel's association with romance, a genre then popular with female readers. In *Gulliver's Travels*, Swift refers uneasily to this connection between romance, novels and female readers, attributing the palace fire in Lilliput to a maid who fell asleep while reading a romance. On one level, the anecdote might imply that romances are merely relaxing bedtime reading, that they will put their readers to sleep. But Swift's story also points to other reasons why women were thought to have played such an important role in the early history of the English novel. For one thing, as an emerging form, novels were not at the time considered to be the most important type of literature (dramatic and epic poetry would probably have taken the top spot). Thus, Swift's story about the romance also reflects an anxiety about how his own work will be received. Classical learning in Greek and Latin still dominated university education during the Restoration and the eighteenth century, and university education was reserved for men. Novels, of course, were written in English, and were already therefore thought to be the domain of the uneducated, the less completely literate. Not only did this reduce the novel's value at the time; it also created the impression that it was simply too easy to read novels. There was a critical sense at the time that novels were therefore bad for readers. Thus, in Swift's anecdote of the palace fire, the reading is so easy the maid falls asleep, and out of such easy reading a fire ensues. Of course, it is also true that by the time Swift wrote *Gulliver's Travels*, women had already been writing 'romances' before men began writing 'novels'. Often, then, men wound up writing women's lives in novels, in what has recently been called narrative transvestism. Defoe, for example, wrote *Moll Flanders* (1722) and *Roxana* (1724); Richardson wrote

Pamela; Or, Virtue Rewarded (1740) and *Clarissa, or the History of a Young Lady* (1747–8). Women also wrote in reaction to such novels, e.g., Eliza Haywood's *Anti-Pamela: or, Feign'd Innocence Detected; In a Series of Syrena's Adventures* (1741). Such responses are already a kind of literary criticism, but women also published more free-standing literary criticism as well during the eighteenth century (e.g., Eliza Haywood, *The Female Spectator* (1744–6), Elizabeth Cooper, *Preface to The Muses Library* (1737)). This public and published discussion of literature across the genders was a constitutive feature of Restoration and eighteenth-century literary culture, although the various texts that made up the discussion have only begun to be uncovered and republished in the last few decades.

Literary Criticism

Modern English literary criticism emerges during the Restoration and eighteenth century. There were literary-critical texts in English long before the Restoration, of course, as for example Sir Philip Sidney's *An Apology for Poetry* (1595). And there would be much more extensive networks of academic and published criticism after the eighteenth century. Nonetheless, major Restoration and eighteenth-century figures such as John Dryden, Joseph Addison and Richard Steele, and Samuel Johnson represent important changes in the status of criticism during the period. From Dryden's *An Essay of Dramatic Poesy* (1668) to Addison and Steele's *The Tatler* (1709–11) and *The Spectator* (1711–12) to Johnson's *Lives of the English Poets* (1781), the Restoration and eighteenth century was a pivotal, maybe even formative, stage in the development of English literary criticism. There is a debate over approaches and methods, literary-critical terms are developed and disseminated as periodical criticism spreads, and across the period a literary canon is developed, refined and debated.

As we saw in the Drama section above, Dryden's *An Essay of Dramatic Poesy* turned the differences between English theatre and the French classical tradition into an advantage for the English. Across the essays of the *Spectator*, as they reflected on literature, Addison and Steele acknowledge Dryden's vision of a writing suited to the English, claiming in *Spectator* no. 62 to 'endeavour as much as possible to establish among us a Taste of polite Writing'. For example, they distinguish between true and false wit – 'the resemblance of ideas' versus 'the resemblance of words' (*Norton Anthology*, p. 2203 [A]), rejecting linguistic self-consciousness and density of metaphor. Through a series of essays focused on *Paradise Lost*, the *Spectator* reappraised Milton's work, situating it in a literary-historical framework, and taking it out of the political contexts in which it had so frequently been understood until then. In 1711, Addison describes what he calls the pleasures of the imagination, located somewhere between the pleasures of sense and those of understanding. For the developing sense of the autonomy of the aesthetic, this will be an important development. (Three decades later, Mark Akenside would name his 1744 series of poems *The Pleasures of the Imagination* after this series of essays.) With *An Essay on Criticism* (1711), Pope addresses Addison's wish to 'give some Account of it, and to lay down Rules how we may acquire that fine Taste of writing, which is so much talked about among the polite world' (*Spectator* 409, ed. Bond, III:527 [A]). For Pope, critics who are also authors are best able to represent this fine taste. In 'Of the Standard of Taste' (1757), David Hume suspects that there are 'certain general principles of approbation or blame' that can be traced in a work of art, and that there are individuals with sufficient 'delicacy of imagination' to trace them – the critics (Hume, p. 234 [A]).

If there was one person who represented for the eighteenth century the delicacy of imagination and the standard of literary taste, it was Samuel Johnson – with the signal exception that he did not wish to articulate a standard of taste. Indeed, in numbers 60 and 61 of Johnson's journal *The Idler*, it is the mock critic Dick Minim who 'often wishes for some standard of taste' (*Johnson*, ed. Greene, p. 294 [A]). Like Steele's Tatler, Dick Minim 'frequented the coffee houses' (p. 291). If both Hume's and Steele's well-known positions are parodied by Johnson, readers might wonder what Johnson offers as an alternative. In part, Johnson's point here is like Pope's: both would agree that 'the power of invention has been conferred by nature upon few' (p. 290), as Johnson puts it in *Idler* 60 (p. 290). Such a claim seems like the height of presumption, arrogance even. But Johnson means something humbler by it than might first appear. For Johnson, the critics ought to have a kind of humility; criticism hurts, he reminds us, and writing well is not easy. Johnson proposes, therefore, that readers rely on the collective insights of many readers over the generations. In his 'Preface to the Plays of William Shakespeare', Johnson defends such accumulated wisdom: 'what has been longest known has been most considered, and what is most considered is best understood' (p. 420). But what is best understood is not, for Johnson, therefore settled; in fact, it can be unsettling. What is so interesting about Johnson is his defence of the emotional power reading can have over the reader. In *Rambler* 4, for example, Johnson contends that 'the power of example is so great as to take possession of the memory by a kind of violence' (p. 176). A generation or two earlier, such a violent capture of memory by image would have prompted attacks on literature, as for example was the case with Collier's *Short View* (1698). For Johnson, such an effect on the psychology means that we ought to refer only to the best examples – in other words, a canon, but a canon of unsettling, powerful, aesthetic pleasures.

There are many different, albeit overlapping, explanations for why this modern English literary criticism emerges during the Restoration and eighteenth century. By the middle of the seventeenth century, it is difficult to overlook the sheer quantity of publication, especially in comparison to the publishing pattern that preceded it. Between the 1630s and the second decade of the eighteenth century, the number of titles published annually grew from 6,000 to 21,000, and the number would rise to about 56,000 titles published per annum by the 1790s, according to *The Practice and Representation of Reading in England* (Raven et al. [Cii]). With such an unprecedented rise in the number of titles published, it is understandable that a need would arise for post-publication readers who might sift through the new books and guide readers to what they considered to be the most important. In other words, the sheer volume of new publication calls for critics. The conclusion to the first issue of Steele's *Tatler* (1709) is particularly illustrative in this regard. Steele explains how he will separate different genres into different categories, represented by coffee houses: 'All accounts of gallantry, pleasure, and entertainment shall be under the article of White's chocolate-house; poetry, under that of Will's coffee-house; learning, under the title of the Grecian; foreign and domestic news, you will have from Saint James's coffee-house.' Such categories have the advantage of organising the total volume of titles, reducing it into a more manageable list, sorted by genre or topic. Through Steele's reference to the coffee houses we can see another way in which the eighteenth-century emergence of literary criticism is understood: the public sphere, as described by Jürgen Habermas in *The Structural Transformation of the Public Sphere* (1962 [B]). For the coffee house is one of Habermas's examples of a newly accessible, informed openness that he believes characterises the eighteenth century. According to Habermas, what has come to be known as literary criticism is central to the development of this new openness.

Habermas's vision of criticism contributing to the Enlightenment is not only inspirational; it is also an important corrective to the familiar Romantic model of criticism which puts a premium on textual unity (Keats's well-wrought urn) and the centrality of the authorial experience (e.g., Wordsworth's 'I wandered lonely as a cloud'). However, Habermas does not address the degree to which this early form of modern English literary criticism is a Restoration project through and through, concerned at root about how to avoid the political violence of the 1640s which many Restoration and eighteenth-century authors associated with democratised access to print. In his 'Life of Addison', for example, Johnson sketches a history of Restoration and eighteenth-century literary criticism:

> The Royal Society was instituted soon after the Restoration to divert the attention of the people from public discontent. The *Tatler* and the *Spectator* had the same tendency; they were published at a time when two parties, loud, restless, and violent, each with plausible declarations, and each without any distinct termination of its view, were agitating the nation; to minds heated with political contest they supplied cooler and more inoffensive reflections.
>
> (Johnson, *Lives*, II:94 [A])

Where Habermas might have us see these figures as struggling heroically to create a public sphere that protects democratic free expression, Johnson casts them as quelling dissent, concerned about democracy.

The Enlightenment

Criticism has been seen as a defining element in that aspect of the eighteenth century known as 'the Enlightenment'. This label has been the source of substantial and defining controversy of late, both in considerations of the eighteenth century, and in how the eighteenth century relates to and has an impact upon the present. Provisionally, it can be said that the Enlightenment is associated with the rise of science and the decline of religion, with a rejection of both enthusiasm and fanaticism, and with a defence of reasoned debate and open critique. Generally, the major figures of the Enlightenment are French *philosophes* and German philosophers, e.g., Voltaire,

Montesquieu and Kant. It may be surprising then to see the Enlightenment included in a literary overview of Restoration and eighteenth-century English literature. But the Habermas version of the eighteenth-century rise of criticism is in essence an Enlightenment model; indeed, the Enlightenment has sometimes been considered an age of criticism. Moreover, seventeenth- and eighteenth-century Britain set the terms for, and featured the key figures of, the Enlightenment. Bacon, Newton and Locke make major contributions to emerging discourses of modern science, democracy and toleration. Voltaire's *Letters on England*, for example, indicate both the importance of letters in the eighteenth century and his sense that what will come to be known at the end of the century as the Enlightenment is already emerging at the beginning of the century in Britain.

The last few decades of the twentieth century saw a wide-ranging debate over the nature and consequences of post-modernism. In one version of this debate, post-modernism is not opposed to, nor even simply after, the modernism of the early twentieth century but is, rather, said to be opposed to the modern itself. In other words, in this sense, the post-modern is also the post-Enlightenment. Thus, the recent 'rise of religion', the return of new age enthusiasms and scepticism towards science are all part of an undoing of the Enlightenment's legacy, the argument goes. In this, though, the literature of the Restoration and eighteenth century can make an important contribution to the discussion. For in the work of, say, Jonathan Swift and Laurence Sterne (both perhaps not coincidentally Anglo-Irish) there is a strong critique of the Enlightenment contemporary with the Enlightenment itself. This has led some to argue that the eighteenth century sees not one Enlightenment, but many 'Enlightenments', plural. But the tension between Swift and the Royal Society that can be seen in Book 3 of *Gulliver's Travels* might also help remind us that the modern, as the breakdown of consensus (and thus of the emergence of public debate and increasingly mass democratisation), always exists alongside its critique.

Central to the contemporary debate over the Enlightenment is the question of reason. In part, this question has to do with the status of religion during the Enlightenment, as tolerance, the separation of Church and state, and therefore secularism are considered among the most important contributions of the Enlightenment – and of the eighteenth century – towards shaping the experience of modernity itself. Related to the matter of religion is the definition and role of the irrational and the superstitious. But even the briefest review of the definition of the term 'reason' from the mid-seventeenth century into the second half of the eighteenth century shows the complexity of the issue at the time. For example, because Locke's *A Letter Concerning Toleration* (1689) is best known for Locke's secularising claim that it is 'above all things necessary to distinguish exactly the business of civil government from that of religion', it is surprising to notice the degree to which Locke situated this vision within Christianity (*Political Writings*, p. 393 [A]). Toleration is 'agreeable to the Gospel of Jesus Christ, and to the genuine reason of mankind' (p. 393), Locke contended. Although the Gospel and reason may have offered Locke two different tests for toleration, the sentence nonetheless implied thereby a similarity between them, a similarity that is at odds with the familiar story about a secularising Enlightenment. Still later, during the middle of the eighteenth century, David

Hume took a different approach to reason: he involved the passions in his definition of reason. Perhaps building on this combination of reason and the passions, Samuel Johnson created an allegory in *The Rambler* no. 96 (1751) to explain the relationship between Fiction, Truth and the passions. Johnson contended that the Muses created clothes, called Fiction, for Truth, with which Truth 'demanded entrance of the passions' (*Rambler*, ed. Bate and Strauss, II:152 [A]). Once admitted by the passions into the mind of the reader, Truth reveals herself to Reason. Thus, for Johnson at mid-century, reason requires passion, and truth requires deception, in order for us to be able to see accurately. This theory of fiction's passionate, corrective effect on reason would later be associated with the eighteenth-century 'sentimental' approach to literature (and to other people).

The story usually told about the Enlightenment recounts a shift from a sixteenth- and seventeenth-century democracy of belief to an eighteenth-century democracy of reason, the Enlightenment. At the beginning of the period, reason was not so secularised; at the end of the period, it was not so dispassionate either. Therefore, another way of explaining the tension in the current debate over the Enlightenment would point to the difference between considering the Enlightenment as a conceptual ideal on the one hand, and as a historical period on the other. There may have been a push for the separation of Church and state, and a shift from reason and religion to reason and the passions (which may itself be a form of secularisation, if not rationalisation). But countervailing tendencies – including the persistence of a theological framework – pulled against these changes during the Restoration and the eighteenth century. Not too long ago, in the debates over the Enlightenment, a focus on these countervailing forces might have been described as Tory (because 'conservative') or post-modern (because not 'secular'). More recently, though, with an apparent, worldwide rise of politicised religion, there has been agreement that it has become particularly important to examine the Enlightenment concepts in the light of their historical contexts. Consequently, the political and terminological boundaries between these formerly contrasted approaches have been somewhat blurred over the last few years.

Texts and Issues

The Royal Society and the Institutions of Modern Science

On 28 November 1660, at Gresham College, London, a group of twelve people, including Robert Boyle and Christopher Wren, who were interested in what was then called natural philosophy (and what is today called science) agreed to form a group that would meet weekly to discuss recent developments and experiments. By the following year, they were called the Royal Society. By 1663, a Royal Charter refers to the group as 'The Royal Society of London for Improving Natural Knowledge'. Like Francis Bacon, they were concerned about the accuracy and limits of words in recording observations of the physical world. Indeed, the Royal Society took 'Nullius in Verba' – 'in the words of no one' – as its motto. The Royal Society was part of the larger Restoration. Its members returned to the development of an emerging modern scientific method interrupted by the Civil Wars and Interregnum. Within a few years, the Royal Society had received approval for publishing the results of their experiments. In the process, the Royal Society demonstrated a commitment to empiricism, reason and access to information that would become hallmarks of the Enlightenment. Through its concern about the political violence of the preceding two decades, the Royal Society is a Restoration project in another sense as well – hoping to avoid a repeat of the Civil Wars, in part by moving from words and towards scientific observation.

Among the first books published by a member of the Royal Society after the founding of the group was *Micrographia* (1665) by Robert Hooke, who had been working as the Royal Society's 'Curator of Experiments' since 1662. An illustrated record of observations made possible with a microscope, *Micrographia* provided engraved illustrations of various objects as they were seen under the microscope, along with Hooke's descriptions of these objects. In the very first of Hooke's observations he examines books and printing, although he begins with not just any book, but with a miniature Bible. That is, he chooses what contemporaries would have considered the most important book. Seen under the microscope, nothing less than the Bible appears 'like a great splatch of London dirt' (*Micrographia*, pp. 3–4 [A]). For Hooke, the dirty irregularities of texts represent 'the dangers in the process of human reason, the remedies of them all can only proceed from the real, the mechanical, the experimental philosophy' (A2r). That is, Hooke argues that readers ought to turn away from books and towards the instruments through which the natural world might be observed. Hooke clears away the book and opens up the space for the natural world that makes up the remainder of *Micrographia*. Of course, books are still with us, so one could argue that Hooke's argument fails. But Hooke does help to distinguish the study of the physical world from the study of texts, and thereby contributes to the emerging split between modern science and texts. In this, Hooke's work is particularly influential for, and indicative of, the approach of the Royal Society.

In 1667, Thomas Sprat published *The History of The Royal Society*. For Sprat, natural philosophy offers a way of acquiring knowledge without the interference of metaphor. Rather than Hooke's technological insight into the messiness of words printed, Sprat complains about words' figurative dimension. 'Who can behold, without indignation', Sprat asks, 'how many mists and uncertainties, these specious tropes and figures have brought on our Knowledge?' (*History*, ed. Cope and Jones, p. 112 [A]). Sprat's approach would seem to be a familiar, neo-Platonist argument about the deception implicit in imagery, with the mists and uncertainties representing images that distract people from the truth. But Sprat ties the problem of tropes to the experience of the Civil Wars, which represent for him a break in an otherwise continuous development of the English language. The Royal Society, Sprat contends, aims 'to return back to the primitive purity, and shortness, when men deliver'd so many things, almost in an equal numbers of words' (113). Sprat calls this one-to-one correspondence between word and object 'Mathematical plainness' (113). Setting aside the likelihood that Sprat's theory might require an infinite number of words for an infinite number of things, the advantage of 'Mathematical plainness' is that one word would not represent a variety of different things (113). With a one-to-one relationship between words and things, words could refer directly to things both in and outside of language; there would be a profound symmetry between language and the world, and thinking would almost become a matter of operating with whole numbers.

John Milton, *Paradise Lost*

Today, John Milton's *Paradise Lost* (1667, 1674) is considered one of the masterpieces of English literature. This epic poem, c. 12,000 lines long, divided into twelve books of blank verse, sets out to 'justify the ways of God to men' (*Norton Anthology*, p. 1477, 1.26 [A]). In the process, the story recounts Satan's Fall from Heaven, God's response, and Adam and Eve's Fall from innocence in the Garden of Eden on earth. With extraordinary ambition and on a grand scale, the poem raises basic and difficult questions about free will and choice, about good and evil, and about relationships between men and women. With its impact on Blake, Mary Shelley and other major English-language authors, the importance of *Paradise Lost* to the canon of English literature cannot be overstated. The impact of *Paradise Lost* on what we might call the cultural and moral imagination of English-language speakers is perhaps even more widespread. It sometimes seems as if Milton's version of events in the book of Genesis in the Bible is more familiar than the Bible itself. During the Restoration, though, *Paradise Lost* did not fare well. It is not clear how popular a 12,000-line epic about Adam and Eve would have been. Samuel Johnson would later say, 'none ever wished it longer' (*Lives*, I.183 [A]). But in the Restoration, prospective readers were familiar with Milton from his defence of regicide during the Civil Wars and his participation in Cromwell's Interregnum government. Indeed, across the first three printings of the poem, the name John Milton gets smaller and smaller until it is simply 'J. M'. – nearly anonymous – in the third printing. By the end of the seventeenth century, though, the critical position of the poem changed.

When *Paradise Lost* opens, the narrator invokes the muse, a generic convention of epic poems, although in this case the implication is that the narrator may be conversing with the same muse who spoke to Moses, i.e., the Judaeo-Christian God. Satan and other angels recently fallen from heaven wake up, finding themselves in Hell, 'such place Eternal Justice had prepared / for those rebellious' (*Norton Anthology*, p. 1478, 1.70 [A]). The angels debate how to proceed, and ultimately decide on pursuing a new type of creature about whom they've heard: humans. Satan, taking it upon himself to find and pervert them, leaves Hell, passing his daughter, Sin (and her child Death), on his way out. God, seeing that Satan is heading towards Eden, explains that humans are 'sufficient to have stood, though free to fall' (p. 1521, 3.99), and his son offers to intervene on behalf of the soon-to-be-fallen humans. On earth, as Satan approaches, Adam and Eve recount different versions of their first days. Eve, for example, describes how she fled Adam the first time she saw him, thinking him 'less winning soft, less amiably mild' than the image of herself she had just seen

(p. 1543, 4.479). Eve reports that Adam caught up to her and 'seized' (p. 1543, 4.489) her hand. Adam later claims that Eve ran because she 'would be wooed' (p. 1563, 8.503). The archangel Raphael tells Adam about the war in heaven that preceded the scenes with which the epic began. Left alone, Adam and Eve debate whether or not to work together, and whether working alone would leave them vulnerable. Eve does go off to work by herself and meets a talking snake that repeatedly invites Eve to look and gaze at him for proof that animals can move up a presumed chain of being. Eve eats the forbidden fruit, and offers it to Adam as well, who chooses to join her in the act. Cursed with exile, Adam is given a tragical history tour by the archangel Michael, a survey of Adam's future, which is to say, humanity's past (from Milton's sense of our later perspective). After this tour, Adam reunites with Eve who claims, 'with thee to go / Is to stay here' (p. 1609, 12.615). With that Adam and Eve step forward, and 'With wandering steps and slow, / Through Eden took their solitary way' (p. 1610, 12.648–9).

Paradise Lost brings together an extraordinary range of precedents, combining them into a new whole. In the first few lines, the narrator claims to be writing something 'unattempted yet in prose or rhyme' (*Norton Anthology*, p. 1476, 1.16). An epic, *Paradise Lost* self-consciously refers back to the Greek epics of Homer. First published in a 10-book edition in 1667, *Paradise Lost* was revised for a second edition in 1674. There are only a handful of new lines in the second edition, but the number of books has gone from 10 to 12. Virgil's *Aeneid* also had twelve books, and it is possible that Milton's revision signals a connection to the Roman epic. In the carefully balanced oppositions between Heaven, Hell and Earth one can hear echoes of Dante's *Divine Comedy*. The mixing of allegory and epic that Spenser attempts to achieve in *The Faerie Queene* can be seen in Milton's *Paradise Lost* as well. At the same time, Milton's epic is a retelling and rereading of the Bible, most prominently Genesis, but other sections as well. That is, Milton recasts the biblical story of creation in the form of the classical epics, while weaving in allegory. Through it all, *Paradise Lost* repeatedly begins again, each time claiming to know more about origins than anyone before, so much in fact that readers are left wondering whether origins can ever be recounted. The result was influential and controversial from the beginning. It would be cited, examined, and contested by such writers as John Dryden, Joseph Addison, Jonathan Swift, Samuel Johnson, Mary Wollstonecraft, William Blake, Mary Shelley, Karl Marx and Sigmund Freud, to name but a few of the diverse and influential subsequent authors who addressed Milton's epic.

Paradise Lost has engaged its readers in a wide range of critical debates. If Hell had already been prepared in advance for 'those rebellious', then there is from the first lines of the first book the question of free will: did God know that the angels (and later man) would fall? If so, can the knowledge of an omniscient and omnipotent God not imply that the fall was destined to happen? In Book 3, God claims that his foreknowledge had no influence on their fault, but that's a complicated position at best: how could God's foreknowledge not influence events? Moreover, God indicates that he would receive no pleasure from mere obedience, which suggests that God might get some pleasure from the fall, or from the resulting prospect of his subjects having to choose between good and evil. For the Romantics, the focus of Milton's poem is Satan, who, along with other fallen angels, occupies the first two books, and who will be seen intermittently through Book 9. It could be that the attractiveness of Satan is part of the poem's theological justification: if Satan is intriguing to those who presumably believe they know better, how would he have seemed to the first two humans? At the same time, at least from Mary Wollstonecraft onwards, there is a critical tradition that accuses the poem of a profound bias against women, through its treatment of Eve, in a state of 'implied / submission' (*Norton Anthology*, p. 1539, 4.307–8). In response, another critical tradition contextualises such claims, seeing, just to take this case as an example, that such a description of Eve might be the narrator's characterisation of Satan's first seeing her.

For still other readers, the inequitable treatment of Eve stands out too much for it not to be part of the point, inviting readers to reflect on whether this is a good relationship, on whether Paradise was paradise for Eve. After all, Milton is the same author who defended divorce – including divorce for women – a quarter of a century earlier, and more than a century before it would be allowed by anything less than an Act of Parliament in England. It could be that Eve's inequitable treatment is part of a fortunate fall: it is good that Eve disobeyed, as her then current order was not good, some might say. But it is also important to note that Eve chose experience. For, as others point out, if it were not for the knowledge of good and evil that their act is said to have given us, we readers would not know that such an inequitable relationship is not good.

The inequity in Adam and Eve's relationship noted by feminist critics might also be an entry into another way of reading *Paradise Lost*, one that takes the poem as an allegory for a political history of the seventeenth century. In this reading, Adam initially acts like a divine-right monarch, presuming that his relationship with God meant that he could claim Eve as his own. Adam and Eve, then, could come to stand for king and people. Such a possibility gives a different meaning to the Romantic sense that Milton was of Satan's party without knowing it: Satan makes Eve's decision to disobey possible. To this way of thinking, there are parallels between Satan and Cromwell. As a political allegory from Milton the defender of regicide and opponent of the Restoration, the title *Paradise Lost* might refer to the democratic possibilities of the 1640s. Some might argue that by Book 3, the narrator asks for forgiveness in the invocation because he now knows that he has been in Hell with Satan. As an epic and an allegory, *Paradise Lost* does what epics do, generally: narrate national origins. For this reading, the important development is in the ending of *Paradise Lost*, as Adam and Eve have learned to live together. After 1688, the reputation of *Paradise Lost* rose as Adam and Eve seem to represent England making a choice, as it had just done in the Glorious Revolution.

Locke: Philosopher of Modernity

John Locke is among the most important English-language philosophers, and the most important of the last several decades of the seventeenth century. His work affected areas as disparate as philosophy of language, money, political philosophy and psychology. In two remarkable years, 1689–90, he published three major works on Church and state, on cognition and on government: *A Letter Concerning Toleration* (1689), *An Essay Concerning Human Understanding* (1690) and *Two Treatises of Government* (1690). During the 1690s, he would publish essays on coins and coinage that would provide both support and theoretical justification for an early version of a credit economy. These works are almost cross-referenced. For example, the discussion of value in the *Two Treatises* will matter for the later work on coins, and is not entirely separate from the discussion of words in *An Essay on Human Understanding*. These different works also share a common assumption and a common, consequent development: across his thinking, Locke presumes the same kind of *tabula rasa* or blank slate that he specifies as the natural state of human consciousness. In response, what ties Locke's proposals together is a central interest in the benefits of conventions and contracts. Through it all, there is a presumption that it is possible to start over, contractually. This profoundly modern premise can be seen, for example, in the shift from the state of nature to the origin of government that Locke lays out in the *Second Treatise*.

There is a debate over contractual theory across the seventeenth century. It can be seen in some of the oppositional, republican arguments in the 1640s, but receives its fullest treatment in Hobbes's *Leviathan* (1651). Locke takes this contractual theory and applies it to new fields. According to Locke, coins, government, minds and words are all the result of convention. Consequently, for Locke, government, the mind and money are each negotiable, and to that extent free-standing rather than tied to a natural order. Unlike Hobbes, though, Locke sees these contractual arrangements as increasing possibilities without increasing instability. For Hobbes, the drafting of the contract is the democratic act; afterwards the resulting sovereign is totally empowered. For Locke's sense of government, religion and finance, the contract allows for continuing democratic options, essentially permanently.

Locke suited the eighteenth-century sense of itself as open and conversant. In *A Letter Concerning Toleration*, Locke offered a position regarding the relationship between Church and state that would come to be associated not only with the Whigs but with the Enlightenment itself as well. Locke argues that state and Church are separate, at a time when they were still connected as far as English law was concerned. Locke's argument here is a variation of his argument in the *Second Treatise*. For Locke, unlike Hobbes, humans have a natural interest in fellowship; churches, like governments, are contractual, voluntary, agreements. The state that might try to compel a particular religious belief, then, acts like the person in the *Second Treatise* who threatens the peace of those around them. At the beginning of *A Letter*, Locke argues, 'Everyone is orthodox to himself' (*Political Writings*, p. 390 [A]). Democracies, then, would allow for the differences that flow from this equality of belief. Against those who worry about those souls that might founder or become spiritually lost under such an arrangement, Locke argues that the care of souls is not a matter for the government, even with the consent of the governed. This does not mean, for Locke, that religion is not important; rather, Locke distinguishes between commanding and persuading. The difference has to do with force: there is less force – and some would say no force at all – in persuading. Evidence is forceful enough. This claim will become a particularly important distinction for the French *philosophes* (and a central issue in the post-modern debate over the continued relevance of the Enlightenment). Locke's separation of Church and state went on to become a defining element of governments in modernity, as different countries and constitutions worked out different relationships with secularism. But it is therefore important to note that Locke sees the separation of Church and state as a religious position, toleration being 'chief characteristical mark of the true Church' (p. 390).

In the *Second Treatise*, Locke distinguishes between four types of value – 'intrinsick', 'use', 'exchange', and 'overplus', each building on the other (*Political Writings*, pp. 279, 285, 286 [A]). For Locke, intrinsic value represents the worth of an object prior to any intervention of human labour, because ''tis Labour indeed that *puts the difference of value* on everything' (p. 281). Those plants, for example, that can be used for food acquire use value, in the eating. Once people have accumulated large amounts of things with use value, they then agree to settle on a scale of exchange value, Locke argues, according to which some other objects are taken in exchange for the desired objects. The objects that are exchanged in the stead of the objects desired are called money, and with it people can acquire more than they can use. Through the differences between intrinsic value, use value and exchange value, there is the possibility of what Locke calls an overplus, or what would now be called profit. This theory of value is also a theory of how money works as a representation of other units of value. From this, Locke is able to move to his explanation of money and coinage in the essays on money that he published in the 1690s. At the time, English coins were worth their weight of the material from which they were made; it was a version of what has been called the 'gold standard', except that it was built into every coin. The problem was, though, that as the coins circulated, people would remove pieces of them, melt them down and sell the metal. This clipping meant that the coins were worth less and that money was being lost. Locke argued for moving beyond this model of money and coinage, and for treating the coins as *representations* of value, not the value itself. To some, this meant severing the connection between the coins and their value, although to Locke it meant only recognising that this connection had already been severed. It was as if Locke's theory of money brought to coins the political consequences of the Glorious Revolution: politics and currency were both based on conventions. The value of coins depended on what people believed the coins were worth, for what they could be exchanged, and, thereby, in what they stood for. Because Locke is here defining both a representational system and a credit system for currency, this shift in the frame of assumptions regarding value was part of what made possible the 1694 creation of a Bank of England, a mechanism for extending credit.

Spectator no. 69 and Enlightenment Cosmopolitanism?

Since 1567, international traders and merchants had been meeting to sell their wares in central London, in the City, in a building known since 1570 as the Royal Exchange. Consumed by the Fire of London in 1666, the Royal Exchange was rebuilt starting in

1667 and reopened in 1669. The layout of the new building was quite similar to that of the previous Exchange: an open-air rectangle bordered and created by two-storey walls, the ground floor of which had a portico on all four sides. But in 1711, this building became more than a market, more than a facility for buying and selling. For in an early issue of the *Spectator*, in one of the most famous essays in that journal, Addison transformed this space into a metaphor, representing all that was new about Britain's position in the world, and, relatedly, about how the globe was then being understood in new ways. Describing people who come together in London from all over the world to sell their wares, Addison casts the Royal Exchange as nothing less than a new world order – one which through a combination of Locke's theories of value, Newtonian physics, and an early sentimentalism understands the Exchange as a new political possibility for the whole world. Consequently, this essay is a central, early English statement of what later came to be known as the Enlightenment project. For Addison, the market redresses inequities, and represents new freedoms, not only to purchase goods, but also to become another person. The essay has been taken as a hopeful statement of Enlightenment cosmopolitanism. Those same elements, though, will remind other readers of subsequent developments in British (and world) history: nationalism, colonialism, globalisation.

Addison begins by telling the reader that there is no place he enjoys going as much as he does the Royal Exchange. There, Addison can mingle, largely unknown, among merchants who come to London, he reports, from Armenia, Egypt, Holland, Japan and Moscow. There, he sees different fashions and different ways of walking, and hears different languages. Mixing among the representatives of these people, Addison is 'A Dane, Swede, or Frenchman at different times' (*Spectator* 69, ed. Bond, I:294 [A]). The way Addison sees it, Nature distributed her benefits unequally across the globe, and these traders address this inequity, redistributing natural benefits to places that would otherwise go without them. Indeed, Addison points to the islands of the United Kingdom as representing precisely the kind of place not blessed with natural advantages – 'barren uncomfortable', as he puts it (p. 295). He lists fruits and vegetables that did not naturally grow in Britain, and would not have taken root there were it not for their having been transported. The point is not only agricultural. Addison reminds readers that, for instance, 'the single dress of a woman of quality is often the product of an hundred climates' (p. 295). Nature provides what is necessary, commerce the variety. The way Addison sees it, this process means that France becomes Britain's 'Gardens', the Spice Islands of south Asia its 'Hot-Beds', the Persians its 'Silk Weavers' and the Chinese Britain's 'Potters' (p. 296). Thus, Addison argues, trade gives Britain an empire without increasing its holdings.

Addison's essay speaks to a developing consumer culture, and to a global interconnectedness that sustains it. After all, the merchants who run this trade 'knit Mankind together' (p. 296). *Spectator* 69 also points towards a vision of something like a world government, as the market is 'a great Council, in which all considerable Nations have their Representatives' (p. 293). Today, some might believe that either the differences between governments and markets or the supports between governments and markets are lost on Addison. But for Addison writing in the early eighteenth

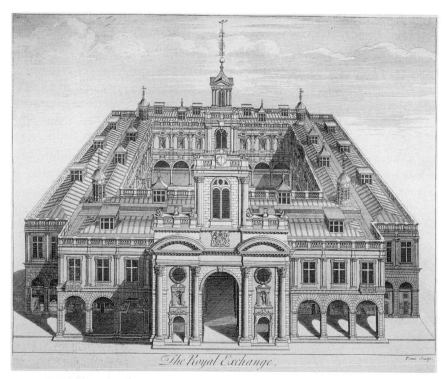

3.13 Royal Exchange (c. 1750).

century, the cooperation required for international trade represents a new political possibility, quite different from international wars over, say, monarchical succession. For Addison, that is, markets represent a new degree of interdependency and stability. At the same time, this new, world government of international trade creates a new kind of citizenship, known best to those who participate in markets such as the Royal Exchange – the citizen of the world. At the same time, Addison's sense of the Royal Exchange reflects Locke's understanding of exchange – people agreeing to trade what they have in abundance for what they need, and thereby achieving a better state. But one can also hear other influences as well.

In Addison's description of a market that circulates the extremes from one area of the world to another so as to achieve an overall balance, we have a Newtonian model of equal oppositions – a lack in one place is balanced by a surplus elsewhere. For Addison, Nature has set this inequality up quite specifically, 'with an Eye to this mutual Intercourse and Traffic among Mankind' (p. 294). Natural differences exist to increase the possibility of our connecting, rather than to necessitate separation. These differences between regions require compensating for the seemingly unequal distribution of goods. The market acts as a regulatory mechanism at the centre of global forces arrayed as opposing extremes. The differences of region and culture can meet in the market, where they will be moderated by the mutual need of one side for what the other offers. Without extremes, there is no need for the market,

Slavery

Before Columbus arrived in the New World, Portuguese traders had for several decades been trafficking in slaves acquired from Africa, shipping them to the Iberian peninsula in southern Europe. But Columbus's arrival on the western edge of the Atlantic opened the door to a larger, transatlantic trade in African slaves. By the end of the eighteenth century, more than 5 million Africans would be transported to the New World. In the colonies, these slaves would provide knowledge and labour for the agricultural economies that went with the colonial plantations. For more than a century, this trade had been dominated by the Portuguese, who transported slaves both to Portuguese and to Spanish colonies. In the seventeenth century, Britain began to become involved in the trade, shipping slaves to the American colonies and British possessions in the West Indies. Slaves arrived in a Dutch ship in Virginia in 1619, and slavery unfolded as a de facto part of life in the British colonies. By 1670, slaves and slave-ownership were written into *The Fundamental Constitution of the Carolinas* drafted by the Lords Proprietors of the Carolinas (to which board John Locke was Secretary). Once involved, the British made the system more efficient, with special ships, and faster routes (see Figure 3.14). By the middle of the eighteenth century, Britain became the world's leading slave-trading nation, a position it would not relinquish until the abolition of the overseas slave trade in 1807. In the process, Britain alone transported more than 3 million Africans to the New World, as many as 45,000 a year towards the end of the eighteenth century. It was during the Restoration and eighteenth century that Britain was most involved in the slave trade. It was also during the eighteenth century, though, that abolitionists began to clamour for an end to the practice: an abolition society began in Philadelphia in 1775, and in London in 1787.

but the market also offers Addison a model for modulating extremes. It is not far from this position to Adam Smith's later formulation in *The Wealth of Nations* (1776) of the 'invisible hand' of the market. But in Addison there is the sense that the market achieves this balancing act only by keeping goods, money and people in circulation. In a way, then, Addison's thinking reflects Harvey's mid-seventeenth-century discovery of the circulation of blood. But in this model of balanced opposites (Newton) kept in circulation (Harvey) by exchange (Locke), Addison's description of the Royal Exchange turns London, and maybe Britain, into something like a heart for the global body, with British shipping serving as the transoceanic 'vessels'. Although it is not Addison's focus, it is not difficult to see how such a model could lead to precisely the colonial empire Britain actually acquired by the end of the century. In other words, this essay offers both a rich defence of the Enlightenment, and the materials for its critique.

Eighteenth-Century Slave Narratives

Across the Restoration and eighteenth century, slavery becomes an issue for the texts of English literature. In 1688, for example, Aphra Behn's *Oroonoko, or the Royal Slave* and in 1690 John Locke's *Second Treatise* both address and/or invoke slavery. Although both texts would later be enlisted for abolitionist ends, it is not clear that either author is making an abolitionist claim. For Locke and Behn, slavery seems to work more as a metaphor than as a lived experience. Behn's 'Royal Slave', for example, can be a Royalist representation of James II, not a free monarch but instead forced out by the traders in Parliament. Locke takes the opposite position in the *Second Treatise*, seeing absolute monarchs as turning subjects into slaves, and offering his contractual model of government as ending such slavery. If only because it does not fit with the later Locke's sense that government protects us from those who would accumulate too much, Locke's role in the earlier *Fundamental Constitution of the Carolinas* (1669) is a matter of some debate: why would Locke make slave ownership a constitutive feature of the new colony? For some, this document's conservative bent means Locke's role was minimal; for others, it means that Locke learned from the experience and published an improvement two decades later. Others argue that Locke's two positions – one for Carolina and another for England – represent an emerging double standard that would keep the bulk of slavery at a distance from the British Isles. Of course, there is also the possibility that Locke's later defence of property would just be expanded to include a defence of holding slaves as property. Just such a defence is given by Daniel Defoe's *Robinson Crusoe*. The title character owns slaves – Xury and Friday – at different points in the novel. Moreover, the central image of the novel – creating a life on a deserted island – happens only because Crusoe wrecks his ship while on an expedition to bring slaves into Brazil illegally. By 1740, slavery has become enough of an issue, even if only as a figure of speech, for it to feature prominently in James Thomson's popular poem (and song) 'Rule, Britannia' (1740): 'Britons never will be slaves.' The question is whether that means Britain is opposed to slavery, or whether the British will always be free, and therefore whether there are others whose enslavement remains acceptable.

By the latter third of the eighteenth century, those who had been enslaved begin to be heard from. Slaves and former slaves began to publish autobiographies, essays and poetry. Among the best known of these authors are: Phyllis Wheatley, whose *Poems on Various Subjects, Religious and Moral* was published in 1773; Ignatius Sancho, whose *Letters* were published in 1782; Quobna Cugoano who published his *Thoughts and Sentiments on the Evil and Wicked Traffic of Slaves and Commerce of the Human Species* in 1789; and Olaudah Equiano, whose autobiography, *The Interesting Narrative of the Life of Olaudah Equiano*, appeared in 1794. These works have all been reissued in recent years as part of an increasing interest in and awareness of the multicultural past. While each provides access to the life of a slave in the eighteenth century, these works can be quite surprising. By the eighteenth century, slavery was a long-established fact of life. It shaped the assumptions even of these remarkable people who were able to publish their lives and reflections. The slave owners 'judged ignorance the best and only security for obedience' (Sancho, *Unchained Voices*, p. 79 [A]), and organised their slaves' lives accordingly. The slaves' stories often combine two older forms, the conversion and the captivity narratives. The slaves often find themselves drawn to the clarity of the moral codes of Christianity – often turning those codes against their captors. Cugoano, for example, argues that 'the destroyers and enslavers of men can be no Christians' (Cugoano, *Unchained Voices*, p. 162 [A]).

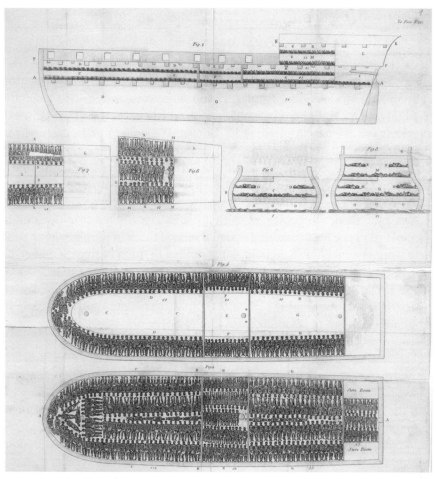

3.14 *Plan of a slave ship*, 1808.

Phyllis Wheatley is an interesting case in this regard. In her poem 'On Being Brought from Africa to America', Wheatley treats her transportation to America not as an enslavement but as a redemption, for how it brought her knowledge of God and the Saviour. 'To the King's Most Excellent Majesty. 1768' can confound today's readers. Wheatley is praising a monarch just as the American Revolution is about to begin. Some see this as evidence of how deeply the experience of subjugation must have affected slaves such as Wheatley. But there is another way of reading it, one that suggests how cleverly subversive Wheatley might have been with this poem. According to the last line, 'A monarch's smile can set his subjects free!'. This could be another statement of Royalist sentiment, unimpeachable in Britain, or a cry for freedom, and in that way popular with those in Wheatley's Boston calling for action against the king. In a way, it is a paradox: why would a monarch set his subjects free? But that question raises the possibility that Wheatley might have been aware of the then-developing sense that slaves who made it to British soil would be treated as free.

Samuel Johnson, *Dictionary of the English Language*

In intellectual history, the eighteenth century is sometimes represented by the dictionary and the encyclopaedia. Access to knowledge is central to the idea of the Enlightenment; the dictionary and encyclopaedia were designed to facilitate this accessibility. In 1728, Ephraim Chambers published *Cyclopaedia, or An Universal Dictionary of Arts and Sciences*. Inspired by it, Diderot, D'Alembert and others began work on a French encyclopaedia, *Encyclopédie, ou Dictionnaire raisonné des sciences, des arts, et des métiers par une société de gens de lettres* (1751–72, 17 vols.; 1776–80, 7 vols.). Between 1768 and 1771, the first edition of the *Encyclopaedia Britannica* was published. Dictionaries were even more numerous. In the last decade of the seventeenth century, the Académie Française published its first dictionary, the result of decades of work by specialists at the Académie (and updated several times in the eighteenth century). There were several English dictionaries compiled in the seventeenth and eighteenth centuries: Henry Cockeram's *The English Dictionarie: Or, An Interpreter of Hard English Words* (1626, 2nd edn); Edward Cocker's *English Dictionary* (1704); Benjamin Defoe's *Compleat English Dictionary* (1735); and Thomas Dyche and William Pardon, *A New General English Dictionary* (1740). Edward Phillips's *The New World of Words: Or, a General Dictionary* went through seven editions between 1658 and 1720.

For English, no dictionary before the *Oxford English Dictionary* (which was completed in the early decades of the twentieth century) would be as influential as the one compiled by Samuel Johnson in the middle of the eighteenth century. The *Dictionary* is probably the most famous of Johnson's works; editions continue to be published today. Although there were English-language dictionaries before Johnson, no previous dictionary included anything like the self-aware prefatory materials featured in Johnson's. In 1747, Johnson published a *Plan* of his proposed *Dictionary*, addressed to Lord Chesterfield (from whom Johnson implicitly hoped for patronage) and claiming that he would 'fix the English language' in three years. It was an audacious plan, of course, especially to those who knew how long it had taken the experts at the Académie Française to complete the French dictionary. But that ambition only added to the significance of the project: one Englishman working efficiently with assistants and independent of the state, as opposed to dozens of experts working slowly for the French monarchy. When Chesterfield refused to provide Johnson with financial support, the project acquired another layer of significance: the *Dictionary* would be produced for the marketplace, with backing from booksellers rather than the aristocracy. When it was published, eight years later, in 1755, Lord Chesterfield came through with public support for the *Dictionary*, publishing two letters in which he regretted the anarchical state of the language and thanked Johnson as a dictator for bringing order. In a letter that could probably stand for the end of the patronage system for literary production, Johnson wrote back to Chesterfield, complaining of how he had originally treated him.

It may also be that part of Johnson's opposition to Lord Chesterfield's belated support for the *Dictionary* arises from how Chesterfield's 1755 letter profoundly misunderstands Johnson's vision for the *Dictionary* as published. For in the Preface, Johnson describes a dictionary and a process of compiling a dictionary that refuses precisely the dictatorial role Lord Chesterfield ascribes to Johnson's *Dictionary*. On the face of it, *any* dictionary would seem to fulfil Chesterfield's wish for order. And in a way, Chesterfield's desire for order is not so different from Thomas Sprat's earlier desire in *The History of the Royal Society* for a language of great precision, or what Sprat calls 'Mathematical plainness' (*History*, ed. Cope and Jones, p. 113 [A]). Like Sprat – and Locke – Johnson claims in the Preface that 'language is only the instrument of science, and words are but the signs of ideas' (*Johnson*, ed. Greene, p. 310 [A]). The difference, though, is that Johnson includes several meanings for each of the words defined in his dictionary. It is as if (to turn a famous phrase from the Preface) the dictionary was begun with the dreams of a scientist doomed at last to wake a poet. In the Preface, Johnson describes how the lexicographer runs the risk of 'reducing to a method'. Johnson's phrase also speaks to the tension between stability and change that characterises his sense of the *Dictionary*, and of the language. The phrase acknowledges the desire for a method, but there is also the sense that to methodise is to reduce, that something is lost in being methodical with language. The fact that Johnson associates method with reduction testifies to the complexity of language that Johnson saw in his survey and is concerned simultaneously to address *and* to capture in the *Dictionary*.

The tension in the *Dictionary* and in reducing words to a method can be seen in the Preface, where Johnson provides two descriptions of words. On the one hand, he argues, 'such is the exuberance of signification which many words have obtained that it was scarcely possible to collect all their senses' (Preface, in *Johnson*, ed. Greene, p. 317 [A]). To call the multiplicity of meaning 'exuberance' is a relatively celebratory way of referring to the entanglements that Johnson saw when he first surveyed his subject. To contain methodically such exuberance would certainly feel like a reduction, or a diminishment. On the other hand, though, Johnson also contends that there are 'spots of barbarity impressed so deep in the English language that criticism can never wash them away' (p. 309). In this case, there seems to be a resignation about the fact of multiple meanings; as spots of barbarity, and as something to be washed away, multiplicity is here cast as a stain on the language, in which case a methodical treatment is the best that can be hoped for. At the same time, though, there is in Johnson's *Dictionary* – as there was not in Sprat's *History* or Chesterfield's letter – an acceptance of the (formerly) metaphorical as the (currently) standard meaning. In the Preface, Johnson claims that 'Tongues, like governments, have a natural tendency to degeneration; we have long preserved our constitution, let us make some struggles for our language' (*Norton Anthology*, p. 2389 [A]). By setting out the principles (e.g., the Preface) and providing the precedents (e.g., the illustrative quotations), there is a way Johnson's *Dictionary* provides a constitution for modern English, in the sense of a written founding document.

Burke, Hastings and Cook: Great Britain Globalises

Some argue that globalisation is a recent phenomenon, made possible by the end of the Cold War, i.e. by the absence of an alternative or an opposition to untrammelled capitalism, and by new communication technologies. But if by globalisation we mean an increasing economic interconnectedness across the world, then Restoration and eighteenth-century Britain made a major contribution to globalisation. Even as it was losing its most prosperous Atlantic colonies, Great Britain was in the process of acquiring new colonies elsewhere, most significantly in India and on the continent they would call 'Australia', or 'southern'. Usually, given Britain's dominance then, people would point to the nineteenth century as Britain's globalised period. But that subsequent dominance required significant seventeenth- and eighteenth-century developments. In 1757, for example, after the Battle of Plassey, the East India Company shifted from trading in Bengal to ruling it. In 1770, Captain Cook reached and began to map the eastern coast of 'Terra Australia'. In this way, the Restoration and eighteenth century offer both major precedents (and instructive parallels) for later events. British globalisation in the eighteenth century is an issue that has many possible texts; *Oroonoko, Robinson Crusoe* and *Gulliver's Travels* would obviously be prominent among them. But if we read with an eye towards this issue, we can find it in seemingly unlikely places. For example, in that mid-century work of domestic fiction, *Clarissa*, the protagonist inherits her grandfather's wealth partly because her uncle has already come into a fortune 'by his East India traffic and successful voyages' (p. 53).

Three texts stand out, though, in the second half of the eighteenth century as having particular relevance for British globalisation: Adam Smith's *An Inquiry into*

3.15 Francis Hayman, *Robert Clive and Mir Jaffar after the Battle of Plassey, 1757* (c. 1760).

the Nature and Causes of the Wealth of Nations (1776), Captain James Cook's *A Voyage Toward the South Pole and Round the World* (1777), and Edmund Burke's 'Speech on Fox's East India Bill' (1783). In May 1768, Cook sets out for the South Pacific, making it to Tahiti in April 1769. Not long after anchoring, Cook finds it necessary to establish rules for trading with the inhabitants of Georges Island (befriend the natives; appoint crew members to do the trading; hold on to tools; do not embezzle; no iron or cloth to be traded unless for food, etc.). A few years later, in 1776, Adam Smith publishes *The Wealth of Nations*, which is known today for its defence of free trade. Less well known is Smith's focus on the effects of colonies, a topic to which he devoted a chapter. For Smith, 'the discovery of America, and that of a passage to the East Indies' are among the most important events in the history of mankind, because – echoing Addison's *Spectator* no. 69 – Smith believes these discoveries make possible 'uniting, in some measure, the most distant parts of the world … enabling them to relieve one another's wants, to increase one another's enjoyments' (Smith, *Wealth of Nations*, II.626 [A]). It is important to note that Smith believes, however, that such benefits of these discoveries 'have been sunk and lost in the dreadful misfortunes which they have occasioned' (II.626). For Smith, these misfortunes spring not from global trading but from arranging global trade into separate monopolies. Thus, for him, free trade can restore the potential benefits unrealised by how global trade had been organised so far. Finally, Edmund Burke continues this theme in his Speech on Fox's East India Bill. Against the East India Company, Burke argues that '*Magna charta* is a charter to restrain power, and to destroy monopoly. The East India charter is a charter to establish monopoly, and to create power' (*On Empire*, ed. Bromwich, p. 290 [A]). Burke would pursue the same line in his 1787 impeachment of Hastings, past Governor-General of India. While these three texts stand for a larger pattern of global colonisation and economic integration in the eighteenth century, their shared attention to the dynamic of free trade means that they continue to be relevant for us today, as analogy or as cause, depending on one's perspective. They also continue to raise questions about the meaning and practice of Enlightenment cosmopolitanism.

Readings

This section offers brief, schematic, synoptic suggestions for some of the ways in which five major works from Restoration and eighteenth-century English literature might be read in context. As such, these readings are not meant to be exhaustive, either for the time period or for the works under consideration. Rather, they are proposals for some of the ways reading in the context of the Restoration and eighteenth century might operate, clues for the kinds of patterns to which one might pay attention in reading contextually, and indications of how one might benefit from doing so. It is hoped that these sketches will induce fuller contextual readings, including contextual readings that convey why these and so many other works of literature have such a powerful effect on readers, across wide ranges of contexts.

Aphra Behn's *Oroonoko, or the Royal Slave* (1688)

Aphra Behn's *Oroonoko, or the Royal Slave* (1688) is sometimes considered the earliest novel in the English language, and certainly offers an excellent introduction to what become some of the central concerns of the novel in the eighteenth century. Like so many novels published through the 1740s, *Oroonoko* is much shorter than the typical nineteenth-century novel. Like the famous eighteenth-century novels that will follow it, *Oroonoko* features a narrator sent across the ocean to new colonies, and takes place at least in part in a new colonial outpost. Moreover, from the beginning, *Oroonoko* will attempt to create the conditions for what will subsequently become the familiar presumption that the novel somehow captures or reflects the real, 'realism' in a word. In the process, Behn's *Oroonoko*, like so many eighteenth-century novels, connects fictional prose narrative to history. That Behn achieves these combinations in this work is part of what makes *Oroonoko* novel. At the same time, though, the topic upon and towards which she makes these contributions, 'the royal slave', is easily equally important.

Oroonoko begins with a remarkable first sentence, one worthy of, indeed seemingly asking for, sustained consideration: 'I do not pretend, in giving you the history of this royal slave, to entertain my reader with the adventures of a feigned hero, whose life and fortunes fancy may manage at the poet's pleasure; nor in relating the truth, design to adorn it with any accidents but such as arrived in earnest to him' (*Norton Anthology*, pp. 1866–7 [A]). The first main clause in that sentence states 'I do not pretend', a striking assertion that places a claim on our belief. From the very beginning of the story, readers are told that the story is true. Of course, many stories claim to tell the truth. But in this same first sentence, the narrator goes on to specify the particular kind of truth being told here, and it is not that of the poet. Rather than casting truth as something to be found behind the embellishments of 'fancy', this story will remain unadorned with anything except what actually happened to the royal slave. In other words, this is not a work of the imagination, not simply a creation of the mind of the author. Rather, the argument is that the procedure will be empirical, the results of observation. The narrator begins the second paragraph 'I was myself an eyewitness to a great part of what you will find here set down' (p. 1867). Thus, the opening of the story connects *Oroonoko* to developments in early modern British science, which was also claiming to focus on how to describe the world without recourse to metaphor, figures or other 'poetic' devices.

'History' is a particularly important word in that first sentence, important both for Behn's *Oroonoko* and for the eighteenth-century English novel. In part, it is related to the French word, 'histoire', or story. But as the narrator does not pretend, in this case the word 'history' seems to be part of the eyewitness, empirical, anti-figurative dimension of *Oroonoko*'s initial development. The narrator is claiming, again, to be relating the actual order of actual events, as histories claim to do. It would seem that readers are supposed to be led to believe the following facts: there was a noble African prince, named Oroonoko, who fell in love with Imoinda (daughter of his foster-father); who refused to enter into battle because an old king takes Imoinda for himself; who is tricked into a slave ship bound for Surinam; who, upon landing there is reunited with Imoinda (and is also introduced to the narrator); who organises the trade between the English colonists and the natives in Surinam; who leads a failed slave uprising; who also fails in a suicide pact with Imoinda; and who is disembowelled, quartered and shipped in pieces around Surinam as an example to other African slaves. And it is quite possible that there was such a person. This also raises the question, of course, of whether the narrator is in some way Aphra Behn herself. The narrator calls attention to her status as a female, worrying that her story might lack credibility among readers. We know that Aphra Behn travelled to Surinam in the 1660s, when her father had been named ambassador there. *Oroonoko*'s narrator's father also dies en route to Surinam. Thus, it could very well be that *Oroonoko* is a history, in the sense of a record of events. Indeed, some of the colonists depicted in *Oroonoko* have the same names as settlers known to have travelled to Surinam during the Restoration.

The narrator believes that Oroonoko was an extraordinary individual, noble in every sense of the word: of good character, well-educated, and able to emerge as a leader from among a wide range of people – English, Native American and African. 'He had', the narrator reports, 'nothing of barbarity in his nature, but in all points addressed himself as if his education had been in some European court' (p. 1870). She contrasts his nobility with the savagery of the plantation owners – the English colonists – a council of whom, the narrator claims 'consisted of such notorious villains as Newgate never transported; and possibly originally were such who understood neither the laws of God or man, and had no sort of principles to make 'em worthy the name of men' (p. 1906). The narrator casts the residents of Surinam as being as innocent as Adam and Eve before the Fall, adding that 'they understand no vice or cunning, but when they are taught by the white men' (p. 1868). It is striking to read such a strong criticism, from the seventeenth century, of what the narrator casts as the unfortunate consequences of European settlement in the New World. With such stark contrasts between the mercenaries running the plantation and the gracious royal slave, Oroonoko (whom the colonists rename 'Caesar' upon his arrival in Surinam), *Oroonoko* was often read as a pioneering and inspiring abolitionist text. According to this way of seeing *Oroonoko*, the miserable treatment to which such a great figure as Oroonoko was subjected clearly indicates the inhumanity of slavery as an institution. For quite some time through the nineteenth century this story was understood in these terms.

It is possible to read the story of *Oroonoko* as history in another sense as well, not just as a true story, but as a record of major events. An early indication of this reading arrives with our first introduction to the character Oroonoko. The narrator tells the reader that Oroonoko 'had heard of the late civil wars in England, and the deplorable death of our great monarch, and would discourse of it with all the sense and abhorrence of the injustice imaginable' (p. 1870). The reference is to the 1649 execution of Charles I (during 'the late civil wars in England'), and the tone is that of a Royalist ('abhorrence', 'deplorable'). Near the end of the novel, at the end of the second-to-last paragraph, after the plantation owners have drawn and quartered Oroonoko, one character decides that he will not attempt to subdue his slaves 'with frightful spectacles of a mangled king' (p. 1910). In 1649, England too witnessed the same spectacle, as the king was executed on a platform in the street outside the Banqueting House in London. It is tempting, then, to read *Oroonoko* as a 'history' of Charles I, the mangled king. However, with its publication in 1688, the year of what is usually known as the Glorious Revolution, it is more likely that *Oroonoko* offers us a Royalist vision of the possible consequences of Parliament's actions on James II. Oroonoko, we are told, was educated by a tutor from France, as, of course James II was, since his family had been in exile in France in the Interregnum. In this case, the subtitle, 'The Royal Slave', might refer not so much to a slave of royal lineage, i.e., Oroonoko, but rather to a royal who has been reduced to a slave, i.e., James II. In this way, the narrator's low regard for the council of plantation owners could be read as a Royalist caricature of the Commons.

Here, though, we come across a powerful paradox: if, like the narrator, Aphra Behn is not pretending, if *Oroonoko* is a history of political events in England in 1688 or the late seventeenth century more broadly, that import is conveyed by a central extended metaphor. The paradox is that the unembellished history is conveyed by an allegory. If there ever was an actual, or historical, Oroonoko in Surinam, he becomes, in Behn's history, a metaphor for what she feared might happen to James II. In this process, as metaphor becomes history, or as history becomes metaphor, we can begin to see what would become a particularly important dynamic for the early English novel. Although this historical connection could be seen as contributing to the novel's familiar relationship with realism, there is another, more specific dimension to it in the case of the early English novels. Many of them use fiction to provide a particular perspective on contemporary, or at least recent, political events. That is, they tell a story to represent a history.

In this tension between story and history, fiction and non-fiction, metaphor and event, we see the hybrid dynamic that characterises the novel as a form. Aphra Behn's *Oroonoko* combines several genres. For example, Oroonoko's sulking refusal to fight for his side because of how the woman he loves has been treated is reminiscent of Achilles in *The Iliad*, and aligns *Oroonoko* with the epic. More importantly, the thwarted, pure love relationship in Africa between aristocratic Oroonoko and Imoinda replays the conventions of medieval romance. In this use of the romance genre, *Oroonoko* can illustrate how the novel emerges from the romance. On the Continent, the development of extended prose narrative is thought to spring so directly out of the romance, that most of the continental languages simply use the word 'roman' to describe what English calls 'the novel'. The difference between the European roman and the English novel can also be seen in Aphra Behn's *Oroonoko*. The claim not only to truth ('I do not pretend') but more importantly to *history* ties the English novel to news, the genre that claims to provide perspective on recent events (and a genre that is starting to emerge with early journalism just then developing). What makes the early English novel 'novel', then, is its ambiguous status as history, both *histoire* (story) and record of significant events. But, crucially, and equally novel, is the attempt to tell such history in one multi-genre book. In a way, as it brings different genres into itself, the early English novel, perhaps especially after Aphra Behn's *Oroonoko*, is a colonising genre, one that in the early decades at least would often discuss directly the experience of colonising itself.

Daniel Defoe, *Robinson Crusoe* (1719)

Daniel Defoe's *Robinson Crusoe* (1719) is one of the most important novels of the eighteenth century, and of English literature. Its success inspired Defoe to write sequels and others to write imitations, so much so that there is a sub-genre known as the 'Robinsonade', the most famous of which is probably Johann Wyss's *Swiss Family Robinson* (1812). *Robinson Crusoe* has clearly become an important part of popular culture. The story has become so pervasive that many readers will be familiar with the setting for most of the story – a deserted island – even if they have not read Defoe's novel itself. Hoping to attract tourists, the government of Chile in 1966 renamed two islands, one after Robinson Crusoe, and the other after Alexander Selkirk, who had been stranded on that island, and whose subsequent narrative provided inspiration for Defoe. Apparently, many readers are intrigued by the back-to-nature challenges faced by someone – someone else, that is – being stranded on a deserted island. It may be difficult, then, in the face of such familiarity to return to the novel, and to consider how it is informed by historical and philosophical developments of the late seventeenth and early eighteenth centuries. Nonetheless, that is what we propose here, because part of *Robinson Crusoe*'s influence can be traced to its relationships to contemporary events, to its context. These relationships shape the details within the story and thereby affect not only its contribution to the development of the novel in English but also to the cultural imagining of modernity itself. Some readers, for example, have made elaborate analogies between Robinson Crusoe and free-market economic theories in the experience of someone thrown back on their own individual resourcefulness (overlooking how much material help Crusoe was able to retrieve from his damaged ship). Perhaps more important than that is the novel's Lockean premise that it is possible to begin anew, both personally and politically, with a blank slate of nature.

Readers familiar with the iconic image of a man alone on an island may be disappointed to learn that in Defoe's narrative it is nearly one-quarter of the way through the novel before Crusoe lands on his island. What precedes his shipwreck is a surprising combination of adventure and religious reflection. When Crusoe does begin to tell the story of his time on the island, there is less adventure than reflection on religion. The question many readers face, of course, is how to reconcile the disparate elements of the novel, or to see how they might have been reconciled at the time. In this, it is particularly important to remember that *Robinson Crusoe* begins with a claim that we are about to read a history. According to the 'Preface', the story to follow is 'a just history of fact; neither is there any appearance of fiction in it' (*Robinson Crusoe*, ed. Ross, p. 25 [A]). As was the case with Aphra Behn's *Oroonoko*, *Robinson Crusoe* is a history in both senses: a story (an *histoire*) and a record of recent events. In the former sense, the novel focuses on the life story of a northerner, born in York as the third son of a German immigrant father and a Yorkshire mother, who leaves home to find his fortune travelling the Atlantic colonial trade routes.

Robinson Crusoe's birth to an immigrant complements Defoe's argument in the 'True Born Englishman', that England has always been composed of immigrants.

The fact that Crusoe is the third son is important as well, because, as he explains, he was consequently 'not bred to any trade' (p. 27). The assumption had been that his older brothers, because more likely to inherit, would have needed to be educated. Looking back on the novel, it would seem that one implication is that the British colonial trade found its workers among those who had not been 'bred' to anything else. On the other hand, though, it must be remembered that Defoe's Robinson Crusoe comes from what Crusoe's father calls 'the middle state, or what might be called the upper station of low life' (p. 28). While it could be another comment on the type of people among whom the colonial enterprises would find their participants, this reference to the middle state is also an important development in itself. Although it might be possible to achieve a middle station without being middle-class, it is difficult not to see this novel as referring to and initially defending the advantages of the English middle class. Despite the transatlantic colonial similarities between them, *Robinson Crusoe*'s focus on the middle state is a sharp contrast with Behn's focus on royalty throughout *Oroonoko*. At least at the beginning, in this discussion with Robinson's father, it seems that the middle class had a story written about them and for them. Subsequent novels will follow Defoe's lead, representing middle-class life and issues to middle-class readers, creating in the process a sense of what it means to be the class in the middle and maybe even a sense that there was a genre for such readers – the novel.

Crusoe decides to go against his father's advice that he stay in the comfortable middle state, and, we are told, 'on the first of September 1651 I went on board a ship bound for London' (p. 31). That ship encounters a violent storm, which Crusoe interprets as 'the judgment of Heaven for my wicked leaving my father's house' (p. 31). The fact that – so early on – there is a concern about the risks of 'leaving my father's house' turns the novel into a religious allegory, about making a choice that results in being ejected from a comfortable, prior middle state (see *Paradise Lost*). Crusoe's religious terms align him with the Dissenters, the name used in the eighteenth century for a diverse group who, although they were Protestant (and in this way were like the state's official Anglican Church) refused to swear allegiance to Anglicanism. There are many reasons for their Dissent, and it is a position with roots in the sixteenth and seventeenth centuries, but generally Dissenters believed that the Anglican Church retained too many ceremonial and structural elements of the Roman Catholic Church. Rather than the formal, ritual aspects of religious observance that characterise both the Anglican and the Catholic churches, Dissenters advocated a personal relationship with God. Crusoe's constant confessional mode is characteristic of this personal relationship with God favoured generally by the Dissenters.

In 1659, in the process of trying to import African slaves into Brazil illegally, or without the '*Asiento*' (p. 59; see p. 200 above), Robinson Crusoe wrecks his ship on the island that will be his home for the next twenty-eight years. Thrown into the water by a storm, Crusoe tells us, 'the wave that came upon me again, buried me at once 20 to 30 foot deep in its own body' (p. 64). Later, after being dragged out to sea and thrown on the beach by a couple of waves, a wave finally 'dashed me against a piece of rock, and that with such force as it left me senseless, and indeed helpless as to my own deliverance; for the blow taking my side and breath, beat the breath as it were quite out of my body' (p. 65). Crusoe is describing the physical act of being caught in the storm-tossed waters. But his being buried in the body of the wave recalls the biblical story of Jonah in the whale. It also sets up an analogy between his being born and his being deposited on the beach: like a newborn, Crusoe is released from the body, 'helpless as to my own deliverance', and unable to breathe. A similar sense of rebirth can be seen in Book V of *The Odyssey*, but in this case, Crusoe's rebirth is imbued with Christian symbolism. As he thanks God for his being saved, we are looking at someone who believes himself to be 'born again', in a Dissenting Christian sense of the phrase, i.e., as personally saved by God's grace.

Crusoe has been on his land alone more than twenty-five years before Friday arrives. Crusoe adopts Friday as a slave, believing in fact that Friday offers himself to Crusoe as a slave specifically. Why Crusoe should think that Friday meant to be his slave is an interesting question, with a range of related answers. Particularly important in this question, as throughout this novel, is the work of John Locke. In his *Second Treatise of Government*, published within two years of Behn's *Oroonoko*, Locke expanded on a developing seventeenth-century theory of contractual government. Focusing on protection of property, Locke distinguishes between four types of value: intrinsic, use, exchange and overplus (see p. 242). In *Robinson Crusoe*, Crusoe invokes use value, mentioning that money is worthless on a desert island (paradoxically, because it cannot be *exchanged*). Crusoe contends that 'all the good things of this world are no farther good to us than they are for our use' (p. 140). If we take Crusoe at his word, if 'everything' in the world is good only if it is useful, the point would apply to humans as well, and could justify slavery, as it treats people for their usefulness, without regard to what Locke calls intrinsic value.

If Crusoe's successful experience of starting over in a state of nature represented by the island reflects John Locke's *Second Treatise*, Crusoe's discussion of government after a Spanish captain joins Crusoe and Friday on the island reflects another work by Locke: *A Letter Concerning Toleration*. 'We had but three subjects', Crusoe notes, 'and they were of three different religions … However, I allowed liberty of conscience throughout my dominions' (p. 241). In allowing liberty of conscience, Crusoe's position is similar to that articulated by Locke in his *Letter*. That 'however' is interesting, because with it Crusoe contrasts his island with the situation in England, where toleration, such as it was, left Dissenters still unable to be elected to office. At the same time, Crusoe's use of the word 'subjects' indicates that he has created not just any kind of government, but a monarchy in particular: 'My island was now peopled, and I thought my self very rich in subjects; and it was a merry reflection which I frequently made, how like a king I looked' (p. 240). That is, on this formerly deserted island that has become his colony, Crusoe recreates the English class system. It is as if the political map has preceded the territory, carried to the island by someone from England's middle state who puts himself in a new position on the formerly deserted island, this new world. There is also a sense that those who joined in the eighteenth-century British colonial expansion believed they could achieve in the colonies something they could not in Britain – not only a religiously tolerant government, but also a change in their class position. On the other side of the Atlantic,

Crusoe moves from the middle state to the top, from the middle class to being the monarch, albeit a tolerant one, himself. Given the history in Britain's American and West Indian colonies, it is interesting that slavery helps to make Crusoe's new class position possible. It is as if the colonies allow a feudalism whose operation is beginning to be diminished in Britain.

Seen from this perspective, Defoe's Crusoe is exactly the kind of person Behn's narrator so disliked in *Oroonoko*: a colonial plantation owner who not only owns slaves but who also puts himself in a position he could not have had in Britain. This also points to another defining feature of the eighteenth-century English novel: dialogue. Usually, the dialogism of the novel is associated with the plurality of voices contained within any particular novel's capacious form. In the eighteenth-century English novel, the dialogue also occurs across novels. The period is known for pairs of novelists responding to each other, e.g., Defoe to Behn, and also Swift to Defoe, and Fielding to Richardson. Between *Oroonoko* and *Robinson Crusoe*, part of the implicit dialogue has to do with their shared claim to 'history'. In *Robinson Crusoe*, the history, at least in the sense of a record of important events, is indicated by the key dates: departure in 1651, shipwreck in 1659 and return to England in 1687. That is, Crusoe leaves England at the beginning of the Interregnum, runs aground on the island just before the Restoration and stays there until just before the Glorious Revolution. Where Behn publishes a novel in which the narrator worries about the frightful spectacle of a mangled king in 1688, Defoe, by contrast, publishes one in which the protagonist returns to England a wealthy landowner in 1687. Defoe's history is much more positive about the Glorious Revolution's transfer of power in 1688 than was Behn's. Thus, the central metaphor of *Robinson Crusoe* might be said to represent a Dissenter's sense that life in England during the Restoration or prior to the Glorious Revolution was like being stranded on a deserted island. In this way, Defoe's *Robinson Crusoe* offers a Whig vision of the history of the second half of the seventeenth century, celebrating the Glorious Revolution, connecting it to the democratic moment of the 1640s, and creating a lineage between that decade's range of Puritans and early eighteenth-century Dissenters.

Robinson Crusoe's date of publication, 1719, provides another angle on the novel's status as history. At the time, the South Sea Bubble was fully inflated (see pp. 200–1). As Defoe himself recounted in his weekly journal, *The Review*, what was later known as the Bubble was related to the South Sea Company, formed to sell slaves to Spanish colonies after the *Asiento* had been granted as part of the Treaty of Utrecht in 1713. The company sent thousands of slaves to South America for several years in the decade. Consequently, its stock became popular, and wildly popular by the end of the decade. The problem was that in fact the company was having trouble getting Spanish colonial administrators to recognise the *Asiento* of the Treaty. Therefore, slaves were often left in South America, neither sold nor welcome. Rather than determine an effective plan in South America, the company let the resale of stock drive the company's value up. By 1719, insiders knew that there was trouble at the company. It is an interesting question as to whether Defoe's *Robinson Crusoe* might have been intended to demonstrate the financial advantages of a South Sea trade.

Regardless, the novel was still not sufficient to save the company, which collapsed, of course, in the South Sea Bubble of 1720.

The outlines of the story of Robinson Crusoe – a man who travels by sea, and spends twenty-eight years stranded, unable to get home, and who has many adventures along the way – connects *Robinson Crusoe* to Homer's *Odyssey*, where, again, a man travelled across the sea, and took twenty years to return home. It may be a coincidence, but both stories are eponymous, meaning that they take their names from their central character. The relationship between the two stories is also a relationship between two genres: epic (*The Odyssey*) and the novel. That is, *Robinson Crusoe* makes a connection between the epic and the novel that has come to be seen as defining the novel as a genre. Both genres focus on the adventures of an often wayward central protagonist, usually have a connection to a story of national origins and are lengthy. Some scholars have called the novel the modern epic; others see the novel as a prose epic. While it is difficult to tell which was the first novel, even in English, to make the connection between the novel and the epic, *Robinson Crusoe* is easily the best known, and illustrates the connection nicely. Still, Robinson Crusoe's origins in the middle state also offer an important contrast between the modern and the ancient epics: the difference in the ages of the protagonists. In the ancient epic, Odysseus has a son at home who is at least twenty years old, and, although we are not told how old Odysseus is, we can assume he would be at least thirty-eight or forty when we first see him in *The Odyssey*. In the modern epic, the protagonists are younger, and often grow up during the novel itself (a process sometimes referred to by the German name of a novelistic genre – *Bildungsroman*). Thus Robinson Crusoe begins his narrative with his childhood in his family home, but ends decades later with his return to England a wealthy man.

Jonathan Swift, *Gulliver's Travels* (1726)

With a story whose outlines would become as famous as Robinson Crusoe's, *Gulliver's Travels* invites being read as Swift's response to Defoe's *Robinson Crusoe*. Like Crusoe, Gulliver, too, is born the third son, although, unlike Crusoe, Gulliver does study at Cambridge. After his parents have trouble affording Gulliver's education, Gulliver, like Crusoe, decides to travel. With his education and further training at Leyden, Gulliver is able to join ships' crews as a surgeon. Like Crusoe, Gulliver winds up shipwrecked, although in Gulliver's case he is shipwrecked on several different islands, basically one for each of the novel's four parts. And unlike Crusoe, Gulliver is never stranded on a deserted island. Quite the contrary – each island is populated with types of people who differ greatly from those on the other islands on which he lands. In the first case, for example, Lilliput, the residents are very short, and relatively urban. In the second case, they are towering giants, and rural. With his third stranding Gulliver meets an ingenious group of socially awkward people who fly their island, sometimes over another island from which they extract revenue. On the fourth island, Gulliver meets a society of talking horses, the Houyhnhnms, who dislike a group, the Yahoos, who physically resemble humans quite closely.

In the prefatory 'A Letter from Captain Gulliver', Gulliver complains that some 'are so bold as to think my Book of Travels a mere Fiction' (*Gulliver's Travels*, ed. Turner, p. xxxviii [A]). A subsequent statement from 'The Publisher to the Reader' reassures readers that 'there is an Air of Truth apparent through the whole' (p. xl). From the very beginning, with the 'Letter from Captain Gulliver', readers are told that Gulliver has been forced to 'say *the thing that was not*' (p. xxxv). This expression comes from Gulliver's time among the Houyhnhnms, a truthful society that cannot abide stating anything other than what is. Gulliver wants to be understood as someone telling the truth. This novel thus recalls the histories of Behn, Defoe and other early novelists. But in this case, the narrator is protesting that the form of his story is at odds with the truth. As the story begins then, we have a narrator who insists that he wants to tell the truth, and that any passages that are not true are the responsibility of a publisher who cares for neither the truth nor for the reputation of the frustrated narrator, who never intended to say the thing that was not. *Gulliver's Travels* begins, then, with a tension over the text's truthfulness. Read with a double consciousness, though, the reader is invited to wonder whether this narrator is saying the thing that is, i.e., whether we are to believe this narrator. This question of the narrator's veracity haunts *Gulliver's Travels* from its first paragraph. Like the narrators of Behn's *Oroonoko* and Defoe's *Robinson Crusoe*, Gulliver claims that he is trying to tell the truth. The difference is that Gulliver claims he has been thwarted. Gulliver's very phrase, 'say the thing that was not', can stand as a fine definition of irony, a figure of speech by which a speaker can say one thing and mean its opposite. In *A Modest Proposal*, Swift made devastating use of irony, famously arguing that landlords ought to eat the children of the poor. From the beginning, *Gulliver's Travels* shares this ironic approach. Gulliver, the narrator and main protagonist, complains that he has been forced to say the thing that is not. In a sense, through irony, Gulliver has been forced to say things he had not intended by the author of the novel who has something different to say.

In the novel's first paragraph, we are told that after leaving Cambridge Gulliver became apprenticed to Mr Bates. By the third paragraph, the implication that Gulliver's status as apprentice means Mr Bates would be Gulliver's 'master' is stated directly, for an ironic implication sometimes overlooked by readers. Gulliver has apprenticed to 'Master Bates' (p. 4), a name that has a homophonic association with 'masturbates'. This ironic pun, through which Gulliver says one thing and the text means an opposite, is more than a lewd joke, although it is that, too (and the first of many such jokes in the novel). By implication, we are reading a story told by a particularly self-involved and socially unaware narrator, as there is perhaps nothing more self-involved than an apprenticeship to 'Master Bates', and little that is more unaware than Gulliver's telling us 'my good Master Bates dying in two Years after, and I having few Friends, my Business began to fail' (p. 4). Gulliver is trying to tell us why he took to the sea for trips to the East and West Indies, the kinds of trips that would lead to his well-known adventure. But he is also telling us that his apprenticeship to Master Bates left him with few friends, which would be understandable if an apprentice were to devote him- or herself to that subject. Once Master Bates dies, Gulliver's business begins to fail, the pun raising questions of course about what his business was.

Gulliver's sexual self-involvement can be seen across the novel. In Lilliput, for example, in chapter 2, while meeting with their diminutive King and Court, Gulliver tells us 'the Ladies and Courtiers were all most magnificently clad, so that the Spot they stood upon seemed to resemble a Petticoat spread on the Ground' (p. 16). On one level, when seen from Gulliver's height, their clothes blurred into a single piece of colourful fabric; on the other, though, he sees people as if they were undergarments. In chapter 3, Gulliver reports that the Lilliputian Emperor wanted to march his troops through an arch to be formed by Gulliver's legs. Although the soldiers had been commanded not to look up, this order 'could not prevent some of the younger Officers from turning up their Eyes as they passed under me. And, to confess the Truth, my Breeches were at that Time in so ill a Condition, that they afforded some Opportunities for Laughter and Admiration' (p. 28). The soldiers were able to see through the rips in Gulliver's trousers, and Gulliver believes the soldiers admired what they saw. It is as if Gulliver hears the laughter *as* admiration – again, an image of his self-involvement. There is a similar lack of awareness when Gulliver tells the story of his extinguishing a fire in the palace by urinating on it; as he congratulates himself on his quick thinking he nonetheless reports that the 'Empress conceiving the greatest Abhorrence of what I had done, removed to the most distant Side of the Court' (p. 43). Among the giant Brobdingnagians, the situation may be reversed, but Gulliver's fascination with physiological and sexualised detail remains. He reports, for example, 'a pleasant frolicksome Girl of sixteen, would sometimes set me astride upon one of her Nipples; with many other Tricks, wherein the Reader will excuse me for not being over particular' (p. 112).

The disturbing impoliteness of Gulliver's descriptions raises questions about what Swift might be getting at through this novel. Gulliver's attitudes strike many readers as misogynist, and some have attributed the misogyny to Swift, especially with reference to some of Swift's poetry. It is also possible to read his attitude as a satire created by Swift. In this way, satire would be connected to the ironic delivery of saying one thing and meaning the opposite. Generally, a satire is a way of presenting material so as to criticise comically, by making fun of the object of critique. The question, of course, is what Swift's object might be if *Gulliver's Travels* is a satire. When considering the rudeness of *Gulliver's Travels*, it is important to remember that there is a long-standing association between the mode of satire and a Greek mythological figure, the Satyr, half-human and half-animal. Satire involves the Satyr's undoing of neat distinctions between the human and the animal. If we see *Gulliver's Travels* in dialogue with other early English novels such as *Robinson Crusoe*, then much of what is provocative, and usually physiological, about *Gulliver's Travels* could be seen as Swift's satire/Satyr of the other novelists' claim to truth. While Robinson Crusoe goes twenty-eight years without reporting on any need to urinate, that is one of the first things Gulliver does after finding himself beached on Lilliput. Or, while we might focus on how Gulliver put out the fire in the palace, there is the equally satirical reason that the fire was ignited in the first place: 'by the carelessness of a Maid of Honour, who fell asleep while she was reading a Romance' (p. 42). For some, Swift is here complaining about women's inattentive reading. It is also possible that he is satirising the inattentive reading produced by the genre of romance.

Most importantly, though, the bawdy 'satyr' side of Swift's satire has profound implications for Swift's understanding of Britain's early colonial development. On each of these islands, Gulliver meets highly developed cultures, each different from the preceding or other ones. And in each case, Gulliver – able to adjust fairly gracefully to extraordinarily difficult and demanding differences among cultures – adapts, learning languages and seeing the advantages of each culture that he visits. For people raised in an age of commercial jetliners, accustomed to crossing datelines and cultures with the ease of fast transportation, Gulliver would seem to be a good, early role model. On a first reading, *Gulliver's Travels* seems to be a story of a figure travelling the world and learning from presumed others, an Enlightenment cosmopolitan. Upon closer inspection, though, it can be seen that *Gulliver's Travels* criticises such Enlightenment cosmopolitanism. That means, however, reading with a kind of doubleness of vision: the narrator's (Gulliver's) and the author's (Swift's). To invoke a distinction that Kwame Anthony Appiah makes in his 2005 book *The Ethics of Identity*, we could say that Gulliver is the rootless cosmopolitan, being criticised by the 'rooted cosmopolitan', Jonathan Swift (Appiah, pp. 213–72 [B]).

The more he travels, the more Gulliver's adjustments to the next new culture shift him from the human to the animal side of the Satyr. By the end, Gulliver prefers horses to humans, and his cosmopolitanism has left him utterly rootless. As we have seen, Swift satirises this participant in Britain's colonising as self-involved, apprenticed to Master Bates. By the end of Part II, though, after being stranded on two very different islands, Gulliver has gone from seeing himself as towering to seeing himself as one of those over whom he used to tower. Consequently, when he is plucked out of the water by a passing ship, he talks to the crew by standing in front of them, head tilted back, and yelling. Of course, within the story, Gulliver's odd behaviour can be explained by his unusual experiences on Brobdingnag. But his behaviour also indicates that Gulliver has returned from his trip less able to speak directly to other humans, whom he says he sees as 'the most contemptible little Creatures I ever beheld' (p. 143). Of course, Gulliver is one of those creatures himself, and by the end of Part II, he is no longer able to face himself in the mirror: 'after mine Eyes had been accustomed to such prodigious Objects ... the Comparison gave me so despicable a Conceit of my self' (p. 143). That is, by the middle of the novel, and after only his second stay on an island, Gulliver is unable to see himself for what he is, another human. Although he cites it as evidence of prejudice, his family probably had a point when they 'concluded I had lost my Wits' (p. 145). By the end of the novel, after he has returned from his time with the Houyhnhnms, Gulliver faints when his wife tries to kiss him. For a year he will not allow her or his children in his presence. He buys two horses and spends four hours every day talking to them instead.

Gulliver may leave England self-involved, but in the end he returns from his travels completely unable to relate to other humans; he prefers the company of horses, because they are more rational. Exploration and travel have reinforced the same inability to deal with others that made Gulliver travel in the first place. At a time when Britain is administering the western edge of the Atlantic from the Equator north, Swift is making a pointed and potentially devastating critique of the effects

of colonies on the colonisers. Although this critique can be seen in the slow psychological breakdown that Gulliver undergoes, usually it is Part III that is seen as
the centre of Swift's attack on early colonialism. In this part of the novel, Gulliver
arrives on an island, 'Laputa', whose name means 'the whore' in Spanish. This flying
island hovers around, and sometimes descends directly upon another island community, Balnibarbi. The relationship between the two is like that between Britain
and Ireland, when seen from the perspective of Ireland, whence Swift is writing.
When Gulliver claims 'I never knew a Soil so unhappily cultivated, Houses so ill
contrived and so ruinous, or a People whose Countenances and Habit expressed so
much Misery and Want' (p. 174), the impoverished people and depleted soil remind
readers of Ireland. But the analogy between Britain and Laputa holds the 'superior'
island responsible for the deprivations of those below. The 'Academy of Projectors'
(p. 176) on Laputa, devoted to fantastic schemes for making and saving money (e.g.,
'Sun-Beams out of Cucumbers'), represents the sometimes similarly wild experiments of the Royal Society. There is also an implication that Britain is similarly
extracting the sunlight and the profits out of Ireland, that the colonial and scientific projects are not unrelated. In both cases, it is about putting the possibility of
getting more money before all else, thus a possible connection to the name of the
island.

Like Defoe's *Robinson Crusoe*, the narrative of *Gulliver's Travels* is punctuated by
specific dates throughout, indicating thereby that we are again reading a history
in the sense of a record of major events. Gulliver's travels are bracketed by two
years: Gulliver leaves for his first trip in 1701 and returns from his final one in 1715.
Gulliver is out of the country for most of Queen Anne's reign (1702–14). He leaves in
the same year as the passage of the Act of Settlement, 1701, and returns in the first
full year of the reign of George Ludwig, Elector of Brunswick-Lüneburg, brought to
the throne by the Act of Settlement in 1714. The time also coincides with what turns
out to be the Tories' last period of high political influence for almost another forty
years. Some might say that Gulliver represents Swift's exile under the Tories. Others
argue that Gulliver's changes from island to island represent the kinds of changes
that the party went through during the period. Taking these two readings together,
we might say that Swift believed that he was in exile as a Tory precisely because of
how the party was run during those years.

Alexander Pope, *Essay on Man* (1733)

Today, the eighteenth-century contribution to literature is understood largely with
reference to the emergence of the novel and of professional literary criticism. But it
was also a period in which poetry was particularly important. Alexander Pope, for
example, was able to move to the fashionable Twickenham district near London and
build a villa for himself there after the popular, commercial success of his translations of Homer's epics. At a time when poetry was that important, Alexander Pope
was perhaps the most important poet. His influence on the English language can still
be heard today in phrases such as 'hope springs eternal', 'fools rush in', and 'a little

learning is a dangerous thing'. The Academy Award-nominated film, *Eternal Sunshine of the Spotless Mind* (2004), takes its title from a line in Pope's poem 'Eloise to Abelard'. Still, Pope's poetry can be difficult for readers today: less playful than the dense work of the seventeenth-century 'Metaphysicals' and more formally structured than the poetry of the Romantics of the late eighteenth and early eighteenth centuries, Pope can seem quite foreign and old-fashioned to today's readers. Nonetheless, that formality makes a major contribution to the interest and importance of Pope's poetry, in its historical context.

While several of his works stand out in literary history, none is quite as ambitious as *An Essay on Man*, published in four anonymous instalments, or 'Epistles', during 1733 and 1734 (Pope, *Poems* [A]). Initially intended to be one of four major works on philosophical topics, *An Essay on Man* is the only one of the series that was completed. Perhaps a poem devoted to the topic of 'man' turned out to be sufficiently ambitious all by itself. As it is, each of *An Essay on Man*'s four 'Epistles', or letters, addresses a different aspect of 'the Nature and State of Man': 'Universe', 'Individual', 'Society' and 'Happiness'. In its impressive scale, some might say *An Essay on Man* takes its place among the works of the Enlightenment that aimed to reimagine society on a more rational basis. As 'Epistles', which Pope describes as a 'way of writing [that] hath prevailed much of late', *An Essay on Man* is consistent with the popularising impulse of the Enlightenment. In a prefatory statement on 'The Design', Pope cites Bacon and 'the Science of Human Nature', thus aligning the poem with the Enlightenment through and through. At the same time, though, the poem is profoundly uneasy about empiricism and what it casts as the related limits of the human ability to understand the natural world. In this way, the poem could also be read as being opposed to the Enlightenment.

Throughout *An Essay on Man*, Pope is at pains to reconcile the various incidences of life, usually its trials, with a larger, beneficent order. 'A mighty maze! But not without a plan', he claims at the beginning of the first epistle (line 6). In a sense, *An Essay on Man* addresses what has come to be known as 'the problem of pain': if there is a good God, why is there so much suffering? In taking up this question, Pope's *An Essay on Man* follows, quite self-consciously, a path pursued earlier by Milton's *Paradise Lost* (1667/74). At the beginning of *Essay on Man*, Pope signals the affiliation. His claim that he will 'vindicate the ways of God to Man' reworks Milton's phrase from Book I of *Paradise Lost*, 'justify the ways of God to men' (I.26). In both cases, the poets claim to be able to explain the problem of pain, but there is a difference between justifying and vindicating: the latter term, vindicate, implies even more certitude than the former, justify. To vindicate presumes that the action need not be justified, or, more to the point, that it already is justified. For Milton, the justification involves a defence of free will, that people make choices that can leave them unhappy, until they discover 'A Paradise within thee, happier far' (*Norton Anthology*, p. 1609, 12.587 [A]). For Pope, by contrast, the vindication hinges on our realising that our perspective on the whole picture is narrow and insufficient. ''Tis but a part we see, and not a whole' (I.60). For Pope, our focus on our conflicts, our discomfort, simply means that we do not see the harmony and comfort somewhere else.

'What wrong we call, / May, must be right, as relative to all' (I.51–2). If we could see everything, as God does, then we would know, Pope believes, that all is right with the world.

Pope's argument is summarised by his claim that 'Whatever is, is RIGHT' (I.294). Of course, it is precisely this attitude towards disasters that Voltaire satirises in *Candide*. How is the 1755 Lisbon earthquake, in which 100,000 people were killed, 'right'? In his *Confessions*, Augustine (b. 354) had argued 'whatever is, is good', and so some might see a relationship between Pope and Augustine. It is quite likely that there is such a connection. However, their reasons for thinking that 'what is is all right' differ significantly. Augustine's remain within the realm of moral evaluation. The fact that things could get worse means that there is still good in them. For Pope, by contrast, 'the first Almighty Cause / Acts not by partial, but by general laws' (I.146). The connections to Roman Catholicism are clear enough. Pope's God is 'the first Almighty Cause', a variation on the uncaused cause described by St Thomas Aquinas (c. 1225–74). Moreover, in its assumption that ethics can be codified, Pope's argument follows the practice of the Catholic Church, a practice to which many contemporary Protestants would have objected. However, Pope invokes a surprising ally in his moral philosophy: Newton. It was Newton, of course, who had in the last few decades just revealed those laws. In his poem, Pope is putting Newton's discovery of those general physical laws to use in ethics. For the implication is that Pope is proposing a Newtonian physics of ethics: for every bad there is an equal and opposite good, so that the whole is right and balanced overall. At the same time, Pope's sense that there is a reasonable way to approach ethics can also be seen reflected, later, in the obviously much more systematic work of Immanuel Kant.

Pope's Newtonian model of general laws governing events also fits with a then current rediscovery and simplification of classical artistic principles. Known as Palladianism in architecture, this early eighteenth-century movement preferred stylistic simplicity – relatively free of ornamentation – balance and symmetry. In this, the argument was that the arrangement of the building, its façade and plan, reflected natural, universal laws. Pope himself designed his home at Twickenham (on the reverse of his translation of Homer) along these Palladian lines. In *Essay on Man*, Pope's poetic form does the same work of balancing that occurs in both Palladian architecture and Newtonian physics. Known as the heroic couplet, Pope's form consists of rhyming pairs of iambic pentameter lines, i.e., couplets of lines, each ten syllables long, with five sets of unstressed/stressed syllabic units, which end with rhyming syllables. The systematic patterning of these lines is already open to Newtonian applications. However, Pope uses them in a way that increases the balance, symmetry and proportion that reflect both the Newtonian and the Palladian approaches. The last lines of the First Epistle are excellent examples of Pope's remarkably balanced technique: 'All Nature is but Art, unknown to thee; / All Chance, Direction, which thou canst not see' (I.289–90). Balanced on either side, across a caesura, the lines balance rhetorical opposites, between what we see and what we do not see. The balance of the lines reflects Pope's argument that the events of the world are also balanced.

Samuel Richardson, *Clarissa, or the History of a Young Lady* (1747–1748)

Printer Samuel Richardson (1689–1761) had already published several books, including his first novel, *Pamela* (1740) by the time he published *Clarissa* in seven volumes during 1747 and 1748. In its influence, in its timing and in the issues it addressed, *Clarissa* was one of the most important English novels of the eighteenth century. Richardson's novel inspired almost fanatical devotion and direct responses from readers. After the novel was first published, many readers wrote to Richardson, and he responded to their readings of the novel in subsequent editions, so much so that the third edition became hundreds of pages longer than the first. Many testimonials to the novel's powerful emotional effect on its early readers are recorded; many report they were reduced to tears by it. Demand was so high that pirated copies were printed in Ireland. *Clarissa* would be cited by and influential for a wide range of major figures in the late eighteenth and early nineteenth centuries, including novelist Henry Fielding, *philosophes* Diderot and Rousseau, American 'Founding Father' John Adams, and Romantic literary critic William Hazlitt. From the middle of the nineteenth century until the last third of the twentieth, however, the novel fell out of favour, for a variety of reasons. There are many reasons for the decline in its critical standing: changes in the definition of and expectations for the novel genre, *Clarissa*'s didactic tone and, not least, its extraordinary length (probably the longest novel in English until the twentieth century) did not help. During the last few decades of the twentieth century, however, *Clarissa* underwent a literary critical revival, and, ironically, partly *because* of some of the features for which it used to be criticised. The tensions between public and private, between presence and absence in its epistolary form, its acute sensitivity to class relations, its situation in the middle of the century, and even its sheer length, to take but a few examples, generated interest in *Clarissa* again. More than anything, though, the prominence of feminist literary criticism helped return *Clarissa* to a position within eighteenth-century literary studies that is somewhat proportionate to the extraordinary effect the novel had in the eighteenth century itself.

Like so many other novels of the eighteenth century, *Clarissa* is a 'history', according to the 'Preface' purportedly written by the fictional editor who supposedly compiled the materials of the novel (Richardson, *Clarissa*, p. 35 [A]). It is a history told through what the 'editor' calls a 'double yet separate correspondence' of letters sent between Clarissa Harlowe and her friend Anna Howe on the one hand and Robert Lovelace and his friend John Belford on the other (p. 35). These characters use what the editor calls a technique of 'instantaneous description' to record events and their impressions of them as they happen. Sometimes, we are told, their hands shake as they write, or the ink is smudged by tears that fall to the page. Through this epistolary form, we learn what happens to Clarissa Harlowe after the death of her grandfather and the reading of his will, in which he gave his estate to Clarissa (instead of his three sons – her father and uncles – and instead of his grandson, her brother James).

Clarissa's parents arrange a marriage between herself and the thoroughly unattractive, but wealthy, James Solmes. Clarissa begs her father not to be forced to marry Solmes, even getting on her knees in front of her father to make her impassioned case. Meanwhile, her brother's college acquaintance, Robert Lovelace, has tried and failed in his wedding proposal to Clarissa's sister, Arabella. As it is clear that Clarissa will refuse Solmes and therefore her parents' wishes for her, Clarissa's family increasingly shuns her, isolating her, and making her life at home very difficult. Lovelace provides Clarissa with the chance to escape. Clarissa accepts Lovelace's arrangements and flees her parents' house. The new situation is no more liberating than the one she left, as Lovelace attempts to seduce and control Clarissa, who claims no interest in marriage to anyone. Eventually, a little after the mid-point of the novel, Lovelace drugs and rapes Clarissa, although the letters cannot bring themselves to say it in so many words. Clarissa loses the will to live. She gives up eating. Within a month she is writing about returning to her Father's house (which, of course, Lovelace misunderstands as referring to Mr Harlowe's home). A month later, Clarissa is dead, declared a saint and martyr by all her friends. Lovelace, shunned, goes to France. There, he dies as the result of a duel. His friend Belford writes a conclusion, updating readers about the subsequent lives of the characters. Finally, Richardson provided a postscript that discusses the preceding history in terms of tragedy.

In two senses of the word 'form', the form of the work, both its shape (size, in this case) and its use of letters, attracts a lot of the critical attention. The work comes to 1,500 pages in the tall paperback edition currently available, and took up multiple volumes when it was first published. By the time he wrote *Clarissa*, Richardson had become the head of the Stationers' Company; he probably could not have done more to help printers and papermakers. Difficult as the novel's length may be for us today, perhaps especially as we try to imagine reading it for a literature course, it is an important part of why *Clarissa* is such an effective novel. Readers experience Clarissa's captivity at what seems to be almost the same pace that she does, so that the very length of the novel increases the likelihood of readers understanding Clarissa's unfortunate situation as it unfolds in front of them in real time. The use of the letters to build a novel of this size is equally important. It points towards the heteroglossia, the multiple voicings, that will come to characterise the novel starting in the nineteenth century.

There is a way in which the epistolary form fits with the Postscript's claim that the story is a tragedy, i.e., a type of drama or theatre. The letters are written by a lengthy cast of characters, each of whom has different things to say about the development of the narrative. The dialogue of the characters conveys the narrative, as is also the case in plays, and there is then a tension between the novel and the drama throughout *Clarissa*. In this novel, the principal contest of voices is that between Clarissa and Lovelace. Clarissa claims the 'clarity' espoused by Sprat and the Royal Society, while Lovelace spins a web of educated allusions and figures reminiscent of rakes and libertines such as John Wilmot, second Earl of Rochester (1647–80). In part, the difference in their writing styles is supposed to stand for differences in their character, in the sense of *ethos*. In part, the difference in their styles has to do with the differences in their educations, he having been educated at college at a time when she could not have been. And in part, the difference might have to do with a dissenting Protestant claim to directness and lack of obfuscation; in this sense, it is interesting that Lovelace dies in Catholic France. There is also a way in which the novel stages a contest between a late classical allusive mode of writing and a spontaneous overflow of emotions, a writing of the heart that will inform the approach of the Romantics fifty years later. In this case, the story ends in a draw; neither is writing for their time, Lovelace being too late and Clarissa being too early.

Part of the interest in the differences between their writing styles has to do with the fact that it is Clarissa who is constant and direct, and Lovelace the one who is ornate and flowery, a reversal of familiar gender stereotypes. But that difference is a subset of the larger reversal that initiates the narrative: the prospect of Clarissa's independence, made possible by her grandfather's generosity in his will. In other words, *Clarissa* narrates the story of an independent woman at a time when women's independence was not yet accepted. Or more to the point, *Clarissa* treats as a tragedy the fact that women – even and perhaps especially women who could be financially independent – are not necessarily allowed to choose for themselves. Some wonder whether Richardson, as a man, ought to have told the story of a woman scorned by family and raped by a friend just because she wanted to make her own choice over whom, and whether, to marry. Romances, such as those by Aphra Behn, had been telling variations on this story for nearly a century. For others, the fact that a man could tell the story may itself show a change in the position of women. It could be argued that Richardson's adoption of Clarissa's story makes this novel a major contribution to the Enlightenment, to spreading democratic choice to more people. At the same time, this novel also represents an apparent change in ideas about women between the seventeenth century and the eighteenth century: if Eve and Clarissa are similar in that they both choose independence, Eve chooses experience, while Clarissa, by contrast, chooses innocence. For others, this novel narrates a political allegory, about democratic choice more specifically in the British context. Some say that Clarissa's brother James plays the role of the Stuart James II as seen by the Whig opposition. We could also say that Clarissa's grandfather, being from the generation of 1688, tries to bequeath a legacy of independence and choice but is thwarted by an intervening generation of the aristocracy. What is interesting in this case, though, is how Richardson treats the lack of choice as a tragedy. It is part of how he uses sentimentalism to sell a vision of the Enlightenment that ties it to seventeenth-century English political history.

Reference

A Primary Texts and Anthologies of Primary Sources

Akenside, Mark. *Pleasures of the Imagination* (1744). In *The New Oxford Book of Eighteenth-Century Verse*. Ed. Roger Lonsdale. Oxford University Press, 1984, pp. 260–2.

Beauchamp, Virginia Walcott, et al., eds. *Women Critics, 1660–1820: An Anthology*. Bloomington: Indiana University Press, 1995.

Burke, Edmund. *On Empire, Liberty, and Reform: Speeches and Letters*. Ed. David Bromwich. New Haven, CT: Yale University Press, 2000.

Defoe, Daniel. *Moll Flanders* (1722). Ed. David Blewett. New York: Penguin, 1989.
Robinson Crusoe (1719). Ed. Angus Ross. New York: Viking Penguin, 1985.
Roxana (1724). Ed. David Blewett. New York: Penguin, 1982.
A Tour Through the Whole Island of Great Britain (1724–6). 2 vols. New York: Dutton, 1966.

DeMaria, Robert. *British Literature, 1649–1789: An Anthology*. Malden, MA: Blackwell, 1996.

Eliot, T. S. 'Milton II'. In *On Poetry and Poets*. London: Faber & Faber, 1969, pp. 146–61.

Fielding, Henry. *The History of Tom Jones, A Foundling* (1749). Ed. R. P. C. Mutter. New York: Penguin, 1985.

Harris, Brice, ed. *Restoration Plays*. New York: Modern Library, 1953.

Haywood, Eliza. *Anti-Pamela* (1741). Ed. Catherine Ingrassia. Orchard Park, NY: Broadview Press, 2004.
Selections from 'The Female Spectator' (1744–6). Ed. Patricia Meyer Spacks. New York: Oxford University Press, 1999.

Hooke, Robert. *Micrographia, or, Some Physiological Descriptions of Minute Bodies Made by Magnifying Glasses with Observations and Inquiries Thereupon* (1665). Reprint. New York: Dover Publications, 1961.

Hume, David. *Essays: Moral, Political, and Literary*. Ed. Eugene F. Miller. Indianapolis: Liberty Fund, 1987.

Johnson, Samuel. *Samuel Johnson: The Oxford Authors*. Ed. Donald Greene. Oxford University Press, 1984.
The Lives of the English Poets (1779–81). Ed. George Birkbeck Hill. 3 vols. Reprint. New York: Octagon Books, 1967.
The Rambler (1750–2). Ed. W. J. Bate and Albrecht B. Strauss. 3 vols. New Haven, CT: Yale University Press, 1969.

Locke, John. *Political Writings*. Ed. David Wootton. Indianapolis, IN: Hackett Books, 2003.

Milton, John. *The Tenure of Kings and Magistrates* (1749). In *John Milton*. Ed. Stephen Orgel and Jonathan Goldberg. Oxford University Press, 1990, pp. 273–307.

The Norton Anthology of English Literature. Vol. 1. Ed. M. H. Abrams and Stephen Greenblatt. 8th edn. New York and London: Norton, 2006.

Oster, Malcolm. *Science in Europe, 1500–1800: A Primary Sources Reader*. New York: Palgrave, 2002.

Pope, Alexander. *The Poems of Alexander Pope: A One-Volume Edition of the Twickenham Text With Selected Annotations*. Ed. John Butt. New Haven, CT: Yale University Press, 1963.

Richardson, Samuel. *Clarissa, or the History of a Young Lady*. New York: Penguin, 1985.

Shaftesbury, Third Earl of (Anthony Ashley Cooper). *Characteristics of Men, Manners, Opinions, Times* (1711). Ed. Lawrence E. Klein. Cambridge University Press, 1999.

Sherman, Stuart. *The Longman Anthology of British Literature, Vol. 1c: The Restoration and the Eighteenth Century*. 2nd edn. Danvers, MA: Addison-Wesley, 2003.

Smith, Adam. *An Inquiry into the Nature and Causes of the Wealth of Nations* (1776). Indianapolis: Liberty Fund, 1981.

The Spectator (1711–12). [Joseph Addison and Richard Steele.] Ed. Donald Bond. 4 vols. Oxford: Clarendon Press, 1965.

Sprat, Thomas. *History of the Royal Society*. Ed. Jackson I. Cope and Harold Whitmore Jones. St Louis: Washington University Press, 1958.

Swift, Jonathan. *Gulliver's Travels* (1726). Ed. Paul Turner. New York: Oxford University Press, 1986.

Tillotson, Geoffrey, Paul Fussell and Marshall Waingrow. *Eighteenth-Century English Literature*. San Diego, CA: Harcourt Brace Jovanovich, 1969.

Unchained Voices: An Anthology of Black Authors in the English-Speaking World of the Eighteenth Century. Ed. Vincent Carretta. Lexington: University of Kentucky Press, 1996.

B Introductions and Overviews

Appiah, Kwame Anthony. *The Ethics of Identity*. Princeton University Press, 2005. Last chapter draws important distinctions between different ideas of cosmopolitanism, engaging the Enlightenment ideal.

Black, Jeremy, and Roy Porter. *A Dictionary of Eighteenth-Century World History*. Malden, MA: Blackwell, 1994.

Damrosch, Leopold. *Modern Essays on Eighteenth-Century Literature*. Oxford University Press, 1988. Major statements on the period, including a synopsis of Michael McKeon's approach to the origins of the English novel.

Day, Gary, and Jack Lynch, eds. *The Encyclopedia of British Literature, 1660–1789*. 3 vols. Malden, MA: Wiley-Blackwell, 2015.

Dickinson, H. T. *A Companion to Eighteenth-Century Britain*. Malden, MA: Blackwell, 2002. Excellent synthetic essays on various aspects of eighteenth-century history, each with further readings.

Engell, James. *Forming the Critical Mind: Dryden to Coleridge*. Cambridge, MA: Harvard University Press, 1989. Thorough history of restoration and eighteenth-century literary criticism.

Gay, Peter. *The Enlightenment: An Interpretation*. 2 vols. New York: Norton, 1966, 1969. Detailed intellectual history of the Enlightenment, with some of the most well-established assertions about its importance.

Habermas, Jürgen. *The Structural Transformation of the Public Sphere: An Inquiry into a Category of Bourgeois Society*. Trans. Thomas Burger. Cambridge, MA: MIT Press, 1989.

'The Public Sphere'. In *Contemporary Political Theory*. Malden, MA: Blackwell, 1997, 150–8.

Jones, Vivien, ed. *Women in the Eighteenth Century: Constructions of Femininity*. New York: Routledge, 2000. Pioneering anthology of eighteenth-century English literature by women.

Langford, Paul. *Eighteenth-Century Britain: A Very Short Introduction*. Oxford University Press, 2000. A good, compact history of the period.

A Polite and Commercial People: England, 1727–1783. Oxford University Press, 1992. Excellent, detailed history of the period. Very thorough.

Lynch, Jack, ed. *Samuel Johnson in Context*. Cambridge University Press, 2012. Short essays on Samuel Johnson and the eighteenth century.

Nussbaum, Felicity A., and Laura Brown, eds. *The New Eighteenth Century*. London: Methuen, 1987. Important anthology of new historicist essays on the eighteenth century, then a period resistant to such approaches.

Plumb, J. H. *England in the Eighteenth Century*. New York: Penguin, 1950. Largely political history of the period; very readable.

Pocock, J. G. A. *The Discovery of Islands: Essays in British History*. Cambridge University Press, 2005. Collection of essays reimagining the British Isles as an Atlantic Archipelago.

Porter, Roy. *The Creation of the Modern World: The Untold Story of the British Enlightenment*. New York: Norton, 2000. Argues for the importance of England to the subsequent Enlightenment among continental *philosophes* who are usually taken to define the period.

English Society in the Eighteenth Century. New York: Penguin, 1982. Approachable social history of the period.

Richetti, John. *The New Cambridge History of English Literature, 1660–1780*. Cambridge University Press, 2005. Synthetic essays about various aspects of Restoration and eighteenth-century English literature, with suggestions for further reading.

Rivers, Isabel. *Reason, Grace, and Sentiment: A Study of the Language of Religion and Ethics in England, 1660–1780*. 2 vols. Cambridge University Press, 1991, 2000. The most detailed treatment available of the intellectual history of theology in Restoration and eighteenth-century Britain.

Schama, Simon. *A History of Britain, Vol. II: The Wars of the British, 1603–1776*. New York: Hyperion, 2001. Narrative history of the seventeenth and eighteenth centuries.

Siskin, Clifford, and William Warner, eds. *This is Enlightenment*. University of Chicago Press, 2010. Collection of essays on the Enlightenment updating the 'public sphere' vision of the eighteenth century.

Todd, Janet. *A Dictionary of British and American Women Writers, 1660–1800*. Totowa, NJ: Rowman & Littlefield, 1987.

Weinreb, Ben, and Christopher Hibbert. *The London Encyclopedia*. Bethesda, MD: Adler and Adler, 1986.

C Further Reading

i The Novel

Bakhtin, M. M. *The Dialogic Imagination: Four Essays*. Ed. Michael Holquist. Trans. Caryl Emerson and Michael Holquist. Austin: University of Texas Press, 1982.

Doody, Margaret Anne. *The True Story of the Novel*. New Brunswick, NJ: Rutgers University Press, 1996.

McKeon, Michael. *The Origins of the English Novel, 1600–1740*. Baltimore, MD: Johns Hopkins University Press, 1987.

Moretti, Franco. *Modern Epic: The World System from Goethe to García Marquez*. New York: Verso, 1996.

   'Slaughterhouse of Literature'. *Modern Literature Quarterly* 61.1 (March 2000): 207–27.

Watt, Ian. *The Rise of the Novel: Studies in Defoe, Richardson and Fielding*. Berkeley: University of California Press, 1957. Influential account of the rise of the novel, from a matrix that included the middle class and empiricism.

ii Cultural History

Bender, John. *Ends of Enlightenment*. Stanford University Press, 2012.

Brewer, John. *Consumption and the World of Goods*. New York: Routledge, 1993.

   The Pleasures of the Imagination: English Culture in the Eighteenth Century. New York: Farrar, Straus, Giroux, 1997.

Ford, Boris. *Eighteenth-Century Britain: The Cambridge Cultural History*. Cambridge University Press, 1992.

Gray, John. *Enlightenment's Wake: Politics and Culture at the Close of the Modern Age*. New York: Routledge, 1995.

Hoskins, W. G. *The Making of the English Landscape*. Baltimore, MD: Penguin, 1970.

Jones, Stephen. *The Eighteenth Century: Cambridge Introduction to the History of Art*. Cambridge University Press, 1985.

McKendrick, Neil, John Brewer and J. H. Plumb. *The Birth of a Consumer Society: The Commercialisation of Eighteenth-Century England*. Bloomington: Indiana University Press, 1982.

Raven, James, Helen Small and Naomi Tadmor, eds. *The Practice and Representation of Reading in England*. Cambridge University Press, 1996.

Summerson, John. *Architecture in Britain, 1530–1830*. New Haven, CT: Yale University Press, 1993.

Tavernor, Robert. *Palladio and Palladianism*. New York: Thames and Hudson, 1991.

Tarabra, Daniela. *European Art of the Eighteenth Century*. Trans. Rosanna M. Giammanco Frongia. Los Angeles: The J. Paul Getty Museum, 2008. Richly illustrated continental and thematic overview of eighteenth-century art, artists, centres and terms.

Waterhouse, Ellis. *Painting in Britain, 1530–1790*. New Haven, CT: Yale University Press, 1994.

iii Political History

Clarke, J. C. D. *English Society, 1660–1832: Religion, Ideology and Politics during the Ancien Régime*. Cambridge University Press, 2000.

Revolution and Rebellion: State and Society in the Seventeenth and Eighteenth Centuries.
       Cambridge University Press, 1986.
De Bolla, Peter. *The Architecture of Concepts: The Historical Formation of Human Rights.* New
       York: Fordham University Press, 2013. A new history of Enlightenment political
       philosophy.
Wootton, David. *Republicanism, Liberty, and Commercial Society, 1649–1776.* Stanford
       University Press, 1994.

iv Social History

Brewer, John. *An Ungovernable People: The English and Their Law in the Seventeenth and
       Eighteenth Centuries.* New Brunswick, NJ: Rutgers University Press, 1980.
Coster, Will. *Family and Kinship in England, 1450–1800.* Cambridge University Press, 2001.
Daunton, M. J. *Progress and Poverty: An Economic and Social History of Britain, 1700–1850.*
       Oxford University Press, 1995.
De Vries, Jan. *The Economy of Europe in an Age of Crisis, 1600–1750.* Cambridge University
       Press, 1976.
Hay, Douglas, et al. *Albion's Fatal Tree: Crime and Society in Eighteenth-Century England.* New
       York: Pantheon, 1975.
Hay, Douglas, and Nicolas Rogers. *Eighteenth-Century English Society: Shuttles and Swords.*
       New York: Oxford University Press, 1997.
McKeon, Michael. *The Secret History of Domesticity.* Baltimore, MD: Johns Hopkins
       University Press, 2005. A cultural and literary history of a domestic sphere
       emerging in the eighteenth century.
Picard, Liza. *Dr Johnson's London: Everyday Life in London, 1740–1770.* London: Phoenix, 2000.
Porter, Roy. *London: A Social History.* Cambridge, MA: Harvard University Press, 1995.
Stone, Lawrence. *The Family, Sex and Marriage in England 1500–1800.* London: Weidenfeld
       & Nicolson, 1977.

v Science

Cohen, I. Bernard, and George E. Smith. *The Cambridge Companion to Newton.* Cambridge
       University Press, 2002.
Feingold, Mordechai. *The Newtonian Moment: Isaac Newton and the Making of Modern
       Culture.* New York Public Library/Oxford University Press, 2004.
Sobel, Dava. *Longitude: The True Story of a Lone Genius Who Solved the Greatest Scientific
       Problem of his Time.* New York: Penguin, 1996.

vi Colonialism

Marshall, P. J., ed. *The Oxford History of the British Empire: The Eighteenth Century.* Oxford
       University Press, 1998.
Nussbaum, Felicity A. *The Global Eighteenth Century.* Baltimore, MD: Johns Hopkins
       Uinversity Press, 2003.

vii Web Resources

andromeda.rutgers.edu/~jlynch/18th/. A portal to a wide range of online materials from
       and about eighteenth-century cultural history.

4 The Romantic Period, 1780–1832

PETER J. KITSON

This overview of the history of the Romantic period provides a narrative of the major social, political and cultural trends which occurred between the years 1780 and 1832 and which impacted on the literature produced by the men and women who lived through them. The Romantic period witnessed enormous political and social upheaval with such political events and social processes as the American and French Revolutions, the Revolutionary and Napoleonic Wars, the prosecution and criticism of the transatlantic slave trade, the Great Reform Act of 1832, the Industrial Revolution and much more. In this period Britain relinquished its American Colonies but found a new empire in other parts of the world, transforming itself into a global superpower. The Romantic Age saw a wholesale change in the ways in which many people lived and this was reflected in the culture of the time. It was a time when Britons forged a new national and imperial identity defined against the cultures and peoples of the world that they encountered in accounts of travel, exploration and colonial settlement.

Chronology

	HISTORY AND CULTURE	LITERATURE
1776–84	American War of Independence	
1784	Act for regulating East India Company	Charlotte Smith, *Elegiac Sonnets*
1785	William Pitt introduces Bill for reform of Parliament William Paley, *Principles of Moral and Political Philosophy*	William Cowper, *The Task* Robert Merry (Della Crusca), *The Florence Miscellany* Sir William Jones, 'A Hymn to Na'ra'yena'
1786	Thomas Clarkson, *An Essay on the Slavery and Commerce of the Human Species* Wolfgang Amadeus Mozart, *The Marriage of Figaro* Impeachment proceedings against Warren Hastings John Boydell's Shakespeare Gallery	Robert Burns, *Poems, Chiefly in the Scottish Dialect* William Beckford, *Vathek*
1787	Formation of a Society for Effecting the Abolition of the Slave Trade Mozart, *Don Giovanni*	
1788	*The Times*	

	HISTORY AND CULTURE	LITERATURE
1789	Fall of the Bastille *Bounty* mutiny Wilberforce introduces twelve resolutions against the slave trade Richard Price, *Discourse on the Love of Our Country*	William Blake, *Songs of Innocence*
1790	Edmund Burke, *Reflections on the Revolution in France* Immanuel Kant, *Critique of Judgment* James Bruce, *Travels to Discover the Source of the Nile*	Ann Radcliffe, *Sicilian Romance* Joanna Baillie, *Poems*
1791	Thomas Paine, *Rights of Man*, Part One Birmingham Church and King Riots Louis XVI flees to Varennes Galvani publishes results of electrical experiments with frogs' legs	Erasmus Darwin, *The Botanic Garden* Mary Robinson, *Poems* (–1793)
1792	Abolition of French monarchy and Republic declared September massacres London Corresponding Society formed Commons resolves on gradual abolition of slavery by 1796 Boycott of sugar begins Thomas Paine, *Rights of Man*, Part Two William Gilpin, *Essay on Picturesque Beauty* Mary Wollstonecraft, *A Vindication of the Rights of Woman*	Smith, *Desmond* William Blake, engravings for John Gabriel Stedman, *Narrative, of a five years' expedition, against revolted Negroes of Surinam*
1793	Execution of Louis XVI Britain and France at war Beginning of French Terror Macartney's embassy to China William Godwin, *Political Justice* Hannah More, *Village Politics* Board of Agriculture established	Blake, *America; Visions of the Daughters of Albion* Smith, *The Old Manor House* William Wordsworth, *Descriptive Sketches; An Evening Walk*
1794	Execution of Robespierre French Republic outlaws slavery in all French colonies Treason trials Habeas corpus suspended	Blake, *Songs of Innocence and of Experience* Godwin, *Caleb Williams* Radcliffe, *The Mysteries of Udolpho*
1795	French Directory established Food riots George III's carriage stoned at opening of Parliament Treasonable Practices and Seditious Meetings Acts Methodist secession Joseph Haydn, *London* Symphony James Hutton, *Theory of the Earth*	Maria Edgeworth, *Letters for Literary Ladies* Hannah More, *Cheap Repository Tracts*
1796	Napoleon's Italian campaign Turner's first oil paintings exhibited Edward Jenner's first smallpox vaccination Beckford builds Fonthill Abbey	S. T. Coleridge, *Poems on Various Subjects* Matthew Lewis, *The Monk* Robinson, *Sappho and Phaon* Anna Seward, *Llangollen Vale* Anne Yearsley, *The Rural Lyre*
1797	Naval mutinies at Spithead and Nore Invasion scares British naval victories at Camperdown and Cape St Vincent	Radcliffe, *The Italian* Smith, *Elegiac Sonnets* (new edition)

	HISTORY AND CULTURE	LITERATURE
1798	France invades Switzerland Napoleon's expedition lands in Egypt; Battle of the Nile Irish rebellion suppressed Thomas Malthus, *Essay on the Principle of Population* Edgeworth, *Practical Education* Haydn, *The Creation* Godwin, *Memoirs of the Author*	Baillie, *A Series of Plays* Coleridge, *Fears in Solitude; France: An Ode;* *Frost at Midnight* Wordsworth and Coleridge, *Lyrical Ballads*
1799	Napoleon becomes First Consul Six Acts against radical activities Introduction of income tax Rosetta Stone discovered	Lewis, *Tales of Terror* Seward, *Original Sonnets* Wordsworth, *Two-Part Prelude* (MS)
1800	Act of Union with Ireland (takes effect 1801) Volta generates electricity Beethoven, First Symphony	Robinson, *Lyrical Tales* Wordsworth and Coleridge, *Lyrical Ballads* (2nd edn with 'Preface') Edgeworth, *Castle Rackrent*
1801	Pitt resigns over Catholic Emancipation Henry Addington becomes Prime Minister First census of England and Wales Thomas Jefferson elected President of the USA	Robert Southey, *Thalaba the Destroyer* Robinson, *Memoirs*
1802	Napoleon restores slavery in the French empire Peace of Amiens *Edinburgh Review* founded Paley, *Natural Theology*	Walter Scott, *Minstrelsy of the Scottish Border* (–1803) Baillie, *Plays of the Passions* (II)
1803	War resumes with France Richard Trevithick builds first working railway steam engine	Darwin, *Temple of Nature* Thomas Chatterton, *Collected Works*
1804	Pitt returns as Prime Minister Napoleon crowned Emperor	Blake, *Milton* Ann and Jane Taylor, *Original Poems for Infant* *Minds*
1805	Napoleon victorious at Austerlitz Battle of Trafalgar Death of Horatio Nelson William Hazlitt, *Essay on the Principles of Human Action* Richard Payne Knight, *Principles of Taste*	Scott, *Lay of the Last Minstrel* Wordsworth *The Prelude* (completed in MS) Mary Tighe, *Psyche; or, The Legend of Love*
1806	Death of Pitt Ministry of All the Talents formed Death of Fox Napoleon defeats Prussians and establishes trade blockade of Britain	Robinson, *Poetical Works*
1807	Act passed for the Abolition of the Slave Trade in the British Colonies France, Russia and Prussia conclude Treaties of Tilsit Humphry Davy isolates sodium and potassium Geological Society founded	Wordsworth, *Poems in Two Volumes* Lord Byron, *Hours of Idleness* Thomas Moore, *Irish Melodies* Smith, *Beachy Head* Charles and Mary Lamb, *Tales from Shakespeare*
1808	Peninsular War begins Adam Dalton, *New System of Chemical Philosophy* Davy isolates magnesium, strontium, barium and calcium	Scott, *Marmion* Felicia Hemans, *England and Spain*
1809	*Quarterly Review* founded First use of gas-lighting in central London	Byron, *English Bards and Scotch Reviewers* More, *Coelebs in Search of a Wife*
1810	George III permanently insane	Baillie, *The Family Legend* George Crabbe, *The Borough* Scott, *The Lady of the Lake* Seward, *Poetical Works*

	HISTORY AND CULTURE	LITERATURE
1811	Prince of Wales becomes Regent Luddite Riots Percy Shelley, *The Necessity of Atheism*	Jane Austen, *Sense and Sensibility* Tighe, *Psyche with Other Poems*
1812	Assassination of Prime Minister Spencer Perceval Napoleon invades Russia United States declares war on Britain Elgin marbles arrive in London Toleration Act	Baillie, *Plays of the Passions* (III) Anna Laetitia Barbauld, *Eighteen Hundred and Eleven* Byron, *Childe Harold's Pilgrimage* I and II Crabbe, *Tales* Hemans, *Domestic Affections*
1813	Napoleon loses at Leipzig East India Company monopoly ended Toleration Act for Unitarians Execution of Luddite leaders Leigh Hunt imprisoned for libelling Prince Regent	Austen, *Pride and Prejudice* Shelley, *Queen Mab* Byron, *The Giaour; The Bride of Abydos* Coleridge, *Remorse*
1814	Napoleon abdicates and exiled to Elba Restoration of French monarchy Congress of Vienna George Stephenson builds steam locomotive	Austen, *Mansfield Park* Byron, *The Corsair; Lara* Leigh Hunt, *Feast of the Poets* Scott, *Waverley* Wordsworth, *The Excursion*
1815	Napoleon escapes from Elba Battle of Waterloo Corn Law passed Davy designs safety lamp	Byron, *Hebrew Melodies* Wordsworth, *Poems* Thomas Love Peacock, *Headlong Hall*
1816	Economic depression Spa Fields Riots Elgin marbles purchased by British Museum Amherst Embassy to China William Cobbett, *Political Register*	Austen, *Emma* Byron, *Childe Harold's Pilgrimage III* Coleridge, *Kubla Khan* Scott, *The Antiquary* Shelley, *Alastor*
1817	Pentridge uprising Habeas corpus suspended Manchester 'Blanketeers' march to London *Blackwood's Edinburgh Magazine* David Ricardo, *Principles of Political Economy* James Mill, *History of British India*	Byron, *Manfred* Coleridge, *Sibylline Leaves; Biographia Literaria* Hazlitt, *Characters of Shakespeare's Plays* John Keats, *Poems* Thomas Moore, *Lalla Rookh* Shelley, *Laon and Cythna* Southey, *Wat Tyler*
1818	Habeas corpus restored Defeat of Sir Francis Burdett's motion for parliamentary reform	Austen, *Northanger Abbey; Persuasion* Byron, *Beppo; Childe Harold's Pilgrimage IV* Hazlitt, *Lectures on the English Poets* Keats, *Endymion* Mary Shelley, *Frankenstein*
1819	'Peterloo Massacre' Six Acts Factory Act William Lawrence, *Lectures on Physiology, Zoology and the Natural History of Man* Théodore Géricault, *The Raft of the Medusa* Schubert, *The Trout Quintet*	Byron, *Don Juan I and II* Crabbe, *Tales of the Hall* Hemans, *Tales and Historic Scenes in Verse* Scott, *Ivanhoe; The Bride of Lammermoor* Shelley, *The Cenci* Wordsworth, *Peter Bell; The Waggoner*
1820	Death of George III Accession of George IV Trial of Queen Caroline for adultery Cato Street Conspiracy Hans Christian Oersted discovers electromagnetism Royal Astronomical Society founded	John Clare, *Poems Desciptive of Rural Life* Keats, *Lamia and Isabella; The Eve of St Agnes and other Poems* Lamb, 'Essays of Elia' Charles Robert Maturin, *Melmoth the Wanderer* Shelley, *Prometheus Unbound* Wordsworth, *The River Duddon*

	HISTORY AND CULTURE	LITERATURE
1821	Greek War of Independence	Baillie, *Metrical Legends of Exalted Characters* Byron, *Cain; Sardanapalus; Don Juan* III–V Clare, *The Village Minstrel* Thomas De Quincey, *Confessions of an English Opium-Eater* Shelley, *Adonais; Epipsychidion*
1822	Castlereagh commits suicide	Byron, *The Vision of Judgement* Hemans, *Welsh Melodies;* 'Songs of the Cid' Shelley, *Hellas* Wordsworth, *Ecclesiastical Sketches*
1823	Mechanics Institute founded *The Lancet* appears Royal Asiatic Society of Great Britain and Ireland meets	Byron, *The Age of Bronze; The Island; Don Juan VI–XIV* Hazlitt, *Liber Amoris* Hemans, *The Siege of Valencia and Other Poems* Mary Shelley, *Valperga* Scott, *Quentin Durward*
1824	Repeal of Combination Act gives trade unions right to exist National Gallery founded Royal Society for the Prevention of Cruelty to Animals founded *Westminster Review*	Byron, *Don Juan XV–XVI* James Hogg, *Confessions of a Justified Sinner* L. E. L. (Letitia Elizabeth Landon), *The Improvisatrice* Scott, *Redgauntlet*
1825	Stockton–Darlington Railway opens Society for the Diffusion of Useful Knowledge founded	Barbauld, *Works* Hazlitt, *The Spirit of the Age* Hemans, *The Forest Sanctuary* L. E. L., *The Troubadour*
1826	London Zoological Society founded	Hazlitt, *The Plain Speaker* M. Shelley, *The Last Man* Scott, *Woodstock*
1827	George Canning becomes Prime Minister Death of Canning University of London founded	Clare, *The Shepherd's Calendar* Alfred Tennyson, *Poems by Two Brothers*
1828	Duke of Wellington becomes Prime Minister Repeal of the Test and Corporations Acts Schubert's Ninth Symphony	Hemans, *Records of Woman* Hunt, *Lord Byron and Some Contemporaries*
1829	Catholic Emancipation Robert Peel creates metropolitan police force	Hogg, *The Shepherd's Calendar*
1830	Death of George IV and accession of Willam IV Earl Grey's Whig reforming government 'Captain Swing' rural riots Opening of Manchester–Liverpool Railway Foundation of the Royal Geographical Society July Revolution in France Greek independence secured Coleridge, *On the Constitution of the Church and State* Cobbett, *Rural Rides* Charles Lyell, *Principles of Geology* vol. I	Hemans, *Songs of the Affections* Scott, *Tales of Grandfather*, Part III Tennyson, *Poems, Chiefly Lyrical*
1831	National Union of the Working Classes founded Slave revolt in Jamaica Michael Faraday discovers electromagnetic induction	M. Shelley, *Frankenstein* (2nd edn) L. E. L., *Romance and Reality* Ebenezer Elliot, *Corn-Law Rhymes* Peacock, *Crotchet Castle* Mary Prince, *The History of Mary Prince, a West Indian Slave*
1832	Passage of the Great Reform Act Morse invents the telegraph	Tennyson, *Poems* De Quincey, *Klosterheim, or The Masque*

Historical Overview

Culture and Society

At the beginning of the Romantic period, Britain was still an agrarian economy with much of the population employed as rural workers or in domestic service; by the end of the period it was a rapidly industrialising nation with mushrooming towns and cities. In the eighteenth century there was no real class-consciousness; Britain had a limited aristocracy (much smaller than most European nations), a substantial rural gentry and what were referred to as the 'middling sorts': professional people, merchants and rural and urban workers. By 1830 something like a modern class-consciousness had emerged with more clearly identifiable upper, middle and working classes. Notions of rank, order, degree and station based on birth became supplanted by groupings of landlords, capitalists and labourers. In the late eighteenth century the population of the British Isles began to grow dramatically. Between 1771 and 1831, the population of England more than doubled from 6.4 million to 13 million. In Scotland the population rose from something like 1.3 million in the mid-eighteenth century to 2.4 million by 1831. Never before had the population risen so markedly over such a short period of time. Historians still argue about the reasons for this explosion but whatever the reason it changed British society for ever. The increasing size of the population expanded the labour force, as well as the demand for goods and services. Economically this was beneficial, as a larger labour force reduced the cost of labour and of the goods and services produced, which, in turn, accelerated the industrial process. As well as aiding industrialisation, the growth in population also contributed to the process of urbanisation, or the phenomenon of the increasing concentration of the population in large cities and towns. In 1770 less than one-fifth of the population lived in an urban community; by 1801 the proportion had risen to over one-third and by 1840 it was almost one-half. In the 1750s London and Edinburgh were the only cities in Britain with in excess of 50,000 inhabitants; by 1801 there were eight towns of over that size and by 1841 there were twenty-six. The great commercial, industrial and manufacturing cities of London, Manchester, Glasgow, Birmingham, Sheffield, Leeds and Bradford increased exponentially in size. By the mid-nineteenth century, for good or for ill, Britain had become the world's first urbanised society. The factory towns of England tended to become rookeries of jerry-built tenements, while the mining towns became long, monotonous rows of company-built cottages, furnishing minimal shelter. The unhealthy living conditions in the towns can be traced to lack of good brick, the absence of building codes, and the lack of machinery for public sanitation; but they were also due to the factory owners' tendency to regard workers as commodities, or 'hands', and not as a group of human beings.

In addition to a new factory-owning bourgeoisie, the Industrial Revolution created a new working class. The new class of industrial workers included all the men, women and children labouring in the textile mills, pottery works and mines. Often,

The Industrial Revolution

The Industrial Revolution is defined as the application of power-driven machinery to the manufacturing of goods and commodities. In the eighteenth century all western Europe began to industrialise to some extent, but in Britain the process was most highly accelerated. The reasons for this are several. Britain had large deposits of coal still available for industrial fuel. There was an abundant labour supply to mine coal and iron, and to man the factories. From its established commercial empire, Britain had a fleet and possessed colonies to furnish raw materials and act as captive markets for manufactured goods. Tobacco merchants of Glasgow, and tea and sugar merchants of London and Bristol, had capital to invest and the technical expertise to exploit it. By the beginning of the eighteenth century the use of machines in manufacturing was already widespread. In 1762 Matthew Boulton built a factory which employed more than six hundred workers, and installed a steam engine to supplement power from two large waterwheels which ran a variety of lathes and polishing and grinding machines. In Staffordshire an industry developed giving the world good cheap pottery; chinaware brought in by the East India Company often furnished a model. Josiah Wedgwood was one of those who revolutionised the production and sale of pottery. Improvements in the textile industry also occurred. In 1733 John Kay patented his flying shuttle allowing weaving to proceed more quickly. In 1771 Richard Arkwright's 'water frame' was producing yarn. About the same time, James Hargreaves patented a spinning jenny on which one operator could spin many threads simultaneously. Then in 1779 Samuel Crompton combined the jenny and the water frame in a machine known as 'Crompton's mule', which produced quantities of good, strong yarn. By 1840 the labour cost of making the best woollen cloth had fallen by at least half. The first modern steam engine was built by Thomas Newcomen in 1705 to improve the pumping equipment used to eliminate seepage in tin and copper mines. In 1763 James Watt began to make improvements on Newcomen's engine, changing it from an atmospheric to a true 'steam engine'. In 1774 Matthew Boulton took Watt into partnership, and their firm produced nearly five hundred engines before Watt's patent expired in 1800. The factory was now freed from reliance on water power.

skilled artisans, such as the 'handloom weavers', found themselves degraded to routine process labourers as machines began to mass produce the products formerly made by hand. Generally speaking, wages were low, hours were long and working conditions unpleasant and dangerous.

The transport system improved considerably throughout the period. The spread of turnpike roads made it possible to transport goods and materials quickly throughout the year. From the 1760s onwards, the canal system reduced the costs of haulage. The revolution in transportation was completed by the beginnings of the railway system. By the mid-nineteenth century railway trains travelling at 30 to 50 miles an hour were not uncommon, and freight steadily became more important than passengers.

There were substantial changes in agriculture as the countryside was transformed. Agrarian capitalism reached a period of development and crisis in the early nineteenth century with the growth of a class of agricultural workers who possessed only their labour to sell to tenant farmers. The period sees the decline of the independent smallholder (often idealised as the 'yeoman' class), movingly presented in Wordsworth's representations of what he referred to as 'Cumbrian statesmen', such as Matthew from his *Lyrical Ballads*. The open-field system of cultivation gave way to compact farms and enclosed fields. Bogs and fens were drained, adding to the

4.1 Industrial Revolution: Joseph Wright (1734–97), *An Iron Forge*, 1772, from an engraving made in 1773 by Richard Earlom (1743–1822). This picture shows men at work in a small iron-forge, with the forge-master's extended family looking on. At a time when most artists presented a thoroughly nostalgic vision of rural work, focusing on traditional agricultural tasks, Wright was quite exceptional in depicting scenes of modern industry. Its dramatic light effects create an almost religious atmosphere, and by showing the various generations of the family together Wright alludes to the traditional theme of the 'ages of man'.

availability of land suitable for cultivation. Propaganda for the new agriculture was largely the work of Arthur Young. In 1793 the Board of Agriculture was established with Young as its secretary. Although a failure as a practical farmer, he was a great success as a publicist for scientific agriculture. Changes to the lifestyle of the rural worker were often bitterly resented. The loss of customary rights, occasioned by enclosure, and the reduction in the value of wages led to dissatisfaction and unrest, culminating in resistance, rioting and rick-burning. Alternatives to this form of agrarian capitalism were broached. Thomas Paine's *Agrarian Justice* (1796) claimed that land rights derived from commonality and argued for a land tax to militate against rural poverty. Radicals like Thomas Spence and his followers went further, arguing for the redistribution of land and the wealth derived from it.

Eighteenth-century Britain became a society with a marked difference between two spheres of activity, the public and the private. There developed an expanding public sphere of political, civil and intellectual life, typified, in particular, by the growth of the coffee house as a venue for reading and debating information. In contrast, the private sphere involved family life and the care and education of children. These two spheres were gendered as masculine and feminine. Notions of gender also underwent a redefinition in the period, largely due to the growth in the mode

Enclosure

Enclosure refers to the conversion of common land and strip-based open-field farming into compact and contained holdings enabling more efficient and sustained farming. This process, which occurred piecemeal and incrementally, had begun in the late medieval period (see p. 115) but was vastly accelerated in the eighteenth century and especially in the Romantic period. Each action of enclosure required parliamentary approval, and between 1762 and 1844 more than 2,500 Enclosure Acts were passed, encompassing over 4 million acres of land. The enclosing of common lands contributed vastly to the increase in agricultural productivity, but this was only achieved with massive dislocation and distress to large numbers of the rural population. The process benefited the larger farms and landowners who saw rents increase with the productivity of their lands. Large sections of the rural population were increasingly vulnerable to pauperisation with the increase of seasonal unemployment and the lessening of opportunities for female and child labour. The customary access of the landless to grazing land, gleaning, peat-cutting, firewood, fishing and game was lost. This loss was especially hard when rural wages were in decline, and it was bitterly resented. The poetry of Clare, Goldsmith, Crabbe and Wordsworth articulates a strong dissatisfaction with the process and its implications for the rural poor. The process was also sometimes violently resisted with rioting, the destruction of hedgerows and the burning of ricks.

of sensibility, which influenced all aspects of culture. Sensibility was very much a middle-class and commercial culture which stressed the fineness of feelings. Women were possessed of sensibility to a greater extent than men, because their nerves were considered to be finer and thus capable of delivering more delicate feelings. Likewise, it was argued that women should devote themselves to the domestic life and not interfere in the public sphere. They were the guardians of morality but not of political action. It was also feared that sensibility, with its stress on fine feeling and emotion, might lead to men becoming feminised. Similarly with the growth of Evangelical religion in the latter half of the century, the stress on the woman at the centre of family life increased. Denied participation in the world of public affairs, women were nevertheless meant to act as the moral guides to men and to set the moral and religious tone for the household. The period is also generally known as one in which the authoritarian and patriarchal family gave way to a more closely entwined unit held together by the values of affective individualism, based on respect, loyalty and filial obedience. While retaining patriarchal control and authority, fathers were obliged to take more interest in their children's lives and education.

Some argue that popular culture came under threat in the early nineteenth century. Not only did the gap between elite and plebeian culture appear to widen, but popular pastimes, customs and morality were scrutinised by a bourgeois class possessed of reforming zeal, both utilitarian and Evangelical. The culture of sensibility, with its concomitant attempt at the reformation of manners, is important here, as is the religious revivalism of the Evangelicals and their commitment to good works and strict morality. There were attempts to regularise and control activities such as pugilism, bull-baiting and cockfighting, and increasing regulation of public spaces, including the coffee house, dramshop and inn. Popular festivities such as the maypole and morris dancing were discouraged and Sunday Schools and religious processions encouraged. The Society for the Suppression of Vice (1802) targeted gambling and drinking as activities to repress. Popular culture was a wide-ranging field of activity which crossed notions of polite and vulgar, elite and plebeian, pre-industrial and modern. It was formed from both print and oral cultures, the Bible, hymns, chapbooks, almanacs, newspapers, romances, gallows speeches and so on. It manifested the survival of superstitions and beliefs involving popular millenarian thought of vulgar prophets such as Richard Brothers and Joanna Southcott, as well as activities for self improvement, especially in the artisan classes by such figures as the radical tailor Francis Place.

The place and function of visual art in an increasingly commercial and industrialised world also troubled the age. The market for some kinds of artworks began to spread beyond affluent aristocratic circles. The Royal Academy was founded in 1768 with Sir Joshua Reynolds as its first president. It became the nation's most powerful institution for the visual arts with forty full and twenty associate members. The Academy organised classes for its students as well as an annual exhibition of paintings, sculpture and drawings by British artists in the splendid halls of Sir William Chambers's neo-classical masterpiece, Somerset House. It sought to support young artists and raise the standard of public taste. In 1805 the British Institution was founded to showcase the works of contemporary British artists. Various commercial galleries were also established, reflecting the commodification of art for a middle-class market. The most notable of these was John Boydell's Shakespeare Gallery, which opened in 1786 in Pall Mall, exhibiting new paintings from Shakespeare that were then engraved for prestigious editions of the plays.

The highest genre of oil painting was that of the history painting, what Reynolds called 'the grand style', depicting figures from the Bible, mythology, or national history. In particular, the period saw a number of contemporary subjects reflecting Britain's military and naval success. Benjamin West's *The Death of General Wolfe* (1770) is often regarded as an exemplar of this. In France, Jacques-Louis David produced works commemorating recent events in the grand style such as *The Tennis-Court Oath* (1791), the *Death of Marat* (1793) and *Napoleon at St Bernard* (1800). Other genres such as portraiture, landscape and still life also increased in prestige. The genre of landscape painting was elevated in the period. The two most important British landscape painters were John Constable and J. M. W. Turner. Constable developed a series of agricultural landscapes from his native Stour valley in Suffolk, the most famous of which are *Flatford Mill* (1817) and *The Hay Wain* (1821). Turner produced a huge opus of incredible variety. He began his career painting in the style of Claude Lorrain, the model for picturesque theorists, and was known for his extensive landscape paintings. He later pioneered a visual style evoking the sublime and apocalyptic (as opposed to Constable's continued predilection for picturesque beauty). Turner's main rival in the sublime was the Newcastle painter John Martin, who, in the 1820s and 1830s, produced spectacular works illustrating, among other things, the Bible, Milton and Byron, such as *Belshazzar's Feast* (1826), *Manfred on the Jungfrau* (1837, see Figure 4.10), *Paradise Lost* (1827) and *The Fall of Babylon* (1831). Philippe Jacques de Loutherberg essayed a series of sublime industrial landscapes, including his *Coalbrookdale by Night* (1801). Another key artist of the period, Henry Fuseli, was Professor of Painting at the Royal Academy for two periods (1799–1805 and 1810 to his death). His work eschewed the concern with history and the public for a depiction of the tragic, sublime and extreme emotions of love, hate, revenge, jealousy and alienation, such as his paintings for Boydell's Shakespeare Gallery and his famous pre-Freudian depiction of the *Nightmare*. The Academy was dominated by male artists but females such as Maria Cosway, Mary Moser and Angelica Kauffman did exhibit there. Many artists chafed against what they saw as the Academy's dominance of the art world. Both James Barry and the engraver William Blake decried the stultifying influence of those like Reynolds who prescribed rules for art. Blake produced his small and highly symbolic experimental pictures for sale to his select patrons.

Although not a part of the fine art market as such, topical political prints were extremely popular and contributed substantially to the political debate of the 1790s and beyond. Key caricaturists such as James Gillray, George and Isaac Cruikshank and Thomas Rowlandson, though not known as individual artists, produced large numbers of hand-coloured etchings on political events, sold to the public in print-shop windows and exhibitions. Typically such prints would contrast British freedoms, with a well-fed John Bull, against French liberty, with its vicious and starving *sans-culottes*. They demonstrated a fear of French democracy and popular movements at home, savagely caricaturing Whig leaders such as Charles James Fox and other contemporary reformers.

Belief and Thought

The canonical Romantic poets were building upon and reacting against the thought of their predecessors, sometimes breaking with the major trends or alternatively pushing that body of thought into more extreme positions than were usual in the Enlightenment. The writers and thinkers of the Enlightenment imagined themselves as emerging from centuries of darkness and ignorance into a new age enlightened by reason, science and a respect for humanity. The most celebrated exponent of this doctrine in the late seventeenth century was the British physician and philosopher John Locke. Locke's *Essay Concerning Human Understanding* (1690) laid the foundations of an Enlightenment theory of mind. Locke dismissed the notion of both neo-Platonists and Rationalists that there existed in the human mind certain innate or *a priori* ideas. He compared the human mind to a blank sheet of paper upon which experience writes, or to an empty cabinet which experience fills. The human mind is thus originally passive, and knowledge is arrived at by relating the ideas left in the mind by sensation. Locke distinguished two types of experience: sensation, the mind's perception of the world, and reflection, the mind's perception of its own operation. By reflecting upon simple ideas the mind is able to generate ideas. To account for this process, Locke developed the theory of the 'association of ideas', by which knowledge of an object is built up from the simple ideas of perception.

Immanuel Kant is said to have effected a 'Copernican revolution' in European thought and laid the foundations for the Romantic idealism of Coleridge, Thomas De Quincey and Thomas Carlyle in Britain. In his *Critique of Pure Reason* (1781) Kant argued by an exhaustive process of deduction that all knowledge derives from experience yet it is dependent on *a priori* or, in his terms, 'transcendental' structures in the mind, such as the concepts of space and time. For Kant, such concepts were present in the mind and not absolutes of experience. He was thus led to distinguish between that which is knowable, the representation of the object in the human mind, and that which is unknowable, the pure object or the 'thing-in-itself' (*Ding an sich*). As well as the concepts of space and time, Kant argued that notions of God, freedom and eternity were likewise part of the transcendent realm, unknowable in themselves, but necessary for us to make sense of reality. The attraction of Kant's philosophy for Coleridge and the Romantics was that it assigned an active and creative role to the mind in the formation of human knowledge. Furthermore, Kant allowed an important role for the artistic imagination which had been somewhat restrained in the empiricist tradition. He distinguished between three kinds or powers of imagination. The first is the *reproductive imagination*, which is close to the Lockeian mode of the association of ideas. The second is the *productive imagination*, which operates between sense perception and allows us to carry on the work of discursive reasoning. The third is the *aesthetic imagination*, which is free of the laws which govern the understanding and which works through symbols. Kant's three-fold distinction corresponds to Coleridge's famous division of the powers of the mind in chapter XIII of *Biographia Literaria* into the *fancy*, the *primary imagination* and the *secondary imagination*.

The Romantic period likewise witnessed a transformation in ideas about science. In the eighteenth century, this body of thought and practices was known as 'natural philosophy', an enquiry into the powers and phenomena of the natural world, demonstrating the splendours of God's creation. By the end of the period the modern term 'scientist' had been coined (by William Whewell) and the notion of the scientist as a professional investigator of the natural world, working in a specialised discipline with institutional support and a network of colleagues, was accepted. The nineteenth century saw the divergence of knowledge into separate disciplines, supported by discrete associations and bodies with distinct and specialised agendas and instruments. The Royal Society, under the presidency of Sir Joseph Banks, conservatively continued to prefer applied science over theoretical questioning and resisted the creation of individual bodies such as the Linnean Society (1788), the Geological Society (1807), the Astronomical Society (1820) and the Zoological Society (1826). In 1831 the British Association for the Advancement of Science was formed with the intention of coordinating the work of the separate societies. The period witnessed many key developments in scientific discovery. There were major advances in the fields of mathematics, physics, chemistry, optics, electromagnetism and biology. Natural philosophy became a battle ground for conservatives and reformers. Joseph Priestley famously allied science with political reform when commenting that 'the English hierarchy (if there be anything unsound in its constitution) has equal reason to tremble even at an air pump, or an electrical machine'. Similarly, French science, especially chemistry, was anathematised by Edmund Burke as seditious.

In the field of the physical sciences unity of electricity, chemistry and magnetism was demonstrated. A 'chemical revolution' was under way, with the identification of new varieties of airs and the discovery of their different chemical properties. In the 1790s, John Dalton proposed that the proportions of gases mixed in the atmosphere depended on their 'atomic weights'. His insights led him to the atomic theory of matter for which he would be remembered. Alessandro Volta's invention of the electric pile, or battery, in 1800 created a device capable of delivering a steady stream of current through material substances. This development was taken up by Sir Humphry Davy, who, in a series of barnstorming lectures at the newly founded Royal Institution, demonstrated the spectacular powers of electricity in breaking down physical materials. Davy, a poet and friend of Coleridge, believed in a dynamical chemistry, holding that power rather than matter was the fundamental force in the universe. In 1820 Hans Christian Oersted proved the long-suspected link between electricity and magnetism. Davy's disciple Michael Faraday discovered the crucial link between electricity and magnetism by making an electric wire rotate around a magnet. William Sturgeon took this discovery further when he later developed the tool of the electromagnet. Back in the 1780s Luigi Galvani, in a series of experiments at the University of Bologna, investigated the relationship between electricity and animation by applying an electric current to the leg of a frog. He coined the term *animal electricity* to describe whatever it was that activated the muscles of his specimens. The phenomenon was dubbed 'Galvanism'. Galvani's nephew, Giovanni Aldini, popularised his discoveries in a series of sensational lectures in London.

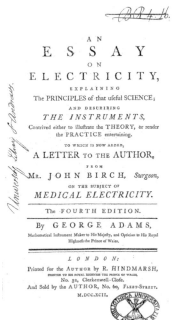

4.2 With the development of batteries and electrical machines and instruments, electric currents were put to a variety of uses. Here a small girl is being given electric therapy. Frontispiece of George Adams, *An Essay on Electricity, Explaining the Theory and Practice of that Useful Science; and the Mode of Applying it to Medical Purposes* (London, 1799).

Geology was a comparatively new science in the period and underwent rapid development. The subject was still dominated by biblical chronology, and major thinkers were interested in reconciling the geological record with the history of the world and its peoples as set out in scripture. This was becoming a more difficult task. The history of the earth was increasingly revealed to be much older than the four thousand or so years suggested by the Bible. To explain the formation of the earth there were also various hypotheses. The 'Neptunists' led by Abraham Gottlob Werner argued that the rock formations were a product of precipitation by an ancient ocean over a long period of time. This argument could be reconciled to the biblical notion of the Flood. The 'Vulcanists' believed that some of the rocks of the earth's surface were formed more quickly by igneous or volcanic action, although they stopped short of entirely contradicting Neptunist thought. The 'Plutonists', led by the Scottish geologist James Hutton, argued that, although rocks might be formed by sedimentation, it was the force of pressure and heat below the surface of the earth which accounted for the present geological structure of the world. For Hutton, geological time was immeasurably long and not confined by the dictates of scripture.

The origins of human life and the place of humanity in the natural order also vexed natural philosophers. The science of comparative anatomy made great strides, with detailed studies of the relationship of human beings to the rest of the natural world. Unorthodox ideas concerning evolution were advanced. In France, Jean-Baptiste Lamarck argued that organisms could slowly adapt to their environment, and that modifications of their organs and biological structure could be passed on through heredity. In Britain such controversial notions were more tentatively broached. Lord Monboddo, for instance, believed that humans had evolved from apes and lost their tails in the process. The chief proponent of the evolutionary hypothesis, however, was the remarkable polymath, Erasmus Darwin. Darwin was a member of the progressive Lunar Society of Birmingham

Methodism

Methodism was a movement begun in the eighteenth century as a religious society that wished to reform the Church of England from within. By force of circumstance it became separate from the Anglican Church and took on the characteristics of an autonomous institution. The movement was founded by John Wesley, an Anglican clergyman. Wesley, along with his brother Charles, had undergone an intensely emotional religious experience in 1738. Some months later John Wesley was invited to come to the city of Bristol and help to preach to the colliers of Kingswood Chase, just outside the city, where living conditions were poor. This open-air preaching marked the beginning of the Methodist Revival. Under the leadership, at first of George Whitefield and afterwards of Wesley, the movement rapidly gained ground among those who felt themselves neglected by the Church of England. Wesley claimed to have reinstated the biblical doctrines that a man may be assured of his salvation and that, by the power of the Holy Spirit, he is capable of attaining perfect love for God and his fellows in this life. In spite of Wesley's wish, conflicts, chiefly over the right to ordain ministers, led to the separation of Methodism from the Church of England in 1795, four years after his death. The Wesleyan Methodist Church grew rapidly throughout the nineteenth century, the growth being largest in the expanding industrial areas. The fervid emotionalism of the brand of Christianity practised by John and Charles Wesley has often been likened to the stress on feeling and passion to be found in all the canonical Romantic poets. In religious thought there was a renewed stress on the individual's personal relation to God.

The Evangelical Revival

Evangelicalism, or the renewed faith in a Gospel-based Christianity, had its origins in the early to mid-eighteenth century. Evangelicals believed in the importance of preaching the Word to all. This was, in part, a response to the growing attractions of deism (the belief in a rational deity deduced from the evidence of nature) as well as a broadly latitudinarian Anglican theology which stressed the importance of achieving salvation through good works. Evangelicals, by contrast, believed passionately in the scriptures and in the fallen state of humanity and its essentially sinful nature. They stressed the importance of an emotional experience of being born again through Christ, emphasising the importance of grace and of their personal relationship with God. They possessed a strong belief in the fundamental tenets of Christianity, such as the resurrection and the virgin birth. In the Romantic period, the most significant Evangelical group within the Anglican Church was the Clapham Sect, centred on the church of Clapham in south London. Its members included John Venn, the Rector, William Wilberforce, Henry Thornton, James Stephen and Zachary Macaulay. Many were Members of Parliament, where, in addition to their abolitionism, they worked for prison reform, prevention of cruel sports, and the suspension of the game laws and the lottery. They supported several missionary and Bible societies, financed Hannah More's schools and pamphlets, and published their own journal, *The Christian Observer*. The Claphamites, mostly wealthy Anglicans, were politically conservative and appealed to the rich as the Methodists did to the poor. Derisively nicknamed the 'Saints', they exerted a powerful influence on the governing circles of English society and were, in part, responsible for the reformation of manners that occurred within the Regency period. Evangelicals were also strongly opposed to the transatlantic slave trade.

which included in its membership Thomas Day, Richard Edgeworth, Matthew Boulton, James Watt and Joseph Priestley. In a series of publications, *The Loves of the Plants* (1789), *The Economy of Vegetation* (1791) and his treatise *Zoonomia* (1794), he hypothesised that humanity had evolved over a period of millions of years from simple organisms or 'filaments'. The anatomist and surgeon William Lawrence, in his *Lectures on Physiology* (1819), developed the analogy between humans and animals bred to further certain physical characteristics, deemed to be valuable. Evolutionary ideas, though regarded with great suspicion, if not horror, by the scientific establishment were being discussed as an alternative account of the natural world to that provided in scripture.

The institution of the established Church itself was also considered as under threat in the later eighteenth century. There was a strong perception that it had become inert and remote from people's lives, staffed by absentee clerics who accepted generous stipends and spent their time in leisure pursuits. In many ways the Romantics responded to the new currents of feeling that arose in the last quarter of the eighteenth century as a reaction to the aridity of much enlightened rationalist thought.

The late eighteenth century was also a time when religious sects, usually organised around charismatic individuals and espousing apocalyptic brands of mystical thought, multiplied. William Blake was, for a time, attracted to the writings of the Swedish mystic Emanuel Swedenborg and attended the New Jerusalem Church of his disciples in Eastcheap before repudiating Swedenborgian teachings in *The Marriage of Heaven and Hell* (1790–3). Various millenarian prophets and sects arose in the 1790s, identifying the French Revolution with the prophecies of Daniel and Revelation. Most notable were the popular prophets Richard Brothers and Joanna Southcott, but they were only two of many. This reading of political events in terms of biblical prophecy attracted both plebeian and polite audiences. Enlightenment notions of deism and scepticism also continued throughout the Romantic period. Thomas Paine's *The Age of Reason* (Part I (1794); Part II (1795)) demystified Christian orthodoxy, seeking to establish a pure deism. Paine regarded the Bible as a mixture of poetry and 'trash'. Joseph Priestley, in numerous works, attempted to purge Christianity of its 'corruptions' and re-establish a pure Christianity which was fully compatible with the dictates of reason. Priestley became a Unitarian Christian who believed in the full humanity of Christ. His work was profoundly influential on the early Coleridge. More radical thinkers such as William Godwin and Erasmus Darwin proposed a materialist and deterministic account of nature and of the mind, and they regarded religion as the response of primitive societies to the forms of a nature whose workings they could not comprehend.

Politics, Power and Ideologies

In the late eighteenth century a growing consensus for the reform of the British political system was beginning to emerge. In the 1780s Britain was still a mainly agrarian country and the landed interest was predominant, despite the rapid growth of urban centres. The country was governed in the interests of some two hundred powerful aristocratic families (represented in the House of Lords) and below them a landed gentry (the 'country gentlemen') of some 12,000 families. These families effectively controlled government at central and local levels. The executive element of government involved the monarch, who nominated the prime minister, who in turn had at his disposal substantial powers of patronage to buy and reward supporters of the government. Substantial numbers of parliamentary seats were decided by nomination or influence. The electoral system was inconsistent and had numerous anomalies, with the effective disenfranchisement of the growing urban centres. In over fifty of the borough seats, the electorate was composed of fewer than fifty people. Defenders of the constitution argued that, despite its failings, the system worked and represented virtually, if not in reality, the key interests of the country. Our modern notion of political parties did not exist; instead, governments were formed by a coalition of alliances, often based on personal followings and enhanced by the power of patronage. A number of attempts to begin the process of reform of the system were made. These were overshadowed by events across the Channel when, in 1789, the French Revolution appeared to end for ever absolute monarchy and feudalism in France. At first the Revolution was welcomed in Britain, but with the increase in political violence, followed by the outbreak of war, many turned against the Revolution and its democratic principles.

After 1792, those in Britain who supported the ideals of the Revolution and political reform more generally were claimed as 'English Jacobins' and subject to persecution. Faced with the growing extremism of the Revolution and the rise of popular radicalism at home in the form of groups such as the London Corresponding Society, the Whig opposition split and its more conservative members, under the Duke of Portland, formed an alliance with the Prime Minister, William Pitt, leaving around fifty or so more radical reformers led by Charles James Fox. Pitt's government became increasing preoccupied with the possibility of revolution at home, leading it to institute the 'treason trials' of 1794 in which of a number of leading radicals were unsuccessfully arraigned for high treason. Despite this failure a number of repressive measures such as the 'Two Acts' which extended the law on treason and which attempted to clamp down on public meetings were passed into law in 1795. The government was also preoccupied with events in Ireland, where the United Irish Society, under the leadership of Wolfe Tone, had been formed to press for reform of Irish constitutional arrangements. In Ireland a Catholic peasantry was exploited by a largely absentee Protestant landowning class, and ruled by a corrupt parliament that mainly took care of British interests. In 1796, an intended French invasion of Ireland failed to materialise but led to a policy of brutal repression in 1797–8, in turn occasioning an abortive rebellion by the United Irishmen. A further consequence of the rebellion was the Act of Union of 1800 which brought Ireland under the auspices of the British Parliament.

4.3 James Gillray, *Un petit Souper à la Parisienne: or A Family of Sans Cullotts refreshing after the fatigues of the day* (H. Humphry, 1792). Gillray's horrific depiction of a family of French *sans-culottes*, a lower-class revolutionary family, takes up Edmund Burke's charge against the Revolutionaries as cannibals, consuming the ordered fabric of society. Gillray's cartoon was composed in response to the slaughter of the Swiss Guards at the Tuileries in 1792.

From 1793 to 1815, with only a brief hiatus, Britain was at war with revolutionary France. This was a new kind of war; one fought as much on political and ideological lines as for territorial gain. The armies of the French republic, at first, had little success but after the victory of the largely citizen army at Valmy in 1792 a new force in world politics emerged, a revolutionary army charged with spreading, by force of arms, republican and revolutionary principles throughout Europe. In Britain those sympathising with reformist or radical agendas were declared, at best, as unpatriotic, and, at worst, as traitors. British society became militarised in a way that was unprecedented in earlier conflict. At their peak the armed forces constituted over three-quarters of a million men, about half of whom were locally trained militia. The demand for seamen was especially acute, leading the Admiralty to rely more and more upon impressments, with all their unpopularity. Fluctuations in the wartime economy meant that many women were led to rely on their parish for poor relief. Additionally, the recurrent threat of a French invasion was ever present. From October 1797 to May 1798, Napoleon was assembling his 'Army of England'

The Slave Trade and Abolitionism

'Abolitionism' generally refers to the political and cultural movement directed against the British Atlantic trade in slaves. This activity was at its height during the period from roughly 1780 to 1807 (when the trade was formally abolished within the British colonies). Between 1680 and 1783 more than two million African slaves were transported to the British colonies alone, and it is estimated that British ships were carrying over 50,000 slaves a year to the Americas between 1791 and 1800 to work in the sugar plantations of the Caribbean and the rice, cotton and tobacco plantations of North America. Most of the slaves went to the sugar colonies, which were believed to account for a substantial portion of Britain's commercial prosperity. The various opponents of the slave trade combined to form the Committee for Effecting the Abolition of the Slave Trade in 1787. Although the times might have appeared propitious for the speedy abolition of the trade, the campaign was to last a further twenty years. The Committee distributed abolitionist literature; it also encouraged the production of literary writings in opposition to the trade, including poems by Hannah More and William Cowper. The Committee encouraged a grass-roots organisation of those opposed to the trade by creating a network of sympathisers to organise petitions in the provinces. Thomas Clarkson was to develop this provincial abolitionist network when he spent the autumn of 1787 in the hazardous task of collecting reliable first-hand information against the slave trade, interviewing sailors in Bristol and Liverpool. In April 1791 Wilberforce's motion against the trade came to a vote, only to be defeated by 163 to 88. It was not until abolition of the foreign trade in slaves became, for various reasons, part of the national interest that the campaign revived. In June 1806 a general motion for abolition was introduced into the Commons which became law on 25 March 1807. From 1 May 1807 the British slave trade was formally abolished, but this did not, however, mark the end of the global trade in slaves which continued and, in fact, increased in the 1820s.

on the other side of the Channel. The nature of the threat changed once Napoleon became First Consul and then, in 1804, Emperor. France was now seen as an aggressive imperial power which it was a national duty to oppose. Patriotic meetings and festivals were frequent, especially in the royal jubilee year of 1809 and at the end of the war in 1814. The threat of invasion receded with Nelson's annihilation of the French fleet at the Battle of Trafalgar in 1805. With the subsequent French economic blockade of Britain, military activity shifted to supporting the Portuguese and the Spanish in the Peninsular War. After the abdication of Napoleon in 1814, and his subsequent return and defeat at Waterloo, Britain attempted to return to a peace-time society, though the dislocation caused by the war would continue and the years that followed the Emperor's fall would be socially troubled and violent.

Post-Waterloo Britain saw a time of economic depression and hardship. Dissatisfaction with the Tory government's handling of the situation was substantial. The 1815 Corn Laws, which protected the price of corn by prohibiting foreign imports until prices reached a certain level, was largely viewed as legislation favouring the landed interest. The campaign against the Corn Laws was well orchestrated by middle- and working-class radicals, utilising petitions, pamphlets and meetings. The phenomenon of the political rally, in which audiences were addressed by a new breed of radical demagogue, such as Henry 'Orator' Hunt, was especially troubling to the

Negro woman, who sittest pining in captivity, and weepest over thy sick child : though no one seeth thee, God seeth thee ; though no one pitieth thee, God pitieth thee; raise thy voice, forlorn and abandoned one ; call upon Him from amidst thy bonds, for assuredly He will hear thee.

4.4 First published in 1781, Barbauld's *Hymns in Prose for Children* was addressed to children, seeking to awaken in them an awareness of God and His works. Hymn VIII assures its readers that God takes care of all His children including the Africans held in slavery. This Hymn can be compared with Blake's 'Little Black Boy'. The illustration here is taken from an illustrated edition of Barbauld's *Hymns* from 1880.

government. In 1819 at St Peter's Field, Manchester, the local magistrates attempted to disperse a peaceful gathering of some 60,000 people with troops. The action resulted in 400 dead and the event became notorious as the 'Peterloo Massacre'. In 1820 political tensions rose when a band of extreme republicans attempted to assassinate the cabinet and establish a provisional government in its place, in what became known as the 'Cato Street conspiracy'. Lord Liverpool's Tory government responded to this popular unrest with a series of repressive measures, including the suspension of habeas corpus. The alleviation of the economic situation in the later 1820s somewhat eased political unrest, but the government remained unpopular and pro-reform sentiment increased. In 1828 Wellington's Tory administration was pressured into passing a bill for Catholic emancipation, removing civil restrictions for Catholics (see pp. 195–7). In the wake of severe political agitation, followed by a change in the government from Tory to Whig, a bill for the reform of Parliament was passed in 1832 which allowed the enfranchisement of the middle classes and rationalised the electoral system. Power was still kept in the hands of the property owners, and the working classes were entirely excluded from the franchise. The process of reform, however, had begun and the worst excesses of the old system had been removed. The Whig government of Earl Grey subsequently initiated a whole series of reforms of national and local government, as well as finally legislating for the abolition of slavery within the British colonies in 1833 (after a six-year period of indenture).

Literary Overview

Introduction

Literary starting points for the Romantic period are difficult to determine; however, the period is often described as covering the years between the 1780s and the 1830s, although some critics may refer back to the 1760s and others forward to around 1850 as significant dates. Defining the period is difficult because the word 'Romantic' refers to a kind of writing which has been defined in opposition to the literature which came before it. Romanticism is thus antithetical to eighteenth-century neo-classicism, rather than a continuation of already established literary and artistic trends. For some criticism, informed by the idealist thought of the major nineteenth-century German philosopher, G. W. Hegel, 'Romanticism' is defined in terms of a move from the outer to the inner, and the growth of a new self-consciousness in literary writing combining a stylistic concern with metaphor and symbol. Other scholars, however, arguing that such formulations were not widely known or especially influential in Britain at the time, prefer to take a 'Romantic period' of writing as the object of their study, by which they mean work that is written, published or read in the period 1780–1835 or so, whatever forms its 'Romanticism' may take. Others still prefer to discriminate between different kinds of 'Romanticism', positing, for instance, a 'female Romanticism' which is alternative to the 'male Romanticism' of the canonical poets. This chapter will use 'Romantic' as a descriptor for the period and its writing, focusing on the historical context of that writing.

It is important to grasp that the word 'Romantic' itself was not used in the way we use it today by the writers of the time, for whom it meant something pertaining to 'romance'; nor did the writers collected under its rubric regard themselves as forming a coherent group. Several critics, notably Stuart Curran, have reminded us that the etymological root of Romanticism is in the word 'romance' and have gestured to the period's enormous interest in, and its revival of, the medieval English ballad, notably in Thomas Percy's influential collection, *Reliques of Ancient English Poetry* (1765). They emphasise its generic relationship to Wordsworth and Coleridge's later publication of their collection, *Lyrical Ballads*, in 1798, often seen as a manifesto of Romantic poetry. The revival of romance and its re-writings are central to Romantic poetry. When the British Romantic writers of this period actually use the term 'Romantic' they generally mean to signify a resurgence of the wild narratives popular in high medieval and early modern Europe: the works of Spenser, Tasso and Ariosto; the quest narratives, tales of the heroic, the marvellous, the magical and the supernatural. When Coleridge wrote in 1817 of his contributions to the *Lyrical Ballads*, and explained that efforts had been directed 'to persons and characters supernatural, or at least romantic', he seems to have this meaning predominantly in mind. The word 'Romantic' was also used in the period in a more specialised way, but in a markedly different sense to our modern usage, by the German critic August Wilhelm Schlegel in his *Course of Lectures on Dramatic Art and Literature*, translated into English in 1815. For Schlegel, the key distinction to be made was that between Classic Greek and Ancient Roman art and a modern Romantic art that coincided with Judaeo-Christian culture; for example, for Schlegel, Shakespeare was the great exemplar of the modern or Romantic artist.

So at the outset it is important to bear in mind that the terms 'Romantic' and 'Romanticism' are subject to several different definitions and often change emphasis and meaning as we shift our focus from the national to the European (and transatlantic) and take into account not just literary artists, but also the dramatic, visual, and musical arts. Some critics, informed by historical models of understanding the period, dispense with the term altogether as an adequate descriptor, preferring instead to emphasise continuities with eighteenth-century writing, situating the work of the period in a 'Long Eighteenth Century' that runs from 1660 (with the Restoration of Charles II) to the passage of the Great Reform Act of 1832. Such critics tend to study the literature and culture of the period in an expansive view, taking into account popular culture in addition to the 'High Romanticism' of the canonical British and European poets.

By critical consensus the canonical British Romantic poets are the six male poets: William Blake, William Wordsworth, Samuel Taylor Coleridge, Percy Bysshe Shelley, John Keats and Lord Byron. Together, it has been argued, they formed a literary and artistic movement known as 'Romanticism', which marked a profound shift in sensibility. Generally Romanticism was seen as marking a violent reaction against eighteenth-century Enlightenment thought with its emphasis on 'reason' as the predominant human faculty. It was often said that Romanticism was inspired by the political revolutions of America in 1776 and France in 1789, and that the products of Romanticism tended to be radical or revolutionary. Writers of the Romantic Age demonstrate the characteristics outlined in the box.

This traditional model has been problematised over the last twenty years or so, chiefly by the emergence of feminist and later new historicist criticism, which has changed the field of study as we know it. Women, self-taught and working-class poets are currently still in the process of being recovered. No longer is there a concentration on the work of six male poets (who may or may not have had that much in common; instead a huge variety of writing, most of which does not fit the standard definition of Romanticism, is now studied. New historicist critics have expressed great suspicion over the whole concept of Romanticism, arguing that, in its espousal of transcendence and mysticism (chiefly in the later writings of Wordsworth and Coleridge), it deliberately evades or ignores material reality and social concerns in what is a manifestly political strategy.

> **Romanticism as an Aesthetic Category**
>
> - Romantic poets affirm the creative powers of the imagination.
> - Romantic poets introduce us to a new way of looking at Nature, which becomes the main subject of their work. The Romantics often argue that the possibility of transcendence or 'unity of being' can be achieved through communion with Nature. Their work exhibits a preference for Nature in its sublime aspects: mountains, glaciers, chasms, storms, as well as strange and exotic settings.
> - Romantic poets tend to explain human society and its development in terms of an organic model, or a model borrowed from Nature, and they reject materialist and mechanistic philosophies.
> - Romantic poets write about the nature of the individual self and the value of individual experience.
> - Romantic thought shows a high regard for the figure of the artist, who is variously described as sage, philosopher, prophet and religious saviour.

Continuities, Innovations and Influences

Traditionally Romanticism was seen to begin around the time of the Revolution in France and to develop certain stylistic and linguistic innovations. These innovations are reflected in the works of a number of writers. William Blake produced his prophetic and apocalyptic illuminated books during the 1790s. Blake's personal vision, expressed in a highly symbolic language and form, was seen by many to inaugurate a new kind of revolutionary writing. Similarly, the publication in 1798 of Wordsworth and Coleridge's *Lyrical Ballads*, which contained, in addition to Coleridge's 'The Rime of the Ancient Mariner', a series of experimental ballads and lyric poems treating rustic subjects and their distress in an elevated and tragic manner, can be seen as a rejection of eighteenth-century poetics. Wordsworth's later apologia for his poems, the 'Preface of 1800', defended the serious treatment of such subjects and could be seen as a manifesto for a revolutionary kind of poetry, for a revolutionary age. Wordsworth also claimed that the *Ballads* ushered in a stylistic revolution in poetry, banishing the allegedly stilted diction of earlier neo-classical poets, preferring instead a language closer to that of contemporary usage. Similarly, notions of genre and hierarchy were transformed by the Romantics. There are, however, other works published in the 1780s and 1790s which might make the claim for the revolutionary nature of Blakean and Wordsworthian Romanticism seem less convincing. In 1785 William Cowper's long blank-verse poem, *The Task*, also dealt with simple homely subjects, its descriptions of the sights and sounds of country life foreshadowing those of nineteenth-century Romanticism. Robert Merry and the group of poets that gathered round him (including Mary Robinson and Hannah Cowley) were known as the Della Cruscans; they produced a series of rhetorically ornate and emotional poems of sensibility published in *The Florence Miscellany* (1785) and the *British Album* (1790), which may well have influenced the young Romantics. Wordsworth's and Coleridge's concern with low and rustic life, and their stress on emotion, had been pre-empted by Robert Burns, whose *Poems Chiefly in the Scottish Dialect* of 1786 demonstrates a similar interest in humble, rural life and poetic language. Similarly, Charlotte Smith's *Elegiac Sonnets* of 1784 and William Lisle Bowles's sentimental *Fourteen Sonnets* of 1789 manifested an intensely emotional response to the natural world, which one might think of as Romantic. Our contemporary critics have tended to place less emphasis on the revolutionary aspects of 'Romantic' literature and more stress on its continuities with the thought, literature and art of preceding decades. One such important trend was the vogue for sensibility.

Sensibility was an eighteenth-century movement that stressed the importance of the emotions and feelings in human relationships. From around the 1740s onwards a number of thinkers argued that humans possessed an innate moral sense or sensibility which manifested itself through the emotions in feelings of sympathy and benevolence for others. This movement has been linked to the rise of the middle classes in the eighteenth century and their growing concern with the reformation of manners. The origins of sensibility are complex. It was a movement which combined an empiricist notion of human knowledge derived from philosophers such as John Locke with the belief, expressed by the radical Enlightenment philosopher Jean-Jacques Rousseau, that humanity in a state of nature is naturally good and benevolent, but is corrupted by society and civilisation. Rousseau stressed the importance of the natural and the

4.5 Gillray's print, published in the *Anti-Jacobin Review* (1798), satirises contemporary radical intellectuals. Sensibility is one of a trinity of idols, along with Justice and Philanthropy, worshipped by writers and politicians including S. T. Coleridge, Robert Southey, Charles Lamb, Erasmus Darwin, Joseph Priestley, John Thelwall and Gilbert Wakefield. The Goddess Sensibility weeps over a dead bird, holds a book by Rousseau and has her right foot on the severed head of Louis XVI.

power of feeling. Very early on sensibility was gendered as a female property, as, it was claimed, women were possessed of a more delicate constitution and therefore were more susceptible to emotion. The Methodist theology of John Wesley and his adherents also contributed to the movement by stressing the primacy of feeling in religious experience, the importance of a heavily emotional and excessive language of sin and rebirth, and the need for a personal encounter with Christ the redeemer. The fictions of Samuel Richardson and Laurence Sterne exploited sensibility and employed male characters who wept copiously over the plights of distressed women, captive slaves and prisoners, and hurt and dying animals. Sensibility also confused gender roles for many, as some men cultivated feeling and sensitivity as in Henry Mackenzie's novel *The Man of Feeling* (1771).

By the 1790s sensibility had become politicised by its association with radical and reformist politics, as demonstrated by James Gillray's satire 'The New Morality', in which British reformers and rad-

The Gothic

Like 'Romantic', 'Gothic' is a word that can mean many different things. By the late eighteenth century the term had come to symbolise the 'medieval' or the 'Dark Ages' prior to the Reformation and the Scientific Revolution, denoting that which was barbaric, disordered, irregular. In the mid-eighteenth century there appeared a number of works idealising medieval culture and architecture in opposition to neo-classical form and design. The irregularity of the medieval cathedral or garden came to be prized above neo-classical Palladian architecture, and the ruin, whether real or faked, became a source of aesthetic delight. Edmund Burke's *Enquiry into the Origin of Our Ideas of the Sublime and Beautiful* (1757) provided a justification for its aesthetics by arguing that terror was an expression of the sublime. The melancholy and, often, morbid poetry of the eighteenth-century 'Graveyard School' similarly created a climate and readership for Gothic subjects. Though it began as an antiquarian and architectural trend, the Gothic became associated with the novel form with the publication in 1764 of Horace Walpole's medieval romance, set in eleventh-century Spain, *The Castle of Otranto*. *Otranto*, with its southern Mediterranean setting, its aristocratic and patriarchal villain Manfred, its persecuted heroine Isabella, its Castle, garrulous servants and supernatural events, set the pattern for future novels. Walpole's followers included Clara Reeve, William Beckford, Matthew Lewis, Ann Radcliffe, William Godwin, Charlotte Dacre, Mary Shelley and Charles Maturin. Many subsequently abandoned Walpole's medieval settings; some, like Radcliffe, avoided the explicitly supernatural, preferring suggestion to outright horror. The Gothic was not confined only to the novel form but encompassed drama and poetry as well.

icals (including Paine, Fox, Coleridge and Southey) worship at the shrine of the new trinity, Philanthropy, Sensibility and Benevolence, established by Enlightenment and revolutionary ideology. Sensibility was thus identified with a potentially dangerous mode of life. Too much sensibility might lead to hysteria and disorder; it might lead to the over-cultivation of the senses at the expense of the reason and judgement; it might lead to men behaving like women; and, most pernicious of all, following one's feeling might lead to sexual impropriety and ruin.

The growing interest in and approbation of the primitive and the wild played a large part in Romantic-period writing and can be located in the Gothic concern with the past. In the mid-eighteenth century Thomas Warton, Richard Hurd and others began to argue, against the norms of eighteenth-century neo-classicism, that the art and culture of the medieval and ancient past was authentic and closer to human nature, certainly more relevant than the stultifying decorums of social life. Thomas

4.6 One of the most influential paintings of the Romantic period, Henry Fuseli's *The Nightmare* caused a sensation on its first showing at the Royal Academy of Arts in 1782. Fuseli's powerfully disturbing canvas explores such Gothic themes as the supernatural, sexual repression, dreaming and the use of narcotics.

Gray had a strong interest in Welsh bardic poetry, James Macpherson composed a series of poems which he claimed were translations of the imaginary Gaelic poet 'Ossian', and Thomas Chatterton claimed to have discovered the medieval manuscripts of the fifteenth-century poet Thomas Rowley, which he published in 1768–9. Bishop Thomas Percy collected and published in 1765 his *Reliques of Ancient English Poetry*, which was to be hugely influential on later Romantic writers. In the 1740s a group of poets known as the 'Graveyard School' published several impressive works, including Edward Young's *Night Thoughts* (1742–5), Robert Blair's *The Grave* (1743) and Thomas Gray's *Elegy in a Country Churchyard* (1751). Such works reflected on death and the frailties of human life in a sombre and often morbid tone. The neo-classical emphasis on reason is increasingly replaced by feeling and the sublime.

Modes of Production and Consumption: the Literary Marketplace and the Periodical Review

The period 1780–1830 presents a transitional phase in the literary marketplace as the commercial publishing practices of the earlier century give way to the fully industrialised and technology-driven production process of the Victorian period. Certainly the publication of titles increased throughout the century. In the 1820s there were several thousand registered printing presses. James Raven estimates that annual publication totals for *all* titles increased from c. 1,900 in 1740, to c. 3,000 in 1780, to over 6,000 by 1800 (Raven, *Judging New Wealth* [Cx]). William St Clair estimates that *book* annual publications in England were c. 500 in 1700–50, rising to 600 during 1750–89, to 800 from 1790 to 1810 and around 1,000 by 1827 (St Clair, *Reading Nation* [Cx]). St Clair states that, from the 1780s to the 1830s, records exist for some 5,000 new books of poetic verse written by something like 2,000 living poets in addition to the reprinting of older canonical writing. The number of new novels printed was similarly large with 3,000 new titles recorded as published between 1790 and 1830. Newspapers and periodicals similarly grew in numbers, increasing from something like 9,464,790 copies in 1760 to 29,387,843 copies in 1820. The processes of book production were gradually mechanised with the introduction of Earl Stanhope's iron platen press, which

4.7 A typical printing press of the early nineteenth century, similar to one William Blake may have used for his engravings.

superseded the traditional printing method of the wooden hand press. Subsequently the steam-driven cylinder press was introduced in the second decade of the nineteenth century. The process of lithography was invented in 1798. This is a mechanical process in which the printing and non-printing areas of the plate are all at the same level, as opposed to intaglio and relief processes in which the design is cut into the printing block. Lithography allowed the printing of pictures in colour.

Many of these innovations were to be perfected later in the century and the printing business remained very much a craft rather than an industry, using specialised artisans, such as the engraver William Blake. Newspapers such as *The Morning Chronicle* (1769), *The Morning Post* (1772), and *The Times* (1788) appeared for the first time.

During the period publishing became an increasingly specialised trade whereby production, wholesaling and retailing came to be handled by separate firms. Roles in the larger firms became more specialised with the emergence of 'readers' and 'literary agents' (notably John Ballantyne, Scott's agent). The size of the reading public itself has been variously estimated as 80,000, by Edmund Burke in 1790, and 'probably not less than 200,000' by the *Edinburgh Review* in 1814 (St Clair, *Reading Nation* [Cx], pp. 478–79). The consensus is that figures of around 65 per cent for male literacy and 50 per cent for female literacy were achieved. Such levels were much higher in Scotland (probably 90 per cent male literacy) due to its national and compulsory elementary educational system. Certainly the Methodist and dissenting stress on the culture of the word meant that there was a strong imperative to literacy, as did the growth in leisure culture, especially among middle-class women. The importance of the commercial circulating libraries was crucial. These increased dramatically in the latter half of the eighteenth century and it has been estimated that there were probably some 1,000 such libraries in Great Britain by 1801 and 1,500 by 1821. It was often claimed, perhaps not reliably, that the libraries' main customers were females whose chief interest was sensational fiction. Some of the larger libraries rented texts other than novels, but for many the latest fiction was the commodity in which they specialised, increasingly in the three-volume duodecimo format. After 1814 the major items lent by the libraries were Scott's Waverley novels, confirming his pre-eminence as the most popular novelist in the period.

Pirated editions were common on the domestic market and significantly influenced the cultural landscape. Pirates, such as William Benbow, claimed, with much justice, that publishers had established a monopoly to restrict the spread of knowledge to the lower classes by inflating the price of books. Famously, William Godwin's radical treatise *Enquiry Concerning Political Justice* of 1793 was not prosecuted for sedition because Pitt believed that its high price of 3 guineas would keep it out of the hands of the impressionable and discontented. Taxes such as the stamp duty on pamphlets and newspapers, as well as the 3-shilling tax on books below a certain size, were an attempt to control and restrict the flow of information and knowledge. The taxes were ruthlessly enforced on those selling unstamped publications. The Seditious Societies Act of 1799 was designed to prevent the circulation of inexpensive political tracts among the lower orders.

A crucial element of the literary scene was the literary journal, which included essays, reviews, poetry, parliamentary reports and so on. The most important in the eighteenth century was the *Gentleman's Magazine* (1731–1818). Two newer journals important for the Romantic period were the *Monthly Review* (1749–1845) and the *Critical Review* (1756–90), the former appealing to a liberal Whig readership and the latter to a conservative Tory readership. With the explosion in reading and debate occasioned by the revolutionary decade of the 1790s, the periodical came to be more partisan and appealed to a distinct reading community, cultivated by promoting certain key values and ideas. New journals catering for the Dissenting, Reformist and radical cause emerged, including the *Monthly Magazine* (1796–1843), the *Analytical Review* (1788–98) and the *English Review* (1783–96). Such journals were countered by pro-government vehicles such as the *British Critic* (1793–1843) and *The Anti-Jacobin, or Weekly Examiner* (1797–8), a satirical review produced by William Gifford and George Canning. During the conservative backlash of the post-revolutionary period many radical journals suffered, but John and Leigh Hunt's *Examiner* (1808–81) maintained production despite Leigh Hunt's imprisonment for seditious libel against the Regent. After the conclusion of the Napoleonic War other political journals emerged.

The *Edinburgh* and the *Quarterly*

The most significant innovation in the history of the periodical press in the period was the arrival of the two leading literary reviews of the nineteenth century, the quarterly *Edinburgh Review* (1802–1929) and the *Quarterly Review* (1809–1967). These were followed by the Tory *Blackwood's Edinburgh Magazine* (1817–1980) and the utilitarian *Westminster Review* (1824). Rather than reviewing large numbers of works, the editors of the two journals would review around fifteen books in depth per quarter emphasising the reviewer's literary accomplishment, sometimes at the expense of the author reviewed. The *Edinburgh* was sympathetic to the Whig, professional and liberal intellectual audience; its editor, Francis Jeffrey, was a liberal secular progressive. Infused with the values of the Scottish Enlightenment, the journal regarded the French Revolution as a necessary, though calamitous, event in the freeing of the commercial and professional classes of the nation, promoting the notion of a commercialised civil society. The *Quarterly*, set up to counter the influence of the elder journal, was sympathetic to the conservative and Tory cause, regarding itself as the 'literary police'. It was supportive of the 'Lake School' of Wordsworth, Southey and Coleridge, and vituperative about both the 'Cockney School' of Leigh Hunt, among which it included Hunt's protégé John Keats, and the 'Satanic School' of Byron and Shelley, as well as about the essayist William Hazlitt. John Wilson's *Blackwood's* proved to be an important journal for the development of the Romantic prose essay (notably De Quincey) as well as for its translation of German Romantic and idealist philosophy. The *London Magazine* printed some of the best prose of Hazlitt, De Quincey and Lamb. In the early years the quarterlies had a circulation of 3,000–4,000, yet by 1817 this had jumped to around 12,000–14,000. Following on the success of the middle-class quarterlies, a new generation of cheap, mass-produced journals for the working classes began to emerge in the 1820s, with titles such as *The Mirror of Literature, Amusement and Instruction* (1822–49), which would reach circulations of up to 250,000.

Most famous was William Cobbett's weekly *Political Register*, priced at twopence (his 'tuppeny trash'), but other radical weeklies included T. J. Wooler's *Black Dwarf* (1817–24), John Wade's *Gorgon* (1818–19) and Richard Carlile's *Republican* (1819–26). Such journals indicated the growing level of 'class' consciousness that began to emerge as the process of the Industrial Revolution gathered pace.

Essay and journal writing was a prominent feature of the literary marketplace. Coleridge wrote a great deal for newspapers such as the *Morning Chronicle* and *Post* as well as for journals and reviews. He also published, for a time and not too success-fully, his own journals, *The Watchman* of 1796 and *The Friend* (1811–12). The chief prose essayist of the period wrote primarily for the reviews. William Hazlitt published in a wide range of periodicals, including the *Political Register*, *The Times*, the *Edinburgh Review* and the *London Magazine*. He preferred the form of the familiar essay, his pieces collected in *Table Talk* (1821–2) and *The Plain Speaker* (1826). Hazlitt showed himself as a powerful and influential literary critic in his *Characters of Shakespeare's Plays* (1817) and his *Lectures on the English Poets* (1818). His most influential work was his series of essays on the key writers and thinkers of the period, *The Spirit of the Age* (1825). Thomas De Quincey, probably the most accomplished prose stylist of the period, was variously a journalist, essayist, novelist and autobiographer. His essays largely appeared in *Tait's* and *Blackwood's* magazines and covered an enormous range of sub-jects from political economy, history and diplomacy to literary criticism. Notable pieces include his essay 'On the Knocking on the Gate in Macbeth' (1823), 'On Murder as One of the Fine Arts' (1827) and 'The English Mail-Coach' (1849). His writings on Wordsworth, Coleridge and Southey were collected as *Recollections of the Lakes and the Lake Poets* (1834–9). Charles Lamb produced his humorous and ironic *Essays of Elia* in 1833. He also wrote several works for children including (with his sister Mary) *Tales from Shakespeare* (1807). Leigh Hunt was also a master of the familiar essay. In numer-ous pieces for the journals the *Examiner* and the *Indicator* (which he edited with his brother John) he commented on the political and cultural scene of Regency Britain.

Authors, Texts and Subjects

The First Generation of Romantic Poets: Blake, Wordsworth, Coleridge

It was against the background of the French Revolution and the debate it initiated that much of the writing of the first generation of Romantic poets appeared. Blake's illuminated *Songs of Innocence* was printed in 1789. Blake developed a technique of engraving and printing his own designs to accompany his poetry. His *The French Revolution* of 1791 transformed the political events in France into a visionary apoc-alypse. His *Songs of Innocence and of Experience* was produced in 1794. Blake's concern with the dialectic of two stages of life, innocence and experience, through which the individual must pass, has come to be regarded as a deeply Romantic notion. The *Songs* contain many of Blake's most famous lyrics, 'London', 'The Tyger', 'The Chimney Sweeper' poems, 'The Fly', 'The Lamb' and 'Holy Thursday'. Blake continued to develop his personal radical philosophy which countered the present establishment in a series of prophecies during the 1790s, such as *Europe* and *America*, championing the idea of a spirit of revolutionary energy (sometimes represented in the figure Orc) battling against the zealous controller of Energy and Thought in the material world, Urizen. Blake's energies after 1800 would be taken up with his major epics, *The Four Zoas, Milton* (1804) and *Jerusalem*.

The late 1790s saw the emergence of other leading poets of the first generation of Romantic writers. In 1798 the influential collection of *Lyrical Ballads, with a Few*

Other Poems was published anonymously. The volume contains much quintessential Romantic poetry, including the first version of Coleridge's 'Rime of the Ancient Mariner', Wordsworth's great Romantic lyric 'Tintern Abbey', and ballads such as 'The Thorn', 'The Idiot Boy' and 'Simon Lee'. The collection was reissued in two volumes in 1800 under Wordsworth's name, with some additional poems and the famous 'Preface' defending the poets' use of the 'language really used by men' and the rustic nature of their subjects (*Norton Anthology*, ed. Greenblatt et al., p. 264 [A]). Wordsworth's attack on eighteenth-century poetic diction, with its ornateness and artificiality, marked out both his and Coleridge's poetry from that of some of their contemporaries. During 1797–8, the *annus mirabilis* of their relationship, Coleridge and Wordsworth composed much of their most celebrated poetry, including the 'Ancient Mariner', Coleridge's 'Conversation Poems', 'Kubla Khan', and the first part of the uncompleted *Christabel*. In 1799 Wordsworth also began the process of composing the long poem that would become *The Prelude* after his death and which would come to be regarded by many as the quintessential Romantic poem. In that year he completed what is known as the 'Two-Part Prelude'; two books of blank verse describing his early childhood in the northern Lake District and the visionary intensity of his relationship with nature. This poem would be continually revised throughout his life, expanding to thirteen books in 1805 and fourteen by the time of his death.

With the French invasion of Switzerland in 1798 and the subsequent rise of Napoleon, sectors of radical and dissenting opinion moved away from opposing the war against France. Coleridge, Wordsworth and their friend and fellow poet Robert Southey all drifted in different ways to a position of conservatism. Southey was probably the most strident in his opinions, especially after his association with the Tory *Quarterly Review* from about 1810 onwards. Southey's literary output, of both poetry and prose, was phenomenal. In particular he was known for his contribution to the eighteenth-century vogue for Oriental romance. His Arabian verse epic, *Thalaba the Destroyer* (1801) set a fashion for such verse tales which would be exploited by Scott and Moore. Southey's scholarly and imaginative interest in comparative religion fuelled his interest in Thalaba's Islamic context and his *Madoc* (1805) and *The Curse of Kehama* (1810) similarly explored Aztec, Celtic and Hindu mythology. Certainly Southey's innovations in Orientalism and the verse narrative, exploited more successfully by others, were crucial to the literature of the period.

Two poets less closely associated by later critics with the aesthetic of Romanticism, Sir Walter Scott and George Crabbe, also published in this period. Although now known chiefly as a novelist (see below), Scott began his literary career first as a translator of German ballads, then as a collector of the chivalric ballads of the Border region which he published in his *Minstrelsy of the Scottish Border* (1802–3), a three-volume annotated collection. His first original work, the romance, *The Lay of the Last Minstrel*, which focused on the Border's historical past, appeared in 1805, to be followed by further ballad epics concerning the historical and political rivalry between Highland and Lowland Scotland. Other less popular romances followed and Scott realised that he could not match the new verse romances of Byron, just then appearing, in terms of popularity. He decided to turn his attention to the novel, with spectacularly

The Lake School

Wordsworth, Coleridge and Southey were grouped together as the 'Lake School of Poets' by Francis Jeffrey in a review of Coleridge's *Biographia Literaria* for the 1817 *Edinburgh Review*. This notion of a group of poets who, at one time or another, all lived in the Lake District of north-west England and formed, in some way, a coherent school of poetry had gained currency since about 1807. The group were attacked by liberal and radical poets, essayists and reviewers such as Jeffrey, Hazlitt and, most famously, Byron in the 'Preface' to Canto I of *Don Juan*. It was felt that they had turned their backs on their radical youth and had abandoned progressive politics, preferring, instead, to advocate a quasi-mystical relationship with nature instead of an active engagement with politics. Wordsworth had moved to the north of England and settled in Grasmere in 1799, and he was followed there by Southey and Coleridge. From this period Coleridge gained an insight into Kantian and German idealist philosophy, which converted him from empiricism to a form of idealism in which the human mind is itself active in the creation of knowledge. He attempted to explain his ideas in a series of later publications including the periodical *The Friend* (1812) and *The Lay Sermons* (1816–17). Wordsworth composed many of his greatest lyrical poems at Grasmere, including 'The Brothers', 'Michael', 'Resolution and Independence' and the 'Ode (Intimations of Immortality)'. He developed here a pantheistic philosophy of nature which functioned as a compensation for the failure of the revolutionary cause as he saw it. From 1813 he served the government in the lucrative sinecure of Distributor of Stamps for Westmoreland. He published his long philosophical poem, *The Excursion* (1814), which presented a conservative philosophy, and his two-volume *Poems* in 1815.

successful results. George Crabbe had attacked the idealisations of rural life in his *The Village* of 1783; his subsequent poetry, beginning with *Poems* (1807), was more successful and significantly more prolific. Crabbe preferred a poetic style closer to Alexander Pope, employing the form of the heroic couplet in a series of works, 'The Parish Register' (published in his *Poems*) and *The Borough* (1810), which describes life in an imaginary seaport closely based on a number of Suffolk towns he knew well. His poetry was both popular and fully engaged with contemporary social and cultural issues.

The Second Generation of Romantic Poets: Byron, Shelley, Keats

The younger generation of Romantic poets born after the French Revolution, while maintaining many 'Romantic' beliefs such as the importance of passion, the celebration of sublime nature, and spontaneity in poetry, reacted against the elder poets in a number of ways. This generation were associated with liberal or radical ideas in opposition to the alleged 'apostasy' of their predecessors. In the 'Dedication' to *Don Juan*, Byron excoriated the 'Lake School' as a group of turncoats:

> Bob Southey! You're a poet – Poet Laureate,
> And representative of all the race;
> Although 'tis true you turned out a Tory at
> Last. Yours has lately been a common case;
> And now, my epic renegade, what are ye at,
> With all the Lakers in and out of place?
> A nest of tuneful persons to my eye
> Like 'four and twenty blackbirds in a pie'.

(Wu, *Romanticism*, p. 933 [A])

Byron further developed the persona of the alienated 'Byronic hero' in a series of highly popular Eastern Tales, the most famous of which are *The Giaour* (1813) and *The Corsair* (1814), and the poetic drama *Manfred* (1816), which hinted at Byron's incestuous love of his half-sister Augusta, as well as Cantos III (1817) and IV (1818) of *Childe Harold*. Byron subsequently abandoned the romantic persona of his earlier works in a series of extremely accomplished and often biting satires, *Beppo* (1818), *The Vision of Judgement* (1822) and the gentler narrative romance, *The Island* (1823), based on the story of the *Bounty* mutiny. His greatest work, however, was his unfinished masterpiece *Don Juan*, the first two Cantos of which appeared in 1819 followed by Cantos III–V (1821),

> ### Byron and Byronism
>
> The most popular poet of the Romantic age was George Gordon, Lord Byron. His romances were extremely successful in commercial terms and his comic epic masterpiece *Don Juan* (thanks in part to cheap pirated editions) was read by numbers in excess of anything with the exception of Thomas Paine's *Rights of Man*. His celebrity and notoriety was encapsulated in the personality cult of Byronism, which swept Europe before and after his death, made him one of the century's most significant writers. It was his verse romance *Childe Harold's Pilgrimage*, the first two cantos of which appeared in 1812, which made him famous and secured his massive readership. The cynical, alienated and solitary Harold wandering around Europe and the Levant, musing moodily on the wastes of time and the vanity of human aspirations, was irresistibly attractive to his post-revolutionary generation. Byron became the centre of fashionable Regency society until the scandalous separation from his wife in 1816 necessitated his self-imposed exile in Italy and then Greece. The myth of the Byronic hero was established for the next generation by the poet's death at Missolonghi in 1824 while engaged in the struggle for Greek independence from the Ottoman empire.

Cantos VI–XIV (1823) and Cantos XV–XVI (1824). The poem tells the story of the adventures of the young Spanish nobleman Don Juan, involving shipwreck, cannibalism, the carnage of the Siege of Ismail, the court of Catherine the Great and follies and fashions of Regency society.

Robert Southey, in the *Quarterly Review*, had identified Byron and Percy Shelley as constituting the 'Satanic School' of poetry. Byron and Shelley were very different kinds of poet but they shared an Enlightenment scepticism and a liberal (in Shelley's case radical) oppositional stance to the Tory government of their day, as well as a strong predilection for movements for national independence, notably in Greece. Shelley, however, was always more of an optimist about humanity's capacity for improvement than the more pessimistic Byron and this shows in the visionary nature of much of his writing. Shelley was something of a scandalous figure for Regency England; he was famously expelled from Oxford as a consequence of his pamphlet (written with his friend T. J. Hogg), *The Necessity of Atheism* (1811) and his first wife, Harriet Westbrook, committed suicide after he sensationally eloped with Mary Godwin. His first major publication was his radical philosophical poem *Queen Mab* (1813) with its extensive footnotes from Enlightenment thinkers. The pirated publishing of the poem assured its lasting success and influence. Increasingly associated with Byron (whom he met in Switzerland in 1816) and the liberal circle of writers associated with Leigh Hunt and his journal *The Examiner*, Shelley returned to England in 1816 and supported the revival of the reform movement. His bitter and satirical *The Masque of Anarchy* was written in anguished protest at the 'Peterloo Massacre' in 1819.

4.8 Frontispiece to *The Poetical Works of Lord Byron* (London, 1859). This nineteenth-century engraving of Byron, after the portrait by Thomas Phillips, shows the poet wearing Ottoman dress in suitably Byronic manner. The original portrait was painted at the height of the fashion for 'Byronism' and identifies the poet with the hero-villains of his popular Oriental Tales. See the discussion of his *The Giaour* in the Readings section.

Shelley was also one of the greatest lyric poets of the age, producing some of the most accomplished Romantic shorter poems, including 'To a Skylark', 'The Sensitive Plant' and, most famous of all, the 'Ode to the West Wind'. In 1821 he wrote his elegy on Keats's death, *Adonais*, claiming that the poet had been killed off by a cruel review of *Endymion* (1817) in the *Quarterly*. Shelley was drowned a month before his thirtieth birthday in a boating accident in the Bay of Lerici off the coast of Italy. The burning of his body on a funeral pyre by Byron, Leigh Hunt and others remains one of the iconic moments of the Romantic age. Shelley left one important work, 'The Triumph of Life', unfinished.

Unlike Byron and Shelley, who were both aristocrats, John Keats was from a humble, though not a poor background; his father managed a prosperous livery stable. He was educated at the Clarke School in Enfield and set to take up the profession of surgeon and licensed apothecary, which he gave up for poetry. His first volume of *Poems* was published in 1817. Keats made the acquaintance of the poet and journalist Leigh Hunt and his circle of friends, including the artist B. R. Haydon and fellow poet John Hamilton Reynolds. Keats's work was championed by Leigh Hunt in the pages of the *Examiner* and from this association Keats became one of the members of what the Tory *Quarterly* and others described as the 'Cockney School' of poets, a pejorative term suggesting a middle-class, suburban and metropolitan kind of writing. His first major work was the long, poetic romance *Endymion* (1817) which tells the story of the shepherd with whom the moon goddess Cynthia falls in love (among other myths and legends). The poem was written in loose, flowing heroic couplets and in a sensuous style. It was vilified by the conservative reviewers of the *Quarterly*, *Blackwood's* and the *British Critic*. In 1819, known as Keats's *annus mirabilis*, he produced much of the poetry that he is best known for. He began work on his projected Miltonic epic *Hyperion* which recounts the story of the battle between the failing Titans and the rising Olympian gods which he would abandon to rework as the visionary poem *The Fall of Hyperion* later in the year. In February he completed the medieval romance, *The Eve of St Agnes*, with its complex and ambiguous tale of star-crossed love written in Spenserian stanzas, as well as the ballad-like poem 'La Belle Dame Sans Merci'. In the spring of 1819 Keats wrote what many consider as his greatest works, and ones which have become synonymous with Romanticism: the Odes 'To Psyche', 'To a Nightingale', 'On a Grecian Urn', and his last extended narrative, *Lamia* (revised in 1820). He famously died of consumption at the age of twenty-five.

Women Romantic Poets

Women wrote and published huge amounts of poetry in the Romantic period. Much of their writing was extremely popular and influential. Because their work does not so easily fit into the aesthetic of 'Romanticism', as it has been traditionally defined, and also because their periods of activity do not dovetail so neatly with the traditional periodisation of Romanticism, it is helpful to discuss their work under the separate heading; however, it is important to understand that women writers were publishing at the same time as their male counterparts, and often in creative dialogue with them, and that any sense of grouping of male and female writers has to remain hesitant.

Anna Laetitia Barbauld was a prominent dissenter, the daughter of John Aikin, a tutor at the Warrington Academy. In 1773 she published her *Poems* and her *Miscellaneous Pieces in Prose* to great acclaim. Establishing herself as a teacher, she published *Lessons for Children* (1778) and *Hymns in Prose for Children* (1781). From the late 1780s she wrote pamphlets on political subjects such as the slave trade and the war with France, as well as an important verse 'Epistle to William Wilberforce' (1791). Her last published poem, the powerful satire, *Eighteen Hundred and Eleven* (1812) presented an apocalyptic view of the consequences of the current war. The poem was unpleasantly criticised as unpatriotic and Barbauld never published poetry again. Mary Robinson was an actress, courtesan, poet, novelist and memoirist. Known as 'Perdita' after her performance in David Garrick's adaptation of Shakespeare's *The Winter's Tale*, she became the mistress of the Prince of Wales. Her first volume of poems was published in 1775 and her two-volume *Poems* in 1791–3. Her sonnet sequence *Sappho and Phaon* appeared in 1796, the same year as Coleridge's *Poems on Various Subjects*. The fine late ballad 'The Haunted Beach' from her *Lyrical Tales* (1800) is a response to 'The Rime of the Ancient Mariner' and her 'Poem to Coleridge' to his 'Kubla Khan'. A major novelist of the period as well as a poet, Charlotte Smith's important collection of poems of sensibility, the *Elegiac Sonnets*, was first published in 1784. Her affective perception of nature and her strong sensibility influenced Coleridge, Keats and Wordsworth. The *Sonnets* combined a powerful poetry of sensibility with a strong Gothic tone, as well as a fine feeling for the natural world. The collection was an immediate success but, faced with expensive legal battles concerning her father's will and the separation from her husband, Smith turned increasingly to the novel to provide literary earnings to support her family. At the time of her death she was completing the collection *Beachy Head with Other Poems* (1807), the title poem being an evocation of her childhood, comparable with Wordsworth's 'Tintern Abbey'. Anna Seward, or 'the Swan of Lichfield', was a largely self-educated poet and letter-writer, known for the ornateness and sentimentality of her verse. Seward disliked Smith's experimentation with the sonnet, preferring the form of the 'epic elegy' which her friend Erasmus Darwin credited her with inventing, including her *Elegy on Captain Cook* (1780) and her *Monody on the Death of Major Andre* (1781). Seward, unlike many woman writers of the time, was aggressively competitive and a noted public critic of Samuel Johnson.

Helen Maria Williams was a poet and novelist who published a number of poems of sensibility in the 1780s. Writing from Paris, she became, from the 1790s onwards, a key political commentator on the Revolution in France. The most popular poet of the period 1820–35, after Byron, was Felicia Dorothea Hemans. Known, in particular, for her depiction of domestic subjects and manners, Hemans wrote to help with her household expenses. She published her first volume of poetry at the age of fourteen, wisely rejecting the subsequent offer of correspondence with an admiring Shelley. Hemans published prolifically: notable among her many works are her *Tales and Historic Scenes* (1819), 'Songs of the Cid' (1822), the tragedy, *The Siege of Valencia* (1823) and *Records of Woman* (1828). Numerous of her lyrics, including 'Casabianca', 'The Homes of England' and 'The Graves of a Household', were memorised by schoolchildren, and her focus on domesticity ensured her substantial popularity with a later Victorian audience and the reprinting and anthologising of her work. Almost as popular and prolific as Hemans was Laetitia Elizabeth Landon (known as 'L. E. L.'). She published a number of novels and volumes of poetry: the most significant are *The Fate of Adelaide* (1821), *The Improvisatrice* (1824), *The Troubadour* (1825), *The Golden Violet* (1827) and *The Venetian Bracelet* (1829), in which she often assumed the persona of the innocent but rejected lover. Other notable works by female poets of the period include Mary Blanchford Tighe's *Psyche; or, The Legend of Love* (1805), an allegorical retelling of the story of Cupid and Psyche which may have influenced Keats; Mary Russell Mitford's romance based on the *Bounty* story, *Christina, or the Maid of the South Seas*, and her series of sketches of rural life, *Our Village*, published between 1824 and 1832; Eleanor Porden's scientific romance, *The Veils: or Triumph of Constancy* (1815); and Ann and Jane Taylor's numerous collections of verse for children including *Original Poems for Infant Minds* (1804) which contains Jane's evocative lyric, 'The Star', or 'Twinkle, Twinkle, Little Star' as it is more commonly known.

Labouring Poets

Romantic poets often wrote about rural nature, but also popular in their day, though since excluded from the canon of 'high' Romanticism, were poets actually identified as 'peasant' or labouring. This category of writer was a fixture of the literary culture of the day and functioned as an acceptable, though heavily circumscribed, opportunity for working people to be published and address a wider public. Patrons desirous of unearthing authentic and unschooled creative genius were ever on the lookout for promising candidates. Robert Burns was packaged as a poetical ploughman absorbed in the poetical minutiae of his local rural world in the 1786 Kilmarnock edition of his *Poems, Chiefly in the Scottish Dialect*, though he was clearly a highly sophisticated and intellectual writer. Burns published two further volumes of poetry in 1787 and

1793. James Hogg, known as the 'Ettrick shepherd', was also a rural labouring-class poet who worked as shepherd until his mid-thirties. Hogg, known mainly for his powerful Gothic fiction *Confessions of a Justified Sinner* (1824), published substantial amounts of poetry for *Blackwood's*. His *Poetic Mirror* (1816) also revealed him as a gifted parodist of mainstream Romantic poetry. John Clare was similarly represented as the 'Northamptonshire Peasant Poet' and marketed as such by his publisher John Taylor in a series of collections, including *Poems Descriptive of Rural Life and Scenery* (1820), *The Village Minstrel* (1821), *The Shepherd's Calendar* (1827) and the *Rural Muse* (1835). Clare, like Burns, was a major poet who found the limitations imposed upon him as a 'peasant poet' crippling. Both Burns and Clare are now regarded and taught as important canonical Romantic poets. Robert Bloomfield, known as the 'Farmer's Boy' (actually by then a shoemaker) produced rural poetry; his first volume of poems sold 40,000 copies. Ann Yearsley, known as 'Lactilla' or 'the Bristol Milkwoman', was championed by Hannah More as an example of a working poet. Her *Poems on Several Occasions* was published in 1785 and further collections followed, despite her public and bitter rupture with More. Other poets, such as Samuel Bamford, the 'weaver's boy' and Ebenezer Elliot (1781–1849), the 'corn law rhymer', produced explicitly social and political verse.

The Romantic Novel

The Romantic period was one in which the novel assumed a new seriousness. The eighteenth-century debate concerning realism and romance in fiction continued. The Gothic romance established by Walpole remained extremely popular. Generally the Gothic novel has been identified as a British, Protestant, middle-class form which located its 'others' among tyrannical and gloomy Catholic aristocrats and violent, unruly plebeians. Its obsessions were very much bourgeois ones, dealing with superstition, tyranny and violence. From its inception, incest and disordered family relations were among its dominant themes. Although Ann Radcliffe's novels were admired, there were other popular fictions and dramas which were viewed with suspicion by polite society, including novels by Eliza Parsons, Regina Maria Roche, supernatural tales like those published by Matthew Lewis as *Tales of Wonder* (1801), and Gothic dramas, such as Lewis's *The Castle Spectre* (1798). Certainly by the early decades of the nineteenth century there was a conservative backlash against the 'low' fiction of Gothic. One thing that troubled polite reviewers was the sheer popularity of the form.

Clara Reeve's *The Old English Baron* (published in 1777 as *The Champion of Virtue*) minimised Walpole's supernaturalism and emphasised historical realism, beginning a genre of writing which critics from Ellen Moers onwards have referred to as 'female Gothic' (*Literary Women*, p. 9 [Cix]). Sophia Lee's historical romance, *The Recess* (1785), had strong Gothic overtones with its depiction of the persecutions visited on two forgotten daughters of Mary Queen of Scots, as did Charlotte Smith's *Emmeline, the Orphan of the Castle* (1788) and *The Old Manor House* (1793) which pre-empted Radcliffe's concern with the explained supernatural. William Beckford's *Vathek* (1786), though more properly regarded as an Oriental tale, located its terrors in the time of the

Arabian Nights with its despotic Caliph Vathek and his quest for the treasures of the pre-Adamite Sultans. Radcliffe was the period's most accomplished Gothic novelist. Her second novel, *A Sicilian Romance* (1790), pioneered what was to become her characteristic plot of the persecuted motherless female, subject to threats and imprisonment by older tyrannical males, amid an Italianate and picturesque landscape; a plot she would develop to greater effect in the *Mysteries of Udolpho* (1794) and her masterpiece *The Italian* (1797), with its towering and influential Gothic villain, Schedoni. Radcliffe famously eschewed Walpole's marvellous occurrences and explained all her uncanny happenings away. Although *Udolpho* is set in the late sixteenth century, the events of *The Italian* take place only forty years from the novel's present. In 1796 Matthew Lewis's sensational tale of Satanism, incest, rape and mob violence, *The Monk*, appeared to a scandalised reading public. Lewis accepted the supernatural on its own terms, drawing inspiration from German folk tales and legends. His novel of excess established an alternative tradition of Gothic writing to that of Radcliffe and, in turn, occasioned her rebuke in the form of her *Italian*.

William Godwin took the form in new directions, developing a series of reformist political arguments in his *Things as They Are; or the Adventures of Caleb Williams* (1794) a novel about the tyranny of the class and legal systems and the importance of truth and free communication. Education and crime were also important themes in this novel of the control and manipulation of one man by another. Another key writer was Charlotte Dacre, whose *Confessions of the Nun of St Omer* (1805) and the extraordinary *Zofloya, or the Moor* (1806) confounded stereotypes of polite female Gothic. Dacre's *Zofloya* rewrote Lewis's *Monk* from a female perspective, featuring an amoral and lustful female protagonist, Victoria, and her demon lover, Zofloya. Dacre's full-blooded tales of murder, revenge and diabolic temptation had little in common with the fictions of Radcliffe or Reeve. It was left to Mary Shelley to combine the excess of Lewis with the novel of ideas of her father, Godwin, in *Frankenstein* (1818). By the end of the second decade of the nineteenth century the Gothic was showing increasing signs of staleness and was frequently parodied, most notably in Jane Austen's *Northanger Abbey* (1818) and Thomas Love Peacock's *Nightmare Abbey* (1818). The last 'classic' Gothic novel of the period is generally thought to be C. R. Maturin's *Melmoth the Wanderer* (1820), an extremely influential tale involving the Gothic stereo type of the wandering immortal through a series of tales of extreme events.

A number of novelists in the 1790s deployed the novel form to participate in the political debate of the time. Numerous 'Jacobin novels' were published. Many of the novels involved plots where innocent individuals are pursued and imprisoned under an unjust social system; several have strong female characters. Charlotte Smith's novels are hard to categorise. They are sentimental fictions with strong links with both the Jacobin and the Gothic novel. Her early novels are very much in the mode of radical sensibility, but her subsequent fiction, *Desmond* (1792), *Marchmont* (1796), *The Young Philosopher* (1798) and, her most popular novel, *The Old Manor House* (1793), all develop political themes about the nature of society and the treatment of women. The increasingly repressive political climate of the late 1790s led to a conservative backlash of anti-Jacobin novels celebrating the traditional values of hearth and home, including Jane West's *A Gossip's Story* (1797) and *A Tale of the Times* (1799),

Elizabeth Hamilton's *Memoirs of Modern Philosophers* (1800) and, more ambivalently, Amelia Opie's *Adeline Mowbray, or Mother and Daughter* (1805).

Novels dealing with courtship and marriage were also common in the period. Frances or Fanny Burney remained a significant novelist of sensibility well into the Romantic period. Her later novels, *Cecilia* (1782), *Camilla, or, a Picture of Youth* (1796) and *The Wanderer* (1814), all deal with social and domestic issues. Susan Ferrier's *Marriage* (1818) tackled the theme of the education and development of two sisters, and was extremely successful. It was, however, Jane Austen who developed this mode of novel to its highest state. In a series of complex and engaging comedies, Austen proved herself to be one of the most sophisticated and ironic commentators on the manners and mores of Regency England. *Northanger Abbey* (1818) satirised the conventions of female Gothic writing using the device of the naive heroine; *Sense and Sensibility* (1811) adopted the familiar narrative of two contrasting sisters as a way of outlining the dangers and pitfalls of a mode of sensibility, radicalised in the 1790s; *Pride and Prejudice* (1813) brilliantly evoked the romance of Elizabeth Bennet and Mr Darcy against the conventions of class and social decorum; *Mansfield Park* (1814) explored the values and mores of the English landed gentry; *Emma* (1816) the relationship between an active and imaginative young woman and her social obligations; and *Persuasion* (1818) dealt with the responsibilities and duties of the gentry.

Novels of regional and national manners were also a feature of the period. Maria Edgeworth, probably the period's most highly respected novelist before Scott, initiated the form with her *Castle Rackrent* of 1800. Another important writer of Irish regional fiction, Sydney Owenson, Lady Morgan, wrote a series of flamboyant novels including *The Wild Irish Girl, A National Tale* (1806), and *O'Donnel: A National Tale* (1814), as well as the important Orientalist romance, set in the seventeenth-century Indian subcontinent, *The Missionary* (1811). The Scottish novelist John Galt published a series of what he called 'theoretical histories' set in the western lowlands of Scotland, and James Hogg also published, in addition to his *Confessions of a Justified Sinner* (1824), two other studies of superstition in Scottish life, *Three Perils of Man* (1822) and *Three Perils of Woman* (1823). Sir Walter Scott dominated the Romantic novel after 1814. His first novel, *Waverley* (1814), was set against the Jacobite Rebellion of 1745, pitting lowland, Enlightenment Edinburgh against the Romantic highland clan system, viewed through the eyes of the naive Romantic hero, Edmund Waverley. Other novels set in recent Scottish history followed. Scott's interests subsequently widened to take in a larger historical survey, though his theme was often the emergence of the organic nation, in novels such as *Ivanhoe: A Romance* (1819), *Quentin Durward* (1823), and *The Talisman* (1825). Scott's identity as the author of the Waverley Novels was kept secret until the 1820s. Mention should also be made of the satirical and historical romances of Thomas Love Peacock (1785–1866) which are hard to categorise as straightforward novels. Peacock developed the form of 'satirical-conversation' novel employing both the dialogue and the chorus (from drama) within novelistic discourse. Characteristically his novels described the conversations of a number of representative characters of the period and their foibles. In a series of novels, the most well known being *Nightmare Abbey* (1818), Peacock satirised Romantic-period poets and writers such as Coleridge, Shelley and Byron, as well as political economists, craniologists and other contemporary intellectual types.

Romantic Drama

Traditional accounts of the period have given less importance to drama and theatre than to poetry and fiction. Those figures who dominated the literature of the age did not, on the whole, produce good-quality drama capable of strong performance, although theatre was a large part of the culture of the period. The major theatres in London were Covent Garden and Drury Lane, which, since the Stage Licensing Act, held exclusive rights to stage spoken drama and opera; smaller theatres could only present plays which mixed speech and song. The most notable stage plays of the latter half of the eighteenth century were sentimental comedies such as Goldsmith's *She Stoops to Conquer* (1773), Sheridan's *The Rivals* (1775) and *The School for Scandal* (1777). Other prominent dramas include Thomas Holcroft's *The Road to Ruin* (1792), Elizabeth Inchbald's *Every One Has His Faults* (1793) and her adaptation of the German playwright August Friedrich von Kotzebue's play, as *Lover's Vows* (1798) (which features in the amateur theatricals depicted in Austen's *Mansfield Park*) as well as Hannah Cowley's *A Bold Stroke for a Husband* (1783). Gothic melodramas were also commonplace, including George Colman the Younger's dramatisation of Godwin's *Caleb Williams* as *The Iron Chest* (1796), Matthew Lewis's *The Castle Spectre* (1798), C. R. Maturin's *Bertram* (1816), Thomas Holcroft's *A Tale of Mystery* (1802) and James Robinson Planché's adaptation of John William Polidori's 1819 tale *The Vampyre* (1820). The period also saw the emergence of the costume drama, with W. T. Moncrieff's *Rochester, or Charles the Second's Merry Days* (1818) as well as the beginnings of farce in Colman's *Love Laughs at Locksmiths* (1802).

A few of the canonical Romantic writers attempted to write plays to be performed on stage. Wordsworth's psychological drama *The Borderers* was turned down by Covent Garden. Coleridge and Southey wrote *The Fall of Robespierre* in 1794 and Coleridge wrote a tragedy, *Osorio*, which was rejected for performance by Drury Lane in 1797 but later produced as *Remorse* in 1813 with some success. Shelley's *The Cenci* was also rejected by Covent Garden in 1819. Keats wrote two historical dramas intended for the theatre, *Otho the Great* (1819) and the fragmentary *King Stephen* (1819). Byron's Venetian tragedy, *Marino Faliero* was acted in 1821. Scott also wrote a series of plays for the theatre.

'Mental Theatre'

The major dramatic form for Romantic writers was that of the 'closet drama' or what Byron referred to as 'mental theatre'; drama to be read but not performed. As the stage was censored by the Examiner of Plays, closet drama allowed the writer more freedom to develop ideas. The most influential of such drama was probably Joanna Baillie's three-volume *A Series of Plays in which it is attempted to delineate the stronger passions of the mind* (or *Plays on the Passions*). Pre-empting some of the psychological concerns of Wordsworth and Coleridge's *Lyrical Ballads*, Baillie used the form of closet drama to analyse the effects of the predominance of one passion, or monomania, on a single person. Her drama *De Monfort*, for instance, explores the passion of hatred, and *Count Basil* that of love. *De Monfort* was produced successfully with John Philip Kemble in the title role and Sarah Siddons playing Jane De Monfort. It was probably Byron, however, who developed furthest the notion of closet drama, or 'mental theatre' as he termed it. While Baillie used the form to try and understand overwhelming and irrational passions, Byron is more concerned with challenging conventional morality and outlining the paradoxes of orthodox thought. He does this in a series of dramas, *Manfred* (1817), *Marino Faliero* (1821), *Sardanapalus* (1821), *The Two Foscari* (1821), *Cain* (1821) and *The Deformed Transformed* (1824).

Texts and Issues

Class, Power and Politics

Literary texts of the Romantic period were shaped and informed by a number of social and political issues. Many have argued that the work of the Romantics is a response to the disruptive social and economic changes in the normal patterns of life occasioned by the growth of the factory system, the disappearance of whole classes of workers in traditional crafts, and the increasing population in cities. It is often argued that Romantic poetry shows a concern with the dignity of the individual person and a psychological concern for the distressed and alienated state of mind. Many of the Romantics believed that the disruptions in the patterns of life occasioned by the commercial and industrial process, and its impersonal abstraction of the economic interests of the individual, blunted the mind and made it solitary. Against this sense of social disintegration, the Romantics demonstrated a concern with the whole, with integration, and with unity: 'The One Life', in Coleridge's phrase.

Similarly, the literature of the period reflects the turbulent political debates informed by what Percy Shelley referred to as 'the master-theme of the epoch in which we live', the French Revolution. Wordsworth, who visited France a year after the fall of the Bastille, captured his sense of youthful excitement at the potential of the event in *The Prelude*:

> Bliss was it in that dawn to be alive,
> But to be young was very heaven! O times,
> In which the meagre, stale, forbidding ways
> Of custom, law, and statute took at once
> The attraction of a country in romance.

> *(The Prelude* (1805) IX.692–6)

In 1790 Edmund Burke's *Reflections on the Revolution in France* initiated a debate among supporters and opponents of the French Revolution in Britain. The initial response to the Revolution had been largely positive, the general view being that the French were freeing themselves from the tyranny of absolute monarchy and approximating their constitution to the British model of limited monarchy. This was very much the argument of the dissenting minister Richard Price's *Discourse on the Love of Our Country* (1789), which compared the French Revolution to that of England in 1688. Burke, however, argued that the revolutionaries' lack of respect for tradition and authority, and their desire to subject everything to the test of reason rather than of experience, could only lead to political anarchy and violence. Initially, most enlightened opinion regarded Burke's book as alarmist. Mary Wollstonecraft responded with her *A Vindication of the Rights of Men* (1790), then her *A Vindication of the Rights of Woman* (1792); the latter influentially extended the discussion to take in the political rights of women, arguing for the importance of equality of a rational education and opportunity for both sexes. Numerous other responses to Burke were penned, the most famous of these being Thomas Paine's *The Rights of Man* (Part 1, 1791; Part 2, 1792) and William Godwin's *Enquiry Concerning Political Justice* (1793) which both argued the reformist and liberal case. It is estimated that the two parts of Thomas Paine's *The*

Rights of Man, in its several editions, sold more than twenty thousand copies. The debate was reflected in cultural terms in a number of ways, including pamphlets, poems, dramas, novels, satires in verse and prose, cartoons and caricatures. The poet and novelist Helen Maria Williams, who had arrived in Paris in 1790, reported back on events and surveyed the prime tourist locations in her *Letters Written in France* (1790). Williams kept a salon at Paris, which Wordsworth and Wollstonecraft visited, until she was imprisoned by Robespierre during the Terror. Libertarian and materialist ideas were also disseminated in the poetry of Erasmus Darwin, whose *The Loves of the Plants* (1789), *The Botanic Garden* (1791) and *Temple of Nature* (1803) versified contemporary scientific theories presenting radical views of sexual equality in the plant world. By 1794, however, the conservative response in Britain to the Revolution was gaining the upper hand; Hannah More's *Cheap Repository Tracts*, aimed at the labouring classes, disseminated conservative notions in simple story forms, and the periodical the *Anti-Jacobin* mercilessly castigated radicals and reformers in verse satires.

Romantic-period writers responded to this debate. As well as the series of Jacobin and anti-Jacobin novels, Romantic poetry engaged in one way or another with the debate. Both Wordsworth and Coleridge were supporters of the Revolution up until around 1798 and they both wrote overtly political poetry. *Lyrical Ballads*, for instance, eschews a concern with fashionable life, featuring, instead, subjects from common life which could be found in every village. Wordsworth claimed that the collection expressed the belief that 'men who do not wear fine clothes can feel deeply' (Wu, *Romanticism*, p. 512n [A]). He affirmed that the *Ballads* are written in the language of ordinary men. William Blake sympathised with the Revolution, which he regarded as an outburst of freedom against the repressive forces of monarchy and established religion. He expressed his radical and free-thinking ideas in a series of visionary poems. In his *Songs of Innocence and of Experience*, he castigated social evils and political repression. The 'Chimney Sweeper' poems criticise a society which condones the use of children to undertake potentially lethal employment, which praises 'God and his priest and king' who 'make up a heaven' of the boys' 'misery'. The narrator of 'Holy Thursday' of *Experience* angrily demands, when confronted by the spectacle of charity boys and girls herded into St Paul's to give thanks to their benefactors:

> Is this a holy thing to see,
> In a rich and fruitful land,
> Babes reduced to misery,
> Fed with cold and usurous hand?
>
> (*Norton Anthology*, p. 90 [A])

The poem 'London' presents an apocalyptic vision of the British empire's capital city, a place of fear and terror in the grip of political and psychological repression by the 'mind-forged manacles' of empiricist philosophy. It presents a searing indictment of the hypocrisies and cruelties of the political and religious establishment:

> How the Chimney-sweeper's cry
> Every blackning Church appalls,
> And the hapless Soldier's sigh
> Runs in blood down Palace walls.
>
> (*Norton Anthology*, p. 94 [A])

However, it is the institution of 'the marriage hearse', which creates a property in people, akin to slavery, and represses free desire, for which the narrator reserves his most scathing language. In the *Songs*, Blake is possibly arguing that both the states of a child-like and giving Innocence, and of an adult selfishness and materialist Experience, are necessary to human development. Although the world is currently dominated by cold and hypocritical materialists (personified by Blake's mythological figure Urizen), there is a possibility that revolutionary energies may break out and imaginatively transform the world. This visionary apocalypse may be present in Blake's 'The Tyger' which presents an enigmatic and sublimely terrifying creature at a moment of cataclysmic metamorphosis:

> When the stars threw down their spears
> And water'd heaven with their tears,
> Did he smile his work to see?
> Did he who made the Lamb make thee?
>
> (*Norton Anthology*, p. 93 [A])

The poets of the second generation of Romantic writers, however, maintained a faith in liberal and reformist politics. Most engaged was Percy Shelley who developed his political ideas in a number of works. His 'Ode to the West Wind', for instance, envisions the autumnal wind as a cleansing force, removing the diseased and corrupt, and transforming the world for a new spring and awakening. His sonnet 'England in 1819' (*Norton Anthology*, p. 771 [A]) presents a nation ruled by 'An old, mad, blind, despised and dying King'. For Shelley, princes are like mud polluting a stream, they are like parasites sucking the blood of their country, 'Till they drop, blind in blood, without a blow', like satiated leeches. Referring to the 'Peterloo Massacre', he accuses the government of killing the liberty of the people but, with characteristic optimism, implies that the system of things may contain the seeds of its own destruction as the military is a two-edged sword which could be used against the established order. 'England in 1819' is a graveyard of corpses from which the glorious phantom of liberty may appear. Shelley has here vividly and comprehensively compressed national ills into fourteen packed lines, savaging the establishment of king, government and established Church as parasitic, polluting, corrupt, hypocritical and murderous.

Land and Landscape

Changes in the rural and urban landscapes were reflected in the writing of the time. Oliver Goldsmith had expressed sentimental regret at rural depopulation in his *Deserted Village* (1770), and George Crabbe's *The Village* (1783) complained of the neglect of rural life. Crabbe opposed Goldsmith's sentimental idealisations with a more critical depiction of the lives of rural people, depicting their laziness and dishonesty as well as their poverty and suffering: 'The Muses sing of happy swains, / Because their Music never knew their pains' (*Norton Anthology*, p. 2887 [A]). Wordsworth and Coleridge's *Lyrical Ballads* can also be read as a response to the changing conditions of rural life. In a letter of 1801 to the Whig politician Charles James Fox, Wordsworth claimed that 'by the spreading of manufactures through every part of the country, by the heavy taxes upon postage, by workhouses, Houses of Industry, and the invention of soup-shops ... the bonds of domestic feeling among the poor ... have been weakened, and in innumerable instances entirely destroyed'. The *Ballads* take as their subject 'low and rustic life' (*Norton Anthology*, p. 264 [A]). They describe the plight of people who are on the very margin of existence: shepherds, rural labourers, the old and infirm, vagrants, beggars, abandoned women, hysterics, the insane and, perhaps most notoriously, those like Johnny Foy, a mentally challenged child or 'Idiot Boy'. Among other things, Wordsworth draws attention to the industrial process (the spreading of manufactures), the fall in rural earnings and the rising cost in provisions occasioned by the war with France, which led to the sufferings of the rustic people. Goody Blake, in the poem 'Goody Blake and Harry Gill', is a victim of the long hours and poor returns of eighteenth-century cottage industry:

> All day she spun in her poor dwelling,
> And then her three hours' work at night –
> Alas, 'twas hardly worth the telling,
> It would not pay for candlelight.
>
> (Wu, *Romanticism*, p. 363 [A])

During winter Goody Blake must forage for wood for her fire because 'in that country coals are dear' (Wu, *Romanticism*, p. 364 [A]). The Shepherd in 'The Last of the Flock' is forced to sell his sheep one by one to pay for food for his children, 'Ten children, sir, had I to feed – / Hard labour in a time of need!' (p. 383). Wordsworth writes of the break-up of families and of the disappearance of that class of rural worker who owns a small tract of land; a process movingly fictionalised in the poem 'Michael', which concerns an elderly shepherd who through circumstance is forced to remortgage his land and, as a consequence, lose the property when his son fails to return home after having made sufficient money to rescue it. At the end of the poem Wordsworth describes how Michael's land and family are alienated from their traditional owners, while the community within which he lived is effaced by the forces of change and improvement, 'Great changes have been wrought / In all the neighbourhood' (p. 522). Wordsworth voices a key complaint of the time about the dispersal of local rural communities into the larger national and global networks of urbanisation, colonialism and empire.

The poetry of the Northamptonshire rural labourer John Clare is deeply sensitive to the changes in the rural environment, which he writes about from the perspective of an insider. Clare was hostile to 'improvement' and enclosure; he was aware of the ecological aspects of the changes in reducing woodlands all over the country as well as destroying breeding grounds for wildlife: 'Ye banishd trees ye make me deeply sigh / Inclosure came and all your glories fell' (Clare, 'The Village Minstrel', *Early Poems*, p. 170 [A]). Clare highlights the tolls which enclosure has taken on the lives of rural workers. In his poem, 'Remembrances', he writes how:

> And cross berry way and old round oaks narrow lane
> With its hollow trees like pulpits I shall never see again

Inclosure like a Buonaparte let not a thing remain
It levelled every bush and tree and levelled every hill
And hung the moles for traitors – though the brook is running still
It runs a naked brook cold and chill

(Clare, *Major Works*, p. 260 [A])

In 'The Mores' Clare bewails the loss of the people's traditional rights to the enclosure movement:

Inclosure came and trampled on the grave
Of labour's rights and left the poor a slave
And memory's pride ere want to wealth did bow
Is both the shadow and the substance now.

(Clare, *Major Works*, p. 168 [A])

Clare's poetry protests against such changes and improvements as enclosure, and bewails the loss of both the common lands and the people's customary rights, which caused numerous labourers to leave the countryside for work elsewhere. For him, enclosure is symptomatic of a new order antithetical to a communitarian view of the world, one which respects the place of wildlife and plants as well as the rights of human beings.

Throughout the period the notion of 'improvement', or the more efficient management and cultivation of land to increase its profitability, became a key concern. The improvement of the landed estate became a key theme of the time. This led to a series of debates among landscape gardeners, including Richard Payne Knight, Lancelot 'Capability' Brown and Humphry Repton, concerning the best way for art to mimic nature. Sunken fences or 'hahas' were used to mark boundaries without spoiling the vista; Arcadian temples and bogus ruins were added to please the eye.

The improvement of the grounds of estates features prominently in Jane Austen's *Mansfield Park*, where the traditional virtues of Sir Thomas Bertram's country estate are contrasted to the fads and whimsies introduced by Mr Rushworth at Sotherton. For Austen, 'improvers' were allied with the ethically unstable characters, Henry and Mary Crawford, who bring disorder and potential tragedy to Sir Thomas's family circle. Similarly, the reader becomes fully aware of Mr Darcy's virtues and Elizabeth's prejudices in *Pride and Prejudice* (1813) when the former's well-managed estate of

The Sublime, the Beautiful and the Picturesque

In aesthetic terms the categories of the sublime, the beautiful and the picturesque were applied to the landscape. Edmund Burke famously defined the sublime in opposition to the beautiful in his *A Philosophical Enquiry into the Origin of Our Ideas of the Sublime and Beautiful* (1757), arguing that the sublime is occasioned by great and terrible objects whereas the beautiful is a product of small and pleasing ones. The picturesque was an eighteenth-century theory which stressed notions such as variety, irregularity, ruggedness, singularity and chiaroscuro (patterns of light and dark) in the appreciation of landscape. In this theory, landscape should be viewed as a painting, framed and mediated by the connoisseur. Ruins and beggars were especially favoured by picturesque writers. The key theorists of the movement were William Gilpin, Uvedale Price and Payne Knight. Gilpin published a series of tourist guidebooks to picturesque landscapes, popularising areas such as the Lakes, the Wye Valley, North Wales and Scotland. Picturesque notions were also applied to landscape parks.

4.9 Picturesque image of a Scottish landscape from William Gilpin's *Observations on Several parts of Great Britain, particularly the High-lands of Scotland, relative chiefly to Picturesque Beauty*. Third edition (London, 1808).

Pemberley is viewed through Elizabeth's admiring eyes. Certainly improvement was something that many viewed with suspicion as an index of disordered moral values. In his *Rural Rides* (1830), the Tory radical William Cobbett commented upon places where new plans of 'enclosure and plantation have totally destroyed the beauty of the estate'.

The canonical Romantic writers tended to eschew the picturesque appreciation of nature for the full-blooded sublime, exemplified by the mountains, crags and torrents of the Lake District and the Alps. Although sharing their appreciation of the topographical sites made famous by picturesque theorists, Romantic poets disliked the notion of nature as framed as in a picture, and as mediated by the practitioner of picturesque beauty. They also objected to the idea that nature could be improved by the addition of formulaic beauties, preferring, instead, a sublime and solitary encounter which became a quasi-mystical or, even, religious experience. Typical of this view of nature and the mind is that developed at length in Wordsworth's epic spiritual autobiography, *The Prelude*. This work grew from a two-part discussion of its author's childhood in the northern Lake District and the peculiar affinity between the child and his natural environment (1799), to a thirteen- (1805) and then fourteen-book (1850) discussion of the growth and development of the poet's mind. Wordsworth stressed the importance of the sublime natural scenery in developing his spiritual, moral and imaginative nature. For instance, when describing how he borrowed a boat for a night-time adventure, he feels rebuked and threatened by an imagined reciprocity in the world around him:

> When, from behind that craggy Steep, till then
> The horizon's bound, a huge peak, black and huge,
> As if with voluntary power instinct,

Upreared its head. – I struck, and struck again,
And, growing still in stature, the grim Shape
Towered up between me and the stars, and still,
For so it seemed, with purpose of its own
And measured motion, like a living Thing
Strode after me.

(Norton Anthology, p. 332 [A])

Returning the boat, the young Wordsworth is troubled for many days 'with a dim and undetermined sense / Of unknown modes of being', of 'huge and mighty Forms' that moved through his days and troubled his dreams (p. 333). Wordsworth argues that as he develops he becomes aware of his self, but also a self or presence apart from himself, that of animated nature. Nature works to purify the mind by stimulating its spiritual and imaginative responses, through intense emotional experiences, often those of terror. A poem like Coleridge's 'This Lime-Tree Bower My Prison' similarly plays with the key categories of landscape (*Norton Anthology*, pp. 428–30 [A]). It begins in picturesque mode with the poet lamenting his inability to join his friends on a walk through the Quantock Hills, due to an accident. Self-consciously luxuriating in the affectations of sensibility ('Friends, whom I never more will meet again.') and the framed picturesque delights of roughness, variety and chiaroscuro, Coleridge's mode is unconsciously heightened as he is led to contemplate his friends enjoying the sublime landscape:

gazing round

On the wide landscape, gaze till all doth seem
Less gross than bodily; and of such hues
As veil the Almighty Spirit, when yet he makes
Spirits perceive his presence.

This awareness of nature as the symbolical language of God is too excessive to sustain indefinitely and Coleridge returns to where he began, the lime-tree bower. Having vicariously experienced the sublime, he is now able to see the interpenetration of nature and self in the bower, celebrating the importance of the beautiful, 'Nature ne'er deserts the wise and pure.'

The sublime is also celebrated in the work of the second generation of Romantic poets, though in a markedly different way. Byron exploits the fashion for sublime alpine landscape, especially in *Manfred* and the third Canto of *Childe Harold's Pilgrimage*. Percy Shelley frequently uses the sublime in such poems as 'Mont Blanc' (*Norton Anthology*, pp. 762–6 [A]), although his sublime revises that of his predecessors in a libertarian mode. He questions whether the sublime impact made on the mind by the mountain is inherent in the object itself or is a projection of the human mind's imagining:

… how hideously

Its shapes are heaped around! rude, bare, and high,
Ghastly, and scarred and riven. – Is this the scene
Where the old Earthquake-daemon taught her young
Ruin? Were these their toys? or did a sea
Of fire envelop once this silent snow?
None can reply – all seems eternal now.

4.10 Sublime image: John Martin, *Manfred on the Jungfrau* (1837). Romantic artists and writers were fascinated by the relationship of man to Nature and this was frequently expressed through the image of figures on clifftops. Manfred is about to throw himself from the cliff but is restrained by a chamois hunter who leads him to safety. The episode is taken from Act I scene II of Byron's dramatic poem *Manfred*.

Shelley is ambiguous about our feelings of the sublime. Unlike Wordsworth and Coleridge, he does not believe that sublime landscape reveals a spiritual or divine presence, the intimations of which may derive from human fantasy, rather than any divine glimmerings. Shelley sees the sublime as a powerful and destructive experience which is as likely to lead to agnosticism as belief. He implies that this scepticism and doubt of itself might undermine what were, for him, repressive forms of orthodox Christian belief and systems of political repression.

Feminist critics of Romantic writing, such as Anne Mellor, have argued that the sublime is essentially a masculine Romantic mode seldom present in the writings of female poets and novelists. Certainly, when women writers exploit the sublime, they often do it in a hesitant or apologetic way. This is true of a poem such as Barbauld's 'A Summer Evening's Meditation' (Wu, *Romanticism*, pp. 35–8 [A]) which includes an imagined tour of the universe:

> To the dread confines of eternal night,
> To solitudes of vast unpeopled space,
> The deserts of creation, wide and wild,
> Where embryo systems and unkindled suns
> Sleep in the womb of chaos?

Barbauld apologetically recedes from this flight of fancy, preferring 'the known accustomed spot' to 'flight so daring'. Neither does she experience the loss of self and connection with another reality which Wordsworth and Coleridge claim.

Science

The Romantics are often caricatured as opposed to scientific discovery and progress. In fact, most of the writers of the period were deeply interested in scientific
enquiry. Coleridge was a friend of both the natural philosophers Thomas Beddoes
and Humphry Davy, and he, Wordsworth and the Shelleys were deeply interested
in the latest scientific ideas and theories. It was not so much science as such that
the Romantic poets were suspicious of, but a narrow utilitarian and empirical
application of science. In many ways it was the Newtonian orthodoxy which they
opposed as materialist and reductive. What Newton effectively did was to banish
the divine from nature and empty the world of its mystery. It was this demystifica-
tion of nature that they resented. Although the vehemence of Blake's denunciation
of Newtonianism is not typical, its general drift is. Blake showed a constant and
total opposition to Newton and his works. This can be seen in the well-known plate
of Newton sitting on a rock, examining on the floor in front of him a geometrical
figure of a triangle within a circle and measuring the base of the triangle with
a pair of compasses, thus ignoring the wonders of the stars and the heavens to
concentrate on abstract reasoning. In *The Song of Los* (c. 1795), Blake mythologises
the institution of Enlightenment thought, whereby 'a philosophy of five senses'
is given 'into the hands of Newton and Locke' by a weeping Urizen, while 'Clouds
roll heavy upon the Alps round Rousseau and Voltaire' (*Complete Poems*, pp. 244–5).
In *Jerusalem* Blake writes of the 'Loom of Locke' being washed by 'the Waterwheels
of Newton'. Almost as hostile is Keats's dismissal of Newton's science of optics in
Lamia (1817):

> Do not all charms fly
> At the mere touch of cold philosophy?
> There was an awful rainbow once in heaven:
> We know her woof, her texture; she is given
> In the dull catalogue of common things.
>
> (II. 229–33; *Norton Anthology*, p. 924 [A])

Keats's criticism of contemporary science's tendency to demystify the world may
have echoed Wordsworth's warning against an overweening analytical faculty in *The
Tables Turned*, whereby 'Our meddling intellect / Misshapes the beauteous form of
things – / We murder to dissect' (Wu, *Romanticism*, p. 402 [A]). Yet Wordsworth also
had a high regard for 'great Newton's own etherial self' (*Prelude* (1805) III.270) and
for his achievements in natural philosophy. His main anxiety was that such scientific triumphs might obscure the higher truth of poetry. In Book V of *The Prelude*,
he describes an apocalyptic dream of Coleridge's where the dreamer encounters a
Bedouin Arab who carries a stone and a shell, respectively symbols of science and of
poetry. Both are precious and are to be saved from the oncoming deluge. The stone
represents 'the adamantine holds of truth / By reason built', but the shell, the Arab
tells, 'Is something of more worth ... A God – yea, many Gods' (ll. 38–9, 71–114;
Norton Anthology, pp. 357–9 [A]).

4.11 Blake's imaginative depiction of Sir Isaac Newton making geometrical measurements on the shore of the ocean of truth, encapsulates his dismissal of eighteenth-century empirical science in favour of the creative imagination.

The Romantic poets preferred a notion of matter which was active and alive and not passive, fixed and dead as in the Newtonian system. This notion that matter is active, made up from forces of energy, attracted the young Coleridge. Although intensely admiring of Newton, he was critical of those trends in Newtonian thought which banished the first cause to the realm of the unknowable and thus provided an encouragement for materialism and atheism. Coleridge never accepted Newton's materialist assumptions about matter, preferring instead a vitalistic theory. In coming to his belief in a vitalistic universe Coleridge may have had the work of Priestley in mind. Priestley's *Disquisitions concerning Matter and Spirit* (1777) argued that every atom was a point of force, acting by means of attraction and repulsion on its neighbours. These *foci* of energy were organised by the Deity, and the physical world was made up of his energy. Like Priestley, the young Coleridge denied that matter and spirit were distinct properties. This sense of nature as vital leads in the direction of pantheism, where God is immanent in nature and not transcendent. In *The Eolian Harp* Coleridge asks,

> And what if all of animated nature
> Be but organic harps diversely framed,
> That tremble into thought, as o'er them sweeps,
> Plastic and vast, one intellectual breeze,
> At once the Soul of Each and God of all?

(*Norton Anthology*, p. 427 [A])

For Coleridge, pantheism was always a tempting option but one which he struggled to resist all his life. The speculations of the Shelley circle concerning the origins and nature of the vital force were reflected in Mary Shelley's Gothic novel *Frankenstein* (1818, revised 1831) which functions as a critique of Enlightenment scientific aspiration. It is important to stress that such intellectual enquiries as those of Coleridge and Percy and Mary Shelley represent as much an engagement with the substantial body of scientific thought that had arisen from debates within the Enlightenment as a rejection of it.

The poet closest of all to the Enlightenment scientific project was probably Erasmus Darwin. Darwin was a polymath, a theorist as well as a botanist, a doctor as well as an inventor, who numbered James Watt and Joseph Priestley among his friends. He translated Linnaeus' *The System of Vegetables* and *The Families of Plants*. Darwin marshalled the best available botanical scholarship to present Linnaeus as accurately as possible to the British public, but it was as a poet that he succeeded in popularising the science. *The Botanic Garden* (1791) was a tribute to the power of the Linnaean system since, like the Swedish botanist, Darwin defined plants by their sexual characteristics. He also personified them so that he could portray their reproduction by analogy with human behaviour. Darwin's plants loved, courted, married and had sex with each other, sometimes in groups, sometimes in what he called 'promiscuous marriage', as in this passage:

> A *hundred* virgins join a *hundred* swains,
> And fond Adonis leads the sprightly trains;
> Pair after pair, along his sacred groves
> To Hymen's fane the bright procession moves;
> Each smiling youth a myrtle garland shades,
> And wreaths of roses veil the blushing maids;
> Light Joys on twinkling feet attend the throng,
> Weave the gay dance, or raise the frolic song;
> – Which, as they pass, exulting Cupids sting
> Promiscuous arrows from the sounding string;
> On wings of gossamer soft Whispers fly,
> And the sly Glance steals side-long from the eye.
>
> (Darwin, *The Botanic Garden*, II. 236–7 [A])

The Botanic Garden proved so popular that it made the science a fashionable pursuit. Blake, Coleridge, Crabbe and Wordsworth all took ideas and images from it. *The Botanic Garden* was not a Romantic poem in the sense that Darwin wrote playfully but made no attempt to explore the inward self in relation to what scientific exploration revealed about the world outside.

Gender and Sexuality

Scholars of Romanticism have only recently begun to pay attention to the role of women writers within the period. In actual fact there were thousands of women writing. It is also becoming apparent that with the rise of the novel in this period, poetry was becoming increasingly marked out as the preserve of male poets, which required birth and breeding, as well as a common education and certain exclusive standards of shared taste. Some women wrote satires as well as sonnets and tragedies in addition to the comedy of manners; but there was a pressure to conform to notions of what was appropriate for women to write, policed by the periodicals and publishers. This is certainly the case with the epic, which, although some were written by a few women, became increasingly identified as a masculine form. Those women who did attempt to become poets often stuck to the forms of romance and the sonnet, though there are still many exceptions to this. The Romantic revival of the sonnet form, often attributed to Coleridge and Wordsworth, was actually occasioned by the publication of Charlotte Smith's popular and influential *Elegiac Sonnets* of 1784. Women writers specialised in the novel, which became an increasingly female form. This is not to say that men did not write novels, but the novels written by Scott and Godwin were described as serious historical or philosophical works, removed from the domestic subject matter of novelists like Jane Austen or Fanny Burney. Certainly there were dangers of straying too far from the accepted modes of female writing. John Wilson Croker's sarcastic review of Barbauld's satire *Eighteen Hundred and Eleven* (1812) warned its author 'to desist from satire, which indeed is satire on herself alone; and of entreating, with great earnestness, that she will not, for the sake of this ungrateful generation, put herself to the trouble of writing any more party pamphlets in verse'. Croker's review, though not necessarily representative of male thinking in the period, was serious enough to occasion Barbauld's retirement from poetry.

Romanticism as practised by the canonical male poets has been identified with a series of concerns which are not those of the female writers of the period. Women tended to write about their own sensibility, about feminine instinct and female duty. Women writers celebrated not the achievements of the imagination and not the spontaneous overflow of powerful feelings, but the workings of the rational mind in both male and female. They stressed not so much the alienated self of the male writer but instead showed a concern with family and community care and attendant practical responsibilities. This has led Stuart Curran to argue that female writers were interested more in the 'quotidian' or the domestic. Such popular women poets as Felicia Hemans and L.E.L. became synonymous with ideas of the home and hearth and God and country (Curran, 'The "I" Altered' [Cxi]). One characteristic sub-genre of female poetry, for instance, is the flower verse which celebrates the particular scent, texture and colour of flora, rather than a Wordsworthian concern with memory and transcendence. This concern with the quotidian can be seen in many poems; a good example is Barbauld's 'Washing-Day' which details the domestic ceremony of the weekly laundry.

> Come, Muse; and sing the dreaded Washing-Day.
> Ye who beneath the yoke of wedlock bend,
> With bowed soul, full well ye ken the day
> Which week, smooth sliding after week, brings on
> Too soon; – for to that day nor peace belongs

> Nor comfort; – ere the first gray streak of dawn,
> The red-armed washers come and chase repose.
>
> (ll. 8–14, *Norton Anthology*, p. 37 [A])

It is unlikely any male writer would understand the regular tedium of the washing day, its relationship to the married life, its gendered specificity, and the way such domestic chores mark the passage of time, 'week, smooth sliding after week', for women who undertake 'to wash, to rinse, to wring, / To fold, and starch, and clap, and iron, and plait'. Such detailed enumeration of the business of the day argues for the gendered view of the poet, a change in the expected Romantic perspective, what Curran refers to as 'The "I" Altered'.

This difference in outlook has led Anne Mellor to argue that there are two 'Romanticisms' in the period, one 'masculine' the other 'feminine'. This for her is a gender bias not a biological distinction. Mellor argues that the 'masculine' Romantic poets have attempted to assimilate the female into their own male selves. For Mellor, more typical perhaps of the female response to nature may be Dorothy Wordsworth's 'The Floating Island'. Here Dorothy describes a 'slip of earth' loosed into the middle of a lake which provides 'the warbling birds' that visit, and the insects that live there, with food and shelter, 'a peopled *world*'. The life of the island is transient and fragile, passing away to be buried 'beneath the glittering lake'. In the metaphor of the floating island, Mellor argues that Dorothy finds a metaphor for her female self: nurturing, kind, but wandering and insecure, in contrast to the more confident 'egotistical sublime' of her brother (Mellor, *Romanticism and Gender*, pp. 154–7 [Cxi]).

Romantic poetry contains several alluring and destructive females. They feature prominently in Coleridge's verse, including the 'Nightmare Life in Death' of his 'Rime of the Ancient Mariner', who, like Beatrice in Lewis's *The Monk* 'thicks man's blood with cold' (*Norton Anthology*, p. 435 [A]). The character is explored in a more complex and sophisticated way in *Christabel*, which features an ambiguously beautiful woman rescued by the young girl of the poem's title, who subsequently preys on her and takes over her mind, rather like a vampire. Coleridge's poem contains a scene in which Geraldine reveals her true nature to Christabel before the two women sleep together:

> Her silken robe and inner vest,
> Dropped to her feet, and full in view,
> Behold! Her bosom and half her side –
> A sight to dream of, not to tell.
>
> (ll. 250–3; *Norton Anthology*, p. 455 [A])

Feminist critics have also accused him of demonising female sexuality with such obvious hints of lesbianism. Geraldine's seduction of Christabel is a parody of the normative male and female romance, where the elder female adopts the role of the male seducer, rather than the preferred role for the period of nurturing wife and mother. A similar character appears in Keats's richly ambiguous poem of the serpent woman, *Lamia*. Lamia, a transformed snake, seduces and captures the youth she loves and together, away from the public gaze, they enjoy a sensual and loving idyll, only destroyed when Lycius's tutor, Apollonius, reveals her true nature, resulting in the death of both lovers. Keats's depiction of Lamia is remarkable for the sympathy accorded to her. In some ways she is the Keatsian ideal woman, a mixture of saint and whore. As a freshly transformed creature she is virgin, but she is also extremely knowledgeable of the arts of love:

> A virgin purest lipp'd, yet in the lore
> Of love deep learned to the red heart's core:
> Not one hour old, yet of sciential brain
> To unperplex bliss from its neighbour pain;
> Define their pettish limits, and estrange
> Their points of contact, and swift counterchange;
> Intrigue with the specious chaos, and dispart
> Its most ambiguous atoms with sure art;
> As though in Cupid's college she had spent
> Sweet days a lovely graduate, still unshent,
> And kept his rosy terms in idle languishment.

> (I.189–99; *Norton Anthology*, pp. 914–15 [A])

She is a 'virgin purest lipp'd' yet 'in the lore of love deep learned to the red heart's core'. Her double nature is important in the poem as a whole. Is she here nothing more than a male fantasy? It is also important to note that Lamia is not just a predator, but the answer to Lycius's prayers to Jove. He has been praying at Jove's sacrificial altar for love and Jove heard his vows, and 'better'd his desire'. He is not an unwilling victim.

Nationhood, Empire and the Orient

What we describe as the Romantic movement coincided with the beginnings of a modern British imperialism which involved the governance and exploitation of increasingly large portions of the globe as the nineteenth century wore on. It also involved conflict with other imperial formations of the time, some expansive and others in decline: European empires such as the French and Russian, and non-European empires such as the Turkish Ottoman and the Qing empire of China. Romantic writers were not themselves imperialists in the literal sense of the term, though some of them became implicated in the imperial process: Coleridge, for instance, acted as a civil servant for the Governor of Malta, Sir Alexander Ball, and Charles Lamb and Thomas Love Peacock both worked for the British East India Company. Many Romantic-period writers – the Wordsworths, Coleridge, De Quincey, and Jane Austen – had family who were involved in colonial trade or empire in one way or another, and it certainly impinged on their consciousness as a pressing fact of life. This was also the period in which, historians like Linda Colley argue, the idea of the British nation was 'forged' (in both senses of the word). Colley claims that Britishness was defined against the 'others' of Catholic religion and the French nation (*Britons* [Ciii]). We could widen this also to include the various other peoples, races and religions that the British encountered in their imperial history. The novels of Sir Walter Scott, for instance, depict the formation of the modern British state against a series of others, notably highland Scotland. Many of Scott's novels are about conflicts between opposing cultures: *Ivanhoe* (1819) is about war between Normans and Saxons and *The Talisman* (1825) is about conflict between Christians and Muslims. His novels about Scottish history deal with clashes between the new English culture and the older Scottish ways.

The extent to which Romantic writing was complicit with or critical of the processes of colonialism and empire is difficult to gauge. William Cowper attacked the rapaciousness and irresponsibility of colonial greed in his *The Task* of 1785:

> Doing good,
> Disinterested good, is not our trade.
> We travel far 'tis true, but not for nought.
>
> (I.673–5; Fairer and Gerrard, *Eighteenth-Century Poetry*, p. 503 [A])

The responsibility and accountability of the metropolitan government for the treatment of other cultures was becoming a cause of increasing concern and was an important issue in the trial of Warren Hastings for his administration of Bengal from 1786 onwards. The speeches of Edmund Burke, who prosecuted the case against Hastings, were among some of the manifestations of colonial guilt at the centre of British political life. Certainly there are many affirmations of the manifest destiny of Britons to civilise the world in Romantic writers. Wordsworth's *Excursion* (1814) contains the Wanderer's vision:

> So the wide wide waters, open to the power,
> The Will, the instincts, and appointed needs
> Of Britain, do invite her to cast off
> Her swarms, and in succession send them forth;
> Bound to establish new communities
> On every shore whose aspect favours hope
> Of bold adventure …
>
> Your Country must complete
> Her glorious destiny. Begin even now.
>
> (Wordsworth, *Excursion*, pp. 295, 299 [A])

The Wanderer predicts that the world will look to Britain for moral and cultural as well as political leadership, and that the country's imperial future will be glorious. Coleridge, in later life, similarly argued that 'Colonisation is not only a manifest expedient – but an imperative duty on Great Britain. God seems to hold out his finger to us over the sea.' Similarly, a political opponent of the Lake poets, Anna Laetitia Barbauld, argues for the identical linkage between colonisation, language and culture in *Eighteen Hundred and Eleven*:

> Wide spreads thy race from Ganges to the pole,
> O'er half the western world thy accents roll:
> … Thy stores of knowledge the new states shall know,
> And think thy thoughts, and with thy fancy glow;
> Thy Lockes, thy Paleys shall instruct their youth,
> Thy leading star direct their search for truth;
> Beneath the spreading Platan's tent-like shade,

Or by Missouri's rushing waters laid,
'Old father Thames' shall be the poet's theme,
Of Hagley's woods the enamoured virgin dream,
And Milton's tones the raptured ear enthral,
Mixt with the roar of Niagara's fall.

(ll. 81–96; Wu, *Romanticism*, p. 46 [A]).

Here Barbauld anticipates nineteenth-century British cultural imperialism, a process by which the colonised accept the hegemony of the culture of the coloniser. Certainly the Romantic canon of Shakespeare, Milton and Wordsworth did become a key part of the cultural imperialism of Britain's domination of nearly one-quarter of the terrestrial globe.

Robert Southey's Oriental epic *Thalaba* (1801) can be seen as an Orientalist text which uses the East to explore western concerns. The poem describes how its militant Muslim hero suppresses the older superstitious religions of his lands. His iconoclastic destruction of the satanic sorcerers of the Domdaniel Cave is a metaphor for Southey's militant Protestant abhorrence of Catholicism. Similarly, *The Curse of Kehama* (1810) details the Indian superstitions of the Hindus as an idolatry to be suppressed by a civilising Protestant form of colonialism. Byron also exploited the current fashion for the Oriental in his 'Turkish Tales'. He prided himself on the authenticity of these tales and the accuracy of their detail or costume. There is no doubt, however, that he understood the marketability of poetry on Oriental subjects. In a letter of 1813 to Thomas Moore he advised the Irish poet who would write the important Oriental romance, *Lalla Rookh* (1817), to 'stick to the East' as the 'only poetical policy'.

Byron was aware of what we might call the commodification of culture and of the market forces which drive the process. He was investing his cultural capital in an expanding market driven by imperial and colonial imperatives. His Tales were commercially extremely successful: *The Giaour* (1813) ran into thirteen editions and sold over 12,000 copies and *The Corsair* (1814) sold an

Orientalism

The Romantic Age has been described as the 'Oriental Renaissance' as the growing European fascination with, and discovery of, Eastern languages and literatures fuelled the interest of writers and their readers for Oriental subjects. *The Thousand and One Nights* (which became known as *The Arabian Nights*) were tales collected and translated by Antoine Galland into French from 1704 (and English translations appeared immediately). The *Nights* established a fascination with an East that was magical, paradisial, sensual, but also cruel and despotic; the abiding symbol for which was the harem or seraglio. This exoticised and often eroticised East easily became confused in the reader's mind with the actual East. Many Orientalist writers, such as Sir William Jones in his many translations as well as original compositions modelled on Hindu writing, regarded the East as a source of imaginative and creative renewal, a reading of the East we might find in Coleridge's 'Kubla Khan'. In recent years, however, what was once viewed as a sympathetic engagement with the East, or alternatively dismissed as escapism and exoticism, has come to be considered in a much more suspect, if not sinister light. Postcolonial critics such as Edward Said (*Orientalism* [Ciii]) have argued that Europeans use the East oppositionally to define their own self image as rational and modern. Orientalism was not simply a literary movement but is present in many art forms of the period, including music, theatre, visual art and architecture.

unprecedented 10,000 copies on the first day of its publication. The critical reception of the Tales was also, on the whole, favourable, with reviewers praising the accuracy and local colour of the poems. Postcolonial criticism, however, argues that Byron's construction of the East is simply that, a construction, a projection of the subject's desires and anxieties, though such critics differ as to the extent that this is complicit or resistant to the contemporary processes of empire which Byron

I N the eleventh year of the reign of Aurungzebe, Abdalla, King of the Lesser Bucharia, a lineal descendant from the Great Zingis, having abdi-

4.12 Thomas Moore's *Lalla Rookh* of 1817 was an extremely popular work of Romantic Orientalism. This illustration of the opening of the frame tale is taken from an Edwardian edition published in 1904.

opposed. Percy Shelley also exploited the East in a series of visionary poems and dramas, including *The Revolt of Islam* (1818), *Hellas* (1822), 'The Witch of Atlas' (1824), and *Prometheus Unbound* (1820) which stressed the redemptive aspects of Prometheus' soulmate, Asia. Like Sir William Jones and Coleridge, Shelley in such poems genders the East as female and represents it as a source of renewal, if not redemption; an alternative to a northern and increasingly puritanical Christianity, as represented in Southey's Oriental works. An important oriental sub-plot also features in Mary Shelley's *Frankenstein* (1818) and her prophetic novel *The Last Man* (1823) envisions the end of the world brought about by a plague from the East. The fascination and fear occasioned by the East, exploited by these writers, finds its culmination in Thomas De Quincey's powerful *Confessions of an English Opium Eater* (1821) which recounted the events of his life and his entanglement with the drug opium in sensational detail. The *Confessions* contain a series of Oriental opium nightmares complete with vengeful Asiatic deities and vicious crocodiles delivering cancerous kisses to their victims. De Quincey's obsession with the East as place of both desire and dread is often explained as a displacement of the anxieties of his own psychopathology.

Slavery and the Transatlantic Slave Trade

Many Romantic-period writers wrote against the transatlantic slave trade. Blake's 'The Little Black Boy' from his *Songs of Innocence* (*Norton Anthology*, p. 84 [A]), for instance, raises issues about the representation of slaves and the limits of the abolitionists' sympathy. His black boy accepts the hierarchies of colour which the poem's readership affirms despite their humanitarian feelings:

> My mother bore me in the southern wild,
> And I am black, but O! my soul is white;
> White as an angel is the English child,
> But I am black, as if bereav'd of light.

Blackness, rather than having any positive associations, is equated with bereavement in the traditional Christian semiotics of Evangelical abolitionist writing. The boy has imbibed this view of colour from his mother who ascribes their shared blackness to the action of the sun, a kind of degeneration from an original and untarnished white. The poem concludes with a vision of interracial fraternity round the 'tent of God' with the black boy shading the white English boy from the searing and coruscating radiance of God's love:

> I'll shade him from the heat till he can bear
> To lean in joy upon our father's knee.
> And then I'll stand and stroke his silver hair,
> And be like him, and he will then love me.

The boy has assimilated a Eurocentric view of the world, accepting the Christian notion of a white male father as God, whom he desires to resemble, to 'be like him' and be loved by him. Blake's poem represents a speaker in a state of innocence and the poem may function, as other poems in the series, as an ironic rebuttal of the hypocritical Christian Evangelicalism the poet so despised.

4.13 The first plate of Blake's illustrated poem 'The Little Black Boy' from his *Songs of Innocence and Experience* (1794).

Blake's illuminated poem, *Visions of the Daughters of Albion* (1793), made more explicit the connections between racial and gender oppression. Blake may here be elaborating on Mary Wollstonecraft's comments on the exclusion of race and gender from the eighteenth-century notion of the rational. In her *A Vindication of the Rights of Woman* (1792) she comments:

> Is sugar always to be produced by vital blood? Is one half of the human species, like the poor African slaves, to be subjected to prejudices that brutalize them, when principles would be a surer guard, only to sweeten the cup of man? Is this not indirectly to deny woman reason?

> (p. 235 [A])

Blake elaborates on the psychology of the colonialist Theotormon's mental impris-onment as well as on his oppression of both woman and African in the person of Oothoon, a victim of colonial and sexual violence. Oothoon is raped by the slave-driver Bromion to impregnate her and thus increase her market value. Theotormon represents the wavering opponent of slavery, disgusted by the practice but unable to extricate himself from the false ideology of the time into opposing the practice out-right. Certainly Bromion's boast encapsulates the slaver's desire for total ownership of the slave, with the physical and sexual domination symbolised by the branding of his name into their flesh:

> Thy soft American plains are mine, and mine thy north & south:
> Stampt with my signet are the swarthy children of the sun:
> They are obedient, they resist not, they obey the scourge:
> Their daughters worship terrors and obey the violent.
>
> (plate 1. ll. 20–3; *Norton Anthology*, p. 104 [A])

Wollstonecraft's equation between women and slavery was not shared by all, but it did indicate a female sensitivity to the slave trade. This was because the dictates of sensibility allowed women to be possessed of finer feelings and a more acute moral awareness than men, while debarring them from the public and political sphere. Anti-slavery, which was deemed a moral issue, was an area of public concern where women could legitimately express their feelings. Additionally, women were the primary pur-chasers and domestic managers of the produce of the slave trade, sugar. Women were certainly prominent in the boycott of sugar and other produce of slave labour during the popular campaign of 1792 and many wrote against it. Hannah More's celebrated poem *Slavery* of 1788 was a strong attack on the trade with its depiction of horrors such as the 'burning village', the separation of families, the resulting slave suicides and so on. Her argument against the trade is that it is unnatural to sell human beings:

> What wrongs, what injuries does Oppression plead,
> To smooth the horror of th' unnatural deed?
> What strange offence, what aggravated sin?
> They stand convicted of a darker skin!
> Barbarians, hold! Th' opprobrious commerce spare,
> Respect His sacred image which they bear.
> Though dark and savage, ignorant and blind,
> They claim the privilege of kind;
> Let malice strip them of each other plea,
> They still are men, and men should still be free.
>
> (ll. 131–40; Wu, *Women Romantic Poets*, p. 46 [A])

More's attack on the trade concedes so much to racial thinking that it damns the Africans to a state of savagery and benightedness, excluded from rationality; they, like animals, can feel but cannot think. Throughout, More develops the Christian semiotics of light and darkness to create a vision of Africa as lacking in light and civilisation. Ultimately, More places her faith in two things: Christianity and com-merce. The light of the Gospel will civilise the Africans, until then devoted to pagan superstition, and capitalist endeavour will convert their chattel status to that of

Olaudah Equiano and the Slave Narrative

The most important text about slavery in the period is one published by a former slave known, in his lifetime, as Gustavus Vassa, *The Interesting Narrative of the Life of Olaudah Equiano, or Gustavus Vassa, the African* (1789). Equiano's *Narrative* is, by far, the most sophisticated piece of writing by an eighteenth-century black British writer, and one of the most interesting of all autobiographies of the period. Equiano tells the story of his life as an Igbo villager (now Nigeria), kidnapped and sold into slavery by Africans from another village. Sold on to the coast, Equiano experiences the horrors of the Middle Passage, afterwards working as a slave on a plantation in Virginia. He is later sold to a lieutenant in the Royal navy, Michael Pascal, who renames him Gustavus Vassa. Equiano's narrative tells of his visits to Britain, his service in the Royal Navy during the Seven Years' War and his slavery in the West Indies, after which he purchases his freedom in 1746. In 1776, he takes part in Constantine Phipps's voyage to reach the North Pole, along with Midshipman Horatio Nelson. The *Narrative* is also a spiritual autobiography which charts Equiano's conversion to an Evangelical form of Christianity. The *Narrative* is the first by a black writer to be penned personally, rather than dictated. Although Equiano's biographer, Vincent Carretta, has recently questioned the authenticity of the earlier chapters of the narrative, presenting evidence that Equiano may have been born in South Carolina, the *Narrative* is a fascinating reconstruction of the hybrid subjectivity of a slave writing in a language not his own and expressing himself though the genre of Protestant spiritual autobiography. Equiano's narrative of his childhood depicts a society which is civilised and ordered, with its customs and rituals, a far cry from the dark savagery represented by More and other Evangelical writers. The 'slave narrative' was a special and popular form of autobiography. Several important life stories by former slaves were published in addition to Equiano's, including Ignatius Sancho's *Letters* (1782), Ottobah Cugoano's *Thoughts and Sentiments on the Evil and Wicked Commerce of the Human Species* (1787), John Jea's *The Life, History, and Unparalleled Sufferings of John Jea* (1815), Robert Wedderburn's *The Horrors of Slavery* (1824) and Mary Prince's *The History of Mary Prince, A West Indian Slave* (1831).

free labourers hired and fired at the whim of the market. More upholds the notion of colonialism as the white man's burden, bringing the light of the gospel to each benighted soul and making them free.

Readings

William Wordsworth, 'Lines Composed a Few Miles above Tintern Abbey, on Revisiting the Banks of the Wye during a Tour, July 13, 1798' (1798)

William Wordsworth's 'Tintern Abbey' (*Norton Anthology*, pp. 258–62 [A]), is one of the most celebrated and discussed poems of the Romantic period. It typifies what M. H. Abrams regarded as one of Romanticism's quintessential forms, the 'greater Romantic lyric', but also corresponds to an older and established kind of poem, the loco-descriptive or prospect poem. For more recent historically minded critics it has become the site of a fierce controversy between those who regard it as an exemplary poem about the relationship between the mind and nature, and those who see it as a deliberate attempt to evade the social and political realities of the time. To understand the poem and the controversies surrounding it we need to know something of its composition. By 1798 Wordsworth (then twenty-eight) was living with his sister Dorothy in Somerset, with Coleridge as a close neighbour. It is thought that around this time both Wordsworth and Coleridge began to lose their commitment to their shared radical beliefs and become more conservative in outlook. In 1801 they both were able to support the continuance of the war against France and, in later years, they both became supporters of the government. Their poetry stressed the restorative and beneficial powers of nature to heal and make well the divided mind. This concern with the powers and influence of nature and its interaction with the individual self came to be regarded as one of the hallmarks of what we call Romantic poetry, often defined in terms of its interest in nature, the self and the imagination.

In 1798 the two poets published a collection of verse entitled *Lyrical Ballads*, which contained the poem, 'Lines Composed a Few Miles above Tintern Abbey, on Revisiting the Banks of the Wye during a Tour, July 13, 1798'. Unlike many of the other poems in the volume, which concerned themselves with rural issues such as poverty and unemployment and which were written in a ballad form, 'Tintern Abbey' is a meditative poem in measured blank verse which deals with the inner life of the poet. The poem was written on a walking tour of the Wye Valley made by Wordsworth on 10–13 July 1798. The site was a common tourist stopping-off place, made famous by William Gilpin's picturesque guidebooks of the region. This was not the first time that Wordsworth had visited the area around the abbey. Five years earlier, in 1793, he had arrived at the spot during a period of mental turmoil. He had just returned from revolutionary France and become separated from his lover, Annette Vallon, by whom he fathered a daughter. Britain was then at war with

4.14 This illustration from William Gilpin's popular tour guide to the Wye Valley features the ruin of Tintern Abbey as a key picturesque site complete with vagrants in the foreground.

revolutionary France and Wordsworth felt alienated from his own country because of his sympathies for the Revolution, as well as depressed by the increasingly violent turn which the Revolution had taken. The poem is an intensely personal examination of Wordsworth's own inner thoughts (it is hard to separate speaker from poet in this case) and is concerned with the growth and development of his moral and imaginative self. The poem celebrates Wordsworth's rediscovery of the capacity to feel.

The poem begins in the present and refers to Wordsworth's first visit to Tintern Abbey in 1793: 'Five years have passed; five summers, with the length / Of five long winters!' (ll. 1–2). The first twenty lines or so suggest the tranquillity and harmony that the poet has now achieved in the present. The signs of human activity, the cottages, the pastoral farms, the orchards and the wreaths of smoke, all blend in with the landscape as human and natural activity coalesce and merge: 'Green to the very door' (l. 17). The opening few lines evoke a calm and meditative mood. Wordsworth now moves from the external landscape to describe his own inner state of consciousness. He describes what he has gained personally since his first visit to the Wye Valley. He has been able to carry the landscape he first saw in his mind and this has calmed and healed his psyche. The memory of the landscape first glimpsed in 1793 has brought him restoration in his 'hours of weariness'. This 'weariness' is associated, rather vaguely by the poet, with the materialism of city or urban life (ll. 23–30). More than this, Wordsworth claims that the memory of the landscape has led to a growth in his moral sense. It has made him a better man (ll. 30–5). He says that he has also attained a sense of spirituality from the vision he had of the Wye Valley those five years ago. He describes a state of heightened perception in which he is no longer aware of the physical and material forms of nature but is instead aware of an inner, spiritual force which permeates the natural world and exists within humanity as well. The experience comes through sense but transcends the senses; the physical eye is 'made quiet by the power / Of harmony'. At such moments, Wordsworth claims that we achieve spiritual insight and that we see 'into the life of things' (ll. 33–48); a 'blessed mood' in which we lose our sense of self and become aware of a transcendent sense of unity, and of ourselves as a part of that unity. Thus Wordsworth claims he has gained three things since his first visit to the Wye Valley: the soothing influence that the landscape has had on his mind, making him feel less stressed and alienated; his moral sense has been increased almost unconsciously; and he has received the gift of spirituality. The experience of the landscape has been absorbed into the mind and contemplated upon over a period of years, what Wordsworth referred to as 'recollection in tranquility' in the 'Preface' to *Lyrical Ballads*.

The poem now moves back in time by five years. Wordsworth remembers how, in July 1793, he had visited the Wye Valley. He remembers his state of mental anguish, describing himself as behaving 'more like a man / Flying from something that he dreads' than someone seeking 'the thing he loved' (ll. 70–1). His attitude to nature has changed from the days of his childhood when the forms of nature are an appetite, something desired and consumed without thinking; an animal passion (ll. 76–80). He is here dimly aware of another presence in nature than that of himself, but not aware of what it is. We thus move in nature from the thoughtless enjoyment of nature in childhood to the consciousness of the reality of nature's presence in adulthood. Since 1793 he claims to now look on nature with a consciousness of the problems and troubles of the world: 'The still, sad music of humanity' (l. 91). Such problems (which include the social and political) are aestheticised as timeless and ever recurring. Wordsworth argues that we move from a childlike and unthinking joy in our relationship with nature to a state where we become aware of the ties we have to other people, and from that state to a mystical awareness of the sense of the divine presence in nature. This inevitably means the loss of the child's vision of the unity of man and nature. Nevertheless, he claims that he has been recompensed for this loss of that original paradisial state by a sense of the visionary intensity he occasionally experiences when contemplating the natural landscape:

> A presence that disturbs me with the joy
> Of elevated thoughts; a sense sublime
> Of something far more deeply interfused,
> Whose dwelling is the light of setting suns,
> And the round ocean and the living air,
> And the blue sky, and in the mind of man:
> A motion and a spirit, that impels
> All thinking things, all objects of all thought,
> And rolls through all things.
>
> (ll. 94–101)

Wordsworth describes a sublime moment of vision, of the interaction between the outer world of the landscape and the inner world of the poet: the subjective poet and the objective world of nature. It is an interpenetration of man and nature achieved through sense perception. It is by perceiving 'the light of setting suns', 'the round ocean' and the 'blue sky' that we gain an impression of the spiritual, glimpsing the divine through natural objects. The spiritual is imaged as a motion, a movement and a power, something active. By a deliberate syntactic ambiguity the motion and the spirit is made to belong to both the external world and to the 'mind of man'. The poem takes the two worlds, the inner and the outer, at the point of their intersection. Wordsworth is claiming that it is such moments as these, moments of visionary intensity when we see into the 'life of things', which have restored him to sanity and balance. Love of nature thus leads to love of man, it reconciles us to humanity. Nature is described as 'the anchor of his purest thoughts' and the 'nurse, guide and guardian of his moral being' (ll. 109–10). Wordsworth is restored as a person, mentally, morally and socially, by the power of nature.

The final verse paragraph of the poem returns us to 1798, when the poem was written, and looks forward to the future. The poet imagines his sister Dorothy, who accompanied him on his second visit to the Wye Valley, as a kind of 'second self' for the poet. We return to the details of the landscape that are described in the first few lines, to the external scene it began with: 'the green pastoral landscape', the 'steep woods', the 'lofty cliffs' (ll. 157–8), which echo the opening description. The poem ends where it began, a unified and circular journey in time from the present to the past, then into the future and back to the present.

This is the scope of the poem. Wordsworth argues that the human self is essentially unified, unified over time by the power of memory. It is through communion with nature that this self is developed, made better, and perfected. This is a message Wordsworth puts into his poetry and passes on to his readership. Up until recently this is very much how the poem has been interpreted. In the 1980s, however, a number of critics opposed this reading of the poem and attempted to demonstrate how the poetry tries to present an 'ideology' or system of ideas, which is conservative and oppressive. The new historicist critic Jerome McGann argued that 'the scholarship and criticism of Romanticism and its works are dominated by a Romantic Ideology, by an uncritical absorption in Romanticism's own self-representations' (McGann, *Romantic Ideology*, p. 1 [Ci]). He claimed that a poem like 'Tintern Abbey' fabricates a false view of the life of the time by presenting an idealistic image of society, which serves the interests of the then ruling classes and helps to maintain the status quo. Wordsworth is, according to McGann, claiming that problems such as human suffering and poverty, 'the still sad music of humanity', are evaded or displaced into the realm of the aesthetic, or the world of imagination. Rather than trying to improve things socially and politically, the solution to all our problems is imaginative and not political. The strongest criticism of 'Tintern Abbey' as an act of deliberate bad faith, however, was made by Marjorie Levinson, who pointed out that although 'Tintern Abbey' features in the title, the abbey itself is not described and is absent from the poem (Levinson, *Wordsworth's Great Period Poems*, pp. 14–57 [Ci]). Why, she asks, would a poet draw attention to the famous ruin and then ignore it? Possibly because the abbey was ruined in the time of Henry VIII when the monarch took over its lands during the Reformation, when England broke away from the Church of Rome, an intrusion of the political and historical into the poem Wordsworth might wish to avoid. The abbey in Wordsworth's day was not in fact a picturesque and pleasing prospect. William Gilpin, describing the scene in his influential picturesque travel book, *Observations on the River Wye* (1782), noted that 'the poverty and wretchedness of the inhabitants were remarkable. They occupy little huts, raised among the ruins of the monastery, and seem to have no employment but begging; as if a place once devoted to indolence could never again become the seat of industry.' Wordsworth's poem avoids mentioning the beggars. Instead, he dwells on the 'wreathes of smoke' (l. 17) seen from a distance which might 'seem' to come from the fires of 'vagrant dwellers in the houseless woods, / Or of some Hermit's cave' (ll. 20–1). Wordsworth poeticises the facts of poverty. More than this the Wye Valley itself was not simply the beautiful and unspoilt landscape which the poet claimed to encounter but a busy industrial scene. Gilpin comments that within 'half a mile of it are carried on great iron-works; which introduce noise and bustle into these regions of tranquillity' and that the Wye becomes 'ouzy, and discoloured' with 'sludgy shores'. The industrial furnaces on the banks of the Wye consumed charcoal, sending up wreaths of smoke, and the river itself was full of shipping, carrying coal and timber from the Forest of Dean.

Levinson believes that Wordsworth has deliberately excluded these signs of poverty and wretchedness and of the great industrial activity going on a mere half a mile away down river, which is soiling and polluting the river, because it would ruin his idealistic picture of a mind experiencing harmony with nature. She argues that Wordsworth has falsified the scene he describes in an attempt to exclude all those historical and industrial things which would destroy the pastoral effect he is trying to create: 'We are bound to see that Wordsworth's pastoral prospect is a fragile affair, artfully assembled by acts of exclusion' (p. 32). His poem is thus ideological; it displaces all the problems and difficulties of an agricultural society in the early throes of industrialisation into the realm of the artistic and imaginative. It is an act of 'false consciousness' which functions to maintain the present system of society by directing people's discontent not into the area of the political but into the realm of the transcendent and the natural. The poem draws attention to that which is excluded from the poem: to absences and evasions. It is a more interesting poem to her because of those very exclusions.

Jane Austen, *Sense and Sensibility* (1811)

Regarded by many as the most significant novelist of the Romantic period, Jane Austen bears a complicated relationship with the literature of the time. In many ways her literary models and enthusiasms were the writers of the eighteenth century, with whom she has much in common, rather than the new forms of Romanticism, with its privileging of emotionalism, freedom from restraint and wild and solitary landscapes; however, in more recent years her work has been more firmly located in the ideas and debates of the time. *Sense and Sensibility* (Austen [A]) was projected as an epistolary novel, entitled *Elinor and Marianne*, in 1795, at the height of the debates about sensibility and its relationship to politically radical ideas. The 1790s were the period when the 'Jacobin' novel of ideas was current and, from 1793 onwards, the beginnings of the anti-Jacobin backlash in Britain were evident. Austen worked on the novel but did not publish it until 1811 as *Sense and Sensibility*, when debates about sensibility had become rather dated. In the 1790s the topic was certainly in the public consciousness. Mary Wollstonecraft's *A Vindication of the Rights of Woman* (1792) had caused a political sensation because of its author's attitude to the status of women. Her opponent Richard Polwhele had referred to her as 'a hyena in petticoats' and an 'unsex'd female'. Wollstonecraft's own life was itself sensational, with her tempestuous affair with the adventurer Gilbert Imlay (whose daughter she bore), her obsession with the painter Fuseli, and her subsequent attempted suicide, all unwisely revealed in her husband William Godwin's *Memoirs* of her life of 1798. Wollstonecraft's novel *Maria, or the Wrongs of Woman* (1798) added to her notoriety by courageously discussing the issue of female desire. Austen's Marianne Dashwood shares many of Wollstonecraft's ideas and attitudes and it is very tempting to conclude that elements of her character are, to some extent, based on that of Wollstonecraft.

The novel takes the very familiar plot-line of the parallel, but contrasted, lives and temperaments of two sisters, Elinor and Marianne Dashwood, who, at first glance, seem to embody the opposing qualities of reason and emotionalism or sensibility. In fact, the characterisation of the sisters is much more complex than this suggests, and both sisters demonstrate mixed and contrary qualities in their behaviour. Austen, however, privileges Elinor by making the narrative of the novel correspond to her consciousness. By a technique known as 'free indirect speech', Austen presents much of the action of the novel from Elinor's perspective, sharing Elinor's thoughts and feelings with the reader. The two leading men in the novel, the dashingly handsome John Willoughby and the shy and dutiful Edward Ferrars, who court Marianne and Elinor respectively, are also similarly contrasted in terms of their behaviour. Nevertheless, the novel is a satire on the fashionable sensibility of the 1790s, as well as a warning about the dangers it could pose if taken too far. As we have seen, by the 1790s sensibility had become radicalised and identified with the democratic politics of the French Revolution and those who supported it in Britain, the 'English Jacobins'. By looking at certain key themes in the novel we can better see how it relates to the context in which it was produced.

The Romantic period has been characterised as one where nature is given a new sense of importance and becomes a key subject for art. Austen also is a writer who deals with nature, but rather than the sublime natural environment of the Lakes or the Swiss Alps, it tends to be the managed English country estate or park that

4.15 An illustrated title page of an 1833 edition of Austen's *Sense and Sensibility* showing two contrasting scenes from the novel involving Elinor and Marianne.

excites her. Austen is also interested not in the details of nature but the person's response to it. Marianne is identified with an emotional and sentimental view of the natural world, which was one of the hallmarks of sensibility. A preference for the natural over the artificial also indicates a political preference for primitive and unspoilt humanity, which the philosopher Rousseau had argued is tarnished by society. This issue was very much a part of the debate about the French Revolution, with the English Jacobins, like Paine and Wollstonecraft, arguing for the natural goodness and benevolence of humanity and its oppression by government and society, while conservatives, like Burke, argued that humanity is naturally fallen and that government is needed to improve and civilise it.

Marianne is very much the heroine of sensibility. She is individualistic, emotional, impatient, rude, indiscreet, passionate, indulgent and enthusiastic. Like her lover Willoughby, she prefers the natural and unadorned to the formal and restrained. When leaving the family home of Norland, Marianne expresses her feelings in an open and excessive way, '"And you, ye well-known trees! ... No; you will continue the same; unconscious of the pleasure or the regret you occasion, and insensible of any change in those who walk under your shade! – But who will remain to enjoy you?"' (p. 29). Later in the novel, after Willoughby's desertion of her, Marianne expresses her melancholy in remembering the autumns at Norland, reminding Elinor of her emotional delight at the falling of the autumn leaves there, '"How have I delighted, as I walked, to see them driven in showers about me by the wind! ... Now there is no one to regard them."' To which she receives a somewhat tart response: '"It is not everyone', said Elinor, 'who has your passion for dead leaves"' (p. 87). The debate about landscape is epitomised in an exchange between Marianne and Edward. Marianne argues that landscape must be experienced personally and that one should respond to it intuitively, arguing that the 'admiration of landscape' has become formulaic and a matter of fashion and 'jargon': 'Everybody pretends to feel and tries to describe with the taste and elegance of him who first defined what picturesque beauty was.' Edward's appreciation of landscape, however, is anti-picturesque:

> I call it a very fine country – the hills are steep, the woods seem full of fine timber, and the valley looks comfortable and snug – with rich meadows and several neat farmhouses scattered here and there. It exactly answers my idea of a fine country, because it unites beauty with utility – and I dare say it is a picturesque one too, because you admire it; I can easily believe it to be full of rocks and promontories, grey moss and brush-wood, but these are all lost on me – I know nothing of the picturesque.
>
> (p. 95)

Edward's notion of a 'fine country' is based on the use to which that country is put; he prefers the prospect of a well-managed and peopled landscape, with farms and labourers, rejecting picturesque notions of beauty derived from ruins and poverty. His vision here is a social one rather than the individual and emotional response called for by Marianne, for whom the picturesque itself has become too formulaic. Marianne's preference for picturesque wildness is also dangerous. It is on one of her 'delightful twilight walks', when she strays to the wilder parts of the estate, where the 'trees were the oldest, and the grass was the longest and wettest', that she contracts a serious fever (p. 286).

Sensibility, while it stressed spontaneity and emotion, was also a very literary fashion, and an appreciation of literature was a required accomplishment for its adherents. Marianne, who is an admirer of Cowper and Scott, compares Edward unfavourably to Willoughby for the lack of emotion he displays when reading. She tells Elinor it would have broken her heart to hear her lover 'read with so little sensibility' (pp. 19–20). She argues that an utter identity of feelings must subsist between two lovers. Willoughby, it appears, has views and tastes exactly similar to Marianne's: 'The same books, the same passages were idolized by each' (p. 49). Despite her stress on spontaneity, Marianne has learnt much of her sensibility from books, a paradox which remained at the heart of the fashion. The performative nature of sensibility is humorously demonstrated in Austen's depiction of Marianne's reaction to Willoughby's initial desertion of her. Marianne is clearly performing a role; the sleeplessness, the weeping and the sighing are all part of a convention of behaviour she must follow. Her doleful playing of Willoughby's favourite songs and her reading of their favourite books is described as the 'indulgence of feeling' undertaken until 'her heart was so heavy that no further sadness could be gained'. This is a 'nourishment of grief' and a courting of 'misery'. Marianne is, however, basically good-natured and good-humoured and unable to support such 'violence of affliction' which lapses into a 'calmer melancholy' (pp. 83–4). This comic scene contrasts with Marianne's genuine and serious illness later in the novel, brought on by the realisation of Willoughby's callous, final betrayal and her subsequent mental anguish.

Marianne believes that first impressions are more likely to be true than second thoughts, as such impressions are spontaneous and therefore derive from our innate moral sense. She argues that there could be nothing improper about what she has done, for if there had been, she would have known so at the time: 'we always know when we are acting wrong, and with such a conviction I could have had no pleasure' (p. 69). Similarly, Marianne, at the beginning of the novel, does not accept the possibility of 'second attachments' in love. For Elinor what is worrying about her views is the 'unfortunate tendency of setting propriety at nought' (p. 57). What is ethically dangerous for Austen in Marianne's behaviour is that she stresses the individual over the communal and social and this has potentially tragic consequences. Furthermore, because sensibility is a performed role, as Hannah More put it: 'these fair marks, reluctant I relate, / These lovely symbols may be counterfeit' ('Sensibility', ll. 275–6; Wu, *Romanticism*, pp. 29–30 [A]). While Marianne may be sincere in her expressions of feeling, others may not, and the role of the man of sensibility is easy to fake by unscrupulous libertines. John Willoughby acts this part with superb accomplishment. He is immensely attractive, alluring and charismatic, especially in contrast to the shy and despondent Edward and the thoughtful and reflective Colonel Brandon. He makes his initial heroic appearance rescuing Marianne when she twists her ankle unwisely racing down a hill. The impression he makes on everyone is immediate: he speaks 'in a manner so frank and so graceful, that his person, which was uncommonly handsome, received additional charms from his voice and expression' (p. 44) and is 'exactly formed to engage Marianne's heart' (p. 50). He is, unlike Edward, an excellent reader. Beneath his charm, however, he conceals a callous and selfish nature. He has already abandoned and ruined one girl, the pregnant Eliza Williams, and when his financial irresponsibility leads him to court and marry an heiress he cruelly deserts Marianne. Willoughby is no one-dimensional villain and even Elinor is in danger of succumbing to his charms during his final visit. Her judgement, however, is that his education and upbringing had been flawed with 'too early an independence and his consequent habits of idleness, dissipation, and luxury' had served to make him 'cold-hearted and selfish' (p. 308).

If Marianne represents the dangers to which an attachment to the principles of sensibility may lead, Elinor rather demonstrates the importance of restraint and reflection. Elinor is aware of the dangers of excessive emotion and the improprieties it might lead to in a society where women who transgress norms of behaviour, however hypocritical, can be ruined. Hers is the central role, not least because much of the reader's understanding of the events of the novel comes mediated by her perspective. Elinor, in contrast to Marianne, possesses 'a strength of understanding, and coolness of judgment'. She is not emotionless but is possessed of an 'excellent heart', and her 'feelings were strong; but she knew how to govern them' (p. 8). Elinor values the order and support of social conventions and knows the importance of abiding by them. Unlike her sister, she understands the necessity of 'telling lies when politeness required it' (p. 118). For much of the novel (a period of four months) Elinor experiences the same inner turmoil as Marianne because the man she loves is bound to another, a deceitful and devious woman, Lucy Steele, who takes cruel delight in psychologically torturing her with details of their engagement in the full knowledge of her feelings. The contrast between her silent suffering and Marianne's indulgence is marked. The strength of Elinor's emotions is shown in the key scene in which she breaks down and confesses her secret grief to her sister: 'Her narration was clear and simple; and though it could not be given without emotion, it was not accompanied by violent agitation, nor impetuous grief. – *That* belonged to the hearer, for Marianne listened with horror, and cried excessively' (pp. 244–5).

The novel closes with the double marriage of Elinor and Edward and Marianne and Colonel Brandon, the man she had previously rejected as too old and too dull for her. Many readers find the romance between Marianne and Brandon hard to swallow, and the humiliation of Marianne a little hard to take: 'She was born to discover the falsehood of her own opinions, and to counteract, by her conduct, her most favourite maxims' (p. 352). The strength of Marianne's humbling may reflect the very real dangers that Austen perceives sensibility might incur, a fashion which is not simply the silly affectation of a seventeen-year-old girl but a philosophy, which, for many, challenged the very basis of British government and society in a revolutionary decade. To see Austen's novel in the context of the times in which it was written is, then, to appreciate its author as a woman seriously engaged with her social and cultural context and to understand that her art conceals a wealth of political significance, accessed by indirection and allusion rather than overt commitment and enthusiasms. *Sense and Sensibility* is clearly a novel fully connected to the times which formed its author's mind.

Lord Byron, *The Giaour* (1813)

The most notable exponent of the Oriental tale in the Romantic period was Lord Byron, a major practitioner of the form of the Romantic verse narrative. Byron's 'Turkish Tales' were extremely popular. They described exotic lands and featured glowering and tormented Byronic heroes and the glamorous objects of their loves. It was a winning formula, irresistible because of the persona of the poet who penned them and the readers' knowledge that he had travelled in the lands he described. In 1809–11, Byron had undertaken a tour of the Eastern Mediterranean, visiting Greece and the Ottoman (Turkish) capital of Constantinople. As well as witnessing sublime natural scenery, he also encountered mosques, palaces, towers, coffee houses, slave markets and bazaars. The territory though which he travelled was then part of the declining but still powerful Ottoman empire. In British liberal circles there was a strong sympathy for the plight of the Greek nation with its past glories, a sympathy shared by Byron who later lost his life in its struggle for national independence in 1824. The territory was a much-contested one; it marked the boundary between European Christendom and Islam. The first of Byron's Eastern Tales, *The Giaour* (Byron [A]), has been variously interpreted as a poem about the clash of world-views between Muslim and Christian and their struggle over the contested territory of Greece.

The Giaour is narrated not in a simple linear narrative but through a series of disjointed fragments told from differing points of view, although these points of view may be unified if the poem is seen as analogous to the performance of a coffee-house storyteller, as Byron indicated it might. It tells the tale of the flight of the Giaour, or 'Infidel', from the court of a Turkish despot, Hassan. The Giaour has had an adulterous affair with a slave of Hassan's harem, a beautiful woman called Leila. Hassan has Leila sewn into a sack and drowned, a traditional Turkish punishment for infidelity and one that Byron claimed to have witnessed and prevented during his travels. The Giaour takes his revenge by ambushing and killing Hassan, but he gains no peace from this act, suffering anguish and torment afterwards. Retreating to a monastery, he remains an alienated and isolated figure haunted by visions of Hassan's severed hand, and unable to accept absolution of his guilt, despite the actions of a concerned and kindly friar.

Like Byron's other Turkish Tales, *The Giaour* exploits the taste for exotic landscape and local colour. Details of the mosques, religious festivals ('the Bairam's feasts begun') and culturally specific language ('high *jerreed*', 'silversheaved ataghan', 'the jewel of Giamschid') (ll. 229, 251, 355, 479) are present to heighten the authenticity of the tale. This is a land of fakirs and dervishes, harems and festivals, where people appeal to Allah and to genies; all these details place the reader in an unfamiliar world, one where the poet is our guide. Byron's extensive notes to the poem serve to reinforce his authority as someone who has travelled and studied in the area. The Greek islands, 'Edens of the eastern wave' (l.15), where the poem is set, are presented as a place of past glory rather than of present importance (ll. 103–7). Quickly Byron establishes the tale within a temporal frame in which modern Greece is degraded in favour of a classical past; a privileging of the Hellenic and neo-classical emphasising a Eurocentric notion of civilisation deriving from ancient Greece. The tale is framed by the hostility between the differing religions, epitomised in the poem's title. When the Muslim fisherman who narrates a part of the poem witnesses the Giaour for the first time he expresses his vision in terms of visceral hatred and disgust: 'I know thee not, I loathe thy race' (ll. 191, 198–9). The young Venetian, with 'his Christian crest and haughty mien' (l. 256) is clearly identified by his religious and ethnic status. It is easy to read the poem in terms of the Orientalist stereotyping which Edward Said accused the West of indulging. Hassan is presented as a typical Oriental despot presiding with jealous pride over his harem (l. 439); he is a local chieftain who is violent, proud and vindictive, demonstrating an Eastern excess of passion, often viewed as the preserve of the inhabitants of this feminised East. Betrayed, as he sees it, by his slave, Leila, he has little compunction in carrying out the terrible punishment according to his laws and customs: an event that is obliquely represented in lines 352–87 of the poem. This event is put in the context of an alleged Islamic misogyny which believes 'that woman is but dust, / A soulless toy for tyrant's lust' (ll. 487–90). Byron's note to these lines informs us that the belief that women have no souls is a 'vulgar error' and a misreading of the Koran but, nevertheless, one he claims is held by many Muslims of his time. Leila is seen as a 'faithless slave' but the worst aspect of her crime for Hassan's people is that she deserts him for 'a Giaour' (l. 535). Hassan's fury and violence is seen as a trait of his religion,

> ... as true an Osmanlie
> As e'er at Mecca bent the knee;
> As ever scorn'd forbidden wine,
> Or pray'd with face towards the shrine ...
> Who falls in battle 'gainst a Giaour,
> Is worthiest an immortal bower.
>
> (ll. 729–32, 745–6)

In contrast to Hassan, the Giaour plays a chivalric role, and though he fails to rescue Leila, he exacts a murderous vengeance for the crime. He is also conflicted and flawed. Unlike Hassan, he is not a participant in any extensive social network. After his death the loss of Hassan is deeply and poignantly mourned by his mother; he receives an honourable funeral and the community of which he was the head subsequently disintegrates: 'For Courtesy and Pity died / With Hassan on the mountain side' (ll. 288–351). The Giaour is from the start an alienated and solitary Byronic figure. He is pictured with an 'evil eye', and resembling 'a demon of the night', tortured by his memories of the death of Leila and his killing of Hassan, his mind brooding over these 'guilty woes ... like the Scorpion girt by fire' (ll.196, 422–3). The Giaour's own Christian faith is problematic: for the Muslim fisherman, he is doubly damned as an 'Apostate from his own vile faith' (l. 616). The second half of the poem from line 787 onwards is taken up with the Giaour's retirement to a monastery and his subsequent inner torment. Haunted by mental visitations of Leila and Hassan's severed hand, he finds no peace in the comforts of conventional religion. To the monks he is an outcast and pariah figure, 'some stray renegade,

/ Repentant of the change he made' (l. 812; 802–7). The Giaour's moral frame of reference is unstable. He actually believes the Friar will absolve him from the deed of murder because the man he killed was hostile to Christianity (ll. 1038–9). More than this, he effaces any moral superiority he may have over Hassan by making himself hypothetically as guilty as the Turk:

> Yet did he but what I had done
> Had she been false to more than one;
> Faithless to him – he gave the blow,
> But true to me – I laid him low.

(ll. 1062–5)

The Giaour is certainly a hybrid or mixed character, one who is capable of culturally cross-dressing and ambushing Hassan's party 'in Arnaut garb' (l. 615). He is alienated from both Christendom and Islam, caught somewhere in between the two in the 'contact zone' of the Levant. Whether the Giaour's ability to pass in both cultures reflects a cosmopolitan ideal or is simply an aspect of a homogenising Orientalist impulse is a key question. The ability to culturally cross-dress is not always a liberating thing. It is something the Western imagination usually reserves for Europeans who may impersonate the culture of the other with some skill, yet also, at the same time, despise the other (the explorer Richard Burton was able to dress and speak as an Arab and undertake the Hajh, or pilgrimage to Mecca, and at the same time maintain his strong sense of ethnic superiority). That this skill is seldom, if ever, vouchsafed to those of the other cultures, privileges a Eurocentric perspective.

The triangular relationship between the Giaour, Hassan and Leila is highly significant for those who see the poem in postcolonial terms. At the heart of the poem is a struggle between two men for a woman. In some ways Leila is simply an absent counter in this struggle, opening the poem to readings in which the homosocial and the homoerotic predominate. The Giaour is certainly as

4.16 'A Turkish Female Slave' by John Cam Hobhouse, who accompanied Byron on his tour of Greece and the Levant in 1811. This illustration from his published account of his travels gives some impression of how Hassan's Leila might have looked.

much obsessed by his hatred for Hassan as his love for Leila, 'The maid I love – the man I hate' (l. 1018). Certainly the Levant was for Byron a place where he could more easily indulge in the homosexual liaisons which were an important facet of his complicated sexual identity. It was also a place where, in his Eastern tragedy about an effeminate ruler *Sardanapalus* and the Turkish cantos of *Don Juan*, he could explore role reversals and cross-gender and cultural identities.

The role of the silent and absent Leila in the poem is fascinating. Leila is a slave in Hassan's harem, the harem being a place of imagined sexual pleasures and tyrannies which obsessed European travellers and readers. She is 'Circassia's daughter' (l. 505), originating from the Crimea, a place reputed by travellers and natural historians in the period to be the source of the most beautiful of the human races, the prize acquisitions of the harem. Leila is imaged as the 'Kashmeer butterfly', a 'lovely toy so fiercely sought', the passive victim chased and destroyed, 'with wounded wing, or bleeding breast' (ll. 388–421). Certainly she is accorded no voice or real presence in the poem. Postcolonial critic Gayatri Spivak has famously characterised British representations of the Indian Hindu rite of Sati prior to its formal abolition in 1829, as 'white men … saving brown women from brown men' (Spivak, 'Can the Subaltern Speak?', p. 271 [Ciii]). She argues that the voice of the woman is lost in this debate between men. Others have seen Leila as a synecdoche for the contested Greek nation, both of which are imaged as beautiful corpses in the poem. While this does make schematic sense, the racial origin of Leila, as European rather than Eastern, creates ambiguity. While Orientalist and postcolonial critics see the poem as involved in the stereotyping of Eastern cultures necessary to establish a Western sense of superiority and political dominance, others can point to the ambiguities, contradictions and paradoxes in this rather bleak fable in which East and West collide and which provides no obviously normative standpoint from which to judge the actors in its tragedy.

Mary Shelley, *Frankenstein or the Modern Prometheus* (1818; Revised 1831)

Mary Shelley's *Frankenstein* was first published anonymously in 1818 and revised for its third edition in 1831. Shelley added an important 'Introduction' which influenced the reader in how to read her story, as well as a number of significant textual changes. This reading uses the 1831 edition as text (Shelley, *Frankenstein* [A]). The novel clearly belongs to the Gothic genre of writing, although it has certain key features of its own. It eschews the medievalism of Walpole's *Castle of Otranto* and Lewis's *Monk* for a nearly contemporary setting some time in the 1790s, and is concerned with recent developments in scientific thought, as well as contemporary exploration and discovery. *Frankenstein* is not concerned with the supernatural but with the future possibilities of current ideas, so much so that many claim it as an early work of science fiction. It is also a novel which contains sensational events and excessive emotion; on its first publication it was assumed by many that the author must be male. *Frankenstein* avoids much of the cliché of Gothic writing, dealing with serious issues, such as education, environment, crime and responsibility. Contemporary reviewers identified the novel as belonging to the school of Godwin (to whom it was dedicated), and it shows many similarities with William Godwin's adaptation of Gothic as a novel of ideas. Godwin was Mary Shelley's father and Mary Wollstonecraft was her mother. She was the product of these two notable revolutionary thinkers. She had a modern education, brought up by her father on Wollstonecraft's programme of a rational female education. In 1814, she met the unconventional young poet Percy Shelley who was estranged from his wife, and by whom she then had two children (both of whom died soon after birth). Percy and Mary were married in 1816 following the suicide of Percy's first wife. It was during the couple's visit to Byron's rented Villa Diodati on the shores of Lake Geneva in 1816 that the ideas for the novel took shape after those present agreed to try their hand at each writing a tale of terror.

Frankenstein has an unusual narrative structure, in that the novel is composed of several embedded narratives (rather like concentric circles) and we have no omniscient narrator to provide an obvious scheme of moral values against which to judge the extraordinary events of the novel; hence the reader is left in a place of moral uncertainty, and has to exercise her or his own judgement. Most encounter the novel in modern texts based on the 1831 Standard Novels edition (though the 1818 text is increasingly popular) and begin reading with the author's 'Introduction'. This was written some twelve years after the composition of the novel and eight years after Percy Shelley's tragic drowning. Shelley was earning a living from her writing as well as trying not to alienate her very conservative and hostile father-in-law, Sir Timothy Shelley. Her 'Introduction', as many have pointed out, contains several inaccuracies or misrememberings. She claims that her main intentions in writing the novel were to 'speak to the mysterious fears of our nature, and awaken thrilling horror', and to 'curdle the blood, and quicken the beatings of the heart' (pp. 7–8), deflecting the reader from some of the more serious questionings of the anonymously published 1818 text. She places the novel in a very clear moral framework, describing 'the pale student of unhallowed arts kneeling beside the thing he had put together', mocking 'the stupendous mechanism of the Creator of the world' (p. 9). Readers, at the outset, should be wary of Shelley's attempt to provide a later and conventionally moral framework in which to read the novel as being about a man 'playing God', an interpretation far more suited to the various stage and cinematic adaptations than to the original text.

The reader next encounters the reprint of the 1818 'Preface' written anonymously by Percy Shelley. He, conversely, places the novel in the context of contemporary natural philosophy. He claims that the novel is not 'merely weaving supernatural terrors' and is exempt from 'the disadvantages of a mere tale of spectres or enchantment' (p. 11), identifying its chief purpose as not the condemnation of a man playing God, but 'the exhibition of the amiableness of domestic affections, and the excellence of human virtue' (p. 12). This would seem to imply that Victor Frankenstein's crimes, if such they are, are committed against society and family, rather than God, and that human virtue, however twisted by social forms, is, as the Godwinian reformers would have it, 'universal'. The reader next encounters the outermost framing narrative of

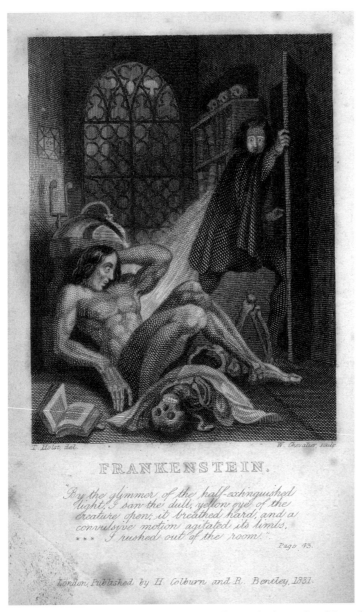

FRANKENSTEIN.

"By the glimmer of the half-extinguished light, I saw the dull, yellow eye of the creature open; it breathed hard, and a convulsive motion agitated its limbs.
⁂ I rushed out of the room."

Page 43.

London, Published by H. Colburn and R. Bentley, 1831.

4.17 Frontispiece and title page to the English Standard Novels edition of *Frankenstein* (1831). The representation of the Creature on the left of the page is the only one authorised by Mary Shelley in her own lifetime.

the story. Captain Robert Walton writes four letters to his sister, Margaret Walton Saville (who shares the same initials as Mary Wollstonecraft Shelley), concerning his departure from the family circle to undertake a voyage of exploration to the North Pole, in the double quest for the 'wondrous powers which attract the needle' (p. 15) and the passage across the top of the globe to the Pacific Ocean. Walton feels isolated and alienated, desiring the 'company of a man who would sympathise with me' (p. 19).

In his fourth letter, Walton describes his imprisonment by the ice and the sighting of two figures, the second of which is the dying Victor Frankenstein engaged in a self-destructive pursuit of the being he has created and animated.

The first ten chapters of the novel proper are Victor's first-person account of his childhood, his education and the creation of the monstrous being he now pursues. The next six chapters contain Victor's account of his Creature's narrative, which tells of its abandonment and the adventures it has experienced since its 'birth'. The Creature claims to have been born benevolent and sympathetic, but has become violent, criminal and aggressive as a result of his treatment by society (rather as Rousseau claimed for humanity as a whole). The Creature describes how, in a fit of rage, he murdered Victor's brother, the child William, and pleads with Victor to create a mate for him. The following seven chapters return the reader to Frankenstein's main narrative telling how he fails in this promise to create a female mate, of the Creature's revengeful murder of his wife Elizabeth on their wedding night, and the subsequent pursuit to the Arctic. The novel closes with Walton's account of Victor's death, the remorse of the Creature and his desire to journey to the Pole to destroy himself on a funeral pyre. When the ice does break Walton abandons his quest and returns home to his sister and the comforts of domesticity. It is important to realise that all the narrators in the text (and there are other embedded narratives like those of the De Lacey family and of Elizabeth Lavenza to consider) are seeking to persuade their auditors to act in a certain way (and thus the reader to judge them in a certain way). There is no omniscient narrator to judge the actions of the characters or corroborate the truth of what they say; only the perspective of other characters whose own moral judgements may be suspect or biased.

Frankenstein as a novel is completely up to date with regard to its treatment of scientific discovery, anachronistically so for its setting in the 1790s. Captain Robert Walton presents himself as a natural philosopher and explorer, a man inspired by travel narratives to investigate the secrets of the North Magnetic Pole and search for a passage through the Arctic Ocean. He accepts the then current hypothesis (to our contemporary understanding absurd) of an open and temperate sea at the pole:

> I try in vain to be persuaded that the pole is the seat of frost and desolation; it ever presents itself to my imagination as the region of beauty and delight ... the sun is for ever visible, its broad disk just skirting the horizon, and diffusing a perpetual splendour ... sailing over a calm sea, we may be wafted to a land surpassing in wonders and in beauty every region hitherto discovered on the habitable globe.
>
> (p. 15)

The most obvious predecessor of Walton's voyage is that of Constantine Phipps, who commanded an expedition of the Royal Navy to sail to the North Pole in 1773; it also just pre-empts the major polar exploratory activity of John Franklin (the man who famously ate his boots in 1819, and, equally notoriously, whose men ate each other when lost in the Canadian Arctic during the expedition of 1845), William Edward Parry, and the later activities of Sir John Ross and his nephew James Clark Ross. Walton is undertaking 'a voyage of discovery towards the northern pole', presumably hoping to sail directly across it. Only by undertaking such a journey, he tells his sister, can 'the secret of the magnet' be attained (p. 16). It is quite possible that

Walton is seeking to locate the magnetic North Pole as well as the geographic Pole, and so discover the causes of magnetic variation and dip which puzzled mariners and scientists for generations.

Similarly Victor's experiments are equally current. Luigi Galvani had coined the term *animal electricity* to describe whatever it was that activated the muscles of his frogs when he passed a current through their legs. Along with contemporaries, Galvani regarded their activation as being generated by an electrical fluid that is carried to the muscles by the nerves. Galvani's nephew, Giovanni Aldini, popularised his discoveries in a series of sensational lectures in London (from 1802) in which he applied electric currents from the Voltaic pile to recently slaughtered animals, and, most spectacularly, to the corpse of a newly executed criminal, who showed terrifying signs of renewed vitality. Discoveries and speculations such as these led to a very public debate between two prominent surgeons, which became known as the 'Vitalist Debate'. The more orthodox faction in this debate argued that life was the product of some extra essential force or spiritual substance applied to the body rather as Jehovah communicates the spark of life into Adam's fingertip in the panel on Michelangelo's Sistine Chapel. Others argued, in a more materialist mode, that life is a product of the assemblage of the parts of the organism, a property of its material organisation. These positions were politicised, with the Vitalist party identified with the traditions of a Christian British science and their opponents with a materialist French science. In 1814 the debate developed in Great Britain into a heated controversy between two of the country's leading surgeons, John Abernethy and his former pupil William Lawrence. Abernethy argued that some form of substance similar to electricity was needed to explain vitality. Lawrence, on the other hand, identified life with the functional interdependence of the organised body itself. Lawrence was Percy Shelley's personal physician and the Shelley circle were well aware of these debates. This context has led scholars such as Marilyn Butler to argue that Victor Frankenstein is a parody of the Abernethy position, infusing life into his creature, in a parody of the Christian God ('Introduction' to Mary Shelley, *Frankenstein* (1818 text), xv–xxxiii [A]).

The novel also raises social and political questions about the reality of crime and guilt. Rousseau had claimed that all humans were born free, virtuous and benevolent but were corrupted by society. Mary Shelley's father's treatise *Political Justice* (1793) famously argued that crime was the result of a flawed environment and education rather than the consequence of any original sin or capacity for depravity. Godwin argued that one might as well blame the knife as the murderer. Generally, this was the argument of the French revolutionaries in their attempt to reform government and society through democracy (and many critics argue that the Creature is a metaphor for the violent actions of the revolutionary masses). The Creature tells us how he was naturally sociable, greeting his creator with a smile before the latter flees from him in horror, appalled by his physical ugliness. Subsequently, the Creature seeks acceptance; aware that his physique is monstrous, he hides himself away and secretly helps a poor family, the De Laceys. Although befriended by the blind father, who cannot see his ugliness, he is driven away by the son, who regards him with fear and horror. Seeking to adopt an unprejudiced child as his friend, he is enraged to murder when the child, who calls him an 'Ogre', reveals that he also is a member of Frankenstein's family. The Creature claims that he is 'malicious' only because he is 'miserable' and that 'if any being felt emotions of benevolence' for him he would 'return them an hundred and an hundred fold; for that one creature's sake' and 'make peace with the whole kind!' (p. 148). At the centre of the novel is the worst crime society can imagine, the murder of a child; nevertheless, the reader may maintain a sympathy for the Creature and attach the blame and responsibility to his creator and society at large. The extent to which individuals are responsible for the crimes they commit against society is raised by the Creature's actions. This issue, for the Shelley circle, had a wider application in the understanding of political violence by the masses during the French Revolution.

If the Creature's actions do not derive from any intrinsic evil, what then is Frankenstein's error? He certainly fails to take responsibility for his creation. After infusing life into the Creature during a period when he is undergoing extreme mental stress, he collapses and when awakened by his creation which grins and reaches out to him, he flees and abandons it. Victor is a damaged being; he shuns his family, friends and fiancée and is the indirect cause of all their deaths. He is obsessed by the drive to discover the secrets of life itself. Some have argued that Victor's obsession results from the early death of his mother and the trauma occasioned by it; when he falls asleep on the night of the creation he dreams of meeting Elizabeth in the streets of Ingolstadt and kissing her, only for her to metamorphose into the corpse of his dead mother complete with Gothic 'grave-worms crawling' in the folds of her shroud (pp. 58–9). This seems to indicate that his giving life to his creation will lead to Elizabeth's demise. It also argues for a pronounced Oedipal obsession with maternity and death. Similarly, his absence from the marital chamber on his wedding night is occasioned by what may be a wilful misreading of the Creature's threat to be with him at that time. Freudian critics have influentially argued that the Creature may be considered as Victor's dark self, carrying out those murderous desires he harbours in his own subconscious.

If Victor commits a crime then it is that of being a negligent parent in abandoning his 'child'. More than this, critics such as Anne Mellor have influentially argued that *Frankenstein* is a feminist text in which male science, in the person of Victor, usurps the female role of giving birth. What Frankenstein does is thus unnatural. Science or natural philosophy is defined in the text as a masculine activity. Waldman, Victor's tutor, tells him how the modern masters of science 'penetrate into the recesses of nature, and show how she works in her hiding-places. They ascend into the heavens: they have discovered how the blood circulates, and the nature of the air we breathe' (p. 49). The image Waldman uses is one of a female nature penetrated or raped by a male science. Similarly, Victor tells how in 'his secret toil' among 'the unhallowed damps of the grave' he 'pursued nature to her hiding places'. He 'tortured the living animal to animate the lifeless clay'. He collects materials for his new being from 'the dissecting room and the slaughter house' (p. 55), which would argue that his Creature is not fully human but a hybrid of human and animal parts. The context of the novel would certainly argue that what Victor does is unnatural and a crime against nature, rather than a crime against God. If we read the text this way, we locate it more firmly in the free-thinking and radical circle of minds and ideas amid which it was created.

Reference

A Primary Texts and Anthologies of Primary Sources

Austen, Jane. *Sense and Sensibility* (1811). Harmondsworth: Penguin, 1995.

Blake, William. *Blake: The Complete Poems*. 2nd edn. Ed. W. H. Stevenson. Harlow: Longman, 1989.

Bromwich, David. *Romantic Critical Essays*. Cambridge University Press, 1987. Introduction to the Romantic period through selections from prose writings with an excellent general introduction.

Butler, Marilyn, ed. *Burke, Paine, Godwin, and the Revolution Controversy*. Cambridge University Press, 1984. A selection of key documents written during the revolutionary and war years.

Frankenstein, or The Modern Prometheus: The 1818 Text. Oxford University Press, 1994.

Byron, George Gordon, Lord. *The Giaour* (1813). In *Byron, The Oxford Authors*. Ed. Jerome J. McGann. Oxford University Press, 1986, pp. 207–46.

Clare, John. *Major Works*. Ed. Eric Robinson and David Powell. Oxford University Press, 2004.

The Early Poems of John Clare, 1804–1822. Vol. II. Ed. Eric Robinson and David Powell. Oxford: Clarendon Press, 1989.

Cox, Jeffrey N., and Michael Gamer, eds. *The Broadview Anthology of Romantic Drama*. Peterborough, Ontario: Broadview, 2003. Selection of key dramas of the period by male and female writers.

Darwin, Erasmus. *The Botanic Garden, a Poem. In Two Parts. Part I. Containing the Economy of Vegetation; Part II. The Loves of the Plants*. 2 vols. 4th edn. London: J. Johnson, 1799.

Fairer, Davis, and Christine Gerrard, eds. *Eighteenth-Century Poetry: An Annotated Anthology*. Oxford: Blackwell, 1999. Has an excellent selection of key pre-Romantic poets with substantial headnotes.

The Norton Anthology of English Literature. Vol. II. Ed. Stephen Greenblatt et al. 8th edn. New York and London: Norton, 2006.

Richardson, Alan, ed. *Three Oriental Tales*. Boston: Houghlin Mifflin, 2002. Excellent introduction to the Oriental tale.

Shelley, Mary. *Frankenstein* (1818; rev. 1831). Ed. Maurice Hindle. Rev. edn. Harmondsworth: Penguin, 2003.

Wollstonecraft, Mary. *A Vindication of the Rights of Men and A Vindication of the Rights of Woman*. Ed. Sylvana Tomaselli. Cambridge University Press, 1995.

Wordsworth, William. *The Excursion. Vol. V of The Poetical Works of William Wordsworth*, ed. Helen Darbishire. Oxford University Press, 1949 (1972).

Wu, Duncan, ed. *Romanticism: An Anthology*. 3rd edn. Oxford: Blackwell, 2006. Contains lengthy headnotes on biographical and critical approaches to each author.

Women Romantic Poets: An Anthology. Oxford: Blackwell, 1997. Contains important works by women poets of the period.

B Introductions and Overviews

Bloom, Harold. *The Visionary Company: A Reading of English Romantic Poetry*. Ithaca, NY: Cornell University Press, 1973. Visionary study of the 'Big Six' Romantic poets.

Burwick, Frederick. *Romanticism: Keywords*. Oxford: Wiley-Blackwell, 2015. Entries on seventy-three keywords frequently discussed by European Romantic authors.

Butler, Marilyn. *Romantics, Rebels and Reactionaries 1760–1830*. Oxford University Press, 1981. Crucial overview of the period by leading historicist scholar of Romanticism.

Chaplun, Sue, and Joel Faflak, eds. *The Romanticism Handbook*. London: Continuum, 2011. Accessible and comprehensive introduction to literature and culture of the period.

Curran, Stuart, ed. *The Cambridge Companion to British Romanticism*. Cambridge University Press, 1993. Outstanding collection of contextual essays about the period.

Faflak, Joel, and Julia M. Wright, eds. *A Handbook of Romanticism Studies*. Oxford: Wiley-Blackwell, 2012. Collection of more advanced essays examining literature of the period through the lens of critical and cultural theory.

Ferber, Michael. *Romanticism: A Very Short Introduction*. Oxford University Press, 2010.

Ford, Boris, ed. *The Romantic Age in Britain*. The Cambridge Cultural History. Cambridge University Press, 1992. Well-illustrated and wide-ranging collection of essays on all aspects of the period's culture.

Gaull, Marilyn. *English Romanticism: The Human Context*. New York and London: Norton, 1988. Highly detailed and scholarly study of the intellectual context of the period.

Jarvis, Robin. *The Romantic Period: The Intellectual and Cultural Context of English Literature 1789–1830*. Harlow: Longman, 2004. Excellent introduction to the various contexts of Romantic-period writing. Good starting point.

Kelly, Gary. *English Fiction of the Romantic Period 1789–1830*. Harlow: Longman, 1989. Sound introduction to the Romantic and Gothic novel.

Kitson, Peter J., ed. *Coleridge, Keats and Shelley*. Basingstoke: Macmillan, 1990. Collection of essays illustrating major theoretical approaches to Romanticism.

McCalman, Iain, ed. *An Oxford Companion to the Romantic Age: British Culture 1776–1832*. Oxford University Press, 1999. Essential reference work.

Moore, Jane, and John Strachan. *Key Concepts in Romantic Literature*. Basingstoke: Palgrave Macmillan, 2010. Accessible scholarly guide to the literature, criticism and history of the era.

Roe, Nicholas, ed. *Romanticism: An Oxford Guide*. Oxford University Press, 2005. Excellent collection of essays on contexts and readings of individual works.

Ruston, Sharon. *Romanticism*. London: Continuum, 2007. Detailed and comprehensive survey of the literature of the Romantic period and its social, historical and intellectual contexts.

Stabler, Jane. *Burke to Byron, Barbauld to Baillie, 1790–1830*. Basingstoke: Palgrave, 2002. Extremely useful introduction to both male and female writers during the period, organised by genre.

Stafford, Fiona. *Reading Romantic Poetry*. Oxford: Wiley-Blackwell, 2012. Introduction and exemplary readings of writers of the era.

Watson, J. R. *English Poetry of the Romantic Period 1789–1830*. 2nd edn. London: Longman, 1992. Sound traditional study of the canonical poets, but has no coverage of female writers.

Wu, Duncan, ed. *Romanticism: A Critical Reader*. Oxford: Blackwell, 1995. Critical essays (1980–95) dealing with Romanticism.

    A Companion to Romanticism. Oxford: Blackwell, 1998. A collection of over fifty short essays on the subject. Useful starting place.

    30 Great Myths About the Romantics. Oxford: Wiley-Blackwell, 2015. Engaging collection of essays that address a range of commonly held misconceptions and beliefs about key figures of the Romantic era and about Romanticism.

C Further Reading

Note

Books contained in this section are usually written for an informed audience and are more advanced than introductory writing. Useful journals in the area include *Studies in Romanticism, Romanticism, The Wordsworth Circle, European Romantic Review, The Byron Journal*, the *Keats–Shelley Journal. Romanticism and Victorianism on the Net* is an electronic journal available at www.ravonjournal.org

i Romanticism and General

Armstrong, Nancy. *Desire and Domestic Fiction: A Political History of the Novel*. Oxford University Press, 1987. Key work about the domestic sphere, essential for Austen.

Abrams, M. H. *The Mirror and the Lamp: Romantic Theory and the Critical Tradition*. New York: Norton, 1953. The standard and scholarly account of Romantic ideas and aesthetics.

Barrell, John. *English Literature in History 1730–80: An Equal Wide Survey*. New York: St Martin's Press, 1983. Comprehensive study of the writing of the period in historical context.

Chandler, James. *England in 1819: The Politics of Literary Culture and the Case of Romantic Historicism*. University of Chicago Press, 1998. Major study arguing that Romantic writers were themselves historicists.

Cox, Jeffrey. *In the Shadows of Romance: Romantic Tragic Drama in England, Germany and France*. Athens: Ohio University Press, 1987. Good introduction to Romantic drama.

Curran, Stuart. *Poetic Form and British Romanticism*. Oxford University Press, 1986. Key study of the ways Romantic writers adapted traditional forms.

Dart, Gregory. *Metropolitan Art and Literature, 1810–1840: Cockney Adventures*. Cambridge University Press, 2012. Study explores an alternative metropolitan Romanticism.

Gigante, Denise. *Life: Organic Form and Romanticism*. New Haven, CT: Yale University Press, 2009. Examines how major writers of the Romantic period strove to produce living forms of art on an analogy with biological form.

Levinson, Marjorie. *Wordsworth's Great Period Poems*. Cambridge University Press, 1986. Concentrates on Wordsworth but contains major new historicist readings of the poems.

Liu, Alan. *Wordsworth: The Sense of History*. Stanford University Press, 1989. Substantial and unified study of major Romantic poet from new historicist perspective.

McGann, Jerome J. *The Romantic Ideology: A Critical Investigation*. University of Chicago Press, 1983. Polemical study arguing that Romanticism's critics have uncritically absorbed the ideas of the canonical Romantic poets.

Morton, Timothy. *Ecology without Nature: Rethinking Environmental Aesthetics*. New Haven, CT: Yale University Press, 2009. Major eco-critical reappraisal of Romantic constructions of nature.

O'Neill, Michael. *Romanticism and the Self-Conscious Poem*. Oxford: Clarendon Press, 1997. Rich and complex readings of the canonical Romantics.

Richardson, Alan. *A Mental Theatre: Poetic Drama and Consciousness in the Romantic Age*. University Park: Pennsylvania State University Press, 1988. Excellent study of Romantic drama and especially useful on Byron's poetic dramas.

Roe, Nicholas. *The Politics of Nature: William Wordsworth and Some Contemporaries*. Basingstoke: Palgrave, 2002. Authoritative and scholarly account of the political context for Wordsworth and his contemporaries.

Rowland, Ann Wierda. *Romanticism and Childhood: The Infantilization of British Literary Culture*. Cambridge University Press, 2015. Study of Romantic representation and conceptualisation of childhood.

Simpson, David. *Wordsworth, Commodification and Social Concern: the Poetics of Modernity*. Cambridge University Press, 2009. Romantic poetry as response to massive changes occurring in industry and technology.

Siskin, Clifford. *The Work of Writing: Literature and Social Change in Britain, 1700–1830*. Baltimore, MD: Johns Hopkins University Press, 1998. Reassessment of the role of print culture on the relationship between Romanticism and modernity.

Watkins, Daniel P. *A Materialist Critique of English Romantic Drama*. University Press of Florida, 1993. Political reading of the key Romantic dramas.

Wolfson, Susan. *Formal Charges: The Shaping of Poetry in British Romanticism*. Stanford University Press, 1997. Concentrates on the Big Six poets and combines new historicist and formalist approaches.

ii Political and Economic Context

Barrell, John. *Imagining the King's Death: Figurative Treason, Fantasies of Regicide, 1793–96*. Oxford University Press, 2000. Covers the key political background to the 1790s.

Bugg, John. *Five Long Winters: The Trials of British Romanticism*. Stanford University Press, 2013. Argues that the British government's repression of the 1790s rivals the French Revolution as the most important historical event for our understanding of the development of Romantic literature.

Chase, Malcolm. *'The People's Farm': English Radical Agrarianism 1775–1840*. Oxford: Clarendon Press, 1988. Study of enclosure and radical ideas.

Christie, Ian. *War and Revolution: Britain, 1760–1815*. London: Edward Arnold, 1982. Key background study.

Daunton, M. J. *Progress and Poverty: An Economic and Social History of Britain 1700–1850*. Oxford University Press, 1995. Sound historical overview.

Deane, Seamus. *The French Revolution and the Enlightenment in England, 1789–1832*. Cambridge, MA: Harvard University Press, 1988. Key study of political and intellectual context.

Derry, John W. *Politics in the Age of Fox, Pitt and Liverpool: Continuity and Transformation*. Basingstoke: Macmillan, 1990. Excellent brief introduction to the political history of the period.

Dickinson, H. T. *British Radicalism and the French Revolution 1780–1815*. Oxford: Blackwell, 1985. Key study of radical ideas.

Emsley, Clive. *British Society and the French Wars, 1793–1815*. Basingstoke: Macmillan, 1979. An invaluable source book for all aspects of the war.

Haughton, Hugh, Adam Phillips and Geoffrey Summerfield, eds. *John Clare in Context*. Cambridge University Press, 1994. Wide-ranging collection of engaging essays on Clare and Romantic agrarianism.

McCalman, Iain. *Radical Underworld: Prophets, Revolutionaries, and Pornographers in London, 1795–1840*. Oxford: Clarendon Press, 1993. Ground-breaking historical study concentrating on subversive writers and figures. Profoundly influential on historical readings of Romanticism.

Neeson, J. H. *Commoners: Common Right, Enclosure, and Social Change in England, 1700–1820*. Cambridge University Press, 1993. Sound study of enclosure.

Payne, Christina. *Toil and Plenty: Images of the Agricultural Landscape in England, 1780–1890*. New Haven, CT: Yale University Press, 1993. Key and informative study.

Smith, Olivia. *The Politics of Language 1791–1819*. Oxford University Press, 1984. Key study of the language of political discourse in the period.

Snell, K. D. M. *Annals of the Labouring Poor: Social Change and Agrarian England, 1660–1900*. Cambridge University Press, 1985. Standard account.

Thompson, E. P. *The Making of the English Working Class*. 2nd edn. Harmondsworth: Penguin, 1968. Classic study of working-class consciousness, history and culture.

White, Simon. *Romanticism and the Rural Community*. Basingstoke: Palgrave Macmillan, 2013. Discussion of Romantic representations of the rural.

Williams, Raymond. *The Country and the City*. London: Chatto and Windus, 1973. Influential study of the representations of urban and rural experience.

Worrall, David. *Radical Culture: Discourse, Resistance and Surveillance, 1790–1820*. New York and London: Harvester Wheatsheaf, 1992. Important study of radicalism, especially agrarian ideas.

iii Colonialism, Orientalism and Empire

Aravamudan, Srinivas. *Tropicopolitans: Colonialism and Agency 1688–1804*. Durham, NH and London: Duke University Press, 1999. Heavily theoretical and advanced but important in widening the scope of the Romantic representations of colonial others.

Enlightenment Orientalism. Resisting the Rise of the Novel. University of Chicago Press, 2012. Reappraisal of impact of oriental fictions on eighteenth-century British culture.

Barrell, John. *The Infection of Thomas De Quincey: A Psychopathology of Imperialism.* New Haven, CT: Yale University Press, 1991. Bravura and ground-breaking study of the Romantic anxieties about the East.

Bayly, C. A. *Imperial Meridian: The British Empire and the World 1780–1830.* London: Longman, 1989. Excellent historical overview from global perspective.

Cavaliero, Roderick. *Ottomania. The Romantics and the Myth of the Islamic Orient.* London: Tauris, 2013. Engaging and full overview of this subject.

Cohen-Vrignaud, Gerard. *Radical Orientalism: Rights, Reform, and Romanticism.* Cambridge University Press, 2015. Study of ways in which the orientalism of Byron and Shelley is linked to the radical press.

Colley, Linda. *Britons: Forging the Nation, 1707–1837.* New Haven, CT: Yale University Press, 1992. Essential reading about ideas of Britain and the nation in the period.

   Captives: Britain, Empire and the World 1600–1850. London: Jonathan Cape, 2002. Stresses the weaknesses and anxieties of British colonialism.

Fulford, Tim, and Peter J. Kitson, eds. *Romanticism and Colonialism.* Cambridge University Press, 1998. Important collection of essays; an essential starting point.

   Travels, Explorations and Empires, 1770–1835. 8 vols. London: Pickering and Chatto, 2001–2. Essential collection of primary sources with introductions and annotations.

Garcia, Umberto. *Islam and the English Enlightenment, 1670–1840.* Baltimore, MD: Johns Hopkins University Press, 2012. Examines how sympathetic representations of Islam contributed significantly to Protestant Britain's national and imperial identity in the eighteenth century.

Higgins, David. *Romantic Englishness: Local, National and Global Selves, 1780–1850.* Basingstoke: Palgrave, 2014. Investigates how narratives of localised selfhood in English Romantic writing are produced in relation to national and transnational formations.

Irwin, Robert. *The Lust for Knowing: The Orientalists and Their Enemies.* London: Allen Lane, 2006. Anti-Said and an excellent survey of the field and the current debate.

Kitson, Peter J. *Romantic Literature, Race, and Colonial Encounter.* New York: Palgrave, 2007. Study of the 'race idea' and Romantic period writing.

   Forging Romantic China: Sino-British Cultural Exchange, 1760–1840. Cambridge University Press, 2013. Study of the impact of China on British Romantic period writing and culture.

Leask, Nigel. *British Romantic Writers and the East: Anxieties of Empire.* Cambridge University Press, 1992. Essential study of representations of the East in Romantic writing.

   Curiosity and the Aesthetics of Travel Writing 1770–1840. Oxford University Press, 2002. Major study of Romantic period travel writing.

MacKenzie, John M. *Orientalism: History, Theory and the Arts.* Manchester University Press, 1995. Argues against Said, detailed and authoritative.

Makdisi, Saree. *Romantic Imperialism: Universal Empire and the Culture of Modernity.* Cambridge University Press, 1992. Romantic writing as complicit with modernity and empire.

Making England Western: Occidentalism, Race, and Imperial Culture. University of
Chicago Press, 2012. Major examination of ways in which British 'others' were
orientalised.

Marshall, P. J., and Glyndwr Williams. *The Great Map of Mankind: British Perceptions of the World in the Age of Enlightenment.* London: Dent, 1992. Classic scholarly account.

Nussbaum, Felicity. *The Limits of the Human: Fictions of Anomaly, Race, and Gender in the Long Eighteenth Century.* Cambridge University Press, 2003. Study of racial attitudes in the period.

Richardson, Alan, and Sonia Hofkosh, eds. *Romanticism, Race and Imperial Culture, 1780–1834.* Stanford University Press, 1996. Key collection of essays on the subject.

Said, Edward W. *Culture and Imperialism.* New York: Knopf, 1993. Romantic novelists and empire.

Orientalism. London: Pantheon Books, 1978. Key and influential polemical account of the subject.

Sardar, Ziauddin. *Orientalism.* Buckingham: Open University Press, 1999. Polemical and committed but good introduction to subject.

Simpson, David. *Romanticism and the Question of the Stranger.* University of Chicago Press, 2013. Major discussion of cultural encounters and representations of strangers and others in the period.

Spivak, Gayatri Chakravorty. 'Can the Subaltern Speak?' in Cary Nelson and Lawrence Grossberg, eds. *Marxism and the Interpretation of Culture.* Urbana, IL: University of Illinois Press, 1988, pp. 271–313.

Warren, Andrew. *The Orient and the Young Romantics.* Cambridge University Press, 2014. New evaluation of orientalism and second-generation Romantic poets.

White, Daniel. *From Little London to Little Bengal: Religion, Print, and Modernity in Early British India, 1793–1835.* Baltimore, MD: Johns Hopkins University Press, 2013. Traces the traffic in culture between Britain and India during the Romantic period.

Wilson, Kathleen, ed. *A New Imperial History: Culture, Identity and Modernity in Britain and the Empire 1660–1840.* Cambridge University Press, 2004. Important collection of new essays.

iv Black Writers and the Transatlantic Slave Trade

Carretta, Vincent. *Equiano, the African: Biography of a Self-Made Man.* Athens: University of Georgia Press, 2005. Authoritative biography of the most important black writer of the period.

Coleman, Deirdre. *Romantic Colonization and British Anti-Slavery.* Cambridge University Press, 2005. Fascinating examination of the links between anti-slavery and colonialism.

Ferguson, Moira. *Subject to Others: British Women Writers and Colonial Slavery 1670–1834.* London and New York: Routledge, 1992. Key text in establishing this subject.

Hochschild, Adam. *Bury the Chains: The British Struggle to Abolish Slavery.* London and New York: Macmillan, 2005. Attractively written account of anti-slavery.

Kitson, Peter J., and Debbie Lee, eds. *Slavery, Abolition and Emancipation.* 8 vols. London: Pickering and Chatto, 1999. Essential collection of primary texts and documents.

Lee, Debbie. *Slavery and the Romantic Imagination*. Philadelphia: University of Pennsylvania Press, 2001. Fascinating reading of Romantic poetry and slavery.

Thomas, Helen. *Romanticism and Slave Narratives: Transatlantic Testimonies*. Cambridge University Press, 2000. Good overview of the subject.

Wood, Marcus. *Slavery, Empathy and Pornography*. Oxford: Clarendon Press, 2002. Challenging readings with chapters on Romantic poetry and Romantic writers.

Wood, Marcus, ed. *The Poetry of Slavery: An Anglo-American Anthology*. Oxford University Press, 2003. Essential anthology of texts.

v Visual Art, Landscape and Aesthetics

Andrews, Malcolm. *The Search for the Picturesque: The Landscape, Aesthetics and Tourism in Britain, 1760–1800*. Stanford University Press, 1990. Standard account.

Barrell, John. *The Dark Side of the Landscape: The Rural Poor in English Painting*. Cambridge University Press, 1980. Important study.

Bermingham, Ann. *Landscape and Ideology: The English Rustic Tradition 1740–1846*. Berkeley: University of California Press, 1987. Key work on the picturesque.

Copley, Stephen, and Peter Garside, eds. *The Politics of the Picturesque: Literature, Landscape and Aesthetics since 1770*. Cambridge University Press, 1994. Important collection of essays on the picturesque.

Donald, Diana. *The Age of Caricature: Satirical Prints in the Reign of George III*. London and New Haven, CT: Yale University Press, 1996.

Duckworth, Alastair. *The Improvement of the Estate*. Baltimore, MD: Johns Hopkins University Press, 1994. Important study of landscaped gardens, especially good on Austen.

Eaves, Morris. *The Counter-Arts Conspiracy: Art and Industry in the Age of Blake*. Ithaca, NY: Cornell University Press, 1992. Important reading of the material processes of producing art.

Fulford, Tim. *Landscape, Liberty and Authority: Poetry, Criticism and Politics from Thomson to Wordsworth*. Cambridge University Press, 1996. Important and accessible study of categories of landscape.

Hipple, W. J. *The Beautiful, the Sublime and the Picturesque in Eighteenth-Century British Aesthetic Theory*. Carbondale: University of Illinois Press, 1957. Major study.

Janowitz, Anne. *England's Ruins: Poetry and the National Landscape*. Oxford: Blackwell, 1990. Important study of Romantic period aesthetics and communitarian ideas.

Myron, Martin, Christopher Frayling and Marina Warner. *Gothic Nightmares: Fuseli, Blake and the Romantic Imagination*. London: Tate Publishing, 2006. Catalogue of Gothic art.

Paulson, Ronald. *Representations of Revolution (1789–1820)*. Baltimore, MD: Johns Hopkins University Press, 1983. Illustrated study of how the French Revolution furnished representations for the visual and literary arts.

Thomas, Sophie. *Romanticism and Visuality: Fragments, History, Spectacle*. New York: Routledge, 2008. Study of Romantic visual culture.

Vaughan, William. *Romanticism and Art*. London: Thames and Hudson, 1994. Good general introduction.

vi Science, Medicine and Technology

Bewell, Alan. *Romanticism and Colonial Disease*. Baltimore, MD: Johns Hopkins University Press, 2000. Fascinating study of medical theories from the Romantic period.

Caldwell, Janis McClarren. *Literature and Medicine in Nineteenth-Century Britain: From Mary Shelley to George Eliot*. Cambridge University Press, 2008. Key study of medical theories and practice in the period.

Cunningham, A., and N. Jardine, eds. *Romanticism and the Sciences*. Cambridge University Press, 1990. Important collection of essays.

Fairclough, Mary. *The Romantic Crowd: Sympathy, Controversy and Print Culture*. Cambridge University Press, 2015. Reads Romantic writers alongside contemporary political, medical and philosophical discourse.

Fulford, Tim, Debbie Lee and Peter J. Kitson. *Literature, Science and Exploration in the Romantic Era: Bodies of Knowledge*. Cambridge University Press, 2004. Accessible and important study of the interrelationships between science, exploration and politics.

Gascoigne, John. *Science in the Service of Empire: Joseph Banks, the British State and the Uses of Science in the Age of Revolution*. Cambridge University Press, 1998. Important discussion of Banks as central figure in the scientific culture of his time.

Golinski, Jan. *Science as Public Culture: Chemistry and Enlightenment in Britain, 1760–1820*. Cambridge University Press, 1992. Classic study of Priestley, Davy and electrochemistry.

Heringman, Noah, ed. *Romantic Science: The Literary Forms of Natural History*. Buffalo: State University of New York Press, 2003. Major collection of essays on Romanticism and Science.

Jordanova, Ludmilla. *Nature Displayed: Gender, Science and Medicine, 1760–1820*. London: Longman, 1999. Key essays on gender and medicine.

Kelley, Theresa M. *Clandestine Marriage: Botany and Romantic Culture*. Baltimore, MD: Johns Hopkins University Press, 2012. Major exploration of botanic thought and practice in the context of British Romanticism.

Knight, David. *The Age of Science: The Scientific World-View of the Nineteenth Century*. Oxford: Basil Blackwell, 1986.

Levere, Trevor. *Poetry Realized in Nature: Samuel Taylor Coleridge and Early Nineteenth-Century Science*. Cambridge University Press, 1981. Major study of Romantic science.

Mahood, M. M. *The Poet as Botanist*. Cambridge University Press, 2008. Explores botanical thought and Romantic poets, among others.

Richardson, Alan. *British Romanticism and the Science of the Mind*. Cambridge University Press, 2005. Important study of Romantic theories of the mind.

Ruston, Sharon. *Shelley and Vitality*. Basingstoke: Palgrave, 2005. Essential for the debate about vitalism.

   Creating Romanticism: Case Studies in the Literature, Science and Medicine of the 1790s. Basingstoke: Palgrave, 2013. Argues for the importance of scientific and medical ideas that helped shape some of the key concepts of the period.

Uglow, Jenny. *The Lunar Men: The Friends Who Made the Future, 1730–1810*. London: Faber & Faber, 2002. Eminently readable and scholarly account of Priestley, Darwin and the Lunar Society of Birmingham.

vii Religion

Canuel, Mark. *Religion, Toleration and British Writing, 1790–1830*. Cambridge University Press, 2002. Argues that Romantic writers were in favour of toleration in religion.

Hempton, David. *Religion and Political Culture in Britain and Ireland: From the Glorious Revolution to the Decline of the Empire*. Cambridge University Press, 1996. Good overview.

Hole, Robert. *Pulpit, Politics and the Public Order in England, 1760–1832*. Cambridge University Press, 1989. Important work about Church and dissent.

Priestman, Martin. *Romantic Atheism: Poetry and Freethought, 1780–1830*. Cambridge University Press, 1999. Important study of freethinkers.

Ryan, Robert. *The Romantic Reformation: Religious Politics in English Literature, 1789–1824*. Cambridge University Press, 1997. Sees Romanticism as a religious and Protestant movement.

Ward, W. R. *Religion and Society in England 1790–1850*. London: B. T. Batsford, 1972. Sound general overview of the subject.

White, Daniel. *Early Romanticism and Religious Dissent*. Cambridge University Press, 2006. Major discussion of Romantic poetry and Unitarianism.

viii Sensibility

Barker-Benfield, G. J. *The Culture of Sensibility: Sex and Society in Eighteenth-Century Britain*. University of Chicago Press, 1992. Detailed and authoritative account of the movement and its relationship to consumerism.

Jones, Chris. *Radical Sensibility: Literature and Ideas in the 1790s*. London and New York: Routledge, 1993. Excellent discussion of the radicalisation of sensibility in the 1790s.

Kowalski-Wallace, Elisabeth. *Consuming Subjects: Women, Shopping and Business in the Eighteenth Century*. New York: Columbia University Press, 1997. Linking of sensibility to consumption; an important study.

McGann, Jerome J. *The Poetics of Sensibility: A Revolution in Literary Style*. Oxford: Clarendon Press, 1996. Sees poetry of sensibility as alternative tradition to conservative, male-dominated Romanticism.

Pinch, Adela. *Strange Fits of Passion: Epistemologies of Emotion, Hume to Austen*. Stanford University Press, 1996. Stresses continuities between sensibility and Romanticism.

Todd, Janet. *Sensibility: An Introduction*. London: Methuen, 1986. Excellent starting point for studying the movement.

ix The Gothic

Botting, Fred. *The Gothic*. London and New York: Routledge, 1996. Excellent starting point for study.

Clery, E. J. *The Rise of Supernatural Fiction 1762–1800*. Cambridge University Press, 1995. Supernatural linked to new technologies and consumerism.

Women's Gothic: From Clara Reeve to Mary Shelley. Tavistock: Northcote, 2000. Useful starting point for female Gothic.

Ellis, Kate Ferguson. *The Contested Castle: Gothic Novels and the Subversion of Domestic Ideology*. Urbana: University of Illinois Press, 1989. Influential feminist study of female Gothic writing.

Gamer, Michael. *Romanticism and the Gothic: Genre, Reception, and Canon Formation*. Cambridge University Press, 2000. Historicist account of Gothic as underside of Romanticism.

Hoeveler, Diane Long. *Gothic Feminism: The Professionalisation of Gender from Charlotte Smith to the Brontës*. Philadelphia: Penn State University Press, 1998. Argues that female Gothic novelists helped define femininity for women of the British middle class.

Gothic Riffs: Secularizing the Uncanny in the European Imaginary, 1780–1820. Columbus: Ohio State University Press, 2015. Comprehensive study of genres – operas, ballads, chapbooks, dramas and melodramas – that emerged out of the Gothic novel tradition.

Hogle, Jerrold, ed. *The Cambridge Companion to Gothic Fiction*. Cambridge University Press, 2002. Excellent essays.

Kilgour, Maggie. *The Rise of the Gothic Novel*. London and New York: Routledge, 1995. Readable and accessible study argues that Gothic was a form of social critique.

Miles, Robert. *Gothic Writing 1750–1820: A Genealogy*. London and New York: Routledge, 1993. Foucauldian reading identifies Gothic as 'discourse' before the novel.

Moers, Ellen. *Literary Women*. London: Women's Press, 1976. Early and influential account of the female Gothic.

Punter, David. *A Companion to the Gothic*. Oxford: Blackwell, 2000.

The Literature of Terror. Vol. 1: The Gothic Tradition. Vol. 2: The Modern Gothic. London and New York: Longman, 1996. Reworking of an original study which founded the Gothic as a serious object of critical study.

Williams, Anne. *Art of Darkness: A Poetics of Gothic*. University of Chicago Press, 1995. Important discussion of key Gothic issues, especially male and female Gothic.

Wright, Angela. *Britain, France and the Gothic: The Import of Terror, 1764–1820*. Cambridge University Press, 2015. Explores the development of Gothic literature in Britain in the context of the fraught relationship between Britain and France.

Wright, Angela, and Dale Townshend, eds. *Romantic Gothic*. Edinburgh University Press, 2015. Collection of essays on the relationship of Romantic and Gothic.

x Literary Marketplace

Altick, R. D. *The English Common Reader: A Social History of the Mass Reading Public 1800–1900*. University of Chicago Press, 1957. Classic study.

Klancher, Jon. P. *The Making of English Reading Audiences, 1790–1832*. Madison and London: University of Wisconsin Press, 1987. Influential discussion of periodical literature.

McGann, Jerome J. *The Textual Condition*. Princeton University Press, 1991. McGann applies a socialised model of literary production to Romantic writing.

Newlyn, Lucy. *Reading, Writing, and Romanticism: The Anxiety of Reception*. Oxford: Clarendon Press, 2000. Relates major Romantics to the growth of the reading public and the rise of criticism.

Raven, James. *Judging New Wealth: Popular Publishing and Responses to Commerce in England, 1750–1800*. Oxford University Press, 1992. Study of popular presses in the period.

St Clair, William. *The Reading Nation in the Romantic Period*. Cambridge University Press, 2004. Recent authoritative study which will become the standard work on the subject.

Twyman, Michael. *The British Library Guide to Printing: History and Techniques*. London: British Library, 1998. Succinct guide to changing printing technologies.

xi Women Poets and Gender

Curran, Stuart. 'The "I" Altered', in Mellor, ed., *Romanticism and Feminism* [Cxi], pp. 185–207.

Favret, Mary A., and Nicola J. Watson, eds. *At the Limits of Romanticism: Essays in Cultural, Feminist, and Materialist Criticism*. Bloomington and Indianapolis: Indiana University Press, 1994. Good collection of revisionary feminist essays.

Fay, Elizabeth. *A Feminist Introduction to Romanticism*. Oxford: Blackwell, 1998. Useful introductory account.

Feldman, Paula R., and Theresa M. Kelley, eds. *Romantic Women Writers: Voices and Countervoices*. Hanover, NH: University Press of New England, 1995. Good collection of revisionary feminist criticism.

Landes, Joan B. *Women and the Public Sphere in the Age of the French Revolution*. New York: Cornell University Press, 1988. Important study.

Mellor, Anne K., ed. *Romanticism and Feminism*. Bloomington: Indiana University Press, 1988. Key collection introducing the study of Romantic women writers.

Mellor, Anne K. *Romanticism and Gender*. New York: Routledge, 1993. Challenging attempt to discriminate between two gendered forms of Romanticism. Essential reading.

Ross, Marlon. *The Contours of Masculine Desire: Romanticism and the Rise of Women's Poetry*. Oxford University Press, 1989. Seminal work on Romantic women writers.

Smith, Orianne. *Romantic Women Writers, Revolution and Prophecy: Rebellious Daughters, 1786–1826*. Cambridge University Press, 2015. Explores how Romantic women writers assumed the role of the female prophet.

Wilson, Carol Shiner, and Joel Haefner, eds. *Re-Visioning Romanticism: British Women Writers, 1776–1837*. Philadelphia: University of Pennsylvania Press, 1994. Important collection of revisionary essays on this subject.

5 The Victorian Age, 1832–1901

MARIA FRAWLEY

Progress, expansion, mobility – these keynotes of Victorian history and culture evoke in their different ways a society keenly attuned to and preoccupied with transformations in nearly every arena of daily life. 'Your railroad starts the new era', Thackeray wrote in *The Roundabout Papers* (1863), and, indeed, the opening of railway lines from 1830 onwards and their rapid spread throughout Britain captures the period's ethos of energetic pursuit, advancement, growth and diffusion. The evolution of industrial society, the rise of great towns and cities, and dramatic increases in population enabled, maybe even forced, government activities to expand exponentially; literacy rates increased, print culture proliferated, information abounded, the circulating library took hold, and a mass reading public was born; the franchise was extended through a series of key parliamentary reform measures; technological developments broadened and quickened opportunities for travel and communication; uncharted lands were explored and mapped, and, for much of the century, Britain enjoyed an expansion of commerce with the wider world – all this outreach making for what Robin Gilmour has described as 'a dynamo hum in the background of Victorian literature' (*The Victorian Period*, p. 2 [B]).

These transformations and the optimistic embrace of progress upon which they depended inevitably wrought their fair share of anxious response. The central metaphors of Dickens's fiction – fog, contagion, the prison – evoke the capacity of disease, both literal and figurative, to spread throughout modern society, eventually to immobilise it. Moreover, if fundamentally outward-looking, the trademark Victorian emphases on progress, expansion and mobility (and the celebratory display of their fruits) also helped to produce a corollary preoccupation with interiority, what the poet Matthew Arnold called 'the dialogue of the mind with itself'. Victorians were nothing if not inquisitive – one can find everything from 'The Irish Question' to 'The Oyster Question' discussed in the press – and curiosity itself is arguably the premise of major works as different as *Jane Eyre, Little Dorrit* and *Alice in Wonderland*. Preoccupation with the idea and ideal of transformation is no less central to the Victorian study of self than of society. Although Scrooge redeems himself with an eleventh-hour promise to change, figures such as Dr Jekyll and, still later in the century, Dracula, embody a deep-seated uncertainty about the stability of identity itself in a changing and modern world. The contradictions and complexities of Victorian Britain account in no small measure for its enduring appeal. The chronology and overview that follow provide a point of entry into this complex and fascinating period in British history.

Chronology

	HISTORY AND CULTURE	LITERATURE
1819	Queen Victoria born	
1824	*Westminster Review* founded	
1829		Thomas Carlyle, 'Signs of the Times'
1830	Passenger railway line opens between Liverpool and Manchester *Fraser's Magazine* founded Charles Lyell, *Principles of Geology* (–1833)	Edward Bulwer, *Paul Clifford* Alfred, Lord Tennyson, *Poems, Chiefly Lyrical*
1831	Reform Bill introduced Cholera outbreak in England British Association for the Advancement of Science founded	John Stuart Mill, 'The Spirit of the Age' Robert Surtees, *Jorrocks' Jaunts and Jollities* (–1834)
1832	First Reform Act *Chambers' Edinburgh Journal* and *Penny Magazine* (–1837) begin Harriet Martineau, *Illustrations of Political Economy* (–1834)	
1833	Factory Reform Act First of John Henry Newman's *Tracts for the Times* issued Abolition of Slavery Act	
1833	*Penny Cyclopaedia* (–1843)	Carlyle, *Sartor Resartus* (–1834)
1834	Poor Law Amendment Act	
1836		Charles Dickens, *Sketches by Boz; The Pickwick Papers* (–1837)
1837	Victoria succeeds to throne Smallpox epidemic Brunel, Great Western Railway	Carlyle, *The French Revolution* Dickens, *Oliver Twist* (–1838)
1838	People's Charter issued Anti-Corn Law League formed	Dickens, *Nicholas Nickleby*
1839	Charles Darwin, *The Voyage of the Beagle* Sarah Stickney Ellis, *The Women of England: Their Social Duties and Domestic Habits*	
1840	Victoria marries Albert Penny post established	Dickens, *The Old Curiosity Shop* Frances Trollope, *Michael Armstrong, Factory Boy*
1841	Peel becomes Prime Minister William Henry Fox Talbot awarded patent for calotype process (positive/negative photographical process) *Punch* begins	
1842	Mudie's Lending Library opens Chadwick's *Report on the Sanitary Condition of the Labouring Population* Poor Law renewed *Illustrated London News* begins Copyright Act	Tennyson, *Poems* (2 vols.) Robert Browning, *Dramatic Lyrics*
1843	Theatre Regulation Act	Dickens, *A Christmas Carol* Carlyle, *Past and Present* John Ruskin, *Modern Painters* (vol. 1) Wordsworth named Poet Laureate

	HISTORY AND CULTURE	LITERATURE
1844	Factory Act (women and children) Railway mania Robert Chambers, *Vestiges of the Natural History of Creation* J. M. W. Turner, *Rain, Steam and Speed – the Great Western Railway* Henry Fox Talbot, *The Pencil of Nature*	Benjamin Disraeli, *Coningsby, or The New Generation*
1845	Onset of the Irish potato famine	Disraeli, *Sybil, or The Two Nations* Dickens, *Dombey and Son* (–1848)
1846	Corn Laws repealed Lord John Russell, Prime Minister	George Eliot translates *Das Leben Jesu*
1847	Ten Hours' Factory Act	Charlotte Brontë, *Jane Eyre* Emily Brontë, *Wuthering Heights* Anne Brontë, *Agnes Grey* Disraeli, *Tancred* W. M. Thackeray, *Vanity Fair* (–1848)
1848	Chartist rebellion Marx and Engels, *Communist Manifesto* Cholera epidemic Public Health Act Pre-Raphaelite Brotherhood founded	Elizabeth Gaskell, *Mary Barton* John Henry Newman, *Loss and Gain*
1849	Henry Mayhew, *London Labour and the London Poor* (series begun in *Morning Chronicle*) Bedford College for Women founded	Dickens, *David Copperfield* (–1850)
1850	Public Libraries Act	Tennyson named Poet Laureate Tennyson, *In Memoriam* Dickens, *Household Words* founded *The Germ* founded (literary magazine of the Pre-Raphaelites) Elizabeth Barrett Browning, *Sonnets from the Portuguese* Charlotte Brontë, *Shirley* Charles Kingsley, *Alton Locke*
1851	Great Exhibition at the Crystal Palace Harriet Taylor Mill, *The Enfranchisement of Women*	Gaskell, *Cranford* Ruskin, *The Stones of Venice*
1852		Dickens, *Bleak House* (–1853)
1853	Cholera epidemic	Matthew Arnold, *Poems* Charlotte Brontë, *Villette* Charlotte Yonge, *Heir of Redclyffe*
1854	Onset of Crimean War	Coventry Patmore, *The Angel in the House* Dickens, *Hard Times* Gaskell, *North and South* (–1855)
1855	*Daily Telegraph* Repeal of stamp duty on newspapers	Browning, *Men and Women* Dickens, *Little Dorrit* (–1857)
1856	First exhibition of Holman Hunt's *The Scapegoat*	Barrett Browning, *Aurora Leigh* (post-dated 1857 on title page) Dinah M. Craik, *John Halifax, Gentleman*
1857	Indian Mutiny Divorce and Matrimonial Causes Act David Livingstone, *Missionary Travels and Researches In South Africa* Social Science Association founded	Anthony Trollope, *Barchester Towers* Mary Seacole, *The Wonderful Adventures of Mary Seacole in Many Lands* George Eliot, *Scenes of Clerical Life* Thomas Hughes, *Tom Brown's Schooldays*
1858	Medical Act	Robert Ballantyne, *Coral Island* *English Woman's Journal* begins

	HISTORY AND CULTURE	LITERATURE
1859	Darwin's *On The Origin of Species*	Wilkie Collins, *The Woman in White* Samuel Smiles, *Self-Help* Eliot, *Adam Bede* Mill, *On Liberty* Dickens, *All the Year Round* founded Dickens, *A Tale of Two Cities* David Masson, *British Novelists and their Styles*
1860	*Cornhill Magazine* begins	Eliot, *The Mill on the Floss* Ruskin, essays published in the *Cornhill*, later collected as *Unto This Last* (1862) Dickens, *Great Expectations* (–1861)
1861	Isabella Beeton's *Book of Household Management* *Hymns Ancient and Modern* Prince Albert dies	Mrs Henry Wood, *East Lynne* Eliot, *Silas Marner*
1862		Mary Braddon, *Lady Audley's Secret* Collins, *No Name* Christina Rossetti, 'Goblin Market' Tennyson, *Idylls of the King*
1863	World's first underground railway, the steam-operated Metropolitan line, opens in London Charles Lyell, *Antiquity of Man* Thomas Henry Huxley, *Man's Place in Nature*	Charles Reade, *Hard Cash* Kingsley, *The Water-Babies* Thackeray, *The Roundabout Papers*
1864	First Contagious Diseases Act	John Henry Newman, *Apologia Pro Vita Sua* Dickens, *Our Mutual Friend* (–1865) Tennyson, *Idylls of the Hearth* Trollope, *Can You Forgive Her?* (–1865)
1865	Women's Suffrage Campaign Transatlantic cable laid Joseph Lister establishes antiseptic surgery St Pancras railway station completed	Lewis Carroll, *Alice in Wonderland* Arnold, *Essays in Criticism (First Series)*
1866	Cholera epidemic	Ruskin, *The Crown of Wild Olives* Algernon Charles Swinburne, *Poems and Ballads* Eliot, *Felix Holt*
1867	Second Reform Act Marx, *Das Kapital* Fenian Rising in Ireland	Hesba Stretton, *Jessica's First Prayer*
1868	Disraeli, Prime Minister (Feb.) Gladstone, Prime Minister (Dec.) Huxley, *On the Physical Basis of Life* (lecture)	Eliza Linn Linton, *The Girl of the Period* Browning, *The Ring and the Book* (–1869) Collins, *The Moonstone*
1869	Girton College, Cambridge, founded *The Graphic* founded Suez Canal opened John Stuart Mill, *The Subjection of Women*	Arnold, *Culture and Anarchy* R. D. Blackmore, *Lorna Doone*
1870	First Married Women's Property Act Forster's Education Act Herbert Spencer, *Principles of Psychology*	Dickens, *The Mystery of Edwin Drood*
1871	Trade Union Act Darwin, *The Descent of Man* Stanley meets Livingstone	Eliot, *Middlemarch* (–1872)
1872	Darwin, *The Expression of Emotions in Man*	Thomas Hardy, *Under the Greenwood Tree* Samuel Butler, *Erewhon* George MacDonald, *The Princess and the Goblin*
1873		Mill, *Autobiography* Walter Pater, *Studies in the Renaissance*
1874	Disraeli, Prime Minister	Hardy, *Far From the Madding Crowd* James Thomson, 'The City of Dreadful Night'

	HISTORY AND CULTURE	LITERATURE
1876	Telephone invented Queen Victoria named Empress of India	Eliot, *Daniel Deronda*
1877		Harriet Martineau, *Autobiography*
1878	Whistler vs Ruskin libel trial Gilbert and Sullivan, *HMS Pinafore*	Hardy, *The Return of the Native*
1879	Electric lightbulb invented	Browning, *Dramatic Idylls*
1880	Gladstone, Prime Minister Cecil Rhodes elected to Cape Parliament	
1881	First Anglo-Boer War	Robert Louis Stevenson, *Treasure Island* Mark Rutherford, *Autobiography of Mark Rutherford*
1882	Married Women's Property Act	
1883	Fabian Society founded	Olive Schreiner, *The Story of an African Farm* John Addington Symonds, *A Problem in Greek Ethics*
1884	Third Reform Act	Ruskin, *Storm Cloud of the Nineteenth-Century*
1885	Salisbury, Prime Minister	Rider Haggard, *King Solomon's Mines* Pater, *Marius the Epicurean*
1886	Gladstone, Prime Minister (Feb.) Salisbury, Prime Minister (Aug.) Repeal of Contagious Diseases Acts	Stevenson, *Dr Jekyll and Mr Hyde* Hardy, *The Mayor of Casterbridge*
1887	Queen Victoria's Golden Jubilee	Conan Doyle, *A Study in Scarlet* Haggard, *Allan Quatermain* Pater, *Imaginary Portraits*
1888	Jack the Ripper murders five women in London Arts and Crafts Exhibition Society	Hardy, *Wessex Tales* Mary Augusta Ward, *Robert Elsmere* Arnold, *Essays in Criticism* (Second Series) Rudyard Kipling, *Plain Tales from the Hills*
1889		George Gissing, *The Nether World*
1890	William Booth, *In Darkest England and the Way Out* Moving-picture shows appear William James, *Principles of Psychology* The electrically operated City and South London line becomes world's first deep-tunnel ('tube') underground railway Sir James Frazer, *The Golden Bough* (first two vols.; complete 13 vols., –1915)	William Morris, *News from Nowhere* Oscar Wilde, *The Picture of Dorian Gray*
1891	William Morris, Kelmscott Press	Gissing, *New Grub Street*
1892		Wilde, *Lady Windermere's Fan*
1893	Independent Labour Party formed	George Bernard Shaw, *Mrs Warren's Profession* (first produced 1902) Wilde, *A Woman of No Importance*
1894		*The Yellow Book* begins
1895	Oscar Wilde arrested and imprisoned for homosexuality	Wilde, *The Importance of Being Earnest; An Ideal Husband* Hardy, *Jude the Obscure*
1897	Queen Victoria's Diamond Jubilee	Bram Stoker, *Dracula* Mona Caird, *The Morality of Marriage*
1898		Hardy, *Wessex Poems*
1899	Irish Literary Theatre founded Second Anglo-Boer War (–1902)	
1901	Death of Queen Victoria Marconi's transatlantic wireless radio message	Kipling, *Kim*
1902		Joseph Conrad, *Heart of Darkness*
1903		Butler, *The Way of All Flesh*
1907		Edmund Gosse, *Father and Son*

Historical Overview

Transformation and the Victorian Age

Given the dramatic changes in daily life that would occur throughout Victoria's long reign (1837–1901), it is fitting that 1832 – the year that the first Reform Act was passed – is often taken to mark the beginning of the period. Coming five years before Victoria succeeded William IV to the throne, the 'Great' Reform Act focused on providing parliamentary representation to industrial centres such as Manchester and Leeds and extending the right to vote to a broader array of property-owning men. Its capacity to inaugurate the period resides less in its status as a specific piece of legislation, however far-reaching (or not) its consequences, than in its indication of the new era's fundamental orientation towards change and reform. In this sense, the introduction of passenger railways in 1830 (the year the Liverpool and Manchester line opened) is an equally appropriate marker of the beginning of the Victorian era. It revolutionised the economy and helped to foster a new sense of interconnectedness; its speed and reliance on schedules combined to transform perceptions of time itself. Perhaps equally significant is the fact that in 1832 the *Penny Magazine*, a mass-circulation publication, was first distributed. The penny post, an affordable mail service, came into being in 1840. If railway lines, popular magazines and mail spread throughout the country and fostered new awareness of interconnectedness between regions, populations and classes, so too did disease: the first outbreak of cholera occurred in Sunderland in 1831, the same year the Reform Bill was introduced, and a serious smallpox epidemic ensued in 1837, the year Victoria became queen. For all of the pride fostered at the end of the Napoleonic Wars, Victorian Britain encountered its fair share of challenges, most dramatically in terms of public health, but also in international and domestic politics, religion and finance.

Queen Victoria

The death of King William IV, on 20 June 1837, brought an eighteen-year-old woman, Victoria – the only daughter of Edward, Duke of Kent – to the throne as Queen of England. During her reign of sixty-four years she came to embody both domestic virtue and imperial power and was widely perceived as a refreshing change from her uncles and their scandal-ridden reigns. In 1840 she married Prince Albert of Saxe-Coburg-Gotha, with whom she had nine children, and with him learned to accept the ideal of a constitutional monarchy, that is, one independent of political party affiliation. Grief-stricken after Albert died of typhoid in 1861, Victoria became largely reclusive, although with the help of Benjamin Disraeli she eventually returned to public view, again undertaking official duties. Her years in seclusion had cost her substantial public favour, but she regained status in the 1870s, in part because of the strength of her support for the empire. Like many of her subjects, Victoria held views not easily characterised as conservative or liberal; against, for example, the right of women to vote, she supported many initiatives designed to better the lives and educational opportunities of the labouring classes. The lavish displays and ceremonies marking her Golden and Diamond Jubilees (1887 and 1897, respectively) suggest that she ended her reign with much the same level of support that had marked its beginnings (see Figure 5.1).

HER MAJESTY'S GRACIOUS SMILE.

Charles Knight,
Court Photographer,

26, Queen's Road,
. . . Aldershot.

5.1 Queen Victoria. This photographic portrait by Charles Knight, Court Photographer, was issued in February 1898.

Government, the Reform Acts, and the Beginnings of Mass Democracy

Although the French Revolution was long over by the time the Victorian era began, its continuing influence should not be underestimated. That the Tories maintained governmental control for several decades leading up to the early 1830s reflects in part a fear of radical movements and a corollary belief in the power of the monarchy to provide stability. Confidence in the Tories abated as frustration with their ability to ensure economic prosperity increased. The alternative party, the Whigs, were able to unite various groups dissatisfied with the status quo – Tories disengaged from their own party, Cobbett-like advocates of the rights of commoners, and followers of Jeremy Bentham's views regarding individual liberty – in the fight for major reform.

Behind the calls for reform of an electoral system that had been in place since the 1680s was the Industrial Revolution, which since the latter decades of the 1700s had dramatically altered the economy and social order. While industrial cities such as Manchester, now home to the factories on which the British economy increasingly depended, had no political representation, small towns with few inhabitants (often referred to as 'rotten boroughs') might benefit from the representation of two MPs in the House of Commons. In addition, only landowners – at the time, little more than 5 per cent of the population – could vote. Discontent with the system had grown over time, but not until the landowning Tory government was voted out over debates about Catholic emancipation in 1829 was the more progressive Whig party, led by Earl Grey, able to advance their reform interests. Like the Tories an essentially aristocratic party, the Whigs recognised the benefits of achieving moderate reform without capitulating to the radical demands of the working classes and risking wholesale revolution comparable to what had happened just decades before in France.

First presented in March 1831, the Reform Bill was defeated in the House of Commons. After a general election increased the Whig majority, a revised bill was submitted to and passed by the House of Commons in October of the same year. Its defeat in the House of Lords spawned riots throughout the country. A further revised bill was passed in March of the following year and, after a series of dramatic measures that included Earl Grey resigning, the Great Reform Act – what Norman

Benjamin Disraeli

Both novelist and statesman, Benjamin Disraeli's fame emanated as much from his leadership of the Conservative Party at the height of Britain's imperial power as from his status as a man who overcame what at the time was the stigma of being born into a Jewish family to become one of Queen Victoria's acknowledged favourites. Twice prime minister (1868 and 1874–80), he was first elected to the House of Commons in 1837. Disappointed at not being given a seat in Robert Peel's government and opposed to Peel's repeal of the Corn Laws in 1846, Disraeli spearheaded an opposition wing within the Conservative Party and garnered considerable public attention through promotion of the Young England movement, which articulated a paternalistic vision of the nation in which the working classes were united with the aristocracy in a cohesive and peaceful hierarchy, with the Church of England as spiritual head (ideals apparent in the novels he authored in the 1840s – *Coningsby, or the New Generation, Sybil, or The Two Nations* and *Tancred, or the New Crusade*). Disraeli battled, often unsuccessfully, with his rival, the Liberal Party leader William Gladstone, for decades, but his status as leader of the Conservative Party was secured in 1867 through his successful management of the Second Reform Bill. His victory was short-lived, though, largely because the Conservative Party was divided over issues regarding Ireland. In 1874 he again became Prime Minister and this time held office until 1880. In this position, Disraeli promoted a variety of social-reform measures, perhaps most notably trade-union legislation that decriminalised striking. His legacy resides also in foreign affairs – i.e., in his efforts to secure a considerable stake in the Suez Canal Company, his promotion of Victoria as Empress of India and his handling of the controversy regarding the Turkish empire. Although Disraeli's party lost power in 1880 and he died the following year, the Conservative Party was soon galvanised in opposition to Irish Home Rule, and Disraeli's advocacy of Young England ideals found new momentum.

McCord calls 'one of the century's most important political events' (*British History 1815–1906*, p. 134 [B]) – became law in 1832. The Reform Act successfully eliminated small constituencies and gave more appropriate representation to a variety of counties and cities that represented national strengths and interests. The number of men eligible to vote doubled to include many more of the middle class. More significantly, the passage of the Act seemed to demonstrate the capacity of the House of Commons and of voting people generally to take precedence over the desires of the House of Lords and even the sovereign. Aristocrats lost politically and economically, and the Whigs – or Liberal Party from the 1850s – retained a majority in the House of Commons for most of the elections held until 1874.

Victoria's reign saw two additional Reform Acts. In 1867, Benjamin Disraeli helped to ensure the passage of the Second Reform Bill, which enfranchised all male householders who satisfied a one-year residential qualification and those who occupied property rated at £12 or more annually. In effect, the electorate of England and Wales doubled again. John Stuart Mill attempted to substitute the word 'person' for 'man' in this bill, but the motion was defeated. By applying the principle of household suffrage across the board and throughout the United Kingdom, a third Reform Act in 1884 enfranchised still more men. Victorian Britain started the ball rolling towards electoral democracy, but not until 1918 were women granted the right to vote.

Legislative Initiatives and Social Reform

Reform in a less tangible sense also characterises the ethos of the Victorian period. Historians generally see the decades between the passage of the Great Reform Act and the election of the Tories in 1874 as a time of prosperity and progress, some of it an outgrowth of the Benthamite emphasis on individualism. The establishment of free trade and legalisation of trade unions, the repeal of the Corn Laws, passage of the Poor Law Amendment Act, gradual improvements in the position of the working classes and conditions of factory life, and the passage of the Education Act of 1870 are among the many noteworthy achievements of this period.

The New Poor Law refers to the Poor Law Amendment Act of 1834, which, propelled by utilitarianism, dramatically changed how welfare was provided to those in need of public assistance. Since the sixteenth century, it had generally been the case that the poor were supported in their own homes by their local parishes. The New Poor Law now organised 15,000 parishes into some 600 poor law unions with responsibility for overseeing a new system of relief centred on workhouses, of which 350 new ones were built at this time. The law aimed at reducing the expense of providing relief to the poor by rehabilitating those able to work. It did this by invoking the principle of less eligibility, which mandated that workhouses have conditions and a standard of living less attractive than would be found elsewhere by the lowest-paid worker. The 'able-bodied' could get assistance only by entering the workhouse, where they would be grouped by age and sex and could not leave unless they were able to support themselves. Many prominent writers seized the opportunity to decry the many ways the conditions of the workhouse degraded its inhabitants (see

Figure 5.2). Describing the 'ghastly kind of contentment' he saw in workhouses in his essay, 'A Walk in a Workhouse', Dickens concludes, 'Upon the whole, it was the dragon, Pauperism, in a very weak and impotent condition; toothless, fangless, drawing his breath heavily enough, and hardly worth chaining up' (Haight, *The Portable Victorian Reader*, p. 85, [Aii]). It was not until much later in the century that the stigma of pauperism came to be replaced by a more sensitive concern for poverty.

The New Poor Law was one of several acts of legislation that indicate just how central social and economic problems were to the early and middle years of Victoria's reign. In 1833, Parliament had passed its first significant Factory Reform Act, which restricted the working week for children under thirteen years of age to forty-eight hours and mandated that those children also attend school for at least two hours a day. It also made it illegal for any child under the age of nine to work in textile factories (with the exception of silk). An agricultural depression in the early 1840s, followed by a potato blight and famine in Ireland (which in turn sent hundreds of

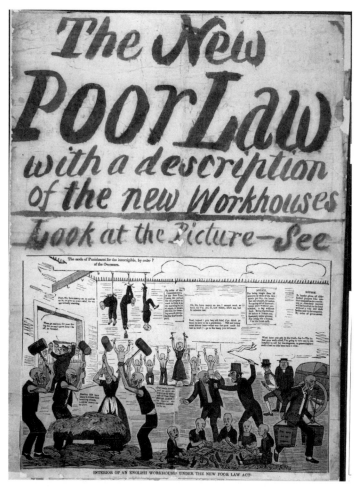

5.2 This anti-New Poor Law poster dates from 1837. The strength of popular feeling against the 1834 Poor Law Amendment Act provoked widespread rioting.

starving Irish people to the already overcrowded cities of England), prompted additional forms of legislation designed to improve the daily lives of the working classes. Several years of agitation resulted in the repeal of the Corn Laws in 1846 ('corn' in this case refers to wheat, rye, barley and oats). These laws had taxed imported grain, thereby protecting the income of landowners while making food expensive both for the working classes and for the manufacturers who had to pay their wages. Despite strong opposition, Robert Peel, advocating the benefits of free trade, led the successful effort to repeal the Corn Laws.

Chartism, the name given to groups who supported the petition known as the People's Charter, emerged concomitantly with the activism surrounding the movement for repeal of the Corn Laws and was propelled by anger over the realities of the workhouses created by the New Poor Law. Chartist activity was particularly strong in northern areas of Great Britain and in South Wales – those hardest hit by economic recession and unemployment – and focused in large measure on preparation and presentation of a charter to Parliament. Designed to redress the social, political and economic injustices of the working classes, the People's Charter had six primary goals: annual parliaments; universal suffrage (for men); the abolition of the property qualification for members of the House of Commons; a secret ballot; equal electoral districts; and salaries for Members of Parliament. Despite some 1,280,000 signatures, it was rejected by the House of Commons in 1839; 2 million more signatures appeared on a petition presented three years later (which was also rejected). Another charter was rejected in 1848. These failings notwithstanding, many of the Chartist demands were satisfied over the course of the century, and the movement helped to create within the working classes a political consciousness. Karl Marx began work at mid-century on the critique of capitalism that would prove so influential to the development of socialism later in the period (in organisations such as the Fabian Society as well as myriad other groups committed to political and economic reform).

Additional legislative measures taken by Parliament in 1855 and 1862 helped to improve the plight of the working classes and to alleviate tensions that had peaked during the Chartist years. Trade unions emerged out of local clubs and guilds of craftsmen, many of whom were unhappy with the supposed advances of the first Reform Bill, and were legalised in 1871. In 1844 workers at Rochdale started a successful cooperative enterprise on which others were soon modelled; many of these included women. Encouraging members to take advantage of insurance companies and credit unions, cooperative societies preached self-reliance, thrift and independence, values touted by Samuel Smiles in *Self-Help* (1859).

The need to improve sanitary conditions, especially in the cities, was another focus of reform initiatives. Four major epidemics of cholera (1831, 1848, 1853 and 1866) hit working-class communities especially hard, primarily because of inadequate measures to ensure a safe supply of water. *A Report on the Sanitary Condition of the Labouring Population*, published in 1842 by Edwin Chadwick (secretary of the Poor Law Commission), led to the Public Health Act of 1848, which created a Central Board of Health with the power to supervise street cleaning and waste removal and responsibility for the water supply. The 1870 Education Act is still another significant piece of mid-Victorian legislation oriented towards reform. The very poor had some access to education before 1870, principally through 'ragged schools' (essentially charitable education), but the Forster Education Act (named after W. E. Forster, a Liberal MP in Gladstone's administration) provided for a national system of elementary education, at least for England and Wales. The sense of urgency that led to these and other reform measures abated as the century wore on, but a drive to confront the social problems of a newly industrialised society pervades the period through to its end.

Women were often at the forefront of a variety of Victorian Britain's most visible public reform movements. Florence Nightingale is an icon not only as 'the Lady with the Lamp' who cared for Britain's soldiers during the Crimean War but as a leader for all sorts of reforms addressing issues such as training for army doctors, the need for improved barracks, and the role of nurses in the military. Mary Seacole, a free-black Jamaican woman who authored *The Wonderful Adventures of Mary Seacole in Many Lands* in 1857 also braved Crimean War battlefields and, despite encountering discrimination, cared for British soldiers at a hotel she ran in Turkey. Nightingale's fame in particular has overshadowed the role that many other women played in forcing forward reform of the educational, political, legal and economic institutions or practices in the period. Women like Clementina Black, a labour reformer, Helen Taylor, an early advocate of suffrage for women, Emily Faithfull, founder of the Victoria Press and tireless proponent of remunerative opportunities for women, Edith Simcox, a journalist who took on topics like 'The Capacity of Women' and argued for women's economic rights, and Emily Davies, founder in 1869 of Girton College, Cambridge, the first residential women's college in Britain, were key players in these and other reform efforts. They kept what came to be known as 'The Woman Question' at the forefront of social reform discussion and debate. The remarkable achievements of women in both social and literary arenas was hampered by prevailing medical myths that perpetuated the belief that women were 'by nature' weaker, more prone to disease and debility, and suited to quiet lives within the domestic sphere. True, domestic ideology (especially the ideal of woman as ministering angel) granted women substantial (if only symbolic) power as moral authorities, but that moral authority was largely restricted to the confines of the home. Published in 1839, Sarah Stickney Ellis's bestselling conduct book, *The Women of England: Their Social Duties and Domestic Habits*, extolled the 'moral beauty' and selflessness of women who devoted themselves to sanctifying the lives of their children or husbands and improving themselves through the exercise of accomplishments in music, art and craft.

Scholars today tend to exercise caution about over-emphasising the impact of the Victorian gendered division of labour and activity into 'separate spheres'. Nevertheless, women throughout the period never tired of keeping the public attuned, often through the periodical press, to the ways women were disadvantaged economically, legally, politically and in terms of access to education. While women moved and worked within the public sphere in many ways, we should not be too quick to dismiss the significance of 'The Woman Question'. Despite achievements like the passage of the Divorce and Matrimonial Causes Act in 1857, which protected women against assault, cruelty and desertion and created a civil divorce court in London, and the Married Women's Property Acts of 1870 and 1882, which provided women with the right to possess the wages they earned after marriage, Victorian women encountered enormous obstacles in achieving the rights they were due.

Religion

Religion played a key role in many of the reform initiatives undertaken in Victorian Britain. An Evangelical wing within the Church of England (sometimes referred to as 'Low Church', as opposed to the 'High Church' or 'Broad Church' factions of the Church of England) supported such organisations as the Society for the Promotion of Christian Knowledge and the Society for the Propagation of the Gospel in Foreign Parts – groups easily mocked by writers like Dickens and Trollope. Bible, religious-tract and missionary societies prospered under the influence of an Evangelical revival inherited from the eighteenth century. One noteworthy leader was Lord Ashley, the Earl of Shaftesbury, a vocal critic of slavery in the colonies who also worked to improve conditions of factory work, to provide education for poor children, and to treat the mentally incompetent with humanity. With its overarching emphasis on the personal experience of sin and the promise of salvation, Evangelicalism prospered outside of the Church of England in dissenting and non-conformist religious denominations. Readers of Victorian literature might take away a skewed impression of Evangelicals, one that unduly emphasises their excessively strict restrictions on amusements and entertainment, their sometimes misplaced efforts to suppress 'vice' (through ludicrous initiatives like placing fig-leaves on nude statues at the Crystal Palace) and their campaign against violations of the Sabbath. Yet, Evangelical movements launched some of Victorian Britain's most significant charitable and social-reform endeavours. Moreover, as Norman McCord notes, 'genuine religious fervour exercised a major influence upon the lives of millions of men, women, and children drawn from all levels of society – not only from Evangelical quarters' (*British History*, p. 241 [B]).

The High Church segment of the Church of England saw its share of strife in the nineteenth century. Those affiliated with the High Church valued the traditions, sacraments and rituals associated with Catholicism; they believed that the authority of the Church derived from God (as opposed to the state) and was transmitted by the apostolic succession of bishops. Although High Church tendencies had diminished during the long eighteenth century, they resurfaced in England in the 1830s in Oxford, primarily because of the upset caused by the admission of non-Anglicans to Parliament and by other perceived threats to Church authority. Leaders of the 'Oxford Movement' (Oxford University clergy that included John Keble, John Henry Newman and Richard Froude) galvanised opposition within the Church to Evangelicalism. Especially influential were *Tracts for the Times*, written by Newman and others, between 1833 and 1844, which argued that the Church of England rightfully occupied the middle way (or *via media*) between Roman Catholicism and Protestantism. Not surprisingly, Newman's ideas (especially his argument that the Thirty-Nine Articles – which summarised the beliefs of the Church of England on basic matters of individual, corporate and national religion – were compatible with many Roman doctrines) produced a backlash reaction among Protestants who feared full-fledged conversion to the Catholic Church. Newman did convert in 1845, but many others, led by Edward Pusey, stayed within the Church of England to fight for the Anglo-Catholic cause. Within the Church of England there also existed a substantial segment of people who would have identified most closely with Broad Church, or latitudinarian, tenets; eschewing the doctrinal issues that divided those embracing High Church doctrines from Evangelicals, they stressed the inclusiveness of the Church and valued open-minded intellectual inquiry such as that spawned by biblical criticism. Religious toleration increased in the latter half of the nineteenth century, but Jews and Catholics continued to be treated sceptically (despite the fact that Jews were admitted to the House of Commons in 1858 and to the House of Lords in 1866).

Richard Altick finds irony in the fact that 'in strengthening the Church's historical foundations, [the Oxford Movement] neglected to protect its fabric from the coming winds of intellectual challenge' (*Victorian People*, p. 219 [B]). Challenge came in many forms. Biblical scholarship, for example, much of it originating in Germany, approached the Old and New Testaments not as divinely inspired but rather as products of human endeavour and aspiration. David Friedrich Strauss's *Das Leben Jesu*, translated into English by Mary Ann Evans ('George Eliot') in 1846 and Ernest Renan's *La Vie de Jesus*, of 1860, were influential studies of the relationship between the suspect historicity of the Bible and its indubitable spiritual and moral legacy. Still more challenges to the religious authority and timescales of the Bible and of Christianity came from scientific study – particularly from advances in geology, natural history and palaeontology.

Science, Technology and Innovation

With the founding of the British Association for the Advancement of Science in 1831, it comes as little surprise that science was at the forefront of much public discussion and activity during Victoria's reign. Both amateurs and professionals were engaged in scientific discovery, and the relationship between the two was continually a matter of debate. Learned societies devoted to nearly every dimension of scientific understanding proliferated in this period. The Natural History Museum epitomises the convergence of Victorian Britain's investment in scientific understanding and its urge to conquer and contain; as Richard Owen, its original curator, proclaimed, 'Birds, shells, minerals, are … to be seen in any museum; but the hugest, strangest, rarest specimens of the highest class of animals can only be studied in the galleries of a national one' (quoted in Black, *On Exhibit*, p. 107, [Ciii]). By the century's end, science had entered the curriculum in Britain's major universities. A. S. Weber points to a variety of factors to explain the extraordinary scientific activity of the Victorian era: 'cheaper and more widespread access to printed materials, the recognition of science as a profession, greater government support for scientific endeavour, a strong relationship between industry and the sciences, and greater literacy rates which brought about increased public knowledge and support of science in Europe and America' (*Nineteenth-Century Science*, p. xi [Aii]).

Charles Darwin's *On the Origin of Species by Means of Natural Selection* deserves its status as a landmark in the history of science, but many of its ideas were in circulation before its publication in 1859. Darwin developed his ideas on natural selection while aboard HMS *Beagle* from 1831 to 1836 and published his studies, *Voyage of the Beagle*, soon after. Robert Chambers's controversial but widely read *Vestiges of the Natural History of Creation* (1844) plotted the evolution of earth from clouds of interstellar gas through a series of geologic ages and, though flawed, helped to pave the way for Darwin's argument. In his concluding remarks, for instance, Chambers emphasises how species might become extinct without the proper conditions for their existence. Published in the early 1830s, Charles Lyell's *Principles of Geology* posited a view of the earth's development over an extended period of time that undercut the biblical story of creation, and other scholars explored the implications of evolution. Darwin's work crystallised much of this thinking, and his methods – his accumulation of data and presentation of argument – were as significant as his ideas about natural selection, the adaptive habits of plants and animals to their environments, and the 'survival of the fittest'. Although *The Origin of Species* concludes with references to 'the grandeur in this view of life' and to the role of 'the Creator' that seem to leave open the possibility of intelligent design, Darwin's later work, *The Descent of Man, and Selection in Relation to Sex* (1871), more forthrightly brought human life into the models drawn earlier from plants and animals. At roughly the same time, Thomas Henry Huxley, a strong proponent of scientific naturalism, began making major contributions to ethnology and physiology; in his lecture *On The Physical Basis of Life* (1868), he urged his readers to accept that 'there is some one kind of matter which is common to all living beings, and that their endless diversities are bound together by a physical, as well as an ideal, unity' (Haight, *The Portable Victorian Reader*, p. 530 [Aii]). The application of evolutionary ideas to emerging social sciences was not long in coming. Anthropology drew on Darwin's model of time and on the work of

The Great Exhibition

Sometimes heralded as 'the first world's fair' the Great Exhibition of the Works of Industry of All Nations epitomised Britain's pride in its industrial supremacy at mid-century. It was organised by Prince Albert and Henry Cole, both members of the Society of Arts, and lasted for five months. The icon most often associated with the Great Exhibition was the spectacular Crystal Palace, an enormous greenhouse-like structure designed by Joseph Paxton (see Figure 5.3). Made of glass and metal and located in Hyde Park, the Crystal Palace was large enough to house thousands of exhibits, roughly half representative of Britain and its colonies. Within this space, objects were grouped according to the following categories: raw materials, machinery, manufactured goods, and the fine arts. Many of the objects on display were essentially useless gadgets, but exhibits included everything from exotic art, jewels and stained glass, to furniture and household items, to printing presses, telegraphs and other machinery, large and small. The Exhibition attracted millions of visitors to London, many travelling by rail and many taking advantage of the 'shilling days' that made for more affordable admissions. (The phrase 'spending a penny' also has its origins in the Great Exhibition, where it referred to the charge exacted to use the public lavatories in the Crystal Palace!) The Great Exhibition can be seen to mark the beginning of modern consumerism and the rise of the commodity and to embody the optimistic embrace of progress so characteristic of the middle years of Victoria's reign.

5.3 'Centre Transept, Crystal Palace', Sydenham, south London, 1855. The original building used for the 1851 Great Exhibition at Hyde Park had been reassembled at Sydenham in 1854.

Herbert Spencer, a philosopher now known as the 'father of social Darwinism'. According to Philip Davis, Spencer 'took the evolutionary system as far as it could possibly go' (*The Victorians*, p. 70 [B]). Positing evolution as a transformation from simple to complex forms, Spencer drew clear demarcations between the religious embrace of mystery and scientific admission of what cannot be known. Not only did his laws of progress help anthropologists to develop a paradigm of man's relation to primate forebears, but they enabled some to promote the adoption of agnosticism as public policy (Fichman, *Evolutionary Theory and Victorian Culture* [Ciii]).

Scientific discoveries of various sorts were behind the many technological innovations that occurred throughout the period. The justly famous 'Great Exhibition of the Works of Industry of All Nations' displayed thousands of exhibits, many of them representing Britain and its colonies (the 'workshop of the world'), when it opened in 1851. As Roy Porter describes it, the 19,000 exhibits 'formed the greatest array yet seen by men', and included 'the largest pearl ever found and the Kohi-Noor diamond, engines of every description, carriages, china, glass and cutlery, including a knife with 300 blades' (*London: A Social History*, p. 291 [B]).

Among the noteworthy inventions during the period was Henry Fox Talbot's production of a photographic negative. In the mid-1830s, Talbot produced images by placing sensitised paper under lace and leaves and then exposing them to sunlight; in the early 1840s, with the help of Daguerre's invention ('daguerreotype' photographs were made from polished copper plates coated with iodine vapour and heated), Talbot developed calotype prints, essentially creating the first multi-copy photographic process. His book, *The Pencil of Nature*, published in 1844, was the first collection of photographs to be published for profit. Charles Babbage's invention of machines capable of calculating mathematical problems earned him a reputation as the 'father of the modern computer'. Scientific research also facilitated the development of important forms of medical technology in the nineteenth century; the stethoscope and microscope were steadily improved and more widely used and, by the late 1840s, the invention of anaesthesia dramatically improved the practice of surgery. Louis Pasteur's study of germ theory at mid-century likewise proved enormously influential, enabling Robert Koch, for example, accurately to identify the organisms that caused tuberculosis.

The Victorian zest for scientific discovery can be measured in many ways. Both men and women took up what might be thought of as scientific hobbies – collecting and studying various specimens of plant and animal life, studying fossils, sketching plants, animals, and native populations while travelling, and joining societies of like-minded individuals. Characters like Job Legh in Elizabeth Gaskell's *Mary Barton* and the Reverend Farebrother in George Eliot's *Middlemarch* exemplify the type of amateur scientist found within many a Victorian family. Works with titles such as *The Note-Book of a Naturalist* and *Glimpses of Plant Life* flourished throughout the Victorian period. E. P. Thompson's *The Notebook of a Naturalist* trumpets the private collections, 'perfect almost as regards the British species', of the 'many practical and zealous florists and ardent followers of Natural History in Great Britain' (pp. vii–viii [Ai]). In her study *Kindred Nature* [Ciii], Barbara Gates charts the extraordinary activity of Victorian women in pursuing all avenues of popular science, their writing shaping modern thinking about the natural world. Featuring the work of women like Arabella Buckley, Marianne North, Beatrix Potter and Gertrude Jekyll, among many others, Gates demonstrates just how essential, if little acknowledged, were women's contributions to natural history – particularly in the areas of collection, illustration and close observation. Her study provides a useful supplement to Samuel Smiles's *Self-Help*, stocked as it is with mini-biographies celebrating the discoveries of male amateur and professional scientists. Whatever the differences in how scientific achievements of the period were recorded for posterity, scientific discovery and technological innovation were clearly a source of national pride – one linked, inevitably, with Britain's evolving imperial identity.

Technologies of Travel, Commerce and the British Empire

The opening of railway lines early in the era spawned a construction boom that created a kind of national circulation system – transporting people, goods and, inevitably, texts of all sorts from one hitherto remote part of the country to another in speedy and predictable fashion. Indeed, in *Sartor Resartus* Carlyle writes that 'Books, like invisible scouts, permeate the whole habitable globe, and Timbuctoo itself is not safe from British literature' (*A Carlyle Reader*, p. 185 [Ai]). Literature provides ample evidence of the ambivalence with which Victorians faced the inevitable and irrevocable alteration of the landscape. In 'On the Projected Kendal and Windermere Railway' Wordsworth asked, 'Is then no nook of English ground secure / From rash assault?' (Cunningham, *The Victorians*, p. 15 [Aii]). The year 1837 saw the creation of the Great Western Railway, designed by I. K. Brunel (who two decades later would design the *Great Eastern*, the largest steam ship of the century). In 1838, the *Great Western* paddle steamer crossed the Atlantic in just under three weeks. By the middle of the century, some 8,000 miles of railway track were in place. Underground rail travel is also a product of the nineteenth century; the London Metropolitan line opened for passenger business in 1863, and by the end of the century the underground network was fairly well established.

The railway was only one of many innovations that led to faster and safer modes of communication and travel – on local, national and worldwide scales. Improvements in roads and travel services gave men and women unparalleled opportunities to move beyond their own communities throughout the era. The sense of connectedness fostered by road and rail travel was enhanced by telecommunication – the telegraph, first, and, in the latter 1870s, the telephone. The transatlantic telegraph cable was ready for use by the middle of the 1860s. Steady improvements in steam-engine technology led also to dramatic changes in ocean transport; by the early 1860s, Britain had iron-hulled warships at its disposal. By 1888, London boasted the first electric power station. The century-long technology boom had numerous implications, especially in economic and commercial realms of activity; trade with China, Australia, India and the United States exponentially increased. Small wonder that the entrepreneur, Thomas Cook, the man behind the famous 'Cook's Tours', is a product of this moment in history, as is John Murray III, publisher of the popular and profitable series of tourist-oriented guidebooks.

Travel and tourism were commercial enterprises, and they prospered in part because of the momentum of expansion generated by a culture of imperialism. Victorian imperialism did not see its heyday until the latter third of the century, but the expansion of the empire occurred gradually, if haphazardly, throughout the nineteenth century, and for several centuries before then. Still, it is worth noting that by the end of the century, Britain's colonies took up more than a quarter of the world's land. The confidence inspired by Britain's technological leadership and domination of world markets no doubt helped contribute to the impulse to explore and settle in many parts of a now far more accessible world – with resources that many Victorians were eager to appropriate and capitalise on. Jennifer Wicke reports that by the end of the Victorian period, Britain's 'imports exceeded even her massive exports', testimony not only to the nation's status as 'commercial colossus' but also to the growing power of the middle classes ('Commercial', in Tucker, *A Companion to Victorian Literature and Culture*, p. 63 [B]). With characteristic acerbity, Dickens spoofs the impulse to capitalise on world resources at the beginning of *Dombey and Son*: 'The earth was made for Dombey and Son to trade in, and the sun and moon were made to give them light' (p. 2 [Ai]). The imperial confidence that Britain's trade inspired, however well founded, shaded easily into a dubious moral superiority (as in Rudyard Kipling's idea of 'the white man's burden') and nurtured a kind of attendant anxiety about the ability of the nation to sustain its power and about contradictions in the national stance.

India dominated Britain's colonial landscape and was effectively controlled by the commercial East India Company and the British Government for much of the century. When the Suez Canal opened in 1869, travellers could journey from Britain to India in just a few weeks. An important rebellion against British rule that erupted in 1857 and 1858 would not have commanded so much attention if there had not already been concerns about the fragility of the British presence abroad. Known in Britain as 'The Indian Mutiny' (and in India as the 'First War for Independence'), it began when a group of Hindu and Muslim soldiers decided to disobey British orders after they had been commanded to do things precluded by or offensive to their religious beliefs: specifically, they were asked to use rifles whose cartridges had been greased with pork and beef fat. Were it not for an already existing fund of discontent – one based on hostility to Britain's administrative posture, economic policies and embrace of Christian Evangelicalism – the opposition would not have escalated, as it did, into a full-scale rebellion, the largest threat to British rule in the nineteenth century. Peasant uprisings, rapes and murder in various communities, and the seizure of Delhi engrossed and, for the most part, enraged, the public at home. British forces regained the city, using force equal to or worse than what had been used against them, and eventually took over rule of India from the East India Company, but the influence of the mutiny can hardly be reduced to structural or governmental changes that ensued. As Heather Sheets has written, 'British narrative accounts that emerged out of the conflict helped to shape beliefs and perceptions about colonialism, gender, and race in both Britain and India, the legacies of which still haunt historical interpretation in the present' ('The Rebellion of 1857: Origins, Consequences, and Themes', n.p. [Ciii]). The fact that Queen Victoria took on the mantle of 'Empress of India' after an Act of Parliament in 1876 bestowed it on her speaks volumes about the continuing role of India in Britain's national identity for decades after the rebellion.

Africa was another major arena for colonisation and missionary activity, and African exploration a manifestation of Victorian Britain's troubled relationship to the idea and reality of empire. Britain was certainly not alone in participating in the so-called Scramble for Africa; it competed actively with Belgium, France and Germany for its perceived share of African resources. By the mid-1860s, Britain's expansion inland into Africa was such that it occupied land in every quarter of the continent, although the historian Andrew Porter contends that its presence in Africa at this point was 'territorially immense but – with the exception of the Cape Colony and the Transvaal – economically insignificant' (*Oxford History*, p. 6 [B]). David Livingstone, a Scottish missionary and doctor, published *Missionary Travels and Researches in South Africa* in 1857 to wide acclaim. In the Boer Wars at the end of the century Britain sought to enhance its access to South Africa's depositories of gold and diamonds; over 20,000 Afrikaner civilians died and Britain lost more of its imperial prestige.

By the end of Victoria's reign, Britain had colonies or occupied territory not just in India and Africa but throughout the world – e.g., the Caribbean, New Zealand and Australia, Hong Kong, Newfoundland and Canada. Much contemporary scholarship has sought to better understand the reality and consequences, both practical and symbolic, of Victorian Britain's embrace of imperialism. Edward Said's *Orientalism* and *Culture and Imperialism* have been especially influential in exposing the pernicious effects of a predominantly Western view of Eastern cultures and nations as fundamentally primitive and passive. Such a view is clearly applicable to many late-century novels, among them Conrad's *Heart of Darkness* (1902), whose narrator, Marlow, describes his group of fellow travellers to Africa as 'wanderers on a prehistoric earth'. Recently Andrew Porter has written that historians 'no longer see in Empire the simple products of metropolitan designs imposed on comparatively inert indigenous peoples. They are much more alive to the varied processes of interaction, adaptation, and exchange which shaped the Imperial and colonial past' (*Oxford History*, p. 4 [B]). As his comment implies, it is necessary to recognise the distinctions between the acquisition of land and governance of people and the many other sorts of global activities and interests that drove Victorian Britons to explore (if not colonise) the world.

'Mightier Than Either Pulpit or Cannon': Print Technology and the Press

The technology that facilitated so much activity beyond Britain also transformed daily life within its borders. Simply put, mechanisation dramatically changed the nature and function of the press. Newspapers began to use steam power for printing in the Romantic era; high-speed presses, innovative mechanisms for reproducing illustrations and, later in the century, advanced typesetting technology followed. In *Victorian People and Ideas*, Richard Altick goes so far as to say that 'To the Victorians, the printing press driven by a steam engine was … the most pregnant emblem of their achievement and aspirations' (p. 64 [B]). Improvements in transportation and communication in the Victorian age combined with rapid urbanisation, entrepreneurial capitalism and growth in literacy to help propel the literary market and periodical press into a formidable industry and cornerstone of Victorian culture. Many other factors converged to change the experience of reading itself, not least of which were the introduction of wood pulp (replacing rags) for paper production and the transition to gas lighting. The introduction of telegraph technology later in the century dramatically changed the nature of news coverage. Economic measures such as the repeal of the remaining penny stamp duty on newspapers in 1855 were also crucial in enabling a popular press to emerge in service to Victorian Britain's expanding readership. Andrew King and John Plunkett note that the removal of the stamp duty enabled 'price reductions, rises in circulation, and an increase in the frequency of publication', all signs that a cheap national press had been born (*Victorian Print Media*, p. 340 [Aii]). All of the above allowed the press to generate relatively affordable reading material, and, not surprisingly, that very material came to be increasingly heterogeneous both in form and function. As Sally Mitchell summarises, 'the Victorians virtually invented mass literature' (*Daily Life in Victorian England*, p. 233 [B]), and the fact that the term 'bestseller' came into being late in the century reflects this reality.

Urban centres, increasingly well served by railways, offered readership markets for publishers, bookshops, libraries and newsagents. Publishers developed ways to cater to particular audiences and to make various types of reading material affordable for a broader spectrum of people. Such formidable firms as Longman, Bentley and Macmillan competed in a frenzied market with those run by John Murray, George Smith, Edward Moxon, and Charles Kegan Paul (and with organisations such as the Society for the Diffusion of Useful Knowledge) to produce print. Libraries played a key role and enjoyed close affiliation with (and substantial discounts from) the burgeoning publishing industry. From mid-century on, free libraries serving the working and middle classes emerged throughout the country. The triple-decker volume that was standard format for so many novels, if unaffordable to the average reader, was sold at discount to circulating libraries such as Mudie's Select Library and W. H. Smith's. Charles Edward Mudie's name was made not just by his sharp business acumen, but also by the influence (and arguably censorship) he exerted in determining which books to market through his 'Select' line. Cheap reprints of popular fiction, history and biography made reading material even more accessible. Religious and learned societies produced and published inexpensive tracts and a wide range of improving literature; an array of sensational literature (sometimes referred to as 'penny dreadfuls' or 'shilling shockers') and broadsides also prospered.

Although circulating libraries made book borrowing relatively affordable, and free libraries even more so, serialisation practices brought still more readers into the literary market. The publication of Dickens's *Pickwick Papers* (1836–7) has long been heralded as a watershed moment in the history of fiction and Victorian reading because of the spectacular success of its instalment format. Not only did publication in parts (whether weekly or monthly instalments) make the purchase of books affordable to a far wider spectrum of consumers, but it engaged readers in the process of following plot and character development in entirely new and exciting ways. Eventually magazine serialisation usurped the market that part-publication of instalments commanded throughout much of the early and middle years of the Victorian era. Elite quarterly magazines such as the *Edinburgh Review*, the *Westminster Review*, and the *Quarterly Review* came into existence several decades before Victoria came to the throne and remained influential venues for intellectual and political discussion, but they were soon outnumbered by new-to-the-market monthly and weekly magazines such as *Blackwood's*, *Bentley's Miscellany*, *Fraser's* and the *Cornhill*. In *Punch*, which began publication in 1841, readers could delight in humorous commentary on nearly every aspect of domestic life and international affairs. Far from simply being vehicles for the production and dissemination of popular fiction and poetry, these and hundreds of other magazines carried a heterogeneous mix of non-fiction, authored by men and women, and directed to the wide-ranging interests of their myriad readers. Richard Altick observes that 'If the intellectual history of the Victorian era is a record of constant ferment and debate, the entrepreneurial, competitive spirit of publishing can be thanked' ('Publishing', in Tucker, *Companion to Victorian Literature and Culture*, p. 301 [B]).

Many periodicals were amply illustrated. *The Illustrated London News*, which began publication in 1842, reproduced thirty-two woodcut illustrations in each of its sixteen-page instalments (see Figure 5.4). Enormously successful from the start, it

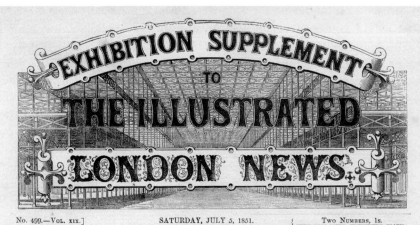

EXHIBITION SUPPLEMENT TO THE ILLUSTRATED LONDON NEWS

No. 499.—Vol. xix.]   SATURDAY, JULY 5, 1851.   { Two Numbers, 1s.
                                                              { WITH HALF-SHEET SUPPLEMENT GRATIS.

THE GREAT EXHIBITION.

GENERAL AND MISCELLANEOUS MODELS.

THE art of modelling, as applied to landscape, is one which we believe to be susceptible of more improvement and more advancement than is generally considered possible. It has never yet been treated as an art, and it has been in general only pursued as a matter of individual whim or scattered members of that ingenious body of amateur wielders of their fingers who are continually producing specimens of that class of nondescript articles which we admire for their ingenuity, and very often not the less for that ingenuity having been singularly misplaced. The tribe of industrials to whom we refer are the running workmen who love to astonish the world by constructing either anomalous objects, or commonplace objects made of anomalous material. One genius will arrange shells into the shape of fruit or flowers. Another—and he has sent his work to the Exhibition—will construct such a monstrosity as a ship fully rigged—her ropes, sails, and spars all cut out of cork. Again, we shall have a cunning workman carving wonderful things out of pith, or shaping a lamp, which is the rapturous admiration of the neighbouring provincial journal, out of a turnip. Anon, we find a man devoting his life to writing the Lord's Prayer and the Ten Commandments within the compass of a fourpenny bit; while his neighbour in these unappreciated arts sends up to the Queen, as an appropriate present, a walking-stick, carved all over with the figures of the Zodiac, or a scene from "Paradise Lost," or, perhaps, a wonderful watch, containing a snuff-box; an almanack; a set of toothpicks; directions for the preservation of health; and a steam for breeding horses. Any attentive reader of the newspapers—and who is there who is not?—will recognise in a moment the class of nondescript ingenuity to which we refer. The neat-handed monstrosities thus produced generally attain an immortality of a fortnight or so, while the laudatory paragraph goes the rounds, until they are supplanted by some more recent and even still more wonderful intelligence touching an enormous gooseberry, or a shower of frogs, in a remote district of England. Now, what we want to enforce is, that modelling as applied to landscape, or to those degrees of the art which lie between raised map making on the one hand, and the representation of rocks and ruins and trees upon the other, has been in general only pursued by the class of nondescript industrials whose master-pieces we have characterised; and the natural consequence is, that the art, in its ordinary manifestations, is in a state of utter desolation and tasteless rudeness. Of this the Exhibition affords several curious proofs; amongst which we may mention at once a model of Tynemouth Priory and rock, which would have disgraced a sugar baker, and a model of a grand allegorical procession of the Shaksperian characters

WAITING HER MAJESTY'S ARRIVAL.

The above Engraving represents the waiting-room erected for the reception of Her Majesty near the North entrance of the Building, having particular reference to the surrounding group of anxious spectators, on the occasion of the inauguration of the Crystal Palace, on the 1st of May. This elegant little apartment is chiefly composed of rich tapestry, the interior being lined with pale light blue and white silk, fluted. The furniture is of a very costly character, combining lightness of appearance with splendour of effect. The sofa and chairs are carved and gilt, and covered with light blue silk damask. The carpet of rich Brussels, is a flowered pattern. Flowers, tastefully disposed, add a pleasing and lively effect to the picture. In the rear of the principal room is a smaller apartment, separated from it merely by a draped partition, in which is a handsome cheval glass, in a gilt frame and stand. Crowds of persons daily throng to view this little bijou of a boudoir, at a respectful distance however—a cordon being drawn around it, guarded by a policeman.

5.4 This 'Exhibition Supplement' of *The Illustrated London News* was published on 5 July 1851. The large illustration depicts the waiting room constructed for the reception of Queen Victoria.

garnered special attention for its spectacular pictorial coverage of major domestic and international events, such as the Crimean War and the Great Exhibition.

Commodities themselves, papers and magazines were also often filled with advertisements for everything from medicinal treatments and cures, soap and other cleansers, to books, writing utensils, clothing, baby equipment, and inventions and gadgets galore (see Figure 5.5). They provide, not surprisingly, a record of the emergence of a consumer culture and the realities and aspirations of the middle classes.

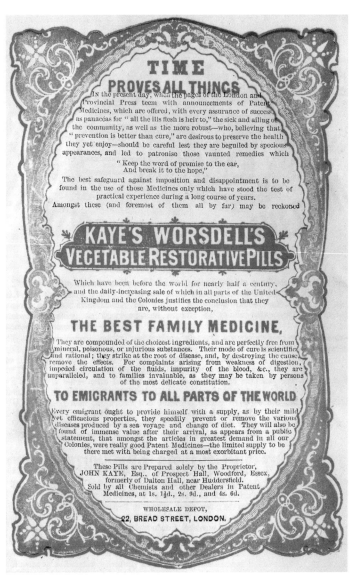

5.5 'Kaye's Worsdell's Vegetable Restorative Pills'. This advertisement appeared on the wrapper to the first instalment of Dickens's *Our Mutual Friend* in 1864.

It is fitting that Rudyard Kipling's late-century and well-known poem, 'Recessional: A Victorian Ode', so often taken to mark the end of the era (and occasioned by Queen Victoria's 1897 Jubilee celebration), first appeared in a newspaper. Kipling writes of 'our pomp of yesterday' and gloomily warns of a people 'drunk with sight of power' (*Longman Anthology of British Literature*, pp. 1770–1 [Aii]). Each stanza of 'Recessional' ends with the line, 'Lest we forget', Kipling's plea that the lessons of the day be not lost. Without saying so, the poem laments the end of an era. If this overview gives the impression that Victorian Britons were wrapped up in the considerable achievements, discoveries and challenges of their own day, then it has done a disservice to the equally formidable record of their preoccupation with the past – a category that includes everything from the 'deep time' of geological history to the nostalgic longing for one's most recent past, yesterday. A preoccupation with the past undergirds the Gothic Revival and the Pre-Raphaelite Brotherhood and informs a wide range of intellectual movements. Perhaps its most intriguing manifestation, though, is in the emergence of aestheticism, through which so much that signified 'the Victorian' came to be seen as 'the past'.

It is no coincidence that aestheticism's most significant founding father, Walter Pater, was a historian, author of *Studies in the History of the Renaissance* (1873) whose conclusion famously argued that 'not the fruit of experience, but experience itself, is the end' (*Longman Anthology*, p. 1670 [Aii]). Pater's language and tenets armed an array of writers and artists, including Oscar Wilde, with the ammunition to reject their culture's philistine mixture of middle-class moralism and didacticism. Robin Gilmour aptly describes the aesthetic movement as 'a mixture of straightforward rebellion against Victorianism, new theorising, and extravagant posing – all meeting in unstable fusion in the symbolic rise and fall of Oscar Wilde' (*The Victorian Period*, p. 237 [B]). The Victorian era may well have ended, in this sense, before Victoria herself died in 1901. To attempt to locate the beginning of the end with an influential cultural movement, such as aestheticism, or with the publication of critical works like *The Way of All Flesh* (1903), Samuel Butler's satire of family life, or *The Importance of Being Earnest* (1895), Wilde's rout of all things Victorian, or, more soberly, with the Boer Wars at the end of the century, which made the fragility of the empire so painfully apparent, is an exercise in futility, however, one that disregards the considerable complexities of Victorian history and literature.

Literary Overview

In an 1858 essay on Dickens, the journalist Walter Bagehot wrote 'London is like a newspaper. Everything is there and everything is disconnected' ('Charles Dickens', p. 87 [Ai]). If his metaphor resonates, it is because the Victorian era was so deeply associated with the proliferation of print. The sheer variety of texts that went into circulation as publishing became a major industry shaped, inevitably and in diverse ways, more traditional literary forms. Print culture in its kaleidoscopic variety became the lens through which Victorians saw their world and understood themselves. In numerous ways, the literature of the Victorian period reflects its sometimes uneasy relationship to the culture of print on which it depended for its astonishing diversity and reach.

Continuities and Influences

Victorian literary history provides many examples of innovative appropriation of both forms and themes inherited from the eighteenth century and the Romantic era. Even the two works most often cited as signalling the arrival of new literary sensibilities and styles – *The Pickwick Papers* and Carlyle's *Sartor Resartus* – are indebted to their predecessors. *The Pickwick Papers* owes something to the popularity of sporting-life stories, most notably Robert Surtees's *Jorrocks' Jaunts and Jollities* (1831–4). First published serially in *Fraser's Magazine*, Carlyle's *Sartor Resartus* (1833–4), a hybrid work of fiction, social criticism and biography, adapts the satirical modes of Swift and Sterne and has didactic tones that hark back to eighteenth-century moralists. Writers throughout Victoria's reign clearly continued to be influenced by, even as they developed in new directions, the work of Romantic-era authors who, in their preoccupation with issues of liberty, individualism, the nature of subjectivity, the function of the past and the relationship between man and the natural world, provided ideas and inspiration a-plenty for the generations that succeeded them.

It goes almost without saying that Shakespeare, too, was an enormous influence on Victorian writers, and not simply as filtered through Dr Bowdler's notoriously sanitised *Family Shakespeare*. Not only were there hundreds of editions, anthologies and productions of Shakespeare's work, but many authors – including Carlyle and Dickens – were indebted to Shakespearean modes of characterisation and use of language. Victorians also developed numerous ways to commodify Shakespeare; his image and his language found their way onto everyday household objects like teacups, towels and silverware in the period. Observing that 'the Victorian Shakespeare is above all a national poet, essential to Englishness', David Latané quotes Carlyle's remark that the 'Indian Empire will go, at any rate, some day; but this Shakespeare does not go, he lasts forever with us; we cannot give-up our Shakespeare!' ('Literary Criticism', in Tucker, *Companion to Victorian Literature and Culture*, p. 393 [B]).

Many literary developments, trends and even publication formats straddle the Romantic and Victorian periods. Keepsake books and annuals remained popular well beyond the heyday of the Romantic era and included work by major Victorian poets. Interest in the Gothic modes of the late eighteenth century percolated throughout the Victorian age. Victorian writers extended in new directions not just the forms and techniques, but also the themes, of their predecessors; the French Revolution, for example, continued to surface for reconsideration, most prominently in Dickens's *A Tale of Two Cities* but also in works like Matthew Arnold's essay, 'The Function of Criticism at the Present Time'.

However influential were generations past on Victorian literary sensibilities, Carlyle's command in *Sartor Resartus* to 'Close thy Byron; open thy Goethe' helps to illustrate a distinctive shift between the two literary periods. Carlyle bemoaned the self-absorption he believed characteristic of Romantic writers and advocated the rigorous embrace of duty he associated with Goethe. Much Victorian literature, pre-occupied with work and practical solutions to the myriad social problems facing the industrial nation, suggests that Carlyle was preaching to the converted. Clearly, the radical fervour once inspired by the French Revolution was supplanted, in a lot of Victorian writing, by concerns to redress social, economic and political problems through mechanisms of reform that seem decidedly modest by comparison.

Modes of Production and Consumption: the Literary Marketplace

Paraphrasing Virginia Woolf's well-known claim that 'on or about December 1910 human character changed', we might say that 'on or about March 1836 nineteenth-century literature changed'. When the firm of Chapman and Hall began advertising an intention to release monthly numbers of *The Posthumous Papers of the Pickwick Club* priced at one shilling each, they little knew that a publishing phenomenon was to be born. *The Pickwick Papers*, as the publication came to be known, was the brainchild of Robert Seymour, a well-known caricaturist, but it was Dickens (then Seymour's junior partner) who was recruited to 'edit' the papers. Having established his name through a variety of publications (collected in *Sketches by Boz*, 1836), Dickens soon garnered a substantial readership, for, in the course of its twenty-month run, *The Pickwick Papers* sold at an astonishing rate of 40,000 a month. No sooner had it been published than it recirculated through reprints of extracts, public readings and stage adaptations. *Pickwick* and Dickens had alike become commodities, and the literary market was transformed. The parts publication format of *Pickwick* has been credited with 'democratizing and enormously expanding the Victorian book-reading and book-buying public' (Patten, p. 45 [Cv]).

The ample illustrations of much serialised fiction, including that of Dickens, contributed also to its popularity; artists like George Cruikshank, Hablot Browne ('Phiz'; see Figure 5.6) and, later in the century, John Everett Millais became almost as well known to readers as the authors themselves. Critics link Dickens's success in particular not just to the affordability of the format and his effective use of illustrations, but also to the ways serialised structure opened up interpretive possibility – the interval between instalments allowing for reviews to further stir speculation among the novel's community of readers. In addition, through his use of seasonal and social references, Dickens devised new ways to link the lives and times of the fiction to those of his readers (Mark Turner, 'The Material Culture of the Victorian Novel', in O'Gorman, *Concise Companion to the Victorian Novel*, p. 117 [B]), and his distinctive voice and narrative persona (coming through not only in the novel but in the many prefaces to various editions that Dickens authored) further encouraged intimacy between author and reader.

Although they were 'the indispensable middlemen between authors and readers', as Richard Altick puts it ('Publishing', in Tucker, *Companion to Victorian Literature and Culture*, p. 289 [B]), publishers exerted enormous influence in determining the direction of literary publication. A handful of firms dominated the literary market for much of Victoria's reign: Chapman and Hall, Bradbury and Evans, Macmillan's,

5.6 Frontispiece to the first edition of *The Pickwick Papers*, with an illustration by 'Phiz' (Hablot Browne).

Richard Bentley, Blackwood's, and Smith, Elder. These firms monopolised the field for much of the fiction now thought of as canonical, but many other publishers fought for a share of the broader literary market. Edward Moxon, for example, made inroads through the publication of poetry (including lavishly illustrated editions of Tennyson). Publisher for the Society for the Diffusion of Useful Knowledge, Charles Knight – who Richard Altick calls 'the very symbol of the cheap-book movement' – helped to circulate a wide range and vast quantity of improving literature, almanacs, encyclopaedias and the *Penny Magazine* (*The English Common Reader*, p. 281 [B]).

Still further outside the mainstream were publishers like G. W. M. Reynolds; author of *Mysteries of London*, Reynolds published various penny-dreadful novels and managed profitable businesses 'in London's lower depths' (*The English Common Reader*, p. 292 [B]).

Both meeting and helping to create the demand generated by the aesthetic movement, a number of smaller, new firms emerged in the last quarter of the century with high-brow speciality interests – among them Elkin Mathews and

> **From Dickens's Preface to *The Posthumous Papers of The Pickwick Club***
>
> The almost unexampled kindness and favour with which these papers have been received by the public will be a never-failing source of gratifying and pleasant recollection while their author lives. He trusts that, throughout this book, no incident or expression occurs which could call a blush into the most delicate cheek, or wound the feelings of the most sensitive person. If any of his imperfect descriptions, while they afford amusement in the perusal, should induce only one reader to think better of his fellow men, and to look upon the brighter and more kindly side of human nature, he would indeed be proud and happy to have led to such a result.

John Lane, who published books by avant-garde artists. Mathews and Lane published the quarterly magazine *The Yellow Book*, which was also receptive to women writers whose works might otherwise not have found a home. Avant-garde publishing emerged concomitantly with modern fine printing and book-making, as evidenced by William Morris's Kelmscott Press in 1890. Driven by a desire to counter what he believed to be the crass and aesthetically unappealing productions of a commercial press, Morris promulgated the value of the human hand to craft

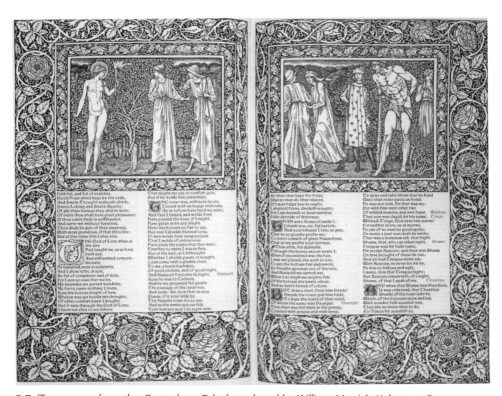

5.7 'Two scenes from the *Canterbury Tales*', produced by William Morris's Kelmscott Press.

5.8 Kate Greenaway. *Marigold Garden: Pictures and Rhymes*. London, New York: George Routledge and Sons, 1885. Frontispiece.

books with more beauty and spirit than anything a machine could produce. The Kelmscott Press produced more than fifty books before Morris died in 1896, including an extraordinary edition of Chaucer's *Canterbury Tales* that was four years in the making (see Figure 5.7). Many dozens of printers and publishers, including the Ashendene Press, responded favourably to Morris's views and helped an era of fine printing to prosper.

That the Victorian era is considered a golden age for children's literature (this is, after all, the era that produced *Alice in Wonderland*, *The Princess and the Goblin* and *The Water-Babies*) also owes much to developments in print culture. Early in the period, the Religious Tract Society and the Society for the Promotion of Christian Knowledge were dominant forces in this market. Much of the literature published for youthful readers betrays its association with Evangelical publishers, both in form (i.e., an affiliation with Sunday school 'reward books' and tracts oriented towards proper, Christian conduct) and substance (e.g., characters who live austere, pious lives, who endure periods of suffering that enable conversions, or who undergo protracted deathbed scenes). The form and function of children's literature in the latter half of the century was indelibly shaped by technologies of illustration. John Tenniel's drawings for *Alice in Wonderland* are almost as well known today as the novel itself. Kate Greenaway was recognised for her distinctive, nostalgic approach to illustration (see Figure 5.8). Her books (such as *Marigold Garden*) and illustrations for other authors (such as those done for Robert Browning's *The Pied Piper of Hamelin*) relied on the contemporary engraving techniques made possible by the famous colour-printer and wood-engraver Edmund Evans.

Publishing firms worked not only with authors and illustrators, but also with circulating libraries. Through fee-based libraries and book clubs, relatively well-to-do readers had access to a wide range of reading material, but circulating libraries – able to pay the exorbitant fees for bulk orders of newly published, in-demand, fiction – enjoyed the most commercial success and connected to the widest range of readers. With help from public-library initiatives of the 1830s and 1840s, free libraries began to open up in urban centres.

The largest and most influential lending library in Victorian Britain was operated by Charles Edward Mudie. His library began lending books in London in 1842 and within a relatively short time span had established branch offices in Manchester and Birmingham. Extolling its virtues in an article for *Once A Week* in 1863, Andrew Wynter claimed that Mudie's has 'superseded half the labour of country book-clubs, athenaeums, and literary societies' and estimated that 'no less than 10,000 volumes are circulating diurnally through this establishment' ('Mudie's Circulating Library', in King and Plunkett, *Victorian Print Media*, pp. 278, 279 [Aii]). The typical three-volume format characteristic of much Victorian fiction was a luxury beyond the reach of many readers, so publishers came to rely on Mudie's to make profitable the distribution of literature. Mudie facilitated the circulation of vast quantities of poetry, fiction and prose, and he set the standards for what type of literature his 'Select' library would allow to circulate. Dickens was certainly not alone in his anxious invocation of the spectre of the young girl's blush in justifying his own supposed desire not to give any affront to his readership. Trollope wrote in his *Autobiography*: 'I do believe that no girl has risen from the reading of my pages less modest than she was before, and that some may have learned from them that modesty is a charm well worth preserving' (p. 8 [Ai]). Mudie believed that the sensibility of the young lady set the standard for family reading. That the character of 'Mrs Grundy' (originally alluded to in the Romantic-era play, *Speed the Plough*, by Thomas Morton) would enjoy lasting fame as a symbol of the censorious nature of Victorian life is testimony to the enormous influence that Mudie's Select Library exerted on the literary market (see Figure 5.9).

The emergence of the popular press played still another role in shaping the literary market. Especially key was a battle against the 'taxes on knowledge', which at mid-century resulted in substantial reduction of the price of newspapers and magazines (which, in turn, carried advertisements for new fiction, critical reviews, and interviews with authors). Papers such as *Lloyd's Weekly* (1848) and the *Daily Telegraph* (1855) garnered huge readerships and paved the way for the 'new journalism' of the 1880s, when magazines like the *Pall Mall Gazette* (1865), led by entrepreneur William

5.9 'Mudie's Select Library'. This advertisement, typical for Mudie's Select Library, appeared in the wrapper to *Our Mutual Friend*.

T. Stead (author in 1885 of 'The Maiden Tribute of Modern Babylon', a graphic exposé of child prostitution), introduced such features as women's columns, sports coverage and crime reports. Begun in 1881 by George Newnes, *Tit-Bits* similarly pioneered a model of journalism for mass circulation (aimed at the newly literate lower middle classes) that relied upon haphazard presentation of short, often sensational, items. Newnes found in the American magazines *Harper's* and *Scribner's*, carriers of much fiction from both sides of the Atlantic, models on which to base another magazine,

The Strand, which he began in 1891 (and which carried Conan Doyle's Sherlock Holmes stories). Coverage of the Jack the Ripper case helped circulation figures of these papers skyrocket. By the end of the century, it was impossible to separate the commercial interests of 'The Fourth Estate' (the term appropriated by Carlyle to denote a powerful press) from its mandate to convey with objectivity the news.

George Gissing – author of the unpublished book *Mrs Grundy's Enemies* – made the literary market the subject of his 1891 novel, *New Grub Street*. In it he excoriates the supremacy of cheap, sensational writing and depicts with gritty realism the social and economic barriers that compromise the integrity of authors struggling to establish their reputations. Gissing describes the despondency of one such author in the character of Marian, who is disheartened to be 'exhausting herself in the manufacturing of printed stuff which no one even pretended to be more than a commodity for the day's market'. Gissing continued,

> She herself would throw away the pen with joy but for the need of earning money. And all these people about her, what aim had they save to make new books out of those already existing, that yet newer books might in turn be made out of them? This huge library, growing into unwieldiness, threatening to become a trackless desert of print – how intolerably it weighed upon the spirit.
>
> (p. 138 [Ai])

A variety of forces converged late in the century not only to enable more people to buy, rather than borrow, books, but also to fuel discontent with the three-volume novel and to facilitate the publication of more affordable one-volume novels. Guinevere Griest cites the rise of free libraries in the provinces, the increasing availability of cheap reprints and a flood of new novels on the market as key features of this changing literary market (*Mudie's Circulating Library*, pp. 168–70 [Cv]). When Mudie's finally relinquished (or lost) the control on the market it exerted via its determination of what books to market as its Select Library, publishers became more receptive to alternative forms, content and writers.

Language, Forms, Genres and Styles

The Victorian Novel

To name just a handful of the major fiction writers of the Victorian period – e.g. Charlotte Brontë, Charles Dickens, William Makepeace Thackeray, Anthony Trollope, George Eliot, Robert Louis Stevenson and Thomas Hardy – is to grasp why the era is invariably associated with the ascendancy of the novel. The literary market that Dickens, via *The Pickwick Papers*, helped to create was one of novel readers. The novel as genre did not, of course, spring full-grown from Dickens's head, but Romantic poetry clearly commanded the literary stage during the first few decades of the nineteenth century. In the years between the heyday of Sir Walter Scott and Jane Austen at one end and Charles Dickens at the other – *terra incognita* to most students of the period – certain types of fiction prospered, most notably depictions of high society (the 'silver-fork novels') and narratives of criminal life (often referred to as 'Newgate novels'). Inspired in part by the social vision and idealism of Carlyle, Dickens entered this scene eager to experiment in new ways with representing the social realities of urban life.

He was not alone. In the late 1830s and throughout the 1840s, 'Condition of England' and social-problem novels appeared. With this literature writers sought overtly to reflect and respond to the wide-ranging problems encountered by a newly urban and industrial nation; their narratives of family and domestic crisis unfold against backdrops of urban squalor. References abound to socio-economic problems of urban life such as prostitution, drug addiction, starvation, slum conditions and crime. In works such as Frances Trollope's *Michael Armstrong, or, The Factory Boy*, Disraeli's *Sybil; or The Two Nations*, Charles Kingsley's *Yeast* and *Alton Locke*, Charlotte Brontë's *Shirley* and Elizabeth Gaskell's *Mary Barton* and, later, *Ruth* and *North and South*, novelists addressed complex problems of economic and social strife, often providing solutions by representing resolutions within the domestic sphere. Looked at this way, the social-problem fiction of the 1840s seems less distinctively linked to the historical moment of the Hungry Forties and Chartist fervour and more integral to the development of an art form that throughout the Victorian era would grapple with the relationship between romantic and realist impulses and agendas. Indeed, in her preface to *Mary Barton*, Elizabeth Gaskell explains her decision to focus on Manchester in language that conflates the two modes: 'I bethought me how deep might be the romance in the lives of some of those who elbowed me daily in the busy streets of the town in which I resided' (p. 37 [Ai]).

The tension between romantic and realistic impulses is everywhere evident in the novels of William Makepeace Thackeray, who, like Dickens, began work as a journalist. In his earliest work Thackeray indulged a penchant for the comic sketches of burlesque, but his later works depict men and women confronting personal failure and disappointment. His best-known novel was *Vanity Fair*. Published in monthly parts in 1847 and 1848, the novel is what Henry James famously (and derisively) termed a 'loose and baggy monster' – that is, a multi-volume work casting its representational net over a panoramic cast of characters. Many dozens of Victorian novels fit this bill, among them Dickens's *Bleak House* and *Little Dorrit* and George Eliot's *Middlemarch* and *Daniel Deronda*. The multi-plot novel may well owe some of its success to its status as a profitable format for publishers working in concert with circulating libraries, but clearly it appealed for other reasons as well. Some literary historians contend that it enabled

---

David Masson on Realism/Romance

A Romance originally meant anything in prose or in verse written in any of the Romance languages; a Novel meant a new tale, a tale of fresh interest. It was convenient, however, seeing that the two words existed, to appropriate them to separate uses; and hence, now, when we speak of a Romance, we generally mean 'a fictitious narrative, in prose or verse, the interest of which turns upon marvellous and uncommon incidents'; and when we speak of a Novel, we generally mean 'a fictitious narrative differing from the Romance, inasmuch as the incidents are accommodated to the ordinary train of events and the modern state of society'. If we adopt this distinction, we make the prose Romance and the Novel the two highest varieties of prose fiction, and we allow in the prose Romance a greater ideality than in the Novel.

(*British Novelists and Their Styles*, David Masson, 1859 [Ai]).

novelists both to mirror and to critique the spectacular nature of commercial society at mid-century – that the genre itself was exhibitionist at just the moment that the Great Exhibition was celebrating the inventions of the industrial nation. Other critics, including George Levine, associate complexly plotted narratives with the metaphor of entanglement so crucial to emerging Darwinian models of understanding species and their development. Peter Brooks offers a more psychological perspective when he writes that 'it was part of the triumph of the nineteenth-century novel in its golden age to plot with a good conscience, in confidence that the elaboration of plot corresponded to, and illuminated, human complexities' (*Reading for the Plot*, p. 114 [Cii]).

Multi-plotted works such as *Vanity Fair*, *Bleak House* and *Middlemarch* are also characteristically Victorian in their didactic function and overtones. Throughout *Vanity Fair*, for example, Thackeray makes heavy-handed and frequent use of an intrusive narrator, the 'Manager of the Performance'. Thackeray's narrator is often a spokesperson for the work's moral message, as when near the narrative's end he proclaims, 'Ah! Vanitas Vanitatum! Which of us is happy in the world? Which of us has his desire? Or, having it, is satisfied?' (p. 666 [Ai]). In his *Autobiography*, Thackeray's fellow novelist Anthony Trollope wrote that he 'always thought of [himself] as a preacher of sermons' (p. 8 [Ai]), and many other Victorian novelists (including Dickens, Gaskell, Charlotte Brontë and George Eliot) might have said the same. Comments like 'Falsehood is so easy, truth so difficult', in *Adam Bede* (p. 151 [Ai]), flow thick and fast through much of George Eliot's fiction. In his study of the novel's emergence as a dominant form in nineteenth-century England, Michael Wheeler rightly points out that such moral teaching – what Carlyle in *Sartor Resartus* referred to as 'a wish to proselytise' (Carlyle, p. 328 [Ai]) – helped to placate Evangelical critics who, early in the century, were particularly suspicious of the novel (Wheeler, *English Fiction*, p. 10 [B]).

The relationship of novelistic form to the religious and moral impulses of the author reveals itself in many other ways as well, perhaps most overtly in Evangelical literature in the first half of the century. Evangelical writers and publishers exerted an especially forceful emphasis on the development of children's literature, for example, with stories published by the Religious Tract Society and the Society for the Promotion of Christian Knowledge often featuring horrifying child deathbed scenes and dramatic moments of conversion. At a crucial moment in Hesba Stretton's bestseller of 1867, *Jessica's First Prayer*, for example, the character of Daniel Standring 'felt his heart turning with love to the Saviour, and he bowed his head upon his hands, and cried in the depth of his contrite spirit, God be merciful to me, a sinner' (p. 63 [Ai]). John Bunyan's *Pilgrim's Progress* (from which Thackeray took the title for *Vanity Fair*) was widely considered essential family reading in the period. Many Victorian authors sought to disseminate its values of self-discipline and pious endurance of life's challenges. As importantly, the idea of the religious quest, or pilgrimage, shaped narrative structure itself. Focusing on the power of Bunyan's story to provide novelists with a rich repository of allusions and with an organising framework to represent the individual's troubled journey through life, Barry Qualls claims that 'both writers and readers were determined to shape the facts of this world into a religious topography, making a path toward social unity in this world an analogue to Christian's progress toward the Celestial City' (*Secular Pilgrims of Victorian Fiction*,

p. 12 [Civ]). The journey through troubled childhood and adolescence is central to the *Bildungsroman* (a novel of formation), a form adapted in different ways in novels such as Brontë's *Jane Eyre* and *Villette*, Dickens's *David Copperfield* and *Great Expectations*, Eliot's *The Mill on the Floss* and Meredith's *The Ordeal of Richard Feverel*.

Tensions between romance and realism present themselves especially forcefully in the novels of the Brontë sisters (Charlotte, Emily and Anne), who also began their careers as novelists in the late 1840s. Charlotte Brontë in particular was drawn to novels of education, and crafted female versions of the classic *Bildungsroman*; her heroines struggle not only with the educational and occupational limitations imposed on women at the time, but also, more fundamentally, with the competing demands of reason and feeling. Although some literary critics have studied *Jane Eyre*, as well as Anne Brontë's novel *Agnes Grey*, as 'social-problem' novels that use the condition of the governess to stage critiques of the political, economic and social conditions that restrict women, the label fails to capture the complicated ways novels by each of the Brontë sisters depict the relationship between social and spiritual experience. For all of the psychological realism that underpins novels like *Jane Eyre*, *Wuthering Heights* and *Villette*, supernaturalism also plays a key role. In *Jane Eyre*, for example, Charlotte Brontë signals a divide in her heroine's psyche when a lightning bolt splits in half a chestnut tree on the night Jane first becomes engaged to Rochester. In a crucial early episode of *Wuthering Heights*, the narrator, Lockwood, confronts the ghost of Catherine Earnshaw in the window of his room.

In a review written in 1858, the critic George Henry Lewes declared realism to be 'the basis of all art'. Conventional histories of the novel in the Victorian age argue for the 'rise' of realism, with novels centred on modern, ordinary life supplanting works where the imaginative propensities of character or author predominated, or where the author's investment in the sentimental, the sensational and melodramatic, or the psychologically aberrant directed the plot or theme. Yet, the meanings of romance and realism (and the relation of the two to representations of suffering and invocations of sentiment) to nineteenth-century writers and readers are notoriously difficult to pin down, as they shifted according to the different contexts in which they were invoked. Nevertheless, there were undoubtedly many works of fiction against which novelists who sought to represent ordinary, everyday life could contrast their works. The enormously popular 'penny dreadfuls' – which sold by the million in the 1860s – packaged their stories of the bizarre, fantastic, and criminal under a sensational engraving on their cover (Bristow, *Empire Boys*, p. 11 [Cii]). The sensation fiction of the 1860s is another case in point; if critics today recognise works like Mrs Henry Wood's *East Lynne* or Mary Braddon's *Lady Audley's Secret* as subtly addressing a variety of real problems afflicting a modernising and consumer-driven society, many of the novel's contemporary critics focused on the adultery, the attempted murder, and the disguise at the heart of their plots. Scorning the appetite of readers who consumed this type of fiction, Henry Mansel wrote in the *Quarterly Review*:

> Excitement and excitement alone seems to be the great end to which [sensation novels] aim … And as excitement, even when harmless in its kind, cannot be produced without becoming morbid in degree, works of this class manifest themselves as belonging, some more, some less, but all to some extent, to the

morbid phenomena of literature – indications of a widespread corruption, of which they are in part both the effect and the cause; called into existence to supply the cravings of a diseased appetite, and contributing themselves to foster the disease, and to stimulate the want that they supply.

('Sensation Novels', *Quarterly Review*, p. 482 [Ai])

One has to wonder whether such critical commentary, pervasive as it was, had any real impact on reading preferences or on authorial thinking about the need either to pander to, or, alternatively, to redirect reading habits. Charles Reade, author of such popular novels as *It Is Never Too Late to Mend, Hard Cash* and *A Woman-Hater*, referred to his brand of social realism with the seemingly paradoxical label 'matter-of-fact romance'. A penchant for melodrama, both in fiction and in the theatre, seems to have flourished despite (and possibly because of) critical alarms about morbidly dangerous literary trends. As Andrew Sanders writes, 'Throughout the mid-century the novel fed the theatre and the theatre the novel, generally to the detriment of both' (*The Short Oxford History of English Literature*, p. 437 [B]). Detective fiction also, especially as mastered by Wilkie Collins in works such as *The Woman in White*, appeals to interest in the criminal and typically deploys a range of narratological devices to manipulate suspense.

Against this backdrop, works such as George Eliot's *Scenes of Clerical Life* (first published in *Blackwood's Magazine* in 1857) certainly seem distinctive in relentlessly calling attention to the mundane. Eliot sounds the clarion call of literary realism early on when her narrator offers the following explanation of purpose:

For, not having a lofty imagination, as you perceive, and being unable to invent thrilling incidents for your amusement, my only merit must lie in the truth with which I represent to you the humble experience of ordinary fellow-mortals. I wish to stir your sympathy with common-place troubles – to win your tears for real sorrow: sorrow such as may live next door to you – such as walks neither in rags nor in velvet, but in very ordinary, decent apparel.

(*Scenes of Clerical Life*, p. 56 [Ai])

Eliot's self-conscious embrace of the ordinary pervades all of her fiction. In *The Mill on the Floss* she tells an implied middle-class audience that 'the pride and obstinacy of millers, and other insignificant people, whom you pass unnoticingly on the road every day, have their tragedy too; but it is of that unwept, hidden sort, that goes on from generation to generation, and leaves no record' (p. 197 [Ai]). Many of Eliot's works concern themselves with the rural (or provincial) and the past. *Adam Bede* and *Silas Marner* invoke the pastoral mode in their idyllic representation of the countryside, yet Eliot is also careful to depict her settings as distanced temporally and psychologically from her own urban, modern world. In *Silas Marner* the narrator muses that 'In that far-off time superstition clung easily round every person or thing that was at all unwonted, or even intermittent and occasional merely, like the visits of the pedlar or the knife-grinder' (p. 5 [Ai]). Later works, such as *The Mill on the Floss* and *Middlemarch*, more critically treat the idea of the provincial, focusing on the narrowness of minds as communities contemplate large-scale change (such as would be wrought by the coming of the railway) or lesser forms of change (such as accepting new forms of medical treatment). Eliot's works focus on the conditions that restrict or undermine human ambition and the painful, tragic, loss of idealism within a society that strongly directs, even determines, one's options. The novelist's famous 'religion of humanity' is directly related to her choice of subject matter and narrative technique. Describing the 'swift-advancing shame' soon to overtake Hetty Sorrel in *Adam Bede*, for example, she concludes:

> Such things are sometimes hidden among the sunny fields and behind the blossoming orchards; and the sound of the gurgling brook, if you came close to one spot behind a small bush, would be mingled for your ear with a despairing human sob. No wonder man's religion has much sorrow in it: no wonder he needs a Suffering God.
>
> (pp. 305–6 [Ai])

In *Middlemarch* especially, Eliot's narrator plays a prominent role in urging readers to sympathy with a cast of characters who are diminished by the petty or hypocritical values of those with whom their own lives are entangled (and, indeed, a web is one of the novel's most prominent metaphors).

In this way, Eliot's fiction offers more consolation than do the works of her fellow realist, Thomas Hardy, whose novels, situated in Wessex (Hardy's name for a semi-fictional region of south-west England) focus similarly on a vanished or vanishing rural world. In works such as *Under the Greenwood Tree, The Return of the Native, Jude the Obscure* and *Tess of the d'Urbervilles*, Hardy depicts a rural world where shared values, however sustaining to many in the community, ostracise outsiders, and where nostalgia for old ways cannot compete with what Angel Clare in *Tess of the d'Urbervilles* calls the 'ache of modernism'. Francis O'Gorman offers an insightful contrast between the two novelists when he writes that 'Eliot's plot combines determinism with teasing suggestions of how things might be different; Hardy's offers a sternly ineluctable movement toward sorrow with the continual recognition of how it could be averted with the smallest assistance from chance or prior knowledge' ('Emotion in the Victorian Novel', David, *Cambridge Companion to the Victorian Novel*, p. 266 [B]). While Hardy would seem to fall squarely within a realist tradition, he rejected the label, writing that 'Art is a disproportioning – i.e. distorting, throwing out of proportion – of realities, to show more clearly the features that matter in those realities, which, if merely copied or reported inventorially, might possibly be observed, but would more likely be overlooked. Hence "realism" is not Art' (quoted in Wheeler, *English Fiction of the Victorian Period*, p. 198 [B]). Much of his subject matter – sexual victimisation in *Tess of the d'Urbervilles* and unhappy marriage in *Jude the Obscure* – exposed him to the wrath of reviewers bent on measuring his fiction against the standards of circulating-library morality. Margaret Oliphant's comments on *Jude the Obscure* reveal well what Hardy was up against. 'There may be books more disgusting, more impious, as regards human nature more foul in detail, in those dark corners where the amateurs of filth find garbage to their taste', she wrote, 'but not, we repeat, from any Master's hand' (Cox, *Thomas Hardy: The Critical Heritage*, p. 257 [Ai]). Hardy was not the only major novelist to find himself a sinner in the hands of an angry critic. Mudie's censored George Meredith's novel, *The Ordeal of Richard Feverel*, for its supposedly offensive and immoral treatment of divorce. Still, the excess of Oliphant's vitriolic language might be read to reflect her anxious awareness that the days were numbered when circulating-library moralism could control the market. N. N. Feltes attributes the demise of booksellers and circulating libraries (and the triple-decker novel that was their life-blood) to the tide of cheap books flowing in alongside the new journalism of the last few decades of the period (*Modes of Production* [Cv]). Although the triple-decker did not die out until the middle of the 1890s, much of the fiction of the last third of the century is notably shorter and more experimental, suggesting a nascent modernism within the history of the genre.

Robert Louis Stevenson's fiction, which enjoyed both popular and critical appeal, illustrates the way form itself could accommodate shifting values and aesthetics. *Strange Case of Dr Jekyll and Mr Hyde* combines elements of Gothic, detective and science fiction in a complex narrative form that stylistically reinforces the novel's theme of fragmented, fluctuating identity. Works like *Treasure Island* and *Kidnapped* equally evidence Stevenson's interest in subverting the preconceptions of his readers, especially with appealing 'amoral' characters like Long John Silver of *Treasure Island*. Influential essays such as 'A Gossip on Romance' and 'A Humble Remonstrance' situated Stevenson at the centre of a rejuvenated romance/realism debate – in effect rescuing the beleaguered romance from the grip of realism.

That so many authors in the latter third of the Victorian era, like Stevenson, turned to or experimented with children's literature owes something to the capacity of fantasy and fairy tale to assert the power of romance to comment on reality. In 1851, John Ruskin published a precursor to this tradition with *The King of the Golden River*. Kingsley's *The Water-Babies, A Fairy-Tale for a Land Baby* yokes a critique of child labour to broad themes of evolution and sanitation in its evocation of the moral education of the main character, Tom, a chimney sweep who encounters the idea(l)s of cleanliness and purity when he enters a magical underwater world. George Macdonald (author of such works as *The Princess and The Goblin*) and Rudyard Kipling (in *Just So Stories for Little Children*) also developed ways for the fantastical or fairy-tale-like to commingle with the didactic. Even *Alice in Wonderland* and *Through the Looking Glass*, which rely so much on linguistic play and the nonsensical, are political in their rendering of the whimsical Queen and in their subtle references (through the characters of the Unicorn and Lion) to the well-known animosity between Disraeli and Gladstone.

The 'death' of the triple-decker would seem to be foreshadowed by the arrival not only of fantastical children's literature but of a wide range of substantially shorter fiction from the 1870s onwards. Stevenson was not alone in writing fiction that seems proto-modernist in its preoccupation with fractured identity and with psychological interiors. *Marius the Epicurean*, published in 1885 by Walter Pater, whose work on the history of the Renaissance and essays on the non-utilitarian value of art would prove so influential to writers in his day, evoked the sensual experiences of the aesthete. Arthur Conan Doyle's Sherlock Holmes stories focus on the hero's mind – that is, his ability to outfox all others (including the police) in the pursuit of criminals through his scientific and logical understanding of coded behaviour. Wilde's *The Picture of Dorian Gray*, yet another slim novel of the period, was first serialised in *Lippincott's*

The New Woman

The New Woman was a recognisable literary figure and a social reality long before the novelist Sarah Grand used the term in an essay in the *North American Review* in 1894. Rejecting the assumptions of separate spheres ideology that consigned woman to the home and circumscribed her power to that space, new women typically demonstrated their independence from restrictive domestic ideology by flouting conventional feminine behaviour – e.g. by wearing clothing that allowed greater freedom of movement or by riding bicycles. While new women embraced a variety of social and political causes, they were particularly preoccupied with the sexual double standard and with inequality within marriage relationships. Mona Caird, an important participant in the New Woman movement, collected a series of articles exposing the problems of marriage laws, *The Morality of Marriage* (1897). Some of the most influential New Woman literary figures were created by male authors – one thinks, for example, of Nora in Ibsen's *A Doll's House* and of Hedda Gabler, and of Mina Harker in Bram Stoker's *Dracula*.

Monthly Magazine in 1890 (just after it had published Doyle's *Sign of Four*). The literature of the 'New Woman' arguably began with Olive Schreiner's *The Story of an African Farm* in 1883 and, with publishers feeling newly liberated from the grip of circulating-library morality, it prospered throughout the 1890s, not only in full-length novels such as Sarah Grand's *The Heavenly Twins* and *The Beth Book* but in an array of short stories (e.g., Netta Syrett's 'The Heart's Desire', Ella D'Arcy's 'White Magic' and Mabel Wotton's 'The Hour of Her Life'). As Carolyn Nelson summarises, 'With its feminist heroines who directly challenged society's construction of the feminine and demanded their emancipation, and its greater emphasis on a psychological exploration of women's inner lives, this fiction provided more authentic depictions of women for its readers' (*A New Woman Reader*, p. xiv [Aii]).

The 1890s alone cannot wholly be credited with putting to rest the 'loose and baggy monsters' of the era it capped. Plenty of short fiction circulated in popular monthly magazines throughout the Victorian era, and collaboratively authored collections of stories like *A House to Let* (1858) and *The Haunted House* (1859), both published as Christmas numbers of Dickens's magazines, enjoyed popular success. Still, most of the influential advocates of aestheticism from the 1870s onwards focused their energies not just on cultivating in the public an appreciation for beauty, but also on rejecting the association of literature with didactic, moral purpose – in doing so, they edged aside a form that, until then, had dominated the literary market.

Poetry

In her introduction to *Victorian Poetry: Poetry, Poetics, and Politics*, Isobel Armstrong warns of the danger of seeing Victorian poetry as 'on the way to somewhere'. 'Whether on the way from Romantic poetry, or on the way to modernism', she writes, 'it is situated between two kinds of excitement, in which it appears not to participate' (p. 1 [B]). Armstrong is right, for Victorian poets engaged in complicated and innovative ways with the same issues of subjectivity and individuality that preoccupied generations both before and after them. Tennyson's poetry is especially instructive in this regard. His *Poems, Chiefly Lyrical*, published in 1830, attracted the attention of Arthur Henry Hallam (who, after his death in 1833, would be elegised by Tennyson in *In*

Memoriam). Hallam recognised Tennyson's striking ability to convey intense emotion and to render the distinctive character of various poetic personas. At the same time, he warned the poet against indulgence in melancholic mood, against too-ready acceptance of Romantic-era poetry of sensation. Certainly, Tennyson's early poetry justified Hallam's critique. Poems like 'Mariana' (with its repetitive refrain 'She said, "I am aweary, aweary, / I would that I were dead!"') and 'The Lotos-Eaters' (in which Tennyson's band of mariners eschew a life of labour and conclude, 'surely, surely, slumber is more sweet than toil') (both poems in *Longman Anthology*, pp. 1139–41 and 1146–50, respectively [Aii]) seem positively antithetical to the embrace of work and the duties of the everyday that by mid-century would seem central to the ethos of Victorian culture. So, too, they stand in sharp contrast to the Chartist poetry written in the late 1830s and throughout the 1840s. Ernest Jones's 'The Silent Cell', for example, strongly endorses commitment to everyday struggle:

> But never a wish for base retreat
> Or thought of a recreant part,
> While yet in a single pulse shall beat
> Proud marches in my heart.

(ursulastange.com/chartistpoetry.html)

During the course of his career, Tennyson garnered a reputation and audience comparable to that of Dickens, and his poetry offers special insight into the complicated and sometimes paradoxical tastes and sensibilities of the Victorian reading public. Set against Chartist poetry of the 1840s, Tennyson's *The Princess: A Medley*, hardly seems evidence of what Andrew Sanders calls his 'new commitment to a poetry of social purpose' (*The Short Oxford History*, p. 426 [B]), for although purportedly concerned with women's lack of access to higher education it turns uneasily to a hazy medieval past to advance its claims. Its power derives, ultimately, not from any real sense of social or political commitment, but from its lyrical devotion to emotional states not unlike those characteristic of Tennyson's earliest poetry. *In Memoriam, A. H. H.* – a poem that Queen Victoria compared to the Bible in its consolatory powers – is actually far more expressive of doubt than of faith. In its relentless representation of emotional and intellectual ambiguity, it offers our best evidence of Tennyson's appeal. Expressing in a range of ways his grief and the crisis of identity that ensued as he grappled with the death of his beloved friend, the poem also complicates its representation of self-in-seclusion by probing, over the course of 133 lyrics, such topics as the function of poetry writing, the challenges to belief posed by scientific knowledge, man's relationship to nature, and the differences between qualitative and quantitative experience of time. The poem functions, in short, as an extended meditation on questions of truth, doubt, belief, faith and knowledge.

Almost all Victorian literature concerns itself with the troubled relationship of the public and the private and in this, too, Tennyson's poetry is representative. In poetry written after he became Poet Laureate, he often urges unity among his diverse readership. In 'Ode on the Death of the Duke of Wellington', for example, he writes, 'A people's voice! We are a people yet' (Cunningham, *The Victorians*, p. 255, Aii) and 'The Charge of the Light Brigade' ends with an appeal to

Honour the charge they made!
Honour the Light Brigade,
Noble six hundred!

(*Longman Anthology*, p. 1196 [Aii])

Generations of men and women committed these lines – and many others of Tennyson's poetry – to memory. Tennyson deserves a central place in any overview of Victorian poetry not just because of his distinctive contributions to the genre but also because of his indubitable influence on fellow poets of the era as well as on his readership. His poetry provided central inspiration, for example, to the Pre-Raphaelite Brotherhood, which formed in 1848. Christina Rossetti's contributions to *The Germ* – the short-lived magazine of the Pre-Raphaelite Brotherhood – reveal her engagement with Tennyson's poetry as well.

The Pre-Raphaelite Brotherhood

The Pre-Raphaelite Brotherhood refers first and foremost to John Everett Millais, William Michael Rossetti, Dante Gabriel Rossetti, James Collinson, Thomas Woolner, Ford Madox Brown and William Holman Hunt. These seven young men – painters, poets and sculptors – banded together in 1848 to form the Pre-Raphaelite Brotherhood (PRB) and sought in their shared commitment to the close study of nature to counter what they believed was the Royal Academy's slavish deference to the formalism typified by the late Renaissance masters who followed Raphael/Rafaello (b. 1483?). The PRB harked back to earlier Italian Renaissance painting and drew inspiration from medieval artists, seeking to emulate the simplicity of their vision and the sincerity of their religious devotion (see Figure 5.10). In their choice and careful delineation of subject matter, use of bright colour and reverence for the highly symbolic, Pre-Raphaelite paintings created a splash in the Victorian art world. Their paintings, exhibited first in an 1849 exhibition, garnered the most attention, but they turned in subsequent years to book and periodical illustration and graphic art. Their magazine *The Germ: Thoughts Toward Nature, Poetry, and Art*, although only surviving for four issues, includes critical statements on their values as well as reviews, poems and stories. Christina Rossetti, sister of Dante Gabriel, began publishing (pseudonymously) in *The Germ*. Although the PRB lost momentum relatively soon after its formation, its work was influential. The arts and crafts and aesthetic movements of the last third of the century can be seen as extensions or revisions of the ideals espoused variously by PRB members. Dante Gabriel Rossetti was one of several artists who worked for William Morris's design company in the 1870s, and *The Germ* provided a model for many magazines in the 1890s.

The kind of daring challenge to tradition that mobilised the Pre-Raphaelite movement finds expression in other ways in Victorian poetry. Many women poets of the period wrote, as critic Angela Leighton puts it, 'against the heart' – that is, against an over-prescriptive and highly moralised sentimental mode. Elizabeth Barrett Browning appropriated the masculine tradition of the sonnet sequence for her mid-century *Sonnets from the Portuguese*. Throughout her collection, Browning accords the female voice of her sonnets extraordinary agency in the expression of desire. Barrett Browning proved so influential to a diverse array of contemporary writers because her poetry sought both in form and technique to move beyond the conventionally feminine. Poems such as 'The Cry of the Children', 'The Runaway Slave at Pilgrim's Point' and 'Casa Guidi Windows' are illustrative of her interest in using poetry to address social problems and to engage in politics.

The long, almost novel-length narrative poems of the period evidence the Victorian propensity,

5.10 *Isabella and the Pot of Basil* (1867–8) by William Holman Hunt. The subject of this painting refers to a poem by John Keats which, in turn, was inspired by a work of the Italian Renaissance poet Giovanni Boccaccio. The work also reflects Holman Hunt's travels and enthusiasm for Middle Eastern culture.

especially after mid-century, to experiment with poetic form. Three prominent examples of this sub-genre of Victorian poetry can be found in Robert Browning's *The Ring and the Book* (1868–9), Tennyson's *Idylls of the King* (1862) and Elizabeth Barrett Browning's *Aurora Leigh* (1856). Barrett Browning's blank verse novel, *Aurora Leigh*, uses elements of the *Bildungsroman* to structure its revolutionary and epic presentation of the woman artist's journey towards social, artistic and financial independence. The twelve idylls that comprise Tennyson's poem represent the coming of King

Arthur, the disintegration of the Round Table and Arthur's passing. Twelve books long, *The Ring and the Book* uses a complex narrative form and representation of a seventeenth-century murder trial to foreground Robert Browning's psychological, philosophical and religious interests.

Browning's more crucial legacy lies with the dramatic monologue, though he did not invent the form. Writing of the Victorian love affair with the dramatic mono-logue, E. Warwick Slinn notes that 'from its inception in the 1830s and 1840s, its use spread rapidly, flooding the literary market and requiring puzzled reviewers to learn to describe its idiosyncrasies and implications' ('Poetry' in Tucker, *Companion to Victorian Literature and Culture*, p. 313 [B]). The form is especially interesting in the way it reflects an emerging understanding of the nature of identity. Browning gravitated to disturbed psyches and in poems included in *Dramatic Lyrics* (1842) and *Men and Women* (1855) readers are invited to reckon with their hidden histories, sordid secrets and immoral thoughts – revealed both wittingly and unwittingly so that authenticity itself is always at issue. Whether concentrating his portrait on real personages (as in 'Andrea del Sarto' and 'Fra Lippo Lippi'), or literary characters (as in 'Childe Roland') or on a fiction of his own (as in the murderous duke in 'My Last Duchess' or the monk in 'Soliloquy of the Spanish Cloister'), Browning was interested in representing the performative and theatrical nature of identity. The closing stanza of the 'Soliloquy' illustrates especially well Browning's playful exuberance and robust use of language:

> Or, there's Satan! – one might venture
> Pledge one's soul to him, yet leave
> Such a flaw in the indenture
> As he'd miss till, past retrieve,
> Blasted lay that rose-acacia
> We're so proud of! *Hy, Zy, Hine* …
> 'St, there's Vespers! *Plena gratiâ*
> *Ave, Virgo!* G-r-r-r – you swine!
>
> (*Longman Anthology*, p. 1311 [Aii])

Where Browning's poetry conveys energy and ebullience, Matthew Arnold's pro-jects what he called in 'The Study of Poetry' a 'high seriousness'. Well known for his emphasis on 'the dialogue of the mind with itself', Arnold would seem to share with Browning, and, indeed, with almost every other Victorian poet, an interest in exploring and representing subjective states of mind. Yet, as Isobel Armstrong notes, over the course of his career Arnold became increasingly suspicious of 'the danger-ous jouissance of introspective feeling' and sought to 'recentre English poetry in a moral tradition' (*Victorian Poetry*, p. 208 [B]). Arnold's reputation resides equally in works of criticism (such as *Culture and Anarchy*), to which he turned after mid-cen-tury. However disenchanted Arnold became with the power of poetry to inspire and instruct, there is little doubt that in its expressions of doubt, resignation and isola-tion, his poetry reached an audience deprived of (yet 'longing for', as he writes in 'To Marguerite – Continued') reassuring certitudes of faith and knowledge.

In the last third of the century poets still more forcefully found ways to chal-lenge dominant ideologies of society and conventions of poetry. Inspired by the development of French symbolism and the credo of art for art's sake, poets of the aesthetic movement were energised not only by their shared sense of commitment to art but by the new opportunities to circulate their ideas made possible by the parallel rise of a press hospitable to their ideas. Algernon Charles Swinburne and Arthur Symons, among others, became known as 'Yellow Book poets', because their work was a staple of the *Yellow Book*, the leading journal of aestheticism that had Aubrey Beardsley as its art director. Other late-century poets, including William Butler Yeats, Lionel Johnson and Ernest Dowson (also a frequent *Yellow Book* contributor) found community by gathering together under the auspices of the Rhymers' Club, where, meeting in pubs, they would eat, drink and recite poetry together.

However tempting it might be to turn, as literary historians so often do, to the rise of the aesthetic movement to locate the end of 'traditional' Victorian poetry and to find the incipient beginnings of modernist impulses, such a manoeuvre falsely posits a homogeneous, conformist and conventional genre that simply did not exist during Victoria's reign. Certainly aesthetic poets such as Swinburne (influenced by the sensuous imagery of the mid-century Pre-Raphaelite poets) seized the opportunity to flout through their poetry what they believed were oppressively restrictive standards for appropriate behaviour and to reject the assumption (as espoused by such influential critics as Matthew Arnold or John Ruskin) of art as having moral ends. In collections such as *Poems and Ballads, Series 1* (1866), Swinburne circulated overtly erotic and occasionally blasphemous poetry. The work would not have been scorned as a 'morbid deviation' in Robert Buchanan's 1871 disdainfully titled essay, 'The Fleshly School of Poetry', if it did not have the power to offend the moral sensibilities of some readers. However audacious their content or use of imagery, these poets cannot be said to have been any more stylistically experimental than Gerard Manley Hopkins, or more sensuous than Tennyson, or, really, more daring than Elizabeth Barrett Browning, Emily Brontë or Christina Rossetti. Throughout Victoria's reign, in other words, writers approached poetry as a genre amenable to experiment, receptive to heterogeneous content and capable of functioning simultaneously as a vehicle for, and tool of, their interest in language and representation.

Drama

Victorian theatre, and the melodrama that characterised it, tends to elicit defensive commentary from the few critics who in recent years have tried to take it seriously, as when Elaine Hadley encourages readers to 'suspend aesthetic evaluation and to accept the fact that stage melodrama no longer epitomizes an embarrassing century in English drama's otherwise illustrious chronology' (*Melodramatic Tactics*, p. 8 [Cii]). And yet, as Nina Auerbach has written, 'Theatricality was not only a spirit of Victorian culture; it was a cultural fact' (*Private Theatricals*, p. 12 [Cii]). Understanding the development of Victorian drama (broadly considered to include not only plays but also pantomime, musical pieces, burlesques and *tableaux vivants*) helps to shed light on the many ways that theatre influenced those living and writing in nineteenth-century Britain.

While a strict division between major and minor theatres had been in effect since the 1737 Licensing Act and would be superseded by the 1843 Theatre

Regulation Act (which made all theatres subject to censorship), the Victorian period witnessed the arrival of numerous new theatres to counter the hegemony of major theatres such as Covent Garden and Drury Lane. The influence of these theatres can be measured by the consumer-driven increase of productions with sensational content and techniques. Plays incorporated many popular dramatic modes, including *tableaux vivants* (the acting out, typically in 'freeze frames', of scenes from famous paintings) and pantomime, which by the 1840s was less exclusively a genre of low comedy and was often used to convey social values. Victorian theatre provided a home for other popular forms of entertainment, including extravaganza, farce and burlesque, but melodrama was the form of choice. By the time the popular productions of Gilbert and Sullivan began in the mid-1870s, musical theatre and light opera had adapted to accommodate a wide range of techniques and purposes; in *HMS Pinafore, The Pirates of Penzance* and *Princess Ida* melodrama gives way to social and topical satire. *HMS Pinafore*, for example, spoofs Sir Joseph Porter, the First Lord of the Admiralty, who was commonly thought to be based on W. H. Smith himself (and who had gained the position through influence rather than any naval experience).

The theatrical and the literary were yoked in numerous ways during Victoria's reign. Charles Dickens and Wilkie Collins collaborated both as actors and authors of such productions as Collins's *The Frozen Deep* and Dickens's *Mr Nightingale's Diary*, and many other major authors were deeply indebted to the theatre, either writing for it, or incorporating its ethos and values into their works (Auerbach, *Private Theatricals*, p. 13 [Cii]). Novels were routinely adapted for the stage (including the sensation novels *Lady Audley's Secret* and *East Lynne*) and many Victorian novels themselves make use of such features of dramatic culture as private theatricals or the *tableau vivant* (the latter form appearing in crucial scenes in *Jane Eyre* and, later in the century, *Daniel Deronda*). Some of the most insightful scholarship on the connections between drama and other forms of Victorian literature focuses on the ways the novel handled and represented the theatricality so flamboyantly on display in theatres and music halls. Joseph Litvak, for example, emphasises the novelistic resistance to theatricality, arguing that much-heralded values such as 'inwardness, privacy, propriety, and sincerity, attempt to suppress or to conceal theatrical energies, images, and techniques, even as they appropriate them' (*Caught in the Act*, pp. 109–10 [Cii]).

Whereas literary historians typically turn to the latter portion of the Victorian period to locate the end of something, drama historians most often look there to identify a beginning. The renaissance of Irish theatre – as heralded by such figures as Lady Gregory, Edward Martyn and William Butler Yeats – belongs squarely to the 1890s, although Dion Boucicault, hitherto Ireland's most prominent playwright, made a monumental contribution to Irish theatre well before the decade. Boucicault's Irish Trilogy (*The Colleen Bawn* of 1860, *Arrah-na-Pogue* of 1864 and *The Shaughraun* of 1874) features stock characters, sensational scenes capped by highly melodramatic moments, and effusive displays of Irish patriotism. Boucicault did not create single-handed the stereotypical Irish stage character, one who was either a drunken buffoon or a hollow braggart; indeed, this dimension of Irish theatre was widespread enough to inspire Lady Gregory and others late in the century to want to bring new credibility and respect to Ireland through better representation in the theatres. The momentum of the Home Rule movement from the 1870s onwards helped to foster an audience for many nationalistic plays.

Oscar Wilde, the pre-eminent playwright of the 1890s, was also Irish, but his contributions to drama centre on his creation of comedies of modern life. *Lady Windermere's Fan* (1892), *A Woman of No Importance* (1893) and *An Ideal Husband* (1895) expose well (and not always comically) the way love relationships become complicated by contemporary social pressures, especially those created by class consciousness and domestic ideology. The living embodiment of the aesthete, Wilde's interest in aestheticism is most explicitly in evidence in his symbolist play *Salomé*, which was written in French; though initially denied a licence for performance because of a prohibition on representing biblical characters on stage, it was translated in 1894 and published with drawings by Aubrey Beardsley (see Figure 5.11).

The Importance of Being Earnest, now widely acknowledged as a monumental achievement on Wilde's part, suffered by opening in theatres just as a scandal erupted related to Wilde's pressing charges against the Marquess of Queensberry

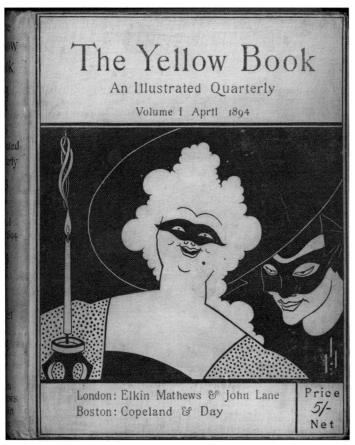

5.11 This Beardsley drawing graced the cover of the first issue of *The Yellow Book: An Illustrated Quarterly* when it came out in April 1894.

for criminal libel. Later in the year, Wilde was convicted of 'gross indecency' and forced to undergo two years of hard labour. So remarkable was the course of Oscar Wilde's career that literary historians sometimes overlook the significance of another late-century playwright. George Bernard Shaw (1856–1950), who also hailed from Ireland, crafted plays designed to disturb the complacent assumptions and expectations of their audiences. Writing over fifty plays that straddle the late Victorian and early modern periods, Shaw tackled prostitution in *Mrs Warren's Profession* (1893), various ideals of masculinity in *Arms and the Man* (1894) and evolution in *Man and Superman* (1903). Contemporaries of Wilde and Shaw knew them also for their prose writings – Wilde for such essays as 'The Decay of Lying' and 'The Critic as Artist' and Shaw for essays such as 'The Quintessence of Ibsenism', and as theatre critic for the *Saturday Review*. Working across genres was par for the course for many other writers throughout the period.

Essays

To turn at the end of this literary overview to the many forms of non-fiction writing that circulated in Victorian Britain is to have come full circle, because the expansion of print culture enabled a wide range of prose writing to flourish. Major periodicals such as the *Edinburgh Review*, the *Quarterly Review*, the *New Monthly Magazine* and *Fraser's Magazine* were established before Victoria came to the throne, but their circulations rose dramatically and by mid-century they were in active competition with a burgeoning commercial press whose periodicals were less defined by political affiliation. Many important works of non-fiction were published in book form, of course, but the expansion of the periodical press influenced authorship of non-fiction in numerous ways – by facilitating the emergence of a professional category of writers, critics and reviewers, for example, and by enabling women writers both to enter the mainstream as professionals and, in some cases, to create alternative publications for the distribution of their views. Readerships expanded too, and the press responded with a dizzying array of choices – e.g. quarterly, monthly or weekly publications, some comic, some satiric and some intensely serious in tone. Content was as likely to be authored anonymously (at least until the 1860s) or pseudonymously, as to be by well-known writers. Often using the term 'miscellany' to characterise an eclectic array of content, Victorian magazines were truly miscellaneous – an attribute that helps to explain the many variations in form and function of the non-fiction writing that saturated Victorian Britain.

The reform-oriented *Edinburgh Review*, the conservative *Quarterly Review* and the radical *Westminster Review* (all influential quarterlies) were associated in readers' minds with distinct political leanings that directed the way their content was read. Thomas Babington Macaulay, for example, published essays on Milton, Southey and Bacon in the *Edinburgh Review* that articulate his beliefs about progress and the principles of utilitarian liberalism. The hold of these periodical titans gradually waned as publications like *Blackwood's Edinburgh Magazine* brought more entertaining content into their mix of offerings, but their legacy was significant. Writing that 'higher journalism, the journalism of the more dignified organs of opinion, the reviews, the superior magazines, and the quality newspapers, was one of the most characteristic cultural manifestations of nineteenth-century Britain', Christopher Kent points out that 'a great many significant works – Arnold's *Culture and Anarchy*, Bagehot's *The English Constitution*, and Ruskin's *Unto This Last* are three that come to mind – first appeared serialized in periodicals rather than as books' ('Higher Journalism and the Mid-Victorian Clerisy', p. 181 [Civ]). Most of the writers who adopted the rhetorical position of the 'sage' were closely, if not exclusively, associated with major quarter-lies. Carlyle wrote 'Signs of the Times' and 'Characteristics' for the *Edinburgh Review*. John Stuart Mill was a regular contributor to *Tait's Edinburgh Magazine* and in 1861 published his *Considerations on Representative Government and Utilitarianism* in *Fraser's Magazine*, although he published much of his work, including *Principles of Political Economy, On Liberty* and *The Subjection of Women* in volume form.

Not all critics who adopted the rhetoric or embraced the stature of the sage identified their ideas with particular political parties. Integrating his art criticism into his analysis of social problems, John Ruskin used works like *Modern Painters* and *The Stones of Venice* to advocate the moral principles on which he believed art, architecture and aesthetic theory should rest.

Ruskin's ardent expressions of the value and potential pleasure of work, and especially its ability to express the creativity and humanity of the worker, directly influenced the arts and crafts movement. His later writing relies heavily on Christian rhetoric in its blending of the political and the prophetic; in work like *Unto This Last* (1862) and *The Crown of Wild Olives* (1866), Ruskin critiques the principles of laissez-faire economics and excoriates the mechanistic nature of urban life.

Throughout the century, 'sages' like Ruskin and Carlyle competed with many other voices eager to educate, to influence, to share experiences (especially those gleaned from abroad) or to popularise and make more understandable the ideas of others. Non-fictional essays or tracts with didactic, improving purposes came hot off the presses of the Religious Tract Society and the Society for the Propagation of Christian Knowledge in addition to appearing within the pages of various miscellanies. The familiar essay was a regular feature of magazines such as *Punch* and *Ainsworth's Magazine*. Essays about experiences in the wider world, intended to inspire the imaginations of arm-chair travellers at home, appeared in nearly every type of magazine. Essays and articles providing information and advice on topics such as courtship, health and domestic economy were standard fare in mass-circulation magazines for girls and women such as the *Monthly Packet*, the *Christian Lady's Magazine* and the *Englishwoman's Domestic Magazine*. Magazines with specialist interests in religion or emerging areas of science helped to publish the work and views of amateurs and professionals alike.

From the enormously varied mix of material that came into print, it hardly seems possible or even necessarily desirable to impose order. Nevertheless, there are important strands of non-fiction writing, such as literary criticism, that deserve special consideration. It would not have been possible for Matthew Arnold to take stock of the field and proclaim that criticism 'ought simply to know the best that is known and thought in the world, and by in its turn making this known, to create a current of true and fresh ideas' in his seminal essay of 1864, 'The Function of Criticism at the Present Time', were it not for a vast field of political, religious and literary criticism against which to make his claims. Victorian critics approached the study of literature with distinct standards of judgement; notions of 'sympathy' and 'sincerity' often dominated discussion of a literary work's appeal to readers, and concepts such as 'colour' were frequently used to describe a work's style. George Henry Lewes established himself as a leading literary critic with essays such as 'The Principles of Success in Literature' and for myriad book reviews that linked his appreciation for a work to its basis in psychological reality. Leslie Stephen, father of both Virginia Woolf and the *Dictionary of National Biography*, produced an enormous array of scholarship on English literature, both during and after his stint as editor of the *Cornhill Magazine*. Yet Stephen was only one among hundreds of critics during the century who sought to study, understand and evaluate literature both past and, increasingly, present. That literary criticism flourished, despite the cynicism about the tastes of the reading public, is testimony to the seriousness with which debates about literary art and its connection to social reality were undertaken throughout the period.

Only on the surface less tethered to specific developments in Victorian print culture is another major strand of non-fictional writing – that of autobiography, biography and memoir. In distinct ways, works as varied as Carlyle's *Sartor Resartus*, Samuel Smiles's *Self-Help*, J. A. Froude's *Thomas Carlyle: A History of the First Forty Years of His Life* and Elizabeth Gaskell's *The Life of Charlotte Brontë* reveal an ongoing interest in biography that is also evidenced by the hundreds of mini-biographical accounts of politicians, inventors and authors that were part of many a magazine's repertoire. Autobiographical writing proliferated (with John Stuart Mill, John Henry Newman, John Ruskin and Harriet Martineau among the many to publish full-length works), and an autobiographical spirit informs novels by Dickens, Brontë and Eliot, and poems by Tennyson, Elizabeth Barrett Browning and Christina Rossetti, among others. Wilde's *De Profundis*, which adopted the epistolary form, melds qualities of the *apologia*, or defence, with other modes, among them testimony, confession and eulogy.

In his influential 'Conclusion' to *Studies in the History of the Renaissance*, Walter Pater proclaimed the aim of the true student of aesthetics to be the definition of beauty. Pater idealised flux, associating the 'inconstant' of the modern, physical life with 'perpetual motion' of elements, and the 'inward world of thought and feeling' with a 'whirlpool' of sensation. At one point he concludes that

> It is with this movement, with the passage and dissolution of impressions, images, sensations, that analysis leaves off – that continual vanishing away, that strange, perpetual weaving and unweaving of ourselves.
>
> (*Longman Anthology*, p. 1670 [Aii])

Whether one agrees or disagrees with Pater, there can be little doubt that his keywords – *experience, personality, voice* – resonated with his readers, entrenched as they were in a literature that foregrounded, sometimes to consolidate and sometimes to destabilise, their meanings. Pater wrote for and about the 'moment', but in pointing to a 'strange, perpetual weaving and unweaving of ourselves', he could not have found better terms with which to characterise the broad and varied tapestry of Victorian literature or the constantly changing press that produced it.

Texts and Issues

Class Relations, Conflict and the Condition of England

'Really, if the lower orders don't set us a good example, what on earth is the use of them? They seem, as a class, to have absolutely no sense of moral responsibility', quips Algernon near the beginning of *The Importance of Being Earnest* (*Longman Anthology*, p. 1886 [Aii]). Wilde mocks the insidious assumption that with the upper classes resides the ability and responsibility to model exemplary values and behaviour to those who work for them. Wilde's humour presupposes a hierarchical society, an 'upstairs/downstairs' world of masters and servants, aristocrats and commoners. In this imaginary world the division between classes is easily identifiable and rigidly maintained. It is undoubtedly true that for Victorians birth, family, education, source of income, as well as speech and manners, combined to position one as a member of a particular class. Yet it is equally true that much Victorian literature also expresses, sometimes paradoxically, the permeability of the boundaries between and within classes.

The trademark concern for the experience of working-class men, women and children that much early Victorian literature demonstrates reveals these tensions. In his novel *Sybil; or the Two Nations*, Benjamin Disraeli famously contended that between the rich and the poor, the so-called two nations, 'there is no intercourse and no sympathy', but the fact that so much ink was spilled on the Condition of England suggests otherwise (Haight, *Portable Victorian Reader*, p. 22 [Aii]). In *The Condition of the Working-Class in England*, Friedrich Engels prompts his hypothetical reader to 'imagine the consequences for yourself' of the conditions that men, women and children encounter in the dark mines (Haight, *Portable Victorian Reader*, p. 69 [Aii]). Henry Mayhew incorporated the testimony of hundreds of working-class men, women and children in the news articles from 1849 that eventually became his four-volume study, *London Labour and the London Poor* (1861–2). Many politicians and writers who addressed the problems of the poor were often equally concerned to reach those responsible for correcting the problems, and the hallmark social-problem novels were both written by, and addressed to, members of the middle classes. Moreover, the categories of the 'working class' and 'the poor' were by no means homogeneous, as was made clear by the Poor Law Amendment Act of 1834, which sought to differentiate between the deserving and the undeserving. If the Factory Act of 1833 solved some problems by regulating the number of hours children could work in factories, the Poor Law Amendment Act of the following year created many more. In *Oliver Twist* Dickens satirises the act's spawning of workhouses as 'rather expensive at first, in consequence of the increase in the undertaker's bill, and the necessity of taking in the clothes of all the paupers, which fluttered loosely on their wasted, shrunken forms, after a week or two's gruel. But the number of workhouse inmates got thin as well as the paupers; and the board were in ecstasies' (p. 12 [Ai]). The Poor Law Amendment Act inspired a similarly angry response in Carlyle, who in *Past and Present* compared the workhouse to the Bastille:

'A Poor-law, any and every Poor-law, it may be observed, is but a temporary measure; an anodyne, not a remedy' (*Longman Anthology*, p. 1036 [Aii]).

Given the dramatic increase in the numbers of poor suffering from overcrowded living conditions and in need of financial support, factory conditions in need of regulation, and the proliferation of workhouses in the early part of the century, it is not surprising that the concept of the urban assumes a central place in social and political analysis of the period as well as in the literature. As summarised by Roy Porter, 'London was spawning pauperism, misery, crime, [and] disease' (*London: A Social History*, p. 259 [B]). The rapid urbanisation of the late eighteenth and early nineteenth centuries – the mass migration of people from the country in search of work in the manufacturing cities such as Manchester, Leeds, Birmingham and Glasgow – was clearly partly to blame for the social and economic problems faced by early Victorians. As Carlyle put it in *Past and Present*, 'Industrial work, still under bondage to Mammon … is a tragic spectacle' (Bradshaw and Ozment, *The Voice of Toil*, p. 45 [Aii]). In Disraeli's novel *Sybil*, readers are informed that while working people struggle everywhere, 'in cities that condition is aggravated. A density of population implies a severer struggle for existence, and a consequent repulsion of elements brought into too close contact' (Haight, *Portable Victorian Reader*, p. 22 [Aii]). Carlyle focused on a related dimension of industrialisation and urbanisation – the mechanisation of labour – in much of his writing on the social and economic conditions of his country. In his seminal essay 'Signs of the Times', he invokes the spectre of 'the living artist … driven from his workshop, to make room for a speedier, inanimate one' and he predicts the enormous influence mechanisation would have on the social system (*Carlyle Reader*, p. 34 [Ai]). Using language that Disraeli would echo in *Sybil*, Carlyle observes how 'wealth has more and more increased, and at the same time gathered itself more and more into masses, strangely altering the old relations, and increasing the distance between the rich and the poor' (*Carlyle Reader*, p. 35 [Ai]).

The preoccupation with the living conditions and economic vulnerability of the labouring classes living in cities and working in the factories is everywhere evident in literature of the 1830s and 1840s. Indeed, nowhere in the Victorian period is the connection between social and literary history so powerfully made than in the Condition of England literature that dominates the literary landscape of the 1840s, a decade that witnessed an agricultural depression, widespread unemployment, and inflated food prices, and the influx of thousands of needy emigrants from Ireland. Large numbers of poorly paid factory workers, subjected in their jobs to abhorrent conditions, began over the 1830s and 1840s to form unions, demanding better working conditions, decent pay and political representation.

Chartism took root at this time not just because of the rampant socio-economic distress, but also because its advocates reached a broader community of sympathisers through song, chant, ballad and hymn. Taking advantage of the radical press to spread its message, Chartism inspired a significant body of writing, much of it designed to promote working-class activism. Chartist poetry in particular builds upon the democratic ideals that the Romantic poets Blake and Wordsworth expressed in their writing. Poets, among them Thomas Cooper, Gerald Massey and Ernest Jones, published their works in Chartist newspapers and magazines such as *The Labourer* and *The Northern Star*. Although not written until 1852, Ernest Jones's 'The Song of the Lower Classes' is representative of Chartist poetry more generally in its appeal to solidarity as well as in its commingling of anger, threat and hope. Its last stanza reads:

> We're low, we're low – we're very, very low
> And yet when the trumpets ring,
> The thrust of a poor man's arm will go
> Through the heart of the proudest king
> We're low, we're low – our place we know
> We're only the rank and file,
> We're not too low – to kill the foe
> Too low to touch the spoil.
>
> (Cunningham, *The Victorians*, p. 480 [Aii])

Chartists were not the only poets to express working-class consciousness or to convey concern for working-class conditions. The enormously popular poet Felicia Hemans published her poem 'The Factory' in *The Christian Lady's Magazine* in 1838. Thomas Hood, editor of the *London Magazine* and *The New Monthly Magazine*, in 1843 published 'The Song of the Shirt' to bring attention to the plight of seamstresses. Included in the 1843 Christmas Number of *Punch*, Hood's poem renders with characteristic pathos the plodding, dulling and debilitating qualities of repetitive labour.

> Work – work – work!
> From weary chime to chime,
>   Work – work – work –
> As prisoners work for crime!
>
> (Cunningham, *The Victorians*, p. 64 [Aii])

Hood's poem inspired several paintings, including Richard Redgrave's *The Seamstress* of 1844 and George Frederic Watts's *The Song of the Shirt* of c. 1850, and helped to make the seamstress an iconic figure. Elizabeth Barrett Browning's poem 'The Cry of the Children', originally published in 1843 in *Blackwood's Edinburgh Magazine*, documents the toll of industrial labour on children:

> For, all day, we drag our burden tiring
>   Through the coal-dark, underground –
> Or, all day, we drive the wheels of iron
> In the factories, round and round.
>
> (Leighton and Reynolds, *Victorian Women Poets*, pp. 73–6 [Aii])

Works like 'Song of the City Artisan', published by the self-educated Eliza Cook in her 1845 collection *Poems, Second Series*, idealise the labourer who, though 'meanly born', is 'content to be among [the] poor' (Bradshaw and Ozment, *The Voice of Toil*, p. 555 [Aii]).

Scholars have come increasingly to focus attention on working-class poetry as an expression of emerging class consciousness in Victorian Britain, but a handful of influential novels continue to exert a powerful hold on scholarly understanding of the literary response to industrialism and the plight of the labourer. Published in the revolutionary year of 1848, Elizabeth Gaskell's novel *Mary Barton*, subtitled 'A Tale of Manchester Life', was set just a few years earlier, at a time when the *Manchester Times* reported 'hungry and half-clothed men and women' to be 'stalking through the streets begging for bread'. Gaskell's success in securing the sympathy of her readers through her yoking of realistic detail and regional dialect to a story both sentimental and sensational in flavour can be measured in the often quoted *Fraser's Magazine* article on 'The Manufacturing Poor', unsigned but now attributed to Charles Kingsley, published soon after. Its author advised readers who 'want to know why poor men, kind and sympathizing as women to each other, learn to hate law and order, Queen, Lords and Commons, country-party, and corn-law leagues, all alike – to hate the rich in short – to do one thing – read *Mary Barton*' (Kingsley, 'Review' [Ai]). Dramatically rendering the poverty and malaise of working-class life in the city, the deep didactic impulses of Gaskell's novel surface in her repeated address to readers, as when she exhorts them to 'Remember, too, that though it may take much suffering to kill the able-bodied and effective members of society, it does not take much to reduce them to worn, listless, diseased creatures, who thenceforward crawl through life with moody hearts and pain-stricken bodies' (*Mary Barton*, p. 160 [Ai]).

Gaskell found in *North and South*, published from 1854 to 1855 in *Household Words*, an opportunity to readdress issues of urban industrialism and working-class consciousness, but many other influential novelists sought to study and represent the Condition of England. Charles Kingsley's *Alton Locke, Tailor and Poet*, for instance, focuses on the appeal of Chartism to a young man growing up in London's horrific slums and surviving a cholera epidemic. Frances Trollope based her *The Life and Adventures of Michael Armstrong, the Factory Boy* (1839–40), often credited as the first industrial novel, on work done in child-labour campaigns and research conducted in Manchester and Bradford. Its stark representation of the suffering and tribulation of exploited children and factory workers inspired some critics to worry that it would incite violence in the working class, a concern exacerbated by Trollope having opted to publish it in the more affordable monthly parts rather than a single volume.

Written in the early 1850s, Charles Dickens's *Hard Times* (1854) belongs also to this category of fiction, for in his creation of Coketown – 'a town of red brick, or of brick that would have been red if the smoke and ashes had allowed it' – and the savage tone that he strikes throughout the narrative, Dickens captures the power of impoverished surroundings to diminish and deform the individual (p. 20 [Ai]). Writing of Dickens's achievement in creating Coketown, George Bernard Shaw observed that 'its rich manufacturers are proud of its dirt, and declare that they like to see the sun blacked out with smoke, because it means that the furnaces are busy and money is being made; while its poor factory hands have never known any other sort of town, and are as content with it as a rat is with a hole' (Dickens, *Hard Times*, p. 358 [Ai]).

Like *Hard Times*, Charlotte Brontë's *Shirley* exemplifies many of the techniques and ideals associated with Condition of England literature. Promising her readers in the opening passage of the novel 'something unromantic as Monday morning', Brontë looks back for her material to the winter of 1811–12 when a bad harvest converged with inadequate or faulty governmental intervention to seriously depress the economy in manufacturing areas of the country (p. 39 [Ai]). Brontë represents the friction between those with Tory and Whig allegiances over how to resolve the conflict with Napoleon and resume trade relations, and she shows how against this backdrop a powerful working-class movement emerged in Nottingham and the manufacturing districts of Yorkshire – the Luddites. Much like the Chartists of a few decades later (Brontë wrote *Shirley* in 1848, in the midst of the European revolutions that made Chartism at home seem especially threatening), Luddites brought attention to the combination of political, economic and social conditions that oppressed workers. While most critics agree that Brontë's heritage and education prevented her from being able to imagine a working-class movement arising organically and succeeding, *Shirley* relates class warfare to injustices and inequalities within the social order more generally.

From the middle of the century onwards, class conflict and the idea of the industrial occupy a decidedly less prominent position in poetry and fiction. True, the eponymous hero of George Eliot's *Adam Bede* (1859) is an artisan whose pleasure in the handwork of carpentry harks back to, and idealises, pre-industrial times. Similarly, *Middlemarch*, written in 1871–2, renders both the multifarious ways class consciousness undergirds the social hierarchy of a provincial town in the early 1830s and the resistance of many in the community to political reform and other manifestations of progress (most notably, the railway). Both novels display Eliot's understanding of the power of class consciousness to create (and limit) desire and to drive behaviour. Neither work can be said to direct itself to specific societal issues facing the underclass in the way of the social-problem novels of the 1840s, though. Literary historians have struggled to understand the reasons behind the decline of the industrial novel after mid-century. Some believe that with the rise of trade unions, the improvement of factory conditions and the elimination of the worst abuses of child labour, the issues so pivotal to the emotional appeal of Condition of England literature were no longer so strikingly relevant. Other critics believe that the genre of social-protest fiction reappeared late in the century in novels focused on the conditions of the East End. Catherine Gallagher contends that emerging models of literary realism, as well as a new emphasis on culture in debates over representation, irrevocably altered the most basic assumptions guiding discourse on the Condition of England. 'The politics of culture can be said to have ended what we call the Condition of England Debate', Gallagher writes in *Industrial Reformation of English Fiction, 1832–1867*. 'It certainly did not put an end to social criticism, but it drastically altered its terms' (p. 265 [Cvi]). For a wide variety of reasons related to the growth of consumerism in Victorian England, the social and economic experiences of the middle classes increasingly occupied centre stage in discussions of literary and political representation. If Condition of England authors presented the problems of, and solutions to, working-class despair through a decidedly middle-class perspective, then the problems inherent to that middle-class perspective and position came increasingly, after mid-century, to command attention in their own right.

Class consciousness and conflict does not, of course, disappear from poetry and prose after the heyday of Condition of England literature. Poets as varied as Henrietta Tindal (author of 'The Cry of the Oppressed'), Mathilde Blind (author of 'Manchester by Night'), and William Morris (author of 'The Voice of Toil') can be seen to carry the torch lighted by an earlier generation, just as late-century works of social criticism like Andrew Mearns's *The Bitter Cry of Outcast London* (1883) and William Booth's *In Darkest England* (1890) manifest a profound concern for the underclasses not unlike Engels and Mayhew decades earlier. Late-century works take the inquiry into class consciousness, conflict and social ills in new directions. George Bernard Shaw's play *Mrs Warren's Profession* (1893), to cite just one example, unearths the economic needs that drive Mrs Warren into prostitution and brothel-keeping. More often than not, though, Victorian literature from mid-century onwards registers its preoccupation with class status and experience through themes tied to the experiences of the middle classes. This preoccupation evidences itself in the exploration of opportunities for women in governess novels like Anne Brontë's *Agnes Grey* and Charlotte Brontë's *Jane Eyre*, just as it informs the attitude towards fallen-women heroines in sensation novels such as *Lady Audley's Secret* and *East Lynne*. Class consciousness shapes the direction of classic novels of education like Dickens's *David Copperfield* and *Great Expectations* and Dinah Craik's *John Halifax, Gentleman*. Samuel Smiles's *Self-Help* celebrates hard work as the cornerstone of gentlemanly respectability.

Indeed, class consciousness permeates nearly every dimension of Victorian life and is inevitably at play in the literature the era produced, whether in works (like Dickens's *A Tale of Two Cities*) where entire classes figure threateningly as angry, implacable crowds or in works focused on the ordinary struggles of individuals to position themselves socially. Robert Louis Stevenson evokes the intense anxiety that attached to class status throughout the period in *Dr Jekyll and Mr Hyde*. In this short novel, Jekyll's friends are driven in their pursuit of knowledge by a desire to preserve his social standing. Yet Jekyll, as we know, is equally driven to pursue his relationship with his undignified and deformed counterpart, Hyde. At a key point in the narrative, Stevenson provides readers with a glimpse of Hyde's lodgings in Soho that stand in marked contrast to those of the prosperous, middle-class Jekyll. In the episode, fog lifts to reveal 'a dingy street, a gin palace, a low French eating house, a shop for the retail of penny numbers and two-penny salads, many ragged children huddled in the doorways, and many women of many different nationalities passing out, key in hand, to have a morning glass' (p. 23 [Ai]). The interior of Hyde's apartment speaks to the sanctity of middle-class aspiration and ideals, but its location on a city street in a working-class neighbourhood, where throngs of the poor stream by, betrays the inescapability and, indeed, vitality, of the underclasses. In its sustained attention to the theme of transformation – to Jekyll's desire and ability to become Hyde – the novel is a study of the inescapable desire to understand, and even inhabit, the experiences and perspectives of other selves and other classes.

Cityscapes, Countrysides and Victorian Ruralism

The modernist writer T. S. Eliot referred to London as the 'Unreal City' in his landmark poem of 1922, *The Waste Land*, but to Eliot's Victorian predecessors the nation's capital and the many problems that took root and flowered there were all too real. Victorian preoccupation with the social problems of industrialism informs a host of poems that foreground the landscape of London – the city as scene of urban desolation, crime, disease and fog-draped squalor. James Thomson prefaced his 'The City of Dreadful Night' (serialised in the *National Reformer* in 1874) with a passage from Dante's *Inferno* that, translated, reads 'This way for the sorrowful city'. Likening the city to a necropolis, he writes:

> The street-lamps burn amidst the baleful glooms,
>   Amidst the soundless solitudes immense
> Of ranged mansions dark and still as tombs.
>
> (Cunningham, The Victorians, p. 739 [Aii]).

Thomson's key motifs, metaphors and techniques – his use of 'street-lamps' to illuminate darkness within the city and his juxtaposition of the troubled individual soul with the anonymous crowd – would have been recognisable to any reader already familiar with the urban topography of Dickens's fiction. As Paul Davis writes, 'what Paris was to Balzac and Petersburg to Gogol, London was to Dickens' (*Dickens A to Z*, p. 218 [B]). An avid walker of the streets, Dickens evokes the sights, sounds, and smells of the city in many of his essays and almost all of his novels, perhaps most vividly in the opening paragraph of *Bleak House* and the closing paragraph of *Little Dorrit*, with its imagery of 'roaring streets' where 'the noisy and the eager, and the arrogant and the froward and the vain, fretted, and chafed, and made their usual uproar' (p. 855 [Ai]). The city offered Dickens a means to foreground the isolation of the individual; after confessing to his penchant for roaming the city streets by night, the narrator of *A Tale of Two Cities* comments, 'In any of the burial-places of this city through which I pass, is there a sleeper more inscrutable than its busy inhabitants are, in their innermost personality, to me, or than I am to them?' (p. 9 [Ai]).

London was not the only city to attract the attention of writers keen to represent the capacity of the urban landscape to create heart-crushing anonymity among inhabitants. George MacDonald's 'A Manchester Poem', to cite just one example, describes a 'chimneyed city' where 'faces gray glide through the darkened fog' (Cunningham, *The Victorians*, pp. 578–9 [Aii]).

The metropolis was also – even for those writers intent on rendering its dreadful nature – a site of energy, heterogeneity and imaginative potential. Thomas Hughes wrote in *Tom Brown's Schooldays* that although his hero had never been in London, he would have liked to have gone 'roving about those endless, mysterious, gas-lit streets, which, with their glare and hum and moving crowds, excited him so that he couldn't talk even' (pp. 70–1 [Ai]). Later in the century, the poet Amy Levy captures the voyeuristic appeal of the city in her 'Ballade of an Omnibus', where the speaker, untroubled by desire, can watch as 'the city pageant, early and late / Unfolds itself' (Cunningham, *The Victorians*, p. 1008 [Aii]). In still another way, Alexander Smith pays homage in 'Glasgow', a poem published in *City Poems*, to the aesthetic experience of the troubled urban world: 'In thee, O City! I discern / Another beauty, sad and stern' (Cunningham, p. 676 [Aii]). Smith compares the city that he knows, with its 'ebb and flow of streets', to the rural world more typically paid homage to by poets, one where 'great mornings shine', untarnished by 'thy noise and smoky breath' (Cunningham, p. 676 [Aii]). One of the most telling gestures of the poem is its repeated reference to

From *Bleak House*

London. Michaelmas Term lately over, and the Lord Chancellor sitting in Lincoln's Inn Hall. Implacable November weather. As much mud in the streets, as if the waters had but newly retired from the face of the earth, and it would not be wonderful to meet a Megalosaurus, forty feet long or so, waddling like an elephantine lizard up Holborn-hill. Smoke lowering down from chimney-pots, making a soft black drizzle, with flakes of soot in it as big as full-grown snow-flakes – gone into mourning, one might imagine, for the death of the sun. Dogs, undistinguishable in mire. Horses, scarcely better; splashed to their very blinkers. Foot passengers, jostling one another's umbrellas, in a general infection of ill temper, and losing their foot-hold at street corners, where tens of thousands of other foot passengers have been slipping and sliding since the day broke (if the day ever broke), adding new deposits to the crust upon crust of mud, sticking at those points tenaciously to the pavement, and accumulating at compound interest.

(p. 4 [Ai])

the city as site of the poet's formative years and experiences; in this way Smith evokes a kind of lost childhood: 'Ne'er by the rivulets I strayed, / And ne'er upon my childhood weighed / The silence of the glens' (Cunningham, p. 677 [Aii]).

'Glasgow' depends, like many of the cityscapes rendered by Victorian writers, upon familiar, even clichéd, thematic polarities. As Kate Greenaway writes in 'The Little London Girl', 'For oh, I love the country – the beautiful country. / Who'd live in a London street when there's the country?' (*Marigold Garden*, p. 27 [Ai]; see Figure 5.12). The country and city stand in symbolic opposition to one another, signifying in a range of ways innocence and experience, the natural and unnatural, the unchanging and the transient. For Elizabeth Gaskell, these ideas fell under the rubric of a geographic opposition. In *North and South*, the heroine travels by train from the northern, industrial city to which she has been transplanted back to the country village of her youth and finds herself 'seeing the old south country towns and hamlets sleeping in the warm light of the pure sun, which gave a yet ruddier colour to their tiled roofs, so different to the cold slates of the north' (p. 349 [Ai]).

Victorian writers appropriated the formula of country versus city from their Romantic forebears. In 'The Prelude', Wordsworth characterises as 'blank confusion' the experience of living amidst the bustle and perpetual whirl of London. The Dorset-born poet William Barnes began 'Rustic Childhood', from his *Poems, Partly of Rural Life* (1846), this way:

No city primness train'd my feet
To strut in childhood through the street,
But freedom let them loose to tread
The yellow cowslip's downcast head.

(Cunningham, *The Victorians*, p. 83 [Aii])

Elizabeth K. Helsinger notes the ironic but revealing fact that 'a rather turbulent and unsettled period in British history produced what we are likely to take today to be the serenities of Tennyson's English Idylls (most written in the 1830s and 1840s), the five volumes of Mary Russell Mitford's best-selling *Our Village* (1824–32), and Constable's *English Landscape Scenery* (1830, 1833)' (*Rural Scenes and National Representation*, p. 8 [Cvi]). Although well stocked with imagery that depicts rural England as stable, serene and prosperous, many of these works subtly express concerns about social unrest and the plight of rural labourers and dissatisfaction with complacent assumptions of national progress.

THE LITTLE LONDON GIRL.

IN my little Green House, quite content am I,
When the hot sun pours down from the sky ;
For oh, I love the country—the beautiful country.
Who'd live in a London street when there's the country?

I live in a London street, then I long and long
To be the whole day the sweet Flowers among.
Instead of tall chimney-pots up in the sky,
The joy of seeing Birds and Dragon Flies go by.

27

5.12 'The Little London Girl'. This illustration and poem, both by Kate Greenaway, appeared in *Marigold Garden: Pictures and Rhymes* (London, New York: George Routledge and Sons, 1885).

While it has become almost commonplace to dismiss the opposition between city and country as just one more manifestation of misplaced nostalgia for a coherent national identity that many now contend never existed – a nostalgia that Raymond Williams claims in *The Country and the City* has been an obsessive preoccupation of English writing for over 300 years – it is important to remember that major cities such as London, Manchester and Birmingham were quite dramatically and visibly transformed by technology and development throughout Victoria's reign. As Sally Mitchell summarises, 'There was constant building and rebuilding. Older areas became slums and were then cleared away for new commercial buildings or rail lines' (*Daily Life*, p. 79 [B]). With omnipresent reminders of transformation in the city, it is hardly surprising that the long-standing association of the country with the stable and unchanging resonated with Victorian Britons or that writers gravitated to the rural when wanting to grapple with issues of social, political and economic change.

Although Elizabeth Gaskell established herself as a major novelist by representing the slums of Manchester in *Mary Barton*, she was arguably more committed in the whole of her career to depicting rural landscapes and ways. Some of her earliest journalistic writings were submitted to William Howitt's *The Rural Life of England* (1840), and she later contributed articles on such topics as 'Cumberland Sheep-Shearers' to *Household Words*. 'The Last Generation in England' – the title of the story that eventually evolved into the short novel *Cranford* – is indicative of an important dimension of Victorian interest in the rural. Like many others preoccupied with the impact of industrialism on the landscape and lifestyles of the British, Gaskell imagined idyllic country villages as repositories of something ineffably essential to the nation, but soon to be lost. Her narrator in *Cranford* speaks both sardonically and wistfully when she notes that 'the last gigot, the last tight and scanty petticoat in wear in England, was seen in Cranford – and seen without a smile' (*Longman Anthology*, p. 1414 [Aii]). This interest in rendering the waning customs, habits and fashions of rural communities shapes Gaskell's approach in her biography, *The Life of Charlotte Brontë*, as well, for there she takes care to stress the bleak and barren landscape characteristic of Yorkshire, the remoteness of the Brontë home in Haworth, and the fact that the family grew up amidst 'rugged', 'primitive' and 'barbaric' people. An ethnographic imagination informs George Eliot's depictions of rural life as well. She situates *Silas Marner* 'in the days when the spinning-wheels hummed busily in the farm-houses' (p. 5 [Ai]).

Victorian writers did not simply find in rural scenes fodder for proto-anthropological or ethnographic cultural study, however. Many were drawn to landscape as emblematic of psychological terrain and as a way of highlighting the idea of perspective, literal and figural, itself. Early on in *Jane Eyre*, for instance, when Brontë's heroine arrives at Thornfield Hall to begin life as a governess, she confesses to her readers that she has harboured aspirations beyond those promised by her new career: 'Now and then', she writes,

> I climbed the three staircases, raised the trapdoor of the attic, and having reached the leads, looked out afar over sequestered field and hill, and along dim skyline … then I longed for a power of vision which might overpass that limit; which might reach the busy world, towns, regions full of life I had heard of but never seen …
>
> (pp. 140–1 [Ai]).

Landscape provides Brontë with a way to probe her heroine's sense of (and desire to overcome) boundaries, both social and psychological. While the late-century poet and essayist Alice Meynell relies less on the country/city thematic to establish the interest of perspective, she, too, is invested in the idea that some boundaries are self-created and turns to the representation of landscape to make her points. In her poem 'Winter Trees on the Horizon', for instance, Meynell writes:

> O Delicate! Even in wooded lands
> They show the margin of my world,
> My own horizon; little bands
> Of twigs unveil that edge impearled.
>
> (*Selected Poems*, p. 36 [Ai])

Nowhere do the social and psychological converge more forcefully than in the fiction of Thomas Hardy, whose descriptions of Wessex, a landscape that shares the physical features of Dorset, become the novelist's primary tools for exploring the lives of characters who are either 'in touch with' the natural world or who are exiled or dislocated – literally out of place. Not unlike Emily Brontë in her emphasis on the wildness of the heath in *Wuthering Heights*, Hardy foregrounds the dark and desolate in his landscapes, often using them to broach existential and ontological questions about man's nature and place in the universe. In *The Return of the Native*, for instance, the novelist introduces 'the vast tract of unenclosed wild known as Egdon Heath' to his readers and writes that 'from that space the distant rims of the world and of the firmament seemed to be a division in time no less than a division in matter' (p. 53 [Ai]).

If Hardy's name is now almost synonymous with the rural, so too is his writing understood to be invariably tragic. Whether one accepts as tragic the transformations to the landscape and country life that happened over the course of the nineteenth century, or whether one believes such a view to be merely a token of false nostalgia inevitably produced by change (or progress), it is clear that the Victorians could not escape seeing in their cityscapes and countrysides the grounds for debate. Their landscapes may have changed, but not the capacity of those changes to evoke powerful emotional responses.

Science, Nature and Crises of Faith

In the very year that Victoria was crowned Queen, 1837, Thomas Babington Macaulay published a review essay on 'Lord Bacon' for the *Edinburgh Review* in which he praises the achievements of science, concluding that 'it is a philosophy which never rests, which has never attained, which is never perfect'. 'Its law is progress', Macaulay proclaims, adding that 'A point which yesterday was invisible is its goal today, and will be its starting-post tomorrow' (*Longman Anthology*, pp. 1274–5 [Aii]). The very sentiments and language on which Macaulay drew to praise the work of science reverberate in 'Ulysses', Tennyson's poem of 1833, in which the hero 'cannot rest from travel' and idealistically desires 'To follow knowledge like a sinking star, / Beyond the utmost bound of human thought' (*Longman Anthology*, pp. 1150–1 [Aii]). Despite their different purposes, both works rely on the language of endeavour, active searching and, ultimately, unceasing toil to represent what is valuable and honourable about discovery itself.

So well known is the history of Darwin's theory of evolution and natural selection that it too often stands for all of Victorian 'science', that is, as a homogeneous body of knowledge at war with, and emerging victorious over, religious belief (also often misconstrued as homogeneous). Among the many points that such simplistic glossing over multifaceted histories effaces is that science was as directed to processes as it was to outcomes of discovery; its appeal, interest and promise, as Macaulay and Tennyson in their distinctive voices capture, was as a prompt for ceaseless striving.

At the beginning of Victoria's reign, tenets of natural theology – most especially the belief that nature reveals evidence of God's design – continued to enable many to accept that their religious beliefs and the scientific study of natural phenomena could peacefully coexist. Commissioned by the Earl of Bridgewater to illustrate the goodness of God as manifested in the Creation, William Whewell's three *Bridgewater Treatises* (1833–40), which argued for the presence of an active creator behind a rational and well-ordered universe, found a wide and popular readership. Scholars disagree on just how much advances in the study of geology, which undermined the biblical timescale, came also to undermine confidence in natural theology, with some seeing it as the foundation of a widespread crisis of faith and others emphasising the many people who were able to refashion the story of the creation so that their faith remained intact. Even without the new understanding of time and space emerging from the fields of geology and astronomy, mid-Victorians had to contend with an array of other challenges to their faith, among them utilitarian philosophies that questioned the usefulness and rationality of religion and the insights of scholars who advocated the historical and essentially secular approach to the Bible known as Higher Criticism. In 1860, an influential collection of articles, titled simply *Essays and Reviews* and authored almost exclusively by Church of England clergymen, laid out the methods of this new approach to biblical study. Josef Altholz explains, 'After all, Lyell's geology and Darwin's biology, even if absolutely true, affected only a few chapters of Genesis, leaving the rest of the Bible untouched; but biblical criticism, even in the hands of devout clergymen, affected the whole text and inspiration and authority of the Bible and perhaps of the Christian faith' (p. 62 [Civ]).

Given the convergence of these myriad intellectual currents, it is hardly surprising that by the middle of the century those heralding the benefits of science in efforts to expand science education in the universities were met by intense opposition from those eager to preserve religious authority. Published during the heyday of this agitated and anxious activity, Darwin's *On*

The Huxley versus Wilberforce Showdown

The June 1860 meeting of the British Association in Oxford – held six months after the publication of *On the Origin of Species* and devoted to the topic of evolution – has acquired legendary status in the history of science. Among the hundreds of people gathered was the Bishop of Oxford, Samuel Wilberforce, who believed himself well prepared for battle, having been coached by the well-known anatomist, Sir Richard Owen. Although Wilberforce had little scientific expertise of his own, he excoriated Darwin's theories. Turning at one point in his remarks to the agnostic Thomas Henry Huxley, also at the meeting, he mockingly asked him whether it was through his grandfather or grandmother that he claimed descent from a monkey (see Figure 5.13). As the story goes, after whispering the comment, 'The Lord hath delivered him into mine hands', Huxley confidently took the stand not only to explain with disarming simplicity and elegance Darwin's key ideas, but also to parade Wilberforce's ignorance and error. Far from being the least bit concerned about having monkey in his ancestry, he explained, 'he would be ashamed to be connected with a man who used great gifts to obscure the truth'. Huxley won over the crowd, and Wilberforce was humiliated. Although it is probably going too far to claim, as J. R. Lucas does, that 'the flood tide of Victorian faith in all its fulsomeness was turned to an ebb', the encounter symbolises the triumph of Victorian rationality over orthodoxy.

(Lucas, 'Wilberforce and Huxley: a Legendary Encounter', n.p. [Ciii]) the *Origin of Species* (1859) sparked a firestorm of response in intellectual circles, most famously engendering an intellectual 'duel' between Thomas Henry Huxley and the Bishop of Oxford, Samuel Wilberforce, at an 1860 British Association meeting. Huxley, who would later coin the word 'agnostic', authored an influential and entirely favourable review of *The Origin of Species* in the April 1860 issue of the *Westminster Review*, likening science to an imperial power that would eventually infiltrate and conquer 'regions of thought into which she has as yet hardly penetrated' (Huxley, 'Review of *The Origin of Species*' [Ai]). Even within the camps that the two powerhouses, Huxley and Wilberforce, represented (loosely, science versus religion), there were distinct divisions, and the influence of Darwin's evolutionary ideas, particularly those of the mutability of life forms and the possibility of extinction, was not restricted to elite intellectual circles. Natural selection made it difficult to

MONKEYANA.

AM. I. A MAN AND A BROTHER?

5.13 Darwin cartoon, 'Monkeyana', which appeared in *Punch* in 1861.

embrace the idea of God at the helm of creation and in control of the processes by which man and animals adapted to their environments (see Figure 5.13).

Published in 1850, Tennyson's *In Memoriam* provides intriguing evidence of the influence of emerging scientific knowledge before either *On the Origin of Species* or *Essays and Reviews* arrived on the scene. Tennyson is known to have read Lyell's *Principles of Geology* (1830–3) and Chambers's *Vestiges of the Natural History of Creation* (1844), and the influence of these and other scientific studies can be seen in his famous elegy. Tennyson scholars point to lyrics 56 and 123 as illustrative of the poet attempting to come to terms with Lyell's theory of the way fossil records and rock strata revealed steady physical change in the earth that resulted in the extinction of entire species. At times, the poet conveys only his sense of awe and wonder, as when in lyric number 123 he writes

There rolls the deep where grew the tree.
   O earth, what changes hast thou seen!
   There where the long street roars, hath been
The stillness of the central sea.

(*In Memoriam*, p. 91 [Ai])

In this particular section of *In Memoriam*, Tennyson adapts his understanding of the changing earth to a more personal apprehension of relationships transformed into memory; other portions of the poem reveal a struggle to accept a scientific understanding of the world. Lyric number 56 begins:

> 'So careful of the type?' but no.
>   From scarped cliff and quarried stone
>   She cries, 'A thousand types are gone:
> I care for nothing, all shall go.'
>
> (In Memoriam, p. 41 [Ai])

The lyric goes on to posit Man as heroically trusting in a beneficent God whose law is love, 'Tho Nature, red in tooth and claw / With ravine, shriek'd against his creed' (*In Memoriam*, p. 41 [Ai]). Throughout *In Memoriam*, Tennyson makes deliberate use of punctuation to emphasise emotions, raise questions and express resignation. He evokes the resignation of having to live without answers to desperate questions:

> O life as futile, then, as frail!
>   O for thy voice to soothe and bless!
>   What hope of answer, or redress?
> Behind the veil, behind the veil.
>
> (In Memoriam, p. 42 [Ai])

Although many critics find in the poem evidence that religious faith is in conflict with scientific understanding, such an interpretation fails to capture Tennyson's nuanced representation of the kaleidoscopic relationship between faith, belief, knowledge, the unknown, feeling, trust, proof, understanding, truth and wisdom – words that circulate throughout his long poem – in human experience. One of the last sections to be written for the poem appears in published versions as the prologue; here Tennyson frames his elegy as prayer, asking ultimately for forgiveness and wisdom from God and emphasising that though 'we, that have not seen Thy face, / By faith, and faith alone, embrace, / Believing where we cannot prove' (*In Memoriam*, p.5 [Ai]).

To the extent that *In Memoriam* expresses the resilience of faith in the face of uncertainty, Tennyson undoubtedly spoke for legions of his fellow Victorians, and it is worth noting that the devotional poems in John Keble's *The Christian Year* (1827) were almost as popular in mid-Victorian Britain as Tennyson's magnum opus. Conflicts certainly existed within the Church of England and the overall hegemony of that institution was undercut by the rise of non-conformist churches and dissenting religions, the dominance of the Presbyterian Church in Scotland and the growth of Catholicism in England and Wales. Nevertheless, the language of the Bible retained its hold and might well be regarded as the common currency of Victorian Britain. Robin Gilmour characterises the extent to which religious discourse tended to permeate other forms of intellectual and cultural discourse as 'the most remarkable fact of all about Victorian religion' (*Victorian Period*, p.71 [B]), and his point is abundantly illustrated in literature. Biblical allusions can be found interspersed through much Victorian fiction and poetry, as can rhetoric of witnessing, conversion, confession, martyrdom and salvation.

Perhaps more importantly, evidence of a literary investment in religious discourse is frequently not separable from an equally compelling investment in scientific discourse. Charles Kingsley, the Broad Church clergyman who published works espousing the ideals of Christian socialism and Muscular Christianity, was also an amateur naturalist and wrote *The Water Babies*, a work that evocatively synthesises theology, evolution and social criticism. Philip Henry Gosse, the subject of Sir Edmund Gosse's autobiography *Father and Son*, was both a well-regarded zoologist and an Evangelical zealot. These examples remind us to be wary of too hastily assuming that science and religion were locked in combat during Victoria's reign. The poetry of Gerard Manley Hopkins, who converted to Roman Catholicism in 1866, illustrates still another way that interest in nature and science converges with religious purpose in productive, not combative, ways. Sharing with many of his fellow mid-Victorians an enthusiasm for natural history, Hopkins kept a journal of observations of the natural world that reveals his tireless curiosity, eye for detail and sense of wonder about the natural world. Hopkins's poetry focuses on capturing moments of intense natural beauty, which he essentially likens to God. 'The world is charged with the grandeur of God', he proclaims in the opening line of 'God's Grandeur' (Cunningham, *Victorians*, p. 863 [Aii]). For Hopkins, the experience of the natural world is fundamentally one of transcendence.

To acknowledge the significance of religious language in Victorian literature, and to attend to manifestations of religious belief in writers who embraced scientific understanding or methodology, is not to downplay the very real ways that literature of the period records crises of faith. Loss of faith is the central theme of Matthew Arnold's mid-century poem, 'Dover Beach' (c. 1851), in which he writes that 'The sea of faith'

> Was once, too, at the full, and round earth's shore
> Lay like the folds of a bright girdle furl'd;
> But now I only hear
> Its melancholy, long withdrawing roar
>
> (Cunningham, *Victorians*, p. 533 [Aii])

Carlyle, Tennyson, John Stuart Mill, George Eliot, Ruskin, Swinburne, Samuel Butler and Edmund Gosse, among others, each experienced a distinctive version of what is now often considered a classic Victorian paradigm for the loss of belief in religious certainties and authority. The only child of Evangelical parents, Ruskin records in his autobiography, *Praeterita* (the title means 'Of Things Past') a childhood dominated by intense Bible study and rigid moral instruction and a subsequent, gradual loss of faith. In a chapter titled 'The Grand Chartreuse', he writes:

> Of course that hour's meditation in the gallery of Turin only concluded the courses of thought which had been leading me to such end through many years. There was no sudden conversion possible to me, either by preacher, picture, or dulcimer. But, that day, my evangelical beliefs were put away, to be debated of no more.
>
> (*Longman Anthology*, p. 1495 [Aii]).

However unique Ruskin's own career and style of writing, the pattern of his loss of faith holds true for many, and historians have come increasingly to stress that in many cases faith was challenged not by the arrival of new scientific knowledge, paradigm-shattering though it was, but rather by moral and ethical qualms about religious culture, especially as shaped by Evangelicalism. This is what Josef Altholz labels 'the warfare of conscience with theology' (p. 65 [Civ]). In Mary Augusta Ward's best-selling novel *Robert Elsmere*, the hero's crisis of faith, which results in his abandoning his clerical position to take up social service, is prompted by rigorous consideration of Higher Criticism. Ward personalises the story, focusing less on the intricacies of her hero's intellectual journey than on its influence on his marriage and domestic happiness. Victorian writers found many ways to express and represent religious faith, the challenges to its sustenance and the personal impact of its loss.

Science in its many variations played a key role in literature of or about religious belief, but its influence was certainly not restricted to this thematic. Gillian Beer has demonstrated the enormous influence Darwin's own language, narrative strategies and views about such matters as sexual selection and the human struggle for survival had on the fiction of George Eliot, Thomas Hardy and others. Many other branches of science (including astronomy, physiology and anthropology) influenced the content, narrative and poetic techniques of Victorian writers. Medicine is one such area to shape the literary imagination. Clinical medicine, the genre of the case history and the discoveries made by new medical instruments influenced the narrative strategies, techniques and assumptions of many nineteenth-century novelists, including George Eliot and Thomas Hardy. Scientific modes of observation are central to debates over vivisection in the 1870s and 1880s. Wilkie Collins's 1883 novel *Heart and Science*, inspired in part by his reaction against a highly publicised case of live animal experimentation, took on what he called 'the hideous secrets of Vivisection' ('Introduction' to *Heart and Science*, p. 12 [Ai]). Photography – of paramount importance to the culture of realism in the period – was a triumph of emerging scientific technologies in the century; in Robin Gilmour's estimation, it is the most characteristic of Victorian media, for 'it brought together science and art in a novel way, was realistic, inescapably contemporary, incipiently democratic, and promised victory over the Time-Spirit which haunted the age' (*Victorian Period*, p. 218 [B]). A haunting Time-Spirit does, after all, seem to hover behind Macaulay's claims for science, however ebullient his tone. If, as he contends, 'A point which yesterday was invisible is its goal today, and will be its starting-post tomorrow', it is nevertheless debatable at best whether science, in its restless pursuit of progress, will ultimately harness and defeat, or simply be subservient to, Time.

Empire, Race and National Identity

The very ideals cited as cornerstones of Victorian culture – progress, expansion and mobility – take tangible and problematic shape in the history of the British empire during the period. The idea of empire either depends upon, or tacitly accepts, all three concepts as necessary givens. Victorian Britain clearly occupied a pivotal position at the centre of a global economy, but it was in the last three decades of the century, during which Victoria was crowned empress of India (the 'jewel' in the national crown), that a more determined attitude towards expansion and conquest rose to prominence and coloured the nation's sense of its purpose and identity. Britain had accrued colonial power steadily since the seventeenth century and throughout Victoria's reign, but the idea of empire was far more visibly a feature of public discussion and in literature when what has been called 'the new imperialism' emerged in the 1870s. Well-known expressions of imperial arrogance such as Cecil Rhodes's brash declaration in 1877 that the British are 'the finest race' and that 'the more of the world we inhabit the better it is for the human race' (see Figure 5.14) have led, unfortunately, to rather static and homogeneous assumptions about how imperial might was expressed and experienced on the part of the British at home and reflected in literature of the period. Scholars such as Bernard Porter have helped recently to reinvigorate and complicate discussion of the history of colonialism in the nineteenth century, questioning both how much agency the nation exerted

THE RHODES COLOSSUS
STRIDING FROM CAPE TOWN TO CAIRO.

5.14 'The Rhodes Colossus', drawn by Linley Sambourne, which appeared in *Punch* in 1892.

in its acquisition and governance of its colonies and how the empire influenced (or, alternatively, did little to shape) understandings of national identity in the period.

Compared to works like Rudyard Kipling's turn-of-the-century poem 'The White Man's Burden', which beckons readers to 'send forth the best ye breed' and to 'bind your sons to exile / to serve your captive's need', literature of the earlier Victorian period seems to relegate issues of British imperial identity to the back burner (Collins and Rundel, *The Broadview Anthology*, p. 1152 [Aii]). Nevertheless, allusions to the empire can be found percolating in almost any novel and invite consideration. Thackeray, whose father worked for the East India Company and who lived for a time in Calcutta, focused much of his commentary on the empire in *Vanity Fair* through the character of Jos Sedley, the ineffectual government officer who sends his sister cashmere shawls from India but who fails to summon the courage to help his fellow British soldiers defeat the French at Waterloo, and who later dies in poor lodgings while living in Brussels. In another novel from this period, *Jane Eyre*, Charlotte Brontë makes fascinating and disturbing use of her country's colonial heritage through the character of the madwoman in the attic – the Creole woman Bertha Mason and first wife of Rochester (whose fortune derives from the plantation economy of the West Indies). Confronted with Bertha Mason, her nemesis and alter ego, Jane Eyre invokes language akin to that which might have been used by slave-holders, colonists and travellers to describe contact with darker-skinned and exotic non-Europeans, at various points describing Bertha as a 'clothed hyena' and noting her 'shaggy locks' and 'savage face'. Far from simply using racial stereotypes to convey Jane's fear and disgust, however, Brontë connects the figure of Bertha Mason to a broad enquiry into themes of responsibility, subservience and rebellion. In *Bleak House*, Dickens memorably and mockingly links British missionary activity and philanthropic impulse to empire in the figure of Mrs Jellyby, who fails to recognise domestic disarray and distress because her attention is instead focused on the natives of Borrioboola-Gha, on the left bank of the Niger. Even in a novel as seemingly sedate as Elizabeth Gaskell's *Cranford*, empire plays a role, particularly in the reintroduction near the narrative's end of Peter ('Aga') Jenkyns, who, after having banished himself from home as a youth, returns from India with fantastical stories a-plenty to entertain and scare Miss Matty and other Cranfordians. Through his character, Gaskell pokes gentle fun at the lack of real knowledge in the village, a microcosm for all of England, about the wider world that surrounds (and at times penetrates) their own.

One finds more frequent expression of colonial confidence and embrace of the imperialist agenda in literature of the latter half of the century. By then many newspapers and magazines had spread the word of (and illustrated) the natural riches and exotic pleasures to be found abroad that were available to enterprising Britons. Many also, inspired by Social Darwinist beliefs in the nation's fitness not only to survive but to conquer, had taken up the topic of how imperialism related to the nation's 'civilising mission'.

Social Darwinism refers to the idea that people, like plants and animals, are subject to the processes of natural selection. In 1871, Darwin published *The Descent of Man, and Selection in Relation to Sex*, arguing, among other things, that man was descended from lower forms of life. His theory was quickly appropriated by those (especially political conservatives) seeking support for the tenets of competition and laissez-faire capitalism. Even before *The Descent of Man* was published, Herbert Spencer had, in *First Principles of a New System of Philosophy* (1862), applied the idea of evolution to race; more stridently than Darwin, Spencer relied on the rhetoric of civilised (European) society to make his claims about racial difference. The arguments of Darwin and Spencer had seeming applicability to differences in social standing as well; inequalities between classes could be posited as the natural result of purportedly inherent moral attributes such as industriousness, cleanliness and frugality. Social Darwinism clearly helped to direct the developing fields of anthropology and ethnography. Not only did Victorian 'sciences' of race influence many arenas of social thought, but they were deployed to support the nation's imperialist agenda.

Essays, articles and speeches by Gladstone and Disraeli, among others, politicised imperialism, as Liberals and Tories sought to stake out their position on issues of military power, trade policies and practices, patriotism and national pride. With successful passage of the Royal Titles Bill in 1876, Disraeli effectively co-opted imperial confidence and pride for the conservative wing. Many scholars go back further – to the acquisition of rights to the Suez Canal and to the Crimean War and the Indian Rebellion of 1857 (the so-called Indian Mutiny) and their aftermaths – to locate the point at which issues of empire became central to the consciousness of the nation. Tennyson yoked Britain's military presence abroad to masculine heroism and self-sacrifice with his rendition of the Battle of Balaclava in 'The Charge of the Light Brigade', with its famous homage to instinctive duty and honour: 'Their's not to reason why, / Their's but to do and die' (*Longman Anthology*, p. 1195 [Aii]). Patrick Brantlinger, among others, has documented the significance of the torrent of art work, poetry and prose that both depicts the Rebellion and finds in the spectacle evidence with which to justify British governmental and military control of India. Tennyson's 'The Defence of Lucknow' and Christina Rossetti's 'In the Round Tower at Jhansi, June 8, 1857' both reflect British reaction and response to the events in India, Rossetti's in particular invoking the heightened emotion inspired by a much publicised and horrific massacre at Cawnpore. The rhetoric linking national identity to Britain's missions overseas is central to Joseph Chamberlain's late-century work on 'The True Conception of Empire' and speaks to empire's continuing relevance long after these mid-century international crises. 'In carrying out this work of civilization we are fulfilling what I believe to be our national mission', Chamberlain wrote, 'and we are finding scope for the exercise of these faculties and qualities which have made of us a great governing race' (*Norton Anthology*, p. 1630 [Aii]).

Nonetheless, the literary appropriation of, and response to, imperialism and the rhetoric of national duty makes clear the fact that many writers found in the nation's relationship to its empire, and its assertion of colonial might, a powerful issue to critique. Wilkie Collins situates his novel of 1868, *The Moonstone*, around a fabulous yellow diamond stolen from an Indian shrine. Far from presenting the British Raj as the guardians of morality and justice, Collins finds in his detective novel the opportunity to expose the greed that he believes drives his country's imperial stance. Probably no novel is as powerful in its representation of the corruption driving imperialism as is Joseph Conrad's *Heart of Darkness*, which focuses on the moral degradation of those who exploit African resources and people. Not all, of course, were critical of the nation's imperial agenda; for many, empire provided the essential premise for adventure narratives and military dramas, such as those authored by Captain Mayne Reid and Robert Ballantyne. Ballantyne's *Coral Island* begins, 'Roving has always been, and still is, my ruling passion, the joy of my heart, the very sunshine of my existence' (p. 1 [Ai]). Adventure was the keynote of numerous magazines directed at young, mostly male, readers that, as Claudia Nelson has argued, 'minimized introspection in favour of action and unquestioning belief in British superiority' ('Growing Up: Childhood', in Tucker, ed., *Companion to Victorian Literature and Culture*, p. 77 [B]). W. H. G. Kingston, author of over a hundred novels, including *Peter the Whaler*, linked Christian, spiritual meditation to colonial conquest. For many of these writers, the adventures of empire led inevitably to the exaltation of a particular form of masculinity. Peter Hunt notes the 'heady mixture of racial superiority, arrogance, [and] fortitude' that fuelled G. A. Henty's glorification of the military in works such as *With Clive in India; Or the Beginnings of the Empire* (Hunt, p. 71 [Cii]).

No novelist was more firmly ensconced in the public imagination as the author of adventure tales than Rider Haggard. *King Solomon's Mines* (1885) – a novel dedicated by its narrator/hero Allan Quatermain 'to big and little boys' – secured his name, facilitating the success of other adventure narratives such as *She, Allan Quatermain* and *Ayesha*. Haggard's accounts of heroic frontiersmen sought, on the surface at least, to inspire confidence and pride in Britain's so-called civilising mission. More nuanced in his rendering of colonialism was Rudyard Kipling. Drawing on his experiences growing up in India and later working there as a journalist, Kipling's collection *Plain Tales from the Hills* (1888) brought distinctively new attention to the lifestyle of the Anglo-Indians and to the strengths and weaknesses of their culture. The Mowgli stories of the *Jungle Books* (1894, 1895) and the *Just So Stories* (1902) show that, far from being simply an apologist for empire (as works like 'The White Man's Burden' might lead one to assume), Kipling's embrace of imperialism was tempered by significant identification with Indian culture and appreciation for its other-worldly, mystical appeal. Kipling's writing reveals orientalist assumptions about the differences between Eastern and Western cultures but also advocates appreciation for the heterogeneous variety of the landscapes and populations of India.

Robin Gilmour's contention that economic decline, industrial challenges and the rise of competitive powers worldwide helped to make British imperialism 'a creature of anxiety rather than of confidence' is undoubtedly true (*Victorian Period*, p. 182 [B]). That anxiety is most palpable in late-century British literature in which the empire seems to 'strike back'. Appropriating emerging ideas about degeneration, race and crime, late-century works such as Rider Haggard's *She* and Bram Stoker's *Dracula* represent a kind of reverse colonisation that, as James Buzard has written, 'depicts a Britain alarmingly open to penetration by alien, even demonic, forces that insinuate themselves into the fiber of British being' (Tucker, *Companion to Victorian Literature and Culture*, p. 449 [B]). All of these features of late-century imperial anxiety are on display in Bram Stoker's *Dracula*.

If this literature failed to instil anxiety in its readers about the relation between Britain and its empire, coverage of the war in South Africa certainly did. In *Gender, Race, and the Writing of Empire*, Paula Krebs probes the variegated response to the Boer Wars to show that consensus about the empire, and the ideal of the civilising mission, was no longer tenable at the end of the century. Victorian Britons famously invoked the Roman empire at the time of Queen Victoria's Diamond Jubilee in 1897. Expressing as it did both unbounded confidence in their achievements and, paradoxically, anxious awareness of their inevitable decline, the comparison perfectly encapsulates the Victorian tendency to posit a sense of cohesive national identity as stable and secure and yet to experience it as elusive, if not lost.

Gender Roles and Relations

In a review essay titled 'Silly Novels by Lady Novelists', published in the *Westminster Review* in October of 1856, George Eliot condemns novels in which 'the frothy, the prosy, the pious, or the pedantic predominate' (in Robinson, *Literary Criticism*, p. 90

[Aii]). Eliot is scathing in her estimation of critics who bestow lavish praise on such books. By 'a peculiar thermometric adjustment', Eliot writes,

> when a woman's talent is at zero, journalistic approbation is at the boiling pitch; when she attains mediocrity, it is already at no more than summer heat; and if she ever reaches excellence, critical enthusiasm drops to the freezing point. Harriet Martineau, Currer Bell, and Mrs Gaskell have been treated as cavalierly as if they had been men.
>
> (Robinson, *Serious Occupation*, p. 113 [Aii])

Women writers should be judged, she argues, by the same exacting standards applied to men, for no educational restrictions can shut women out from the materials of fiction, and there is no species of art which is so free from rigid requirements (p. 114).

Eliot's essay both assumes and reveals much about gender roles and relations in the period. Her implied condemnation of a domestic ideology that links the feminine to the fatuous, her commentary on real and perceived educational and professional barriers to women, her attention to the rigid requirements not just of genre but also of gender, and the class-laden implications of designating a segment of authors as ladies, capture quite different but significant components of 'The Woman Question'. The three writers that Eliot singles out are also significant. Although throughout her career she was subject to unflattering portrayals as 'manly', Harriet Martineau published most often (at least by mid-century) under her own name. 'Currer Bell' was the pen name of Charlotte Brontë; if its androgynous flavour was intended to deflect gendered reviews of her work, the decision backfired, for speculation about whether the author, especially of *Jane Eyre*, was male or female was rife. 'Mrs Gaskell' seems as an authorial identity to give the symbolic legitimacy of marriage to Elizabeth Gaskell, perhaps protecting her from critics who might object to a woman entering the public sphere to take on the social, political and economic issues of the day as forthrightly as she did. Eliot adopted her own pen name not just so that her work would be reviewed as rigorously as if she were a man, but also to share a name, if not the last name, with George Henry Lewes, the married man and prominent literary and social critic with whom she lived. Mary Ann (later Marian) Evans in fact used her real name on only one published work, her 1854 translation of Feuerbach's *Essence of Christianity*.

Assumptions about gender attributes and differences were crucial components of Victorian self-fashioning and inform literature of the period at multiple levels and in complex ways. Victorian women in particular were saturated with prescriptive literature filled with social instruction on the duties of womanhood and proper feminine behaviour.

The Evangelical press helped to ensure a strong moral overtone to sermons, educational tracts and advice books that sanctified a belief in the separate spheres (which industrialism had helped to solidify) and the resulting duties of women in the maintenance of a tranquil home and the ministering oversight of husband and children. Medical science sought to locate and explain the sources of weakness and fragility within the female body and to warn of the consequences of not respecting that phenomenon as natural.

A relatively small number of Victorian literary works uncritically accept the tenets of separate spheres ideology, however. Sarah Ellis's popular advice book, *The Women*

---

of England, promotes a view of women as little more than self-denying instruments of domestic happiness. But even those works most often trotted out to expose the restrictive and debilitating idealisation of women betray signs of conflict and ambiguity. Coventry Patmore's verse sequence 'The Angel in the House' lauds the wife who 'loves with love that cannot tire', but he also compares woman more generally to 'a foreign land, Of which, though there he settle young, / A man will ne'er quite understand' (Cunningham, *The Victorians*, p. 559 [Aii]). John Ruskin's essay 'Of Queen's Gardens' idealises the home as a sacred place and pits man, who functions as 'the doer, the creator, the discoverer, the defender', against the woman, who is 'wise, not for self-development but for self-renunciation' (*Norton Anthology*, pp. 1587–8 [Aii]). Ruskin's essay ends by lauding the 'true changefulness' of woman, praise that rubs up uneasily against her characterisation as 'incorruptible' (*Norton Anthology*, pp. 1587–8 [Aii]). Move away from these classic standard bearers of the domestic ideal and one finds a veritable army of literary works that take substantial liberty with (and represent with far more complexity) woman – her duties, desires, opportunities, opinions and influence. Florence Nightingale's long autobiographical essay 'Cassandra', first circulated at mid-century, counsels mothers to awake and recognise that 'if this domestic life were so very good, would your young men wander away from it, your maidens think of something else?' (*Longman Anthology*, p. 1512 [Aii]). Equally forceful are the many moments in *Jane Eyre* when Brontë's heroine rebukes Rochester for his idealisation of her, as when she asserts, 'I am not an angel … and I will not be one till I die: I will be myself' (p. 288 [Ai]). Or Barrett Browning's emphasis on the indignation in Aurora Leigh's rejection of Romney:

> You misconceive the question like a man,
> Who sees a woman as the complement
> Of his sex merely.

(*Longman Anthology*, p. 1126 [Aii])

Although in *The Princess*, Tennyson's long narrative poem of 1847, Princess Ida and Prince Florian conclude that her mission to establish a woman's college is doomed to failure (she will instead turn it into a hospital), he counsels her to 'Blame not thyself too much', nor to blame 'Too much the sons of men and barbarous laws; / These were the rough ways of the world till now' (*Longman Anthology*, p. 1164 [Aii]).

Powerful and seemingly progressive as are such pronouncements, they are juxtaposed throughout the era to literature that foregrounds the spectre of the 'fallen woman', who whether as sexual seductress or as victim of the male sexual predator is the symbolic opposite of the pure and purifying angel in the house. Central to the sensation fiction of the 1860s, the fallen woman haunts numerous other works, including Elizabeth Gaskell's *Mary Barton* and 'Lizzie Leigh', Dickens's *Oliver Twist* and *Bleak House*, Eliot's *Adam Bede*, Christina Rossetti's 'Goblin Market' and Hardy's *Tess of the d'Urbervilles*. The figure of the fallen woman could be seen to epitomise a Christian logic, for as daughters of Eve women were assumed to be susceptible to temptation and likely to fall. The fallen woman figures as predominantly in Pre-Raphaelite painting. In *The Awakening Conscience*, a painting of 1853, William Holman Hunt depicts a woman extricating herself from the lap of her lover, her awakening conscience

5.15 *Found.* Rossetti's painting, begun in 1859, depicts a young farmer who, after having arrived in London to sell a calf, finds that his sweetheart, now a prostitute, is destitute on the streets.

rescuing her from an impending fall (*Longman Anthology*, colour plate 13 [Aii]). The first of Augustus Egg's 1858 narrative paintings titled *Past and Present* depicts a woman literally and figuratively fallen; stretched across the floor at her husband's feet, her prostrate posture signifies the degradation she has brought upon herself and the grief she has brought to him (*Longman Anthology*, colour plate 14 [Aii]). Shame is the keynote of yet another Pre-Raphaelite painting to feature the fallen woman, Dante Gabriel Rossetti's *Found* (see Figure 5.15).

The figure of the fallen woman had correlates in social reality, especially the prostitute. As urbanisation increased over the course of the century, prostitution became more visibly a subject of social concern and public debate. Social historians note that the moral panic that invariably accompanied discussion about the predominance of prostitution masked anxiety about the inability of society to control women. As Jan Marsh has written, 'As daughters, employees or servants, young women were subject to male authority; as whores they enjoyed economic and personal independence. The response was a rigorous campaign, in sermons, newspapers, literary and visual art, to intimidate, shame and eventually drive fallen women from the streets by representing them as a depraved and dangerous element in society, doomed to disease and death' ('Sex and Sexuality', n.p. [Ci]). The persistence and influence of Victorian assumptions about the fallen woman are especially apparent in the Contagious Diseases Acts, the first of which, after passing in 1864, required that prostitutes be subject to inspections and, if discovered to be infected with venereal disease, to be held in a 'lock' hospital for up to three months. Punishing only women and essentially allowing men licence for sexual exploitation and dominance, the Contagious Diseases Acts inspired outrage among many individuals, including Florence Nightingale. Groups such as the National Association for the Repeal of the Contagious Diseases Acts and the Ladies National Association organised campaigns of protest. The Acts were repealed in 1886. That Josephine Butler, head of the Ladies National Association, was able to attract substantial support among the organisation's many local chapters for her protests is testimony to the inroads feminism had made from the middle of the century onwards. Although many early nineteenth-century writers, male and female, espoused feminist principles, not until the middle of the century, when the Langham Place Circle and other groups came into being, did the wide-ranging issues that concerned feminists – e.g. access to education, opportunities for remunerative work and economic independence, and legal rights within marriage and property rights after divorce – have institutional support. With the publication of Harriet Taylor Mill's *The Enfranchisement of Women* in 1851, a campaign for the suffrage took hold, and it was further strengthened by John Stuart Mill's ground-breaking promotion of women's rights in *The Subjection of Women* (1869). By the 1880s and onwards, it was the leading cause of many feminists. The fruits of these and other efforts of mid-century feminists can be seen in works by New Woman writers at the end of the century, as in Olive Schreiner's enormously popular and partly autobiographical *The Story of an African Farm* (1883), whose main character, Lyndall, defends her principles with stalwart confidence and opts not to marry her lover even though she is pregnant.

The sheer variety of issues that came to be seen as part and parcel of the Woman Question might well imply cultural consensus and certainty around all things male. While Victorian men of the middle and upper classes certainly had the advantage of the sexual double standard and experienced little political and legal disadvantage compared to women, cultural beliefs about masculine conduct and duty were no less constrictive or likely to provoke anxious response. Works of scholarship such as James Eli Adams's *Dandies and Desert Saints* and Herbert Sussman's *Victorian Masculinities* have shown just how variegated was the terrain of Victorian manhood and how compelling were its cultural mandates. Sussman's basic contention that for the Victorians 'manhood is not an essence but a plot, a condition whose achievement and whose maintenance forms a narrative over time', helps to explain the frequency with which Victorian novels tackle the complicated mix of assumptions about class, gender and character that constituted the gentlemanly ideal (*Victorian Masculinities*, p. 13 [Ci]). Dickens's *Great Expectations* highlights the intrinsic contradictions and debilitating consequences of the gentlemanly ideal through its heart-wrenching evocation of the way Pip abandons his loving father-figure, Joe Gargery, in his ascent to gentility and thereby becomes engulfed in guilt and, ultimately, tainted with the criminal. Many other dimensions of the gentlemanly ideal inform popular works of Victorian fiction. Chivalry is central to the conception of the hero in Charlotte Yonge's *The Heir of Redclyffe*, for example, just as vigour and fortitude are in the 'Muscular Christian' vision of Thomas Hughes in *Tom Brown's School Days*. Dinah Craik's bestselling novel *John Halifax, Gentleman* focuses on the work ethic and genuine goodness of its eponymous hero. The enormous appeal of this particular version of the gentleman – the self-made man, as opposed to the man who, like Pip, arrives at wealth without work, is amply evident in Samuel Smiles's *Self-Help*. All men can aspire to this particular conception of rank and power, however, for the key ingredients of gentlemanly status are ideals available to all – e.g. self-respect, honour and courage. As Smiles summarises, 'The poor man may be a true gentleman – in spirit and in daily life. He may be honest, truthful, upright, polite, temperate, courageous, self-respecting, and self-helping, – that is be a true gentleman' (pp. 327–8 [Ai]).

Anxiety about, if not overt resistance to, ideologies that constructed men as rational exemplars of the moral, the dutiful, the hard-working and the vigorous is manifest in numerous ways in Victorian literature. Bulwer-Lytton, Tennyson, Darwin and Stevenson were only a few of the many prominent writers who identified themselves as invalids, either keeping diaries or publishing accounts of their struggles with nervous disorders, their susceptibility to the trials of overwork, and their experiments with therapies that by reducing them to postures of passivity and prostration brought them, in Janet Oppenheim's words, 'perilously close to the feminine condition' ('*Shattered Nerves*', p. 141 [Ciii]). Even more obviously than the invalid, the dandy – who rose to prominence in society and as a literary figure in the last quarter of the century – subverted the traditionally masculine, embodying instead idleness, irresponsibility and a rejection of conventional morality, in favour of the pursuit of pleasure and the embrace of beauty. Late-century revision of the masculine ethos took other forms as well. Joseph Conrad was one among many writers whose depictions of imperialism reveal scepticism about the idealisation of men as heroic warriors and national saviours.

To the extent that Victorian masculinity was associated, by definition, with the heterosexual, it is worth noting that a homoerotic impulse surfaces in a wide variety of Victorian literature – in Dickens's *David Copperfield* and *Our Mutual Friend*, for example, and in the poetry of Hopkins. Some critics see Tennyson's *In Memoriam* as witness to the homoerotic desire the poet experienced in his youth for Arthur Henry Hallam, the subject of his elegy. In a study of Victorian Britain's investment in the Hellenic ideals, Linda Dowling takes note of the homoerotic religiosity of John Henry Newman's *Tracts for the Times*. Although homosexuality came, over the course of the century, to be pathologised as sexual deviation and eventually to be criminalised, homoerotic friendships flourished before that point. Still, sodomy was a capital offence until the 1860s, and in 1885 the Labouchere Amendment to the Criminal Law Amendment Act defined acts of gross indecency between men as illegal. Lesbian women were spared the prospect of prosecution, probably because, as Linda K. Hughes has written, 'they were not deemed as socially dangerous as male homosexuals and because of their relative invisibility' ('1870', in Tucker, ed., *Companion to Victorian Literature and Culture*, p. 40 [B]). The criminalisation of homosexuality makes works like John Addington Symonds's *A Problem in Greek Ethics* (1883), which looked to ancient Greece for models of man–boy love to legitimise male–male desire, all the more significant.

The most famous victim of the Labouchere Amendment was undoubtedly Oscar Wilde, who went from being dandy-aesthete par excellence to, as he put it in a letter written at the time he was composing *De Profundis*, a 'disgraced and ruined man' (*Selected Letters*, p. 154 [Ai]). Despite the tragic course of his life, Wilde can be credited with insisting upon the centrality of love in homosexual relations. When asked on the witness stand (see Figure 5.16) to explain his reference to the love that dare not speak its name, Wilde responded as follows:

> The love that dare not speak its name in this century is such a great affection of an elder for a younger man as there was between David and Jonathan, such as Plato made the very basis of his philosophy, and such as you find in the sonnets of Michelangelo and Shakespeare. It is that deep, spiritual affection that is as pure as it is perfect. It dictates and pervades great works of art like those of Shakespeare and Michelangelo, and those two letters of mine, such as they are. It is in this century misunderstood, so much misunderstood that it may be described as the Love that dare not speak its name, and on account of it I am placed where I am now. It is beautiful, it is fine, it is the noblest form of affection. There is nothing unnatural about it. It is intellectual, and it repeatedly exists between an elder and a younger man, when the elder man has intellect, and the younger man has all the joy, hope and glamour of life before him. That it should be so, the world does not understand. The world mocks at it and sometimes puts one in the pillory for it.
> (Douglas O. Linder, 'The Trials of Oscar Wilde: an Account', n.p. [Cvii]).

Wilde's declaration is a trenchant reminder that gender not only dictates roles, but it structures relations – most powerfully the love relationship. It is telling that those lines of Victorian poetry most likely to be widely known outside academic

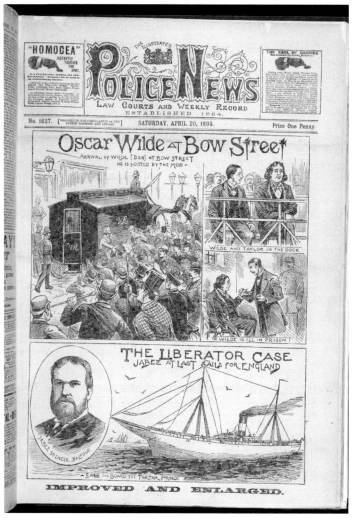

5.16 'Oscar Wilde at Bow Street' appeared in the *Illustrated Police News Law-Courts and Weekly Record* on 20 April 1895.

communities today derive from Elizabeth Barrett Browning's *Sonnets from the Portuguese* (when in Sonnet XLII she asks 'How do I love thee?' and answers, 'Let me count the ways'; *Longman Anthology*, p. 1112 [Aii]) and from Tennyson's *In Memoriam* (when he claims that ''Tis better to have loved and lost, / Than never to have loved at all'; *In Memoriam*, p. 58 [Ai]). Beautiful and resonant as are these lines, they can hardly do justice to the range and complexity of Victorian expressions of love. In Brontë's masterpiece novel *Villette*, the heroine Lucy Snowe angrily scorns easy love, in favour of her own, 'furnace-tried by pain, stamped by constancy, consolidated by affection's pure and durable alloy, submitted by intellect to intellect's own tests, and finally wrought up, by his own process, to his own unflawed completedness, this Love that laughed at Passion, his fast frenzies and his hot and hurried extinction' (*Villette*, p. 576 [Ai]). In Dante Gabriel Rossetti's sonnet sequence, *House of Life*, the poet describes a love relationship in which 'my soul only sees thy soul its own' ('Lovesight', in *Longman Anthology*, p. 1605 [Aii]). Victorian writers turned to love as the *sine qua non* of human experience. In their world of flux, love provided – despite and because of its infinite varieties – a source of stability and certainty, an imaginative ideal to yearn for without having to turn to the past or imagine the future.

Readings

Charlotte Brontë, *Jane Eyre* (1847)

Early on in *Jane Eyre*, the eponymous heroine recalls a time when she, unjustly accused of lying and commanded to leave the room, was prompted by a passion of resentment to respond: '*Speak* I must; I had been trodden on severely, and *must* turn', she writes (p. 68 [Ai]). Brontë's emphasis conveys not simply the urgency of Jane's felt emotions, but also what is arguably the novel's dominant motif and theme – the function of voice, the need for expression, the power of utterance and their connection to the idea and ideal of autonomy. Charting her heroine's journey from a troubled childhood and adolescence through her experiences as a governess to marriage – that narrative end for so many female-centred, early English novels – Brontë's novel appropriates many traits of the *Bildungsroman*, or novel of formation, and in doing so situates itself within a literary trajectory that includes *David Copperfield, The Mill on the Floss* and many other major Victorian novels. By structuring her novel around highly charged moments of silence and speech, however, Brontë enriches and complicates that genre, most especially by foregrounding for her readers not simply the societal institutions or conventions that would silence the heroine (and sometimes, by implication, women more generally) but also the ways that she silences herself, as often in acts of self-censorship as in attempts to control others. In this way, Brontë's novel probes the very complicated relationship between psychological and social dimensions of identity.

Brontë's interest in using speech to grapple with more fundamental issues of self-control is evident early on in the novel, as when Jane records a scarcely voluntary demand made of her evil Aunt Reed and then explains, 'I say scarcely voluntary, for it seemed as if my tongue pronounced words without my will consenting to their utterance: something spoke out of me over which I had no control' (p. 60). Commanded to be silent in the opening episode of the novel, and punished when she is not, Jane uses her narrative as a form of resistance and rebellion against strictures of suppression. If in the early stages of her relationship with Rochester, Jane's refusals to speak on demand reflect her reticence and unwillingness to submit to his authority, by the time she ponders leaving Thornfield she is deeply troubled by the prospect that she will lose the opportunity for conversation: 'I have talked, face to face, with what I reverence, with what I delight in – with an original, a vigorous, an expanded mind', she tells him (p. 281). At one of the narrative's most climactic moments, when Jane lies at death's door, she tries 'to wait His will in silence', and remembers, 'These words I not only thought, but uttered; and thrusting back all my misery into my heart, I made an effort to compel it to remain there – dumb and still' (p. 362).

In so deliberately emphasising her heroine's need both to have and to control powers of utterance, Brontë makes more resonant the implications and reliability of Jane's first-person narration. The reader of *Jane Eyre* is, as the critic Garrett Stewart has written, 'conscripted' into a relationship with the narrator that necessarily complicates interpretation of her relationship with others in her life. If the novel's most famous moment of direct address is when Jane states, 'Reader, I married him', many of her other addresses to the reader open up more complicated understanding of the reader/narrator/author relationship, as when she defensively writes, 'And reader, do you think I feared him in his blind ferocity? – if you do, you little know me' (p. 456).

Brontë's story undoubtedly reverberated for many of the readers who first encountered it in 1847 and thereafter – perhaps especially for her fellow women writers, many of whom documented their own struggles to develop their authorial voices, to go public with their ideas and opinions. Sandra Gilbert and Susan Gubar have influentially posited *Jane Eyre* as the foundational text for understanding the influence of patriarchal literary standards on the nineteenth-century woman writer, arguing that the 'madwoman in the attic' – the phrase refers specifically to Bertha Mason, Rochester's mad wife and Jane's alter ego – can be seen to symbolise the woman writer whose creative impulses cannot be openly expressed (*The Madwoman in the Attic* [Ci]). Compelling as is this reading of Bertha Mason's role, Brontë accomplishes considerably more with her characterisation. Noting the prominence of debates about Britain's position with respect to its colonies, many critics believe that Brontë deliberately draws on the rhetoric of the colonial subject as 'primitive' and 'savage' to convey Jane's deeply conflicted attitude towards her own passions and desire either to control or to be dominated; such readings help to explain why Jane (and others) liken Bertha to a vampire or stress her 'fearful blackened inflation of the lineaments'(p. 311). The colonial context of *Jane Eyre* reveals itself as well in the lengthy section devoted to Jane's stay at Moor House, with people who, in one of the novel's most romantic gestures, will turn out to be her cousins. Jane forcefully resists the pressure exerted by the religious zealot St John Rivers to marry him in order to join him in missionary work in India. His is a model of Christian sacrifice that she cannot embrace, for while she appreciates the power of his sermons and values his commitment and aspiration to Christian glory, she rejects his domestic self: at the fireside, he is 'too often a cold cumbrous column, gloomy and out of place' (p. 419). Brontë is careful to insist that St John's sisters validate Jane's decision – 'you'd be grilled alive in Calcutta', they tell her; Brontë uses the episode to advance Jane's own self-understanding as well: 'I was no apostle – I could not behold the herald – I could not receive his call', she writes (p. 427).

Such moments demonstrate the ways Brontë adapts and critiques the genre of spiritual autobiography in *Jane Eyre* – a work in many ways inspired by *Pilgrim's Progress* – and the multiple ways it explores religiosity (despite the fact that one of the most influential, if unrepresentative, early reviews condemned it as an 'anti-Christian composition'). Brontë is merciless in her representation of the Evangelicalism of Mr Brocklehurst, the hypocritical head of the Lowood School who dictatorially crushes anything smacking of pride or vanity and subjects the girls to numerous privations while parading his own well-fed and highly ornamented daughters. With Helen Burns, a character based on one of Brontë's own sisters, the novelist probes (and ultimately rejects) the notion of Christian stoicism, of resignation in the face of the trials and tribulations that afflict one while on earth. Brontë's entire novel is steeped in the language of the Bible, as when Jane says of her Aunt Reed, 'I ought to forgive you, for you knew not what you did' (p. 52), or when she recognises that St John, for all his earnest embrace of Christian mission, 'had not yet found that peace of God which passeth all understanding' (p. 378).

Indeed, how to reconcile her own desires – for passion and for liberty – with an equally strong desire for service, to God and to her fellow man, is at the core of Jane Eyre's journey. Early on in the novel, Jane voices her need to leave Lowood School as a desire to find 'a new servitude', her language reflecting both the limits of her aspirations and her need to rein in the desire for liberty that haunts her just as emphatically as it stirs her to action. Deeply troubled throughout her narrative by her status as a dependant, and open about her own biases against degraded social status, Jane struggles, Brontë implies, to overcome a debilitating class-consciousness that makes it difficult for her to fully embrace either Christian or secular forms of servitude. At a particularly low point in her childhood years at the Reed home, Jane describes herself as 'a useless thing … a noxious thing' (p. 47). The language that she uses to describe her life as her narrative draws to a close suggests that, in marriage, she can enjoy the feeling of being useful and needed (without needing, as a newly wealthy woman, to depend upon Rochester's money). After explaining that she reads and sees for her now almost-blind husband, Jane tells us, for example, that 'there was a pleasure in my services, most full, most exquisite, even though sad – because he claimed these services without painful shame or damping humiliation' (p. 476). Even more deliberately, she draws on Christian language to express satisfaction with the (inter)dependencies of marriage:

> I know what it is to live entirely for and with what I love best on earth. I hold myself supremely blest – blest beyond what language can express; because I am my husband's life as fully as he is mine. No woman was ever nearer to her mate than I am: ever more absolutely bone of his bone and flesh of his flesh.
>
> (pp. 475–6).

'This is not to be a regular autobiography', Jane notifies her readers early on. Just as Brontë herself deployed the deliberately androgynous pseudonym of 'Currer Bell' to function as 'editor' of Jane Eyre: An Autobiography, so too does her heroine/narrator find numerous ways to explore the meaning and function of identity itself at different junctures in her self-development. Jane Eyre is peppered with deeply painful moments when Jane fails to recognise herself – already feeling like 'nobody' while in Gateshead Hall, she looks in a mirror and sees only a 'visionary hollow' and 'strange little figure' staring back at her when she is banished to the Red Room (p. 46). At a much later point in the narrative Jane derisively refers to herself as 'poor stupid dupe' and forces herself to draw her own self-portrait, labelled 'Portrait of a Governess, disconnected, poor, and plain' (p. 190). The fantastical and other-worldly compete with social realism in Jane Eyre's psyche, just as they do in our lives, Brontë implies. Readers today often find Brontë's use of supernaturalism and melodrama disconcerting, but they cannot fail to appreciate the myriad ways these elements enhance our understanding of the force of her heroine's character. Although Matthew Arnold referred to *Villette* when he denounced Brontë as having 'a mind full of hunger, rage, and rebellion' (*Letters*, 1: 132 [Ai]), his emotional imagery is equally applicable to *Jane Eyre*. The powerful emotions that so rattled Arnold are of course those that have prompted generations of Brontë's readers to admire her honest, courageous and revolutionary (this is, after all, a novel of 1847) exploration of a woman's search for a liberty that will allow her to define for herself the grounds of her pleasure and the terms of her relationships to others.

Charles Dickens, *Bleak House* (1852–3)

Perhaps no Victorian work is more resistant to interpretive summary than Dickens's mid-century masterpiece *Bleak House* (see Figure 5.17), a novel that in modern editions stretches to almost 900 pages and that contrives to contain many hundreds of scenes and varieties of character. Its very expanse, its embrace of the capacious and its audacious intermingling of realism and romance, might seem to make it the apotheosis of a 'loose and baggy monster'. Indeed, Dickens invokes the monstrous in the highly symbolic and suggestive description of a London shrouded in fog and weighed down by mud that introduces the novel; the narrator notes that 'it would not be wonderful to meet a Megalosaurus, forty feet long or so, waddling like an elephantine lizard up Holborn-hill' (p. 3, Ai). Yet if Dickens reaches into deep history for his framing metaphor, his interest throughout *Bleak House* is very much on contemporary manifestations of monstrosity. The illiterate street-sweeper Jo is, for example, 'of no order and no place; neither of the beasts, nor of humanity'. As Dickens explains,

> He is not one of Mrs Pardiggle's Tockahoopo Indians; he is not one of Mrs Jellyby's lambs, being wholly unconnected with Borrioboola Gha; he is not softened by distance and unfamiliarity; he is not a genuine foreign-grown savage; he is the ordinary home-made article. Dirty, ugly, disagreeable to all the senses, in body a common creature of the common streets, only in soul a heathen. Homely filth begrimes him, homely parasites devour him, homely sores are in him, homely rags are on him; native ignorance, the growth of English soil and climate, sinks his immortal nature lower than the beasts that perish.
>
> (*Bleak House*, p. 628 [Ai])

It is easy to see in this passage (vintage Dickens in its urgent and relentless pursuit of his point) why *Bleak House* is often thought to mark a turning point in the novelist's career, when his vision became decidedly darker, harsher and more scornful. For all of the novel's emphasis on the fog that encases this modern world, Dickens demands that his readers see what surrounds them, and he shames them for their reluctance to look.

Vision is, in fact, central to this richly visual novel. Not only does Dickens scorn characters like Mrs Jellyby (and, through her, other blind or hypocritical

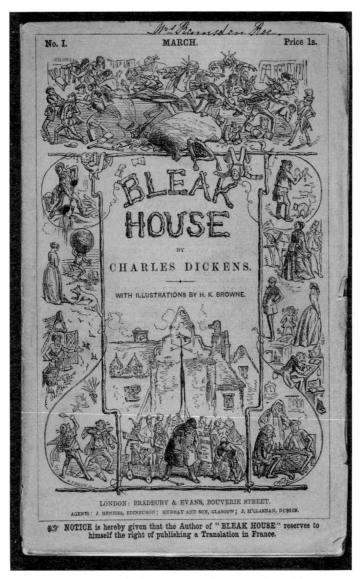

5.17 The title page to *Bleak House*, with illustrations by Hablot Browne ('Phiz').

philanthropists and social ameliorists) whose focus on the imagined needs of Borrioboola Gha is so intense that she is rendered incapable of seeing the realities of her own home and of the life that surrounds her, but he structures the novel's plot, its unravelling of the true identities of Lady Dedlock and Esther Summerson, around key moments of seeing, as when Lady Dedlock sees a piece of handwriting and recognises it (the significance of her own response recognised, in turn, by the lawyer Tulkinghorn), or when Guppy sees Lady Dedlock's portrait and intuits her affinities to Esther, or when Esther sees Lady Dedlock's face and begins to know her own history. The novel's investment in the visual, and in particular its juxtaposition of painted portraits with photographic images, reflects its historical moment in an intriguing range of ways. Although *Bleak House* is set in the early 1830s, just before Fox Talbot's first photographs were made public, it was written in the early 1850s, when photographic images were widely in circulation and a range of optical inventions made technologies of vision crucial to emerging notions of modernity. Photography was also crucial to medical diagnosis of insanity and to the developing field of criminology, for it allowed entirely new modes of identification. Surveillance and the pursuit of identity are major themes of *Bleak House*; the critic Ronald Thomas persuasively argues that Inspector Bucket – central figure of this detective novel – 'stands in the place cleared by the technology of the camera and derives his legal and cultural authority from a professional expertise of image making that is able to authenticate what the ancient court and the traditional oil portraits cannot' (p. 93 [Cvii]).

If Bucket (as well as characters such as Mrs Snagsby, who 'Sees it All') are endowed with expansive powers of surveillance, *Bleak House* nevertheless focuses as much attention on the inscrutable and the invisible. Although Esther gradually recovers her sight after her bout with smallpox, one of the first things that she sees is that the mirrors have been removed from her room. Diseases of all sorts haunt *Bleak House*, often unsusceptible to detection until they have advanced too far to be stopped (and in this way crucial to Dickens's overarching commentary about his own society's self-satisfied belief in progress). Although Dickens hilariously mocks Sir Leicester Dedlock's egotistical belief that his gout is 'a demon of the patrician order and is something exclusive, even to the levelling process of dying' (p. 216), his satire is biting. The vagrant boy Jo carries disease from the slums of Tom-All-Alone's ('a ruinous place', 'a swarm of misery', p. 217) to the Bleak House bedroom of Esther. Contagion was not just a social and medical reality for Victorian novelists like Dickens; it provided them, as Athena Vrettos has shown (*Somatic Fictions* [Ciii]), with a narrative device to link disparate groups of people and to represent the potential instability of biological and social identities.

Disease also stops time – for Esther, for example, by displacing her to the seemingly timeless world of the sickroom, and for Jo by ending his life. In this way, disease is crucial to the most prominent symbol of Dickens's novel – the Court of Chancery – and indeed Dickens describes it as a deeply diseased institution. Chancery has 'its decaying houses and its blighted lands in every shire … its worn-out lunatic in every mad-house, and its dead in every churchyard' (p. 5). The novel depicts men and women of all ages made mad, in both senses of the word, by the insanity of the Chancery Court, and critics have duly taken note of those characters (like the crazy woman Miss Flite or Richard Carstone) who might be seen to display increasing rationality as they descend further and further into their madness. Jarndyce and Jarndyce, the ludicrous lawsuit at the heart of the novel, is, like the Megalosaurus that opens *Bleak House*, monstrous; it is 'a scarecrow of a suit and has grimly writhed into many shapes' (pp. 6, 7). Most of all, like disease itself, the suit (and the court system of which it is only a symptom) functions to endlessly protract time. It symbolises the inertia that Dickens believed to be the most debilitating and defining characteristic of his day.

Nevertheless, it is possible, as Esther's narrative reminds us, to recuperate from disease. For all of its harsh recriminations and its deeply bitter commentary on what impedes the pursuit of justice, *Bleak House* places enormous emphasis on the restorative powers of forgiveness. Taking frequent recourse to the Growlery to vent his frustrations, Esther's guardian John Jarndyce is nevertheless ceaselessly forgiving of those who betray his generosity; his indulgent nature leads him in the end to arrange for Esther to marry the middle-class doctor Allan Woodcourt, instead of himself. In a stroke-induced fog, Sir Leicester Dedlock commands Bucket to find his wife and assure her of his forgiveness. Richard Carstone's parting words to Ada are to ask for forgiveness, for 'having brought her to poverty and trouble and for having scattered [her] means to the winds' (p. 854). Some critics see *Bleak House* as 'apocalyptically warning of a coming day of judgment' (Davis, *Charles Dickens, A to Z*, p.35[B]), but the novel as forcefully affirms in its multiple closing episodes the redemptive potential of humanity.

Yet, however much finality the novel provides once the case of Jarndyce and Jarndyce ends (the will is decided, but the money that all were waiting for has been evaporated in legal costs), the novel just as insistently repudiates closure. Dickens marks the termination of the central lawsuit by having the crazy woman Miss Flite release her birds to liberty. Dickens's greatest achievement in *Bleak House* is in his manipulation of the tension between the human impulse to fixity, the desire for stability, and the reality of how experience in all of its manifestations spurns such longing as futile. Indeed, that futility defines the Condition of England, where social invisibles like Jo will invariably be told to 'move on'. Identity itself, Dickens suggests, is deeply and provocatively unstable. Lady Dedlock, at the top of the social echelon, has, in the end, to be identified with Nemo (the name means 'No one'). Esther Summerson is, as her beloved guardian reminds her, 'Dame Trot, Dame Durden, Little Woman! – all just the same as ever' (p. 860).

Bleak House has long been considered to be the Victorian period's most enduring representation of London in all of its protean nature, and, much like the Great Exhibition that immediately preceded it, the novel makes spectacular use of its urban setting and the restless forces the city struggles to contain. Less noticed, but no less powerful, is the novel's interest in the mind as another kind of container, one that seeks, not altogether successfully, to bring order to chaotic worlds within and without. Dickens embeds this struggle in his very narrative technique, pitting the strong, confident and comprehensive voice of the anonymous third-person omniscient narrative against the diffident and tentative voice of Esther Summerson. Still, Esther has the novel's final words, and her emphasis is on uncertainty. Asked by her loving husband whether she realises that, despite her smallpox-ravaged face, she is prettier than she ever was, Esther responds,

> I did not know that; I am not certain that I know it now. But I know that my dearest little pets are very pretty, and that my darling is very beautiful, and that my husband is very handsome, and that my guardian has the brightest and most benevolent face that ever was seen; and that they can very well do without much beauty in me – even supposing –
>
> (p. 861)

Thus Dickens ends, without ending, *Bleak House*, his open-ended sentence-structure stylistically reinforcing the novel's complex commentary on the nature of knowledge and the pursuit of truth in a world of kaleidoscopic perspectives. Although Esther pauses mid-sentence before she begins to conjecture, Dickens implies that her thoughts, and her life, will go on, beyond the boundaries of a novel whose representational powers cannot hope to contain them any more than a city like London can be comprehended.

Christina Rossetti, 'Goblin Market' (1862)

> Morning and evening,
> Maids heard the Goblins cry,
> 'Come buy our orchard fruits,
> Come buy, Come buy.'

(*Longman Anthology*, p. 1618 [Aii])

With these seductively simple and haunting lines, Christina Rossetti began the highly imaginative and sensuous narrative poem that would secure her fame and give to the Pre-Raphaelite Brotherhood their first commercial success. The irony of this would not have been lost on Rossetti, for her powerful poem is at once a study of sisterhood, in all of its meanings, and a study of the fruits (as in outcomes) of a culture of commerce. If no single Victorian poem has attracted more scholarly criticism in recent years than has 'Goblin Market', that attention is owing to the ways the poem yields multiple interpretations that make it difficult to pin down an overarching didactic purpose. Indeed, to the extent that 'Goblin Market' resists yielding a conclusive interpretation but provides, even as it explores, pleasure, it reveals something of the role played by Pre-Raphaelite literature in helping to fuel the rise of aestheticism in the latter half of the period.

Under the pseudonym of Ellen Alleyn, Rossetti had contributed poems to *The Germ* during the early 1850s and to other literary magazines afterwards, but *'Goblin Market' and Other Poems* (1862) was her first published book of poetry and brought her instant acclaim. Part fairy tale, part allegory, part parable, 'Goblin Market' situates within its story of two sisters a range of Victorian preoccupations – principally economic, sexual and religious. These preoccupations do not simply coexist within the poem, however, but rather function in reciprocal relation, sometimes reinforcing and sometimes complicating one another. Well before the poem's two central players, Laura and Lizzie, are introduced, readers are bombarded with image after image of the lush fruit that goblin men will use to tempt the girls. All are invited, the poem implies, to taste and try fruits that are 'Sweet to tongue and sound to eye' (*Longman Anthology*, pp. 1618–19 [Aii]).

With the introduction of the sisters, however, it becomes clear that these are *forbidden* fruits, and the poem shifts to focus more squarely on the ways Laura and Lizzie try to resist not just the fruits themselves but, more pointedly, the goblin men who hawk them. When Rossetti writes that 'Laura bowed her head to hear / Lizzie veiled her blushes' (*Longman Anthology*, p. 1619 [Aii]), it is clear that it is the goblin men, not the fruits themselves, that threaten the purity of the sisters. As the poem moves forward, Rossetti's interest in distinguishing between the sisters becomes increasingly clear, with 'sweet-toothed' and 'curious' Laura in hot pursuit of pleasure and physical satisfaction and the more conventional and upright Lizzie ready to resist – and armed not just with 'wise upbraidings' but also with a cautionary tale to scare her sister back to the straight and narrow path. Lizzie reminds her of Jeanie, the poem's representative fallen woman, in this way:

> She pined and pined away;
> Sought them by night and day,
> Found them no more, but dwindled and grew grey;
> Then fell with the first snow
> While to this day no grass will grow
> Where she lies low

(*Longman Anthology*, p. 1622 [Aii])

Laura, though, can't resist temptation and 'like a vessel at the launch / when its last restraint is gone' goes off in search of satisfaction (*Longman Anthology*, p. 1620 [Aii]).

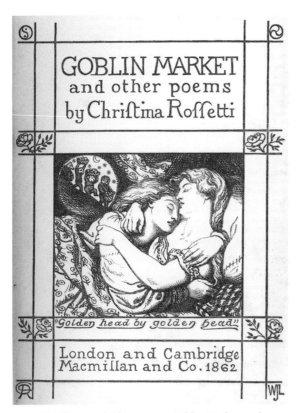

5.18 The illustrated title page to *Goblin Market and Other Poems* (Cambridge: Macmillan, 1862). The illustration of Laura and Lizzie, the two main characters of 'Goblin Market', was done by Christina Rossetti's brother, the Pre-Raphaelite artist Dante Gabriel Rossetti.

Giving up a highly symbolic golden curl in exchange for the opportunity to indulge in their 'fruit globes fair or red', she falls prey, Rossetti implies, to sexual seduction and soon discovers that her 'baulked desire' cannot be satisfied. She is damaged goods. 'Goblin Market' subverts the traditional narrative of the fallen woman, though, in bringing Laura back into the sanctity of the domestic fold through the sacrificial and redemptive efforts of her sister. In this, as in other ways, the sexual and religious implications of the story are inextricably bound to one another. Undergoing what amounts to attempted rape, 'lily-like' Lizzie brings home restorative fruit juices (described as a 'fiery antidote') to her ailing sister, telling her: 'Hug me, kiss me, suck my juices / Squeezed from goblin fruits for you' (*Longman Anthology*, p. 1628 [Aii]).

Here again the religious and sexual inform one another, for the passage's Eucharistic overtones complicate its more dominant sexual flavour. These tantalising lines of the poem have, not surprisingly, prompted scores of readers to detect in Rossetti's poem a subversive interest in the power of lesbian (and some contend incestuous) relationship to counter the poem's more overt narrative of heterosexual contact and exchange. Other critics focus on the contribution this passage makes to the poem's interest in the vampiric. Some feminist critics have found in the poem a concern with hunger, broadly construed, and anorexic response, and identify this moment as a crucial turning point.

Complicating these interpretations is the poem's ending, which can only seem to be one where Lizzie, as Christ-like saviour, redeems her fallen sister and restores her to the sanctity of the domestic sphere. In the concluding episode, Rossetti depicts a female-centred domestic space that barricades itself from contact with the outside world. It is noteworthy that the final lines of the poem that preach sisterly solidarity are enclosed in quotation marks. Like the story of Jeanie, this mini-sermon is a story, a cautionary tale designed to quell female desire and, implicitly, to preach the virtues of abstention (or its religious equivalent, renunciation) (*Longman Anthology*, p. 1626 [Aii]). Did Rossetti mean to affirm that message, or to expose it as one of the malignant features of a patriarchal society that posits women as passionless (as opposed to men, who, like the goblins in the poem, are defined by their animalistic sexual drive)? That question, like so many others raised by the poem, is open to interpretation.

Although 'Goblin Market' had originally been titled 'A Peep at the Goblins', Rossetti's revision to emphasise the significance of the commentary on commerce and commodity culture is noteworthy. 'Come buy, come buy' is so often repeated (and described at one point as an 'iterated jingle / of sugar-baited words') that the poem takes on the mantle of advertisement, with readers, like the sisters themselves, seduced into commercial transaction. The goblins are not just men, they are, as the poem repeatedly reminds us, *merchants*. More than a few critics have argued that Rossetti's poem reflects the dominating presence of capitalism and, more specifically, the marketing practices of advertising, in mid- to late Victorian Britain. As Herbert Tucker writes, 'This was especially true for a poet of Christina Rossetti's age: born in 1830, and cresting the prime of life in 1862 when her "Goblin Market" volume was published, she was young enough to feel the new pitch of Victorian advertisement as keyed particularly to her generation's susceptibilities; yet she was old enough to know better, having grown up under a more naïve promotional dispensation' ('Rossetti's "Goblin Market"ing', p. 118 [Cvii]). Read through the lens of the poem's commentary on consumerism and advertising, Laura can be seen to suck the fruits because she is a 'sucker' – that is, one 'who will never get an even break because no actual commodity can match the consuming appetite that her susceptibility to strong marketing has awakened' (Tucker, pp. 124–5 [Cvii]).

Rossetti's book of poetry was itself a commodity, and however suspicious her title poem might suggest her to be about the seductions of the market, she was alive to the potential to profit, literally and symbolically, from commercial success. She worked closely with her brother, Dante Gabriel Rossetti, on illustrations for the poem, clearly recognising that they were crucial not just to its interpretation but also to the marketing of the volume.

Indeed, one of the poem's most overlooked features is the way it so carefully structures itself around time – 'day after day, night after night', readers are constantly attuned to the shifts from morning to evening, twilight to dawn, summer to winter, and to the eventual passage through 'days, weeks, months, years' that yields an 'afterwards' that can be safely juxtaposed to 'not-returning time' (*Longman Anthology*, pp. 1629, 1630 [Aii]). In this way, perhaps more than any other, 'Goblin Market' is a paradigmatic Victorian poem, for, to invoke Robin Gilmour's phrase about the entire period, it makes rich and imaginative use of a 'Time-haunting Spirit' to place itself in history.

Robert Louis Stevenson, *Strange Case of Dr Jekyll and Mr Hyde* (1886)

Interviewed for a *Scribner's Magazine* series on popular writers in 1888, Robert Louis Stevenson – well known by then as the author of the sensationally thrilling novella, *Strange Case of Dr Jekyll and Mr Hyde* – explained his affinities with the 'penny press' – the term designating affordable and usually sensational popular fiction, sometimes known as 'penny dreadfuls' and 'shilling shockers'. Reared on the pious literature of *Cassell's Family Paper*, Stevenson soon found himself lusting after the more adventurous, if less wholesome, fiction he saw advertised and illustrated in a local stationer's window – and to there he would make a weekly pilgrimage. The language he uses to describe this dimension of his childhood is especially revealing:

> This inexpensive pleasure mastered me. Each new Saturday I would go from one newsvendor's window to another's, till I was master of the weekly gallery and had thoroughly digested 'The Baronet Unmasked', 'So and so approaching the Mysterious House', 'The Discovery of the Dead Body in the Blue Marl Pit', 'Dr Vargas Removing the Senseless Body of Fair Lilias', and whatever other snatch of unknown story and glimpse of unknown characters that gallery afforded.
> (in 'Backgrounds and Contexts', Stevenson, *Dr Jekyll*, p. 122 [Ai]).

Just as Stevenson's remarks highlight a fundamental ambiguity about the nature and addictive power of pleasure, so too do they reveal a crucial tension between the desire (and note the imperial overtones) to master and to be mastered. *Dr Jekyll and Mr Hyde* is, after all, at heart a study of the power of pleasures, inexpensive, illicit and illegal, to overcome both social and psychological mechanisms of restraint. Among the many cultural contexts that help to situate Stevenson's masterpiece within literary history, not least (although often overlooked) is that of print culture. Describing himself as 'a student of our penny press', Stevenson avows the extent to which his conception of authorship and his commitment to romance has been shaped by affiliation with a kind of literature – lurid, sensational and graphic, and undeniably accessible – that spawned substantial anxiety about popular literature and its readerships in the latter third of the century. References to the literary market surface in the novella in intriguing ways – e.g., the 'shop for the retail of penny numbers' that can be found near Hyde's apartment, the circulars (advertisements) that come in the mail to Jekyll's home, etc. Even Jekyll's reference to Hyde as 'a part' instead of a person (p. 61) can be read as an allusion to the mechanisms of print culture that helped to make literature affordable to the masses during the period.

The question of what constitutes a person is, of course, also a matter of debate throughout *Dr Jekyll and Mr Hyde*. Identifying Henry Jekyll early on by a long series of professional affiliations – 'MD, DCL, LLD, FRS' – Stevenson seems to underscore the anxieties of middle-class men to legitimise themselves through their professional identities, which function as nearly impenetrable mantles (p. 52). Stevenson makes clear in his work just how important the idea of respectability is to the middle classes, especially to the group that his novella, almost entirely absent of women, is most preoccupied with – 'well-known men about town'. Some critics, including Elaine Showalter in *Sexual Anarchy: Gender and Culture at the Fin de Siècle*, find evidence of homoeroticism at work in Stevenson's novel, particularly in its focus on blackmail, which 'would immediately have suggested homosexual liaisons' (p. 34 [Ci]). Reading a document of Jekyll's that calls into question the nature of his activities, the lawyer Utterson tells Poole, Jekyll's servant: 'I would say nothing of this paper. If your master has fled or is dead, we may at least save his credit' (p. 41). Indeed, Jekyll himself seeks to redeem his reputation by reminding his readers of his attempt to earnestly embrace work, and of times when he lived a 'beneficent and innocent life' (p. 57). Although his language might have satisfied Samuel Smiles and others eager to advise men on how to build and protect their characters, his commitment cannot withstand the pressures exerted by Hyde. Jekyll's intense desire to escape from the shackles of respectable, mature, masculinity is captured when he explains his initial willingness to give Hyde free rein in his home:

> Men have before hired bravos to transact their crimes, while their own person and reputation sat under shelter. I was the first that ever did so for his pleasures. I was the first that could thus plod in the public eye with a load of genial respectability, and in a moment, like a schoolboy, strip off these lendings and spring headlong into the sea of liberty.
>
> (p. 52)

Jekyll concludes this portion of his full statement of the case by exuberantly proclaiming, 'Think of it – I did not even exist!' (p. 52), a sign of just how engaged Stevenson was in questions of what constitutes identity.

Determining who and what Hyde represents is, of course, central to the interpretive appeal of Stevenson's novel. *Dr Jekyll and Mr Hyde* is a classic *Doppelgänger* tale – he term referring to a story that either revolves around two central characters functioning as doubles of one another or, alternatively, to a fiction about an individual whose personality is divided. This type of narrative appealed to many others who, like Stevenson, appropriated the Gothic tradition, among them Mary Shelley (in *Frankenstein*), James Hogg (in *Confessions of a Justified Sinner*), and Emily Brontë (in *Wuthering Heights*). G. K. Chesterton long ago pointed out that 'the real stab of [Stevenson's] story is not in the discovery that the one man is two men; but in the discovery that the two men are one man' (in 'Backgrounds and Contexts', Stevenson, *Dr Jekyll*, p. 183). It is misreading the novella to identify it as a simple allegory of good versus evil, with one character signifying moral man, the other amoral, or – to use more overtly psychological terms – the ego and the id. Stevenson asks us in a variety of ways to attend carefully to their relationship to one another, which is not always antagonistic (as, for example, when Jekyll expresses pity for Hyde).

Some of the most critically compelling interpretations of Hyde have noted the way Stevenson drew for his characterisation on a fund of late-Victorian (and post-Darwinian) rhetoric associated with degeneration, predatory impulses, and 'the criminal man'. A discourse of degeneration thrived in Stevenson's day, sometimes taking the form of racial anxieties about the threats posed by immigrants to English purity, sometimes of the nation's anxieties about the maintenance of its imperial supremacy, sometimes of biological anxieties about the relationship of man to animal, sometimes of sexual anxieties about the distinctions between male and female, masculine and feminine traits. Cesare Lombroso, a well-known criminologist, described the criminal as an 'atavistic being'. The connections to Stevenson's novella are obvious, for Hyde is consistently described by those who encounter him as deformed, savage, and ape-like, and the process of Jekyll's transformation into Hyde – 'the brute that slept within me' – as a reversion. Patrick Brantlinger argues that Stevenson appropriates the highly racialised stereotypes of the Irish hooligan or 'Paddy' figures to characterise Hyde and that recognising these tropes helps us to locate the novel within the time frame when the Irish Home Rule controversy and concerns about Fenianism were at their height (*The Reading Lesson*, p. 175 [Cv]). Yet Stevenson's descriptions of Hyde are general enough to reach beyond specific races or nationalities. They suggest, on the one hand, the possibility of a 'savage within' that Jekyll struggles to repress and contain and, on the other, of a savage without that Jekyll (in a version of 'going native') desires to appropriate for himself – to inhabit and experience. Studying numerous late-century narratives that invoke the rhetoric of degeneracy, Lyn Pykett articulates a crucial question that Stevenson's novella raises but does not resolve: 'Was degeneration a form of … regression to an earlier primitive state – the Hyde waiting to claim every Jekyll, the savage beneath the skin of civilisation? Or was it the condition towards which civilised societies and the psychological subjects which they produced were tending – Hyde as created by the discontents of Jekyll's civilisation?' (*Reading Fin de Siècle Fictions*, p. 14 [Ci]). Stevenson ultimately seems less committed to probing the answer to these questions than to representing the influence of contact with degeneration on others. Describing his initial impressions of Hyde, Mr Enfield comments, 'It wasn't like a man; it was like some damned Juggernaut', his use of the term hinting at the novel's muted engagement with the imperial, for 'Juggernaut' derives from the Hindu word for 'the lord of the universe' (*Dr Jekyll*, p. 7 [Ai]). Hyde stirs feelings of 'hitherto unknown disgust, loathing and fear' in Utterson (p. 17) and leads the lawyer to believe that 'he must have secrets of his own: black secrets' (p. 19).

Secrecy is one of the novel's key motifs: 'This is a private matter, and I beg of you to let it sleep', Jekyll observes to Utterson early on (p. 20). The impulse to keep secrets, to repress and contain knowledge, is not confined to Dr Jekyll. Indeed, Stevenson adapts some of the features of the detective novel (including a fascination with handwriting as a key to identity) in *Dr Jekyll and Mr Hyde* in order to foreground the drive to uncover secrets, even while so much of the plot revolves around repressing or containing them. Hyde, we learn, 'had never been photographed' (p. 24). Stevenson's work was published shortly before the infamous series of murders by

Jack the Ripper; some even believed that his novel inspired the crimes. As in the best Victorian fiction, Stevenson's narrative technique, involving multiple forms of narration, lends stylistic force to this thematic dimension of his novella. Juxtaposing the traditional third-person omniscient narrative with which the story begins to the more personal and subjective accounts of letters and to Jekyll's confessional (and unreliable) 'full statement of the case', Stevenson makes problematic the notion that all knowledge is ultimately penetrable. Perhaps most crucially, the novel's most closely guarded secret – i.e. what pleasures Jekyll indulges in but conceals – is never revealed. We know that, according to Utterson, Jekyll was wild when he was young, but just how that essential wildness has been made manifest in his adult pursuit of pleasure is unclear. Hastie Lanyon provocatively refers to the 'moral turpitude that man unveiled to me, even with tears of penitence', but he cannot bring himself to articulate with more precision what he knows. Jekyll himself describes his pleasures as 'undignified' and 'monstrous', able to be pursued only when 'his conscience slumbered' (p. 53). What crimes, through Hyde, bring Jekyll his longed-for pleasure, what appetites does he secretly indulge? Stevenson is intent, it is obvious, on piquing the curiosity of his readers.

In fact, like other fantastical works of this period (one thinks, for example, of Lewis Carroll's *Alice in Wonderland*, though *Dr Jekyll and Mr Hyde* is very clearly set in an urban wonderland, the 'wider labyrinths of lamplighted London') the novella has much to say about curiosity itself (p. 15). Jekyll himself taunts Lanyon for letting the greed of curiosity take command of him. Only professional honour and a sense of obligation enable Utterson to overcome the great curiosity that compels him to read a document from Lanyon. In language that explicitly links the theme to the novella's commentary on prohibited pleasures, the narrator notes that 'it is one thing to mortify curiosity, another to conquer it' (p. 31).

The following formula, variously attributed to Dickens, Wilkie Collins, and Charles Reade, was proffered as the key to success as a novelist: 'Make them laugh, make them cry, make them wait.' Humour and sentiment are conspicuously absent in *Dr Jekyll and Mr Hyde*, and Stevenson, well known to be critical of the long novels favoured by circulating libraries, certainly did not ask his readers to wait long for his novella to end, although that ending was ultimately inconclusive. His mantra seems only to have been, 'Make them wonder'. Wonder is, after all, romance's most essential ingredient. If our voyeuristic natures lead us to wonder just what Dr Jekyll was doing as Mr Hyde, *Dr Jekyll and Mr Hyde*, a novel that Richard Altick reports sold over 40,000 copies in its first six months, leads us also to speculate about the pleasures of secrecy, the appeal of disguise, the powers of the subconscious and the difficulties of self-control – in short, about the fascinating, mysterious and mobile nature of identity.

Oscar Wilde, *The Importance of Being Earnest* (1895)

The Victorian period may have officially ended with the death of the queen in 1901, but social and literary historians typically locate points of rupture both before and after that momentous event. In fact, the whole course of Victorian literature provides abundant evidence that the values, conventions, themes and styles often cited as representative of the period were as often under assault as they were on display. Oscar Wilde's achievement as playwright, essayist and aesthete was not to inaugurate censure of the period but rather to fashion a new and highly effective form of critique. A few decades after Wilde's heyday, Lytton Strachey would publish one of the most scathing indictments of the Victorian era. With his biography *Eminent Victorians* (1918), Strachey exposed – through richly sardonic portraits of Florence Nightingale, Thomas Arnold, General Gordon and Cardinal Manning – what he believed to be the period's arrogant hypocrisies. In *The Importance of Being Earnest*, Oscar Wilde did much the same, using his trademark weapon of comedic wit rather than a Strachey-like scorn, and focusing not on real people but on fictional characters who make further fictions of their identities. Unearthing the biography of Jack Worthing, who masquerades as Ernest but is revealed by the end to be more earnestly Ernest than he knew, Wilde's play satirises in order to unsettle many assumptions of Victorian society and its literature.

Just how seriously one should take Wilde's comedy is, of course, an issue; after all, the work is sub-titled 'A Trivial Comedy for Serious People' (a characteristically Wildean inversion of its original sub-title, 'A Serious Comedy for Trivial People'), and taking an overly serious approach to the play clearly risks losing its comedic appeal, missing its considerable pleasures. Appreciating the different functions of Wilde's inversions in *The Importance of Being Earnest* is key. As in much of his writing, Wilde used inversions to advance his essential beliefs and ideals, perhaps most famously in the claim made in his essay of 1889, 'The Decay of Lying', that 'Life imitates Art, that Life in fact is the mirror, and Art the reality' (*Longman Anthology*, p. 1872 [Aii]). Flippant and fleeting remarks like 'Divorces are made in heaven', 'Ignorance is like a delicate exotic fruit; touch it and the bloom is gone', and 'A girl with a simple, unspoiled nature … could hardly be expected to reside in the country', are the stuff that *The Importance of Being Earnest* is made of, and the rapid-fire manner in which Wilde discharges them have the effect, cumulatively, of mitigating the impact of any single shot. Furthermore, while such inversions command the stage in the play, enhancing its performative feel, they run up on occasion against remarks like 'who has the right to cast a stone against one who has suffered?' that are far more difficult to categorise as instances of Wildean wit (especially when pondered in the light of Wilde's biography and the fact that, after unsuccessfully lodging a libel suit against the Marquess of Queensbury, he was found guilty of sodomy and sentenced to prison just months after his play was first performed).

Few topics near and dear to the Victorian heart are not at least alluded to in the course of the play. Wilde takes aim at everything from the popularity of the triple-decker novel to the purview of utilitarian and Evangelical organisations (Chasuble preaches a 'charity sermon' to the 'Society for the Prevention of Discontent among the Upper Orders'). Nevertheless, several keynotes of Wilde's social critique are so consistently struck as to merit additional commentary. The play tends towards marriage, but subjects that institution to more criticism than any other. From the servant Lane's comment that 'in married households the champagne is rarely of a first-rate brand' (to which Algernon responds, 'Good heavens! Is marriage so demoralizing as that?') to Lady Bracknell's remark that the recently widowed Lady Harbury 'looks quite twenty years younger', one can glean Wilde's interest in subverting complacent assumptions about marriage and happiness (*Longman Anthology*, pp. 1886 and 1891, respectively [Aii]). Despite (or because of) its status as one of the essential foundations on which middle-class respectability rested, marriage is scorned in the play as having very much to do with business and correlatively little to do with pleasure.

So deeply interwoven into late-century theories of aestheticism was the concept of pleasure that it comes as no surprise to find commentary on the topic percolating throughout *The Importance of Being Earnest*: 'Oh, pleasure, pleasure! What else should bring one anywhere?' Jack remarks in the play's opening scene, and, much later, Algernon comments that 'My duty as a gentleman has never interfered with my pleasures in the smallest degree' (*Longman Anthology*, p. 1886 [Aii]). In another of those moments when his readers (or audience) must question just how much irony Wilde intends, Gwendolyn, in feisty and contentious dialogue with Cecily, remarks, 'On an occasion of this kind it becomes more than a moral duty to speak one's mind. It becomes a pleasure' (*Longman Anthology*, p. 1906 [Aii]). Pleasure, in other words, trumps morality. Wilde couldn't have made clearer his commitment to disregarding the strictures of realist art or his interest in overturning the mandates of proper behaviour in his society.

Ever since Wilde provocatively contended in 'The Decay of Lying' that the aim of the liar is simply 'to charm, to delight, to give pleasure', critics have been swift to process the implications for understanding his approach to authorship and artistry. All of the characters in *The Importance of Being Earnest* lie as readily as they tell the truth, and in prototypical Wildean fashion, most of their lies tell truths. No lies loom larger, however, than the ones surrounding the identities of Jack Worthing and Algernon Moncrieff. Both men live double lives, a feature of the play that lends itself to reading in the context of late-century confusion of sexual identities and gender roles: Jack, with his invented younger brother Ernest, and Algernon, with his imaginary uncle, the invaluable permanent invalid called 'Bunbury'. Although Jack is, in the interests of marrying Gwendolyn, committed to 'killing off' his invented brother, Algernon contends that 'nothing will induce me to part with Bunbury' (*Longman Anthology*, p. 1890 [Aii]). Wilde questions just how much control the men have over their invented, alternative identities, even as he clearly relishes the fact that they provide both with the excuse to escape from the performance of undesirable gender- and class-bound obligations as gentlemen. Just as they shuttle from town to country and back, Wilde implies that they can shuttle between public and private personas. Who those private personas are is only hinted at in the play, although some critics maintain that 'Bunburying' is, in the context of the play and of Wilde's life, code for homosexual pursuits and pleasures, all of which must be disguised to be enjoyed.

In its end, the play's emphasis on (and celebration of) disguise falls prey to its plot of discovery; Jack's true identity is gradually uncovered as he is revealed to be

Ernest (if not earnest), and also, serendipitously, the older brother of Algernon. Even this dimension of the play, though, is a manifestation of Wilde's satire, as he clearly parodies the formulaic and melodramatic fiction so popular in the Victorian period (works like *Jane Eyre* and *Oliver Twist* that bestowed respectable identity and fortune on their long-suffering orphan heroes and heroines). Indeed, the play's most hilarious moments have to be those when Jack, quaking under interrogation by Lady Bracknell, confesses that he has lost both parents. ('To lose one parent, Mr Worthing, may be regarded as a misfortune; to lose both looks like carelessness', she responds!) Worse still, Jack must admit the nitty-gritty details of his orphan status – he was found in a handbag in a cloakroom at Victoria Station ('To be born, or at any rate bred, in a hand-bag, whether it had handles or not, seems to me to display a contempt for the ordinary decencies of family life that reminds one of the worst excesses of the French Revolution', is Lady Bracknell's priceless retort; *Longman Anthology*, p. 1895 [Aii]).

Making Victoria Station the site of Jack's birth enables Wilde to explain, by the play's end, many of the hidden interconnections between characters, but not least significant is the revelation, from the governess Miss Prism, that it was she who in a moment of mental abstraction put the manuscript of her three-volume novel in a perambulator and, by mistake, put the baby (Jack) in the handbag. The implied parallels between Jack's identity and the work of fiction for which he was a substitute are obvious enough, but Wilde imaginatively extends the symbolic significance of Jack's railway heritage still further. With Lady Bracknell's remark that 'Until yesterday, I had no idea that there were any families or persons whose origin was a terminus', Wilde not only mocks his culture's preoccupation with heritage, but he adapts for his own distinctive purposes the symbolic potential of the railway. If the railway signified the era's most confident and optimistic beliefs about progress, mobility and interconnectedness, in this play about finding, losing and creating identities, it suggests the powerful appeal of transport and exchange. The hustle and bustle of Victoria Station provided Wilde with the appropriate scene to explain the mistaken transaction that begins Ernest Worthing's history, but the railway station itself – where origins are also 'ends' – is a perfect instantiation of Wildean inversion and social commentary at its richest. Thackeray's confident proclamation that 'your railway starts the era' achieves even greater resonance in the light of *The Importance of Being Earnest*, a play that derails so many of the supposed certainties of the period whose ending it helped to mark.

Reference

A Primary Texts and Anthologies of Primary Sources

i Primary Texts

Arnold, Matthew. *Letters of Matthew Arnold*. Ed. George W. E. Russell. New York: Macmillan, 1895.

Bagehot, Walter. 'Charles Dickens' (1858). *The Collected Works of Walter Bagehot*. Ed. Norman St John-Stevas. 15 vols. London: The Economist, 1965–86.

Ballantyne, R. M. *The Coral Island*. Ed. J. S. Bratton. New York: Oxford University Press, 1990.

Braddon, Mary Elizabeth. *Lady Audley's Secret* (1861). New York and London: Penguin, 1998.

Brontë, Charlotte. *Jane Eyre* (1847). Ed. Q. D. Leavis. New York and London: Penguin, 1985.

   Shirley (1849). New York and London: Penguin, 1985.

   Villette (1853). New York and London: Penguin, 1985.

Brontë, Emily. *Wuthering Heights* (1847). Ed. Linda H. Peterson. Boston, MA: Bedford/St Martin's Press, 2003.

Carlyle, Thomas. *A Carlyle Reader: Selections from the Writings of Thomas Carlyle*. Ed. G. B. Tennyson. Cambridge University Press, 1984.

Collins, Wilkie. *Heart and Science* (1883). Ed. Steve Farmer. Peterborough, Ontario: Broadview Press, 1996.

Cox, R. G., ed. *Thomas Hardy: The Critical Heritage*. New York: Barnes and Noble, 1970.

Dickens, Charles. *Bleak House* (1852–3). New York: The Modern Library, 2002.

   Dombey and Son (1846–8). Ed. Alan Horsman. Oxford University Press, 1982.

   Great Expectations (1860–1). Ed. Charlotte Mitchell. New York and London: Penguin, 1996.

   Hard Times (1854). Ed. Fred Kaplan and Sylvère Monod. New York: Norton, 2001.

   Little Dorrit (1857). New York: Random House, 2002.

   The Old Curiosity Shop (1840–1). New York and London: Penguin, 2000.

   Oliver Twist (1838). New York: Bantam Books, 1982.

   The Posthumous Papers of the Pickwick Club (1836–7). Ed. Mark Wormald. New York and London: Penguin, 1999.

   A Tale of Two Cities (1859). Reprint. New York and London: Bantam Books, 1981.

Eliot, George. *Adam Bede* (1859). Ed. John Paterson. Boston: Houghton Mifflin, 1968.

   The Mill on the Floss (1860). Oxford University Press, 1998.

   Scenes of Clerical Life (1857–8). Amherst, NY: Prometheus Books, 2000.

   Selected Essays, Poems and Other Writings. London: Penguin, 1990.

   Silas Marner (1861). New York and London: Penguin, 1996.

Gaskell, Elizabeth. *Cranford* (1853). Ed. Elizabeth Porges Watson. Oxford University Press, 1980.

   Mary Barton (1848). Ed. Stephen Gill. New York and London: Penguin, 1985.

   North and South (1854). Ed. Alan Shelston. New York: Norton, 2005.

Gissing, George. *New Grub Street* (1891). Ed. Bernard Bergonzi. New York and London: Penguin, 1968.

Greenaway, Kate. *Marigold Garden: Pictures and Rhymes*. London and New York: George Routledge and Sons, 1885.

Hardy, Thomas. *Jude the Obscure* (1895). Boston: Houghton Mifflin, 1965.

   The Return of the Native (1878). New York and London: Penguin, 1984.

   Tess of the d'Urbervilles (1891). New York and London: Penguin, 2003.

Hughes, Thomas. *Tom Brown's School Days* (1857). New York: Signet, 1986.

Huxley, Thomas Henry. 'Review of *The Origin of Species*'. *Westminster Review* 17 (April, 1860): 541–70.

Jones, Ernest. 'The Silent Cell'. ursulastange.com/chartistpoetry.html.

Kingsley, Charles. 'Review of *Mary Barton*'. *Fraser's Magazine* 39 (1849). Rptd in *Mary Barton*. Ed. Jennifer Foster. Peterborough, Ontario: Broadview Press, 2000, pp. 515–16.

Mansel, Henry. 'Sensation Novels'. *Quarterly Review* 113 (April 1863): 482–95, 501–6, 512–14.

Masson, David. *British Novelists and Their Styles*. Boston: Gould and Lincoln, 1859.

Meynell, Alice. *Selected Poems of Alice Meynell, 1847–1922*. London: Nonesuch Press, 1965.

Smiles, Samuel. *Self-Help: With Illustrations of Character, Conduct, and Perseverance* (1859). Ed. Peter W. Sinnema. Oxford University Press, 2002.

Stevenson, Robert Louis. *Strange Case of Dr. Jekyll and Mr. Hyde* (1886). Ed. Katherine Linehan. New York: Norton, 2003.

Stoker, Bram. *Dracula* (1897). Ed. Glennis Byron. Peterborough, Ontario: Broadview Press, 2000.

Stretton, Hesba. *Jessica's First Prayer*. London: Religious Tract Society, 1867.

Tennyson, Alfred, Lord. *In Memoriam* (1850). Ed. Erik Gray. New York: Norton, 2004.

   Selected Poems. Ed. Aidan Day. New York and London: Penguin, 1991.

Thackeray, William Makepeace. *The Roundabout Papers* (1863). New York: Dent, Dutton, n. d.

   Vanity Fair (1847–8). Ed. J. I. M. Stewart. New York: Penguin, 1968.

Thompson, E. P. *The Notebook of a Naturalist*. London: Smith, Elder, 1845.

Trollope, Anthony. *An Autobiography* (1883). Ed. Michael Sadleir and Fred Page. Oxford University Press, 1999.

Wilde, Oscar. *Selected Letters by Oscar Wilde*. Ed. Rupert Hart-Davis. Oxford University Press, 1979.

ii Anthologies of Primary Sources

Bower, John Wilson, and John Lee Brooks, eds. *The Victorian Age: Prose, Poetry, and Drama*. New York: F. S. Crofts, 1946.

Bowness, Alan. *The Pre-Raphaelites*. London: Penguin/ Tate Gallery, 1984.

Bradshaw, David J., and Suzanne Ozment, eds. *The Voice of Toil: Nineteenth-Century British Writings about Work*. Athens: Ohio University Press, 2000. A collection of poems, stories, essays and a play organised around categories that reflect dominant Victorian attitudes towards work – e.g., 'work as mission', 'work as opportunity', 'work as oppression'.

Broomfield, Andrea, and Sally Mitchell, eds. *Prose by Victorian Women*. New York and London: Garland, 1996. Represents a variety of non-fiction writing by sixteen women writers, including Harriet Martineau, Frances Power Cobbe, Edith Simcox, Mona Caird, Sarah Grand and Vernon Lee.

Buckler, William E., ed. *Prose of the Victorian Period*. Boston: Houghton Mifflin, 1958. Includes major contributions by Macaulay, Carlyle, Newman, Mill, Ruskin, Arnold, Huxley and Pater.

Christ, Carol, and Catherine Robson, eds. *The Norton Anthology of English Literature*. 8th edn. Vol. E: 'The Victorian Age'. New York: Norton, 2005.

Collins, Thomas, and Vivienne Rundel, eds. *The Broadview Anthology of Victorian Poetry and Poetic Theory*. Peterborough, Ontario: Broadview Press, 1999.

Cunningham, Valentine, ed. *The Victorians: An Anthology of Poetry and Poetics*. Oxford and Malden, MA: Blackwell, 2000. Comprehensive anthology that includes important reviews and studies of poetry with its substantial sampling of the genre.

Doughty, Terri, ed. *Selections from 'The Girl's Own Paper', 1880–1907*. Broadview Reprint Edition. Peterborough, Ontario: Broadview Press, 2004.

Haight, Gordon S., ed. *The Portable Victorian Reader*. Harmondsworth: Penguin, 1976.

Hamilton, Susan, ed. *Criminals, Idiots, Women, and Minors: Victorian Writing by Women on Women*. Peterborough, Ontario: Broadview Press, 1995.

Hearn, Michael Patrick, ed. *The Victorian Fairy Tale Book*. New York: Pantheon, 1988. An effectively illustrated collection of stories and tales, including works by Dickens, Thackeray, Christina Rossetti, Robert Browning and Oscar Wilde.

King, Andrew, and John Plunkett, eds. *Victorian Print Media: A Reader*. Oxford University Press, 2005. Includes an array of little-known primary sources from magazines and newspapers related to the culture of print. Organised around themes such as legal issues and copyright; publishing, printing, communication; and reading spaces.

Leighton, Angela, and Margaret Reynolds, eds. *Victorian Women Poets: An Anthology*. Oxford: Blackwell, 1995. Comprehensive anthology that includes selection of major and little-known women poets representing all of the classes.

Longman Anthology of British Literature. Ed. Heather Henderson and William Sharpe. Vol. 2B: *The Victorian Age*. 2nd edn. New York and London: Longman, 2003.

Mundhenk, Rosemary J., and LuAnn McCracken Fletcher, eds. *Victorian Prose: An Anthology*. New York: Columbia University Press, 1999.

Nelson, Carolyn Christensen, ed. *A New Woman Reader: Fiction, Articles, and Drama of the 1890s*. Peterborough, Ontario: Broadview Press, 2001. Seven complete short stories and a play are supplemented by articles that cover such topics as women's suffrage, the marriage question and the figure of the new woman.

Reilly, Catherine, ed. *Winged Words: Victorian Women's Poetry and Verse*. London: Enitharmon Press, 1994. Eclectic sampling that includes some infrequently anthologised but representative poems by women such as Cecil Frances Alexander, Elizabeth Craigmyle, Anne Ellison and Emily Hickey.

Ricks, Christopher, ed. *The New Oxford Book of Victorian Verse*. Oxford University Press, 1990. Comprehensive volume that includes a sampling of light verse, nonsense and protest poetry among its representations of more major works like

Fitzgerald's 'The Rubáiyát of Omar Khayyám' and Clough's verse-novel 'Amours de Voyage'.

Robinson, Solveig C., ed. *A Serious Occupation: Literary Criticism by Victorian Women Writers*. Peterborough, Ontario: Broadview Press, 2003. A helpful volume that demonstrates women's contributions to the field of literary criticism, with essays covering topics related to specific genres and individual authors, and more general studies of the role of literature.

Rodensky, Lisa, ed. *The Oxford Handbook of the Victorian Novel*. Oxford University Press, 2016. Extremely useful resource tackling such key topics as the emergence of the novel; reading, reviewing and censorship in the period; the novel in relation to travel and technology; the novel and other disciplines; industrialism and the Protestant ethic.

Small, Ian, ed. *The Aesthetes: A Sourcebook*. London: Routledge & Kegan Paul, 1979. Essential source for documents related to the cultures of aestheticism and decadence in late nineteenth-century Britain.

Weber, A. S. *Nineteenth-Century Science: A Selection of Original Texts*. Peterborough, Ontario: Broadview Press, 2000.

B   Introductions and Overviews

Altick, Richard D. *The English Common Reader: A Social History of the Mass Reading Public, 1800–1900*. 2nd edn. Columbus: Ohio State University Press, 1998. Study of the social, political and economic conditions that influenced reading in nineteenth-century Britain, with special emphasis on the reading preferences and habits of the middle and working classes.

The Presence of the Present: Topics of the Day in the Victorian Novel. Columbus: Ohio State University Press, 1991. Overview of the ways Victorian novelists responded to and appropriated what was happening in the world. Examines such topics as 'consumer goods', 'popular entertainments', 'money and occupations', 'new ways of reading and writing'.

Victorian People and Ideas: A Companion for the Modern Reader of Victorian Literature. New York: Norton, 1973. An influential guide to the period that shows how certain issues and debates in the period evidence themes such as the 'utilitarian spirit', the 'Evangelical temper', 'religious movements and crises' and 'the nature of art in society'.

Armstrong, Isobel. *Victorian Poetry: Poetry, Poetics, and Politics*. London: Routledge, 1993. A revisionary literary history of Victorian poetry that places Tennyson and Browning in the context of conservative and Benthamite aesthetics of the avant-garde and that focuses on Clough, Arnold, Browning and others in the context of mid-century revolutionary culture. Substantial chapters on Swinburne, Hopkins, Meredith and James Thomson round out this influential analysis.

Brake, Laurel, and Marysa Demoor, eds. *The Dictionary of Nineteenth-Century Journalism*. Ghent and London: Academia and the British Library, 2009. Comprehensive reference work with entries covering all aspects of periodical and print culture.

Briggs, Asa. *Victorian People: A Reassessment of Persons and Themes, 1851–67*. University of Chicago Press, 1972. Focusing on the period between the Great Exhibition (1851) and the second Reform Act (1867), Briggs assesses the accomplishments and achievements that characterise the Victorian age.

David, Deirdre, ed. *The Cambridge Companion to the Victorian Novel*. Cambridge University Press, 2001. The wide-ranging essays in this collection focus on major novelists as well as on lesser-known writers such as Olive Schreiner and H. Rider Haggard. Highly regarded scholars approach the novel through the lens of such themes as gender, race, empire, science and industrialism.

Davis, Paul. *Charles Dickens, A to Z. The Essential Reference to His Life and Work*. New York: Checkmark Books, 1999. An extremely useful guide to Dickens that identifies characters and locations in his works and provides detailed summaries of the novels, analyses of their themes and techniques and overviews of their critical reception.

Davis, Philip. *The Victorians. Vol. 8: 1830–1880*. Oxford University Press, 2002. A comprehensive and detailed overview of the period that organises its discussion around broad themes such as 'the rural to urban', 'nature', 'religion' and 'mind', and that situates its examination of genres (including sub-genres such as 'the sensation novel' and 'fairy tales and fantasies') within discussion of the conditions of literary production.

Felluga, Dino, Pamela Gilbert and Linda Hughes, eds. *The Encyclopedia of Victorian Literature*. Oxford: Wiley Blackwell, 2015. www.blackwellreference.com. 4-volume print set and online edition that includes over 330 cross-referenced entries on topics related to all major genres as well as a wide variety of themes pertinent to study of the period and its literature.

Gilmour, Robin. *The Victorian Period: The Intellectual and Cultural Context of English Literature, 1830–1890*. Harlow: Longman, 1993. One of the most highly regarded studies of the developments and people that influenced the intellectual climate of the period. Gilmour pays particular attention to the Victorian preoccupation with time and interest in history.

Harris, Jose. *Private Lives, Public Spirit: Britain: 1870–1914*. Harmondsworth: Penguin, 1994. A study of the ways that the latter part of the Victorian period fostered the re-emergence of a spirit of activism that, Harris contends, extended well into the twentieth century.

Hewitt, Martin, ed. *The Victorian World*. New York: Routledge, 2012. A reassessment of Britain's global presence during Victoria's reign, using scholarship from an array of fields, including history, art history, sociology, geography, economics and the history of law.

Houghton, Walter E. *The Victorian Frame of Mind, 1830–1870*. New Haven, CT and London: Yale University Press, 1957. One of several overviews of the period still considered required reading. Focusing on the emotional, intellectual and moral attitudes that characterise Victorians, Houghton argues for their distinctive contributions to the modern mind.

McCord, Norman. *British History 1815–1906*. Oxford University Press, 1991. An extremely detailed and thorough history of the period that pays particular attention to political, economic, administrative and social institutions and developments.

McCord traces the same ideas and themes through four separate periods (1815–30; 1830–50; 1850–80; and 1880–1906).

Mitchell, Sally. *Daily Life in Victorian England*. Westport, CT: Greenwood Press, 1996. An extremely readable and well-illustrated study of everyday life in the era that makes abundant use of its wide-ranging primary sources.

ed. *Victorian Britain: An Encyclopedia*. Garland, 1988. A valuable and comprehensive reference book with entries on an enormous array of people, institutions, movements and ideas, each with suggested further reading.

O'Gorman, Francis, ed. *A Concise Companion to the Victorian Novel*. Oxford: Blackwell, 2005. A collection of original essays by experts in the field that examines the novel in the light of social and historical contexts such as visual culture, empire, sexuality, biology and the law.

Porter, Andrew, ed. *The Oxford History of the British Empire. Vol. III: The Nineteenth Century*. Oxford University Press, 1999. Covering the period from the 1780s to the First World War, Porter's volume studies the ways British expansion facilitated imperial rule and the principal areas of imperial activity overseas. Thirty chapters cover topics as varied as 'British Migration and the Peopling of the Empire', 'Religion, Missionary Enthusiasm and Empire', 'Empire and Metropolitan Cultures', 'Canada from 1815' and 'The British Occupation of Egypt from 1882'.

Porter, Roy. *London: A Social History*. Cambridge, MA: Harvard University Press, 1995.

Sanders, Andrew, ed. *The Short Oxford History of English Literature*. Oxford: Clarendon Press, 1994. Highly useful overview of the period that in its coverage of 'High Victorian Literature, 1830–1880' and 'Late Victorian and Edwardian Literature, 1880–1920' tends to move from author to author rather than from subject to subject.

Sunderland, John. *The Stanford Companion to Victorian Fiction*. Stanford University Press, 1989. A comprehensive reference work that provides factual and biographical entries on a wide array of Victorian writers and works of fiction.

Tucker, Herbert F., ed. *A Companion to Victorian Literature and Culture*. Malden, MA: Blackwell, 1999. A creatively structured reference tool that collects essays written by well-known scholars on key moments in the period (i.e., '1832', '1848', '1870' and '1897') and on broad topics such as stages of life, occupations and kinds of writing. Extensive cross-referencing and a highly detailed index make this a useful research tool.

Wheeler, Michael. *English Fiction of the Victorian Period*. 2nd edn. London: Longman, 1994. Chronologically arranged overview that provides easy-to-digest summaries of such topics as 'silver-fork' and 'Newgate fiction', 'religious and historical novels of the mid-century', 'new realists and the romance revival of late-Victorian fiction'.

C Further Reading

i *Gender, Sexuality and Literature*

Adams, James Eli. *Dandies and Desert Saints: Styles of Victorian Masculinity*. Ithaca, NY: Cornell University Press, 1995. Examines patterns of self-fashioning among

Victorian male intellectuals. Topics include 'Manhood and Abasement in Kingsley and Tennyson', 'Masculine Authority and the Male Body' and 'Masks and Masculinity in Pater's Aestheticism'.

Deane, Bradley. *Masculinity and the New Imperialism: Rewriting Manhood in British Popular Literature, 1870–1914*. Cambridge University Press, 2014. Focusing on the imperialism championed by Disraeli and his successors, this study charts the shifting ideals of masculinity that emerged in the fraught global context of the late century.

Dowling, Linda. *Hellenism and Homosexuality in Victorian Oxford*. Ithaca, NY: Cornell University Press, 1984. Thorough study of Hellenism as a philosophical and literary movement that facilitated a positive interpretation of homosexual identity.

Flint, Kate. *The Woman Reader, 1837–1914*. New York and Oxford: Clarendon Press, 1983. A wide-ranging cultural study of the figure of the woman reader and the history of women's reading practices from the Victorian period to the First World War. Flint draws on representations of reading in fiction, poetry, painting and an array of medical texts and conduct manuals to explore the controversies generated by women's reading.

Gilbert, Sandra, and Susan Gubar. *The Madwoman in the Attic: The Woman Writer and the Nineteenth-Century Literary Imagination*. New Haven, CT and London: Yale University Press, 1979. Dated but still influential analysis of the literary response of nineteenth-century women writers to patriarchal ideology and the cult of domesticity in Britain.

Hall, Donald E., ed. *Muscular Christianity: Embodying the Victorian Age*. Cambridge University Press, 2006. A thorough exploration of Muscular Christianity as a religious, literary, and social movement.

Helsinger, Elizabeth K., Robin Lauterbach Sheets and William Veeder, eds. *The Woman Question: Society and Literature in Britain and America, 1837–1883*. University of Chicago Press, 1989. A three-volume study that organises its discussion under the headings of 'Defining Voices', 'Social Issues' and 'Literary Issues'. Substantial discussion of Queen Victoria and helpful summaries of domestic ideology as reflected in literature and art.

Kestner, Joseph. *Protest and Reform: The British Social Narrative by Women, 1827–1867*. London and Madison: University of Wisconsin Press, 1985. Argues for the influence of women writers in shaping realist narrative as a mode of social reform.

Leighton, Angela. *Victorian Women Poets: Writing Against the Heart*. Charlottesville: University Press of Virginia, 1992. Uses poetry by Felicia Hemans, Laetitia Landon, Elizabeth Barrett Browning, Christina Rossetti, Alice Meynell and others to examine the ways writers distanced themselves from sentimental traditions and embraced strategies of self-displacement.

Marsh, Jan. 'Sex and Sexuality'. www.vam.ac.uk/collections/periods_styles/19thcentury/gender_health/sex_and_sexuality/index.html.

Pykett, Lynn. *The Improper Feminine. The Women's Sensation Novel and the New Woman Writing*. London: Routledge, 1992. A thorough analysis of femininity and the idea of the 'improper' woman in sensation fiction, with attention to the historical contexts that enabled sensation fiction to prosper at various moments in the nineteenth century.

Reading Fin de Siècle Fictions. New York: Prentice Hall, 1996.

Showalter, Elaine. *A Literature of their Own: British Women Novelists from Brontë to Lessing*. Princeton University Press, 1977. Like *The Madwoman in the Attic* by Sandra Gilbert and Susan Gubar, an early but influential study of patterns in nineteenth-century women's writing.

Sexual Anarchy: Gender and Culture at the Fin de Siècle. New York: Viking, 1990. A study of ways late-century aestheticism and the culture of decadence contributed to confusion of sexual identities and gender roles.

Sussman, Herbert. *Victorian Masculinities: Manhood and Masculine Poetics in Early Victorian Literature and Art*. Cambridge University Press, 1995. An exploration of manhood and masculinity that focuses on Carlyle, Browning, the Pre-Raphaelite Brotherhood, Pater and others to identify a 'masculine poetics' that developed in response to industrial and commercial dimensions of the age.

Thompson, Nicola Diane, ed. *Victorian Women Writers and the Woman Question*. Cambridge University Press, 2012. An excellent assessment of non-canonical women writers whose works explore marriage, legal and voting rights and other dimensions of 'The Woman Question.'

Van Remoortel, Marianne. *Women, Work, and the Victorian Periodical: Living by the Press*. Basingstoke: Palgrave Macmillan, 2015. A useful study of women in journalism, covering everything from writing to lesser studied topics such as editing and illustration.

Walkowitz, Judith. *City of Dreadful Delight: Narratives of Sexual Danger in Late-Victorian London*. University of Chicago Press, 1992. A wide-ranging study of various narratives of sexual danger (including newspaper coverage of child prostitution and of the Jack the Ripper murders) that focuses on the mutually constitutive relationship between power, politics and sexuality.

ii Genres: Fiction, Poetry, Drama, Life-Writing, Children's Literature

Auerbach, Nina. *Private Theatricals: The Lives of the Victorians*. Cambridge, MA: Harvard University Press, 1990. A study of the relationship of theatricality (broadly conceived to include role-playing and gesturing) to the Victorian crisis of self. Auerbach studies the ways theatricality threatened the idea of sincerity and the notion of an authentic self.

Bodenheimer, Rosemarie. *The Politics of Story in Victorian Fiction*. Ithaca, NY and London: Cornell University Press, 1988. Focusing on the narrative structure of mid-Victorian novels, Bodenheimer explores literary responses to social upheaval.

Bratton, J. S. *The Impact of Victorian Children's Fiction*. London and Totowa, NJ: Croom Helm, 1981. A study of didactic children's fiction, from its development in the early part of the century to the realist movement in girls' fiction and the adventure movement in boys' fiction.

Bristow, Joseph. *Empire Boys: Adventures in a Man's World*. London: HarperCollins, 1991. A study of the emergence of narratives of heroic adventure and the celebration of empire in the period between 1870 and 1900 and their relationship to juvenile publishing and curriculum design.

Brooks, Peter. *Reading for the Plot: Design and Intention in Narrative*. Cambridge University Press, 1993. Drawing on an array of nineteenth- and twentieth-century novels, Brooks takes a psychological, as opposed to structural, approach to the plot and plotting.

Daly, Nicholas. *Sensation and Modernity in the 1860s*. Cambridge University Press, 2013. An assessment of the various ways that sensation fiction and aestheticism each arose against the backdrop of the Reform Act of 1867.

Garrett, Peter. *The Victorian Multi-Plot Novel: Studies in Dialogical Form*. New Haven, CT and London: Yale University Press, 1980. Influential study of sub-genre of Victorian fiction, with thorough and persuasive readings of major novels such as *Little Dorrit* and *Middlemarch*.

Hadley, Elaine. *Melodramatic Tactics: Theatricalized Dissent in the English Marketplace, 1800–1885*. Stanford University Press, 1995. An analysis of the relationship between theatre, drama and what Hadley terms 'melodramatic modes', and the social and economic forces of market society in nineteenth-century Britain.

Hunt, Peter. *An Introduction to Children's Literature*. Oxford University Press, 1996.

Landow, G. P., ed. *Approaches to Victorian Autobiography*. Athens: Ohio University Press, 1979. Collection of essays examining the development of autobiographical modes during the period. Topics include the influence of Rousseau, the representation of childhood and the emphasis on honesty in Victorian autobiography. Among the many individual writers studied in detail are Ruskin, Newman, Margaret Oliphant and Dickens.

Levine, George. *The Realistic Imagination: English Fiction from Frankenstein to Lady Chatterley*. Chicago University Press, 1981. Study of Victorian fiction (and some modernist novels) that focuses on the use of language to render life realistic and to grapple with the problems of realistic representation.

Litvak, Joseph. *Caught in the Act: Theatricality in the Nineteenth-Century English Novel*. Berkeley: University of California Press, 1992. A study of Jane Austen, Charlotte Brontë, George Eliot and Henry James that focuses on the ways theatricality reveals the social norms that novelists both represented and reacted against.

Miller, D. A. *The Novel and the Police*. Berkeley: University of California Press, 1988. Influential study that uses Foucault to argue for the way Victorian novels function to discipline and police their characters and their readers. Miller pays particular attention to strategies of surveillance and imprisonment.

iii Science, Technology, and Empire

Beer, Gillian. *Darwin's Plots: Evolutionary Narrative in Darwin, George Eliot and Nineteenth-Century Fiction*. Cambridge University Press, 1983. Examines the way Victorian novelists – especially Eliot, Hardy and Kingsley – responded to and, in some cases, incorporated Darwin's theory of natural selection.

Black, Barbara. *On Exhibit: Victorians and Their Museums*. Charlottesville: University Press of Virginia, 2000.

Brantlinger, Patrick. *Rule of Darkness: British Literature and Imperialism, 1830–1914*. Ithaca, NY: Cornell University Press, 1988. An influential study of the imperialist ideology at work in literature ranging from boys' adventure fiction to major novels by Thackeray, Disraeli and others, and personal narratives by explorers.

Chapple, J. A. V. *Science and Literature in the Nineteenth Century*. Basingstoke: Macmillan, 1986. A helpful introduction to a wide-ranging topic, with emphasis on evolutionary psychology and nineteenth-century 'sciences' of race.

Conlin, Jonathan. *Evolution and the Victorians: Science, Culture and Politics in Darwin's Britain*. London: Bloomsbury Academic, 2014. Approaches the discovery of evolution as a collaborative enterprise and contextualises this history in the light of long-standing debates about imagination, faith and knowledge.

Fichman, Martin. *Evolutionary Theory and Victorian Culture*. New York: Humanity Books, 2002. A thoughtful study of scientific discovery and debate that moves beyond Darwin to include Spenser, Huxley and others.

Gates, Barbara T. *Kindred Nature: Victorian and Edwardian Women Embrace the Living World*. University of Chicago Press, 1998. A study of the contributions of women to the scientific study of nature (as well as to movements such as the defence of animal rights and opposition to vivisection) and the relationship of their work and writing to what now is identified as the environmental movement.

Krebs, Paula. *Gender, Race, and the Writing of Empire: Public Discourse and the Boer War*. Cambridge University Press, 1999. Significant study of the ways beliefs about gender and race converged in public discourse about British imperialism and the Boer War of 1899–1902 that makes good use of newspapers and propaganda to help contextualise writing by figures such as Conan Doyle, Olive Schreiner, Rudyard Kipling and H. Rider Haggard.

Lightman, Bernard V., and Bennett Zon, eds. *Evolution and Victorian Culture*. Cambridge University Press, 2014. An impressive collection of essays that explore the impact of evolutionary ideas on a wide range of literary and art forms.

Lucas, J. R. 'Wilberforce and Huxley: a Legendary Encounter'. *Historical Journal* 2, 2 (1979): 313–30.

Oppenheim, Janet. *'Shattered Nerves': Doctors, Patients, and Depression in Victorian England*. Oxford University Press, 1991. Historical account of nervous disorders in Victorian Britain that includes chapters on major figures and issues in the medical and scientific communities as well as chapters on beliefs about nervous disorders and their treatments and consequences for women, men and children.

Sheets, Heather. 'The Rebellion of 1857: Origins, Consequences, and Themes'. In *Teaching South Asia: Internet Journal of Pedagogy* 1, 1 (Winter 2001, www.mssu.edu/projectsouthasia/tsa/VIN1/StreetsPFV.).

Vrettos, Athena. *Somatic Fictions: Imagining Illness in Victorian Culture*. Stanford University Press, 1995.

iv Religion

Altholz, Josef, 'The Warfare of Conscience with Theology'. Available on *The Victorian Web*, an excellent site and resource for students: www.victorianweb.org/religion/altholz/a2. (Chapter reprinted from Althoz's book, *The Mind and Art of Victorian England*. Minneapolis, MN: University of Minnesota Press, 1976.)

Bradley, Ian. *The Call to Seriousness: The Evangelical Impact on the Victorians*. New York: Macmillan, 1976. One of the most highly regarded studies of Evangelicalism and its influence on habits, attitudes and lifestyles in the period, particularly before 1860. Bradley focuses on matters such as beliefs about proper conduct, piety, prudery and attitudes towards philanthropy.

Chadwick, Owen. *The Secularisation of the European Mind in the Nineteenth Century*. Cambridge University Press, 1975. Well-regarded study of the ways urbanisation, technological innovation and changes in print culture converged with evolutionary science and Marxism to undermine the authority of organised religion in the period.

Kent, Christopher. 'Higher Journalism and the Mid-Victorian Clerisy'. *Victorian Studies* 13, 2 (1969): 181–98.

Jay, Elisabeth. *The Religion of the Heart: Anglican Evangelicalism and the Nineteenth-Century Novel*. Oxford University Press, 1979. An influential and highly regarded explanation of Evangelicalism within the Church of England and its representation in a wide array of novels.

Qualls, Barry. *The Secular Pilgrims of Victorian Fiction: The Novel as Book of Life*. Cambridge University Press, 1982. A highly readable study of the influence of Bunyan's *Pilgrim's Progress* and the tradition of spiritual biography on the writing of Thomas Carlyle, Charlotte Brontë, Charles Dickens and George Eliot. Qualls demonstrates how industrial and commercial culture affected the ways these writers revised and responded to the earlier tradition.

v Print Culture, Histories of Reading

Brantlinger, Patrick. *The Reading Lesson: The Threat of Mass Literacy in Nineteenth-Century British Fiction*. Bloomington: Indiana University Press, 1998. Moving from Romantic novels like Mary Shelley's *Frankenstein* to later-century works like Stevenson's *Dr Jekyll and Mr Hyde*, Brantlinger focuses on the ways writers reflect and respond to anxieties about literacy, reading preferences of the working classes and commercialism.

Feltes, N. N. *Modes of Production of Victorian Novels*. University of Chicago Press, 1986. A Marxist approach to the Victorian novel that focuses in particular on the publishing formats and economic histories of *Pickwick Papers*, *Henry Esmond*, *Middlemarch*, *Tess of the d'Urbervilles* and *Howards End*.

Griest, G. L. *Mudie's Circulating Library and the Victorian Novel*. Bloomington: Indiana University Press, 1970. A still indispensable history of Mudie's, covering such topics as the rise of triple-decker novels and circulating libraries, the competition between Mudie's and W. H. Smith's, Mudie's relationship with novelists and with subscribers, the role of circulating-library censorship and the eventual decline of the multi-volume novel.

Hewitt, Martin. *The Dawn of the Cheap Press in Victorian Britain: The End of the 'Taxes on Knowledge', 1849–1869*. London: Bloomsbury, 2014. Major study of the history of the nineteenth-century press, focusing on the impact of the removal of 'taxes on knowledge' on the newspaper industry and journalism more generally.

Hughes, Linda, and Michael Lund. *The Victorian Serial*. Charlottesville: University Press of Virginia, 1991. A helpful study of the many ways that serial publication formats influenced literary representation, with considerable attention to reviews of serialised novels.

Jordan, John O., and Robert Patten, eds. *Literature and the Marketplace: Nineteenth-Century British Publishing and Reading Practices*. Cambridge University Press, 1995.

Patten, Robert. *Charles Dickens and His Publishers*. Oxford: Clarendon Press, 1978. An authoritative study of Dickens's relationship with publishers, with attention to the influence of *The Pickwick Papers* in shaping Dickens's career and relationship with his readers.

Shattock, Joanne, and Michael Wolff, eds. *The Victorian Periodical Press*. University of Toronto Press, 1982. Indispensable overview, focusing on the press as a reflection of Victorian culture as well as on significant developments in publishing history and the influence of the press on literature.

vi Industrialism, Class, and Studies of the Rural and Urban in Literature

Brantlinger, Patrick. *The Spirit of Reform: British Literature and Politics, 1832–1867*. Cambridge, MA: Harvard University Press, 1977. A study of middle-class literature written between the First and Second Reform Bills.

Childers, Joseph. *Novel Possibilities: Fiction and the Formation of Early Victorian Culture*. Philadelphia: University of Pennsylvania Press, 1995. A persuasive account of politics and the early Victorian novel, with sustained attention to the influence of emerging studies of industrialisation and sanitation problems in the urban environment.

Gallagher, Catherine. *Industrial Reformation of English Fiction: Social Discourse and Narrative Form from 1832–1867*. University of Chicago Press, 1985. Considers the content and form of social protest and Condition of England fiction as a response to and intervention in debates about industrialism in the period covered.

Helsinger, Elizabeth. *Rural Scenes and National Representation: Britain, 1815–1850*. Princeton University Press, 1997. Focusing on images of rural Britain as represented by Tennyson, Constable and others, Helsinger studies the power of the idea of the rural to signify conflicting ideas about national identity.

Joyce, Patrick. *Visions of the People: Industrial England and the Question of Class, 1848–1914*. Cambridge University Press, 1991. A study of the social identity of the labouring classes in nineteenth-century England, with attention to language, dialect and forms of culture such as the broadside ballad and the popular theatre.

Sanders, Mike. *The Poetry of Chartism: Aesthetics, Politics, History*. Cambridge University Press, 2012. The most comprehensive collection of Chartist poetry gleaned from the leading paper, *The Northern Star*. Explores the role of poetry in shaping the movement and response to it.

Vanden Bossche, Chris R. *Reform Acts: Chartism, Social Agency, and the Victorian Novel, 1832–1867*. Baltimore, MD: Johns Hopkins University Press, 2014. Excellent study of the ways that tension between reform and revolution shaped understandings of agency in the Victorian novel.

Williams, Raymond. *The Country and the City*. Oxford: Chatto and Windus, 1973. Arguably Williams's most important work, *The Country and the City* charts the changing attitudes towards rural and urban life as reflected in British literature.

vii Miscellaneous Work

Ferguson, Trish, ed. *Victorian Time: Technologies, Standardizations, Catastrophes*. Basingstoke: Palgrave Macmillan, 2013. Thoughtful collection of essays tackling the ways fiction of the period reflects and responds to the emergence of industrial time.

Leary, Patrick. *The Punch Brotherhood: Table Talk and Print Culture in Mid-Victorian London*. London: British Library, 2010. Lively and informative study of major Victorian periodical and the club culture that helped to produce it.

Linder, Douglas O. 'The Trials of Oscar Wilde: an Account', www.law.umkc.edu/faculty/projects/FTrials/wilde/wilde.html.

Markovits, Stefanie. *The Crimean War in the British Imagination*. Cambridge University Press, 2013. A thoughtful and comprehensive study of the influence of the Crimean War on literary culture.

Thomas, Ronald. 'Double Exposures: Arresting Images in *Bleak House* and *The House of Seven Gables*'. *Novel: A Forum on Fiction* 31, 1 (Autumn 1997): 87–113.

Tucker, Herbert F. 'Rossetti's "Goblin Market"ing: Sweet to Tongue and Sound to Eye'. *Representations* 82, 1 (Spring 2003): 117–33. Studies Rossetti's poem in the context of commercial culture and advertisement.

Victorian Research Web. http://victorianresearch.org/ An essential website that provides a comprehensive guide to resources for historical research on the Victorian period and its literature.

6 The Twentieth Century, 1901–1939

PAUL POPLAWSKI

Taking us from the steam age to the nuclear age, the first forty years of the twentieth century saw both the consolidation of a century-and-a-half's industrial growth and development, and a decisive transition towards the now-familiar modernity of our own technologically advanced, mass-democratic and mass-consumerist society. Despite evident continuities from the late-Victorian period up to the First World War, the cumulative effect of the profound changes wrought by industrialisation throughout the nineteenth century gave the twentieth century a wholly new temper and texture almost from the start. Britain was now irreversibly an urban, and increasingly a suburban, nation. The democratic and educational reforms of the late 1800s gave impetus to more radical demands for reform in the 1900s, as did the continuing rise of organised labour and of socialism and feminism. Most dramatically, perhaps, a whole raft of scientific and technological advances had led to striking material expressions of a new age in the form of the motor car, cinema, wireless telegraphy, the aeroplane and electric power. This was 'the seething and teeming of the pre-war period, its immense ferment and its restless fertility' (R. C. K. Ensor, quoted in Johnson (ed.), *Twentieth-Century Britain*, p. 76 [Bi]).

Sadly, it was the devastatingly *destructive* power of the new machine age that was demonstrated in the 'Great War', the cataclysmic event which cuts this period in two, and which cut down the male youth of almost a complete generation. Suddenly, the Edwardian age (let alone the Victorian) became another world, and it is all too easy to read Ensor's final word above as 'futility' – the title also of a famous war poem by Wilfred Owen. The 'roaring twenties' and the 'hungry thirties' – the boom and bust of the jazz age and the great depression – have their own complex histories, but the shadow of the war hung heavily over them as it merged imperceptibly into the dark night of a second, even more devastating, war.

Chronology

	HISTORY AND CULTURE	LITERATURE
1899	Second Boer War begins First petrol motor buses appear in London First wireless transmission across the English Channel Magnetic (tape) recording invented William James, *Talks on Psychology*	Henrik Ibsen, *When We Dead Awaken* Henry James, *The Awkward Age* Arthur Wing Pinero, *Trelawney of the 'Wells'* Arthur Symons, *The Symbolist Movement in Literature* H. G. Wells, *Tales of Space and Time* W. B. Yeats, *The Wind among the Reeds*
1900	Labour Representation Committee established Relief of Mafeking (Boer War) – widespread celebration in Britain Conservative government re-elected (in power since 1895) Most children under eleven attending elementary school *Daily Express* founded Max Planck's quantum theory Sigmund Freud, *The Interpretation of Dreams* Friedrich Nietzsche, *Ecce Homo* Paris Exhibition includes display of major advances in film technology	Joseph Conrad, *Lord Jim* Pinero, *The Gay Lord Quex* Wells, *Love and Mr Lewisham*
1901	Death of Queen Victoria; accession of Edward VII Funeral of Queen Victoria filmed 75 per cent of population lives in towns B. S. Rowntree's *Poverty: A Study of Town Life* suggests a third of urban population living in poverty Britain's first submarine launched First transatlantic radio communication by Marconi Planck's law of radiation	Thomas Hardy, *Poems of the Past and Present* (–1902) Rudyard Kipling, *Kim* G. B. Shaw, *Three Plays for Puritans* Wells, *The First Men in the Moon* Yeats, *Poems*
1902	Boer War ends Balfour Education Act establishes state system of secondary schools Midwives Act William James, *The Varieties of Religious Experience* First transatlantic telegraph from Marconi to King Edward VII Georges Méliès *Voyage to the Moon* makes significant technical advances in film First recordings by singer Enrico Caruso	Arnold Bennett, *Anna of the Five Towns* Conrad, *Heart of Darkness* Walter de la Mare, *Songs of Childhood* Arthur Conan Doyle, *The Hound of the Baskervilles* James, *The Wings of a Dove* Kipling, *Just So Stories* *Times Literary Supplement* Yeats, *Cathleen ni Houlihan*
1903	Workers' Educational Association founded Foundation of the Women's Social and Political Union (WSPU), a militant branch of suffrage movement *Daily Mirror* launched Wilbur and Orville Wright make first powered flight Motor Cars Act increases speed limit from 14 to 20 mph New York–London news service begins using wireless telegraphy	Samuel Butler, *The Way of All Flesh* Erskine Childers, *The Riddle of the Sands* Conrad, *Typhoon* James, *The Ambassadors* Shaw, *Man and Superman*

	HISTORY AND CULTURE	LITERATURE
1904	Government Committee on Physical Deterioration investigates health of urban poor *Entente Cordiale* settles colonial differences between UK and France The Empire, Manchester, is the first large music hall to be used as a cinema Offset printing invented Abbey Theatre, Dublin, founded 8,465 cars licensed in Britain Ernest Rutherford, *Radioactivity* Freud, *The Psychopathology of Everyday Life* Thorstein Veblen, *The Theory of Business Enterprise* *Die Brücke*, Dresden group of Expressionist artists formed First regular motor bus service introduced in London	J. M. Barrie, *Peter Pan* Conrad, *Nostromo* Hardy, *The Dynasts I* (*II* 1906, *III* 1908) James, *The Golden Bowl* J. M. Synge, *Riders to the Sea*
1905	Start of suffragette agitation and first suffragettes imprisoned Demonstrations of unemployed Unemployed Workmen Act Aliens Act restricts immigration Rayon ('artificial silk') first produced Sinn Féin founded; Ulster Unionist Council formed Albert Einstein's special theory of relativity Freud, *Three Essays on the Theory of Sexuality* Havelock Ellis, *Studies in the Psychology of Sex*, I–VI	Doyle, *The Return of Sherlock Holmes* E. M. Forster, *Where Angels Fear to Tread* Harley Granville-Barker, *The Voysey Inheritance* Shaw, *Major Barbara* Wells, *Kipps* Oscar Wilde, *De Profundis*
1906	Liberal landslide in general election; 29 Labour MPs elected and Labour Party constituted Education (Provision of Meals) Act HMS *Dreadnought*, world's largest battleship, launched	de la Mare, *Poems* Everyman's Library series begins publication John Galsworthy, *The Man of Property; The Silver Box* performed *Modern Language Review* Pinero, *His House in Order* William Le Queux, *The Invasion of 1910* Yeats, *Poetical Works*
1907	Education Act allows for medical inspections in schools Qualification of Women Act allows women to stand for local councils *The New Age*, new series, ed. A. R. Orage Robert Baden-Powell founds Boy Scouts Pablo Picasso, *Les Demoiselles d'Avignon*, introduces cubism Henri Bergson, *Creative Evolution* William James, *Pragmatism*	Conrad, *The Secret Agent* Forster, *The Longest Journey* Edmund Gosse, *Father and Son* James Joyce, *Chamber Music* Synge, *The Playboy of the Western World*
1908	Old Age Pensions Act introduces state pensions for the over-seventies Children's Act (or 'Children's Charter') introduces wide-ranging legislation for the protection and welfare of children Unemployed hunger march Ford's first Model T car sold in Britain Pathé's first regular newsreel First aeroplane flight in Britain Edward Carpenter, *The Intermediate Sex*	Bennett, *The Old Wives' Tale* W. H. Davies, *Autobiography of a Super-Tramp* *The English Review* founded by Ford Madox Ford Forster, *A Room with a View* *The Mask* (theatre quarterly) Wells, *The War in the Air*

	HISTORY AND CULTURE	LITERATURE
1909	Lloyd George's 'People's Budget' Trade Boards Act introduces regulations for 'sweated' home-workers C. F. G. Masterman, *The Condition of England* Louis Blériot flies across English Channel North Pole reached by Robert Peary (US) F. T. Marinetti launches futurism with first manifesto	Galsworthy, *Strife* Hardy, *Time's Laughingstocks* Ezra Pound, *Personae* Wells, *Ann Veronica; Tono-Bungay*
1910	Liberals re-elected to minority governments in two general elections; Labour wins 40 seats Edward VII dies; succeeded by George V South Wales miners' strike Suffragette prisoners go on hunger strike First post-impressionist exhibition in London First feature-length films Freud, *On Psychoanalysis* Scott's ill-fated expedition to the Antarctic (–1912)	Bennett, *Clayhanger* *Essays and Studies* (journal) Forster, *Howards End* Galsworthy, *Justice* Wells, *The History of Mr Polly* Yeats, *The Green Helmet*
1911	London dockers' strike and major railway strike paralyses much of the country Parliament Act removes Lords' veto National Insurance Act makes (limited) provision for sickness and unemployment benefit Horse-drawn buses taken out of service in London Ford Model T assembly plant opened in Manchester Rutherford postulates nuclear structure of the atom F. G. Hopkins proves existence and importance of vitamins Beatrice and Sidney Webb, *Poverty* *Der Blaue Reiter* group of expressionist artists formed in Munich Franz Boas, *Primitive Mythology* Sir James Frazer, *The Golden Bough* (11 vols.–1915; first two vols., 1890) Roald Amundsen reaches South Pole	Bennett, *Hilda Lessways* Rupert Brooke, *Poems* Conrad, *Under Western Eyes* D. H. Lawrence, *The White Peacock* Katherine Mansfield, *In a German Pension* Wells, *The New Machiavelli*
1912	Widespread strikes in Britain Irish Home Rule Bill and ensuing Ulster crisis as Unionists mobilise opposition Women's Franchise Bill rejected by the House of Commons; suffragettes riot in London *Daily Herald*, 'The Labour Daily Newspaper', launched *Titanic* sinks on maiden voyage Royal Flying Corps founded Harriet Quimby becomes first female aviator to cross the English Channel Some 400 cinemas in London; establishment of British Board of Film Censors	Robert Bridges, *Poetical Works* de la Mare, *The Listeners* Lawrence, *The Trespasser* Thomas Mann, *Death in Venice* *Georgian Poetry*, ed. Edward Marsh (first of a series of anthologies) *Poetry: A Magazine of Verse* (Chicago), ed. Harriet Monroe *Poetry Review* (London), ed. Harold Munro (who also establishes the Poetry Bookshop in Bloomsbury) Pound, *Ripostes*
1913	Ulster Volunteer Force established Triple Alliance of rail, transport and miners' unions formed Sylvia Pankhurst forms the East London Federation for Working Class Suffragettes; suffragette Emily Davison dies after throwing herself under the King's horse at the Derby Freud, *Totem and Taboo*; also *Interpretation of Dreams* (1900) first translated into English Igor Stravinsky's *The Rite of Spring* provokes riot at first performance in Paris	Lawrence, *Sons and Lovers; Love Poems* Compton Mackenzie, *Sinister Street* Marcel Proust publishes first of the seven volumes of *A la recherche du temps perdu* (*Remembrance of Things Past*) (last volume, 1927)

	HISTORY AND CULTURE	LITERATURE
1914	Home Rule Act passed but later suspended because of war; Ulster Volunteer Force armed; Curragh 'Mutiny' of British army officers in support of Unionists Suffragette riots in London First World War begins (28 June); Britain declares war on Germany on 4 August Defence of the Realm Act gives government emergency powers German sea bombardment of Yorkshire coast	*Blast: A Review of the Great English Vortex*, ed. Wyndham Lewis, announces vorticism (runs only until 1915) *The Egoist* (formerly, *The New Freewoman*) Hardy, *Satires of Circumstance* James, *Notes on Novelists* Joyce, *Dubliners* Lawrence, *The Prussian Officer; The Widowing of Mrs Holroyd* Pound, *Des Imagistes* Wells, *The World Set Free* Yeats, *Responsibilities*
1915	War intensifies with huge losses on all fronts; poison gas used for first time at Second Battle of Ypres; Zeppelin attacks on London German submarine blockade of Britain lifted after sinking of passenger liner, *Lusitania*: over 1,000 killed, including US citizens 'Shells Scandal' (shortage of munitions) leads to collapse of last Liberal administration: coalition government formed under Herbert Asquith Einstein's general theory of relativity	Richard Aldington, *Images* Bennett, *These Twain* Brooke, *1914 and Other Poems* John Buchan, *The Thirty-Nine Steps* Ford Madox Ford, *The Good Soldier* Franz Kafka, *Metamorphosis* Lawrence, *The Rainbow* W. Somerset Maugham, *Of Human Bondage* Dorothy Richardson, *Pointed Roofs*, first in a 13-novel sequence known as *Pilgrimage* (12th novel, 1938; 13th posthumous, 1967) *Some Imagist Poets: An Anthology*, ed. Amy Lowell (further Imagist anthologies followed in 1916 and 1917) Virginia Woolf, *The Voyage Out*
1916	Strike of Clydeside munitions workers Conscription introduced 'Easter Rising' of nationalists in Dublin suppressed; 450 killed; leaders executed Battle of the Somme leaves over 1 million dead Theories of shell-shock develop from the treatment of war casualties Second coalition government formed under David Lloyd George	Bridges, *The Spirit of Man* Harold Brighouse, *Hobson's Choice* Hardy, *Selected Poems* H. D. (Hilda Doolittle), *Sea Garden* Joyce, *A Portrait of the Artist as a Young Man* Shaw, *Pygmalion* Wells, *Mr Britling Sees it Through*
1917	Dada art movement launched in Zurich Carl Jung, *Psychology of the Unconscious* USA enters war Over half a million lives lost during the Third Battle of Ypres (Passchendaele) Russian Revolution (March) Freud, *Introduction to Psychoanalysis*	T. S. Eliot, *Prufrock and Other Observations* Hardy, *Moments of Vision* Lawrence, *Look! We Have Come Through!* Edward Thomas, *Poems* Yeats, *The Wild Swans at Coole*
1918	End of First World War; Armistice, 11 November Representation of the People Act (4th Reform Act) gives the vote to all men over twenty-one and women over thirty, nearly trebling the electorate to around 21 million people Maternity and Child Welfare Act Marie Stopes, *Married Love; Parenthood* Conservative-dominated coalition government re-elected Membership of trade unions peaks at around 8 million Fisher Education Act raises school-leaving age to fourteen Ministry of Health established Influenza pandemic, kills over 21 million people world-wide by 1920 Rutherford splits atom Oswald Spengler, *Decline of the West* (vol. 2, 1922)	Brooke, *Collected Poems* Joyce, *Exiles* Wyndham Lewis, *Tarr* Mansfield, *Prelude* Siegfried Sassoon, *Counter-Attack* Edward Thomas, *Last Poems* Rebecca West, *The Return of the Soldier*

	HISTORY AND CULTURE	LITERATURE
1919	Treaty of Versailles: war settlement imposing reparations on Germany Anglo-Irish War begins Nancy Astor becomes first woman MP Sex Disqualification Removal Act opens professions to women Over 1,000 strikes between 1919 and 1920 First transatlantic flight by John Alcock and Arthur W. Brown	Aldington, *Images of War* *Coterie* (runs only until 1921) *English Studies* Maugham, *The Moon and Sixpence* Shaw, *Heartbreak House* Sassoon, *War Poems* Woolf, *Night and Day*
1920	Government of Ireland Act partitions Ireland Unemployment Insurance Act League of Nations founded (precursor of the United Nations) Communist Party of Great Britain founded Oxford admits women to degrees (1880 at London University) Jung, *Psychological Types*	Agatha Christie, *The Mysterious Affair at Styles* Eliot, *The Sacred Wood* Lawrence, *Women in Love; The Lost Girl* Rose Macaulay, *Potterism* Mansfield, *Bliss* Wilfred Owen, *Poems* Pound, *Hugh Selwyn Mauberley* Lytton Strachey, *Eminent Victorians* Wells, *The Outline of History* Yeats, *Michael Robartes and the Dancer*
1921	Economic slump National Unemployed Workers' Movement (NUWM) established Anglo-Irish Treaty establishes Irish Free State in Southern Ireland Marie Stopes opens first birth-control clinic in London	Aldous Huxley, *Crome Yellow* Luigi Pirandello, *Six Characters in Search of an Author* Shaw, *Back to Methuselah*
1922	Unemployment stands at 2 million; first of many 'hunger marches' organised by the NUWM throughout the 1920s and 1930s. Miners' strike defeated as Triple Alliance fails on 'Black Friday' (15 April) Geddes Committee recommends large cuts in government spending, curtailing post-war reconstruction efforts Conservatives win election; Labour forms official opposition for first time Irish Civil War breaks out (ends 1923) Mussolini comes to power in Italy Radio broadcasting begins; British Broadcasting Company formed Major Jack C. Savage develops skywriting Sir James Frazer, *The Golden Bough* (one-volume abridged edn)	*The Criterion*, ed. T. S. Eliot Eliot, *The Waste Land* Galsworthy, *The Forsyte Saga* Hardy, *Late Lyrics and Earlier* A. E. Houseman, *Last Poems* Joyce, *Ulysses* (published in Paris; banned in the USA until 1933, and in the UK until 1936) Lawrence, *Aaron's Rod; England, My England; Studies in Classic American Literature* Mansfield, *The Garden Party* I. A. Richards, *Principles of Literary Criticism* May Sinclair, *The Life and Death of Harriett Frean* Woolf, *Jacob's Room*
1923	British empire at its largest-ever extent Matrimonial Causes Act allows women to sue for divorce on same grounds as men, including adultery	*The Adelphi*, ed. J. M. Murry Bennett, *Riceyman Steps* E. E. Cummings, *Tulips and Chimneys* Huxley, *Antic Hay* Lawrence, *The Ladybird; Kangaroo; Birds, Beasts and Flowers* Macaulay, *Told by an Idiot* Sean O'Casey, *The Shadow of a Gunman*

	HISTORY AND CULTURE	LITERATURE
1924	First Labour government in Britain under Ramsay MacDonald (January) Housing Act provides for subsidised public housing and generates over half a million new homes by 1932 London tram strike Conservative government re-elected (December) First manifesto of surrealism Freud, *The Ego and the Id*	Ford, *Some Do Not* (first book of *Parade's End* tetralogy) Forster, *A Passage to India* T. E. Hulme, *Speculations* O'Casey, *Juno and the Paycock* Shaw, *Saint Joan*
1925	Pensions Act provides pensions at sixty-five Guardianship of Infants Act gives women equal rights to their children	*Calendar of Modern Letters* Noël Coward, *Hay Fever* H. D. (Hilda Doolittle), *Collected Poems* Scott Fitzgerald, *The Great Gatsby* Ford, *No More Parades* Hardy, *Human Shows* Ernest Hemingway, *In Our Time* Lawrence, *St Mawr* Hugh MacDiarmid, *Sangschaw* *Review of English Studies* Woolf, *Mrs Dalloway; The Common Reader* Yeats, *A Vision*
1926	General Strike Electricity (Supply) Act sets up Central Electricity Board to coordinate supply through a national grid (completed by 1936) Television first demonstrated by John Logie Baird; British Broadcasting Corporation (BBC) established	Ford, *A Man Could Stand Up* Lawrence, *The Plumed Serpent* T. E. Lawrence, *Seven Pillars of Wisdom* MacDiarmid, *Penny Wheep; A Drunk Man Looks at the Thistle* O'Casey, *The Plough and the Stars* Sassoon, *Satirical Poems* Wells, *The World of William Clissold*
1927	Trade Disputes Act makes general strikes illegal Charles Lindbergh, first solo transatlantic flight	Forster, *Aspects of the Novel* Robert Graves and Laura Riding, *A Survey of Modernist Poetry* Joyce, *Pomes Penyeach* T. F. Powys, *Mr Weston's Good Wine* Jean Rhys, *The Left Bank* Woolf, *To the Lighthouse*
1928	Minimum voting age for women in Britain reduced to twenty-one from thirty years Alexander Fleming discovers penicillin (fully exploited from 1940) First films with sound in Britain	Edmund Blunden, *Undertones of War* Ford, *Last Post* Hardy, *Winter Words* Huxley, *Point Counter Point* Christopher Isherwood, *All the Conspirators* D. H. Lawrence, *Lady Chatterley's Lover* (uncensored version banned in the UK until 1960; in the USA until 1959); *Collected Poems; The Woman Who Rode Away* O'Casey, *The Silver Tassie* Rhys, *Quartet* Sassoon, *Memoirs of a Fox-Hunting Man* R. C. Sheriff, *Journey's End* (first produced; published, 1929; film version, 1930) Evelyn Waugh, *Decline and Fall* Woolf, *Orlando* Yeats, *The Tower*

	HISTORY AND CULTURE	LITERATURE
1929	General election returns minority Labour government; Margaret Bondfield becomes first woman Cabinet member Wall Street Crash and start of international economic depression	Aldington, *Death of a Hero* Elizabeth Bowen, *The Last September* Bridges, *The Testament of Beauty* William Faulkner, *The Sound and the Fury* Robert Graves, *Goodbye to All That* Hemingway, *A Farewell to Arms* D. H. Lawrence, *Pansies* L. H. Myers, *The Near and the Far* (title volume of a tetralogy completed in 1940) John Cowper Powys, *Wolf Solent* J. B. Priestley, *The Good Companions* Erich Maria Remarque, *All Quiet on the Western Front* (film version, 1930) I. A. Richards, *Practical Criticism* Woolf, *A Room of One's Own*
1930	Coal Mines Act reduces underground working to 7½ hours per day First solo flight to Australia by Amy Johnson Jet engine invented Freud, *Civilisation and its Discontents*	W. H. Auden, *Poems* Blunden, *Collected Poems* Coward, *Private Lives* Eliot, *Ash Wednesday* Faulkner, *As I Lay Dying* Hardy, *Collected Poems* D. H. Lawrence, *The Virgin and the Gipsy* Lewis, *The Apes of God* Maugham, *Cakes and Ale* Rhys, *After Leaving Mr Mackenzie* Sassoon, *Memoirs of an Infantry Officer* Shaw, *The Apple Cart* Waugh, *Vile Bodies*
1931	Economic crisis and escalating unemployment (up to 3 million this year) brings about collapse of government; MacDonald forms National (coalition) Government which wins general election (October) with large Conservative majority Ford Dagenham plant opens and introduces mass-production of cars to Britain	Bowen, *Friends and Relations* Ivy Compton-Burnett, *Men and Wives* D. H. Lawrence, *Apocalypse* Woolf, *The Waves*
1932	Unemployed hunger march to London Britain's economy begins to recover from depression British Union of Fascists formed by Sir Oswald Mosley	Auden, *The Orators* Eliot, *Sweeney Agonistes; Selected Essays* Huxley, *Brave New World* D. H. Lawrence, *Last Poems* Priestley, *Dangerous Corner* *Scrutiny*, ed. F. R. Leavis Woolf, *The Second Common Reader*
1933	Hitler becomes German Chancellor	Auden, *The Dance of Death* Vera Brittain, *Testament of Youth* Compton-Burnett, *More Women than Men* Walter Greenwood, *Love on the Dole* George Orwell, *Down and Out in London and Paris* Stephen Spender, *Poems* Yeats, *The Winding Stair*

	HISTORY AND CULTURE	LITERATURE
1934	Unemployed hunger march and lobby of Parliament Special Areas Act provides limited assistance to alleviate unemployment in depressed areas UK League of Nations Union organises 'Peace Ballot' (November 1934–June 1935): 11.5 million respondents, most favouring international disarmament	Eliot, *The Rock* James, *The Art of the Novel* D. H. Lawrence, *The Tales* MacDiarmid, *Stony Limits* Orwell, *Burmese Days* Pound, *Make it New* Priestley, *English Journey* Rhys, *Voyage in the Dark* Shaw, *Collected Prefaces* Dylan Thomas, *18 Poems*
1935	National Government re-elected; Labour gains in areas of high unemployment Nylon invented Radar invented Italy invades Ethiopia	Walter Brierley, *Means-Test Man* Compton-Burnett, *A House and Its Head* Eliot, *Murder in the Cathedral* Isherwood, *Mr Norris Changes Trains* Louis MacNeice, *Poems* Orwell, *A Clergyman's Daughter* Penguin Books launched with first ten sixpenny paperbacks
1936	Death of George V and accession of Edward VIII, who abdicates later in the year to marry divorcée, Mrs Simpson; his brother becomes King George VI 'Jarrow March' of unemployed from Tyneside to London Public Order Act bans political uniforms (mainly aimed at Mosley's fascist blackshirts) First regular television broadcasts Spanish Civil War begins with right-wing rebellion, led by General Franco, against government	Auden, *Look, Stranger!* Winifred Holtby, *South Riding* Huxley, *Eyeless in Gaza* Orwell, *Keep the Aspidistra Flying* Sassoon, *Sherston's Progress* Dylan Thomas, *25 Poems*
1937	British Government under Neville Chamberlain pursues policy of appeasement towards Italy and Germany Charles Madge and Tom Harrison start the 'Mass Observation' project to survey and document the lives of the masses	Auden and MacNeice, *Letters from Iceland* Isherwood, *Sally Bowles* David Jones, *In Parenthesis* Lewis Jones, *Cwmardy* Orwell, *The Road to Wigan Pier* Priestley, *Time and the Conways* Woolf, *The Years*
1938	Munich agreement with Hitler claimed by Chamberlain as guarantor of 'peace in our time'	Bowen, *The Death of the Heart* Idris Davies, *Gwalia Deserta* C. Day-Lewis, *Overtures to a Death* Orwell, *Homage to Catalonia* Waugh, *Scoop* Woolf, *Three Guineas*
1939	Germany invades Czechoslovakia, breaking the Munich agreement, and then invades Poland; Britain and France declare war on Germany Madrid falls to Franco's troops bringing the Spanish Civil War to an end Electron microscope invented	Christopher Caudwell, *Studies in a Dying Culture* Eliot, *The Family Reunion* Isherwood, *Goodbye to Berlin* Joyce, *Finnegans Wake* MacNeice, *Autumn Journal* Flann O'Brien, *At Swim-Two-Birds* Orwell, *Coming Up for Air* Rhys, *Good Morning, Midnight* Spender, *Poems for Spain*

Historical Overview

Continuities

While it is tempting, retrospectively, to view the turn of a century as a major historical turning point, bringing with it abrupt and fundamental social changes, it is clear from our own relatively recent experience of the turning of a millennium that nothing necessarily changes simply because of the passing of a landmark calendar date. Just as the 1990s and the 2000s ran into one another with no sudden or profound changes to the structure or fabric of our society, so the 1890s ran into the 1900s; and, though there was a heightened moment of symbolic change in 1901 with the death of Britain's then-longest-reigning monarch, Queen Victoria, the general continuities between the late Victorian and early Edwardian periods are perhaps the first things to note here.

Consonant with the 1890s' rebellious insistence on all things 'new' (the New Woman, the New Unionism, the New Realism, the New Spirit), the new century saw a continuing reaction against what were perceived (rightly or wrongly) as deeply entrenched Victorian values and attitudes, especially in religion and morality. Although there were no major upheavals in organised, institutional religion in this

6.1 'Progress': cartoon by George Morrow (*Punch* 1910).

period in Britain, the profound impact of nineteenth-century science, philosophy and thought (especially Darwinian thought) continued to be widely felt and there was certainly a spreading and deepening crisis of faith among artists and intellectuals, whose questioning and search for alternative systems of belief were now also increasingly influenced by the recently established fields of anthropology and comparative religion.

Politically and ideologically, too, society continued to become more pluralistic and democratic, and the Victorian trend towards a more diverse social-class structure and looser, less deterministic social networks continued apace. Indeed, continuing expansions in educational provision and the gradual restructuring of Britain's industrial base brought about ever greater social mobility and a further increase in the importance and influence of the lower middle classes and sections of the skilled and educated working classes. The growth in relative prosperity of these groups further fuelled the development of a mass consumer society which, as in the Victorian period, included the consumption not only of goods and services but also of literature, arts, entertainment, spectator sports and news media. Rapid advances in science, technology, manufacturing and transport accelerated the rate of material social change as the new century progressed; while the rate of general cultural change was also accelerated by a marked growth of cosmopolitan culture and international influences, especially in the arts, where a veritable explosion of 'isms' – post-impressionism, imagism, expressionism, futurism, vorticism, cubism, dadaism, surrealism – began to revolutionise form, style and subject matter in almost all artistic genres.

In the political arena, there was an obvious continuity from the nineteenth century in the uninterrupted run of a Conservative government from 1895 to 1905, and, though change was in the air with the founding of the Labour Party and the growth of a militant suffragette movement, the institutional and ideological patterns of mainstream political life in Britain would broadly mirror those of the period of Gladstone and Disraeli for a few years yet. More importantly, the key political debates and issues of the early twentieth century remained largely those of the late nineteenth century: Irish Home Rule, female suffrage, economic performance relative to international competition, unemployment, the impact of trade unionism, the distribution of wealth and income, education. The continuing drift of the population into towns (a process that had been accelerated by a major agricultural depression in the 1870s), maintained existing pressure on politicians to address problems of urban planning, housing and health; while, similarly, continuing agitation on the part of socialists, trade unionists and suffragettes ensured that questions of poverty, labour rights and equality stayed firmly on the political agenda across the centuries' divide. On the world stage, the British empire continued to expand from the 1870s through to the end of the First World War and for most of this period Britain remained, in effect, the superpower of the day, dominating the seas and holding sway over more than 400 million people and around one-fifth of the land mass of the globe.

Economically, too, Britain's new century carried over many of the dominant features of the mid- to late Victorian periods. Despite continued widespread poverty and unemployment, stark inequalities between rich and poor, and marked regional variations, the underlying trend of the economy was one of steady, if modest, growth, with an overall general improvement in living standards and a rise in average real incomes. Clearly there were fluctuations throughout the period – during and immediately after the First World War, for example, and especially after the Wall Street Crash of 1929 which was followed by a major economic depression which had devastating consequences for several British regions (most notably the industrial areas of the north, central Scotland and south Wales) – but, on an overall average, the British economy continued the Victorian trend of growth in productivity and prosperity right up to the outbreak of the Second World War. The old staple industries of the Industrial Revolution – coal, steel, mechanical engineering, textiles, clothing – largely maintained their pre-eminence in the new century, alongside buoyant financial and service sectors. Moreover, what some historians have called the Second Industrial Revolution, beginning in the 1880s, had by now gathered pace (especially in the south-east of the country) and had begun to define a more distinctively twentieth-century industrial landscape characterised by an increasing use of electricity, by various forms of light and precision engineering, advanced chemical manufacture, motor-vehicle production and an ever-growing variety of mass-produced consumer commodities, including newspapers and books, soap, tobacco, ready-made clothing, chocolate, domestic appliances and electrical goods.

Internationally, by the start of the twentieth century, Britain, reaping the rewards of early industrialisation, had firmly established itself as the world's greatest trading nation and most influential economy. Sterling was viewed as roughly equivalent to gold and was used as an international currency much as the dollar is today; and this, along with the strength and sophistication of Britain's financial institutions

6.2 Balloon race, Ranelagh, 1906.

and their large and sustained capital investments abroad, meant that Britain was effectively an economic anchor for the rest of the world. As one economic historian puts it:

> In 1900 London was the world's capital city three times over – in political terms as the fulcrum of the British Empire, in commercial terms as the centre of banking and finance with sterling the dominant international currency, and in industrial terms as the largest port in the largest trading nation in the world.
>
> (Paul Johnson, 'Introduction: Britain, 1900–1990', in Johnson (ed.), *Twentieth-Century Britain*, p. 1 [Bi])

On the surface at least, Britain would maintain this position of pre-eminence until the outbreak of war in 1914.

Notes of Discord

Beneath the apparently smooth continuities from the late nineteenth century, however, another story was beginning to unfold and, even at the start of the century, the apparently robust health of the nation was showing signs of failing on a number of fronts. The literal poor health of the many British recruits who were rejected as unfit by the Army for the Boer War (1899–1902) was a stark reminder of widespread poverty and malnutrition in the country, but it also serves as a suggestive image of other underlying weaknesses in Britain's situation at the time. A series of early defeats in the Boer War itself showed that Britain's apparent military might was not unassailable; and the very fact of the conflict (in addition to continuing troubles in Ireland) stood as a significant challenge to the hegemony of an empire that had come to be viewed almost as part of the natural order of things.

Moreover, while Britain's economy was still growing steadily, it was in fact growing more slowly than its major international competitors, Germany, France and America, and its international trade markets were increasingly coming under pressure from these countries. The staple industries mentioned earlier were strong and successful still in their own terms, but they were not making the same rapid productivity and efficiency gains as their competitors abroad. Although the full implications of this relative slow-down would not work themselves out until the economic crises of the post-war period, in retrospect the Edwardian period appears to be the point at which Britain's Victorian economic development finally peaked and began to fall back.

Many Edwardians seem to have sensed this and, notwithstanding the actual (if modest) improvements in their standard of living as compared to the past, believed themselves to be living through a period of serious decline. This somewhat paradoxical perception is frequently mentioned by historians of the period and it can be explained partly by the point above about *relative* international decline, and partly by frustrated expectations in that the great promise of Britain's Victorian successes was not being realised as rapidly or as richly as people had come to hope and expect. A large number of people simply voted with their feet and there was a significant rise in emigration in the first years of the century up to the war, with most emigrants going to America and Australia and, later, Canada. At the same time, there was a significant rise in social and industrial protest, with increasingly militant agitation on the part of suffragettes, socialists and trade unions. More defensive reactions to the underlying sense of decline could be seen in the imperialistic campaign for protectionist tariff reforms which sought to impose duties on goods from outside the British empire, as well as in the spread of a tub-thumping form of patriotism and militarism that had first emerged just before the Boer War and was now becoming institutionalised in organisations such as the National Service League (1902) and the British Brothers League (1903), and in youth organisations like the Boy Scouts (1907). On all sides, though, the optimism and faith in progress that had characterised the Victorian period had clearly begun to give way to something approaching a crisis of confidence – and it was a crisis that, through various forms of disillusioned critique, was given acute expression in much of the literature of the period. Even as early as 1902, for example, the symbolic title and narrative of Joseph Conrad's modernist masterpiece, *Heart of Darkness*, registered a growing sense of malaise over Britain's (and Europe's) imperial adventures.

In fact, the debate about the health of the nation sparked off by the Boer War was matched by a broader political and polemical debate about the social, economic and moral state of the nation, a debate which in many ways reprised the Condition of England discourse of the mid-Victorians (see pp. 396–7, 413–18). In fiction, this gave rise to an Edwardian version of the Condition of England novel, in works such as E. M. Forster's *Howards End* (1910) and H. G. Wells's *Tono-Bungay* (1909), where, for example, Wells sums up the country's apparent 'present colour and abundance' as 'October foliage before the frosts nip down the leaves' (pp. 381–2). For him, Britain represents 'the most unpremeditated, subtle, successful and aimless plutocracy that ever encumbered the destinies of mankind' (p. 258), and he writes, with uncanny prescience:

> A mass of people swelters and toils, great railway systems grow, cities arise to the skies and spread wide and far, mines are opened, factories hum, foundries roar, ships plough the seas, countries are settled; about this busy striving world the rich owners go, controlling all, enjoying all, confident and creating the confidence that draws us all together into a reluctant, nearly unconscious brotherhood … The flags flutter, the crowds cheer, the legislatures meet. Yet it seems to me indeed at times that all this present commercial civilization is no more than my poor uncle's career writ large, a swelling, thinning bubble of assurances; that its arithmetic is just as unsound, its dividends as ill-advised, its ultimate aim as vague and forgotten; that it all drifts on perhaps to some tremendous parallel to his individual disaster …
>
> (pp. 221–2 [A])

Liberal Reform and the Rise of Labour

It is perhaps a further paradox that such an air of pessimism should have engendered such a resounding endorsement of liberalism, free trade and reform in the landslide election victory of the Liberals in 1906. This brought to an end ten years of continuous Tory rule and brought to power one of the most radically reformist governments Britain had ever seen. It also saw the election of the first Labour MPs and the birth of the Parliamentary Labour Party, developments which clearly stiffened the radicalism of the new Liberal ministry but which also heralded a new era of direct Labour representation within Parliament and the end of the old-established two-party system.

Between 1906 and 1914, the Liberal government introduced a series of landmark reforms, including: the introduction of state-funded old age pensions (1908), and state-funded sickness and unemployment benefits (the National Insurance Act, 1911); the provision of free school meals for children of the poor (1906); controls on wages for 'sweated' or unregulated forms of labour (1909); labour exchanges for the unemployed (1909); payment of salaries to MPs (1911) (one of the original demands of the Chartists); and prison reforms such as the introduction of a system of probation (1907). Other radical policies were pursued in the 'People's Budget' of 1909 when, in order to pay for the above and other reforms, the Chancellor of the Exchequer, David Lloyd George, proposed a range of new tax measures which particularly targeted the rich and landed classes (e.g., a tax on profits from the sale of land). As Lloyd George had anticipated, the Conservatives vehemently opposed the budget and the House of Lords, dominated by Tory peers, firmly rejected it and sent it back to the Commons, thus bringing about a constitutional crisis. This gave Lloyd George and his party the chance to take the issue directly to the electorate in what then also became a debate about the power of the unelected upper house. The Liberal government was duly re-elected at the start of 1910 (though with a smaller majority), and the Lords were forced to accept Lloyd George's budget.

Labour Representation

Parliament had long been dominated by the two established parties, the Liberals (or Whigs) and the Conservatives (or Tories). After the failed Chartist campaigns of the 1830s and 1840s, there was a relative lull in large-scale movements and agitation for working-class rights and representation. However, with Forster's Education Act of 1870, and subsequent related Acts in 1876, 1880 and 1891, educational opportunities for the working classes had been greatly expanded and the consequent gradual improvement in educational standards and literacy rates from the 1880s onwards brought a concomitant increase in working-class aspirations, a wider diffusion of socialist ideas, and an increasing determination to organise and agitate for fundamental social and political change. There was now a marked increase in the number of mass-membership industrial trade unions and a mushrooming of socialist organisations such as the Independent Labour Party (ILP) and the more middle-class Fabian Society. In Parliament the cause of labour and the poor had been championed in the past mainly by the radical wing of the Liberal Party, along with a few independent MPs with working-class affiliations who voted as Liberals. In the 1890s, momentum gathered pace for Labour to have its own separate representation and the first major step towards this came with the setting up of the Labour Representation Committee (LRC) in 1900 by, among others, Keir Hardie, a Scottish miners' leader who was a prominent member of the ILP and who had first been elected to Parliament in 1892. The LRC brought together a number of different groups and, crucially, it was supported by the trade unions, who raised a penny per year political levy on their members to help finance Labour candidates for Parliament. Twenty-nine Labour MPs were elected in the 1906 election and they were joined by twenty-four other like-minded MPs to form the first Parliamentary Labour Party with Keir Hardie as leader.

6.3 Soup queue, 1906.

Despite these various parliamentary and legislative successes, other serious social and political problems remained largely unresolved under the Liberals. There was widespread industrial unrest over low wages, poor conditions and uncertain employment, with several crippling rail, dock and coal strikes in the early 1910s and many violent confrontations between workers and the authorities. In 1911, two strikers were shot dead by troops and, indeed, the number of serious industrial disputes immediately preceding the war has led some commentators to suggest that Britain might have seen a revolution if the war had not broken out at that point. There was also increased intensity, audacity and violence in the suffragettes' continuing campaign for the vote, with mass marches and demonstrations, attacks on buildings and property, arson, raids on Parliament, arrests, imprisonments, hunger-strikes (with attempts at force-feeding by the authorities), as well as dramatic individual gestures such as the fatal protest of Emily Davison who died after throwing herself in front of the King's racehorse at the Derby of 1913. And there was the continuing and seemingly intractable problem of Ireland and the issue of Home Rule …

Irish Home Rule

Two earlier Home Rule Bills had failed in 1886 and 1893. Now, partly in return for the support of the Irish Nationalist Party during the constitutional crisis of 1910, the government presented a third, in April 1912. As before, this was resolutely opposed by the Protestants of Ulster (in the north-east of Ireland) who, supported and encouraged

6.4 Sylvia Pankhurst and police escort, 1912.

by English Unionists, began to arm themselves in preparation for a military stand against any attempt to include Ulster within the 'home' rule of the rest of Catholic Ireland. The Irish Nationalists, under pressure from Sinn Féin (who advocated complete independence for Ireland), refused to support a government amendment leaving Ulster out of the agreement, and they too began to arm themselves – so, when the Act was finally passed in early 1914, a bloody civil war seemed inevitable. The so-called Curragh Mutiny of March 1914 – when officers based at Curragh in Dublin indicated they would not cooperate in imposing Home Rule on Ulster – demonstrated that the leaders of the British Army were clearly pro-Unionist and this further constrained the government's scope for manoeuvre at this point. However, there was a reprieve of sorts with the outbreak of the First World War in August when the Home Rule Act was suspended – and later events made it effectively redundant. At Easter 1916, Sinn Féin attempted a rebellion in Dublin. This was suppressed after five days of fighting and the British then executed fifteen of the leaders. This brutal act turned Irish opinion decisively in Sinn Féin's favour – as the poet W. B. Yeats suggested, all had now 'utterly changed', 'A terrible beauty is born' ('Easter 1916') – and support for their cause grew steadily. In the post-war election of 1918 they easily defeated the moderate Nationalists and then refused to take their seats in the British Parliament; instead, they established their own Irish assembly in 1919 and embarked upon a concerted armed campaign against the British. The Government of Ireland Act of 1920 partitioned Ireland into Ulster and the South, but the Anglo-Irish War continued until December 1921 when the Anglo-Irish Treaty finally gave Southern Ireland – now the Irish Free State – the status of a self-governing dominion within the British empire, leaving Ulster separate as an integral part of the United Kingdom.

The First World War

Various complex international tensions led to the outbreak of war in 1914. Western European powers had been competing in trade, industrial development and colonial expansion since before the start of the century. Germany in particular had ambitions to overtake Britain as the world's dominant economic, naval and imperial power and strategic alliances had brought about two loose blocs, the Triple Alliance of Germany, Austria-Hungary and Italy on one side and the Triple Entente of Britain, France and Russia on the other (although, in the war, Italy fought on the side of the Allies). Different, or additional, historic factors were in play in central and eastern Europe, but it was here, in Sarajevo, Bosnia, on 28 June 1914 that the incident which sparked off the war occurred, when the Archduke Franz Ferdinand (the heir to the Austro-Hungarian Emperor Franz Josef), was assassinated by Serbian nationalists. Austria-Hungary declared war on Serbia; Russia mobilised to defend Serbia; Germany declared war on Russia and then also on France when she mobilised in support of Russia; Germany marched on France via Belgium and it was this violation of Belgian neutrality which finally triggered Britain's entry into the war, on 4 August 1914.

Again, as at the start of the Boer War, Britain was engulfed by a huge wave of popular patriotism. There was a frenzied rush of war bombast at recruitment rallies and in the press, 'Land of Hope and Glory' rang out through the streets of London, and some 500,000 men volunteered for the army in the first month, with a million volunteering by the end of 1914, glad, it seems, at last to be allowed to prove themselves on the battlefield: 'Now, God be thanked Who has matched us with His hour', wrote Rupert Brooke, echoing the war-feverish mood, 'And caught our youth, and wakened us from sleeping' ('Peace', 1914). There was, however, a general feeling in the country that 'it would all be over by Christmas' and that Britain's actual involvement in the fighting would be limited – that although troops would be sent to support the Belgians and French, Britain's main role would be to blockade Germany on the seas and provide financial backing for the Allies. In the event, the war went on for more than four years, claiming over 9 million lives, with around 2.5 million British casualties, including almost a million killed. After the Battle of the Marne in September 1914, the war became largely a war of attrition as a death-dealing deadlock quickly established itself, with the opposing forces entrenched along a western front which stretched from the Swiss frontier to the Belgian coast:

> From the end of 1914 until the great offensives of 1918 these lines never varied by more than some twenty miles to east or west, and the small strip of Flanders where many of the attacks took place became a hell in which hundreds of thousands were slaughtered in trying to gain a few acres of pock-marked mud or one of the rare dominating ridges. Defence prevailed over attack; and the machine-gun, the dominating weapon until the last year, took a fearful toll. To counter this power of the defence, attacking forces relied chiefly on terrific artillery barrages. These were intended to flatten the enemy's barbed wire, obliterate his trenches, silence his guns, and allow the infantry to go 'over the top'. But since the opposing trenches were not usually

greatly affected, their occupants brought their machine-guns into play as soon as the barrage lifted, and mowed down the advancing troops by the thousand.

(Richards and Hunt, *An Illustrated History of Britain*, p. 244 [Bi])

Events in the East were much more mobile, if no less destructive of human life (and the war extended also into the Middle East with Turkey's entry into the war on the German side), but there, too, a see-saw of gains and losses tended more or less to cancel each other out over the main part of the war.

As suggested above, the huge losses of life were partly the result of new technology: in addition to the machine-gun and more powerful artillery, this first experience of industrialised warfare on a mass scale also saw the first uses of poison gas in the trenches and, later, tanks (which would prove decisive for the Allies at the end of the war), along with the first major submarine campaigns at sea, aerial bombardment by Zeppelin airships and, increasingly throughout the war, the military use of aeroplanes. This was not at all the sort of war anyone had expected and the idealistic dreams of glory and heroism of the first waves of young volunteers were quickly shattered in the face of brutal and unremitting mechanised slaughter. Rupert Brooke died of blood-poisoning on a troopship before seeing action; but many other equally idealistic young writers survived the trenches long enough to revise their generation's romantic conceptions of war in the starkest possible terms:

If in some smothering dreams you too could pace
Behind the wagon that we flung him in,
And watch the white eyes writhing in his face,
His hanging face, like a devil's sick of sin;
If you could hear, at every jolt, the blood
Come gargling from the froth-corrupted lungs,
Obscene as cancer, bitter as the cud
Of vile, incurable sores on innocent tongues, –
My friend, you would not tell with such high zest
To children ardent for some desperate glory,
The old Lie: Dulce et decorum est
Pro patria mori.

(Wilfred Owen, 'Dulce et Decorum Est', 1917–18)

No one factor was absolutely decisive in Germany's ultimate defeat, but, among other things, Britain's naval blockade of Germany, Russia's reserves of manpower, and the entry into the war of the Americans on the Allied side in April 1917 all played a significant part. The end of what H. G. Wells called *The War That Will End War* (1914) came with the armistice at 11 a.m. on 11 November 1918.

On the home front, the material impact of the war was not immediately great (except in terms of the increasingly long casualty lists, of course). Although this was the first war in living memory in which the British Isles were themselves under direct attack, with early sea bombardments on the east coast and aerial raids by Zeppelins and, later, aeroplanes, such attacks were relatively few and far between, as were the resulting casualties. Food rationing was not introduced until the final year of the war, although prices increased drastically over the four years and many families inevitably suffered from having lost their main breadwinner to the war. There were shortages and hardships of all kinds and to try to conserve fuel Daylight Saving was introduced in 1916, but Britain's existing industrial capacity was generally sufficient to diversify into war production without fundamentally destabilising the civilian industries and economy. Following the 'shells scandal' of May 1915, when there was an outcry over the lack of munitions for British soldiers in France, the newly formed coalition government initiated a massive expansion in the arms industries which helped to maintain full employment and created many new employment opportunities, particularly for women. The government's initial emphasis on 'Business as Usual' for the country and its strong intervention in industry and the economy thereafter seem to have prevented any major crises at home and any substantial loss of morale among the general population. Indeed, in addition to bringing women more widely into the world of paid work (in commerce, the civil service, transport and the service sector as well as in direct war work), one of the most important legacies of the war for British society was the extent to which the state was now *expected* to intervene in the economy and to take direct responsibility for a whole range of social policy such as housing, education and employment. Immediately after the war, for example, the government took direct responsibility for supporting the unemployed (many of whom, inevitably, were returning servicemen), and for providing *either* work *or* maintenance. This pushed the limited pre-war policies on relief and unemployment insurance closer to a full system of unemployment benefits. Just before the end of the war, moreover, the democratising effect of mass mobilisation and sacrifice issued in another crucial legacy, the 1918 Representation of the People Act which extended the franchise to all men over twenty-one and to women ratepayers over thirty, increasing the electorate from 8 million to 21 million.

At the Paris Peace Conference (1919–20) which concluded the war, the Allies imposed punitive reparations on Germany which, many have argued, sowed the seeds of the Second World War by damaging the German economy and creating the conditions for the rise of Hitler and the Nazis. Potentially more positive was the Conference's setting up of the League of Nations which was intended to maintain peace, prevent future wars and work for disarmament. However, the League was weakened from the start when America refused to join and, with the membership including only Britain and France of the other great powers, it never had the necessary authority to impose its will except in minor disputes and remained largely ineffectual in the run-up to the Second World War in the 1930s. Nevertheless, it reflected a widespread desire for peace and disarmament in the aftermath of the horrors of the First World War and later provided a rallying point for anti-war groups in Britain such as the Peace Pledge Union (established in 1934 and with a membership of some 100,000 people by 1936), which in turn influenced Britain's policy of appeasement in the late 1930s.

Britain between the Wars: Politics, Economy, Social Change

At the 1918 general election, held immediately after the war, the wartime coalition government (led since December 1916 by Lloyd George) swept the board on an ambitious platform of national reconstruction whose aim was to build 'a land fit for heroes'. Many of the planned reforms were not carried through at the time because of mounting economic problems, but, in addition to the Unemployment Insurance Act of 1920 already mentioned, other important pieces of legislation which would have significant ramifications for the future were the Housing Act of 1919, which for the first time provided state subsidies for house-building and prepared the ground for similar, more effective Acts in 1923 and 1924; and the Fisher Education Act of 1918 which laid many of the foundations for the modern education system, raising the school-leaving age to fourteen and proposing, among other things, provision of public nursery education and continuation schools. The coalition government collapsed in 1922 when the Conservatives withdrew their support and the Liberal Party was now split between those who had supported the post-war coalition with the Conservatives and those (led by the former Prime Minister, Herbert Asquith) who had opposed it. At the general election in that year, this disunity gave the Conservatives an easy victory and helped the Labour Party to second place for the first time. At the next election, at the end of 1923, the Conservatives lost their majority and, with the support of the Liberals, the Labour Party formed their first (minority) government in 1924 under Ramsay MacDonald. This was clearly a reflection of major changes in the British political landscape since the start of the century and, although this Labour government was only short-lived and the Conservatives regained power under Stanley Baldwin later in 1924, the result of *that* election confirmed Labour's increasing support in the country and the definitive demise of the Liberals as the country's second major party. The Labour Party again came to power as a minority government in 1929, defeating the Conservatives partly because of the latter's failure to deal adequately with the continuing problems of unemployment; but the new government was almost immediately faced with the beginnings of a major economic depression and finally collapsed during the international economic crisis of 1931 when members of the cabinet refused to agree to a programme of major cuts in government expenditure (including, crucially, a cut of 10 per cent in unemployment benefit). In the face of bitter opposition from the rest of the Labour Party, Ramsay MacDonald formed a coalition government to see the cuts through. A general election later in the year gave the coalition a large majority, with a predominance of Conservative members, and the so-called National Government then remained in power till the end of the decade (led by Stanley Baldwin from 1935 and Neville Chamberlain from 1937).

Britain lost many key export markets during the war, largely to America, and from that point on America effectively took over Britain's position of dominance in the world economy. There was a brief economic boom in Britain immediately following the war in response to newly released demands for goods that had become scarce over the war years; but, as normal international trading conditions re-established themselves and the underlying structural weaknesses of Britain's economy were exposed, the boom was quickly followed by one of the worst-ever economic collapses in British history, between 1920 and 1921, from which the old staple industries of textiles, mechanical engineering, shipbuilding, coal, iron and steel would never fully recover to their pre-war levels. The slump was actually deeper for Britain than the second depression of 1929–32, following the Wall Street Crash, and the above industries were to remain depressed for most of the 1920s and 1930s.

Britain began to restructure its economy in the 1920s with the development of new industries focused more on the domestic market than on exports, with particular expansion in the fields of motor-vehicle production, chemicals, consumer goods and electric power, and, though recovery was uneven, the British economy did pick up again and grew modestly through the 1920s. One of the main costs of such restructuring, however, was a large increase in unemployment in the older industries and all that that implied for the regions where such industries were concentrated. Employment levels increased in the areas where the 'new' industries prospered – Greater London, the south-east, the west Midlands and parts of the east Midlands – but unemployment and industrial strife were widespread elsewhere throughout the decade. There was a culmination of discontent and class antagonism in the General Strike of 1926 when workers in all sections of British industry were called out by the Trades Union Congress (TUC) in support of the miners, who were facing demands from their employers for a longer working day and less pay: 'not a minute on the day, not a penny off the pay' was the miners' slogan. The General Strike threatened to paralyse the country, but the government had made careful preparations to deal with the situation and, using, among other things, radio broadcasts to rally support from middle-class volunteers, it was able to maintain some essential services and lessen the impact of the action; the TUC failed to provide strong leadership and Britain's only ever general strike lasted for just nine days before collapsing – a failure which weakened the union movement for many years to come. The miners remained on strike for a further six months, before they too were forced to accept longer hours and lower wages.

The international depression of 1929–32 again knocked Britain back. Unemployment in 1929 was already high at 1.5 million, and this rose to 3.4 million, or 17 per cent of the labour force, by 1932, while industrial output fell by 9 per cent. However, things were much worse for Germany, France and the USA, and, again, the most vulnerable areas were the regions associated with the old industrial staples of iron and steel, coal, shipbuilding, cotton and mechanical engineering: south Wales, Lancashire, the north-east and central Scotland were all particularly badly affected and, in those regions, there were massive levels of unemployment and extreme poverty and hardship throughout the 1930s. Overall, however, low import prices of food, caused by a sharp reduction in prices internationally, meant that, for the 19 million or so who did not lose their jobs, real incomes actually rose and standards of living held up – and, as these consumers maintained demand at home, industries which were not dependent on exports continued to prosper reasonably well. Also, there was no financial collapse in Britain as there was in other countries (partly because Britain came off the Gold Standard in 1931 to stop a run on the pound). So, although the depression was extremely hard for the millions of unemployed in the north of England, central Scotland and south Wales, it was relatively mild in comparison to America, Germany and France. Unemployment remained high (there were still 2.2 million unemployed in 1938), but the depression had eased by the autumn of 1932 and output in Britain recovered to its 1929 level by 1934, with the terms of international trade moving in Britain's favour.

6.5 *The British Worker*, 12 May 1926, and the *British Gazette*, 13 May 1926: newspaper front pages announcing the end of the General Strike and presenting the point of view of the Trades Union Congress and the government respectively. The *British Gazette* was published by the government under the supervision of the Chancellor of the Exchequer, Winston Churchill.

The popular image of the 1920s as a carefree, frivolous, even anarchic 'jazz age' is partly coloured by the popular image of the American 1920s – but that is a significant point in its own right, as this was the first decade when America began to exert a strong influence on British and European popular culture: 'Our Twenties did not roar quite as America's did. And yet this was the decade in which the American way of life invaded Europe as never before – in films, songs, dancing, drinks, language, vitality' (Alan Jenkins, *The Twenties*, p. 12 [Bi]). Indeed this was the decade when popular culture began to take on its typically modern forms, with the rapid growth in popularity of the cinema in particular spreading other popular fashions in, for example, clothes, hair, speech and manners, interior decoration and music. But, as Alan Jenkins says, the twenties in Britain were not the same as in America. Although it was certainly a period of psychological release after the war and there was something of a hedonistic mood of 'living for the moment' – among the middle and leisured classes at least – these years clearly had their grimmer side too, with a major economic depression, mass unemployment, constant industrial unrest and an underlying sense of war-trauma. Virginia Woolf's *Mrs Dalloway* (1925) is in this sense a brilliant analysis of the divided nature of the 1920s, where, on a glorious June morning in London, an upper-class woman exults in ordering beautiful flowers for her carefully planned dinner party while, in the park over the way, a former soldier relives the horrors of the trenches as he begins his chaotic slide into a suicidal nervous breakdown.

Just as the twenties were not all cocktails and cheek-to-cheek dancing, the thirties were not as unremittingly grim and gloomy as they are often made out to be. This is a decade where its writers have perhaps had a disproportionate influence on the later historiography of the period, with much of the socially committed literature of the time contributing significantly to the abiding picture of the decade as one of unrelieved depression and deprivation, and of bitter class conflict constantly threatening to erupt in violent upheaval. In fact, although there was certainly a good deal of political agitation, and both communist and fascist activity in Britain, there seems never to have been any significant threat from either left or right to the established political and economic order; and, although the mass hunger marches were real enough, and chronic hardship and poverty did indeed exist for millions of people in the depressed industrial areas, these were, as Stephen Constantine explains, 'far from being uniformly years of suffering':

Sectors of unemployment: men, per 1,000, unemployed for a year or more in June 1936	
Coal miners	123
Ship-builders and repairers	95
Cotton workers	67
Seamen	59
Iron and steel workers	57
Pottery workers	54
Workers in textile-bleaching, dyeing, etc.	37
Waiters and other workers in hotels, restaurants, etc.	33
Gas, water, and electricity workers	33
Boot and shoe workers	31
General engineering	31
Dock and harbour workers	27
Workers in distributive trades	27
Workers in bread, biscuits, cakes, etc.	26
Tailoring workers	25
Furniture workers	21
Printers, bookbinders	14
Workers in motor vehicles, cycles, etc.	10
All workers	41

(Table slightly adapted from Stephen Constantine, *Unemployment in Britain between the Wars*, p. 89 [Bi]; original source, the Pilgrim Trust, *Men Without Work*, Cambridge University Press, 1938, pp. 17–18)

> Greatly helped by a fall in the cost of living in the 1920s and early 1930s, average real wage earnings between the wars went up, until by 1938 they were perhaps one-third higher than in 1913 ... parents were limiting the size of their families and with fewer mouths to feed incomes went further. On average, hours of work were also down ... The consequence was a conspicuous improvement in the living standards of the majority of people in Britain. For some it brought real affluence, perhaps the opportunity to own a sparkling mass-produced motor car, an Austin or a Morris, or a chance to buy a semi-detached house with a garden and modern conveniences in one of the new estates being laid out in the suburbs. For many more people it meant at least some additional domestic comforts. Better equipped, newly built council houses were available for rent; modern furniture, radios, labour-saving household equipment such as electric cookers and other consumer goods could be bought. There was more cash left over for entertainments. Audiences packed the cinemas and dance halls ... more people were taking annual holidays, many in the holiday camps which sprang up on the coast in places like Skegness and Pwllheli.
>
> (*Unemployment in Britain between the Wars*, pp. 1–2 [Bi])

Improvements in diet and in medical and social services also brought improvements in the overall state of the nation's health, with a consequent fall in death rates and an increase in life expectancy. All this was no consolation for the long-term

The Face of a 1930s Industrial Slum

The train bore me away, through the monstrous scenery of slag-heaps, chimneys, piled scrap-iron, foul canals, paths of cindery mud criss-crossed by the prints of clogs. This was March, but the weather had been horribly cold and everywhere there were mounds of blackened snow. As we moved slowly through the outskirts of the town we passed row after row of little grey slum houses running at right angles to the embankment. At the back of one of the houses a young woman was kneeling on the stones, poking a stick up the leaden waste-pipe which ran from the sink inside and which I suppose was blocked. I had time to see everything about her – her sacking apron, her clumsy clogs, her arms reddened by the cold. She looked up as the train passed, and I was almost near enough to catch her eye. She had a round pale face, the usual exhausted face of the slum girl who is twenty-five and looks forty, thanks to miscarriages and drudgery; and it wore, for the second in which I saw it, the most desolate, hopeless expression I have ever seen … She knew well enough what was happening to her – understood as well as I did how dreadful a destiny it was to be kneeling there in the bitter cold, on the slimy stones of a slum backyard, poking a stick up a foul drain-pipe.

(George Orwell, *The Road to Wigan Pier* (1937), pp. 14–15 [A])

unemployed of the 1930s, of course – and it was particularly the long duration of periods of unemployment for individuals which became the outstanding issue of the decade – but such an unusually positive overview of these years set against the more sombre portraits provided by classic texts such as Walter Greenwood's *Love on the Dole* (1933), Lewis Jones's *Cwmardy* (1937) and George Orwell's *The Road to Wigan Pier* (1937) can usefully remind us of the need to approach all historical constructions (including this one) as inevitably partial and selective.

J. B. Priestley captured something of the complexity of the changing social picture of the 1930s in his *English Journey* (1934) when, at the end of his journey in 1933, he talks of many different Englands, 'variously and most fascinatingly mingled in every part of the country' – though he singles out three in particular which he calls 'the Old, the Nineteenth-Century and the New':

> There was, first, Old England, the country of the cathedrals and minsters and manor houses and inns, of Parson and Squire; guide-book and quaint highways and byways England … Then … there is the nineteenth-century England, the industrial England of coal, iron, steel, cotton, wool, railways; of thousands of rows of little houses all alike, sham Gothic churches, square-faced chapels, Town Halls, Mechanics' Institutes, mills, foundries, warehouses … The third England … was the new post-war England, belonging far more to the age itself than to this particular island. America, I supposed, was its real birthplace. This is the England of arterial and by-pass roads, of filling stations and factories that look like exhibition buildings, of giant cinemas and dance-halls and cafés, bungalows with tiny garages, cocktail bars, Woolworths, motor-coaches, wireless, hiking, factory girls looking like actresses, greyhound racing and dirt tracks, swimming pools, and everything given away for cigarette coupons.
>
> (pp. 397–401 [A])

Priestley goes on to talk of an increasingly egalitarian England where 'the very modern things, like the films and wireless and sixpenny stores, are absolutely democratic, making no distinctions whatever between their patrons'; for the first time in history, he suggests, this is an England 'without privilege' (402). There is clearly

6.6 Granada Cinema, Tooting, with Gothic Revival interior, 1931 – one of the 'picture palaces' of the period.

some wishful thinking here, but Priestley's point neatly links us back to the start of this overview and underlines the trend suggested there of a continuing and accelerating extension of equal opportunities and democracy in the first four decades of the twentieth century. Anticipating and advocating even greater such advances for the second half of the century, George Orwell, writing early in the Second World War, made essentially the same optimistic assessment as Priestley in his essay, 'England Your England' (1941):

> One of the most important developments in England during the past twenty years has been the upward and downward extension of the middle class … To an increasing extent the rich and the poor read the same books, and they also see the same

films and listen to the same radio programmes. And the differences in their way of life have been diminished by the mass production of cheap clothes and improvements in housing … There are wide gradations of income but it is the same kind of life that is being lived at different levels, in labour-saving flats or council houses, along the concrete roads and in the naked democracy of the swimming-pools … This war, unless we are defeated, will wipe out most of the existing class privileges.

(pp. 87–9 [A])

Literary Overview

Introduction

The literature of the first third or so of the twentieth century is usually defined in terms of its thoroughgoing rejection of the cultural values, attitudes and practices of the immediately preceding Victorian age – or at least of those aspects of the age that had come to stand for a 'Victorianism' defined, among other things, by hypocrisy and puritanical narrow-mindedness. Reaction against such Victorianism had been gathering pace since at least the 1880s, but after Queen Victoria's death reaction became outright rebellion as a new age of scepticism and searching critique began to assert itself and all the assumed Victorian verities were challenged and questioned. Indeed, this questioning spirit is perhaps the outstanding characteristic of early twentieth-century literature, and it is a characteristic that was clearly acknowledged at the time, as reflected in the subtitle of one of the earliest literary-critical surveys of the period, by A. C. Ward: *Twentieth-Century Literature 1901–1925: The Age of Interrogation* (1928). Interestingly, the sub-title was dropped for subsequent revised editions of this popular book as the years covered by the survey lengthened to include the 1930s, 1940s and early 1950s, but even then Ward's introduction continued to stress what he saw as the determining aspect of early twentieth-century literature:

> From 1901 to 1925 English literature was directed by mental attitudes, moral ideals, and spiritual values at almost the opposite extreme from the attitudes, ideals, and values governing Victorian literature. The old certainties were certainties no longer. Everything was held to be open to question: everything – from the nature of the Deity to the construction of verse-forms.
>
> (*Twentieth-Century Literature 1901–1950*, pp. 1–2 [Bii])

The wars of the period inevitably added impetus and edge to anti-Victorian critique, and if the experience and consciousness of war, with all the ramifications of its newly realised potential for destruction, was an all-pervasive feature of the history of the early twentieth century, so too was it an all-pervasive feature of the literature of the period. Especially after 1914 (although the Boer War should not be forgotten), war itself supplied the direct and indirect subject matter for innumerable literary texts, but the shock of mass mechanised warfare – and all that it meant for civilisation – also helped to engender both radically new forms of writing and a type of discursive warfare among writers and critics themselves as to what should be the appropriate literary response to this brave new world of modernity. The resulting literary experiments and debates (also galvanised, as mentioned earlier, by developments in science, philosophy, psychology and the visual and other arts) gave rise to an extraordinarily rich and diverse range of writings, and this has meant that there is still no entirely settled 'map' of the literature of the period. For some writers, even towards the end of the period, it was effectively 'business as usual' where, although issues may well have changed, the tried and tested techniques of the Victorians would still more or less suffice. For others, nothing short of a literary revolution would do, not just in subject matter, but also in form, style and technique. Markets changed and certain forms such as the triple-decker novel soon disappeared, but more significant than any single change in itself was the fact of a general diversification of market forces which allowed comfortably for both continuity *and* radical experimentation and innovation.

In the second half of the twentieth century, the standard model of literary-critical classification

Modernism

Modernism is a complex and contested label within literary studies and some critics now prefer to talk of disparate 'modernisms' rather than of one overarching 'modernism'. It is a loose retrospective label which, though used much earlier, only came into regular use in literary studies in the 1960s, and there was never any single 'movement' or grouping of writers who actually identified themselves as modernists. In fact, in a rather circular fashion, the term tends to encompass a range of *other* discrete literary and artistic movements (or tendencies) whose various elements together help to define what we mean by modernism. These movements include naturalism, symbolism, imagism, futurism, cubism, vorticism, expressionism and surrealism – and, in the light of such a list, it is useful to bear in mind a well-known description of modernism as 'an appallingly explosive fusion' of many different and often contradictory trends (Malcolm Bradbury and James McFarlane, 'The Name and Nature of Modernism', in Bradbury and McFarlane (eds.), *Modernism*, p. 48 [Bii]). English-language modernism is usually defined as the experimental and innovative literature of the period roughly between 1890 and 1939, and, traditionally, critics have emphasised *formal* or technical experimentation over newness of theme or content (although form and content are not always easy to disentangle: are modernist novels innovative because they foreground psychology and sexuality as themes or because they develop new techniques for doing so?). For some critics, modernism (or 'high modernism') has meant only James Joyce and a handful of other radical innovators such as Ezra Pound, T. S. Eliot, Virginia Woolf and Dorothy Richardson, while others have a more expansive view of the term and apply it to a much wider range of writers (and across a broader period).

for these years, especially in the field of fiction, has been one which identifies two major trends or modes of writing, defined principally by their different stylistic and technical features (though also to some extent by their subject matter): experimental modernism on the one hand and a more or less traditional social realism on the other.

This model certainly has merit and is particularly useful as a means of discriminating between *general* trends of writing, especially at the modal extremes; but, apart from a few outstanding examples at those extremes, once one begins to study specific individual works and individual writers, any absolute distinction along these lines becomes difficult to sustain: many 'modernists' still rely quite heavily on traditional techniques of realism, and many 'realists' incorporate elements which elsewhere would be described as modernistic. Moreover, definitions of modernism and realism have been frequently contested anyway, especially over recent years, so while the broad modernist/realist distinction is still important and has general currency in literary studies, it is useful to approach it with a critically open mind.

The literature of the 1930s is often considered separately from that of the earlier twentieth century as representing a general reversion to traditional modes of realist writing in response to a highly politicised decade which seemed to many writers to demand a 'literature of commitment' that could engage directly, even didactically, with major social issues. But here, too, there is a danger of oversimplifying matters, as the earlier decades also had their own socially committed literature in, for example, the works of H. G. Wells and George Bernard Shaw, and even in the thirties such work was itself by no means homogeneous or lacking in formal inventiveness. Moreover, more obviously experimental modernist writing clearly continued throughout this decade, too, in the work of writers such as Dylan Thomas, David Jones and, most famously, James Joyce, whose *Finnegans Wake* (1939) is often considered the apogee of modernism. It can be admitted that the predominant literary tendency of the thirties was one which sought common ground with the masses rather than the individualistic epiphanies typically associated with modernism, but modernistic voices and visions left their mark too.

Continuities, Influences and Innovations

Late-Victorian literature had already begun to question Victorianism in no uncertain fashion. Even as early as 1872, Samuel Butler, influenced like many of his contemporaries by Darwinian and related thought, had comprehensively satirised the values of his age in his anti-Utopian novel *Erewhon* (an anagram for 'nowhere'). Butler's attack on Victorian hypocrisies continued into the twentieth century with *Erewhon Revisited* (1901) and, perhaps most memorably, with his autobiographical novel, *The Way of All Flesh* (published posthumously in 1903, though begun much earlier); and the attack was consolidated and diversified in roughly that same scope of years by the works of several other notable writers such as George Meredith, George Gissing, Oscar Wilde, Olive Schreiner, Thomas Hardy, George Moore, Sarah Grand and George Egerton (Mary Chavelita Dunne). These writers provide one important immediate background to early twentieth-century literature, as well as a literal line of continuity, given that some of them survived into the new century and influenced other, younger writers. Their importance is principally related to their criticism of society and their advanced views on religion, morality, sexuality and gender, rather than to any major innovations of form or technique, although, for example, the strikingly proto-modernistic form of Schreiner's *The Story of an African Farm* (1883) should be noted, along with the channelling of elements of French naturalism into the English novel by Gissing and Moore.

More important for long-term literary innovation were the key transitional figures of the period, Henry James (1843–1916), W. B. Yeats (1865–1939) and G. B. Shaw (1856–1950). None of these writers was English by birth (James was American, Yeats and Shaw Irish), but each of them, within their own generic spheres, played a major role in the development of English literature as it moved from the nineteenth into the twentieth century.

Changes in the world of British theatre were slow-moving in the period we are considering, and one might argue, from our present vantage point, that the general literary and artistic ferment of these decades did not impact on serious drama as forcefully as it did on fiction and poetry, and that it was not until later in the twentieth century that any real sense of innovation made its mark in this field. However, looking at Shaw's career in its contemporary context, it becomes clear that he precipitated major changes in the nature of dramatic writing and in the expectations of audiences as to what the theatre could or should do. Shaw came to London from Dublin in 1876 and worked for a time as a journalist and a music and drama critic. In the 1880s, he became an ardent socialist and a leading member of the Fabian Society, and he wrote several unsuccessful novels before turning to the theatre in the 1890s. He was strongly influenced by the Norwegian playwright, Henrik Ibsen (1828–1906), particularly by his realism, his direct dramatisation of ideas and his bold treatment of important social issues. At a time when serious theatre was dominated by relatively conservative drawing-room drama and the 'well-made play', Shaw felt that Ibsen's was just the sort of drama needed to revitalise the British theatre and to bring it up to date with developments elsewhere in Europe. Shaw championed Ibsen's work in Britain in his polemical study, *The Quintessence of Ibsenism* (1891), and this also effectively served as a blueprint for his own play-writing career in subsequent decades. Starting with *Widowers' Houses* (1892), a critique of slum landlordism, he adapted Ibsen's dramatic model for British audiences to produce his own uniquely witty brand of socially engaged theatre over the course of some thirty full-length plays, including *Mrs Warren's Profession* (written 1893, produced 1902), *Arms and the Man* (1894), *Man and Superman* (1903) and *Major Barbara* (1905). Shaw's aim in his plays was to shock audiences out of their conventional views and attitudes and to encourage them to think rationally and critically, without preconceived ideas, about all aspects of their society, and particularly about its inequalities and injustices. To do this, Shaw used all the theatrical devices available to him, including witty dialogue, clever stagecraft, plot surprises and sudden reversals, but he became known particularly for his use of unorthodox characters and scenarios, his use of paradox in speech and situation and, above all, for his direct presentation of ideas in the carefully weighed speeches and discussions of his characters. Among other things, although his characters are often criticised for being merely mouthpieces for his ideas, Shaw shifted the focus of attention in drama from conventionally well-made plots to the dynamic interrelations between character, speech, action and ideas. Moreover, for all that he was an avowed realist, even in his earliest plays he experimented freely with non-realistic elements where he felt these could help to convey his message, and, in this, he has often been seen to anticipate the techniques of later modern dramatists such as Brecht and Bond, while his use of witty argument and paradoxical humour could also be seen to anticipate certain elements in Beckett and Pinter. Finally, we should also note that Shaw was one of the first writers for the theatre to exploit the potential (commercial, artistic and didactic) of publishing his plays as texts to be read as serious literature in their own right – and this too had the effect of raising the profile of drama and of altering people's perceptions of its function.

Henry James was born in America but settled in England in 1876, eventually becoming a naturalised British citizen in 1915, a year before his death. In their broad social realism and their detailed depiction of the mores and manners of polite society, his novels exhibit many of the traits of the conventional nineteenth-century novel, and this applies even to some of the works he wrote in the twentieth century. However, James's highly self-conscious concern with style and form, his experiments with narration, his interest in psychology, and his fascination with the involved complexities of consciousness, perception and interpretation make his work also acutely modern and directly relevant to an understanding of how the art of fiction, particularly in its modernist line of development, began to change in the twentieth century. All the features just mentioned are closely interrelated, but the fundamental questions of narration and consciousness lie at the heart of James's importance as an innovator in fiction.

Especially in his later phase, with novels such as *What Maisie Knew* (1897), *The Wings of a Dove* (1902), *The Ambassadors* (1903) and *The Golden Bowl* (1904), James made his most important advances with the refinement of a technique of narration which, while still using a third-person narrator, limited the narrative point of view almost totally to one focal character or 'centre of consciousness'. In this technique, all narrative information is filtered through the eyes and mind of the focal character without any obvious intervention of the narrator, thus creating the illusion that the story is telling itself, with events unfolding before us just as they are perceived and made sense of by the central character. The shaping and organising influence of the narrator is still there, of course, but it is not immediately evident because the narrator remains wholly detached and impersonal, and because the reader is made to feel so close to the perceiving centre of consciousness. Part of the beauty of the technique, then, is that it avoids the evident artifice and intrusiveness of traditional third-person omniscient narration without becoming entirely constrained by the often similarly evident artifice of first-person narration. Equally important for future developments in fiction was that, by foregrounding the workings of consciousness, the technique merges almost imperceptibly into the very subject matter of James's fiction, in the sense that the structuring consciousness of the principal character to all intents and purposes *becomes* the story.

The processes of consciousness, the structuring of perception, meaning and identity, became for James not only an informing principle of narration but the principal theme of his late narratives; and it would become a principal theme too for the novelists who followed him, just as it had already become a growing area of interest more generally in society with the rise of psychology and psychoanalysis. In seeking a new psychological dimension of realism in the depiction of the workings of consciousness, Henry James pushed fictional realism to a limit at which no further development was really possible without moving into the sort of experimentation associated with later novelists such as Dorothy Richardson, James Joyce and Virginia Woolf. James had clearly paved the way for these modernists and, appropriately enough, it was his psychologist brother, William James, who, in his *Principles of*

Psychology (1890), coined the phrase by which *their* fictional technique would become known: 'stream of consciousness'.

In his youth and early adulthood, W. B. Yeats was strongly influenced by the resurgence of Irish nationalism in the campaign for Home Rule and in the Irish Literary Revival of the 1880s, of which Yeats soon became a leading member – and for most of his life he was directly involved in some way or other with Irish cultural (and, to a lesser extent, political) nationalism. The title of his collection of stories and anecdotes, *The Celtic Twilight* (1893), became a byword for the supposed romance and mysticism of Celtic culture, and, throughout his career, he would draw extensively on the ancient folklore and mythology of Ireland, informing this also with his interests in theosophy, spiritualism and the esoteric. For the first decade of the twentieth century, moreover, Yeats, with others, was heavily involved with the setting up and running of an Irish national theatre, establishing it in 1904 at the Abbey Theatre, Dublin. Yeats here promoted Irish subject matter and poetic over realistic drama, and he wrote and staged his own plays, most notably *Cathleen ni Houlihan* (1902). Following a brief period of disillusion over Irish independence, Yeats (like many others), was drawn firmly back to the cause by the Easter Rising of 1916 and its brutal aftermath, and he would later go on to serve as a senator in the Irish Free State.

To simplify a hugely complicated and varied career, it is possible to see Yeats's development as a poet progressing in three broad phases (roughly 1886–99, 1900–18, 1919–39) – from a lush late-Romanticism, deeply imbued with Celticism, aestheticism, symbolism, and esoteric doctrine (e.g. *The Wind among the Reeds*, 1899), through a transitional period of proto-modernistic austerity and impersonality of style (e.g., *Responsibilities*, 1914), to a final phase of fully developed modernism, where previous elements of his art feed into a highly complex, self-defining system of mythological thought built on an often obscure visionary symbolism (e.g., *The Tower*, 1928). As Linda Williams elaborates:

> He had begun his writing career as a writer of the Victorian *fin de siècle*, and ended it as a key figure of modernist anti-decadence. His early poems are infused with an elegiac quality and peopled with mythological and heroic figures from an 'old Ireland' of ephemeral, supernatural beauty … This is Yeats the 'last romantic'.
>
> But Yeats is also arguably the first modernist of poetry, his feeling of alienation from his time strengthening his later apocalyptic poems, which 'sing amid our uncertainty' ('Per Amica Silentia Lunae'; 1917). The cultural crisis of the early 20th century turned the task of re-thinking the limits and drives of language into one of almost world-historic importance for many poets, impatient that the untenable realist notion of a shared common experience between writer and reader be exposed. If Yeats's early work is marked by a bygone aesthetic, and is metrically and syntactically conventional, his later work – particularly that written from *The Wild Swans at Coole* (1919) until his death in 1939 – would strongly assert his modernity.
>
> ('"Rule and Energy in View": the Poetry of Modernity', in Williams (ed.), *The Twentieth Century*, pp. 65–6 [Bii])

In his pioneering use of what T. S. Eliot called 'the mythical method', in his experiments with impersonal voices or 'masks' for the poetic persona, and in his striving for an organically self-contained art of vision and symbolism, Yeats mapped out

The Mythical Method

In 1923, T. S. Eliot wrote a short essay on James Joyce's novel *Ulysses* (1922), commenting in particular on Joyce's use of Homer's *Odyssey* to provide a structural background and counterpoint to his contemporary narrative. In identifying this 'mythical method', Eliot struck a keynote of the period and made a seminal statement about modernism. What is often overlooked in the piece is that Eliot picked out Yeats as probably the first writer to experiment with the method.

> In using the myth, in manipulating a continuous parallel between contemporaneity and antiquity, Mr Joyce is pursuing a method which others must pursue after him ... It is simply a way of controlling, of ordering, of giving a shape and a significance to the immense panorama of futility and anarchy which is contemporary history. It is a method already adumbrated by Mr Yeats, and of the need for which I believe Mr Yeats to have been the first contemporary to be conscious. It is a method for which the horoscope is auspicious. Psychology ... ethnology, and *The Golden Bough* have concurred to make possible what was impossible even a few years ago. Instead of narrative method, we may now use the mythical method. It is, I seriously believe, a step toward making the modern world possible for art.
>
> ('*Ulysses*, Order, and Myth', first printed in *The Dial* (1923),
> reprinted in Ellman and Fiedelson (eds.), *The Modern Tradition*, pp. 679–81 [A])

much of the terrain of modernist literature and his development represents almost the complete cycle of the evolution of modernist poetry from its nineteenth-century antecedents. We see in it also a more general evolution of literary sensibility as related to historical context in the way Yeats carried forward and transformed into modern terms the late-Victorian critique of urban industrialism and materialism.

Modes of Production and Consumption: the Literary Marketplace

As touched on earlier, economic and social factors began significantly to change patterns of cultural production and consumption at the end of the nineteenth century. Of most relevance to literature (and fiction in particular) were changes in publishing practices and increased levels of literacy, education and disposable income among the general population. As paper became much cheaper on the world market, as faster and more efficient printing presses were developed and refined, and as distributive, retail, marketing and advertising networks were consolidated and expanded, so books and other printed materials became easier and cheaper to produce and to sell in large quantities, at lower prices. More people than ever before had sufficient disposable income to buy consumer goods and, with key educational reforms and developments from 1870 onwards, more people than ever before had the ability and the inclination to read and to buy books, periodicals, magazines and newspapers. There was a new reading public, vastly increased and vastly more varied than in the past, representing a potentially massive new demand for reading material of all kinds; and there was a new set of economic conditions which meant that publishers could meet that demand, especially if, as they now did, they broke with the big circulating libraries such as Charles Mudie's (see Chapter 5, pp. 393–5) and distributed more books directly themselves at a price people could afford. As the circulating libraries had had a monopoly on the market for new fiction since the mid-nineteenth century, they had been able largely to dictate their own terms to publishers (and through them to authors), and to establish a set of relatively rigid conventions as to the standard form and content of the books circulated (as with the 'triple-decker' novel, for example). Often, too, they would act as self-appointed guardians of public morality and censor or ban works they disapproved of (or which they felt might offend the public and damage business). Now, however, publishers could afford to negotiate more freely with authors as to the type of books they might publish, and the supply side of the market was increasingly free to diversify in direct interaction with consumer demand.

Economic factors are always in a complex relationship with other cultural developments, of course, and the above changes came about also as a response to intellectual and artistic pressures coming from writers themselves. While the previous chapter has clearly demonstrated the richness and complexity of Victorian culture, it is useful here to contrast what was nevertheless a *relatively* unified culture with the rapidly diversifying – or, some might say, fragmenting – culture of the late nineteenth and early twentieth centuries, and to see in this contrast some of the reasons behind the literary realignments we are discussing. In mainstream Victorian society, one could say that there was a broad consensus on Christian morality and on the existing social and political order. This meant, among other things, that Victorian writers and readers could largely assume a common culture and a shared language of values, attitudes and cultural reference. Mudie's and the other circulating libraries played their part in sustaining this broad consensus by promoting writers and works that tended to reflect and reinforce the perceived standards of the dominant culture. However, as those standards and that culture began to be questioned in the last quarter of the nineteenth century, writers began also to challenge the literary conventions that had become associated with them (at least partly because of the circulating libraries). The interrogative spirit discussed above, along with a new sense of the relativity and complexity of life, led serious writers more and more to express their frustration with the artificial constraints placed upon their art by the currently dominant system of publication and circulation. George Moore made an important intervention on behalf of writers in 1885 when he published a withering attack on the circulating libraries, *Literature as Nurse, or Circulating Morals*, and when, in the same year, he had a new novel, *The Mummer's Wife*, issued in one volume by Vizetelly, the English publisher of Emile Zola. This was a direct challenge to the convention – closely associated with the circulating libraries – of initially publishing new novels in three separate, expensively priced volumes; and, in fact, it sounded the death-knell of the triple-decker novel, as other English publishers soon followed Vizetelly's example, and this new trend then undermined the monopoly of the circulating libraries generally.

The demise of the triple-decker novel neatly illustrates how economic and artistic factors combined at this time to bring about change both in the literary marketplace and in literary form. One of the main complaints about the triple-decker had been that it encouraged a lot of padding and the use of stock devices. Now, however, with the possibility of single-volume publication, novelists gained a greater degree of free-dom over the length and structure of their work and this contributed to a developing trend towards shorter, often more poetic or symbolic fiction. Writers also gained greater freedom to experiment with style, to deal with unconventional topics and to express unconventional views. They were not entirely free in this respect, of course, as publishers still had to consider the censors and public opinion, but publishers, too, were now freer to take their own commercial risks, and they were generally happy to support a greater range of writing and a continuing diversification of the market.

As should be clear by now, such diversification helps to explain a good deal about the changes in literature from the Victorian period to the Edwardian and beyond. It went hand in hand with new freedoms of literary form and expression; but it also represented a fundamental change in the position of the writer and in the relation-ship between writers and readers. The relatively stable Victorian consensus gave its major writers their own relatively stable sense of moral or intellectual authority at the heart of public opinion, as framed by institutions like the circulating libraries; with the breakdown of that consensus and the institutions which supported it, how-ever, and with the rise of a much more complex and segmented society, it was rather the *lack* of shared values and experience that began to define literary relations, and writers inevitably lost some of their authority as they lost their sense of a unified audience and of a common language they could confidently share with such an audi-ence. Twentieth-century writers would be freer to develop their own personal artistic visions – and modernist writers did so with a vengeance – but they were destined to become more isolated, more detached from their readership, and to lose the public prestige and influence of their eminent Victorian predecessors. From now on, rather than appealing to a single, known (or imagined) audience, they would have to take their chance on the open market, appealing possibly to many different audiences, possibly to none.

Shaw might have exploited the expanding market for novel-sized books by pub-lishing his play-scripts, supplemented by long prefaces and other material, but oth-erwise, as a performance art, drama was subject to different market factors from those applying to fiction and poetry. There was no nationally subsidised theatre at this time and, apart from music hall and variety, most dramatic activity at the start of the century was concentrated in a small number of commercial theatres in London. Plays had to be popular to be profitable and there was little incentive for theatre managers to experiment with new techniques or with controversial subject matter that might alienate their predominantly middle-class audiences. In the 1890s there had been some efforts to provide outlets for intellectually and artistically more challenging forms of drama – as, for example, in the case of J. T. Grein's Independent Theatre, which staged Ibsen's *Ghosts* in 1891 and Shaw's first play, *Widowers' Houses*, in 1892; and, at the start of the twentieth century, the Irish theatre movement in Dublin and the birth of a repertory movement in England (which began to spread nationally from London's Court Theatre and Manchester's Midland and Gaiety Theatres) brought some decentralisation of theatrical activity and some loosening of the artistic constraints associated with conventional commercial theatre. However, despite a certain dramatic revival in the 1890s and 1900s with the emergence of real-istic social-problem plays by Shaw and others, and despite the impact of Shaw him-self, the theatre in England remained relatively conservative throughout our period and developments in drama were modest as compared to the radical changes afoot in the other genres.

Forms, Genres and Styles

We have already seen that critics traditionally identify modernism and realism as the two main lines of stylistic development within this period. In the past, and for some still today, there has also often been an implied value judgement in this division. From one point of view, experimental modernist writing has been seen as the genu-inely new, original and authentic art of the century while realist art has been consid-ered as simply a plodding continuation of worthy but outmoded nineteenth-century forms. From another point of view, modernist art has been considered obscure, elitist and out of touch with everyday experience, while realist art has been embraced (in the thirties, for example) for its direct relevance to people's lives in striving to pres-ent an accurate and truthful representation of historical and political actuality. Such value judgements have become increasingly problematic as the precise meanings of 'modernism' and 'realism' have been questioned and modified and, in particular, as the appropriate grouping of writers and works within each camp has been debated. Nevertheless, as a broad categorisation of stylistic tendencies at least, it can be help-ful still to distinguish between these two 'modes of modern writing', to use David Lodge's terms (*The Modes of Modern Writing* [Ci]) – the one typified by poetic density and an extensive use of metaphor (or imaginative analogy), and the other typified by a striving for transparency of meaning and a preference for the use of metonymy (or imagery linked by direct logical connection – as in 'crown' used for 'queen').

Lodge helpfully elaborates on the distinction between modernism and realism as follows:

> Modernism turned its back on the traditional idea of art as imitation and substituted the idea of art as an autonomous activity. One of its most characteristic slogans was Walter Pater's assertion, 'All art constantly aspires to the condition of music' – music being, of all the arts, the most purely formal, the least referential … The fundamen-tal principle of aesthetics before the modern era was that art imitates life … but by the end of that [nineteenth] century it had been turned on its head. 'Life imitates art', declared Oscar Wilde, meaning that we compose the reality we perceive by mental structures that are cultural, not natural in origin, and that it is art which is most likely to change and renew those structures when they become inadequate or unsat-isfying … [T]raditional realism … does not aspire to the condition of music; rather it aspires to the condition of history … It regards literature as the communication of a reality that exists prior to and independent of the act of communication.
>
> ('Modernism, Anti-Modernism and Postmodernism', pp. 5–6 [Ci])

In the work of archetypal modernists such as Yeats, Eliot and Pound, modernism produced a 'poetry that distinguishes itself from ordinary referential discourse by violently dislocated syntax and bewildering shifts of register … in which there are no narrative or logical climaxes but instead vibrant, suggestive, ambiguous images and symbols' ('Modernism, Anti-Modernism and Postmodernism', p. 6); and parts of this description apply equally to the modernist novels of writers such as Conrad, Woolf, Lawrence and Joyce; for, as Lodge continues in the same essay:

> Pursuing reality out of the daylight world of empirical common sense into the individual's consciousness, or subconscious, and ultimately to the collective unconscious, discarding the traditional narrative structures of chronological succession and logical cause-and-effect, as being false to the essentially chaotic and problematic nature of subjective experience, the [modernist] novelist finds himself relying more and more on literary strategies and devices that belong to poetry, and specifically to Symbolist poetry, rather than to prose: allusion to literary models and mythical archetypes, for instance, and the repetition of images, symbols, and other motifs – what E. M. Forster described, with another gesture towards music, as 'rhythm' in the novel.
>
> (p. 6)

In addition to those mentioned above, other important British modernists in either poetry or fiction, or both, include Richard Aldington, W. H. Auden, Elizabeth Bowen, Hilda Doolittle (H. D.), Ford Madox Ford, E. M. Forster, T. E. Hulme, David Jones, Percy Wyndham Lewis, Hugh MacDiarmid, Katherine Mansfield, Charlotte Mew, Jean Rhys, Dorothy Richardson, May Sinclair, Edith Sitwell and Dylan Thomas.

On the predominantly realist front, the most important writers of fiction of the period are Arnold Bennett, Ivy Compton-Burnett, Rudyard Kipling, John Galsworthy, Graham Greene, W. Somerset Maugham, George Orwell and H. G. Wells. The satirical novels of Aldous Huxley and Evelyn Waugh, while technically closer to the realist tradition, also have affinities with modernism in their subversive view of modern society, while the fiction of Christopher Isherwood could be said to have begun in the modernist mode but then developed towards realism. The growth of a mass market for fiction meant, perhaps above all, a growth in popular genres such as the family saga, light comedy, detective fiction and the adventure thriller, and some of the most widely read novelists of the time were John Buchan, Agatha Christie, Compton Mackenzie, Hugh Walpole, P. G. Wodehouse and Dorothy L. Sayers.

In poetry, it is more difficult to categorise writers definitively as 'realist', and few writers of the age were not influenced by some of the aspects associated with modernism. However, poets like Kipling, Hardy, Robert Bridges, W. H. Davies, Walter de la Mare and John Masefield stand out most strongly in contrast to the modernists for largely continuing to use metrical verse forms rather than free verse. The war-poets – for example Wilfred Owen, Siegfried Sassoon, Isaac Rosenberg, Edmund Blunden – and the poets of the thirties such as C. Day-Lewis, Louis MacNeice and Stephen Spender (Auden is usually seen as part of this group, too) tend to be seen in categories of their own largely defined by the traumatic experiences of war on the one hand and the politically charged climate of the thirties on the other. As this suggests, despite many modernistic technical innovations in their poetry, both these groups clearly aspire to a relatively direct representation of the felt history of their time – in Lodge's terms, they aspire to the condition of history rather than of music – and they can thus be counterposed, at least to some extent, against modernism.

In the theatre, Shaw is a transitional figure between the nineteenth and twentieth centuries partly because he is also ambiguously positioned on the modernist/realist divide. Clearly, his discursive didacticism places him firmly on the realist side, while, as we have seen, his iconoclasm and his technical innovations place him closer to the modernists. Even so, stylistically, it would be difficult to recognise Shaw in the characterisation of modernism just given, and this reinforces the sense that in this period English drama was largely distinct from poetry and fiction in continuing, despite Shaw, to be largely dominated by realist or naturalist modes, as best represented by the serious social plays of Henry Arthur Jones, Arthur Wing Pinero, John Galsworthy and Harley Granville-Barker. Comic drama and sentimental and musical fantasy were well represented in the period by the plays of J. M. Barrie, W. Somerset Maugham and Noel Coward, but, apart from Shaw, the few serious departures from the dominant realism in the English theatre came in the thirties. J. B. Priestley experimented with time and expressionist modes in plays such as *Time and the Conways* (1937) and *Johnson Over Jordan* (1939), and T. S. Eliot carried over his poetic modernism into the theatre with his verse dramas *Murder in the Cathedral* (1935) and *The Family Reunion* (1939), while W. H. Auden and Christopher Isherwood together also experimented with verse dramas such as *The Dog Beneath the Skin* (1936). A more significant dramatic dialogue between modernism and realism took place in Ireland from the start of the century in developments at the Abbey Theatre in Dublin, where a cross-fertilisation of modes is evident in the continuum from the symbolist verse dramas of Yeats and A. E. (George Russell), through to the more realistic romances of J. M. Synge – *Riders to the Sea* (1904) and *The Playboy of the Western World* (1907) – and the grittier social realism of Sean O'Casey in his famous trilogy *The Shadow of a Gunman* (1923), *Juno and the Paycock* (1924) and *The Plough and the Stars* (1926). Interestingly, too, O'Casey then moved towards non-naturalistic techniques in his later plays, experimenting with expressionism for example in his 1928 play, *The Silver Tassie*.

Texts and Issues

The First World War

Given the number of major conflicts that took place within the space of these forty years (including the Boer War, the Anglo-Irish War, the Irish Civil War, and the Spanish Civil War) and the fact that they encompassed the First World War and the build-up to the Second World War, it would be difficult to overestimate the impact of war – and all the ramifications of war – on the culture and literature of this time. The First World War in particular represented a shattering end to the nineteenth century's optimistic faith in human progress, and there was a permeating consciousness of the war as a defining reality for modern civilisation. As D. H. Lawrence suggested in 1924, everywhere, it seemed, 'the dead hand of the war lay like a corpse decomposing' (*St Mawr*, p. 90 [A]). Although Lawrence was a non-combatant, his works are symptomatic of that permeating consciousness, especially as it grappled with the moral and spiritual implications of the underlying tendencies which had led to and supported the war and its mass mechanised destruction. In a famous chapter of his novel *Kangaroo* (1923), entitled 'The Nightmare', Lawrence reflected on what he saw as a fundamental debasement of humanity brought about by the war and by the bellicose attitudes it engendered: 'It was in 1915 the old world ended. In the winter of 1915–16 the spirit of the old London collapsed, the city, in some way, perished, perished from being a heart of the world, and became a vortex of broken passions, lusts, hopes, fears, and horrors. The integrity of London collapsed, and the genuine debasement began, the unspeakable baseness of the press and the public voice, the reign of that bloated ignominy, John Bull' (p. 216; *John Bull* was a jingoistic periodical of the time). Lawrence's use here of the word 'vortex' is possibly ironic in its echo of the avant-garde art movement, vorticism, which celebrated the creative energy of modernity, often through expressionistic depictions of machinery and industry; but the 'vortex of broken passions, lusts, hopes, fears, and horrors' also effectively out-lines much of the psychological terrain explored by Lawrence and other modernist writers in their artistic representations of how human relationships had internalised the conditions of war-torn modernity.

The focus on internal factors – on the ways in which the underlying *forms* of life had influenced and been influenced by the war – also reflects a central tenet of modernism: that form embodies meaning and can often reveal underlying truths about life more effectively than explicit statements or descriptions can. And, indeed,

6.7 'No comfort at all': war widow, 1917.

modernist art dealt with the war as much by the implications of its fragmented forms and its embedded symbolism as by the explicit logic of its surface meanings. T. S. Eliot's *The Waste Land* (1922) is probably the pre-eminent example of this, but Lawrence's work, too, is again symptomatic. His outstanding modernist novel, *Women in Love* (1920), was composed largely contemporaneously with the First World War and it clearly registers the pressures of war in its fractured episodic structure, its sudden outbursts of violence, and its highly wrought language of emotional and sexual conflict – and yet it contains not a single explicit reference to the war. In fact, Lawrence consciously excluded such reference as his aim was not to record the external circumstances of war, but rather to analyse its 'internal' consequences for the individual and society, and to embody these in the internal dynamics of the text. As he explained in the separately published 'Foreword to *Women in Love*' (1920), 'I should wish the time to remain unfixed, so that the bitterness of the war may be taken for granted in the characters' (*Women in Love*, pp. 485–6 [A]); and, as Mark Kinkead-Weekes further explains in his introduction to the novel:

> *Women in Love* is … a war novel, even though its society is apparently at peace and its date left deliberately vague. Uncovered in the depths of all the characters is violence, threatening to destroy the self and others, and this is because the novel was written at a time when all over Europe people had thrown themselves – at first with enthusiasm – into the First World War, and in that most terrible year of Verdun and the Somme, 1916, when slaughter reached an appalling peak that had never been known before … [The novel's] art, in language and form, must be such as can render and explore violence, disintegration, deadly excess.
>
> (*Women in Love*, pp. xv–xvi [A])

Almost every scene of the novel contains examples of such violence, disintegration and deadly excess and, as other critics have noted, much of Lawrence's language quite directly evokes images of battle and war. Even the apparently innocuous activity of throwing stones into a pond is thus linguistically transformed into a symbolic enactment of war's shattering of society, as Jack Stewart points out in his analysis of Birkin's stoning of the moon's reflection in the chapter 'Moony' (*The Vital Art of D. H. Lawrence*, p. 87 [Ci]).

There was of course a mass of literature in the period which dealt much more directly with the First World War, much of it written by combatants who wanted – or needed – to express their feelings about the war and to record something of the day-to-day realities of their experience. The earliest poetic responses of many of the best-known war-poets – Brooke, Julian Grenfell, Sassoon, Owen, Rosenberg – were written in a heroic mode of patriotism and idealistic enthusiasm for a war seen as an opportunity for the country's youth to demonstrate its valour in a self-evidently righteous cause. Even Sassoon, soon to become one of the war's most bitter critics, excoriating the authorities and the officer class for their incompetence, and throwing into question the whole purpose of the war, even he could write, in mid-1915:

The anguish of the earth absolves our eyes
Till beauty shines in all that we can see.
War is our scourge, yet war has made us wise,
And, fighting for our freedom, we are free.

…
We are the happy legion, for we know
Time's but a golden wind that shakes the grass.

…
What need we more, my comrades and my brothers?

('Absolution')

For most, this heroic mode did not survive the first large battles of the war, where previously unimaginable numbers of lives were lost for no immediately obvious gains. At best, one might say that the heroic mode of war poetry was later transmuted into an elegiac memorialising of lost comrades and of the courage and camaraderie shown by ordinary fighting men in the face of extreme adversity; but for many of the soldier-poets such as Sassoon, the dominant tone inevitably became one of disillusioned protest and bitter satire:

'Good-morning, good-morning!' the General said
When we met him last week on our way to the line.
Now the soldiers he smiled at are most of 'em dead,
And we're cursing his staff for incompetent swine.
'He's a cheery old card,' grunted Harry to Jack
As they slogged up to Arras with rifle and pack.

But he did for them both with his plan of attack.

(Siegfried Sassoon, 'The General', 1917)

For almost all the poets, though, there clearly developed a need to bear witness, as simply and sincerely as possible, to the devastating loss of life, and to the terrible pity or tragedy of war; and it is really this sort of poem, usually lyrical or dramatic in form, which has come down to us as the most memorable and moving testament of that time:

Move him into the sun –
Gently its touch awoke him once,
At home, whispering of fields half-sown.
Always it woke him, even in France,
Until this morning and this snow.
If anything might rouse him now
The kind old sun will know.

(Wilfred Owen, 'Futility', 1918)

The poetry of the war has been widely anthologised since the period of the war itself and is still widely studied in British schools, colleges and universities. It has therefore been influential in shaping popular cultural perceptions of the war and is likely to be fairly familiar to most readers. Novels about the war are less well known, however, despite the fact that a large number were published both during the war and throughout the post-war period, with a peak in 1928–30 during what became known as the war-books controversy. Around 172 war novels were published in Britain between 1914 and 1918, and, according to Martin Ceadel, 'Although most romanticized the war, not all did so: in particular, Henri Barbusse's *Under Fire* (1917), a translation of the novel published in Paris the previous year as *Le Feu*, was in many respects the prototype of the "realistic" trench novel … And, as the poet Edmund Blunden later noted, from 1917 there was a markedly more critical spirit in war-time literature' ('Pacifism and Collective Security', in Johnson (ed.), *Twentieth-Century Britain*, p. 225 [Bi]). H. G. Wells's *Mr Britling Sees It Through* (1916), though set mainly on the home front, might be added here as an unusually early example of a (partially) critical war novel.

In the first part of the 1920s, as people tried to put the trauma of war behind them, the output of war books diminished somewhat. However, as post-war disenchantment grew through the 1920s in the face of economic and international problems, and of the apparent failure of successive governments to build a land (and homes) 'fit for heroes', so people began more and more to doubt what they had been told about the war and to ask questions about why, and for what, so many people had lost their lives. This mood was given expression in C. E. Montague's critical polemic of 1922, *Disenchantment*, and it can also be seen reflected in Virginia Woolf's disturbing presentation of the shell-shocked Septimus Smith in her 1925 novel, *Mrs Dalloway*. The number of war novels thus started to creep up again in the mid-twenties. Eight such novels appeared in 1927 and ten in 1928, the tenth anniversary of the Armistice and 'an apt time for the war generation to take stock':

> The first of the successful war books was an elegantly understated memoir by Edmund Blunden, *Undertones of War*, which appeared in November 1928 … December 1928 saw the first production of R. C. Sheriff's play *Journey's End* (with Laurence Olivier in the lead). Victor Gollancz at once snapped up the text for publication; and the following month the play moved to the Savoy Theatre where it ran for 594 consecutive performances … [I]n January 1929 Erich Maria Remarque's *All Quiet on the Western Front* was published in book form in Germany … an English edition followed in March 1929.
>
> These books sold well: the *Publisher and Bookseller* announced at the end of 1929 that 'Sheriff's *Journey's End* was easily the most popular book throughout the year'; and … Remarque's English edition sold 300,000 copies in six months. These successes created a breakthrough which was soon exploited by a second wave of war books published in 1929–30 … twenty-five appeared in 1929, and thirty-six in 1930 … This second wave also reached the cinema where its impact was increased by the introduction of sound: in 1930, films of *All Quiet on the Western Front* and *Journey's End* were released, as well as other realistic war films such as the German director G. W. Pabst's *Westfront 1918*.
>
> (Martin Ceadel, 'Pacifism and Collective Security',
> in Johnson (ed.), *Twentieth-Century Britain*, pp. 230–2 [Bi])

Most of the war novels were so grittily realistic about life in the trenches that they came to be known as 'the latrine school of War-fiction' by some critics; and because they pulled no punches in their depiction either of the mud, blood and guts of warfare or of the often far from ideal behaviour of men and officers, they inevitably served to undermine any romantic notions about the heroic or noble nature of the war, even when they were not also openly critical of it, as many of them were – Richard Aldington's 'jazz novel', *Death of a Hero* (1929), being perhaps the most prominent example (Frederic Manning's *Her Privates We* (1930) and the memoirs of Robert

Graves, *Goodbye To All That* (1929), and Siegfried Sassoon, *Memoirs of an Infantry Officer* (1930), might also be mentioned in this light). Unsurprisingly, then, there was a strong reaction against these novels in nationalist sections of the press and among those who still believed that, in the broader scheme of things, Britain's involvement in the war had been necessary and honourable. Some more positive depictions of the war were produced – for example, Charles Edmonds's *A Subaltern's War* (1929) – and a lively public debate ensued. However, as A. C. Ward suggested in 1930 (*The Nineteen-Twenties*, pp. 145–9 [Bii]), this 'war books controversy' was not just an academic debate about the rights and wrongs of a war that was past and done – it also involved an opposition of principles of immediate relevance for the future, as much of the debate boiled down to fundamental oppositions between pacifism and militarism and between individualism and collectivism, issues which would become ever more pressing on both the domestic and the international front in the thirties. Interestingly, then, we see here an unusually direct example of literature engaged in dialogue with past, present and emerging historical contexts.

Two important modernist works which (like Lawrence's *Women in Love* and Woolf's *Mrs Dalloway*) are notable for their innovative narrative techniques and use of psychology, but which should certainly not be overlooked in any consideration of war literature, are Rebecca West's early Freudian study of shell-shock, *The Return of the Soldier* (1918) (significantly, adapted for stage in 1928), and Ford Madox Ford's tetralogy, *Parade's End* (1924–8), especially the middle two novels, *No More Parades* (1925) and *A Man Could Stand Up* (1926), both of which present powerful depictions of the experience of war at the battlefront.

The Position of Women

If war was one permeating issue of the period, so too was the different sort of combative struggle represented by the continued rise of feminism and the intensifying campaigns of the suffragist, suffragette and socialist movements for greater rights and freedoms for women. The 'New Woman' literature of the last part of the nineteenth century had already played a significant role in reflecting and advancing debates about women's issues. Now, in the first decades of the twentieth century, those debates themselves had come to constitute an integral part of the historical context within which all writers were working and it was inevitable that they would engage with those issues and debates in ever-more complex and varied ways.

As with the issue of war, though, a broad distinction can be made between realist works which more or less directly dramatised feminist and suffrage issues as part of their explicit subject matter – as in Elizabeth Robins's campaigning play *Votes for Women* (1907) and H. G. Wells's forthright portrayal of a New Woman and sometime suffragette, *Ann Veronica* (1909) – and modernist works which explored the nature, role and status of women more indirectly through poetic suggestion, symbolism or experimental narrative technique. The latter approach is exemplified in the finely crafted, lightly glancing stories of Katherine Mansfield, the stream-of-consciousness fiction of Dorothy Richardson, May Sinclair and Virginia Woolf, and the

Feminism and the Suffrage Movement

By the 1880s women's organizations had become an important element in the Labor movement. Working-class activists became particularly prominent in the Women's Cooperative Guild (founded in 1883), and went on to form the Women's Trade Union League, Women's Industrial Council, Women's Labour League and Fabian Women's Group. In the 1890s there was a massive surge in cross-class and cross-party feminist campaigns for full citizenship. By 1897 coordination of these organizations produced a federation, the National Union of Women's Suffrage Societies. The constitutionalists, under the leadership of Millicent Garrett Fawcett were termed 'suffragists'. More militant 'suffragettes', willing to take direct action, looked to Emmeline Pankhurst, who in 1903 founded the Women's Social and Political Union in Manchester …

World War I brought a lessening of suffragist activism because some feminists divided their time with supporting the peace campaign, while many concentrated on working for the war effort. In recognition of female patriotic support … [in February] 1918, British women over thirty with a property qualification were enfranchised. This partial success contributed to some lessening of urgency and the relative disunity over priorities which characterized the post-war women's movement. It faced an uphill task, for there was a strongly antifeminist backlash. Despite the 1919 Sex Disqualification Removal Act, a marriage bar was introduced in many professions to rid the workplace of the women who had replaced men during the war. Women were now expected to choose between a career and marriage …

By the mid-1920s it was apparent that there was a clear divergence in the British women's movement between old equal rights feminism and new welfare feminism … The former … concentrated on political emancipation and entry to the professions. But the National Union of Women's Suffrage Societies now changed its name to the National Union of Societies for Equal Citizenship and, led by Eleanor Rathbone, aimed for a broader appeal by focusing on women's particular needs in their domestic role … They campaigned for family allowances, birth control advice, and the raising of the age of consent. Achievements of the decade included the Equal Franchise Act (1928), the Matrimonial Causes Act (1923) which equalized divorce, and the Guardianship of Infants Act (1925) which allowed divorced women custody of their children.

(Caroline Franklin, 'Feminism 1890–1940' in Poplawski (ed.),
Encyclopedia of Literary Modernism, pp. 106–7 [Bii])

allusive, imagistic poetry of H. D. (Hilda Doolittle). As suggested earlier, however, sharp distinctions between realism and modernism are difficult to sustain, with most authors incorporating both modes into their writing – and there are also many writers from this period who treated a range of women's issues through an integrated blend of realism and modernism (for example, E. M. Forster, D. H. Lawrence and Jean Rhys, in novels such as *Howards End* (1910), *The Rainbow* (1915) and *After Leaving Mr Mackenzie* (1930)).

Indeed, perhaps the more important distinctions in this context are between the different types of feminist emphasis which started to emerge in the period – between, for example, 'equal rights' feminism and 'welfare feminism' (see textbox) and, more importantly from a literary point of view, between a feminism which predicated its claims to equality on the basis of a common human nature with men, and one which, while continuing to advocate equal rights, celebrated the positive *difference* of women as a form of resistance and challenge to the established patriarchal structures of society. A seminal statement of the latter position was Virginia Woolf's long polemical essay *A Room of One's Own* (1929) where, for example, she writes:

But it is obvious that the values of women differ very often from the values which have been made by the other sex; naturally, this is so. Yet it is the masculine values that prevail. Speaking crudely, football and sport are 'important'; the worship of fashion, the buying of clothes 'trivial'. And these values are inevitably transferred from life to fiction. This is an important book, the critic assumes, because it deals with war. This is an insignificant book because it deals with the feelings of women in a drawing-room. A scene in a battlefield is more important than a scene in a shop – everywhere and much more subtly the difference of value persists.

(p. 74 [A])

Woolf developed her ideas further along these lines in *Three Guineas* (1938) and her own fiction largely devoted itself to defining a distinctively feminine style through which to explore what she saw as the distinctive consciousness and experiences of women – 'these infinitely obscure lives' which 'remain to be recorded' in all their 'profundities and … shallows' (*A Room of One's Own*, p. 89). Other important theoretical works of the period that cut across the feminist continuum include Eleanor Rathbone's *The Disinherited Family* (1924), 'Ray' Strachey's *The Cause* (1928) and Winifred Holtby's *Women in a Changing Civilisation* (1935).

There was of course strong and widespread opposition to the suffrage movement and to feminism generally at this time, from both men and women. From the literary world, for example, the best-selling novelist Mary Ward (1851–1920) helped to set up the Women's National Anti-Suffrage League in 1908, and Rudyard Kipling appeared in the *Anti-Suffrage Review* as a prominent supporter; his barbed poem 'The Female of the Species' (' … is more deadly than the male') was published in the *Morning Post* in 1911. But in their late-Victorianism, writers like this were clearly fighting against the tide and their views were becoming rapidly outdated and easy to mock. Perhaps more damaging to women (and to women writers) in the long term was a more disguised reaction to the women's movement in the rise of what has been termed a 'masculinist' modernism 'which prized aesthetic innovation over accessibility and objective precision over sensibility' (Caroline Franklin, 'Feminism 1890–1940', in Poplawski (ed.), *Encyclopedia of Literary Modernism*, p. 108 [Bii]). This was the form of modernism that later came to be canonised by the (largely male) literary establishment as 'High Modernism', and it was made up almost entirely of male writers – Joyce, Yeats, Eliot, Pound, Lewis and Lawrence – many of whose works are highly ambivalent in their representation of women and several of whom have been accused of misogyny by later generations of feminists. Interestingly, too, as Franklin also points out, the male literary reaction to women's growing empowerment helped (with the war) to bring about a 'crisis of masculinity' which showed itself in 'the depiction by male modernists of weak male protagonists at the mercy of complex external forces, ironized or ridiculed as incapable of the romantic heroism of the past (Joyce's Bloom in *Ulysses*, T. S. Eliot's J. Alfred Prufrock, Lawrence's Clifford Chatterley in *Lady Chatterley's Lover*, Chaplin's tramp, Kafka's K, Beckett's Hamm in *Endgame*)' (p. 108). This is another good example of how historical contexts can be seen operating within the formal or structural elements of literature as much as in its surface themes and explicit statements.

Psychology, Perception and the Question of Meaning

If one of the fundamental questions underlying much art and literature is 'What is the meaning of life?' the modernist age put forward an equally fundamental supplementary question – '*How* do we create meaning in the first place?' Influenced by recent and developing scientific, philosophical and psychological theories, artists and writers of the day were deeply preoccupied with this and related questions of knowledge, perception and language. Indeed, a large part of the art and literature of the period can be properly understood *only* in the light of such questions, as they underpin so many of the technical experiments and thematic concerns of the time.

What are the processes of perception by which we apprehend and understand the world and our experiences in it? How do we assimilate and order those perceptions to create the everyday meanings of our lives, as well as a sense of life's overall 'meaning'? How can art and literature best reflect these processes of meaning-making while at the same time striving to make meaning themselves? These are the sorts of questions modernists, in particular, grappled with. In the visual arts, the superimposed planes of cubism provide perhaps the pre-eminent example of how artists had started to probe the underlying dynamics of how we make sense of our interactions in and with the external world; while rhythmic or spatial forms of narrative, rapid changes of point of view and various 'stream of consciousness' effects represent a roughly equivalent form of experimental probing in modernist fiction.

And with all the modernists, these questions of how meaning or meanings are constructed help to explain their highly self-conscious (and frequently self-reflexive) concern with the methods and media of artistic expression. For literature, of course, this meant a particular concern with the medium of language itself. What Michael Bell has described as 'the enigma of language' was a 'near obsession' for the modernists and a pervasive theme throughout their works, as well as throughout the intellectual culture of the time, as Bell explains:

The human creation of meaning is ... focused in the period's interest in language; an interest whose cardinal significance is now sometimes referred to as the 'linguistic turn.' ... By the early teens of the century, it was becoming possible to see language no longer as merely describing or reflecting the world, but actually forming it as world; a viewpoint that was later to be developed by the American linguist Benjamin Lee Whorf. A key turning point was the work of the Swiss linguist Ferdinand

> **Cubism**
>
> [I]n Cubism, instead of one subject looking at and painting one object, there is a shift to a position of relativity and interaction ... The founding Cubists, Pablo Picasso (1881–1973) and Georges Braque (1882–1963) ... showed several sides to the object, maybe from five or six angles, and, because they dispensed with a fixed perspective, the Cubists did not paint to size either ... The resulting paintings are composite images and perhaps Picasso's most influential effect was to introduce collage techniques ... Cubism ... suggested to writers new ways of constructing both narrative and 'character' as composites, as not singular but an assembly of fragments.
>
> (Peter Childs, *Modernism*, pp. 111–14 [Bii])

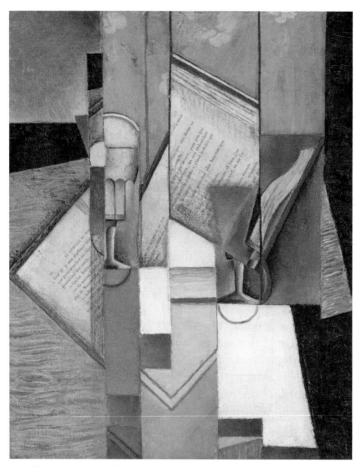

6.8 *The Book*, 1913, by Juan Gris: cubist painting.

de Saussure. Whereas nineteenth-century study of language was predominantly historical, concerned with origins and development, de Saussure's *Course in General Linguistics*, published in 1916 after his death, emphasized the synchronic and structural dimension. He showed how the linguistic sign stands in an arbitrary relation to its external referent while meaning is created relationally within the system of language itself. Whereas Adam in Eden gave names to all the existing objects, on this model we only *have* recognizable objects by creating names for them. Wittgenstein in the *Tractatus Logico-Philosophicus* (1921) was to develop a related point: 'The limits of my language mean the limits of my world.' Stephen Dedalus's philosophical ruminations while walking the beach in the 'Proteus' episode of *Ulysses* begin with a cognate thought … 'Signatures of all things I am here to read.'

('Thought, Language, Aesthetics and Being 1900–1940', in Poplawski (ed.), *Encyclopedia of Literary Modernism*, p. 424 [Bii])

Modernist writers had an acute appreciation of this constructive or formative power of language, especially in terms of its shaping of cultural views and values (and Eliot and Pound, for example, 'had a crusading interest in precision of language as the means of cultural health', Bell, p. 425); but they also often engaged with the paradoxical sense that language constantly gestures beyond itself to meanings that do indeed appear to be beyond its own referential or representational limits, and it is part of the definition of modernism that it tended to push language beyond those limits in order to generate moments of apparently non-linguistic revelation or 'epiphany' (in Joyce's term).

> **Epiphany**
>
> By an epiphany he meant a sudden spiritual manifestation, whether in the vulgarity of speech or of gesture or in a memorable phase of the mind itself. He believed that it was for the man of letters to record these epiphanies with extreme care, seeing that they themselves are the most delicate and evanescent of moments.
>
> (James Joyce, *Stephen Hero* (an early draft of *A Portrait of the Artist as a Young Man* (1916)), cited in Ellmann and Fiedelson (eds.), *The Modern Tradition*, p. 136 [A])

In this sense, the modernists drew attention to a type of unconscious side to language, which 'like the female moons in Joyce's "Ithaca" episode and Lawrence's "Moony" chapter of *Women in Love*, is rather an inscrutable surface sustained by an invisible body whose dark side cannot be known' (Bell, p. 426). In their own very different ways, writers like Joyce and Lawrence, Eliot, Pound, Yeats, Richardson and Woolf all made radical experiments with language which both reflected back on language as the very element of meaning in our lives *and* drew attention to forms and meanings it yet seemed unable to encompass. Lawrence captures something of this double-sidedness of language, and its importance to modernist art, when he writes in his 'Foreword to *Women in Love*': 'Man struggles with his unborn needs and fulfilment. New unfoldings struggle up in torment in him, as buds struggle forth the midst of a plant ... This struggle for verbal consciousness should not be left out in art ... *It is the passionate struggle into conscious being*.' One of the themes of the novel itself is precisely this struggle with language and its 'other' side – 'She listened, making out what he said. She knew, as well as he knew, that words themselves do not convey meaning, that they are but a gesture we make, a dumb show like any other ... There was always confusion in speech. Yet it must be spoken' (*Women in Love*, pp. 485–6; p. 186 [A]).

Clearly linked to the growing influence in society of the discourses of psychology and psychoanalysis, and largely inseparable from the 'linguistic turn' of modernism, was the 'psychological turn' that we have already touched on in our discussion of Henry James's pioneering treatment of consciousness in his fiction. His work provides a key early example of a growing fascination in the literature of this period with the inner life of the individual and with new techniques for exploring and depicting that life, particularly in relation to questions of language, perception and meaning. This was the golden age of the psychological novel and there was a rapid development (following James's lead) of new narrative techniques such as interior monologue and stream of consciousness, along with innovative uses of rhythm, repetition and symbolism, to try to represent the hidden workings of the conscious and unconscious mind. One important statement of this new understanding of consciousness and its implications for fiction comes in Virginia Woolf 's influential essay, 'Modern Fiction' (1919), where she announces that for the 'moderns' the focal point of interest 'lies very likely in the dark places of psychology':

> Examine for a moment an ordinary mind on an ordinary day. The mind receives a myriad impressions – trivial, fantastic, evanescent, or engraved with the sharpness of steel. From all sides they come, an incessant shower of innumerable atoms ... so that, if a writer were a free man and not a slave, if he could write what he chose, not what he must, if he could base his work upon his own feeling and not upon convention, there would be no plot, no comedy, no tragedy, no love interest or catastrophe in the accepted style ... Life is a not a series of gig lamps symmetrically arranged; life is a luminous halo, a semi-transparent envelope surrounding us from the beginning of consciousness to the end. Is it not the task of the novelist to convey this varying, this unknown and uncircumscribed spirit, whatever aberration or complexity it may display ... Let us record the atoms as they fall upon the mind in the order in which they fall, let us trace the patterns, however disconnected and incoherent in appearance, which each sight or incident scores upon the consciousness ... every feeling, every thought; every quality of brain and spirit is drawn upon; no perception comes amiss.
>
> (In Ellman and Fiedelson (eds.), *The Modern Tradition*, pp. 123–6 [A])

Woolf was writing here partly after the event, for her argument is informed by the psychological fiction that was already widespread prior to 1919. She makes specific reference in the essay to Joyce's *A Portrait of the Artist as a Young Man* (1916) and *Ulysses* (1922) (which had begun to appear serially from 1918), but, in addition to early works like James's *The Turn of the Screw* (1898), two other seminal modernist novels of consciousness had also had a major impact by that time: Marcel Proust's *A la recherche du temps perdu*, a seven-volume sequence of novels (or *roman fleuve*) published between 1913 and 1927, and Dorothy Richardson's *Pilgrimage*, another novel sequence, this time of thirteen novels, twelve of which were published between 1915 and 1938, with the final volume appearing posthumously in 1967. Strong currents of thematic and formal interest in psychological analysis are also evident in, for example, Joseph Conrad's *Heart of Darkness* (1902) and *The Secret Agent* (1907), Lawrence's *Sons and Lovers* (1913) and *The Rainbow* (1915), and the short stories of Katherine Mansfield, appearing from 1910 onwards. Virginia Woolf herself then became one of the leading exponents, with Richardson and Joyce, of the stream of consciousness novel, with works such as *Mrs Dalloway* (1925) and *To the Lighthouse* (1927).

Cutting across the linguistic and psychological 'turns' of modernism was the age's fundamental concern with the relativity of knowledge and meaning. All the works just mentioned exhibit a cubist-style questioning of the relationships between observer and observed and subject and object, and between perception, point of view, language and interpretation. Traditional concepts of truth, objectivity and human rationality had been challenged by thinkers like Nietzsche, Einstein and Freud and an unprecedented sense of the complexity of life and the relativity of meaning was the order of the day. Modernist art engaged with that complexity and relativity partly by throwing attention onto the very means by which we experience and strive to understand the world: perception, language, and our conscious and unconscious processes of thought and feeling. *Heart of Darkness* and *The Turn of the Screw* are classic examples of how modernist writers began to manipulate language, plot, narrative voice, perception and point of view to create dense multifaceted narratives which are resistant to any single, clear-cut interpretation and which more or less force the reader to reflect on how meanings and interpretations come about in the first place. This is one of the sources of difficulty or obscurity often associated with modernist art, and Conrad himself, in *Heart of Darkness*, provided a typically elliptical image of the sort of elusive meanings to be expected from such art:

> But Marlow was not typical ... and to him the meaning of an episode was not inside like a kernel but outside, enveloping the tale which brought it out only as a glow brings out a haze, in the likeness of one of these misty halos that sometimes are made visible by the spectral illumination of moonshine.
>
> (p. 8 [A])

As mentioned much earlier in this chapter, Conrad's novel engages directly with its historical context in raising questions about imperialism; but it is no coincidence, in what we have called an age of interrogation, that the self-reflexive questioning of narrative meaning illustrated here should go hand in hand with that broader sense of political or ideological self-questioning. In fact, Conrad's novel seems purposely to bring together 'imperialism' and 'meaning' as subtly interrelated historical issues of the day, and it thus provides a good example of how literary texts do not simply 'reflect' their historical contexts but also help actively to define them.

Readings

H. G. Wells, *Tono-Bungay* (1909)

In any consideration of modern English literature seen in relation to its contexts, the writings of H. G. Wells (1866–1946) stand out as quintessentially representative of the type of literature that carries its historical contexts on its sleeve. In her essay 'Modern Fiction', Virginia Woolf famously grouped Wells together with Arnold Bennett and John Galsworthy as social realists or, in her negative terms, 'materialists', who, in striving so hard to depict the surface actuality of contemporary life, often ended up missing the deeper *spirit* of life: 'they write of unimportant things ... they spend immense skill and immense industry making the trivial and the transitory appear the true and the enduring' (in Ellmann and Fiedelson (eds.), *The Modern Tradition*, p. 122 [A]). Woolf softens her criticism of Wells to some extent by describing him as 'a materialist from sheer goodness of heart' and she captures something of his Dickens-like zeal for social reform when she continues that, with his 'plethora of ... ideas and facts', he takes 'upon his shoulders the work that ought to have been discharged by Government officials' (p. 122). To be sure, in their historical sweep and often comic social critique, there is indeed a Dickensian quality in the novels of H. G. Wells, and one could do far worse than to read a selection of them – he wrote more than fifty – to gain a lively imaginative overview of the history of his time.

Tono-Bungay is perhaps Wells's outstanding example of an early twentieth-century Condition of England novel. As we have seen, there were deep-seated structural changes in train within Britain's economy at this time; and, where mid-Victorian

Condition of England novels focused on social problems thrown up by the rapid rise of heavy manufacturing industries, *Tono-Bungay* is equally a product of its period in concentrating on the growing dominance in the economy of the commercial and financial sectors and on the related expansion of a consumerism increasingly influenced by modern mass-media techniques of marketing and publicity. The novel also clearly reflects the reforming political climate of the 1900s and comments extensively on a full range of social issues, including urban planning and housing, social class, unemployment, poverty, divorce laws, education, the power of the press, imperialism and the arms race.

In its first serial publication in Britain (between December 1908 and March 1909 in the *English Review*), the novel was ironically sub-titled 'A Romance of Commerce'; and, in its rags-to-riches story of how the quack medicine 'Tono-Bungay' becomes the mass-selling foundation of Edward Ponderevo's huge financial empire, the novel presents a cutting satire on the corrupt and corrupting nature of much modern business practice, shown as being underwritten by often fraudulent advertising claims, by the often groundless 'confidence' of investors and share-dealers, and by the general gullibility of the buying public. By selling 'slightly injurious rubbish at one-and-three-halfpence and two-and-nine a bottle, including the Government stamp', Ponderevo gains untold wealth and influence and the 'respect, the confidence of endless people' (p. 147). As the nephew-narrator George Ponderevo says at the height of his uncle's power and wealth:

> I cannot claim that a single one of the great businesses we organized added any real value to human life at all. Several, like Tono-Bungay, were unmitigated frauds by any honest standard, the giving of nothing coated in advertisements for money ... You perceive now ... the nature of the services for which this fantastic community gave him unmanageable wealth and power and real respect. It was all a monstrous payment for courageous fiction, a gratuity in return for the one reality of human life – illusion. We gave them a feeling of hope and profit; we sent a tidal wave of water and confidence into their stranded affairs ... The whole of this modern mercantile investing civilization is indeed such stuff as dreams are made of ... and beneath it all, you know, there was nothing but fictitious values as evanescent as rainbow gold.
>
> (pp. 220–2)

There are innumerable such critical glances at the contemporary world of commerce in the novel, but the world of advertising is clearly singled out as the key factor in the success of Tono-Bungay. Wells's cynical view of this all-pervasive aspect of modern life is comically summed up by the fatuous enthusiasm of one of his characters, Ewart:

> Advertisement has revolutionized trade and industry; it is going to revolutionize the world. The old merchant used to tote about commodities; the new one creates values. Doesn't need to tote. He takes something that isn't worth anything – or something that isn't particularly worth anything, and he makes it worth something. He takes mustard that is just like anybody else's mustard, and he goes about saying, shouting, singing, chalking on walls, writing inside people's books, putting it everywhere, 'Smith's Mustard is the Best.' And behold it *is* the Best!
>
> (p. 159)

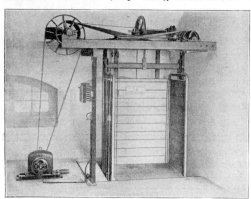

6.9 Advertisements, 1921.

The comic-grotesque figure of Uncle Ponderevo is something like one of his own advertisements – full of empty, valueless bluster – and the very story of his preposterous rise and semi-tragic fall embodies a critique of what Wells saw as the aimlessness and moral vacuity at the heart of modern British society. In effect, his story plays out what the narrator refers to early on as 'the broad slow decay of the great social organism of England' (p. 66).

Stylistically or formally, the novel positions itself from the start in the tradition of classic social realism by drawing attention to its focus on representative character 'types' from a broad social range (though concentrating on the middle classes), as well as by stressing its accumulative, or naturalistic, method. The first-person narrator, George Ponderevo, tells us that he is a privileged observer of an 'extensive cross-section of the British social organism' (p. 10) because he was 'jerked out' of his normal 'stratum' to live 'crosswise' (p. 9), or across different classes:

> Yes, I've seen a curious variety of people and ways of living altogether. Odd people they all are, great and small, very much alike at bottom and curiously different on their surfaces. I wish I had ranged just a little further both up and down, seeing I have ranged so far … my contacts with princes have been limited to quite public occasions, nor at the other end of the scale have I had what I should call an inside acquaintance with that dusty but attractive class of people who go about on the high roads drunk but *en famille* (so redeeming the minor lapse), in the summertime, with a perambulator, lavender to sell, sun-brown children, a smell and ambiguous bundles that fire the imagination.
>
> (p. 10)

He also warns us that 'this book is going to be something of an agglomeration': 'I want to trace my social trajectory (and my uncle's) as the main line of my story; but … I want to get in too all sorts of things that struck me, things that amused me and impressions I got – even although they don't minister directly to my narrative at all' (p. 11). And, although this is a first-person narrative (therefore with a limited point of view), the narrator nevertheless stakes his claim to a type of traditional omniscience and objectivity. He refers to his 'bird's-eye view of the modern world' (p. 11) and says:

> And it isn't a constructed tale I have to tell but unmanageable realities … if only I can keep up the spirit of truth-telling all through as strongly as I have now, you shall have it all.
>
> (p. 13)

These opening narrative gambits are common in the history of the novel form in their attempts to gain the reader's acceptance of the 'truth' or 'reality' of the fiction being presented. However, there is also something new and modernistic in Wells's self-conscious reflections on the art of narrative fiction here, as well as in his attempts to define a new type of novel through which to render life and society:

> I've read an average share of novels and made some starts before this beginning, and I've found the restraints and rules of the art (as I made them out) impossible for me … I fail to see how I can be other than a lax, undisciplined storyteller. I must sprawl and flounder, comment and theorize, if I am to get the thing out I have in mind.
>
> (p. 13)

Virginia Woolf half-recognised Wells's point here when, in the essay mentioned above, she distinguished between the all-too-solid constructions of Bennett's 'embalming' craftsmanship as a novelist and Wells's more 'generous' sympathies, which prevented him from enclosing his characters in too 'shipshape and substantial' a structure. Interestingly, A. C. Ward, writing in 1930, identified Wells as 'the first important modernist experimenter in English fiction' precisely for this breaking away from the conventions of the well-constructed novel. Ironically enough, Ward suggests that Wells in fact led the way for novelists such as Virginia Woolf 'to free the novel from … artificial limitations … and to release it for new and larger activities' (*The Nineteen-Twenties*, pp. 51–2 [Bii]). So, while *Tono-Bungay* does clearly sit within the broad social realist tradition for its explicit attempts to outline the economic, political and cultural contours of early twentieth-century British society, we should not overlook the many fruitful ways in which it also incorporates emerging modernist trends.

Indeed, the novel's insistent narrative self-questioning and its surface looseness of structure are both directly functional to the novel's social critique in raising issues of order, meaning and truth. For one thing, the speculative nature of the narrative can be seen to echo the unstable business speculation which sits at the heart of the plot surrounding Tono-Bungay, a product which to all intents and purposes is a pure fiction, sustained only by market confidence in the claims made for it by clever marketing and publicity campaigns. In that sense, Tono-Bungay is somewhat like a story in a novel, whose credibility is also largely dependent on how well it is 'sold' (or told) to the reader. In suggesting a sense of provisionality and instability in narrative meanings and values, then, the form of the novel imitates some of its themes in best modernist fashion.

The reliability – or otherwise – of the narrator, George Ponderevo, is also bound up with this, of course. For, although he is disarming in his apparent honesty and openness in laying bare his struggles with narrative accuracy and 'truth-telling', and although he often voices many of the obvious moral objections to the massive confidence trick represented by Tono-Bungay, he is undoubtedly implicated in that trick from beginning to end, and we are bound to ask questions about his integrity and trustworthiness. Our doubts about him are also seriously compounded by such episodes as the mock-colonialist expedition to the aptly named Mordet Island in Africa where he is involved in the murder of one of the natives and in the out-and-out theft of the heaps of 'quap' (equally aptly named). In fact this particular episode is replete with symbolic meanings of relevance to the whole novel and to the whole of Wells's analysis of British society as a diseased and decaying social organism, for while the radioactive quap promises great monetary wealth on the world's markets as a source of rare heavy metals, it is in itself a type of valueless anti-matter, a degenerative cancerous material. Wells makes an explicit parallel between the decaying quap and the decay of culture when he has his narrator musing, 'It is in matter exactly what the decay of our old culture is in society, a loss of traditions and distinctions and assured reactions'; and, as he continues, Wells brings together both literal prophecy about the dangers of radioactivity and his metaphoric view of the moral direction of his society when he writes, 'I am haunted by a grotesque fancy of the ultimate eating away and dry-rotting and dispersal of all our world' (p. 329).

D. H. Lawrence, *The Rainbow* (1915)

Perhaps more obviously than *Tono-Bungay*, Lawrence's The *Rainbow* can be seen as a transitional novel incorporating both continuities with, and radical departures from, the nineteenth-century novel of social realism. Initially it presents itself as a traditional family chronicle or saga, beginning with a type of genealogy of the Brangwen family and a history of their farm; but it then quickly establishes its modernist credentials through its pronounced use of symbolism and poetic prose, and through its sustained expressionistic attempt to invent a new language for the feelings and for unconscious impulses and intuitions. It deals directly and candidly with questions of class, gender and sexuality, and its plot in fact incorporates its own social historical survey of England at the end of the nineteenth century and the start of the twentieth century, including detailed reflections on religion, education, feminism, industrialism, empire and war. In a sense, it thus both directly re-presents its historical context and symptomatically *represents* its period through its typically modern emphases and its experimental modernist style.

The novel opens in deceptively familiar style – at first glance this could be George Eliot, or perhaps Thomas Hardy, setting the historical rural scene through a conventional omniscient third-person narrator:

> The Brangwens had lived for generations on the Marsh Farm, in the meadows where the Erewash twisted sluggishly through alder trees, separating Derbyshire from Nottinghamshire. Two miles away, a church-tower stood on a hill, the houses of the little country town climbing assiduously up to it.
>
> (p. 9)

This is part of a first short section which is actually a prelude to the main first chapter, which itself begins in a style that is, if anything, even more reminiscent of a traditional social-realist novel, with its precise cause-and-effect presentation of external 'historical' facts:

> About 1840, a canal was constructed across the meadows of the Marsh Farm, connecting the newly opened collieries of the Erewash Valley. A high embankment travelled along the fields to carry the canal, which passed close to the homestead, and, reaching the road, went over in a heavy bridge … Then, a short time afterwards, a colliery was sunk on the other side of the canal, and in a while the Midland Railway came down the valley at the foot of the Ilkeston hill, and the invasion was complete. The town grew rapidly, the Brangwens were kept busy producing supplies, they became richer, they were almost tradesmen.
>
> (p. 13)

In fact, comparing this to the 'prelude', one can see that the latter is markedly more poetic or metaphoric, as if it has been strategically placed by Lawrence to prepare the reader for the *true* modernist style and themes of the main part of the novel. The rhythmic, incantatory style, for example, later used to evoke characters' psychological and sexual impulses, appears here for the first time in the description of the ancestral Brangwen men's pulsing relationship with the land (pp. 9–10); and symbolic oppositions are established which then recur rhythmically throughout the rest of the novel as types of leitmotif (a typically modernist strategy for picking out key themes). In particular, we have the opposition introduced here between the male-coded 'blind intercourse of farm-life' and the female-coded 'spoken world beyond' – the traditional inward-looking 'blood-intimacy' of the Brangwen men and the outward-facing Brangwen women who wish 'to discover what was beyond, to enlarge their own scope and range and freedom' (pp. 10–11). This opposition prepares us for the New Woman narrative of Ursula Brangwen, who, in the third generation of Brangwens, breaks decisively with Victorian expectations of women by single-mindedly pursuing her own intellectual, economic and sexual independence; but it also introduces the novel's concern with language, expression and meaning in its contrast between the 'blind' and the 'spoken'. In the terms used earlier from *Women in Love*, the Brangwen women, and Ursula in particular, as their modern outrider, are engaged in the 'passionate struggle into conscious being', just as Lawrence himself struggles in this novel to develop a new narrative language for inner psychological, emotional and sexual states.

Lawrence's sustained focus on the position and experience of women and his fundamental concern with consciousness and the subconscious clearly define two key areas in which *The Rainbow* relates directly to its historical context. (This is unsurprising given that Lawrence began his career as a novelist in the heyday of the suffragette movement and in early adulthood mixed in progressive circles of socialists, feminists and early psychoanalysts.) The story of Ursula Brangwen's quest for self-fulfilment, though complex in its details, can be left largely to speak for itself in the broad ways in which it represents women's struggles at this time to affirm their freedom and independence and to exploit to the full the new opportunities gradually opening up for them in the fields of education and employment. However, Lawrence's individual approach to the psychology of his characters warrants a little further discussion.

Defending an early draft of the novel in a much-quoted letter of June 1914, Lawrence declared a new approach to characterisation which, while unique to him in its particular details, clearly reflects the wider contemporary interest in psychology, consciousness and the unconscious as discussed earlier:

> You mustn't look in my novel for the old stable ego of the character. There is another ego, according to whose action the individual is unrecognisable, and passes through, as it were, allotropic states which it needs a deeper sense than any we've been used to exercise, to discover are states of the same single radically unchanged element.
>
> (*Letters* ii, p. 183 [A])

Part of the explanation for Lawrence's idiosyncratic language here, however, is that his understanding of consciousness and the unconscious was always somewhat different from that of most other thinkers and writers of the time, in that he felt that the non-mental impulses of the body and the feelings should also be given their full due in any consideration of human experience and behaviour – that 'consciousness' had to mean bodily, emotional and mental consciousness all together. This is also why his experiments in writing about 'the other ego' became intimately bound up with his experiments in writing about sex and sexuality (although the latter was also motivated by a more straightforward historical protest against repressive Victorianism and narrow-minded censorship). In many ways, Lawrence was ahead of his time in experimenting with a type of 'writing of the body' through which he tried to give integrated expression to the full experience of mind, body and feelings as they interact naturally in daily life. Lawrence had already taken some steps in this direction in *Sons and Lovers* (1913) and other of his early works, but, as the letter above suggests, he seems to have gained a new sense of what he was striving for while writing *The Rainbow*.

In this novel, combining a free indirect style of narration with a rhythmic patterning of language and imagery, Lawrence developed his own version of a stream of consciousness technique – though it is probably better to talk of a stream of *unconsciousness*, given that part of his point in the above letter is that 'the other ego' is 'unrecognisable' or inaccessible to the everyday 'stable ego'. Conventionally, a free indirect style means that a third-person narrator retains control of the narration, but that the point of view is filtered (or focalised) through the consciousness of a character, so that there is a temporary impression of first-person narration (in simple terms, it is a blend of third-person and first-person narration). Here, however, because of Lawrence's complicating view of consciousness as something at least partly unconscious, one has to qualify the meaning of saying that the point of view is filtered through the 'consciousness' of characters – as they themselves, in their 'normal' state of self-consciousness, would obviously be unable to express a point of view that was unconscious to them. This then is where Lawrence uses what has been called a 'psychology of rhythm' to create an effect of imitating not the conscious verbal thought processes of his characters, but the total rhythm of their being, both conscious and unconscious. This was clearly an ambitious undertaking on Lawrence's part (how *can* anyone know what such a rhythm might be for another person?), but it is another notable example of how writers in this period were variously pushing back the boundaries of literary technique (and content) partly in response to evolving theories and debates elsewhere in society about human thought, behaviour and consciousness.

Perhaps the most obvious example of this aspect of Lawrence's technique comes in the sheaves-stacking scene in chapter 4 of the novel (pp. 113–17) where Will and Anna stack corn sheaves together in the moonlight in a type of ritual courtship dance which symbolises their growing passion and desire for one another. Neither character in the scene is fully conscious of the true depth of his or her feelings for the other but as the rhythm of the prose gradually builds up the rhythmic action of their movements across the field, so we are also given a sense of a complex emotional and sexual rhythm being clarified within and between them:

> They worked together, coming and going, in a rhythm, which carried their feet and their bodies in tune … He worked steadily, engrossed, threading backwards and forwards like a shuttle across the strip of cleared stubble, weaving the long line of riding shocks, nearer and nearer to the shadowy trees, threading his sheaves with hers.
>
> And always she was gone before he came. As he came, she drew away, as he drew away, she came. Were they never to meet? Gradually a low, deep-sounding will in him vibrated to her, tried to set her in accord, tried to bring her gradually to him, to a meeting, till they should be together, till they should meet as the sheaves that swished together.
>
> (pp. 114–15)

The balance here, in the narrative technique, is initially with the third-person narrator who appears to be describing the action from a purely external vantage point. However, on closer analysis (especially over the whole episode), it becomes clear that the first-person perceptions and feelings of both characters are constantly mediating the narration – most clearly, in this brief extract, in the second paragraph where, for example, the question, 'Were they never to meet?', represents Will's own direct (if possibly subconscious) thought. But, working across third- and first-person points of view, the key innovation is the rhythmic effect which attempts to capture a full bodily response that includes unconscious feelings and intuitions as well as conscious mental processes. Later in the novel, as the focus of attention settles on Ursula Brangwen (a more articulate and more highly self-conscious character than the earlier Brangwens), the balance in Lawrence's free indirect style shifts to the first person and there is a greater sense of Ursula as a Jamesian 'centre of consciousness' filtering narrative events. Nevertheless, the psychology of rhythm remains a key factor in characterising Ursula and especially those aspects of her inner nature which are unconscious to her.

Ursula's encounter with the horses at the end of the novel is a prime example of how Lawrence symbolically counterpoints the rhythms of external nature with the inner psychological rhythms of his characters, for he presents there a powerful expressionistic parallel between the rhythmically pounding horses and the pounding of deep impulses within Ursula which, against her conscious inclination to settle for a conventional life with Skrebensky, unconsciously urge her on in her struggle for a life of full independence 'beyond' social convention:

> She knew the heaviness on her heart ... She felt the thud of their heavy hoofs on the ground. What was it that was drawing near her, what weight oppressing her heart? She did not know, she did not look ... In a sort of lightning of knowledge their movement travelled through her, the quiver and strain and thrust of their powerful flanks, as they burst before her and drew on, beyond.

> (pp. 451–2)

T. S. Eliot, *The Waste Land* (1922)

With its bewilderingly fragmented, imagistic evocation of a sterile and broken civilisation, and its relativistic 'shoring up' of fragments from many myths and cultures, Eliot's *The Waste Land* has long been considered an archetypal text of literary modernism, providing a conveniently concentrated example of almost all the major features associated with that label. Although the poem's wide range of cultural reference suggests many other relevant contexts too (urbanisation, popular culture and entertainment, and the developing fields of anthropology and comparative religion), the First World War is perhaps its most obvious shaping context.

The war is explicitly alluded to in the semi-comic repartee of the women in the pub in Part II of the poem, and literal echoes of the war can be heard in lines like 'Cracks and reforms and bursts in the violet air' (Part V, l. 373); but the impact and aftermath of the war is deeply embedded in the poem's all-pervasive and many-faceted sense of death and loss, fracture and disorientation. The imagery of death and desolation is everywhere, from the very first section sub-title, 'The Burial of the Dead', through to the fourth, 'Death by Water'. The land is dead, trees are dead, the bones of dead men lie in garrets and alleys, 'Rattled by the rat's foot only, year to year' (Part III, l. 195):

> He who was living is now dead
> We who were living are now dying
>
> (Part V, ll. 328–9)

As this last line suggests, though, the poem is not in any simple way a memorial to the men who literally died in the war. It is also, if not more so, a lament for the living death that the war symbolically bequeathed to the world in marking the end of a cultural cycle and the shattering of its fundamental values, beliefs and aspirations. The city of modernity is now an 'Unreal City', a hellish ghostly waste land, full of 'Falling towers' and the walking undead –

> A crowd flowed over London Bridge, so many,
> I had not thought death had undone so many
>
> (Part I, ll.62–3)

As the recurrent imagery of dryness and sterility makes clear, the poem is in this sense actually about the spiritual death of western civilisation, and the poem's fragmented web of allusions to Christianity and to various other religions, myths and rituals is intended to evoke the anguished modern search for new sources of faith and meaning in the world – these, for the poetic persona, are the 'fragments' 'shored against my ruins' (Part V, l.431).

The narrative disjunctions and the sudden shifts of location and language in the poem are clearly functional to this sense of profound spiritual disorientation in the modern world. There is a countervailing motif of quest for new directions, partly indicated by the allusions to the Grail legend which Eliot himself pointed out in his notes to the poem, but this too emerges only haltingly through indirections and glancing associations within a patchwork of apparently disconnected images and ideas. With its incantatory ending – 'Shantih shantih shantih' – the final part of the poem certainly brings a sense of rhythmic and atmospheric resolution, and the suggestions of rain and springtime hint at the possibilities of spiritual regeneration; but the symptomatic modernist *difficulty* of interpretation and understanding remains probably the overriding impression one takes away from a first reading of the poem. And this, of course, makes perfect sense in the light of a war whose often aimless carnage had come to seem incomprehensible to many, especially in the disillusioned atmosphere of the post-war peace (which perhaps gives an ironic twist to Eliot's gloss on the meaning of 'shantih' as 'The Peace which passeth understanding'). Eliot's waste land may be primarily a spiritual one, then, even when mapped onto London or other major cities, but it is difficult not to see the desolate battlefields of Flanders as its underlying material model.

Virginia Woolf, *Mrs Dalloway* (1925)

Like Wells and the young Lawrence, Woolf was a keen social critic with progressive liberal and feminist sympathies, and *Mrs Dalloway* shares many of the social and political themes found in the other two novels discussed here – while its pronounced modernist technique (as well as its city setting and its treatment of the war) also aligns it clearly with Eliot's *The Waste Land*.

The novel was written between 1922 and 1924 and is set mainly in 1923 so historically it is situated within a period of important change in British political life, with the demise of the two-party dominance of the Tories and Liberals and the coming to power for the first time ever of a Labour government (in January 1924). This context is evident within the novel in the satirical treatment of the British upper classes and, in particular, the governing classes as represented by characters like Richard Dalloway (a Conservative MP), Hugh Whitbread and Lady Bruton; and there is a stark critique of class inequalities in the contrasts between their pampered lives and the lives of characters like Rezia and Septimus Smith and the 'degradingly poor' Miss Kilman (p. 135). A whole host of other contextual issues are evident in the novel too. It reflects in close detail on the different social roles of men and women at the time, and presents a subtle analysis of gender differences in its carefully staged character contrasts and comparisons, celebrating in particular a feminism of 'difference' in the portrayal of Clarissa Dalloway, while also giving voice to equal-rights feminism through the figure of Sally Seton. Peter Walsh, just back from India, hints at contemporary debates about empire, and the narrative deals directly with the impact of the war, both through the nightmarish visions and ultimate suicide of the shell-shocked Septimus Smith, and through the contrasts between Clarissa's (and Peter Walsh's) pre-war memories of gentrified country life at Bourton and the changing social scene of post-war London in the novel's present. General social and cultural transformations brought about by new technologies such as the car and aeroplane are registered too, perhaps most entertainingly at the start of the novel in the extended descriptions of the (possibly royal) motorcade (pp. 15–20) and the advertising aeroplane's cryptic sky-writing (pp. 21–31); and there are frequent references to the mass media and to popular entertainment such as the cinema – indeed, the novel's own technique has been described as cinematic in its use of flashbacks, shifting points of view, and montage-like cutting from scene to scene.

As with Lawrence's *The Rainbow*, however, what is perhaps most distinctive about *Mrs Dalloway* is its typically modern psychological treatment of character and consciousness.

Changing Conceptions of Character and Identity

Not only the conventions for representing character had changed for Woolf's generation, but also the very concept of character and personality. The human personality was not one given fixed monolithic entity, but a shifting conglomerate of impressions and emotions. Psychoanalysis was uncovering a multi-layered self, in which dreams, memories, and fantasies were as important as actions and thoughts. Philosophers were describing the self as a receiver of a tumult of sensations. Artists and painters were experimenting with versions of perception and reality. The Woolfs' Hogarth Press began to publish Freud's works in 1921, and although she was overtly dismissive of psychoanalysis, Woolf developed her own acute psychological method of explaining sensation, memory and repression, one which resembles Freud's in many respects and which uses a similar model of the levels of human consciousness.

(Elaine Showalter, 'Introduction', *Mrs Dalloway*, p. xviii [A])

Woolf's experiments in depicting consciousness in fiction are rather different from Lawrence's, though, and here the 'stream of consciousness' label is much more straightforwardly applicable. Woolf's previously cited comments from her essay 'Modern Fiction' effectively sum up what is usually meant by the technique: the 'ordinary mind on an ordinary day' receives 'a myriad impressions' like 'an incessant shower of innumerable atoms', and it is the task of the novelist to capture this effect of consciousness by recording the atoms 'in the order in which they fall'. The aim, then, is to convey a sense of the continuous flow of consciousness in all its complex multiplicity and frequent randomness – 'no perception comes amiss', she says. The effect in *Mrs Dalloway* is evident from the very first page, where we are asked to follow the impressionistic association of ideas running through Clarissa Dalloway's mind as she steps out on the streets of London to buy flowers:

> What a lark! What a plunge! For so it had always seemed to her when, with a little squeak of the hinges, which she could hear now, she had burst open the French windows and plunged at Bourton into the open air. How fresh, how calm, stiller than this of course, the air was in the early morning; like the flap of a wave; the kiss of a wave; chill and sharp and yet (for a girl of eighteen as she then was) solemn, feeling as she did, standing there at the open window, that something awful was about to happen; looking at the flowers, at the trees with the smoke winding off them and the rooks rising, falling …
>
> (p. 3)

We can see here that the usual balance of a free indirect style of narration has been tipped significantly away from the third-person narrator in favour of the more or less direct perceptions and perspectives of the first-person character-narrator (although third-person references to 'she' and 'her' remain); and we can also see that the loosely structured presentation of those perceptions and perspectives is intended to evoke a realistic sense of the free-wheeling nature of moment-by-moment consciousness. Moreover, a large part of the passage relates to Clarissa's memories, sparked off by the similarity of the present June morning to the one at Bourton when she was eighteen (she is now fifty-three). This draws attention to an important additional element in Woolf's technique and to her underlying realisation that the stream of consciousness is always inevitably partly a stream of memories too, which constantly impinges on our present experience. In this, like other experimental novelists of the time, Woolf was reflecting current theories of time and consciousness put forward by thinkers like William James and Henri Bergson (who, for example, stressed the difference between objective clock-measured time and our subjective experience of time as a constant flow or sense of 'duration'), and it led her to incorporate in the novel what she referred to as 'caves' of memories in her portrayal of each of the main characters: 'my discovery: how I dig out beautiful caves behind my characters; I think that gives exactly what I want; humanity, humour, depth. The idea is that the caves shall connect, & each comes to daylight at the present moment' (quoted in Showalter, 'Introduction', *Mrs Dalloway*, pp. xxviii–xxix).

What this also draws attention to, however, is the paradoxically systematic nature of Woolf's technique; for, while her aim at the micro-level of the novel may have been to create an effect of the disordered randomness of consciousness, what she clearly wanted to achieve overall was a significant *ordering* of the lives and experiences of her characters. Stepping back, as it were, from the immediate texture of the novel's presentation of character consciousness, we can immediately appreciate the highly structured and patterned nature of the novel, not least in its careful scene-by-scene construction and balanced alternation between one point of view and another. As Leon Edel points out, 'However much Mrs Woolf might assert the need to record the shower of atoms "in the order in which they fall," she neither accepted that order, nor believed in describing their frequent incoherence.' Woolf's aim is not *merely* to recreate the fleeting effects of consciousness (even if that were entirely possible in language) and her method, for Edel, is less that of the naturalistic novelist and more that of the lyric poet who selects and orders her material for concentrated effect – 'She was interested in the sharpened image, the moment, the condensed experience' (*The Psychological Novel*, p. 130 [Ci]). In other words, like many modernists, Woolf was concerned to use her art to generate moments of epiphany or transcendence which might breathe some order and meaning into the apparent chaos of contemporary existence. *Mrs Dalloway* presents both sides of this modernist coin in the novel's double climax, with the life-affirming order and 'assembly' of Clarissa's party precariously counterbalanced against the sundering 'chaos' of Septimus Smith's madness and suicide.

Reference

A Primary Texts and Anthologies of Primary Sources

Conrad, Joseph. *Heart of Darkness*. 1902. Harmondsworth: Penguin, 1977.

Dowson, Jane, ed. *Women's Poetry of the 1930s: A Critical Anthology*. London: Routledge, 1996. Fills an important gap in most other anthologies of the thirties with the previously neglected work of twenty women poets.

Eliot, T. S. *The Waste Land*. 1922. In Alexander W. Allison, et al., eds. *The Norton Anthology of Poetry*. 4th edn. New York and London: Norton, 1996, pp. 1344–56.

Ellman, Richard, and Charles Fiedelson, Jr, eds. *The Modern Tradition: Backgrounds of Modern Literature*. London: Oxford University Press, 1965. A huge compendium, with substantial extracts from a wide range of primary sources of relevance to the whole of the period. Not readily available now, however, but useful to know about as a potential supplement to the anthologies by Kolocotroni et al. and Rainey.

Faulkner, Peter, ed. *A Modernist Reader: Modernism in England 1910–1930*. London: Batsford, 1986. A focused collection of documents from the period stated (letters, articles, manifestos), along with seminal critical essays; put into context by the editor's introduction and commentaries.

First World War Poetry Digital Archive. http://www.oucs.ox.ac.uk/ww1lit/. Based at the University of Oxford but with open access, this is a rich multimedia resource focused on primary texts from the poets themselves but including a wide range of other materials on the war and its literature.

Glover, Jan, and Jon Silkin, eds. *The Penguin Book of First World War Prose*. London: Penguin, 1990.

Kendall, Tim, ed. *Poetry of the First World War: An Anthology*. Oxford University Press, 2013. A fresh, well-balanced new anthology, including a selection of music-hall and trench songs, and with helpful notes and biographies, and a comprehensive select bibliography of poets' works, general anthologies and critical studies.

Kolocotroni, Vassiliki, Jane Goldman and Olga Taxidou, eds. *Modernism: An Anthology of Sources and Documents*. Edinburgh University Press, 1998. An excellent starting point for sampling the many and various ideas, theories and debates that have gradually shaped our sense of what modernism is. Provides a strong sense of intellectual context and includes extracts from a range of texts dating from the mid-nineteenth to the mid-twentieth centuries.

Lawrence, D. H. *The Letters of D. H. Lawrence, Vol. II: 1913–16*. Ed. George Zytaruk and James T. Boulton. Cambridge University Press, 1981.

The Rainbow. 1915. Ed. Mark Kinkead-Weekes. London: Penguin, 2006.

St Mawr. In *The Woman Who Rode Away, St Mawr, The Princess*. Ed. Brian Finney, Christa Jansohn and Dieter Mehl. London: Penguin, 2006.

Women in Love. Ed. David Farmer, Lindeth Vasey and John Worthen. Harmondsworth: Penguin, 1995.

Orwell, George. *The Road to Wigan Pier*. 1937. Harmondsworth: Penguin, 1989.

'England Your England'. 1941. In *Inside the Whale and Other Essays*. Harmondsworth: Penguin, 1962, pp. 63–90.

Priestley, J. B. *English Journey: Being a Rambling but Truthful Account of What One Man Saw and Heard and Felt and Thought during a Journey through England during the Autumn of the Year 1933*. 1934. London: Mandarin, 1994.

Rainey, Lawrence, ed. *Modernism: An Anthology*. London: Blackwell, 2005. A comprehensive anthology of works by the major Anglo-American modernist writers, with a selection of critical and polemical texts.

Rhys, Jean. *After Leaving Mr Mackenzie*. 1930. Harmondsworth: Penguin, 2000.

Scott, Bonnie Kime, ed. *The Gender of Modernism*. Bloomington: Indiana University Press, 1990. An anthology of extracts and articles by women. A seminal re-drawing of the traditional 'map' of modernism.

Silkin, Jon, ed. *The Penguin Book of First World War Poetry*. 2nd rev. edn. London: Penguin, 1996. A generous selection, including non-British poets, with a critical introduction by the editor.

Skelton, Robin, ed. *Poetry of the Thirties*. Harmondsworth: Penguin, 1964. A representative selection from all the major poets of the decade, with a critical introduction by the editor.

Smith, Angela K., ed. *Women's Writing of the First World War: An Anthology*. Manchester University Press, 2000.

Stallworthy, Jon. *Anthem for Doomed Youth: Twelve Soldier Poets of the First World War*. London: Constable/Imperial War Museum, 2002. Movingly illustrated mixture of poems and biographical commentary, with a carefully selected list of further reading.

Wells, H. G. *Tono-Bungay*. 1909. Harmondsworth: Penguin, 2005.

Woolf, Virginia. *Mrs Dalloway*. 1925. Harmondsworth: Penguin, 1992.
A Room of One's Own. 1929. Harmondsworth: Penguin, 1945.

B Introductions and Overviews

i History and Culture

Constantine, Stephen. *Unemployment in Britain between the Wars*. Harlow: Longman, 1980. Part of a series of 'Seminar Studies in History', this short book provides a crisp analytical overview of the title's subject and a separate section of supporting documentary material, useful for discussion purposes.

Dewey, Peter. *War and Progress: Britain 1914–1945*. London and New York: Longman, 1997. A clearly written economic and social history of the period with an abundance of detailed tabular information.

Gardiner, Juliet, and Neil Wenborn, eds. *The History Today Companion to British History*. London: Collins and Brown, 1995. A handy and reliable dictionary-style work of reference with a wealth of intelligently cross-referenced entries on all aspects of British history – thus of value to the whole of the present book, but also often neatly summarising ongoing developments such as the women's suffrage campaign and the Irish Question which relate particularly to this chapter. See also the website, www.historytoday.com which has a range of relevant themes to explore in its archive section.

Haigh, Christopher, ed. *The Cambridge Historical Encyclopedia of Great Britain and Ireland*. Cambridge University Press, 1985. See especially chapter 7, but the whole book is a useful historical counterpart to the present book, using roughly similar period divisions. Ideal for quick reference and well illustrated.

Horne, John, ed. *A Companion to World War I*. Oxford: Wiley-Blackwell, 2010.

Hughes, Robert. *The Shock of the New: Art and the Century of Change*. 2nd edn. London: Thames and Hudson, 1992. First published 1980. A compelling introduction to the art of the twentieth century which, while concentrating on the visual arts, casts abundant light on the other arts too, including literature, and illuminates the modernist period particularly well. The book grew out of Hughes's superb BBC TV series of the same name (1980) but this appears not to be readily available today.

Jenkins, Alan. *The Twenties*. London: Peerage Books, 1974. An evocative popular social-historical survey of the decade, organised into short, loosely themed chapters, richly illustrated and entertainingly written.

Johnson, Paul, ed. *Twentieth-Century Britain: Economic, Social and Cultural Change*. London and New York: Longman, 1994. A scholarly collection of clearly written essays, helpfully subdivided into short thematic sections and covering a wide range of topics of direct relevance both to this chapter and the next one. A rich and reliable source of information, analysis and discussion, with focused suggestions for further reading attached to each essay. An excellent starting point for study of the period.

Richards, Denis, and J. W. Hunt. *An Illustrated History of Modern Britain 1783–1964*. 2nd edn. London: Longman, 1965. A little dated, but still largely reliable and particularly valuable for its clear organisation and crisp, concise and incisive treatment of events.

Strachan, Hew, ed. *The Oxford Illustrated History of the First World War*. Oxford University Press, 1999. An authoritative source of reference.

Taylor, A. J. P. *The First World War: An Illustrated History*. Harmondsworth: Penguin, 1966. Orig. pub. 1963. A straightforward and readable factual account of the war on all fronts.

Westwell, Ian. *The Complete Illustrated History of World War I: A Concise Authoritative Account of the Course of the Great War, With Analysis of Decisive Encounters and Landmark Engagements*. London: Hermes House (Anness Publishing), 2015. The title is accurate; and, with over 500 photographs, maps and battle plans in 256 detailed, clearly organised and lucidly written pages, difficult to beat as a concentrated and vivid overview.

Williams, Raymond. *Culture and Society 1780–1950*. London: Chatto and Windus, 1958. A classic overview of the period indicated, particularly useful for tracing continuities in thought and literature through to the twentieth century. (See also his *The Long Revolution* (London: Chatto and Windus, 1961) and *Keywords: A Vocabulary of Culture and Society* (London: Fontana, 1983) both of which continue and complement the work of the first book.)

ii Literature

Bradbury, Malcolm, and James McFarlane, eds. *Modernism: 1890–1930*. Harmondsworth: Penguin, 1976. Rptd with new preface, 1991. A seminal collection of essays, providing a comprehensive initial overview of international modernism, with a strong emphasis on social and intellectual contexts in the first part of the book. Also contains a detailed chronology of events, brief biographies of a hundred key figures of modernism and an extensive general bibliography. An excellent source of reference, though several of the essays are quite demanding and some are a little dated now.

Bradbury, Malcolm. *The Social Context of Modern English Literature*. Oxford: Blackwell, 1971. A sociological approach to the production and consumption of literature in the first half of the twentieth century; a little heavy going at times, but providing a detailed insight into socio-economic issues that are often neglected or glossed over by generalisations.

Bradshaw, David. *A Concise Companion to Modernism*. Oxford: Blackwell, 2003.

Bradshaw, David, and Kevin J. H. Dettmar, eds. *A Companion to Modernist Literature and Culture*. Oxford: Blackwell, 2006. Comprehensive coverage of the field through sixty-two well-focused short essays, including a large section of readings of key texts and a valuable final section on 'other' modernisms which neatly encompasses a range of new critical approaches to the subject.

Brooker, Peter, ed. *Modernism/Postmodernism*. London: Longman, 1992. A challenging but carefully selected anthology of key critical essays, with contextualising introductions and a useful general introduction by the editor. Includes an extensive bibliography.

Carey, John. *The Intellectuals and the Masses: Pride and Prejudice among the Literary Intelligentsia, 1880–1939*. London: Faber, 1992. A lively polemic which neatly sketches in the social background of the period while exploring writers' attitudes to prominent aspects of mass culture and society.

Chapple, I. A. V. *Documentary and Imaginative Literature 1880–1920*. London: Blandford Press, 1970. A clearly written contextual study of the literature of the stated period, with a strong emphasis on social history and drawing on many lesser-known contemporary writers and commentators.

Childs, Peter. *Modernism*. London and New York: Routledge, 2000. (New Critical Idiom Series.) Lucidly written and carefully explained, with a good sense of contemporary critical debates and many useful examples drawn from a wide range of material. Includes a short glossary of key terms. An excellent primer for undergraduate study.

Cunningham, Valentine. *British Writers of the Thirties*. Oxford University Press, 1988.

Faulkner, Peter. *Modernism*. London: Methuen, 1977. (Critical Idiom Series.) An earlier and briefer introduction in the same series as Childs's book above, with a narrower range and focus, but useful for an initial impression of 'classic' Anglo-American modernism.

Ford, Boris, ed. *The New Pelican Guide to English Literature, Vol. 7: From James to Eliot*. 3rd edn. Harmondsworth: Penguin, 1973. Orig. pub. 1961. Now inevitably a little old-fashioned, but still a valuable source of reference and historical perspective, with a good deal of contextual matter in Parts 1 and 2, many useful critical essays, and extensive primary and secondary bibliographies.

Hamill, Faye, Esme Miskimmin and Ashlie Sponenberg, eds. *Encyclopedia of British Women's Writing, 1900–1950*. Basingstoke: Palgrave Macmillan, 2006. Dictionary-style work with detailed entries on 185 authors and related contextualising topics. Excellent source of reference, including an annotated bibliography.

Joannou, Maroula, ed. *The History of British Women's Writing, 1920–1945*. Basingstoke: Palgrave Macmillan, 2013. (The History of British Women's Writing, vol. 8.) This and its companion volume below (under Laird), provide a comprehensive and critically up-to-the-minute account of women's writing for the whole of the period covered by this chapter. Each volume includes a helpful timeline and bibliography and is organised clearly into thematic sections with expert essays on a wide range of topics that map out the period in a stimulating new way.

Kemp, Sandra, Charlotte Mitchell and David Trotter. *Edwardian Fiction: An Oxford Companion*. Oxford University Press, 1997. A usefully focused and comprehensive source of reference.

Kern, Stephen. *The Modernist Novel: A Critical Introduction*. Cambridge University Press, 2011. An outstandingly clear and comprehensive introductory account of the modernist novel (and of modernism generally), and one which systematically contextualises modernism within the political, social and economic history of the period 1900–40. Each chapter focuses on a key element of literary narrative such as character, event, space, time and narration, and explores in close detail the major formal innovations of the leading 'high' modernists and how these innovations engaged with the history of the period. A sophisticated work and an excellent critical introduction for students.

Laird, Holly A. ed. *The History of British Women's Writing, 1880–1920*. Basingstoke: Palgrave Macmillan, 2016. (The History of British Women's Writing, vol. 7.)

McCulloch, Margery Palmer. *Scottish Modernism and Its Contexts: 1918–1959*. Edinburgh University Press, 2009.

Poplawski, Paul, ed. *Encyclopedia of Literary Modernism*. Westport, CT and London: Greenwood Press, 2003. Alphabetically organised entries on key authors, texts, contexts and movements, straightforwardly written, with focused suggestions for further reading and a general bibliography. Ranges widely across the period 1890–1940, with entries on Wales, Scotland and Ireland, a strong international dimension, and entries surveying the historical and cultural developments of the time. An accessible starting point for the period, complementing the anthologies by Kolocotroni et al. and Rainey [A].

Sanders, Andrew. *The Short Oxford History of English Literature*. 2nd edn. Oxford University Press, 2000 (chapters 8 and 9). A concise, reliable and readable introductory overview, with a comprehensive guide to further reading.

Stevenson, Randall. *The British Novel Since the Thirties: An Introduction*. London: Batsford, 1986. Particularly useful here for its detailed coverage of the decade of the thirties itself (in chapter 2), especially as this is usefully contextualised by an introductory first chapter on 'The Novel, 1900–1930'. The final chapter, on the experimental novel since 1930, is also valuable for discussing the continuities between modernism and post-modernism.

Modernist Fiction: An Introduction. London: Harvester Wheatsheaf, 1992.

Trodd, Anthea. *A Reader's Guide to Edwardian Literature*. New York: Harvester Wheatsheaf, 1991. A general survey with a helpful emphasis on social and historical contexts.

Women's Writing in English: Britain 1900–1945. London: Longman, 1998. A rich and accessible source of introductory information on women's writing across many different genres during the period, with useful suggestions for further reading. Includes many lesser-known writers and covers areas such as popular fiction, travel writing, children's fiction and autobiography, in addition to the mainstream literary genres.

Trotter, David. *The English Novel in History: 1895–1920*. London: Routledge, 1993. A detailed study of the social and historical context of literature in the period, especially useful for its coverage of popular fiction.

Ward, A. C. *Twentieth-Century Literature 1901–1950*. 12th edn. London: Methuen, 1956. Orig. pub. 1928, as *Twentieth-Century Literature 1901–1925: The Age of Interrogation*. A useful historical text in its own right for being first written within the period covered by this chapter and therefore providing a contemporary perspective *and* an example of contemporary critical discourse. Still eminently readable and insightful, and admirably concise for the amount of ground covered.

The Nineteen-Twenties: Literature and Ideas in the Post-War Decade. London: Methuen, 1930. More expansive on the particular decade than Ward's broader survey above, but the same point applies here that Ward provides a useful, and largely reliable, perspective from the period. Chapter 3, 'Modernist Adventures', is notable as one of the earliest systematic usages of 'modernist' as a literary-critical term.

Williams, Linda R. ed. *The Twentieth Century: A Guide to Literature from 1900 to the Present Day*. London: Bloomsbury, 1992. A very useful and reliable introductory guide combining a small group of compact, accessible critical essays and an A to Z reference section.

C   Further Reading

i Literature: Modernism and General

Bell, Michael, ed. *The Context of English Literature: 1900–1930*. London: Methuen, 1980. A small group of scholarly essays covering a range of contexts, but with an emphasis on intellectual history.

Bell, Michael. *Literature, Modernism and Myth: Belief and Responsibility in the Twentieth Century*. Cambridge University Press, 1997.

Berman, Marshall. *'All That is Solid Melts into Air'. The Experience of Modernity*. London: Verso, 1983. A classic interdisciplinary study of modernity which particularly stresses the urban experience.

Booth, Howard J., and Nigel Rigby, eds. *Modernism and Empire*. Manchester University Press, 2000. A collection of essays taking a broadly post-colonialist view of the modernist period.

Brannigan, John. *Archipelagic Modernism: Literature in the Irish and British Isles, 1890–1970*. Edinburgh University Press, 2015. A detailed, demanding, but rewarding scholarly work, important for challenging traditional Anglocentric and metropolitan versions of modernism.

Collier, Peter, and Judy Davies, eds. *Modernism and the European Unconscious*. Cambridge: Polity Press, 1990. A broad-ranging collection of essays emphasising the importance of psychoanalysis in the development of modernism.

Edel, Leon. *The Psychological Novel 1900–1950*. London: Rupert Hart-Davies, 1955. A succinct, incisive and readable treatment of this important topic. Dated, but still useful, with some close readings of key texts.

Hynes, Samuel. *The Auden Generation: Literature and Politics in England in the 1930s*. London: Bodley Head, 1976.

Kern, Stephen. *The Culture of Time and Space 1880–1918*. Cambridge, MA: Harvard University Press, 1983. Rptd with a new preface 2003. A seminal work of cultural history that cuts across arts and sciences in exploring how changes in technology and culture in this period fundamentally changed our ways of experiencing and thinking about time and space. The book abounds in literary discussion and is of particular relevance to the study of modernism (see also Kern's book in [Bii] above).

Levenson, Michael H., ed. *The Cambridge Companion to Modernism*. Cambridge University Press, 1999. A collection of essays providing wide general coverage of the whole field of literary modernism and including a chapter on further reading.

Lodge, David. *The Modes of Modern Writing: Metaphor, Metonymy and the Typology of Modern Literature*. London: Edward Arnold, 1977. An important collection of essays exploring the formal features of writing in the twentieth century, with a section of detailed readings on key authors. Some challenging ideas, but clearly written and illuminating.

'Modernism, Anti-Modernism and Postmodernism'. In *Working with Structuralism*. London: Routledge, 1981, pp. 3–16. Useful as an introductory outline of some of the main ideas explored in Lodge's book above.

Mao, Douglas, and Rebecca L. Walkowitz, eds. *Bad Modernisms*. Durham, NC: Duke University Press, 2006. A collection of essays viewing modernism from new perspectives (see next item).

Mao, Douglas, and Rebecca L. Walkowitz. 'The New Modernist Studies'. *PMLA* 123, 3 (May 2008): 737–48. In recent years, there has been a veritable explosion of works in what has now come to be known as 'the new modernist studies'. This authoritative essay provides a relatively brief and accessible overview of this development, including a comprehensive list of further references. For an online version, see: www.rci.rutgers.edu/~walkowit/pubs/NewModernistStudiesPMLA.pdf

Nicholls, Peter. *Modernisms: A Literary Guide*. London: Macmillan, 1991. A scholarly overview, important for challenging older canonical constructions of modernism and for emphasising the diversity of 'modernisms'.

Stewart, Jack. *The Vital Art of D. H. Lawrence: Vision and Expression*. Carbondale and Edwardsville: Southern Illinois University Press, 1999. Valuable beyond its single-author focus for its interdisciplinarity and for its close readings of Lawrence's texts in terms of their visual arts contexts.

Timms, Edward, and David Kelley, eds. *Unreal City: Urban Experience in Modern European Literature and Art*. New York: St Martin's Press, 1985.

Waugh, Patricia. *Revolutions of the Word: Intellectual Contexts for the Study of Modern Literature*. London: Hodder Arnold, 1997.

Williams, Raymond. *The Politics of Modernism: Against the New Conformists*. Ed. Tony Pinkney. London: Verso, 1989. A posthumous collection of Williams's essays exploring the cultural and political contexts of modernist literature.

Willison, Ian, et al., eds. *Modernist Writers and the Marketplace*. London: Macmillan, 1996. Usefully complements and updates Bradbury's *The Social Context of Modern English Literature* [Bii].

ii Literature and the First World War

Bergonzi, Bernard. *Heroes' Twilight: A Study of the Literature of the Great War*. 3rd edn. Manchester: Carcanet, 1996.

Cardinal, Agnes, et al., eds. *Women's Writing on the First World War*. Oxford University Press, 1999.

Cecil, Hugh. *The Flower of Battle: British Fiction Writers of the First World War*. London: Secker and Warburg, 1998.

Das, Santanu, ed. *The Cambridge Companion to the Poetry of the First World War*. Cambridge University Press, 2013. A stimulating and wide-ranging contemporary reassessment of a much-studied topic, and particularly valuable for expanding the field to include 'Archipelagic, Colonial and Civilian War Poetry' in Part III. Includes chronologies and a guide to further reading.

Fussell, Paul. *The Great War and Modern Memory*. Oxford University Press, 1975.

Hynes, Samuel. *A War Imagined: The First World War and British Culture*. London: Pimlico, 1990.

Ouditt, Sharon. *Women Writers of the First World War: An Annotated Bibliography*. London: Routledge, 1999.

Sherry, Vincent, ed. *The Cambridge Companion to the Literature of the First World War*. Cambridge University Press, 2005. The essays in the first part of this book provide a good general introduction to the topic, and there is a helpful chronology and guide to further reading; the later essays range more widely and include a discussion of the war and cinema.

Silkin, Jon. *Out of Battle: The Poetry of the Great War*. 2nd edn. Basingstoke: Macmillan, 1998.

Smith, Angela K. *The Second Battlefield: Women, Modernism and the First World War*. Manchester University Press, 2000.

Tate, Trudi. *Modernism, History and the First World War*. Manchester University Press, 1998.

iii Women's Writing and the Women's Movement

Beauman, Nicola. *A Very Great Profession: The Woman's Novel 1914–39*. London: Virago, 1983. A seminal work for its recuperation of many forgotten novels and novelists of the period and its championing of the 'middlebrow' woman's novel. Many of the works discussed have since been reprinted by Beauman's Persephone Books.

Benstock, Shari. *Women of the Left Bank, Paris 1900–1940*. London: Virago, 1987.

Caine, Barbara. *English Feminism 1780–1980*. Oxford University Press, 1997.

Felski, Rita. *The Gender of Modernity*. Cambridge, MA: Harvard University Press, 1996.

Gilbert, Sandra, and Susan Gubar. *No Man's Land: The Place of the Woman Writer in the Twentieth Century*. 3 vols. New Haven, CT: Yale University Press, 1988, 1989, 1994.

Hanscombe, Gillian and Virginia L. Smyers. *Writing for their Lives: The Modernist Women 1910–1940*. London: Women's Press, 1987.

Harrison, Brian. *Prudent Revolutionaries: Portraits of British Feminists between the Wars*. Oxford: Clarendon Press, 1987.

Joannou, Maroula, ed. *Women Writers of the 1930s: Gender, Politics, and History*. Edinburgh University Press, 1998. A collection of historically contextualised critical essays which challenges traditional accounts of the literature of this period.

Law, Cheryl. *Suffrage and Power: The Women's Movement 1918–1928*. London and New York: Tauris, 1997.

Pugh, Martin. *Women and the Women's Movement in Britain 1914–1959*. London: Macmillan, 1992.

Showalter, Elaine. *A Literature of Their Own: British Women Novelists from Brontë to Lessing*. London: Virago, 1978.

iv Cinema and Film

Chanan, Michael. *The Dream that Kicks: The Prehistory and Early Years of Cinema in Britain*. 2nd edn. London and New York: Routledge, 1996.

Christie, Ian. *The Last Machine: Early Cinema and the Birth of the Modern World*. London: BBC Education and British Film Institute, 1994.

Donald, James, Anne Friedberg and Laura Marcus, eds. *Close Up 1927–1933: Cinema and Modernism*. London: Cassell, 1998. A valuable compilation of original articles (many by modernist writers Dorothy Richardson and H. D.) from the avant-garde film journal, *Close Up*, with contextualising introductions and appendices.

Marcus, Laura. *The Tenth Muse: Writing About Cinema in the Modernist Period*. Oxford University Press, 2007. An important study of the impact of cinema on the literature and culture of the early twentieth century.

Metropolis. Dir. Fritz Lang (1927). A classic and highly influential early sci-fi movie, particularly notable here for its expressionist style and its modernist vision of the city as a place of mechanisation and alienation. The city in the film is a decidedly futuristic one but it was inspired by Lang's visit to New York in 1924. The film is available in different versions, but the most complete is the restored one issued in the Masters of Cinema series in 2010.

Morris, Nigel. 'Film and Modernism'. In Poplawski, ed., *Encyclopedia of Literary Modernism* [Bii], pp. 110–20.

7   The Twentieth and Twenty-First Centuries, 1939–2015

JOHN BRANNIGAN

This chapter brings the story of English literature in its historical context from the beginning of the Second World War in 1939 to the present day. As we approach the contemporary, it is more difficult to say with any accuracy what are the determining contexts and prevailing trends of English literature. This is partly because it is more difficult to settle on what are the major texts and major issues of this period. It is possible, however, to recognise that there have been huge changes in British society and culture since 1939, most notably the effects of the Second World War, the decline of the British empire, the rise and fall of the welfare state, the liberalisation of sexuality and gender roles, and the influence of migration, devolution and globalisation on contemporary meanings of English and British national identity. These changes have affected English literature since 1939 in various ways, most notably in the turn against modernism after the war, the waxing and waning of post-modernism, the increased significance of women's writing and writing by ethnic minorities in Britain, and the renewed emphasis on the Condition of England. This chapter is an attempt to explain the relationship between these new trends in English writings and their historical contexts.

Chronology

	HISTORY AND CULTURE	LITERATURE
1939	Outbreak of Second World War British forces arrive in France Evacuation of children from London	T. S. Eliot, *The Family Reunion* Robert Graves, *The Long Weekend* James Joyce, *Finnegans Wake* Jan Struther, *Mrs Miniver*
1940	Winston Churchill succeeds Neville Chamberlain as British Prime Minister (PM) British forces forced to evacuate from France through Dunkirk Battle of Britain – the battle for air supremacy	Dylan Thomas, *A Portrait of the Artist as a Young Dog* Graham Greene, *The Power and the Glory*
1941	USA and USSR (Allies) enter the war against Germany and Japan (Axis) Rowntree Report on Poverty	Noel Coward, *Blithe Spirit*
1942	Battle of El Alamein – British forces defeat the Germans in North Africa Beveridge Report on Social Security, which forms a blueprint for the post-war welfare state	Eliot, 'Little Gidding'

	HISTORY AND CULTURE	LITERATURE
1943	Allied invasion of Italy Fall of Mussolini	Coward, *This Happy Breed* Henry Green, *Caught* Greene, *The Ministry of Fear*
1944	D-Day invasions of Normandy Allies recapture France Butler Education Act Michael Tippett, *A Child of Our Time* (oratorio) Miners' Strike	H. E. Bates, *Fair Stood the Wind for France* Ivy Compton-Burnett, *Elders and Betters* Eliot, *Four Quartets* Aldous Huxley, *Time Must Have a Stop*
1945	First atomic bombs dropped on Nagasaki and Hiroshima End of Second World War, celebrated by VE and VJ Days Labour form new government under Clement Attlee Benjamin Britten, *Peter Grimes* (opera)	John Betjeman, *New Bats in Old Belfries* Norman Collins, *London Belongs to Me* Green, *Loving* Philip Larkin, *The North Ship* Nancy Mitford, *The Pursuit of Love* George Orwell, *Animal Farm* Elizabeth Taylor, *At Mrs Lippincote's* Evelyn Waugh, *Brideshead Revisited*
1946	National Health Act Bank of England nationalised Bertrand Russell, *History of Western Philosophy* Arts Council founded	Keith Douglas, *Alamein to Zem Zem* Larkin, *Jill* Eric Linklater, *Private Angelo* Taylor, *Palladian* D. Thomas, *Deaths and Entrances*
1947	India becomes independent from Britain USA provides Marshall Aid for European recovery Coal industry nationalised	Compton-Burnett, *Manservant and Maidservant* Patrick Hamilton, *The Slaves of Solitude*
1948	End of British rule in Palestine British Nationality Bill defines all Commonwealth and empire citizens as British subjects Railways nationalised National Health Service (NHS) founded	T. S. Eliot, *Notes Towards the Definition of Culture* Christopher Fry, *The Lady's Not for Burning* Greene, *The Heart of the Matter* F. R. Leavis, *The Great Tradition* Terence Rattigan, *The Browning Version* Waugh, *The Loved One*
1949	North Atlantic Treaty Organisation (NATO) formed China becomes communist under Mao Tse Tsung Iron and steel industries nationalised	Elizabeth Bowen, *The Heat of the Day* Eliot, *The Cocktail Party* Mitford, *Love in a Cold Climate* Orwell, *Nineteen Eighty-Four*
1950	Britain sends troops to join UN forces in Korea, attempting to prevent communist insurgency supported by China Labour returned to government, with small majority	William Cooper, *Scenes from Provincial Life* Greene, *The Third Man* Doris Lessing, *The Grass is Singing* Barbara Pym, *Some Tame Gazelle* Waugh, *Helena* Antonia White, *The Lost Traveller*
1951	British communist spies Burgess and Maclean defect to USSR Atomic energy produces electricity Festival of Britain Conservatives form new government, with Churchill returning as PM	Keith Douglas, *Collected Poems* Larkin, *Poems* Olivia Manning, *School for Love*
1952	King George VI dies Britain produces its own atomic bomb First contraceptive tablets made State of emergency in Kenya	Agatha Christie, *The Mousetrap* Donald Davie, *Purity of Diction in English Verse* David Jones, *The Anathemata* Lessing, *Martha Quest* Rattigan, *The Deep Blue Sea* D. Thomas, *Collected Poems* Angus Wilson, *Hemlock and After*

	HISTORY AND CULTURE	LITERATURE
1953	Coronation of Queen Elizabeth II Hillary and Tenzing climb Mount Everest (Himalayas)	L. P. Hartley, *The Go-Between* Ian Fleming, *Casino Royale* Rosamund Lehmann, *The Echoing Grove* John Wain, *Hurry on Down*
1954	End of post-war food rationing	Kingsley Amis, *Lucky Jim* William Golding, *Lord of the Flies* George Lamming, *The Emigrants* Lessing, *A Proper Marriage* Rattigan, *Separate Tables* D. Thomas, *Under Milk Wood*
1955	Treaty for European Union (EU) Equal pay for women in civil service Churchill retires Conservatives returned as government, and Anthony Eden becomes PM State of emergency in Cyprus	Samuel Beckett, *Waiting for Godot* Bowen, *A World of Love* Greene, *The Quiet American* Larkin, *The Less Deceived* R. S. Thomas, *Song at the Year's Turning*
1956	Suez crisis – Britain forced to withdraw from invasion of Egypt USSR crushes insurrection in Hungary Transatlantic telephone service started Colin Wilson, *The Outsider* Anthony Crosland, *The Future of Socialism*	Brendan Behan, *The Quare Fellow* Robert Conquest (ed.), *New Lines* C. S. Lewis, *The Chronicles of Narnia* John Osborne, *Look Back in Anger* John Petty, *Five Fags a Day* Sam Selvon, *The Lonely Londoners* J. R. R. Tolkien, *The Lord of the Rings* Wilson, *Anglo-Saxon Attitudes*
1957	Eden resigns as PM Harold Macmillan becomes PM Britain tests its first nuclear bomb European Economic Community is formed Ghana becomes independent Richard Hoggart, *The Uses of Literacy* Wolfenden Report on sexuality, which recommends decriminalisation of homosexuality Tom Maschler (ed.), *Declaration* – a collection of political essays by prominent writers in Britain	John Braine, *Room at the Top* Ted Hughes, *The Hawk in the Rain* Larkin, *A Girl in Winter* Colin MacInnes, *City of Spades* Iris Murdoch, *The Sandcastle* V. S. Naipaul, *The Mystic Masseur* Osborne, *The Entertainer* Taylor, *Angel* Waugh, *The Ordeal of Gilbert Penfold*
1958	Race riots in Nottingham and Notting Hill J. K. Galbraith, *The Affluent Society* First stereo recordings Campaign for Nuclear Disarmament (CND) founded Raymond Williams, *Culture and Society*	Bates, *The Darling Buds of May* Behan, *The Hostage* Betjeman, *Collected Poems* Shelagh Delaney, *A Taste of Honey* Ann Jellicoe, *The Sport of My Mad Mother* Errol John, *Moon on a Rainbow Shawl* Bernard Kops, *Awake for Mourning* Rose Macaulay, *The World My Wilderness* Murdoch, *The Bell* Harold Pinter, *The Birthday Party* Paul Scott, *The Alien Sky* Alan Sillitoe, *Saturday Night and Sunday Morning*
1959	Aldermaston demonstration against nuclear weapons Conservatives returned as government First section of M1 motorway opened, the first motor- way in Britain C. P. Snow, *The Two Cultures*	John Arden, *Serjeant Musgrave's Dance* Malcolm Bradbury, *Eating People is Wrong* E. R. Braithwaite, *To Sir, With Love* P. H. Johnson, *The Unspeakable Skipton* Laurie Lee, *Cider with Rosie* MacInnes, *Absolute Beginners* Mervyn Peake, *Gormenghast Trilogy* Sillitoe, *The Loneliness of the Long Distance Runner* Keith Waterhouse, *Billy Liar* Arnold Wesker, *Roots*

	HISTORY AND CULTURE	LITERATURE
1960	CND demonstrations in Trafalgar Square Demonstrations in Trafalgar Square against South Africa's apartheid regime *New Left Review* begins Heart pacemaker invented The TV soap opera *Coronation Street* begins The *Lady Chatterley* trial – Penguin wins the right to publish D. H. Lawrence's *Lady Chatterley's Lover*, banned since 1928, and it sells 3 million copies this year alone	Lynne Reid Banks, *The L-Shaped Room* Stan Barstow, *A Kind of Loving* Lawrence Durrell, *The Alexandria Quartet* Wilson Harris, *The Palace of the Peacock* Lessing, *In Pursuit of the English* Pinter, *The Caretaker* Sylvia Plath, *The Colossus* Rattigan, *Ross* Andrew Salkey, *Escape to an Autumn Pavement* David Storey, *This Sporting Life*
1961	Commonwealth Immigrants Bill ends the right to free entry of Commonwealth citizens South Africa leaves the Commonwealth DNA structure detected The satirical magazine *Private Eye* begins	Roy Fisher, *City* Thom Gunn, *My Sad Captains* Osborne, *Luther* Muriel Spark, *The Prime of Miss Jean Brodie* Waugh, *Sword of Honour Trilogy*
1962	Jamaica, Trinidad and Uganda become independent End of national military service Anthony Sampson, *The Anatomy of Britain*	Al Alvarez (ed.), *The New Poetry* Anthony Burgess, *A Clockwork Orange* Lessing, *The Golden Notebook*
1963	President J. F. Kennedy assassinated in the USA Nuclear Test Ban Treaty signed CND demonstrations in Trafalgar Square Macmillan resigns as PM Alec Douglas-Home becomes PM Kenya becomes independent Britten, *War Requiem* Robbins Report on Higher Education	Nell Dunn, *Up the Junction* B. S. Johnson, *Travelling People* Naipaul, *Mr Stone and the Knights Companion* Plath, *The Bell Jar* Theatre Workshop, *Oh! What a Lovely War*
1964	Labour forms government under Harold Wilson Herbert Marcuse, *One-Dimensional Man*	Christine Brooke-Rose, *Out* Larkin, *The Whitsun Weddings* Joe Orton, *Entertaining Mr Sloane* Selvon, *The Housing Lark* Wilson, *Late Call*
1965	Race Relations Bill attempts to curb racial discrimination in public places Abolition of the death penalty CND demonstrations in Trafalgar Square against Vietnam War State of emergency in Aden (now Yemen) Rhodesia declares independence The Beatles awarded MBE	Edward Bond, *Saved* Margaret Drabble, *The Millstone* Manning, *The Balkan Trilogy* Osborne, *A Patriot for Me* Pinter, *The Homecoming* Plath, *Ariel*
1966	Labour returned as government Guyana becomes independent The Colonial Office is merged into the Commonwealth Office England wins World Cup (soccer) *Cathy Come Home* televised	Basil Bunting, *Briggflatts* John Fowles, *The Magus* Greene, *The Comedians* Orton, *Loot* Jean Rhys, *Wide Sargasso Sea* Tom Stoppard, *Rosencrantz and Guildenstern are Dead*
1967	Abortion legalised Homosexuality decriminalised First heart transplant Widespread use of the contraceptive pill	Angela Carter, *The Magic Toyshop* Dunn, *Poor Cow* Henri, McGough, Patten, *The Mersey Sound* Elizabeth Jennings, *Collected Works* Naipaul, *The Mimic Men* Wilson, *No Laughing Matter*

	HISTORY AND CULTURE	LITERATURE
1968	Commonwealth Immigration Bill attempts to control the immigration of Kenyan Asians Race Relations Bill makes racial discrimination illegal Enoch Powell's Birmingham speech inciting racial division May Uprising in Paris Anti-Vietnam War demonstrations in London Commonwealth Office merged into Foreign Office Theatre censorship ends in Britain	Bond, *Early Morning* C. Day Lewis succeeds John Masefield as Poet Laureate Barry Hines, *A Kestrel for a Knave*
1969	Northern Ireland 'troubles' begin, with nationalist insurgents demanding independence from Britain Largest miners' strike since 1944 US astronauts walk on the moon Human eggs fertilised *in vitro* Booker Prize (fiction) started	Fowles, *The French Lieutenant's Woman* Greene, *Travels with my Aunt* Michael Horovitz (ed.), *Children of Albion* B. S. Johnson, *The Unfortunates* Lessing, *Children of Violence* Bernice Rubens, *The Elected Member*
1970	Equal Pay Bill Conservatives form government under Edward Heath Voting age reduced to eighteen Computer 'floppy' disks invented The Beatles disband Formation of the Women's Liberation Movement	Hughes, *Crow* C. P. Snow, *Strangers and Brothers* novel sequence completed (begun 1940)
1971	Immigration Bill attempts to distinguish alien immigrants from those with UK lineage Greenpeace founded Decimalisation of sterling currency Miners' strike leads to State of Emergency	Bond, *Lear* Geoffrey Hill, *Mercian Hymns* Naipaul, *In a Free State* Taylor, *Mrs Palfrey at the Claremont*
1972	Northern Ireland placed directly under Westminster rule (the end of regional government in Northern Ireland)	John Berger, *G.* John Betjeman succeeds C. Day Lewis as Poet Laureate Carter, *The Infernal Desire Machines of Doctor Hoffman* Drabble, *The Needle's Eye* Stoppard, *Jumpers*
1973	Britain enters the European Economic Community Oil and energy crisis Fishing disputes begin 'the cod war' with Iceland Health Minister Keith Joseph unveils controversial plans to introduce private health care within the NHS	Martin Amis, *The Rachel Papers* J. G. Ballard, *Crash* Greene, *The Honorary Consul* B. S. Johnson, *Christy Malry's Own Double Entry* Murdoch, *The Black Prince* Peter Shaffer, *Equus*
1974	First election results in no majority A Labour government forms under Harold Wilson A second election confirms Labour government First evidence of erosion of the ozone layer	Ballard, *Concrete Island* Burgess, *The Enderby Novels* Larkin, *High Windows* Lessing, *The Memoirs of a Survivor* Murdoch, *The Sacred and Profane Love Machine*
1975	Sex Discrimination Bill Inflation reaches 25 per cent Extraction of oil from the North Sea	M. Amis, *Dead Babies* Bradbury, *The History Man* Trevor Griffiths, *Comedians* Ruth Prawer Jhabvala, *Heat and Dust* David Lodge, *Changing Places* Anthony Powell, *A Dance to the Music of Time* novel sequence completed (begun 1951) Salman Rushdie, *Grimus* Selvon, *Moses Ascending* Iain Sinclair, *Lud Heat* Scott, *The Raj Quartet*

	HISTORY AND CULTURE	LITERATURE
1976	Race Relations Act strengthens anti-discrimination laws Wilson retires as PM James Callaghan becomes PM Riots in Notting Hill Concorde begins passenger service National Theatre completed	David Edgar, *Destiny* Lehmann, *A Sea-Grape Tree* Storey, *Saville* Emma Tennant, *Hotel de Dream*
1977	Anti-racist riots in Lewisham First AIDS deaths recognised in New York Punk becomes popular Tom Nairn, *The Break-Up of Britain* Virago Press publishes first book	Carter, *The Passion of New Eve* Scott, *Staying On* Stoppard, *Professional Foul*
1978	The first 'test-tube' baby	David Hare, *Plenty* Hill, *Tenebrae* Ian McEwan, *The Cement Garden* Murdoch, *The Sea, The Sea* Tennant, *The Bad Sister* Fay Weldon, *Praxis*
1979	Workers' strikes and bad weather conditions make up the 'winter of discontent' Anti-racist protester, Blair Peach, is killed at a National Front rally Conservatives form government under Margaret Thatcher Medical profession confirms that smoking causes cancer	Caryl Churchill, *Cloud Nine* Golding, *Darkness Visible* Naipaul, *A Bend in the River* Craig Raine, *A Martian Sends a Postcard Home* Tennant, *Wild Nights*
1980	Zimbabwe becomes independent Riots in Bristol British Airways and British Aerospace privatised Worst recession in 50 years E. P. Thompson and Dan Smith, *Protest and Survive*	Howard Brenton, *The Romans in Britain* Burgess, *Earthly Powers* Golding, *Rites of Passage* L. K. Johnson, *Inglan is a Bitch* Manning, *The Levant Trilogy* Caryl Phillips, *Strange Fruit* Tom Phillips, *The Humument* Graham Swift, *The Sweet-Shop Owner*
1981	British Nationality Bill restricts the definition of British citizenship Riots in London, Liverpool and Manchester CND demonstrations in London IBM launches the personal computer	Fisher, *Poems 1955–80* Rushdie, *Midnight's Children* Swift, *Shuttlecock* D. M. Thomas, *The White Hotel*
1982	War against Argentina in the Falkland Islands Women demonstrate against nuclear weapons at Greenham Common Compact disc players introduced	Pat Barker, *Union Street* Churchill, *Top Girls* Alasdair Gray, *Lanark* Timothy Mo, *Sour Sweet* Morrison and Motion (eds.), *Contemporary British Poetry* C. Phillips, *Where There is Darkness*
1983	Conservatives returned as government US cruise missiles deployed in Britain	Susan Hill, *The Woman in Black* Rushdie, *Shame* Selvon, *Moses Migrating* Swift, *Waterland* Weldon, *The Life and Loves of a She Devil*

HISTORY AND CULTURE	LITERATURE
1984 Miners' strike and aggressive police response create deep divisions British Telecom privatised IRA attempt to assassinate Thatcher in Brighton First successes of gene cloning	K. Amis, *Stanley and the Women* M. Amis, *Money* Ballard, *Empire of the Sun* Ian Banks, *The Wasp Factory* Julian Barnes, *Flaubert's Parrot* Carter, *Nights at the Circus* Ted Hughes succeeds John Betjeman as Poet Laureate Lodge, *Small World* Raine, *Rich* Michele Roberts, *The Wild Girl*
1985 Riots in London and Birmingham Public buses are privatised TV soap opera *EastEnders* begins Live Aid pop concerts for famine relief in Ethiopia	Peter Ackroyd, *Hawksmoor* Brenton and Hare, *Pravda* Tony Harrison, *v.* Hill, *Collected Poems* C. Phillips, *The Final Passage* Jeanette Winterson, *Oranges Are Not the Only Fruit*
1986 British Gas is privatised Laptop computers introduced	K. Amis, *The Old Devils* Barker, *The Century's Daughter* Jim Crace, *Continent* Kazuo Ishiguro, *An Artist of the Floating World*
1987 Conservatives returned as government Storms cause massive destruction Stock market crash Paul Gilroy, *There Ain't No Black in the Union Jack*	Ackroyd, *Chatterton* Bruce Chatwin, *The Songlines* Churchill, *Serious Money* Drabble, *The Radiant Way* Penelope Lively, *Moon Tiger* McEwan, *The Child in Time* Winterson, *The Passion*
1988 Stephen Hawking, *A Brief History of Time*	Allnutt et al. (eds.), *The New British Poetry* Chatwin, *Utz* Crace, *The Gift of Stones* Alan Hollinghurst, *The Swimming-Pool Library* Larkin, *Collected Poems* Lodge, *Nice Work* Michael Moorcock, *Mother London* Rushdie, *The Satanic Verses* Swift, *Out of this World* Alan Warner, *The Lost Father*
1989 Revolutions in Eastern Europe The end of the Cold War Iranian death threats against Salman Rushdie National Curriculum introduced in schools Ruins of Shakespeare's theatres discovered in London Rave parties become popular	Ackroyd, *First Light* M. Amis, *London Fields* Ishiguro, *The Remains of the Day* Winterson, *Sexing the Cherry*
1990 Thatcher resigns as PM John Major becomes PM Germany reunified Human gene experimentation	Beryl Bainbridge, *An Awfully Big Adventure* A. S. Byatt, *Possession* Hanif Kureishi, *The Buddha of Suburbia* Nigel Williams, *The Wimbledon Poisoner*
1991 Britain and the USA go to war against Iraq on United Nations mission Britain opts out of European single currency Francis Fukuyama, *The End of History*	M. Amis, *Time's Arrow* Carter, *Wise Children* Mo, *The Redundancy of Courage* Ben Okri, *The Famished Road* C. Phillips, *Cambridge* Sinclair, *Downriver*

HISTORY AND CULTURE	LITERATURE
1992 Conservatives returned as government Europe creates the single market Government forced to devalue sterling currency	Crace, *Arcadia* Gunn, *The Man with Night Sweats* Harrison, *The Common Chorus* Victor Headley, *Yardie* Nick Hornby, *Fever Pitch* Roberts, *Daughters of the House* Barry Unsworth, *Sacred Hunger*
1993 Racist murder of Stephen Lawrence in south London	Fred D'Aguiar, *British Subjects* Sebastian Faulks, *Birdsong* Hulse, Kennedy and Morley (eds.), *The New Poetry* Trevor Johnson, *Hysteria* C. Phillips, *Crossing the River*
1994 Northern Ireland Peace Process begins The National Lottery commences – a weekly televised lottery, part of the proceeds of which go to fund charities and public amenities The Church of England ordains its first women priests	Ackroyd, *Dan Leno and the Limehouse Golem* Jonathan Coe, *What a Carve Up!* D'Aguiar, *The Longest Memory* Romesh Gunesekera, *Reef* Hollinghurst, *The Folding Star* Terry Johnson, *Dead Funny* Sinclair, *Radon Daughters*
1995 The Channel Tunnel opens between Britain and France	Barker, *Regeneration Trilogy* M. Amis, *The Information* Sarah Kane, *Blasted* Rushdie, *The Moor's Last Sigh*
1996 'Mad Cow Disease' (BSE) outbreak Successful cloning of sheep at Roslin Institute, Edinburgh	Bainbridge, *Every Man for Himself* Pinter, *Ashes to Ashes* Helen Fielding, *Bridget Jones's Diary* Mark Ravenhill, *Shopping and Fucking* Swift, *Last Orders*
1997 Labour form government under Tony Blair Hong Kong reverts to Chinese authority Princess Diana killed in car crash Referenda on devolution of Scotland and Wales	Crace, *Quarantine* McEwan, *Enduring Love* C. Phillips, *The Nature of Blood* Sinclair, *Lights Out for the Territory*
1998 The 'Belfast Agreement' signals progress towards a political settlement in Northern Ireland	Barker, *Another World* Barnes, *England, England* Hughes, *Birthday Letters* John King, *England Away* McEwan, *Amsterdam* Andrew Motion, *Selected Poems 1976–1997* Andrew Motion succeeds Ted Hughes as Poet Laureate
1999 Macpherson Report on Racism in the Police Force Racist bombs in London The Scottish Parliament and Welsh Assembly open (regional government for Scotland and Wales)	Ackroyd, *The Plato Papers* Simon Armitage, *Killing Time* Melvyn Bragg, *The Soldier's Return* Rushdie, *The Ground Beneath Her Feet* Sarah Waters, *Tipping the Velvet*
2000 Millennium celebrations feature 'The Dome' in Greenwich, and 'The London Eye'	D'Aguiar, *Bloodlines* Ishiguro, *When We Were Orphans* Matthew Kneale, *English Passengers* Newland and Sesay, *IC3* Zadie Smith, *White Teeth*
2001 9/11 Terrorist attacks in USA Labour returned as government	Barker, *Border Crossing* McEwan, *Atonement* Rachel Seiffert, *The Dark Room*

	HISTORY AND CULTURE	LITERATURE
2002	British and US forces invade Afghanistan	Michael Frayn, *Spies* Sarah Hall, *Haweswater* Z. Smith, *The Autograph Man* Waters, *Fingersmith* Alice Oswald, *Dart*
2003	British and US forces invade Iraq	Monica Ali, *Brick Lane* M. Amis, *Yellow Dog* Swift, *The Light of Day*
2004	10 countries join the European Union, bringing the total to 25 member countries	Barker, *Double Vision* S. Hall, *The Electric Michelangelo* Hollinghurst, *The Line of Beauty* Andrea Levy, *Small Island* David Mitchell, *Cloud Atlas*
2005	Labour returned as government Terrorist attacks on London kill 52 people	Barnes, *Arthur and George* Chris Cleave, *Incendiary* Ishiguro, *Never Let Me Go* McEwan, *Saturday* Z. Smith, *On Beauty* Ali Smith, *The Accidental* Leila Aboulela, *Minaret*
2006	Terrorist threats continue, with a major plot to blow up planes from the UK disrupted Russian dissident Alexander Litvinenko is murdered in London Mandarin Chinese surpasses English as most widely used internet language UK repays last instalment of Anglo-American loan of 1946	Tom McCarthy, *Remainder* Mitchell, *Black Swan Green* Anthony Neilson, *Realism*
2007	Tony Blair is replaced as PM by Gordon Brown Northern Ireland Assembly forms, with Unionist and Nationalist partners in government Scottish Nationalist Party wins Scottish parliamentary elections UK hit by major storms and floods, the worst in sixty years Global banking crisis begins	McEwan, *On Chesil Beach* S. Hall, *The Carhullan Army* Sean O'Brien, *The Drowned Book* Oswald, *A Sleepwalk on the Severn* Bola Agbaje, *Gone Too Far!* Polly Stenham, *That Face*
2008	Global recession begins, lasting until 2012, and causing sharp rise in unemployment, credit crises, and housing market collapse UK government announces £400 billion to bail out failing banks	Gordon Burn, *Born Yesterday* Philip Hensher, *The Northern Clemency* Simon Stephens, *Pornography*
2009	Parliamentary expenses scandal Henry Allingham and Harry Patch, two of the last surviving veterans of the First World War, die within days of each other in July Unemployment reaches 2.5 million Protests against G20 summit in London	Hilary Mantel, *Wolf Hall* S. Hall, *How to Paint a Dead Man* John Burnside, *Glister* S. Stephens, *Punk Rock* Carol Ann Duffy succeeds Andrew Motion as Poet Laureate
2010	Conservatives and Liberal Democrats form a coalition government, with David Cameron as PM Student protests in UK against rising costs of tuition	Jon McGregor, *Even the Dogs* Laura Wade, *Posh* Howard Jacobson, *The Finkler Question* Levy, *The Long Song* Will Self, *Walking to Hollywood*

	HISTORY AND CULTURE	LITERATURE
2011	Anti-austerity protests in London Riots in English cities British troops withdrawn from Iraq	A. Smith, *There But For The* Burnside, *Black Cat Bone* Barnes, *The Sense of an Ending*
2012	London hosts the Olympic Games Child sexual abuse scandals, with allegations investigated against former TV celebrities and former government ministers	Z. Smith, *NW* Mantel, *Bring Up the Bodies* Lucy Kirkwood, *NSFW* Self, *Umbrella*
2013	Succession to the Crown Act ends the 1701 ban on monarchs married to Roman Catholics, and ends male primogeniture in royal succession	Crace, *Harvest* Kirkwood, *Chimerica*
2014	Scottish independence referendum held, with 55 per cent against independence Same-sex marriage legalised in UK, except Northern Ireland British troops withdraw from Afghanistan	Mitchell, *The Bone Clocks* Rona Munro, *The James Plays* A. Smith, *How To Be Both*
2015	Queen Elizabeth II becomes the longest reigning monarch in British history Conservatives form government, with David Cameron as PM	McCarthy, *Satin Island* Sarah Howe, *Loop of Jade* Mitchell, *Slade House*

Historical Overview

Introduction

This overview of the history of the post-war and contemporary periods in Britain provides an introductory narrative of the major social, political and cultural trends which might be considered the defining contexts of recent British literature. Life in Britain since the Second World War has changed considerably, and while many changes are comparable to those experienced in other countries, some are distinctive. The war lived on in the British cultural imagination perhaps longer than was the case for other combatant nations. The declining world power of Britain, and the loss of its empire, resulted in a complex process of redefining and revisiting ideas of national identity. The attempts, in the early 2000s, by Prime Minister Tony Blair to establish the idea of 'Cool Britannia' and 'New Britain' were perhaps indicative of the struggle to reimagine what it means to be English or British after the war and after the empire. The Scottish Independence Referendum in 2014, and the UK European Union Referendum in 2016, indicated that key questions about what constituted 'British' national identity, and what forms of international alliance were desired in Britain, remain unresolved.

Britain and the Post-War World

The Second World War began in September 1939, at the end of a decade of economic depression, and after a series of wars and invasions across Europe in which fascism emerged as a triumphant power in Germany, Italy and Spain. After the German invasion of France in 1940, Britain stood alone, awaiting the seemingly imminent invasion of its shores by German forces. Russia had made a pact with Germany which lasted until 1941. It took the Japanese attack on Pearl Harbor in 1941 finally to persuade the USA to enter the war against fascism in Europe. It took the combined forces of these three world powers, along with many smaller allies, to defeat the 'axis' forces of Germany, Italy and Japan by 1945.

For many people in Britain since 1945, the Second World War represented the last great theatre of heroism and glory. Boys in particular immersed themselves in watching films like *The Dam Busters* (1954), *The Longest Day* (1962), and *A Bridge Too Far* (1977), reading 'comics' like *Victor* (1961–92), *Valiant* (1962–76), *Battle* (1975–88) and *Commando* (1961–), collecting toy soldiers representing the 'Desert Rats' against the 'Afrika Korps', or making scale models of the Spitfire and the Messerschmitt 109. The war – and winning the war – made a deep and lasting impression on British culture. It was represented as the victory of a determined, proud and stubborn people against the evil of fascism. It placed Britain on the side of moral righteousness, in contrast to the bitter and grubby roles Britain had played and continued to play after the war in its colonies. It placed Britain, too, at the centre of world affairs, the saviour of oppressed peoples from the terror of Nazism. In many ways, the stories that Britain told itself about the war can now be seen as somewhat mythic, or at least exaggerated. The economic, industrial and military power of the USA and Russia won the war, not the personality traits of British people. Alongside Britain's heroic role in sending the expeditionary force in 1939, the air war in 1940, the North Africa campaign, and the D-Day landings, there runs an alternative narrative of humiliation and defeat at Dunkirk, Arnhem and Singapore, and the widespread devastation of the Blitz on the civilian population. The stories of national unity and resilience also mask the more complicated realities of a society deeply divided, especially along class lines, and often serve to silence some of the more telling accounts of how, for many working-class people, the poverty, mechanisation and rationing of wartime was a continuation of, and not a contrast to, their experiences of the depression in the 1930s. Although the war has been conventionally represented as a glorious chapter in modern British history, then, it is also in many ways symptomatic of Britain's declining role in world affairs, its dependence on the burgeoning superpower of the USA, and its increasingly visible social divisions and problems.

Britain was no longer secure in its place as a world leader, and that was increasingly evident in the management of its empire. In 1944, as British troops were taking part in the Allied forces' invasion of occupied France, the British empire could claim some 760 million inhabitants outside the British Isles. After Hong Kong was returned to Chinese control in 1997, what remained of the empire overseas consisted of less than 170,000 people, mostly living in remote islands like the Falklands or Pitcairns. The statistic symbolises for many historians the immense change in Britain's role in the world. The decline of the British empire can be traced further back, of course, to the Boer War (1899–1902), the War for Irish independence (1919–22), or the Statute of Westminster in 1931, which granted political and legal independence to Commonwealth countries. The seeds of Indian independence were already present in the Government of India Act of 1935. But the spectacle of the end of empire was to be played out in the post-war

7.1 London in the Blitz. The 'Blitz' was the conventional term for the German aerial bombardment of Britain during the Second World War. Around 42,000 people are estimated to have died, with over two million houses destroyed.

period, with Indian independence enacted in 1947, numerous rearguard colonial wars fought out in the 1950s and 1960s, along with negotiated withdrawals from territories across Africa, Asia and the Caribbean, and the 'last post' melodrama of the return of Hong Kong to Chinese authority in 1997. The idea of the Commonwealth remains, but it has long been overshadowed by Britain's relationships with the USA and Europe. Some would argue that the empire and the Commonwealth have little or no significance to how British people, in the main, have seen themselves. George Orwell, for example, distinguished the upper-class, landowning English who ruled over an 'unEnglish' empire, from the 'common' English people, who were quietly patriotic and behaved as if they were not aware of the empire. On the other hand, one could argue that both Englishness and Britishness have been hugely, if not wholly, defined in relation to the colonial enterprise, and that colonies (within as well as outside the British Isles) served at a symbolic level to provide a foil against which to identify white, English identity. There is, it might be argued, a direct relationship between the racial typology of Victorian imperialism and the experiences of racist discrimination and violence in post-war society. The decline of the empire, however, has also meant a dramatic shift in how Britain is imagined, from the 'mother' or centre of a global family of far-flung, sometimes obstreperous children, to the insular, island race, desperate to protect its shores from the invasion of foreign migrants.

The story of Britain's declining imperial role was intricately related to the rise of American and Russian global power, and the 'Cold War' between them, which involved localised conflicts between rival factions supported by the superpowers, but a global 'peace' maintained by the threat of nuclear war. Britain's attempts to suppress colonial insurrections since 1945 have been mostly interconnected with its alliance with America against the spread of communism. However, when British colonial interests clashed with American Cold War policies, the latter prevailed. The most dramatic instance of this occurred in the 'Suez crisis' of 1956. The British government worked with France and Israel to recapture the Suez canal, a vital shipping link between Europe and the East, which had been nationalised by the Egyptian government. To do this, Israel invaded Egypt, and Anglo-French forces were then deployed supposedly to maintain peace, but actually to control the canal. However, US President Eisenhower objected, especially as the invasion weakened his criticism of Russia's invasion of Hungary earlier in the year. Threatened with US economic sanctions, Britain was forced to withdraw, thereby indicating that American approval was necessary for the pursuit of British foreign policy. Britain's former role as a global power guaranteed it a certain prominence in the post-war world, however. It has had a permanent seat on the security council of the United Nations (UN) since its inception in 1945, and played an important role in the formation of the North Atlantic Treaty Organisation (NATO) with the USA and other western European states in 1949. Between 1947 and 1960 Britain retained a policy of compulsory military service (called National Service), and in 1952 and 1957 tested atomic and hydrogen bombs as part of its pledge to develop and maintain its own nuclear deterrence capability. For much of the post-war period, the British public were encouraged by government information bulletins to prepare for survival after a nuclear war, and the images of the apocalyptic destruction of Hiroshima and Nagasaki in 1945 were stark reminders of the horrific potential which lay behind the cat-and-mouse games of the Cold War. But throughout the 1960s and 1970s, Britain scaled down its military forces and commitments, amalgamating traditional regiments, handing over control of its naval and military facilities overseas to its allies, and undertaking defence reviews in 1966 and 1968 which promised to all-but eliminate any commitments to stationing forces outside of Europe and the Mediterranean. Britain became a close partner and ally to the USA in the Cold War, engaging in joint exercises, sharing intelligence, military forces and facilities, but Britain also became less capable during this time of pursuing the global deployments necessary for the war against Russian and Chinese influence. It was also evident that Britain and the USA did not always share the same objectives – Britain refrained from any significant involvement in Vietnam, for example, while the USA discouraged the British determination to recapture the Falkland Islands in 1982, and has often been ambivalent about Britain's policies in Northern Ireland. With the fall of communism in Russia and the Eastern Bloc in 1989, Britain had further cause to review its international commitments. Ironically, perhaps, the 'new world order' pursued by the USA since that time has found Britain partnering America in closer military and political alliance than ever, fighting in Iraq side by side both in 1991 and 2003, in Afghanistan in 2002, and with NATO in the former Yugoslavia in the 1990s. British prime ministers have

7.2 Atomic bomb devastation in Nagasaki, 1945.

consistently valued the 'Special Relationship' with the USA as a guarantor of security and national 'interests', never more so than in the 'War on Terror' pursued since the terrorist attacks on New York and Washington in 2001.

This 'Special Relationship' continues to define Britain as a global power, although critics have often seen the relationship as one in which Britain merely serves to help America to legitimate the pursuit of its interests across the globe. The British Prime Minister, Harold Macmillan (1957–63), once famously told President Kennedy that Britain would play Greece to America's Rome, and the patrician notion that Britain is passing on the keys of imperial power to its cherished successor has persistently coloured the relationship between the two countries. In 1972, Britain became a member of another international alliance, the economic and increasingly political alliance of the European Community. Formed as a means of achieving greater economic cooperation between western European states in 1957, the European Union (EU), as it became known, was also conceived more implicitly as a political mechanism for avoiding the rivalries between major European states which had resulted in the two world wars. Britain's involvement in Europe has always been somewhat hesitant, however, showing reluctance to cede any power over its own sovereignty to the institutions of European integration. It is partly because Britain retains the notion of itself as capable, through its relationship with America, of continuing to have global influence, that the 'Special Relationship' has frequently prevented Britain from becoming more closely tied to its European partners. As the European Community expanded, and became more interested in issues of economic, political and even cultural unity, in the 1990s and 2000s, British politicians were markedly divided about the European issue. Britain 'opted out' of European endeavours towards common social policies, a single currency, and common approaches to immigration. The idea of European integration has often been represented in British political discourse as a threat, not just to political sovereignty but also to cultural identity, and as an unattractive and problematic alternative to the USA. The refusal of France and Germany to join with US and British forces in Iraq in 2003 served further to compound the sense that alliances with Europe and America are competing, rather than compatible, commitments in British foreign policy. The debt crisis in several European countries after the banking crash of 2008 has served to weaken the appeal of further economic and political integration with Europe for British voters. In addition, the entitlement of all EU citizens to live and work in any other member state meant that citizens from many of the poorer regions of eastern and southern Europe were able to move freely to Britain, and this has contributed to concerns that Britain is not able to control its own borders. The choice between America and Europe, as the vehicles for maintaining Britain's role as a global power, was the central, divisive issue in post-war British foreign politics. In 2016, however, a referendum in Britain returned a narrow majority in favour of leaving the European Union.

Social, Political and Economic Change

The experiences of people in Britain during the Second World War marked a watershed in ideas of society and political organisation. In contrast to the mass unemployment, food queues and slum housing of the depression in the 1930s, the government proved capable during the war of organising full employment, an effective system of rationing food and other necessities, and providing accommodation of some kind for those whose houses were destroyed or damaged. The war proved that centralised and planned government control could deliver (to a large extent) the basic needs of its population, at least when politicians had the will to do so. When Ernest Bevin, the trade-union leader, joined Winston Churchill's government in 1940, he famously declared that if the labour movement and the working class 'now rise with all their energy and save the people of this country from disaster, the country will always turn with confidence to the people who saved them'. It was implicit in this statement, and in many others of the time, that a debt was owed to the working class in Britain for sacrifices suffered in the war, that the poverty and injustices of the 1930s could not be allowed to happen again. Instead of the unfettered market economics of the thirties, Britain would adopt a system of welfare-capitalism for the immediate post-war period, on the implicit understanding that there had to be state intervention to protect the poor from unemployment, hunger, homelessness or slum conditions, sickness and illiteracy. In the general election of 1945, the Labour Party commanded the vast majority of working-class support, winning some 12 million votes. On the back of that support, Labour engineered much of the social reform and welfare provision which has cushioned the impact of unemployment and poverty in post-war British society. The National Health Service, a commitment to full employment, universal full-time secondary education, pension rights and public provision of affordable housing were all introduced in British society in the late 1940s. They represented a promise that society had to be structured along more egalitarian lines, and that government had a social responsibility to protect the poor from the capitalist drive for wealth.

Historians often refer to this promise as the basis for a social consensus which lasted for over three decades in British politics. Both Labour and Conservative governments pursued, to varying degrees, the aim of regulating or offsetting capitalism with welfare reforms. In some cases, this produced a gradual inclination towards social harmony. Class divisions were eroded a little by common experiences of the health service, for example, or for men in the national military service. Even by the late 1940s, however, Labour had ceased to endorse fully the ideology of welfare capitalism, and had shifted towards an acceptance of market economics as the motor of generating wealth. The consensus concerning welfare provision remained broadly in place until the 1980s, but the Conservative Party won the election in 1951 on the promise that the 'bad old days' of Labour rationing and restrictions would be replaced by affluence and consumer goods. The Festival of Britain in 1951 also marked a departure from the gloom of the war and the austerity of the forties by imagining Britain as a modern, bright society, driven by technological advancement and affordable new material goods. The fifties have since become known as a decade of ideological conservatism, in which women were encouraged, sometimes even compelled, to become housewives, and leave the world of public work to men, and in which the timidly socialist commitment to welfare became subordinate to the drive towards greater production and consumption. One explanation for the anti-feminism of the fifties, for example, is that women were needed in the home not primarily as housewives or mothers, but as consumers, supposedly with the leisure time to spend their husband's disposable income on a greater range of foods, household goods and labour-saving devices. But this could not have taken place, of course, had it not been for the economic boom which brought an increase in living standards for the majority of people in Britain. Successive Conservative governments in the fifties were able to turn voters' minds away from the fear of poverty (which fuelled a desire for social and welfare reforms) by appealing to consumer desires for televisions, refrigerators, washing machines and cars. The rise in living standards was also greatly enhanced by the advent of the credit society, in which private ownership of houses, as well as the purchase of all sorts of material goods and services, became more accessible to greater numbers of people through an expansion of mortgage lending and financial credit schemes. This meant that relatively low-earning households could buy into the consumer economy, by placing themselves in long-term debt. From this point onwards, one could argue, consumerism and free-market economics were bound to come into conflict with the promise of social reform.

In the late fifties and early sixties it was possible to believe that Britain was becoming a classless society. The expansion of secondary and university education, and the availability of scholarship schemes for working-class children to go on to higher education, meant that there was a certain amount of opportunity to move upwards on the social ladder. At the same time, many working-class households could afford televisions and even cars. The quality of housing improved, as did the working conditions of many people, and Britain looked a brighter, cleaner place, with high-rise accommodation, motorways, and sleek, fast cars giving the country a more modern ambience. In the sixties, the high-profile international success of British rock and pop music gave the impression that the country had shrugged off the shackles of its past, and was the fashionable centre of a modern, even post-modern world. On the evidence of the cultural products of the first post-war generation, who came of age in the sixties – the Beatles, the Rolling Stones, 'Carry On' films, Monty Python comic sketches, and the pop art of Richard Hamilton and David Hockney, to cite some examples – the decade marked a new era of confidence and innovation. The spirit of rebellion against the 'establishment', which perhaps began with teenage teddy boys and rock 'n' roll in the fifties, blossomed in the sixties. Women felt empowered to demand more in terms of social equality, and by the end of the sixties, the women's liberation movement had begun to organise campaigns to end gender inequality. The women's liberation movement grew out of the experiences of the post-war generation, many of whom had benefited from educational and employment opportunities which would not have been possible for their mothers, but the movement also served to illustrate that there were deeply divisive social issues beneath the signs of economic and cultural success. For some commentators, the flashy symbols of affluence in those boom years masked more deeply rooted problems, which became increasingly apparent in the 1970s.

The Welfare State

The development of welfare-state provisions in Britain after the war is broadly in line with trends in many democracies in Europe and abroad. Sweden and New Zealand, for example, had already developed welfare-state policies in the 1930s. The Labour government of 1945–51 is generally credited with introducing a welfare state in Britain, although its measures were widely based on the recommendations of the Beveridge Report of 1942, which argued the case for the welfare state. In successive acts of legislation, and involving substantial investment, the Labour government introduced the National Health Service (1946), national insurance scheme (1946), unemployment and low income assistance (1948), and a commitment to more publicly owned housing. Arguably, one could include the nationalisation of major industries as part of the government's welfare reforms in the sense that this allowed greater state control of employment and income levels also. Several planks of the welfare state remain in altered and diminished forms today, but since the 1980s, an increasing trend towards the USA's model of minimal welfare services has taken hold in Britain. In particular, untested American arguments that welfare makes people dependent and lazy have influenced both the practice and rhetoric of British policies on social-welfare provision.

Britain had enjoyed more or less steady economic growth and social stability between 1945 and 1970, and the political consensus on welfare-capitalism served to secure the idea that the country was working towards greater social harmony. The 1970s, however, would become, at least for subsequent generations, iconic of Britain's decline. Indeed, the titles of several books published in this period, and surveying its crises, paint a dismal picture: *The Break-Up of Britain* (Tom Nairn, 1977), *Is Britain Dying?* (Isaac Kramnick, 1979), *Britain in Agony* (Richard Clutterbuck, 1980), and *Britain Against Itself* (Samuel H. Beer, 1982), are just some examples. In the 1980s, Margaret Thatcher and the Conservative Party capitalised on the idea that the seventies had been a disaster, to argue that the country had been in terminal decline, misled by the Labour Party and the trade unions, and had only been rescued by Thatcher's election victory in 1979. This was an expedient myth, of course, which ignored the global recessionary trends brought about by the oil crisis of 1973, and the consequent, irreparable damage inflicted by monetary inflation on manufacturing industries. Nevertheless, the folk memories of the 1970s foreground the industrial strikes, the power cuts, the constant war between government and unions, the tax increases and huge price inflation. The eruption of war in Northern Ireland, and the growth of nationalist movements in Scotland and Wales, also asked serious and troubling questions about the stability of Britain as a political entity. The decade seems marred by political and social discontent. Its successes, in terms of more progressive legislation on race and gender equality, and in terms of managing the impact of a global economic crisis, are seldom recalled. The decade culminated in the famous 'winter of discontent' of 1978–9, in which the Labour government's attempt to limit wage demands sparked successive waves of industrial and public-service strikes, forcing the government to back down and thus appear unable to govern effectively.

The Conservative government in 1970 had come to power on the promise that it would end the social consensus on welfare reform, and that Britain 'would stand on its own two feet'. It had to give up this pledge when faced with slowing economic growth, rising unemployment, and pressure to increase wages. A strong element within the Conservative Party deeply regretted having to return to the interventionist politics of welfare-capitalism thereafter, and the election victory in 1979 brought

7.3 The Beatles receiving the MBE award.

a more determined, right-wing and free-market-oriented party into power. In the course of the 1980s under Thatcher's leadership, and the 1990s under her successor, John Major, what became known as 'Thatcherism' meant abandoning any notion of regulating capitalism or of a social contract between government and the working class, and the withdrawal of the state from economic and social intervention. Nationalised industries like British Airways, British Gas, British Petroleum and British Telecom were systematically privatised. Failing industries were, with some exceptions, allowed to fail. Trade unions were subjected to stringent regulation, and effectively had their power broken in the divisive miners' strike of 1984. Council-owned housing was made available for private purchase. Healthcare was reorganised into public and private sectors, so that those who could afford it could pay for better quality, private healthcare. Public funding was squeezed for education, health, welfare and cultural services. At the same time, unemployment rose above 4 million in the 1980s, which contrasted starkly with Edward Heath's government in 1971 which backed down when unemployment came close to 1 million. Thatcher countered the progressive race legislation of the 1970s with anti-immigration legislation of her own. The 1980s witnessed an economic boom, fuelled in particular by the growing success of financial industries which were strongly oriented towards foreign investment, but the decade was also one of deepening social divisions. Mass unemployment, violent riots, rising crime, homelessness and increasing poverty, existed alongside the flaunted, 'new' wealth of city traders and entrepreneurs. 'Society' had been abandoned, effectively, in pursuit of wealth, on the premise that increasing wealth would 'trickle down' to the poor.

In the 1990s, and into the twenty-first century, Thatcherism was pursued as an almost unarguable approach to governing Britain. Privatisation continued under John Major as vigorously as under Thatcher. Perhaps even more surprising to those who had been used to characterising the Labour party as a left-wing political movement was the fact that the Labour governments elected in 1997, 2001 and 2005 with considerable majorities continued, by and large, with Conservative policies of curbing public spending, deregulated market economics, and schemes to privatise state-controlled public services. Under Major, the Conservatives introduced waves of draconian legislation to prevent immigration and to curb civil liberties, including the right to free assembly and the right to silence for the accused in criminal investigations. Tony Blair's Labour governments more or less continued with this trend, although Blair's appeal to the electorate was based on the assumption that voters want Conservative policies pursued, but less aggressively and more equitably. The eighteen years of Conservative rule in Britain between 1979 and 1997 left Labour supporters desperate for social, political and economic reform, for left-wing values put into political practice, but Tony Blair marked his departure from the politics of left-wing Labour movements of the past by habitually referring to the slogan 'New Labour, New Britain', and by repealing the famous 'Clause Four' of Labour's founding principles, which called for common ownership of the means of production, distribution and exchange. For some, this marked the end of idealism in British politics, in that both major parties now contended for the right to steer the country towards the same pragmatic goals, adopting similar policies, but vying for who could manage the economy more effectively. The Conservative government under John Major had begun to appear deeply divided by their stance on European integration, corrupted by several political scandals, and too aggressive, even nasty, when it came to social issues. Under Tony Blair, the Labour government managed the economy with considerable success, broadly pursued the same Conservative policies on education, healthcare and public services, and followed similar approaches to foreign policy. This was a new political consensus, to all intents and purposes, based on the endorsement of free-market economics, a strong emphasis on the rule of law and order, and the abandonment of progressive social intervention. Labour offered a friendlier face than the Conservatives of the 1980s and 1990s, a lesson that by 2007 even the Conservatives professed to have learned. The Labour governments from 1997 introduced measures to ensure a minimum wage for low-paid employment and better pensions for the elderly, and there was a substantial increase of women members of parliament in 1997. There were more women ministers, and openly gay cabinet ministers, in Tony Blair's governments. Despite these important changes, however, the politics of Thatcherism remained intact in the policies pursued under successive governments in the 1990s and the twenty-first century.

The banking crisis of 2008 and subsequent recession deepened an already pronounced division in Britain between the wealthy and the poor. While successive governments since the 1970s have refused to subsidise or rescue the industries upon which working-class communities depend, and privatised many publicly owned industries, both Labour and Conservative governments between 2007 and 2011 provided over £1 trillion of taxpayers' money to bail out or prop up failing banks and financial companies. Governments defended the use of taxpayers' money as a necessary prevention of a collapse of the national financial system, and to ensure some

7.4 Tony Blair on Remembrance Sunday, 2005, with Margaret Thatcher looking over his shoulder.

measure of economic stability, yet it was also a transfer of wealth on an unprecedented scale from public revenue to private financial companies. At the same time, it was accompanied by declining provision of social housing for people unable to afford to buy property, falling or frozen rates of pay in low and middle income jobs, and rising unemployment. The recession of 2008–12 was not just a British economic problem, of course. It was global, and it reinforced the perception that the financial stability and economic prosperity of Britain was more dependent than ever before upon a global system of speculative capitalism which promised wealth but which was also capable of spectacular failure. It also reinforced the perception that both the successes and failures of financial capitalism were dependent upon social inequalities, upon a small percentage of people benefiting enormously from the increasingly straitened masses. Protests against the austerity measures introduced by governments erupted in 2009, 2010, and 2011, and signalled growing discontent with a society in which such inequality of wealth, and inequality of opportunity, was becoming more and more visible. The re-election of the Conservative government to office in 2015, however, indicated that these protests did not translate into any sizeable shift in political support for the neo-liberal economic policies which have dominated British politics since the 1970s.

Culture and Identity

In the post-war period, there has been much confusion about, and many attempts to redefine, what it means to be English, and especially what it means to be British. Britishness had for some time been an elastic identification tied up with the empire, whereas Englishness implied something more exclusive. The 1948 British Nationality Act, for example, defined all Commonwealth citizens as British subjects. You were British whether you lived in Bombay, Barbados, Belfast or Basingstoke. However, this 'inclusive' understanding of Britishness was later perceived by anti-immigration lobbyists and politicians as permitting an 'open-door' policy of immigration from former colonies, and legislation introduced since then, especially since the 1970s, has increasingly defined Britishness in such a way as to severely restrict immigration. Large numbers of migrant workers were required to boost the workforce after the war, and some sectors of public-service employment in particular recruited staff directly from the Caribbean and India, for example. Immigrants from the Commonwealth countries received an ambivalent welcome, however. On the one hand, they were employed in jobs badly needed in British society, and were supposedly 'British', but on the other hand, they were often badly paid and subject to racist discrimination in housing, employment and society generally. Many people have argued that underlying tighter immigration controls are implicitly racist distinctions between 'white' Britons and 'black' and 'Asian' others, and that such controls are an extension of the ways in which black and Asian people living in Britain have been racially abused and socially deprived. Racist attacks and race riots have been a recurrent problem in British society, with the most serious taking place in London and Nottingham in 1958, Bristol in 1980, London, Liverpool and Manchester in 1981, and again in London and Birmingham in 1985, and in Oldham, Burnley and Bradford in 2001. Many of these riots were caused by tensions between right-wing racist organisations like the National Front (founded in 1967) and the British National Party (founded in 1982), and racially disadvantaged groups, or between the latter and police, when racist policing practices were suspected. Immigration and racism have also been fairly constant, if never quite decisive, issues in post-war political history, and Conservative politicians such as Enoch Powell, Norman Tebbit and Margaret Thatcher have followed an often explicit agenda of defining Britishness in such a way as to exclude ethnic minorities, or at least to compel them into identifying with a conservative and exclusivist idea of Britishness. Paul Gilroy surveys this problematic relationship between race and national identity in contemporary Britain with exemplary lucidity in his book, *There Ain't No Black in the Union Jack* (1987 [Cii]). In the heated debates about the relationship between security and immigration which have taken place since the 9/11 attacks in the USA, an equally divisive issue surrounds Islamic communities and people in Britain, about whether religious identity is compatible with national identity. It is a controversial and often misleading issue, which replays centuries-old confrontations in Britain involving Catholics and Jews.

If the history of 'Britishness' in the post-war period is one of shrinking from the strained inclusiveness of an imperial nation to the anxious attempt to define Britishness according to its more insular, island territories on the northwest of Europe, then it has also come under pressure from within these islands. Northern Ireland, which had existed as a devolved statelet under a majoritarian democracy, erupted into civil war and a terrorist campaign against the British state in 1969. The same political party, the Unionist Party, based overwhelmingly on Protestant support, had been in power since 1920, and had routinely discriminated against Catholics on social issues. When a civil-rights campaign was repressed in the late 1960s, a paramilitary campaign emerged from the nationalist community to wage war against Unionism (which spawned its own paramilitary forces), and against the British state in an attempt to win nationalist demands for independence. In politics on 'mainland' Britain, Northern Ireland was at best an ambivalent issue, a seemingly foreign place in which British troops were fighting and dying in a colonial war with questionable moral credibility, but also supposedly a part of Britain, the streets of which looked as though they could be any English streets, except for the soldiers, barricades and bomb blasts. The war lasted for almost thirty years, and all sides were involved in protracted negotiations towards a peace settlement after 1994. The Belfast Agreement of 1998 provided the mechanisms for a form of government which would ensure that power was shared between nationalist and Unionist parties, and since 2007 this has provided relatively stable regional government. The contentious issue of whether Northern Ireland is British or Irish remains unresolved, perhaps even irresolvable, but power-sharing has at least enabled the solution to this question to be sought by peaceful political means. Since the early 1970s, nationalist campaigns for Welsh and Scottish independence have also put pressure on the meaning of Britishness, and the viability of British political and cultural identity. The Labour government introduced limited forms of legislative devolution in Scotland and Wales in 1997, and the narrow margin by which Scottish voters decided to remain part of the United Kingdom in 2014 is perhaps an indication that the break-up of British political union is only a matter of time. Various suggestions have been made since 1997 for devolved regional assemblies in parts of England, but whether these constitute reform of British political institutions or a dissolution of the cultural meaning of Britishness is as yet difficult to discern. It remains a peculiar situation that England, often regarded as synonymous with Britishness, and certainly the dominant member of the United Kingdom, is the only part of that Union which is not formally constituted as a state.

Englishness has been relatively less slippery a term than Britishness, and somewhat less elastic. The commonly adopted term for black people born and raised in England, for example, is 'Black British'. Englishness seems a more insular idea, associated therefore with white skin, and often more easily stereotyped and caricatured. Like any other national identity, of course, Englishness is a mass of contradictions. England, on the one hand, is associated with aristocracy, tradition, elitism, the 'stiff upper lip', emotional restraint, and genteel cultural pursuits. On the other hand, it is also the home of the Beatles, punk, football fandom, the 'swinging sixties', stand-up comedy and political satire. In some cases, these contradictions represent the ways in which 'culture' is class-inflected in specific ways, and, since the emergence of 'the teenager' in the fifties, the ways in which a distinctive 'youth' culture has departed from 'official' forms of cultural identification. These contradictory notions of English culture do not necessarily map onto separate groups of people, however, and often exist in a dialectical relation with each other. The continued existence of the monarchy perhaps illustrates the contradictions in the meanings of Englishness further. The monarchy is outmoded as an effective political institution, and recent reforms of the political system have replaced aristocratic, hereditary 'Lords' in the Houses of Parliament with 'Lords' appointed on the basis of life achievements. But any serious proposals for abolishing the monarchy have failed to garner popular political support, which would suggest that the monarchy retains a vital symbolic, even fetishistic, function in English national identity. The monarchy symbolises English tradition, and nostalgia for an imagined past unity and glory, without which England (and Britain) would simply be just another modern democracy, on the margins of American and European power. In the symbolic union with tradition through the monarchy, then, England maintains the idea of itself as exceptional and distinctive, precisely because of its imperial past and the sense of historical continuity provided by the notion of aristocratic genealogy. The remarkable wave of mourning for Princess Diana when she died in 1997 was suggested at the time as perhaps the precursor to abolishing the monarchy, since Diana had become a controversial outcast from the Royal Family. But the monarchy has survived, without any serious proposals for abolition since, and mourning for Diana now looks as if it was an expression of ambivalence about the monarchy, not objection to it. The public relationship with the monarchy, then, registers the complexity of cultural identifications with 'traditional' notions of Englishness, since it is both anachronistic, and, for that reason, a vital link with an imagined idea of Englishness as distinct and glorious in the past.

Belief and Thought

The intellectual and religious history of post-war Britain is perhaps typical of many western democracies. Britain became a much more secular society throughout the twentieth century, and the clash of faiths characteristic of previous times all but dissipated. Arguably, contemporary religious conflicts in twenty-first-century Britain involving Islamic believers are, in fact, between the secular and the religious, rather than between Christian and Islamic religious beliefs. The controversies surrounding the fatwa, or death threat, issued in 1988 against Salman Rushdie for his novel *The Satanic Verses* are perhaps indicative of this. The Christian churches are by far the largest faith group, representing 60 per cent of the population according to 2011 census statistics. However, the largest denomination, the Church of England, estimates that only 1 million people attend its services every week. Catholics are estimated to number about 5 million believers in Britain, although less than 1 million are active worshippers. The fastest-growing faith group in Britain is Islam, whose believers in 2011 accounted for almost 5 per cent of the population, partly as a result of immigration trends. A growing portion of the British population register no religious affiliation, with the British Social Attitudes survey of 2015 finding that 49 per cent of British adults declared themselves non-religious, and there are organisations such as the National Secular Society and the British Humanist Association which actively campaign for the further reduction of religious influence on British society. Political rhetoric in Britain also tends to emphasise a language of civic responsibilities and humanist values rather than religious beliefs, although the governments led by both Tony Blair and David Cameron continued to give special status to so-called 'faith schools' in the education system.

Britain has continued to play a fairly substantial part in the world's intellectual and scientific developments. Successive programmes of expanding higher education since the war have facilitated the growth of a highly literate population, and consequently the development of research, information and technology industries. Almost half of the population of 25–34-year-olds in Britain have studied in higher education programmes, which is relatively high compared to the USA, France and Germany. About one-sixth of the top-ranked universities in the world are British, and many of the world's leading global corporations have research and development operations based in the UK. Britain has pioneered many technological innovations in engineering, aerodynamics, telecommunications and weapons design, and played a leading role in genetics and medical research. At the same time, it can boast of many renowned writers, architects, fashion designers, film-makers and music industrialists. The innovations in science, technology and the arts have all been part of the intellectual culture of post-war Britain, but increasingly, as C. P. Snow was to identify in his Rede lecture in 1959, humanities and the sciences were in fact 'two cultures' (*The Two Cultures* [A]) with little, it seemed, to say to each other. The scientists, Snow believed, had come to see writers and artists, who seemed now to monopolise the term 'intellectual', as increasingly preoccupied in an insular manner with the forms and techniques of art, rather than its social relevance. The writers equally seemed to see scientists as having become technocrats, falsely optimistic about the role of science in the world, and devoid of moral responsibility for their inventions. Although Snow's warning about the dangers of this divided culture is rooted in the specific contexts of the 1930s and 1950s, those 'two cultures' have more or less continued to exist separately. For their part, scientists mainly remain outside of the literary and artistic circles of post-war society, and largely unconcerned about cultural trends and debates. In literature, the huge popularity of science fiction and catastrophe fiction, in which scientists are often depicted as unwittingly or indeed deliberately unleashing disaster on humanity, represents anxieties about the power of science, and fears that scientific progress has become the master narrative of post-war society.

To speak of two cultures is perhaps, as Snow was aware, to miss the wider point that intellectual work began to become more and more specialised throughout the twentieth century, so that one might talk of a gradual breakdown of anything approaching a common intellectual culture. The proliferation of forms of media and communications means, for example, that whereas the immediate post-war generation might have had one common source of cultural information and intellectual stimulation in something like the BBC (although arguably even then this was divided according to class and cultural identity), people living in Britain today have a huge range of information sources. The role that culture plays in people's lives has probably not changed in the post-war period – it is distracting entertainment for some, and intellectual stimulation for others – but the means and forms of cultural entertainment and education have increased vastly. This is particularly the case with new technologies such as satellite, digital and interactive television and broadband internet, which have created a complex and varied range of cultural services. The number of television channels, for example, has grown from four in 1988 to over four hundred now available through digital technology. While this increase may be regarded as merely a matter of quantity rather than quality, the capacity for interaction with digital technology also means that people are using television differently, and part of the future envisioned for the BBC as a digital platform, for example, is that its interactive services will play some role in encouraging its viewers to become active citizens who participate in public debate. Access to Internet technology also promises greater choice for individuals both as consumers and citizens, and is making possible new forms of social interaction and belonging which are not dependent on the accidents of geographical proximity. Throughout the post-war period, governments supported to varying degrees the notion of public culture, through funding the arts and community cultural projects, for example, or through public-service outlets like the BBC and the National Theatre. Such a commitment demonstrates the currency of the idea that Britain should have a common sense of its cultural and intellectual life, even if it is a common sense of the country's cultural diversity, but it is by no means without its critics, who argue that Britain has become too diverse in its interests to support a uniform culture. That same debate continues in relation to the possibilities afforded by the digital and Internet revolutions. Are these new technologies enabling new forms of community and belonging, or are they making it possible for a greater individualism and consumerism to take hold? In the twenty-first century, especially in the economic recession which followed 2008, the idea of providing financial subsidies to support the arts and public culture has come under renewed pressure. Public service broadcasting is regarded by some, along with the National Health Service, as one of the last bastions of a democratic vision of post-war Britain, but criticised by others as an expensive monopoly which should be subject to the same market forces as the provision of other goods and services.

Literary Overview

Introduction

In a simple telling of the story of English literature, the Second World War might represent the end of modernism and the beginning of a new period, often called the post-war, and usually associated with post-modernism. The profound changes in English literary history since 1939, however, are much more difficult to characterise. The war made a deep impact on English culture, but it did not produce an easily identifiable body of writing as did the First World War. Many of the major figures in English modernism (Woolf, Ford, Lawrence) died before or during the war, but literary modernism did not end, and may even be seen to continue in the work of some contemporary writers. It is also hard to identify with any certainty the significance of the term post-modernism to contemporary English writing, and especially problematical to identify post-modernism as the aesthetic or cultural mainstream in the post-war or contemporary periods. Both modernism and post-modernism were supposed to signify a critical attitude towards, and surpassing of, the apparently naive aesthetics of realism, yet many contemporary English novelists, for example, are committed to representing a changing social world within a broadly realist form of narrative. A more complex story of English literature since 1939 has to take account, therefore, of the relative lack of satisfactory terminology with which to identify and describe its constituent parts, and of the plural and hybrid forms of post-war and contemporary writing.

Continuities, Innovations and Influences

Literature and the Second World War

It could be argued that the Second World War had the potential to unify the nation behind a common cause to a far greater extent than the so-called 'Great War' of 1914–18. In ideological terms, Hitler and Nazism in the 1930s represented more palpable enemies, more obvious villains, than the Kaiser and German imperialism had done twenty to thirty years earlier. The British cinematic representations of the Second World War, both then and since, reflect this story of a common and heroic struggle against the evil tyranny of Nazism, of the fight against genocide, militarism and dictatorship. More than any other of the arts, perhaps, film used the war as the epic setting for the individual struggle for meaningful and ethical action. In contrast, literary representations of the war often cast suspicion, if not indeed ridicule, on the notion of the war as epic, heroic or even meaningful. The Second World War produced its own 'war poets', in particular Keith Douglas, Alun Lewis and Sidney Keyes, who were equal to, if less well known than, the poets of the First World War. Douglas's poetry especially registers the futile and unheroic nature of war, often through images of rotting corpses which seem to mock the living, and the loot robbed greedily from the dead. While films told stories of courageous battle against the enemy in torturous conditions, Douglas's poetry shows the war to be like childish games in the sand, yet grotesquely spotted with the undignified spectacle of grimacing corpses. Douglas's most famous poem, perhaps, is 'Vergissmeinnicht', in which a dead enemy soldier is discovered 'abased' and 'sprawling in the sun'. There is no glory in his death, just the pathetic observation of 'how on his skin the swart flies move; / the dust upon the paper eye / and the burst stomach like a cave' (in *Complete Poems* [A]).

The lack of heroic representation characterises the literary response to the war and this is perhaps clearest in the most significant fictional treatment of the war, Evelyn Waugh's *Sword of Honour* trilogy. The protagonist of the trilogy, Guy Crouchback, searches for 'honour', for the medieval chivalric role of the knight on a crusade against evil. Such an image was pervasive in the political rhetoric of the war, but what Crouchback finds instead is banality, lies, folly and disgrace. *Sword of Honour* is not short on deaths and injuries, but they are almost always the consequence of senseless accidents or mechanical failures. Nor is it short on 'heroes', but their heroism is invented by war propaganda out of trivial, often farcical, mistakes. The war

7.5 Victory in Europe (VE) Day celebrations, 1945.

is shown to be not a moral crusade, but a very modern, bureaucratic muddle. The significance of Waugh's trilogy is that it shows sufficient conviction in the ingloriousness of the war, and the moral vacuity of the modern age, to depict what has been constructed historically as one of the most tumultuous and decisive events in human history as a pointless, dishonourable farce. Waugh was keen to emphasise that the war was not the story of good versus evil, but of systematic destruction and inhuman depravity on all sides. In this regard, he was by no means alone. For very different reasons, and in very different ways, numerous writers including George Orwell, Dylan Thomas, Graham Greene, Angela Thirkell, Elizabeth Bowen, T. S. Eliot and Cyril Connolly registered disillusionment with the 'glorious' narrative of wartime Britain, which in defeating Germany and Japan had resorted to totalitarian measures itself, and, with its allies, had adopted weapons of mass destruction which equalled and even surpassed those used by its enemies.

Realism, Modernism, Post-Modernism

The literary response to the war did not, therefore, represent a substantial departure from that of an earlier generation of writers to the First World War. If anything, the fact that writers who were influenced by the First World War writers found themselves repeating the same despairing reaction to war threatened to make their writing seem merely imitative. If it now appears that the war was the signal for a shift in literary values or styles, that change is most evident in the reactions to modernism which followed the war. Although there was a brief flourishing of neo-Romantic and decadent writing in the late 1940s, which can be understood in some ways as a reaction against the austerity imposed by the war, the twenty years after the war were dominated by an apparent rejection of modernism by the emerging generation of British writers. Robert Conquest's anthology of new poetry, *New Lines* (1956 [A]), best exemplifies this anti-modernist strain within post-war British culture. The poets Conquest selected, including Philip Larkin, John Wain, Kingsley Amis, Elizabeth Jennings, Donald Davie and Thom Gunn were heralded, somewhat unfairly, as the harbingers of a new poetic mode of common sense, formal conservatism and empiricism. Amis provided a poetic manifesto for what became known as 'the Movement' in his poem 'Against Romanticism', included in Conquest's selection, in which he wrote 'Better, of course, if images were plain, / Warnings clearly said, shapes put down quite still.' Poetry should provide 'visions that we need', and not, the poem implied, the esoteric ramblings of

The Decline of English Literature

The reaction against experiment acquired such publicity in the fifties that it has affected the reputation of post-war English literature as a whole, which has often been accused of parochialism, insularity and backwardness, of writing as if the modernists had never written, ignoring problems of existence, perception and narration, and resting content with minute accounts of class distinctions and other cosy social realities. It seems to many English critics that the avant-gardes of Europe and the Americas have, by humiliating contrast, continued to make energetic and exciting progress.

(Harry Ritchie, *Success Stories: Literature and the Media in England, 1950–1959*. London: Faber & Faber, 1988, p. 213 [Ci])

Romanticist poetry. Davie provided a critical manifesto in his book, *Purity of Diction in English Verse* (1952), which celebrated the neo-classical form of Augustan poetry over the excesses of Romanticism and modernism. Davie privileges 'logic', 'honesty', 'dignity', 'responsibility', 'urbanity' and 'conservation' as the values proper to post-war poetry. Experimentalism and modernism were to be avoided, since they 'would drive the poet further than ever into a private wilderness and alienate more and more potential readers'. The Movement poets, in retrospect, can be seen as embodying many of the values of a common culture and social equality that went into the making of institutions like the National Health Service and the BBC.

The critique of modernism by young British writers in the 1950s appeared to be based on this conception of modernism as escapist, elitist and obscure, and therefore antithetical to the democratic and populist values of the post-war social consensus. In this respect, the anti-modernism of the fifties might be understood as specifically concerned with class politics. This has led many commentators to see the Movement poets as intimately connected with the social realism of fiction and drama, which was understood to represent the emerging cultural self-consciousness of the working class. John Braine, David Storey, Alan Sillitoe and Stan Barstow were the key novelists associated with working-class writing, while the emergence of working-class characters and settings in the plays of John Osborne, Arnold Wesker and Shelagh Delaney represented a departure from drawing-room comedies and verse drama. The turn to realism in literature in the fifties seemed to be the dominant trend, but it is important to recognise that modernist aesthetics were not rejected wholesale in post-war writing. Many writers did in fact continue to reflect the modernist concern with language as a medium of representation, and with the subjective and contingent nature of knowledge. In poetry, Basil Bunting's *Briggflatts* (1966) and David Jones's *The Anathemata* (1952) are the most obvious and highly regarded modernist poems of the post-war era. In fiction, Christine Brooke-Rose, B. S. Johnson, James Hanley and Wilson Harris are just some of the writers who continued the modernist experiment with narrative form and subjectivism. Perhaps equally worth noting is the tendency in the post-war English novel to absorb the techniques of modernism within a broadly realist aesthetic, as is evident in the writings of Henry Green, Angus Wilson, Margaret Drabble, Doris Lessing, Elizabeth Taylor, David Lodge and Malcolm Bradbury, among others.

Precisely what constitutes post-modern literature is notoriously difficult to define, but it is habitually associated with stylistic characteristics such as self-reflexivity, parody, pastiche and meta-fiction, and with epistemological claims that reality is preceded by and dependent on language, and that we can only know the real through its textual traces. It may be possible, for example, to describe the work of Harold Pinter, perhaps Britain's most significant post-war dramatist, as post-modern, in the sense that his plays consistently highlight the ways in which language conceals truth. His characters provide no explanation of their own past experience or present motivations, thus appearing to live in a world of multiple surfaces and infinitely various actions, a world without definitive meanings or causes. The term post-modern is also usefully applied to certain novelists in contemporary England, particularly Martin Amis, Salman Rushdie, Jeanette Winterson, Angela Carter, Julian Barnes, Graham

---

The Post-Modern Novel

This is a true story but I can't believe it's really happening.

It's a murder story, too. I can't believe my luck.

And a love story (I think), of all strange things, so late in the century, so late in the goddamned day.

This is the story of a murder. It hasn't happened yet. But it will. (It had better.) I know the murderer, I know the murderee. I know the time, I know the place.

I know the motive (*her* motive) and I know the means.

I know who will be the foil, the fool, the poor foal, also utterly destroyed. And I couldn't stop them, I don't think, even if I wanted to. The girl will die. It's what she always wanted. You can't stop people, once they *start*. You can't stop people, once they *start creating*.

What a gift. This page is briefly stained by my tears of gratitude. Novelists don't usually have it so good, do they, when something real happens (something unified, dramatic and pretty saleable), and they just write it down?

(Martin Amis, *London Fields*. London: Penguin, 1990, p. 1)

Swift, John Fowles, Peter Ackroyd and Iain Sinclair (although it may be that in many cases the label 'historiographic meta-fiction' used by Linda Hutcheon in *A Poetics of Postmodernism* [B] is more appropriate). If there is a common link between these novelists it is that their work frequently comments on its own fictionality, interrogates the relationship between narrative and representation, and dissolves or at least questions the possibility of epistemological norms. It also frequently does so in ways which comically subvert the high pretensions and artistic seriousness of modernism, while radically undermining the philosophical assumptions of classical realism. The post-modern is often equated mistakenly with the contemporary, and those writers who are committed to the idea of artistic experiment as a serious project, or the idea of art having a referential function, might unfairly be seen as lagging behind the times. This notion of the relationship between realism, modernism and post-modernism as a series of progressive stages in literary history should be resisted, since such labels, however convenient, frequently misrepresent the complex, mixed and various nature of literary writing. While it may have been convenient to use the term 'post-modern' to label some of the most widely regarded British novelists of the 1980s and 1990s, it has lost all descriptive or explanatory meaning in relation to twenty-first century writing.

The Twenty-First Century Novel

As yet, no satisfactory descriptive term has emerged to characterise the main literary trends of the twenty-first century. Linda Hutcheon, who had developed the currency of the term 'post-modern' in literary studies in the late 1980s, declared that it was no longer useful in 2002, writing that 'Postmodernism needs a new label of its own', and challenged her readers to 'find it – and name it for the twenty-first century'. Several critics have attempted to do this, describing the literature of the twenty-first century as 'post-post-modernism', 'cosmodernism', 'metamodernism', 'digimodernism', 'new sincerity', and 'critical realism'. As is perhaps evident from some of these labels, at the same time as literary critics have grown more sceptical and dismissive of the descriptive value of 'post-modernism', they have been expanding and extending the significance of 'modernism'. Modernism has become almost synonymous in cultural history with the twentieth century. While this may be simplistic, it is clear that many twenty-first-century writers are still preoccupied with the artistic impact of modernism. The novelist Tom McCarthy, for example, has said that 'The task for contemporary literature is to deal with the legacy of modernism'. His own work might certainly be read as doing this, particularly the novel *C* (2010), but it is also evident in Julian Barnes's *The Sense of an Ending* (2011), Zadie Smith's *On Beauty* (2005), and Will Self's *Umbrella* (2012). Contemporary writers may still be working out the implications and consequences of modernism, but it is also clear that this is not in the spirit of nostalgia, but in the search for new beginnings. The millennial anxieties about the end of the last century have given way in the early twenty-first century to a renewed preoccupation with the possible sources of a transformative aesthetics. As David Glover and Scott McCracken wrote of the 'bad new days' of the new century, 'We know we are in it, but the full implications of the new age are not yet clear' ('The Bad New Days', p. 8 [A]).

That the early twenty-first century entails 'bad new days' might be easily discerned from the themes which preoccupy its novelists. Ecological crises and the pauperising effects of global capitalism are important themes in David Mitchell's *Cloud Atlas* (2004), Sarah Hall's *The Carhullan Army* (2007), and Tom McCarthy's *Satin Island* (2015), for example. In each case, the form registers something of our contemporary crises also. Hall's novel takes the form of the penal files of a female insurgent who has been interrogated for her part in an uprising against an Orwellian 'English Authority', set in a near future of food and energy rationing, martial law and climate catastrophe. Mitchell's novel interweaves six stories which consist of journal entries, letters and interviews, including the testimony of a post-apocalyptic clone worker 'genomed' to work as a corporate slave in an underground diner. *Satin Island* is structured into sections which resemble a corporate report, and tells the story of an anthropologist hired as a corporate executive, named U, who is obsessed by random images of global turmoil – oil spills, a dead parachutist, zombie parades, islands consisting of waste dumps, traffic jams in Lagos. The formal rendering of character in each of these novels reveals that any sense of individuality is dependent upon authoritarian surveillance, corporate regimes and consumer ideologies. 'Forget family, or ethnic and religious groupings', U tells us in *Satin Island*, 'corporations have supplanted all these as the primary structure of the modern tribe' (p. 39).

A dystopian sensibility is evident in much twenty-first century British fiction. The death, disappearance, or neglect of children is a recurring dystopian trope in the work of John Burnside, for example, in his novels, *The Dumb House* (1997), *Glister* (2009), and *A Summer of Drowning* (2012). In *Glister*, a disused and polluted chemical works provides the scenic and symbolic landscape for the murders of several children, which are falsely reported by the local policeman as disappearances to protect a developer's bogus 'regeneration' scheme. The children are not the only victims, however, in a town wrecked by illness, poverty, and hopelessness, and the novel ponders the existence of a malevolent force hanging over the place. As the early twenty-first century has witnessed a series of revelations of the dark history of child abuse and child murders in post-war Britain, with claims of, for example, paedophile networks involving senior figures in the establishment, it is perhaps inevitable that this has become a significant trope of contemporary fiction. David Peace plumbs the depths of historical abuse and corruption in his *Red Riding Quartet* (1999–2002). In Gordon Burn's *Born Yesterday* (2008), the disappearance of Madeleine McCann on holiday with her family in Portugal is interwoven with the other 'news' of 2007 – car bombs, floods, the change of prime minister from Tony Blair to Gordon Brown – and tells a story of a disturbed country obsessed with media imagery and social power, and haunted by the legacies of Thatcherism and misguided foreign wars. Yet, in hovering dangerously close to real 'news', these novels also exhibit great confidence in the power of fiction to reveal, to connect, and possibly also to transform the meaning of the disparate events they depict.

Post-Imperial and Post-Colonial English Writing

An alternative narrative of post-war literary history might be organised around the response to the decline of the British empire. If the empire defined and stabilised a certain myth of British identity, the dwindling of imperial power has precipitated an interrogation of the meanings of Britishness, and more narrowly, Englishness. As British authorities were compelled to withdraw from their various dominions in Asia and Africa, the many immigrants from those former colonies who came to Britain also changed the nature of British society, and prompted new questions about what constituted a British and English citizen. It could be argued that these two forces – decolonisation and immigration – have had the most significant impact on writing in England since the Second World War. On the one hand, numerous writers in England have been concerned to explore the legacy of imperial decline, most notably Paul Scott in *The Raj Quartet* (1966–75) and *Staying On* (1977), and V. S. Naipaul in *The Mimic Men* (1967) and *The Enigma of Arrival* (1987). In some cases, the end of empire has prompted a revisionary perspective on British history, and numerous writings have explored the more complicated and murky past than the official imperial vision of British history could have countenanced. Timothy Mo's *An Insular Possession* (1986), for example, traces how English traders came to establish themselves as colonisers in China. David Dabydeen and Fred D'Aguiar have both written long poems about the slave trade, the 'middle passage' which took African peoples to enslavement and death in the Caribbean and the Americas. Caryl Phillips's novel, *Crossing the River* (1993), is perhaps one of the most inventive and far-reaching explorations of the legacies of slavery, spanning the historical and geographical range of the slave trade across the Atlantic, and suggesting in its conclusion that the meanings of Englishness after the war are inseparable from the racial politics and economics of slavery and colonialism.

At the same time, immigration from former colonies has registered in various forms on English writing. Many of the writers involved in the Caribbean literary renaissance in the 1950s were based in London, for example, including most notably Sam Selvon, George Lamming, Andrew Salkey, Una Marston, Errol John and V. S. Naipaul. One may infer from this that London remained the metropolitan cultural centre for many writers hailing from former colonies. But it also provokes a most important question for the meanings of English literature. Is Sam Selvon an English writer because he lived and wrote in England for much of his life, and based some of his writings in England? Or is he Trinidadian from having been born and educated there, and having set some of his writings there? The 'Englishness' of English literature has become harder to define, but if this sounds like a problem, it has had very rich consequences for literature in England since the war. Such writers as Salman Rushdie, Hanif Kureishi, Caryl Phillips, Linton Kwesi Johnson, Fred D'Aguiar, David Dabydeen, Zadie Smith, Doris Lessing, V. S. Naipaul, Timothy Mo and Leila Aboulela either emigrated to Britain, or are the children of immigrants, and their writings are an essential part of the story of English literature since the war. The significance of the colonial legacy, both for these writers and for many other writers in England, is to open up for literary exploration the meanings of Englishness, both in the past and the present. As the industrial transformations of the nineteenth century prompted the Condition of England novel, the colonial and migratory legacies of the post-war period have brought renewed literary attention to the state of the nation.

Modes of Production and Consumption

Although increasingly Britain, like the rest of the industrialised world, appears to be a society obsessed with the visual technologies of film, television and, later, video, computer games and Internet entertainment, the post-war and contemporary periods should also be renowned as a time of unprecedented levels of literacy and unprecedented access to literature. Two reasons for this are particularly noteworthy. One is the continuous expansion since 1944 of the mass-education system, enabling greater access to secondary and university education. English Literature as an academic discipline has been a core component of the secondary-school curriculum throughout this time, and a popular and widely accessible choice for students at university level. This in itself has created not only a huge demand for literary books as texts for study, but generations of people who have learned to enjoy and appreciate reading literature, both for entertainment and for gaining knowledge and understanding. 'Literature' has come to mean, at least for universities, booksellers and publishing houses, a discrete category of high-quality and culturally valuable writing, rather than simply denoting everything in written form. Alongside the growth of mass education, another reason for the greater significance of 'Literature' since before the war is the 'paperback revolution' in publishing. In particular, Penguin publishers, founded in 1935 by Allen Lane, began the practice of publishing 'serious' literary fiction in easily affordable paperback editions, and helped to establish a wider demand for literature. Although the war interrupted the growth of

> **The Trouble with the English...**
>
> ... the trouble with the English was their ... *In a word*, Gibreel solemnly pronounced, *their weather*.
>
> Gibreel Farishta floating on his cloud formed the opinion that the moral fuzziness of the English was metereologically induced ...
>
> 'City', he cried, and his voice rolled over the metropolis like thunder, 'I am going to tropicalize you.'
>
> (Salman Rushdie, *The Satanic Verses*. London: Vintage, 1988, p. 354)

this phenomenon, largely due to the shortage of paper and workers, greater levels of affluence since the 1950s have fuelled the market for reading literary fiction.

Ironically, the enormous expansion of the demand for literary fiction has coincided with repeated warnings about the 'death of the novel'. *Granta* magazine published a symposium on the death of the novel in 1980, and yet just three years later the same magazine published the first collection of the 'Best of Young British Novelists', which included the work of Martin Amis, Pat Barker, Julian Barnes, Kazuo Ishiguro, Ian McEwan, Salman Rushdie and Graham Swift. These novelists enjoyed considerable success, which can be measured in sales figures as well as prestigious awards and prizes. To a degree, their success is evidence that 'good' literature can survive in the capitalist marketplace, that the quality of literary writing need not be a casualty of the economics of mass-market publishing. Q. D. Leavis, in her *Fiction and the Reading Public* (1932), had warned that publishers would be driven by the need for maximum sales, and would seek out a homogenised, formula 'product' which would increasingly make good-quality, literary writing unpublishable. Although it could be argued that the publication of literary fiction is still dependent on publishing houses which offset potential losses with the publication of formula fiction (and throughout the 1980s and 1990s literary publishing houses became increasingly parts of huge transnational corporations), the evidence to be gleaned from booksellers, newspaper review supplements, prestigious award ceremonies and publishing companies is that more literary fiction is being read in contemporary Britain than ever before. The availability of literary fiction on digital reading devices might be regarded as a new means by which fiction is proliferating, but it has not changed significantly the idea of what constitutes a novel.

7.6 Authors shortlisted for the Man Booker Prize, 2012 – Tan Twan Eng, Deborah Levy, Hilary Mantel, Alison Moore, Will Self, Jeet Thayil.

In comparison to the highly visible ways in which the novel is publicised and celebrated, the production and consumption of poetry and drama are less easy to gauge. Poets can only dream of the sales figures and royalty payments achieved by the most successful novelists, but there are some notable successes. Ted Hughes's *Birthday Letters* made the bestseller lists and won several awards, including the Whitbread Book of the Year, when it was published in 1998. Philip Larkin's *High Windows* sold out its first printing of just over 6,000 hardbound copies in just three weeks in 1974, and his *Collected Poems* (1988) ran to almost 60,000 hardbound and 95,000 paperbound copies. Aside from a few such notable exceptions, however, poetry is published in relatively small print runs or in small magazines, and most poets must earn their living through teaching posts and residencies. There have been attempts to popularise poetry, such as the 'Poems on the Underground' campaign since 1986, a radio series on the 'nation's favourite poems', and the campaign to launch the 'new generation' poets in 1994. But none have succeeded in making poetry anywhere near as successful as fiction.

In some respects, the history of theatre in Britain for much of the post-war period might be characterised as an attempt to break the association of theatre with like-minded middle-class audiences. With the decline of the music hall in the 1930s, theatre became renowned as a predominantly middle-class form of entertainment. Several generations of dramatists since the 1950s have attempted to widen the appeal of drama. John Osborne's *Look Back in Anger* (1956) was heralded, somewhat erroneously, as the beginning of working-class theatre in Britain, and was followed by the so-called 'New Wave' of social realist dramatists, such as Arnold Wesker, Shelagh Delaney and John Arden. However radical were the claims of the new drama, its audiences still derived predominantly from the professional and managerial occupations, who earned incomes above the national average. Playwrights with radical socialist or feminist ideas found it difficult to reach suitable audiences. In addition, theatre performances could only be performed under licence prior to 1968, which meant in practice that the text for every play had to be submitted to and censored by the Lord Chamberlain's office. Plays were frequently amended to avoid blasphemy or 'foul' language, or banned altogether if deemed unsuitable. The socialist theatre company led by Joan Littlewood, Theatre Workshop, attempted in the fifties and early sixties to test the limits of censorship with plays like Brendan Behan's *The Hostage* (1958) and Littlewood's *Oh! What a Lovely War* (1963). It was Edward Bond's play, *Saved* (1965), however, which was widely credited with undermining the authority of the Lord Chamberlain's office, and causing the withdrawal of theatre censorship in 1968. Bond was one of a number of Marxist and feminist playwrights who, in the sixties and seventies, attempted to take drama out of the West End and into small community theatres which might attract working-class and radical student audiences. Some experiments were briefly successful, but community theatres needed substantial financial subsidies from government-funded or sponsored organisations. Under the Conservative governments of the 1980s, such ventures were increasingly unlikely to receive official support, and community theatres were especially vulnerable to cutbacks. What Q. D. Leavis warned about the fate of fiction under market capitalism was more evidently a threat to theatre: in 1954 Kenneth Tynan observed that in the

7.7 The Penguin edition of D. H. Lawrence's *Lady Chatterley's Lover*, which was ruled to be not obscene by a jury at the Old Bailey in 1960.

twenty-seven West End theatres, only three new, serious plays were being shown, the rest being made up of musicals and light comedies. Tynan believed that the balance was tipped more in favour of 'serious' drama in 1956. It is a moot point whether this was due to the arrival of brilliant new dramatists, such as Osborne, or might have more general, structural causes, such as post-war government commitments to subsidise theatre heavily as an art form.

Of all the literary art forms, theatre is perhaps the one most directly susceptible to economic pressures, since drama costs considerable amounts of money to produce, and to be successful a play needs rapidly to attract sufficient numbers of people willing to pay for tickets. A play might have just a few days to make an impact, whereas a book might sit on booksellers' shelves for months or years before becoming successful. Political dramatists had sought to achieve an effect by taking plays to the communities which they thought might be inspired or mobilised to political action, but the economics of theatre production and consumption meant that only the large, well-attended West End theatres and, from 1976, the National Theatre on the South Bank in London could afford to support new drama fully. The lesson from the fifties generation was that television and film was a more effective way of reaching popular audiences.

The Generation without Purpose

JIMMY: I suppose people of our generation aren't able to die for good causes any longer. We had all that done for us, in the thirties and forties, when we were still kids. There aren't any good, brave causes left. If the big bang does come, and we all get killed off, it won't be in aid of the old-fashioned grand design. It'll just be for the Brave New-nothing-very-much-thank-you. About as pointless and inglorious as stepping in front of a bus.

(John Osborne, *Look Back in Anger*. London: Faber & Faber, 1957, pp. 84–5)

The films of *Look Back in Anger* and *A Taste of Honey* reached hundreds of thousands of people, many more than was possible even with extended West End runs. The working-class dramatists of the fifties arguably were more influential on the development of television dramas like the long-running soap, *Coronation Street* (1960–), the series, *Boys from the Blackstuff* (1982), and films, *Cathy Come Home* (1966) and *Raining Stones* (1993), than they were on the evolution of the theatre. It might be suggested that by the late 1980s theatre was still as much a middle-class bastion of entertainment as it had been before *Look Back in Anger*. This might explain the development in the 1990s and 2000s of what has been characterised as 'In-Yer-Face' theatre, in which playwrights such as Sarah Kane, Mark Ravenhill, and Anthony Neilson sought to shock audiences out of a perceived complacency about the kind of society they lived in. Theatre remains in economic terms the domain of a privileged minority who can afford to attend it, even though in terms of content and form it has supported some of the most obvious attempts at radical aesthetic and political experiment in post-war literary history.

An alternative narrative of the history of post-war British drama might begin not with the production of John Osborne's *Look Back in Anger* in 1956, but with the London premiere of *Waiting for Godot* by Samuel Beckett in 1955. Beckett was an Irish playwright who lived in France and wrote mostly in French, but arguably no British playwright had such influence on the development of post-war British drama as Beckett. After *Waiting for Godot*, Beckett's plays figured prominently in the theatre scene in Britain, and had profound influence on several playwrights, most notably Harold Pinter. Beckett stripped his plays of social reference points, so that bare scenes of often grim, unexplained lives stood symbolically for the wretched condition of human existence. His plays have often been explained in terms of existentialist explorations of the meanings of humanity shown without the trappings of civilisation and culture. Since the Holocaust laid bare the horrific potential of human cruelty, and the threat of nuclear war made modern civilisation seem a precarious veneer, it could be argued that Beckett's plays were thoroughly historical in their exploration of the post-war human condition. It is Beckett's style, however, as much as his central theme, that has been influential. No other playwright has used the bare stage to such effect, nor experimented so radically with minimalist language, imagery, character and action.

Language, Forms, Genres and Styles

Language: Whose English?

The period under survey in this chapter began with the publication of James Joyce's *Finnegans Wake* (1939), the most formally and linguistically inventive text ever produced in English, but its play upon a diverse range of languages and upon the etymological roots of English make it difficult to define simply as an 'English' literary work (even aside from the complications of having an Irish author). The 'Movement' poets of the 1950s saw such linguistic dexterity as a product of the excesses of modernist experiment, and Donald Davie argued in particular that English poets after the war were instead seeking to 'purify' rather than 'expand' the language. In the twentieth and twenty-first centuries English has continued to expand as a language in the way that it has always done, through cultural interaction with a diverse range of languages, and through the localised inventions reflected in dialectal usage. In literary texts, arguably, dialect has been most notably deployed in writings produced by immigrants. Sam Selvon uses a modified Trinidadian dialect of English in his *The Lonely Londoners* (1956), for example, to give a particular cultural inflection to his immigrant characters. Rushdie frequently does the same with Indian dialects of English in his novels. At the same time, there have been attempts by working-class writers to reflect the patterns of regional, working-class speech, usually in dialogue. Usually with omniscient narration, a 'standard' English dialect is used, but it is a consistent feature of Pat Barker's early novels, for example, to bring the language of the narrator closer to that of the regional dialects of the characters. In England, perhaps more so than in many other countries, dialect is a marker of class identity, and that has been a concern of many working-class writers in post-war Britain. Other writers have been interested in the cultural politics of language in different ways: George Orwell's *Nineteen Eighty-Four* (1949), for example, reflects anxieties about the ideologies engendered in political language, while Anthony Burgess's *A Clockwork Orange* (1962) features an invented dialect to reflect the influence of youth sub-cultures on language use.

Post-Modern Fiction

The post-modern is usually associated with post-war scepticism about the emancipatory claims of enlightenment modernity, particularly in the aftermath of atrocities like the Holocaust and Hiroshima. Instead of a narrative of progress, post-modern writing and art tends to reflect pessimism about the fate of modern society, and cast doubt on the idea that human life is meaningful or purposeful. The post-modern sense of cultural exhaustion and impending demise is evident in Martin Amis's *London Fields* (1989), in which the dying narrator remarks that even the babies in England are dressed as if they are old, and the marks of decay and death are present everywhere. Graham Swift's novels abound with this feeling of exhaustion, and particularly of an England spiritually and morally shattered by two world wars and the demise of its imperial glory. *Last Orders* (1996) tells the story of a funeral procession, which tours through the symbolic garden of England to its battered channel coast-line, and on the way the friends of the deceased recall their own stories of post-war English decline. David Gervais observed that 'Modern England is in danger of becom-ing a museum of itself', and many contemporary English novels reflect this notion that England is a place receding into the past, none more so than Julian Barnes's novel, *England, England* (1998), in which 'England' is a heritage theme park.

This is one key way in which the strongly elegiac tendencies of much post-war English fiction can be understood as conforming to a post-modern notion of the end of history, of scepticism towards the narratives of progress and enlightenment which have dominated Western culture since the eighteenth century. Indeed, it is worth reflecting that much post-modern British fiction is set in the past, and plays subversively with the possibility of truthful historical narratives. In many novels, that 'play' takes the form of theoretical explorations of the very grounds of fictional and historical narratives, most notably in John Fowles's *The French Lieutenant's Woman* (1969) and Barnes's *Flaubert's Parrot* (1984), where narrators digress on the subject of how narratives are constructed. Post-modern texts tend to reflect on the difficulty of the act of representation itself, and understand the world as made up of signs, often difficult or impossible to read truthfully. In Iain Sinclair's *Lights Out for the Territory* (1997), for example, the city is understood metaphorically as a palimpsestic text, lay-ered with meaning, while the palimpsest takes visual form in Tom Phillips's artistic rewriting of a Victorian novel as *The Humument* (1980).

It is a recurrent feature of the post-modern text to question the nature of the real, and to blur the distinction between the fabulous and the real. Thus in Angela Carter's *Nights at the Circus* (1984), Fevvers has wings which enable her to soar above the chains of reason, but not without Carter's ironic subversion of the emancipa-tory potential of such wings. So too, Jeanette Winterson's *Sexing the Cherry* (1989) fea-tures a monstrous 'dog-woman' capable both of great destruction and love. Salman Rushdie is perhaps most accomplished as a magic realist, making believable and everyday the world of the supernatural, with characters capable of flight, telepathy and miraculous metamorphoses. Alongside these examples of the fascination with the conflation of the fantastic and the real, the post-modern novel also entails a cri-tique of modernity, as in some of J. G. Ballard's fiction, such as *Crash* (1973) or *Concrete Island* (1974), in which the bright, fast settings of modernity reveal disturbing cracks and fissures.

Political Drama

It could be argued that drama was always the most political art form in Britain, and since Elizabethan times monarchs and governments have feared the effects that cer-tain plays might have on the masses, and they therefore maintained censorship laws to police theatre performances until 1968. In the post-war period, theatre became even more explicitly political. Osborne's *Look Back in Anger* (1956), however confusing the direction of its anger, was perceived as an assault on the establishment. Harold Pinter's plays explored the relationship between language and violence, and the power struggles which take place even in the most mundane and domestic settings.

Whose English?

helluva hard tay read theez initstull
if yi canny unnirston thim jiss clear aff then
gawn
get tay fuck ootma road

ahmaz goodiz thi lota yiz so ah um
ah no whit ahm dayn
tellnyi
jiss try enny a yir fly patir wi me
stick thi bootnyi good style
so ah wull

(Tom Leonard, 'Good Style', *Intimate Voices: Selected Work 1965–1983*. London: Vintage, 1995, p. 14)

In the late 1960s and early 1970s in Britain, a new generation of experimental political dramatists came into prominence. The emergence of a distinctive youth culture in the fifties gave rise to dreams of political change, hopes that young people could shake off the shackles of capitalism and institutionalised communism, but the collapse of the student uprising in Paris in 1968, and the Soviet crushing of the Czech uprising in Prague in the same year, extinguished those dreams. Marxist playwrights shifted their attention from the creation of drama designed to generate a greater consciousness of working-class identity to the disruption of dominant political ideologies. Feminist drama of the period might be understood in the same way, as switching from consciousness-raising to political critique. John Bull, the foremost historian of political drama in Britain, argued that writers such as David Hare, Howard Brenton, David Edgar, Trevor Griffiths, Caryl Churchill and Edward Bond were 'frequently and violently in disagreement about the forms and aims of the new drama, but in agreement on one thing, the desire to create a drama that would stand in the vanguard of political and social change' (p. 1). Contemporary

7.8 Harold Pinter in his study, 1983.

dramatists continue to see their work in this vanguard role, and to experiment with theatrical form, although arguably the political orientations of recent drama are less obvious or overt than previous generations of modern dramatists. Anthony Neilson's *Realism* (2006), for example, is both provocative and innovative – dramatising the inner life of a lonely man – but its provocations do not have any obvious political significance. Simon Stephens's *Pornography* (2008) is daringly topical, set in July 2005 and encompassing the G8 summit of world political leaders, the celebration of London winning the bid to host the Olympic Games, and the 7 July suicide bombings which killed fifty-two people. It is a moving play, with a loose, lively structure, but if its tragic depictions of alienation and loss are underpinned by any political ideology, that can only be described as a rather weak sense of shared humanity.

Diversity in the Face of Poetry

In contrast to the vanguardist pose of many post-war British dramatists, the most celebrated and successful poets in the period often appear to be more interested in the valedictory. The poetry of Philip Larkin, Geoffrey Hill, Ted Hughes and Tony Harrison, although the work of each poet is very different from the others, has in common a prevailing sense of living in a time overshadowed by the past, pale in comparison to the richness and unity evoked only as a distant memory. None could be described as nostalgic, but there is certainly a strong sense of lament for the state of the present. This is perhaps most obvious in the sardonic and glum conservatism of Larkin's later poetry, particularly 'Going, Going' (1972), often quoted in this context, but often also described as one of Larkin's weakest poems. It is notable in different forms, however, in long poems like Harrison's *v.* (1985), in which an unemployed skinhead serves as a contrast against the worthy working-class occupations inscribed upon the gravestones he defaces, or Hill's *Mercian Hymns* (1971), which explores the ancient Mercian King Offa as a figure of English nationalism. Hughes might be bracketed with such valedictory poets on the basis of his displacement of the urban chaos and global terror of post-war politics into the savage intimacies of rural and animal life, and the surprising conservatism of some of his work as Poet Laureate.

This might be considered the dominant line in post-war poetry, but it belies the sheer diversity of poetry since the war. Since the late sixties, with the emergence of the Mersey poets, the influence of Northern Irish poets like Seamus Heaney, and the establishment of poetry presses like Carcanet and Bloodaxe outside the traditional London-Oxbridge centres, poetry in England has been rich in the plurality of its voices, forms and styles. This diversity certainly takes the form of cultural and regional differences, from the West Indian inflections of dub poets like Benjamin Zephaniah and Linton Kwesi Johnson, to Tom Leonard's Glaswegian-accented poetry, or Peter Reading's use of demotic English. It is also a formal diversity, from the concrete poetry of Bob Cobbing, the neo-modernist experimentation of J. H. Prynne and Roy Fisher, to the popular comedy of John Hegley, the conversational directness of Selima Hill or the spry rhythms of Simon Armitage. Perhaps most illustrative of this diversity is the anthology *The New British Poetry, 1968–1988* (1988), which was edited in four sections by separate editors to cover the range of social, cultural, ethnic, gender and aesthetic differences within contemporary poetry. The explosion of women's poetry since the 1970s is also of particular note. In their time, Elizabeth Jennings, Sylvia Plath and Elizabeth Bishop seemed isolated and remote from the male-dominated generation of the fifties and sixties. In contrast, several anthologies of contemporary women's poetry were published in the 1980s and 1990s, although the idea of anthologies specifically showcasing women's poetry became problematic for many women writers who increasingly came to see such collections as ghettoising. What constitutes the dominant or mainstream tendency in contemporary British poetry is not debatable simply on the basis of its contemporaneity, therefore, for the proliferation of new poetries since the 1960s has also been the product of a much wider political and cultural contest about British society, history and identity.

One notable contrast between the most celebrated poetry of the immediate post-war decades and that of the twenty-first century has been the renewed importance of place and environment in recent poetry. Whereas Larkin could dismiss his birthplace in a line – 'Nothing, like something, happens anywhere' – there is a strong emphasis in much contemporary poetry on the importance of local ecologies and communities. Alice Oswald's collection, *Dart* (2002), is an exemplary instance of this tendency, telling the story of the river Dart in Devon from multiple perspectives, including swimmers and boatmen, poachers and farm workers. *A Sleepwalk on the Severn* (2009) similarly constructed a poem for voices about the river Severn using the effects of the moon on people and water as a focal point. Of more industrial landscapes, Robert Hampson's *Seaport* (2008) is an important work for its extraordinary poetic account of the history and development of Liverpool. Hampson's work draws upon documentary sources, just as Oswald draws upon interviews and conversations with local dwellers, a technique which emphasises the extent to which poetry is 'found' and made in local habitations. This tendency in contemporary poetry to represent community and ecology in sensitive and ethical ways has been described as 'ecopoetics'.

Environmental Prose, or the New Nature Writing

In the arts in Britain generally, the growing recognition since the 1960s that advanced economies have depended upon a destructive and potentially catastrophic relationship to nature has led to creative endeavours to re-imagine our environment. Ecopoetics is one manifestation of this attention to the environment, but perhaps a more significant development in contemporary literature is the emergence of a strong genre of non-fictional 'nature writing'. The key works of the genre include Robert Macfarlane's *The Wild Places* (2007) and *The Old Ways* (2012), Roger Deakin's *Waterlog* (1999) and *Wildwood* (2007), Helen MacDonald's *H is for Hawk* (2014), Tim Dee's *The Running Sky* (2009) and *Four Fields* (2013), and Kathleen Jamie's *Findings* (2005) and *Sightlines* (2012). There is a great variety of styles, tones and themes, as well as environments, addressed in these works, but what links them as examples of the genre is a commitment to a personal experience and reckoning of the distinctiveness of place, and humility about our relations with non-human species and natural environments, as well as our relations with other human beings. Many of these works take the form of narratives of journeys, although often to places not very far away, in which the journeys themselves are exemplary of ethical and reverent ways of relating to the world. For Deakin in *Waterlog*, for example, swimming the rivers, lakes, and seas around Britain places the swimmer '*in* nature, part and parcel of it … on equal terms with the animal world around you: in every sense, on the same level' (p. 4). The means of travel is also a mode of being in the world, as Robert Macfarlane writes in *The Old Ways* of 'ways of walking that were also ways of thinking' (p. 23). The books listed above might be regarded as not properly literary, and categorised instead as topographical, or indeed as the work of naturalists and bird-watchers, but what distinguishes them as literature is that they are also works of beautiful prose, and often bring to prose the elegance of poetry, as for example when Macfarlane writes 'Paths are the habits of a landscape' (p. 17). Kathleen Jamie's essays are formal masterpieces; indeed many of the new nature writers may be credited with reviving the literary art of essay writing.

The sudden popularity of the genre in the twenty-first century perhaps obscured the extent to which naturalist prose already had a long and distinguished history in English writing, from Gilbert White's *The Natural History of Selborne* (1789), to Richard Jefferies, Edward Thomas, Ian Niall, Kenneth Allsop and Frank Fraser Darling in the nineteenth and twentieth centuries. Since the 1960s, Richard Mabey, Sue Clifford and Angela King have explored and celebrated the rich environmental history and local particularities of many parts of England, and Tim Robinson's extraordinary prose mappings of the Aran Islands and Connemara in the west of Ireland have been profoundly influential on the shape and ambition of contemporary environmental writing. The American tradition of nature writing from Thoreau's *Walden* (1854) to the work of Rachel Carson in the 1950s and Barry Lopez since the 1970s, has also been influential. Much of this environmental writing in modern literature has been produced in a context of deep and often disturbing environmental change, in which the landscape and ecosystems of which we are a part have been irrevocably altered and diminished. The popularity of contemporary examples of the genre, and the republication of classics of nature writing by Little Toller Press, may be substantially explained by widespread concerns that industrialised societies like Britain have alienated themselves from the environments upon which we all depend.

Texts and Issues

Introduction

What have been the major issues in English literature since 1939? There was no radical change in the issues which preoccupied post-1939 writers from those which preoccupied writers of the earlier twentieth century, the nineteenth century and before. Writers even in the early twenty-first century continue to be concerned with questions of social structure, gender relations, national identity, the impact of technological change, and the relationship between humanity and the natural environment in ways which might be easily recognisable to Charles Dickens, William Wordsworth or Jane Austen. And yet the scale and speed of change in the contemporary period, and the global and instantaneous impact of new technologies, from the nuclear bomb to electronic communication, have altered the social fabric profoundly. Some would argue that literature struggles to keep up with the fictions created by politicians and the media. Even a novel like George Orwell's *Nineteen Eighty-Four* (1949), which imagines a futuristic dystopian world of authoritarianism and social control, falls behind the possibilities of media manipulation and political illusion available today. Arguably, also, contemporary writers remain preoccupied with older forms of community and belonging, and have not yet fully imagined, or brought to literary expression at any rate, the new forms of social connection made possible through email, chat-rooms, on-line gaming, computer viruses, spam, text-messaging, video-phones and other new technologies. Does literature lag behind technology? Does it do so deliberately?

Class, Culture and Society

Social class became a central issue in British politics and culture in the immediate aftermath of the war. Both Labour and Conservative Party politicians promised in various forms to abolish poverty, to provide decent wages, housing, education and healthcare, and even to create a classless society. Such promises, of course, were at best idealistic, and at worst simply cynical lies to sway the electorate, but there were two key times in the period since the war which ostensibly offered greater opportunities for working-class people to climb the social ladder. In the 1950s and 1960s, the achievement of full employment and an international trade boom created higher wages and standards of living; at the same time improved access to higher education seemed to allow some working-class people the opportunity to enter middle-class professions. This became known as the affluent society, and was reflected in the vastly increased numbers of people who could afford televisions, cars, holidays, and to own a house. In the 1980s, the privatisation policies pursued by Thatcherite governments seemed to create similar opportunities: people living in publicly owned housing could buy their own properties, working- and middle-class people were encouraged to buy shares in the newly privatised public utility companies, like British Gas, British Telecom, and so on, and, much more obviously than in the 1950s, the new apparent hero of Thatcherist economics was the working-class man turned aspiring millionaire, famously satirised as 'Del Boy' in the TV series *Only Fools and Horses* (1981–91). What politicians meant when they talked about a classless society, of course, was a highly limited notion that the old ideas of social rank and inherited power were giving way to a social structure based on slightly more permeable (but by no means open) tiers. It was possible for a working-class man or woman to rise to the top, but it was rare and by no means easy, and, of course, the other side of the prosperity of the eighties was the sharp rise in unemployment, which reached over 4 million before the end of the decade.

Fictions of social mobility and newly earned affluence were popular in the 1950s and early 1960s, as were literary and cinematic representations of class difference and class relations more generally. Kingsley Amis's *Lucky Jim* (1954), essentially a campus novel about a lower-middle-class young man who pricks fun out of the paraphernalia and pomposity of upper-middle-class academia, was largely understood to be a fiction of rising up through the social structure. To a large extent, the writers of the late fifties accepted and promoted the political myth of greater social mobility and increased opportunities for the working class to join the affluent society. Joe Lampton in Braine's *Room at the Top* (1957 [A]) realises that money, power and glamour are there for the taking, if only one has the will to succeed. Lampton contrasts the grim, cold world of his upbringing in the thirties in the town of Dufton with the fresh possibilities presented by his new life in Warley, a place where he imagines 'every door in the town would be wide open and the grades wouldn't matter'. What is interesting about both novels in their representation of social climbing, however, is that neither Jim Dixon nor Joe Lampton achieves success through hard work or educational merit, but through a sexual relationship with a woman of higher social standing. It is only when Joe Lampton ingratiates himself with the daughter of a wealthy Warley businessman that he finds himself welcomed into a new affluent position. In this sense, both novels, as well as the famous play by John Osborne, *Look Back in Anger* (1956), are more about cross-class sexual relationships than social mobility.

Alan Sillitoe's *Saturday Night and Sunday Morning* (1958) does not show as much faith in the possibility of its working-class male protagonist, Arthur Seaton, 'reaching the

7.9 Tony Ray-Jones, 'Brighton Beach, 1966'.

top'. Seaton is markedly more anti-authoritarian and cynical about the distractions of television and cars, but he is also a new kind of working-class protagonist, one with plenty of money in his pocket to enjoy himself, and a sense of freedom from any responsibilities to raise a family, or to 'better himself'. He is the affluent worker, who will soon be able to buy his own house and car, but what makes the novel more interesting than a fairy-tale story of comfortable living is Arthur's relative indifference to such affluence. His antagonism towards the police and army authorities is understood to be a long-standing trait of his community, and the rhythm of working-class life, centred around the factory, the pub and the street, appear timeless and unaffected by the glitzy promises of social transformation. There are comparatively few texts which represent women's experiences of the period, but those which do, like Shelagh Delaney's *A Taste of Honey* (1958) and Nell Dunn's *Up the Junction* (1963), show that women's lives remained the same. There were other writings by men, too, which showed that the working class as a whole did not by any means become affluent and carefree in the fifties. While Joe Lampton is climbing the social ladder and enjoying the small luxuries which he can afford, Dunn's women are running pies under cold water to make them swell up, and Sam Selvon's immigrants are catching pigeons in London for dinner to keep from starving. While Arthur Seaton is working hard and earning £14 a week, Jack Petty in *Five Fags a Day* (1956) is fighting with the rats to pick scrap metal from slag heaps, and Mike Lewis in Bernard Kops's *Awake for Mourning* (1958) is seizing his chance to steal a wallet from a passing stranger.

While the novels and plays by Braine, Sillitoe, Osborne and Delaney became successful films in the early 1960s, it is the darker side of working-class life which increasingly came to dominate British writings about class. The slums did not disappear, and the social problems caused by poverty, unemployment, and gross economic inequalities were increasingly evident. Films like *Cathy Come Home* (1966), *A Clockwork Orange* (1971), and *Scum* (1977) would, of course, make the earlier films of social mobility and success look sentimental and naive. In literature, two texts from the early 1980s would highlight the depth of Britain's social problems with class division. Caryl Churchill's play, *Top Girls* (1982), for example, begins with an apparent triumph for feminism and socialism: Marlene, a working-class woman, rises to the top of her profession as a successful businesswoman, analogous to the rise to power of Prime Minister Margaret Thatcher in 1979. In an opening fantasy scene, Marlene celebrates this success at a restaurant with a group of women from previous centuries who have broken social taboos and barriers, but while they congratulate each other on their successes, a waitress serves them silently, ignored by them as if she didn't exist. As the play progresses, it becomes clear that Marlene has achieved success at the expense of others – her daughter, her sister, her employees – and by imitating the values of patriarchial power. Her rise to the top is thus not a story of social transformation, but simply of individual ambition, success at the cost of marginalising and exploiting others. Pat Barker's *Union Street* (1982) returns to the same kind of working-class community featured in Sillitoe's novel, but after the collapse of the manufacturing industries, the mass unemployment of working-class men, and the dereliction of many working-class streets, Barker's depiction of such a community is almost unrecognisable from Sillitoe's. Barker tells the story of the women of this community, beginning with an eleven-year-old girl who is raped in the abandoned yard of a steel factory, and ending with an elderly woman who elects to die on a park bench rather than be evicted from her condemned home. In between, there is no hope of social mobility for her protagonists, and it is implied that the young girl's life is mapped out for her through a low-paid factory job, teenage pregnancy, marriage to a terminally unemployed man who will beat her because of his own frustration, premature ageing, and the cold, hunger and poverty of old age. There are small windows of hope in *Union Street*, but on the whole the working-class women of the novel are as condemned as the houses they live in, surrounded by prostitution, drug-addiction, violence and despair. In particular the novel is grim about class relations. There are no sympathetic middle- or upper-class characters in the novel, and when the young girl breaks into a middle-class home, she experiences it as an alien, unfathomable place.

By the early twenty-first century, class divisions had arguably widened even further compared with the 1980s, with the gap between the richest and poorest in British society more marked than ever. The vested interests in keeping British society so divided were partly satirised in Jonathan Coe's *What a Carve Up!* (1994), a political comedy about the divisive legacy of Thatcherism. In Chris Cleave's novel, *Incendiary* (2005), what begins as the angry letter of a grieving working-class woman to Osama bin Laden, the leader of the Al Qaeda terrorist network, turns into a probing examination of contemporary British class divisions. The woman, who is unnamed, has lost her husband and young son in a horrific terrorist explosion in London, and she demands to know why her family, who are the poor inhabitants of an East End council estate, have been killed. But she discovers later in the novel that police knew in advance about the bomb that killed her husband, son and a thousand other football supporters, and decided to allow it to go off so as to protect their terrorist informers and so help them to prevent the 'real' threat of a bomb in the financial district. 'A thousand City suits die and it's goodbye global economy. A thousand blokes in Gunners T-shirts die and you just sell a bit less lager', observes one character sardonically, at which point it is clear that the terrorist theme of the novel functions as an allegory for the ways in which working-class people in contemporary Britain are routinely abandoned to the contingencies of 'sink' housing estates, failing schools, overcrowded hospitals, and the accidents of free-market economics. Sociologists have argued recently that class structures in Britain have radically changed since the 1950s, and that the three-tiered structure of working, middle and upper classes has been further stratified under the pressures of neo-liberal capitalism into an increasingly disenfranchised and impoverished 'precariat' at the bottom, an increasingly empowered elite at the top, and more 'fuzzy' and complicated intersections of economic, social and cultural capital in the middle. There is greater recognition among contemporary sociologists that class is not just measured by economic measures, but also by access to cultural and social capital. There is a strong correlation between people who engage in the approved forms of cultural activities – going to the theatre, opera, or art galleries, reading 'great' books and the review sections of Sunday newspapers – and the ownership and acquisition of economic capital. Although there is evidence that what constitutes 'good' culture is changing, and that there are emerging forms of cultural capital which do not map so easily on to economic wealth, nevertheless Cleave's allusion to football and lager as markers of low social status remains a stable indicator of the ways in which social divisions in Britain are strongly tied to cultural divisions.

Gender and Sexuality

The period since 1939 has also been a time of significant change for issues relating to gender and sexuality. The war placed many women into jobs customarily regarded as men's work, and might have helped to loosen previously rigid stereotypes of masculine and feminine spheres of activity. After the war, however, there followed a period of considerable ideological pressure on women to stay at home and raise children, while men were expected to pursue careers and enter public life. Women had won the right to vote in 1918, albeit restricted to those over thirty who were ratepayers or married to ratepayers. By the late 1960s, there was talk of sexual revolution, and female sexuality was supposedly no longer a taboo subject for public discussion. In 1957, the Wolfenden Report recommended the decriminalisation of homosexuality as a private act, and this seemed to lay the ground for more liberal attitudes towards sexual identity and relations. Abortion was legalised and the contraceptive pill made available in the 1960s, which also seemed to give women greater choice about sexual activity and pregnancy. In 1975, legislation was introduced which purported to guarantee equal pay for men and women doing the same jobs, and, in 1979, Britain elected its first female prime minister, Margaret Thatcher. These steps recognised that women had an important place in the workforce and in political life. One could from such details construct a narrative of gradual political liberation and equality for women, and for gay men and women, in Britain, with some retrenchments along the way. Literary representations of, and responses to, such a narrative, are often highly sceptical of any claims of a general emancipation of women and homosexuals from sexual and social oppression, however.

In women's writing of the fifties, there is ample evidence of discontent with the stereotypes of femininity and the restrictions of domesticity, although this takes a modest form. There are very few literary examples of successful professional women, female adventurers, or women experimenting with alternative lifestyles or sexual identities, but writers such as Lynne Reid Banks, Doris Lessing, Elizabeth Taylor, Barbara Pym, Rose Macaulay and Rosamund Lehmann did provide images and stories of female characters who were markedly dissatisfied with the expected lot of contemporary women. Perhaps even more obviously, homosexuality found muted form in the literature of the fifties, masquerading through heterosexual relations in Terence Rattigan's plays *The Deep Blue Sea* (1952) and *Separate Tables* (1954), for example, and, when expressed openly in Rattigan's *Ross* (1960) and Osborne's *A Patriot for Me* (1965), it was represented as a fatal flaw or weakness. Male homosexuality also found itself too often expressed through farce, in Brendan Behan's *The Hostage* (1958) and later Joe Orton's *Loot* (1966), while female homosexuality could hardly be found in literary representations at all. If heterosexual marriage is the socially endorsed ideal for sexual relations, it has frequently appeared strained and inadequate, from Elizabeth Taylor's portrait of a marriage in which her protagonist, Julia Davenant, feels like nothing more than her husband's baggage, in *At Mrs Lippincote's* (1945), to the more comic treatment of marital strain in Nigel Williams's *The Wimbledon Poisoner* (1990).

One of the most ambitious fictional explorations of gender and sexual identity in the post-war period is Doris Lessing's *The Golden Notebook* (1962). Lessing's heroine, Anna Wulf, divides her life into four notebooks – black, red, yellow and blue – each of which represents and contains different aspects of her experience and self-aware-ness. The fifth notebook, the golden notebook of the title, is her attempt to resolve her diffused and fragmented identities into a meaningful whole. These notebooks are themselves interspersed with a realist narrative entitled *Free Women*, a novel within the novel, which tells the story of Anna and her friend Molly, and their attempts to find love and happiness. The presumption of *Free Women* is that narrative can order life into a continuous and coherent stream, but the other notebooks, written in the form of diary, memoir, scribbled ideas, fragments of thoughts, introspective questioning, and which are frequently punctuated by lines, subdivisions and editor's notes commenting on changes of style, reveal that Anna's life is too fragmented and disjunctive to find coherent literary expression. Lessing uses such incoherent frag-ments to reflect on the instability of Anna's sense of self, and ultimately to imply a profound sense of disillusionment with the possibilities of liberal feminism, with

7.10 Woman reads as baby sleeps, about 1949. Advertising images such as these were power-ful ways of persuading women to accept that their roles were as wives and mothers within the domestic sphere.

its reliance upon a stable, centred subjectivity. *The Golden Notebook* anticipates the disenchantment of Western feminism's 'first wave' – the 'rights and votes'-based approach in the sixties – and the emergence of second-wave feminism, with its focus on the discursive and ideological foundations of patriarchy. The illusion of female liberation in the sixties is also the subject of Ruth Prawer Jhabvala's *Heat and Dust* (1975), which tells the story of two English women, Olivia, the wife of a colonial official, whose story is set in 1923; and the unnamed narrator, fifty years later, who arrives in India to retrace Olivia's life. Olivia seems constrained to bend to the will of men, while the narrator is supposedly a free woman, sexually liberated and independent. Yet, the narrator ends up being used sexually by a young man, and like Olivia, pregnant and compelled to live out what appear to be unchanging social and sexual conditions for women, as objects of exploitation and manipulation. So too, in Caryl Churchill's play, *Cloud Nine* (1979), the sexual oppression of the Victorians is contrasted with the apparent liberation of the post-1960s generation, only to reveal that although sexuality is more openly discussed and practised, the social and sexual status of women has hardly changed at all.

Sexuality for women and for gay men has become more overt, more publicly acknowledged, in Churchill's play. But if the love that dared not speak its name is now shouting it from the rooftops, it seems that this is no indication of changing social and sexual structures. The same is evident in fictional representations of gay and lesbian sexuality. Alan Hollinghurst's *The Swimming-Pool Library* (1988), for example, shocking in its depictions of violent gay sex, is ambivalent about the degree to which any form of liberation is taking place. Hollinghurst's narrator, Beckwith, is gradually becoming less aggressively hedonistic, and he learns more about the social and historical contexts of male homosexuality which give him a limited sense of solidarity with a wider gay community, but homosexuality remains as covert and marginalised as it appears to have been in the past. In contrast, Jeanette Winterson's exploration of lesbian identity in *Oranges Are Not the Only Fruit* (1985), seeks out the possibility of an ideal sisterhood through which lesbianism might find inclusion. Both Winterson and Angela Carter explored the degree to which patriarchal discourses might be subverted through fantasy and the creation of new feminist mythologies, and their work was emblematic of a more radical feminist approach to gender identity and sexuality than was possible, even conceivable, it seems, in the fifties.

Since the early 1990s it has become conventional, if often misguided, to refer to a postfeminist era. 'Postfeminism' is a term which implies that the struggle for rights for women has been broadly successful, and that women born since the 1960s do not have to contend with the same hardships,

> ### Women's Liberation
>
> And once the old world has turned on its axle so that the new dawn can dawn, then, ah, then! all the women will have wings, the same as I. This young woman in my arms, whom we have found tied hand and foot with the grisly bonds of ritual, will suffer no more of it; she will tear off her mind forg'd manacles, will rise up and fly away. The dolls' house doors will open, the brothels will spill forth their prisoners, the cages, gilded or otherwise, all over the world, in every land, will let forth their inmates singing together the dawn chorus of the new, the transformed –.
>
> (Angela Carter, *Nights at the Circus*. London: Picador, 1985, p. 285)

7.11 The *Empire Windrush*, bringing Caribbean immigrants to England in 1948.

inequalities, and prejudices that their mothers and grandmothers endured. In literature, Helen Fielding's *Bridget Jones's Diary* (1996) is often read as an expression of this postfeminist sensibility, in which the eponymous heroine has a career, independence, and freedom, but as a single woman in her thirties still hankers after marriage to a successful man as the only means of attaining happiness. Fielding's novel is in many ways a more sophisticated parody of this fantasy than this reading implies, but it captures a key aspect of postfeminism which is its danger of taking the achievements of feminism so much for granted as to have forgotten the need for feminism at all.

Empire, Race and National Identity

The dissolution of the British empire and the influx of immigrants from former colonies have prompted repeated attempts politically and legally to redefine the meanings of English and British national identity. The post-war period in this respect represents a fundamental change in the notion of national identity, for in the imperial period, as Simon Gikandi argues, 'the essence of British identity was derived from the totality of all the people brought together by empire; in the postimperial period, in contrast we find a calculated attempt to configure Englishness as exclusionary of its colonial wards' (*Maps of Englishness*, p. 71 [Cii]). In literature and culture, it might be argued that the end of empire and the changing ethnic demography of the nation have prompted the return to a Condition of England mode of representation and examination (see pp. 413–18, 483). This is evident in many forms in the literature of the period. In Doris Lessing's *In Pursuit of the English* (1960 [A]), the English are a myth, impossible to define and know, an island minority persecuted for 'their cooking, their heating arrangements, their love-making, their behaviour abroad and their manners at home' (p. 7), but at the same time an imperial nation, pervasive and powerful. Lessing describes her pursuit of the English as a 'grail', and many other writers from former colonies came to England in search of the myths and stereotypes of Englishness they had been taught to admire and aspire towards. In the literature of several migrant writers, then, there is a palpable sense of disappointment and disillusionment with the gulf between the colonial myths of Englishness and the grim realities, especially with the bombed-out cities and dilapidated slums in evidence in the forties and fifties. In George Lamming's *The Emigrants* (1954), E. R. Braithwaite's *To Sir, With Love* (1959), and Andrew Salkey's *Escape to an Autumn Pavement* (1960), just to cite a few examples, Caribbean immigrants learn painful lessons about English society which dislodge the romantic ideals of Englishness familiar from their colonial childhoods. Thereafter, black and Asian British literature tends to register not this disjunction between romantic illusions and stark realities, but the increasingly difficult negotiations of racial difference and social structure for subsequent generations. Caryl Phillips's plays, *Strange Fruit* (1980) and *Where There is Darkness* (1982) examine the psychological impact of the discourses of racialisation in post-war Britain through figures of dislocation, for instance, while Victor Headley's *Yardie* (1992) depicts an entrenched and embattled network of Caribbean ghettoes in London, struggling with street gangs and drugs wars, and so alienated from English national culture as to be almost oblivious of its existence. Monica Ali's *Brick Lane* (2003) is narrated by a Bangladeshi housewife, Nazneen, who is becoming conscious through the novel of the complex relations between the enclosed Bangladeshi community in Tower Hamlets in London and the racialised discourses of English society. The novel is illuminating for its treatment of the experience of social marginalisation experienced by immigrants, and it is equally insightful about perceptions of white, working-class Englishness. Problematically, the novel ends with a rather hasty optimism about the freedoms of English society – 'This is England … You can do whatever you like' (p. 492), which seems to belie the difficulties experienced by the characters throughout the novel in finding a way of integrating into English society, a topic made especially current in the early twenty-first century in its juxtaposition of Islam and Englishness. Leila Aboulela's novel, *Minaret* (2005), tells a different story about Islam in England. Aboulela's narrator is a westernised Sudanese woman, Najwa, who has been raised in a wealthy and powerful family in Khartoum, but exiled from her homeland she is now reduced to cleaning and childcare jobs in London. Initially, Najwa experiences the same sense of freedom in London as Ali's narrator, that she can do what she likes. Such freedoms, however, as sitting alone in a restaurant as a woman, unthinkable in the Khartoum of her childhood, are also alienating. Instead, it is in London that she discovers the consolations of religious faith, and a supportive Islamic community. The hijab gives her confidence on the city's streets; the minaret of the novel's title is her beacon of belonging. London is just one of the many global cities in which Najwa might find herself living, and hence Islam provides her with a sense of stability which her enforced mobility has denied her.

The writings of immigrants and many others who have experienced social and racial discrimination have been especially germane to an understanding of the complex and changing meanings of Englishness and Britishness in the post-war period, mainly by making central the figure of the migrant as a dislocated presence in British society. There have also been a number of literary explorations of figures who appear to be more central to the iconography of English and British national identity. Kazuo Ishiguro's *The Remains of the Day* (1989) is a classic exploration of the identity crisis of an English butler, Stevens, who towards the end of his career in 1956 re-examines the ideals of Englishness by which he has tried to live his life, and glimpses the painful realisation that they are inadequate. A similar sense of the self-repressive nature of ideals of Englishness – emotional restraint, devotion to work and duty, and awareness of social station – is evident in Graham Swift's *The Sweet-Shop Owner* (1980). In both Ishiguro's and Swift's novels, Englishness is understood to some extent as an inhabited or lived role or mask, which has in some ways damaged or warped the humanity of their characters. As such, it is also implied, especially in *The Remains of the Day*, that Englishness is dead or at least dying as a viable, felt identity. This is not the case, although somewhat problematically, in a novel like John King's *England Away* (1998), the third in King's trilogy of football hooligan novels, in which his characters experience Englishness as a vibrant and positive identity, but one which is associated with xenophobic violence, misogyny and white working-class masculinity. Arguably, for positive representations of cultural identity in English literature since 1939, if we set aside those patriotic writings associated with wartime itself, we have to turn to the ways in which regions or cities have become a more affirmative source of identification than the nation. London in the novels of Maureen Duffy, Peter Ackroyd and Iain Sinclair, for example, is a complex site of psychic energies and cross-temporal voices which, although it contains dark resonances, makes the epithet of Londoner stable and dynamic. Scottish and Welsh identities in particular are also much more positive in literary writings than seems possible for Englishness or Britishness. Undoubtedly the taint of imperial history, and its association of Englishness with xenophobia, monarchy and militarism, makes it difficult to reimagine national culture and national identity in literary writing in positive terms, and much of post-war English writing, as illustrated above, was concerned with deconstructing the imperial ideologies of Englishness. In twenty-first century literature, arguably, the meanings and legacies of globalisation have overshadowed the imperial past as the key contexts for England's relations with the world. In Zadie Smith's *NW* (2012), for example, the cosmopolitanism and ethnic diversity of London are no longer simply accountable to post-colonial migration, and questions of national identity make little sense in such globalised spaces. David Mitchell's work is perhaps even more exemplary of this preoccupation with the global. *Ghostwritten* (1999) and *Cloud Atlas* (2004), just to take two of his novels, range across diverse places around the globe, including Japan, Mongolia, Hawaii, Belgium, California and Korea, with which Britain has little or no imperial connection, and strive to give fictional form to the idea of globality. Such developments as the global novel or cosmopolitan novel put pressure on the idea that the term 'English literature' has any stable or coherent referent beyond the English language.

Readings

Introduction

In this chapter of the book, it is perhaps more difficult to say with any certainty what have been the major literary achievements of the period covered. It takes time to assess whether the writers who appear most significant in their own lifetime turn out to be so after the dust settles on their work. The canon of English literature is constantly unstable and hotly contested in every period, but it could be argued that for the period since 1939 no canon has even been established. Philip Gaskell's *Landmarks of English Literature* (1998), for example, which proposes a list of what to read to acquaint oneself with the history and development of literature, stops with Conrad, Eliot and Joyce in the modernist period. It would be difficult to get experts on the post-1939 period even to agree on such a shortlist of what to read. This section of the chapter proposes to read several texts from the period as significant literary landmarks. In doing so, it cannot help but propose a canon, although it will be immediately obvious that it is an especially tentative canon given the difficulty and inadvisability of arriving at definitive judgements of contemporary literature.

George Orwell, *Nineteen Eighty-Four* (1949)

Novels which are set in the future, commonly called science fiction, are routinely discussed in terms of their claims to prophecy. The year 1984 may have come and gone, but even in the twenty-first century Orwell's most famous novel can seem prescient in many respects: flat-screened panel televisions mounted on the walls of every home, able to transmit as well as receive; a national lottery, which with 'its weekly pay-out of enormous prizes, was the one public event to which the proles paid serious attention' (George Orwell, *Nineteen Eighty-Four*, p. 89 [A]); wars being fought against bitter enemies who had until recently been staunch allies; a surveillance society, capable of monitoring every word and action. Such novels, however, are not written about the future, or at least not about the future as such. They are written about the present, and the omens of a dark future which are contained as possibilities in the present. In 1946 when Orwell began to write *Nineteen Eighty-Four*, there were many contexts which could and did provide for Orwell the basic material for the situations imagined in the novel: the purges in Stalinist Russia in the 1930s, the

The End of the English Novel

The English novel has been characterized by the self-depictions of its maker's dominance: the novel of sense and sensibility is informed by the authority of belonging. Today, however, the imagination resides along the peripheries; it is spoken through a minority discourse, with the dominant tongue re-appropriated, re-commanded, and importantly reinvigorated. It is, at last, the end of the English novel and the beginning of the British novel.

(Bill Buford, 'Introduction: the End of the English Novel', *Granta*, 3 (1980), p. 16)

death camps and mass hysteria of Nazi Germany, the swift transfer of hostility by the USA from Germany to Russia, the austerity and propaganda of wartime Britain, of which Orwell obviously had personal experience. Orwell's own experiences as a colonial policeman in Burma would also have fuelled his sense that twentieth-century political ideologies had an unprecedented capacity for making real O'Brien's vision of the future as 'a boot stamping on a human face – for ever' (p. 280), and of justifying such terror in the name of freedom, justice or progress.

As Orwell served the interests of imperial ideologies in Burma, and disseminated the misinformation of wartime Britain, Winston Smith is at the front line of the totalitarian state of Oceania, rewriting the documents of the past so as to tell the story demanded by his superiors in the present. At the command of Winston's pen, allies become enemies, traitors are now friends, and unwanted dissidents are airbrushed out of history. The willing revisionist by day, Winston seeks to record his true memories and feelings by night, and against the puritan, anti-human ideologies he serves, he begins to engage in sexcrimes and thoughtcrimes with Julia, and to plan for resistance against Big Brother and the thought police. In his sleep he dreams of the 'Golden Country', an imagined haven of peace and freedom to which he might escape. Winston's attempts at resistance and dreams of escape are shown at the end to be illusions, not only countered by the Party and its totalitarian state, but created by them in order to crush Winston all the more effectively. Perhaps the most compelling scenes in the novel are those in which Winston is being tortured by O'Brien into recognising obvious lies as truths. O'Brien explains in these scenes the differences between the totalitarian ideologies possible in the late twentieth century and those that went before, that whereas others believed they were terrorising in order to create better societies, Big Brother is based upon the premise that 'The object of persecution is persecution. The object of torture is torture. The object of power is power' (p. 276). Power is its own end, but it is only visible by inflicting suffering on others: 'Power is in tearing human minds to pieces and putting them together again in new shapes of your own choosing' (p. 279). Winston is forced to abandon his remaining illusions about his own dignity and honour, about the possibility of being human in the face of such inhuman terror, when he betrays Julia, and when O'Brien shows Winston to a mirror where he sees how decrepit he has become under torture.

As an analysis of the forms of power made possible by the social structures and technologies of the twentieth century, *Nineteen Eighty-Four* is one of the most important literary works of the century, and it enjoys widespread popularity. Many of its ideas have also found currency in bizarre forms, such as the television 'reality' programme, 'Big Brother', popular at the time of writing, which televises game-show contestants who are locked in a house together, ordered to perform tasks, and voted off the show by audiences, and another television programme, 'Room 101', in which celebrities are invited to discuss things that they find annoying or distasteful. The phrase 'Big Brother', as well as the words 'new-speak', 'doublethink' and 'thoughtcrime', have become more widely used, even by people who have never read the novel, to refer to the tendency in modern political states, even and perhaps especially democratic states, to monitor and manipulate their citizens. To contextualise the novel historically, however, it is important to assess not how accurate it was at guessing the political future, but how it was fuelled into being by the horrific capacity for destruction, inhumanity and lies which was blatantly in evidence at the time Orwell was writing. So, too, the novel is usually considered to offer a bleak depiction of the futility of resistance, but arguably the full force of the novel is geared towards underlining the importance of memory and historical research, and of countering the fashionable philosophical dictum that 'Nothing exists outside of human consciousness' (p. 278). Orwell is perhaps the most politically conscious writer in twentieth-century Britain, and his writings are best understood as interventions in the urgent political debates of his time.

Sam Selvon, *The Lonely Londoners* (1956)

After the war, Britain needed to rebuild, and to do so, many of its new and newly nationalised employers such as the National Health Service, London Transport and British Railways urgently required workers. Some recruited directly from the colonies in the Caribbean, Africa and Asia. Others benefited from the arrival from the colonies of thousands of immigrants, whose British citizenship had been sanctioned by the British Nationality Act of 1948. It soon became obvious to many of the immigrants that a contradiction lay deep in British society, that although their labour was needed, there was also a large degree of resentment and racial discrimination against black immigrants. This was evident in the explicit racism of signs on shop and house windows advertising 'no coloureds', and it erupted into violence in the race riots in Notting Hill and Nottingham in 1958. The supposedly tolerant 'Mother Empire', which extended the virtues of Britishness to the four corners of the globe, appeared in the 1950s less than comfortable with the growing numbers of black settlers. Perhaps the best and clearest literary expression of the experiences of Caribbean immigrants during this period is Sam Selvon's third novel, *The Lonely Londoners* [A]. Selvon arrived from Trinidad in 1950 in search of work, and published two novels set in the Caribbean, and wrote many talks and stories for the BBC before *The Lonely Londoners* appeared in 1956. In his earlier novels Selvon had sought to show for English readers the realities of island life in the Caribbean, but in *The Lonely Londoners* he sets out to tell the story of several black immigrants in London, struggling to get by, but all the while entranced by the glamour and romance of the city. The novel is written in a modified Trinidadian dialect, deliberately brought closer to 'standard' English in order to induce English readers to become familiar with the lives of the immigrants. At the same time, it includes characters who are from Jamaica, Trinidad and Nigeria, self-consciously making connections between black immigrants from very different societies and backgrounds. At the heart of its concerns is the evident injustice of racism, most memorably captured in the poignant scene where a distraught Galahad is found 'talking to the colour Black, as if is a person, telling it that is not *he* who causing botheration in the place, but Black, who is a worthless thing for making trouble all about' (p. 88). The narrator continually refers to the black characters as 'spades', a term which he uses as a positive affirmation of collective identity, but which was frequently used as a term of racial abuse.

7.12 Poster for the film *1984*, based on Orwell's novel.

Selvon's characters are intoxicated with London, in love with the idea of living in 'that place that everybody in the world know about' (p. 84), in contrast with the image of Trinidad on the map in Piccadilly Circus tube station, where 'the island is so small it only have a dot and the name' (p. 91). Selvon juxtaposes the naivety of newly arrived immigrants with the wiser, more cynical voice of the narrator and the central character, Moses Aloetta, for whom London is now nothing special. Moses serves as a kind of unofficial welfare officer to some new immigrants, guiding them towards where to get jobs, where he knows houses will not discriminate against them for their skin colour, where they can meet other immigrants. He serves as the principal viewpoint character, through whom we see the lives of many others, as he comes to feel 'as if he live each of their lives' (p. 139). The novel tells the stories of the various immigrants through an episodic and balladic form – Sir Galahad who braves the London winter in a tropical suit, Cap who flits from hostel to hotel across the city, and disappears, Bart who becomes possessive and guarded and searches the city for his lost girlfriend, Harris who dresses in bowler hat and umbrella to imitate the English 'gent', and Tolroy, whose whole family turn up unannounced at Waterloo station to live with him. Selvon's narrator conveys the stories with humour and evident warmth, but the novel is ultimately sombre about the fate of the new immigrants: 'Under the kiff-kiff laughter, behind the ballad and the episode, the what-happening, the summer-is-hearts, he could see a great aimlessness, a great rest-less, swaying movement that leaving you standing in the same spot' (p. 141). Moses is seen at the end of the novel lonely and unsettled, even if he is still dreaming about the possibilities of success. Although the novel reflects a time of some optimism about the possibilities for integration, suggesting, for example, a communal feel-ing among the immigrants and the working class, the narrative viewpoint indicates racial division in never accessing the interior perspectives of any white characters. It also reflects a time when Caribbean immigrants were mostly male and single, and women are represented in the novel for the most part as sexual objects. *The Lonely Londoners* is sometimes seen as the first of a loose trilogy, to be followed by *Moses Ascending* (1975) and *Moses Migrating* (1983), which steadily mark the decline in race relations in post-war Britain, and the increasing difficulties of settlement and inte-gration for black people.

Philip Larkin, *The Whitsun Weddings* (1964)

Philip Larkin is arguably the most popular and highly regarded poet in England since 1939, although he is also deeply controversial for the conservatism of his writing and the bigotry of some of his personal views. He acquired his reputation as a poet in the 1950s, when he was associated with 'The Movement' poets, but he was at the height of his powers with the collection which he published in 1964, *The Whitsun Weddings* [A]. Larkin may seem somewhat tangential, even antagonistic, to the dominant ten-dencies associated with twentieth-century writing. He came to eschew the influence of modernism and neo-Romanticism, for example, and his poetry shows little affin-ity with the emerging beat and post-modern poetry of the sixties. Larkin's poetry is broadly realist in style and conventional in technique. Its subject is usually the mundane experiences of everyday life, experiences which yet afford the poet reasons for meditation, and impel him to recognise that fundamental questions about iden-tity, time, sex, age and death lie behind the everyday. Set against the alienating and apparently aloof tendencies of modernism, and the sometimes forbidding experi-mentalism of post-modernism, it is no wonder in this respect that Larkin gained a readership only rivalled in the period by John Betjeman. Larkin's poetry celebrates the ordinariness of human life, and treats even the seemingly most banal lives and places of provincial England as worthy of our imaginative attention, and for that his popularity is richly deserved.

As a collection, *The Whitsun Weddings* [A] contains some of Larkin's best-known and loved poems, such as 'Mr Bleaney', 'MCMXIV', 'Dockery and Son', 'The Arundel Tomb', and, of course, the title poem, 'The Whitsun Weddings'. Larkin's biographer, Andrew Motion, has written that the collection 'did more than confirm Larkin's reputation; it turned his voice into one of the means by which his country recognised itself' (*Philip Larkin: A Writer's Life*, 343 [Ci]). That Larkin spoke to the concerns of post-war England, and became as a result a national poet, can be seen in several of the poems in the collection. 'MCMXIV', for example, dramatises the moment in August 1914 when 'long uneven lines' of men with 'moustached archaic faces' waited to volunteer for the First World War, a moment which the poem goes on to mark as a rupture from the continuous England, its 'fields / Shadowing Domesday lines', which had gone before. 'Never such innocence again', the poem concludes, as Larkin holds up this frozen moment of waiting for war as a point of no return, the end of an England which is lost for ever. The first impression of this poem is that it appears to be nostalgic for the lost continuity of a pastoral England, a mythic ideal, with its precisely observed snapshot of the men 'leaving the gardens tidy', and the 'shut shops' with 'bleached / Established names on the sun-blinds'. The poem renders England in 1914 a place of stillness, silence and tradition, which in its evocative detail appears to embrace it as a more desirable world. But the final line is ambivalent. Does the speaker mean to lament the loss of such innocence? Or does he mean that we should never fall prey again to such innocence, a rallying cry made particularly ironic, of course, for coming after the Second World War? The Roman numerals of the title, of course, powerfully suggest the cenotaphs and memorials to the war dead which can be found in every village, town and city throughout England.

'The Whitsun Weddings', the longest poem in the collection, also renders its vision of a sunlit railway journey from Hull to London in striking and impeccable detail. The speaker locates himself and his reasons for being on this 'three-quarters-empty train' precisely, and the scene is depicted from his viewpoint: 'Wide farms went by, short-shadowed cattle, and / Canals with floatings of industrial froth; / A hothouse flashed uniquely: hedges dipped / and rose.' Larkin dispenses here with the self-deprecation which he frequently brings to his speakers in other poems. Instead, this speaker is comfortable, confident, and secure that his observations, and the reflections they prompt, are worth noting. As the train stops in 'the next town, new and nondescript', the speaker almost fails to notice that in the shade of the platform are the 'whoops and skirls' of wedding parties, waving off the bride and groom. Larkin's gift for caricature is evident: 'The fathers with broad belts under their suits / And seamy foreheads; mothers loud and fat; / An uncle shouting smut.' So too, however, is his capacity to show the scene from other points of view: 'as we moved, each face seemed to define / Just what it saw departing'. As the train hurries towards London, the speaker pictures the newly-weds 'sitting side by side', and this depiction gives way to the reflection that 'none / Thought of the others they would never meet / Or how their lives would all contain this hour.' The scene observed by the speaker is about a 'frail / Travelling coincidence', the accidental coming together on a train of a dozen couples newly married, with common experiences which are yet unshared, a moment of possible connection which stands 'ready to be loosed with all the power that being changed can give'. Like 'MCMXIV', 'The Whitsun Weddings' closes with the notion of a rupture, about which the poem is ambivalent: 'there swelled / A sense of falling, like an arrow-shower / Sent out of sight, somewhere becoming rain.' For whom did this sense swell? The speaker, or the married couples, or all the people on the train? The implication is that the sunlit moment of the Whitsun weddings is already fading into the distance, and now a rather more overcast future is being glimpsed.

Despite the more ominous conclusion to the poem, it is the momentary coming together of these people on a train, and the possibility of connection, which the speaker is impelled to think about. The association with Whitsun, a religious festival of merry-making of ancient provenance, gives the scenes observed by the speaker a sense of tradition and continuity. At each station, different couples get on the train, but they are performing the same ritual in time-honoured fashion. Larkin suggests a sense of commonality or unity, even when 'none / Thought of the others they would never meet'. When Larkin wrote the poem between 1955 and 1958, there was argu-ably an increased consciousness of common forms of social experience in England, through such institutions as the national military service, the National Health Service hospitals, compulsory secondary-school education, and BBC radio and tele-vision. The train was still a more affordable and popular form of transport than the car, and through the experience of train travel, Larkin's speaker can feel a connec-tion with strangers, and see that they have common feelings and common lives, even though they do not know each other. They are all embarked upon the same journey, literally and metaphorically, and this provides a sense of symbolic union. As the poem draws to a close, however, this sense of union dissipates. London is described as 'spread out in the sun / Its postal districts packed like squares of wheat'. The ear-lier descriptions of hedges, the smell of grass, and wide farms in the countryside contrasts starkly with this image of London as 'packed like squares of wheat', just as the slow gathering of couples along the way, with fathers, mothers, uncles seen waving them off, contrasts with the 'postal districts' – EC1, SE9, NW6 – which denote the anonymity of life in London. The poem thus suggests that this moment in time is delicately poised between an older, traditional way of life, based on continuity and ritual, and a newer, nondescript and anonymous future, towards which the train hurries, 'shuffling gouts of steam'. Ironically, just a few years later, even the steam would be associated nostalgically with a bygone age, as British Railways withdrew all steam locomotives four years after Larkin's collection was published. Through such poems, Larkin became renowned as the poet of a peculiar kind of English national melancholy, who spoke for a symbolic unity of experience and feeling, all the more keenly realised because this England was depicted as receding.

Pat Barker, *Union Street* (1982)

Union Street is a contemporary Condition of England novel, even though Englishness is barely registered as an issue in its pages. Barker's first novel tells the story of the inhabitants of one working-class street in north-eastern England, in seven chapters which each focus on one character, from the youngest, Kelly Brown, in the opening chapter, to the oldest, Alice Bell, who is dying in the final chapter. It is perhaps the bleakest depiction of working-class life in post-war fiction, its female characters raped, beaten, abused and ignored, and its few male characters unemployed, disempowered, or, if they are sympathetically depicted, like John Scaife and Joss, dying and stunted. The novel is structured as a *Bildungsroman*, in the sense that the seven women whose stories form the chapters represent different stages or possibilities in one life lived in this community under impoverished social conditions. Each of the women experiences a moment of recognising her life reflected in older or younger characters, so that Kelly Brown, as an eleven-year-old, recognises that her life is mapped out for her in the lives of women she watches emerging from the cake bakery, as Alice Bell at the end of the novel thinks that 'She had been so many women in her time' (Pat Barker, *Union Street*, p. 263 [A]). Through this device, the novel produces an ambivalent image of the women collectively: on the one hand, the sense in which their lives are intertwined and interchangeable fuels a positive idea of female community and symbolic unity; on the other hand, the idea that Kelly will inevitably follow a path predetermined for women of her class, through poverty, abuse, violence and neglect, without hope of escape, is a profoundly disturbing and frank account of life for working-class women.

The novel is informed principally by the social and political climate of the 1970s, at which time it became obvious that the post-war promises of social reform, of class and gender equality, and a revivified industrial economy were not merely undelivered, but were being rescinded altogether. Moreover, Barker makes it clear that the hopes of social mobility and a better deal for working-class people which fuelled the social-realist fictions of the fifties and sixties had almost no bearing on the lives of women, and the particular sections of the working class featured in her novel, who were almost an underclass. Barker's characters are all the products of industrial capitalism – the wage-slaves of mechanised factories who are abandoned when the factories close. At the heart of the community depicted in the novel lies an abandoned, derelict steelworks, which symbolises the social and cultural dereliction left in its wake. In their movements and routines they come to resemble the industrial process, as if they are cyborgs. Kelly is described as 'turning into a machine. Her legs, pumping up and down the cold street, had the regularity and power of pistons. And her hands ... were as heavy and lifeless as tools' (p. 64). The sound of women talking is described as like 'sharp, electric clicks' (p. 65). Sex is described as being used by an 'impersonal, machine-like passion' (p. 101). The birth of Lisa Goddard's baby is also 'mechanical', the pains coming with 'remorseless regularity' which felt like 'extreme heat, as though she were being forced to stand too close to a furnace' (p. 128). The very subjectivity of Barker's characters is determined by the industrial processes on which their lives as economic subjects depend, a point clearly illustrated in the scenes set in the cake factory in which the women are forced into silence and solipsism as a result of the deafening mechanical noise. Instead of being part of a social process, every woman on the assembly line functions as a monadic unit, operating only in harmony with the mechanical process she is paid to serve.

Although the novel is born out of the devastating experiences of industrial collapse and unemployment characteristic of the late 1970s and increasingly the case in the 1980s, then, it is also profoundly critical of the ways in which working-class men and women have been commodified as economic subjects, and abandoned to the tidal cycles of liberal capitalism. Against the despondency which this depiction of the economic and social realities of life in such a community sets up, however, Barker pits a symbolic vision of women transcending these social conditions, albeit in severely limited ways, through their interdependence on one another. The title of the novel hints at the never-realised dream of earlier working-class communities, of creating a union powerful enough to fight collectively for a better way of life. The dream is emblazoned in the name of the street, but it now serves merely to mock the very idea. The characters are shown to be more vulnerable than ever, and even the houses which offer basic protection are pocked with holes, cracks and broken windows. This is contrasted with the middle-class home which Kelly breaks into, where 'everything seemed to stir around her, resenting the intrusion', and where her rough skin seems to catch on the soft and silky textures which characterise the interior of the house (p. 52). At eleven years old, Kelly has been violently initiated into adult sexuality through a brutal rape, and this makes her seem completely alien to the middle-class home in which the woman's bedroom is described as 'a temple to femininity' (p. 53). In her rage, Kelly vandalises her school, scoring out 'the worst word she knew' – 'cunt', the slang for female genitalia. It is the mark of her sex, and the mark therefore of the degradation and exploitation of her sex. Through such scenes, Barker brings the stratifications of the British social system in the post-war period to vivid and disturbing life. The novel makes clear that the differences between the classes is not simply one of relative income, or relative comfort, but of an almost unbridgeable gulf between separate, parallel worlds. Since *Union Street* was published, decades of liberal economics have further increased the gulf between rich and poor in Britain, and further isolated the poor from any meaningful forms of social and political recourse.

Sarah Kane, *Blasted* (1995)

Sarah Kane was the *enfant terrible* of theatre in the 1990s. Her first play, *Blasted* [A], shocked and outraged audiences and critics when it was first performed in the Royal Court Theatre in London in January 1995. The *Daily Mail* called it 'this disgusting feast of filth'. The *Daily Telegraph* deplored its 'gratuitous welter of carnage'. The *Spectator* called it 'a sordid little travesty of a play'. The artistic director, and several prominent playwrights, came out to support Kane's work against its detractors. The hostile reception of the play served a useful purpose, however, in raising questions about the function of contemporary theatre. Are contemporary dramatists compelled to resort to gratuitous scenes of sex and violence in order to attract attention? Had the modern dramatic tendency to shock audiences reached its furthest extremes? Why would audiences pay for theatre designed to provoke its audience? On the other hand, what use is a theatre which cannot depict scenes of sexual abuse and violence which are routine items of news? Did Kane's play show on stage anything which was unfamiliar from those dark events in Bosnia and Rwanda of the mid-1990s? Is it not one role of contemporary theatre to bridge the gap between the horrors of contemporary events and the passive, fleeting ways in which such events are narrated to us in newspapers and the broadcast media?

Blasted is a series of dark, spectacular tableaux, depicting habitual but shocking scenes of modern violence, from the casual abuse and 'domestic' violence of the first half of the play, to the torture and war of the second half. The first half of the play is concerned with a disturbing relationship between a middle-aged journalist, Ian, and a young woman, Cate, who suffers repeatedly from fits and recurrent mental illness. Kane's characters are unable to articulate the destructive motives which drive them to abuse. Cate is represented from the outset as childlike, sucking her thumb, smelling the flowers in the hotel room, and giggling at Ian's absurd actions. She communicates with Ian as much through gestures as language, and even then, her verbal expressions are short, frequently stammered, and often confused. Ian carries a gun, and is constantly anxious for his security and desperate for sexual gratification. He forces Cate to masturbate him, and simulates sex with her as she lies unconscious, pointing a gun to her head all the time. She is not simply Ian's passive victim, however, for, after she has been raped, she begins to perform oral sex on him, only to bite down hard on his penis as he comes. Sex is associated throughout the play with violence and violation. Ian is repeatedly abusive to Cate, as he is abusive about what he calls 'wogs', 'Pakis', 'retards', 'lesbos', and many others. Ian is a rapist and bully in the first half of the play, but when the soldier enters in the second half of the play, Ian becomes the raped victim. The soldier holds Ian captive and scared, tortures him, rapes him, and then eats Ian's eyes out of their sockets before shooting himself. Ian is left scrabbling in the darkness, and, after Cate has returned with a dying infant, and leaves again in search of food, is seen in various stages of deprivation – masturbating, defecating, crying, weak with hunger and then devouring the body of the dead baby. In the final scene of the play, Ian is buried alive in a hole in the floor, only his head visible, and Cate has returned with food, having probably been raped outside. *Blasted* is a play which collects all the most shocking images and characters of modern theatre – the verbal assaults of Jimmy Porter in *Look Back in Anger* (1956), the stoning to death of a baby in a pram in Edward Bond's *Saved* (1965), the homosexual rape in Howard Brenton's *The Romans in Britain* (1980) – and exaggerates them even further.

What *Blasted* refuses to do is to give its audiences any sense of social context for what takes place in the play. The play also offers audiences no explanation about the shift of tone and setting, from the expensive hotel in Leeds of the first half, in which Ian can order champagne, gin and breakfast from the hotel staff, and the hotel

---

Post-Realist Theatre

A character on stage who can present no convincing argument or information as to his past experience, his present behaviour or his aspirations, nor give a comprehensive analysis of his motives, is as legitimate and as worthy of attention as one who, alarmingly, can do all of these things.

(Harold Pinter, Programme Notes for *The Caretaker*, 1960)

appears to be fully functional in a fully functioning society, to the war-torn, dysfunctional setting of the second half. The hotel is bombed, soldiers are rampant, and we learn from the soldier that the war has been going on for some time. The only context for the violence presented in the play is violence. These gaps in the play might be framed as criticisms – unexplained violence and sexual abuse might be seen as a sensationalist ploy to attract attention; the shift in setting and tone, again unexplained, might be the mark of a badly formed play; the sometimes crudely overt references to and borrowings from other plays, particularly those of Beckett, Bond and Brenton, might make the play seem derivative and, more pointedly, confused in its hasty conflation of theatrical influences.

But these criticisms would not do the play justice, would not give sufficient credit to the radical intervention it makes in the relationship between contemporary theatre and society, and would not do enough to account for its impact in the 1990s. How then do we make sense of this play? How might we understand its intervention in contemporary theatrical forms? Kane's contemporary Mark Ravenhill argued that Kane was essentially drawing upon classical models of theatre, that Kane's model of theatre is indebted to the visceral forms in which Greek tragedy presents situations like incest, rape and murder. They are presented without social or psychological explanation, not because the dramatists don't see such occurrences as socially or psychologically explicable, but because theatre is not a sociological study. It does not achieve its effects by explaining the causes of the events it depicts. *Blasted* does not aim to provide understanding. It is an exemplary instance of what Kane called 'experiential theatre', which sets out to make the audience feel as if they have experienced what has been presented on stage. Kane's play does not just represent scenes of violence or trauma, but makes the audience experience scenes of violence or trauma. What she sought to achieve was what the critic Aleks Sierz calls 'in-yer-face theatre', a theatre which brought audiences closer to feeling, experiencing and, therefore, understanding the horror and the pain of this world. Kane doesn't conclude the play on this note, however. She concludes with what is perhaps a typically Beckett-like gesture of human affirmation. Cate feeds Ian, for which he says, in the final line

---

The Final Scene of *Blasted*

CATE *enters carrying some bread, a large sausage and a bottle of gin. There is blood seeping from between her legs.*

CATE You're sitting under a hole.

IAN I know.

CATE Get wet.

IAN Aye.

CATE Stupid bastard.

She pulls a sheet off the bed and wraps it around her.
She sits next to IAN's *head.*
She eats her fill of the sausage and bread, then washes it down with gin.

IAN *listens.*

She feeds IAN *with the remaining food.*
She pours gin in IAN's *mouth.*
She finishes feeding IAN *and sits apart from him, huddled for warmth.*
She drinks the gin.
She sucks her thumb.
Silence.
It rains.

IAN   Thank you.

Blackout.

(Sarah Kane, *Blasted* (1995). London: Methuen, 2002, pp. 60–1)

of the play, 'Thank you'. Kane's vision is bleak and unyielding, but it is honest, and it finds affirmation and hope in the depths of despair. *Blasted* also sets out to define a particular role for theatre, perhaps more generally for good literary writing, too, of reaching beyond the fleeting headlines of the news, beyond the superficial ways in which we interact with stories of human pain and loss through the media, and of deepening our engagement with the meanings and forms of contemporary life.

Alice Oswald, *Dart* (2002)

Dart is Alice Oswald's most renowned and celebrated poem. It won the coveted T. S. Eliot Prize for Poetry when it was published in 2002. As a river poem, and a poem written for many voices, it might invite comparison indeed with T. S. Eliot's modernist masterpiece, *The Waste Land* (1922). However, in its conception and in how it might be read and interpreted, it is very different from Eliot's work. Oswald's poem is already regarded as a classic example of eco-poetry. The poem tells the stories of the River Dart in Devon, and of the people who live and work on the river. It was commissioned as part of the Poetry Society's 'Poetry Places' scheme funded by the Arts Council, and as such involved working with schoolchildren and local community members by or near the river. Oswald writes in the preface to the poem that it draws from 'conversations with people who know the river ... linking their voices into a sound-map of the river, a songline from the source to the sea' (p. iii). Her reference to 'songline' is to Aboriginal beliefs that ancestors had recorded navigational paths, including landmarks and water sources, in songs which if performed correctly would enable the singer to navigate the same paths, as well as retaining the history and lore of the land. Bruce Chatwin described the tradition in his book, *The Songlines* (1987), as 'singing the world into existence'. Oswald's reference may be taken as indicative of a strong sense of affinity in eco-poetry with Aboriginal concepts of being interdependent with nature. From the beginning of *Dart*, with its opening focus on a hill-walker in search of the source of the river, who is depicted as 'rustling and jingling his keys/ at the centre of his own noise' (p. 1), the poem strives to dilute the conventional anthropocentric concentration of Romantic nature poetry by commingling human voices with the mutterings of the river and its non-human habitants. The subsequent voices of a naturalist, a fisherman, eel watcher, a drowned canoeist, a mill worker, and others, dissolve into the voices of the river itself, sometimes almost imperceptibly. It is clear throughout the poem that the river is the central and sacred presence, the source of the life and sometimes of the death of the characters we meet. Behind the named geography of the river's course, and fleeting references to the histories of the river's users and neighbours, there is also a mythology of water nymphs, river-gods, and the ghostly presence of 'Jan Coo', whose name we are told means 'So-and-So of the Woods' and who haunts the river.

Dart is exemplary of several key trends in environmental writing. It is a work of co-creation, drawing from the language of inhabitants and workers of the river, and drawing from the folklore of the river communities in ways which are sensitive and harmonious. It is also a form of 'nature poetry' which seeks to avoid the tradition of representing nature as subservient to human will, or representing nature as an idyllic haven. Oswald's river brims with the histories of how it has been manipulated and exploited, but the human presence is ultimately fleeting and anonymous. Even lines such as this – 'I know who I am, I/ come from the little heap of stones up by Postbridge' – which articulate a confident sense of identity and belonging, are ambiguously voiced, unclear as to whether we are hearing the words of the old man walking, the ghost of Jan Coo, or the river itself. *Dart* has been especially celebrated, however, as a work which draws from an environmental tradition of localism, or more particularly, bioregionalism. A bioregion is a geographical unit defined by natural features, boundaries, or constituencies such as a watershed, mountain range, or sea. Greg Garrard in his book on *Ecocriticism* describes bioregionalism as 'a politics of "reinhabitation" that encourages people to explore more deeply the natural and cultural landscape in which they already live'. Reinhabitation may take many forms, such as experiencing the natural features of one's local area through walking or swimming, or buying locally sourced produce, or getting involved in local efforts to restore public rights of way. However, a crucial part of reinhabitation is an imaginative engagement with the histories, ecologies, and folklore of local places, and poetry can play a key role in deepening our engagement with and understanding of place.

Dart may be regarded as a bioregional poem for the obvious reason that it charts the geography and 'sound-map' of the river course. The bioregionalism of the poem goes deeper than this, however. The poem abounds with the names of the flora and fauna distinctive to the river's bed and banks. It names the river's varieties of water, and the sounds of water, from the source down to the sea. It delights too in the words distinctive to Devonian dialects of English, words such as 'slammicking', 'shrammed', and 'spickety' (p. 21), which chart a close relationship between a community and its regional environment. Within the bioregion, the poem traces the differences between upriver and downriver. As we near the sea, we encounter a more industrial scale of activity – milk production plants, sewage treatment works, water extraction facilities – which seem far removed from the forester and hill-walker upriver. Nonetheless, the river retains a sense of mystery; even as it thickens and deepens to become 'this jostling procession of waters/ its many strands overclambering one another', a voice still wonders 'why is this river not ever/ able to leave until it's over?' (pp. 42–3).

Oswald's poetry is deeply immersed in a long tradition of nature writing. She frequently draws inspiration from and alludes to Greek and Roman classics in which mythology is tied closely to the natural world. She draws too from the Romantics, particularly Wordsworth, but usually as exemplary of a lamentable tendency to see nature as detached and idealised. In her depiction of the inseparability of the human from the natural, of humans-in-nature, and in her retention of folkloric aspects of the sacredness of the natural world, she is often regarded as closer to the work of Ted Hughes, and perhaps even D. H. Lawrence. Like Hughes and Lawrence, Oswald's work implies a dark warning about the consequences of disconnection from our natural habitats, but in seeking to inspire a re-imagination of the fuller ecological sense of the places we call home, it is ultimately work of profound hopefulness and ingenuity.

Ali Smith, *How to Be Both* (2014)

In keeping with its title, Ali Smith's *How To Be Both* resists easy categorisation. It is a novel, but might equally be read as two intertwined novels. It is captivating fiction, but it is spun upon the bare facts of art history. It is an inventive and skilful work of historical fiction, but weaves its story of the mesmerising art of Francesco del Cossa in Ferrara into a moving and witty depiction of the life of a twenty-first-century teenager mourning the death of her mother in Cambridge. The title also resonates with its story of indeterminate gender – Francesco masquerades as a man, and her twenty-first century mirror-image is called George as a shortened version of Georgia. In both the fifteenth-century story and its present day pairing, love between women flowers easily, and sexual desire defies fixed classification. Smith's novel, like the fresco paintings of Francesco, is an artful demonstration of 'how to tell a story, but tell it more than one way at once, and tell another underneath it up-rising through the skin of it' (p. 51). The image is one of art, of identity, and of biology, since the novel recurrently alludes to the double helix of the human genome. As a work of ekphrasis (writing which is inspired by or comments upon art), which is reflexive about its own artifice as fiction, and which relentlessly dissolves the boundaries between life and death, art and reality, male and female, past and future, Smith's novel could superficially be seen to conform to definitions of post-modernism. The two sections, both numbered 'one', were also printed interchangeably, so that some readers start with Francesco's story and others with George's, a neat gimmick which exemplified the post-modern tendency to play on the randomness of structures and the contingency of beginnings and endings. There is a telling difference, however, between Smith's novel and the classics of post-modern fiction. Smith has absorbed and made ingenious use of many of the innovations which we have come to call post-modernism, and indeed those of modernism, but her work restores and renews faith in the capacity of art to connect, communicate, and to resist authority.

There are no forced comparisons between the fifteenth and twenty-first century contexts. Francesco's greatest work is commissioned by a Duke who believes he should be shown as the embodiment of justice, while all the while he impoverishes, brutalises and murders his subjects. George's mother is a feminist and social activist whom George suspects has been under the clandestine surveillance of government agents, and whom George finally resolves to emulate by making sure that 'whoever's watching know she's watching' (p. 371). The most compelling connection between Francesco and George is their discovery of the power of truth-telling, of 'someone with no power, no social status to speak of, who'd take it upon themselves to stand up to the highest authority when the authority was unjust or wrong, and would express out loud the most uncomfortable truths' (p. 367). In Francesco's case, this takes the form of a room full of fresco paintings which manage to both flatter and subvert the authority of the Duke, and which preserve their subversive implications for those who know how to look. In George's case, however, we are left with the hopeful sense that she will embody this determination to know how to look for the future. This final resolution in the novel to refuse to allow authority the vain image of itself to go unchecked is a turning point for George, which countermands her earlier certainty that history was appalling and 'well and truly over' (p. 290).

A persistent theme in contemporary writing is the challenge of understanding the many and diverse forms of our connections with other people and other living species, a theme often contextualised in relation to globalisation, environmental crises and migration. In *How to Be Both*, this theme extends to our connections with the past, with other times. The narrative about George's mother constantly corrects itself from present to past tense. Francesco is telling her story from beyond the grave, watching George in the art gallery half a millennium into the future, in what she imagines is purgatory. An instructive moment in the novel dwells on this theme of contemporaneity. George is watching a programme on television about an old steam train, the Flying Scotsman, while simultaneously watching the same programme on her laptop from an earlier point in the film (she has missed the beginning on television), and while also looking up photobombs on her phone. Her mother reprimands George for what she sees as an abstracted kind of behaviour: 'You are a migrant of your own existence' (p. 227). It is a familiar scene of inter-generational strife about attentiveness, the addictiveness of visual media, and anxieties that young people are dangerously disconnected from the world around them. Yet the novel gently nudges us towards an appreciation of the capacities of the teenager in this instance. George is perhaps demonstrating a fuller appreciation of the demands of the contemporary world to think in terms of simultaneities, ambiguities, and multiplicities, and to inhabit a world of complex interconnections and interdependencies. At the same time, the world she inhabits is one fraught with ethical dangers and conundrums. This is illustrated in one of the most disturbing scenes in the novel when George watches a pornographic film involving a girl who is possibly under the age of sexual consent, and tells her father that she is doing so to witness the injustice perpetrated on the girl. For George's father, it is a film he cannot and does not wish to see, and he complains to George that her watching it will not alter what has happened to the girl. George insists that her watching is different, and counters the exploitative actions of the film. George is aware that her compulsion to watch might in itself be a sign of psychological damage, and yet there remains the possibility that her watching, but watching differently, may be an act of bravery and honesty, of admitting the cruelty and injustice of our world in order to better understand and testify to its inequities. Her sharp sense of wit and her appreciation of linguistic precision and the problems of translation are sure indications of a young woman equipped to speak up and speak back to a world in which so many are deprived of a voice. Smith's novel is not utopian in any sense, but both Francesco's and George's narratives end in the future tense, with the promise of the life, love and art to come. There are many contemporary fictions which envision the future through sinister and malevolent figures of authority, surveillance, and conspiracy. David Mitchell's *Slade House* (2015) and China Mieville's *This Census Taker* (2016) are compelling examples. However, Smith's *How To Be Both* acknowledges this potential for menace in our present social and political structures, and yet avows a tentative belief that the future of human society can be imagined and shaped differently if we can learn to think with (and not against) the complexity, ambiguity, and plurality of our contemporary condition.

Reference

A Primary Texts and Anthologies of Primary Sources

Allnutt, Gillian, et al., eds. *The New British Poetry, 1968–1988*. London: Paladin, 1988. Probably the most innovative and inclusive anthology of contemporary British poetry.

Barker, Pat. *Union Street*. London: Virago, 1982.

Braine, John. *Room at the Top* (1957). Harmondsworth: Penguin, 1959.

Conquest, Robert, ed. *New Lines*. London: Macmillian, 1956.

Douglas, Keith. *The Complete Poems*. London: Faber & Faber, 1964.

Glover, David, and Scott McCracken, 'The Bad New Days', *New Formations*, 62 (Autumn 2007): 7–9.

Kane, Sarah. *Blasted* (1995). London: Methuen, 2002.

Larkin, Philip. *The Whitsun Weddings*. London: Faber & Faber, 1964.

Lessing, Doris. *In Pursuit of the English* (1960). London: Granta, 1980.

Longley, Edna, ed. *The Bloodaxe Book of Twentieth-Century Poetry from Britain and Ireland*. Tarset: Bloodaxe, 2000. A good range of poetry is included, across the geographical and historical span of its title, which enables some useful connections to be made between diverse poets and poetic traditions.

McCarthy, Tom. *Satin Island*. London: Jonathan Cape, 2015.

Morrison, Blake, and Andrew Motion, eds. *The Penguin Book of Contemporary British Poetry*. London: Penguin, 1982. Generous selections from each of the poets it includes, but controversial because of the limited number and range of poets.

Newland, Courttia, and Kadija Sesay, eds. *IC3: The Penguin Book of New Black Writing in Britain*. London: Penguin, 2000. A striking anthology which makes a statement about black Britain as well as black British writing, and organises its generous selection into settlers, explorers and crusaders, representing three generations of black Britons of African descent.

Orwell, George. *Nineteen Eighty-Four* (1949). London: Penguin, 1989.

Oswald, Alice. *Dart*. London: Faber, 2002.

Selvon, Sam. *The Lonely Londoners* (1956). Harlow: Longman, 1985.

Sierz, Aleks, ed. *The Methuen Drama Book of Twenty-First Century British Plays*. London: Methuen, 2010. This collection includes *Blue/Orange* by Joe Penhall, *Elmina's Kitchen* by Kwame Kwei-Armah, *Realism* by Anthony Neilson, *Gone Too Far!* by Bola Agbaje, and *Pornography* by Simon Stephens.

Smith, Ali. *How To Be Both* (2014). London: Penguin, 2015.

Snow, C. P. *The Two Cultures and the Scientific Revolution*. Cambridge University Press, 1959.

B Introductions and Overviews

Bradbury, Malcolm. *The Modern British Novel*. London: Penguin, 2001. Standard textbook of the history of the British novel since 1945, which covers an interesting range of both major and less well-known authors.

Brannigan, John. *Orwell to the Present: Literature in England since 1945*. Basingstoke: Palgrave, 2003. This book attempts to give an overview of the ways in which we might conceptualise and map the key developments in literature in England since 1945.

Broom, Sarah. *Contemporary British and Irish Poetry: An Introduction*. Basingstoke: Palgrave Macmillan, 2006. A compelling introduction which combines insightful close readings with detailed accounts of poetic and literary contexts, and which ranges widely from Tony Harrison to Patience Agbabi, from Seamus Heaney to Tom Raworth.

Chambers, Colin, and Mike Prior. *Playwrights' Progress: Patterns of Postwar British Drama*. Oxford: Amber Lane, 1987. This book provides a useful overview of post-war drama. It is divided into two parts, the first of which considers themes of class, gender, national identity and social change in relation to a wide range of drama. The second part contains chapters on playwrights Osborne, Wesker, Arden, D'Arcy, Bond, Brenton, Hare and Churchill.

Connor, Steven. *The English Novel in History, 1950–1995*. London: Routledge, 1996. An excellent study, which provides a lucid explanation of the relationship between literary texts and historical contexts, and analyses some of the historical themes and concerns of post-war fiction.

Corcoran, Neil. *English Poetry since 1940*. London: Longman, 1993. A valuable critical introduction to poetry from 1940 to the early 1990s divided into considerations of the late modernism of the forties, the neo-Romanticism of the late forties, the Movement in the fifties, the neo-modernism and counter-cultural poetry of the sixties, women's poetry, Northern Irish poetry and a diverse range of later twentieth-century work. Chapters are brief, but Corcoran provides useful critical analyses of a wide range of poetry.

Draper, R. P. *An Introduction to Twentieth-Century Poetry in English*. Basingstoke: Macmillan, 1999. A balanced introduction to an impressive array of poets and poetry, which argues that the upheavals of the twentieth century have produced a diverse and heterogeneous range of poetry.

Head, Dominic. *The Cambridge Introduction to Modern British Fiction, 1950–2000*. Cambridge University Press, 2002. A survey of a wide range of novels and novelists, which provides a one- or two-page summary of each novel, and groups them under various headings such as gender, class and multiculturalism.

Hutcheon, Linda. *A Poetics of Postmodernism: History, Theory, Fiction*. London: Routledge, 1988.

Mengham, Rod, ed. *An Introduction to Contemporary Fiction*. Cambridge: Polity Press, 1999. An engaging collection of essays which surveys fiction in English from 1970 to the end of the century.

Parker, Peter, ed. *The Reader's Companion to the Twentieth-Century Novel*. London and Oxford: Fourth Estate/Helicon, 1994.

The Reader's Companion to Twentieth-Century Writers. London and Oxford: Fourth Estate/Helicon, 1995. Invaluable reference books. The companion to the novel is organised chronologically and provides descriptions of the plots and contexts of a huge range of novels. The companion to writers is organised alphabetically.

Rabey, David Ian, ed. *English Drama since 1940*. London: Longman, 2003. A comprehensive introductory guide to drama in England.

Shellard, Dominic. *British Theatre since the War*. New Haven, CT: Yale University Press, 2000. A detailed, balanced and thoughtful introduction to the history of theatre since the war.

Sinfield, Alan, ed. *Society and Literature, 1945–1970*. London: Methuen, 1983. A groundbreaking collection of essays which surveyed the engagement between literature and politics in the post-war period.

Sinfield, Alan. *Literature, Politics and Culture in Post-War Britain*. London: Continuum, 2004. The landmark study of literature and culture since the war in relation to a wide-ranging and brilliant analysis of historical contexts.

Taylor, D. J. *After the War: The Novel and England since 1945*. London: Flamingo, 1994. A readable tour through the history of the novel in the second half of the twentieth century, although Taylor is keen to cast the period's fiction as the poor relation of its Victorian ancestors.

C Further Reading

i *Studies of Literature and Culture Since 1939*

Acheson, James, and Sarah C. E. Ross, eds. *The Contemporary British Novel*. Edinburgh University Press, 2005. A collection of essays on key British novelists of the 1980s and 1990s.

Bell, Ian, ed. *Peripheral Visions: Images of Nationhood in Contemporary British Fiction*. Cardiff: University of Wales Press, 1995. A collection of essays which addresses a wide range of regional and national representations in British fiction.

Bentley, Nick. *Contemporary British Fiction*. Edinburgh University Press, 2008. An authoritative study of fiction from 1975 to 2005, this book combines concise digests of the key historical contexts with close analysis of major novels grouped under the themes of narrative form, ethnicities, gender and sexuality, history and memory, and cultural space.

Bloom, Clive, ed. *Literature and Culture in Modern Britain: Vol. Three, 1956–1990*. London: Longman, 2000. A good collection of essays which surveys the dramatic changes in British society and culture as reflected in its literary production during the period surveyed.

Bradley, Jerry. *The Movement: British Poets of the 1950s*. New York: Twayne, 1993. This book offers a detailed and incisive analysis of British poets in the 1950s associated with the Movement.

Brannigan, John. *Literature, Culture and Society in Postwar England, 1945–1965*. Lampeter: Edwin Mellen Press, 2002. Chapters in this book tackle the emergence of new-right Conservatism, the representation of working-class life, gender, sexuality and the impact of postcolonial writers, particularly from the Caribbean, on literature and culture in post-war England.

Brook, Susan. *Literature and Cultural Criticism in the 1950s: The Feeling Male Body*. Basingstoke: Palgrave Macmillan, 2007. One of the most original and perceptive books on post-war English literature and criticism, which argues that the link between the Angry Young Men and New-Left cultural criticism was a common attention to the 'feeling male body' as a means of reasserting masculine power.

Brooker, Joseph. *Literature of the 1980s: After the Watershed*. Edinburgh University Press, 2010. A lively and probing analysis of the 1980s through its literature, which is reflexive also about how the decade continues to exercise influence on the twenty-first century.

Bull, John. *New British Political Dramatists*. Basingstoke: Macmillan, 1994. The ground-breaking study of the new dramatists who emerged in the seventies to challenge the establishment, particularly Edgar, Hare, Brenton and Griffiths.

Davies, Alastair, and Alan Sinfield, eds. *British Culture of the Postwar*. London: Routledge, 2000. A collection of essays which combines discussion of general themes and trends with consideration of particular authors. Essays are grouped around four themes: imperial and post-imperial Britain; welfare state and free market; Britain, Europe and Americanisation; and class, consumption and cultural institutions. There are essays on: cinema; the Institute of Contemporary Arts (ICA); the influence of Auden; drama; and on authors Pat Barker, Penelope Lively, Salman Rushdie, Angus Wilson and Alan Hollinghurst.

Day, Gary, ed. *Literature and Culture in Modern Britain: Vol. Two, 1930–1955*. London: Longman, 1997. A lively synthesis of literary and historical change is provided in this collection of essays which takes the unusual range of immediately before and after the war.

Dowson, Jane, and Alice Entwistle. *A History of Twentieth-Century British Women's Poetry*. Cambridge University Press, 2005. An insightful and detailed study of a comprehensive range of women poets in twentieth-century Britain.

Elsom, John. *Post-War British Theatre*. London: Routledge and Kegan Paul, 1976. Elsom's introduction to the prevailing trends in theatre since the war.

Elsom, John, ed. *Post-War Theatre Criticism*. London: Routledge and Kegan Paul, 1981. Selection of reviews of theatre productions.

Ferrebe, Alice. *Literature of the 1950s: Good, Brave Causes*. Edinburgh University Press, 2012. An authoritative and insightful study of the literature of the decade which took Britain from austerity to affluence.

Gąsiorek, Andrzej. *Post-War British Fiction: Realism and After*. London: Edward Arnold, 1995. Gąsiorek's argument is that post-war writing has blurred the distinctions between realism and modernism, and this book examines many instances of fictions which are not so easily labelled. The book includes discussion of writers Ivy Compton-Burnett, Henry Green, V. S. Naipaul, George Lamming, John Berger, Doris Lessing, Angus Wilson, John Fowles, Angela Carter, Sara Maitland, Graham Swift, Salman Rushdie and Julian Barnes. These writers provide ample evidence for Gąsiorek of the necessity of rethinking critical concepts of realism and experimentalism in fiction.

Gervais, David. *Literary Englands: Versions of 'Englishness' in Modern Writing*. Cambridge University Press, 1993. Interesting analysis of the shifting conceptions of Englishness as represented in modern writing.

Holmes, Frederick. *The Historical Imagination: Postmodernism and the Treatment of the Past in Contemporary British Fiction*. Victoria, BC: English Literary Monographs, 1997.

A useful study of the particular form of historiographic meta-fiction found in contemporary British fiction.

Lacey, Stephen. *British Realist Theatre: The New Wave in Its Context 1956–1965*. London: Routledge, 1995. A key history and analysis of the new wave, which brilliantly examines the diverse forms and interests of the dramatists who followed in the wake of *Look Back in Anger*.

Luckhurst, Roger, and Peter Marks, eds. *Literature and the Contemporary: Fictions and Theories of the Present*. Harlow: Longman/Pearson Education, 1999. An exciting collection of essays which addresses the philosophy and cultural history of the contemporary.

Middeke, Martin, Peter Paul Schnierer and Aleks Sierz, eds. *The Methuen Drama Guide to Contemporary British Playwrights*. London: Methuen, 2011. Twenty-five chapters cover the key dramatists in contemporary Britain, from Richard Bean to Roy Williams.

Middleton, Peter, and Tim Woods. *Literatures of Memory: History, Time and Space in Postwar Writing*. Manchester University Press, 2000. An ambitious and challenging study of post-war literature, which examines themes of history, memory, time, realism and cultural geography. Part 1 begins with post-modern concerns with the representation of the past, and includes four chapters on more general issues of recent historical fiction. Part 2 follows generic concerns with chapters on theatre, poetry, science fiction and urban fiction.

Morrison, Blake. *The Movement: English Poetry and Fiction of the 1950s*. Oxford University Press, 1980. The first major study of the Movement poets and novelists.

Motion, Andrew. *Philip Larkin: A Writer's Life*. London: Faber & Faber, 1993.

Piette, Adam. *Imagination at War: British Fiction and Poetry 1939–1945*. London: Macmillan, 1995. Excellent history and analysis of the writing of the Second World War.

Rebellato, Dan. *1956 and All That: The Making of Modern British Drama*. London: Routledge, 1999. Challenging and persuasive analysis of the contexts for the emergence of new British drama in the fifties.

Ritchie, Harry. *Success Stories: Literature and the Media in England, 1950–1959*. London: Faber & Faber, 1988. Rewarding and accessible study of the relationship between the iconoclastic writers of the fifties and the media.

Roberts, Philip. *The Royal Court Theatre and the Modern Stage*. Cambridge University Press, 1999. Detailed history of the most significant theatre in post-war Britain.

Russell Taylor, John. *Anger and After: A Guide to the New British Drama*. Harmondsworth: Penguin, 1963. The first and still very useful study of the new dramatists to emerge in Britain in the fifties.

Shank, Theodor, ed. *Contemporary British Theatre*. Basingstoke: Macmillan, 1994. A good collection of essays by scholars and practitioners which surveys the range of new British drama in the eighties and early nineties.

Sierz, Aleks. *In-Yer-Face Theatre: British Drama Today*. London: Faber & Faber, 2001. The key study of the new, shocking dramatists of the 1990s, such as Sarah Kane and Mark Ravenhill.

Rewriting the Nation: British Drama Today. London: Methuen, 2011. Sierz's follow up to *In-Yer-Face Theatre* which surveys the proliferation of drama in the first decade of the twenty-first century, and argues that theatre remains central to exploring national identity in Britain.

Taylor, D. J. *A Vain Conceit: British Fiction in the 1980s*. London: Bloomsbury, 1989. A detailed outlook on the emerging generation of novelists in the 1980s.

Waugh, Patricia. *Harvest of the Sixties: English Literature and Its Background 1960 to 1990*. Oxford University Press, 1995. As its title implies, Waugh's book considers the sixties as a defining period for contemporary literature, and examines the legacy of the sixties on subsequent writing. Waugh provides an authoritative and lucid introduction to the political and cultural contexts of post-1960 literature, and focuses attention in her discussion of literary texts on themes of metaphysics, rationality, national identity and the end of social consensus.

Wheatley, David. *Contemporary British Poetry*. Basingstoke: Palgrave Macmillan, 2014. An intelligent and wide-ranging discussion of the key critical contexts of contemporary British poetry, which considers post-colonial, gender, and eco-critical frameworks, as well as the role of anthologies and poet-critics.

ii Studies of Race, Empire, and Post-Empire

Baucom, Ian. *Out of Place: Englishness, Empire and the Locations of Identity*. Princeton University Press, 1999. An original and eloquent analysis of the literary and cultural expressions of English national and imperial identity since the nineteenth century.

Gikandi, Simon. *Maps of Englishness: Writing Identity in the Culture of Colonialism*. New York: Columbia University Press, 1996. An impressive study of the shifting cartography of Englishness, and especially insightful on the conceptualisation of post-imperial writing.

Gilroy, Paul. *There Ain't No Black in the Union Jack*. London: Routledge, 1987. The landmark analysis of black British culture, and the forms of racism evident in British politics.

Lee, A. Robert, ed. *Other Britain: Other British: Contemporary Multicultural Fiction*. London: Pluto, 1995. A good collection of essays on the multicultural nature of contemporary fiction in Britain.

Pearce, Lynne, Corinne Fowler and Robert Crawshaw, eds. *Postcolonial Manchester: Diaspora Space and the Devolution of Literary Culture*. Manchester University Press, 2013.

Pitcher, Ben. *The Politics of Multiculturalism: Race and Racism in Contemporary Britain*. Basingstoke: Palgrave Macmillan, 2009. An incisive study of the contemporary politics of race in Britain, with sustained attention to the complex politics and practices of multiculturalism.

Proctor, James. *Dwelling Places: Postwar Black British Writing*. Manchester University Press, 2003. Excellent study of the topographies of black British writing.

Schoene, Berthold. *The Cosmopolitan Novel*. Edinburgh University Press, 2009. The book traces the emergence of a relatively new trend in the novel of imagining global community, particularly in the work of David Mitchell, James Kelman, and Ian McEwan.

Webster, Wendy. *Imagining Home: Gender, 'Race' and National Identity, 1945–64*. University College London Press, 1998. An impressive and detailed social and cultural history of the intersections of gender, race and nation in the period of large-scale immigration after the war.

iii Studies of Gender and Sexuality

Alexander, Flora. *Contemporary Women Novelists*. London: Edward Arnold, 1989. A useful, broad-ranging study of contemporary women's fiction, which begins with an analysis of the feminist politics of the sixties and seventies before examining the work of Pat Barker, Angela Carter, Margaret Drabble, A. S. Byatt, Fay Weldon and Anita Brookner.

Baker, Niamh. *Happily Ever After? Women's Fiction in Postwar Britain, 1945–1960*. New York: St Martin's Press, 1989. A useful study of the history of women's fiction immediately after the war which is especially attentive to fiction as a popular cultural production.

De Jongh, Nicholas. *Not in Front of the Audience: Homosexuality on Stage*. London: Routledge, 1992. An original and stimulating study of the representation of homosexuality on stage since the late nineteenth century.

Dowson, Jane, ed. *Women's Writing, 1945–1960: After the Deluge*. Basingstoke: Palgrave Macmillan, 2003. An exciting and lively collection of essays which reassesses the significance of women's writing in the fifteen years after the war.

Duncker, Patricia. *Sisters and Strangers: An Introduction to Contemporary Feminist Fiction*. Oxford: Blackwell, 1992. A feminist reading of feminist fiction since 1970, which introduces the principal concerns and problems of second-wave feminism.

Eagleton, Mary, and Emma Parker, eds. *The History of British Women's Writing, 1970–Present*. Basingstoke: Palgrave Macmillan, 2015. An ambitious collection of essays which charts the diverse forms and achievements of contemporary women's writing.

Entwistle, Alice. *Poetry, Geography, Gender: Women Rewriting Contemporary Wales*. Cardiff: University of Wales Press, 2013. Particularly attentive to post-devolutionary contexts, this book combines close readings and cultural historical analysis to examine how contemporary women writers are redefining the relationship between gender and nation in Wales.

Greene, Gayle. *Changing the Story: Feminist Fiction and the Tradition*. Indianapolis: Indiana University Press, 1991. Interesting analysis of the ways in which contemporary feminist novelists interact with notions of tradition.

Greer, Stephen. *Contemporary British Queer Performance*. Basingstoke: Palgrave Macmillan, 2012. A study of how theatre and performance have enabled explorations of LGBT identities in contemporary Britain, with a particular focus on collaborative and community ventures.

Griffiths, Trevor R., and Margaret Llewellyn-Jones, eds. *British and Irish Women Dramatists since 1958*. Milton Keynes: Open University Press, 1993. Excellent collection of essays on women dramatists, which usefully addresses the ways in which women have sought to find a space for public expression through the theatre.

Joannou, Maroula. *Contemporary Women's Writing: From 'The Golden Notebook' to 'The Color Purple'*. Manchester University Press, 2000. One of the best and most lucid studies of contemporary women's writing, which takes the twenty-year span, 1962–82, between the two novels of its subtitle as a set of artificial parameters within which to examine the relationship between women's writing and women's lives. The study is informed throughout by a lively engagement with the politics of women's liberation.

Komporaly, Jozefina. *Staging Motherhood: British Women Playwrights, 1956 to the Present*. Basingstoke: Palgrave Macmillan, 2007. This book uses the representation of motherhood as a way of examining the impact of feminism on women's writing for the theatre.

Philips, Deborah, and Ian Haywood. *Brave New Causes: Women in Postwar British Fictions*. London: Leicester University Press, 1998. Excellent cultural history of the representation of women in a wide range of popular literary texts, including magazine fiction and romances.

Sage, Lorna. *Women in the House of Fiction: Post-War Women Novelists*. Basingstoke: Macmillan, 1992. An indispensable study of the ways in which post-war women writers subverted the conventions of fictional form.

Wandor, Michelene. *Look Back in Gender: Sexuality and the Family in Post-War British Drama*. London: Methuen, 1987. Brief chapters which explore the representation of various aspects of sexuality, the family, gender relations and feminist politics.

Watkins, Susan. *Twentieth-Century Women Novelists: Feminist Theory into Practice*. Basingstoke: Palgrave, 2000. A good introduction to feminist theoretical approaches to twentieth-century women's fiction.

iv Studies of Class

Haywood, Ian. *Working-Class Fiction: From Chartism to Trainspotting*. Plymouth: Northcote House, 1997. An accessible and interesting analysis of the fictional representations of working-class life in Britain.

Hill, John. *Sex, Class and Realism: British Cinema 1956–63*. London: British Film Institute, 1986. Although this book addresses a short period in the history of British cinema, it provides an invaluable overview of the significance of social realism to the representation of class in post-war Britain.

Jones, Owen. *Chavs: The Demonization of the Working Class*. London: Verso, 2011. A fascinating and thoughtful account of contemporary representations of the working class in Britain.

Laing, Stuart. *Representations of Working-Class Life, 1957–1964*. Basingstoke: Macmillan, 1986. Laing covers a similar period to John Hill, but this book is more attuned to the literary and dramatic representations of working-class life.

Savage, Mike. *Social Class in the 21st Century*. London: Pelican, 2015. This book reports on the findings of a BBC-sponsored survey, the Great British Class Survey, the largest ever undertaken in Britain, which examined the state of class divisions in the twenty-first century and proposed a new typology of classes to replace the old three-tier structure of working, middle and upper classes.

v Social, Cultural and Political History

Alibhai-Brown, Yasmin. *Who Do We Think We Are? Imagining the New Britain*. London: Penguin, 2000. This book examines the impact of large-scale immigration on British society, and the entrenched attitudes towards race and foreigners which pose obstacles to the imagination of a pluralist society.

Appleyard, Brian. *The Pleasures of Peace: Art and Imagination in Postwar Britain*. London: Faber & Faber, 1989. An insightful and detailed study of the arts in post-war Britain, which gives an impressive overview of the relationship between literature, criticism, art, sculpture, architecture and other forms of creative endeavour. Appleyard identifies some less obvious trends and themes in post-war writing, such as the influence of Graham Greene on the Angry Young Men.

Childs, David. *Britain since 1945: A Political History*. London: Routledge, 2012. Indispensable chronological survey of the political history of Britain since the war, now in its seventh edition.

Gardiner, Juliet. *Wartime: Britain 1939–1945*. London: Headline, 2004. A readable and lively account of the difficulties faced by Britain during the war.

Harrison, Brian. *Seeking a Role: The United Kingdom 1951–1970*. Oxford University Press, 2009.
Finding a Role? The United Kingdom 1970–1990. Oxford University Press, 2010. Brian Harrison's two volumes in the *New Oxford History of England* provide a synoptic account of the social, political and economic changes in Britain since 1951.

Hewison, Robert. *Under Siege: Literary Life in London 1939–45*. London: Weidenfeld & Nicolson, 1977.
In Anger: Culture in the Cold War 1945–60. London: Weidenfeld & Nicolson, 1981.
Too Much: Art and Society in the Sixties 1960–75. London: Methuen, 1986.
Culture and Consensus: England, Art and Politics since 1940. London: Methuen, 1995. Hewison is the best cultural historian of the post-war period, and has written extensively about the period in *Under Siege, In Anger, Too Much* and *The Heritage Society. Culture and Consensus* is an attempt to synthesise the broader concerns of his work into one book, which is divided into chapters on each decade. An informative and persuasive view of the period is offered here.

Hobsbawm, Eric. *Age of Extremes: The Short Twentieth Century 1914–1991*. London: Michael Joseph, 1994. A cogent and lively narrative of twentieth-century history, which is useful for providing a historical overview.

Marwick, Arthur. *British Society since 1945*. London: Penguin, 2003. The standard social-history textbook of the period, newly updated to cover up to 2002.

Morgan, Kenneth O. *Britain Since 1945: The People's Peace*. Oxford University Press, 2001. Engaging analysis of post-war Britain, which is one of the standard textbooks of the period. This edition also examines the rise of New Labour.

Nairn, Tom. *After Britain*. London: Verso, 2000. Brilliantly polemical study of the fate of Britain at the millennium, particularly in the context of Labour's introduction of limited attempts at devolution in Scotland and Wales.

Nehring, Neil. *Flowers in the Dustbin: Culture, Anarchy and Postwar England*. Ann Arbor: University of Michigan Press, 1993. Wonderful cultural history of the period, particularly on the history of sub-cultures.

Sandbrook, Dominic. *Never Had It So Good: A History of Britain from Suez to the Beatles*. London: Abacus, 2005.
White Heat: A History of Britain in the Swinging Sixties. London: Abacus, 2006.
State of Emergency: The Way We Were, Britain 1970–1974. London: Penguin, 2011.
Seasons in the Sun: The Battle for Britain, 1974–1979. London: Penguin, 2012. Sandbrook's four books on the post-war decades provide compelling accounts of social, cultural and political change in Britain.

Turner, Alwyn W. *Crisis, What Crisis? Britain in the 1970s*. London: Aurum, 2008.
  Rejoice! Rejoice! Britain in the 1980s. London: Aurum, 2010.
  A Classless Society: Britain in the 1990s. London: Aurum, 2013. Alwyn Turner's trilogy
    of books provides an entertaining and incisive account of the social, cultural
    and political history of Britain through the 1970s, 80s and 90s. It is particularly
    valuable for its interweaving of popular culture and political change.
Wilson, Elizabeth. *Only Halfway to Paradise: Women in Postwar Britain, 1945–1968*. London:
    Tavistock Press, 1980. An accessible and thorough study of the history of
    women from the end of the war to the height of the swinging sixties.

8 Postcolonial Literature in English

PAUL POPLAWSKI

Some of the most compelling and innovative writing in the English language over the past eighty years or so has emanated from far beyond the British and Irish Isles – from, for example, Australia, Barbados, Canada, the Indian subcontinent, Jamaica, Kenya, New Zealand, Nigeria, South Africa, Trinidad and Zimbabwe. The literature from these and other English-speaking countries is now commonly referred to as 'postcolonial literature', a term which clearly announces a connection to the history of British colonialism, which (among other things) established English as a principal language in these countries and thus as a language available for literary production. While their literary and cultural identities are by no means defined by their links to Britain, these countries were all once colonised by Britain and were all formerly part of the British empire, so the stories of how their English literatures have developed are inevitably bound up with the story of the rise and fall – and after-effects – of that empire.

Accordingly, this chapter begins with a detailed survey (in the chronology and the historical overview) of the development, growth and decline of the British empire, from Britain's earliest colonial adventures in the sixteenth century to the empire's zenith in the early years of the twentieth century and on to the period of decolonisation after the Second World War which led to independence for almost all the former colonies by the 1980s.

To the extent that these colonies shared at least *some* similar experiences within this overarching historical context, one can identify some common factors in the emergence of their individual traditions of literature in English, along with some common characteristics and concerns. So while, to do full justice to the unique character and complexity of each country's own literature, it may be preferable to talk in the plural of 'postcolonial literatures' (and perhaps better still simply to refer to a country's literature by its own national name), it can be helpful, for the purposes of general analysis and comparison, to posit a singular field of postcolonial literature in which texts are seen to have important elements in common in their critical and creative engagements with the processes of colonialism, decolonisation and post-colonial independence. This chapter, then, allows for both singular and plural perspectives, but its very nature as a *general* introduction means that the predominant stress will be on the former.

Note

The topics and time-span of this chapter inevitably overlap somewhat with those of preceding chapters in this book. I have tried to avoid substantially repeating earlier material here, so the following pages from those chapters can be consulted as a valuable supplement to the present chapter, as these all deal with issues (or provide references) of direct relevance to postcolonialism: Ch. 2, pp. 159–62; Ch.3, pp. 189, 245–7, 249–63, 273; Ch. 4, pp. 291, 326–33, 343–6, 356–9; Ch. 5, pp. 380–3, 428–32, 440–3, 465–6; Ch. 6, pp. 480–3, 485–6; Ch. 7, pp. 550–5, 561–3, 572–3, 591–3, 596–8, 614.

Chronology

Note

In order to present the relevant colonial history without repeating entries for literature from the chronologies in earlier chapters, this chronology has no column for literature until 1930 (though one or two literary items are included in the historical column before then). Also, as the main historical focus of the chapter is on the British empire and its demise, entries for the historical column end at 1997 with Britain's handing back of Hong Kong to China. The aim of this part of the chronology is to provide a 'backbone' of factual information to support the discursive historical overview which follows.

	HISTORY AND CULTURE
1421	Henry ('the Navigator') of Portugal establishes school of navigation and inaugurates age of global maritime exploration by European nations
1430s	Portuguese navigators explore west coast of Africa; African slaves first introduced into Portugal (1434)
1480s	Fishing fleets from west of England probably visiting Newfoundland cod fisheries by this time
1490	Portugal has begun to ship slaves from Benin to work on sugar plantations on Atlantic islands of São Tomé and Madeira
1492	Arrival of Columbus in the Caribbean; he lands at San Salvador (12 October) and then Cuba and Hispaniola (Haiti); three further voyages in next ten years with landfalls at, e.g., Jamaica, Antigua, Puerto Rico (1494), Grenada, Trinidad, St Vincent (1498), St Lucia, Honduras, Costa Rica (1502), Panama (1503)
1497	John Cabot, on voyage of exploration for Henry VII, sights and names Newfoundland
1498	Spanish settlement established on Hispaniola; colonists send 600 indigenous Caribs back to Spain to be sold as slaves
1501	Amerigo Vespucci voyages to the New World (–1502); his later account is basis of the name 'America' and realisation that it is a separate continent First African slaves brought to Santo Domingo, Hispaniola
1501–11	Portuguese establish trading stations in East Africa and colonise Mozambique, their naval supremacy in Indian Ocean giving dominance of lucrative spice trade with the east
1507	At Saint-Dié, France, 'America' appears for first time in print and on a map as a new continent, when German cartographer Martin Waldseemüller, drawing on Vespucci's discoveries, publishes world map and a pamphlet, *Cosmographiae introductio*
1510	Spain grants royal charter for the trade of African slaves to the New World
1536	Union of England and Wales
1537	Henry VIII claims sovereignty over Newfoundland
1541	Henry VIII proclaims himself King of Ireland
1542	*Declaration, Conteyning the Just Causes and Consyderations of This Present Warre with the Scottis* issued by Henry VIII: first in series of Tudor propaganda pamphlets arguing for Anglo-Scottish union and invoking concepts of an empire of 'Great Britain'
1562	Privateer Sir John Hawkins leads first British participation in growing transatlantic slave trade between West Africa and the New World
1577	Sir Francis Drake begins circumnavigation of the globe (–1581)

	HISTORY AND CULTURE
1578	Elizabeth I grants royal patent to Sir Humphrey Gilbert allowing for the colonisation of any 'remote, heathen and barbarous lands' not already owned by 'any Christian prince or people'
1582	Richard Hakluyt, *Diverse Voyages*
1583	Gilbert formally claims Newfoundland and sets up short-lived colony at St John's; after his death on the return voyage, his patent is transferred to Sir Walter Ralegh
1584	'Virginia' named by Ralegh after Elizabeth I as he sponsors abortive attempt at first settlement in America, at Roanoke Island, Virginia
1584–5	Ralph Fitch becomes first recorded British traveller to India
1585–6	Drake sails to West Indies to attack Spanish; on return voyage, rescues survivors of failed Virginian colony
1587	William Camden, *Britannia*
1595	Ralegh sails to South America and explores the River Orinoco (in present-day Venezuela); on his return, he publishes his *The Discoverie of the Large, Rich and Beautiful Empire of Guiana* (1596)
1599	There are at least 700,000 African slaves in the New World by this time
1600	East India Company chartered
1603	Death of Elizabeth I and accession of James VI of Scotland to English throne as James I
1605	Newfoundland Company chartered
1606	Virginia Company chartered
1607	Colony of Virginia established with the founding of Jamestown, the first permanent British settlement in America
1608	East India Company begins to petition Mughal rulers for trade concessions in India; first trading stations or 'factories' established on east and west coasts by 1613; further factories emerge on both coasts throughout the century, with fortified settlements at three major 'Presidencies' at Madras (1639), Bombay (1661) and Calcutta (1691), each with its own army
1609	British settlement of Bermuda (under Crown rule from 1684)
1610	Newfoundland colony established (under Crown rule from 1713) English navigator Henry Hudson explores present Hudson Bay (Canada)
1611	Performance of Shakespeare's *The Tempest*
1612	Cultivation of tobacco transforms economic prospects of Virginia as exports begin in this decade East India Company establishes first trading posts in Burma
1614–15	Transportation of convicts begins from Britain to Virginia (and, later, to other colonies) as condition of pardon from death sentence; after 1718, also used as sentence for non-capital offences; from the mid-1600s, some transportation of political prisoners too
1620	*Mayflower* Pilgrims sail to America and settle at Plymouth, Massachusetts; migration from Britain to 'New England', often for religious reasons, increases steadily from now as further colonies are established on America's north-eastern seaboard; the population of these settlements is around 30,000 by 1660
1621	Nova Scotia ceded to Britain by France and settled mainly by Scots, but sovereignty continues to be contested by France (until 1713)
1624	St Kitts (St Christopher) becomes first British settlement in the Caribbean (under Crown rule from 1663)
1625	British settlement of Barbados (under Crown rule from 1663); planters experiment with tobacco, cotton and indigo before discovering the potential of sugar in the early 1640s; initial labour supplied by indentured labourers escaping poverty from England and Scotland
1628	North Carolina colony established
1629	New Hampshire colony established First British settlers in Bahamas (under Crown rule from 1717, formally confirmed 1783)
1630	Massachusetts colony established
1632	Settlement of Montserrat and Antigua Maryland settled by Catholics (colony chartered in 1634)
1633	Connecticut colony established
1636	British Honduras (Belize) first settled but a formal colony only from 1862 Rhode Island colony established
1641	First settlement of Tobago (subsequently held by both Holland and France, until British control confirmed in 1763)

	HISTORY AND CULTURE
1642	Dutch navigator Abel Tasman explores seas of what he calls 'New Holland' (Australia); identifies island later named Tasmania, which he now calls Van Dieman's Land (after governor of the Dutch East Indies)
1650s	Sugar cultivation on Barbados, with exports of refined sugar, molasses and rum, proves highly profitable and makes Barbados wealthiest colony in New World; sugar cultivation spreads rapidly to Jamaica, the Leeward and other Caribbean islands in a 'sugar revolution' that sparks economic boom and huge increase in related slave trade from West Africa – in Barbados alone, c. 135,000 slaves arrive between 1640 and 1700
1651	Atlantic island of St Helena annexed by Britain (settled by East India Company in 1661 and under Crown rule from 1834) Navigations Act: first of series to protect Britain's monopoly on trade with its colonies (and on the shipping of that trade), especially in what are, from 1660, specified as 'enumerated goods' such as sugar, tobacco, indigo, ginger and, later, coffee and raw silk
1652	First Dutch settlers at Cape of Good Hope, South Africa; predominantly of Calvinistic background, the original 'Boers' (farmers)
1655	Britain seizes Jamaica from Spain; hundreds of fugitive slaves take to mountains and form basis of the 'Maroons' who harry the British until the end of the next century
1663	Company of Royal Adventurers to Africa (later, Royal Africa Company), founded. South Carolina colony established
1664	Delaware colony established
1665	Britain acquires New Netherlands (New York) from Dutch New Jersey colony established
1666	Settlement begins of what becomes the British Virgin Islands
1670	Hudson's Bay Company chartered by Charles II with rights over huge areas of Canada (France disputes these until 1713); begins fur-trading from coastal areas
1673	Royal Africa Company establishes forts on West African coast, trading in slaves and gold
1680	Pennsylvania colony established
1685	Charles II dies, James II accedes
1688	'Glorious Revolution': James II replaced by William and Mary (–1702)
1689– 97	King William's (or Nine Years') War, principally against France but also against Jacobites in Scotland and Ireland seeking restoration of James II
1690	Battle of the Boyne in Ireland: William defeats James II and Catholic Irish
1692	Kingston founded in Jamaica
1694	Establishment of Bank of England eases government borrowing and helps finance war
1702	William dies; Queen Anne accedes War of the Spanish Succession (–1713) involves Britain once more in wide-ranging war with France and Spain
1707	Act of Union between England and Scotland
1713	Treaties of Utrecht between Britain and both France and Spain: France formally accepts British sovereignty over Newfoundland, Nova Scotia, Hudson's Bay territory and St Kitts, and Spain cedes Minorca and Gibraltar to Britain and transfers its slave trade contract from France to Britain
1714	Queen Anne dies; George I accedes
1718	Transportation Act extends sentence of transportation to non-capital offences
1719	Daniel Defoe, *Robinson Crusoe*
1727	George I dies; George II accedes
1728	First Maroon War in Jamaica: after long conflict, the Maroons are granted freedom and autonomy within designated areas in treaties of 1738–9
1730	Britain is the world's main slave-trading nation by around this time and will have transported c. 3 million slaves by 1807
1733	Georgia established, the thirteenth of Britain's North American colonies
1740–8	Anglo-French conflicts in India
1745	Jacobite Rebellion in Scotland
1756–63	Seven Years' War – Britain allied with Prussia against France, Austria, Russia and, later, Spain, with fighting in Europe, India and the Americas; Britain's victory establishes naval supremacy and makes it leading world power; at the Treaty of Paris in 1763, France formally cedes Canadian territories to Britain along with Caribbean islands of Dominica, Grenada, Tobago, and St Vincent; Britain consolidates dominant position in India

	HISTORY AND CULTURE
1757	Battle of Plassey – British victory over French and Indian forces gives East India Company control of Bengal and signals beginning of overall British rule in India; Robert Clive becomes Governor of Bengal (–1760)
1759	Wolfe conquers French Canada (Quebec) for Britain
1760	Jamaica: widespread slave rebellions with the deaths of some 1000 slaves and 60 whites, with much damage and brutal reprisals George II dies; George III accedes
1765	East India Company acquires *Diwani*, the power to collect taxes, in Bengal (marking a shift from expanding trade to expanding governance in India) First settlement of Falkland Islands – contested by France and Spain; Britain prevails but withdraws in 1774 until 1832, when a colony is established to thwart Argentinian claims
1768–71	During three-year voyage of circumnavigation, Captain James Cook charts the coasts of New Zealand, eastern Australia and southern New Guinea; on later voyages he charts parts of Antarctica (1772–5) and the Pacific coast of America (1776–9)
1770	Cook sails into (and names) Botany Bay, near present-day Sydney
1771	First edition of *Encyclopaedia Britannica*
1772	Lord Mansfield, in the Somerset case, rules that slaves are free on English soil
1773	Regulating Act establishes post of Governor-General of India to increase governmental oversight of East India Company; Warren Hastings is first appointee (–1785) East India Company gains monopoly over Indian opium production and rapidly expands illicit trade to China from now, generating huge profits by early nineteenth century – and major social problems of addiction in China
1774	Quebec Act defines governance of colony and aims to reconcile French inhabitants to British rule
1775–83	American War of Independence ends in defeat for Britain and loss of its thirteen American colonies British also at war with the Maratha states in western India (until 1782)
1778–1814	Caribbean island of St Lucia changes hands several times between France and Britain, until finally annexed by Britain in 1814
1778	Scottish court rules slavery illegal Vernacular printing press established in India and publishes a *Grammar of the Bengali Language* by Nathaniel Halhed
1780–1800	c. 750,000 slaves shipped by Britain from West Africa to the Caribbean
1784	India Act establishes London Board of Control for East India Company Sir William Jones founds Bengal Asiatic Society to promote study of Indian culture
1785	Hastings resigns as Governor-General of India and returns to Britain amid accusations of corruption; after an impeachment trial lasting seven years (1788–95), he is acquitted Sir Charles Wilkins translates *Bhagavad Gita* from Sanskrit
1787	Society for the Abolition of the Slave Trade founded; major public campaign for abolition begins in Britain Sierra Leone founded by British abolitionists for settlement of freed slaves (comes under Crown rule, 1807)
1788	First settlement established at Botany Bay in New South Wales, Australia, as a penal colony, although free settlers also soon arrive; transportation to independent America no longer possible and some 160,000 British convicts transported to Australia by 1852; there are c. 750,000 Aboriginal inhabitants on the continent at this time The African Association established to promote exploration of Africa
1789	Start of French revolution Mutiny on the *Bounty* (–1790): mutineers set up colony on Pitcairn Islands (comes under Crown rule in 1838) William Jones translates Indian drama, *Shakuntala*, by Kalidasa
1790–2	British acquire territory in southern India after victory over Tipu Sultan in third Mysore War
1791	Canada Act divides Quebec into Upper and Lower Canada and establishes representative assemblies for both Major slave insurrection in French colony of Saint Domingue (Haiti) begins the Haitian revolution (–1804), led by Pierre Toussaint l'Ouverture
1792	Baptist Missionary Society founded William Carey, *An enquirey into the obligations of Christians, to use means for the conversion of the heathens*
1793	French Revolutionary Wars begin (–1802) Britain launches abortive campaign to seize Saint Domingue and suffers heavy losses to l'Ouverture's forces (and to yellow fever) before eventually withdrawing in 1798

	HISTORY AND CULTURE
1794	Britain conquers Seychelles from France French Republic outlaws slavery in its colonies
1795	Britain seizes Dutch Cape Colony in South Africa; colony contested by Dutch until formally ceded to Britain in 1814 Jamaica: 2nd Maroon War ends with a negotiated treaty but its terms are later ignored by the British who deport the Maroons via Nova Scotia to Sierra Leone London Missionary Society (non-denominational) established Malay state of Malacca seized from Dutch and formally ceded to the East India Company in 1824 Lime juice first introduced by British navy to combat scurvy
1796	British conquest of parts of Guiana from Dutch (whole territory formally ceded to Britain, 1815; colony of British Guiana established, 1831)
1797	Trinidad seized from Spain (formally ceded to Britain, 1815)
1798	Church Missionary Society (Anglican) founded
1799	Victory over French-backed Tipu Sultan of Mysore, at Seringapatam, gives Britain control over most of south and west India
1800	Baptist mission at Serampore, India, establishes printing press and is soon printing translations of the Bible and grammars and dictionaries in several Indian languages
1801	Act of Union with Ireland creates United Kingdom of Great Britain and Ireland.
1802	Napoleon restores slavery in French empire and dispatches large force to retake Saint Domingue (Haiti); after a bloody war there, his forces are defeated by the end of 1803
1803	British settlement in New South Wales extends to Van Dieman's Land (Tasmania) In India, British territory extended after second Maratha War (–1805) Napoleonic Wars begin (–1815)
1804	Saint Domingue formally declares itself an independent republic under new name of Haiti; its constitution of 1805 abolishes slavery forever; some half a million lives have been lost since the start of the revolution British and Foreign Bible Society formed to support ongoing work in the empire on vernacular translations
1806	Britain annexes Cape of Good Hope; in addition to the indigenous Khoikhoi, there is a population of c. 30,000 Boers here
1807	Abolition of the slave trade in the British empire
1810	Britain seizes Mauritius from the French (formally annexed, 1814)
1813	In India, East India Company monopoly ends but Company continues as agent of government for British Crown; monopoly in China continues Wesleyan Methodist Missionary Society founded
1814	Britain annexes territory in Nepal in Gurkha War (–1816) and a British Resident appointed to Nepalese court; Gurkhas recruited to British Indian army from this time Missionaries arrive in New Zealand from this time Napoleon defeated and banished to Elba
1815	Napoleon escapes to raise French army again but finally defeated at Battle of Waterloo; Congress of Vienna peace treaty confirms Britain's possession of Cape Colony, Ceylon, Mauritius, Guiana, Trinidad, Tobago, Malta and Heligoland From now to 1914, c. 21.5 million Britons will emigrate to the colonies First major Chinese–English dictionary (6 vols.) compiled by Robert Morrison of the London Missionary Society
1816	Shaka becomes King of Zulu nation in South Africa as period of Zulu ascendency begins Bussa's Slave Rebellion in Barbados suppressed by troops and militia with c. 1000 rebels killed or executed
1818	Defeat of Pindaris in central India and victory in third Maratha War decisively consolidates British control over India
1819	British trade settlement established on Singapore which comes under East India Company rule from 1824
1820	Glasgow Missionary Society established at eastern Cape of South Africa: missionary John Bennie learns Xhosa and develops an orthography; a printing press is established in 1823 and begins to print in the vernacular
1820–38	Liberia first settled by freed slaves sent by philanthropic American Colonisation Society
1823	Anti-Slavery Society founded
1824	Settlement of Queensland begins (colony formally established, 1859) Robert Wedderburn, *The Horrors of Slavery*

	HISTORY AND CULTURE
1824–6	Britain defeats Burma (Myanmar) in war and annexes Assam
1825	Van Dieman's Land becomes separate colony
1826	Malacca, Penang and Singapore brought together as the Straits Settlement under East India Company rule (under Crown rule from 1867) Settlement begins in Western Australia (Swan River Colony established, 1829)
1827	Fourah Bay College founded in Sierra Leone, one of Africa's earliest universities
1829	South African College founded in Cape Town
1830s	Australian colonies have become major suppliers of wool to British textile industry by this time
1830	Charlotte School founded in Sierra Leone and provides education for African girls Royal Geographical Society founded and soon becomes influential in promoting exploration of Africa
1831–2	'Baptist War' for emancipation – massive rebellion of slaves in Jamaica led by Baptist preacher Sam Sharpe: c. 200 slaves shot and hundreds more later executed (including Sharpe) Mary Prince, *The History of Mary Prince, a West Indian Slave*
1833	Abolition of Slavery Act passed and enacted within British empire in August 1834; £20 million is paid in compensation to slave owners; from now, alternative labour for plantation colonies like Trinidad, Guyana and Mauritius largely supplied from India by system of indenture (often seen as another form of slavery): e.g. c. 450,000 indentured Indian labourers go to Mauritius between 1834 and the early twentieth century India Act lays foundation for reforms of education and law in India overseen by Thomas Babington Macaulay and along strongly British lines
1834	South Australia colony founded; settlement begins in Victoria (colony established, 1851)
1835	Dutch Boers in South Africa begin 'Great Trek', partly in protest over British abolition of slavery; over the next ten years, c. 10,000 Boers migrate from the Cape Colony to found the Orange Free State and Transvaal Macaulay's Minute on Education establishes English as India's official language for government and education, aiming to create a class of people 'Indian in colour and blood' but English in tastes, opinion, morals and intellect
1838	Boer trekkers defeat King Dingale's Zulu army at Blood River in Natal
1839–42	First Opium War as China fails to stop Britain's illegal trade of opium into the country: British warships shell and seize several ports and, in the Treaty of Nanking (1842), China is forced to cede Hong Kong (which becomes a Crown colony in 1843) and to open five further ports to British trade, including Canton (Guangzhou) and Shanghai First Afghan War: Britain's abortive attempt to annex Afghanistan ends in disaster with the loss of entire British army of 15,000
1839	Aden (on southern Arabian peninsula and today part of Yemen) annexed for Britain by East India Company; ruled by Company until 1858, then as part of British India; becomes key refuelling port after opening of Suez Canal in 1869 Durham Report on governance of British North America recommends union of the two Canadas and makes landmark proposal of granting Canada 'responsible government' – i.e., internal self-government by an executive directly responsible to a democratically elected legislature; although not fully realised in Canada until 1867, the devolutionary principle of 'responsible government' becomes a key element of Britain's colonial policies from now
1840	Treaty of Waitangi with Maori chiefs establishes British rule in New Zealand in return for safeguarding Maori land and other rights Canada Act unites Upper and Lower Canada (renamed as West and East Canada – to become Ontario and Quebec in 1867)
1841	Scottish missionary and explorer, David Livingstone, sent by London Missionary Society to Bechuanaland (later Botswana); his many expeditions in central Africa from now till his death in 1873 galvanise British public interest in Africa and inspire later missionaries and explorers Sultan of Brunei appoints James Brooke Rajah of Sarawak (Malaysia); the Brooke family rule until replaced by Crown rule in 1946
1843	Britain annexes Natal in South Africa – Boers move northwards into Transvaal British conquest of Sindh in north-west India
1845	First Sikh War begins British annexation of the Punjab in India
1845–72	Land Wars in New Zealand as Maori people resist land claims by British settlers
1846	Nova Scotia granted responsible government

HISTORY AND CULTURE	
1847	Colony of British Kaffraria established in South Africa after British conquer Xhosa people; colony incorporated into Cape Colony in 1866 Liberia becomes officially independent
1848	Second Sikh War (–1849) completes conquest of Punjab Start of period of intensive 'westernisation' in India under Governor-General Dalhousie (–1856) with many reforms and the building of roads, irrigation canals, new harbours, the introduction of the telegraph, a postal service and the first railways; policy also introduced whereby princely states whose rulers leave no heir 'lapse' to Britain First British missionaries in East African territory later to become Kenya
1850s	First major gold rush in Australia, in Victoria and New South Wales, brings large influx of European migrants and Chinese labourers and increases non-Aborigine population of Australia to over a million by 1861
1851	Britain establishes consulate in Lagos (in modern-day Nigeria)
1852	Britain annexes further territories from Burma after another war
1852–6	In Africa, Livingstone explores the upper Zambezi and crosses the central continent, east to west, seeing and naming the Victoria Falls; back in Britain in 1856–7, his lecture tours generate huge interest and excitement in opening up Africa for 'commerce and Christianity'
1853	Crimean War (–1856) (Britain enters in 1854)
1854	In Britain, the position of Colonial Secretary first formally introduced, with Sir George Grey as first incumbent (the post lapses in 1966)
1855	Newfoundland granted responsible government; the Australian colonies of New South Wales, Victoria and Southern Australia granted responsible government
1856	New Zealand granted responsible government; Van Dieman's Land renamed Tasmania and granted responsible government In India, Britain annexes the independent northern state of Oudh (Awadh) and introduces widespread changes; this annexation is often cited as one contributory cause of the rebellion of 1857
1856–60	Second Opium War: China defeated by Britain (with France) by 1858 and forced to sign Treaty of Tianjin agreeing to open further ports to foreign trade, to guarantee free movement for missionaries within China, and to pay a large security in silver; when treaty is not ratified, hostilities resume in 1860 and China is forced to give way after Peking (Beijing) is entered and the Imperial Summer Palace sacked; treaty paves way for Britain to become dominant force in Chinese commerce for at least next sixty years
1857	Indian Rebellion (–1858): massive uprising against British rule across northern central India, eventually suppressed after much destruction and bloodshed, with atrocities committed on both sides; a landmark event in the history of the British in India, resulting immediately in a restructuring of government by the India Act of 1858 David Livingstone, *Missionary Travels and Researches In South Africa* Mary Seacole, *The Wonderful Adventures of Mary Seacole in Many Lands*
1858	India Act abolishes East India Company and places India under direct Crown rule
1859	Queensland granted responsible government Bible translated into Xhosa (first published in one volume in 1864)
1861	Britain formally annexes Lagos (Nigeria) and gradually extends control in this region over next twenty-five years
1864	Britain conquers border territory from Bhutan
1865	Jamaica Insurrection (or Morant Bay Rebellion): a rising by sugar plantation workers leads to imposition of martial law and brutal punishments – some 439 people hanged, 600 flogged, and thousands of homes set on fire
1867	British North America Act creates Dominion of Canada, a self-governing confederation of provinces; Canada is first of Britain's colonies to become largely autonomous within the empire and provides a model for future development of a Commonwealth of independent nations Transportation of convicts to Australia (by now, only to Western Australia) ceases
1868	In southern Africa, Basutoland becomes British Protectorate (until 1966)
1869	Diamond rush in South Africa following discovery of diamonds in 1867 in Griqualand where Kimberley is founded (1873) and soon established as a principal centre for diamond mining Suez Canal opens, drastically reducing sailing time from Europe to Asia (e.g., journey from London to Bombay roughly halved compared to the route round the Cape)

	HISTORY AND CULTURE
1870s	British companies begin to send steam trading vessels up the Niger First missionaries arrive in Kingdom of Buganda (later part of Uganda)
1872	Cape Colony granted responsible government
1873	Britain acquires territory in southern Arabian peninsula inland from Aden to form Aden Protectorate
1873–4	British–Asante war in West Africa; Asante capital, Kumasi, captured
1874	British-controlled territory along West African coast formally becomes Gold Coast colony
1874–1914	Britain negotiates treaties of protection over nine Malay states; the Federated Malay States formed in 1896
1875	British government buys a controlling 40 per cent of shares in the Suez Canal
1876	Royal Titles Act makes Queen Victoria Empress of India (proclaimed 1877) Church of Scotland mission founded in south-east Africa at Blantyre (in today's Malawi), named after Livingstone's birthplace Last surviving Aborigine in Tasmania dies – there were some 5,000 people on the island when first settled
1877	British annexation of the Transvaal (leads to first Boer War in 1880) 5–6 million die in famine in India
1878	Britain claims Walvis Bay in South-West Africa (annexed to Cape Colony in 1884) By treaty with Turkey, Cyprus becomes British protectorate (annexed in 1914 and under Crown rule from 1925)
1879	Britain invades Zululand and, after initial serious defeat at Isandlwana, conquers Zulu nation, thus decisively consolidating control in southern Africa (Zululand incorporated into Natal in 1897) Second Afghan War (–1881): Britain fails a second time to annex Afghanistan United African Company formed for trade on the Niger – forerunner of the Royal Niger Company
1880–1	First Boer War; British forces defeated at Majuba Hill and internal autonomy of the Transvaal restored by the Treaty of Pretoria
1881	'The scramble for Africa' begins as European powers compete for new colonial territories throughout the continent (–1914) Islamic uprising against Egyptian rule in Sudan led by the 'Mahdi', Mohammed Ahmed bin Abdullah
1882	Britain invades Egypt, defeats Egyptian army at battle of Tel el-Kebir, and then occupies and effectively rules the country until 1922 (as a British Protectorate from 1914); British troops to remain in control of the Suez canal until 1956
1883	In Sudan, the Mahdi's forces defeat British-Egyptian army Olive Schreiner, *The Story of an African Farm*
1884	Protectorate of British Somaliland established in Horn of Africa
1884–5	Berlin Conference: European powers agree rules for territorial claims in Africa and begin to draw lines of partition for the continent; actual annexation of territory on the ground gathers momentum from now
1885	British Indian army invades Burma (Myanmar) and, after war (–1886), annexes it to British India (–1936); Burmese resistance continues for several years policed by c. 40,000 British forces In Sudan, the Mahdi captures Khartoum and General Gordon is killed (he becomes an iconic imperial hero in Britain) Niger Districts Protectorate established around Niger delta Founding of the Indian National Congress
1886	Royal Niger Company chartered to secure trade and territory on Niger Gold rush in the Transvaal centred on the Witwatersrand goldfields ('the Rand') near Johannesburg, which rapidly develops into the largest and richest city in South Africa; by 1902, there are 120 mining companies in the region using c. 12,500 white and c. 100,000 tightly regulated black workers; gold rush increases British–Boer tensions in region
1887	British South Africa Company founded by Cecil Rhodes and given royal charter in 1889 to colonise area of south-central Africa (later, Southern and Northern Rhodesia / Zimbabwe and Zambia)
1888	Imperial British East Africa Company chartered to colonise and commercially develop regions later to become Kenya and Uganda King Lobengula of Matabeleland in Southern Rhodesia agrees mining rights with British South Africa Company Trinidad and Tobago joined to form single Crown colony
1890	Rhodes's 'Pioneer Column' invades Mashonaland in Southern Rhodesia and establishes base at future capital of Salisbury (Harare)
1891	British Central African Protectorate established, known from 1907 as Nyasaland (later Malawi) Joseph Jeffrey Walters (of the Vai people of Liberia), *Guanya Pau: The Story of an African Princess*, probably the first published novel in English by an indigenous African

HISTORY AND CULTURE
1892	Gilbert and Ellice Islands (in the Pacific) become a joint British Protectorate (and a Crown colony from 1916)
1892–3	Start of gold rush in Western Australia – takes population here from c. 35,000 to c. 200,000 within ten years
1893	British forces provoke war with Matabele and easily defeat them with vastly superior weaponry (e.g. Maxim machine-gun); whole of Southern Rhodesia now largely controlled by British South Africa Company
	Gandhi in South Africa until 1915; campaigning against racism and segregation, he develops principles of civil disobedience later used in India
	Yorubaland in western Nigeria annexed by Britain
	Women gain the vote in New Zealand
1894	Kingdom of Buganda in East Africa becomes British Protectorate
1895	Jameson Raid: failed attempt, by an associate of Cecil Rhodes, to overthrow Boer government in Transvaal; Jameson is tried and briefly imprisoned in Britain for his illicit actions and Rhodes is forced to resign as Prime Minister of Cape Colony for organising conspiracy; parliamentary inquiry exonerates Colonial Secretary, Joseph Chamberlain
	British East Africa Protectorate (Kenya) established under Crown rule
	Serious famines in India from now to 1905; plague also strikes, 1896–8, killing one million
1895–6	British–Asante war: King Prempeh deposed and Asante becomes British Protectorate (annexed to the Gold Coast colony in 1901)
1896–7	Second war in Southern Rhodesia results again in decisive victory for British over joint forces of Matabele and Mashona peoples
1897	British troops invade and sack Benin in West Africa, looting 2,500 of its bronze treasures
	Further British protectorates established around Buganda
	Mary Kingsley, *Travels in West Africa* (positive depictions of indigenous West African culture, based on travels in 1893–4 and 1894–5, challenge prevailing imperialist stereotypes of 'inferior races')
1898	British expeditionary force led by Kitchener defeats Mahdist regime in Sudan and establishes Anglo-Egyptian condominium (–1956)
	Britain granted lease of the strategic port and territory of Weihaiwei in northern China (after gathering war-ships off the coast)
	Victoria University College, New Zealand
1899	Second Boer War begins
1900	Relief of Mafeking – widespread celebration in Britain; Britain defeats main Boer armies and occupies key towns by autumn 1900, but determined guerilla warfare continues till May 1902; Britain interns Boer civilians in 'concentration' camps – in which, by the end of the war, over 20,000 have died from disease
	Sol T. Plaatje writes his *Diary* of the siege of Mafeking (published posthumously in 1973), a unique view of the war from a black African
	Northern Nigeria and Southern Nigeria established as separate protectorates and pass from Royal Niger Company to Crown rule; Frederick Lugard, High Commissioner for Northern Nigeria until 1906, here develops his influential model of 'indirect rule', working through traditional local leaders
	India has a population at this time of c. 300 million, governed by c. 5000 British officials
1901	Death of Queen Victoria; accession of Edward VII
	Australian Commonwealth Act (1900) brings into being a federated Australia formed by union of six separate colonies; an Immigration Restriction Bill is passed as part of a 'White Australia' policy
1902	Treaty of Vereeniging ends Boer War: Boer republics acknowledge British sovereignty and are promised future self-government
	Queen Victoria's birthday (24 May) adopted as 'Empire Day' in honour of the c. 55,000 colonial forces from the broader empire who fought for Britain in the Boer War
	Joseph Conrad, *Heart of Darkness*
1904	Building of Panama Canal begins (–1914); a key source of employment for the Caribbean, drawing c. 20,000 workers from Barbados, for example, who, on their return, can buy land from white planters, thus altering patterns of land ownership by 1930s
1905	Colony of Uganda created from Buganda and surrounding protectorates
	British Somaliland becomes separate colony
	Lord Curzon, Viceroy of India, partitions Bengal in face of strong Bengali protests and the start of the *swadeshi* ('home-produced') movement, boycotting all imported goods (especially British); movement soon spreads throughout India as a broader nationalist campaign
	Russo-Japanese War: Japan's victory over a European power helps fan nationalism in India
	Sinn Féin founded; Ulster Unionist Council formed

	HISTORY AND CULTURE
1906	Transvaal granted responsible government Founding of the Indian Muslim League
1907	New Zealand becomes a Dominion within British empire Orange Free State granted responsible government
1909	In India, Morley-Minto reforms increase Indian representation on legislative councils and allow for a separate Muslim electorate
1910	Union of South Africa established as a Dominion within the British empire by union of Cape Colony, Natal, Orange Free State and Transvaal
1911	In India, Bengal reunited as Curzon's partition of 1905 is reversed Britain grants internal autonomy to Bhutan in return for control of its foreign policy J. E. Casely-Hayford (Gold Coast/Ghana), *Ethiopia Unbound*, probably the second African novel in English
1912	African National Congress (ANC) founded by, among others, Sol T. Plaatje Irish Home Rule Bill
1913	Native Land Act in South Africa restricts land rights of black Africans (more than two-thirds of the population) to only 7.5 per cent of the land
1914	Start of First World War Northern and Southern Nigeria united to form single colony with Lugard as first Governor-General ANC sends delegation to London to protest about Native Land Act
1915	Abortive anti-colonial uprising in Nyasaland (Malawi) led by Rev. John Chilembwe Gandhi returns to India and begins to forge Indian National Congress into a mass movement for home rule ('swaraj'), seeking also to unite Hindus and Muslims in this endeavour (reflected formally in the Lucknow Pact of 1916)
1916	Easter Rising of nationalists in Dublin suppressed; 450 killed; leaders executed Sol T. Plaatje, *Native Life in South Africa* – political critique of policies such as the Native Land Act of 1913
1917	Russian revolution
1918	End of First World War; over 2.6 million people from the colonies have participated as combatants, carriers, labourers and porters, with at least 200,000 dead and over 400,000 wounded; in addition, c. 90,000 Chinese labourers from Weiheiwei serve in France, and c. 1 million African porters serve in East Africa with c. 10,000 deaths, largely from disease Influenza pandemic kills over 21 million people worldwide by 1920; c. 17 million die in India
1919–22	In India, Rowlatt Acts (1919) extend repressive wartime measures and spark first wave of Gandhi-inspired campaigns of large-scale strikes and civil disobedience
1919	In Egypt, major anti-British uprising suppressed after weeks of fierce fighting, with over 1,500 Egyptians killed Riots in British Honduras, Jamaica and Trinidad Some 400 people killed and 1,200 injured when British troops fire on demonstrators in Amritsar in the Punjab: the 'Amritsar Massacre' further galvanises anti-British Indian nationalism Government of India Act makes partial concessions towards self-government for India and provides for elected majorities on both central and provincial legislatures; but some seats remain for non-elected nominees and many key powers are reserved by Britain Anglo-Irish War begins
1920	League of Nations first meets (precursor of the United Nations (1946)) As agreed at the 1919 Versailles Peace Conference, the following League of Nations' mandates to Britain come into effect: British Cameroons (–1961), Iraq (–1932), Palestine (–1948), Tanganyika (Tanzania) (–1961), Togoland (–1957), and Transjordan (Jordan) (–1946) British East Africa Protectorate becomes Crown colony of Kenya; political movements here for African rights, especially land rights, develop from around this time with the emergence of influential leaders like Harry Thuku and Jomo Kenyatta Arab uprising in Iraq: c. 8,000 Iraqis and c. 2,300 British and Indian troops die after six months of conflict Government of Ireland Act partitions Ireland
1921	Anglo-Irish Treaty establishes Irish Free State in Southern Ireland
1922	Egypt regains independence Irish Civil War breaks out (ends 1923) In Kenya, Harry Thuku's imprisonment sparks mass protest in Nairobi, violently suppressed by police
1923	British empire at its largest-ever extent Southern Rhodesia passes from South Africa Company to the Crown and is granted responsible government (though Britain reserves powers – rarely used in fact – to control racially discriminatory legislation)

	HISTORY AND CULTURE
1924	Northern Rhodesia passes to Crown rule; major development of the rich copper belt begins from now as region becomes one of world's major copper producers First political party in Barbados, the socialist Democratic League, founded by Charles Duncan O'Neale First Labour government in Britain
1926	Balfour Definition of Dominion status refers to a 'British Commonwealth of Nations' and paves way for 1931 Statute of Westminster Empire Marketing Board established to promote trade within the British empire (–1933)
1929	Jomo Kenyatta in exile from Kenya (–1946) Violence in Palestine leaves over 200 dead Wall Street Crash and start of international economic depression

	HISTORY AND CULTURE	LITERATURE Note: *Titles without annotation are novels unless the title indicates otherwise.*
1930	Britain returns Weihaiwei to China Uprising in Burma against British rule (–1932)	Sol T. Plaatje, *Mhudi* (written 1920)
1930–1	Gandhi leads mass campaign of civil disobedience in India in protest at salt taxes – thousands are imprisoned, including Gandhi	
1931	Statute of Westminster gives legislative autonomy over all internal affairs to self-governing Dominions of Australia, Canada, the Irish Free State, Newfoundland, New Zealand and the Union of South Africa; Britain retains control of defence and foreign affairs but this is a key shift from empire to Commonwealth Land Apportionment Act in Southern Rhodesia divides land massively in favour of white minority and effectively bars black people from towns	
1932	Iraq becomes independent	
1933		Claude McKay (Jamaica), *Banana Bottom*
1934		George Orwell, *Burmese Days* (essays) Christina Stead (Australia), *Seven Poor Men of Sydney*
1935	Government of India Act introduces further democratic reforms with increased franchise and provincial self-government; Britain retains control of central government, foreign and defence policy and most revenues Italy invades Ethiopia	Mulk Raj Anand (India), *Untouchable* R. K. Narayan (India), *Swami and Friends* Jinadasa Vijayatunga (Sri Lanka), *Grass for My Feet*
1936	Arab revolt over Jewish settlement in Palestine gathers pace with attacks on British troops In Jamaica, militant trade union organisation established by Alexander Bustamente	Anand, *Coolie* C. L. R. James (Trinidad), *Minty Alley*
1937	In first Indian elections under the new constitution of 1935, Congress Party wins c. 50 per cent of seats and forms government in seven of eleven provinces Widespread labour riots in Caribbean colonies (–1938) Burma granted limited self-government Irish Free State renamed Eire with new republican constitution	Narayan, *The Bachelor of Arts*

	HISTORY AND CULTURE	LITERATURE Note: *Titles without annotation are novels unless the title indicates otherwise.*
1938	Continuing Arab revolt in Palestine brutally suppressed by British Treaties with local rulers (–1939) in south Arabian peninsula establish British protectorate of South Arabia Barbados Progressive League (later, Labour Party) established, led by Grantley Adams People's National Party established in Jamaica, led by Norman Manley	James, *The Black Jacobins* (history) Narayan, *The Dark Room* Raja Rao (India), *Kanthapura*
1939	Start of Second World War In India, provincial governments resign in protest at Britain's failure to consult on declaring India at war	Anand, *The Village*
1940	Winston Churchill succeeds Neville Chamberlain as British Prime Minister Trade Unions legalised in Barbados	Stead, *The Man Who Loved Children*
1941	Start of Holocaust Sino-Japanese War Pearl Harbor Allies declare war on Japan Germany and Italy declare war on USA Surrender of Hong Kong to Japanese	
1942	Battle of El Alamein – British forces defeat the Germans in North Africa Jamaica Labour Party founded by Bustamente Japan overruns Singapore, occupies British Malayan territories and Burma (–1945) and reaches eastern borders of India Britain's Sir Stafford Cripps fails to win over Gandhi and Congress with offers of post-war independence; Congress launches Quit India campaign; rebellion is suppressed, Congress banned and Gandhi and other leaders imprisoned (–1944)	
1943	Representation of the People Act in Barbados extends voting rights and enables election of black majority to the (non-executive) Assembly in 1944	
1944	National Congress of Nigeria and Cameroons formed by pro-independence leader Nnamdi Azikiwe Jamaica becomes first Caribbean colony to have a legislature elected by full adult suffrage	Stead, *For Love Alone*
1945	Defeat of Germany and end of War in Europe Atomic bombs dropped on Hiroshima and Nagasaki (respectively, c. 100,000 and c. 75,000 killed at once) End of Second World War; over 5 million people from the dominions and colonies have participated: of these, c. 100,000 died and c. 400,000 wounded Labour form new British government under Clement Attlee; Attlee sets 1948 as date for Indian independence Fifth Pan-African Congress, Manchester, attended by over 200 delegates and leaders-in-exile such as Kwame Nkrumah (Ghana) and Jomo Kenyatta (Kenya); calling for an end to colonial rule, this an important rallying point for independence movements emerging over next two decades Nyasaland African Congress (later Malawi Congress Party) established to press for independence; Hastings Banda to emerge as leading figure In Palestine, armed Zionist campaign against British gathers pace	Narayan, *The English Teacher*

	HISTORY AND CULTURE	LITERATURE Note: *Titles without annotation are novels unless the title indicates otherwise.*
1946	In Barbados, further constitutional reforms give Assembly right to appoint members of British Governor's Executive Committee Jomo Kenyatta returns to Kenya and leads intensifying campaign for land-rights, political representation and equality In India, thousands killed in clashes between Hindus and Muslims in Calcutta and Bombay and, with the security situation rapidly deteriorating, Britain accelerates moves towards Indian independence In Palestine, militant Zionist organisation, the Irgun, bomb British headquarters at King David Hotel, killing 91 people First meeting of United Nations	Peter Abrahams (S. Africa), *Mine Boy* Es'kia Mphahlele (S. Africa), *Man Must Live* (stories) Judith Wright (Australia), *The Moving Image* (poems)
1947	15 August: India and Pakistan become independent; partition causes millions of people to flee their homes and hundreds of thousands are killed in intercommunal violence across northern India Britain refers Palestine mandate back to the United Nations	
1948	Ceylon (Sri Lanka) gains independence; Burma (Myanmar) becomes independent from India Britain withdraws from Palestine; Arab–Israeli war follows and state of Israel established on Israel's victory Riots in Accra on the Gold Coast (Ghana) push Britain to accelerate moves towards independence Assassination of Gandhi by Hindu extremist Federation of Malaya established, including the Straits Settlement (apart from Singapore) – but armed communist insurgency begins shortly afterwards and state of emergency declared (–1960) In Kenya, militant elements of the Kikuyu, frustrated by lack of political progress for land-rights, form underground Land and Freedom Army, later commonly referred to as the 'Mau Mau' Formal end to the title of Emperor/Empress of India used by British monarchs since 1877 British Nationality Act defines all Commonwealth and empire citizens as British subjects; *Empire Windrush* brings first 492 Jamaicans to work in Britain; immigration from the Caribbean and, later, South Asia, grows over next two decades In South Africa, Dr Malan's 'purified' Afrikaner National Party comes to power and inaugurates era of nationwide apartheid with raft of racist segregation laws (many long-established in the Transvaal), including Pass Laws (1952), which prevent free movement of non-whites, and enforcement measures such as the Suppression of Communism Act (1950); ANC becomes an increasingly radical voice of protest from now, led, amongst others, by Nelson Mandela Ibadan University College, Nigeria, founded	G. V. Desani (India), *All About H. Hatterr* Alan Paton (S. Africa), *Cry, the Beloved Country*

	HISTORY AND CULTURE	LITERATURE
		Note: *Titles without annotation are novels unless the title indicates otherwise.*
1949	London Declaration allows for independent republics to remain members of what is now the Commonwealth of Nations (i.e., no longer the 'British Commonwealth') Eire becomes the Irish Republic and leaves Commonwealth Gold Coast Convention People's Party established under leadership of Kwame Nkrumah – calls for rapid move to independence Newfoundland federates with Canada	Nadine Gordimer (S. Africa) *Face to Face* (stories) Narayan, *Mr. Sampath* Vic Reid (Jamaica), *New Day* Wright, *Woman to Man* (poems)
1950	Nkrumah imprisoned as he calls for a campaign of civil disobedience Universal suffrage established in Barbados and Labour Party under Grantley Adams wins majority in first fully representative elections of 1951 In Kenya, the Mau Mau movement is made illegal	Doris Lessing (S. Rhodesia), *The Grass is Singing*
1951	First free elections in the Gold Coast lead to large majority for Convention People's Party; Nkrumah released from prison and shortly becomes Prime Minister ANZUS security pact between Australia, New Zealand and US – reflects changes in post-war world order and in Britain's relations with former colonies	
1952	In Kenya, the Mau Mau begin armed campaign against white settlers and fellow Kikuyu people considered to be collaborating with settler regime; a state of emergency is declared; Jomo Kenyatta is (wrongly) accused of organising the rebellion and is imprisoned (–1961)	Narayan, *The Financial Expert* Samuel Selvon (Trinidad), *A Brighter Sun* Amos Tutuola (Nigeria), *The Palm-Wine Drinkard*
1953	Britain establishes Central African Federation (CAF) to try to force union of the colonies of Southern Rhodesia, Northern Rhodesia and Nyasaland under central government from Salisbury (Harare); strongly resisted by the black majorities of the latter two colonies	Abrahams, *Return to Goli* (autobiography) Nissim Ezekiel (India), *Sixty Poems* Gordimer, *The Lying Days* Attia Hosain (India), *Phoenix Fled and Other Stories* George Lamming (Barbados), *In the Castle of My Skin* Paton, *Too Late the Phalarope*
1954	In preparation for full independence, a transitional constitution is agreed for Nigeria as a federation of three large regions – Northern (predominantly Hausa), Western (predominantly Yoruba) and Eastern (predominantly Igbo) Tanganyika African National Union formed, led by Julius Nyerere	Abrahams, *Tell Freedom* (autobiography) Martin Carter (Guyana), *Poems of Resistance* Cyprian Ekwensi (Nigeria), *People of the City* Lamming, *The Emigrants* Tutuola, *My Life in the Bush of Ghosts*
1955	State of emergency in Cyprus with Greek-Cypriot insurgency seeking union with Greece (–1959)	Carter, *Poems of Shape and Motion* A. D. Hope (Australia), *The Wandering Islands* (poems) Ray Lawler (Australia), *Summer of the Seventeenth Doll* (play) Narayan, *Waiting for the Mahatma* Patrick White (Australia), *The Tree of Man*
1956	Suez crisis: following agreed withdrawal of British troops, Egypt nationalises Suez Canal and Britain attempts to reinvade but forced to withdraw under pressure from US and others In Kenya, main military leader of Mau Mau, Dedan Kimathi, is captured and this effectively ends the war, though state of emergency continues until 1960 In South Africa, Nelson Mandela and other ANC leaders are imprisoned and tried for treason, but case collapses after several years	Abrahams, *A Wreath for Udomo* Selvon, *The Lonely Londoners* Khushwant Singh (India), *Train to Pakistan*

	HISTORY AND CULTURE	LITERATURE Note: *Titles without annotation are novels unless the title indicates otherwise.*
1957	Gold Coast becomes independent as Ghana Malaya gains independence In Aden, Arab nationalist unrest begins (attacks on British troops gradually escalate to emergency of 1965) Britain tests its first nuclear bomb European Economic Community is formed	Janet Frame (New Zealand), *Owls Do Cry* V. S. Naipaul (Trinidad), *The Mystic Masseur* White, *Voss*
1958	British West Indies Federation of island colonies established (dissolved, 1962) Empire Day (24 May) formally renamed as Commonwealth Day (date changed in 1967 and subsequently) Military coup in Pakistan brings Mohammed Ayub Khan to power and begins period of military rule (–1971) In Britain, race riots in Nottingham and Notting Hill Oil discovered in south-eastern region of Nigeria Uganda gains internal self-government	Chinua Achebe (Nigeria), *Things Fall Apart* Errol John (Trinidad), *Moon on a Rainbow Shawl* (play) Dom Moraes (India), *A Beginnning* (poems) Mphahlele, *Down Second Avenue* (autobiography) Narayan, *The Guide* Nayantara Sahgal (India), *A Time to Be Happy*
1959	Major uprising throughout Nyasaland (Malawi) in protest at CAF; state of emergency declared and some fifty people killed by police and over 1000 detained, including Hastings Banda, leader of the Congress Party Kenya: 11 Mau Mau detainees are beaten to death by prison guards at the Hola Camp detention centre Britain establishes South Arabian Federation of Emirates	Geoffrey Drayton (Barbados), *Christopher: A Novel of Childhood in the West Indies* Naipaul, *Miguel Street*
1960	Nigeria gains independence within Commonwealth British Somaliland becomes independent and unites with Italian Somaliland to form Somalia Ghana becomes republic within Commonwealth with Nkrumah as first president Cyprus becomes independent republic within Commonwealth with Britain retaining military bases on the island Sharpeville Massacre in South Africa as police fire on anti-Pass Laws protesters at township near Johannesburg, killing some 67 people and wounding around 200; the South African government makes ANC illegal and most leaders are soon exiled or imprisoned In Nyasaland, state of emergency lifted and Banda released; he now plays central role in dissolution of CAF and in securing independence for Nyasaland; in Northern Rhodesia (Zambia), the leading voice against CAF, Kenneth Kaunda (also recently released from prison) founds the United National Independence Party State of emergency in Kenya ends; thousands have been killed during this period (mainly Africans), and possibly as many as 150,000 have been held in British detention camps where torture has been rife; first moves towards Kenyan independence are agreed at Lancaster House conference in London; trade unionists Tom Mboya and Oginga Odinga establish Kenya African National Union (KANU) as main independence party Uganda People's Congress formed, led by Milton Obote	Achebe, *No Longer at Ease* Anand, *The Woman and the Cow* (reissued as *Gauri* 1976) Wilson Harris (Guyana), *The Palace of the Peacock* (first of a 'Guyana Quartet') Margaret Laurence (Canada), *This Side Jordan* Dom Moraes, *Poems* Andrew Salkey (Jamaica), *Escape to an Autumn Pavement*

	HISTORY AND CULTURE	LITERATURE Note: *Titles without annotation are novels unless the title indicates otherwise.*
1961	Sierra Leone and Tanganyika become independent South Africa leaves Commonwealth and becomes a republic, determined to preserve minority white rule and system of apartheid in face of sustained condemnation by Commonwealth and UN over past decade; ANC now changes policy of passive resistance to one of strategic armed struggle In Southern Rhodesia, resistance to apartheid-style government of white settler regime gathers pace from now with founding of Zimbabwe African People's Union (ZAPU) by Joshua Nkomo in1961 and of more militant Zimbabwe African National Union (ZANU) by Revd. N. Sithole and Robert Mugabe in 1963; both organisations soon banned and leaders imprisoned Jomo Kenyatta released from prison and becomes leader of KANU Abortive US invasion of Cuba	Carter, *Conversations* Ekwensi, *Jagua Nana* Frame, *Faces in the Water* Hosain, *Sunlight on a Broken Column* Mphahlele, *The Living and the Dead* (stories) Naipaul, *A House for Mr. Biswas* Narayan, *The Man-Eater of Malgudi* White, *Riders in the Chariot*
1962	Jamaica, Trinidad & Tobago and Uganda become independent Kenyatta leads delegation to London to negotiate new constitution for Kenya Tanganyika becomes republic with Julius Nyerere as first President Commonwealth Immigration Act ends the right of free entry to Britain of Commonwealth citizens US–Soviet Cuban missile crisis	Achebe, *The Sacrificial Egg and Other Stories* Ekwensi, *Burning Grass* Frame, *The Edge of the Alphabet* Alex La Guma (S. Africa), *A Walk in the Night* (stories) Mphahlele, *The African Image* (criticism) Christopher Okigbo (Nigeria), *Heavensgate* (poems) Derek Walcott (St. Lucia), *In a Green Night* (poems)
1963	Organisation of African Unity founded (becomes African Union in 2001) KANU wins first fully representative elections in Kenya and Kenyatta becomes Prime Minister; Kenya now gains full independence and becomes a republic in 1964 Nigeria becomes a republic with Dr Nnamdi Azikiwe its first President In South Africa, Nelson Mandela and other ANC leaders are put on trial; he and others are sentenced to life imprisonment in 1964 CAF dissolved as Nyasaland and Northern Rhodesia secede; the independence parties in both countries, led by Hastings Banda and Kenneth Kaunda respectively, gain clear majorities at free elections and new constitutions are agreed for their countries' independence Malaya joins with Singapore, North Borneo and Sarawak to form Malaysia Aden becomes part of South Arabian Federation Uganda becomes a republic with the hereditary ruler of Buganda, Sir Edward Mutesa, as president	Dennis Brutus (S. Africa), *Sirens Knuckles Boots* (poems) Carter, *Jail Me Quickly* Anita Desai (India), *Cry the Peacock* Athol Fugard (S. Africa), *Blood Knot* (play) Gordimer, *Occasion for Loving* Naipaul, *Mr Stone and the Knights Companion* Hal Porter (Australia), *The Watcher on the Cast-Iron Balcony* (memoir) Wole Soyinka (Nigeria), plays, *A Dance of the Forests, The Lion and the Jewel, Three Short Plays*
1964	Malta, Zambia and Malawi become independent Republic of Tanzania formed from union of Tanganyika and Zanzibar In (Southern) Rhodesia, Joshua Nkomo and Robert Mugabe are imprisoned (–1974)	Achebe, *Arrow of God* La Guma, *And a Threefold Cord* Laurence, *The Stone Angel* Ngugi wa Thiong'o (Kenya), *Weep Not, Child* Gabriel Okara (Nigeria), *The Voice* Selvon, *The Housing Lark*

HISTORY AND CULTURE	LITERATURE Note: *Titles without annotation are novels unless the title indicates otherwise.*
1965 The Gambia and the Maldives become independent; Singapore secedes from Malaysia and becomes independent state Island dependencies of Mauritius and the Seychelles come under British administration as British Indian Ocean Territory Unilateral Declaration of Independence (UDI) by government of Rhodesia, led by Ian Smith and right-wing Rhodesian Front who reject Britain's conditions for independence (i.e., democratic majority rule and racial integration); UDI deemed illegal by Britain and the UN and sanctions imposed from 1966, with support from rest of Commonwealth Emergency in Aden and South Arabia as armed insurgency by Arab nationalists intensifies (–1967)	Ama Ata Aidoo (Ghana), *The Dilemma of a Ghost* (play) Michael Anthony (Trinidad), *The Year in San Fernando* Desai, *Voices in the City* Ezekiel, *The Exact Man* (poems) Tsegaye Gabre-Medhin (Ethiopia), *Oda-Oak Oracle* (play) Modrooroo/Colin Johnson (Australia), *Wild Cat Falling* Ngugi, *The River Between* Soyinka, *The Road* (play), *The Interpreters* Walcott, *The Castaway* (poems) White, *Four Plays*
1966 Barbados, Basutoland (as Lesotho), Bechuanaland (as Botswana) and British Guiana (as Guyana) become independent British Colonial Office merged into Commonwealth Office In Ghana, military coup overthrows Nkrumah's government while he is out of country; he remains in exile until his death in 1972; military rule continues until 1969 Indira Gandhi becomes Prime Minister of India In Nigeria, complex political and inter-regional tensions have been mounting since independence and come to a head with an attempted military coup in which Prime Minister Balewa and other government figures are killed; a counter coup follows and Colonel (later General) Gowon emerges as head of a military government; the situation deteriorates even further as intercommunal violence erupts in the north with the massacre of thousands of easterners In Kenya, constitutional changes move country towards one-party rule by Kenyatta's KANU In Uganda, President Mutesa is ousted by Prime Minister Milton Obote, who now becomes President and ends the autonomy of Buganda in a new constitution (–1967)	Achebe, *A Man of the People* Elechi Amadi (Nigeria), *The Concubine* Ekwensi, *Iska* Fugard, *Hello and Goodbye* (play) Gordimer, *The Late Bourgeois World* Hope, *Collected Poems 1930–65* Flora Nwapa (Nigeria), *Efuru* Grace Ogot (Kenya), *The Promised Land* Okot p'Bitek (Uganda), *Song of Lawino* (poems) Jean Rhys, *Wide Sargasso Sea* White, *The Solid Mandala* Wright, *The Other Half* (poems)
1967 British troops withdraw from Aden and South Arabian Federation which become an independent republic as South Yemen (this, in 1990, unites with North Yemen to form Republic of Yemen) In Nigeria, three eastern states secede from federation as Biafra and civil war breaks out (–1970); writer Wole Soyinka imprisoned for opposing war (–1969) Aborigines granted citizenship in Australia after referendum	Anthony, *Green Days by the River* (Edward) Kamau Brathwaite (Barbados), *Rights of Passage* (poems) Kamala Das (India), *The Descendants* (poems) Mphahlele, *In Corner B* (stories) Naipaul, *The Mimic Men* Narayan, *The Vendor of Sweets* Ngugi, *A Grain of Wheat* David Rubadiri (Malawi), *No Bride Price* Soyinka, *Idanre and Other Poems*, *Kongi's Harvest* (play)

HISTORY AND CULTURE	LITERATURE Note: *Titles without annotation are novels unless the title indicates otherwise.*
1968	Mauritius and Swaziland become independent Caribbean Free Trade Area (CARIFTA) established among Commonwealth countries; forerunner to Caribbean Community (CARICOM) established 1973 In federal Nigeria, political reforms are introduced to address perceived causes of civil war, including reorganising federation into twelve smaller states with devolved governments In South Africa, anti-apartheid activist Steve Biko establishes South African Students' Organisation, a proving ground for development of influential 1970s Black Consciousness movement	Margaret Atwood (Canada), *The Animals in that Country* (poems) Ayi Kwei Armah (Ghana), *The Beautiful Ones Are Not Yet Born* Brathwaite, *Masks* (poems) Brutus, *Letters to Martha and Other Poems from a South African Prison* Frame, *The Rainbirds* Alice Munro (Canada), *Dance of the Happy Shades* (stories) Ogot, *Land Without Thunder* (stories) Peter Palangyo (Tanzania), *Dying in the Sun*
1969	In Kenya, the murder of prominent politician, Tom Mboya, nearly sparks civil war Ghana: civilian rule returns with election of President Kofi Busia Northern Ireland 'troubles' begin In Somalia, dictatorship of General Siyad Barre begins (−1991)	Amadi, *The Great Ponds* Atwood, *The Edible Woman* Brathwaite, *Islands* (poems) Ezekiel, *Three Plays* Fugard, *Boesman and Lena* (play) Bessie Head (S. Africa/Botswana), *When Rain Clouds Gather* Taban lo Liyong (Uganda), *Fixions and Other Stories* Ian McDonald (Trinidad/Guyana), *The Hummingbird Tree* Mphahlele, *The Wanderers* Les Murray (Australia), *The Weatherboard Cathedral* (poems) Sahgal, *Storm in Chandigargh* Sahle Sellassie (Ethiopia), *The Afersata: An Ethiopian Novel* Robert Serumaga (Uganda), *Return to the Shadows* Walcott, *The Gulf* (poems)
1970	Fiji becomes independent Civil war ends in Nigeria as Biafra surrenders and is reintegrated into twelve-state federal republic Rhodesia declares itself a republic and continues to follow lines of South Africa's apartheid regime	Aidoo, *Anowa* (play) Jared Angira (Kenya), *Juices,* (poems) Armah, *Fragments* Nuruddin Farah (Somalia), *From a Crooked Rib* Harris, *Ascent to Omai* Merle Hodge (Trinidad), *Crick Crack, Monkey* Nwapa, *Idu* p'Bitek, *Song of Ocol* Walcott, *Dream on Monkey Mountain and Other Plays* White, *The Vivisector*
1971	Bangladesh becomes independent from Pakistan; civil war and then Indo-Pakistan war follow; defeat for Pakistan leads to end of military rule there and elections bring Zulfikar Ali Bhutto to power Uganda: President Obote overthrown in military coup by General Idi Amin and nine years of brutal dictatorship follow	Achebe, *Beware, Soul Brother* (poems) Aidoo, *No Sweetness Here* (stories) Kofi Awoonor (Ghana), *Night of My Blood* (poems); *This Earth, My Brother* Desai, *Bye-Bye Blackbird* Head, *Maru* Munro, *Lives of Girls and Women* Okigbo, *Labyrinths* p'Bitek, *Two Songs* Naipaul, *In a Free State* Soyinka, *Madmen and Specialists* (play) Wright, *Collected Poems*

	HISTORY AND CULTURE	LITERATURE Note: *Titles without annotation are novels unless the title indicates otherwise.*
1972	Sheikh Mujibur Rahman becomes first prime minister of Bangladesh Guerrilla warfare against white rule intensifies in Rhodesia President Kaunda of Zambia suspends constitution and creates one-party state under United National Independence Party Ghana: military coup ousts President Busia In Uganda, the Amin regime summarily expels some 60,000 Asians, without any compensation; Uganda is expelled from the Commonwealth	Achebe, *Girls at War and Other Stories* Angira, *Silent Voices* (poems) Armah, *Why Are We So Blest?* Atwood, *Surfacing* Buchi Emecheta (Nigeria/UK), *In the Ditch* (essays) Witi Ihimaera (New Zealand), *Pounamu Pounamu* Joe de Graft (Ghana), *Muntu* (play) Thomas Keneally (Australia), *The Chant of Jimmie Blacksmith* Mphahlele, *Voices in the Whirlwind* (criticism) Murray, *Poems against Economics* Peter Nazareth (Uganda), *In a Brown Mantle* John Ruganda (Uganda), *The Burdens* (play) Soyinka, *The Man Died, Prison Notes*
1973	Bahamas become independent Caribbean Community (CARICOM) established as a common market and for liaising with international organisations such as the European Union Britain joins European Union	Anthony, *Cricket in the Road and Other Stories* Armah, *Two Thousand Seasons* Brathwaite, *The Arrivants* (poems) Das, *The Old Playhouse and Other Poems* Head, *A Question of Power* Meja Mwangi (Kenya), *Kill Me Quick* Danichew Worku (Ethiopia), *The Thirteenth Sun* Soyinka, *Season of Anomy* Walcott, *Another Life* White, *The Eye of the Storm*
1974	Grenada becomes independent In Cyprus, abortive coup by Greek nationalists followed by invasion of northern Cyprus by Turkey and, in 1975, the proclamation of a Turkish Cypriot Federation In Rhodesia, the recently released Joshua Nkomo and Robert Mugabe lead guerrilla armies from neighbouring Zambia and Mozambique in sustained war of liberation against Smith regime (–1979)	Thea Astley (Australia), *The Kindness Cup* André Brink (S. Africa), *Looking on Darkness* J. M. Coetzee (S. Africa), *Dusklands* Fugard, *Statements* (three plays: *Sizwe Bansi is Dead* (1972), *Statements after an Arrest under the Morality Act, The Island*) Gordimer, *The Conservationist* Ihimaera, *Whanau* Munro, *Something I've Been Meaning to Tell You* (stories) Mwangi, *Carcase for Hounds* Sellassie, *Warrior King* Serumaga, *The Elephants* (play) Soyinka, *Collected Plays* (2 vols)
1975	Lomé Convention, first in series of special agreements for trade and aid between EU and Commonwealth nations of Africa, Caribbean and Pacific (further agreements, 1979, 1984, 1989) Military coup in Bangladesh and murder of Prime Minister Rahman State of emergency declared in India by Indira Gandhi (–1977) Military coup in Nigeria as General Gowon is ousted by Brigadier Murtala Mohammed; his government reorganises the federation into nineteen states Racial Discrimination Act in Australia ends 'White Australia' policy begun in 1901	Achebe, *Morning Yet on Creation Day: Essays* Jessica Anderson (Australia), *The Commandant* Desai, *Where Shall We Go This Summer?* Hope, *A Late Picking: Poems 1965–74* Ruth Prawer Jhabvala (India), *Heat and Dust* Linton Kwesi Johnson (Jamaica/UK), *Dread Beat and Blood* (poems; on disc, 1978) David Malouf (Australia), *Johnno* Mwangi, *Taste of Death* Nwapa, *Never Again* Salman Rushdie (India), *Grimus* Selvon, *Moses Ascending* Soyinka, *Death and the King's Horseman* (play)

	HISTORY AND CULTURE	LITERATURE
		Note: *Titles without annotation are novels unless the title indicates otherwise.*
1976	Seychelles becomes independent and regains islands of British Indian Ocean Territory (apart from the Chagos islands) In South Africa, large anti-government demonstrations in the black township of Soweto, near Johannesburg, fired on by police with hundreds of people killed and over a thousand injured; protests spread throughout the country Nigerian military leader Brigadier Mohammed assassinated in failed coup attempt; replaced by Lieutenant-General Olusegun Obasanjo who begins gradual process of return to civilian rule (–1979)	Ekwensi, *Survive the Peace* Emecheta, *Bride Price* Ezekiel, *Hymns in Darkness* (poems) Farah, *A Naked Needle* Mwangi, *Going Down River Road* Murray, *Selected Poems* Narayan, *The Painter of Signs* Ngugi *The Trial of Dedan Kimathi* (play co-authored with Micere Githae Mugo) Rebecca Njau (Kenya), *Ripples in the Pool* Ogot, *The Other Woman* Soyinka, *Ogun Abibiman* (long poem), *Myth, Literature and the African World* (essays) Walcott, *Sea Grapes* (poems) White, *A Fringe of Leaves*
1977	Death of Steve Biko in police custody further galvanises anti-apartheid militancy within South Africa and strengthens international calls for tougher sanctions against government In India, Gandhi and Congress Party defeated in elections for first time since independence In Kenya, President Jomo Kenyatta dies and is succeeded by Daniel arap Moi (who will remain in power until 2002) Military coup in Pakistan brings General Zia-ul-Haq to power	Aidoo, *Our Sister Killjoy* Brathwaite, *Mother Poem* Carter, *Poems of Succession* Desai, *Fire on the Mountain* Gabre-Medhin, *Collision of Altars* (play) Helen Garner (Australia), *Monkey Grip* Head, *The Collector of Treasures and Other Botswana Village Tales* Ihimaera, *The New Net Goes Fishing* (stories) Ngugi, *Petals of Blood*
1978	Dominica, Solomon Islands, and Ellice Islands (as Tuvalu) become independent Ian Smith's Rhodesian Front government concedes need to negotiate settlement to civil war; agrees elections for transitional government but these are boycotted by ZANU and ZAPU; a new government led by Bishop Abel Muzorewa is set up but not recognised internationally; the war continues until following year Edward Said, *Orientalism*	Amadi, *The Slave* Anderson, *Tirra Lirra by the River* Desai, *Games at Twilight and Other Stories* Fugard, *Orestes* (play) Malouf, *An Imaginary Life* Okara, *The Fisherman's Invocation* (poems) Ngugi imprisoned in Kenya and later deported Walcott, *The Joker of Seville and O Babylon* (plays)
1979	St Lucia, St Vincent & Grenadines, and Gilbert Islands (as Kiribati) become independent Rhodesia–Zimbabwe peace talks at Lancaster House in London which lead to all-party agreement and a new constitution, with elections scheduled for 1980 Ghana: government ousted by military council led by Flight Lt. Jerry Rawlings; Dr H. Limann then elected as head of state Nigeria: civilian rule restored with election of President Alhaji Shehu Shagari Tanzanian and Kenyan forces invade Uganda and help in overthrow of Idi Amin; elections in 1980 return Milton Obote to presidency	Brathwaite, *Soweto* (poems) Brink, *A Dry White Season* Emecheta, *The Joys of Motherhood* Farah, *Sweet and Sour Milk* Gordimer, *Burger's Daughter* Festus Iyayi (Nigeria), *Violence* La Guma, *Time of the Butcherbird* Earl Lovelace (Trinidad), *The Dragon Can't Dance; The Wine of Astonishment* Dambudzo Marechera (Zimbabwe), *The House of Hunger* (stories) Mphahlele, *Chirundu* David Mulwa (Kenya), *Master and Servant* Naipaul, *A Bend in the River* Walcott, *The Star-Apple Kingdom* (poems)

	HISTORY AND CULTURE	LITERATURE
		Note: *Titles without annotation are novels unless the title indicates otherwise.*
1980	Antigua and Vanuatu become independent	Coetzee, *Waiting for the Barbarians*
	ZANU wins first Zimbabwe election and Robert Mugabe	Desai, *Clear Light of Day*
	becomes Prime Minister of newly independent nation	Ekwensi, *Divided We Stand*
	Serious sectarian unrest in northern Kano region of	L. K. Johnson, *Inglan is a Bitch* (poems)
	Nigeria suppressed by federal troops, with c. 1,000 people	Marechera, *Black Sunlight*
	killed	Murray, *The Boys Who Stole the Funeral* (poems)
		Ogot, *The Graduate; The Island of Tears*
		Caryl Phillips, *Strange Fruit*
1981	Belize (British Honduras) becomes independent	Farah, *Sardines*
	Ghana: Jerry Rawlings seizes power in his second military	Frame, *Living in the Maniototo*
	coup	Fugard, *A Lesson from Aloes* (play)
	Nigeria: oil slump and economic austerity measures	Gordimer, *July's People*
	introduced	Head, *Serowe: Village of the Rain Wind* (social history)
		Malouf, *Selected Poems*
		Jack Mapanje, *Of Chameleons and Gods* (poems)
		Mphahlele, *The Unbroken Song* (stories)
		Ngugi, *Detained: A Writer's Prison Diary; Writers in Politics: Essays*
		Nwapa, *One Is Enough*
		Lenrie Peters (Gambia), *Selected Poetry*
		Rushdie, *Midnight's Children*
		Soyinka, *Opera Wonyosi* (Brechtian musical play), *Aké: the Years of Childhood* (autobiography)
		Tutuola, *The Witch-Herbalist of the Remote Town*
		Walcott, *The Fortunate Traveller* (poems)
		Archie Weller (Australia), *The Day of the Dog*
		Wright, *The Cry for the Dead* (poems)
		White, *Flaws in the Glass*
1982	Falklands War	Brathwaite, *Sun Poem*
	Abortive military coup in Kenya leads to state clamp-	Brink, *A Chain of Voices*
	down, banning of opposition parties, and consolidation of	Keneally, *Schindler's Ark*
	autocratic rule by President Moi	Narayan, *Malgudi Days* (stories)
	Joshua Nkomo sacked from Robert Mugabe's govern-	Ngugi, *Devil on the Cross* (originally written in Gikuyu,
	ment in Zimbabwe; rebellion by pro-Nkomo supporters	1980, translated by Ngugi)
	suppressed by government forces	Michael ('Mikey') Smith (Jamaica), *Mi Cyaan Believe It* (recorded album of dub poetry)
1983	St Kitts & Nevis become independent	Achebe, *The Trouble With Nigeria*
	President Shagari re-elected in Nigeria, but Major-General	Brathwaite, *Third World Poems*
	Muhammad Buhari seizes power in bloodless military	Coetzee, *The Life and Times of Michael K*
	coup	Shashi Deshpande (India), *Roots and Shadows*
	Turkish Republic of Northern Cyprus proclaimed but not	Ezekiel, *Latter Day Psalms* (poems)
	recognised internationally	Farah, *Close Sesame*
		Jamaica Kincaid (Antigua), *At the Bottom of the River*
		Narayan, *A Tiger for Malgudi*
		Grace Nichols (Guyana/UK), *i is a long memoried woman* (poems)
		Rushdie, *Shame*
		Selvon, *Moses Migrating*

	HISTORY AND CULTURE	LITERATURE Note: *Titles without annotation are novels unless the title indicates otherwise.*
1984	Major confrontation between Indian army and Sikh extremists in Amritsar; Indira Gandhi assassinated later in year	Desai, *In Custody* Farah, *Maps* Head, *A Bewitched Crossroad: An African Saga* Nichols, *The Fat Black Woman's Poems* Soyinka, *A Play of Giants* (play) Walcott, *Midsummer* (poems)
1985	Famine in Ethiopia kills c. 500,000 Another coup in Nigeria, as Ibrahim Babangida seizes power (Nigeria then remains under military rule until 1999) In Tanzania, President Nyerere retires, replaced by President Ali Hasan Mwinyi Military coup in Uganda deposes President Obote	Aidoo, *Someone Talking to Sometime* (poems) Zaynab Alkali (Nigeria), *The Stillborn* Atwood, *The Handmaid's Tale* Peter Carey (Australia), *Illywhacker* Jack Davis (Australia) *No Sugar* Fred D'Aguiar (Guyana/UK), *Mama Dot* (poems) Harris, *Carnival* (first of 'Carnival' trilogy of novels) Keri Hulme (New Zealand), *The Bone People* Amryl Johnson (Trinidad/UK), *Long Road to Nowhere* (poems) Kincaid, *Annie John* Caryl Phillips (St Kitts/UK), *The Final Passage* Sahgal, *Rich Like Us* Ken Saro-Wiwa, *Sozaboy: A Novel in Rotten English* Walcott, *Collected Poems 1948–84*
1986	Further coup in Uganda and Yoweri Museveni installed as president	Brathwaite, *Jah Music* (poems) Coetzee, *Foe* Ekwensi, *Jagua Nana's Daughter* Amitav Ghosh (India), *The Circle of Reason* Lorna Goodison (Jamaica), *I Am Becoming My Mother* (poems) Iyayi, *Heroes* B. Kojo Laing (Ghana), *Search Sweet Country* Adewale Maja-Pearce (Nigeria), *Loyalties and Other Stories* Marjorie O. Macgoye (Kenya), *Coming to Birth* Nichols, *Whole of a Morning Sky* Ngugi, *Decolonising the Mind (polemic)* Nwapa, *Women Are Different* Ben Okri (Nigeria/Britain), *Incidents at the Shrine* (stories) Niyi Osundare (Nigeria), *The Eye of the Earth* (poems) Michael Smith, *It a Come* (poems) Stead, *I'm Dying Laughing* Tutuola, *Yoruba Folktales* Wole Soyinka wins Nobel Prize for Literature
1987	In Zimbabwe, Mugabe and Nkomo merge rival parties to form single ZANU-PF; constitution changed to create executive presidency: Mugabe elected to this position and Nkomo becomes a vice-president	Achebe, *Anthills of the Savannah* Abdulrazak Gurnah (Tanzania/Britain), *Memory of Departure* Awoonor, *Until the Morning After: Collected Poems* Brathwaite, *X/Self* (poems) Dom Moraes, *Collected Poems 1957–1987* Keneally, *The Playmaker* Naipaul, *The Enigma of Arrival* Tutuola, *Pauper, Brawler, and Slanderer* Walcott, *The Arkansas Testament* (poems)

	HISTORY AND CULTURE	LITERATURE Note: *Titles without annotation are novels unless the title indicates otherwise.*
1988	Burma changes name to Myanmar Pakistan returns to civilian rule with election of Benazir Bhutto	Achebe, *Hopes and Impediments: Selected Essays 1965–1987* Jean 'Binta' Breeze (Jamaica), *Riddym Ravings* (poems) Brink, *States of Emergency* Carey, *Oscar and Lucinda* Tsitsi Dangarembga (Zimbabwe), *Nervous Conditions* Deshpande, *The Long Silence* Fugard, *A Place with the Pigs* (play) Ghosh, *The Shadow Lines* Gordimer, *The Essential Gesture* (criticism) Kate Grenville (Australia), *Joan Makes History* Gurnah, *Pilgrim's Way* A. Johnson, *Sequins for a Ragged Hem* (travel) Laing, *Woman of the Aeroplanes* Mphahlele, *Renewal Time* (stories) Rushdie, *The Satanic Verses* Sahgal, *Mistaken Identity* Bapsi Sidhwa (Pakistan/US), *Ice-Candy-Man* Soyinka, *Mandela's Earth and Other Poems*
1989	Revolutions in Eastern Europe and continuing liberalisation in USSR signal end of the Cold War P. W. Botha resigns as President of South Africa and is replaced by F. W. de Klerk who embarks on programme of reform that will lead to dismantling of apartheid system	Brutus, *Airs and Tributes* (poems) Shimmer Chinodya (Zimbabwe) *Harvest of Thorns* D'Aguiar, *Airy Hall* (poems) Laing, *Godhorse* (poems) Gita Mehta (India), *Raj* Narayan, *A Story-Teller's World: Stories, Essays, Sketches* Nichols, *Lazy Thoughts of a Lazy Woman* (poems) M. G. Vassanji (Kenya/Tanzania/Canada), *The Gunny Sack*
1990	Release of Nelson Mandela (11 February) and unbanning of ANC and other opposition groups in South Africa signals end of apartheid era and beginning of process towards fully representative democracy	Brathwaite, *Shar/Hurricane Poem* Brink, *An Act of Terror* Syl Cheney-Coker (Sierra Leone), *The Last Harmattan of Alusine Dunbar* Fugard, *My Children! My Africa!* (play) Gurnah, *Dottie* Head, *Tales of Tenderness and Power* Kincaid, *Lucy* Tutuola, *The Village Witch Doctor and Other Stories* Walcott, *Omeros* (epic poem)
1991	Multi-party constitution re-established in Zambia and Frederick Chiluba elected president	Aidoo, *Changes: A Love Story* Nadine Gordimer wins Nobel Prize Okri, *The Famished Road* Rushdie, *Imaginary Homelands: Essays and Criticism* Vassanji, *No New Land* Tim Winton (Australia), *Cloudstreet*

	HISTORY AND CULTURE	LITERATURE Note: *Titles without annotation are novels unless the title indicates otherwise.*
1992	Multi-party democracy partially restored in Kenya: President Moi returned to power for fourth term Ghana: military rule ends and Jerry Rawlings elected President Tanzania: multi-party elections introduced	Aidoo, *An Angry Letter in January and Other Poems* Awoonor, *Comes the Voyager at Last* Brathwaite, *Middle Passages* (poems) Breeze, *Spring Cleaning* (poems) Ekwensi, *King Forever!* Gordimer, *Why Haven't You Written: Selected Stories 1950–72* Murray, *Translations from the Natural World* (poems) Michael Ondaatje (Sri Lanka/Canada), *The English Patient* Soyinka, *From Zia, with Love* (play) Vassanji, *Uhuru Street* (stories) Yvonne Vera (Zimbabwe), *Why Don't You Carve Other Animals?* (stories)
1993	Nigeria: Chief Moshood Abiola claims victory in elections, but military declares results invalid; despite general strikes and protests in favour of Chief Abiola, General Sani Abacha seizes power, suppresses opposition and begins period of autocratic rule; Abiola is arrested in 1994 and dies in prison in 1998 Nelson Mandela and F. W. de Klerk share Nobel Peace Prize In Australia, the Native Title Act formally recognises Aboriginal land rights following a high-court ruling in 1992 that such rights were in existence in 1788 (something always previously denied)	Brutus, *Still the Sirens* (poems) D'Aguiar, *British Subjects* (poems) Mehta, *A River Sutra* Farah, *Gifts* Malouf, *Rembering Babylon* Phillips, *Crossing the River* Sidhwa, *An American Brat* Vera, *Nehanda* Walcott, *The Odyssey* (play) Derek Walcott wins Nobel Prize
1994	First fully democratic multi-racial elections in South Africa give clear victory to the ANC: Nelson Mandela becomes President Civil war in Yemen Northern Ireland Peace Process begins	Anderson, *One of the Wattle Birds* Brathwaite, *Barabajan Poems* D'Aguiar, *The Longest Memory* Emecheta, *Kehinde* Romesh Gunesekera, *Reef* Gurnah, *Paradise* Rushdie, *East, West* (stories) Vassanji, *The Book of Secrets* Vera, *Without a Name*
1995	Nigeria: Abacha military government executes Ogoni civil and environmental rights activists, including writer Ken Saro-Wiwa; sanctions imposed by EU and Nigeria expelled from Commonwealth (−1998)	Rushdie, *The Moor's Last Sigh* Carey, *The Unusual Life of Tristram Smith*
1996	In Uganda first direct elections for president return President Museveni to power	Aidoo, *The Girl Who Can and Other Stories* Angira, *Tides of Time: Selected Poems* Atwood, *Alias Grace* Breeze, *Riding on de Riddym* (poems) Gurnah, *Admiring Silence*
1997	Britain returns Hong Kong and New Territories to China; Britain retains some small territorial dependencies overseas, but this hand-over generally seen as the final act of the British empire	Carey, *Jack Maggs* Carter, *Selected Poems* Vikram Chandra (India), *Love and Longing in Bombay* Richard Flanagan (Australia), *The Sound of One Hand Clapping* Kincaid, *The Autobiography of My Mother* Mehta, *Snakes and Ladders: A View of Modern India* Phillips, *The Nature of Blood* Arundhati Roy (India), *The God of Small Things* Walcott, *The Bounty* (poems)
	Entries for this column end here	

HISTORY AND CULTURE	LITERATURE Note: *Titles without annotation are novels unless the title indicates otherwise.*
1998	D'Aguiar, *Bill of Rights* (poems) Murray Bail (Australia), *Eucalyptus* Kiran Desai (India), *Hullabaloo in the Guava Orchard* Farah, *Secrets* Eva Sallis (Australia), *Hiam* Vera, *Butterfly Burning* Walcott, *What the Twilight Says* (essays) Weller, *Land of the Golden Cloud*
1999	Astley, *Drylands* Coetzee, *Disgrace* Anita Desai, *Fasting, Feasting* Grenville, *The Idea of Perfection* Rushdie, *The Ground Beneath Her Feet*
2000	Achebe, *Home and Exile* (essays) Atwood, *The Blind Assassin* Brathwaite, *Words Need Love Too* (poems) Breeze, *The Arrival of Brighteye* (poems) D'Aguiar, *Bloodlines* (poems) Ghosh, *The Glass Palace* Jhumpa Lahiri (India/UK/US), *Interpreter of Maladies* (stories) Ondaatje, *Anil's Ghost* Osundare, *The Word is an Egg* (poems) Walcott, *Tiepolo's Hound* (poems)
2001	Brathwaite, *Ancestors* (poems) D'Aguiar, *An English Sampler: New and Selected Poems* Gurnah, *By the Sea* Naipaul, *Half a Life* Naipaul wins Nobel Prize
2002	Coetzee, *Youth* L. K. Johnson, *Mi Revalueshanaray Fren: Selected Poems* Murray, *Poems the Size of Photographs*
2003	Chimamanda Ngozi Adichie (Nigeria/US), *Purple Hibiscus* J. M. Coetzee wins Nobel Prize Gordimer, *Loot and Other Stories* Lahiri, *The Namesake* Phillips, *Distant Shore* Sahgal, *Lesser Breeds*
2004	Achebe, *Collected Poems* Ghosh, *The Hungry Tide* Andrea Levy (UK/Jamaica), *Small Island* Naipaul, *Magic Seeds* Walcott, *The Prodigal: A Poem*
2005	Brathwaite, *Born to Slow Horses* (poems) Coetzee, *Slow Man* Gurnah, *Desertion* Phillips, *Dancing in the Dark* Rushdie, *Shalimar the Clown*

HISTORY AND CULTURE	LITERATURE Note: *Titles without annotation are novels unless the title indicates otherwise.*
2006	Adichie, *Half of a Yellow Sun* Kiran Desai, *The Inheritance of Loss* Sidhwa, *Water: A Novel* Breeze, *The Fifth Figure* (poems) Dangarembga, *The Book of Not*
2007	Chinua Achebe wins Man Booker International Prize
2008	Aravind Adiga (India), *The White Tiger* Cheney-Coker, *Stone Child and Other Poems* Ghosh, *Sea of Poppies* Lahiri, *Unaccustomed Earth* (stories)
2009	Achebe, *The Education of a British-Protected Child* (memoir) Adichie, *The Thing Around Your Neck* (stories) Ngugi, *Something Torn and New: An African Renaissance* (polemic)
2010	Brathwaite, *Elegguan* (poems) Walcott, *White Egrets* (poems)
2011	Breeze, *Third World Girl: Selected Poems* (with DVD of live performance) Ghosh, *River of Smoke*
2012	Achebe, *There Was a Country: A Personal History of Biafra* Soyinka, *Of Africa* (polemic)
2013	Adichie, *Americanah* NoViolet Bulawayo (Zimbabwe/US), *We Need New Names* Eleanor Catton (New Zealand), *The Luminaries*. Lahiri, *The Lowland*
2014	Flanagan, *The Narrow Road to the Deep North* Walcott, *The Poetry of Derek Walcott, 1948–2013*
2015	Ghosh, *Flood of Fire* Marlon James (Jamaica), *A History of Seven Killings* (winner of Man Booker Prize)

Historical Overview

The Compass of the British Empire

In the first half of the twentieth century almost every schoolchild in the British empire would have been familiar with some such map as the one presented here (Figure 8.1). Famously painted red or pink in coloured prints, Britain's territories would have stood out immediately as a dominant block of colour, clearly proclaiming Britain's pre-eminence as a world power. Around a fifth of the world's land surface was map-red for most of that half-century and this encompassed about a quarter of the world's population. In 1913, for example, this equated, roughly, to 11.5 million square miles of land and 421 million people. Clearly, though, one needs only to ponder those two statistics for a moment to realise that such a blanket representation

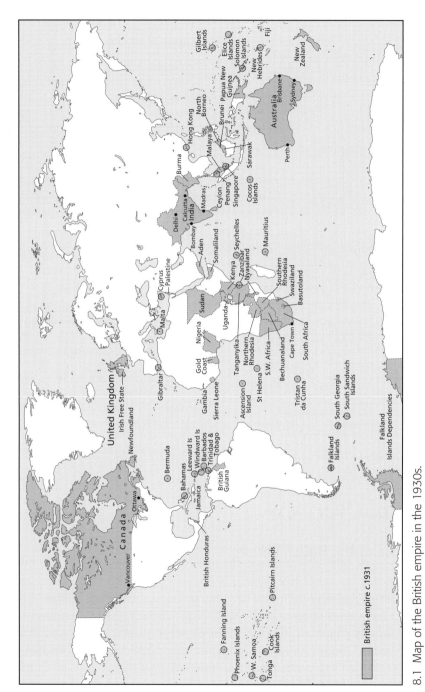

8.1 Map of the British empire in the 1930s.

of the empire quite obviously smooths over a huge degree of variation and diversity in terms of peoples, cultures and geographical terrain and that it inevitably presents a very deceptive sense of unity and homogeneity across all the red-coloured areas. 'Imperialist' maps like this began to circulate widely only in the late nineteenth century during a relatively short-lived period of heightened enthusiasm for the empire in Britain – sometimes referred to as the 'Age of Imperialism' (roughly 1870–1914) – but, without comparative maps from other periods in the empire's long and complex history, such a map might also project a deceptive sense of stability, perhaps even of permanence, in the borders of the empire. In fact, those borders were rarely constant throughout the empire's history and they certainly changed significantly during the first half of the twentieth century, before effectively fading away altogether in its second half.

The British empire's complexity at any particular time, and its great variability over some four centuries, are thus fundamental points to note from the outset, and ones that should always temper any summary judgements or generalisations on the topic (including any that might appear here, of course). The protean nature of the empire is neatly evoked by Keith Robbins, when he writes that:

> The British Empire, at the turn of the [twentieth] century, was an extraordinary concoction, embracing under one flag a great diversity of territories and peoples. So far-flung and so heterogeneous was it that it is difficult to discern a single 'imperial system'. The complexity of India, the aspirations of the self-governing colonies of settlement, and the 'undeveloped estate' of Africa were the chief ingredients ... while the Empire could look solid, especially if one's main acquaintance with it was on a map, there was a mass of only half-disclosed uncertainty amongst its guardians.
>
> ('From Imperial Partner to European Partner 1901–1975: Overview', in Haigh (ed.), *Cambridge Historical Encyclopedia*, p. 289 [Bi])

The heterogeneity of this 'extraordinary concoction' was partly the result of the long history of its creation and partly the result of its piecemeal and often unplanned, if not entirely haphazard, growth. While there was certainly *some* system in its development, and almost always some clear economic, political or military advantages to be gained from colonial expansion, there were relatively few periods in the empire's history when its development was strongly guided by any overarching strategy imposed from the centre, either by the Crown or by Parliament. Those few periods mainly coincided with times of war, when coordinated military strategies were required, but even then, particularly before the advent of steamships and telegraph communications in the mid-nineteenth century, the simple logistics of distance tended to militate against tight centralised control. There was a much more concerted effort to manage colonial affairs by the government in the technologically enhanced twentieth century, but, ironically, that came just as the empire was slipping decisively *out* of Britain's control anyway.

An often-repeated comment about the empire was made in 1883 by J. R. Seeley, who said, 'We seem, as it were, to have conquered and peopled half the world in a fit of absence of mind' (cited in David Armitage, *The Ideological Origins of the British Empire*, p.16 [Ci]). Such a casual sweep of history obviously glosses over many unpleasant realities, but it does nevertheless capture something of the British empire's apparently adventitious growth.

Britain's Global Mosaic

The empire – Kipling's 'dominion over palm and pine' – was a global mosaic of almost ungraspable complexity and staggering contrasts. At one end of the scale there was India, an ancient civilisation and an empire in its own right, where the British ruled grandly … as heirs to the Mughals. At the other end, there was Pitcairn, remote and tiny, 1.75 square miles in extent, with a peak population of 233 in 1937, descendants of eighteenth-century mutineers … Some countries were dauntingly big artificial complexes like Nigeria, 350,000 square miles, made up of hundreds of 'tribes', each with its own language, animists in religion[;] of elegant Muslim emirs in the north, and entrepreneurial Ibos in the south[;] and, in between, miniscule clans lost deep in rain-forests. By contrast, Gambia was little more than the banks of a 200-mile stretch of river, embedded in French Senegal. One quarter of Nyasaland was a lake, while British Guiana was held in the embrace of four mighty rivers, with spectacular rapids and falls. Fiji was made up of 844 islands, about one hundred of them permanently inhabited … There were countries with thousands of miles of railway (India pre-eminently), but Basutoland with just three-quarters of a mile, and some without even that, such as Cyprus, the Bahamas, and British Honduras … There were places where Europeans could sleep with the natives, like Sarawak and the Solomon Islands, and places where they most definitely could not, like Simla and Salisbury.

(Ronald Hyam, *Britain's Declining Empire*, pp. 3–5 [Ci])

Some Origins of Empire

To the extent that there was any dominant pattern to how Britain acquired and developed its empire, this was established in the early days of Britain's – or, at that time, mainly England's – maritime explorations, when, in the late sixteenth century and early seventeenth century, colonial interests beyond the British and Irish Isles were advanced mainly by individual 'knight adventurers' such as Sir Humphrey Gilbert and Sir Walter Ralegh, or by joint-stock companies such as the East India Company (1600) and the Virginia Company (1606). These were granted royal licences (or charters) to explore particular areas for territorial or trade advantages and, where possible, to lay claim to them as possessions of the Crown. However, the immediate organisation and exploitation of any such settled territories remained in the hands of the licence holders, and, in general, it was only later – and in some cases much later – that the colonies which arose from such ventures (when successful) formally came under the direct rule of the British Crown. For example, Newfoundland was initially colonised by Humphrey Gilbert in 1583 and more permanently settled later in 1610 by the Newfoundland Company, but it came under Crown rule only in 1713. It was such relatively uncoordinated, if officially sanctioned, private endeavours that initially drove the growth of the British empire, and this was a pattern, with important variations, that would persist through to the end of the nineteenth century. An example from that period would be Rhodesia (Zimbabwe), which was conquered and settled in 1890–3 by the British South Africa Company (chartered in 1889) and which then came under Crown rule some thirty years later, in 1923.

While in retrospect, then, one might want to suggest that a distant overseas British empire 'began' with the first permanent settlements in Virginia and Newfoundland in 1607 and 1610 respectively, there was in fact no particularly premeditated or concerted national policy (let alone strategy) to establish such an empire at that time – and, as already suggested, it remains debatable as to how much centralised direction of British colonial expansion there ever was subsequently. On the other hand, the *concept* of a British empire had certainly begun to take shape among the ruling classes by this time, through important political and ideological debates taking place from the 1540s onwards. These debates were initially more to do with domestic state-formation and with Tudor attempts to claim sovereignty over an 'empire' that would unite the three kingdoms and four nations of England, Scotland, Ireland and Wales, but they soon became interrelated with colonial developments further afield which led to an expansion in the meaning of empire. Following hard on the heels of the Statute of Wales (1536) and the Irish Kingship Act (1541), military campaigns were launched in the 1540s, first under Henry VIII and then under Edward VI, to force Scotland into a union with England, and Tudor propaganda pamphlets were produced at the same time (the first in 1542) to try to justify such a union by arguing for the legitimacy and advantages of an 'empire' constituted by a 'greater Britain'. These arguments continued to evolve throughout Elizabeth I's reign and beyond and the notion of a greater British empire helped to consolidate moves towards Anglo-Scottish union in 1707 as well as towards the broader union with Ireland in 1801 which established the United Kingdom of Great Britain and Ireland. However, as a more extensive overseas territorial empire began to emerge from the seventeenth century onwards, *that* empire increasingly served as a significant 'other' to give further self-definition to the gradual yoking together of the British and Irish nations. In that sense, while early notions of a 'home' empire helped to create a unitary notion of a greater Britain, it was the subsequent growth of an overseas empire which retroactively confirmed that unitary identity and helped put the 'British' into 'the British empire'. By the eighteenth century, 'Britain was coming to be defined for many of its citizens by possession of an empire … [E]mpire did more than reflect the Britishness of the British in Britain; it helped to focus and develop it' (P. J. Marshall, 'Imperial Britain', in Marshall (ed.), *The Cambridge Illustrated History of the British Empire*, p. 319 [Bi]).

In both conceptual and material ways, then, the British empire gained initial definition in relation to the emergence of a composite British state over a period of about two centuries. This process of definition was clearly very gradual, uneven and uncertain and it was probably not until the first half of the eighteenth century that strong and relatively stable notions of Britishness and empire became established.

'Protestant, Commercial, Maritime and Free': Some Motifs of Empire

By the mid-eighteenth century, too, the identity of the British empire (as, indeed, of Britain itself) had become strongly associated with a fourfold conception that it was 'Protestant, commercial, maritime and free' (Armitage, *The Ideological Origins of the British Empire*, p. 174 [Ci]). Despite certain inherent tensions and paradoxes within such a view, it is one which continued to shape perceptions of the empire (both in Britain and in the colonies) throughout much of the rest of its history. Each of the interconnected elements of this conception certainly reflects important truths about the empire, though each needs to be carefully qualified too.

As we have seen, the empire undoubtedly emerged from a period of Protestant reformation and self-assertion; this was inevitably linked to anti-Catholicism both at home and in foreign affairs, where geopolitical competition and conflict with Portugal, Spain and France in particular became inextricably linked to Britain's colonial expansion across the Atlantic and in the Caribbean, as well as in India. The desire for greater religious freedoms on the part of non-conformist Protestants also directly motivated colonial settlement in north America – but this fact in itself, along with that of widespread Catholic emigration from Britain too (to the Catholic colony of Maryland for example), immediately complicates the denominational situation and argues against any simple characterisation of the empire in Anglican Protestant terms. The promotion of broadly Christian ideals always remained an important ideological justification for the empire, of course, and Evangelical Protestant missions in particular became a major force throughout the empire from the late eighteenth century onwards, taking a leading role in the abolitionist movements and spreading not only the Christian word but education and literacy generally. The case for a broadly Protestant empire might perhaps also be made in conjunction with the 'commercial' view of empire in the light of economic theories which see Protestantism and its ethics of individualism and self-improvement as intimately linked to the rise of capitalism.

The pursuit of trade and economic gain as a motivation for colonial development was not unique to Britain, of course, but, for Napoleon's 'nation of shopkeepers', it is not surprising that the British would particularly want to cast their empire in a commercial mould and to construe it as primarily a global trading network. Indeed, developing coterminously with the rise of capitalism and in close interaction, later, with the Industrial Revolution, it certainly *was* that, and, for a large part of its history, the biggest and most successful such network in the world – and, plainly, the empire could not have flourished at all without some economically viable commercial basis. However, it is equally plain that the empire was not established *solely* for or on legitimate trade and commerce. The naked pursuit of military and political power was obviously involved too and rapacious conquest and plunder often played as big a part of the empire's 'commerce' as fair trade did. Moreover, prior to the nineteenth century, much of the most profitable business of the empire (such as the trade in sugar and tobacco) was conducted on the back of slavery and the slave trade's cruel commerce in people – and, thereafter, it often depended on an almost equally cruel exploitation of indentured and similar 'tied' forms of labour.

It goes almost without saying that, as an island, Britain's overseas empire was established by seafaring means. Portugal and Spain had led the way in maritime navigation and exploration – and in transatlantic colonialism and empire-building – in the fifteenth and sixteenth centuries; but Britain had gradually overtaken them as the world's dominant sea-power by the eighteenth century and had gained more or less unassailable control over the oceans with the final defeat of Napoleonic France in 1815. Britain's increasing mastery of the seas over these centuries facilitated ever greater colonial expansion supported by increasing control of sea-trade and merchant shipping. In these ways, Britain's empire was unarguably a maritime-based one. On the other hand, Britain did not actually rule anything so nebulous as just the waves, of course, but, rather, specific colonial *lands* and *peoples*, which, although separated from Britain by the seas, still required substantial levels of investment of the nation's human and material resources. The maritime 'myth' of empire, that is, conveniently served to celebrate Britain's far-flung power and the various material advantages it brought, while at the same time playing down all the costs, commitments and responsibilities that such a vast range of physical territories inevitably brought with them. In addition, by submerging the concrete particularities of many different peoples and places beneath one 'oceanic' perspective, such a myth served further to reinforce that deceptive image mentioned earlier of the empire as some sort of homogeneous unity.

> ### Britannia Rules the Waves
>
> The conventional chronology of the Empire's origins … located them in the reign of Elizabeth I … and anchored it in a particular maritime history. The originating agents of empire were the Elizabethan sea-dogs, Gloriana's sailor-heroes who had circumnavigated the globe, singed the King of Spain's beard, swept the oceans of pirates and Catholics, and thereby opened up the sea-routes across which English migrants would travel, and English trade would flow, until Britannia majestically ruled the waves.
>
> (Armitage, *The Ideological Origins of the British Empire*, p.100 [Ci])
>
> When Britain first at Heaven's command
>   Arose from out the azure main,
> This was the charter of the land
> And guardian angels sang this strain:
> Rule Britannia! rule the waves!
>   Britons never will be slaves.
>
> (James Thomson, 'Rule, Britannia' (1740))

The idea of the empire as a force for freedom might be seen as a complementary myth here, and it is certainly the most paradoxical part of this fourfold conception of empire, given that the underlying meaning of 'empire' is power and rule over others. Nevertheless, it was a fairly constant boast of the British for most of the empire's history that, through her colonies, Britain was sharing and spreading the benefits of its civilisation and institutions, amongst which its religion, its parliamentary democracy, its system of common law, and its championing of freedom took pride of place. Britain's parliament, in particular, was a potent symbol of freedom within the empire and was in fact always a possible source of redress over grievances or injustices in the colonies: 'Although it was somewhat removed from the routine control of dependent territories … Parliament could, for instance, call to account unruly colonial officials, as it did in the case of Robert Clive in the 1770s or the prison officers guilty of atrocities in Kenya's Hola Camp two centuries later. It was through parliamentary action that slavery was eventually outlawed in the British empire … By setting standards, no matter how loose and ill-defined, Parliament scrutinized the activities of the British overseas and justified imperial rule to the world at large' (A. J. Stockwell, 'Power, Authority, and Freedom', in Marshall (ed.), *The Cambridge Illustrated History of the British Empire*, pp. 171–2 [Bi]).

It is undoubtedly true that the British empire did, institutionally and ideologically, embed within its colonies many of Britain's best traditions of democracy, civil liberties and equality before the law. This was most straightforwardly the case in the white 'colonies of settlement' of pre-independence America, Canada, Australia and New Zealand, where the original British settlers and their descendants (if not the indigenous populations they displaced) could generally assume similar rights and freedoms as in Britain itself, and where the colonies fairly quickly achieved some democratic self-government on the British model. But even in the non-settled 'colonies of rule' in India and Africa, and in the plantation colonies of the Caribbean, such traditions were sufficiently rooted by the mid-twentieth century positively to facilitate the struggle for independence *from* Britain by anti-colonial nationalist movements which often used the available legal and democratic structures to advance their causes (even when armed struggle also played a part). It was commonly the case, too, that the post-colonial states which emerged out of these independence struggles chose largely to retain their British-derived models of governance and law (even if these were later changed or modified). Having noted all this, however, it is also undoubtedly true that in many parts of the empire, and for most of its history, there was a racist double standard in operation whereby the hallowed principles of freedom, equality and democratic representation applied only to a privileged, mainly white European minority and by no means at all to the majority of non-white subject peoples. This was overwhelmingly the case in the slave-era plantation colonies, of course, and mostly the case in all the colonies of rule, including the colonies of settlement *and* rule, like South Africa and Southern Rhodesia, where minority white settler regimes systematically denied civil rights to their non-white majorities. Clearly, 'Britons' were never to be slaves, but freedom for other British subjects in the empire was a much less certain matter. As Lord Salisbury (later Britain's prime minister) stated in 1878, 'If our ancestors had cared for the rights of other people, the British empire would not have been made' (cited in Hyam, *Understanding the British Empire*, p. 30 [Ci]).

One or Two – or Three – Empires?

Ironically, no sooner had a relatively stable conception of Britain's empire emerged in the eighteenth century than it was deeply shaken by Britain's loss of her thirteen American colonies after defeat in the American War of Independence (1775–83) at the hands not only of the American 'rebels' but also of their allies, the French, Spanish and Dutch. This first dramatic instance of decolonisation within the empire dealt a serious blow to Britain's power and prestige, left its economy with a massive debt (of around £243 million), and unceremoniously deflated the burgeoning imperial confidence that had been inspired by Britain's now starkly contrasting successes in the earlier Seven Years' War (1756–63). The loss of the American colonies immediately changed the map of the British empire at that point and some historians have even suggested that it represented a watershed between two quite distinct phases of empire, sometimes distinguished as the 'First' and 'Second' British empires. According to this view, the First empire, developed between the sixteenth and eighteenth centuries, was focused westwards across the Atlantic to

North America and the West Indies, and was established more by migration and trade than by conquest; while the Second empire, from the eighteenth to the twentieth centuries, was oriented much more towards the east (India in particular), Australasia and Africa, and was marked by a greater degree of expansion by military conquest rather than by migration and trade. Such a division is perhaps useful for a shorthand mapping of the empire over its four centuries, but it is difficult to sustain systematically, not least because of the many overlaps and continuities between the two suggested phases.

Most obviously, the Caribbean colonies and the territories of what would later become Canada were still within the empire after 1783 and remained of primary economic and strategic importance to Britain. Britain actually saw a major boom in overall transatlantic trade in the last quarter of the eighteenth century (helped also by the fact that the newly independent American colonies continued to trade with Britain much as before, despite their political secession). Trade with India, on the other hand, while increasing, rose at an appreciably slower rate during the same period. The British had been establishing their influence in India since the early 1600s, so one can hardly argue that further expansion there in the eighteenth century represented an entirely new 'swing to the east' for the empire – and, in any case, that particular expansion had begun well before the American War of Independence.

On the whole, then, one cannot say that the American War of Independence caused an especially sharp sea-change in the always-uneven development of the British empire, even if the loss of the American colonies was a traumatic event for Britain and inevitably changed *some* of the dynamics of the empire. What does seem incontrovertible, however, is that the nature of Britain's involvement in India, through the East India Company, underwent a major change in the second half of the eighteenth century and became less concerned with trade *per se* and more with extending territorial control for the direct taxation revenues this could entail.

Even from its earliest days, the East India Company was an *armed* trading company and had used force, or the threat of force, to secure commercial advantages in India, but territorial expansion by military means had been relatively limited before the mid-eighteenth century, partly because trade had been sufficiently profitable and partly because of the modest size of the Company's armed forces. As the once-great Mughal empire in India began to fragment in the eighteenth century, and as Anglo-French conflicts there (as elsewhere) escalated, so the opportunities for territorial gain by military means increased and the East India Company began to expand its armies very substantially from mid-century onwards (and these were supported on land and at sea by regular British forces sent to fight the French). A policy of military annexation of territory by Company forces was not initially sanctioned either by the Company's governors in London or by the British government, but, at a time when dispatches to and from Britain could take between six to twelve months to arrive, leaders on the ground in India were often difficult to control and it seems as if it was the ambitions of people like Robert Clive, Warren Hastings and Lord Wellesley which, between the 1750s and early 1800s, shaped a *de facto* policy of territorial conquest which transformed the Company's role in India from one of trade to one of imperial rule and administration. The unmistakable rapacity underlying those ambitions and that policy are revealed in a letter of 1759 from Robert Clive to the British prime minister of the day, William Pitt the elder. Making capital on his victory at the Battle of Plassey of 1757, Clive writes:

> The great revolution that has been effected here by the success of the English arms, and the vast advantages gained to the Company by a treaty concluded in consequence thereof, have, I observe … gained the public attention; but much more may yet in time be done, if the Company will exert themselves … I have represented to them in the strongest terms the expediency of sending out and keeping up constantly such a force as will enable them to embrace the first opportunity of further aggrandising themselves … Now I leave you to judge, whether an income yearly of two millions sterling, with the possession of three provinces [Bengal, Bihar and Orissa] abounding in the most valuable productions of nature and of art, be an object deserving the public attention and whether it be worth the nation's while to take the proper measures to secure such an acquisition … which … would prove a source of immense wealth to the kingdom …
>
> (Cited in Simon C. Smith, *British Imperialism 1750–1970*, pp. 22–3 [Bi])

By about 1818, although a nominal Mughal empire still existed, most of India was effectively ruled by the East India Company (albeit indirectly in some places through

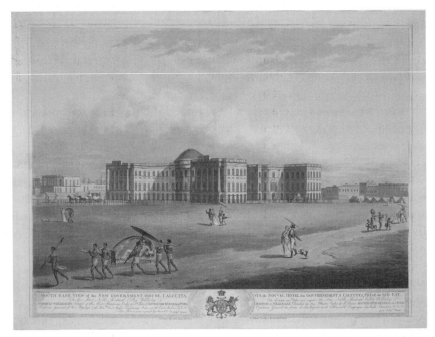

8.2 Government House, Calcutta, 1805. Modelled on Kedleston Hall, Derbyshire, the grandiose design here reflects a common tendency of the British in their empire, particularly in India, to try to project an image of imperial power, pomp and circumstance in their government buildings, and, of course, as evident here, to try, wherever possible, to export British styles of architecture and landscape design to the colonies.

local rulers under British 'protection'). This rule was consolidated by further annex-ations and wars in the period up to 1857 and was also marked by increasingly direct, and increasingly anglicising, intervention in India by the British government itself. In the aftermath of the momentous Indian Rebellion of 1857–8, the East India Company was finally abolished entirely and Britain established direct Crown rule, inaugurating the period later often referred to as the 'Raj', which lasted until India gained its independence in 1947.

India was almost entirely different from any of the other individual colonies in the British empire in terms of both its own nature (its sub-continental size, its rich ancient history, its cultural complexity) and the uniquely intricate and varied nature of Britain's involvement with it over a period of nearly three and a half centuries. India was literally an empire itself for much of the time that it 'belonged' to the British empire and it is perhaps best viewed in such light, not principally as part of a 'first' or 'second' British empire, but as a separate Indo-British entity in its own right (in a sense, then, a 'third' British empire). It seems relevant that the last of the Mughal Emperors was formally deposed in 1858 when Britain imposed Crown rule, and that, in 1876–7, Queen Victoria was proclaimed 'Empress of India', as these things suggest that the British saw themselves as heirs to the Mughals and did, indeed, view India as something of a self-contained empire.

The Scramble for Africa and the Age of Imperialism

As the industrial revolution gathered pace in the nineteenth century so Britain's demand for raw materials and produce increased, along with a growing need to expand markets for her manufactured goods. The existing colonies of the empire were crucial to the fulfilment of both requirements, but there was also now a stron-ger motivation to continue to expand the empire and its influence wherever pos-sible – and the nineteenth century has sometimes been called Britain's 'imperial century' in recognition of a newly aggressive phase of colonial activity. As we have seen, after 1815, Britain was the dominant military power in the world and this remained the case until a newly unified Germany began to challenge her position in the last quarter of the nineteenth century. Thus, for around seventy years during the most intense period of her industrial development, Britain had pretty much free rein in seeking to shape global trading conditions in her own interests; and one of her main interests at the time was to promote free trade as a means of opening up more markets for her industries and as a catalyst for capitalism generally. China was one important field for British expansionism in the mid-Victorian era, with the Opium Wars and 'gun-boat diplomacy' securing Hong Kong as a new British colony in 1842 and establishing a number of treaty ports that eased commercial access to internal Chinese markets and safeguarded Britain's illicit but lucrative exports of Indian opium into China. Also in the east, a staged conquest of Burma took place through three wars between 1824 and 1885 and the British presence in Malaysia was also gradually consolidated throughout the century with, for exam-ple, the establishment of the Straits Settlement in 1826 (Singapore, Malacca and

Penang) and of the protectorate of Federated Malay States in 1896. South Africa, too, was another key area of expansion at this time as the British pushed outwards from Cape Colony to establish the colony of Natal after a series of wars with the Xhosa, to dispute territory with the Boers in what would later become the Orange Free State, and, in 1868, to annex Basutoland (Lesotho). Further substantial military consolidation of territory would take place in South Africa later in the century (in the Zulu war of 1879, for example) – and Africa more generally would become the major area for British colonial expansion in the second half of the nineteenth century and into the twentieth century.

The last quarter of the nineteenth century in particular was the period of what is generally referred to as 'the scramble for Africa', when intensifying economic and political competition amongst the major European powers spread into Africa, with Britain, France, Belgium, Germany and others vying with one another to maximise the extent of their territories and influence there. Although European colonial activity in coastal areas of Africa dated back to the earliest days of Portuguese maritime exploration and developed through the long centuries of the transatlantic slave trade, expansion into the interior was largely a nineteenth-century phenomenon and began to accelerate from the middle of that century (partly along the lines of routes established by explorers like David Livingstone, Richard Burton, J. H. Speke, and H. M. Stanley). Britain had been steadily developing new colonial footholds in all parts of the continent but this activity was spurred on from the late 1870s by the new interest in Africa shown by the other European powers. By 1884, amongst other developments, France had extended its claims in western Africa eastwards from Senegal to the upper Niger and it had occupied Tunisia; both Belgium and France had established a major presence in the Congo; and Germany had declared protectorates over Togo, Cameroon, South West Africa and German East Africa (later Tanganyika/Tanzania). One of Britain's biggest acts of military intervention in Africa at this time was her occupation of Egypt in 1882, carried out purportedly to restore order after a revolt there, but also to protect Britain's substantial financial and strategic interests in the country, including those related to the Suez Canal, which was a vital conduit for Britain's trade to India and the East. Egypt never became a formal colony as such, but it remained to all intents and purposes under thoroughgoing British rule until 1922 and provided a springboard for the later (re-) conquest of the Sudan in 1898.

But the most aggressive phase of the race for colonial advantage in Africa began after the Berlin Conference of 1884–5 which sought to regulate and formalise claims to African territories by the European nations. The conference ratified several existing claims, agreed matters of protocol and, perhaps unwittingly, gave a direct inducement to further colonial conquest by stipulating that future claims needed to be based on evidence of 'effective occupation'. The conference was 'the first public signal that tropical Africa was up for grabs' (Roland Oliver, *The African Experience*, p. 178 [Ci]). It laid the foundations for the eventual wholesale partition of the continent on the basis of borders of political expedience determined largely in Europe by Europeans who had little regard for the impact of their decisions on the thousands of African communities they were parcelling up. In the 1880s, the colonial annexation of territory in Africa proceeded relatively peaceably as the European powers at first advanced through the use of treaties and concessions granted by local African rulers and were generally content to consolidate existing spheres of influence without treading on each other's toes. However, in the 1890s, as the Europeans moved towards the uncharted territory of the interior, which seemed less conditionally 'up for grabs' to whichever power could occupy it first, so the 'scramble' became a more savage race and more inclined to the use of arms. A savage enough example is that of Cecil Rhodes's British South Africa Company in its establishment of Rhodesia through the machine-gun-aided suppression of the Shona and Ndebele (Matabele) peoples in military campaigns of 1890, 1893 and 1896.

With the end of the Boer War in 1902, the main lines of the European partition of Africa were in place and the process was broadly complete by the outbreak of the First World War in 1914. In the relatively short time since the Berlin Conference, the political map of a whole continent had been transformed, as can be seen by comparing the two versions of the map in Figure 8.3. Although the map has undergone many further changes of detail since that time, the essential configuration of nations and borders established in that period has remained roughly the same up to the present day – and the colonial partition of Africa has therefore continued to exert its influence in the post-colonial era. Roland Oliver makes a truly arresting observation about the scale of change involved in this partition for African communities at the grass roots, when he writes:

> Above all, it has to be remembered that the 'partition of Africa' is a phrase that has meaning only in relation to the actions of outsiders in respect of other outsiders. Seen from the inside, in the deeper perspective of African history, the so-called 'partition' was on the contrary a ruthless act of political amalgamation, whereby something of the order of ten thousand units [of community] was reduced to a mere forty.
>
> (*The African Experience*, p. 184 [Ci])

It is worth stressing here that Oliver's 'ten thousand units' is not a loose rhetorical generalisation but a realistic estimate of actual communities. This is made clearer as he explains his main point further while also reminding us of Europe's 'pin on the wall' approach to the drawing of the partition map:

> It has become a commonplace of political polemic that the diplomats of Europe, equipped with pencils and rulers, drew straight lines across the largely blank interior regions shown on African maps, bisecting and sometimes trisecting the territories of African peoples. The accusation is true so far as it goes, but by constant repetition it has obscured the larger truth that African polities were mostly very small, and that nearly all of the new European colonies comprised within their frontiers many times more indigenous groups than they divided. It was quite normal for a single one of the newly defined colonies to comprise two or three hundred earlier political groupings, even after discounting those societies which recognized no authority wider than that of the extended family.
>
> (Oliver, pp. 184–5)

Supporters of imperial expansion and of Britain's so-called 'civilising mission' abroad were particularly vociferous and militant – indeed, often downright jingoistic – in

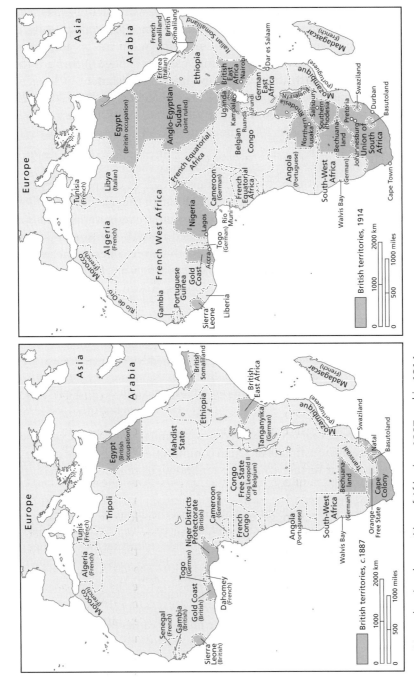

8.3 Maps showing the partition of Africa in c.1887 and in 1914.

precisely the same period as the scramble for Africa, from around 1875 to the out-break of the First World War in 1914. As this period coincided with the rise of mass communications, popular journalism and advertising, this proved to be a heyday of patriotic tub-thumping for an inflated notion of an empire which, till that time, had been only a relatively vaguely realised phenomenon for most British people not directly involved in it. Often referred to as the 'Age of Imperialism' (or 'new imperi-alism', as discussed by Maria Frawley earlier in Chapter 5 (p. 428–32)), and presided over by advocates of empire such as Benjamin Disraeli (Prime Minister, 1874–80) and Joseph Chamberlain (Colonial Secretary, 1895–1903), the period created a somewhat romanticised, heroic image of the empire that gave it, for a short time at least, a widespread popular appeal:

> The new-found reverence for empire coalesced around monarchism, militarism and notions of racial superiority, or Social Darwinism … Indeed, the monarchy became increasingly associated with imperial imagery. This reached a remarkable climax when representatives from throughout the empire came to London in 1897 to celebrate Victoria's diamond jubilee. The second half of the nineteenth century also witnessed a growth in popularity of the armed forces, with military figures such as General Gordon, killed at Khartoum in 1885, raised to the status of national heroes. The depiction of such figures as representatives of a master people fuelled notions of racial superiority.
>
> (Smith, *British Imperialism 1750–1970*, p. 79 [Bi])

Decolonisation and the End of Empire

The new imperialism was relatively short-lived, however, and, in retrospect, can be seen as something of a swan-song for the empire. As John O'Farrell has quipped, 'you can almost date the British Empire going into crisis from the point at which the English start going on about how great it is' (*An Utterly Impartial History of Britain*, p. 403 [Bi]). Britain's decidedly un-emphatic victory in the Boer War had in fact rather dented her imperial confidence and had raised serious questions about her ability, militarily and economically, actually to defend all her far-flung territorial possessions – while the subsequent carnage of the First World War largely put paid to any lingering popular romance about colonial military conquest. The victory over the Boers in 1902 was in any case somewhat pyrrhic, as the Boers were granted concessions at the ensuing Treaty of Vereeniging which helped them gain political dominance later in the decade and enabled them to dictate the (proto-apartheid) nature of the new Union of South Africa which was formed in 1910 as a self-govern-ing dominion. Although South Africa remained within the empire, along with the other colonies of settlement which had already gained dominion status (Canada, Australia and New Zealand), its establishment under Afrikaner leadership confirmed what the Boer War had already suggested, that Britain was starting to lose its grip over the empire. Another clear sign of this was a renewed nationalist momentum, from the start of the 1900s, towards home rule in Ireland. This was a momentum that had been partly inspired by the Boer resistance to the British in South Africa, and one which eventually led, through the Easter Rising in Dublin of 1916 and the Anglo-Irish War of 1919–21, to the partition of Ireland and the establishment, in 1922, of the Irish Free State, again as a self-governing dominion within the empire. However, in this case, there was a much stronger opposition than in South Africa to remaining subject to British sovereignty, as demonstrated by the Irish Civil War of 1922–3 which was caused by the intensity of nationalist divisions over this and related issues.

If the examples of South Africa and Ireland represented the first visible cracks in the British empire, the First World War probably contributed more, in the long run, to its overall breakdown – despite the fact that, after the war, the empire seemed to be stronger than ever and was actually enlarged for a time by the granting to Britain of a number of League of Nations mandates over former German and Turkish territories (including Iraq, Palestine, Tanganyika and Transjordan). In fact, Britain's economy and international economic position had been greatly weakened by the war (and the above enlargement of the empire would eventually only compound the problem); and, though it was not immediately apparent, the war had also called the nature of Britain's relationship with its colonies into question, in a way that would have long-term consequences. Britain's economy before the war had already been struggling in comparison to its main competitors and it lost important export markets during the war; it now emerged from the conflict hugely in debt to America and with its old staple industries struggling to re-establish themselves within an increasingly harsh international economic climate. America was effectively overtaking Britain as the world's leading economic, industrial and military power and 'Britain found herself in the invidious position of needing imperial resources as never before to bolster her foundering economy, while lacking the means to cover her increased colonial commitments' (Smith, *British Imperialism 1750–1970*, p. 111 [Bi]). The colonies had rallied robustly to Britain's aid during the conflict and had already contributed massively to the war effort, in terms of finance and resources, and in terms of direct participation and human lives lost (at least 2.6 million people participated). This inevitably called for some readjustment in Britain's attitudes to her colonies and some greater recognition for them as collaborative partners rather than exploitable possessions. War survivors from the colonies – particularly non-white participants – also now had a range of new perspectives from their war experiences, including mixing with other nationalities, through which to reassess their lives back home as subject peoples. Attitudes on both sides of the colonial relationship could never be quite the same again and, in particular, in the inter-war years, 'the fundamental incompatibility of a democracy based on participation and consent ruling an empire by command became steadily more evident' (Keith Robbins, 'From Imperial Partner to European Partner 1901–1975: Overview', in Haigh (ed.), *Cambridge Historical Encyclopedia*, p. 289 [Bi]).

Britain did make some efforts to address this incompatibility, though not equally or sufficiently in all parts of the empire. Britain's relationship with the white dominions was decisively re-defined at the imperial conference of 1926 and in the Statute of Westminster of 1931, where the hierarchical language of empire gave way to a language of commonality and partnership, as the equal status of all the members of the new-formed British Commonwealth was proclaimed (and, from now, the dominions were to all intents and purposes independent). But the pace of democratic change for other colonies remained woefully slow and significant progress for most of them would not be made until after 1945, although there were some limited extensions of political representation before then (as under a new constitution in Jamaica in 1944, for example). In India, in particular, nationalist leaders 'were able to use the liberal wartime rhetoric of Britain and her allies to appeal to the masses and demand greater freedoms' (Smith, *British Imperialism 1750–1970*, p. 63 [Bi]). Campaigns led by Gandhi helped to force Britain to concede major democratic advances through the Government of India Acts of 1919 and 1935, and the latter was followed by general elections for provincial assemblies in 1937 which brought the India National Congress Party to power in seven out of eleven provinces, thus paving the way for Congress to press even harder, throughout the 1940s, for the full independence that was achieved in 1947.

The Second World War was a very different war from the First, but its consequences for Britain and its empire were in some ways very similar, though on a magnified scale. Britain's economy had been weakened by the first war but it had been positively devastated by the second and Britain was more or less bankrupt by 1945 and ever more in debt to America. The colonial contribution of resources and people to the war effort was again unstinting, but the numbers of participants were much greater, at over five million, and spread across a wider range of roles (though

8.4 Empire Marketing Board poster, 1927. The Board was set up in 1926 to promote imperial trade and produce and the economic benefits of the empire generally. Here, the figures for 1915 indicate the importance of the colonies to Britain during the war – but the banner headlines and the imagery of the poster (including the ship) can also be fruitfully analysed for what they suggest about the nature and history of the empire.

the numbers of combatants and battle casualties were lower because it was a more technological war). Again, those colonial peoples who had few rights and privileges at home would have their views and expectations of the world significantly altered by their war experiences (and their training in arms would, in some cases, find redeployment later in armed opposition to British colonialism). The contradictions of the imperial situation, particularly in its racial dimension, loomed more largely in this war too, with so many obviously subject peoples of the empire fighting for the empires's freedom from fascist subjection. Those contradictions were thrown into sharp relief early on by one of the main principles of the Atlantic Charter, issued by President Roosevelt and Winston Churchill in 1941, which stated that all peoples had a right to self-determination and that sovereign rights and self-government should be restored 'to those who have been forcibly deprived of them' (cited in Smith, *British Imperialism 1750–1970*, p. 112 [Bi]). Although Churchill himself was clearly uncomfortable – in fact, downright indignant – at the thought of such a principle being applied within the British empire (later insisting that it was intended to apply only to those countries in Europe 'now under the Nazi yoke'), the tide of American and other international opinion was such that it was inevitable that it *would* be so applied in the years after the war. In Britain, too, that tide of opinion would generally be supported in the same new egalitarian spirit which swept Churchill aside and put Clement Attlee's Labour Party into power immediately after the war.

The independence of India and Pakistan in 1947 set the mood, as it were, for a post-war period of surprisingly rapid and widespread decolonisation which brought the British empire to an effective end by the late 1960s (though several individual colonies remained dependent on Britain well beyond that time). As with the initial growth of the empire, there was nothing particularly systematic or planned about its demise and there was precious little pattern to how it unravelled in different places. The economic and military unsustainability of such a large empire in the modern world, the internal pressures of independence movements within the colonies, the external pressures of international censure over the curtailment of freedoms and of the rights of peoples to self-determination, and the global dynamics of the Cold War and its nuclear dangers, all played a key part in Britain's overall retreat from empire – as did the fact that other European nations were also shedding their empires over the same period, particularly in Africa.

From now on, after India and Pakistan (and Ceylon and Burma in 1948), British policy would be directed towards a gradual preparation of all her other colonies for future self-government and eventual independence. However, 'eventual' was still clearly the operative word in the 40s and early 50s, when there remained an expectation in government circles that some sort of British empire – although perhaps reconfigured on the lines of partnership rather than rule – would continue to exist and to play a major role on the world stage, and in Britain's economic and strategic interests, for many years to come. There was, for example, a new development programme for the colonies, initiated with the Colonial Development and Welfare Act of 1940 and substantially enlarged in 1945, along with an ill-fated attempt in 1953 at promoting colonial partnership and development by uniting Southern Rhodesia (Zimbabwe), Northern Rhodesia (Zambia) and Nyasaland (Malawi) in a new Central

African Federation. Such plans suggested that nobody really envisaged the end of empire just yet. In the end, though – as illustrated by the breakdown of that Central African Federation in 1964 and by the protests in the Gold Coast which hastened its independence as Ghana in 1957 – events in the colonies often spiralled out of Britain's control, and internal demands for freedom intensified to such a pitch (sometimes violently, as in Malaya, Cyprus, Aden and Kenya, for example) that there came to be no viable alternative for Britain except to grant independence and withdraw as soon as possible. It was also the case, it seems, that the British government had come to realise by the late 1950s that there were no longer any compelling economic – or other – advantages for Britain in sustaining the empire, and that its long-term interests would be better served through nurturing closer relations with Europe and America. In terms of status on the world stage, the loss of an empire would in any case be cushioned by a continuing (but less costly and less burdensome) association with the former colonies through the Commonwealth. If the empire began with an adventurous quest for overseas profits, it ended with an emphatic cutting of overseas losses, as Simon C. Smith suggests:

> **Howzat!**
>
> Historians have offered four main options for explaining the end of empire. These may be put in the form of a cricketing analogy. Either the British were bowled out (by nationalists and freedom-fighters), or they were run out (by imperial over-stretch and economic constraints), or they retired hurt (because of a collapse of morale and 'failure of will'), or they were booed off the field (by international criticism and especially United Nations clamour) … 'Failure of will' is perhaps the weakest of the explanations … Ever wary of monocausal theories, most historians opt for a judicious balance or interlock of metropolitan, colonial-nationalist, and international influences …
>
> (Hyam, *Britain's Declining Empire*, pp. xiii–xiv [Ci])

> Britain's approach to empire was firmly rooted in a clear conception of her own national interest. Although the rhetoric of empire changed … the underlying pragmatism rarely wavered. Britain pursued her imperial path not out of a sense of altruism, or even primarily concern for indigenous peoples, but for profit, whether in economic, political or military terms. When the balance of advantage shifted, and the burdens of empire outweighed the assets, Britain withdrew. The transfer of power to a partitioned India in 1947 is perhaps the best example of this … by 1957 the value of Britain's remaining dependencies also began to be questioned. Within days of becoming prime minister, Harold Macmillan was requesting 'something like a profit and loss account for each of our Colonial possessions, so that we may be better able to gauge whether, from the financial and economic point of view, we are likely to gain or lose by its departure'.
>
> (Smith, *British Imperialism 1750–1970*, p. 121 [Bi])

Neo-Colonialism

Each of Britain's many former colonies has its own detailed and distinctive post-colonial history and there is clearly no room to consider each of those individually here. However, one important element in common that is worth restating, to conclude this brief overview of the British empire, is that most of Europe's post-war decolonising activity was played out in complex interaction with the Cold War between the United States and Soviet Russia, which ended only in 1989. The nature and outcomes of many independence struggles – and, indeed, the immediate histories of many of the newly independent nation states which emerged from those struggles – were shaped by the global contest for dominance between these two super-powers. Clearly, Britain was opposed to communism and bore allegiance to the United States in this contest, and these were key factors in Britain's approach to negotiating the independence of its colonies, as well as in Britain's post-war outlook generally. Ensuring a pro-Western stance in the former British colonies was not particularly difficult in the short term, as the independence settlements for most of them generally involved adopting a British-style constitution and remaining within the Commonwealth. It also generally involved a fairly wholesale inheritance of most of the existing colonial structures of government, administration and policing (often along with many of the existing personnel too, though some of these came, by that time, from an emerging *indigenous* elite of educated and trained people). Inevitably, also, the economies of

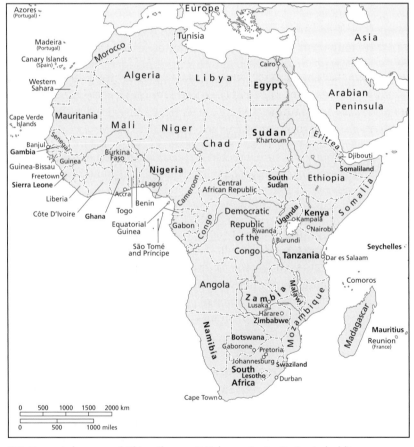

8.5 Present-day map of Africa (former British empire territories in bold).

most of the new states would for a time continue to be structurally bound to Britain and her financial and trading markets. Even after independence, therefore, most of the former colonies saw a phase of continued colonial, or neo-colonial, influence – and the question of how far any of the colonies have wholly shed such influence (especially in an increasingly intermeshed and globalised world) remains an important one within postcolonial studies and recurs as a major issue in much postcolonial literature.

Literary Overview, Texts and Issues

Introduction

With such a large field of study and such varied literary traditions, it is clearly not possible in a short chapter like this to provide anything more than a mere sketch of the main lines of development within postcolonial literature and within the academic discourse surrounding it. This chapter therefore adopts a fairly generalised approach that aims to give newcomers to the field a broad sense of its nature and of the main issues that postcolonial writers, critics and scholars are typically concerned with. Moreover, in order to provide a realistic overview that will best serve the practical needs of students and teachers engaged in undergraduate courses in literature where postcolonial literature will be included as only a relatively small element of a much broader programme of study, I have generally restricted my range of reference to writers and works from the areas which I believe are most often studied at this level – that is, Africa, India and the Caribbean (though some mention is made of works from elsewhere and the chronology at the start of the chapter includes a wider range of reference). The four detailed textual analyses that follow in the section of 'Readings' are a little more substantial than in other chapters of the book partly to counterbalance the broad-sweep nature of this section and partly also to allow for a fuller elaboration of some of the leading themes that are introduced here. The readings are thus intended to follow on organically from the discussion within this section, and for that reason, too, they focus on the period of rapid decolonisation between 1960 and 1980 when postcolonial literary studies first came to prominence.

Although theoretical issues are touched on here, there is no space to engage with the full range of (often complex) theoretical debates that have informed postcolonial studies. However, it is important to be aware of such debates and the Reference section provides guidance to relevant further reading in this area. In particular, anthologies such as *The Post-Colonial Studies Reader* (Ashcroft et al. [Bii]) should be consulted for convenient introductory access to the seminal ideas of writers and critics such as Frantz Fanon, Edward Said, Raja Rao, Ngugi wa Thiong'o, Chinua Achebe, Wilson Harris, Kamau Brathwaite, Gayatri Chakravorty Spivak, Homi K. Bhabha and Benita Parry.

Postcolonial Literature: Defining the Field

As the foregoing historical overview has suggested, the British empire was a complex and sprawling global patchwork which encompassed a huge diversity of territories and peoples that often had very little in common with one another, *except* for their subordination to British rule and all that this entailed (which was quite a lot, of course). By definition, postcolonial literatures in English emanate from the former colonies of the empire, and these therefore naturally reflect the above diversity and also often have little in common with one another, apart from that shared British colonial background and its legacy of the English language. It is perhaps useful at this point, then, to recall the suggestion made at the start of this chapter about balancing a sense of the diversity and distinctiveness of particular postcolonial literatures against a sense of a singular postcolonial literature whose texts can be seen to share at least some common elements and concerns relating to colonialism, regardless of their many other differences. This latter focus is after all part of the point of the label 'postcolonial', in that it defines what unifies and gives analytical direction to the field of study in its reference to the common denominator of the experience of colonialism (the prefix, 'post', adds the senses of 'coming after' colonialism and, more subtly, of opposition to it, as, in academic circles, 'postcolonial' generally implies a critical stance towards colonialism). But the singular and the plural forms of 'literature' both carry certain dangers in this context. With the singular, the risk is of suggesting that there might be a simple 'one size fits all' model of postcolonial literature which is then used to impose an artificial uniformity on the field – which in turn runs the risk of marginalising and subordinating significant cultural differences which do not neatly conform to the model (much as colonialism itself tended to do in 'civilising' its colonies). With the plural, the danger is of over-exaggeration and mystification, of suggesting that the differences between bodies of English literature from different cultures are more extreme and categorical than they actually are, and thus suggesting that only experts and initiates in individual specialised fields can properly understand them. There is, moreover, just a hint of something denigratory in the plural form, as if one might be suggesting that these bodies of work are a subset of literature proper, not in fact *truly* literature – just 'literatures'.

The term 'postcolonial', too, is problematic and has been – and continues to be – hotly contested amongst critics. Frankly, it is not a term whose meaning is immediately clear, especially in the sense that it has come to be used in literary and related cultural studies. For historians, the usually hyphenated form of 'post-colonial' does have an immediately unambiguous meaning as a period marker denoting (obviously enough) the period *after* colonialism – that is, the period after colonial rule has ended. However, within the academic field of (generally non-hyphenated) postcolonial literary studies, this common-sense logic has always been blurred by the need to recognise important writings produced *during* the period of colonialism; and, as the theoretical rationale for postcolonial studies developed around theories of resistance to, and critique of, colonialism, so the focus of those studies inevitably had to incorporate the period of colonialism itself, in order to analyse the oppressive dynamics of colonialism and the ways in which these were resisted and challenged and, eventually, overcome in the processes of decolonisation. Thus, the 'post' came to imply not after the *end* of colonial rule but after its *beginnings*, and so 'postcolonial' came to imply the whole range of experience from the beginning to the end of colonialism and beyond it into a period 'after colonialism'. Taken literally, this creates a huge and somewhat vague field of inquiry. For literary studies, it could in principle mean considering almost five centuries of literature while also losing an important distinction between the colonial and imperialist writings of British authors on the one hand and the 'postcolonial' writings of indigenous authors on the other. At the same time, there is, indeed, a sense in which postcolonial studies has introduced not a new *period* of study, but a new form of criticism or critical strategy which reads texts in the light of the phenomenon of European colonialism since the fifteenth century – so, in that sense, yes, all sorts of texts throughout this period might be read from a postcolonial perspective, whether or not they have their material origins in an explicitly colonial situation. However, in practice, the focus or content of the academic study of Anglophone 'postcolonial literature' has tended to encompass mainly indigenous (and diasporic) writings from the former colonies produced in the twentieth century from around the 1930s onwards – that is, in the years immediately leading up to and included in the central period of decolonisation within the British empire between 1947 and the 1970s, and then in the ensuing years up to the present. In this sense, then, postcolonial literary study is concerned with how such writings have registered and engaged with the experiences of colonialism, decolonisation, and 'postcolonialism' understood not just as a period after colonialism but also as a state of affairs marked by the legacies of colonial rule.

But that latter point, and the open-ended nature of the 'after-ness' of the term 'postcolonial', raises a further question here. For how long after the end of colonialism does it remain relevant or accurate to talk of a nation, a culture, or a literature as postcolonial? Are the former colonies of the British empire doomed to be forever just a paler shade of red on the map, their identities eternally defined by the legacy of colonialism – or is there some end in sight, a point at which it will seem entirely anachronistic to keep defining a culture by its postcoloniality? After all, on the whole, we do not talk, today, of mainstream contemporary American literature as postcolonial, even though America was once part of the British empire (and aspects of its literature have certainly been discussed in postcolonial terms in the past). In fact, today, that could be seen as an insult, implying that American literature was not a fully developed and independent literature of its own, that it was still in some ways dependent on, subordinate to, the literature and culture of its old colonial master. And there is the rub, too, for a continued labelling of the literature of other former colonies as 'postcolonial', as this can be construed as just another subtle way of implying Britain's cultural superiority in that, as always, the definition places Britain in the defining role. Defining the field of study in relation to empire, that is, smacks of an attempt to perpetuate the cultural power of the imperial centre over the former colonial 'margins'. Many indigenous writers themselves resist the label of 'postcolonial' for these very reasons. C. L. Innes provides a useful example to elaborate the point: 'The Indian writer Nayantara Sahgal ... dislikes the term because she considers that it implies that colonization by the British is the only important thing that has happened to India, and that it denies the history that precedes British colonization and the continuing traditions stemming from those earlier periods' (*The Cambridge Introduction to Postcolonial Literatures in English*, p. 2 [Bii]). One justification for continuing to use the label, however, is that, even after independence, former colonies have often remained under the economic and cultural sway of Britain and, increasingly, of the United States, so that it has been possible to argue that their independence has not been fully achieved and that their economies in particular continue to be largely controlled by a new form of colonialism, or 'neo-colonialism' – one that does not involve any level of formal rule, but which nonetheless ensures a pervasive structural and ideological influence over the affairs of a nation. In the light of this, the anti-colonialist rationale of postcolonialism clearly continues to have relevance well beyond a nation's formal achievement of independence.

To consider the possible meanings and ambiguities of the label 'postcolonial literature' is not to split hairs over terminology, but a useful means of introducing some important issues in the field of postcolonial studies and of beginning to consider some of its theoretical underpinnings – and something of these underpinnings can also be gleaned from a brief consideration of the origins of the field.

One might say that, like sex in Britain (according to Philip Larkin), postcolonial literature began, probably, some time between the *Lady Chatterley* ban and the Beatles' first LP. Only, at that time, it was called 'Commonwealth literature' – and I am referring, of course, to the beginnings of the *study* of postcolonial literature as a formal academic discipline. By 1964 (the year after the Beatles' first LP) there was clearly a sufficiently developed level of interest within British academic circles to occasion a major conference on the subject of Commonwealth literature (held at the University of Leeds) along with the launch of a new *Journal of Commonwealth Literature*, the first issue of which was published in 1965 (the journal is still current today and a useful source of reference). From this time on, the study of Commonwealth literature became increasingly common within higher education in Britain and gradually became established in university English departments throughout the actual Commonwealth too. However, a cross-fertilisation with a range of traditional and new academic subjects with overlapping interests (anthropology, geography, sociology, politics, African studies, Black studies, Third World studies, etc.), along with the emergence in the 1970s of a much stronger theoretical orientation within literary and cultural studies in the wake of the impact of French post-structuralism, contributed to a questioning, by the 1980s, of both the name and nature of 'Commonwealth studies' in literature and more widely. The 'Commonwealth' label obviously defined the field by reference to the organisation that had come to replace the British empire, first as the British Commonwealth and then as simply the Commonwealth – so, clearly, despite the apparently benign and egalitarian nature of the Commonwealth organisation, there was always a vestigial sense in this label of the imperial power continuing to define and control the field of academic inquiry, while at the same time conveniently avoiding any explicit reference to the political realities of the colonial and imperial past. Paradoxically, the label was thus both politically 'incorrect' *and* insufficiently political for the mood of the times; and, as already hinted at, as a loosely descriptive label, it contained no clear theoretical orientation by which one might begin to structure and unify the field analytically and critically. Moreover, in restricting the field to Commonwealth countries, the label in principle excluded some English-speaking nations (like America and Ireland) and did not provide a ready interface for relating to the wider community of non-British scholars interested in developing global and comparative perspectives on postcolonialism beyond just the Commonwealth.

An alternative to both 'Commonwealth' and 'postcolonial' labels that has sometimes been preferred is 'New literatures in English'. This avoids defining the field solely by reference to colonialism and is less restrictive politically and geographically than the other two terms, but, again, it offers no theoretical or comparative dimension, the precise meaning of 'new literatures' is rather vague, and there remains an implied suggestion of 'junior' literatures that are defined by a senior master-literature. Perhaps the decisive factor in establishing 'postcolonial' as the dominant scholarly designation for this field of studies over the past twenty-five years, was the publication, in 1989, of the seminal critical work, *The Empire Writes Back: Theory and Practice in Post-Colonial Literatures*, by Bill Ashcroft, Gareth Griffiths and Helen Tiffin. In exploring, explaining and synthesising many of the key discussions in the field over the preceding forty years or so, and in developing a clear theoretical framework and rationale for that field, this book gave a clear lead to scholars and teachers in the establishment of postcolonial literary studies as a standard subject area within the university English curriculum from the early 1990s onwards. Explaining their choice of the term 'post-colonial', the authors write:

> 'Post-colonial' seems to be the choice which both embraces the historical reality and focuses on that relationship which has provided the most important creative and psychological impetus in the writing. Although it does not specify that the discourse is limited to works in english, it does indicate the rationale of the grouping in a common past and hints at the vision of a more liberated and positive future. In practical terms, the description … is less restrictive than 'Commonwealth'; it shares with 'new literatures in English' the ability to include, for example, the english literature of the Philippines or of the United States as well as that of 'pakeha' (white) or Maori writing in New Zealand, or that of both Blacks and whites in South Africa.
>
> However, the term 'post-colonial literatures' is finally to be preferred over the others because it points the way towards a possible study of the effects of colonialism in and between writing in english and writing in indigenous languages in such contexts as Africa and India, as well as writing in other language diasporas (French, Spanish, Portuguese).
>
> (p. 24[Bii])

(Note that the lower case 'e' for 'english' is used deliberately by the authors to distinguish variants of English which challenge the cultural hegemony of Standard English.) Even as Ashcroft, Griffiths and Tiffin make their argument for the term 'postcolonial', however, they acknowledge its limitations and suggest that 'better terms may still emerge' (p. 24). As suggested earlier, the term does continue to be contested and it remains to be seen how long a future it may have, but it has certainly survived since 1989 and, as those 'better terms' have not yet emerged, it remains the pre-eminent term for defining this field within the academic and literary-critical world.

Continuities, Influences and Innovations

Types of Colony

In approaching postcolonial literature in English in terms of its engagement with the complex after-effects of British colonisation, we first need to remind ourselves about the different types of colonies that were involved. Although each individual situation was different and had its own particular characteristics, there were three broad types of British colony and each type can be said to have had its own distinctive implications for the literature it has engendered. These three types were: colonies of settlement; colonies of rule; and colonies of *both* settlement and rule. The *colonies of settlement* or settler colonies, involved the permanent migration or transplantation of people from Britain to other lands – and the three main colonies of this sort that are usually included within postcolonial literary studies are Canada, Australia and New Zealand. Obviously, America was also originally in this category, but its initial settlement was so long ago that it tends not to be considered under the aegis of postcolonial studies and its literature is now almost always studied as an entity in its own right (or as part of a programme of American Studies, for example). The *colonies of rule* were those where the British generally did not settle permanently but established systems of direct or indirect rule – and the main colonies of this type were India (which included what are now Bangladesh, Burma and Pakistan) and most of the African colonies. In the category of *colonies of both settlement and rule*, there are two distinct sub-types, as it were. On the one hand, there were the colonies of the Caribbean, which were settled by people migrating permanently from Britain but which were then established as plantation economies and populated by slaves forcibly transported from West Africa who were thereafter, obviously, ruled by the white settlers. After the abolition of the slave trade, large numbers of indentured labourers, mainly from India, were also brought into the Caribbean and came to form a significant part of the population in Guyana and Trinidad in particular. On the other hand, there were a group of African colonies – South Africa, Rhodesia and Kenya – where Europeans settled permanently in large numbers and who, mainly by conquest, established rule over the majority populations of the many existing indigenous nations and peoples. However, within that broad pattern, the situation for each of these countries was quite different and that of South Africa, in particular, was hugely complicated by the fact that there were two colonising groups, the Dutch Boers (the first to settle) and the British. This meant that, over time in South Africa, there came to be two distinct colonising cultures – Afrikaner (as the Boers came to be known) and British – along with their own languages, Afrikaans and English. Eventually, it was an Afrikaner-dominated South Africa that became independent of the British empire in 1910 and which later left the Commonwealth in 1960. Although there would be some intermingling of Boers in the other two colonies of Rhodesia and Kenya, these were more straightforwardly British, with English as the colonising language. In Rhodesia, settlement was earlier and more extensive than in Kenya, and was based much more on initial violent conquest – and, while both colonies shared many colonial features, Rhodesia developed somewhat more like South Africa in establishing an authoritarian, apartheid-based white regime that became increasingly independent of Britain and which did eventually, and illegally, declare unilateral independence in 1965.

As these last examples show, once one begins to look more closely at the particular circumstances of each colony within each of the broad types, differences and complications begin to proliferate. A moment's reflection on the 'New World' colonies of America, Canada, Australia and New Zealand will remind us that, just as with the colonies of rule, all of these involved the disruption, conquest, rule (and sometimes extermination) of long-established indigenous cultures – Amerindian, Aboriginal and Maori – and this clearly makes more complex the senses in which we can talk of these places as being postcolonial. Moreover, as with South Africa, there were always two colonising cultures in Canada also, as Canadian territories were first substantially colonised by the French. Amongst other things, this means that (as with South Africa) two rich European linguistic and literary cultures have become established alongside one another. In the Caribbean, too, intense rivalry, over several centuries, amongst several European colonial powers – Portugal, Spain, France, Holland, Britain – meant that most of the islands and territories were exposed to multiple European influences over time, and some islands like Dominica, St Lucia and Trinidad have double European heritages alongside the heritages introduced from West Africa and India. Colonisation in this region also involved the disruption – and near-extermination by warfare, enslavement and disease – of long-established indigenous Amerindians (usually broadly grouped as Arawaks and Caribs). The postcolonial permutations of the Caribbean are, thus, amongst the most complex of all the regions under consideration. One might also add that, while it is true that there were never numerically significant levels of permanent British settlement on the Indian subcontinent (and even at the height of British rule, the vast majority of Indian people would never have encountered a white person), Britain's presence in India spanned more than four centuries and many Britons clearly did live there for prolonged periods (especially, but not only, during the so-called 'British Raj' after 1857), so that there is a sense of the British having been 'in' India in a more settled way than is suggested by the idea of a colony of rule. The situation becomes even more complicated when one takes into account the large-scale emigration of peoples from the former British colonies throughout the twentieth century, particularly to Britain itself from the late 1940s onwards (memorably described by the Jamaican poet, Louise Bennett, as 'colonizin in reverse'), but also to America and Canada. Thus, for some time now, there has been a large diaspora, in all these countries, of people of African, Indian and Caribbean heritage. This provides yet another important dimension to the meanings congregating around the term 'postcolonial', especially in relation to literature, as many writers in this diaspora are commonly categorised as postcolonial writers even though they do not permanently live in (and may not have been brought up in) the former colonial countries of their family heritage. Moreover, often for economic reasons, many postcolonial writers divide their time between their own countries and Britain or America or elsewhere and it has become increasingly common to read of the cosmopolitan credentials of contemporary authors in the biographical notes that are usually printed with their books. For instance, to choose two random examples: 'Gita Mehta … divides her time among India, England, and the United States' (biographical note, *A River Sutra*, 1993) and 'Vikram Seth was born in India and educated there and in England, California and China' (dustjacket, *Two Lives*, 2005). Such an internationalisation of authors' lives can be related to broader processes of globalisation in economics, politics, media and communications, and it further complicates our understanding of the conditions that shape postcolonial literature – to borrow Kazuo Ishiguro's novel title of 1986, we are now often dealing with writers of a floating world where 'local' and 'global' elements interpenetrate.

Languages, Styles and Local Cultures

When one comes to consider literary influences and continuities within Anglophone postcolonial literature, then, one can see immediately from the above that these are likely to be complex and multiple and, indeed, that innovations, crossovers and *dis-continuities* are just as likely to be the order of the day. One clearly needs always to bear in mind the richly diverse and often multilingual contexts out of which post-colonial writing emerges and, ideally, to give due weight, where relevant, to partic-ular local influences deriving not only from other European languages but from oral and scribal traditions in indigenous languages (traditions that are often closely bound up with belief-systems, of course). In India, for example, English is but one of many languages in which literature has been produced and one should not assume that Indian writers in English are somehow insulated from important literary influences from these other language traditions (some of which are much older than the English tradition). Much, if not most, of the Anglophone literature from the Caribbean is inflected to some degree by Creole forms of English and, as the Barbadian writer Kamau Brathwaite in particular has maintained, because of the slave trade's roots in West Africa, there are also continuities from there in black Caribbean language and culture which feed into its literature. In the Caribbean, also, spoken and sung oral traditions have been important influences on the development of its written litera-ture and both literature and 'orature' continue to develop in close interaction with one another. The rich traditions of oral storytelling in most parts of Africa have had a strong influence on African writing in English and, naturally, the styles and structures of African languages are often informing elements of how English is used by African writers in their work. There are large bodies of literature written in different African languages too, of course – Gikuyu and Swahili in East Africa, Igbo and Hausa in West Africa, Shona, Sotho, Xhosa and Zulu in Southern Africa, to mention just a few – and these are a further source of potential interactions with writings in English.

A flavour of the sort of multifaceted artistic negotiations amongst languages, gen-res and cultures that many postcolonial writers find themselves engaged in (whether consciously or not) is given here by the prominent Nigerian poet Niyi Osundare:

> I am painfully aware of the difference between the Yorùbá chant in my mind, and
> the English poem that is born after laborious midwifing, of the long journey between
> a song summoned from memory by the urgency of the human voice and a poem

committed to cold print with its scribal rigidity. I am aware of the liberty I am taking with English syntax, of the expansion and liberalization that must take place before a structural space ... can concede some room to the vibrant lyricism of the song of the marketplace and the village square. ... Most times I inhabit the interface between these two tongues ... keenly aware of the pragmatic necessity of English without losing sight of the vital primacy of Yorùbá.

('Yorùbá Thought, English Words', pp. 29–30 [Cii])

While readers cannot be expected to recognise all the background influences that might have gone into the shaping of every single individual postcolonial text, it is important to be aware that such a creative 'interfacial' process is often at work, fusing and transforming diverse linguistic and cultural materials from both sides of the interface into something hybrid and new. Such a hybridising process can produce effects for the reader that are initially disconcerting and perhaps difficult to make sense of immediately, but that is part of the challenge of postcolonial literature and what makes it distinctive and different from more familiar 'home-grown' writing in English. Even if the precise sources of difference in a particular text may be obscure until explored further, a general appreciation of why that difference might be there in the first place can be helpful in an initial reading to carry us through any immediate difficulties of sense or significance. For example, the opening sentence of *Season of Anomy* (1973), a major novel by another Nigerian author of Yorùbá background, Wole Soyinka, is perfectly understandable in its broad meaning, but I suspect most readers will feel the need to read it at least twice to come to terms properly with the unusual syntax:

A quaint anomaly, had long governed and policed itself, was so singly-knit that it obtained a tax assessment for the whole populace and paid it before the departure of the pith-helmeted assessor, in cash, held all property in common, literally, to the last scrap of thread on the clothing of each citizen – such an anachronism gave much patronising amusement to the cosmopolitan sentiment of a profit-hungry society.

(p. 2 [Ai])

As suggested, this might be slightly disconcerting at first, but even if we are not aware of Soyinka's precise background, a postcolonial openness to hybrid styles will incline us to assume that the narrator's style here is intended to reflect something of the style of an African language and/or manner of speech that would be appropriate to the African setting: if we know something about Soyinka, then we might assume that setting to be Nigeria and the style to be influenced, probably, by Yorùbá.

Soyinka himself makes a slightly different but directly pertinent point in his 2014 introduction to what has become a classic of African and Nigerian literature, Amos Tutuola's *The Palm-Wine Drinkard* (1952), where Soyinka explains Tutuola's highly unconventional and idiosyncratic style in terms of a 'polyglot' 'neither-nor' *invention* that is neither standard English nor local patois but nevertheless 'intuitively' attuned to the specific context of communal 'sounds':

Tutuola was not shut off from the 'correct' usage of the English language; he simply chose to invent his own tongue, festooned with uproarious images, turning it into a logical vehicle of the colonial neither-nor (or all-comer) environment. This was a polyglot proletariat – market traders, motor-park touts, farmers, office clerks and factory workers, Pentecostal Christians and proselytising Muslims, traditional *orisa* worshippers and all … Tutuola intuitively realised that the more common 'broken English', or patois, would not suffice to capture the sounds of such a community – a world that was too realistic to be liminal, too paranormal to be realistic, each segment intersecting with others according to its own laws – to impose a congruous existence on the imagination.

(p. vi [Ai])

What Soyinka also helpfully reminds us of here is that, as with all writing, Tutuola's style is inevitably an artfully *crafted* one (despite the fact that Tutuola was originally criticised for his apparent artlessness). Writing is a semiotic system and there can be nothing inherently 'natural' or straightforwardly direct in its correspondence to the world it depicts or to the language sounds it attempts to represent. Every piece of writing has to 'invent' and craft anew a language or style appropriate to its specific purpose. Nevertheless, as Soyinka implies later in the same introduction, Tutuola's loosely flowing language does structurally echo elements of traditional Yorùbá culture and is therefore well-suited to the Yorùbá folklore which the novel largely deals with: 'the Yoruba metaphysical world shies away from rigid compartmentalisation. The world of the living flows into the ancestral domain and into the fragile world of the Unborn' (p. vii). Where early critics had suggested that the novel was merely 'an extended folk tale in search of syntax' (p. v), Soyinka seems to counter that they had simply missed the significance of the hybrid Yorùbá syntax that was there all along.

Soyinka's reference above to 'broken English' is an allusion to Ken Saro-Wiwa's experimental novel in 'rotten English', *Sozaboy* (1985), which provides one of the clearest examples of how postcolonial writing often performs its own 'reverse colonisation' on the English language by investing it with the patterns of locally evolved variants of English, in this case the anarchic energies of what Saro-Wiwa himself describes as a 'disordered and disorderly' mixture of 'Nigerian pidgin English, broken English and occasional flashes of good, even idiomatic English' ('Author's Note', n. p. [Ai]). The result is a particularly marked hybrid form of English that obviously registers the grammar of a British colonial past at the same time as 'disordering' it with the day-to-day speech styles of the postcolonial present:

> So, although everyone was happy at first, after some time, everything begin to spoil small by small and they were saying that trouble have started … Radio begin dey hala as 'e never hala before. Big big grammar. Long long words. Every time.
>
>   Before before, the grammar was not plenty and everybody was happy. But now grammar begin to plenty and people were not happy. As grammar plenty, na so trouble plenty. And as trouble plenty, na so plenty people were dying … We motor people begin to make plenty money. Plenty trouble, plenty money. And my master was prouding. Making *yanga* for all the people, all the time.

(p. 3)

The novel remains 'a unique literary construct', of course, as William Boyd stresses in his introduction to the 1994 edition cited here – as he says, 'No one in Nigeria actually speaks or writes like this' (n.p.) – but the style gives us a *feel* for how ordinary people actually speak and also, importantly, for how the unsophisticated young narrator, the 'soldier boy' of the title, struggles to make sense of what, in the words of Saro-Wiwa's note, is a 'dislocated and discordant society'.

Modernism, Christianity and the Bible

I have emphasised the importance of attending to the 'local' material and cultural contexts of postcolonial writings partly to warn against moving too quickly to assimilate them to an Anglo-centric perspective that sees them predominantly as offshoots or outgrowths of the traditional canon of English (or Anglo-American) literature and which therefore runs the danger of obscuring significant elements of cultural difference and distinctiveness. Ashcroft, Griffiths and Tiffin give an interesting example of this danger when they point out that

> European critics have generally regarded the Malawian novelist David Rubadiri's *No Bride Price* (1967) as a simple, sociological account and a classic realist text. Yet criticism informed by an understanding of African oral performance and orature has shown how it reflects the pattern of traditional drum narratives which have been built into the structural features of the text.
>
> (*The Empire Writes Back*, p. 188 [Bii])

Having said that, we *do* also need to give due weight to postcolonial literature's complex dialogue with British culture and with 'mainstream' English literature, as this unquestionably provides one important dimension of continuity and interrelationship through which we can both better understand individual texts and traditions *and* make connections, comparisons and theoretical generalisations across many different cultural terrains. As discussed earlier, this is part of the point of describing the literature as 'postcolonial' in that it relates it, critically, to the former colonial culture.

   We can begin by noting a certain felicitous conjunction here in the fact that T. S. Eliot was responsible for negotiating the publication of Amos Tutuola's *The Palm-Wine Drinkard* by Faber & Faber in 1952. It is convenient to note this now because Eliot's poetry and the modernist tradition of the first half of the twentieth century that he is particularly associated with were important influences on many postcolonial writers. As we shall see later in the section of 'Readings', Eliot was a major influence on Kamau Brathwaite and Anita Desai, whose novel, *Clear Light of Day* (1980), amongst other things, carries an immediately explicit acknowledgement of influence in its opening epigraph from Eliot's *Four Quartets* (1944). Caryl Phillips's novel about 1950s migration from the Caribbean to England, *The Final Passage* (1985), also carries an epigraph from *Four Quartets*; and one of the most renowned of early postcolonial novels, Doris Lessing's Rhodesia-based *The Grass is Singing* (1950), takes its title from a line in Eliot's *The Waste Land* (1922) (and also prints a long extract from the poem as an epigraph). Chinua Achebe's second novel, *No Longer at Ease* (1960), takes its title from Eliot's 'The Journey of the Magi' (1927). These are just a few examples where Eliot's particular influence is explicit, but modernist influences generally are pervasive throughout postcolonial writing, in terms of both substance and style. Probably the single most famous postcolonial novel is Achebe's *Things Fall Apart* (1958), and this takes *its* title from W. B. Yeats's modernist poem, 'The Second Coming' (1921). The lines in the poem which contain this phrase are used by Achebe as an epigraph, too. They have particular thematic implications within the novel and also neatly conjure up something of the precise situation of the British empire's 'falling apart' in the 1950s when Achebe was writing the book (in the lead-up to Nigeria's own independence in 1960, amongst other things) – but, for present purposes, they can be used to give a clue to at least one of the reasons for the attraction of modernism for postcolonial writers:

> Turning and turning in the widening gyre
> The falcon cannot hear the falconer;
> Things fall apart; the centre cannot hold;
> Mere anarchy is loosed upon the world.

Neatly encapsulating modernism's typical sense of living through a period of fundamental change that augured a sharp break with the past, these lines would clearly offer a focus of strong identification for anyone interested in breaking with the past of colonialism, especially with the images of a falcon wheeling away from its master, no longer hearing (or heeding) his orders, and of a centre of power no longer able to maintain control over its peripheries. Modernism, that is, in its radical break with the past, both in dealing with unconventional subject matter and in pushing the bounds of established forms, provided postcolonial writers with an inspiring literary model for their own creative struggle to achieve a sharp break from the past – the colonial past.

Another relevant 'coincidence' here is that one of the novels that is often seen as an important precursor of modernism, if not one of its earliest actual manifestations, is also sometimes seen as one of the earliest postcolonial novels, too – Olive Schreiner's *The Story of An African Farm* (1883). For its period, the style and structure of Schreiner's novel were highly unconventional, as were her advanced evolutionary ideas and her radical feminist approach to sexuality and gender. These are the features that are usually adduced in claiming the novel for modernism. However, the book is set mainly on the high Karoo of the Eastern Cape in South Africa and presents a vivid and subtly critical picture of the rather unsettled dislocations of British and Boer settler life in the mid-nineteenth century (there is also an allegorical critique of colonising behaviour in the character of Bonaparte Blenkins), and, in that light, it qualifies as a postcolonial novel too. Here, though, we cannot sensibly say that Schreiner has been influenced by the later phenomenon of modernism and this is one of those instances where it is important to give due weight to local influences before reaching for more cosmopolitan perspectives. Indeed, one might say that the postcolonial dynamics of Schreiner's text are a large part of what later made it come to seem modernistic – a case of postcolonialism influencing modernism, rather than the other way round. And I have in mind here the way that the episodic and discontinuous structure of the narrative reflects not a modernist sensibility so much as the sensibility of a colonial consciousness of estrangement from the land, the European settler's sense of not-quite-belonging in the 'new world' environment. As Joseph Bristow concisely puts it in his introduction to the novel, 'Stretching out towards the horizon, Africa exceeds the explanations offered by the world-view brought by those invaders who have settled there' (p. xv [Ai]). This sense of estrangement and the concomitant search for 'grounding' in the new environment are central and recurring themes in the literature of all the settler colonies. Canadian Margaret Atwood's novel *Surfacing* (1972) and Keri Hulme's *Bone People* (New Zealand, 1985) are two examples among many – and the partial sense of resolution offered at the end of Schreiner's novel by Waldo's final quiet communing with nature, as his spirit passes peacefully away into the sunshine, foreshadows a similar resolution to this issue in Patrick White's *The Tree of Man* (1955), where the farmer, Stan Parker, becomes one with his environment at his death as he contemplates his spittle commingling with the Australian earth.

In noting the dialogue between postcolonial writing and modernism, it is worth also pointing out that many works of postcolonial literature have been categorised as 'post-modernist' because of their apparently experimental subversion of the conventions of *both* realism and modernism. However, critics continue to debate this issue and it is often argued that postcolonial writing is not so much post-modernist as reflective of indigenous traditions and conventions that simply do not conform to those of the West.

The use of dream-visions or mystical allegories within Schreiner's novel is another feature that is often cited as part of its experimental style, but these also relate to another important context for the novel which was shared by many other early (and some later) postcolonial writers. This is the context provided by Christianity and the Bible, for, of course, much of the education in British colonial territories was provided by Christian missionaries and many Anglophone postcolonial writers, from a wide spectrum of former colonies, were educated in mission schools and show clear evidence in their works of a common heritage in the stories, language and imagery of the Bible. Kenya's Ngugi wa Thiong'o, for example, who had his early schooling at a Church of Scotland mission school, reflects such an influence in his early novels *Weep Not, Child* (1964) and *The River Between* (1965), as does, in a very different way, Vic Reid in his highly rhythmical, semi-vernacular historical novel *New Day* (1949) which deals with the Jamaican Morant Bay rebellion of 1865. Schreiner herself was the daughter of missionaries and although she shed her Christian beliefs very early on in life, she clearly retained a predilection for a biblical style and used this especially in those sections of her novel where she wanted to suggest visionary alternatives to present reality through dreams or allegories. In this vein, the first chapter of Part II of the novel, 'Times and Seasons', is particularly replete with biblical language and allusion (though adapted for non-Christian purposes):

> And so, it comes to pass in time, that the earth ceases for us to be a weltering chaos. We walk in the great hall of life, looking up and round reverentially. Nothing is despicable—all is meaning-full; nothing is small—all is part of a whole, whose beginning and end we know not. The life that throbs in us is a pulsation from it; too mighty for our comprehension, not too small.
>
> (p. 118 [Ai])

Another South African writer whose language is particularly marked by biblical rhythms and images is Alan Paton, whose most famous and still widely read novel, *Cry, the Beloved Country* (1948), was highly influential in its time for its protest against the racial injustices of South Africa (and see also his intense and finely wrought *Too Late the Phalarope* (1953)). The opening description of *Cry, the Beloved Country* illustrates the style well and shows how Paton adapts the rhythms of the language to the landscape:

> There is a lovely road that runs from Ixopo into the hills. These hills are grass-covered and rolling, and they are lovely beyond any singing of it. The road climbs seven miles into them, to Carisbrooke; and from there, if there is no mist, you look down on one of the fairest valleys of Africa. About you there is grass and bracken and you may hear the forlorn crying of the titihoya, one of the birds of the veld ... Stand unshod upon it, for the ground is holy, being even as it came from the Creator. Keep it, guard it, care for it, for it keeps men, guards men, cares for men. Destroy it and man is destroyed.

(p. 11)

It has often been noted, also, that Tutuola's *Palm-Wine Drinkard* and other of his novels draw on the spiritual pilgrimage structure of Bunyan's *Pilgrim's Progress*. Indeed, as Gareth Griffiths says in his excellent chapter on missionary influences on writing in Africa, Bunyan's work 'had a powerful effect as a role model on much English and indigenous language writing in Africa', including on the very first indigenous African novel in English, *Guanya Pau* (1891) by Joseph Jeffrey Walters (Gareth Griffiths, *African Literatures in English*, pp. 63–4 [Bii]).

In noting a broad Christian framework of influence on postcolonial literature, we might of course trace a degree of continuity back to the early slave narratives of the eighteenth century, as these too were strongly shaped by biblical models absorbed from missionaries and the abolitionist Christian discourses of the period (see the discussions earlier in this book by Lee Morrissey and Peter Kitson, pp. 245–7 and 291, 330–3). These discourses were clearly important at that time in providing a space for the voices of slaves to be heard and the material structures supporting those discourses also obviously supplied the practical means for the writing, publication and circulation of the narratives. However, in his important essay on poetry and history in the Caribbean, 'The Muse of History' (1974), the St Lucia poet, Derek Walcott, comments interestingly on the transplanted slave culture's ambiguous inheritance from the Bible, when he writes, 'While the Old Testament epics of bondage and deliverance provided the slave with a political parallel, the ethics of Christianity tempered his vengeance and appeared to deepen his passivity ... the Christian treachery that seduces revenge' (Walcott, *What the Twilight Says: Essays*, pp. 45–6 [Ai]). What this should remind us of in terms of continuities into the nineteenth and twentieth centuries is that the Christianising and 'civilising' mission of the Church can also be seen as a hegemonic ideological influence that often supported and bolstered colonial rule, just as it could operate to 'passive-y' slaves. I turn to this idea here because the Bible and Christianity – and indeed modernism and other literary influences from the 'centre' that cannot hold – have often served as types of counter-influences on postcolonial literature too. That is, they have elicited critical or oppositional responses within postcolonial writing, a literal 'writing back' to the centre of empire designed to challenge all the many ways in which it has worked to colonise not just the bodies but also the hearts and minds of the colonised, through such things as religion and literature. We have already seen something of this in Olive Schreiner's appropriation of a biblical style which is then turned on the Bible itself as part of her critique of the Christian religion. In that instance, however, Schreiner's primary target *is* religion in that she is attacking what she considers to be an irrational system of faith in favour of her own evolutionary beliefs (although she is also attacking the ideological support that religion gives to a way of life that subordinates women). What later postcolonial writers like Ngugi and Chinua Achebe seek to challenge is not so much the religion *per se*, but what has been done by, and in the name of, that religion to displace and denigrate the traditional indigenous systems of belief and cultural order that were dominant prior to colonisation.

Achebe's *Things Fall Apart* – initially conceived as one work with *No Longer at Ease* – is probably the seminal instance of this sort of challenge, and he strongly consolidates the challenge in his later novel, *Arrow of God* (1964). As a response to the pervasive colonialist myths that Africa was a place of darkness and savagery and had no civilisation of its own worthy of the name, Achebe set out in these novels to represent traditional Igbo culture in detail from the inside, from its own point of view, and in its full richness and complexity. In *Things Fall Apart*, in particular, he also builds in a strategically structured comparison between Igbo and British traditions in that, after the long first part of the book in which he firmly establishes the Igbo way of life, he then has two much shorter parts in which he presents the arrival in the region of British missionaries and a British colonial government. While Achebe never oversimplifies matters with his contrastive technique, and he is careful to illustrate the shortcomings of Igbo culture as much as its strengths and to make clear some of the attractions of Christianity to the Igbo, the general effect of the novel's structure (and narrative point of view) is to turn the tables on traditional colonial discourse by introducing the Igbo in depth from the inside and the British in relatively shallow ways from the outside – as well as from the point of view of an Igbo consciousness which struggles to make sense of the strange ways of the white interlopers and their alien and (to some Igbo) plainly 'mad' religion: '"You told us with your own mouth that there was only one god. Now you talk about his son. He must have a wife, then" … At the end of it Okwonkwo was fully convinced that the man was mad' (p. 122) [Ai]. Thus, the British are in a sense made strange for the reader, and their religion and culture are exposed in bare outline, as it were, while, on the other hand, we come to gain a deep insight into the intricate workings of traditional Igbo society.

Writing Back to the Canon

Things Fall Apart is also a seminal example of postcolonial 'writing back' to the traditional canon of English literature and to the problematic images it has often constructed of colonised peoples and places. Achebe's novel, as already suggested, is a type of history of Igbo civilisation designed to counter self-serving colonialist stereotypes and simplifications. In its original conception, the novel was planned by Achebe partly as a response to Joyce Cary's colonial novel *Mister Johnson* (1939) (whose scenario is now more directly echoed in *No Longer at Ease*), but it is also, famously, a counterblast to Joseph Conrad's influential vision of Africa in his classic modernist novel *Heart of Darkness* (1902), which Achebe has also attacked more directly in his critical writings and, most notably, in the essay 'An Image of Africa: Racism in Conrad's *Heart of Darkness*' (1977), where he writes: '*Heart of Darkness* projects the image of Africa as "the other world", the antithesis of Europe and therefore of civilization, a place where man's vaunted intelligence and refinement are finally mocked by triumphant bestiality' (Achebe, *Hopes and Impediments: Selected Essays 1965–87*, p. 2 [Ai]). In the same essay, Achebe goes on to make the important point that 'Conrad did not originate the image of Africa which we find in his book. It was and is the dominant image of Africa in the Western imagination and Conrad merely brought the peculiar gifts of his own mind to bear on it' (p. 12). In bringing the peculiar gifts of *his* mind to bear on Conrad's (and Cary's) representative 'dehumanization of Africa' (p. 8), Achebe, in *Things Fall Apart*, might be said to have inaugurated the postcolonial tradition of 'writing back' to the canon mentioned above.

Such a strategy of writing back has been an important means in postcolonial literature of challenging and subverting the dominant discourses of colonialism and neo-colonialism – and, therefore, of contributing to the general postcolonial struggle to 'decolonise' minds, imaginations and sensibilities. As a widespread strategy amongst writers, moreover, it has helped to establish what Helen Tiffin has described as a field of 'post-colonial counter-discourse'. As she explains this important idea further, Tiffin places what might otherwise sometimes appear as isolated instances of literary 'borrowing' within a clear theoretical framework, and she also helpfully emphasises that writing (and reading) back is *not* colonisation in reverse, but a nuanced process of dialogue premised on an inevitable hybridity:

> Post-colonial cultures are inevitably hybridised … Decolonisation is process, not arrival; it invokes an ongoing dialectic between hegemonic centrist systems and peripheral subversion of them; between European or British discourses and their post-colonial dis/mantling. Since it is not possible to create or recreate national or regional formations wholly independent of their historical implication in the European colonial enterprise, it has been the project of post-colonial writing to interrogate European discourses and discursive strategies from a privileged position within (and between) two worlds; to investigate the means by which Europe imposed and maintained its codes in the colonial domination of so much of the rest of the world.
>
> Thus the rereading and rewriting of the European historical and fictional record are vital and inescapable tasks. These subversive manoeuvres … are what is characteristic of post-colonial texts, as the subversive is characteristic of post-colonial discourse in general.
>
> ('Post-colonial Literatures and Counter-Discourse', pp. 95–6 [Bii])

Chinua Achebe is by no means the only postcolonial writer to have 'replied' to Joseph Conrad, as C. L. Innes indicates:

> Nadine Gordimer's short story 'The African Magician' (1965) rewrites Conrad's story of a voyage up the Congo, and [Abdulrazak] Gurnah's *Paradise* [1994] also carries Conradian echoes, as its protagonist Yusuf (Joseph) journeys into the interior of the African continent. Parallel journeys into the interior of Guyana and Australia have been written by Wilson Harris in the *Palace of the Peacock* (1960) and other novels belonging to his Guyana Quartet, and Patrick White in *Voss* (1957) … Ama Ata Aidoo's *Our Sister Killjoy: or Reflections from a Black-eyed Squint* (1977) … can be read as a seriously playful and experimental reversal of Conrad's novel that engages with questions of history and its modes of narration.
>
> (*The Cambridge Introduction to Postcolonial Literatures in English*, p. 48 [Bii])

At the same time, Conrad is by no means the only canonical writer to have served as a source of counter-discourse for postcolonial writers. In fact, there are so many, that one might say that there is now a postcolonial canon of canonical writers who have been written back to (as John Thieme's wide-ranging study, *Postcolonial Con-Texts: Writing Back to the Canon* (2002), amply illustrates). Leading that canon, ahead of Conrad, are William Shakespeare and Daniel Defoe for the importance of their texts, *The Tempest* (first performed, 1611) and *Robinson Crusoe* (1719), as sites of postcolonial debate, dialogue and creative transformation. The fundamental importance of both texts to colonialism has been thoroughly explored by Peter Hulme in his magisterial study, *Colonial Encounters: Europe and the Native Caribbean 1492–1797* (1986). Hulme here shows in detail how these works were instrumental in establishing an anxiety-ridden myth of first encounter between 'civilised' Europe and the 'virgin' but 'savage' native Caribbean. This was a myth focused on 'the classic colonial triangle' of 'European, native and land' which, Hulme argues, became an integral part of the dominant discourse of colonialism through which 'large parts of the non-European world were *produced* for Europe' (pp. 1–2; [Cii]). With Prospero and Caliban on the one hand and Crusoe and Man Friday on the other, both these texts involve a basic master–slave relationship in an island setting clearly evocative of early colonial encounters in the Caribbean; and both texts have provided rich material for postcolonial rewritings, rereadings, and adaptations. Ashcroft, Griffiths and Tiffin note a wide range of these for *The Tempest* – for example, Barbadian George Lamming's influential postcolonial rereading of Shakespeare's play in his *The Pleasures of Exile* (1960), and the reworking of the play in an African context, in 1969, by the Francophone Martinique poet, Aimé Césaire (one of the main voices of the Négritude movement from the 1930s) – and they write further:

> *The Tempest* has been perhaps the most important text used to establish a paradigm for post-colonial readings of canonical works … In fact, more important than the simple rereading of the text itself by critics or in productions has been the widespread employment of the characters and structure of *The Tempest* as a general metaphor for imperial–margin relations … or, more widely, to characterize some specific aspects of post-colonial reality … Lamming himself has re-written *The Tempest* from a post-colonial perspective in his novel *Natives of My Person* [972].
>
> (*The Empire Writes Back*, pp. 190–1 [Bii])

8.6 Amerigo Vespucci 'discovers' America. A print from c. 1589–93 by Theodoor Galle after an engraving by Jan van der Straet in the Amsterdam Rijksmuseum. Recreating Vespucci's 'first' encounter with the virginal New World in 1501, this is an image replete with colonialist symbolism.

As we shall see later in my reading of Kamau Brathwaite, his poetry, too, draws significantly on *The Tempest*.

Daniel Defoe's novel, meanwhile, has been a regular point of reference for postcolonial writers as a ready metaphor for New World settlement and/or for colonial invasion and domination; it also offers a sharply defined dramatic focus for exploring the relationship between coloniser and colonised. Caribbean writers in particular often allude to the Crusoe scenario – for example, Derek Walcott's second collection of poems was entitled *The Castaway* (1965) and included 'Crusoe's Journal' and other Crusoe-related poems. Walcott has recast the story as a play, *Pantomime* (1980), and has written a critical essay on 'The Figure of Crusoe' (1993) and refers to it several times in other essays (for example, in the earlier- mentioned 'The Muse of History'). Crusoe's island is said to be located within sight of Trinidad, so it is perhaps no coincidence that Trinidadian writers like V. S. Naipaul have a particular interest in the work. In his book of articles *The Overcrowded Barracoon* (1972), Naipaul has six journalistic pieces in a section entitled 'Columbus and Crusoe', and these draw variously on ideas and images from Defoe's novel to provide a valuable sketch of postcolonial life in the Caribbean at the end of the 1960s (the title of one of the essays gives a flavour of Naipaul's wry tone here: 'Anguilla: The Shipwrecked Six Thousand'); and his novel *The Mimic Men* (1967), particularly rich in postcolonial themes generally, has at its heart a sense of the powerlessness arising from marginalisation and a Crusoe-like abandonment – 'We, here on our island … had been abandoned and forgotten. We pretended to be real … we mimic men of the New World' (p. 175 [Ai]). Two other Trinidadian references that might be noted in passing are the poems, 'Crusoe's Thursday' (1994) by John Lyons (in Brown and McWatt, eds. *The Oxford Book of Caribbean Verse*, p. 146 [Ai]), and 'Poem' (1971) by John La Rose, which, in fact, mixes references to both *Crusoe* and *The Tempest* ('Damn Caliban! … Crusoe's accursed cannibal's lot!') (in Salkey, ed. *Breaklight*, p. 38 [Ai]). Defoe's novel has also been reworked in post-modernist style by the South African writer, J. M. Coetzee, in his challenging novel *Foe* (1986), where he blends postcolonial and feminist concerns in exploring whether it is ever possible to give authentic voice to the histories and victims of oppression (the Friday figure in this novel has had his tongue pulled out).

Other notable examples of postcolonial 'writing back' are Jean Rhys's critical reworking of elements of Charlotte Brontë's *Jane Eyre* in *Wide Sargasso Sea* (1966; see my later discussion under Readings); Salman Rushdie's critical echoing of (amongst others) E. M. Forster's *A Passage to India* (1924) in his magical realist narrative of postcolonial India, *Midnight's Children* (1981); Guyanan Wilson Harris's version of Dante's *Divine Comedy* in his *Carnival* (1986); and Australian Peter Carey's recuperation of the history of Dickens's convict, Magwitch, from *Great Expectations*, in his *Jack Maggs* (1997). Such rewritings have also helped to generate a great many postcolonial rereadings of canonical texts aimed at drawing out the ways in which they might be said to participate in colonial discourse. As Ashcroft, Griffiths and Tiffin point out:

> Once this kind of reading strategy is engaged, the possibilities for reconstructing the more or less hidden potentialities of other English literary texts, such as those of Austen, Thackeray, and Swift, are revealed. Yasmine Gooneratne (1986), for example, has reread Jane Austen's *Mansfield Park* to uncover the silences of the text and its repression of the economic basis on which polite society erects its civilized practices. The 'dead silence' which greets Fanny's enquiries to her uncle, Sir Thomas Bertram, as to the slave trade is a resonant reminder of the hidden anguish and torture on which estates like Mansfield Park are raised.
>
> (*The Empire Writes Back*, pp. 192–3 [Bii]).

Edward Said also discusses Austen and other novelists in the above terms in a well-known book that helped to promote just this sort of postcolonial rereading – *Culture and Imperialism* (1993 [Cii]). What such a development suggests is that, as well as being the study of texts produced within postcolonial contexts, postcolonialism can also be understood as a *way* of reading that is informed by postcolonial thinking and which can, in principle, be applied to any text.

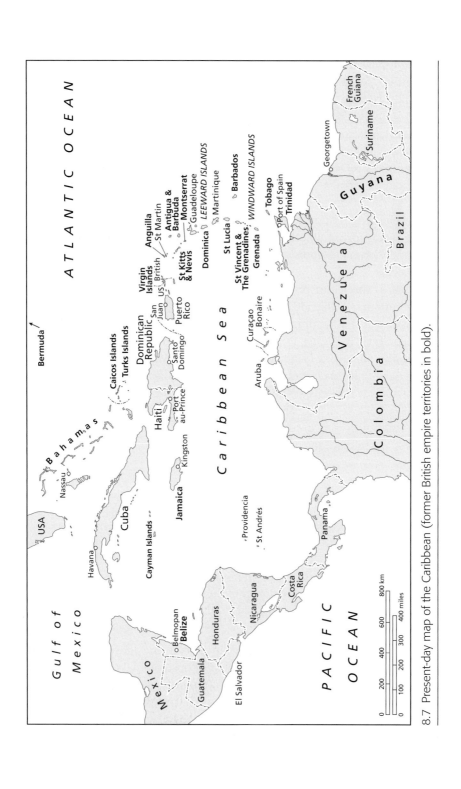

8.7 Present-day map of the Caribbean (former British empire territories in bold).

Readings

Ngugi wa Thiong'o, *Weep Not, Child* (1964)

Ngugi's finely crafted, poetic, and politically charged novel is an exemplar of post-colonial literature in its tightly integrated engagement with a whole gamut of leading postcolonial issues – power, race, class, culture, tradition, beliefs, language, identity, gender – though of particular prominence here are the issues of land and education and the novel's thoroughgoing commitment to anti-colonialist critique. While Chinua Achebe's *Things Fall Apart* is often, with justice, seen as the foundational novel of postcolonial literature for its recuperation of African history and culture and its 'writing back' to the imperialist centre, Ngugi's novel is a landmark of postcolonial writing's characteristic *political* will, not just to recuperate the past from imperialist distortion, but also to engage directly with the injustices of the colonial and neo-colonial present so as to recuperate (so to speak) the possibility of a freer, fairer and more humane future for all.

Weep Not, Child is by no means as explicitly political or ideological as much of Ngugi's later work, but it deals directly with the political realities of colonial Kenya from the post-war 1940s through to the first years of the anti-colonial uprising known as the Mau Mau rebellion (1952–6) which precipitated moves towards Kenya's eventual independence in 1963. Events in the novel are focalised primarily (though by no means exclusively) by the 'innocent eye' of the young Gikuyu boy, Njoroge, as we follow him through the various stages of his education. The novel opens with an immediate focus on that theme, as Njoroge's mother breaks the good news that the family can afford to send him to school. Njoroge can hardly believe his ears and his deep delight is palpable: '*O, mother, you are an angel of God, you are, you are ... Had she been to a magic worker? Or else how could she have divined his child's unspoken wish, his undivulged dream?*' (p. 3). This scene sets the tone for repeated moments throughout the novel where we hear of Njoroge's almost religious faith in education as the key to the future for himself, his family, his village and even his country. It also reflects the high value placed on education by his community: 'Somehow the Gikuyu people always saw their deliverance as embodied in education' (pp. 104–5). Njoroge's experiences at each of his three schools are clearly a major part of his development and they punctuate the narrative throughout (providing, among other things, a useful insight into the nature of the schooling available in colonial Kenya at that time).

Njoroge's story of formation is carefully interwoven with the broader context of the Mau Mau rebellion as this is experienced by Njoroge and his family, along with the rest of his village. Of particular significance are two other families, that of Howlands, the white settler farmer on whose land Njoroge's father, Ngotho, works; and that of Jacobo, the prosperous black landowner on whose land Njoroge's family lives, and whose privileged status derives from his wily collaboration with the British. These three family units operate representatively to reflect the racial and class stratifications in the society, but their internal relationships and the interactions between the families also provide the essential dynamics which drive the narrative. Within Njoroge's family, for example, the clash of generations between Ngotho and his eldest son, Boro, dramatises questions of tradition, belief and political engagement and eventually pushes both men to different forms of radical action that contribute directly to the outcome of the novel. Similarly, the childhood friendship between Njoroge and Mwihaki, Jacobo's daughter, serves to nuance the representative oppositions between the family units (as does a briefer school encounter between Njoroge and Howlands' son, Stephen (ch. 14)) and it also matures into a type of *Romeo and Juliet* scenario that operates in subtle counterpoint to the communal tragedy that slowly envelops the young couple.

A good deal of the relevant historical background to the Mau Mau rebellion is incorporated within the novel itself as part of the lived experiences of the characters, and, although the reader obviously needs to piece this together from the narrative as it unfolds, it clearly serves Ngugi's political purpose of re-presenting colonial history from the point of view of the colonised. Njoroge's village of Mahua is located in the 'White Highlands' of Kenya's Central Province, which, as the name suggests, was the principal area of white settlement. Settlement here was encouraged by the British from 1903 largely to fill an economic vacuum and to generate agricultural freight that might help to pay for the hugely expensive Uganda Railway that had been built in the 1890s (nicknamed the 'lunatic line' because its purpose was never clear). The white settlers were drawn to the region by the favourable climate and fertile land – and by the fact that enormous acreages of land were being offered at absurdly low prices. However, these were in fact the ancestral lands of thousands of indigenous Gikuyu people so that white settlement actually meant the systematic seizure of their land and a gradual 'clearance' of the Gikuyu into overcrowded 'African reserves' on poor agricultural land that could not possibly sustain the density of numbers involved. The Gikuyu were thus dispossessed of their land (which sustained them economically *and* spiritually, according to their traditional beliefs) and at the same time turned into a source of cheap labour for the white settlers. After the First World War, the situation was significantly exacerbated by a further large influx of white settlers under a Soldier Settlement Scheme which again offered land cheaply, this time to British soldiers returning from the war. In *Weep Not, Child*, these events are reflected directly in the experience of Njoroge's family, as his father Ngotho tells them, as he recalls his own 'reward' for service in the war:

> Then came the war. It was the first big war. I was then young, a mere boy, although circumcised. All of us were taken by force. We made roads and cleared the forest to make it possible for the warring white man to move more quickly. The war ended. We were all tired. We came home worn out but very ready for whatever the British might give us as a reward. But more than this, we wanted to go back to the soil and court it to yield, to create, not to destroy. But Ng'o! The land was gone. My father and many others had been moved from our ancestral lands. He died lonely, a poor man waiting for the white man to go.

(pp. 25–6)

Black African grievances over land rights in colonial Kenya were greatly compounded by the existence of an apartheid-style colour bar, by the institution of racially discriminatory laws and by a general lack of basic rights for the majority population. The first black Kenyan political movement was formed in the early 1920s led by Harry Thuku, but this had little impact on a regime determined to maintain white dominance and which at that time was itself threatening to rebel against the British government to avoid having to make reforms. Later, in 1944, the Kenya African Union was established by Joma Kenyatta to renew the political campaign for change but this too failed to make major progress and, in the changed climate after the Second World War, patience in the political process began to run out, especially among younger black Kenyans, some of whom had become radicalised during the war, and for whom armed struggle now seemed to be the only hope.

In the novel, the essence of this situation is dramatised in the story of Njoroge's eldest brother, Boro, who fights for the British in the war and who later becomes a leading Mau Mau fighter during the rebellion. Following on almost immediately from Ngotho's speech above, we are told of Boro:

> He too had gone to war, against Hitler. He had gone to Egypt, Jerusalem and Burma. He had seen things. He had often escaped death narrowly … When the war came to an end, Boro had come home, no longer a boy but a man with experience and ideas, only to find that for him there was to be no employment. There was no land on which he could settle … all these things came into his mind with a growing anger. How could these people have let the white man occupy the land without acting? … To his father, he said, 'How can you continue working for a man who has taken your land? How can you go on serving him?'
>
> He walked out, without waiting for an answer.
>
> (pp. 26–7)

Boro has clearly decided to take his own action; and, indeed, he later plays a decisive role in the grim denouement of the plot through the murder of Howlands and Jacobo, who have come, by the time of the emergency, to represent the colonial order at its most brutal. Until this time, neither man has been presented entirely unsympathetically. However, once Howlands becomes temporary District Officer in charge of security, he seems to lose all restraint and, somewhat like Conrad's Kurtz in *Heart of Darkness*, turns to his own form of barbarism, sadistically torturing Njoroge and Ngotho and revelling in the thought of what he anticipates as a self-inflicted bloodbath of 'savages' (pp. 118–20, 97, 77). Jacobo, meanwhile, now cynically manipulated by Howlands (who secretly despises him), has become the leader of the homeguards and has become universally feared as 'a terror in the land' (p. 91).

In dealing with the period of the rebellion and the British military suppression of it, however, Ngugi is again careful to reflect the true historical situation and to provide different points of view on it. Thus, he conveys a sense of the confusion and terror inspired among the Gikuyu community by the secretive Mau Mau guerillas themselves – 'they cut black men's throats' (p. 72); 'they could slash their opponents into pieces with Pangas' (p. 89) – and it is undoubtedly true that the Mau Mau did target mainly Gikuyu 'collaborators' during the rebellion (killing around 2000) rather than the white settlers (of whom around 32 were killed). On the other hand, summary executions and beatings (pp. 85–6, 101) and the above-mentioned torturing of Ngotho and Njoroge are presented as examples of the now well-attested atrocities carried out by the British security forces during the emergency. These were on a massive scale and Ngugi's examples are relatively restrained – some estimates suggest that around 100,000 Kenyans died through torture, starvation and neglect in British prison camps, and 1,090 Kenyans were hanged by the authorities, often on flimsy charges. But perhaps what the novel demonstrates most clearly through its representation of the violence unleashed in the rebellion is the always potentially brutal and brutalising nature of colonialism and of any social order founded on oppression. It remains for the young – however naively – to offer some hope in the darkness. Thus, we witness Njoroge consoling Mwihaki:

> The sun will rise tomorrow … if you knew even for one moment that this would go on for ever, then life would be meaningless unless bloodshed and death were a meaning. Surely this darkness and terror will not go on for ever.

> (p. 106)

Unfortunately, the terror has only just begun and later, at the end of the novel, Njoroge will reject any easy optimism about the future of his country – "'my tomorrow was an illusion'" (p.132) – as he proposes to Mwihaki that they run away to Uganda. Ironically, it is then the turn of Mwihaki to insist that his vision was not an illusion and that, as young adults now, they have a duty to their families and community to remain resolute for the future. Njoroge is not convinced and contemplates suicide, and the novel ends on a note of ambivalence, certainly. However, *this* 'Romeo and Juliet' does not end in either of the lovers' deaths and Njoroge's attempt at suicide is prevented by his mother, Nyokabi, in a highly symbolic scene which sees her coming to find him in the dark and leading him home to the light: 'He saw the light she was carrying and falteringly went towards it. It was a glowing piece of wood which she carried to light the way' (p. 135).

In drawing attention to Ngugi's commitment to presenting a verifiable (if fictionalised) version of historical events, I do not want to suggest that *Weep Not, Child* is a documentary novel or even a novel of classic social realism. In fact, with its temporally disjunctive and episodic structure, its multi-voiced narration and constantly shifting points of view, with an extensive use of free indirect style and some unusual Brechtian breaks in the narration (as, for example, in the 'Interlude' section, pp. 62–4), the novel is more clearly in the tradition of experimental modernism; and, while the novel may register real historical events, the reader still has to work critically to make sense of what is being presented. There is no traditional omniscient narrator here to interpret things for us. This is a particularly pertinent point in relation to the theme of education, as the novel – again, in true modernist style – counterpoints content and form by matching the explicit thematic focus on education in the story with a narrative technique that, as it were, forces readers into a learning process of their own. Njoroge provides us with one privileged point of view in the novel, but, as the narration operates, this is not just a point of view but also a voice or a style, and it is the style, for much of the novel, of a young and inexperienced child. Both what we 'see' and what we are told thus have the limitations of the child's consciousness and understanding. Other voices and points of view are available to help us to put together a fuller and more rounded picture of events but these all have their own particular limitations of perspective and understanding too – and this includes the 'first' narrator who introduces the characters and other aspects of the story world, as here: 'And the road which ran across the land and was long and broad had no beginning and no end. At least, few people knew of its origin. Only if you followed it it would take you to the big city and leave you there ... ' (p. 5). This narrator, who speaks in a style evocative of one of the Gikuyu villagers, is perhaps best described as a lightly dramatised 'folk' voice, and Ngugi is careful to restrict the range of information that this voice divulges, so that, though it knows a *little* more than the others, it blends in as part of the combined communal polyphony of voices.

Overall, then, it is a strictly limited viewpoint that we are presented with at any one time and there is certainly no unified critical perspective provided on the whole colonial situation in which the novel's voices are embedded. And this, I think, is the point: that just as Njoroge's painful experiences eventually reveal to him his 'false consciousness' and show him that the formal schooling that he has set so much store by has not actually taught him to see the world as it really is – 'all these experiences now came to Njoroge as shocks that showed him a different world from that he had believed himself living in' (p. 120) – so we are led, partly also by Njoroge's 'shocks', to see that the fragmented perspectives offered by the novel's voices ultimately *cannot* be pieced together into a unified whole because these are the voices of a deeply divided society and of an alienated people unable, because un-free, to make whole sense of their lives, either individually or communally. *Weep Not, Child* is thus not just a political novel, but a politicising novel, where we learn *with* the text that the struggle for true understanding cannot be separate from the struggle for freedom and autonomy.

Jean Rhys, *Wide Sargasso Sea* (1966)

As a profound and multifaceted exploration of cultural identity fully enmeshed within the historical contexts of British colonialism in the West Indies, Jean Rhys's *Wide Sargasso Sea* is an outstanding example of a characteristic work of postcolonial literature. Rhys's novel is, of course, a well-established classic of twentieth-century literature generally and often seen as a masterpiece of late literary modernism. It is also well-known for its 'rewriting' of aspects of Charlotte Bronte's nineteenth-century classic, *Jane Eyre* (1847), and in particular for its feminist-inflected recuperation of the identity and history of that novel's character, Bertha Mason, the archetypal 'mad woman in the attic', through Rhys's own character, Antoinette Cosway. As that identity and history are intimately linked to the Caribbean, the postcolonial nature of *Wide Sargasso Sea* has long been recognised by critics. However, the full scope of its engagement with postcolonial issues bears some restatement, I think, especially for new readers.

Perhaps the first thing to note is the novel's almost endless proliferation of cross-cultural elements and its embodiment, therefore, of an inextricably hybridised postcolonial culture. Rhys's own thoroughly multicultural background clearly contributed to her artistic representation of this world. She was born in the Caribbean on the island of Dominica to a white Scottish-Creole mother and a Welsh father, whose own mother, Rhys's paternal grandmother, was Irish. Dominica had origi-nally been colonised by the French and retained a strong French-Catholic culture beside its British Anglo-Protestant culture – which also meant that both English and French were spoken along with patois variants of both languages. Rhys spent the first sixteen years of her life in Dominica (spending three months on St Lucia when she was twelve) but then left for England in 1907; she later lived for a period in Europe (in Holland, France and Austria), before eventually settling back in England where she wrote *Wide Sargasso Sea* over about ten years from the mid-1950s to its pub-lication in 1966. Apart from a brief visit at the end of the 1930s, she never returned to Dominica, although she maintained contact with the island and briefly considered returning to settle there in later life.

Wide Sargasso Sea and *Jane Eyre* clearly share many important features in their nar-ration of the interrelated stories of Bertha Mason and Antoinette Cosway. They both present a young woman's formation from childhood, through adolescent experi-ences at school, to adulthood, love and marriage; they both celebrate passion and spontaneity over cold reason and convention as well as spiritual and personal fulfil-ment over money and status; they share patterns of imagery (fire and the colour red, for example) and make highly symbolic use of descriptions of nature and the envi-ronment; both draw on Gothic elements such as cruelty, injustice, dreams, super-stitions and hints of the supernatural; they are both narrated in the first-person and privilege a female point of view (though the Rochester character narrates part of Rhys's novel). However, we miss much of the point of Rhys's novel if we do not appreciate the clear differences between the two works and see, in particular, that *Wide Sargasso Sea*, to the extent that it is a mirror image of *Jane Eyre*, is a *reversed* mir-ror image, or, rather, a depiction of the *other* side of the mirror. Most obviously, we see the other side of Bertha's story and another side of the Rochester character and, with both characters, we see other sides of 'insanity'; but most importantly for our purposes, we also see a side of social history that is largely (if not entirely) occluded in the earlier novel – that of colonialism and how it fed, and fed into, a class-based, patriarchal society strongly centred on money, power and status. The two novels are clearly formally and technically very different too, and, of course, underlying most of their differences is the fact that they are products of very different periods and approach their subjects from very different cultural paradigms or frameworks.

Wide Sargasso Sea is nothing if not a thoroughly modern – indeed, modernist – novel. Its fundamental concern with the unconscious psychology of its two major characters, and particularly with the identity-crisis of Antoinette, and its use of an intensive psychological focus to illustrate issues of race, gender and class and their interactions in determining power relations in society; its treatment of alienation and social fragmentation, of sexual passion, cruelty, prejudice and violence; its cynicism and fatalism; its impressionistic and elliptical, open-ended style; its fluid use of time in flashbacks and flashforwards, and its shifts and restrictions of nar-rative point of view – all these things clearly reflect Rhys's pedigree as a modernist writer (who had first come to prominence in the 1920s and 1930s). The novel also reflects its period of composition, particularly in relation to its engagement with colonial history, as this was the period of the first main wave of decolonisation within the British empire and overlapped also with the era of Caribbean migration to Britain from 1948 onwards into the 1960s. Rhys must have been acutely aware of these contemporary developments even as she was delving back into nineteenth-century history for the fictional period of her novel (Jamaica, for example, one of the main settings in the novel, attained independence in 1962 – though Dominica remained a British dependency until 1978). Rhys's novel was therefore historically *post*-colonial while, internally, it engages in critical postcolonial dialogue with both the period of its setting, in the 1830s and 40s, after the abolition of slavery in the British empire, *and*, inevitably, with the years of Rhys's own growing up in Dominica at the end of the nineteenth and start of the twentieth centuries, as Rhys clearly draws on these early experiences for her descriptions of the natural and social environments of the Caribbean islands. All these historical contexts are relevant to an understanding of Rhys's complex portrayal of the formation of her character's personal and cultural identity.

But 'formation' is probably something of a misnomer here, as what Rhys actually portrays for much of the novel is the *fragmentation* of Antoinette's sense of identity ('fragmentation' both as a state and as a process), a fragmentation brought about by, and inseparable from, the fragmented nature of her society. The novel is precisely about the interrelationship between social and psychic fracture: it is about Antoinette's psychological self-division and her struggle for an integrated personality, and it is, to some degree, also about the psychological weakness and self-division of the Rochester character – but both characters are also products or 'victims' (in different ways of course) of their particular sociocultural formations, Antoinette as a dispossessed Creole woman of a despised, former slave-owning expatriate community, and 'Rochester' as a younger 'dispossessed' son of the English upper classes forced by circumstance to become a reluctant colonial fortune-hunter. She is a 'white cockroach' to the black community and a 'white nigger' to the non-Creole English, '"So between you I often wonder who I am and where is my country and where do I belong and why was I ever born at all"'(p. 85). 'Rochester', meanwhile, has been emotionally stunted by his conventional upbringing and finds it difficult to recognise any deeper sense of self beneath his prescribed social persona – 'How old was I when I learned to hide what I felt? A very small boy. Six, five, even earlier. It was necessary, I was told, and that view I have always accepted' (p. 85). Divided within themselves, the two characters are almost inevitably divided from others and from each other and their fated relationship stands symbolically for the historical cycle of conflict, internal division and fragmentation within postcolonial West Indian society.

There is an important difference, however, between the types of psychological weakness exhibited by Antoinette and the Rochester character and between what these weaknesses represent. Despite the tragic trajectory of her life, Antoinette's flamboyant Caribbean character always carries some *potential* for self-integration and self-realisation and there is a sense in which her very tragedy enacts a symbolic coming together of her self and her adoptive *black* community. Whereas the Rochester character (certainly by the end of the novel) seems truly incapacitated by his psychological self-division, because it cuts him off from his inner emotions, his inner self,

Antoinette seems throughout to have a strong subjective sense of self, and everything in the novel (including her style of narration) points to an emotional warmth, integrity and vitality that always suggests at least the possibility that she might be able to unify the disparate parts of her fragmented identity: 'She is Creole girl, and she have the sun in her', as Christophene says (p. 130). *Her* psychological weakness derives in fact not precisely from a division from her self but from a divided self-image, not from any lack of inner self, but from a confusion of possible selves, a confusion over identity that reflects the confusion of competing social and cultural forces around her and, crucially, of the competing definitions *by others* of who or what she is. Her instincts tell her that she would like to be black like her black mammie, Christophene, and her friend Tia ('I will live with Tia and I will be like her' (p. 38)), but she has been brought up, effectively, to aspire to being like the picture of 'The Miller's Daughter', 'a lovely English girl with brown curls and blue eyes and a dress slipping off her shoulders' (p. 30). And, as we have seen, the black community will not actually allow her to be 'black' like Tia and parts of the white community will not allow her to be fully 'white'. Antoinette seems never quite able to recognise herself in the mirror that her society holds up to her and when she looks in an actual mirror, 'The girl I saw was myself yet not quite myself' (p. 147). But even in this phrase, there is still a sense that Antoinette can *almost* catch a glimpse of her true self and, initially at least, the relationship with the Rochester character seems to offer her a chance of wholeness.

Rhys also initially suggests that, for him too, their relationship might point the way towards self-integration, but this is a route that he finally rejects when he rejects Antoinette and turns from the 'madness' of Granbois back to the cold 'sanity' and order of conventional society in Jamaica and England: 'All the mad conflicting emotions had gone and left me wearied and empty. Sane' (p. 141). Recoiling from the passionate Antoinette he has experienced within the essentially black culture of their honeymoon island (Dominica), he reasserts his Englishness and uses the power it comes with to construct a new identity for Antoinette, as the mad Creole heiress, Bertha. He extinguishes Antoinette's flamboyance in the change of name and, transplanting her from the vibrant colours and lush vegetation of the Caribbean to the drab cardboard prison of her room at Thornfield Hall, he pronounces her 'insane'. But these are vindictive, cruel and deeply irrational acts that both reflect and compound his inner emptiness. His temporary passion for Antoinette at Granbois and his absorption in the natural landscape there offered him the opportunity, briefly, of connecting with a deeper inner self. His sadistic attempt to 'break' his wife and his subsequent relish in planning and effecting her incarceration represent a flight from true sanity and humanity. This is perhaps the most brilliant of the novel's inversions of *Jane Eyre*: the increasing fragmentation and paranoia evident in Rochester's narration in Part II suggest quite clearly that it is he who should be locked away (see esp. pp. 135–41). Compared to his manic rambling at the end of his narration, Antoinette's final narration is beautifully lucid and serene, and it is so because *her* act of destruction is a positive step of self-integration rather than a spitefully vindictive act of self-abnegation. Her projected destruction of Thornfield Hall represents a positive act of defiance against its world's definition of her, and her imagined jump to Tia represents a reconciliation at last with the 'black' part of her identity which she first recognised as a child in one of the few authentic mirror reflections she experiences: 'We stared at each other, blood on my face, tears on hers. It was as if I saw myself. Like in a looking-glass' (p. 38).

The relationship between the Rochester character and Antoinette clearly exposes the grossly unequal gender power relations that obtained in the nineteenth century; but the relationship can also be seen to reflect, in a displaced or condensed way, the typical power dynamics that operate in a colonial context between coloniser and colonised. The situation in the novel, especially as the scene moves to the relative wilderness of the Granbois Estate on the island that represents Dominica, is redolent of a type of colonial invasion of Antoinette's world in the Englishman's gradual taking over of her space and her identity, even to the point of renaming her as the English 'Bertha' to confirm that she has become fully his own colonial 'possession'. Like all colonised people, she is then expected to conform to his cultural values and norms – his definition of what is 'sane' and 'civilised' – or to face punitive consequences, as she does by being categorised as 'mad' and then transported to England and, effectively, imprisoned. The Rochester character's general denigration of indigenous Caribbean culture and his high-handed manner towards its people are also evocative of typical aspects of British colonial rule – he calls the servant boy at Granbois a 'half-savage', for example, and describes the boy's English as not 'any English that I can understand' (pp. 140–1); also, in his argument with Christophene, his rapid recourse to the law is telling: '"Then I will have the police up, I warn you. There must be some law and order even in this God-forsaken island"' (p. 131). What is perhaps most striking, though, from a postcolonial point of view, in Rhys's dramatisation of the relationship between Antoinette and 'Rochester', is her apparent insight into the dehumanising effects, for both sides, of what is effectively an oppressor–oppressed relationship. This has been an important theme in postcolonial theory and is given clear expression by the radical educationalist, Paulo Freire, in his *Pedagogy of the Oppressed*, where he writes:

> Although the situation of oppression is a dehumanized and dehumanizing totality affecting both the oppressors and those whom they oppress, it is the latter who must, from their stifled humanity, wage for both the struggle for a fuller humanity … However, the oppressed … suffer from the duality which has established itself in their innermost being … They are at one and the same time themselves and the oppressor whose consciousness they have internalized.
>
> (p. 24 [Cii])

Like many of Jean Rhys's heroines, Antoinette exhibits all the traits of an oppressed 'victim' who has internalised and come to accept the belittling judgements of all those who have the power of definition over her. In the Rochester character, too, Rhys presents a compelling study of how the oppressor's denial of full humanity to another person inevitably drains him of his own humanity, leaving him 'wearied and empty' and, in a certain sense, as unfree as Antoinette. As Freire says, it is only the 'oppressed' who can wage the struggle for a fuller humanity, and it is thus left to Antoinette, as she poetically reclaims her own life and identity in her final dream, to take the symbolic (if tragic) step towards a fuller humanity for herself, for Tia's people, *and*, perhaps, for 'Rochester' too.

(Edward) Kamau Brathwaite, *The Arrivants: A New World Trilogy* (1973)

The Arrivants is made up of three long poetic sequences – or 'movements', in Brathwaite's own more appropriately musical and dynamic term – that were first published individually as *Rights of Passage* (1967), *Masks* (1968) and *Islands* (1969). As one might deduce from all these titles, the arrival of peoples from Africa into the 'new' world of the Caribbean makes up the broad subject of the trilogy. No simple summary can do justice to the prodigious richness of rhythms, allusions, linguistic inventiveness, imagery and ideas of this work, but it is, in effect, a kaleidoscopic cultural history of the Caribbean, conjuring up its continuities out of the ancient civilisations of Africa and leading us through the middle passage of the transatlantic slave trade up to the modern era of jazz and decolonisation, of calypso and further diasporic migrations. Indeed, it is precisely a history of journeys – and a journeying through histories – with the focus constantly shuttling back and forth spatially between Africa and the Caribbean islands (with excursions to Britain, Europe and America) and temporally across the span of centuries from before the rise of European colonialism to the late twentieth century. Although the sequence is presented through a very wide range of different voices or personas and is not generally autobiographical in its mode of address, it also represents a sort of spiritual history of Brathwaite's own personal journeys in the 1950s and early 1960s when, reversing the middle passage, he travelled from Barbados to England (to Cambridge University, where he studied History), then from England to Ghana (where he worked as an education officer for eight years), and full circle back again to the Caribbean. But on both personal and cultural levels, *The Arrivants* reflects a search for identity and wholeness for the Caribbean psyche by reclaiming its African heritage from the violent fractures of colonialism and the slave trade.

Brathwaite's aim, as both poet and historian, has been concerned consistently with a type of cultural archaeology of the black diaspora, what he has described as 'the retracing of our people's movement through space and time and the resurrection of their cultural materials' (quoted in editor's introduction, Stewart Brown, ed., *The Art of Kamau Brathwaite* p. 7 [Cii]). In his poetry in particular, a crucial feature of this retracing and resurrection is that it takes place in and through the language (or voice) *of* that people, in a principled procedure of creative resistance to, and transformation of, the 'master' language of colonialism and enslavement. Against the language of oppression, that is, Brathwaite poses what he has dubbed 'nation language', the subversive, self-defining folk-voices of the Caribbean. For it was in language, he argues, 'that the slave was perhaps most successfully imprisoned by his master and it was in his (mis-)use of it that he perhaps most effectively rebelled. Within the folk tradition language was (and is) a creative act in itself' (quoted in Nathaniel Mackey, 'An Interview with Kamau Brathwaite', p. 15 [Cii]). In the terms of the model of postcolonial linguistic resistance proposed by Ashcroft, Griffiths and Tiffin in *The Empire Writes Back*, Brathwaite's characteristic procedure in his poetry is to *abrogate* the standard forms of English in order to *appropriate* them for his own oppositional, creolised – or Calibanised – *english* (pp. 38–9 [Bii]). As in his own description in *Islands* of the spider-hero of West African and Caribbean folklore, the trickster-creator Ananse, Brathwaite's endlessly inventive wordplay and creative typographical display on the page make him, too, a 'word-breaker' so that he can be a better new 'world-maker' (*The Arrivants*, p. 167). Indeed, in Brathwaite's poetry, the medium really is inseparable from the message with his Creolising procedures often ingeniously counterpointing the sense of the lines – though sometimes his meanings are carried even more by his musical rhythms and by the typographical appearance of lines on the page than by the sense of words.

The above reference to Shakespeare's Caliban from *The Tempest* draws attention to one of the many intertextual motifs in *The Arrivants*, and this plays not only on that play's own historical colonial consciousness, but, perhaps more importantly, also on its archetypal encoding of a colonial master–slave relationship in the characters of Prospero and Caliban. Subsequently, in fact, Brathwaite has used the two characters as a type of shorthand to represent, in the case of Prospero, the forces of colonialism and neo-colonialism, and, in the case of Caliban, everything that challenges those forces – as we see here, in Brathwaite's elaboration of the statement about language cited above:

> I mean, it doesn't only mean language in terms of verbs and sentences, but the whole business of the structures, the ideological structures that are built to control the colonial, to control the slave, to control the underclasses of the western world, to control the mind. That is what Prospero constantly attempts to do, be it through television or through comic books or through the books you have in school. But it is the responsibility of Caliban, of the colonized, not only to revolt against that imposition but to discover his own coral, his own roots.
>
> (Mackey, 'An Interview with Kamau Brathwaite', p. 17 [Cii])

These comments post-date *The Arrivants*, and Brathwaite's use there of the Prospero–Caliban relationship is not as pronounced as in his later work. Nevertheless, it is clearly invoked in the long section entitled 'Caliban' in *Islands* (pp. 191–5) and suggested by other repeated allusions to *The Tempest*. It is important to note, though, that Brathwaite does not see Prospero and Caliban (and all they stand for) in simple binary opposition. There is now, inescapably, a symbiotic *relationship* between them, a dialogue, however unequally it began, and 'There is no / turning back' (p. 85), as the last lines of *Islands* state. And it is important that Caliban is not *defined* by opposition to Prospero, as that is tantamount to continuing to be controlled by him and by the master–slave logic of colonialism. For Brathwaite, rather, Caliban stands for the alternative of subverting that logic all together by taking Prospero's language (and all it stands for) and creatively creolising or hybridising it with the African-rooted rhythms of the Caribbean. This is a key transformational idea that is embodied in the very form and process of *The Arrivants* – that a revitalised future for the Caribbean depends on a creative and *dialogic* appropriation of the language and other cultural materials that history has – however painfully – handed down to its people. This implies an engagement with the slavery-ruptured past too, of course, and this is why the celebration of the new New World, sounded in the carnival rhythms of the final poem of *The Arrivants*, includes a 'torn' note right at the end:

Making
with their

rhythms some-
thing torn

and new

(p. 270)

The final emphasis is on the potential of the new, however, and the lack of a full stop leaves the poem open to the future and suggests that the process of creative transformation continues.

Probably the most important and evident literary intertext for *The Arrivants* is the poetry of T. S. Eliot, certainly in relation to the fragmentary organisation of the work into movements, parts, sections and subsections, but also in relation to the imagistic use of recurring motifs (dryness, water, fire, smoke, stones, dust, journeying) and to the 'mythic method' of counterpointing different eras of history to set up chains of association between different cycles of civilisation, culture and beliefs. There are strong echoes of *The Waste Land* in the overall plan and imagery of *The Arrivants* and allusions to this and other of Eliot's poems appear throughout. Brathwaite's 'Wake' (pp. 208–13) has lines which are almost direct quotations from *The Waste Land*, for example, and Eliot's 'Preludes' and other of the *Prufrock* poems of 1917 seem to be directly invoked in Brathwaite's own 'Prelude' (pp. 28–9; and there are two other poems with that same title in the sequence, pp. 4–8, 90–3). Brathwaite plainly shares with Eliot an interest in the operations of time and memory, and there are direct affinities in that with Eliot's *Four Quartets*, too.

Brathwaite also shares with Eliot an interest in incorporating elements of music into his poetry, but Brathwaite takes this interest formally and thematically far beyond Eliot's experiments in evoking the moods and sounds of modern jazz and blues. *The Arrivants* must rank as one of the most musically inflected of all major works of modern poetry in its skilfully integrated and always symbolically reso- nant sounding of so many different musical styles: traditional West African drum- ming, 'Work Song and Blues' (the title of the very first part of the sequence), gospel spiritual, Caribbean folk, calypso, ska, reggae, and, above all, jazz in all its various forms. Clearly, what all these musical traditions have in common, and the reason why they are so central to Brathwaite's work of cultural 'resurrection', is that they are all important expressions of Black culture and, usually, expressions of that alter- native 'Caliban' culture discussed above, which resists and subverts the dominant culture established by colonialism. Jazz has a particular significance for Brathwaite not only for its having recognisably African roots and a tradition, from its beginnings in the early twentieth century, of *positive* affirmation of Black identity and culture, but also for its being an art form defined by its continually creative, innovating and improvisatory nature. In his celebration of jazz as an especially emancipatory art form within Black culture, Brathwaite draws, among other things, on the inspiration of earlier 'jazz' writers in the Harlem Renaissance (Langston Hughes, for example), but his particular achievement, as Louis James points out, 'was to specifically introduce the concept of jazz, already revolutionizing Black culture in the United States, to disrupt the hegemony of British culture in the British West Indies, and open the way for a new development in indigenous culture ('Brathwaite and Jazz', p. 64 [Cii]). Effectively – and he does this also in discursive form in a three-part essay, 'Jazz and the West Indian Novel', published contemporaneously in 1967–8 with the first two movements of *The Arrivants* – Brathwaite posits jazz as the best-suited aesthetic model for a rejuvenated Caribbean culture and we see precisely a sort of jazz-like and performance-based aesthetic operating throughout *The Arrivants* in its constantly shifting and modulating play of syncopated voices.

The linguistic register of those voices varies widely (and sometimes in the same poem) and spans a broad continuum from standard English to a vividly realised spoken creole that exemplifies Brathwaite's notion of a Caribbean nation language. Mervyn Morris has suggested that 'The Dust' (pp. 62–9), which presents a scene of Barbadian women in dialogue reflecting philosophically on life, is one of the Caribbean's finest poems in creole, and that another creole poem, 'Rites' (pp. 197–203), 'is a West Indian classic, our quintessential cricket poem' ('Overlapping Journeys: *The Arrivants*, p. 127 [Cii]). That poem describes a match at the Bridgetown Oval against the English MCC and provides a good comic example of Brathwaite's wordplay when he punningly records a moment of hushed tension when the spectators could have heard 'if de empire fart' (p. 202). It is worth noting that Brathwaite was a pioneer of performance and dub poetry and that, ideally, his work (like that of other Caribbean poets like Louise Bennett, Linton Kwesi Johnson and Jean 'Binta' Breeze) needs to be heard to gain the full effects of its musical rhythms and creole styles. Indeed, *The Arrivants* was a radical new form of poetry altogether and it is probably no accident, historically, that its constituent poems first began to appear in the 1960s, a period particularly associated with radical protest and counter-cultural trends such as the hippies and the Black Power movement, as well as with the rise of popular culture, especially in music. Specific historical events of that era are mentioned by Brathwaite at times, too, with a reference to America's attempted invasion of Cuba and riots in Trinidad, for example (p. 60).

But it is perhaps Brathwaite's principal theme of migration that most reflects the broader post-war contexts of *The Arrivants*, as the period through to the 1960s was a time of particularly high emigration from the Caribbean, and especially to Britain from Barbados and Jamaica from 1948 (the year of the first arrivals in Britain on board the *Empire Windrush*; see Chapter 7, pp. 591–2, 596–8). Brathwaite memorably evokes the anxieties and uncertainties of such migration in a section entitled 'The Emigrants' (pp. 51–6), a title that pays homage to the 1954 novel of the same name by Brathwaite's compatriot, George Lamming, which itself deals memorably with the early experiences of the *Windrush* emigrants in Britain. Brathwaite's 'The Emigrants' is subdivided into seven shorter parts, most of which can be read as distinct poems in their own right and most of which have a contemporary setting (subsection 6 in particular briefly reprises elements of Lamming's novel in a series of imagistic snapshots of immigrant life in Britain). However, as is characteristic of the whole work, there is a spectacular historical 'break-out' in the second poem which, taking its cue from an ironic image in the first, which sees the contemporary migrants as Columbus-like 'New World mariners', transports us suddenly back to the 1490s to present the scene of one of Columbus's first landings on a Caribbean island. This is an outstanding poem in its own right, linguistically beautifully controlled and poignantly mixing luxuriantly sensuous imagery of the island with a sharp sense of the impending brutality of 'Pike / point and musket butt'. Where Brathwaite's engagement with Eliot is not a 'writing back' to the centre of colonial culture so much as a dialogic 'writing forwards' from it, this is more definitely an example of the former strategy in its response to European colonialism's long tradition of presenting New World lands as paradisal *virgin* territory, uninhabited by anyone considered fully human, and preordained by God as the rightful possession of his chosen Christian people (see Figure 8.6; and see Peter Hulme's discussion of this image at the start of his classic account of the tradition just mentioned in *Colonial Encounters* [Cii]). A specific example of this tradition in English literature, and one to which Brathwaite's poem seems to be responding directly, is Andrew Marvell's 'Bermudas' (probably written in the 1650s and first published in 1681), which seems to depict Bermuda's 'dis- / covery' (to use Brathwaite's deliberately broken form in *his* poem) by an 'English boat', and which is presented as a song of praise to God for such a prodigiously bountiful *gift*:

> What should we do but sing his praise
> That led us through the wat'ry maze
> Unto an isle so long unknown
> And yet far kinder than our own? ...
> He gave us this eternal spring
> Which here enamels everything ...

For all its descriptive beauty, Marvell's poem contains absolutely no hint (unless some irony is intended) of the possibility that the island may already be inhabited. Brathwaite's poem, then, in characteristic postcolonial style, effectively reverses Marvell's poem's point of view to restore the written-out existence of the original Amerindian inhabitants of the Caribbean. But this reversal is very subtly and unobtrusively achieved; for, in fact, the Marvellian/colonial viewpoint of Columbus does still largely focalise the island for the reader – until, that is, we realise, through the simplest of touches, that another level of focalisation exists and that Columbus, as he proprietorially takes the measure of the island from his ship, is himself being watched *from* the island by its indigenous inhabitants. Those touches are the simple slipping-in of some personal possessive pronouns which, though few, nevertheless sharply shift the narrative point of view to the island, while also making clear, in protest at the appropriating gaze of colonialism, that the island has already long been another people's home – this is '*my* summer air', '*my* simple water', '*our* land', '*our* farms', '*our* shore' (my emphasis; pp. 52–3).

Anita Desai, *Clear Light of Day* (1980)

Anita Desai was born in India in 1937 to a Bengali father and a German mother and she has lived in Britain and America as well as in India. She was brought up speaking German and Hindi but learnt to read and write through the medium of English and all her works have been produced in English. As such a background might lead us to expect, the theme of hybridity looms large in Desai's writing and in *Clear Light of Day* it relates closely to other important postcolonial themes such as language, memory and history in the novel's intricately worked exploration of cultural identity. Desai is also recognised for the subtly feminist nature of her work which frequently dramatises the frustrations of women who, within the context of a rapidly changing and modernising India, remain caught within the claustrophobic confines of traditional patriarchal structures. *Clear Light of Day*, in particular, represents a searching psychological study of just such female experience in the life of its main character, Bim Das.

As for Kushwant Singh's *Train to Pakistan* (1956) and Salman Rushdie's *Midnight's Children* (1981), the key reference point for the historical context of *Clear Light of Day* is that of independence and partition for India and Pakistan in 1947, along with the violent social upheavals immediately surrounding that time. The modernist style, structure and narrative technique of Desai's novel make it formally quite different from Singh's narrative of documentary realism and Rushdie's work of post-modernist magical realism, however, and, in typically modernist style, the broader historical context is symbolically embedded within the personal domestic drama of the fragmented Das family and filtered to us impressionistically through the dialogue, thoughts and feelings of the main characters. Nonetheless, the atmosphere of the novel is suffused by those historical events and the novel's main themes all crystallise around the tumultuous summer of 1947.

Indeed, the very structure of the novel places that summer literally at the centre of the narrative, as if everything hinges upon and radiates out from it. The novel has four separate parts, each dealing with a specific phase in the life of Bim and her family over a period of around thirty years, from the mid-1930s to the mid-1960s. Bim is the central focalising consciousness of the narrative and it is principally through her memories of the family's life in Delhi, in subtle counterpoint with her present search for meaning in life, that the complex tapestry of personal and communal Indian history is gradually woven. The four parts of the novel do not follow in chronological order, however, and the narrative constantly circles back onto itself as it progresses. Part I begins in the story-present of the 1960s as we are introduced to Bim and her younger sister, Tara, who has just returned on a visit from America with Bakul, her ambassador husband. Bim, middle-aged and unmarried, looks after their autistic younger brother, Baba, and has lived uninterruptedly in the family home in Old Delhi since childhood. There is tension in the air as we sense Bim's bitterness at being left with all the responsibilities of nursing Baba and maintaining the family home and business, though we also sense Tara's guilt at having 'abandoned' her sister in 1947 to marry Bakul. Their elder brother, Raja, also left home at that point to go to Hyderabad to marry the daughter of their Muslim landlord, Hyder Ali, who had had to flee during the partition riots. Despite Bim's erstwhile devotion to Raja, she has not spoken to him for many years since he inherited Hyder Ali's property and wrote her a 'landlordly' letter. Part II takes us back to the period of independence, partition and the assassination of Gandhi in 1947–8. Among other things, we hear of the deaths of the Das parents, of the alcoholism and death of the children's beloved Aunt Mira; of Raja's friendship with the Hyder Ali family and his passion for Urdu poetry and Muslim culture; of Bim's nursing of Raja during a serious illness; and then of the final 'partition' of the family as Tara and Raja leave. Part III takes us back further still to pre-independence India in the 1930s and 1940s and to a range of scenes from the childhood of Bim, Tara, Raja, and Baba. Part 4 brings us full circle back to the story-present of the 1960s. The accumulated family tensions suggested by the preceding narrative come to a head in an angry outburst from Bim, but this then clears the air for her to make her peace with Tara and Raja, and, perhaps most importantly, with herself – and the novel then builds to a powerful epiphany in a magnificently evoked concert of classical Indian music.

The achronological ordering of the plot is clearly designed to set up a sense of dialogue and counterpoint between past and present, with Part II at the heart of it – so that the personal history of the Das family becomes inextricably bound up with the national history of the period leading up to, through and beyond Independence. The rhythm of the novel, too, contributes to this structural emphasis on 1947, in that the pace effectively accelerates in its two middle parts, which deal with a number of key events spread over several years, while Parts I and IV deal with only a few days (in which there is little 'action' as such). The narrative in those parts (framing and focusing the central action) is 'stretched' in a sort of slow-motion effect as Bim haltingly reflects on her life and relationships, struggling inwardly to reconcile the flurried and fleeting past with the apparently stalled present. Bim herself makes an interesting comment about the rhythm of life which might be applied equally well to the novel:

> 'Isn't it strange how life won't *flow*, like a river, but moves in jumps, as if it were held back by locks that are opened now and then to let it jump forwards in a kind of flood? There are these long still stretches – nothing happens – each day is exactly like the other – plodding, uneventful – and then suddenly there is a crash – mighty deeds take place – momentous events … That summer was certainly one of them – the summer of '47 –'

(pp. 42–3)

The stretching of narrative time in order to render 'moments' of consciousness recalls a characteristic feature of modernist fiction, of course, and of the novels of Virginia Woolf in particular. Together with the narrative's non-linear chronology, it also recalls Woolf's characteristic attempts to capture the complexity of 'psychological time' and the ways in which the circling and disjunctive processes of memory and emotion weave patterns of meaning and identity for the individual that are outside the linear logic of mechanical 'clock time'. Thus, in addition to focusing attention on the historical events of 1947, the chronologically disordered and unevenly paced narrative of *Clear Light of Day* also helps to evoke the psychological rhythms of Bim's struggle to make sense of her life out of the tumult of the past.

The novel's evident concern with time, memory and history is signalled even before the start, in Desai's two epigraphs. The first of these, a well-known line by Emily Dickinson, 'Memory is a strange Bell – Jubilee, and Knell', encapsulates the double-edged nature of memory as always potentially both a celebration and a mourning of the past, clearly setting the tone for a novel that places such celebration and mourning (of both personal and public pasts) in close poetic dialogue. The other epigraph, from T. S. Eliot's 'Little Gidding' (*Four Quartets*, 1944), is perhaps more integrally important to the novel, both in its own right – in suggesting how the past can 'become renewed, transfigured, in another pattern' – but also in the clue it gives us to Desai's broader use of the *Four Quartets* as a type of structural and thematic template for her novel. In addition to the obvious echo in the four-part structure of the novel, Eliot's four long poems resound throughout Desai's text, from the initial scene of the rose-garden walk, which draws on the rose-garden imagery of 'Burnt Norton', through to the direct quotation from 'The Dry Salvages' at the end of the novel, when Bim remembers reading 'in Raja's well-thumbed copy of Eliot's *Four Quartets*, the line: "*Time the destroyer is time the preserver*"' (p. 182). Desai's own copy of Eliot's sequence was probably well-thumbed too and many other of Eliot's lines can be detected peeping out palimpsestically from beneath her text. Eliot's concern with time and memory and his carefully wrought interweaving of past and present in *Four Quartets* certainly seems to have been a major shaping influence on *Clear Light of Day* and, although the full significance of Eliot's epigraph at the start of the text does not become clear until its end, in retrospect it provides a succinct poetic gloss on how Desai's novel works to envision future renewal for her characters – and for India – through its transformative grappling with the meanings of the past.

Another thing that does not become entirely clear until the end of the novel is the significance of Bim's hard-won professional independence as a history teacher in a local college. Drawing out the natural links between history and memory, the novel thus casts Bim as a custodian of the communal past as well as of the family past. Just as she is the keeper of the old family home and all its memories, so she is a preserver and interpreter of public history for her students. Her two roles as historian and family memorialist are brought together at the end of the novel in the epiphany Bim experiences as she listens in the garden to the old guru's rapturous song and realises the many intricate ways in which she and her family have been, and continue to be, interwoven threads in the ancient and continually evolving tapestry of life and culture that is India:

> She saw before her eyes how one ancient school of music contained both Mulk, still an immature disciple, and his aged, exhausted guru with all the disillusionments and defeats of his long experience. With her inner eye she saw how her own house and its particular history linked and contained her as well as her whole family with all their separate histories and experiences … giving them the soil in which to send down their roots, and food to make them grow and spread, reach out to new experiences and new lives, but always drawing from the same soil, the same secret darkness. That soil contained all time, past and future, in it. It was dark with time, rich with time. It was where her deepest self lived, and the deepest selves of her sister and brothers and all those who shared that time with her.
>
> (p. 182)

Reference

A Primary Texts and Anthologies of Primary Sources

Achebe, Chinua. *Things Fall Apart* (1958). In *The African Trilogy: Things Fall Apart, No Longer at Ease, Arrow of God*. London: Picador, 1988.
　Anthills of the Savannah. London: Heinemann, 1987.
　Hopes and Impediments: Selected Essays 1965–87. Oxford: Heinemann International, 1988.
Achebe, Chinua, and C. L. Innes, eds. *African Short Stories*. London: Heinemann, 1985. This and the following anthology each contain stories by twenty writers from across the continent and provide an excellent representative sample of the genre.
　The Heinemann Book of Contemporary African Short Stories. London: Heinemann, 1992.
Brathwaite, (Edward) Kamau. *The Arrivants*. Oxford University Press, 1973.
Brown, Stewart, ed. *Caribbean New Wave: Contemporary Short Stories*. London: Heinemann, 1990. Collects twenty-three stories from across the region.
Brown, Stewart, and Mark McWatt, eds. *The Oxford Book of Caribbean Verse*. Oxford University Press, 2005. A rich pan-Caribbean collection with a stimulating introduction and biographical notes on all the poets. Usefully broadens out and updates Burnett's Penguin anthology below.
Brink, André, and J. M. Coetzee, eds. *A Land Apart: A South African Reader*. London: Faber & Faber, 1986. Rich and varied anthology edited and introduced by two of South Africa's leading authors.
Burnett, Paula, ed. *The Penguin Book of Caribbean Verse in English*. Harmondsworth: Penguin, 1986. A comprehensive anthology of both oral and literary traditions, with an excellent introduction surveying the whole of the poetic tradition of the English-speaking Caribbean. Includes detailed biographies and an extensive glossary of Caribbean vernacular terms.
Desai, Anita. *Clear Light of Day*. Harmondsworth: Penguin, 1980.
Donnell, Alison, and Sarah Lawson Welsh, eds. *The Routledge Reader in Caribbean Literature*. London: Routledge, 1996. An excellent compilation of primary and secondary texts, covering the whole of the twentieth century, and with critical introductions to each section.
Ferracane, Kathleen K., ed. *Caribbean Panorama: An Anthology from and about the English-Speaking Caribbean* … University of Puerto Rico, 1999. A thematically organised selection of poems, stories and novel extracts, with, in the introduction, an excellent overview of the history and contexts of the Caribbean. Also contains study questions, biographies and suggestions for further reading.
Gilbert, Helen, ed. *Postcolonial Plays: An Anthology*. London: Routledge, 2001.
Moore, Gerald, and Ulli Beier, eds. *The Penguin Book of Modern African Poetry*. 4th edn. Harmondsworth: Penguin, 1998. (First edn 1963.) A very rich and wide-ranging anthology, representing nearly one hundred twentieth-century poets from twenty-seven countries, including many poems in translation.
Naipaul, V. S. *The Mimic Men* (1967). London: Vintage, 2001.

The Overcrowded Barracoon and Other Articles (1972). Harmondsworth: Penguin, 1976.

Ngugi wa Thiong'o. *Weep Not, Child*. London: Heinemann, 1964.

Paton, Alan. *Cry, The Beloved Country: A Story of Comfort in Desolation* (1948). London: The Reprint Society, 1949.

Rhys, Jean. *Wide Sargasso Sea*. Harmondsworth: Penguin, 1966.

Ross, Robert L., ed. *Colonial and Postcolonial Fiction: An Anthology*. New York: Garland, 1999. An excellent and unusually wide-ranging resource with thirty-five pieces by major writers from throughout the Commonwealth.

Salkey, Andrew, ed. *Breaklight: An Anthology of Caribbean Poetry*. London: Hamish Hamilton, 1971.

Saro-Wiwa, Ken. *Sozaboy: A Novel in Rotten English* (1985). Harlow: Longman, 1994.

Schreiner, Olive. *The Story of an African Farm* (1883). Oxford University Press, 1992.

Soyinka, Wole. *Season of Anomy* (1973). London: Arena, 1988.

Stafford, Jane, and Mark Williams, eds. *The Auckland University Press Anthology of New Zealand Literature*. Auckland University Press, 2013.

Thayil, Jeet, ed. *The Bloodaxe Book of Contemporary Indian Poets*. Tarset: Bloodaxe Books, 2008.

Thieme, John, ed. *The Arnold Anthology of Postcolonial Literatures in English*. London: Hodder Arnold, 1996. Presents a large and wide-ranging selection of texts.

Tutuola, Amos. *The Palm-Wine Drinkard* (1952). London: Faber & Faber, 2014.

Walcott, Derek. *What the Twilight Says: Essays*. London: Faber & Faber, 1998.

B   Introductions and Overviews

i   The British Empire and Decolonisation

Faught, C. Brad. *The New A –Z of Empire: A Concise Handbook of British Imperial History*. London: I. B. Taurus, 2011. A convenient source of quick reference and particularly helpful in providing two suggestions for further reading for each entry as well as a general bibliographical note on relevant scholarship.

Haigh, Christopher, ed. *The Cambridge Historical Encyclopedia of Great Britain and Ireland*. Cambridge University Press, 1985. See especially chapter 7, 'From Imperial Power to European Partner 1901–1975', which provides a detailed summary of the immediate historical contexts for Britain during the period leading to the end of empire.

Jackson, Ashley. *The British Empire: A Very Short Introduction*. Oxford University Press, 2013. An engaging, critically balanced and reliable contemporary overview, drawing on a wide range of authoritative sources and with a helpful short guide to further reading.

James, Lawrence. *The Rise and Fall of the British Empire*. London: Little, Brown, 1994. A substantial narrative account of the full history of the empire – detailed, reliable and readable. Reprinted in an abridged illustrated edition in 1999.

Marshall, P. J., ed. *The Cambridge Illustrated History of the British Empire*. Cambridge University Press, 1996. Scholarly, balanced, helpfully structured and clearly written, with superb illustrations, this is probably the most thorough single-volume overview of the history of the empire and its demise. The book provides detailed, reliable and incisive coverage of all the main historical facts and developments, but also devotes separate chapters to particular themes in the study of empire (e.g., imperial ideology, art, urbanisation) and systematically draws attention to key issues and debates.

O'Farrell, John. *An Utterly Impartial History of Britain, or 2000 Years of Upper-Class Idiots in Charge*. London: Black Swan, 2008. For 'all those who weren't listening at school' … As the title suggests, an irreverent comic sweep through the whole of British history, and probably not to be cited in examinations, but carefully researched in broad outlines and, the jokes aside, generally accurate. See especially chapter 8, 'Empire 1815–1914'.

Palmer, Alan. *Dictionary of the British Empire and Commonwealth*. London: John Murray, 1996. An excellent quick-reference companion with some 650 cross-referenced entries covering the most important political, social, technological and cultural developments in the history of the empire and Commonwealth. Has helpful maps, a very good select bibliography of further reading, and a comprehensive index.

Smith, Simon C. *British Imperialism 1750–1970*. Cambridge University Press, 1998. Part of a series of 'Perspectives in History', this is a stimulating and concise introduction to some key themes and issues in British imperial history. Each of the ten chapters examines a particular aspect of that history and draws on original documentary sources to encourage and inform further debate and discussion. Has an excellent annotated select bibliography.

ii Postcolonial Literature and Related Studies

Ashcroft, Bill, Gareth Griffiths and Helen Tiffin. *The Empire Writes Back: Theory and Practice in Post-Colonial Literature*. London: Routledge, 1989. A seminal introductory text notable for its careful integration of theory and practice. Includes a comprehensive bibliography and a very helpful annotated readers' guide to both general postcolonial criticism and specific accounts of national and regional literatures.

eds. *The Post-Colonial Studies Reader*. London: Routledge, 1995. An invaluable collection of key writings within the field, many of which might otherwise be difficult for students to access. Contains some ninety items, thematically organised into fourteen sections.

Post-Colonial Studies: The Key Concepts. 3rd edn. London: Routledge, 2013. Helpful dictionary-style overview of the general field with detailed entries for each concept. See also Thieme's *Glossary* below, which is more literature-focused.

Atwood, Margaret. *Survival: A Thematic Guide to Canadian Literature*. Toronto: Anansi, 1972.

Benson, Eugene, and L. W. Conolly, eds. *Encyclopedia of Post-Colonial Literatures in English*. London: Routledge, 1994. Another very useful anthology to sit with the books by Ashcroft, Griffiths and Tiffin above.

Crow, Brian, with Chris Banfield. *An Introduction to Post-Colonial Theatre*. Cambridge University Press, 1996. An accessible introduction with chapters devoted to seven postcolonial playwrights – from the Caribbean (Derek Walcott), America

(August Wilson), Australia (Jack Davis), India (Badal Sircar and Girish Karnad), West Africa (Wole Soyinka) and South Africa (Athol Fugard).

Crystal, David. *English as a Global Language.* 2nd edn. Cambridge University Press, 2003. A classic text by one of the leading authorities on the English language, this book presents a remarkably concise and comprehensive account of the spread of English as a global language, thus providing an excellent foundation for a fuller understanding of the spread of literature in English in postcolonial contexts.

Gandhi, Leela. *Postcolonial Theory: A Critical Introduction.* New York: Columbia University Press, 1998. A clear account of the intellectual history and leading themes of postcolonial studies.

Griffiths, Gareth. *African Literatures in English: East and West.* London: Longman, 2000. A superb critical introduction to the regions indicated, mapping out the field expertly, providing many close readings of texts, and with an excellent section of further reference.

Heywood, Christopher. *A History of South African Literature.* Cambridge University Press, 2004.

Hughes, Michael. *A Companion to West Indian Literature.* London: Collins, 1979. A useful dictionary-style companion providing details and critical references for authors, texts and journals – though, obviously, only up to the date of publicaton.

Innes, C. L. *The Cambridge Introduction to Postcolonial Literatures in English.* Cambridge University Press, 2007. A finely written, clear and comprehensive introduction that looks closely at a wide range of texts and provides a wealth of insight and relevant information. Ideal for undergraduate study.

Irele, F. Abiola, and Simon Gikandi, eds. *The Cambridge History of African and Caribbean Literature.* 2 vols. Cambridge University Press, 2004. A comprehensive, clearly written and thoroughly contextualised critical history with forty expert essays covering a wide range of languages and literatures from Africa and the Caribbean. An invaluable source of reference.

Keith, W. J. *Canadian Literature in English.* London: Longman, 1985.

Killan, Douglas. *Literature of Africa.* Westport: Greenwood Press, 2004. Very clearly written and organised, with brief introductions to the literature of the main regions followed by developed readings of a number of texts. An excellent resource for students.

Killan, Douglas, and Ruth Rowe, eds. *The Companion to African Literatures.* Oxford: James Currey, 2000. An extensive and richly detailed dictionary-style book of reference with critically nuanced entries that are carefully cross-referenced to provide a coherent overview of the whole field of authors, texts, contexts, genres, regions, cultures and languages.

King, Bruce, ed. *West Indian Literature.* London: Macmillan, 1995.

Loomba, Ania. *Colonialism/Postcolonialism.* London: Routledge, 1998. A refreshingly lively and clearly written overview of the field, critically acute and incisive, providing a wide-ranging and well-balanced discussion of major issues and debates.

Loomba, Ania, Suvir Kaul et al., eds. *Postcolonial Studies and Beyond.* Durham, NC and London: Duke University Press, 2005. A stimulating collection of essays exploring new directions for postcolonial studies.

McLaren, John. *Australian Literature: An Historical Introduction.* London: Longman, 1990.

Mehrotra, Arvind Krishna, ed. *A History of Indian Literature in English*. London: Hurst, 2003. Not a continuous history but a broad mapping out through twenty-four separate essays on specific genres and a range of major authors.

Ramazani, Jahan. *The Hybrid Muse: Postcolonial Poetry in English*. University of Chicago Press, 2001.

Ramchand, Kenneth. *An Introduction to the Study of West Indian Literature*. London: Faber, 1976.

Ramone, Jenni. *Postcolonial Theories*. Basingstoke: Palgrave Macmillan, 2011. An accessible and thoroughgoing introduction that ranges widely over postcolonial theories and contexts and provides a number of close textual readings.

Roberts, Neil, ed. *A Companion to Twentieth-Century Poetry*. Oxford: Blackwell, 2001. Valuable for its excellent long entry on postcolonial poetry (by Jahan Ramazani – see above for his book *The Hybrid Muse*) and for its region-specific entries (West Indian Poetry, etc.).

Robinson, Roger, and Nelson Wattie, eds. *The Oxford Companion to New Zealand Literature*. Oxford University Press, 1998.

Schwarz, Henry, and Sangeeta Ray. *Companion to Postcolonial Studies: An Historical Introduction*. London: Blackwell, 2004.

Thieme, John. *Post-Colonial Studies: The Essential Glossary*. London: Bloomsbury Academic, 2003. A wide-ranging mapping of the subject with a central focus on literature and literary theory.

Tiffin, Helen. 'Post-Colonial Literatures and Counter-Discourse'. In Ashcroft et al., eds. *The Post-Colonial Studies Reader* [Bii], pp. 95–8.

Walder, Dennis. *Post-Colonial Literatures in English: History, Language, Theory*. Oxford: Blackwell, 1998. A clearly written and compelling introductory survey of the field, dealing helpfully with the key issues indicated in the subtitle.

Walsh, William. *Indian Literature in English*. London: Longman, 1990. Clearly and concisely written and skilfully organised to provide a comprehensive introduction in relatively few pages. The introduction sketches in the contextual background and there are useful reference sections.

C Further Reading

i The British Empire and Decolonisation

Armitage, David. *The Ideological Origins of the British Empire*. Cambridge University Press, 2000. An advanced and specialised historical study, but providing deep insight into the closely intertwined processes of British state-formation and British empire-building from the mid-sixteenth to the mid-eighteenth centuries; particularly useful in clarifying the linked histories of England, Wales, Scotland and Ireland in relation to empire.

Darwin, John. *Britain and Decolonisation: The Retreat from Empire in the Post-War World*. Basingstoke: Macmillan, 1988.

Das, Santanu, ed. *Race, Empire and First World War Writing*. Cambridge University Press, 2011. An excellent multi-disciplinary collection of essays ranging widely across the experiences of different racial, ethnic and national groups who participated in the war (mainly, but not solely, those from former British colonies).

Freund, Bill. *The Making of Contemporary Africa: The Development of African Society since 1800*. London: Macmillan, 1984. A clearly written and carefully developed materialist introduction that keeps social and economic contexts closely to the fore.

Hobsbawm, Eric J., *The Age of Empire 1875–1914*. London: Weidenfeld & Nicolson, 1987.

Hyam, Ronald. *Britain's Declining Empire: The Road to Decolonisation 1918–1968*. Cambridge University Press, 2006. Based on detailed archival research into British government policy, this is a thoroughgoing political history of decolonisation throughout the empire, with detailed case studies on all the main regions. An authoritative source for advanced study, but written with a light touch – so also highly readable for anyone wanting to dip into particular aspects of the history.

Understanding the British Empire. Cambridge University Press, 2010. A wide-ranging set of essays on the political, economic and cultural history of the empire, including chapters on humanitarian and missionary activity and on sexuality.

Keay, John. *India: A History*. London: HarperCollins, 2000. A comprehensive and readable account for the general reader covering the entire history from 3000 BC but dealing concisely with the colonial period in the last quarter or so of the book.

Louis, William Roger, et al., eds. *The Oxford History of the British Empire*. 5 vols. Oxford University Press, 1998–9. The most comprehensive and authoritative source for scholarly reference.

Oliver, Roland. *The African Experience*. London: Weidenfeld & Nicolson, 1991. A concise survey of the whole history of Africa from the origins of humanity to the release of Nelson Mandela. Helpfully illustrated by a range of maps and figures, the book provides a solid foundation for an understanding of the development of African cultures across the continent. The second half of the book, which deals with the colonial and post-colonial periods, is of most direct relevance here.

Parry, J. H., P.M. Sherlock, and A. P. Maingot. *A Short History of the West Indies*. London: Macmillan, 1987.

ii Postcolonial Literature and Related Studies

Note

There are now a large number of journals of relevance to postcolonial literature, including *African Literature Today, Ariel, Journal of Commonwealth Literature, Journal of Postcolonial Writing* and *Wasafiri*. A fuller list, with website links, can be found at https://public.wsu.edu/~brians/anglophone/pocojournals.html

Bock, Hedwig, and Albert Wertheim, eds. *Essays on Contemporary Post-Colonial Fiction*. Munich: Max Hueber Verlag, 1986. A well-balanced compilation of twenty-two expert essays on major authors and writings from throughout the Commonwealth.

Brown, Stewart, ed. *The Art of Kamau Brathwaite*. Bridgend: Seren Books, 1995.

ed. *The Pressures of the Text: Orality, Texts and the Telling of Tales*. Centre of West African Studies, University of Birmingham, 1995.

ed. *Kiss and Quarrel: Yorùbá/English, Strategies of Mediation*. Centre of West African Studies, University of Birmingham, 2000.

Bucknor, Michael A., and Alison Donnell, eds. *The Routledge Companion to Anglophone Caribbean Literature*. London: Routledge, 2011.

Fanon, Frantz. *The Wretched of the Earth*. Harmondsworth: Penguin, 1961. Fanon's ideas here and in the following work have been of seminal importance in the development of postcolonial studies.

  Black Skin, White Masks. New York: Grove Press, 1967.

Freire, Paulo. *Pedagogy of the Oppressed*. Harmondsworth: Penguin, 1972.

Huggan, Graham, ed. *The Oxford Handbook of Postcolonial Studies*. Oxford University Press, 2013. A challenging collection of critical essays considering the past, present and future of postcolonial studies.

Hulme, Peter. *Colonial Encounters: Europe and the Native Caribbean 1492–1797*. London: Routledge, 1986. A detailed and challenging but extremely rewarding study of the origins of colonial discourse and its development through canonical texts such as *The Tempest* and *Robinson Crusoe*.

Irele, F. Abiola, ed. *The Cambridge Companion to the African Novel*. Cambridge University Press, 2009.

James, Louis. 'Brathwaite and Jazz'. In Stewart Brown, ed. *The Art of Kamau Brathwaite* [Cii], pp. 62–74.

Kröller, Eva-Marie, ed. *The Cambridge Companion to Canadian Literature*. Cambridge University Press, 2004

Lazarus, Neil, ed. *The Cambridge Companion to Postcolonial Literary Studies*. Cambridge University Press, 2004. An advanced scholarly introduction to the field with a range of challenging perspectives. Lazarus's own chapter on 'The global dispensation since 1945' is of particular relevance to the present chapter.

Mackey, Nathaniel. 'An Interview with Kamau Brathwaite'. In Stewart Brown, ed. *The Art of Kamau Brathwaite* [Cii], pp. 13–32.

Memmi, Albert. *The Coloniser and the Colonised*. New York: Orion Press, 1965.

Morris, Mervyn. 'Overlapping Journeys: *The Arrivants*'. In Stewart Brown, ed. *The Art of Kamau Brathwaite* [Cii], pp. 117–131.

Ngugi wa Thiong'o. *Decolonising the Mind: The Politics of Language in African Literature*. London: James Currey, 1981.

  Something Torn and New: An African Renaissance. New York: Basic Civitas Books, 2009.

Osundare, Niyi. 'Yorùbá Thought, English Words: A Poet's Journey Through the Tunnel of Two Tongues'. In Stewart Brown, ed. *Kiss and Quarrel* [Cii], pp.15–31.

Quayson, Ato, ed. *The Cambridge Companion to the Postcolonial Novel*. Cambridge University Press, 2016.

Said, Edward. *Orientalism*. 1978. Harmondsworth: Penguin, 1991.

  Culture and Imperialism. London: Chatto and Windus, 1993.

Thieme, John. *Postcolonial Con-Texts: Writing Back to the Canon*. London: Continuum, 2002.

Webby, Elizabeth, ed. *The Cambridge Companion to Australian Literature*. Cambridge University Press, 2000.

Index

Note: Page numbers in **bold** denote detailed textual readings; those in *italic* denote topics of boxed insets.